Adobe® InDesign®
CS3 Bible

Adobe® InDesign® CS3 Bible

Galen Gruman

Wiley Publishing, Inc.

Adobe® InDesign® CS3 Bible

Published by
Wiley Publishing, Inc.
10475 Crosspoint Boulevard
Indianapolis, IN 46256
www.wiley.com

Copyright © 2007 by Wiley Publishing, Inc., Indianapolis, Indiana

Published simultaneously in Canada

ISBN: 978-0-470-11938-9

Manufactured in the United States of America

10 9 8 7 6 5 4 3 2 1

For general information on our other products and services or to obtain technical support, please contact our Customer Care Department within the U.S. at (800) 762-2974, outside the U.S. at (317) 572-3993 or fax (317) 572-4002.

Library of Congress Control Number: 2007926381

About the Author

Galen Gruman is principal at The Zango Group, an editorial consulting firm. Currently a frequent contributor to *Layers Magazine*, *Macworld*, *CIO*, and *InfoWorld*, he has also been editor of *Macworld* and *M-Business,* executive editor of *Upside,* West Coast bureau chief of *Computerworld,* and vice president of content for ThirdAge.com. He is author or coauthor of 20 other books about desktop publishing. Gruman led one of the first successful conversions of a national magazine to desktop publishing in 1986 and has covered publishing technology since then for several publications, including the trade weekly *InfoWorld,* for which he began writing in 1986; *Macworld,* whose staff he joined in 1991; and most recently *Layers.* Originally a newspaper reporter in Los Angeles, Gruman caught the production-technology bug in 1979 and hasn't recovered.

Credits

Acquisitions Editor
Kim Spilker

Project Editor
Chris Wolfgang

Technical Editor
Jonathan Q. Woolson

Copy Editor
Lauren Kennedy

Editorial Manager
Robyn Siesky

Business Manager
Amy Knies

**Vice President and Executive Group
Publisher**
Richard Swadley

Vice President and Executive Publisher
Bob Ipsen

Vice President and Publisher
Barry Pruett

Project Coordinator
Adrienne Martinez

Graphics and Production Specialists
Carrie Foster
Brooke Graczyk
Denny Hager
Jennifer Mayberry
Barbara Moore
Heather Pope
Alicia B. South

Quality Control Technicians
John Greenough
Jessica Kramer
Christine Pingleton

Proofreading and Indexing
Aptara

Wiley Bicentennial Logo
Richard J. Pacifico

Contents

About the Author v

Foreword xxxi

Preface. xxxiii

Acknowledgments xxxv

Introduction xxxvii

Quick Start: Building a Document from Start to Finish 1

    Creating a New Document 2
    Working with Frames and Pages...4
    Working with Text 7
    Working with Lines 13
    Creating and Applying Colors 14
    Working with Graphics 17
    Adding Special Effects 18
    Printing a Composite 19

Part I: Welcome to InDesign — 21

Chapter 1: What InDesign Can Do for You. 23

    Understanding Global and Local Control 26
    Summary 28

Chapter 2: Inside the InDesign Interface. 29

    Exploring the InDesign Application Folder 30
        The Presets folder 30
        The Plug-ins folder..30
        The Required folder 31
    Exploring the Document Window 31
        Title bar 31
        Zero point 34
        Scroll bars..34
        Pasteboard, pages, and guides...34
        Show/Hide Structure button...36
        Zoom field and pop-up menu...36

Contents

Version Cue pop-up menu 36

Page controls 37

    Page-turning buttons 37

    Page field and pop-up menu 38

Using Tools 38

    Using Tool Tips and keyboard shortcuts 39

    Opening and closing the Tools panel 40

    Selecting tools 41

    Understanding what the tools do 42

        Selection tool 43

        Direct Selection tool 44

        Position tool 45

        Pen tool 45

        Anchor and direction point tools 45

        Type tool 45

        Type on a Path tool 46

        Pencil tool 46

        Smooth tool 46

        Erase tool 46

        Line tool 46

        Frame tools 47

        Shape tools 47

        Button tool 47

        Scissors tool 47

        Rotate tool 47

        Scale tool 48

        Shear tool 48

        Gradient Swatch tool 48

        Gradient Feather tool 48

        Free Transform tool 48

        Note tool 48

        Eyedropper tool 48

        Measure tool 49

        Hand tool 49

        Zoom tool 49

    Color buttons 49

    View buttons 49

Working with Panels and Docks 50

    Arranging panels 50

    Changing the dock display 52

    Using panels 53

    Checking out the panels 54

Reviewing Menu Commands 68

    InDesign menu 68

    File menu 69

Edit menu 70

Layout menu 71

Type menu 71

Notes menu 73

Object menu...74

Table menu 75

View menu 75

Window menu 76

Help menu 76

Contextual menus 77

How to change your mind 79

Summary 80

Chapter 3: Getting InDesign Ready to Go **81**

Working with Preferences Files..81

InDesign Defaults file 82

Presets folder 82

Using the Preferences Dialog Box 83

General preferences 84

Page Numbering area 85

Font Downloading and Embedding area.........85

When Scaling area 86

Scripting area 86

Reset All Warning Dialogs button 86

Interface preferences...86

Type preferences 87

Type Options area 87

Drag and Drop Text Editing area.....................89

Links area 89

Advanced Type pane 91

Character Settings area 91

Input Method Options area..............................92

Composition preferences 92

Highlight area 93

Text Wrap area 94

Units & Increments preferences 94

Ruler Units area 94

Point/Pica Size area 96

Keyboard Increments area...............................96

Grids preferences 98

Baseline Grid area 98

Document Grid area 100

Guides & Pasteboard preferences 100

Color area 100

Guide Options area..101

Pasteboard Options area 102

Contents

Dictionary preferences 102
    Language area 102
    Hyphenation Exceptions area 103
    User Dictionary area 104
Spelling preferences 104
    Spelling area 104
    Dynamic Spelling area 104
Autocorrect preferences 105
Notes preferences 106
Story Editor Display preferences 107
    Text Display Options area 107
    Cursor Options area 108
Display Performance preferences 109
    Options area 109
    Adjust View Settings area 110
    Scrolling area 110
Appearance of Black preferences 110
    Options for Black on RGB and Grayscale Devices area 110
    Overprinting of [Black] area 111
File Handling preferences 111
    Document Recovery Data area 112
    Saving InDesign files 112
    Snippet Import area 113
    Version Cue area 113
    Images area 113
Clipboard Handling pane 113
    Clipboard area 114
    When Pasting Text and Tables from Other Applications area 114
Setting Other Global Preferences 115
Setting up automatic program updates 115
Customizing keyboard shortcuts 116
    Using and modifying default shortcuts 116
    Viewing and printing shortcuts 119
Customizing menus 120
Color management settings 120
Modifying Defaults for Documents, Text, and Objects 121
Document defaults 121
Text defaults 123
Object defaults 124
Modifying Defaults for Views 125
Setting Color and Style Defaults 127
Reverting Preferences and Defaults 127
Changing Views 127
Zooming and scrolling 128
    The Zoom tool 128
    Zoom options in the View menu 128

The Zoom field and pop-up menu 130
The Hand tool 130
The Navigator panel 131
Object display options 131
Opening Multiple Document Windows 132
Summary 133

Part II: Document Fundamentals   135

Chapter 4: Creating, Opening, and Saving Documents 137

Taking Stock before You Begin 137
Setting Up a New Publication..138
Creating new documents 139
Creating your own document types 142
Opening Documents and Templates..142
Opening documents versus opening templates..147
Working with files in the Bridge file system 148
Converting documents created with other programs....................................149
QuarkXPress 150
PageMaker 150
Recovering a document after a crash or power failure....................................151
Saving Documents and Templates 151
Saving documents versus saving templates 152
Knowing how to not save changes 154
Saving Files in Other Formats 154
Export formats for whole documents 154
Export formats for document elements..155
Working with exported tagged text files 156
Exporting files as graphics 158
Managing File Versions with Version Cue 160
Understanding the Version Cue interface 160
Working with versions 162
Managing files 164
Summary 165

Chapter 5: Working with Pages 167

Working with Multi-page Documents..167
Adding pages 168
Deleting pages 170
Copying and moving pages..170
Working within a document 170
Working across documents 171
Starting documents on a left page..172
Controlling page shuffling 173
Creating gatefold spreads 173

Contents

Working with Page Numbers 175

Dividing a Document into Sections 176

Navigating Documents and Pages..179

    Navigating by page number 179

    Navigating with the menus and shortcuts...................................180

    Navigating with the Pages panel 181

    Using the Navigator panel 181

        Changing view magnification 182

        Scrolling with the Navigator panel 182

        Other options in the Navigator panel 182

Adjusting Page Layouts and Objects..183

Summary 186

Chapter 6: Working with Layers 187

Understanding Layers...187

Creating Layers 191

    Creating a layer..191

Working with Objects on Layers 192

    The active layer 192

    Selecting objects on layers 193

    Placing objects on layers..193

    Moving objects to different layers 194

Manipulating Layers..194

    Selecting layers 194

    Hiding layers 195

    Locking layers 195

    Preventing layers from printing or exporting 196

    Rearranging layers 196

    Combining layers 197

    Deleting layers 197

    Controlling guides 198

Summary 198

Chapter 7: Creating Layout Standards. 199

Creating and Applying Master Pages..200

    The Pages panel 201

    Creating a new master page 205

        Basing a master page on another master page 206

        Creating master pages from document pages 207

    Importing a master page...207

        Duplicating a master 208

        Deleting a master 208

    Laying out a master page 208

    Applying a master page to document pages 210

    Modifying master items on document pages................................212

Using Templates 213

    Creating templates 213

    Modifying templates 215

    Creating documents from templates 215

Storing Objects in Libraries 215

    Adding and deleting library objects 218

    Cataloging library objects 219

    Copying library objects onto document pages 221

Using Ruler Guides and Grids 221

    Ruler guides 222

        Creating ruler guides manually 222

        Creating a set of guides automatically 222

        Working with ruler guides 223

    Working with column guides 225

    Working with the baseline grid 225

    Working with the document grid 227

Summary 228

Chapter 8: Defining Colors, Tints, and Gradients. 229

Defining Color Terms 230

Understanding Process and Spot Color..231

    Identifying methods of color printing 231

    Mixing spot and process colors...232

    Converting spot color to process color 232

Working with Color Models 232

Understanding Paper Variation Models..234

Defining Colors and Tints 236

    Creating colors the ideal way: the Swatches panel 237

        Creating tints 240

        Creating mixed colors..241

    Using the Colors panel 243

    Importing and sampling colors..245

        Importing swatches..245

        Importing colors from graphics....................................245

        Sampling colors 246

Working with Gradients 248

    Creating gradients 248

    Creating unnamed gradients...250

    Adjusting gradient angle and location...................................251

Managing Swatches 253

    Editing swatches..253

    Merging swatches 253

    Deleting swatches 253

    Duplicating swatches 254

Applying Colors, Tints, and Gradients 254

Summary 256

Contents

Part III: Object Fundamentals   257

Chapter 9: Adding Frames and Lines **259**

Creating a Text Frame 260
Creating a Graphics Frame 262
Converting Frames for Specific Content 264
Drawing Straight Lines 265
Summary 267

Chapter 10: Manipulating Objects **269**

Selecting Objects 269
    Understanding the selection tools 270
    Selecting objects 271
    Selecting overlapping objects 273
        The Select submenu 273
        Keyboard shortcuts 275
        Control panel selection buttons 275
    Selecting multiple objects 276
    Deselecting objects 276
Moving Objects 277
Creating Copies of Objects 278
    Copying objects within documents 278
    Copying objects between documents 280
Deleting Objects 281
Preventing Objects from Printing 282
Aligning and Distributing Objects 282
Positioning Objects Precisely with Guides 286
Summary 287

Chapter 11: Transforming Objects **289**

Resizing and Scaling Objects 289
    Resizing methods 290
        Using the mouse 290
        Using the Control or Transform panel 290
    Scaling methods 291
Performing Other Transformations 293
    Rotating objects 293
        Using the Rotate tool 294
        Using the panels 294
    Using the Shear tool 296
    Flipping objects 296
Repeating Transformations 297
Replacing Object Attributes 298
Summary 300

Chapter 12: Applying Effects to Objects **301**

Working with Strokes...302

    Adding strokes 302

    Creating stroke styles 306

Adding Corner Options 309

Applying Lighting Effects 311

    Using the Effects panel 312

    Applying transparency 312

    Applying drop shadows and inner shadows 315

        Applying inner shadows 318

    Applying feathering 318

        Applying basic feathering 319

        Applying directional feathering 320

        Applying gradient feathering..320

    Applying outer and inner glows 321

        Applying an outer glow 321

        Applying an inner glow 322

    Applying beveling and embossing 322

    Applying satin effects 323

Summary 324

Chapter 13: Orchestrating Objects **325**

Stacking Objects..326

Combining Objects into a Group 329

    Using groups within groups 329

    Selecting objects within groups...330

    Ungrouping 331

Locking Objects 331

Nesting Objects within Frames..332

Nesting Frames within Other Frames 332

Creating Inline Frames 333

    Creating an inline frame with the Paste command 334

    Creating an inline frame with the Place command 335

    Creating an inline frame using the Anchored Object command 336

    Adjusting inline frames...338

    Deleting inline frames 339

Setting Up "Follow Me" Anchored Frames 339

    When to use anchored frames 339

    Adding anchored frames..340

    Converting existing frames to anchored frames.................................343

    Adjusting anchored frames 343

    Releasing and deleting anchored frames 343

Wrapping Text around Objects...344

    Using the Text Wrap panel 344

    Setting text-wrap preferences 348

    Changing the shape of a text wrap 349

Contents

Defining and Applying Object Styles 349
    Creating object styles 350
        The General pane 351
        The Fill pane...352
        The Stroke pane 352
        The Stroke & Corner Options pane 353
        The Paragraph Styles pane 354
        The Text Frame General Options pane 355
        The Text Frame Baseline Options pane 355
        The Story Options pane 356
        The Text Wrap & Other pane 356
        The Anchored Object Options pane 357
        The Frame Fitting Options pane 357
    Managing object styles 358
    Using style groups 359
    Understanding predefined styles...360
    Applying object styles...360
        Handling existing formatting 360
        Removing an object style from an object 361
Managing Links 361
    Managing file relations 362
    Managing versions 364
    Navigating directly to files 364
    Getting detailed information...364
    Working with InCopy files 365
    Managing the panel itself 365
Summary 365

Part IV: Text Fundamentals   367

Chapter 14: Importing Text Files. 369

Determining Where to Format Documents...369
Preparing Text Files 370
    Preserving special features in text files 370
        Tables 372
        Headers and footers 372
        Footnotes and endnotes 372
        Hyperlinks 373
        Inline graphics and text boxes 373
    Avoiding text-file pitfalls..373
        Fast save 373
        Software versions 373
Adding Text 374
    Using the Type tool..374
    Pasting text..375

Dragging and dropping text 376

Importing text with the Place dialog box 377

    Import options for Microsoft Word and RTF files 379

    Import options for text-only files 382

    InCopy files 384

    Import options for Microsoft Excel files 384

    Import options for Tagged Text files 385

Summary 386

Chapter 15: Flowing Text through a Document. 387

Working with Text Frames 388

    Creating text frames on master pages 389

        Creating a master text frame 389

        Modifying master text frames 390

    Drawing additional text frames..391

        Creating text frames on master pages 391

        Creating rectangular and variable-shaped text frames 393

Threading Text Frames..394

    Threading frames manually 394

    Threading frames semiautomatically..395

    Threading frames and adding pages automatically 396

        Placing text while autoflowing 396

        Autoflowing after placing text..396

    Breaking and rerouting threads...397

Adjusting Columns 398

    Specifying columns in master frames 398

    Adjusting columns in text frames 398

    Placing rules between columns..399

Managing Spacing and Alignment within Text Frames 400

Working with Overset Text...401

Summary 401

Chapter 16: Editing and Formatting Text 403

Editing Text 403

    Controlling text view 403

    Navigating text 405

    Highlighting text 405

    Cutting, copying, and pasting text 405

    Deleting and replacing text 405

    Undoing text edits 407

Correcting Spelling Mistakes 407

    Fixing spelling on the fly 407

    Checking spelling as you type 409

    Using the Check Spelling dialog box 409

    Working with multiple languages 411

Customizing the Spelling and Hyphenation Dictionaries 413

Contents

Customizing the spelling dictionary 413
Customizing hyphenation points 415
Setting spelling and hyphenation dictionary preferences..............................416
Searching and Replacing...418
Searching and replacing text 419
Changing special characters 425
Searching and replacing formatting 426
Changing fonts globally 427
Working with saved search queries..428
Adjusting Text Appearance in Text Frames 430
Setting text frame options 430
Working with Notes 433
Summary 435

Chapter 17: Specifying Character Attributes 437

Working with Character Formats 438
Changing Font Family, Font Style, and Font Size 441
Selecting fonts 443
Changing font size 445
Applying Other Character Formats...446
Horizontal Scale and Vertical Scale 448
Baseline Shift 448
Skew (false italic) 448
Language 449
All Caps and Small Caps...450
Superscript and Subscript...451
Underline and Strikethrough 451
Ligatures...452
OpenType options 453
No Break 455
Leaving Space between Characters and Lines 456
Kerning 456
Tracking 457
Leading 458
Summary 459

Chapter 18: Specifying Paragraph Attributes 461

Understanding Paragraph Basics..461
Using leading 463
Controlling alignment and indents 465
Alignment...465
Indents 467
Lock to Baseline Grid 468
Adding Space between Paragraphs 469
Adding Drop Caps 470

Adding Automatic Bullets and Numbered Lists 472
Controlling Hyphenation and Justification 473
    Manual hyphenation... 474
    Automatic hyphenation 474
    Justifications controls 476
    Composing text 479
        Adobe Single-Line Composer 479
        Adobe Paragraph Composer 479
Setting Other Paragraph Formats 480
    Keep Options 480
    Paragraph rules.. 482
    Optical margin override 483
Summary 484

Chapter 19: Creating Special Text Formatting 485

Using Bulleted and Numbered Lists 486
    Defining lists 486
    Applying lists 489
    Working with imported lists 489
Formatting Fractions 490
    Applying a fraction typeface 490
    Formatting fractions manually 491
Reversing Type out of Its Background... 492
Creating Sidebars and Pull-Quotes 493
Optical Margin Alignment 494
End-of-Story Markers... 495
Underline and Strikethrough Options 496
    Converting text into shapes 498
Making Text Follow a Path 499
Summary 500

Chapter 20: Setting Up Styles 501

Creating and Applying Styles 502
    Paragraph styles 502
        Creating paragraph styles 503
        Applying paragraph styles... 505
        Overriding existing formatting 505
        Managing paragraph styles 506
        Using style groups 508
    Character styles 509
        Creating and applying character styles 509
        Overriding character styles 511
        Managing and grouping character styles 512
Working with Nested Styles 512

Contents

Changing Styles 514

    Modifying styles 514

    Modifying text that's been styled with a style 515

Importing Styles 516

    Importing styles from InDesign documents 516

    Working with style sheets in imported text files 517

        Editing imported paragraph style sheets 518

        Overriding imported paragraph styles...............................518

        Exporting styles 519

Summary 519

Chapter 21: Using Special Characters. 521

Inserting Glyphs...521

    Using keyboard shortcuts 522

    Using menus 524

    Using the Glyphs panel 524

        Creating glyph sets 526

        Sharing glyph sets 527

Working with OpenType Variants...527

Using Other Tools to Access Special Characters 531

Understanding Special Spaces, Dashes, and Quotes 534

    Using special spaces 534

        Nonbreaking spaces 535

    Fixed-width spaces..535

    Using dashes 536

        All about em dashes 536

        All about en dashes..537

    Using quotes and apostrophes 537

        Entering keyboard quotes 538

        Typing reverse single quotes 538

        Handling adjacent single and double quotes.....................538

Working with Foreign Languages 538

Summary 544

Part V: Business Document Fundamentals   545

Chapter 22: Setting Up Tabs and Tables. 547

Using the Tabs Panel 548

    Tab style buttons 549

    X field..549

    Leader field...551

    Align On field 552

    Tab ruler 552

    Position Panel above Text Frame button 552

    Flyout menu..553

Creating Tables...553
    Creating a table..555
        Table Setup pane...556
        Row Strokes and Column Strokes panes 556
        Fills pane 558
        Headers and Footers pane 558
    Working with rows and columns 559
        Adding and deleting 559
        Manipulating rows and columns 560
    Working with cells 560
        Text pane 561
        Strokes and Fills pane 561
        Rows and Columns pane 563
        Diagonal Lines pane 563
        Other cell options 564
    Using table and cell styles...565
Converting Tabs to Tables 568
Summary 569

Chapter 23: Automating Text **571**
Automating Page Numbers..572
Using Section Markers 572
Using Text Variables 573
    Creating text variables 573
    Formatting text variables 575
    Editing and managing text variables 576
    Inserting text variables 576
Working with Merged Data 577
    Setting up merged data...578
    Creating pages with merged data 579
    Working with multiple records per page..582
Using Tagged Text for Database Publishing...584
Summary 586

Chapter 24: Working with Footnotes, Indexes, and TOCs **587**
Working with Footnotes..587
    Numbering and Formatting pane 589
    Layout pane 590
Indexing Documents and Books 591
    Choosing an indexing style 592
    Using the Index panel...593
        Understanding Reference and Topic modes..593
        Entering index items via the Index panel 594
        Entering index items using keyboard shortcuts.................................597
        Editing index entries..597
        Working with the index 598

Creating Tables of Contents 600
    Planning a TOC 600
    Defining a TOC 601
Summary 605

Chapter 25: Creating Multi-Document Projects 607

Planning Your Book 609
Creating and Opening Books 609
    Adding chapters to books 610
    Opening and editing chapters 610
    Understanding a book panel's status reports 612
Working with Style Sources 612
Working with Page Numbers and Sections 614
    Numbering pages consecutively 614
    Numbering pages with sections 615
        Manual numbering updates 616
    Specifying chapter numbers 616
Printing Chapters and Books 617
Summary 618

Part VI: Graphics Fundamentals   619

Chapter 26: Importing Graphics. 621

Preparing Graphics Files...622
    Graphics embedded in text files 622
    Issues with vector files 624
        Embedded fonts 624
        PostScript files: EPS, DCS, Illustrator, and PDF.........................624
        Other vector formats...626
    Issues with bitmap formats 626
        Professional-level bitmap formats 626
        Web-oriented bitmap formats 628
        Other bitmap formats..629
Identifying Color Issues 629
    Color systems 629
    Calibrated color 630
Exploring Methods for Importing Graphics 630
    Using the Place dialog box 631
    Using import options 633
        Import options for bitmap graphics 634
        Import options for vector file formats 637
    Using other ways to import graphics 639
        Copy and paste 640
        Drag and drop 640
Summary 641

Chapter 27: Fitting Graphics and Frames Together **643**

Fitting Graphics within Their Frames 643
  Resizing a graphic's frame 644
  Moving a graphic in its frame 644
  Using an irregular frame 644
Figuring Out the Fitting Commands 645
Working with Clipping Paths 648
  Using a graphic's own clipping path 648
    Using the clipping path as a mask 649
    Using the clipping path as a wrap boundary 649
  Creating a clipping path in InDesign 650
  Modifying clipping paths 652
  Deleting clipping paths 653
Summary 653

Chapter 28: Drawing Free-Form Shapes and Curved Paths **655**

Finding Out All about Paths 656
  The properties of a path 656
    Closure 656
    Stroke 657
    Fill 657
    Contents 657
  The anatomy of a path 658
Drawing Lines with the Pen Tool 660
  Straight and zigzag lines 660
  Curved lines 662
    Curved segments connected by smooth points 662
    Curved segments connected by corner points 664
  Combining straight and curved segments 665
Drawing Free-Form Shapes 667
Editing Free-Form Lines and Shapes 668
  Adding and deleting anchor points 669
  Modifying segments 671
    Moving anchor points 671
    Converting anchor points 672
    Manipulating direction handles 673
  Working with open and closed paths 674
    Extending an open path and connecting open paths 674
    Closing an open path 675
    Opening a closed path 676
  Using the Scissors tool 676
Working with Compound Paths 678
  Creating compound paths 679
  Editing compound paths 680
  Changing a path's direction 681

Splitting a compound path 681
Using the Pathfinder...682
Using Other Path Effects...683
The Convert Shape options 683
The Smooth tool..684
The Erase tool..684
The Corner Options dialog box 685
Summary 686

Part VII: Output Fundamentals 687

Chapter 29: Preparing for Color Prepress. 689

Managing Color Management...690
Setting up your system 692
Adjusting the on-screen display 694
Setting monitor bit depth 694
Adjusting InDesign's color display settings 694
Adjusting color output settings...695
Setting color management policies 695
Adjusting bitmap images' color...697
Adjusting blackness 697
Applying profiles to images 699
Changing document color settings 701
Managing color during output 704
Saving color-management preferences 704
Working with Color Traps 704
Understanding trap methods 705
Specifying knockout and overprinting 705
Specifying trapping presets...707
Applying trapping to pages...710
Summary 711

Chapter 30: Preparing for Printing 713

Making Initial Preparations 713
Setting up Macintosh printers...714
Setting up Windows printers 716
Windows XP..716
Windows Vista..718
Preflighting Your Document 720
Creating a Document Package 725
Dealing with Service Bureaus 727
Sending documents versus output files.......................................727
Determining output settings 728
Ensuring correct bleeds 729
Sending oversized pages 730
Setting up Booklets..730
Summary 735

Chapter 31: Printing Techniques 737

Selecting InDesign Printing Options 738
  Common options 738
  The General pane 741
  The Setup pane...742
    Paper size and orientation 742
    Scaling, positioning, and tiling options 744
  The Marks and Bleeds pane 745
    Printer's marks 745
    Bleeds and slugs 747
  The Output pane 748
  The Graphics pane 751
  The Color Management pane 753
  The Advanced pane 754
    Bitmap printing 754
    OPI settings 754
    Transparency flattening 755
  The Summary pane 756
Working with Spot Colors and Separations 756
  Managing color and ink output 756
  Adjusting screen angles 759
Working with Transparency 760
  Using transparency the ideal way 760
  Flattening transparency during output 761
    Creating flattener presets 761
    Applying flattener presets 763
    Previewing flattener settings 763
Summary 764

Chapter 32: Creating Prepress Files 765

Selecting the Best Prepress File Option 765
  Exporting to PDF 766
  Exporting to EPS 766
  Printing to EPS or PostScript files 767
Creating PDF Files 767
  Exporting PDF files 767
    Common options 768
    The General pane 769
    The Compression pane 771
    The Marks and Bleeds pane 772
    The Output pane 774
    The Advanced pane 776
    The Security pane 777
    The Summary pane 779
  Using Distiller job options 779
  Printing to PDF files 780

Contents

Exporting EPS Files 782
    The General pane 782
    The Advanced pane 784
Creating Output Files 785
Summary 786

Part VIII: Electronic Publishing Techniques   787

Chapter 33: Creating Electronic Documents 789

Using Hyperlinks 789
    Creating hyperlinks 790
    Modifying and deleting hyperlinks 793
Creating Bookmarks 794
Creating Page Actions..796
    Creating buttons...796
    Creating states 797
    Associating actions 798
Embedding Movies and Sound..800
    The Movie Options dialog box 801
    The Sound Options dialog box 801
Exporting to the Web 802
    General pane 803
    Images pane 804
    Advanced pane 805
    Working with exported files 806
Exporting eBooks 808
Summary 809

Chapter 34: Working with XML 811

Importing and Creating XML Tags 812
    Importing tags 812
    Creating tags...815
    Mapping tags and styles 816
Applying Tags...816
Taking Advantage of Other XML Options...817
Exporting XML Files 820
Summary 822

Part IX: Workgroup Publishing Techniques   823

Chapter 35: Working with Others 825

Sharing Elements with Other Users 826
    Where InDesign stores what 826
    Preference files 828

Color definitions..828
Paragraph, character, table, cell, and object styles.....................828
Spelling dictionaries 829
Graphics and text files 830
Libraries 830
Snippets 830
Templates 831
Output settings 831
Master pages 831
InDesign documents 832
Interface preferences 832
Mixing Mac and Windows Environments 833
InDesign differences 833
Which elements transfer 834
Which elements don't transfer 835
Platform differences 836
Filenames 836
Font differences 836
Transfer methods 838
Working with Other Creative Suite Applications 838
Working with graphics and colors 838
Working with Web content..838
Working with Adobe Bridge 839
File context...839
Bridge interface 841
Suite functionality 841
InDesign-specific functionality 841
Summary 842

Chapter 36: Workgroup Editing with InCopy **843**
Setting up Workgroup Assignments 843
Identifying the user 844
Preparing story files for InCopy 844
Creating story assignments 845
Adding stories to assignments...846
Exporting InCopy story files 847
Packaging assignments 848
Editing and manipulating assigned stories 848
Using the InCopy Program 849
Story views 849
Story checkout, check-in, and saving 850
Revisions tracking..850
Special features..852
Summary 853

Contents

Part X: Extending InDesign   855

Chapter 37: Using Plug-Ins 857

Using the Default Plug-Ins 857
Purchasing Special-Purpose Plug-Ins 859
Understanding How Plug-Ins Work within InDesign 859
Managing Plug-Ins 860
Summary 861

Chapter 38: Using Scripts 863

Using Scripts 864
   Script locations..864
   Scripting principles 865
Exploring JavaScript 867
   Learning the language..867
   What you need to write and run scripts 868
      Running your script 868
      Saving your script 869
Exploring AppleScript 869
   Learning the language..869
   What you need to write and run scripts 869
      Checking for syntax errors 869
      Running your script 870
      Saving your script 870
   Locating more AppleScript tools..871
Exploring VBA 872
   Learning the language..872
   What you need to write and run scripts 872
      Running your script 873
      Saving your script 873
Creating and Running Scripts...874
   Writing simple scripts..874
      JavaScript 875
      AppleScript..875
      VBA 876
   Labeling items 877
      JavaScript 877
      AppleScript..877
      VBA 877
   Writing conditional scripts 877
      JavaScript 878
      AppleScript..878
      VBA 878
      JavaScript 878
      AppleScript..879
      VBA 879
Summary 879

Part XI: Appendixes   881

Appendix A: Installing or Upgrading InDesign 883

Appendix B: What's New in InDesign CS3 889

Appendix C: Switching from QuarkXPress 907

Appendix D: Switching from PageMaker 923

Appendix E: More Resources. 931

Appendix F: Shortcuts Cheat Sheet 933

Index 945

Foreword

InDesign CS3 has undergone some dramatic changes with this new version, enhancing its integration and streamlining its interface. While new capabilities can be exciting, they are often equally disconcerting and confusing — both to beginners and to longtime users.

In recent years, the market for desktop publishing programs has widened. Once considered an exclusive tool for publishing pros and high-end graphic artists, DTP now appeals to folks who want to design anything from a résumé to a flyer to a self-published book. Today, even simple products call for a refined, polished presentation, and products like InDesign are on hand to provide the tools.

That's where *Adobe InDesign CS3 Bible* steps in. While many users depend on product documentation to guide them through the basics, an application's online help files go only so far. A program's documentation may give you a broad overview, but there is little elaboration about the subtleties and complexities of what an application lets you accomplish. *Adobe InDesign CS3 Bible* offers in-depth treatment, giving you a complete picture of everything you need to know about this program, and, of course, does its best to answer all your questions. It's not called a Bible for nothing!

You couldn't have a better InDesign guide than author Galen Gruman. For 20 years, Galen has specialized in reviewing and publishing instructional books about desktop publishing applications. As the author of the *InDesign Bible* series, Galen has been writing about this program since its inception. Whenever I have any questions about InDesign, I know whom to ask.

Jackie Dove
Senior Reviews Editor

Preface

The turning point was sometime in 2005, when InDesign became the leading desktop publishing program. References to InDesign as a scrappy underdog struggling to compete with the established QuarkXPress began to wane, just as the number of QuarkXPress users did. That's why chances are that InDesign CS3 is not the first version of InDesign that you have used.

Whether you used a previous version of InDesign or a program like QuarkXPress or PageMaker, you'll find that InDesign CS3 — the program's fifth version — takes a little getting used to. Adobe has updated the interface throughout (as part of an ongoing reinvention of its Creative Suite software). Adobe has also enhanced many of InDesign's capabilities, in some cases by simplifying how they work and in other cases by extending existing functionality in useful new ways, such as through the newfound support of multiple file import, master page import, saved searches, table and cell styles, and style groups.

But don't think for a minute that InDesign CS3 is only about refining how the software works; the newest version adds some major new capabilities such as variable text, a redesigned user interface, object-level search, new lighting effects, inclusion of some InCopy group-editing features, and XHTML export. The program will be both familiar and unfamiliar.

Although Adobe has made many features work a little more intuitively, the fact remains that InDesign does a lot of things for a wide range of users, so it remains daunting. The software is certainly more complex than ever, a whopping collection of capabilities that you may never glimpse more than a fraction of in your daily use. I'm very much reminded of the Louvre: You just can't take it all in during one or even a few visits.

Layout artists have an incredibly powerful tool in the form of InDesign to let them deliver on their creative aspirations and vision. I can only hope that this book helps you achieve and indeed increase those ambitions.

Acknowledgments

Thanks to the development and product marketing staff at Adobe for providing early versions of the InDesign CS3 software, providing insights into their thinking as they brought in new features, and listening to suggestions on making it even better. Thanks to the editors and production staff at Wiley Publishing for their efforts in making this book possible, especially to project editor Chris Wolfgang and technical editor Jonathan Woolson for their improvements to the book's content and clarity.

The InDesignCentral.com Web site and its contents are copyrighted by The Zango Group.

Original photographs are copyrighted by Galen Gruman and Ingall W. Bull III, unless otherwise credited.

Introduction

Welcome to *Adobe InDesign CS3 Bible* — your personal guide to a powerful, full-featured publishing program that offers precise but flexible control over all aspects of page design. My goal is to guide you each step of the way through the publishing process, showing you how to make Adobe's InDesign CS3 work for you. You'll also learn tips and tricks about publishing design that you can use in any document, whether it was created in InDesign or not.

Taking the best from the two schools of thought on desktop publishing, InDesign merges the highly structured approach of programs such as QuarkXPress and Ventura Publisher with the more naturalistic approach of Adobe PageMaker, which InDesign all but replaced in 1999. Thus, InDesign offers a wide range of desktop-publishing capabilities for sophisticated designers who develop magazines, books, ads, and product brochures. It also gives the power of the press to individuals and groups who use the program's impressive set of publishing tools to communicate their thoughts, dreams, and philosophies.

Version CS3 of InDesign takes that strong basis and makes it even better, often in subtle ways meant to make the workflow process easier and more intuitive. While InDesign's abundance of features necessarily makes its interface complex, Adobe continues to find ways to simplify it. The latest version brings in some major changes to how the controls are managed, adopting some of the thinking of Macromedia Dreamweaver, which Adobe acquired in 2006. And it has also added new features, from small enhancements in space options and file import to significant additions like lighting effects, XHTML export, and variable text. Many existing features are extended with new capabilities, such as the ability to create style groups for easier management and the ability to search-and-replace object attributes and special symbols in addition to text formatting.

InDesign lets you take advantage of modern electronic publishing's full range of possibilities. Not only can you produce high-quality, lively flyers, newsletters, magazines, and similar publications in InDesign, you can also create rich, colorful documents that can be viewed on the Web, distributed by CD, or set directly to a printing press for faithful print reproduction.

In a nutshell, InDesign is meant to help those who educate, inform, and document today's world. Join me in learning how to use this powerful program.

What This Book Offers

So, because InDesign comes with good documentation that is full of examples, why do you need this book? To see the bigger picture. Publishing design involves much more than understanding a particular program's tools; it involves knowing when, how, and, most importantly, why to use them. In this book, I help you realize the potential of InDesign by applying its tools to real-world publishing design needs. I also identify any weaknesses and explain how to overcome them — something that vendor manuals rarely do.

Some desktop publishers have years of high-end creative, design-intensive experience. Others are just getting started in publishing, perhaps by producing simple newsletters or flyers to advertise a community event. Not a few are exploring the brave new world of Web publishing.

Desktop publishers fall into several classes:

- Designers new to InDesign but familiar with other desktop publishing software
- Designers familiar with print publishing but new to electronic publishing
- Experienced designers new to desktop technologies
- Novice designers new to desktop technologies

No matter which class you're in, this book addresses your needs. You don't need a degree in design or ten years' experience producing national ad campaigns — you can use this book if you're responsible for developing and implementing the look of any document, whether it's a four-page company newsletter or a four-color billboard ad. The basic techniques and issues are the same for both ends of the spectrum. And of course, this book covers in detail the specialized needs — table creation, image control, color output, and electronic publishing for example — of specialty designers. (If you're just learning such advanced techniques, be sure to read the sidebars that explain the underlying issues.) Regardless of your level of experience with desktop publishing, this book can help you use InDesign efficiently, and guide you to discovering more of the program's potential.

What distinguishes this book from the rest of its type is that it does not attempt to be a substitute for the documentation that accompanies InDesign. Instead, it guides you through the *process* of publishing a document, regardless of whether that document is your first or your thousandth.

How to Read This Book

Adobe InDesign CS3 Bible is made up of 38 chapters and six appendixes divided into 11 parts, in addition to the QuickStart that appears just before Part I begins. If you're a novice InDesign user but familiar with desktop publishing, I suggest you read the book in order, because the process of page design is presented in the typical publishing workflow. You first learn how (and why) to create basic pages, containers, placeholders, and templates; then you learn how to work with specific elements (such as text and graphics); and finally, you learn how to use special effects and deal with prepress issues (such as output control, image manipulation, trapping, and printing).

If you're new to publishing, be sure to start with Part VIII, Electronic Publishing Techniques, which teaches novice publishers the basics. Experienced publishers should at least skim this part as well — you're likely to find new ideas and perspectives on how you approach your work.

Whether you're reading the book sequentially or nonsequentially, you'll find the many cross-references helpful. Publication design is ultimately successful because the result is more than the sum of its parts, and the tools used to create and implement your designs cannot be used in isolation. Because this is true, having one "right" order or grouping of content is impossible. The cross-references let you know where to get additional information when what you're seeking to understand or learn doesn't fit the way I've organized this book.

Following is a brief description of the parts in *Adobe InDesign CS3 Bible*.

InDesign QuickStart

This guide walks you through the creation of a document to give you a quick tour of the program, from creation to printing. It's a convenient way to see the main InDesign features in action and quickly get a sense of how they work, whether you're new to publishing or new to InDesign.

Part I: Welcome to InDesign

This part walks you through the initial steps of using InDesign to create your publications. I give you a basic introduction to InDesign itself, explaining the concepts it uses in its layout approach. I also highlight what's special about InDesign in general and about InDesign CS3 in particular. But most of the part focuses on understanding all the tools and panels available to you and all the preferences you can set, so you can see the big picture all in one place.

Part II: Document Fundamentals

This part explains how to create the basic containers — documents, pages, and layers — of a publishing project and how to set the standards for your documents, from master pages, libraries, and templates to guides and colors. InDesign comes with a set of tools that lets you automate repetitive work, apply common elements to a range of pages, and customize page settings, among other capabilities. This part walks you though the ins and outs of all of them.

Part III: Object Fundamentals

This part explains how InDesign's frame and line tools work so you can create and manipulate layout objects. With these building blocks, you construct and alter almost all the components in a layout, from the frame containers that hold text and pictures to original artwork you create in InDesign. You'll also learn how to move, group, copy, and lock such objects and how to automate repetitive object actions to save time. You can learn about the many transformations and effects you can apply objects, from skews to drop shadows, from text wrap to transparency. You can also learn how to manage the relationships between imported objects and their original files.

Part IV: Text Fundamentals

This part shows you how to import and work with text files, including the application of typographic features to really jazz up your layout and the tools to ensure that spelling and hyphenation are always correct. You can learn how to set up styles to automate the application of typography to document text, as well as how to use the insanely wide range of special symbols and characters available in InDesign.

Part V: Business Document Fundamentals

This new part covers the features — old and new — that appeal most to business document creators, from annual reports to product manuals. But of course you don't have to create these kinds of documents to take advantage of features such as tables, text variables, footnotes, indexes, tables of contents, and multi-chapter projects, so don't let the part's title intimidate you.

Part VI: Graphics Fundamentals

This part explains how to use InDesign to manipulate and work with graphics in your layout, whether imported from another program or created within InDesign. Although text carries the message, a picture is what gets your attention and often can say more than any collection of words. This part helps you get the most out of your graphics in InDesign. It also shows you how you can use the tools in InDesign to create a variety of shapes that can be used as original artwork or as specialty containers for text and images.

Part VII: Output Fundamentals

This part walks you though the output steps of publishing. You'll learn what you need to be aware of as well as how to output your documents for printing, whether to a local printer or through a service bureau.

Part VIII: Electronic Publishing Techniques

InDesign lets you create all sorts of documents for electronic distribution, such as on the Web or on CDs. This new part explains how to create to take advantage of hyperlinks, video, audio, and interactive buttons for use in PDF files, as well as how to create Web pages and eBooks using the new XHTML export features. Finally, you can learn the basics of working with XML, the structured content system widely used by Web-oriented content engines. InDesign can both create XML files and use XML files to turn templates into completed InDesign documents for automated publishing systems.

Part IX: Workgroup Publishing Techniques

Very few publishers work by themselves, and most have a whole raft of tools to work their miracles. The chapters in this new part expose you to key insights in working beyond InDesign, covering workgroup issues and the InCopy add-on program for multi-user editing. InDesign CS3 brings in several InCopy features directly into InDesign, so even if you don't buy InCopy, you'll still be using some of its features.

Part X: Extending InDesign

This part helps you expand your InDesign horizons through the use of plug-ins to add new capabilities, and the use of scripts to automate your work.

Part XI: Appendixes

The appendixes in this book take you through the ins and outs of how to install Adobe InDesign, what is new in version CS3, and how QuarkXPress and PageMaker users can more easily make the switch to InDesign. Appendix F includes all the shortcuts for both Macs and PCs in one place.

The companion Web site

No application exists in a vacuum. A publishing program is especially dependent on other applications: those that create the source files, those that manage printing, and those that manage fonts, for example. And applications change — sometimes, a vendor like Adobe adds features to a shipping product or fixes ones that don't work as expected. The companion site, www.InDesignCentral.com, is where you can keep current on the InDesign ecosystem, with links to related software tools, the sample files used in this book's QuickStart chapter, links to helpful resources such as usergroups, and if needed, updates to this book.

Conventions Used in This Book

Before I begin showing you the ins and outs of InDesign, I need to spend a few minutes reviewing the terms and conventions used in this book.

InDesign commands

The InDesign commands that you select by using the program menus appear in this book in normal typeface. When you choose some menu commands, a related pull-down menu or a pop-up menu appears. If this book describes a situation in which you need to select one menu, and then choose a command from a secondary menu or list box, it uses an arrow symbol. For example, "Choose Layout ⇨ Margins and Columns" means that you should choose the Margins and Columns command from the Layout menu.

Dialog boxes, panels, and panes

Like most modern programs, InDesign uses dialog boxes to offer up a bunch of related features in one place. It also uses a similar mechanism called a panel, which is essentially a dialog box that you can always keep open for easy access. Both of these mechanisms use an interface feature that has proved to be quite popular called *tabbed panes*. This is a method of stuffing several dialog boxes into one dialog box or several panels into one panel. You see tabs, like those in file folders, and by clicking a tab, the pane of options for that tab comes to the front of the dialog box or panel. This book will tell you to go to the pane, which you do by clicking the tab where the name of the pane is to display the pane. For example, "Go to the General pane" means click the General tab in the current dialog box or panel.

Dealing with Computer-Platform Appearance Issues

InDesign CS3 runs on Mac OS X 10.4 (Tiger), Mac OS X 10.5 (Leopard), Windows XP with Service Pack 2 or later installed, and Windows Vista. Most desktop publishers use Apple Computer's Mac, and thus most readers of this book will likely be Mac-based. That's why I use Mac screenshots in the illustrations throughout this book. (Plus, Adobe uses Windows screen shots in its documentation.) But the minority in publishing who use Microsoft's Windows continues to grow, especially for business-oriented and personal publishing, so I do show Windows screenshots when notable differences exist. Adobe has done a good job of ensuring that the interface for InDesign is almost identical — within the natural differences between Mac and Windows — on the two platforms.

Keyboard conventions

This book provides both the Macintosh and Windows shortcuts throughout, with the Mac shortcut first. In most cases, the Mac and Windows shortcuts are the same, except for the names of the keys, as follows.

InDesign for Mac's user interface uses symbols to indicate special keys in shortcuts, such as ⌘, whereas the Windows version uses the actual key names, such as Ctrl.

- The Mac's Command key (⌘) is the most-used shortcut key. Its Windows equivalent is Ctrl. (This key is sometimes known as the Apple key, since the key has both the ⌘ symbol and an open Apple logo [⌘] printed on it. But because there is also the Apple menu, indicated by a solid Apple logo [], in the Mac OS, it's best not to call this key the Apple key and then get confused with the Apple menu.)

- Shift is the same on the Mac and Windows. In many Mac program menus — including InDesign — Shift is displayed by the symbol ⇧.

- The Option key on the Mac is usually the same as the Alt key in Windows. In many Mac program menus — including InDesign — you see the symbol ⌥ used.

- The Control key on the Mac has no Windows equivalent (it is not the same as the Windows Ctrl key). Many Mac programs — including InDesign — indicate it with the symbol ⌃ in their menus.

- The Tab key is used both to move within fields in panes and dialog boxes and to insert the tab character in text. InDesign and many other Mac programs indicate it in menus with the symbol →|.

- The Return key (Mac) or Enter key (Windows) is used to apply a dialog box's settings and close the dialog box (equivalent to clicking OK or Done), as well as to insert a hard paragraph return in text. In InDesign and many other Mac programs, it is indicated in menus by the symbol ↵. Note that there is another key labeled Enter on most keyboards, in the numeric keypad. This sometimes works like the regular Return or Enter, but in InDesign text, it inserts a column break. I refer to it as *keypad Enter* in this book. In InDesign and many other Mac programs, it is indicated in menus by the symbol ⌤.

- The Delete key (Mac) and Backspace key (Windows) deletes text, one character at a time, to the left of the text-insertion point. Windows also has a separate Delete key that deletes text, one character at a time, to the right of the text-insertion point. The Mac's Clear key, although in the same position on the keyboard, does not delete text. In InDesign and many other Mac programs, the Delete key is indicated in menus by the symbol ⊠.

If you're supposed to press several keys at the same time, I indicate that by placing plus signs (+) between them. Thus, Shift + ⌘ + A means press and hold the Shift and ⌘ keys, then press A. After you've pressed A, let go of all three keys. (You don't need to hold down the last letter in the sequence.)

I also use the plus sign (+) to join keys to mouse movements. For example, Option + drag means to press and hold the Option key while dragging the mouse on the Mac, and Alt+drag means to press and hold the Alt key while dragging the mouse in Windows.

Also note that InDesign lets you change the shortcuts associated with menu and other commands (by choosing Edit ➪ Keyboard Shortcuts). Throughout the book, I assume the shortcuts in use are the default ones and that you haven't altered them.

Icons

I've used special graphic symbols, or *icons,* throughout this book. These icons call your attention to points that are particularly important or worth noting.

NEW FEATURE The New Feature icon indicates a technique or action that is new to or revised in InDesign CS3.

TIP The Tip icon indicates a technique or action in InDesign that will save you time or effort.

NOTE The Note icon indicates information that you should remember for future use — something that may seem minor or inconsequential but will, in reality, resurface.

CAUTION The Caution icon is used to warn you of potential hang-ups or pitfalls you may encounter while using InDesign (and how to avoid them).

CROSS-REF The Cross-Reference icon points you to different parts of the book that contain related or expanded information on a particular topic.

PLATFORM DIFFERENCES The Platform Difference icon alerts you to differences using InDesign on the Macintosh versus in Windows.

QUARKXPRESS The QuarkXPress icon alerts QuarkXPress users who are switching to InDesign to significant differences in function and approach between the two programs.

Quick Start

Building a Document from Start to Finish

Although InDesign CS3 is a complex program that lets you do everything from designing a fashion magazine to indexing a book to generating separation plates for professional printing, you can get started building documents with just a few simple skills. If you're in a hurry to get started on a document — or you have a job interview tomorrow based on your proficiency in InDesign — work through the steps in this section. You can learn the basic building blocks of documents (frames and lines) and the two primary tools (Selection and Direct Selection).

By all means, do not assume that these steps provide all you need to know about InDesign CS3. From here, head to related sections of the book and explore the full functionality of the program. If you're not sure where to start, figure out what you'll be doing the most. For example, if you'll be flowing text into a newsletter template, head to Part IV.

To create the sample document shown in Figure QS.1 — from my book *QuarkXPress to InDesign: Face to Face* (Wiley, 2005) — you need InDesign, a text file from a program such as Microsoft Word, a graphic file such as a TIFF file, and a laser or inkjet printer. You can follow the steps exactly (substituting your own text, graphic, and fonts), or you can vary the design as much as you want.

> **TIP** You can download the text and graphics used in this QuickStart example at www.InDesignCentral.com/QS.html. You have to supply your own fonts, however.

IN THIS CHAPTER

Creating a new document

Working with frames

Working with text

Working with lines

Creating and applying colors

Working with graphics

Applying lighting effects

Printing a composite

FIGURE QS.1

Combining formatted text and several graphics with a few simple frames and lines produces a completely designed book.

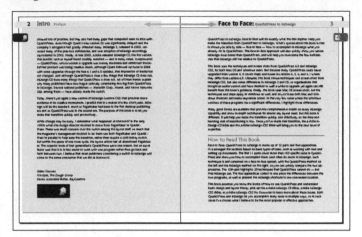

Creating a New Document

In this QuickStart, I assume that your copy of InDesign has been set with picas as the default measurement for vertical and horizontal measurement, one of two typical settings for publications. (The other is to set horizontal measurements at picas and vertical measurements at inches.) But for those who think in inches, I also provide values in inches. You set measurement defaults in the Ruler Units section of the Units & Increments pane of the Preferences dialog box, which you access by choosing InDesign ➪ Preferences ➪ Units & Increments or pressing ⌘+K on the Mac, or by choosing Edit ➪ Preferences ➪ Units & Increments or pressing Ctrl+K in Windows.

I also assume that your coordinates are set for the entire spread, not for individual pages. To make sure they are set for the spread, go to the Units & Increments pane of the Preferences dialog box and be sure that Spread is selected in the Origin pop-up menu.

When you create a new document in InDesign, you're actually specifying the final size and setup of the pages in the document.

1. **Start InDesign.**

2. **Choose File ➪ New ➪ Document, or press ⌘+N or Ctrl+N.**

   The New Document dialog box appears (see Figure QS.2).

3. **In the Width field, enter** `44p3` **or** `7.375 in` **(based on your preferences for picas or inches).** In the Height field, enter `55p6` or `9.25 in`. (Notice how the Page Size pop-up menu changes to Custom.)

Set up the page size and other attributes for your document in the New Document dialog box.

4. **Enable the Facing Pages check box, because this is a book printed on two sides, thus it needs both left- and right-page versions.**

5. **Enable the Master Text Frame check box.**

6. **Set the number of columns to 1.**

7. **In the Margins area, click the Make All Settings the Same iconic button (the chain icon) so the broken chain changes to an unbroken chain.** (This lets you set the margins independently.) Set the Inside margin to 7p6 (or 1.25 in if you prefer inches), Top to 5p9 (0.95833 in), Bottom to 4p3 (0.70833 in), and Outside to 5p (0.833 in).

8. **Click the Save Preset button and give these specifications a name, such as *Book*.**

   Assigning a name to these specifications lets you select these exact settings for future documents for this publication by choosing the preset name from the Document Preset pop-up menu.

9. **Click OK to create the new document's layout.**

   InDesign creates one page.

10. **Choose File ➪ Save As or press Shift+⌘+S or Ctrl+Shift+S.**

11. **In the Save As field, type** Book Intro.indd, **as shown in Figure QS.3.** Choose a location for the file, and then click Save.

FIGURE QS.3

Use the Save As dialog box to save and name a new document.

CROSS-REF For more information about creating a new document, see Chapter 4.

Working with Frames and Pages

By using the automatic text frame, you've already created the frame for the article text. But the article has colored frames at the top for the story title that you need to create via frames.

NOTE All measurements in this QuickStart are from the upper-left corner of the frames. In the Control panel, be sure that the upper-left square in the array of nine squares (the reference points) is black, which makes that point the *control point* from which all dimensions and transformations are applied. If it's not black, simply click it to make it the control point.

Frames can exist on document pages or on master pages. A master page is essentially an internal page template that you can apply to document pages, adding all the master page's attributes to any document pages you prefer. This speeds formatting of repetitive elements such as footers, headers, and folios.

To create a master page:

1. **Go to the Pages panel.** (If it is not available at the right-hand side of your screen, open it by choosing Window ➪ Pages, or by pressing ⌘+F12 or Ctrl+F12.)
2. **From the panel's flyout menu (the icon below the panel's close box), choose New Master.**

3. **In the New Master dialog box, enter a name for the master page that will help you remember what it is used for (such as *Intro* in this case).** Make sure Number of Pages is set to 2, so InDesign creates a master spread. Click OK.

    InDesign opens the master spread for you.

You're now ready to add objects to the master spread. You start with the page background, then add the folio at the top, and finally place the logos on the outside margins.

1. **Select the Rectangular Frame tool.** To see the names of tools, point at them until a Tool Tip displays.

2. **On the left-hand page, click and drag to create a frame that is approximately 43p3 (7.20833 in) wide and 49p9 (8.291667 in) tall, as shown in Figure QS.4.** You fine-tune the size and placement in the next steps. The new frame is selected, as indicated by the white handles. If the frame becomes deselected in the following steps, click on it to select it.

3. **Highlight the X field in the Control panel (Window ➪ Control, or Option+⌘+6 or Ctrl+Alt+6), which specifies the item's origin across (placement from the left edge of the page).** Type 1p (or 0.1667 in if you prefer inches) in this field.

FIGURE QS.4

Use any of the frame tools to create background shapes into which you can import a picture. Use the Control panel (at top) to precisely control position and size.

4. **Tab to the Y field, which specifies the item's origin down (placement from the top of the page).** Type 3p (0.5 in) in this field.

5. **Tab to the W field, which specifies the item's width.** Type 41p3 (7.20833 in) in this field.

6. **Tab to the H field, which specifies the item's height.** Type 49p9 (8.291667 in) in this field.

7. **Press Return or Enter to reposition.** Resize the frame according to the values entered.

8. **Choose Item ➪ Duplicate, or press Option+Shift+⌘+D or Ctrl+Alt+Shift+D.** If necessary, first click on the new frame to select it.

9. **Highlight the X field in the Control panel.** Type 44p3 (7.375 in), as shown in Figure QS.5

10. **Tab to the Y field.** Then type 3p (0.5 in). You add color to this frame later.

Now, create the frames for the icons that hang outside the margins:

- **Left-hand icon frame:** X: −1p6, Y: 4p6, W: 4p, and H: 2p3. (Or X: −0.25 in, Y: 0.75 in, W: 0.667 in, H: 0.375 in.)
- **Right-hand icon frame:** X: 86p6, Y: 4p6, W: 4p, and H: 2p3. (Or X: 14.41667 in, Y: 0.75 in, W: 0.667 in, H: 0.375 in.)

In Figure QS.1, you may have noticed that the corners of these icon frames are slightly rounded. That's easy to do in InDesign:

1. **Select the two folio frames (click one, Shift+click the other).**

2. **Choose Object ➪ Corner Options to open the Corner Options dialog box.**

3. **Choose Rounded from the Effect pop-up menu and enter 0p6 (0.5 in) in the Size field.** Click OK.

With the basic master spread created, it's time to add some pages to your document and apply the master spread to them:

1. **Add as many pages as you think you might need by choosing Insert Pages from the Pages panel's flyout menu.** Enter the number of pages desired in the Insert Pages dialog box's Pages field — enter 5 in this example — and click OK.

   You can always add more pages or delete extra ones later.

2. **In the flyout menu, choose Apply Master to Pages.** In the Apply Master dialog box, choose the master spread you just created from the Apply Master pop-menu and enter 1–6 in the To Pages field. Then click OK.

3. **Choose File ➪ Save, or press ⌘+S or Ctrl+S, to save your work.**

CROSS-REF For more information about working with frames, see Part III. For more on master pages, see Chapter 7.

FIGURE QS.5

Resizing and repositioning the second frame with the Control panel

Working with Text

In InDesign, text goes inside a text frame. You can type text into the frame or import a text file in various formats. Once text is inside the frame, you can change the font, size, color, and many more options.

> **TIP** What's nice about InDesign is that you can put text in any frame, whether it started life as a text frame or not. The only catch: If the frame has a graphic in it, then you can't make it into a text frame without first clearing out the graphic, as I describe in Chapter 10.

Now you create the frames for the folios on the master page you created in the last section:

1. **Select the Type tool.** (You can also use the Rectangle tool or the Rectangular Frame tool.)

   Now that you've created these two frames, use the same process to create the two folio frames at top. The dimensions for each are in Step 2.

   Also set both frames to have rounded corners, using the same settings as for the icon frames, as I describe in the previous section.

2. Follow the frame creation steps from the previous section and create two frames with the following positions and dimensions:

   ▪ **Left-hand folio frame:** X: –1p, Y: 1p3, W: 40p3, and H: 1p9. (Or X: –0.1667 in, Y: 0.208333 in, W: 6.45833 in, and H: 0.291667 in.)

   ▪ **Right-hand folio frame:** X: 51p9, Y: 1p3, W: 38p9, and H: 1p9. (Or X: 8.625 in, Y: 0.208333 in, W: 6.875 in, and H: 0.291667 in.)

3. **Be sure to select the Type tool.** Click in the left-hand folio frame to enter its folio. Type a tab character, then choose Type ➪ Insert Special Character ➪ Markers ➪ Current Page Number (or press Option+Shift+⌘+N or Ctrl+Alt+Shift+N). Type a tab character, the text Intro, an em space (Shift+⌘+M or Ctrl+Shift+M), and the text Preface. Don't worry about text alignment for now.

4. **Click in the right-hand folio frame and type** Face to Face: QuarkXPress to InDesign, **then type a tab character, and finally enter an automatic current page number by pressing Option+Shift+⌘+N or Ctrl+Alt+Shift+N.**

   Note how the page number appears as a letter — the same letter as the master page number, in fact.

5. **First in the left-hand frame and then in the right-hand frame, highlight the entire phrase and choose a font from the Control panel's Font menu (be sure the A iconic button is selected); the example uses Formata).** In the Font Size field, choose or enter 12 pt. Highlight the automatic page number and set the Font Size to 19 pt.

6. **In the left-hand frame, highlight the text until the word** Intro **and choose a font style from the Control panel's Font Style menu (the example uses Bold).** Also choose or enter 19 pt in the Font Size field. In the right-hand frame, highlight *Face to Face:*, then apply Bold as the Font Style and 19 pt as the Font Size. Highlight the automatic page number and set the Font Size to 19 pt. Figure QS.6 shows an example.

Now you put text in the text frame that was created through the automatic text frame feature earlier:

1. **Go to the document page by double-clicking the desired page in the Pages panel.** In this case, go to page 1.

2. **Choose File ➪ Place, or press ⌘+D or Ctrl+D.** The Place dialog box (shown in Figure QS.7) appears.

3. **Check Show Import Options.**

4. **Locate a text file in a format such as Microsoft Word.**

5. **Click to select the text file, then click Open.** The Microsoft Word Import Options dialog box appears.

6. **Be sure that Use Typographer's Quotes is checked.** In most cases, you want the Import Styles Automatically radio button selected, with both the Paragraph Style Conflicts and Character Style Conflicts pop-up menus set to Use InDesign Style Definition. You can save Word import settings for reuse later by clicking the Save Preset button. Then click OK to import the file.

FIGURE QS.6

When text is highlighted, you can format it using controls on the left side of the Control panel.

FIGURE QS.7

Choose File ⇨ Place, or press ⌘+D or Ctrl+D, to import text from a word processor.

InDesign shows the loaded-text icon (it looks like a tiny paragraph and also shows the first few words of the text) that indicates a file ready to be placed into a frame, as shown in Figure QS.8.

FIGURE QS.8

The loaded-text icon has a preview of the file you are importing.

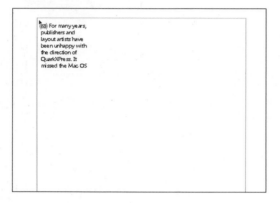

7. **Shift+click at the upper-left corner of the master text frame on page 1 to tell InDesign to pour the text into it and to all subsequent pages' master text frames.**

    If you were placing the text in another frame, you would just click the frame.

8. **Choose File ➪ Save, or press ⌘+S or Ctrl+S, to save your work.**

If the text file you import does not fit in the frame, a red square in the lower-right corner indicates that text is overflowing. There is no need to worry about that for these purposes. If you do not have a text file, simply type another sentence in the frame.

With the text placed, you now need to format it. Ideally, your Word file would use styles, so the imported text would have Word's styles associated with it. You then can edit those styles in InDesign to change the formatting globally.

Assuming that your Word text uses styles, modify them in InDesign as follows:

1. **Go to the Paragraph Styles panel (Type ➪ Paragraph Styles, or ⌘+F11 or Ctrl+F11).**

2. **Using the Type tool, click in any text whose formatting you want to change.**

    The current style applied, if any, is highlighted in the panel's style list. (If there is no style, [Basic Paragraph] is highlighted instead.)

3. **Double-click the style name to edit it.** Go through the various panes' options and click OK when done.

    All text using that style is updated automatically.

4. **Repeat Steps 2 and 3 for all styles that you want to edit.**

5. **Create any needed styles by choosing New Paragraph Style from the Paragraph Styles panel's flyout menu.** Go through the various panes to set the desired formatting, and click OK when you're done.

6. **Apply styles to paragraphs with no styles, or to text with the wrong styles, by clicking the appropriate paragraphs (or by highlighting a range of paragraphs) using the Type tool.** Then click the desired style from the Paragraph Styles panel, or choose it from the Control panel, as shown in Figure QS.9.

   If you want to override all local formatting applied within the paragraphs, Option+click or Alt+click the style name instead.

7. **Choose File ➪ Save, or press ⌘+S or Ctrl+S, to save your work.**

You can also create additional styles in InDesign and apply them to text by placing the text cursor anywhere in the desired paragraph and then clicking the desired style from the Paragraph Styles panel; to apply character styles, highlight the text with the Type tool, and then click the desired style from the Character Styles panel.

FIGURE QS.9

After you import text and apply styles, your first page should look something like this.

This is a good time to clean up the positioning of text in the folios, which involves setting tab stops:

1. **Open the Tabs panel by choosing Type ⇨ Tabs or pressing Shift+⌘+T or Ctrl+Shift+T.**

2. **With the Type tool, click in the left-hand page's folio text.**

3. **Enter** 3p3 **(or** 0.541667 in **if you prefer inches) in the X field to set the first tab stop.**

4. **Click on the tab ruler in the band above the numbers near the 6p (1 in) position.** Enter 5p (0.833 in) in the X field to move the tab to that location if necessary. Figure QS.10 shows the result.

FIGURE QS.10

Setting tabs in the Tabs panel

5. **Now click in the right-hand page's folio using the Type tool.**

6. **Enter** 34p3 (5.70833 in) **the X field.**

7. **Then click the right tab iconic button (the third from the left) at the top of the Tabs panel to right-align the page number.**

8. **To move the folio away from the arrowhead, enter** 2p3 (0.375 in) **in the Left Indent field in the Control panel (be sure the ¶ iconic button is selected).**

9. **Choose File ⇨ Save, or press ⌘+S or Ctrl+S, to save your work.**

CROSS-REF For more information about entering, importing, and formatting text, see Part IV. For more on tabs, see Chapter 22.

Working with Lines

You can create lines of any shape and size, and then change the style, width, and color. Here, I'm adding two arrowheads to the document's master page, so it appears on all pages. To work on a master page, double-click a master page icon in the Pages panel (Window ➪ Pages, or ⌘+F12 or Ctrl+F12).

Here's how to add the arrows:

1. **Select the Line tool.**

2. **Be sure the Stroke iconic button in the Tools panel or Swatches panel is set to [Black] — click the icon, then go to the Swatches panel (Window ➪ Swatches or F6), and finally click the [Black] swatch.**

3. **Position the mouse where you want to draw the line (here, starting at the gutter above the master text frame on the left-hand page), and then click and Shift+drag it to the left about 10p (1.667 in) to create a line, as shown in Figure QS.11.** (Pressing the Shift key while you drag constrains the Line tool to drawing a horizontal or vertical line.)

FIGURE QS.11

Use the Line tool to create lines at any angle.

Once you release the mouse, the new line is selected, as indicated by the white handles. If the line becomes deselected in the following steps, click on it to select it.

4. **Now set the line thickness and the arrowhead using the Stroke panel (Window ➪ Stroke, or ⌘+F10 or Ctrl+F10).** Enter 6 in the Weight field and choose Triangle in the End pop-up menu.

   The arrow should point to the left. If it is pointing the wrong way, choose Triangle in the Start pop-up menu and choose None in the End pop-up menu. (Note that you can also set the weight in the Control panel.)

5. Now go to the right-hand page and draw another arrow, also from the gutter, but this time Shift+drag it to the right about 10p (1.667 in).

   It's okay that the right-hand pages arrow overlaps the folio text on that page.

6. Precisely place and size the lines using the Control panel, as follows:

   ▪ **Left-hand line:** X: 34p3, Y: 1p6, and L: 10p. (Or X: 5.70833 in, Y: 0.25 in, and L: 1.667 in.)

   ▪ **Right-hand line:** X: 44p3, Y: 1p6, and L: 10p. (Or X: 7.375 in, Y: 0.25 in, and L: 1.667 in.)

   Figure QS.12 shows the result.

7. Choose File ⇨ Save, or press ⌘+S or Ctrl+S, to save your work.

CROSS-REF For more information about working with lines, see Chapter 9.

FIGURE QS.12

How the arrowhead lines should look

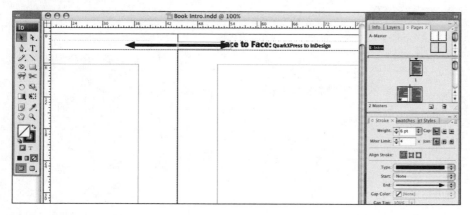

Creating and Applying Colors

To apply the color you want to an item or text, first you need to create that color. By default, InDesign provides a few colors: cyan, magenta, yellow, [Black], red, blue, green, [Paper] (white), [None], and [Registration]. (The names that InDesign puts in brackets are colors that cannot be deleted or modified.) In most cases, you will create additional colors to suit your documents.

1. To open the Swatches panel, where you create, modify, and apply colors, choose Window ⇨ Swatches or press F5.

2. From the flyout menu, choose New Color Swatch to open the New Color Swatch dialog box shown in Figure QS.13.

FIGURE QS.13

Select the color mode that contains the ink you want, then choose the desired ink from the list or, if you know its number, enter it.

3. **From the Color Mode pop-up menu, choose Pantone Solid Uncoated, then type** `1675` **in the field after labeled Pantone.** Now click OK.

   This adds the pre-mixed ink Pantone 1675U to the Swatches panel, to be printed as a spot color (separate ink). Note that if you wanted to create more colors, click Add instead. Click OK only when you want to close the dialog box.

You can apply colors to frame backgrounds, lines, strokes, some imported images, and text. Here's how you'd apply colors to the frames you created in the master spread in the previous section.

1. **Be sure the Swatches panel is open (Window ➪ Swatches or F5).**

2. **Using the Selection tool, select the left-hand page's large frame.**

3. **Make sure the Fill iconic button is selected in the Tools panel or Swatches panel, as it is in Figure QS.14.**

   This tells InDesign what you want to color the object, not any strokes it may have.

4. **Click the name of the color you created in the previous section.** In this example, select [Black].

   The selected frames now fill with the color.

5. **Now lighten the solid black to a light shade of gray by entering** `10` **in the Swatch panel's Tint field.**

6. **Be sure there is no colored stroke (outline) around the frame.** To do so, select the Stroke iconic button in the Tools panel or Swatches panel, then select the [None] swatch.

   You can also go to the Stroke panel (Window ➪ Stroke, or ⌘+F10 or Ctrl+F10) and enter 0 in the Weight field.

7. **Repeat Steps 3 through 6 for the right-hand page's large frame.** However, this time, apply the color Pantone 1675U to it, also with a 10 percent tint.

FIGURE QS.14

Click a color to apply it to the background of a frame.

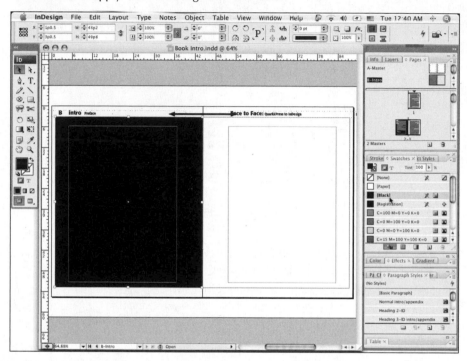

8. Using the same process, apply a 10 percent tint of Pantone 1675U to the left-hand page's folio frame and a 10 percent tint of [Black] to the right-hand page's folio frame.

9. Click the Stroke iconic button in the Tools panel or Swatches panel, then apply a 40 percent tint of Pantone 1675U to the left-hand page's arrow and a 40 percent tint of [Black] to the right-hand page's arrow.

   Yes, this means that the gray folio and arrow appear on the page with the light orange background and vice versa.

10. Choose File ➪ Save, or press ⌘+S or Ctrl+S, to save your work.

CROSS-REF For more information about creating and applying colors, see Chapter 8, as well as the special color insert.

The process is the same for text, except that you highlight the text with the Type tool before applying a color to its fill. For this exercise, set the folios' text color as follows:

- On the left-hand page, set all the text except the automatic page number to Pantone 1675U. Apply a 70 percent tint to the word *Preface*.

- On the left-hand page, apply a 70 percent tint of [Black] to the text *QuarkXPress to InDesign*, and set the automatic page number to Pantone 1675U.

Working with Graphics

In InDesign, any image that you import into a layout — whether it's a digital photograph, chart, or line drawing — is referred to as a graphic. Graphics go inside graphics frames, either ones you create before you place graphics or ones that InDesign creates automatically when you import graphics but have no frames selected. Once a graphic is inside a frame, you can change its size and placement.

> **TIP** Another thing that's nice about InDesign is that you can put a graphic in any frame, whether it started life as a graphics frame or not. The only catch: If the frame has text in it, then the graphic gets inserted as an inline graphic, making InDesign treat it as if it were text, as described in Chapter 13.

Earlier, you created frames for the icons that appear on the outside margins of pages. Now you import the graphics into them:

1. **To import a graphic, choose File ➪ Place, or press ⌘+D or Ctrl+D.**

   The dialog box is essentially the same as the one you used to import the text file, though the import options differ significantly.

2. **Locate the graphics file (in formats such as a TIFF, JPEG, GIF, or EPS); select each one (Shift+click for a range; ⌘+click or Ctrl+click individual items) and click Open.** For the left-hand page, choose `quark icon bw.tif`. For the right-hand page, choose `indesign icon bw.tif`.

   The loaded graphic icon appears, with a numeral 2 indicating there are two graphics to be placed.

3. **Click first in the icon frame on the left-hand page to place the QuarkXPress icon.** Click in the icon frame on the right-hand page to place the InDesign icon.

4. **Now adjust the placement of the icons in the frame.** Using the Direct Selection tool, click in the left-hand page's icon frame, and enter 15 in the Control panel's Scale X Percentage field and –1p6 (or –0.25 in if you prefer inches) in the X+ field. Then click on the right-hand page's icon frame and enter 15 in the Scale X Percentage field.

   Note how the Y Percentage field changes to match the X Percentage field. If it does not, click the Constrain Proportions for Scaling iconic button (the chain icon) so that it becomes a solid chain. Then reenter the desired scale. You can also resize the image to fit the frame by choosing Object ➪ Fitting ➪ Fit Content Proportionally (Option+Shift+⌘+E or Ctrl+Alt+Shift+E). Figure QS.15 shows the result.

5. **Choose File ➪ Save, or press ⌘+S or Ctrl+S, to save your work.**

> **CROSS-REF** For more information about working with pictures, see Part VI. For more on manipulating objects, see Part III.

FIGURE QS.15

The placed graphics, scaled to fit

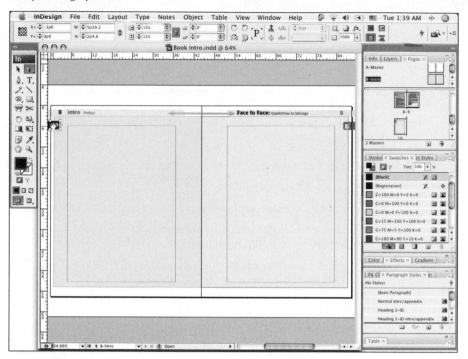

Adding Special Effects

InDesign CS3 has lots of special lighting effects such as transparency, drop shadows, and embossing. It's easy to add them using the Effects panel:

1. **Select the object to which you want to add one or more effects using the Selection tool.**

2. **Go to the Effects panel (Window ➪ Effects, or Shift+⌘+F10 or Ctrl+Shift+F10).**

CROSS-REF   For more information about special effects, see Chapter 12.

3. **From the flyout menu, choose Effects and then the desired effect from the submenu.**

   I chose Bevel and Emboss for the effect shown in Figure QS.16.

4. **In the Settings For pop-up menu, select what to apply the effect to: Object, Stroke, Fill, or Text.** I chose Object for this exercise.

   You can apply different effects to different components of an object by using the Settings For pop-up menu and then selecting the effects from the list at left. You can also apply multiple effects at once to the object and/or any of its components.

FIGURE QS.16

A bevel effect applied to the icon

5. **Experiment with the effects and settings — be sure the Preview check box is enabled so you can see how they look.**

   Here, I chose the defaults: Inner Bevel as the Style, Smooth as the Technique, Up as the Direction (for the light), 0p7 for the Size, 120° for the Angle, 30° for the Altitude, Screen for the Highlight, Multiply for the Shadow, and 75% for the Opacity of both the highlight and shadow.

6. **Click OK when you are done.**

7. **Choose File ⇨ Save, or press ⌘+S or Ctrl+S, to save your work.**

Printing a Composite

Whether you're designing a document for black-and-white photocopying, color printing, professional printing, or even a PDF, you need to review drafts. By default, InDesign is set up to your system's default printer with just a few clicks.

1. Choose File ➪ Print, or press ⌘+P or Ctrl+P.

TIP If you press Return or Enter as soon as the Print dialog box displays, chances are that InDesign will print a usable draft on your laser printer. However, if you've selected a different page size, orientation, or other option, you may want to confirm the other settings.

2. At the top of the dialog box, the Printer pop-up menu is usually set to your system's default printer.

   You can leave this setting or locate and select the printer you're actually using. It's best to select your actual printer.

3. Go to the Output pane and make sure the Color pop-up menu is set to Composite Grayscale if you're printing to a black-and-white laser printer and to Composite CMYK if you're printing to a color inkjet or laser printer.

4. Look at the page preview at the lower-left of the dialog box and make sure the page (indicated by the light-gray rectangle) fits within the printer paper (indicated by the blue line), as shown in Figure QS.17.

5. Click Print.

CROSS-REF For more information about printing, see Part VII.

FIGURE QS.17

The Print dialog box lets you confirm that your document fits on the paper in the selected printer, as well as set the appropriate print settings for your document and target printer.

Part I

Welcome to InDesign

IN THIS PART

Chapter 1
What InDesign Can Do for You

Chapter 2
Inside the InDesign Interface

Chapter 3
Getting InDesign Ready to Go

Chapter 1

What InDesign Can Do for You

InDesign CS3 is the fifth version of Adobe's flagship publishing tool, a product that came into its own with the third version (CS, which stands for Creative Suite). Widely regarded as the best layout tool today, InDesign CS3 continues to benefit from ongoing improvement from its makers at Adobe Systems.

Every new version of InDesign has brought significant new capabilities to your fingertips, and CS3 is no different. This new version introduces several key additions that make it easier to produce flexible documents, such as the ability to create text variables so the same document can have different versions of, say, a chapter heading or copyright line. Catalog publishers, for example, will love these additions. Adobe has also improved lots of features — some big, some small — to both simplify the product's use and to enhance its capabilities. For example, a retooling of the feature palettes helps reduce interface clutter, while the introduction of new lighting effects extends design options.

CROSS-REF For a quick overview of what's new in InDesign CS3, Appendix B puts it all in one place.

InDesign users fall into two camps: recent converts from QuarkXPress or even the long-defunct PageMaker, and people who've used at least one previous version of InDesign. If you're an experienced user of previous InDesign versions, you already know the InDesign approach. That's great — you're a step ahead! Feel free to skip this chapter or just skim it for a refresher. But if you're new to InDesign, please read on.

IN THIS CHAPTER

Learning what InDesign can do

Understanding global and local control

Identifying InDesign terminology

23

CROSS-REF If you're switching to InDesign from QuarkXPress or PageMaker, be sure to check out Appendix C or Appendix D, respectively.

NOTE My book *QuarkXPress to InDesign: Face to Face*, also published by Wiley, provides a detailed step-by-step transition guide for QuarkXPress users.

So what can InDesign do for you? A lot. For years, layout designers had to choose between a free-form but manual approach to layout (PageMaker) and a structured but easily revised approach (QuarkXPress). For years, most chose the latter. But with InDesign, you can choose both, which is a key reason why it is now so widely acknowledged as the best publishing tool. InDesign's flexible approach is important for both novice and experienced users because there is rarely a one-size-fits-all answer for all your design challenges. Sometimes (for example, if your project is a onetime publication or an experimental effort), creating a layout from scratch — almost as if you were doing it by hand on paper — is the best approach. And sometimes using a highly formatted template that you can modify as needed is the best approach because there's no need to reinvent the wheel for common documents.

InDesign can handle sophisticated tasks such as magazine and newspaper page layout, but its simple approach to publishing also makes it a good choice for smaller projects such as flyers and newsletters. InDesign is also a good choice for corporate publishing tasks such as proposals and annual reports. Plug-in software from other vendors add extra capabilities; for example, Virginia Systems offers several plug-ins that make InDesign a good tool for books and academic papers.

CROSS-REF For more on plug-in software, see Chapter 37.

But InDesign is not merely a merger of QuarkXPress and PageMaker — though it may seem that way to experienced users. It is designed from the ground up as an electronic publishing tool. That means you can easily send documents to service bureaus and printing presses for direct output, saving you lots of time and money. It also means you can create documents for electronic distribution, particularly using the Adobe Portable Document Format (PDF) or the Web's XHTML format, though the latter capability assumes you'll redesign the content's appearance in a Web editing program like Adobe Dreamweaver. These electronic files can include interactive features such as forms and sounds. And InDesign uses a whole bunch of automation techniques — from text variables through sharable styles and swatches — to ease the effort required to produce and maintain your documents.

CROSS-REF For more in-depth coverage of output and electronic-document fundamentals, see Parts VII and VIII, respectively.

In this chapter, I detail the wide range of uses and features of InDesign, point out the ways in which InDesign can be useful to you, and describe the basic metaphor on which the program is based. I also provide a comprehensive list of the terms, clearly and concisely defined, that I use throughout the book. So whether you're an expert or novice, read on and prepare yourself for a great InDesign adventure.

What Makes InDesign Special

The release of PageMaker in 1986 launched the desktop-publishing revolution, and in the following years, PageMaker and its competitors added tons of cool features. It may be hard to imagine that there's anything new to add to this publishing toolkit.

Well, InDesign's creators have managed to add a few new features. Following are the significant additions to the desktop-publishing toolkit, courtesy of InDesign (note that this list doesn't include enhanced versions of features found in competitors such as QuarkXPress or in PageMaker):

- **Paragraph composer:** This lets InDesign adjust the spacing and hyphenation over an entire paragraph at once — rather than, as typical of other programs, one line at a time — to achieve the best possible spacing and hyphenation. (See Chapter 18.)

- **Optical margin alignment:** This actually moves some characters past the margin of your columns to create the optical illusion that all the characters line up. It works because some characters' shapes fool the eye into thinking they begin before or after where they really do, so although they're technically aligned, they appear not to be. Optical margin alignment fixes that. (See Chapter 19.)

- **Optical kerning:** This adjusts the spacing between characters based on their shapes, which provides for the most natural look possible without resorting to hand-tuning their spacing. (See Chapter 17.)

- **A menu for inserting special characters:** This makes it so you no longer have to remember codes or use separate programs like the Mac's Character Palette or the Windows Character Map to add special symbols like bullets (•) and section indicators (§). Your word processor has likely had this feature for a few years, but this is a first in desktop publishing. (See Chapter 21.)

- **Glyph scaling:** This lets InDesign stretch or compress characters to make them fit better on a line. (A *glyph* is a character.) This works in addition to tracking and kerning, which adjust the spacing between characters to make them fit better on a line. (See Chapter 17.)

- **Custom strokes for characters:** This lets you change the look of characters by making their outlines thicker or thinner. You can also give the part of the characters inside the outlines a different color to create an outline effect. (Typically, the part inside the stroke is the same color as the stroke, so the reader sees a normal, solid character.) (See Chapter 12.)

- **EPS display:** This feature lets you see the detailed contents of an EPS file rather than rely on a poor-quality preview image or, worse, see an X or gray box in place of the image. (See Chapter 26.)

- **Illustrator and Photoshop file import:** This lets you place these graphics files directly in your layout. (See Chapter 26.)

- **Multiple views of the document:** This lets you have several windows open for the same document, enabling you to see different sections at the same time. (See Chapter 3.)

continued

continued

- **Lighting effects:** This set of features lets you give dimensional effects to text through the use of custom drop shadows and other effects. (See Chapter 12.)

- **Transparency:** This lets you make objects fade to create special effects as they overlap or for ghost-like visuals. (See Chapter 12.)

- **Automated spell-checking and text correction:** This is similar to Microsoft Word's noninvasive correction tools. (See Chapter 16.)

InDesign also includes a few features that aren't new in desktop publishing history but have not been available to mainstream programs for many years:

- **Object styles:** This lets you apply a range of attributes, such as fill and stroke, to an object and reuse those same settings on other objects. (See Chapter 13.)

- **Table and cell styles:** These let you apply consistent formatting to entire tables or to individual cells, as well as reuse those settings in other tables and cells. (See Chapter 22.)

- **Text variables:** This feature lets you have InDesign automatically insert and keep updated information such as chapter numbers, filenames, creation dates, and anything you choose to define as a variable. (See Chapter 23.)

- **Footnotes:** This is similar to how word processors handle this annotation method. (See Chapter 24.)

- **Follow-me anchored objects:** This lets you keep items such as figures and sidebars with text as it flows throughout a document. (See Chapter 12.)

Understanding Global and Local Control

The power of desktop publishing in general and InDesign in particular, is that it lets you automate time-consuming layout and typesetting tasks while letting you customize each step of the process according to your needs. This duality of structure and flexibility — implemented via the dual use of the frame-based and free-form layout metaphors — carries over to all operations, from typography to color. You can use *global controls* to establish general settings for layout elements and then use *local controls* to modify those elements to meet specific publishing requirements. The key to using global and local tools effectively is to know when each is appropriate.

Global tools include:

- General preferences and application preferences (see Chapter 3)
- Master pages (see Chapter 7)
- Text styles (see Chapter 20)
- Table and cell styles (see Chapter 22)
- Object styles (see Chapter 13)
- Stroke styles (see Chapter 12)

- Text variables (see Chapter 23)
- Sections of page numbers (see Chapter 5)
- Color definitions (see Chapter 8)
- Hyphenation and justification (see Chapter 18)
- Libraries (see Chapter 7)

NOTE Styles and master pages are the two main global settings that you can expect to override locally throughout a document because — although the layout and typographic functions that styles and master pages automate are the fundamental components of any document's look — they don't always work for all of a publication's specific content.

Local tools include:

- Frame and shape tools (see Part III and Chapters 27 and 28)
- Character and paragraph tools (see Chapters 17, 18, 19, and 20)
- Graphics tools (see Part VI)

In many cases, it's obvious which tool to use. If, for example, you maintain certain layout standards throughout a document, then using master pages is the obvious way to keep your work in order. Using styles is the best solution if you want to apply standard character and paragraph formatting throughout a document. When you work with special-case documents, such as single-page display ads, it doesn't make much sense to spend time designing master pages and styles — it's easier just to format one-of-a-kind elements on the fly.

In other cases, deciding which tool is appropriate is more difficult. For example, you can create a *drop cap* (a large initial letter set into a paragraph of type, like the one that starts each chapter in this book) as a character option in the Character panel, or you can create a *character style* (formatting that you can apply to any selected text, ensuring the same formatting is applied each time) that contains the drop-cap settings and apply that style to the drop cap. The method you choose depends on the complexity of your document and how often you need to perform the action. The more often you find yourself doing something, the more often you should use a global tool (such as character styles).

Fortunately, you don't have to decide between global and local tools right away while designing a document. You can always create styles from existing formatting later or add elements to a master page if you find you need them to appear on every page.

Another situation in which you can choose between local or global controls is specifying measurement values. Regardless of the default measurement unit you set (and that appears in all dialog boxes and panels), you can use any unit when entering measurements in an InDesign dialog box. If, for example, the default measurement is picas, but you're accustomed to working with inches, go ahead and enter measurements in inches.

CROSS-REF Chapter 3 covers how to apply measurement values and how to set your preferred defaults.

InDesign Vocabulary 101

InDesign comes with its own terminology, much of it adopted from other Adobe products. The general terms include the following:

- **Frame:** The container for an object, whether text, graphic, or color fill.

- **Link:** The connection that InDesign makes to an imported file; the link contains the file's location, last modification date, and last modification time. A link can reference any image or text file that you have imported into a layout. InDesign can notify you when a source text or graphics file has changed, so you can choose whether to update the version in your layout. (A *hyperlink*, often also abbreviated to *link* in casual conversation, connects elements in a Web page to other Web pages or other resources such as PDF files.)

- **Package:** The collecting of all files needed to deliver a layout for commercial printing.

- **Pane:** A section of a dialog box or panel whose options change based on what set of controls you've selected in the dialog box or panel.

- **Panel:** A container for controls that stays on-screen even when you aren't using it (unlike a dialog box, which appears only while you are using it). Panels, which used to be called *palettes*, can be docked to the right edge of the screen or free-floating. Panels can be combined into a single container called a *panel group*.

- **Path:** A shape in which the endpoint and start point are separate, keeping the shape "open." Lines are a straight type of path.

- **PDF:** The Adobe Portable Document Format is the standard for electronic documents. No matter what kind of computer it is viewed on (Windows, Macintosh, Palm, or Unix), a PDF document retains high fidelity to the original in typography, graphics representation, and layout. InDesign can both place PDF files as if they were graphics and export its own pages as PDF files.

- **Place:** To import a graphics file or text file.

- **Plug-in:** A piece of software that loads into InDesign and becomes part of it, adding more capabilities.

- **Stroke:** The outline of an object (whether a frame, a line, or an individual text character).

- **Thread:** The links between text frames that route stories among them.

Summary

InDesign offers a strong set of features for professional publishers working on brochures, magazines, advertisements, and similar publications. It offers many unique features such as a multiline composer, glyph scaling, and customer character strokes.

Chapter 2

Inside the InDesign Interface

The first time you use a program, it can be overwhelming. You're not sure what you can actually do with the program, and each program has its own interface idiosyncrasies. InDesign is no different. If you're familiar with other Adobe applications, such as Dreamweaver or Photoshop, the InDesign software interface will be familiar to you. Even if you've been using QuarkXPress, you'll be able to translate much of what you see in InDesign to QuarkXPress terms.

But because every program is unique, each has its own style and approaches. So now that you're ready to start using InDesign, follow through this chapter to find out where InDesign puts its capabilities and how to access them. When you first launch InDesign, you see the Tools panel on the left, and you may see several other panels on the right. InDesign is ready and waiting for you to open a document and start working.

However, taking a few minutes to familiarize yourself with the interface is invaluable to learning new software. After all, without a basic understanding of what you're looking at on-screen, it's difficult to begin working in InDesign. And even if you've used InDesign before, Adobe has made lots of changes to its interface in this version, so it's worth your while to peruse this chapter to see what's changed.

IN THIS CHAPTER

Discovering what's inside the application folder

Exploring the document window

Using tools, panels, and docks

Reviewing menu commands

How to change your mind

Exploring the InDesign Application Folder

Often, users simply launch an application from an alias or shortcut and never even look in the application folder. This is just fine, until it comes time to install a new plug-in or to share important information with other users. Familiarizing yourself with the basic contents helps ensure that you're not throwing away anything important and that you're working with the correct files and folders.

If you locate the InDesign application folder on your hard drive and open it, you see it's chock-full of stuff you may not even recognize. The three subfolders you need to know about in this application folder are entitled Presets, Plug-ins, and Required.

The Presets folder

The Presets folder contains seven kinds of standards: shortcut sets, color swatch libraries, scripts, workspaces, glyph sets, auto-correction tables, find-change tables, and stored document sizes. InDesign lets you create shortcut sets so different users can have their own shortcut definitions; these preferences are stored in the InDesign shortcut sets folder in the Presets folder. Because these preferences are stored in files, they can be copied to other users' Presets folder to help ensure consistent options among all users in a workgroup.

 Chapters 3 and 35 cover the Presets folder in more detail.

The Plug-ins folder

The Plug-ins folder contains small software modules, called *plug-ins*, that add both core features and additional, optional features to InDesign. The Plug-ins folder contains a variety of subfolders such as Dictionaries, Filters, and Graphics that make locating files easy.

To install additional plug-ins from Adobe or other companies, add them to the Plug-ins folder. Follow the instructions provided by each vendor — some have an installation program, while others have you copy the plug-in file to the Plug-ins folder.

To remove a plug-in, simply click and drag it out of the subfolder of the Plug-ins folder and store it someplace else or delete it.

TIP   **To keep track of required files and plug-ins versus optional ones, you may want to create an Optional Plug-ins folder and install any optional plug-ins there. As long as the Optional Plug-ins folder is inside the Plug-ins folder, InDesign loads them when it starts up.**

You also use the Plug-ins folder to access any customizations you make to the spelling or hyphenation dictionaries in InDesign. These custom settings are saved in the files inside the Dictionaries folder. If you're in a workgroup, the only way to ensure that everyone is working with the same spelling and hyphenation standards — so that text flows the same way on everyone's computer — is to share the dictionary files.

CROSS-REF See Chapter 35 for more information on maintaining standards across workgroups. See Chapter 37 for details on managing plug-ins.

The Required folder

The Required folder is similar to the Plug-ins folder in that it contains components of InDesign. The difference is that the components in the Required folder are necessary for InDesign to function, so you should not modify this folder or its contents.

Exploring the Document Window

When you're running InDesign, the first thing to do is create a new, empty document by choosing File ➪ New ➪ Document, or pressing ⌘+N or Ctrl+N, and clicking OK immediately. This gives you a document window so you can start exploring the application. (Never mind the settings for now — you're just exploring.)

No matter what size document you're dealing with or how many pages it has, all documents are contained within a standard window. The window provides controls that help you create and place objects, change the view scale, and navigate between pages. Figure 2.1 shows all the standard elements of a new document window.

Title bar

The bar across the top of the window is known as the *title bar*. InDesign's title bar not only reports the name of the document, but also the magnification at which you're viewing it. For example, the words "Portugal-Lisbon Area.indd @ 74%" centered in the title bar mean that you're looking at an InDesign document file called "Portugal-Lisbon Area.indd" and you're viewing it at 74 percent — a typical percent value when choosing View ➪ Fit Page in Window (⌘+0 [zero] or Ctrl+0 [zero]) on a 17-inch monitor (at the typical screen resolution of 1,024 x 768 pixels). The title bar also includes three buttons for manipulating the document window, as shown in Figure 2.1.

TIP Double-clicking the document title bar on the Mac minimizes the window. In Windows, it maximizes the window (or restores the window if it is already maximized).

Slight differences exist between the Mac and Windows interfaces for document windows. The Windows controls for window sizing appear in the upper-right corner rather than in the upper-left corner. In Windows, the Maximize button performs the same role as the Mac's Zoom button. Note that the Maximize button becomes the Restore button when the document window is *maximized* (made to fill the screen); the Restore button returns the window to its previous size. Also, in Windows, you can resize a window by clicking and dragging any side or corner, not just by clicking the Size button at the lower right. Figure 2.2 shows the Windows window-sizing controls.

FIGURE 2.1

The standard document window provides controls for managing documents on-screen, changing the view scale, displaying different pages, and placing objects on pages.

Reference points
Control panel
Close button
Tools dock
Minimize button
Tools panel
Restore button
Zero point
(ruler origin)
Rulers
Title bar

Panel flyout menu
Main dock
Panel
Panel tab
Panel group

Pasteboard
Page margins
Page boundary
Page-turning
buttons
Show/Hide
Structure button
Zoom field
Zoom pop-up menu

Pasteboard Size box
Scroll buttons
Scroll bars
Version Cue pop-up menu
Version Cue status
Page pop-up menu
Page field

FIGURE 2.2

The window-sizing controls for Windows XP (left) and Vista (right)

New document windows always display a horizontal ruler across the top and a vertical ruler down the left side. The horizontal ruler measures from the top-left corner of the page across the entire spread; the vertical ruler measures from the top to the bottom of the current page.

You can use these rulers to judge the size and placement of frames and lines on your page. Although InDesign provides more precise methods for placing objects — such as the Control panel, in which you can enter exact values — designers often use the rulers for rough placement while they experiment with a design, as shown in Figure 2.3.

FIGURE 2.3

This frame's top is aligned with the 9-pica mark on the vertical ruler.

By default, both rulers display increments in picas, but you can change the measurement system for each ruler in the Units & Increments pane of the Preferences dialog box (choose InDesign ➪ Preferences ➪ Units & Increments or press ⌘+K on the Mac, or choose Edit ➪ Preferences ➪ Units & Increments or press Ctrl+K in Windows). If you do this while no documents are open, the rulers in all new documents appear in your preferred measurement systems. If a document is open, the rulers are changed only in that document.

CROSS-REF   Chapter 3 explains ruler increments in more detail.

If you need more space on-screen or want to preview a design without all the layout tools, you can hide the rulers by choosing View ⇨ Hide Rulers, or by pressing ⌘+R or Ctrl+R. Most users show the rulers all the time out of habit, but the rulers aren't really necessary in template-driven documents such as magazines where all the placement decisions are indicated by guides and master pages. If you're editing text on a smaller monitor, you might appreciate the space gain of not having rulers, minimal though it might be.

Zero point

The intersection of the rulers in the upper-left corner of the page is called the *zero point*. Known as the *ruler origin* in other applications, this is the starting place for all horizontal and vertical measurements. If you need to place items in relation to another spot on the page (for example, from the center of a spread rather than from the left-hand page), you can move the zero point by clicking and dragging it to a new location. The X and Y values in the Control panel and Transform panel update as you click and drag the zero point so you can place it precisely. The zero point is document-wide, so it changes for all pages or spreads in the document. To restore the zero point to the upper-left corner of the left-most page, double-click the intersection of the rulers in the upper-left corner.

After the zero point is moved, all the objects on the page display new X and Y values even though they haven't moved. Objects above or to the left of the zero point have negative X and Y values, and the X and Y values of other objects do not relate to their actual position on the page or spread.

All this can be confusing, especially in a workgroup when other users may change the zero point and forget to restore it to the upper-left corner. To solve this problem, you can lock the ruler origin, making it more difficult for users to change it. Ctrl+click or right-click the ruler origin and choose Lock Zero Point from the contextual menu. Granted, the Unlock Zero Point command is right there as well, so users can just as easily unlock it. But even though unlocking it is easy to do, it's still worth using this feature, because some users won't know how to unlock it and others will be reminded that you don't want them messing with the zero point.

Scroll bars

Standard scroll bars run down the right side and across the bottom of the document window. As in most applications, you can either click and drag the scroll bars or click the scroll buttons to move around on a page or move to other pages in the document.

Pasteboard, pages, and guides

Inside the rulers, you see a white area surrounding the black, drop-shadowed outlines of your pages (see Figure 2.1). The work area surrounding the page is called the *pasteboard,* and it's

Keep Your Bearings Straight

A powerful but confusing capability in InDesign is something called a *reference point*. InDesign lets you work with objects from nine reference points — any of the four corners, the middle of any of the four sides, or the center — such as when you're positioning the object precisely or rotating the object. You choose these reference points in the Control panel or Transform panel, using the grid of nine points arranged in a square.

By default, InDesign works with the central reference point, which is great for rotating an object but can lead to confusion when you enter in the X and Y coordinates to place it precisely. That's because most people use the upper-left corner of an object when specifying its coordinates, not the center of the object. So be sure to change the reference point to the upper left whenever entering X and Y coordinates in the Control or Transform panels. (I use the upper-left reference point in this book unless otherwise indicated.)

How do you change which reference point is active? That's easy: Just click the point in that preview grid. The active reference point — called the control point — is black, while the others are white.

designed as a workspace for creating, experimenting with, and temporarily storing objects. You can also use the pasteboard to bleed objects off a page so they print to the edge of a trimmed page. Unlike PageMaker (and like QuarkXPress), each page or spread in InDesign has its own paste-board. There's 1 inch of pasteboard above and below each page, and a space equal to the page width to the left and right of each page or spread. For example, a spread consisting of two 4-inch pages has 4 inches of pasteboard to the left and 4 inches of pasteboard to the right.

Pages, drawn with black outlines, reflect the page size you set up in the New Document dialog box (File ➪ New ➪ Document, or ⌘+N or Ctrl+N). If it looks like two pages are touching, you're looking at a multipage spread. By default, you see magenta lines across the top and bottom of each page showing the top and bottom margins you specified when you created the document. Violet-colored lines indicate the left and right margins (for single-page documents) or inside and outside margins (for facing-page documents). These lines are nonprinting guides that can help you position objects.

You can change the placement of these guides by choosing Layout ➪ Margins and Columns, and you can create additional guides by clicking and dragging them off the horizontal and vertical rulers.

CROSS-REF   I cover guides in detail in Chapter 7.

If you can't see the guide colors well, you can change them for all new documents. When no documents are open, choose new colors in the Guides & Pasteboard pane of the Preferences dialog box (choose InDesign ➪ Preferences ➪ Guides & Pasteboard or press ⌘+K on the Mac, or choose Edit ➪ Preferences ➪ Guides & Pasteboard or press Ctrl+K in Windows). The Margins color changes the horizontal guides and the Columns color affects the vertical guides.

Show/Hide Structure button

The dual-arrow iconic button at the bottom of the document window (see Figure 2.1), called the Show/Hide Structure button, opens and closes the XML Structure window, which is used in Web-oriented documents based on XML.

 I cover XML in Chapter 34.

Zoom field and pop-up menu

The lower-left corner of the document window contains the Zoom field and pop-up menu that let you change the document's view scale. The view scale can be as small as 5 percent and as large as 4,000 percent, and you can modify it in 0.01 percent increments. You have three options for using the Zoom field and pop-up menu:

- To change the view to a preset value, click the arrow on the field and choose an option from the pop-up menu, as shown in Figure 2.4.

FIGURE 2.4

You can choose from a list of preset view percentages using the list in the Zoom pop-up menu.

- To change the view to a specific value, highlight the value in the field, type a new value, and press Return or Enter.

- To jump into the field quickly and type a specific value, press Option+⌘+5 or Ctrl+Alt+5, type a new value, and press Return or Enter. This method lets you change the view without taking your hands off the keyboard.

Version Cue pop-up menu

As Figure 2.5 shows, InDesign uses the Version Cue pop-up menu to show you the status of your document in the Version Cue version-management system that comes with InDesign CS3 and other Creative Suite 3 programs. For example, it lets you see other versions of a document, revert to the project's version of the file, and show the source file in the Adobe Bridge browser window or in the Finder (Mac) or Explorer (Windows) interface. At left of the pop-up menu is an information display that indicates the document's current Version Cue status.

NOTE If Version Cue is not enabled, or if the current document has not been saved to a Version Cue folder, most options are grayed out.

CROSS-REF Chapter 4 covers Version Cue in detail.

FIGURE 2.5

An unlabeled pop-up menu at the bottom of the document window lets you open other versions of your document, find the file in the Adobe Bridge browser (or in the Mac Finder or Windows Explorer), or revert to the project's master version. To the left of this pop-up menu, InDesign displays the document's current Version Cue status.

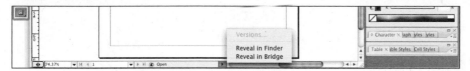

Page controls

InDesign has several controls for maneuvering through pages: page-turning buttons, and the Page field and pop-up menu. There are also controls for entering prefixes for sections' page numbers and for indicating absolute page numbers in a document that contains multiple sections.

Page-turning buttons

Next to the Zoom pop-up menu, you can find a combined page-number field and pop-up menu encased by two sets of arrows, shown in Figure 2.6. These arrows are page-turning buttons, which let you turn pages sequentially or jump to the first or last page in the document. From left to right, clicking these arrows takes you to the first page, the previous page, the next page, and the last page.

FIGURE 2.6

Buttons on the bottom of the document window let you flip from page to page. You can also use the Page pop-up menu to select a specific page.

Page field and pop-up menu

The document window also provides a control for jumping to a specific page or master page in a document. To jump to a specific page number, highlight the current number in the Page field, type a new page number, and press Return or Enter. A shortcut to highlighting the field is ⌘+J or Ctrl+J.

To jump to a master page, type the first few characters of the master page's name in the field. Jumping to document pages can be a little more complicated. Because the page number that displays and prints on the document page does not have to match the position of the page in the document — for example, the third page might be labeled *iii* instead of 3 — there are two methods for entering the page number you want to jump to: section page numbers and absolute page numbers.

You can also use the pop-up menu to the right of the Page field to get a list of available pages, including master pages (see Figure 2.6).

CROSS-REF   Chapter 5 covers page navigation in more detail.

Using Tools

InDesign by default displays a docked panel on the left side of the screen called the *Tools panel* (longtime users also know it as the *Toolbox,* the name used in early InDesign documentation), which contains 32 tools plus 13 other functions. It appears by default at the upper-left of the screen (see Figure 2.7). The tools let you create and manipulate the objects that make up your pages. The tools work similarly to those in other Adobe products (such as Photoshop, Illustrator, and Dreamweaver), and they work somewhat like the tools in QuarkXPress. But the tools do not work like the toolbars in your word processor, which are more like macros that make something happen. With InDesign's tools, for the most part, you select the tool and do something with it — draw a new frame, rotate a line, crop an image, and so on.

The one tool not directly accessible from the Tools panel is the Marker tool. But you can switch to it from the Eyedropper tool by holding Option or Alt. (Chapter 8 and the special color insert explain its use.)

With so many tools, all of which perform limited functions, understanding what each tool does is imperative. When it comes to tools, InDesign has little intuition — it requires you to select the precise tool for the action you want to complete. The software is unable to predict that you might want to make a box slightly larger while you're editing text, or that you might want to reshape a frame at the same time you're resizing it. You need to learn which tool to use and get used to switching tools — a lot.

QUARKXPRESS   In recent years, QuarkXPress has made its equivalent tools more flexible so users don't have to switch as often when they go from, for example, editing content to resizing the frame to better fit that content. If you're a QuarkXPress user, pay special attention to the tool definitions that follow so you can translate the InDesign tools to ones that you understand.

Using Tool Tips and keyboard shortcuts

To start getting familiar with the tools, first make sure that the Tool Tips pop-up menu is set to Normal or Fast in the Interface pane of the Preferences dialog box (choose InDesign ⇨ Preferences ⇨ Interface or press ⌘+K on the Mac, or choose Edit ⇨ Preferences ⇨ Interface or press Ctrl+K in Windows). Point at each tool to learn its official name, as shown in Figure 2.7; let the pointer rest on the tool for a few seconds (if Tool Tips is set to Normal) and a Tool Tip appears, telling you the name and shortcut key of that tool. Knowing the actual name is the key to learning about any tool — after all, neither the InDesign documentation's index nor this book's index lists tools by the way they look (for example, *little black pointer* or *empty square*); instead, if you want to look up a tool, you need to know the tool's name (Selection tool or Rectangle tool, for example).

NEW FEATURE The Tool Tips display settings have moved from the General pane of the Preferences dialog box to the new Interface pane.

FIGURE 2.7

Tool Tips provide the names of tools along with the shortcut key (in parentheses) that you can use to select that tool.

While you're learning the tool names, you may notice a single letter in parentheses next to each tool name. This is the shortcut key to selecting that tool. For example, the (T) next to the Type tool indicates that pressing T selects the Type tool. The Tools panel's shortcuts don't use modifier keys like ⌘ and Ctrl. If you're editing text or otherwise have the Type tool selected — or if you're in a text-entry field in a pane or dialog box — typing these shortcuts simply inserts the text where your cursor is.

CAUTION If you're not careful, you can type nonsense text in your articles because of the way the Tools panel's shortcuts work (without having to press ⌘ or Ctrl).

TIP To avoid typing these extra letters into your text, always use ⌘+click or Ctrl+click to click anywhere on the page or pasteboard. This "releases" the live text that you were working on before typing a single-letter keyboard shortcut.

After you learn all the keyboard commands, you can create and refine a layout without ever reaching for the Tools panel. In no time, you'll be switching from the Scale tool to the Rotate tool with a quick punch of the R key, and then hitting T to add a text frame. Now, obviously, you can't use the keyboard commands for selecting tools while typing or editing text, but they are worth remembering for switching tools while designing a layout. In many production environments, copy editors handle text changes, while layout artists handle design issues. In such environments, the layout artists would learn these shortcuts, while the copy editors would avoid them.

Opening and closing the Tools panel

Opening and closing the Tools panel is easy. One method of opening (or closing) the Tools panel is to choose Window ⇨ Tools. The other method of opening (or closing) the Tools panel is more obscure: Pressing the Tab key (with any tool but the Type tool selected) closes all open panels, including the Tools panel. To reopen those panels, press Tab again. To reopen just the Tools panel, choose Window ⇨ Tools.

You can change the Tools panel's width by clicking the double-arrow iconic button in the dock that contains the Tools panel. The first click converts the Tools panel to be two icons wide rather than the default one icon wide. If the panel is not docked, a second click rotates the Tools panel to horizontal orientation. (If it is docked, you cannot click the double-arrow icon to make the panel horizontal.) The next click restores the panel to the standard one-icon-wide vertical orientation. You can also set the display to any of these three settings — whether the panel is docked or not — in the Interface pane of the Preferences dialog box, using the Floating Tools Panel pop-up menu. Figure 2.8 shows the three display options.

NEW FEATURE Adobe has changed how the Tools panel, as well as other panels, work. By default, the Tools panel is now encased in a dock, from which you can drag it out to be free-floating. When docked, the Tools panel's position is fixed and it cannot overlap a document window; when it's free-floating, you can move the Tools panel anywhere, and it can obscure or be obscured by a document window. Also, the default layout for the Tools panel is now one icon wide, rather than two icons wide.

FIGURE 2.8

By clicking the toggle iconic button (the double-arrow icon) in the Tools panel, you toggle among double-column vertical, single-column vertical, and single-column horizontal display (the horizontal option is available only if the Tools panel is not in its dock, as shown at right). These options are also available in the Preferences dialog box.

Toggle button for Tools panel display

Tools panel inside its dock

Tools panel outside the dock

Selecting tools

To select a tool and start using it, click it in the Tools panel. As long as you're not using the Type tool, you can also press a keyboard shortcut displayed in parentheses in the Tool Tips.

In addition to the tools you can see, the Tools panel contains a few hidden tools that are consolidated into little pop-out menus. Any tool with a small arrow in its lower-right corner is hiding one or more similar tools, as shown in Figure 2.9. To access hidden tools, click and hold on a tool that has a pop-out indicator. When the pop-out displays, click one of the new tools to replace the standard tool with the pop-out tool.

FIGURE 2.9

The Tools panel: If a small triangle appears in the lower-right corner of a tool, you can click and hold on it to display pop-out tools. Pop-outs appear for all tools that have them, with the tool at the top the default for the Tools panel.

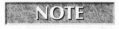 Many of the pop-out tools also have keyboard shortcuts, as Figure 2.9 shows.

Understanding what the tools do

In real life, you can often get by using the wrong tool for a job — using a flat screwdriver instead of a Phillips, or a shoe instead of a fly swatter. This doesn't work in InDesign. Whether you're typing text, reshaping an object, or applying a color, there's one — and only one — tool for each job. Loosely organized with the most commonly used tools at the top, the Tools panel includes tools for creating and manipulating frames and lines — the objects that make up your designs (see Figure 2.9).

NOTE Frames are shapes and containers that you can size, position, and reshape with precision. InDesign has three types of frames: empty (unassigned) frames for blocks of color, text frames for type, and graphics frames for imported images. By default, most frames are empty but you can easily convert them to text or graphics frames. Other frames are created specifically as text or graphics frames.

NEW FEATURE Gone from the Tools panel is the Adobe tool (where the product logo is displayed); it used to launch the Adobe Web site. You now access the Shear tool from the Scale tool's pop-out menu, making space for a new tool: Notes. A few tools — Button, Scissors, Gradient, Measure, and Eyedropper — have moved within the panel. And the Gradient Feather tool is new.

Selection tool

The Selection tool (shortcut V) lets you select objects on the page and move or resize them. You might want to rename this tool in your mind as the Mover tool because it's the only tool that lets you drag objects around on-screen.

QUARKXPRESS Think of the Selection tool as half of your Item tool.

TIP If you're working with text and have the Type tool selected, you can switch to the Selection tool by holding down ⌘ or Ctrl, instead of using the Tools panel.

Here's how the Selection tool works:

- **To select any object on a document page, click it.** If you can't seem to click it, it might be an object placed by a *master page* (a preformatted page used to format pages automatically) or it might be behind another object.

- **To select an object placed by a master page, press Shift+⌘ or Ctrl+Shift while you click.**

- **To select an object that is completely behind another object, ⌘+click it or Ctrl+click it.**

- **To select multiple objects, click and drag around the objects or Shift+click them individually.** Because you need to press the Shift key anyway while selecting objects placed by master pages, you can always multiple-select those objects.

- **To move selected objects, click somewhere within the objects and drag the mouse.**

- **To resize a selected object, click and drag any handle.** Press Shift+⌘ or Ctrl+Shift while you drag to maintain the proportions of the object.

- **To resize both a selected frame and its graphic, press ⌘ or Ctrl while you drag.** Press Shift+⌘ or Ctrl+Shift to keep things proportional.

TIP   To resize multiple objects simultaneously, you must first group them (choose Object ➪ Group, or press ⌘+G or Ctrl+G). Otherwise, only the object whose handle is being dragged will resize. Ungroup by choosing Object ➪ Ungroup, or pressing Shift+⌘+G or Ctrl+Shift+G.

Direct Selection tool

The Direct Selection tool (shortcut A) lets you select individual handles on objects to reshape them, and it lets you move graphics independently of their frames.

QUARKXPRESS   Think of the Direct Selection tool as the other half of your Item tool and also as the Content tool for graphics.

Here's how the Direct Selection tool works:

- **To select an object to reshape it, click it to display anchor points on the edges.** (The anchor points are hollow handles that you can select individually, as shown in Figure 2.10.) You can drag the anchor points to reshape the object.
- **To select objects placed by a master page, Shift+⌘+click or Ctrl+Shift+click, as with the Selection tool.** The Direct Selection tool lets you easily select objects behind other objects and select items within groups.
- **To select multiple objects, click and drag around the objects or Shift+click them.** Because you need to press the Shift key anyway while selecting objects placed by master pages, you can always multiple-select those objects.
- **To move a graphic within its frame, click inside the frame and drag the graphic.**
- **To move a frame leaving the graphic in place, click an edge of the frame and drag it.**

NOTE   In addition to using the Selection tool for *threading* (linking) text frames (see Chapter 15), you can use the Direct Selection tool. This is one of the few cases where you have more than one tool to handle a task.

FIGURE 2.10

Clicking and dragging a hollow anchor point with the Direct Selection tool lets you reshape items.

Position tool

The Position tool (no shortcut) is a renamed version of PageMaker's Crop tool. You access it from the pop-out menu in the Direct Selection tool. The Position tool combines some aspects of the Selection tool with some aspects of the Direct Selection tool:

- As with the Selection tool, you can resize an object's frame by dragging its handles.
- As with the Direct Selection tool, you can click a graphic and reposition it (crop it) within the frame by dragging.

Pen tool

The Pen tool (shortcut P) lets you create paths consisting of straight and curved segments. Modeled after the Pen tools in Illustrator and Photoshop, this is the tool for creating simple illustrations within InDesign. (See Chapter 28.)

If a path you create with the Pen tool is left open, the object is essentially a line that you can color or adjust stroke settings for. If the path is closed, the object is basically an empty frame. You can import text or graphics into the paths using the Place command (choose File ➪ Place, or press ⌘+D or Ctrl+D) or you can type into the path using the Type tool. If you decide to place text or graphics in an open path, the path closes automatically and becomes a frame. (To place text on a path, first select the Type on a Path tool [shortcut Shift+T], and then click the path.)

Here's how the Pen tool works:

- **To create straight segments of a path, click to establish an anchor point, move the mouse to the next location, click again, and so on.** To move an anchor point after clicking, press the spacebar and drag the segment.
- **To create curved segments of a path, click and drag, and then release the mouse button to end the segment.**
- **To close a path and create a frame, click over the first anchor point created (the hollow one).**
- **To leave a path open and create a line, ⌘+click or Ctrl+click away from the path or select another tool.**

Anchor and direction point tools

The Pen tool includes a pop-out menu containing three additional tools for reshaping lines and frames: Add Anchor Point (shortcut =), Delete Anchor Point (shortcut – [hyphen]), and Convert Direction Point (shortcut Shift+C). (See Chapter 28.)

 For more information about using the Pen and anchor point tools, see Chapter 28.

Type tool

The Type tool (shortcut T) lets you type, edit, and format text. The Type tool also lets you create rectangular text frames as you need them. (See Chapters 9, 14, and 15.)

QUARKXPRESS Think of the Type tool as a combination of the Rectangle Text Box tool and the Content tool for text — except remember that by itself, it doesn't let you do anything else such as resizing a frame. However, if you press and hold the ⌘ or Ctrl key, the frame's reference points appear, allowing you to resize it. When you are done resizing it, release the ⌘ or Ctrl key to return to editing text in the frame.

Here's how the tool works:

- To create a rectangular text frame, click and drag; hold the Shift key to create a perfect square.
- To begin typing or editing text, click in a text frame or in any empty frame.
- To highlight text so you can format it, cut and paste it, drag-move it, and so on.
- To select a word, double-click anywhere in the word.
- To select a paragraph, triple-click anywhere in the paragraph.
- To select all the text in a *story* (a series of threaded text frames), choose Edit ➪ Select All or press ⌘+A or Ctrl+A.

You can place or drag and drop text files, and you can *thread* (link) text frames with either of the selection tools, but the tools won't let you touch the text.

Type on a Path tool

The Type tool has a pop-out menu to select the Type on a Path tool (shortcut Shift+T), which lets you select a path or frame and type text onto it so it follows the path or frame's outline. (See Chapter 19.)

Pencil tool

The Pencil tool (shortcut N) lets you draw freeform shapes by having InDesign trace your mouse movements, creating a curve based on that automatically. (See Chapter 28.)

Smooth tool

The Pencil tool has a pop-out menu to select the Smooth tool, which lets you smooth lines, curves, and shapes. It has no shortcut. (See Chapter 28.)

Erase tool

The Pencil tool also has a pop-out menu to select the Erase tool, which lets you erase portions of an object. It has no shortcut. (See Chapter 28.)

Line tool

The Line tool (shortcut E) lets you draw free-standing lines (rules) on your page. To use this tool, simply click it and drag the mouse. You can use the rulers, the Control panel, or the Transform panel to size and position the line precisely. Pressing the Shift key while you click and drag constrains the line angle to 45-degree increments, which is useful for creating straight horizontal and vertical lines. (See Chapter 9.)

Frame tools

InDesign has three frame tools: Rectangle Frame (shortcut F), Ellipse Frame, and Polygon Frame. Their icons are distinguished by a large X inside. The latter two tools, which have no shortcuts, are available from the Rectangle Frame tool's pop-up menu. The frames created by these tools are meant to hold either graphics or text. To create frames with these tools, click and drag using the rulers or information in the Control panel or Transform panel to judge the size and placement. To create a perfect circle with the Ellipse Frame tool or a perfect square with the Rectangle Frame tool, press the Shift key while you click and drag. (See Chapter 9.)

You can fill and stroke the empty frames for use as design elements or you can import text and graphics into them using the Place command (File ⇨ Place, or ⌘+D or Ctrl+D). You can also click in an empty frame with the Type tool to begin typing in it. (See Chapters 14 and 26.)

QUARKXPRESS The InDesign frame tools are the same as picture-box and text-box tools in QuarkXPress, except that InDesign's boxes (frames) can hold either type of content, so there are not two variants of these tools in InDesign as there are in QuarkXPress.

Shape tools

If you'd rather create actual graphics frames, use the Rectangle (shortcut M), Ellipse (shortcut L), or Polygon tools. (The Ellipse and Polygon tools are pop-out tools available from the Rectangle tool.) The tools are meant to create shapes that you use as artwork, rather than as containers. But you can place text or graphics into one of these shapes the same way as you would a frame. (See Chapter 9.) Essentially, the shape tools are superfluous and you can ignore them.

Button tool

The Button tool, which has no shortcut, creates rectangular frames that are used as buttons in interactive Acrobat documents, which you can create in InDesign. (See Chapter 33).

Scissors tool

The Scissors tool (shortcut C) lets you cut paths into separate paths. When you cut an open path (a line or curve), you get two separate lines. When you cut a closed path in one place, you get an open path. When you cut a closed path (a frame) in two places, you get two closed paths containing the same contents. Note that you cannot cut paths containing text. (See Chapter 28.)

Rotate tool

The Rotate tool (shortcut R) lets you change the angle of selected items visually. To use the Rotate tool, first select an item with the Selection tool or the Direct Selection tool, and then select the Rotate tool. Or ⌘+click or Ctrl+click an object with the Rotate tool. Click and drag in any direction. The object rotates from the location of the active reference point, as shown in Figure 2.12.

The active reference point is indicated through the nine boxes in the upper left of the Control panel or Transform panel — the black square is the active reference point (also called *control point*) from which the rotation pivots and from which all coordinates originate. Just click whatever square you want to be the active reference point. You can also click and drag the active reference point to a new location for a custom rotation.

To rotate an object in 45-degree increments, press the Shift key while you click and drag.

Scale tool

The Scale tool (shortcut S) lets you grab any object and resize it horizontally, vertically, or proportionally. When you scale text or graphics frames, the size of the text and image are resized as well. As with the Rotate tool, the Scale tool doesn't let you select items to scale. You either need to select an object first with a selection tool, or ⌘+click or Ctrl+click it with the Scale tool. (See Chapter 11.)

Shear tool

Available through the Scale tool's pop-out menu, the Shear tool (shortcut O) works much the same as the Scale tool. Instead of resizing the object and contents, the Shear tool slants selected objects in the direction you drag. But it also rotates the object, creating a more 3-D-like perspective effect. (See Chapter 11.)

Gradient Swatch tool

The Gradient Swatch tool (shortcut G) lets you change the direction of existing gradient fills or strokes applied to objects. To apply gradients to objects, you use the Gradient panel. (See Chapter 8.)

 The Gradient Swatch tool had been called the Gradient tool in previous versions of InDesign.

Gradient Feather tool

Available through the Gradient Swatch tool's pop-out menu, the new Gradient Feather tool (shortcut Shift+G) acts just like the Gradient Swatch tool except that it applies fades the gradient to transparent, a quick way to apply a feathering effect. (See Chapter 12.)

Free Transform tool

The Free Transform tool (shortcut E) is handy because it lets you move, rotate, and reshape objects all with one tool. If you click and hold the mouse within the object, you can drag it. If you click any of the handles on the object frame, you can resize it. If you click and hold on any edge (except where there is a handle) or anywhere outside the object, you can rotate the object. (See Chapter 11.)

Note tool

The Note tool lets you insert a nonprinting note (such as a reminder to yourself or another designer) in text. After selecting the tool, click in any text to insert the note. The Notes panel displays, where you can type the note and navigate to other notes. Formerly part of the add-on InCopy program, this tool is now standard in InDesign. (See Chapter 16.)

Eyedropper tool

The Eyedropper tool (shortcut I) samples the color settings for the object at the location you click with it. This is handy way to find out the color makeup of imported graphics so you can then create a color swatch that matches it exactly or apply that sampled color to other objects. If the

Eyedropper tool is selected, pressing Alt or Option switches to the Marker tool, which lets you apply the color you just sampled to any object. (See Chapter 8.)

Measure tool

Available through the Eyedropper tool's pop-out menu, the Measure tool (shortcut K) opens the Info panel and lets you draw a line whose dimensions appear in that pane so you can measure an arbitrary distance. You can see objects' dimensions in the Control, Transform, and Info panels, but the value of the Measure tool is that it determines the distance between objects rather than the dimensions of objects. It can also come in handy when you're measuring the distance across multiple objects. (See Chapter 10.)

Hand tool

The Hand tool (shortcut H) lets you scoot pages around to view a different portion of a page or another page entirely. The Hand tool is an entirely visual method of scrolling, allowing you to see the page contents at all times. To use the Hand tool, click and drag in any direction. You can access the Hand tool temporarily without actually switching tools by pressing Option+spacebar or Alt+spacebar. (See Chapter 3.)

Zoom tool

The Zoom tool (shortcut Z) lets you increase and decrease the document view scale. You can highlight a specific area on a page to change its view or you can click on-screen to change the view scale within InDesign's preset increments (shown in the Zoom field and pop-up menu in the lower-left corner of the document window). (See Chapter 3.)

Color buttons

The bottom portion of the Tools panel contains buttons for applying colors to the edges of objects (*strokes*) and the insides of objects (*fills*). You use these buttons with the Stroke, Color, Gradient, and Swatches panels to apply and experiment with the colors applied to objects. (See Chapter 8.) See Figure 2.9 for an illustration of these buttons.

View buttons

At the very bottom of the Tools panel are the two view-oriented iconic buttons: Normal View Mode and Preview Mode. The first shows the pasteboard, margins, and guidelines, while the second hides those to give an unadorned preview of the final document. (They are also accessible by choosing View ➪ Screen Mode and then the desired option from the submenu.)

There are two preview options available via a pop-up menu in the Preview Mode iconic button: Bleed Mode and Slug Mode. Bleed Mode shows any objects that bleed beyond the page boundaries, while Slug Mode shows the space reserved for information such as crop marks and color separation names used in final output, as covered in Chapters 4 and 31. You set these up when you create new documents or by choosing File ➪ Document Setup (Option+⌘+P or Ctrl+Alt+P).

Working with Panels and Docks

Initially, software developers used floating palettes to provide convenient access to commonly used options such as swatches, fonts, and styles. Palettes provide a more interactive method of working with features, because the screen is not obscured by a large dialog box and you can access the controls quickly. Eventually, palettes started to move away from serving as a convenient alternative to commands and became the primary method — often the *only* method — for performing many tasks.

NEW FEATURE In InDesign CS3, Adobe has revamped its palettes. Now called *panels*, they serve the same purpose and work pretty much the same way in terms of the functions they provide. But how you arrange them has changed, as well as how some appear visually. The dock that many are placed into by default is also new to InDesign CS3. Figure 2.11 shows the default panel interface.

Arranging panels

By default, InDesign places 13 panels in a dock at the right edge of your screen: Pages, Layers, and Info in the top panel group; Stroke, Swatches, and Object Styles in the next panel group; Color, Effects (the new name for the Transparency panel), and Gradient in the third panel group; and Character, Paragraph, Character Styles, and Paragraph Styles in the bottom panel group. The goal of this dock is to keep panels in a self-contained area, minimizing interface clutter.

NOTE Because the Tools panel resides in its own dock, I call the one containing the 13 panels the *main dock.*

As in previous versions of InDesign, you access a panel by clicking its tab (if it is on-screen) and/or by choosing the desired panel from the Window menu. If you choose a panel from the Window menu that is not already in the dock, that selected panel displays onscreen as a free-floating panel.

Also, as in previous versions of InDesign, you can move panels in and out of panel groups, dragging them by their tabs. You can drag panels within the main dock, or outside the dock (which makes them free-floating). You can also drag free-floating panels into the dock.

TIP To drag an entire panel group — all the panels whose tabs are in the same row in the dock — hold Option or Alt when you drag one of its panels' tab.

Again, as in previous versions of InDesign, some panels have additional fields that you can display by clicking the up/down arrow iconic button in its tab. Clicking the icon again returns the panel to the normal display. But you can no longer minimize the panel to just its tab.

Unlike previous versions of InDesign, you can now close a panel inside the main dock, using the Close box on its tab. (To bring it back, select it from the Window menu.) In previous versions, you could close only free-floating palettes, so to close a docked pane meant you dragged it out to be its own free-floating palette, then closed it. In InDesign CS3, you can close all panels — whether docked or not. And you can close entire free-floating panel groups.

NEW FEATURE To return to InDesign's standard presentation of panels, including which are grouped together and which are docked, choose Window ➪ Workspace ➪ Reset Panels.

What you can no longer do is dock individual panels to the side of your monitor. In InDesign CS3, they're either in the main dock or they're free-floating. When docked, a panel cannot overlap a document window; when free-floating, a panel can be moved anywhere, whether obscuring or being obscured by a document window.

The tabs are now always along the top of the panel. In previous versions, they would appear on the left of the palette if the palette was docked to the side of the monitor but on top if they were free-floating. Similarly, the flyout menus (the new name for palette menus) are now always at the upper right of a panel. (The flyout menus' icon has also changed from a triangle to a miniature menu.)

There are exceptions to InDesign's treatment of panels: First, the Tools panel lives in its own dock, from which it cannot be removed. Second, the Control panel is *not* in a dock, but it does continue to dock to the top of the screen by default. Third, the Quick Apply and Command Bar panels also do not reside in a dock, they are just free-floating panels. Fourth, you cannot close the Tools, Control, and Command Bar panels from the panels themselves; you must use the Window menu. (You can also use the keyboard shortcut Option+⌘+6 or Ctrl+Alt+6 to open and close the Control panel.)

There are so many panels in InDesign CS3 — even more than in previous versions — that you might want to consider hooking up a second monitor for displaying them. And break out the computer glasses and your decoder ring, because the panels are small and laden with mysterious icons.

As with the tools, if you make sure Tool Tips is selected in the Interface pane of the Preferences dialog box (choose InDesign ➪ Preferences ➪ Interface or press ⌘+K on the Mac, or choose Edit ➪ Preferences ➪ Interface or press Ctrl+K in Windows), you can get some pretty good hints as to what the panel icons and fields do.

To try to gain some control over InDesign's panel profligacy, you can create *workspaces,* which are essentially memorized panel collections. Display the panels you want, where you want them, and create a new workspace by choosing Window ➪ Workspace ➪ Save Workspace. Give it a name that makes sense, such as Text Panels. That workspace is now available by clicking Window ➪ Workspace ➪ *workspace name*, and automatically displays just those saved panels in their saved locations. By having several such workspaces, you can quickly switch among collections of panels based on the tasks you're focused on.

NEW FEATURE InDesign CS3 comes with several predefined workspaces, including Basic, and Printing and Proofing, to give you a sense of how you might use this feature.

To go back to the standard InDesign workspace, choose Window ➪ Workspace ➪ Default Workspace. (This menu sequence used to be Window ➪ Workspace ➪ [Default] in previous versions of InDesign.)

Also use the Control panel as your first stop — keeping the other panels collapsed — because it provides access to most common functions. Even better, the Control panel adjusts its display based on what the current object is, so you get just the relevant options. For example, when you select a text frame, the Control panel provides the most functions of the Transform, Character Style, Character, Paragraph, Paragraph Styles, and Stroke panels.

Anatomy of a panel. Panels contain a flyout menu that provides additional options. Their tabs also have a Close box to remove them from the dock. Some have a hide/show options button to display and hide additional fields.

Changing the dock display

Although you can't move the main dock, you can adjust how it displays. You can widen or narrow the dock by dragging the resize icon at upper right. You can also collapse the dock into a series of icons by clicking either the double-arrow icon at the upper left of the dock or the dark rectangle at the top of the dock — I find this the best way to work with the panels, as it leaves you the most space onscreen. You expand the dock back by clicking the double-arrow icon again. Figure 2.12 shows the main dock collapsed, expanded, and widened.

FIGURE 2.12

Three views of the main dock, from left to right: normal, collapsed, and widened.

Using panels

To use a panel, first you need to activate it. You can do this by clicking its tab (if the panel containing it is open) or by choosing its menu command in the Window menu (if the panel is not open or if another pane in that palette is active). You need to be on the lookout here — if a menu command brings a panel forward in the main dock or in a free-floating panel group, you might not even notice.

When a panel is active, its controls have the following characteristics:

- Click a pop-up menu to display and select an option, or click an icon to select an option; the changes take effect immediately.

- Highlight a value in a field to enter a new value. To implement the value, press Shift+Return or Shift+Enter. Or you can press Tab to move to the next field or Shift+Tab to the previous field. Or just click in a different field or elsewhere in the document. To get out of a field you've modified, leaving the object unscathed, press Esc.

- Some fields include up and down arrows that you can click to increase or decrease the value in the field.

- Fields accept values in all different measurement systems. (I cover this in detail in Chapter 3.)

- In addition to typing values in fields, you can enter calculations. You can add to, subtract from, multiply, and divide values in fields using the following operators: +, −, * (multiply), and / (divide). For example, to reduce the width of a frame by half, you might type /2 next to the current value of 4.5 inches in the Width field. Or, to increase the length of a line by 6 points, you can type +6 next to the current value in the Length field.

 You can also use percentages in fields, such as 50%, which adjusts the current value by that percentage.

- Most panels provide a pop-up menu that you can display by clicking the iconic button in the upper-right corner. The flyout menu (formerly called the palette menu) that appears provides commands related to the current panel's contents (for example, the Color panel provides a command for changing the color model, as shown in Figure 2.11).

Checking out the panels

Like the tools in InDesign, each panel has a distinct function. I cover the use of each panel in detail in the appropriate chapters throughout this book (for example, the Layers panel is covered in Chapter 6). But with the help of Tool Tips and a quick introduction to their primary purpose, you can start using many of the panels to begin performing basic functions.

Customizing the Control Panel

InDesign CS3 adds the ability to customize the Control panel, using the Customize flyout menu option. This is especially useful if you are working with a monitor with a screen resolution set at less than 1152 x 872 pixels, since InDesign automatically removes options from the Control panel at smaller screen sizes. By customizing the Control panel, you can keep the options you want and remove the ones you don't, rather than accept what InDesign thinks you should have.

In the Customize Control Panel dialog box that appears when you select Customize from the flyout menu, you can select and deselect sets of iconic buttons to control which ones display. These objects are grouped into five categories — Object, Character, Paragraph, Tables, and Other. You can control individual buttons within these categories by clicking the right-facing arrow icon to the left of each group's name; you'll get a list of options within that group that you can individually control.

The Control panel also adds several functions to its options if you have a widescreen monitor. For example, with a monitor set at 1280-pixel width, you see both the character and paragraph options at once, rather than have to toggle between them. When you've selected an object with the Selection tool at that resolution, you'll see extra controls such as frame alignment and frame fitting.

TIP All but one of the text-oriented panels are available from the Type menu: Character, Character Styles, Glyphs, Index, Paragraph, Paragraph Styles, Tabs, and Table. (The Table panel and its related Table Styles and Cell Styles panels are not available here, but that's because they have their own Table menu for accessing their controls.) This provides faster access than accessing them through the Window ⇨ Type & Tables submenu.

Here is a quick summary of the InDesign panels (all available through the Window menu unless otherwise indicated). Note that in the figures of the various panels, the full panel is shown for any that have the option of showing just some options; these panels have an up-down arrow iconic button to the left of the panel name.

- **Tools panel:** As I covered earlier in this chapter, the Tools panel is the mechanism by which you select the appropriate tool to accomplish various layout tasks.

- **Control panel (Option+⌘+6 or Ctrl+Alt+6):** The Control panel is one of the most useful features in InDesign. It combines many attributes for the currently selected object so you can minimize the use of other panels and menu items. The panel changes based on what you select, as seen in Figure 2.13.

QUARKXPRESS By default, the Control panel is docked to the top of the screen. QuarkXPress users might want to float it at the bottom to mimic QuarkXPress's interface.

FIGURE 2.13

From top to bottom, the default Control panel for frames with graphics, lines, and text paths; frames with text selected with the Selection or Direct Selection tool; and frames and text paths with text selected with the Type tool (with each of the two variations of the Control panel for text displayed). Extra options display if your monitor resolution is 1280 pixels or wider.

- **Links panel (shortcut Shift+⌘+D or Ctrl+Shift+D):** The Links panel shows the original location of imported graphics and text files (see Figure 2.14).

- **Character panel (Type ⇨ Character or Window ⇨ Type & Tables ⇨ Character, or press ⌘+T or Ctrl+T):** Use the Character panel (shown in Figure 2.15) to change common attributes of highlighted text such as the font, size, leading, kerning, tracking, and scaling.

- **Paragraph panel (Type ⇨ Paragraph or Window ⇨ Type & Tables ⇨ Paragraph, or press Option+⌘+T or Ctrl+Option+T):** Use the Paragraph panel (shown in Figure 2.15) to change common attributes of selected paragraphs such as the alignment, indents, space before and after, and hyphenation.

- **Character Styles panel (Type ⇨ Character Styles or Window ⇨ Type & Tables ⇨ Character Styles or press Shift+⌘+F11 or Ctrl+Shift+F11):** Use the Character Styles panel (shown in Figure 2.16) to create and apply styles consisting of character-level formats.

- **Paragraph Styles panel (Type ⇨ Paragraph Styles or Window ⇨ Type & Tables ⇨ Paragraph Styles or press ⌘+F11 or Ctrl+F11):** Use the Paragraph Styles panel (shown in Figure 2.16) to create and apply styles consisting of paragraph-level formats.

- **Object Styles panel (Window ⇨ ⇨ Object Styles, or press ⌘+F7 or Ctrl+F7):** Use the Object Styles panel (shown in Figure 2.16) to create and apply styles for frames, lines, and other objects.

FIGURE 2.14

The Links panel

- **Tabs panel (Type ⇨ Tabs, or press Shift+⌘+T or Ctrl+Shift+T):** The Tabs panel (shown in Figure 2.17) lets you create tab stops for selected paragraphs; you can also specify alignment, position, and leader characters for the tabs. Note that Adobe calls this a dialog box, but it does not work like any other dialog box. There are no OK or Cancel buttons, and — unlike when a regular dialog box is open — you can select items in your layout while it is open. It really is a panel, except that it uses a nonstandard Close box and has no Minimize box. So I'm still calling it a panel.

FIGURE 2.15

The Character panel (left) and the Paragraph panel (right)

FIGURE 2.16

The Character Styles panel (left), Paragraph Styles panel (right), and Object Styles panel (bottom)

NEW FEATURE The Tabs panel is no longer available from the Window ⇨ Type & Tables submenu.

■ **Story panel (Type ⇨ Story or Window ⇨ Type & Tables ⇨ Story):** It's small but important — the Story panel (shown in Figure 2.17) lets you specify hanging punctuation for all the frames in a story by checking Optical Margin Alignment. You can also change the type size at which alignment begins if the need arises. (Note that the Story panel has no flyout menu.)

FIGURE 2.17

The Tabs panel (left) and the Story panel (right)

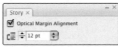

■ **Glyphs panel (Type ⇨ Glyphs or Window ⇨ Type & Tables ⇨ Glyphs, or press Option+Shift+F11 or Alt+Shift+F11):** The Glyphs panel lets you access special characters within a font. Figure 2.18 shows the Glyphs panel.

FIGURE 2.18

The Glyphs panel

■ **Text Wrap panel (shortcut Option+⌘+W or Ctrl+Alt+W):** The Text Wrap panel (shown in Figure 2.19) provides iconic buttons for controlling how text runs around selected objects.

■ **Transform panel (Window ⇨ Object & Layout ⇨ Transform):** The Transform panel (shown in Figure 2.19) lets you specify size, placement, scale, rotation, and shear of selected objects.

- **Align panel (Window ⇨ Object & Layout ⇨ Align or Shift+F7):** The Align panel (shown in Figure 2.19) provides buttons that let you evenly distribute or realign multiple-selected objects with one click.

FIGURE 2.19

The Text Wrap panel (top), the Transform panel (middle), and the Align panel (bottom)

- **Pages panel (shortcut ⌘+F12 or Ctrl+F12):** Use the Pages panel (shown in Figure 2.20) to create master pages and to add, rearrange, and delete document pages. You can also create sections of page numbers using the Pages panel's flyout menu.

- **Layers panel (shortcut F7):** The Layers panel (shown in Figure 2.20) provides access to vertical slices of a document that you can use to control the stacking order of objects, to isolate specific portions of a design, or to store revisions of the same document.

- **Navigator panel (Window ⇨ Object & Layout ⇨ Navigator):** The Navigator panel (shown in Figure 2.20) shows a color proxy version of pages and lets you isolate a portion of any page to display in the document window.

FIGURE 2.20

The Pages panel (top), the Layers panel (middle), and the Navigator panel (bottom)

■ **Swatches panel (shortcut F5):** The Swatches panel (shown in Figure 2.21) lets you create named colors such as those using Pantone, Focoltone, and Toyo inks, and apply the colors to text, strokes, and fills.

■ **Stroke panel (shortcut ⌘+F10 or Ctrl+F10):** Use the Stroke panel (shown in Figure 2.21) to outline the edges of frames and lines; you have control over the thickness and the pattern of the outlines.

■ **Color panel (shortcut F6):** The Color panel (shown in Figure 2.21) lets you create Lab, CMYK, and RGB colors, and apply the colors to text, strokes, and fills. (Lab, CMYK, and RGB are all composite color models, in which all colors are made by mixing a small number of primary colors.) Chapter 8 describes these models in detail.

■ **Attributes panel:** The Attributes panel (shown in Figure 2.21) lets you specify that the stroke or fill in selected objects overprints the background. (Note that the Attributes panel has no flyout menu.)

■ **Gradient panel:** Use the Gradient panel (shown in Figure 2.21) to create a stroke or fill consisting of a graduated blend between two colors.

■ **Table panel (Window ⇨ Type & Tables ⇨ Table or Shift+F9):** The Table panel (shown in Figure 2.22) lets you adjust table settings.

■ **Table Styles panel (Window ⇨ Type & Tables ⇨ Table Styles):** The Table Styles panel (shown in Figure 2.22) lets you specify and apply styles for tables.

■ **Cell Styles panel (Window ⇨ Type & Tables ⇨ Cell Styles):** The Cell Styles panel (shown in Figure 2.22) lets you specify and apply styles for table cells.

NEW FEATURE   The Table Styles and Cell Styles panels are new to InDesign CS3.

■ **Index panel (Window ⇨ Type & Tables ⇨ Index or Shift+F8):** The Index panel (shown in Figure 2.23) lets you add and manage index entries.

■ **Data Merge panel (Window ⇨ Automation ⇨ Data Merge):** The Data Merge panel (shown in Figure 2.23) lets you import data for use in form letters, labels, and other documents that use the same layout for variable text.

■ **Assignments panel:** The Assignments panel (shown in Figure 2.24) lets you make individual stories in your layout available to a user of the InCopy add-on program. For example, with InCopy, a copy editor can check out a story from your layout to proofread it while you're still working on the layout.

■ **Notes panel:** The Notes panel (shown in Figure 2.24) — formerly part of InCopy but now standard in InDesign — lets you insert and manage nonprinting notes used as reminders for yourself or other people working on the layout.

NEW FEATURE The Assignments and Notes panels are new to InDesign CS3.

■ **Scripts panel (Window ⇨ Automation ⇨ Scripts, or press Option+⌘+F11 or Ctrl+Alt+F11):** The Scripts panel (shown in Figure 2.25) shows available AppleScripts, VBA scripts, and Java scripts in the Scripts folder in the InDesign folder.

FIGURE 2.21

Top row: the Swatches and Stroke panels. Middle row: the Color and Attributes panels. Bottom row: the Gradient panel

FIGURE 2.22

The Table panel (left), the Table Styles panel (right), and the Cell Styles panel (bottom)

FIGURE 2.23

The Index panel (left) and the Data Merge panel (right)

FIGURE 2.24

The Assignments panel (left) and the Notes panel (right)

■ **Script Label panel (Window ➪ Automation ➪ Script Labels):** The Script Label panel (shown in Figure 2.25) lets you change the label of an object for use by scripts. (Note that the Script Label panel has no flyout menu.)

FIGURE 2.25

The Scripts panel (left) and the Script Label panel (right)

■ **Pathfinder panel (Window ➪ Object & Layout ➪ Pathfinder):** The Pathfinder panel (shown in Figure 2.26) lets you manipulate paths, enabling you to combine, separate, and otherwise work with open and closed paths. It also now lets you convert shapes. (Note that the Pathfinder panel has no flyout menu.)

■ **Effects panel (shortcut Shift+⌘+F10 or Ctrl+Shift+F10):** The Effects panel (shown in Figure 2.27) lets you adjust the solidity of images to create fading and overlap effects.

NEW FEATURE   The Effects panel replaces the Transparency pane in previous versions of InDesign, as well as adds many new lighting effects.

FIGURE 2.26

The Pathfinder panel

■ **Flattener Preview panel (Window ➪ Output ➪ Flattener):** The Flattener Preview panel (shown in Figure 2.27) lets you see what page items (typically those with transparency) are *flattened* (made solid) during printing or exporting to Encapsulated PostScript (EPS), Scalable Vector Graphics (SVG, a vector format for the Web), or Portable Document Format (PDF) formats. Flattening occurs for printing devices and graphics export formats that don't support transparency.

FIGURE 2.27

The Effects panel (left) and the Flattener Preview panel (right)

■ **Separations Preview panel (Window ➪ Output ➪ Separations or Shift+F6):** The Separations Preview panel (shown in Figure 2.28) lets you see page items with various color plates enabled, as well as preview the effects of different ink densities.

■ **Trap Presets panel (Window ➪ Output ➪ Trap Presets):** The Trap Presets panel (shown in Figure 2.28) lets you set and apply different trapping settings to objects, which controls how abutting and overlapping objects print to avoid gaps caused by paper-feed variations during printing.

FIGURE 2.28

The Separations Preview panel (top) and the Trap Presets panel (bottom)

■ **Info panel (press F8):** The Info panel (shown in Figure 2.29) shows some of the characteristics — such as size, position, and cropping — of selected objects. It also displays the results of using the Measure tool.

The Info panel

■ **Bookmarks panel (Window ⇨ Interactive ⇨ Bookmarks):** The Bookmarks panel (shown in Figure 2.30) creates the bookmarks used in PDF files to create clickable indexes and tables of contents.

■ **Hyperlinks panel (Window ⇨ Interactive ⇨ Hyperlinks):** The Hyperlinks panel (shown in Figure 2.30) lets you set up hyperlinks from and to document objects and pages, as well as to Web locations.

■ **Tags panel:** The Tags panel (shown in Figure 2.30) lets you add XML tags and map them to paragraph and character styles. XML tags determine the formatting for XML data sources used in XML documents.

■ **States panel (Window ⇨ Interactive ⇨ States):** The States panel (shown in Figure 2.30) sets button actions for PDF files.

■ **Command Bar panel (Window ⇨ Object & Layout ⇨ Command Bar):** The Command Bar panel (shown in Figure 2.31) gives you one-button access to a variety of controls, such as ones for opening files, formatting text, and launching Adobe Photoshop. If you hover over a button, a Tool Tip displays, indicating its function. The Command Bar is based on a PageMaker feature. (Note that the Command Bar panel has no flyout menu.)

NEW FEATURE   The Command Bar in InDesign CS3 was called the PageMaker Toolbar in previous versions of InDesign.

■ **Quick Apply panel (Edit ⇨ Quick Apply, or ⌘+Return or Ctrl+Enter):** The Quick Apply panel (shown in Figure 2.32) lets you access paragraph, character, object, and other styles from a single location; as well as menu commands and scripts. Plus it lets you use the keyboard to select and apply them, making it easier to apply styles to text when editing with the keyboard (no need to switch to the mouse and back). Note that the Quick Apply panel does not have a flyout menu but it does have an unnamed pop-up menu that you use to control which types of settings may be quick-applied.

FIGURE 2.30

Top row: the Bookmarks and Hyperlinks panels. Bottom row: the Tags and States panels.

FIGURE 2.31

The Command Bar panel

FIGURE 2.32

The Quick Apply panel and its pop-up menu

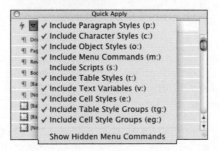

The Quick Apply Option

A fast way to apply various attributes to layout elements is by using the Quick Apply panel. Quick Apply is a consolidated list of styles, scripts, text variables, and other attributes that you access by choosing Edit ⇨ Quick Apply, by clicking the Quick Apply button (the lightning-bolt icon) in many panels, or by pressing ⌘+Return or Ctrl+Enter. The Quick Apply panel presents all available options in an alphabetical list. You can scroll down to the one you want or type the first few letters of the attribute in the text field at the top to jump to attributes beginning with those letters, and then navigate to the one you want and press Return or Enter, which brings you back to where you were working and closes the Quick Apply panel.

This feature can be handy if you're working on layouts from your keyboard — perhaps you're a layout artist working on a notebook while commuting. For example, you can switch to the Quick Apply panel, apply a style, and return to your object or text, all without touching the mouse.

InDesign CS3 adds a lot more attributes to the Quick Apply panel, so it can quickly get overwhelming. (InDesign CS2 just had styles in this panel.) To remove attributes you likely will never use in this panel — such as scripts and menu customizations — choose the unnamed pop-up menu at the top of the panel, and deselect unwanted attributes (the checkmarks indicate attributes that will display).

Reviewing Menu Commands

With so many panels, menu commands take on a more secondary function in InDesign. Many menu commands do nothing but display a panel or bring it forward — this is especially true in the Type and Table menus. But to get comfortable in InDesign, you need to know the basic function of each menu.

 If you're switching from QuarkXPress, you might get lost in the menus, so the charts in Appendixes C and D of this book — which cover how to make the move from QuarkXPress or PageMaker to InDesign — show the equivalent menus.

InDesign menu

Available only on Mac OS X, the InDesign menu, shown in Figure 2.33, contains preference and plug-in settings, as well as the command to exit the program and to hide it. The Services menu option contains Mac OS X functions, not any InDesign-specific options. Note that none of these menu items' functions are available in panels.

 The InDesign menu is available only on the Mac. In Windows, the About InDesign and Configure Plug-ins menu options reside in the Help menu, the Preferences menu option resides in the Edit menu, and the Quit InDesign menu option resides in the File menu. The other InDesign menu options are Mac OS X-specific.

FIGURE 2.33

The InDesign menu (in Mac OS X only)

File menu

The File menu (shown in Figure 2.34) lets you perform actions on entire documents, libraries, and books, including creating, opening, saving, closing, exporting, and printing. The Place command lets you import graphics and text files, and the Export command lets you save documents in different formats such as EPS, HTML, and PDF. The Windows version also includes the Quit menu option. Note that none of these menu items' functions are available in panels.

FIGURE 2.34

The File menu

The File menu now includes the User option for use by InCopy, as well as the Cross-Media Export options. The InBooklet SE menu has been renamed Print Booklet. And the File menu no longer has the Package for GoLive option; that feature no longer exists.

Edit menu

InDesign's Edit menu (shown in Figure 2.35) provides access to its invaluable multiple undo and redo features, as well as the standard Cut, Copy, Paste, and Clear commands. You can find Duplicate, and Step and Repeat here, even though you might be searching the Object menu for them. The Edit menu also provides commands for searching and replacing text and formats, checking spelling, and editing spelling and hyphenation dictionaries, as well as for opening the Story Editor text-editing feature and setting up stories for the InCopy add-on program. It also provides access to color settings and keyboard shortcut preferences. The Windows version also contains the Preferences menu option. Note that these menu items' functions, except for Quick Apply, are not available in panels.

 The Edit menu has some new options: One is the InCopy menu for setting up story assignments for use by InCopy. Another is the Menus option to customize InDesign menus.

FIGURE 2.35

The Edit menu

Layout menu

With the Layout menu (shown in Figure 2.36), you can change the position of the column and margin guides you established in the New Document dialog box, create guides at specific locations, and resize an entire document proportionally. You can also turn pages in a document and insert automatic page numbers using Layout menu commands. Finally, this menu contains the commands for setting up tables of contents. Note that these menu options' functions — except for the Pages, page-navigation, and Numbering & Section Options menus — are not available in panels.

FIGURE 2.36

The Layout menu

Type menu

The Type menu (shown in Figure 2.37) provides all your controls for formatting text — character formats, paragraph formats, tabs, and styles. The Story command lets you specify hanging punctuation for all the frames in a story. You can also convert text to a frame and insert special characters using a dialog box rather than keyboard shortcuts. Note that the Find Font, Change Case, Type on a Path, Document Footnote Options, Text Variables, Insert Character, Fill with Placeholder text, and Show Hidden Characters menu items' functions are not available though panels.

NEW FEATURE The Type menu adds two new menu options — Text Variables and Bulleted & Numbered Lists — to accommodate InDesign CS3's new text variables feature and to make bullets and numbering more accessible.

Revised Shortcuts

InDesign CS3 has changed a few shortcuts that users of previous versions of InDesign should know, so they can adapt accordingly:

- Type ➪ Paragraph Styles: The new shortcut is ⌘+F11 on the Mac, but the old shortcut of F11 still works. In Windows, the shortcut remains F11, but Ctrl+F11 also works.

- Type ➪ Character Styles: The new shortcut is Shift+⌘+F11 on the Mac, but the old shortcut of Shift+F11 still works. In Windows, the shortcut remains Shift+F11, but Ctrl+Shift+F11 also works.

- Type ➪ Paragraph: The new Windows shortcut is now Ctrl+Alt+T, no longer Ctrl+M, to match the Mac's Option+⌘+T. Adobe let Ctrl+Alt+T work as an alternative in InDesign CS2; now the menu has changed to make Ctrl+Alt+T the official shortcut. But the old Ctrl+M continues to work if you want to still use it.

- View ➪ Show/Hide Frame Edges: The new shortcut for the Mac only is Control+⌘+H. The Windows shortcut remains ⌘+H.

- View ➪ Display Performance ➪ Fast Display: The new shortcut is Option+Shift+⌘+Z or Ctrl+Alt+Z, replacing Shift+⌘+0 or Ctrl+Shift+0.

- View ➪ Display Performance —>High Quality Display: The new shortcut, for the Mac only, is Control+Option+⌘+H. The Windows shortcut remains Ctrl+Alt+H.

- Window ➪ Effects: The new shortcut to the renamed Transparency panel is Shift+⌘+F10 on the Mac, but the old shortcut of Shift+F10 still works. In Windows, the shortcut remains Shift+F10, but Ctrl+Shift+F10 also works.

- Window ➪ Pages: The new shortcut is ⌘+F12 on the Mac, but the old shortcut of F12 still works. In Windows, the shortcut remains F12, but Ctrl+F12 also works.

- Window ➪ Stroke: The new shortcut is ⌘+F10 on the Mac, but the old shortcut of F10 still works. In Windows, the shortcut remains F10, but Ctrl+F10 also works.

For consistency, this book uses the new shortcut for both Mac and Windows for the new shortcuts involving the F10, F11, and F12 keys, such as ⌘+F10 and Ctrl+F10 for opening the Stroke panel. They changed to accommodate Mac OS X's Exposé program, which uses the F10, F11, and F12 keys in its shortcuts, causing it to launch when InDesign users entered shortcuts using them. The new InDesign shortcuts don't step on Exposé's toes.

New shortcuts include the following:

- Type ➪ Glyphs: Option+Shift+F11 or Alt+Shift+F11.

- Type ➪ Insert Special Character ➪ Quotation Marks ➪ Straight Double Quotation Marks: Command+Shift+' or Alt+Shift+'.

- Type ➪ Insert Special Character ➪ Quotation Marks ➪ Straight Single Quotation Mark (Apostrophe): Command+' or Alt+'.

- Notes ➪ Notes Mode: ⌘+F8 or Ctrl+F8.

- Window ➪ Automation ➪ Scripts: Option+⌘+F11 or Ctrl+Alt+F11.

Appendix F lists InDesign's many shortcuts in one handy place.

FIGURE 2.37

The Type menu

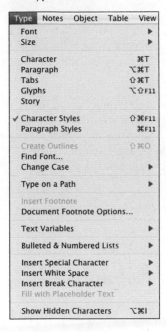

Notes menu

The Notes menu (shown in Figure 2.38) lets you insert and manage notes in your layout that do not print.

FIGURE 2.38

The Notes menu

NEW FEATURE   The Notes menu is new to InDesign CS3. This feature used to be available only if you bought the InCopy add-on.

Object menu

Use the Object menu (shown in Figure 2.39) for layout functions such as controlling the stacking order of lines and frames, grouping objects together, locking objects to the page, and wrapping text around objects.

You can manipulate objects, such as changing the number of columns and text inset in the Text Frame Options dialog box or fine-tuning the corners of a frame using the Corner Options dialog box. For working with graphics, the Object menu lets you fit graphics to frames and frames to graphics, create clipping paths, merge and separate paths, convert shapes, apply colors to some types of images, and create drop shadows and apply other lighting effects. It also lets you insert movies and audio files for interactive PDF documents.

Note that the Text Frame Options, Anchored Object, Corner Options, Clipping Path, and Convert Shape menu items' functions are not available through panels.

NEW FEATURE   The Effects option replaces the Drop Shadow and Feather options in the InDesign CS2 Object menu, and the Compound Paths menu item in InDesign CS3's Object menu used to be provided through submenu items in the InDesign CS2 Paths menu. And Corner Options is the new name for what previous versions called Corner Effects.

FIGURE 2.39

The Object menu

Table menu

The Table menu (shown in Figure 2.40) contains the controls to create and edit tables. Using commands from this menu, you create tables, modify them, convert text into tables and vice versa, manage table cells, and control row and column spacing. Note that this menu's functions are available through panels.

The Table menu

View menu

With the View menu (shown in Figure 2.41), you can change the view scale of the document, choose whether objects placed by master pages appear, and specify which layout tools are visible: *threads* (links between text frames), the edges of frames, rulers, guides, the baseline grid, and the document grid. You can also specify whether guides are locked and whether items snap to guides and the document grid. Note that none of these menu items' functions, except for Screen Mode and the zoom controls, are available in panels.

 If you're expecting to use the View menu to show and hide invisible characters such as spaces and tabs, look in the Type menu instead.

NEW FEATURE The View menu adds the Show/Hide Assigned Frames and Show/Hide Notes options to accommodate the InCopy features added to InDesign CS3.

FIGURE 2.41

The View menu

Window menu

For the most part, the Window menu (shown in Figure 2.42) opens panels or brings panels forward within their panel group. Other commands let you manage document windows, opening additional windows for the same document and redistributing document windows on-screen. Currently open documents are listed at the bottom of the menu. The window display and workspace functions are not available via panels.

NEW FEATURE   The Window menu adds the Assignments and Notes options, as well as the Cell Styles and Table Styles options to the Type & Tables submenu. It removes the Tabs option from the Type & Tables submenu. (You can still access the Tabs panel by choosing Type ➪ Tabs.)

Help menu

The Help menu (shown in Figure 2.43) contains links to Adobe's HTML help files, as well as to Adobe's program update, registration, and activation functions. The Windows version also contains the About InDesign and Configure Plug-ins menu options. Note that none of these menu items' functions are available in panels.

FIGURE 2.42

The Window menu

FIGURE 2.43

The Help menu

Contextual menus

The final interface element you'll find useful in InDesign is the contextual menu. By Control+clicking or right-clicking the document, an object, the rulers, items listed in a panel, and so on, you can display a menu of options for modifying whatever it is you're clicking. Figures 2.44 through 2.46 show eight contextual menus: two variants of one contextual menu for frames (whether containing text or graphics), two variants when you're using the Type tool one for when nothing is selected, two affecting the rulers, and two examples of contextual menus for panels.

FIGURE 2.44

From left to right, the contextual menus for a text frame, for a graphics frame, and for a text-insertion point

FIGURE 2.45

From left to right, the contextual menus for a selection of text and for when nothing is selected

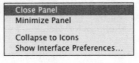

FIGURE 2.46

From left to right, the contextual menus for rulers, for the zero point, and for a panel group

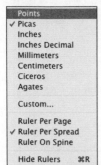

FIGURE 2.47

Many panels offer contextual menus for listed items, such as the Pages panel (left) and Swatches panel (right).

How to change your mind

Sometimes, you do something you didn't mean to — or you did mean to do it but don't like the results. InDesign gives you several ways to change your mind:

- Choose Edit ⇨ Undo or press ⌘+Z or Ctrl+Z for most actions. (Some actions, particularly actions such as scrolling that do not affect any items or the underlying document structure, are not undoable.) You can undo multiple actions in the order they were done by choosing Edit ⇨ Undo or pressing ⌘+Z or Ctrl+Z — each time you undo, and the previous action is undone.

- If you change your mind while InDesign is still completing the action, pressing Esc usually cancels the operation.

- When working in most dialog boxes, you can revert all settings to what they were when you opened the dialog box. Just press Option or Alt, which changes the Cancel button into a Reset button, and then click Reset.

If you've undone something that you decide you didn't want to undo, InDesign has a way to help here as well: Choose Edit ⇨ Redo or press Shift+⌘+Z or Ctrl+Shift+Z. This redoes whatever you undid via Edit ⇨ Undo, or ⌘+Z or Ctrl+Z. It does not reinstate a canceled operation or a reverted dialog box.

Alternately, choosing Undo and Redo is a handy way of seeing a before/after view of a particular change. As with undo, you can redo multiple undone actions in the order in which they were undone. If you've made lots of changes to your document and you want to jettison them, you can choose File ⇨ Revert to reopen the file as it was when you last saved it.

Summary

InDesign stores its preferences in a file that you can copy and send to other users to ensure you use a standard interface in workgroups. It offers its functionality through a variety of interface methods: tools, panels, menu options, and contextual menus, as well as through some navigation controls in the document window. Panels are the primary vehicle for accessing InDesign features, while tools are the primary vehicle for determining what actions are possible.

The variety of panels can be overwhelming, so InDesign lets you save different workspace sets that let you specify which panels to display and where to display them in each set. You can move panels into the main dock to keep them self-contained at the right side of your screen. You can also move, separate, and combine panels into panel groups of your choice, both within the main dock or as free-floating panel groups. New panels are Assignments, Notes, Cell Styles, and Table Styles.

The Control panel is a great timesaver, grouping many functions into one panel, showing only the relevant options for different kinds of objects as they are selected.

You can undo and redo most actions, giving you greater ability to experiment.

Chapter 3

Getting InDesign Ready to Go

IN THIS CHAPTER

Knowing where preferences are stored

Setting preferences for documents and the application

Customizing keyboard shortcuts and menu options

Setting defaults for documents, text, and objects

Creating default colors and styles

Changing the view scale

Although you may not realize it, Adobe has made a variety of educated guesses about the way you work. For example, it assumes you work in picas, that you prefer low-resolution previews of images, and that you use typographers' quotes. Adobe has also made decisions about the default properties of text, the default color swatches included with documents, and the default attributes of some objects. In all cases, Adobe tried to make the defaults appropriate for most publishers.

But no matter how much thought Adobe put into making these educated guesses, they don't work for everybody. In fact, it's unlikely that every single setting is appropriate for you. So no matter how tempted you are to jump in and start working, take a minute to prepare InDesign for the way you actually work. Otherwise, you end up conforming the way you work to InDesign's decisions, making it more difficult to learn the program and get your work done; or you end up making the same changes to document after document, wasting time in the process.

Working with Preferences Files

InDesign stores preferences in several places. Some are stored in the documents themselves, so they work as expected as they are moved from user to user. Others are stored in files on your computer and affect only you.

InDesign Defaults file

The preferences you set in InDesign, from measurement units to color-calibration settings, are all stored in the InDesign Defaults file:

- On the Mac, this file is in the Users: *current user*:Library:Preferences:Adobe InDesign:Version 5.0 folder on the drive that contains the Mac OS X System folder.

- In Windows XP, it is in the \Document and Settings*current user*\Application Data\Adobe\InDesign\Version 5.0 folder on the drive that contains Windows.

- In Windows Vista, it is in the \Users*current user*\AppData\Local\Adobe\InDesign\Version 5.0 folder on the drive that contains Windows.

CROSS-REF In Windows, these folders may be hidden. Chapter 35 explains how to make them accessible.

To specify these defaults, you modify settings in the Preferences dialog box when no documents are open. All new documents you create are based on these settings.

Because some of the information affects how text flows and how documents look, you may want to standardize it for a workgroup by setting preferences once and sharing the InDesign Defaults file. (Sharing the file is a simple matter of giving copies of the file to other InDesign users to place in the appropriate system folder.)

TIP To return to a blank slate, you can delete the InDesign Defaults preference files when opening InDesign. Press Control+Option+Shift+⌘ or Ctrl+Alt+Shift when launching InDesign.

NOTE If you make changes to preferences while a document is open, the changes save with that document and not in the InDesign Defaults file. The document remembers its own preference settings so it looks the same when it's opened on other computers running InDesign.

Presets folder

The Presets folder contains seven kinds of stored preferences: shortcut sets, color swatch libraries, workspaces, glyph sets, auto-correction tables, find/change tables, and stored page sizes. Because these preferences are stored in files, they can be copied to other users' Presets folders to help ensure consistent options among all users in a workgroup. Here are the six folders that contain the stored preferences:

- **Shortcut Sets:** InDesign lets you create custom shortcut sets, so if you don't like the shortcuts that Adobe assigned to various commands — or if you want to add shortcuts to features when Adobe doesn't provide them — you can make InDesign work your way. This also lets different users have their own shortcut definitions on the same computer.

- **Swatch Libraries:** This folder contains color-swatch libraries — both those that come with InDesign and any you might add yourself.

- **Workspaces:** This folder contains workspace definitions; a *workspace* is a set of panels and panel positions that you can save for easy switching among different interfaces optimized for different layout tasks. For example, you can have all text-editing panels appear when you're working on text, and graphics and object-handling panels appear while you're laying out elements.

- **Glyph Sets:** This folder contains any *glyph sets* — collections of special characters that you use frequently and want one-panel access to — that you've created in InDesign. Chapter 21 explains how to create these.

- **Autocorrect:** This folder includes XML documents that store the automatic text-correction rules that display in the Autocorrect pane of the Preferences dialog box — both those that come with InDesign and those you add yourself (see Chapter 16). If you are knowledgeable in XML, you can edit this file to add more correction rules outside of InDesign (helpful for a production programmer, for example).

- **Find-Change Queries:** This folder includes XML documents that store common find/change queries, such as replacing two paragraph returns with one, as shown in the Query pop-up menu of the Find/Change dialog box (see Chapter 16). If you are knowledgeable in XML, you can edit this file to add more correction rules outside of InDesign.

The Presets folder contains the seventh stored setting, the New Doc Sizes.txt file. It contains any custom page sizes you have created; you edit this text file in any text editor to create your own. These custom page sizes display in the New Document and Document Setup dialog boxes' Page Size pop-up menus. An example would be building a custom page size for every standard ad size for a magazine or newspaper to ensure correct dimensions on new ad documents. Just add a new line in the New Doc Sizes.txt file for each document style as follows: name→width→height. For example: Business card→3.5"→2". (The → character here indicates a tab; you should press the Tab key.)

NEW FEATURE Stored find/change queries and glyph sets are new to InDesign CS3. Also, the Scripts folder has been moved out of the Presets folder into the main InDesign folder.

CROSS-REF I cover workspaces in Chapter 2; shortcut sets later in this chapter; document creation in Chapter 4; swatch libraries in Chapter 8; search and replace and auto-correction in Chapter 16; glyph sets in Chapter 21; and scripts in Chapter 38.

Using the Preferences Dialog Box

Preferences are settings that affect an entire document — such as what measurement system you're using on rulers, what color the guides are, and whether substituted fonts are highlighted. In InDesign, you access these settings through the Preferences dialog box (choose InDesign ⇨ Preferences ⇨ *desired pane* or press ⌘+K on the Mac, or choose Edit ⇨ Preferences ⇨ *desired pane* or press Ctrl+K in Windows). They are stored in the InDesign Defaults file in your InDesign application folder.

NOTE   You must select a specific pane from the Preferences submenu. For example, you might choose InDesign ⇨ Preferences ⇨ Composition on the Mac or Edit ⇨ Preferences ⇨ Composition in Windows. If you use the keyboard shortcut ⌘+K or Ctrl+K, you will get the General pane, from which you can then select the desired pane from the list on the left.

InDesign has two methods for changing preferences: You can change preferences when no documents are open to create new settings for all future documents, or you can change preferences for the active document, which affects only that document. Your strategy for changing preferences depends on the way you work and the needs of specific documents. For example, if you generally prefer to work in points, you might change the default measurement system to points with no documents open. However, you might have a design such as an envelope that makes more sense in inches, so you can change the measurement system for that specific document.

The Preferences dialog box provides 17 types of settings divided into panes: General, Interface, Type, Advanced Type, Composition, Units & Increments, Grids, Guides & Pasteboard, Dictionary, Spelling, Autocorrect, Notes, Story Editor Display, Display Performance, Appearance of Black, File Handling, and Clipboard Handling. The steps for setting preferences stay the same, regardless of the changes you need to make.

NEW FEATURE   The Interface and Clipboard Handling panes are new, taking controls previously available in the General and File Handling panes, respectively. The Notes pane is completely new.

When using the Preferences dialog box:

1. **Determine whether the change is for a specific document or for all future documents, and then open or close documents accordingly.** If no documents are open, the changes are stored in your preferences file and will be remembered for all new documents. If a document is open, the changes are in effect for that document only.

2. **Choose InDesign ⇨ Preferences ⇨ General on the Mac or press ⌘+K, or choose Edit ⇨ Preferences ⇨ General or press Ctrl+K in Windows, to open the General pane.**

3. **To switch to a specific pane, click an option from the list at the left of the dialog box, as shown in Figure 3.1.**

4. **Change any settings in any of the panes, and then click OK.** The changes are saved with the active document or in the InDesign Defaults file.

NOTE   In this section, I take a comprehensive look at all the preferences in InDesign. I explain references that affect specific features again in the relevant chapters. For example, I cover Dictionary preferences in Chapter 16.

CAUTION   Unlike most actions you perform in InDesign, you cannot reverse changes to preferences using the Undo command (choose Edit ⇨ Undo, or press ⌘+Z or Ctrl+Z). If you change your mind about a preference setting, open the Preferences dialog box and change the setting again.

General preferences

Options in the General pane (see Figure 3.1) affect the operation of several InDesign features.

Page Numbering area

In the Page Numbering area of the Preferences dialog box, the View pop-up menu controls how page numbers appear in the fields such as the page number field on the document window. Here are the controls:

- **Section Numbering:** This is the default setting, which means that InDesign shows the page numbers according to the information in the Section Options dialog box accessed through the Pages panel's flyout menu. When Section Numbering is selected, by default you need to type section page numbers, such as Sec2:3, in fields.

- **Absolute Numbering:** This option, which I prefer, shows page numbers according to each page's position in the document. For example, the first page is 1, the second page is 2, and the third page is 3, even if the pages display the Roman numerals i, ii, and iii. When this option is selected, you can always jump to the first page in a document by typing 1 in the Page Number box.

FIGURE 3.1

The General pane of the Preferences dialog box

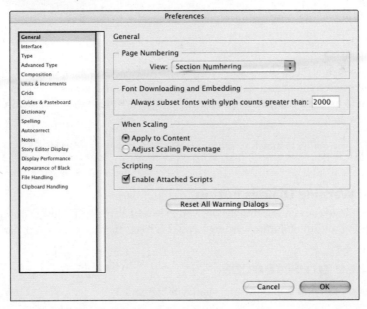

Font Downloading and Embedding area

The Always Subset Fonts with Glyph Counts Greater Than field is used for OpenType fonts that have many special characters, such as accented letters, symbols, and diacritical marks. To prevent output files from getting clogged with very large font files, this option lets you set the maximum number of characters (glyphs) that can be downloaded from a font file into an output file. Any characters actually used are always downloaded; the reason you might want to download an entire font is so someone could edit the file as a PDF or EPS file and have access to all characters in the proper fonts for such editing.

When Scaling area

When the Apply to Content radio button is enabled and you resize an object with no stroke, InDesign displays the new scale whether you select the *object* using the Selection tool or Position tool or you select its *content* using the Direct Selection tool or Position tool — this option makes it easy to see which objects have had their content scaled when selected with the Selection tool.

When the Adjust Scaling Percentage option is enabled instead, InDesign shows the resized object as 100% when you select it with the Selection tool or Position tool, but show the actual new scale only when you select its content using the Direct Selection tool or Position tool — this has always been InDesign's standard behavior. (If the object has a stroke, then InDesign shows the new scale no matter what tool you select it with — also InDesign's longstanding normal behavior.)

 The When Scaling area is new to InDesign CS3. This control used to be in the Type pane and called Adjust Text Attributes While Scaling. It now applies to both textual and graphics contents, not just text.

CROSS-REF Chapter 11 explains how to scale objects and their contents.

Scripting area

If checked (which is the default status), the Enable Attached Scripts option lets scripts run automatically whenever you open a specific menu. This lets script developers write scripts that don't require you to explicitly run them from the Scripts panel; instead they run themselves as you select certain menu items.

NEW FEATURE The ability to attach script to menu actions is new to InDesign CS3.

Reset All Warning Dialogs button

Use this button to turn on warning dialogs you may have turned off. Most warning dialog boxes have an option to turn off future warnings, and this resets them so they all appear again.

Interface preferences

InDesign has four options in this pane, shown in Figure 3.2:

- The Floating Tools Panel pop-up menu lets you set the Tools panel as single-column width, single row, or the default double-column width. This is a matter of personal preference. The default is a single column.

- The Tool Tips pop-up menu has three options: Normal, Fast, and None. None turns off *Tool Tips*, the labels that pop up when the mouse hovers over a panel's icons. Fast makes the labels appear faster, which is best for new users learning the interface. Normal is the default setting and is the best for experienced users because it waits a bit before displaying the label so they don't pop up if you're just moving the mouse slowly.

- The Show Thumbnails on Place option, if checked, shows you a small preview icon of an imported text or graphics file when you use the Place command to bring them into InDesign.

- If the Auto-Collapse Icon Panels option is checked, InDesign automatically closes an open panel once the mouse is no longer within that panel. But this feature works only if the main dock has been collapsed and you are accessing the panels from it in that collapsed view. (Free-floating panels are not affected.)

NEW FEATURE The ability to see a preview of a placed file and the use of a collapsible dock are both new to InDesign CS3.

FIGURE 3.2

The Interface pane of the Preferences dialog box

Type preferences

Options in the Type pane of the Preferences dialog box, shown in Figure 3.3, affect how several character formats work, whether you use typographer's quotes, and how text appears on-screen.

Type Options area

These options control how InDesign handles character formatting behind the scenes as you work. Note that the first four of the seven Type Options that control different aspects of InDesign's character handling are selected by default.

■ **Use Typographer's Quotes:** When you press the quote key on the keyboard with Use Typographer's Quotes selected, InDesign inserts the correct typographer's quotes (often called *curly quotes*) for the current language in use. For example, for U.S. English, InDesign inserts typographic single quotes (' ') or double quotes (" ") rather than straight quotes. For French and some other languages, InDesign inserts double angle brackets (« »). InDesign knows what language's characters to use based on the Language pop-up menu in the Character panel (choose Type ➪ Character, or press ⌘+T or Ctrl+T), or in the Paragraph Style and Character Style panels' Advanced Character Formats pane (choose Type ➪ Paragraph Styles, or press ⌘+F11 or Ctrl+F11, and choose Type ➪ Character Styles, or press Shift+⌘+F11 or Ctrl+Shift+F11, respectively).

FIGURE 3.3

The Type pane of the Preferences dialog box

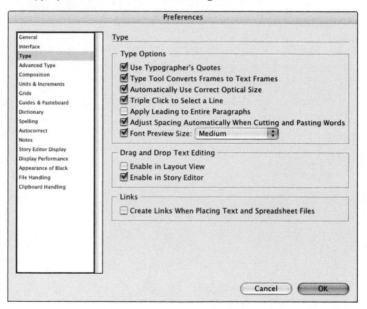

■ **Type Tool Converts Frame to Text Frames.** Checked by default, this option has InDesign automatically convert an empty frame to a text frame if you click it with the Type tool. If unchecked, you would have to choose Object ➪ Content ➪ Text to convert a selected graphics or unassigned frame to a text frame.

NEW FEATURE   The ability to control whether a graphics or unassigned frame is automatically converted to a text frame is new to InDesign CS3. In past versions, this behavior was automatic.

- **Automatically Use Correct Optical Size:** Use this option when it's selected. It automatically accesses OpenType and PostScript fonts that include an optimal size axis, which ensures optimal readability at any size.

- **Triple Click to Select a Line:** When this option is selected, InDesign lets you triple-click anywhere in a line to select the whole line. This used to be a standard shortcut in Mac applications but has fallen into disuse recently.

- **Apply Leading to Entire Paragraphs:** If this option is selected, InDesign applies leading changes to the entire paragraph as opposed to the current line. In most cases, you want the leading to be applied to all paragraphs, so I recommend that you click this option (it is not selected by default in InDesign).

QUARKXPRESS QuarkXPress rightfully treats leading as a paragraph attribute, so be sure to select the Apply Leading to Entire Paragraph option in InDesign to make it work like it should. But note that InDesign does not support QuarkXPress's additive leading capability (where you type +2 pt to make the leading 2 points more than whatever the current point size is), so leading in InDesign will never exactly match the QuarkXPress approach.

- **Adjust Spacing Automatically When Cutting and Pasting Words:** This option is selected by default and adds or deletes spaces around words when you cut and paste, so words don't abut or have too many spaces next to them.

- **Font Preview Size:** If selected, a preview displays in all menus in which lists of fonts appear. The preview shows the actual font so you can see what you'll get before selecting the font. The pop-up menu at right lets you select the size of the preview. Figure 3.4 shows an example. Note that if you have lots of fonts, the preview menu size quickly becomes unwieldy.

Drag and Drop Text Editing area

The options here control whether you can drag and drop text selections within a document. By default, Enable in Story Editor is selected while Enable in Layout View is deselected. These default settings mean you can drag and drop text in the Story Editor but not when working on a layout, the rationale being that a layout artist could inadvertently move text if it were enabled for the layout view.

Links area

The Create Links When Placing Text and Spreadsheet Files option creates links to your source text files. InDesign can alert you when those files change so you can reimport them if desired. (InDesign always does this for graphics files.) Select this option if you want InDesign to track such links in the Links panel (choose Window ⇨ Links, or press Shift+⌘+D or Ctrl+Shift+D).

FIGURE 3.4

Example of a font menu that appears when Font Preview Size is selected and set to medium size

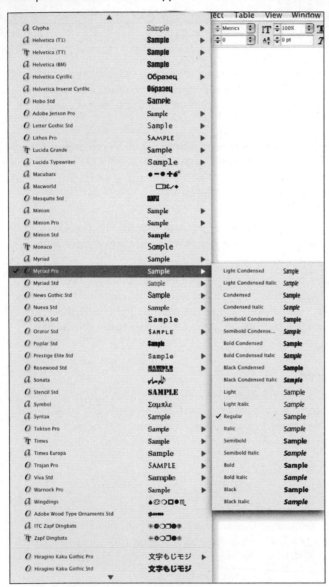

Advanced Type pane

The Advanced Type pane includes additional typographic settings, as seen in Figure 3.5.

The flyout menu on the Character panel (Type ⇨ Character, or ⌘+T or Ctrl+T) lets you format highlighted characters as Superscript (reduced and raised above the baseline), Subscript (reduced and dropped below the baseline), or Small Caps (reduced versions of capital letters). Note that Superscript, Subscript, and Small Caps characters do not need to be reduced — they can actually be enlarged instead. The controls in the Advanced Type pane govern precisely how these characters are placed and resized, as well as control the handling on non-Latin text entry.

FIGURE 3.5

The Advanced Type pane of the Preferences dialog box

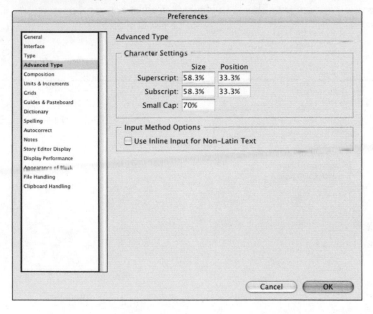

Character Settings area

This area controls the size of subscripts, superscripts, and small caps:

■ The Size fields let you specify how much to scale these characters. The default is 58.3 percent, but you can type a value between 1 and 200 percent. I prefer 60 or 65 percent, depending on the type size and font.

■ The Position fields let you specify how much to shift Superscript characters up and Subscript characters down. The default is 33.3 percent, but you can type a value between −500 and 500 percent. I prefer 30 percent for subscripts and 35 percent for superscripts.

- The Small Cap field lets you specify the scale of Small Caps characters in relation to the actual capital letters in the font. The default is 70 percent, but you can type a value between 1 and 200 percent.

Input Method Options area

The Use Inline Input for Non-Latin Text option enables input method editors (IMEs) from Microsoft, Apple, or other companies, if installed on your computer, for typing Chinese-, Japanese-, and Korean-language (CJK) characters on non-CJK operating systems. It's meant for the occasional use of CJK characters. If you publish regularly in these languages, you should use the appropriate CJK version of InDesign instead.

Composition preferences

In general, preferences in the Composition pane, shown in Figure 3.6, affect entire paragraphs rather than individual characters.

FIGURE 3.6

The Composition pane of the Preferences dialog box

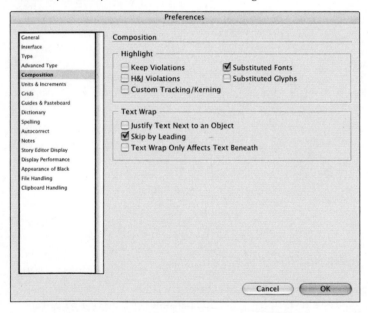

Highlight area

The options in the Highlight area control whether InDesign calls attention to possible typesetting problems by drawing a highlighter pen effect behind the text.

■ **Keep Violations:** This option is deselected by default and highlights the last line in a text frame when it cannot follow the rules specified in the Keep Options dialog box in the Paragraph panel's flyout menu (Type ⇨ Paragraph, or Option+⌘+T or Ctrl+Alt+T). For example, if the Keep Options settings require more lines to stay together than fit in the text frame and, thus, bumps all the text in a frame to the next text frame in the chain, the Keep Options rules are violated and the last line of text is highlighted so you know to change the frame size or the Keep Options rules for that text.

■ **H&J Violations:** When selected, H&J Violations uses three shades of yellow to mark lines that might be too loose or too tight due to the combination of spacing and hyphenation settings. The darker the shade, the worse InDesign considers the problem to be. H&J Violations is deselected by default; you might want to select it while fine-tuning type, and then deselect it when you're finished.

■ **Custom Tracking/Kerning:** If this option is selected, it highlights custom tracking and kerning (essentially, anywhere you override the defaults) in a bluish green. It's handy for copy editors, helping them quickly find such overrides to make sure they're not too tight or loose for readability reasons.

■ **Substituted Fonts:** This option is selected by default and uses pink highlights to indicate characters in fonts that are not available to InDesign. InDesign actually uses Adobe Sans MM or Adobe Serif MM to create a replacement for missing fonts, so the text looks close to the actual font. For editing purposes, the substituted fonts work fine, although the pink highlights can be distracting. But for output purposes, it's important that you have the correct fonts, so you may want to live with the irritation and have InDesign highlight substituted fonts for you.

■ **Substituted Glyphs:** This option highlights in yellow any glyphs (special characters) that are substituted. This usually occurs when you have multiple versions of the same font, with different special characters in each version. For example, a file using the euro (€) currency symbol might have been created in the newest version of, say, Syntax. But a copy editor working on the same file may have an older version of Syntax that doesn't have the euro symbol in it. Selecting Substituted Glyphs ensures that such a problem is highlighted. Substituted Glyphs also highlights characters of an OpenType font that have been changed on the fly by turning on some OpenType features from the Control panel's or Character panel's flyout menu, such as Discretionary Ligatures, Swashes, Small Caps, Slash Zero, and so on. I recommend you select this option.

> **NOTE** InDesign is hypersensitive to fonts (see Chapter 17), so you get such highlighting even when you have the correct font installed but the wrong face applied to it (such as Normal rather than Regular); in these cases, the font style has brackets ([ ]) around it in the Character or Control panel.

Text Wrap area

As the label makes clear, the three options here affect how text wraps:

- **Justify Text Next to an Object:** If this option is selected, it overrides any local justification settings that justify text that wraps around an object. That means the text smoothly follows the object's shape, rather than keeps any ragged margins that can make the wrap look strange. This option comes into play when you wrap ragged (left-aligned or right-aligned) text around objects; I recommend that you avoid wrapping text on its ragged side because it looks awkward. Although this option eliminates the awkwardness of ragged text that wraps around an object, it presents a different awkwardness: having some text ragged (that which is not wrapping) and some text justified (that which is wrapping).

- **Skip by Leading:** When selected, this option uses the text's leading to determine how much space follows an object that it is wrapping. This has an effect only if you choose the Jump Object text-wrap option in the Text Wrap panel. (See Chapter 13 for more on text wrap.)

- **Text Wrap Only Affects Text Beneath:** If selected, this option has only text below an object wrap around that object. This lets some text overlap an image and some text to overwrap it, depending on the text's location in the stacking order.

Units & Increments preferences

The measurement systems you use for positioning items and the way the arrows on the keyboard increase or decrease settings are controlled by settings in the Units & Increments pane shown in Figure 3.7.

Ruler Units area

The Ruler Units area affects three things: the origin point (by page, by spread, or by the spine), the measurement system displayed on the horizontal and vertical ruler on the document window, and the default values in fields used for positioning objects.

The Origin pop-up menu determines the zero point (typically, the upper-left corner of the page) for object positions. If you choose Page, objects' positions are relative to each page's upper-left corner. If you choose Spread, objects' positions are relative to the current spread's upper-left corner. If you choose Spine, objects' positions are relative to the binding spine of each spread — the very top and center of where the two pages meet.

With the Horizontal and Vertical pop-up menus, you can specify one measurement system for the horizontal ruler and measurements and specify another measurement system for the vertical ruler and measurements. For example, you might use points for horizontal measurements so you can use the rulers to gauge tab and indent settings, while using inches for vertical measurements. If you use Inches for both the Horizontal and Vertical Ruler Units, not only do the rulers display inches, but the X, Y, W, and H fields on the Control panel (choose Window ⇨ Control, or press Option+⌘+6 or Ctrl+Alt+6) or Transform panel (choose Window ⇨ Object & Layout ⇨ Transform) display values in inches as well.

FIGURE 3.7

The Units & Increments pane of the Preferences dialog box

NOTE To display the document ruler, choose View ⇨ Show Ruler, or press ⌘+R or Ctrl+R.

TIP The default horizontal and vertical measurement system is picas. If you aren't accustomed to working in picas, be sure to change the default Horizontal and Vertical Ruler Units when no documents are open. This ensures that all future documents use your preferred measurement system. (If you make the change with a document open, the change applies only to the open document.)

To specify the measurement systems you want to use, click an option from the Horizontal pop-up menu and from the Vertical pop-up menu. The following options are available:

- **Points:** A typesetting measurement equal to ¹/₇₂ of an inch. To enter values in points, type a p before the value or pt after the value (p6 or 6 pt, for example).

TIP InDesign doesn't care if you put spaces between numbers and the abbreviations in your measurements — 3 p is read the same as 3p, and 0.4inch is read the same as 0.4 inch, for example.

- **Picas:** A typesetting measurement equal to ⅙ of an inch. To enter values in picas, type a p after the value (for example, 6p).

- **Inches:** An English measurement system that is divided into sixteenths. To enter values in inches, type i, in, inch, or " after the value. For example, 3i, 3in, 3 inch, and 3" are all read by InDesign as 3 inches.

- **Inches decimal:** Inches divided into tenths on the ruler rather than 16ths. To enter values in inches decimal, include a decimal point as appropriate and type i, in, inch, or " after the value.

- **Agates:** Typically used in newspapers, an agate is ¼ of an inch, usually the depth of a line in the small type of classified ads, stock tables, and sports statistics boxes. To enter values in agates, type ag after the value. For example, 10ag.

NEW FEATURE   The use of agates is new to InDesign CS3.

- **Millimeters:** A metric measurement that is ⅒ of a centimeter. To enter values in millimeters, type mm after the value (for example, 14mm).

- **Centimeters:** A metric measurement that is about ⅓ of an inch. To enter values in centimeters, type cm after the value (for example, 2.3cm).

- **Ciceros:** A European typesetting measurement that is slightly larger than a pica. To enter values in ciceros, type c after the value (for example, 2c).

- **Custom:** This option lets you set a custom number of points as your measurement unit, placing a labeled tick mark at every point increment you specify. You get to customize the number of tick marks between the labeled marks by typing a value in the Points field. For example, if you type 12 in the field, you get a tick mark at each pica, because there are 12 points in a pica. A good opportunity to use this is if you need to have the rulers show tick marks at whole-line increments; in that case, if your leading is 8 points, you'd set the Custom field to 8.

TIP   Despite the Ruler Units you specify, you can type values in any fields using any supported measurement system. For example, if you're working in picas, you can type an inch value in the Width field by typing 1 in. InDesign automatically converts the value to picas for you. You can type values in picas and points by placing a p between the two values. For example, typing 1p2 indicates 1 pica and 2 points.

Point/Pica Size area

The Points/Inch pop-up menu lets you specify how a point (pt) is calculated. The default is PostScript (72 pts/in). You can also select Traditional (72.27 pts/in), which had been the standard before electronic publishing took hold in the 1980s, as well as 72.23 and 72.3. You can also enter a value of between 60 and 80. Leave this at PostScript (72 pts/in) unless you or your service bureau has a reason to select a different option.

Keyboard Increments area

The arrow keys on the keyboard let you move selected objects right, left, up, or down. You can also use the arrow keys and other keyboard shortcuts to change some text formatting. You can customize

Keyboard Options for Cursor Movements

Whatever you enter as the values for the Cursor Key fields, when you are working in InDesign, you can use several keys to change how much the values actually change and/or make a copy of the moved object:

- If you press the Shift key while you press an arrow key, the object moves ten times the amount specified in the Cursor Key field.

- Holding the Option or Alt key while you press an arrow key creates a copy of the selected object at the distance specified in the Cursor Key field.

- Holding the Shift key with the Option or Alt key while you press an arrow key creates a copy of the selected object at ten times the amount specified in the Cursor Key field. This last combination is a very simple and quick way to create a grid of text or image boxes with equal spacing between them.

Similarly, you can use keys to modify how the Size/Leading field values are applied:

- To increase the point size of selected text, press Shift+⌘+. (period) or Ctrl+Shift+. (period).

- To decrease the point size, press Shift+⌘+, (comma) or Ctrl+Shift+, (comma).

- Add Option or Alt to the combination to multiply the increment by five.

- To modify leading for selected text, Option+click or Alt+click the up or down arrow on the keyboard.

There are two other ways to use keys to change how cursors are applied:

- In the Character panel's Baseline Shift field, press Shift while clicking to multiply the increment by five.

- In the Character panel's kerning field, hold the ⌘ or Ctrl key to multiply the increment by five.

the way these shortcuts work, for example, by specifying how far each click of an arrow key moves an item.

These preferences are not used consistently to modify the arrow keys or keyboard shortcuts:

- The Cursor Key field works with all four arrow keys.

- The Size/Leading value works with the up and down arrow keys for leading.

- The Kerning field works with the left and right arrows.

- The Size/Leading value works with a regular keyboard shortcut.

- The Baseline Shift field works only while pressing the arrow keys when the Baseline Shift field is highlighted on the Character panel.

The options are:

- **Cursor Key field:** When you select an object with the Selection tool or the Direct Selection tool, you can move it up, down, left, or right using the arrow keys on the keyboard. By default, the item moves 1 point. You can change the increment to a value between 0.001 and 100 points (equal to 8p4 or 1.3888 inches). For example, if you're using a document grid, you might change the increment to match the grid lines.

- **Size/Leading field:** The value you type in this field, which is 2 points by default, specifies how much point size or leading is increased or decreased when implemented with keyboard commands. You can type a value between 1 and 100.

- **Baseline Shift field:** You can shift the baseline of highlighted text up or down by clicking in the Baseline Shift field on the Character panel, and then pressing the up or down arrow on the keyboard. You can change the default value of 2 points to any value between 1 and 100. If you press Shift while clicking, the increment is multiplied by five.

- **Kerning field:** To kern text with keyboard commands, you position the cursor between two letters, and then Option+click or Alt+click the right arrow key to increase kerning or the left arrow to decrease kerning. By default, each click changes kerning by $^{20}/_{1000}$ of an em dash — shown on screen as 20/1000 em. You can change this value to anything between 1 and 100, in increments of $^{1}/_{1000}$ of an em dash. Hold the ⌘ or Ctrl key to multiply the increment by five.

Grids preferences

Grids preferences let you set up a baseline grid, which you commonly use to space text evenly across columns, and a document-wide grid, which you can use for positioning or drawing objects. If you're planning a structured design that uses a grid, you want to set it up before you start working in the document. It's likely that each design you create will have different grid settings based on its individual content, so you probably won't change Grids preferences with no documents open. The Grids pane is shown in Figure 3.8.

NOTE By default, both the baseline grid and the document grid appear on every spread behind all objects; the document grid appears on the pasteboard as well. Both grids cover the entire document and cannot be associated with a specific master page or layer. You can have grids appear in front by deselecting the Grids in Back option.

Baseline Grid area

You can specify the color of the baseline grid, where it starts, how far apart each grid line is, and when it appears. To display the baseline grid for a document, choose View ➪ Grids & Guides ➪ Show Baseline Grid, or press Option+⌘+' (apostrophe) or Ctrl+Alt+' (apostrophe). You have the following options:

- **Color pop-up menu:** The default color of the baseline grid is Light Blue. If this color is difficult for you to see, or if you're accustomed to the pink lines in QuarkXPress, you can select a different color from the Color pop-up menu. Choose Other to access the system color picker and create your own color.

- **Start field:** This value specifies how far down from the top of the page the grid starts. The Start value, which defaults to 3p0, usually matches your top margin.

- **Relative To pop-up menu:** InDesign lets you set where the grid starts, which is at Top of Page or Top Margin.

The Grids pane of the Preferences dialog box

- **Increment Every field:** The amount of space between grid lines is specified in the Increment Every field. The default value of 1p0 usually changes to match the leading of your body text so text aligns with the grid.

- **View Threshold pop-up menu.** You can prevent the baseline grid from appearing when you decrease the view percentage. If you use the default setting, the baseline grid does not appear at views below 75 percent. You can type a value between 5 and 4,000 percent.

TIP You might want to change the View Threshold to match the document's most common Fit Page in Window view. For example, a magazine page on a 15-inch monitor in a full window might display at around 65 percent when you choose View ➪ Fit Page in Window.

Document Grid area

The document grid consists of intersecting horizontal and vertical gridlines, forming a pattern of small squares that you can use for object placement and for drawing symmetrical objects. You can customize the color and spacing of the grid lines. To display the document grid, choose View ⇨ Grids & Guides ⇨ Show Document Grid, or press ⌘+' (apostrophe) or Ctrl+' (apostrophe). You have the following options:

- **Color pop-up menu:** The default color of the document grid is Light Gray. Although this light shade is unobtrusive, you might want to change it to something brighter or darker so you can see it better. You can choose a different color from the Color pop-up menu or choose Other to create your own.

- **Gridline Every field:** The major grid lines, which are slightly darker, are positioned according to this value. The default value is 6p0; in general, you want to specify a value within the measurement system you're using. For example, if you're working in inches, you might type 1 inch in the Gridline Every field. That way, the gridlines match the major tick marks on the ruler. You set the horizontal and vertical settings separately.

- **Subdivisions field:** Although this is a number and not a measurement, it ends up specifying the amount of space between grid lines. The major grid lines established in the Gridline Every field are divided according to the value you type here. For example, if you type 1 inch in the Gridline Every field, and you type 4 in the Subdivisions field, you get a gridline at each quarter-inch. The default number of subdivisions is 8. You set the horizontal and vertical settings separately.

Guides & Pasteboard preferences

When you create a new document, you set up margins in the New Document dialog box (choose File ⇨ New ⇨ Document, or press ⌘+N or Ctrl+N). For more alignment options within a document, you can create guidelines by clicking and dragging them off the rulers or clicking Layout ⇨ Create Guides. Settings in the Guides & Pasteboard pane of the Preferences dialog box, shown in Figure 3.9, control the color and other attributes of the margins and guides.

Color area

In the Color area, the Color pop-up menus for Margins, Columns, Bleed, Slug, and Preview Background let you select colors other than the defaults. If you want to make your own color, choose Custom to access the system color picker. The Margins color (Magenta by default) displays on all horizontal guides; the Columns color (Violet by default) displays on all vertical guides. To display guides in a document, choose View ⇨ Grids & Guides ⇨ Show Guides, or press ⌘+; (semicolon) or Ctrl+; (semicolon).

FIGURE 3.9

The Guides & Pasteboard pane of the Preferences dialog box

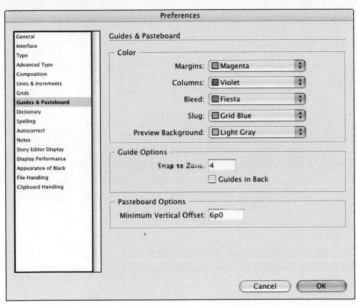

Guide Options area

This area controls guide snap-to and placement:

- **Snap to Zone:** This field's value specifies how close you need to drag an object to a grid line or guideline to make it *snap to* the line (think of it as the line's magnetic field). The default Snap to Zone value is 4 pixels, but you can type a value between 1 and 36. You enable snapping to the grid through the Snap to Document Grid and Snap to Guides commands in the View menu.

- **Guides in Back:** By default, margins and guides appear in front of all objects. If you prefer to have objects obscure margins and guides, select the Guides in Back option in the Guide Options area. Note that baseline grids and document grids always appear behind all objects, regardless of this setting.

QUARKXPRESS The Guides in Back option is for those QuarkXPress 3.3 users who never figured out how to change the unfortunate default of placing guides in back and are therefore accustomed to working with guides this way.

Pasteboard Options area

The Pasteboard Options area has the Minimum Vertical Offset field, where you specify the amount of pasteboard to appear above and below your pages. The default is 6p0 (1 inch).

Dictionary preferences

The Dictionary pane, shown in Figure 3.10, sets options related to hyphenation and spelling dictionaries, as well as to quotation marks.

Language area

The Language area begins with a pop-up menu that lets you select a language. You choose a language when you want to replace the existing, or add new, hyphenation and spelling dictionaries for that language. (This lets you control the dictionaries used by each language separately.) For example, if you want to replace the French dictionaries, choose French in the pop-up menu, and then select the new French dictionaries elsewhere in this pane. The current dictionaries for the selected language appear in the window beneath it, and there are four buttons (from left to right) to link, add, delete, or save dictionary files.

 InDesign lets you associate multiple user dictionaries with each language. Chapter 16 explains how to create, edit, remove, and otherwise manage dictionaries.

FIGURE 3.10

The Dictionary pane of the Preferences dialog box

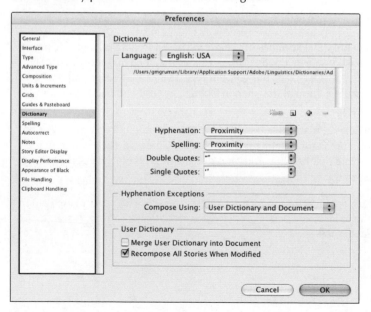

How to Install Dictionaries

To install different dictionaries, place them in the Dictionaries folder inside the Plug-ins folder (inside your InDesign application folder). Press Option+⌘+/ or Ctrl+Alt+/ to update the pop-up menus in the Dictionary pane without restarting InDesign. (In a workgroup, it's important that everyone use the same dictionaries.)

Eventually, you may be able to purchase third-party spelling or hyphenation dictionaries for InDesign — although no third-party commercial dictionaries have been released since InDesign was created in 1999. For example, you might be able to purchase a different Traditional German dictionary with more words than the one InDesign has. In that case, when you check the spelling of a word with Traditional German as its language format, InDesign would consult the third-party dictionary rather than the default. More likely, you will use this feature to create your own project-specific dictionaries, such as a dictionary of technical terms.

In addition, the Language area offers these controls over dictionaries:

- **Hyphenation:** This pop-up menu lets you choose from any hyphenation dictionaries installed for the selected language. Typically, there is only the default dictionary, Proximity, in this pop-up menu.

- **Spelling:** This pop-up menu lets you choose from any spelling dictionaries installed for the selected language. Typically, there is only the default dictionary, Proximity, in this pop-up menu.

The Language area also lets you set the quotation marks you want use. Different languages use different quotation marks, and InDesign adjusts the quotation marks automatically when you switch the language. However, there may be some cases where you might want to override the languages' default quotation-mark settings, which you can do in the Double Quotes and Single Quotes pop-up menus.

Note that changing the quotation-mark options for one language does not affect the settings for others. Each language can have independent settings for the quotation marks used.

CAUTION After you change a language's quotation-mark settings, there's no way to reset them to the language defaults except to choose the proper options from the pop-up menus. That means you need to remember or record what the original, correct setting was.

Hyphenation Exceptions area

The Compose Using pop-up menu has three options that specify what to use for hyphenation exceptions, which override the language dictionary's hyphenation rules. For example, you may choose not to hyphenate a short word like "preset" that has a legitimate hyphenation like "pre-set." And you may correct the hyphenation of specialized terms not in the language's dictionary.

The options here dictate how you manage those exceptions. By default, InDesign stores hyphenation exceptions in an outside file, so multiple users can standardize on the same exceptions list. But you can also store exceptions in a document, perhaps for unique needs. The Compose Using pop-up menu lets you select from Document, User Dictionary, and User Dictionary and Document options. Choose User Dictionary if you want to override any exceptions stored in the document — perhaps they're wrong or the copy editors want to rely only on a standard exception list. Choose Document if you want to ignore exceptions stored in an outside file. Choose User Dictionary and Document if you want to use both.

User Dictionary area

This area has two options that are selected by default and should stay that way:

- **Merge User Dictionary into Document:** If selected, this option copies the user dictionary file into the document, so if the file is sent to someone else who doesn't have access to that dictionary, the hyphenation in the document is preserved. The main reason to deselect this option is if you need to keep your files to a minimum size; otherwise, selecting this option prevents reflow when you pass a document to a service bureau or another designer, especially if you have any custom hyphenations.

- **Recompose All Stories When Modified:** If selected, this option redoes the document's hyphenation to reflect the changed user dictionary.

Spelling preferences

The Spelling pane, shown in Figure 3.11, lets you control what the InDesign spell checker examines when it checks spelling in a document.

Spelling area

There's little reason not to select all four options in this area — Misspelled Words, Repeated Words, Uncapitalized Words, and Uncapitalized Sentences. Note that Uncapitalized Words checks for known proper nouns that aren't capitalized.

Dynamic Spelling area

This area lets you enable whether InDesign checks spelling in your documents as you type and import text. If enabled (by checking the Enable Dynamic Spelling option), InDesign highlights onscreen any errors using the colors selected for the four types of errors it checks for: Misspelled Words, Repeated Words, Uncapitalized Words, and Uncapitalized Sentences. Select the desired color from the appropriate pop-up menu.

FIGURE 3.11

The Spelling pane of the Preferences dialog box

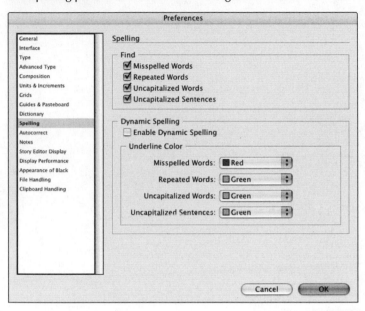

Autocorrect preferences

This pane, shown in Figure 3.12, lets you turn on automatic text correction, select which dictionary to use to detect misspellings, and specify which words are to be replaced in the list below.

Turn on auto-correction by checking the Enable Autocorrect option. If you want the auto-correction feature to also fix capitalization errors, be sure to check Autocorrect Capitalization Errors. Select the dictionary against which to check spelling from the Language pop-up menu.

You can modify the list of words to be automatically corrected using the list below the Language pop-up menu. Click Add to add a misspelled word and its correction. To delete an auto-correction rule, select it in the Misspelled Word list and click Remove.

NOTE You might think you can use the auto-correction feature to have InDesign substitute special characters for codes you enter, to save the hassle of memorizing the keyboard shortcuts or using the Glyphs panel. But you can't: InDesign doesn't let you enter special characters in the Correction field after you click the Add button. That means, for example, you cannot have InDesign change -- to an em dash (—), or change (r) to ® using this feature.

CROSS-REF Chapter 16 explains how to work with InDesign's spell-checking capabilities.

The Autocorrect pane of the Preferences dialog box

Notes preferences

The Notes pane sets up how notes are handled in InDesign. Notes are nonprinting blocks of text that you can insert within the document's text as reminders for yourself or others. Figure 3.13 shows the pane.

The Note Color pop-up menu lets you control the color of notes, to help make them stand out from other layout elements. If checked (the default), the Show Note Tool Tips option controls whether a pop-up box displaying the note appears when your mouse hovers over a note character in text.

The Notes in Story Editor area has three options. The first two, checked by default, are self-explanatory: Include Note Content When Checking Spelling and Include Note Content in Find/Change Operations. The third option, the Inline Background Color pop-up menu, controls whether there is no color (the default) or the note color displayed behind the special, nonprinting character in your text that "anchors" the note. Selecting the note color option makes the notes easier to find, but it can also be distracting.

NEW FEATURE The ability to add notes to documents is new to InDesign CS3. In previous versions, you had to buy the add-on InCopy program to have this capability. Chapter 16 covers notes in more detail.

FIGURE 3.13

The Notes pane of the Preferences dialog box

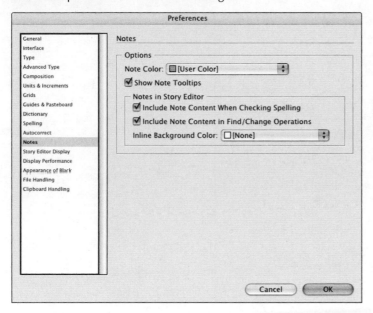

Story Editor Display preferences

The Story Editor Display pane controls how the Story Editor displays text and the text cursor. Figure 3.14 shows the pane.

 Chapter 16 covers the Story Editor in detail.

Text Display Options area

The Text Display Options area determines how text displays in the Story Editor. All options are meant to make it easy to edit text on-screen.

The first set of options lets you customize the text itself in the Story Editor. The Font pop-up menu lets you choose a font that is easy to read — you can use any active font available on your computer — as well as a point size (the default of 12 points is usually quite readable, but you may want to enlarge or reduce that in specific cases). The Line Spacing pop-up menu lets you change the default Singlespace setting to 150%, Doublespace, and Triplespace. You may prefer 150% or Doublespace if you have a wide Story Editor window to help make reading the text easier.

FIGURE 3.14

The Story Editor Display pane of the Preferences dialog box

Two pop-up menus control the basic display: Text Color and Background. You rarely want to change either of these from the default of black for the text color and white for the background. (However, if you do change the background color, you might want to choose a light yellow or green that's a bit easier on the eye.)

The Theme pop-up menu has four predefined text color/background combinations that override any changes you make to the Text Color and Background pop-up menus. Of those four themes, you want to keep Ink on Paper, which is simply black text on a white background. The other three options provide hard-to-read displays modeled after the very first computer displays in the 1970s and early 1980s.

The Enable Anti-aliasing option, if selected, smoothes text display for better readability in the Story Editor. You choose the smoothing type — Default, Best for LCD Display, or Soft — you prefer in the Type pop-up menu. Note that both Windows and the Mac OS offer similar capabilities systemwide, so you may not want to set antialiasing in InDesign if you have already set it for your whole computer.

Cursor Options area

InDesign gives you a choice of the text cursor that appears in the Story Editor. In the Cursor Options area, choose whichever looks best on-screen and is easy to find without obscuring the text under it. That varies based on the font and point size you choose. If you want the text cursor to blink — that might help you find it more easily — be sure to select the Blink option.

Display Performance preferences

The Display Performance pane, shown in Figure 3.15, controls how images and text appear on-screen.

Options area

In the Default View pop-up menu in the Options area, you can choose from three view settings: Typical, Fast, and High Quality. These affect only what appears on-screen, not what is printed. The three options correspond to how you set the options in the Adjust View Settings area of this pane.

If checked, the Preserve Object-Level Display Settings option overrides any global view settings here with those you have set for specific images. Images that have no individual view settings set will still take on the settings in this pane.

You can override these view settings by choosing Object ⇨ Display Performance and then picking Fast Display (Option+Shift+⌘+Z or Ctrl+Alt+Shift+Z), Typical Display (Option+⌘+Z or Ctrl+Alt+Z), or High Quality Display (Command+Option+⌘+H or Ctrl+Alt+H) from the submenu. The new setting remains in effect until you change it or until the next time you launch InDesign. Furthermore, you can set display settings for individual objects by ensuring that Allow Object-Level Display Settings is checked in that submenu (choose it if not) and then selecting the desired objects and applying the desired display settings to them. These settings remain in effect until you change them or clear them all by choosing View ⇨ Clear Object-Level Display Settings.

FIGURE 3.15

The Display Performance pane of the Preferences dialog box

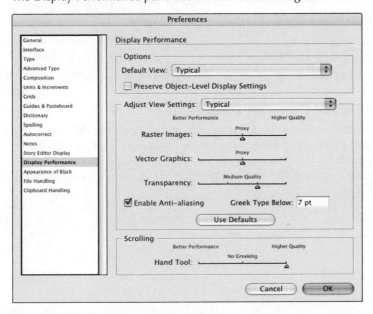

Adjust View Settings area

Use the Adjust View Settings area to determine what Typical, Optimized, and High Quality should mean in your copy of InDesign. Click the tick mark for the quality level you want to set in each of the three graphical view aspects (Raster Images, Vector Images, and Transparency). You can also click and drag the sliders to the desired tick mark. Note that you must move the slider all the way to a tick mark; you cannot choose a setting in-between tick marks.

For *raster* (bitmap) images and *vector* images, you have three options: Gray Out, Proxy, and High Resolution. Proxy means a low-resolution version (72 dpi). For transparency, there are three quality levels available — Low, Medium, and High — as well as Off, which doesn't display objects behind transparent portions of an image.

The Adjust View Settings area also has two controls for text:

- **Enable Anti-aliasing:** When this option is selected, it smoothes text display. Note that you may already have set antialiasing in your Windows or Mac OS X systemwide display preferences, in which case you probably don't need to also set them in InDesign.
- **Greek Type Below:** This field is where you set the size text appears as gray lines rather than as actual characters.

Click Use Defaults to return to InDesign's default setting for this pane.

Scrolling area

You can adjust screen refresh while scrolling by setting your preferred options in the Hand Tool slider. Either click the desired tick mark or move the slider to the desired tick mark. Selecting the leftmost tick mark means you see less detail appear as you scroll. This can speed up scrolling in complex documents. It has no effect on image preview when you stop scrolling, nor on printing quality.

Appearance of Black preferences

InDesign lets you control how black appears on-screen and when printing, as seen in Figure 3.16.

Options for Black on RGB and Grayscale Devices area

This area lets you control the display of blacks, as well as the output when printing and exporting to PDF. Using the On Screen and Printing/Exporting pop-up menus, you can choose Display All Blacks Accurately or Display All Blacks as Rich Black. *Rich black* (also called *superblack*) is created by combining black and magenta to create a darker appearance. Chapter 8 covers this concept in more detail.

The Appearance of Black pane of the Preferences dialog box

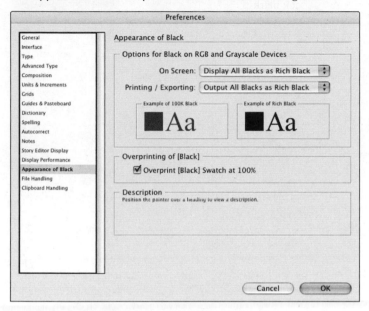

Overprinting of [Black] area

By default, the Overprint [Black] Swatch at 100% option is selected so that any black text, strokes, or fills overprint. This usually results in clearer text and lines. (This option applies to the [Black] color in the Swatches panel, rather than, say, a black swatch that you create.) If you deselect Overprint [Black], all black text, strokes, and fills knock out of their backgrounds, which results in a lighter black and could cause some misregistration when printing.

CROSS-REF See Chapters 8 and 29 for more details on creating colors and trapping colors, respectively.

File Handling preferences

The File Handling pane, shown in Figure 3.17, controls how recovery files and document previews are handled. It also controls how XML snippets are handled, whether the Version Cue system is active, and how image size is handled when an image file is relinked.

FIGURE 3.17

The File Handling pane of the Preferences dialog box

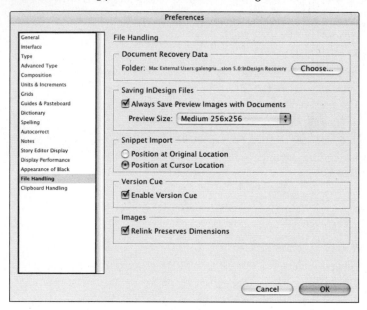

Document Recovery Data area

In this area, InDesign lets you specify the folder that contains auto-recovery files, which are files that let you recover most or all of your work in case of a program or system crash. You can click Choose to select an alternate directory, but there's really no reason to change the default, which places the recovery folder safely inside the appropriate location based on your operating system:

- On the Mac, this directory is Users:*current user*:Library:Preferences:Adobe InDesign:Version 5.0:Caches folder on the drive that contains the Mac OS X System folder.

- In Windows XP, it is \Document and Settings*current user*\Application Data\Adobe\ InDesign\Version 5.0\Caches folder on the drive that contains Windows.

- In Windows Vista, it is \Users*current user*\AppData\Local\Adobe\InDesign\Version 5.0\ Caches folder on the drive that contains Windows.

Saving InDesign files

The Always Save Preview Images with Documents option, if selected, lets InDesign save a thumbnail view of the document's first page. Select a preview size from the Preview Size pop-up menu. That preview appears in the Open a File dialog box instead of the InDesign logo when you select a file. It's handy when you've got a ton of files in a folder and can't remember which is which.

Snippet Import area

Snippets are XML files that contain pieces of an InDesign layout exported for use by others. The radio buttons here give you the choice of having any snippet that you drag into the layout placed at its original coordinates (that is, at the same coordinates it had in its original document) or at the cursor (mouse pointer) location when you drag it to the new document. The default is Position at Cursor Location, which is typically where you'd expect it.

> **NEW FEATURE** The Snippet Import options are new to InDesign CS3. In previous versions, snippets always were positioned at their original location. Snippets are covered in Chapter 10.

Version Cue area

The Enable Version Cue option, if selected, turns on Adobe's Version Cue file-management system. This changes your Open a File, Save, Place, Export, and similar file-handling dialog boxes to enable you to save multiple versions of the same document for workflow publishing.

> **CROSS-REF** Chapters 4 and 36 cover Version Cue in more detail.

Images area

The Relink Preserves Dimensions option, which is checked by default, ensures that if you update a link to a graphics file using the Relink command that any dimensions such as position and scale that you applied to the original file are retained after the relink.

> **NEW FEATURE** This option is new to InDesign CS3. Previously, relinking (as opposed to updating) a link would discard any dimensions previously set. Chapter 13 covers linking in more detail.

Clipboard Handling pane

The Clipboard Handling pane, shown in Figure 3.18, controls how image and text formatting are handled when you copy elements to or from the Clipboard.

> **NOTE** When you choose Edit ⇨ Copy, or press ⌘+C or Ctrl+C, and choose Edit ⇨ Cut, or press ⌘+X or Ctrl+X, in any application, you place a copy on the Mac or Windows Clipboard. This lets items be shared among applications. Such items in the Clipboard are pasted into your current document using the standard Paste commands: Edit ⇨ Paste, or ⌘+V or Ctrl+V.

> **NEW FEATURE** The Clipboard Handling pane is new, but its functions are not. The Clipboard options used to be in the File Handling pane, and the Paste options in the When Pasting Text and Tables from Other Applications area used to be in the Type pane.

Clipboard area

There are three options in this area that control how PDF data is handled between the Clipboard and InDesign.

- **Prefer PDF When Pasting:** Selecting this option converts items copied from Adobe Illustrator into PDF files so that transparency objects, blends, and patterns are preserved during the paste operation into InDesign.

- **Copy PDF to Clipboard:** Selecting this option creates a temporary PDF file when you copy items from InDesign for pasting into applications such as Illustrator.

- **Preserve PDF Data at Quit:** Selecting this option keeps any pasted PDF information in the Clipboard's memory when you quit InDesign. You usually don't need to select this option.

When Pasting Text and Tables from Other Applications area

This area gives you a choice as to how formatting is handled when you paste textual objects from other applications: Using the two Paste radio buttons, you click either All Information or Text Only. The default is Text Only. This can be helpful or a pain, depending on whether you want copied text to preserve its formatting or you prefer copied text to take on the formatting of the destination location's text. The right answer depends on your specific layouts.

FIGURE 3.18

The Clipboard Handling pane of the Preferences dialog box

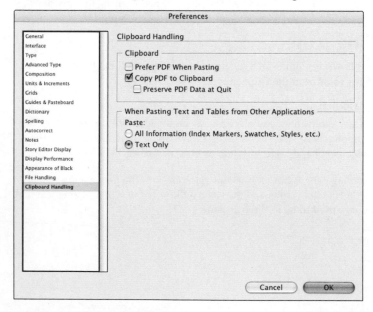

Setting Other Global Preferences

There are several global preferences handled outside the Preferences dialog box.

Setting up automatic program updates

The Adobe Updater Preferences dialog box, shown in Figure 3.19, lets you decide whether to let InDesign connect automatically to Adobe's servers over your Internet connection to download and install product updates.

To open this dialog box, choose Help ➪ Updates. InDesign then displays the Adobe Updater dialog box that displays the status of the update process. Once it has completed its search for any current updates, the Preferences button appears in the Adobe Updater dialog box, along with the Quit button. Click preferences to make the Adobe Updater Preferences dialog box appear.

FIGURE 3.19

The Adobe Updater status dialog box (top) and the Adobe Updater Preferences dialog box (bottom)

In this pane, select the Automatically Check for New Updates Every Month option to enable this feature. You can also determine whether to have InDesign install the updates after they are downloaded or to ask you for permission first. You can also change the download folder for updater files and select which Adobe applications are updated. (This lets you conveniently set automatic updating for all your Adobe applications without having to go to this dialog box in each application.)

The User Preferences pane lets you control Internet proxy server access, for which your network administrator provides the right settings if this is needed on your network. Most users never have to use this pane.

Customizing keyboard shortcuts

InDesign provides keyboard shortcuts for accessing most tools and menu commands, and for many pane options. For the most part, the keyboard shortcuts selected by Adobe either match platform standards — such as ⌘+X or Ctrl+X for Edit ➪ Cut — or they're based on keyboard shortcuts in PageMaker, Photoshop, and Illustrator. Fortunately, you're not stuck with the keyboard shortcuts Adobe decided on — I say fortunately because a few decisions and omissions are a little odd.

QUARKXPRESS You can choose to use shortcuts based on QuarkXPress 4.0 shortcuts, or you can modify a copy of the QuarkXPress set. But I recommend not using QuarkXPress shortcuts in InDesign, as doing so just prolongs the necessary adaptation to InDesign's native interface.

The Keyboard Shortcuts dialog box (choose Edit ➪ Keyboard Shortcuts), shown in Figure 3.20, provides all the tools you need for modifying keyboard shortcuts.

Using and modifying default shortcuts

When you first launch InDesign, you're using the default set of shortcuts, which you can view in menus, in some Tool Tips, and in your documentation. (This book lists default shortcuts as well.) You cannot modify the default set, but you can create a new set based on it, and then modify the shortcuts in that set.

The Keyboard Shortcuts dialog box (Edit ➪ Keyboard Shortcuts), shown in Figure 3.19, provides all the tools you need for modifying keyboard shortcuts. To use the standard keyboard shortcuts after switching to another set, choose Default from the Set pop-up menu at the top of the dialog box, and then click OK.

Here's how to create a new set:

1. **Choose Edit ➪ Keyboard Shortcuts.**
2. **Click New Set.**
3. **In the New Set dialog box, choose Default from the Based On Set pop-up menu.**
4. **Type a different name for the set in the Name field, and then click OK to create the set.**
5. **To start modifying the commands, select a menu or type of shortcut to change from the Product Area pop-up menu.** For example, you can choose File Menu, Object Editing, or Typography.

To Customize or Not to Customize

The ability to customize keyboard shortcuts, letting you work the way you want, is great — or is it? Maybe it is only if you work alone and never talk to others about your work or their work. Modified keyboard shortcuts can lead to confusion when discussing techniques, reading documentation, or sharing computers. While modifying keyboard shortcuts — or even while considering it — keep the following in mind:

■ You can specify keyboard shortcuts for specific fonts and faces that you use frequently, such as a shortcut for, say, Gill Sans Bold Italic. For the font to be listed in the Commands area, you need to make sure it's available to InDesign when you open the Keyboard Shortcuts dialog box.

■ Don't change systemwide conventions such as the shortcuts for New, Open a File, Save, and Print.

■ Don't change common keyboard commands to harmful shortcuts — for example, don't use ⌘+F or Ctrl+F for changing leading rather than invoking Find/Change.

■ If you share computers in any way — even just another user reaching over your shoulder to provide assistance — adding keyboard shortcuts is safer than changing them. Your shortcuts are slightly customized, but other users are able to use your copy of InDesign without unexpected results.

■ If you're at a 24-hour production shop in which two or three people share computers, each person can have his or her own set of named keyboard shortcuts. But this requires each user to remember to activate his or her own set.

■ You can't export keyboard shortcuts to share with other users. If consistency is important, make sure everyone creates the same set.

■ Don't modify keyboard shortcuts for computers in public places such as training centers or photocopy centers.

■ QuarkXPress users coming to InDesign have to learn new software anyway, so they will benefit in the long run from learning new keyboard shortcuts as well. Even though using your old shortcuts would ease the initial transition, the frustration caused by missing or different shortcuts is worse than learning new ones. So don't prolong the switch by using this option.

■ When you're specifying keyboard shortcuts, remember to use a modifier key or keys: ⌘, Option, Shift, or Control on the Mac and Ctrl, Alt, or Shift on Windows. You obviously can't use single-letter or single-numeral commands (which Adobe uses for selecting tools) while you're editing text.

If my words of caution make me seem negative about customizing keyboard shortcuts, I'm really not. Just consider all the ramifications before you do any customizing.

6. **Scroll through the Commands area, and click to select a command so you can change its shortcut.** The Current Shortcuts area shows you the command's existing shortcut (if there is one).

7. **Click in the New Shortcut field.** You have three options at this point:

   ■ If a keyboard shortcut exists for this command, you can click Remove to delete it and free it up for another command.

   ■ If no keyboard shortcut exists for this command, you can press the actual modifier keys and command, and then click Assign.

   ■ If a keyboard shortcut exists for this command, but you want to override it, you can press the actual modifier keys and command, and then click Assign. (The shortcut you are overriding appears below the Assign button.)

8. **Typically, you leave the Context pop-up menu at Default, but if you want the short-cut to be active for a specific context, choose Alerts Dialogs, Tables, XML Selection, or Text.** This context determines when InDesign treats the keyboard shortcut as a short-cut rather than as simple text.

9. **Click Save after modifying a shortcut set.**

10. **When you're finished editing (and saving) keyboard shortcuts, click OK to exit the dialog box.** For the shortcuts that don't appear in menus, you can print a list to use as a reference. See the section "Viewing and printing shortcuts" later in this chapter.

FIGURE 3.20

The Keyboard Shortcuts dialog box lets you create new sets of keyboard shortcuts.

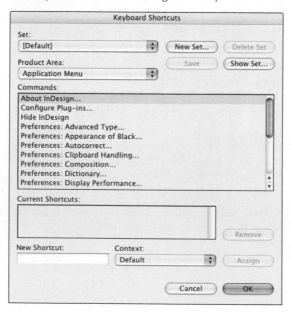

Using and Modifying QuarkXPress Shortcuts

If you're switching to InDesign from QuarkXPress and are not accustomed to using Photoshop or Illustrator, the keyboard shortcuts in InDesign may seem odd. To ease the transition to InDesign, Adobe has provided a set of keyboard shortcuts based on those in QuarkXPress 4.0. I say "based on" because some QuarkXPress commands don't have equivalents and some work very differently, while other QuarkXPress shortcuts conflict with long-established Adobe shortcuts. And commands unique to InDesign still have their own keyboard shortcuts; for example, you can still select tools with the single letters shown in the Tool Tips.

Among the shortcuts you might miss or be confused by are the following:

- Option or Alt for the Page Grabber Hand is missing (use the Navigator panel instead).

- ⌘+K or Ctrl+K for deleting selected objects is missing. (You can always use the Delete key unless the Type tool is selected.) That's because even though InDesign's QuarkXPress 4.0 shortcut set maps the Preferences dialog box to QuarkXPress 4's ⌘+Y or Ctrl+Y shortcut, it also retains the standard Adobe shortcut of ⌘+K or Ctrl+K to open the Preferences dialog box.

If you want to use the QuarkXPress set of keyboard shortcuts, choose Set for QuarkXPress 4.0 from the Set pop-up menu at the top of the Keyboard Shortcuts dialog box (Edit ⇨ Keyboard Shortcuts). You might want to print out the list of keyboard shortcuts and review them so you know what's available and what's different. (See the section "Viewing and printing shortcuts" later in this chapter.)

If you decide to use the QuarkXPress set of keyboard shortcuts, you might want to create a copy and modify some of them. For example, you can assign ⌘+K or Ctrl+K to Clear because you're used to using it for deleting items (rather than leave it set to open the Preferences dialog box). You can also repair the incorrect commands, although in many cases they're assigned to other commands and must be replaced.

 You might consider adding a keyboard shortcut for Layout ⇨ Create Guides, such as the unused Option+Shift+G or Alt+Shift+G.

Viewing and printing shortcuts

After you modify keyboard shortcuts, you may need a list for reference. (In addition, reviewing the entire QuarkXPress set before you start editing it is helpful.)

Click Show Set in the Keyboard Shortcuts dialog box (Edit ⇨ Keyboard Shortcuts) to view a list of shortcuts for the currently selected set. The shortcuts appear in TextEdit (on the Mac) or in WordPad (in Windows). You can then print the list from that application.

Customizing menus

Sometimes, the sheer number of menu options in InDesign—in the standard menus at the top of the screen, in contextual menus, and in panel menus—can be overwhelming. InDesign CS3 lets you hide menu options that get in your way. You can also save different configurations as different sets, so you can switch among them based on the task you are involved with at the moment.

CAUTION   Changing menus can be a bad idea. You might forget about a feature that you later want to use, for example. People sharing a computer may get confused when the interface looks different than they are used to and they can't find the commands they need.

NEW FEATURE   The ability to customize menus is new to InDesign CS3.

If you do decide to customize your menus, the process is simple:

1. Choose Edit ➪ Menus to open the Menu Customization dialog box shown in Figure 3.21.

2. Using the Category pop-up menu, select the category of menu you want to modify: Application Menus or Context & Panel menus.

3. In the list of application menu commands that displays, choose the menu option you want to show or hide, or color. Click the eye icon in the Visibility column to remove a menu option (the icon goes blank); to restore a menu option, click a blank icon in the Visibility column (the icon becomes an eye). You can also give the menu item a color background by choosing a color in the Color column's pop-up menus. Note that to access submenus, you click the right-pointing triangle to the left of a menu's name to expand the list of submenu options.

4. When done, click Save As. Then enter a name in the Save Menu Set dialog box and click OK when you're done.

5. Click OK when you're done changing menus to return to InDesign.

To modify an existing customized menu set, choose it from the Set pop-up menu, make your changes as described previously, and click Save when done. Similarly, to delete a set, choose it from the Set pop-up menu, and then click Delete.

To reset InDesign to use the standard menus, choose Window ➪ Arrange ➪ Reset Menus.

Color management settings

You can customize the way color management works in InDesign and across Adobe Creative Suite applications. The Color Settings dialog box (choose Edit ➪ Color Settings) lets you customize the default color transformations used for viewing and outputting colors.

CROSS-REF   See Chapter 29 for details on color management and how to set the defaults.

The Menu Customization dialog box

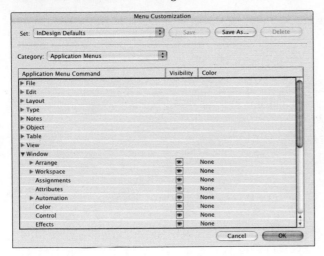

Modifying Defaults for Documents, Text, and Objects

When you create a new document, start typing, or create a new object, it is based on default settings that you can change. For example, by default, a new document is always letter-sized, but if you design only CD covers, you can change the default.

You may need to work with InDesign for a while to determine which of these settings to change and which settings you prefer. When you identify a problem — for example, you realize that you always end up changing the inset for text frames — jot down a note about it or close all documents right then. When no documents are open, change the setting for all future documents.

Document defaults

You can modify the default size, margins, and columns in new documents; the default attributes of guides; and the way layouts are adjusted. To modify document defaults, choose the following with no documents open:

- **File ⇨ Document Setup (Option+⌘+P or Ctrl+Alt+P):** The Document Setup dialog box, shown in Figure 3.22, lets you modify the default settings in the New Document dialog box for the Number of Pages, Page Size, Facing Pages, and Master Text Frame, as well as for bleeds and slugs if you click the More Options button. (When you click More Options, the Bleeds and Slugs area appears, and the button changes to Fewer Options, as shown in the figure.)

- **Layout ➪ Margins and Columns:** The Margins and Columns dialog box, shown in Figure 3.23, lets you modify the default settings in the New Document dialog box for the Margins and Columns areas.
- **Layout ➪ Ruler Guides:** This adjusts the View Threshold and Color for all new guides. It opens the Ruler Guides dialog box, which is shown in Figure 3.24.

FIGURE 3.22

When no documents are open, the Document Setup dialog box lets you customize default settings in the New Document dialog box.

FIGURE 3.23

Use the Margins and Columns dialog box when no documents are open to establish default margins and columns.

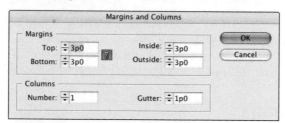

FIGURE 3.24

When no documents are open, the Ruler Guides dialog box lets you customize default settings for ruler display.

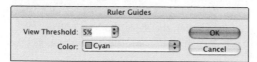

■ **Layout ⇨ Layout Adjustment:** The Layout Adjustment dialog box, shown in Figure 3.25, lets you resize entire layouts and customize how they are resized.

Use the Layout Adjustment dialog box when no documents are open to establish default layout-adjustment settings.

Text defaults

When you start typing in a new text frame, the text is formatted with default character formats, paragraph formats, and story attributes. You can also choose to show invisible characters such as spaces and tabs by default; otherwise you need to activate their display in each text-heavy document. To modify text defaults, choose:

■ **Type ⇨ Character (⌘+T or Ctrl+T):** Select default options for character formats such as font, size, and leading from the Character panel. (You can also choose Window ⇨ Type & Tables ⇨ Character.)

■ **Type ⇨ Paragraph (Option+⌘+T or Ctrl+Alt+T):** Select defaults for paragraph formats such as alignment, indents, spacing, and so on from the Paragraph panel. (You can also choose Window ⇨ Type & Tables ⇨ Paragraph.)

■ **Type ⇨ Paragraph Styles (⌘+F11 or Ctrl+F11):** Select defaults for the [Basic Paragraph] style, which is what all unstyled imported text, as well as text typed in a new text frame in InDesign, will use. (You can also choose Window ⇨ Type & Tables ⇨ Paragraph Styles.)

■ **Type ⇨ Story:** This lets you activate Optical Margin Alignment. Because Optical Margin Alignment works best for display type rather than body type, it's unlikely that you'll make Optical Margin Alignment your default setting. (You can also choose Window ⇨ Type & Tables ⇨ Story.)

■ **Type ⇨ Show Hidden Characters (⌘+Option+I or Ctrl+Alt+I):** Select this option if you often edit in InDesign and always end up turning on Show Hidden Characters.

You can also edit the spelling and hyphenation dictionaries while no documents are open by choosing Edit ⇨ Spelling ⇨ Dictionary. However, because all the edits are saved in the same file, it doesn't matter whether documents are open.

Object defaults

When you create new objects, they're based on some default settings. For example, you can specify how text wraps around objects. To modify object defaults, use the following commands:

- **Object ➪ Text Frame Options (⌘+B or Ctrl+B):** The Text Frame Options dialog box, shown in Figure 3.26, lets you specify the default Columns, Inset Spacing, First Baseline, and Ignore Text Wrap settings for new text frames.

FIGURE 3.26

Use the Text Frame Options dialog box to specify default attributes of new text frames.

- **Window ➪ Object Styles (⌘+F7 or Ctrl+F7):** Select defaults for the [Normal Graphics Frame] and [Normal Text Frame] object styles, which are what all new frames created in InDesign use.

- **Window ➪ Text Wrap (⌘+Option+W or Ctrl+Alt+W):** The Text Wrap panel lets you specify how text wraps around all new objects.

- **Object ➪ Corner Options (⌘+Option+R or Ctrl+Alt+R):** The Corner Options dialog box lets you choose a style for the corners of all new frames except those created with the Type tool.

- **Object ➪ Clipping Path (Option+Shift+⌘+K or Ctrl+Alt+Shift+K):** The Clipping Path dialog box lets you specify the default attributes of clipping paths imported into graphics frames.

■ **Window ⇨ Stroke (⌘+F10 or Ctrl+F10), Window ⇨ Swatches (F5), Window ⇨ Gradient (F6), and Window ⇨ Attributes:** These panels let you specify other default properties of objects. For example, if all objects you create are stroked (framed), specify a weight in the Stroke panel.

■ **Double-click the Polygon tool or Polygon Frame to open the Polygon Settings dialog box (there is no menu command or keyboard shortcut):** This lets you specify the default number of sides and the inset for the first new polygon in a new document. Note that you can set the two tools differently, letting you have two types of polygons remembered for you.

Modifying Defaults for Views

Another way to customize your copy of InDesign is to specify which layout tools appear by default. The lower two-thirds of the View menu, shown in Figure 3.27, lets you do this. If you'd prefer not to view the edges of frames, you can hide them by default. Or if you always want to start with a document-wide grid, you can show it by default. To modify viewing defaults, choose the appropriate menu options. Note that the menu names toggle between Show and Hide each time you select them. (Therefore, if the menu option begins with Hide, it means that attribute is currently being displayed; if it starts with Show, it means the attribute is currently not being displayed.)

FIGURE 3.27

The View menu commands that are available when no documents are open

- **View ⇨ Show/Hide Text Threads (Option+⌘+Y or Ctrl+Alt+Y):** This shows or hides the links between text frames.

- **View ⇨ Show/Hide Frame Edges (Control+⌘+H or Ctrl+H):** This shows or hides the edges of frames.

NEW FEATURE The Mac shortcut for View ⇨ Show/Hide Frame Edges has changed in InDesign CS3 to Control+⌘+H, from ⌘+H in previous versions. The Windows shortcut (Ctrl+H) is unchanged.

- **View ⇨ Show/Hide Rulers (⌘+R or Ctrl+R):** This shows or hides the horizontal and vertical ruler.

- **View ⇨ Grids & Guides ⇨ Show/Hide Guides (⌘+; [semicolon] or Ctrl+; [semicolon]):** This shows or hides margin, column, and layout guides.

- **View ⇨ Grids & Guides ⇨ Show/Hide Baseline Grid (Option+⌘+' [apostrophe] or Ctrl+Alt+' [apostrophe]):** This shows or hides the baseline grid established in the Grids pane of the Preferences dialog box. You can access this pane on a Mac by choosing InDesign ⇨ Preferences ⇨ Grids or pressing ⌘+K; choose Edit ⇨ Preferences ⇨ Grids or press Ctrl+K in Windows.

- **View ⇨ Grids & Guides ⇨ Show/Hide Document Grid (⌘+' [apostrophe] or Ctrl+' [apostrophe]):** This shows or hides the document-wide grid established in the Grids pane of the Preferences dialog box.

In addition to changing which layout tools appear by default, you can control some of their default behavior. Choose the appropriate menu options to enable or disable them. Note that if the menu option is currently enabled, a check mark appears next to its name, in which case choosing it again disables the option and the check mark disappears.

- **View ⇨ Grids & Guides ⇨ Lock Guides (Option+⌘+; [semicolon] or Ctrl+Alt+; [semicolon]):** Disabled by default. When you choose this option to enable it, all ruler guides are locked in place.

- **View ⇨ Grids & Guides ⇨ Lock Column Guides:** Enabled by default. When you choose this option to disable it, all column guides are no longer locked in place.

- **View ⇨ Grids & Guides ⇨ Snap to Guides (Shift+⌘+; [semicolon] or Ctrl+Shift+; [semicolon]):** Enabled by default. When you choose this option to disable it, aligning objects with guides is more difficult, but positioning objects near guides is easier.

- **View ⇨ Grids & Guides ⇨ Snap to Document Grid:** Disabled by default. When you choose this option to enable it, objects are easy to align with document grid lines whether or not they're showing.

CROSS-REF Chapter 7 covers how to use guides and grids in your layout.

Setting Color and Style Defaults

If you find yourself creating the same colors, paragraph styles, character styles, table styles, cell styles, and/or object styles over and over again, create them with no documents open. They will be available to all future documents. To create these elements, use the New command in the flyout menus for the following panels: Swatches (F5), Character Styles (Shift+⌘+F11 or Ctrl+Shift+F11), Paragraph Styles (⌘+F11 or Ctrl+F11), Table Styles, Cell Styles, and Object Styles (⌘+F7 or Ctrl+F7). You can also use the flyout menus' Load commands to import colors and styles from existing documents instead of creating them from scratch.

Reverting Preferences and Defaults

If you inherit a copy of InDesign from another user, or if you've been changing preferences and defaults at random and are unhappy with the results, you can revert InDesign to all its default settings. You particularly want to do this if you're learning InDesign using tutorial files or in a class setting.

TIP To revert all preferences and defaults, deleting the InDesign Defaults preference files when opening InDesign, press Control+Option+Shift+⌘ or Ctrl+Alt+Shift when launching InDesign.

NOTE Keep in mind that you need to re-enable any custom keyboard shortcut set you were using by choosing it from the Set pop-up menu in the Keyboard Shortcuts dialog box (Edit ➪ Keyboard Shortcuts).

Changing Views

Customizing also involves the way you look at your work. InDesign provides a variety of options for magnifying and displaying your work. Understanding these ahead of time and memorizing the ones that work best for your type of work, your eyesight, and your monitor can help you get started with InDesign.

Desktop-publishing pioneers in the late 1980s often worked on publications using 9-inch black-and-white monitors, and they spent as much time zooming in, zooming out, and pushing over-sized pages around on undersized screens as they did formatting text and modifying graphics. The best present you could give yourself — or your employer could give you — is a large monitor (two large monitors aren't bad, either). In this era of proliferating panels, there's no such thing as too much screen space. But even if you have a huge monitor, you're going to find yourself zooming in and out and using InDesign's other display-related features to control what you see on-screen and help you work more efficiently.

Zooming and scrolling

When you begin building a page, it's often easiest to display the entire page (choose View ➪ Fit Page in Window, or press ⌘+0 [zero] or Ctrl+0 [zero]) or spread (choose View ➪ Fit Spread in Window, or press Option+⌘+0 [zero] or Ctrl+Alt+0 [zero]) and work somewhat roughly — creating the required objects and positioning them more or less where you want them. After you add text and graphics to your frames, you probably want to begin polishing the page by modifying individual objects. At this point, seeing a reduced view of an entire page or spread isn't the best way to work. If you need to work on details, it's best to pull out a magnifying glass. With InDesign, this means tapping into the program's view-magnification capabilities.

You can zoom in to magnifications up to 4,000 percent and zoom out to magnifications as small as 10 percent. Like many other features, you have several options for changing view magnification. You can zoom in and out using:

- The Zoom tool
- The zoom commands in the View menu
- The Zoom pop-up menu or the accompanying box at the bottom left of the document window

The Zoom tool

If you're the type of designer who prefers the click-and-drag solution when it's available, you probably want to use the Zoom tool to enlarge a portion of a page. Here's how it works:

1. **Select the Zoom tool or press Z if the Type tool is not selected.**

2. **At this point you have two options:**

   - **You can move the Zoom pointer over the area you want to see and click the mouse.** Each click enlarges the view to the next preset magnification percentage. (To display these percentages, click the pop-up menu next to the Zoom field at the bottom-left corner of the document window.)

   - **You can click and drag a rectangle that encloses the area you want to see.** When you release the mouse, the area is centered in the document window. (When you hold Option or Alt, the plus sign in the Zoom pointer changes to a minus sign. Clicking or clicking and dragging in this situation zooms out instead of in.)

> **TIP** You never have to actually select the Zoom tool. Instead, use its keyboard shortcuts: ⌘+spacebar or Ctrl+spacebar (for zooming in) and ⌘+Option+spacebar or Ctrl+Alt+spacebar (for zooming out).

Zoom options in the View menu

The third group of commands in the View menu, shown in Figure 3.28, lets you change the view magnification. Here's a brief description of each command:

FIGURE 3.28

The zoom commands in the View menu (when a document is open)

- **Zoom In (⌘+= or Ctrl+=):** This enlarges the display magnification to the next higher percentage. (When no objects are active, the Zoom In command is also available in the contextual menu.)

- **Zoom Out (⌘+– [hyphen] or Ctrl+– [hyphen]):** This reduces the display magnification to the next lower percentage. (When no objects are active, the Zoom Out command is also available in the contextual menu.)

 If an object is active when you choose Zoom In or Zoom Out or use the Zoom field or pop-up menu, the object is centered in the document window after the view changes.

- **Fit Page in Window (⌘+0 [zero] or Ctrl+0 [zero]):** This reduces or enlarges the display magnification of the currently displayed page (the current page number is displayed in the page number field at the lower left of a document window) so that the entire page is visible (and centered) in the document window.

- **Fit Spread in Window (Option+⌘+0 [zero] or Ctrl+Alt+0 [zero]):** This is similar to Fit Page in Window, except you use it if you're working on a facing-page document and want the entire spread to be on-screen.

- **Actual Size (⌘+1 or Ctrl+1):** This displays the document at 100 percent magnification. When you choose Actual Size, a pica is a pica and an inch is an inch — if your monitor is appropriately configured.

Double-clicking the Zoom tool is the same as choosing View ⊃ Actual Size; it displays a document at 100 percent magnification.

■ **Entire Pasteboard (Option+Shift+⌘+0 [zero] or Ctrl+Alt+Shift+0 [zero]):** This reduces the display magnification so that the current page or spread and its surrounding pasteboard are visible within the document window.

 To switch back and forth between the last two magnification percentages, press Option+⌘+2 or Ctrl+Alt+2.

The Zoom field and pop-up menu

The Zoom field in the bottom-left corner of the document window and its accompanying Zoom pop-up menu, shown in Figure 3.29, offer two additional methods for changing display magnification. To use the field, simply type a value between 5 percent and 4,000 percent, and then press Return or Enter. To use the pop-up menu, click the arrow, and then choose one of the preset magnification values.

FIGURE 3.29

The Zoom field and the Zoom pop-up menu

 If an object is active when you click Zoom In or Zoom Out (from the View menu) or use the Zoom field or pop-up menu, the object is centered in the document window after the view changes.

The Hand tool

Sometimes after you've zoomed in to work on a particular object, you want to work on a portion of the page that's not currently displayed. You can always zoom out, and then use the Zoom tool or the zoom commands to zoom back in, or you can "push" the page around within the window until you can see the portion of the page you want to work on. To scroll, you can use the scroll bars and boxes on the right and bottom of the document window, or you can use the Hand tool (press H if the Type tools is not selected). Simply select it, and then click and drag to move the currently displayed page or spread around within the document window. When you can see what you want, release the mouse.

> **TIP** To temporarily access the Hand tool when the Type tool is not selected, press the space-bar. The hand pointer appears. Click and drag to move the page within the document window. (This is one of InDesign's most useful keyboard shortcuts!)

The Navigator panel

The Navigator panel (Window ➪ Object & Layout ➪ Navigator), shown in Figure 3.30, is the home of several display-related features, most of which are available elsewhere (and which I've already covered in this chapter).

FIGURE 3.30

The Navigator panel

> **TIP** If you choose View All Spreads from the Navigator panel's flyout menu, the page area at the top of the panel displays all of the document's spreads. The more spreads in a document, the smaller each one appears in the Navigator panel when you select View All Spreads.

Object display options

Generally, you're going to want to display the objects you've placed on your pages. After all, what's displayed on-screen is what gets printed, right? Not exactly. For example, text and graphic frames are displayed on-screen with blue borders, even if they're empty, but the borders don't print. In addition to the six zoom commands (covered earlier in this chapter), there are two other commands that affect how objects appear:

■ **View ➪ Show/Hide Frame Edges (Control+⌘+H or Ctrl+H):** When you click Hide Frame Edges, text and graphics frames are not displayed with a blue border. Additionally, an *X* does not appear in empty graphics frames when frame edges are hidden. You might want to hide frame edges to see how a page will look when printed.

TIP When you move an object by clicking and dragging, you have the choice of displaying the entire object (including the contents of a frame) or displaying only the bounding box. If you begin dragging immediately after clicking to select an object, only the bounding box appears as you drag. If you pause after clicking an object until the stem of the arrow pointer disappears and then begin dragging, the entire object appears.

- **In the Pages panel's flyout menu, choose View ➪ Show/Hide Master Items.** When you choose Show Master Items, any objects on the currently displayed document page's master page appear. When you choose Hide Master Items, master objects on the currently displayed page are hidden. This command is page-specific, so you can show or hide master objects on a page-by-page basis.

Opening Multiple Document Windows

Like most programs, InDesign lets you open several documents at once. It also takes this concept one step further by letting you open multiple windows simultaneously for individual documents. Earlier in this chapter, I recommended using the largest monitor you can get your mitts on. A large monitor makes this feature even more useful. By opening multiple windows, you can:

- **Display two (or more) different pages or spreads at once and work on them at the same time.** Well, you still have to work on them one at a time, but no navigation is required; you have only to click within the appropriate window.

- **Display multiple magnifications of the same page.** For example, you can work on a detail at high magnification in one window and display the entire page — and see the results of your detail work — at actual size in another window.

- **Display a master page in one window and a document page based on that master page in another window.** When you change the master page, the change is reflected in the window in which the associated document page is displayed.

To open a new window for the active document, choose Window ➪ Arrange ➪ New Window. The new window appears in front of the original window. To show both windows at once, choose Window ➪ Arrange ➪ Tile. When you click the Tile command, all open windows are resized and displayed side by side. (If you choose Window ➪ Arrange ➪ Cascade, all open windows appear stacked and staggered on top of each other. The frontmost document window is visible; the title bars of the other windows are visible above the frontmost document.)

When multiple windows are open, clicking on a window's title bar or anywhere within the window activates it. Also, the names of all open documents appear at the bottom of the Window menu. Choosing a document name from the View menu brings that document to the front. If multiple windows are open for a particular document, each window appears (they're displayed in the order in which you created them) in the Window menu.

When you open a document, it appears in the last window you used before you last saved it. Any other windows that were open when you saved the document are not saved.

TIP   To close all windows for the currently displayed document, press Shift+⌘+W or Ctrl+Shift+W. To close all windows for all open documents, press Option+Shift+⌘+W or Ctrl+Alt+Shift+W.

Summary

InDesign provides extensive controls for setting preferences for everything from how objects appear on-screen and how text spelling and hyphenation are managed to how keyboard shortcuts work and how color is handled. You can also reset all preference changes to their defaults with just one command.

Part II

Document Fundamentals

IN THIS PART

Chapter 4
Creating, Opening, and Saving Documents

Chapter 5
Working with Pages

Chapter 6
Working with Layers

Chapter 7
Creating Layout Standards

Chapter 8
Defining Colors, Tints, and Gradients

Chapter 4

Creating, Opening, and Saving Documents

You're pumped up. You've purchased a copy of InDesign, installed it, checked out the interface, and now you're ready to put the program to work. So, what's next? Launch the application and start clicking? Hardly. Creating a publication with InDesign is much like going on a trip. You don't reach your destination unless you've prepared a plan for getting there. And you reach your destination more quickly and more easily if your plan is a sound one.

Remember, too, that most trips don't go exactly according to plan. InDesign is both versatile and forgiving. As you create a publication, you should feel free to change your mind, experiment, and let your creativity roam. As long as you reach your destination (on time!), taking a few detours is acceptable, and encountering a few roadblocks (small ones, you hope) is inevitable.

IN THIS CHAPTER

Planning a publication

Creating a new document

Opening native and foreign documents and templates

Saving documents and templates

Exporting documents and document elements

Using Version Cue for version management

Taking Stock before You Begin

Before you launch InDesign, open a new document, and begin working, you must answer several fundamental questions about the publication you are producing:

- What is the basic nature of the piece? Will it be printed, or will it be distributed over the Internet or an intranet? Is it going to be published as a print, PDF, or Web piece, or perhaps in several formats?

- What are its dimensions?

- How many pages will it have? If it will be a multipage publication, will it have facing pages like a book or a catalog, or will it be single-sided like a flip chart?

- How many columns will each page have? How wide will the margins be?

- Does the budget allow for the use of color? If so, how many colors? What kind of paper will it be printed on? What kind of printer or printing press will be used?

- How will the publication be distributed? Under what circumstances will it be read? What's the life expectancy of the publication?

- If the publication is bound for the Internet, will you create an HTML file (which can be viewed by anybody with a Web browser) or a PDF file (which requires viewers to have the free Adobe Reader application or browser plug-in)?

- And what about the content of your publication? What programs were used to create the text files and graphic files your publication will contain? Did you create the content yourself, or did others? What file formats were used for text and graphic files? What is the most effective way to present the content given the production requirements and budget?

As you answer these questions, a rough image of your publication begins to take shape in your mind. When you're ready to begin turning your ideas into an actual publication, you have a couple of choices. Many designers whose skills date back to the days of traditional paste-up still prefer to use traditional tools — a drawing pad and colored markers or pencils in this case — to create rough sketches before they fire up their page-layout or illustration program. Other designers who were never exposed to such archaic tools are comfortable doing their brainstorming and sketching on the fly, using their favorite software. Whatever method suits you is fine. Keep in mind that, at this early stage, you shouldn't be spending much time fine-tuning details. You can do that later with InDesign.

An overly careful person can plan forever, in which case, nothing actually gets done. At some point, when the image you have of the publication you're creating is clear enough in your mind to begin work, it's time to create a new InDesign document.

Setting Up a New Publication

After you launch InDesign, you have two options: You can choose the Open command (File ➪ Open, or ⌘+O or Ctrl+O) to open a previously created document or template (more on opening documents and templates later in this chapter), or you can choose File ➪ New ➪ Document, or ⌘+N or Ctrl+N, to create a new document.

When you create a new document, the New Document dialog box shown in Figure 4.1 appears. It is here that you implement many of the decisions, including page size, number of pages, number of columns, and margin width you arrived at during the planning stage. Although you're free to change your mind later, you save yourself time and potential headaches by sticking with the basic page parameters you establish in the New Document dialog box.

> **TIP**
> To change the measurement units displayed in the New Document dialog box, choose
> InDesign ⇨ Preferences ⇨ Units & Increments or press ⌘+K on the Mac, or choose Edit ⇨
> Preferences ⇨ Units & Increments or press Ctrl+K in Windows. Next, choose the measurement system
> you want from the Horizontal and Vertical pop-up menus in the Ruler Units area. If you change prefer-
> ences when no documents are open, your changes are applied to all subsequently created documents.

FIGURE 4.1

The settings you make in the New Document dialog box establish the basic framework for the pages in your
publication. This example shows the settings used to create a 48p9-x-65p3 (8⅛-x-10⅞-inch) magazine page.

Creating new documents

Here's how to create a new document:

1. **Choose File ⇨ New ⇨ Document or press ⌘+N or Ctrl+N.**

2. **If you know exactly how many pages your publication will have, type the number
    in the Number of Pages field.** If you don't know for sure, you can always add or delete
    pages later as needed.

3. **Select the Facing Pages option if you're creating a multipage publication that will
    have a spine, such as a book, catalog, or magazine.** You do not need to select this
    option if you're creating a one-page document, such as a business card, an ad, or a poster.
    Some publications, such as flip charts, presentations, and three-ring bound documents,
    have multiple pages but use only one side of the page. For such documents, don't select
    the Facing Pages option, either.

4. **If you want to flow text from page to page in a multipage document, such as a book
    or a catalog, select the Master Text Frame option.** (See Chapter 15 for more informa-
    tion on using master text frames.) When you select this option, InDesign automatically
    adds a text frame to the document's master page and to all document pages based on this

master page. This saves you the work of creating a text box on each page and manually threading text through each frame.

5. **In the Page Size area, you can choose one of the predefined sizes from the pop-up menu.** Your options are Letter (8.5" x 11"), Legal (8.5" x 14"), Tabloid (11" x 17"), Letter Half (5.5" x 8.5"), Legal Half (7" x 8.5"), A4 (210mm x 297mm), A3 (297mm x 420mm), A5 (148mm x 210mm), B5 (176mm x 250mm), Compact Disc (4.7222" x 4.5"), or Custom. Other options may appear in this menu if you've defined your own page sizes as described in Chapter 3.

   If you choose Custom as the page size, you can type values in the Width and Height fields. But you don't have to actually choose Custom: No matter what page size is selected, if you type values in those fields, the Page Size automatically changes to Custom. The minimum height and width is 1 pica (0.1667"); the maximum is 216". Clicking the Portrait iconic button next to Orientation produces a vertical page (the larger of the Height and Width values is used in the Height field); clicking the Landscape iconic button produces a horizontal page (the larger of the Height and Width values is used in the Width field). You can also specify Height and Width values by clicking the up and down arrows associated with these fields.

> **TIP** When you specify page size, make sure the values you type in the Height and Width fields are the size of the final printed piece — and not the size of the paper in your printer. For example, if you're creating a standard-sized business card, type 3.5i in the Width field and 2i in the Height field.

> **TIP** If you want to print *n*-up — meaning several "pages" on one sheet, such as several business cards on an 8½-x-11-inch sheet of paper — you can create a letter-sized document (8.5" x 11"), but you have to arrange the business cards within the page boundary and add your own crop marks for each card.

6. **Specify margin values in the Margins area.** The *margin* is the white area around the outside of the page within which page elements — text and graphics — are placed. A document doesn't have to have margins (you can type 0 into these fields), and if you want you can place text and graphics in the margin area. If the Facing Pages option is selected, Inside and Outside fields are available in the Margins area. Designers often specify larger inside margins for multipage publications to accommodate the fold at the spine. If Facing Pages is not selected, Left and Right fields replace the Inside and Outside fields. You can also specify margin values by clicking the up or down arrows associated with the fields.

7. **Type a value in the Columns field to specify how many columns your pages have.** You can also specify the number of columns by clicking the up or down arrows associated with the Column field.

8. **Specify a gutter distance (the gutter is the space between columns) in the Gutter field.** You can also specify a gutter width value by clicking the up/down arrows associated with the Gutter field.

9. **If you click More Options, the Bleed and Slug area of the New Document dialog box appears (refer to Figure 4.1), and the More Options button changes to Fewer Options.** The More Options button expands the dialog box to provide options to set bleed and slug areas. (The button then changes to Fewer Options, which if clicked hides

the Bleed and Slug area.) A *bleed area* is a margin on the outside of the page for objects you want to extend past the edge of the page — you want them to extend at least ⅛ inch so if there is any shifting of the paper during printing, there's no white space where the image should be (touching the edge of the page). The *slug area* is an area reserved for printing crop marks, color plate names, and other printing information — some output devices cut these off during printing unless a slug area is defined. For both bleed and slug areas, you can set the top, bottom, left, and right margins independently.

10. **Click OK to close the New Document dialog box.** When you do, your new, blank document appears in a new document window. Figure 4.2 shows the window of a newly created document that uses the settings shown in Figure 4.1.

FIGURE 4.2

The magazine page settings in the New Document dialog box shown in Figure 4.1 resulted in the document you see here. The view percentage field in the lower-left corner of the document window shows that the page is currently displayed at 75 percent of actual size.

TIP You can bypass the New Document dialog box by pressing Shift+⌘+N or Ctrl+Shift+N. When you use this method, the most recent settings in the New Document dialog box are used for the new document.

Creating your own document types

InDesign lets you create predefined document types, called *document presets*, to supplement the standard ones such as Letter. Note that a preset is much more than a saved page size; it also includes margins, columns, and the other setting specified in the New Document dialog box.

There are two ways to create document presets:

■ You can save these new-document settings by clicking Save Preset in the New Document dialog box. These saved settings appear in the Document Style pop-up menu in the future.

■ You can choose File ➪ Document Presets ➪ Define to create (by clicking New) a new document style or import (by clicking Load) one from another document. It opens the dialog box shown in Figure 4.3. When you create a new preset, or edit an existing one, you get a dialog box that essentially matches the New Document Setup dialog box in Figure 4.1. Modify the settings as desired and click OK to return to the Document Presets dialog box.

FIGURE 4.3

The Document Presets dialog box lets you create, import, edit, and delete document styles.

Opening Documents and Templates

Opening documents with InDesign is pretty much the same as opening documents with any program. Simply choose File ➪ Open or press ⌘+O or Ctrl+O, locate and click the document on which you want to work, and then click Open. But InDesign offers a few options for opening documents you don't find in every program. For example, you can:

■ Open more than one document at a time.

■ Open a copy of a document instead of the original. This keeps you from overwriting the original file accidentally — very helpful if you're making several variations of one document.

- Open a template under its own name. This makes editing templates easier than it is with other programs, specifically QuarkXPress.

- Open documents created with some versions of PageMaker and QuarkXPress: QuarkXPress and QuarkXPress Passport versions 3.3 through 4.1 and PageMaker versions 6.0 through 7.0.

 TIP InDesign's File menu displays the names of the five most recently saved documents in the Open Recent submenu that appears under the Open option in the File menu after you have opened a file.

To open a file:

1. **Choose File ➪ Open or press ⌘+O or Ctrl+O.** The Open a File dialog box shown in Figures 4.4 and 4.5 appears. The Open a File dialog box differs based on whether you are using Adobe's Version Cue file-management system or not, as I explain later in this chapter. (This book's screen shots have Version Cue enabled because that is InDesign's default setting.)

TIP One downside to using the Version Cue dialog boxes is that you don't see any image previews in their default views when placing graphics, as you will with the standard Mac and Windows dialog boxes. To see image previews in Version Cue dialog boxes, choose Thumbnails, Icons, or Tiles from the Version Cue dialog box's View menu.

2. **Locate and open the folder that contains the documents you want to open.** Click a filename or press and hold ⌘ or Ctrl and click multiple filenames.

    In Windows, the Files of Type pop-up menu offers several options: PageMaker 6.0–7.0 files, QuarkXPress 3.3–4.1 files, InDesign files, InDesign Interchange, GoLive Section, Adobe PDF Creation Settings Files, and All Formats. Choose any of these options to display a specific file format in the file list. (Choose All Files in the Files of Type pop-up menu to display files with no extensions.) Note that InDesign CS3 can open files created by any previous version of InDesign, in addition to CS3-created files. The InDesign Interchange format is a variation of the standard InDesign CS3 format that lets InDesign CS2 read your CS3 file, minus any CS3-specific formatting.

    On a Mac, the Open a File dialog box displays any supported file formats that have filename extension, and the dialog box includes a Preview pane that displays a thumbnail version of the selected file or, more commonly, its icon. (Choose All Documents in the Enable pop-up menu to display files without the filename extensions.)

PLATFORM DIFFERENCES The name of the pop-up menu for selecting file types differs between the Mac and Windows versions of InDesign, as does the menu option for displaying all files (including those with no filename extensions).

3. **Click Open Normal (Mac) or Normal (Windows) at the bottom of the Open a File dialog box if you want to open the original document (rather than a copy of the document); click Open Copy (Mac) or Copy (Windows) to open a copy of a document.** When you open a copy of a document, it's assigned a default name (Untitled-1, Untitled-2, and so on). If you want to use a template to create a new version of a publication, select

Normal; InDesign creates a document based on the template. To open a template under its own name so that you can edit it, click Open Original (Mac) or Original (Windows). Templates are explained in the following section, "Opening documents versus opening templates." (For documents, selecting Open Normal/Normal or Open Original/Original does the same thing: It opens the document for editing.)

FIGURE 4.4

With Version Cue enabled, the Mac (right) and Windows (left) versions of the Open a File dialog box differ slightly. When you open a file, you have the option to open it normally (Open Normal/Normal), open the original copy of a template (Open Original/Original), or open a copy of the file (Open Copy/Copy).

4. Click OK to close the dialog box. Each document you open appears in a separate document window. The page and view magnification displayed when a document was last saved is used when you open the document.

TIP   You can also open an InDesign document or template by double-clicking its file icon. If InDesign is not running, double-clicking a document or template file — as long as it has the proper filename extension (.indd for documents and .indt for templates) — launches the application and opens the document/template. If InDesign is already running, the document appears in a new window.

FIGURE 4.5

With Version Cue disabled, the native Mac (top) and Windows (bottom) versions of the Open a File dialog box also differ slightly from each other.

Displaying Filename Extensions

Both Windows and the Mac OS use icons to show you (and tell programs) what format a file is in. Windows and Mac OS X (but not earlier versions of the Mac OS) use filename extensions to identify the file type. But by default these are hidden from view when you open folders.

InDesign uses the filename extension .indd to denote InDesign documents. Without this filename extension, you won't be able to double-click a file icon to open it, although you can still open the file from InDesign's Open a File dialog box (File ⇨ Open, or ⌘+O or Ctrl+O), as long as you select All Documents from the Enable pop-up menu (on the Mac) or All Files from the Files of Type pop-up menu (in Windows). Note that the Place dialog box for importing text and graphics — covered in Chapters 14 and 26 — does not have the Enable pop-up menu on the Mac; InDesign shows all files, even unsupported ones, in this dialog box.

If filename extensions are hidden in Windows XP, open any folder and then choose Tools ⇨ Folder Options and then select the View tab to make the pane shown in the following figure appear. (You have to have a disk or folder open to have the View menu.) Enable the Show Hidden Files and Folders option, then click OK.

In Windows Vista, choose Start ⇨ Computer, then choose Organize ⇨ Folder and Search Options in the dialog box that appears. Go to the View pane and enable the Show Hidden Files and Folders option, then click OK. You see essentially the same pane as Windows XP uses.

If filename extensions are hidden in Mac OS X 10.4.8 (Tiger) or Mac OS X 10.5 (Leopard), click Finder ➪ Preferences, go to the Advanced pane, and then enable the Show All File Extensions option, as shown in the following figure, and close the dialog box. (You have to be using the Finder, not be in an application, to get this menu.)

Opening documents versus opening templates

Whenever you save a document, you have the option of saving a standard document file or a template (more on saving templates later in this chapter). A *template* is an InDesign file that's used to create multiple iterations of the same publication. For example, if you produce a monthly newsletter, you can save gobs of time and ensure consistency from issue to issue by using a template as the starting point for each edition of the newsletter. A template is essentially the shell of a publication that contains the basic framework — page layout, master pages, styles, and so on — but doesn't contain any actual content.

 For more information about creating templates, see Chapter 7.

When you open a template, you have two choices: You can either open a copy of the file and use it to create a new publication, or you can open the original file, make changes, and then save an updated version of the template.

If you want to use a template as the starting point for a new publication, choose File ➪ Open or press ⌘+O or Ctrl+O, locate and select the template, and make sure Open Normal (Mac) or Normal (Windows) is selected in the Open a File dialog box (refer to Figure 4.4) before you click Open.

If you want to modify a template, click Open Original (Mac) or Open (Windows) at the bottom of the dialog box. If Open Normal (Mac) or Normal (Windows) is selected, clicking Open opens a new document window and assigns the document a default name, Untitled-1, Untitled-2, and so on. If Open Original (Mac) or Original (Windows) is selected, the original file opens and the original name appears in the title bar.

Working with files in the Bridge file system

There's another way to open documents and templates in InDesign CS3: Choose File ➪ Browse (or press Option+⌘+O or Ctrl+Alt+O) to open documents or templates, or choose File ➪ New ➪ Document from Template to open just templates. Choosing either option opens up the Adobe Bridge program, shown in Figure 4.6, where you can browse for a file to open.

Bridge is designed to be a central repository for Creative Suite programs and support files, mainly for use in workgroup situations but also as an Adobe-centric alterative to the standard Mac and Windows file systems. Bridge's biggest attraction is that it lets you see previews of and file information for almost all the files types you'd be working with in your layouts. (And Bridge does come with several canned templates created by Adobe that you might want to consider using.)

NEW FEATURE The Document from Template menu option is new to InDesign CS3.

FIGURE 4.6

You can access files through the Adobe Bridge program, a common file environment for Creative Suite applications.

There's no difference in the documents or templates available via Bridge than those available via the regular Open a File dialog box — it's just a different organizational structure for your files.

If you want to access the template files stored in Bridge's InDesign folder without using Bridge itself, navigate to Library:Application Support:Adobe:Templates:InDesign on the Mac, to Program Files/Common Files/Adobe/Templates/InDesign in Windows. Of course, if you do prefer to use Bridge to store template files, you use InDesign's regular Save As dialog box, select InDesign CS3 Template as the file format, and navigate to the Bridge application's InDesign folder.

You can access Bridge files directly from the Bridge application, using its folder-based interface to find files of interest.

CROSS-REF Most of Bridge's features are oriented to Photoshop users, so chances are you can just ignore Bridge. But it does have some utility in workgroup environments, as I explain in Chapter 35.

Converting documents created with other programs

One of InDesign's hallmarks is its capability to open documents from other programs and convert them to InDesign documents.

CAUTION Because other programs' formats are so different from InDesign's, and their capabilities differ as well, the chances of being able to import a foreign document and have it flawlessly convert to InDesign are small. Use this feature to do the first step in the conversion process, but expect to spend time cleaning up the converted files by hand.

InDesign alerts you to any import issues of PageMaker and QuarkXPress files with a dialog box that appears after the import is complete (see Figure 4.7).

CROSS-REF InDesign cannot import PDF files, but it can bring in PDF files as graphics for placement in your document. Chapter 26 covers this process in detail. It can also import PDF job-option files, so you can reuse the same settings already developed for Adobe Acrobat Distiller when you export to PDF, as Chapter 32 covers.

FIGURE 4.7

InDesign shows the Warnings dialog box if there are any conversion issues when importing foreign file formats.

QuarkXPress

InDesign can read QuarkXPress and QuarkXPress Passport files from versions 3.3, 4.0, and 4.1. (Adobe has no plans to support files in the version 5, 6, or 7 formats of QuarkXPress, though Markzware offers a conversion utility for these formats.)

 For links to Markzware and other providers of InDesign tools, visit this book's companion Web site at www.InDesignCentral.com.

Because there are so many differences between QuarkXPress and InDesign, it's impossible to predict all the conversion issues that may arise. The good news is that a great many things work well, but some don't. Here are some common conversion issues to which you should pay attention:

- If your QuarkXPress document relies on XTensions (a type of plug-in) to add capabilities (such as table creation), it does not convert correctly into InDesign and may not even import at all. Examples include any documents built with QuarkXPress's indexing and book features.

- QuarkXPress's leading model is different than InDesign's, so expect leading to sometimes vary significantly, especially if you use additive leading as the automatic leading method in QuarkXPress.

- InDesign doesn't retain kerning-table adjustments in QuarkXPress files. (It does retain any kerning applied manually.)

- The customizable dashes in QuarkXPress are converted to solid and dashed lines. (Note that stripes do convert properly.)

- Special gradient blends, such as the diamond pattern, are converted to linear blends or circular blends.

- Text on a curved path is converted to regular text in a rectangular frame, even though InDesign supports text on paths.

- H&J sets don't have an equivalent in InDesign, so they do not convert, although any H&J settings are carried over into the converted paragraph styles.

- Libraries don't convert.

- Printer styles don't convert.

CROSS-REF Appendix C covers other issues when moving from QuarkXPress to InDesign.

PageMaker

InDesign can read PageMaker 6.0, 6.5, and 7.0 files. Because PageMaker and InDesign offer many of the same features, there are fewer translation issues between them. Some to take note of include:

- Fill patterns aren't supported.

- Libraries don't convert.

- Printer styles don't convert.

CROSS-REF Appendix D covers other issues when moving from PageMaker to InDesign.

Recovering a document after a crash or power failure

InDesign includes an automatic recovery feature that protects your documents in the event of a power failure or a system crash. As you work on a document, any changes you make after saving it are stored in a separate, temporary file. Under normal circumstances, each time you choose Save, the information in the temporary file is applied to the document. The data in the temporary file is important only if you aren't able to save a document before crashing. A word of warning: Although InDesign's automatic recovery feature is a nice safety net, you should still be careful to save your work often. Here's how it works:

1. **Relaunch InDesign or, if necessary, restart your computer and then launch InDesign.**

2. **If automatic-recovery data is available, InDesign automatically opens the recovered document and displays the word "Recovered" in the document's title bar.** This lets you know that the document contains changes that were not included in the last saved version.

3. **If you want to save the recovered data, choose File ⇨ Save; "Recovered" is removed as part of the filename, and InDesign asks if you want to overwrite the old file.** Overwriting the old file is easier than using File ⇨ Save As and typing a name, unless you do want to save a copy of the file in case you want to go back to the old version later. If you want to use the last saved version of the document (and disregard the recovered data), close the file (File ⇨ Close, or ⌘+W or Ctrl+W) without saving, and then open the file (File ⇨ Open, or ⌘+O or Ctrl+O).

NOTE Sometimes, InDesign can't automatically recover the documents for you. Instead, it gives you the choice of recovering any files open during a crash or power outage, saving the recovery data for later, or deleting the recovery data. You typically want to recover the files immediately.

Saving Documents and Templates

When you open a new document, it's assigned a default name (Untitled-1, Untitled-2, and so on) and the first page appears in the document window. At this point, you're like a painter standing in front of a blank canvas. But painters don't have to worry about system crashes and power failures; you do. Make sure that when you work on InDesign documents, you follow the first rule of safe computing: Save early and often.

The second group of commands — Close, Save, Save As, Save a Copy, Check In, and Revert — in InDesign's File menu provides options for saving the active/frontmost document. Here's a rundown of what each command does:

- **Close (⌘+W, or Ctrl+W or Ctrl+F4):** This closes the active document. If the document has never been saved or if it's been changed since it was last saved, a dialog box appears that lets you save, close without saving, or cancel and return to the document.

- **Save (⌘+S or Ctrl+S):** This saves changes you've made to the active document since you last saved. If you choose Save for a document that hasn't yet been saved, the Save As dialog box appears. This dialog box lets you name and choose a storage folder for the document.

 If you have more than one document open, you can save the documents all at once by pressing Option+Shift+⌘+S or Ctrl+Alt+Shift+S.

 As with the Open a File dialog box, the Save dialog box's appearance differs slightly depending on whether you are using Version Cue or not.

- **Save As (Option+⌘+S or Ctrl+Alt+S):** This lets you save a copy of the active document in a different (or in the same) folder using a different (or the same) name. When you choose Save As and when you choose Save for an unsaved document, the Save As dialog box (see Figure 4.8) appears.

- **Save a Copy:** This lets you create a copy of the active document in a different (or in the same) folder using a different (or the same) name. When you use the Save a Copy command, the original document remains open and retains its original name. It differs from Save As only in that it keeps the original document open.

- **Check In:** This saves the current document as a version with a Version Cue project. This latest save is considered a version of the previously saved file.

NEW FEATURE Check In is the new name for the Save a Version menu option in previous versions of InDesign.

CROSS-REF Version management is covered in later in this chapter.

- **Revert:** This undoes all changes you've made to a document since you last saved it. There is no way to undo this and reinstate all your changes after you revert, so be careful.

Saving documents versus saving templates

Whenever you save a document for the first time or you use the Save As or Save a Copy command, the Save As dialog box lets you save a standard InDesign document file or a template.

In an ideal world, you would create a finished template, save it, and then open a copy of the template and use it to create an actual publication. In the real world, however, templates are often created by yanking the content out of a finished publication and then saving the gutted file as a template. Regardless of how you create your templates, make sure you remember to select the InDesign CS3 Template option in the Save As dialog box. Where you choose the desired format varies based on the operating system and Version Cue status:

- On the Mac, use the Enable pop-up menu. It doesn't matter whether Version Cue is on or off, or whether you've clicked Use Adobe Dialog or Use OS Dialog in the dialog box.

- In Windows with the Use Adobe Dialog button clicked (Version Cue must be on), use the Format pop-up menu.

- In Windows with the Use OS Dialog button clicked (or if Version Cue is disabled) use the Save as Type pop-up menu.

FIGURE 4.8

The Mac version of the Save As dialog box (top) and the Windows version (bottom) are slightly different. If Version Cue were disabled, they would also look slightly different as well (compare Figures 4.4 and 4.5).

If you forget to save a document as a template, it opens under its actual name. If you then make any changes and choose File ➪ Save (⌘+S or Ctrl+S), the changes are saved with the original document. If this happens, simply save the document again and choose the InDesign CS3 Template option.

> **TIP**   Choosing File ➪ Package lets you save a copy of a document along with all files — linked graphics, fonts, and ICC color profiles — required to print the document. This feature is particularly handy if you intend to send an InDesign document to an output provider. (See Chapter 30 for more information about the Package command.)

Knowing how to not save changes

As I mentioned earlier in this chapter, InDesign is a very forgiving program. If you make a mistake, change your mind, or work yourself into a complete mess, you don't have to remain in your predicament or save your work. InDesign offers an escape route.

You can revert to your last saved version. To do this, choose File ➪ Revert. This undoes all changes you made since last saving a document. There is no way to undo this and reinstate all your changes after you revert, so be careful.

Saving Files in Other Formats

InDesign's Save, Save As, Save a Copy, and Check In commands let you save documents and templates using InDesign's native file format. The Export command (File ➪ Export) opens the Export dialog box, from which you can save documents and some individual document elements such as stories and graphics in several other formats. And InDesign has separate menu commands for exporting Web and eBook documents, as Chapter 33 explains.

Export formats for whole documents

To export entire documents, InDesign provides the following options (accessed from the Export dialog box unless otherwise indicated):

- **InDesign Interchange format:** This format lets InDesign CS3 save files readable by InDesign both CS2 and CS3, so users of the previous and next versions of InDesign can exchange files. (Therefore, InDesign Interchange CS3 files will also be readable by InDesign CS4 as well, and CS4 interchange files will be readable by InDesign CS3, when InDesign CS4 becomes available.) The trick is to export, not save as, files to the InDesign Interchange format. Interchange files have the filename extension .inx.

- **Production formats:** You can save the document as an EPS or a PDF file for use by pre-press tools and service bureaus or for import into other applications as a graphic. You get the choice of exporting individual pages and page ranges, not just the whole document. Choose the Adobe PDF or EPS options in the Format pop-up menu (called Save as Type when you use click Use Adobe Dialog in Windows) in the Export dialog box.

■ **Online formats:** You can save the document in XML format for use in online database-oriented content-management systems by choosing the XML option in the Format pop-up menu (called Save as Type when you use click Use Adobe Dialog in Windows) in the Export dialog box, or by choosing File ➪ Cross-Media Export ➪ XML. You can also export your document to the Web's structured HTML format by choosing File ➪ Cross-Media Export ➪ XHTML/Dreamweaver. The XHTML format can be read by both Web browsers and by Web creation tools such as Adobe Dreamweaver and CoffeeCup HTML Editor for further refinement in the Web content. Finally, you can export to the eBook format meant for Web-based distribution of rich-media documents — by choosing File ➪ Cross-Media Export ➪ XHTML/Digital Editions.

NOTE Despite the use of the word *Dreamweaver* in the menu option, you are not restricted to using Dreamweaver to do further work on these files; you can use any modern Web editor.

CROSS-REF Chapter 32 covers how to export PDF files. Part VIII covers the creation of interactive PDF and eBook files, how to export to XHTML and eBook formats, and how to import, export, and use XML files.

NEW FEATURE The Cross-Media Export menu is new to InDesign. So is the ability to export layouts to XHTML/Dreamweaver, which replaces the previous version's Package for GoLive option, which exported documents for use only in Adobe's GoLive Web creation program. The ability to export to XHTML/Digital Editions is an enhanced version of the pervious versions' ability to export eBook-enabled PDF files.

Export formats for document elements

You can also export pieces of your document, such as text files and graphics. Be sure to select the objects (use the Type tool for text and the Direct Selection tool for graphics), and then choose the appropriate options from the Export dialog box (File ➪ Export):

■ **Word processing formats:** If you place the text cursor into a story, you can export its text (select a range of text if you want to export only that selection) into one of three formats: RTF (Rich Text Format) for import into word processors with only basic formatting retained and Text Only for import into word processors that don't support RTF (no formatting is retained). You can also export selected stories to the InCopy or InCopy CS format, for use in that add-on program (see Chapter 36); exported stories appear in the Assignments panel.

NOTE If you need to export several stories from the same document, it's better to use the Assignments panel to create an assignment file that contains multiple stories, as described in Chapter 36. If you export multiple stories to one of the InCopy formats in the Export dialog box, each story is exported to its own file — and that can create a confusing number of files.

NEW FEATURE The ability to export text to the InCopy formats from the Export dialog box is new to InDesign CS3.

- **InDesign Tagged Text format:** Whether you select text using the Type tool or the Direct Selection tool, you can save the story in the InDesign Tagged Text format (for editing in a word processor and later reimporting into InDesign with all InDesign formatting retained).

- **Graphics formats:** You can export individual or multiple graphics as well as entire pages and layouts to either the JPG or Scalable Vector Graphics (SVG) formats by choosing the desired option in the Export dialog box. You can also export text frames, which convert the exported text to an uneditable image.

- **Document snippets:** You can also export selected elements to an XML snippets file; choose InDesign Snippets from the Export dialog box. A snippet contains all the formatting information and contents for whatever you select, so it can be brought into other layouts completely intact. It's a very handy way to share pieces of your layout with other users and other layouts. You can also simply drag objects from your page to the Mac or Windows desktop to create an XML snippet; you import XML snippets by dragging the snippet file (which has the filename extension .inds) into your document from the desktop. (Chapter 10 covers snippets in more detail.)

Working with exported tagged text files

No matter which layout program they use, most people don't use the Tagged Text option because the coding can be tortuous. Because you can't use tagged-text codes with your word processor's formatting, you must code everything with tagged text and save the document as an ASCII file. So why have Tagged Text at all? A good reason is because this format is the one format sure to support all the formatting you do in InDesign as well as make it easy for you to automate the layout of database-derived documents such as catalogs (see Chapter 23 for details on database publishing).

The usefulness of Tagged Text is not in creating text for import, but in transferring files created in InDesign to another InDesign user (including someone working on another platform) or to a word processor for further work. You can export an InDesign story or piece of selected text in the Tagged Text format, and then transfer the exported file to another InDesign user or to a word processor for further editing.

Exporting a Tagged Text file into a word processor makes sense if you want to add or delete text without losing special formatting, such as fonts, kerning, or style tags, that your word processor doesn't support. After you edit the text, you can save the altered file (make sure that it is saved as ASCII text) and reimport it into your InDesign layout.

The best way to understand the Tagged Text format is to export some of your own documents to it, and open the resulting file in a word processor to see how InDesign coded the file. A warning: The Tagged Text format can be complex, especially because most codes have two forms: a short (abbreviated) form and a long (verbose) form; you choose which InDesign form exports from the Export dialog box in InDesign (choose File ➪ Export, and then choose InDesign Tagged Text as the file format). Note that a Tagged Text file is simply an ASCII text file, so it has the filename extension .txt and uses the standard text-only file icon in Windows and on the Mac.

Here's an example of verbose coding (because the code is so long, I had to add line breaks; slightly indented lines are actually part of the same code segment):

```
<ASCII-WIN>
<DefineParaStyle:Normal=<Nextstyle:Normal><cTypeface:Regular>
  <cSize:10.000000><pHyphenationLadderLimit:0><pHyphenation:0>
  <pHyphenationZone:18.000000><cFont:Times New Roman>
  <cColorTint:100.000000>>
<DefineCharStyle:Default Paragraph Font=<Nextstyle:Default
  Paragraph Font>>
<DefineCharStyle:Hyperlink=<BasedOn:Default Paragraph Font>
  <Nextstyle:Hyperlink><cColor:Blue><cTypeface:Regular>
  <cSize:10.000000><cHorizontalScale:1.000000>
  <cBaselineShift:0.000000><cCase:Normal><cStrokeColor:>
  <cUnderline:1><cFont:Times New Roman><cPosition:Normal>
  <cStrikethru:0><cColorTint:100.000000>>
<ColorTable:=<Black:COLOR:CMYK:Process:0.000000,0.000000,0.000000,
  1.000000><Blue:COLOR:RGB:Process:0.000000,0.000000,1.000000>>
<ParaStyle:Normal><pHyphenation:1><CharStyle:Default Paragraph
  Font> <CharStyle:><CharStyle:Hyperlink>www.adobe.com
  <CharStyle:><CharStyle:Default Paragraph Font>.
  <CharStyle:><pHyphenation:>
```

Here is the same text with abbreviated tags:

```
<ASCII-WIN>
<dps:Normal=<Nextstyle:Normal><ct:Regular><cs:10.000000><phll:0>
  <ph:0><phz:18.000000><cf:Times New Roman><cct:100.000000>>
<dcs:Default Paragraph Font=<Nextstyle:Default Paragraph Font>>
<dcs:Hyperlink=<BasedOn:Default Paragraph Font>
  <Nextstyle:Hyperlink><cc:Blue><ct:Regular><cs:10.000000>
  <chs:1.000000><cbs:0.000000><ccase:Normal><csc:><cu:1>
  <cf:Times New Roman><cp:Normal><cstrike:0><cct:100.000000>>
<ctable:=<Black:COLOR:CMYK:Process:0.000000,0.000000,0.000000,
  1.000000><Blue:COLOR:RGB:Process:0.000000,0.000000,1.000000>>
<pstyle:Normal><ph:1><cstyle:Default Paragraph Font>
  <cstyle:><cstyle:Hyperlink>www.adobe.com<cstyle:>
  <cstyle:Default Paragraph Font>. <cstyle:><ph:>
```

What does all that coding mean? It's for a one-page document with one frame that has simply one line of text: This is a hyperlink to www.adobe.com. The text is black, except for the Web address, which is in blue underline.

As you can see, there's a lot to Tagged Text codes. InDesign comes with a complete list of codes in a PDF file called Tagged Text.pdf that you can find in the Tagged Text folder within the Adobe Technical Info folder on the InDesign CD-ROM.

In practical terms, you may not mind editing Tagged Text slightly or leaving the tags in a file when you alter the files text. But you're not likely to forgo the friendly formatting available in your word processor and in InDesign to apply Tagged Text coding to everything in your text files.

Exporting files as graphics

The process for exporting to JPEG or SVG is similar. Select the objects to export, choose File ⇨ Export, choose the desired format in the Export dialog box, and click Save to get the Export JPEG dialog box or Export SVG dialog box (shown in Figure 4.9).

In the Export section of the Export JPEG dialog box, and in the Pages section of the Export SVG dialog box, are identical options for choosing whether to export the selected graphics, entire pages and page ranges, or the entire document using the controls in the Export area Pages area.

 If you select multiple objects and choose Selection, they will be combined into one graphic in the exported file.

FIGURE 4.9

The Export JPEG (top) and Options SVG (bottom) dialog boxes

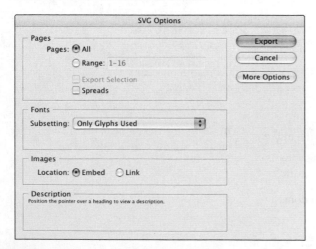

You also can control quality, format, and resolution settings.

For JPEG files, here are the options (all in the Image area):

- The Quality pop-up menu lets you control the image quality, with choices of Low, Medium, High, and Maximum. Note that the higher the quality, the less the JPEG image can be compressed.

- The Format Method pop-up menu controls how the JPEG image displays in a browser. The default Baseline option displays the entire image at once, while the Progressive option has it build up line by line — a good option for very large files, so viewers can tell something is happening as the image loads.

- The Resolution field lets you specify the output resolution in dots per inch (dpi); 72 dpi is appropriate for the Web assuming the image will be used at the same size, but you should pick a value of 300 for images to be published at the same size in print.

NEW FEATURE The ability to specify output resolution for JPEG files is new to InDesign CS3.

For SVG files (and for files saved in the more space-efficient SVG Compressed sibling format), here are the options:

- The Subsetting pop-up menu controls how fonts are embedded into the SVG file to ensure accurate online display. The most efficient option is Only Glyphs Used; the other options embed entire character sets, which lets you edit the text in the SVG file in another program and retain accurate display. The None option embeds no fonts, letting the user's browser determine how text appears.

- The Location radio button options — Embed and Link — determine whether images are embedded into the SVG file or will be linked as separate files in the same folder.

- If you click the More Options button, you see the Preset pop-up menu in the Transparency Flattener area. Here, you choose how transparency is handled during export, as explained in Chapter 31.

- Use the CSS Properties pop-up menu to control how much formatting information is embedded in the SVG file. Most of the time, Presentation Attributes is the best option, because it embeds contextual information that helps you edit the SVG file in other programs. Style Attributes is recommended if you're using the images with Extensible Stylesheet Language Transformation (XSLT) files. (The other two pop-up menu options — Style Attributes (Entity References) and Style Elements — assume that style information is embedded in HTML pages and used by the SVG files — this saves on SVG file size but reduces the flexibility in where you can use the files. Check with your Web master as to which option is appropriate for the ultimate use of the SVG file.

- Follow the Web master's requirements for the Decimal Places and Encoding settings; these affect the technical setup for the CSS files themselves.

For both types of files, click Export when done.

Managing File Versions with Version Cue

Typically, organizations develop their own version-management procedures, such as having layout artists add version numbers or dates to layout iterations. Adobe is hoping that Version Cue, which comes with InDesign and all Creative Suite applications, will eventually replace the do-it-yourself approach.

You can use Version Cue by yourself to manage versions of your documents as you create them or with others in a workgroup to both manage multiple versions of files and share files among users. Either way, the file-versioning steps are the same.

But before you can use Version Cue, you have to enable it. To do so, go to the File Handling pane of the Preferences dialog box, then enable the Enable Version Cue option. (Choose InDesign ➪ Preferences ➪ File Handling or press ⌘+K on the Mac, or choose Edit ➪ Preferences ➪ File Handling or press Ctrl+K in Windows.) This turns on the Version Cue dialog boxes in InDesign and other Creative Suite applications. You must do this to work with Version Cue.

To make your computer available as a server to other users, go to the Version Cue CS3 system preference (Mac) or control panel (Windows) that InDesign or Creative Suite installs for you. On the Mac, choose ➪ System Preferences and then click the Version Cue CS3 iconic button; click Start to turn on the server and enable the Turn on Server When the Computer Starts option to have the server started automatically in the future. Note that if your computer is not set as a server, you can still work with InDesign and other Creative Suite files stored on other Version Cue servers, as well as save files locally for just your own use. You do not have to make your computer a server to work with Version Cue.

 Chapter 35 covers how to work with other users, including how Version Cue supports workgroups.

Understanding the Version Cue interface

Emulating Mac OS X's and Windows' quick-access sidebar, InDesign's Version Cue–enabled dialog boxes have a sidebar that gives you quick access to the local Desktop folder, the local Documents folder (Mac) or My Documents folder (Windows), and the Version Cue folder. (In Windows, you also get access to the My Pictures and My Network Places folders.) In addition, Version Cue provides quick access to the Project Search, Project Trash, and Files in Use functions, the first being a search function that works with Version Cue's folders and the latter two being virtual folders. Finally, you have access to user-chosen favorites at the bottom of the pane; you add them by selecting a folder and then choosing Add to Favorites from the Tools drop-down menu (covered later in this section).

You set the Version Cue defaults using the Adobe Bridge application, which manages Creative Suite 3–wide settings. Choose Bridge ➪ Preferences or press ⌘+K on the Mac, or choose Edit ➪ Preferences or press Ctrl+K in Windows. Figure 4.10 shows the dialog box. At the bottom of the General pane, in the Favorite Items section, you set the default folders to display in Version Cue dialog boxes' Favorites sidebar section.

The Version Cue–enabled dialog boxes in InDesign (and other Creative Suite applications) also have several iconic buttons, as labeled in Figure 4.11. The functions of the first four — Up One Folder, Create New Folder, Refresh, and Delete — are self-explanatory. The fifth, Tools, is a drop-down menu that contains the functions to create projects (shared folders), connect to existing projects, manage sharing and versions, manage project items, synchronize items, and revert to the standard dialog boxes (by choosing the Show OS Dialog menu option). The sixth iconic button, at far right, is the View drop-down menu that offers file view choices of Details, Icons, Thumbnails, and Tiles.

To switch back to the standard Mac or Windows dialog boxes, click Use OS Dialog or choose Use OS Dialog from the Tools drop-down menu. To get the Version Cue–enabled dialog boxes back, click the Use Adobe Dialog button that appears at the bottom of the regular Mac and Windows dialog boxes.

FIGURE 4.10

The General pane of the Preferences dialog box in Adobe Bridge. The Favorites Items section manages Version Cue's default folder display.

Because all local folders — those on your computer or mounted through your computer's network connections — display in the Version Cue–enabled dialog boxes, even if you never use shared workspaces, you still have access to all your local files, as well as to any files accessible over the network. In a nutshell, the trick to using Version Cue is to know whether files are stored in a Version Cue workspace folder or in a regular folder, and then navigate accordingly.

NOTE   Although Version Cue should automatically find shared workspaces for and from any PC or Mac that has Version Cue enabled, you might not find all such workspaces in your copy of InDesign. Ask your network administrator to help if that's the case.

FIGURE 4.11

With Version Cue enabled, the Open a File, Save, Export, and Place dialog boxes in InDesign gain several new features for managing shared projects and controlling file versions, as well as a modified appearance for navigating through both Version Cue and normal folder hierarchies. The Open a File dialog box is shown here.

Working with versions

When you open a file through Version Cue, you are actually working on a copy of the master file. Depending on how you save the file, you get different results:

- **Save (File ⇨ Save, or ⌘+S or Ctrl+S):** All changes are saved locally, and the master version in the project folder is not modified. You can add version comments in the Save dialog box.

- **Check In (File ⇨ Check In):** All changes are saved both locally and to the master project folder, replacing the master file. The filename remains the same as when you opened it. You can add version comments in the Check In dialog box; as shown in Figure 4.12, InDesign automatically increments the version number each time you save a version (so if the file was version 4 when you opened it, it will be version 5 when you save a version).

NEW FEATURE The Check In option in InDesign CS3 replaces the Save a Version option in previous versions of InDesign.

■ **Save As (File ⇨ Save As, or Shift+⌘+S or Ctrl+Shift+S):** If you save in a local folder, all changes are saved locally to a new file (with a different, user-defined name), and the master version in the project folder is not modified. Otherwise, it saves the file into the project folder as a new version of the original file, leaving the original file unchanged. Either way, you can add version comments in the Save As dialog box.

■ **Save a Copy (File ⇨ Save a Copy, or Option+⌘+S or Ctrl+Alt+S):** All changes are saved locally to a new file (with a new name chosen by InDesign: the word "copy" is added to the end), and the master version in the project folder is not modified. You can add version comments in the Save a Copy dialog box.

FIGURE 4.12

The Check In dialog box lets you add comments to the current version of your file.

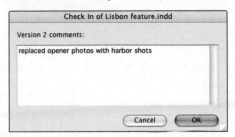

NEW FEATURE When you save a new version of a layout using Version Cue, only the changes are saved, instead of a copy of the original file. This doesn't take up as much disk space, but it does mean you can no longer back up individual version files using the Version Cue system preference (Mac) or control panel (Windows).

CAUTION Version Cue works with files from CS, CS2, and CS3 programs. Because you can open CS and CS2 files with a CS3 application, you could end up with, for example, a file that started in InDesign CS format that is now in InDesign CS3 format, making it inaccessible to InDesign CS and CS2 users.

There is also a menu option in the Tools drop-down list that manages document versions: Versions. This option displays the version comments for a selected file, as well as lets you view any of the versions. It also lets you promote an earlier version so it becomes the current version; this is a handy way to keep layout experiments that you reject and make an earlier version the new starting point for further explorations. Figure 4.13 shows this Versions dialog box.

NEW FEATURE Gone in InDesign CS3 is the ability to save an alternate version of a layout. The idea behind alternates was to create a new set of versions of a layout, to distinguish alternative approaches from historical versions of the same approach. But users didn't get it, opting instead for simply saving a new file with a new name when working on alternative layouts.

Managing files

If you want to take advantage of the Version Cue project management and versioning tools, you use the Tools drop-down menu extensively (refer back to Figure 4.11). Here's a run-through of the Version Cue features for managing shared projects:

- **Reveal in Finder (Mac) or Reveal in Explorer (Windows):** Opens a new window with the folder containing the selected file.

- **Reveal in Bridge:** Opens the Bridge program that Adobe provides to manage project preferences across the Creative Suite and shows the selected file's status there.

- **Add to Favorites:** Adds the selected file to the Favorites or My Favorites list in the Version Cue–enabled dialog boxes.

- **New Folder:** Creates a new folder at the current project's location.

- **Refresh:** Updates the workspace and project information to reflect any deletions, additions, and changes.

- **Synchronize:** Synchronizes project status information between the master project and your locally stored files.

- **Download:** Copies a project file to your local computer.

- **Clear Local Files:** Removes the local copy of the project from your computer, leaving just the file stored in the Version Cue project folder.

- **Versions:** Lets you see all version comments and rearrange the version order as desired.

- **New Project:** Lets you create a new project.

- **Connect to Server:** Lets you connect to another computer or server on which Version Cue projects might reside; you need to know the IP address.

- **Edit Properties:** Lets you set basic project settings, such as folder location within the workspace hierarchy and whether a project is shared.

- **Show Metadata Area:** Displays the metadata — various file and content attributes that you can associate with files via the Adobe Bridge program.

NEW FEATURE Adobe has changed the Version Cue–enabled dialog boxes' Tools menu options considerably in CS3.

The Tools menu's changes include the following:

- The Show File Info Area has been renamed Show Metadata Area, and Connect To has been renamed Connect to Server.

- The Refresh, Download, and Clear Local Files options are new.

- Gone are the old Share Project, Show Deleted Items, Delete, Restore, and Disconnect options. You now manage most of these functions in one of two places: the Bridge program's Tools menu or in the Edit Properties dialog box (accessed by choosing Edit Properties in the

Tools drop-down menu from a Version Cue–enabled dialog box). In the Edit Properties dialog box, you can control whether a project is shared in the Edit Properties menu as well by checking or unchecking the Share This Project with Others option, and you access other Version Cue management features by clicking the Server Administration button.

The Versions dialog box lets you view previous versions of a document as well as promote a previous version to be the new current master version.

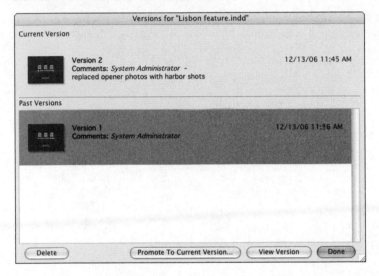

Summary

When you're ready to begin working on a new document, choose File ➪ New ➪ Document, and then use the controls in the New Document dialog box to specify the page size, margins, column format, and any bleed and slug areas for the document. You can also save these settings for easy future use as document styles from the New Document dialog box.

After opening a new document, choose File ➪ Save to save a standard InDesign document file or a template file. (A *template* is a preconstructed document that you use to create multiple versions of a publication.) You can choose File ➪ Save As to save a copy of the current document, or you can choose File ➪ Revert to discard your most recent round of changes. If you want to work on a document you've previously saved, choose File ➪ Open.

In addition to opening InDesign documents and templates, you can open QuarkXPress and QuarkXPress Passport 3.3, 4.0, and 4.1 documents, as well as PageMaker 6.0, 6.5, and 7.0 documents. Choosing File ➪ Export lets you save InDesign documents as InDesign Interchange, EPS,

PDF, and XML formats. (With the InDesign Interchange format, InDesign can export in a format readable by the previous version of InDesign.) You can also save individual stories or text selections in RTF, text-only, InCopy, and InDesign Tagged Text formats. You can export individual objects, groups or objects, individual pages, ranges of pages, or entire documents to the JPEG and SVG formats. You can also export selected objects as XML snippet files that preserve all content and formatting, making it easy to share elements across documents. Last, you can create structured HTML files for use in Web creation programs by choosing File ➪ Cross-Media Export ➪ XHTML/Dreamweaver and rich-media eBook files for the Web by choosing File ➪ Cross-Media Export ➪ XHTML/Digital Editions.

The Version Cue feature lets you save multiple versions of your documents, so you can go back to previous versions as you experiment with your layouts. It also lets you work with files stored on servers accessible to other users, for workgroup environments.

Chapter 5

Working with Pages

It's a rare InDesign user who creates only one-page documents. Even if business cards, ads, and posters are your bread and butter, you'll probably produce at least a few multi-page documents. If you plan to create newsletters, newspapers, books, catalogs, or any other such multi-page publications, you need to know how to add pages to your document, move pages around if you change your mind, and delete pages if necessary.

In addition to letting you create multi-page documents — something that most illustration and image-editing programs don't — InDesign lets you divide multi-page documents into independently numbered sections. As documents grow in size, your ability to navigate quickly to the page you want to work on becomes an important consideration. The longer you spend getting to the page you want, the less time you have to work on it. Fortunately, InDesign provides several navigation aids that make it easy to move around on a page or in a document.

IN THIS CHAPTER

Adding, removing, and rearranging document pages

Adjusting page numbers

Working with sections

Navigating through a document and scrolling in a page

Adjusting page layouts and objects

Working with Multi-page Documents

If you intend to create a multi-page document, you should select the Facing Pages option in the New Document dialog box (File ➪ New ➪ Document, or ⌘+N or Ctrl+N) when you create the document. You also want to display the Pages panel (Window ➪ Pages, or ⌘+F12 or Ctrl+F12), shown in Figure 5.1, because it provides the controls that let you add pages (document and master), delete and move pages, apply master pages to document pages, and navigate through a document.

CROSS-REF For more information about using the Pages panel to work on master pages, see Chapter 7.

NOTE The overwhelming majority of multi-page documents are facing-page publications such as books, catalogs, and magazines. Some exceptions are flip charts, Web pages, and three-hole-punched publications printed on only one side. In this chapter, the figures show examples of a facing-page document. If you're creating a single-sided multi-page document, the techniques are the same as for facing-page documents, but the icons in the Pages panel show only single-sided page icons (the icons aren't dog-eared).

FIGURE 5.1

The Pages panel and its flyout menu. This is how the panel looks when you open a new, facing-page document. (Here, it happens to have one page.)

Adding pages

A document can contain as many as 9,999 pages, although you'd never want to create a document nearly that long. In general, try to break up long publications into logical pieces. For example, if you're creating a book, it's a good idea to create separate documents for the front matter, each chapter, the index, and any other parts (appendixes and so on). Also, if you're producing a long document, you want to take advantages of master pages (covered in Chapter 7), which save you the work of building each page from scratch.

When you create a multi-page document, you're free to add however many pages you want. But be careful. Even though InDesign lets you create a seven-page newsletter, in real life, facing-page publications always have an even number of pages — usually a multiple of 4 and often a multiple of 16 because of the way printers arrange multiple pages on a single sheet of paper.

NEW FEATURE InDesign CS3 now shows a preview image of your pages in the Pages panel, which makes it easier to know you're selecting the right page. You can control the display by choosing Panel Options from the panel's flyout menu. In the Panel Options dialog box, select the desired icon size and make sure Show Thumbnails is checked. You can also set separate view settings for master pages.

Here's how to add pages to a document:

1. **If it's not displayed, open the Pages panel by choosing Window ⇨ Pages or pressing ⌘+F12 or Ctrl+F12.**

2. **From the Pages panel's flyout menu, choose Insert Pages.** The Insert Pages dialog box, shown in Figure 5.2, appears.

3. **In the Pages field, type the number of pages you want to add.**

4. **Select an option from the Insert pop-up menu: After Page, Before Page, At Start of Document, or At End of Document.** Be careful: If you've already started working on page 1, for example, make sure you add new pages after page 1. Otherwise, it isn't page 1 anymore and you have to move the objects you already created.

5. **Type a page number in the field next to Insert or use the arrows to increase or decrease the value in one-page increments.**

6. **From the Master pop-up menu, select the master page you want to apply to the new pages.**

7. **When you're finished, click OK to close the dialog box.**

NEW FEATURE The shortcut for accessing the Pages panel has changed to ⌘+F12 or Ctrl+F12 in InDesign CS3 from just F12 in previous versions. But the old F12 still works, though it could conflict with Mac OS X's Exposé utility.

FIGURE 5.2

The Insert Pages dialog box

You can also add new pages or spreads — spreads are added if a spread is selected in the Pages panel — one at a time at the end of a document, by clicking the Create New Page iconic button at the bottom of the Pages panel. When you use this method, the master page applied to the last document page is applied to each new page. Pages are added after the currently selected page in the panel.

Speedy Page Actions

There is a faster way to add and manipulate pages if you don't happen to have the Pages panel already open: Choose Layout ➪ Pages, and then select the appropriate option, such as Add Pages, from the submenu. The resulting dialog boxes match those accessed from the Pages panel.

If you want to quickly add just one page after the current page, click Layout ➪ Pages ➪ Add Page, or press Shift+⌘+P or Ctrl+Shift+P. Note that this menu shortcut is not available through the Pages panel's flyout menu, although, of course, you can use the keyboard shortcut at any time.

You can also click and drag a master page icon (or both pages in a facing-pages spread to add a spread) from the top of the Pages panel to add a page using a master page's settings (use the [None] page for a plain page) between any pair of document page spreads or to the right of the last document spread. If a vertical bar appears when you release the mouse button, the spread is placed between the spreads on either side of the bar. If a vertical bar does not appear between document page spreads when you release the mouse button, the new spread is placed at the end of the document.

Deleting pages

InDesign offers several choices for deleting pages from a document. You can:

- Select one or more page icons in the Pages panel and either click and drag them to the pane's Delete Selected Pages iconic button (the trashcan icon) or simply click the Delete Selected Pages iconic button. Click a spread's page numbers to select both pages. You can click a page icon or spread number and then Shift+click another page icon or spread number to select a range of pages. Hold down the ⌘ or Ctrl key and click page icons or spread numbers to select multiple, noncontiguous pages.

- Select one or more page icons in the Pages panel and then click Delete Pages or Delete Spreads from the panel's flyout menu.

- Choose Layout ➪ Pages ➪ Delete Pages. Any pages or spreads selected in the Pages panel are deleted. (If one or more spreads are selected, the menu option is Delete Spreads.) This is not a terribly useful option because you have to have the Pages panel open and thus may as well just use its flyout menu to delete pages.

Copying and moving pages

InDesign lets you copy and move pages from one document to another, as well as copy and move pages within a document.

Working within a document

To *duplicate* the current spread within the current document, click Duplicate Spread from the Pages panel's flyout menu or by choosing Layout ➪ Pages ➪ Duplicate Spread. (If you're not working with

The Dangers of Shuffling

Although you can move pages around in a document, do so only with great care, if at all. Generally, if you want to move the *objects* on one page to another page, it's safer to cut (Edit ➪ Cut, or ⌘+X or Ctrl+X) or copy (Edit ➪ Copy, or ⌘+C or Ctrl+C) the objects than to move the page, which might cause subsequent pages to shuffle.

What's the big deal about shuffling? Shuffling moves pages around to make space for the moved page, and that can move what had been left-hand pages to the right-hand side of the spread and vice versa. If you have different alignments on left and right pages — such as having page numbers on the outside of pages — this shuffling can wreak havoc with that alignment.

If you absolutely must move a single page, it's safer to move its spread. (Of course, if you're working on a single-sided facing-page document, shuffling is not an issue.)

spreads because Facing Pages is unchecked in the Document Setup dialog box, the menu option is still named Duplicate Spread.)

To *move* a page within a document, click its icon in the Pages panel and then drag the hand pointer between two spreads or between the pages of a spread inside the Pages panel. A vertical bar indicates where the selected page is placed. Release the mouse button when the vertical bar is where you want to move the page. To move a spread, click the page numbers beneath the icons (rather than on the page icons) before dragging them to the new location.

NEW FEATURE As you drag pages and spreads around the Pages panel, InDesign CS3 now automatically scrolls through the pages. This means you don't have to increase the size of the panel to move pages across larger distances.

NEW FEATURE Also new to InDesign CS3, the mouse pointer changes to the grabber (hand) pointer when it's not over a page in the Pages panel. If you click and drag this pointer within the panel, InDesign scrolls the panel in the direction you move the mouse.

Or you can choose Move Pages from the Pages panel's flyout menu or choose Layout ➪ Pages ➪ Move Pages. Either way, the Move Pages dialog box appears (refer to Figure 5.3). In that dialog box, you can specify where to move the pages: After a specific page, before a specific page, at the beginning of the document, or at the end of the document.

Working across documents

You can also copy and move pages to other documents. Note that the other documents must be open for the following techniques to work.

To copy a page, an easy way is to click and drag the page icon from the source document's Pages panel to the target document's Pages panel. InDesign copies the page in front of the one you release the mouse at. Any master pages associated with the copied document pages are copied as well.

But the easiest way is to select the page in the Pages panel, and then drag its icon to the document you want to copy it to. The Insert Pages dialog box then appears, giving you a choice of where to insert the page in the new document.

To *move* a page rather than copy it, be sure to check the Delete Pages After Inserting Option in the Insert Pages dialog box. You can also use the Move Pages dialog box I described earlier: Just be sure to select the target document in the new Move To pop-up menu.

NEW FEATURE The Insert Pages dialog box is new to InDesign CS3, as is the Move To pop-up menu in the Move Pages dialog box.

Figure 5.3 shows both the Insert Pages and Move Pages dialog boxes.

FIGURE 5.3

The Insert Pages dialog box (top) displays when you drag pages between documents, while the Move Pages dialog box (bottom) displays through a menu option.

Starting documents on a left page

By default, InDesign starts all documents with a right-hand page. As a default, that makes sense, because the first sheet in a document always is a right-hand page. But sometimes, you want documents to start on a left-hand page, particularly if they are a chapter or section in a larger document. For example, magazine articles often start on a left page, giving the introduction a full spread. To start a document on a left page:

1. **Select the first page in the Pages panel and then choose Numbering & Section Options from the panel's flyout menu, or choose Layout ⇨ Numbering & Section Options.**

2. **Select the Start Section option.**

3. **Select the Start Page Numbering at option and enter an even number such as 2 in the field to its right.**

4. **Click OK.**

5. **The Pages panel updates, showing the start page on the left of the spine.**

6. **You may not want to assign a starting page number (for example, if the starting page number is unknown because the number of pages that precede this document is unknown, and you are letting the book feature determine the page numbers later).** In this case, repeat Step 1 but deselect Start Section. This leaves the page as a left-hand page but lets the book feature figure out the page number.

QUARKXPRESS The preceding technique should be familiar to you, except that QuarkXPress does not let you remove the section start — as soon as you do, QuarkXPress would make the page a right-hand page again. InDesign does not.

CROSS-REF For more on the book feature, see Chapter 25. Sections are covered in more detail later in this chapter.

Controlling page shuffling

When you insert new pages, existing pages after the inserted pages are automatically changed from left-hand (*verso*) pages to right-hand (*recto*) pages, and vice versa, as needed when individual pages are added and removed in a facing-pages document. You can prevent that for selected spreads, such as a two-page table, that you don't want to have broken apart when other pages are added or deleted. Of course, for proper printing you may need to move that spread so it follows a complete spread when you're done adding or deleting pages.

To disable shuffling for selected spreads, first select them in the Pages panel and then choose Allow Selected Spread to Shuffle in the flyout menu. By default, this menu option has a checkmark to its left indicating that the spreads can shuffle; choosing it unchecks the option, meaning the selected spreads will *not* shuffle. (If the menu option is already unchecked, choosing it re-enables it and the checkmark reappears.)

NOTE When you designate pages not to shuffle — that is, to be kept together — the page numbers below the spread in the Pages panel are displayed in brackets.

You can also disable shuffling for all spreads by choosing Allow Document Pages to Shuffle in the flyout menu: If the checkmark is not there, the pages will *not* shuffle.

NEW FEATURE InDesign CS3's Allow Selected Pages to Shuffle menu option used to be called Keep Spreads Together in previous versions of InDesign. This name change also changes InDesign's behavior: Now, you have to disable the Allow Selected Pages to Shuffle option to permit keep pages together rather than enable the Keep Spreads Together option.

Creating gatefold spreads

Have you ever seen a publication, a magazine perhaps, that had a foldout page? Often such pages are ads (publishers love advertisers who buy multi-page ads) or special sections. Or maybe you've seen a two-sided, multifold brochure with several panels, each the same size. A multi-page spread of this type is often called a *gatefold spread* or *accordion page*, or (in earlier versions of InDesign) an *island spread*.

When you designate a spread as a gatefold spread, the spread's pages don't move if you add or delete any document pages in front of it. (Normally, when you add or delete pages, all subsequent pages bump backward or shuffle.)

When you create a gatefold spread of three pages in a facing-page publication, you should always create them in pairs because, in an actual printed publication, if you add a third page to a two-page spread, the backside of the page becomes the third page in another three-page spread. Along the same lines, if you create a four-panel, trifold brochure, both the front and the back have four panels. If this is difficult to visualize, take a look at Figure 5.4.

One last word about gatefold spreads: They require special care throughout the production process, and they cost you extra at the printer and bindery. If you're creating a modest, black-and-white newsletter for a local nonprofit organization, throwing in a three-panel gatefold probably isn't an option. On the other hand, if you can find an advertiser with deep pockets, InDesign lets you create gatefold spreads with up to ten pages.

To create a gatefold spread, first select the pages that you want to make into a gatefold, and then deselect the Allow Selected Pages to Shuffle option from the panel's flyout menu. Now, drag any of the pages you just unmarked as Allow Selected Pages to Shuffle to create the gatefold spread; that is, drag pages to the spread that will contain the multiple pages. A vertical bar indicates where the page will be placed. When the bar is where you want to place the page, release the mouse button.

To clear a gatefold, select it in the Pages panel and then reselect the Allow Selected Pages to Shuffle option in the panel's flyout menu.

Figure 5.4 shows a pair of three-page gatefold spreads in a facing-pages publication.

FIGURE 5.4

In this example, pages 2, 3, and 4 are a gatefold, as are pages 5, 6, and 7.

TIP You may want to create a section out of the extra pages in a gatefold so that you can number them separately from the surrounding pages. Sections are covered later in this chapter.

QUARKXPRESS The InDesign gatefold spread is similar to QuarkXPress's capability to place several pages on one spread to create foldouts. Both use the same process: You click and drag a page next to a page in the spread to which you want to add the page. The difference is that in QuarkXPress you don't have to first select the pages and then tell QuarkXPress to keep them together, as you do in InDesign.

Working with Page Numbers

Pages are numbered automatically starting at 1 based on the order in which they appear in the Pages panel. But you can change the page numbering from Arabic numerals to Roman numerals or letters, as well as change the start page to be something other than 1. To do so, select the first page in the document in the Pages panel and choose Layout ➪ Page Numbering & Sections or choose Numbering & Section Options from the Pages panel's flyout menu. Either way, you get the dialog box shown in Figure 5.5. (Its name will be New Section if the page has no section already applied to it. Otherwise, the name will be Numbering & Section Options.)

TIP A quick way to edit an existing section is to double-click its icon — the triangle that appears over the section's starting page in the Pages panel. You then get the Numbering & Section Options dialog box.

To change the initial page number, select the Start Page Numbering at option and type a new starting page number in its field. To change the page numbering style from the default of Arabic numerals (1, 2, 3, 4, . . .), use the Style pop-up menu and choose from I, II, III, IV, . . .; i, ii, iii, iv, . . .; A, B, C, D, . . .; and a, b, c, d, . . .

TIP To have a facing-pages document start on a left-hand page, you must have the starting page number be even.

CROSS-REF InDesign lets you create automatic page numbers, which lets you add the current page number to a folio or to automatically update the page number in a cross-reference such as a continued line. Chapter 23 covers this feature in detail.

It also lets you specify a chapter number for each document for use in book projects so InDesign can use the text variables feature to automatically enter the chapter number in text such as folios for you. Chapter 23 covers text variables and Chapter 25 covers books.

FIGURE 5.5

The New Section dialog box lets you change the starting page number and the types of numerals used. (This dialog box is named Numbering & Section Options if you are working with a page that was previously made a section start.)

Dividing a Document into Sections

Some long documents are divided into parts that are numbered separately from the other parts. For example, the page numbers for the front matter of books are often Roman numerals, while those for the body of the book are standard Arabic numerals. If a book has appendixes, a separate numbering scheme can be applied to these pages. In InDesign, such independently numbered parts are referred to as *sections*.

A multi-page document can contain as many sections as you want (a section has to contain at least one page). If each section of a document uses a different page layout, you probably want to create a different master page for each section. Here's how to create a section:

1. **If it's not displayed, open the Pages panel by choosing Window ➪ Pages or pressing ⌘+F12 or Ctrl+F12.**

2. **Click the icon of the page where you want to start a section.**

3. **Choose Numbering & Section Options from the panel's flyout menu.** If the page is not already a section start, the New Section dialog box, shown in Figure 5.5, appears. Otherwise, the identical Numbering & Section Options dialog box appears. (You can also create a section starting at the current page in your document by choosing Layout ➪ Numbering & Section Options.) By default, the Start Section option is selected. Leave it selected.

Targeting Versus Selecting Spreads

Depending on the task you're working on, you may want to use the Pages panel to *target* a spread or to *select* a spread. The choice you make determines the actions you can perform.

A targeted spread is the spread to which copied objects will be placed when you choose Edit ➪ Paste or press ⌘+V or Ctrl+V, or to which library objects will be placed when you choose Place Items from a library panel's flyout menu. The target spread is the one that's in the center of the document window and is indicated by the page number displayed in the page-number field at the lower-left corner of the document window. Only one spread can be the target spread at any one time. At reduced magnifications, it's possible to display several spreads in the document window. In this case, the number in the page-number field indicates the target spread.

When you select one or more spreads, you can then perform several page-level modifications, such as adjusting margin and column guides, applying a master page, or deleting the pages, in a single operation.

There are several ways to target a spread. You can:

- Modify an object on the spread or its pasteboard.
- Click on a spread or its pasteboard.
- In the Pages panel, double-click the page numbers below the spread's page icons. (This also moves you to the document pages in the spread.)

You also have several options for selecting a page or spread:

- Click once on a page icon to select one page of a spread; click the page numbers to select both pages. If you click twice, the page or spread is selected and targeted.
- Click a page icon or spread number and then Shift+click another page icon or spread number to select a range of pages.
- Hold down ⌘ or Ctrl and click page icons or spread numbers to select multiple, noncontiguous pages.

In the Pages panel, the page numbers of the target spread are displayed reversed, white numbers in a black rectangle, while the page icons are highlighted in a light-blue color.

4. **In the Section Prefix field, type up to eight characters that identify the section in the page-number box at the lower-left corner of the document window.** For example, if you type Sec2, the first page of the section is displayed as Sec2:1 in the page-number box.

5. **From the Style pop-up menu, choose the Roman numeral, Arabic numeral, or alphabetic style you want to use for page numbers.**

6. **For Page Numbering, select the Automatic Page Numbering option if you want the first page of the section to be one number higher than the last page of the previous section.** The new section uses the specified style; the previous section may use this style or another style.

7. **Select the Start Page Numbering at option and type a number in the accompanying field to specify a different starting number for the section.** For example, if a book begins with a section of front matter, you could begin the body section of a book on page 1 by choosing Start At and typing 1 in the field. If you select Continue from Previous Section, the first page of the body section would begin one number higher than the Roman numeral on the last page of the front matter.

8. **In the Section Marker field, type a text string that you can later automatically apply to pages in the section.** You might want to enter something straightforward like Section 2 or, if the section is a chapter, the name of the chapter.

> **TIP** You can insert the section marker name so it prints in folios, chapter headings, and story text by choosing Type ⇨ Insert Special Character ⇨ Markers ⇨ Section Marker. This is a great way to get a chapter name (if you use it as the section marker) in your folio or to have cross-references in text to a section whose name might later change. You can also specify a chapter for automatic insertion into folios or other text. Chapter 23 explains both in detail.

9. **Click OK to close the dialog box.**

When you create a section, it's indicated in the Pages panel by a small, black, inverted triangle over the icon of the first page in the section, as shown in Figure 5.6. (If you move the mouse pointer over the black triangle, the name of the section appears.) The page-numbering scheme you've specified is reflected in the page numbers below the page icons. When you begin a section, it continues until the end of the document or until you begin a new section.

> **TIP** By default, the Pages panel displays section numbers beneath the icons of document pages. To display absolute page numbers — the first page is page 1 and all other pages are numbered sequentially — choose InDesign ⇨ Preferences ⇨ General or pressing ⌘+K on the Mac, or choose Edit ⇨ Preferences ⇨ General or pressing Ctrl+K in Windows, and select Absolute Numbering from the View pop-up menu.

If you decide that you want to remove a section, navigate to the page that begins the section, choose Numbering & Section Options from the Pages panel's flyout menu, or choose Layout ⇨ Numbering & Section Options, and deselect the Section Start option.

FIGURE 5.6
_____

The small inverted triangle above a page icon (page 4, here) represents a section start.

Transparency Alert

InDesign is a pioneer in the use of transparency for layouts, but that feature can trip up some printers. To help you identify pages that use transparency, InDesign CS3 automatically adds an icon to the right of the page number in the Pages panel if that page uses transparency. No transparency, no icon. The figure below shows pages with the transparency icon in the Pages panel.

Navigating Documents and Pages

Moving from page to page in a long document and scrolling around a large or magnified page are among the most common tasks you'll perform in InDesign. The more time you spend displaying the page or page area you want to work on, the less time you have to do the work you need to do. Like most trips, the less time you spend between destinations, the better.

You can always just go to the page you want, but for navigating through the pages of a document when you don't know which page has the content you are seeking, the Pages panel (Window ➪ Pages, or ⌘+F12 or Ctrl+F12) offers the fastest ride. For navigating around in a page, you may want to switch to the Navigator panel (Window ➪ Object & Layout ➪ Navigator).

Navigating by page number

InDesign lets you easily move through pages by just selecting the desired page — if you know its number, of course. To do so, enter the desired page number in the Page field, then press Enter or Return, or select the page from the Page pop-up menu, both of which are at the bottom left of the document window, as shown in Chapter 3.

 TIP Use the shortcut ⌘+J or Ctrl+J to highlight the Page field to make it a little faster to enter the desired page number.

Understanding Special Page Numbers

When entering in page numbers for page navigation, printing, or other functions, you usually can use regular numbers, such as 5 for the fifth page. But there are some occasions where that won't get what you want; these occasions involve the use of sections.

A *section page number,* specified through the Numbering & Section Options dialog box (choose Layout ➪ Numbering & Section Options or choose Numbering & Section Options in the Pages panel's flyout menu) is a customized page number. You use section numbers if your document needs to start on a page other than 1 — for example, if you're working on a magazine and each article is saved in a different document, or if you have a preface using Roman numerals (such as iv). A single document can have multiple sections of page numbers and can use section page numbers to change the format of numbers to Roman numerals, letters, and so on.

If your sections use different numbering styles such as letters, Roman numerals, and Arabic numerals, you can go to the desired page as long as the page number you enter is unique: iii, c, and 3 would represent different pages, and InDesign would know which is which because their numbering is different.

But if your document uses the same page numbers more than once, such as page 51 in two different sections, you can't just enter 51 to get to page 51, since InDesign won't know which page 51 to go to. That's where section page numbers come in. To jump to or print a page with a section page number, you need to indicate which section it is and what page number appears on the page. InDesign provides a default name for sections, starting at Sec1. When you enter a section page number, you must separate the section name and the page number with a colon. For example, if you start the page numbering on page 51, you need to type Sec1:51 in the page number field to jump to that page. Having to include this undisplayed section information makes this option fairly unappealing, so you may prefer to use absolute page numbers

An *absolute page number* indicates a page's position in the document, such as 1 for the first page, 2 for the second page, and so on. To specify an absolute page number in the page number field or other dialog box (such as Print) that involves selecting pages, you type a plus sign before the number that represents the page's position. For example, the first page in the document is always +1, the second page is always +2, and so on. If you don't type a plus sign, the first page with the number 1 is what InDesign will assume you mean — although this may not be the first page in the document. For example, perhaps you have a 5-page section with Roman numerals followed by a 30-page section with Arabic numerals. Type just 1; this goes to the first page in the Arabic-numbered section, while entering +1 goes to the first page in the document (*i*, in this case).

Navigating with the menus and shortcuts

InDesign also offers several menu commands and keyboard shortcuts to quickly navigate your layout, as Table 5.1 details.

TABLE 5.1			

Page Navigation Menus and Shortcuts

Navigation	Menu Sequence	Macintosh Shortcut	Windows Shortcut
Go to a specific page	Layout ⇨ Go to Page	⌘+J	Ctrl+J
Go to first page	Layout ⇨ First Page	Shift+⌘+PgUp	Ctrl+Shift+Page Up
Go back one page	Layout ⇨ Previous Page	Shift+PgUp	Shift+Page Up
Go forward one page	Layout ⇨ Next Page or Layout ⇨ Go Forward	Shift+PgDn or ⌘+PgDn	Shift+Page Down or Ctrl+keypad PgDn
Go to last page	Layout ⇨ Last Page	Shift+⌘+PgDn	Ctrl+Shift+Page Down
Go to last page viewed	Layout ⇨ Go Back	⌘+PgUp	Shift+Page Up or Ctrl+keypad PgUp
Go forward one spread	Layout ⇨ Next Spread	Option+PgUp	Alt+Page Up
Go back one spread	Layout ⇨ Previous Spread	Option+PgDn	Alt+Page Down

Navigating with the Pages panel

When the Pages panel appears, you can use it to quickly move from page to page in a multi-page document and to switch between displaying master pages and document pages. To display a particular document page, double-click its icon. The selected page is centered in the document window. To display a master spread, double-click its icon in the lower half of the panel.

> **TIP** You can reverse the order of master pages and regular pages in the Pages panel by choosing the Panel Options option in the flyout menu. Then select Pages on Top instead of the Default Masters on Top. You can also control whether pages and master pages appear as preview thumbnails, whether they display vertically or horizontally, whether they appear in fixed sizes or in proportion to their actual dimensions, and what size their icons should be.

> **TIP** The Fit Page in Window command (View ⇨ Fit Page in Window, or ⌘+0 or Ctrl+0) and Fit Spread in Window command (View ⇨ Fit Page in Window, or Option+⌘+0 or Ctrl+Alt+0) let you enlarge or reduce the display magnification to fit the selected page or spread in the document window. When you have lots of objects parked on the pasteboard, also useful is View ⇨ Entire Pasteboard (Option+Shift+⌘+0 or Ctrl+Alt+Shift+0).

Using the Navigator panel

Although it's possible to use the Navigator panel (Window ⇨ Object & Layout ⇨ Navigator) to move from page to page in a long document, the Pages panel is better for this task. The Navigator panel is more useful for scrolling within a page, particularly for doing detail work on a page that's displayed at a high magnification. If you're an Illustrator, PageMaker, or Photoshop user, you may already be familiar with the Navigator panel, which works the same in all three applications.

Figure 5.7 shows the Navigator panel and its flyout menu.

FIGURE 5.7

The Navigator panel and its flyout menu

Changing view magnification

You can use the Navigator panel to zoom in or zoom out on the current spread. You have several options for zooming in and out:

- Click the handle on the zoom and drag left to zoom out or right to zoom in.

- Click the zoom-out icon to the left of the zoom slider to zoom out; click the zoom-in icon to the right of the zoom slider to zoom in.

- Type a view percentage in the field at the bottom right of the Navigator panel. Type a smaller value to zoom out; type a larger value to zoom in. Type 100% to display the page at actual size.

 You can also use the Zoom tool or its keyboard shortcuts to zoom in or out (⌘+spacebar or Ctrl+spacebar to zoom in; Option+⌘+spacebar or Ctrl+Alt+spacebar to zoom out).

Scrolling with the Navigator panel

The rectangle displayed in the Navigator panel (on the actual screen it should appear in red) indicates the area that's currently displayed in the document window. When you change the display magnification, the rectangle changes size (it gets larger as you zoom out and smaller as you zoom in). You can display a different area in the currently displayed spread by clicking and dragging the rectangle or by clicking outside it. If you click outside it, the point where you click is centered in the document window.

Other options in the Navigator panel

If red isn't your favorite color, you can change the color of the rectangle displayed in the Navigator panel by choosing Panel Options from its flyout menu, and then choosing a different color from the Color pop-up menu in the Panel Options dialog box.

If you choose Show All Spreads from the Navigator panel's flyout menu, all the document's spreads appear in the panel. The more spreads you have, the smaller they appear and the smaller the rectangle that indicates the area that's displayed in the document window becomes. By clicking and dragging the rectangle from page to page you can navigate to a particular area on a page while remaining at the current display percentage. This can be a handy way of navigating, but if you're working on a document that has many pages, the page icons and rectangle can become too small to work with easily. Figure 5.8 shows the Navigator panel with the View All Spreads option selected.

FIGURE 5.8

The Navigator panel with View All Spreads selected

> **TIP** You can also use the scroll bars at the right and bottom of the document window to move to different areas of a page or to a different page in a document or the keyboard shortcut. (Hold down the spacebar, and then click and drag the hand pointer. Make sure the Type tool is deselected or else this feature does not work.)

Adjusting Page Layouts and Objects

If you've ever created and worked with a document all the way to the finishing touches, and then discovered that the page size was wrong from the beginning, you know the meaning of frustration. Manually adjusting the size and placement of all the objects in a document is an ugly chore, and one you want to avoid at all costs. However, should the unthinkable happen — you have to modify the size, orientation, or margins of a document that is partially or completely finished — InDesign automatically resizes and repositions objects when you change its basic layout.

For example, maybe you've created a magazine for an American audience that subsequently needs to be converted for publication in Europe. Most newsletters in the United States use letter-sized pages (8½ x 11 inches), while in Europe the standard page size for such publications is A4 (210 x 297 mm), which is slightly narrower and slightly taller than U.S. letter size. Of course, you have to change *color* to *colour, apartment* to *flat,* and so on. But you also have to both squeeze (horizontally) and stretch (vertically) every item on every page to accommodate the A4 page's dimensions.

The Layout Adjustment command (Layout ⇨ Layout Adjustment) gives you the option of turning this chore over to InDesign, which automatically adjusts object shape and position according to the new page size, column guides, and margins.

The Layout Adjustment dialog box lets you turn layout adjustment on or off and specify the rules used to adjust objects when you change page size or orientation (via the Document Setup dialog box; File ⇨ Document Setup or Option+⌘+P or Ctrl+Alt+P) or margins or columns (via the Margin and Columns dialog box, accessed via Layout ⇨ Margins and Columns). To adjust a layout:

1. **Choose Layout ⇨ Layout Adjustment to display the Layout Adjustment dialog box, shown in Figure 5.9.**

2. **Select the Enable Layout Adjustment option to turn on the feature; deselect it to turn it off.**

3. **In the Snap Zone field, type the distance within which an object edge automatically snaps to a guideline when layout adjustment is performed.**

4. **Select the Allow Graphics and Groups to Resize option if you want InDesign to resize objects when layout adjustment is performed.** If you don't select this option, InDesign moves objects but does not resize them (the preferred option).

5. **Select the Allow Ruler Guides to Move option if you want InDesign to adjust the position of ruler guides proportionally according to a new page size.** Generally, ruler guides are placed relative to the margins and page edges, so you probably want to select this option.

6. **Select the Ignore Ruler Guide Alignments option if you want InDesign to ignore ruler guides when adjusting the position of objects during layout adjustment.** If you think that objects may snap to ruler guides that you don't want them to snap to during layout adjustment, select this option. If selected, InDesign still snaps object edges to other margin and column guides.

7. **Select the Ignore Object and Layer Locks option to let InDesign move locked objects (either objects locked directly via Object ⇨ Lock Position, or via ⌘+L or Ctrl+L, or objects that reside on a locked layer).** Otherwise, locked objects are not adjusted.

8. **When you're done, click OK to close the dialog box.**

The Layout Adjustment feature works best when the layout is not complex and does not contain more than one or two text frames. But if you radically change a document that you've already done considerable work on, the Layout Adjustment feature usually creates more work than it saves. For example, the switch from a U.S. letter-sized page to an A4-sized page is a relatively minor change and the layout adjustments will probably be barely noticeable. But if you decide to change a tabloid-sized poster into a business card in midstream, well, you're better off starting over.

FIGURE 5.9

The Layout Adjustment dialog box

Here are a few things to keep in mind if you decide to use InDesign's Layout Adjustment feature:

- If you change page size, the margin widths (the distance between the left and right margins and the page edges) remain the same.

- If you change page size, column guides and ruler guides are repositioned proportionally to the new size.

- If you change the number of columns, column guides are added or removed accordingly.

- If an object edge is aligned with a guideline before layout adjustment, it remains aligned with the guideline after adjustment. If two or more edges of an object are aligned with guidelines, the object is resized so that the edges remain aligned with the guidelines after layout adjustment.

- If you change the page size, objects are moved so that they're in the same relative position on the new page.

- If you've used margin, column, and ruler guides to place objects on pages, layout adjustment are more effective than if you've placed objects or ruler guides randomly on pages.

- Check for text reflow when you modify a document's page size, margins, or column guides. Decreasing a document's page size can cause text to overflow a text frame whose dimensions have been reduced.

- Check everything in your document after the adjustment is complete. Take the time to look over every page of your document. You never know what InDesign has actually done until you see it with your own eyes.

TIP If you decide to enable layout adjustment for a particular publication, you may want to begin by using the Save As command (File ➪ Save As, or Shift+⌘+S or Ctrl+Shift+S) to create a copy. That way, if you ever need to revert back to the original version, you can simply open the original document.

Summary

If you're working on a multi-page document, you want to display the Pages panel. It lets you add, move, and delete document pages as well as create multi-page spreads called *gatefold spreads*.

If you're working on a long document with multiple parts and want to number each part separately, you can create sections to manage these multiple page-numbering schemes within the document. You can also have InDesign automatically add the correct page numbers for folios and continued lines, as well as section names in folios and other text.

As you work on a long document, you can use the Pages panel to target a specific page or spread in the document window; to select multiple pages or spreads so that you can move, modify, or delete them collectively; and to navigate from page to page in a multi-page document. If you're doing detail work or working on a large page, you can use the Navigator panel to scroll around the page and to change the view magnification.

If you decide to change the layout of a publication after you've started work, you can use the Layout Adjustment feature to automatically adjust the size and position of objects and guidelines when you change the document's page size, margins, or columns.

Chapter 6

Working with Layers

Publishers seem to spend a lot of time doing the same things: creating several different versions of the same ad for different markets or flowing text in another language into a design. The goal of software is to automate the predictable so you have more time for creativity. Toward this goal, InDesign provides a method for preserving the time you put into creating and editing a layout that is used for more than one purpose: *layers*.

If you've ever seen a series of clear plastic overlays in presentations, understanding layers is easy. In one of those old overhead presentations, the teacher might have started with one overlay containing a graphic, then added another overlay with descriptive text, then added a third overlay containing a chart. Each overlay contained distinct content, but you could see through each one to the others to get the entire message. InDesign's layers are somewhat like this, letting you isolate content on slices of a document. You can then show and hide layers, lock objects on layers, rearrange layers, and more.

IN THIS CHAPTER

Understanding the purpose and use of layers

Creating layers

Working with objects on layers

Manipulating layers

Understanding Layers

Each document contains a default layer, Layer 1, which contains all your objects until you select and create a new layer. Objects on the default layer — and any other layer for that matter — follow the standard *stacking order* of InDesign. (The first object you create is the backmost object, the last one you create is the frontmost, and all the other objects fall somewhere in between. See Chapter 13 for detailed information about stacking orders.)

As with the clear plastic overlays, the order of the layers also affects the stacking order of the objects. Objects on the bottom layer are behind other objects, and objects on the top layer are in front of other objects. In Figure 6.1, the Background Images layer toward the bottom of the list contains the business card's standard graphics and the main text. Two additional layers contain different sets of contact information, in separate text frames, for different people.

FIGURE 6.1

A business card with different layers for each person's card. The graphics common to all cards are on their own layer (Default).

Although layers are often compared to plastic overlays, there's one big difference: Layers are not specific to individual pages. Each layer encompasses the entire document, which doesn't make much difference when you're working on a 1-page ad but makes a significant difference when it comes to a 16-page newsletter. Layers help you enforce the stacking order of your page elements, making it easier to manage them. Layers are essential to grouping chunks of similar elements that can be altered quickly.

The Layers panel (Window ➪ Layers or F7) is your gateway to creating and manipulating layers (see Figure 6.2). Its controls are mostly iconic, but, as with other panels, when Tool Tips are turned on via the Tool Tips pop-up menu in the Interface panel of the Preferences dialog box, you can learn what controls do by pointing at them. (Choose InDesign ➪ Preferences ➪ Interface or press ⌘+K on the Mac, or choose Edit ➪ Preferences ➪ Interface or press Ctrl+K in Windows.) If you know what the controls do, you can intuit a great deal of how to work with layers.

FIGURE 6.2

The Layers panel

Eye icon (indicates visible layer)

Lock icon (indicates locked layer)

Pen icon (indicates active layer)

Object icon (indicates layer associated with selected object)

Delete Selected Layers

Create New Layer

When, Where, and Why to Use Layers

The layers feature is one that you can honestly ignore. If you never looked at the Layers panel, you could continue to do your work in InDesign. But that would be a mistake. So take a look at the possibilities and see if they fit into your workflow. In the long run, using layers can save you time and help you prevent mistakes that can result when you need to track changes across multiple documents.

Say you've created an ad with the same copy in it but a different headline and image for each city where the ad runs. You can place the boilerplate information on one layer and the information that changes on other layers. If any of the boilerplate information changes, you only need to change it once. To print different versions of the ad, you control which layers print.

You might use layers in the following situations:

■ **A project with a high-resolution background image:** For example, a background such as a texture might take a long time to redraw. You can hide that layer while designing other elements, and then show it occasionally to see how it works with the rest of the design.

continued

continued

- **A document that you produce in several versions:** For example, a produce ad may have different prices for different cities or a clothing catalog may feature different coats depending on the climate in each area. You can place the content that changes on separate layers, and then print the layers you need.

- **A project that includes objects you don't want to print:** If you want to suppress printout of objects for any reason, the only way you can do this is to place them on a layer and hide the layer. You might have a layer that's used for nothing but adding editorial and design comments, which you can delete when the document is final. (Even though InDesign CS3 now adds support for nonprinting notes, you can insert them only into text; therefore having a design-comments layer is still useful to be able to make annotations for frames, images, and other nontextual elements.)

- **A publication that is translated into several languages:** Depending on the layout, you can place all the common objects on one layer, and then create a different layer for each language's text. Changes to the common objects only need to happen once — unlike if you created copies of the original document and flowed the translated text into the copies.

- **To experiment with different layouts of the same document:** You can show and hide layers to present different options to your supervisor or client. This strategy lets you use common elements, such as the logo and legal information, in several versions of the same design.

- **A complex design with overlapping objects, text wraps, and grouped objects:** Say the background of a page consists of a checkerboard pattern made up of filled, rectangular frames. You don't want to accidentally select the blocks while you're working with other objects. If you isolate complex objects on their own layer, you can show only that layer to work on it, hide that layer to concentrate on other layers, lock the layer so you can't select objects, and otherwise manipulate the layer.

- **To create bulletproof templates:** Locked layers are a great way to decrease the possibility of items in a template being moved or deleted. Move all the objects you don't want moved or deleted on a layer and lock the layer. Although you can unlock layer, a locked layer keeps the people who use the template from accidentally moving or removing anything too quickly.

- **To ensure folios and the like are never overprinted.** Overall production guru, as well as this book's tech editor, Jonathan Woolson, places folios (the document's page numbers, running headings, and so forth) on their own layer, uppermost in the layer stack. This ensures that they never accidentally obscured by other objects.

- **To help text print properly over transparent elements.** Woolson also find layers useful to isolate text above other objects with transparency effects. This avoids the rasterizing of text during output to plate or film — something that can make the text quality look poor.

When determining whether objects should go on a layer, remember that layers are document-wide and not page-specific.

Creating Layers

Each document contains a default layer, Layer 1, which contains all the objects you place on master pages and document pages—until you create and activate new layers. You can create as many layers as you need. Once you create a new layer, it's activated automatically so you can begin working on it.

Creating a layer

The Layers panel (Window ⇨ Layers or F7) provides several methods for creating new layers. It doesn't matter which document page is displayed when you create a layer because the layer encompasses all the pages in the document. To create a layer, do one of the following:

- To create a new layer *on top of all existing layers*, click the Create New Layer iconic button on the Layers panel to get the New Layer dialog box. The layer gets the default name of Layer *x*.

- To create a layer *above the selected layer*, ⌘+click or Ctrl+click the Create New Layer iconic button. The layer will get the default name of Layer *x*.

- To create a new layer *on top of all existing layers* but *customize its name and identifying color*, Option+click or Alt+click the Create New Layer iconic button, or choose New Layer from the flyout menu. Use the New Layer dialog box to specify options for the layer, as described shortly. (The New Layer dialog box—set with a custom name and color—is shown in Figure 6.3.)

FIGURE 6.3

The New Layer dialog box

NOTE You can create a layer while a master page is displayed. Objects you create on a layer while a master page is displayed are placed on all pages based on that master page. However, the layer is not specific to that master page. It is available for all document pages—even those based on other master pages—and you can place objects on it.

TIP To change a layer's settings, double-click it or choose Layer Options for [Name of Layer] from the flyout menu to display the Layer Options dialog box.

Whether you're using the New Layer dialog box shown in Figure 6.3 or the nearly identical Layer Options dialog box, the customization options work the same:

- **Name field:** Type a descriptive name for the layer. For example, if you're using layers for multilingual publishing, you might have a U.S. English layer, a French layer, and a German layer. If you're using layers so you can hide background objects while you're working, you might have a Background Objects layer.

- **Color pop-up menu and button:** A layer's color helps you identify which layer an object is on. The color appears to the left of the layer name in the Layers panel and appears on each object on that layer. The color is applied to frame edges, selection handles, bounding boxes, text ports, and text wraps. Note that the display of frame edges is controlled by the View ⇨ Show/Hide Frame Edges command (also available through the shortcut Control+⌘+H or Ctrl+H). By default, InDesign applies a different color to each new layer, but you can customize it to something meaningful for your document and workflow. Choose a color from the list or double-click the color swatch to use from the operating system's color picker.

 Note the new Mac shortcut for View ⇨ Show Frame Edges is Control+⌘+H. The Windows shortcut (Ctrl+H) is unchanged.

 I cover the other layer manipulation features in these dialog boxes later in this chapter.

Working with Objects on Layers

Whether you're designing a magazine template from the ground up or modifying an existing ad, you can isolate specific types of objects on layers. You can create objects on a layer, move objects to a layer, or copy objects to a layer.

The active layer

The *active layer* is the one on which you're creating objects — whether you're using tools, importing text or graphics, clicking and dragging objects in from a library, or pasting objects from other layers or other documents. A pen icon to the right of a layer's name means it's the active one (refer to Figure 6.2). Although you can select more than one layer at a time, only one layer can be active. To switch the active layer to another layer, click to the right of the layer name that you want to be active; the pen icon moves, making that the new active layer. Keep in mind that to activate a layer, it must be visible.

 Regardless of which layer is the active layer, you can select, move, and modify objects on any visible, unlocked layer.

Selecting objects on layers

Regardless of the active layer, you can select, move, and modify objects on any visible, unlocked layer. You can even select objects on different layers and manipulate them.

The Layers panel helps you work with selected objects in the following ways:

- To determine to which layer an object belongs, match the color on its bounding box, handles, and so on, to a color to the left of a layer name.

- To determine which layers contain active objects, look to the right of the layer names. A small box — the object icon — next to a layer name (refer to Figure 6.2) indicates that it contains an active object.

- To select all the objects on a layer, Option+click or Alt+click the layer's name in the Layers panel. The layer must be active, unlocked, and visible.

 To select master-page objects as well as document-page objects on a layer, you need to Option+Shift+click or Alt+Shift+click the layer name.

Placing objects on layers

To place objects on a layer, the layer must be active as indicated by the pen icon. To place objects on the layer, use any of these options:

- Use any tools to create paths and frames.

- Use the Place command (File ⇨ Place, or ⌘+D or Ctrl+D) to import graphics or text.

- Use the Paste command (Edit ⇨ Paste, or ⌘+V or Ctrl+V) to paste objects from the Clipboard onto the layer.

- Click and drag objects to the layer from a library or another document.

NOTE When you create objects on master pages, they are placed on the default layer and are therefore behind other objects on document pages. To create objects on master pages that are in front of other objects, place the objects on a different layer while the master page is displayed.

You can cut and paste objects from one page to another, but have the objects remain on their original layer — without concern about the active layer. To do this, use the Paste Remembers Layers command in the Layers panel's flyout menu rather than Edit ⇨ Paste, or ⌘+V or Ctrl+V. You might do this if you're moving the continuation of an article from one page to another but you want the text to remain on the same layer. (For example, if you're working on a multilingual document with separate layers for English, French, and Spanish text, using Paste Remembers Layer ensures that text frames cut or copied from the French layer are pasted onto the French layer on the new location.)

Moving objects to different layers

Once an object is on a layer, it isn't stuck there. You can copy and paste objects to selected layers, or you can move them using the Layers panel. When you move an object to a layer, it's placed in front of all other objects on a layer. To select multiple objects, remember to Shift+click them, and then move them in one of the following ways:

- **Paste objects on a different layer.** First cut or copy objects to the Clipboard. Activate the layer on which you want to put the objects, and then use the Paste command (Edit ➪ Paste, or ⌘+V or Ctrl+V). This method works well for moving objects that are currently on a variety of layers.

- **Move objects to a different layer.** Click and drag the active objects' object icon (to the right of a layer's name) to another layer. When you use this method, it doesn't matter which layer is active. However, you can't move objects from multiple layers to a single layer using this method. (If you select multiple objects that reside on different layers, dragging the icon moves only objects that reside on the first layer on which you selected an object.)

- **Move objects to a hidden or locked layer.** Press ⌘ or Ctrl while you click and drag the active objects' object icon.

- **Copy rather than move objects to a different layer.** Press Option or Alt while you click and drag the active objects' object icon.

- **Copy objects to a hidden or locked layer.** Press Option+⌘ or Ctrl+Alt while you drag the active objects' object icon.

TIP   After designing a new template, you might realize that it would be easier to work with if you had isolated certain objects on layers. You can create new layers, and then move objects to them at this point. Just make sure the layers are in the same stacking order as the original objects.

Manipulating Layers

Using the Layers panel, you can select and manipulate entire layers. These changes affect all the objects on the layer — for example, if you hide a layer, all its objects are hidden; if you move a layer up, all its objects appear in front of objects on lower layers. Functions that affect an entire layer include hiding, locking, rearranging, merging, and deleting.

Selecting layers

The active layer containing the pen icon is always selected. You can extend the selection to include other layers the same way you multiple-select objects: Shift+click for a continuous selection and ⌘+click or Ctrl+click for a noncontiguous selection. When layers are selected, you can move them within the stacking order of layers, modify attributes in the Layer Options dialog box, merge them, or delete them.

Hiding layers

When you hide a layer, none of the objects on that layer display or print. You might hide layers for a variety of reasons, including to speed screen redraw by hiding layers containing high-resolution graphics, to control which version of a publication prints, and to simply focus on one area of a design without the distraction of other areas. To show or hide layers using the Layers panel, do one of the following:

- Click the eye icon in the first column to the left of a layer's name. When the eye's column is blank, the layer is hidden. Click in the column again to show the layer. You can also double-click a layer and select or deselect the Show Layer option in the Layer Options dialog box.

- If no layers are hidden, you can show only the active layer by choosing Hide Others from the flyout menu.

- Regardless of the state of other layers, you can show only one layer by Option+clicking or Alt+clicking in the first column next to its name. All other layers will be hidden.

- If any layers are hidden, you can show all layers by choosing Show All Layers from the flyout menu. You can also Option+click or Alt+click twice in the first column to show all layers.

The new Suppress Text Wrap When Layer Is Hidden option in the flyout menu prevents text wrapping around the layer's objects when the layer is hidden. Be sure to select this option when you use multiple layers for variations of the same content — such as multilingual text or different contacts for business cards. Otherwise, your layer's text cannot display because it is wrapping around a hidden layer with an object of the same size in the same place.

NEW FEATURE The Suppress Text Wrap When Layer Is Hidden menu option is new to InDesign CS3.

Locking layers

When you lock a layer, you cannot select or modify objects on it — even if the locked layer is active. You might lock a layer containing boilerplate text or a layer containing a complex drawing that you don't want altered. Locking and unlocking layers is easy, so you might lock one layer while focusing on another, and then unlock it. To lock or unlock layers using the Layers panel, do one of the following:

- Click the blank box in the second column to the left of a layer's name. When the lock icon appears, the layer is locked. Click the lock icon to unlock the layer; the icon becomes blank. You can also double-click a layer and select or deselect the Lock Layer option in the Layer Options dialog box.

NEW FEATURE The lock icon replaces the crossed-out pencil icon from previous versions of InDesign.

- If no layers are locked, you can lock all but the active layer by choosing Lock Others from the flyout menu.

- If any layers are locked, you can unlock all layers by choosing Unlock All Layers from the flyout menu.

- You can toggle between Lock Others Unlock All Layers by Option+clicking or Alt+clicking the blank box or the lock icon.

NOTE When you lock an object to a page (Object ⇨ Lock Position, or ⌘+L or Ctrl+L), as described in Chapter 10, the object's position stays locked regardless of its layer's lock status.

Preventing layers from printing or exporting

InDesign CS3 now lets you designate layers as nonprinting, separately from being hidden. Select the layers you don't want to print or export, and then choose Layer options from the Layers panel's flyout menu and uncheck Print Layer. Layers that won't print show their names in italics in the Layers panel. (In addition, hidden layers also do not print.)

CROSS-REF When you do print or export, you can override layers' nonprinting status, as explained in Chapters 31 and 32.

NEW FEATURE The ability to specify layers as nonprinting is new to InDesign CS3.

Rearranging layers

Each layer has its own front-to-back stacking order, with the first object you create on the layer being its backmost object. You can modify the stacking order of objects on a single layer using the Arrange commands in the Object menu, as explained in Chapter 10. Objects are further stacked according to the order in which the layers are listed in the Layers panel. The layer at the top of the list contains the frontmost objects, and the layer at the bottom of the list contains the backmost objects.

If you find that all the objects on one layer need to be in front of all the objects on another layer, you can move that layer up or down in the list. In fact, you can move multiple-selected layers up or down, even if the selection is noncontiguous. To move layers, click the selection and drag it up or down in the Layers panel. When you move layers, remember that layers are document-wide so you're actually changing the stacking order of objects on all the pages.

TIP You might be accustomed to moving objects to the front of the stacking order to make them easily editable. Working this way, you might be tempted to bring a layer up to the top of the layer stacking order so you can edit it easily, and then move it back to its original location. Try to get out of that habit, though, and into the habit of simply showing the layer you need to work on and hiding the others.

Combining layers

If you decide that all the objects on one layer belong on a different layer—throughout the document—you can merge the layers. When you're learning about the power of layers, it's easy to create a document that is unnecessarily complex (for example, you might have put each object on a different layer and realized that the document has become difficult to work with). The good news is that you can also merge all the layers in a document to *flatten* it to a single layer. To flatten all layers:

1. **Select the *target layer* (where you want all the objects to end up) by clicking it.**

2. **Select the *source layers* (which contain the objects you want to move) in addition to the target layer.** Shift+click, or ⌘+click or Ctrl+click, to add the source layers to the selection.

3. **Make sure the target layer displays the pen icon and that the target and source layers are all selected.**

4. **Choose Merge Layers from the Layers panel's flyout menu.** All objects on the source layers are moved to the target layer, and the source layers are deleted.

> **NOTE** When you merge layers, the stacking order of objects does not change, so the design looks the same—with one notable exception: If you created objects on a layer while a master page was displayed, those objects go to the back of the stacking order with the regular master-page objects.

Deleting layers

If you've carefully isolated portions of a document on different layers and then find that you don't need that portion of the document, you can delete the layer. For example, if you have a U.S. English and an International English layer, and you decide that you can't afford to print the different versions and one dialect's readers will simply have to suffer, you can delete the unneeded layer. You might also delete layers that you don't end up using to simplify a document.

When you delete layers, all the objects on the layer throughout the document are deleted. To ensure that you don't need any of the objects before deleting a layer, you can hide all other layers, and then look at the remaining objects on each page. If you think you might need them later for this or another document, you can click and drag them to the pasteboard or place them in a library.

Using the Layers panel, you can delete selected layers in the following ways:

■ Click and drag the selection to the Delete Selected Layers iconic button (the trashcan icon).

■ Click the Delete Selected Layers iconic button. (The current layer, the one with the pen icon, is deleted.)

■ Choose Delete Layer from the Layers panel's flyout menu.

If any of the layers contain objects, a warning reminds you that they will be deleted. And, of course, the ubiquitous Undo command (Edit ➪ Undo, or ⌘+Z or Ctrl+Z) lets you recover from accidental deletions.

 To remove all layers that do not contain objects, choose Delete Unused Layers from the Layers panel's flyout menu.

Controlling guides

The New Layer and Layer Options dialog boxes give you control over how guides work for specific layers:

■ **Show Guides option:** This lets you control the display of guides that were created while the selected layer was active. When selected, as it is by default, you can create guides while any layer is active and view those guides on any layer. When deselected, you cannot create guides. Any guides you create while that layer is active are not displayed, but you can still see guides that were created while other layers were active. Note that when guides are hidden entirely (View ➪ Grids & Guides ➪ Hide Guides, or ⌘+; [semicolon] or Ctrl+; [semicolon]), this command has no apparent effect.

■ **Lock Guides option:** This works similarly to Show Guides in that it only affects guides that are created while the layer is active. When deselected, as it is by default, you can move guides on any layer for which Lock Guides is deselected. When selected, you cannot move guides created while that layer was active. You can, however, move guides on other layers for which Lock Guides is deselected. Note that when all guides are locked (View ➪ Grids & Guides ➪ Lock Guides, or Option+⌘+; [semicolon] or Ctrl+Alt+; [semicolon]), this command has no apparent effect.

Summary

If you take the time to integrate layers into your workflow, you can save time and effort in creating multilingual publications, produce multiple versions of a document, and benefit from greater flexibility with objects. Until you create new layers, all the objects are placed on the default layer. Although each layer has its own stacking order, the order of layers also affects stacking order.

You can create objects on the active layer, and you can move objects to different layers. Even though objects are on layers, you can continue to select and modify them as you normally would — provided that the layers are visible and unlocked. Hiding layers suppresses the printout of objects, as well as prevents their display. There's also a separate control to prevent unhidden layers from printing. To streamline a document, you can merge and delete layers.

Chapter 7

Creating Layout Standards

Think for a moment about the publications you produce. Chances are that most of your work involves creating multiple iterations of a basic set of publications, and each publication looks more or less the same from issue to issue. For example, periodicals such as newsletters, magazines, and newspapers don't change much from one issue to the next (disregarding the occasional redesigns that all publications undergo). The ongoing uniformity of such things as page size, margins, page layouts, text formats, even the tone of the writing, gives each publication a unique look and feel.

If you had to start from scratch every time you created a publication, you'd spend the bulk of your time setting up your documents and have little time left to attend to the appearance of the content (you'd probably get terribly bored, too). Few things are less rewarding than doing the same job over and over. Fortunately, InDesign includes several extremely useful features that let you automate repetitive tasks. This chapter focuses on three of them: master pages, templates, and libraries.

IN THIS CHAPTER

Automating repetitive tasks

Working with master pages

Creating templates

Using libraries

Ensuring consistency with rulers, grids, and guides

- A *master page* is a preconstructed page layout that you can use when adding pages to a multi-page document. With master pages, you can design a single background page and then use it as the basis for as many document pages as you want. Without master pages, you would have to create every page from scratch.

- A *template* is a preconstructed document that's used to create multiple iterations of the same design or publication. A template is a shell of a document that contains everything in a publication except content. Each time you need to create a new version of a repeatedly produced publication, you open its template, save the version as a new document file, add the content (text and graphics), tweak as desired, and then print. Next issue, same thing.

Adapting Layout Standards to Your Work

When you combine libraries, master pages, and templates with the capability to create character, paragraph, table, and cell styles (see Chapters 20 and 22) and object styles (see Chapter 13), you have a powerful set of automation tools. Styles automate text and object formatting; libraries automate object creation; master pages automate page construction; and templates automate document construction.

How and to what extent you use these features depends on your personal preferences and the publications you produce. You might think that something as small as a business card wouldn't benefit from any of these features, but if it's a business card for a corporate employee, the chances are that, other than the personal information, it's exactly the same as business cards of every other employee. By creating and saving a business-card template, you can quickly build cards for several or several hundred new employees. All you have to do is open the template; add the name, title, and phone number of the new employee; and then send to the printer.

For other publications, you might use several — perhaps all — of the aforementioned timesaving features. A good newsletter template, for example, contains a set of styles for formatting text, probably a master spread or two (depending on whether all pages share exactly the same design), and perhaps an associated library of frequently used objects — house ads, corporate logos, boilerplate text, and so on.

■   As its name suggests, a *library* is a place where you store things. Specifically, InDesign libraries are files for storing objects that you create in InDesign and that you intend to use repeatedly in multiple documents.

This chapter covers a fourth set of options — rulers, guides, and grids — that don't automate your work but do make it easier to be consistent across pages. Ensuring consistency is a key part of implementing layout standards, and it's easy to overlook these aids when using InDesign.

TIP   Although this chapter begins with master pages, this doesn't mean that you should begin work on a publication by creating master pages. You may prefer to work on text-formatting tasks first and build styles before turning your attention to page-layout and document-construction tasks.

Creating and Applying Master Pages

Before the arrival of personal computers, publications were created by graphics designers who leaned over light tables and, armed with matte knives and waxing machines, stuck galleys of type, halftones, and plastic overlays onto paste-up boards. The paste-up boards were usually oversized sheets of white card paper on which was printed a grid of light blue lines. The blue guidelines indicated such things as the edge of the final, trimmed page; the margins in which text and graphics were placed; column boundaries; and so on. These guidelines helped the designer position elements on a page and also helped ensure consistent placement of repeating page elements, such as page numbers.

Although there are no paste-up boards in the electronic publishing world, the concept has survived in the form of *master pages*. A master page is a building-block page that you can use as the background (that is, as the starting point) for document pages. The master pages themselves don't print, but any pages that use them print the items from their master page, in addition to any unique elements you add to those individual pages. Typically, master pages contain text and graphic elements, such as page numbers, headers, footers, folios, and so on, that appear on all pages of a publication. And like their paste-up board ancestors, master pages also include guidelines that indicate page edges, column boundaries, and margins, as well as other manually created guidelines to aid page designers in placing objects. By placing items on master pages, you save yourself the repetitive work of placing the same items one by one on each and every document page.

NOTE Note that InDesign's menu options and other interface sometimes switch between *master page* and *master spread* based on which is selected, but the steps are the same even if I say *page* and InDesign shows *spread*.

By default, every InDesign document you create contains a master page. Whether you use the master page or create and use additional master pages depends on the kind of publication you're creating. If it's a single-page document, such as a business card or an advertisement, you don't need to worry about master pages at all. (Generally, master pages are of little use for one-page documents.) However, if you're creating a multi-page document like a newsletter, a book, or a catalog, using master pages save you time and help ensure design consistency. It's impossible to overstate the importance of master pages. They're one of InDesign's most powerful features.

The Pages panel

When you work on multi-page documents, you may want to display the Pages panel (Window ➪ Pages, or ⌘+F12 or Ctrl+F12), which is shown in Figure 7.1. The Pages panel displays a thumbnail preview of your document pages (bottom) and master pages (top) in the current document. The controls in the Pages panel and its accompanying flyout menu let you perform several master page-related tasks, including creating and deleting master pages, applying master pages to document pages, and creating master pages out of document pages. The Pages panel also lets you add and remove document pages.

NEW FEATURE InDesign CS3 can display thumbnail views of your pages, making it easier to know which page you're working on within the panel.

NEW FEATURE The shortcut for accessing the Pages panel has changed to ⌘+F12 or Ctrl+F12 in InDesign CS3 from just F12 in previous versions. F12 still works, though using it could interfere with Mac OS X's Exposé software.

QUARKXPRESS Master pages in documents originally created in QuarkXPress will have a slightly different naming convention than those created in InDesign: A-Master A rather than A-Master, for example.

FIGURE 7.1

The Pages panel. The document page icons at the bottom of the panel show that the publication has 34 pages. The master page icons at the top show the default master pages: [None], A-Master, B-Master, and so on.

CROSS-REF See Chapter 5 for more information about adding and removing document pages.

Here's a quick rundown of the controls available in the Pages panel and the commands in its flyout menu:

- The page icons (by default at the top of the panel) represent master pages. Every document includes a master page called [None], which includes only margin guidelines, and A-Master, which reflects the margin and column settings you specify in the New Document dialog box when you create the document. If a letter appears on a master page icon, it indicates that the master spread is based on another (parent) master page; for example, if you have a master page named C-Master and the icons for C-Master have the letter *A*, then C-Master is based on A-Master. A master page's name appears below its icon. If a master page and its name are highlighted, it means that the master page appears in the document window. If a master page name appears in reverse type, it's currently displayed in the document window.

- The page icons (by default at the bottom of the panel) represent document pages. Dog-eared icons represent left and right pages in a facing-pages document. The letter displayed on a page icon indicates the master page it's based on. (If no letter appears, the page is based on the blank master page.) The numbers below the page icons indicate the page numbers, including section numbering, if any (sections are covered in Chapter 5;

automatic page numbers are covered in Chapter 23). If a page and its number are highlighted, it means that page currently appears in the document window. If a page number appears in reverse type (that is, white characters on a black background), it means that it's currently displayed in the document window.

■ The Create New Page iconic button (notepad icon) at the bottom of the panel lets you add a new page with a mouse click. (When a master page is displayed, the button becomes the Create New Master button.)

■ The Delete Selected Pages iconic button (trashcan icon) lets you delete document and master pages. (When a master page is displayed, the button becomes the Delete Selected Masters button.)

■ The Insert Pages flyout menu option lets you add pages to a document and specify the master page on which they're based.

■ The Move Pages flyout menu option lets you move document pages using a dialog box in which you specify which pages to move and where to move them. You can also simply click the pages to select them and drag them to their new location within the Pages panel. When a master page is displayed, the menu option becomes Move Masters.

■ The New Master flyout menu option lets you add a new master page.

■ The Duplicate Spread and Duplicate Page flyout menu options do exactly what the names say. They let you duplicate a page or a facing-pages spread. The name of the command depends on whether a page or spread is highlighted in the panel. (When a master page is displayed, the menu options become Duplicate Master Spread and Duplicate Master Page.)

■ The Delete Page and Delete Spread flyout menu options let you delete single pages and facing-pages spreads. Again, the menu name changes based on what is selected in the panel. When a master page is displayed, the menu options become Delete Master Spread and Delete Master Page.

■ The Select Unused Masters flyout menu option selects all unused master pages and spreads, so you can easily identify and perhaps delete them.

■ The Master Options flyout menu option changes master page attributes, including name and parent master page (if you want to base a master page on another master page).

■ The Apply Master to Pages flyout menu command is used for applying a master page layout to one or more document pages.

■ The Save as Master flyout menu option lets you convert a document page into a master page.

■ The Hide Master Options flyout menu option hides any master page items in your document. The menu option then becomes Show Master Options so you can redisplay them.

■ The Override All Master Page Items flyout menu option lets you have any local changes to the selected pages override the master page settings. This command moves all master items to the document page on the selected pages. You can also use the shortcut Option+Shift+⌘+L or Ctrl+Alt+Shift+L.

■ The Remove All Local Overrides and the Remove Selected Local Overrides flyout menu options return master objects that you've modified on specific document pages to their original condition. If no object is selected and you are displaying a document page, the menu command is Remove All Local Overrides; if one or more objects are selected, the menu command is Remove Selected Local Overrides.

■ The Detach Selection from Master flyout menu option removes any master page items that had been modified on the selected pages from the master page *for those selected document pages* only. Essentially, this command prevents you from using the Remove All Local Overrides or Remove Selected Local Overrides commands for these document pages, permanently changing the master pages for them.

■ The Allow Master Item Overrides on Selection flyout menu option lets you change the object on document pages, by Shift+⌘+clicking or Ctrl+Shift+clicking it and changing attributes such as size, location, or color. If you deselect this option on the master page for any selected objects, then you cannot change the object on any document pages, which is a great way to prevent unauthorized changes for standard elements. Of course, all someone has to do is change the settings on the master page, but that kind of effort is usually enough to hinder unintentional changes this feature is really aimed at stopping.

NEW FEATURE   The Allow Master Item Overrides on Selection command is new to InDesign CS3.

■ If checked, the Allow Document Pages to Shuffle flyout menu option ensures that pages within spreads are not split apart as you add pages. Normally, adding a single page shuffles all subsequent pages so they form new spreads. With this command, existing spreads are maintained, so adding an odd number of pages does not cause them to be reshuffled.

■ If checked, the Allow Selected Spread to Shuffle flyout menu option ensures that pages within this spread do split apart as you add pages.

CROSS-REF   See Chapter 5 for details on how the shuffling controls work.

■ The Panel Options flyout menu option controls icon size, position, and other Pages panel display settings, as shown in Figure 7.2.

NEW FEATURE   InDesign CS3 now displays pages and master pages using thumbnail previews, so you can see the actual contents within the Pages panel. To turn this off, deselect Show Thumbnails in the Panel Option dialog box for document and/or master pages.

■ The Numbering & Section Options flyout menu option lets you establish independently numbered sections in a single document. For example, you can create a section if you want to use a different numbering scheme (Roman numerals, perhaps) for the front matter of a book than for the body.

CROSS-REF   See Chapter 5 for more information about sections.

■ The Spread Flattening flyout menu option lets you control image flattening for specific spreads. *Flattening* is InDesign's term for reducing the resolution of graphics to save disk space and speed output time. Typically, you'd flatten images for Web-oriented documents because the Web displays images at the relatively low resolution of 72 dpi. You might also flatten high-resolution graphics when printing a draft version to speed up printing.

CROSS-REF Chapter 31 covers flattening in more detail.

FIGURE 7.2

The Panel Options dialog box for the Pages panel controls display options.

Creating a new master page

If all the pages in the publication you're creating share essentially the same page design, you don't need to create a new master page. Instead, you can simply use the default master page called A-Master that every document has. But if you intend to use more than one page layout in your document — maybe you're building a magazine and you want some pages to use a three-column format and others to use a two-column format — you need to create additional master pages.

Before you create a new master page, you should have a general idea of how you want it to look. In particular, you should know where you want to place margins, column boundaries, and repeating elements, such as page numbers. (Laying out master pages is covered later in this section.) When you're ready to create a new master page, follow these steps:

1. **If the Pages panel is not displayed, choose Windows ➪ Pages, or press ⌘+F12 or Ctrl+F12.**

2. **From the Pages panel's flyout menu, choose New Master.** You can also press Option+⌘ or Ctrl+Alt and click the Create New Page iconic button at the bottom of the panel. The New Master dialog box, shown in Figure 7.3, appears.

3. **In the Prefix field, specify a one-character prefix that's attached to the front of the master page name and appears on associated document page icons in the Pages panel.** The default is a letter such as B, C, or D.

FIGURE 7.3

The New Master dialog box

4. **In the Name field, type a name for the master page.** Use something descriptive, such as 3-*column Layout*, *Front Matter Layout*, or *Chapter Title Pages*.

5. **If you want to base the master page on another master page you've already created, select the parent master page from the Based on Master pop-up menu.** Basing a master page on another master page is covered in more detail later in this section.

6. **In the Number of Pages field, type the number of pages you want to include in the master spread.** Typically, you type 2 for a facing-pages document and 1 for a single-page document.

7. **When you finish specifying the attributes of the new master page, click OK to close the dialog box.**

After you create a new master page, it appears in the document window. (When a master page is displayed, its name appears in the Page field in the bottom-left corner of the document window.) You can modify any of a master page's attributes at any time by clicking its icon at the top of the Pages panel, choosing Master Options from the panel's flyout menu, and then changing any of the settings in the Master Options dialog box, which is identical to the New Master dialog box.

Basing a master page on another master page

If you find that a particular publication requires more than one master page, you may want to first lay out a base master page (you can use the default A-Master) and then create additional master pages that share the same basic layout but are slightly different. For example, if the magazine you're working on uses two-, three-, and four-column page layouts, you can create the two-column master spread first and include all repeating page elements. You can then create two additional master page spreads, base them on the two-column master, and specify different column formats. The two *children* masters are identical to the parent except for the number of columns. If you subsequently decide to modify, move, or delete a repeating page element, such as the issue date in the folio, you can make the change on the parent master and it is automatically applied to the children masters.

When you create a new master page, the New Master dialog box provides the option to base it on an existing master page. You can also choose or change a master spread's parent by:

- Choosing Master Options in the Pages panel's flyout menu and then choosing a master page from the Based on Master pop-up menu.

- Dragging and dropping the icon of a master spread (the parent) onto the icon of another master spread (the child). Be careful if you use this method. It's possible to base only one page of a master spread on another, but in most cases you want to base both pages of the child master on both pages of the parent master. To do so, make sure that when you release the mouse button both pages of the child are highlighted.

- Clicking the master spread you want to be the child, and then pressing Option or Alt and clicking the master spread you want to be the parent.

When you base a master page on another master page, the prefix of the parent appears in the upper outside corner of the page icon of the child.

TIP   If you base a master page on another master page, you can still modify the master objects (that is, the objects inherited from the parent master) on the child master page. As with regular document pages, you have to Shift+⌘+click or Ctrl+Shift+click on the object inherited from a parent master to release it before you can edit it on a child master.

QUARKXPRESS   In QuarkXPress, one master page cannot be based on another. As a result, InDesign users who are used to QuarkXPress might ignore this feature, but they shouldn't. This feature has the same power that based-on formatting adds to character and paragraph styles in QuarkXPress and InDesign.

Creating master pages from document pages

Generally, if you need a new master page, you begin by choosing New Master from the Pages panel's flyout menu. But you can also create a master page from a document's page (or a master spread from a document spread). To do so, highlight the document page or spread by clicking the page number(s) below the page icon(s) in the Pages panel, and then choose Save as Master from the Pages panel's flyout menu. The new page or master is assigned a default name and prefix. If you want to modify any of its attributes, click its name in the Pages panel, and then choose Master Options from the pop-up menu.

Importing a master page

Sometimes, another document has a master page that you'd like to use in your current layout. InDesign CS3 lets you import those master pages: Just choose Load Master Pages from the Pages panel's flyout menu, and then select the source document in the dialog box that appears. InDesign will import all master pages from that document into your current one. There's no way to select specific master pages.

NEW FEATURE   The ability to import master pages is new to InDesign CS3. Before, you had to create a new master page in your document, and then copy the elements from another document using old-fashioned copy-and-paste.

If any of the imported master pages have the same name as your current document's master pages (such as the default name A-Master), a dialog box appears giving you the choice of replacing the current master pages with the imported ones that use the same name or of renaming the imported master pages, so you keep what you have and add the imported ones. InDesign does the renaming for you, using the next available default name. For example, if your current document has master pages A-Master and B-Master already defined, it renames the imported A-Master to C-Master.

Note that InDesign also alerts you if the imported master pages use different dimensions than the current document's pages. But it won't adjust the imported pages to fit the current document's size, so some items may appear off the page if the imported master page has larger dimensions than the current document.

Duplicating a master

You can create a copy of a master page or spread by clicking its icon and then choosing Duplicate Master Spread from the Pages panel's flyout menu or by clicking and dragging the master page's icon onto the Create New Master iconic button, and releasing the mouse. If you duplicate a master page or spread, there is not a parent/child relationship between the original master and the copy (as there is when you base a master on another master).

Deleting a master

To delete a master page, click its name and then choose Delete Master Page from the Pages panel's flyout menu. You can also click the master page icon, and then click the Delete Selected Masters iconic button (trashcan icon) in the Pages panel or click and drag the master page icon directly to the Delete Selected Masters iconic button.

Laying out a master page

Because a master page is similar to a document page, you can use the same approach for building both master and document pages. Some designers prefer to do a preliminary sketch on paper and then re-create the design in InDesign. You may like to do your creative brainstorming at your computer, in which case you can use InDesign as your sketchpad. The main difference between document pages and master pages is that master pages don't contain any content (other than elements that appear on every page). So, when you're building a master page, you should be thinking more about the page's overall infrastructure than about details.

Here are a few things to keep in mind when designing master pages:

- If you're working on a facing-pages document (most multi-page publications have facing pages), you can create facing-pages master spreads. The left-hand page (used for even-numbered document pages) and right-hand page (used for odd-numbered document pages) of the master spreads you create are more or less mirror opposites of each other. For example, page numbers are generally placed near the outside edge of facing pages so that they're visible when a reader thumbs through the pages. Or you may decide to place the publication name on one side of a spread and balance it by placing the date of publication in the same position on the other side.

■ If you want to automatically place page numbers on document pages, you should add a page number character on each page of your master spreads. To add a page number character, draw a text frame with the Type tool, and then choose Type ➪ Insert Special Character ➪ Markers ➪ Auto Page Number or press Option+Shift+⌘+N or Ctrl+Alt+Shift+N. The prefix of the master page (A, B, C, and so on) is displayed on the master page, but on document pages, the actual page number is used. When you add a page number to a master page, make sure to format the numbers as you want them to look on document pages.

■ Perhaps the most important elements of a master page are the margins and column guides. To specify margins and columns for a master page, make sure the page appears in the document window, and then choose Layout ➪ Margins and Columns. The Margins and Columns dialog box, shown in Figure 7.4, appears. The controls in this dialog box let you specify the position of the margins, the number of columns, and the gutter width (space between columns).

FIGURE 7.4

The Margins and Columns dialog box

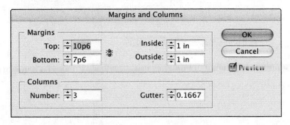

When placing text elements on master pages, you may want to use placeholder text instead of actual text. InDesign makes it easy to do: Just choose Type ➪ Fill with Placeholder Text. InDesign adds fake Latin text to the text frame until it is filled. In some cases, you want to add your own placeholder text. For example, if you produce a monthly magazine and you want to include the name of the month on each spread (perhaps opposite the name of the newsletter on the facing page), you can use placeholder text like [Name of month] or [Add month here] or use the variable-text feature. If you use placeholder text, format it as you want the actual text to appear on document pages. Of course, be sure to replace the placeholder text with the actual text in your final document.

CROSS-REF Note that you can use the Section Marker feature in some cases to have InDesign automatically enter text, such as the issue month. See Chapter 5 for more details. Or you can use the new, more flexible variable-text feature, explained in Chapter 23.

■ If you want to place additional guidelines on a master page, you can add as many custom guidelines as you want. Guidelines are covered later in this chapter.

■ Like objects on document pages, the objects you place on master pages have a stacking order. On document pages, all master objects remain beneath any objects you add to the page.

Figure 7.5 shows a typical master page spread for a newsletter. Whenever you want to make a change to a master page, double-click its icon in the Pages panel to display it in the document window.

TIP To copy a master page from one document to another, display the source document, click the master's name in the Pages panel, drag it to the window of the target document, and then release the mouse button.

QUARKXPRESS The ability to move master pages from one document to another, or even from one layout to another in a QuarkXPress 6 or 7 project, does not exist in QuarkXPress. So QuarkXPress users may be in the habit of using libraries to transfer master page items from one document to another. In InDesign, you don't need to take this circuitous route.

FIGURE 7.5

A typical three-column master layout for a newsletter. The footer at the bottom of the left- and right-hand pages includes a page-number character on the outside. On a master page, the page number appears as the master page's prefix (A, in this case).

Applying a master page to document pages

After you've built a master page, you can apply it to new document pages as you add them or to existing pages (see Chapter 5 for information about adding and removing document pages). For facing-pages documents, you can apply both pages of a master spread to both pages of a document spread, or you can apply one page of a master spread to one page of a document spread. For example, you can apply a master page with a two-column format to the left-hand page of a document spread and apply a master page with a three-column format to the right-hand page.

To apply only one page of a master spread to a document page, click the icon of the master spread and then drag it onto the icon of the document page you want to format. When the target document page is highlighted (framed in a black rectangle as shown in the left side of Figure 7.6), release the mouse button. If both document pages are highlighted, both sides of the master spread are applied to the document spread.

To apply both pages of a master spread to both pages of a document spread, drag the master spread's icon below the right-hand page in the document spread (under its page icon). When both pages of the target document spread are highlighted, as shown in the right side of Figure 7.6, release the mouse button. (You need to move the icon to the corner of a spread for the spread rather than an individual page to be highlighted.)

FIGURE 7.6

Left: Applying a single page of a master spread to a document page. Right: Applying both pages of a master spread to a document spread. I've turned off the preview display for the document pages to make the highlighting more visible.

InDesign also lets you apply a master page to multiple document pages in a single operation. You can:

- **Select the document pages to which you want to apply a master.** Click a page then Shift+click another page to select a range of pages, or you can press ⌘ or Ctrl and click pages to select nonconsecutive pages. After you select the document pages, press Option or Alt and click the master page you want to apply.

- **Choose Apply Master to Pages from the Pages panel's flyout menu.** The Apply Master dialog box, shown in Figure 7.7, appears. Choose the master page you want to apply from the Apply Master pop-up menu, and specify the pages to which you want to apply it in the To Pages field. Use commas to separate page numbers; use a hyphen to specify a range of pages. For example, type 2, 4–6, 8 to apply the selected master to pages 2, 4 through 6, and 8.

- **Choose Layout ➪ Pages ➪ Apply Master to Pages.** This works the same way as the Apply Master to Pages flyout menu option in the Pages panel.

FIGURE 7.7

The Apply Master dialog box

You can also use these techniques to apply a different master page to a document page. If you want to disassociate a document page from its applied master page, you can apply the default [None] master page the same way you apply any other master page.

Modifying master items on document pages

As you work on a document page that's based on a master, you may find that you need to modify, move, or delete a master object. For example, you might apply a master to the first page of a newsletter and then decide that the page number you've placed on the master page isn't necessary for page 1. In this case, you'd select the master object on the document page and delete it. Any change you make to a master object on a local page is referred to as a *local override*.

If you remove a master object from a document page, you sever the object's relationship to the master page object for that document page only. If you subsequently move or modify the object on the master page, it doesn't affect the deleted object on the document page; it remains deleted on that particular document page.

However, you can modify a master object on a document page without completely breaking its relationship to the corresponding object on the master page. For example, if you change the size, position, or content of a master object on a document page, any subsequent size, position, or content change you make to the object on the master page does not affect the object you modified. But any changes you make to the stroke or fill of the object on the master page are applied to the overridden master object on the document page. Similarly, if you use any of the transformation tools or the corresponding controls in the Control panel or Transform panel to modify a master object on a document page, any similar transformation applied to the corresponding object on the master page is not applied to the overridden object.

In other words, any type of attribute applied to the item on a particular document page prevents any changes to the same attribute on the master page from affecting that document page.

> **TIP** The Show Master Items command (choose Show Master Items in the Pages panel's flyout menu) lets you show or hide master objects on document pages. (The name of the menu option is Show Master Items when items are hidden, Hide Master Items when they are not hidden.)

To modify a master object on a document page, you must select it. However, master objects behave slightly differently than other objects on document pages. Specifically, to select a master object on a document page, you press Shift+⌘ or Ctrl+Shift when you click the object with one of the selection tools. After you select a master object on a document page, you can modify it in the same manner as you modify nonmaster objects.

If you modify one or more master objects on a document page and then decide you want to revert back to using the original master objects, you can remove the local overrides. To do so, display the document page that contains the master objects you've modified, select the objects, and then choose Remove Selected Local Overrides from the Pages panel's flyout menu. If no objects are selected, the command name changes to Remove All Local Overrides (if the selected spread doesn't have any modified master objects, the command is not available).

You can prevent master page objects from being modified at all. To do this, select them on the master page, and then choose Allow Master Item Overrides on Selection so that the check mark disappears to its left. Now, you cannot change or even select these objects on the document page unless you come back to the master page and re-enable this option.

But note that if you use this technique in an existing document, any document pages where the selected master page objects have already been modified will retain those modifications and allow additional modifications. Only untouched objects will be made untouchable.

If you want to reset all overridden master page objects, before locking them down with the Allow Master Item Overrides menu option, you must first choose Remove All Overrides from the flyout menu.

NEW FEATURE The Allow Master Item Overrides on Selection command is new to InDesign CS3.

Using Templates

A template is a preconstructed InDesign document that you can use as the starting point for creating multiple versions of the same design or publication. For example, if you are assigned the task of creating a dozen testimonial ads that share the same layout but use different graphics and text, you begin by creating a template that contains all the elements that are the same in every ad — placeholder frames for the graphics and text, guidelines, and so on. Along the same lines, if you produce periodicals like a newsletter or a magazine, you should create a template for each one.

Creating templates

The process of creating a template is much the same as creating a document. You create the required character and paragraph styles, master pages, repeating elements (for example, the nameplate on the first page and mailing information on the back page), and so on. The only thing you don't add to a template is actual content.

It would be nice if designers had the luxury of creating a template up front for each new publication they produced. But in the real world, templates are often created by gutting an existing document. The first time you create a publication such as a newsletter, the main goal during production is getting a finished document to the printer — hopefully on time. After you finish the first issue of a publication (or a prototype), you can open the file, remove all objects and content that aren't repeated in every issue, and then save the gutted file as a template. This is probably how you'll build many of your templates.

Here are the steps in creating a template:

1. **Choose File ➪ Save As or press Shift+⌘+S or Ctrl+Shift+S to display the Save As dialog box shown in Figure 7.8.**

2. **Choose a storage folder and specify a name for the file.** Even though the template has the filename extension .indt as opposed to the .indd extension of a document, it's not a bad idea to add the word Template to the filename, if possible. It lets whoever uses the file quickly know its purpose.

3. **On a Mac, choose InDesign CS3 Template in the Format pop-up menu. On a PC, choose InDesign CS3 Template from the Save As Type pop-up menu.** If you are saving the template in a Version Cue workspace, the pop-up menu is called Format on both the Mac and Windows.

4. **Click Save to close the Save As dialog box and save the template.**

FIGURE 7.8

Saving templates

> **TIP** If you're designing a template that others will use, you might want to add a layer of instructions. When it's time to print a document based on the template, simply hide the annotation layer, or mark it as nonprinting. (See Chapter 6 for more information about layers.)

Modifying templates

A template is almost exactly the same as a standard InDesign document with one major exception: A template is slightly protected from being overridden. When you open a template, it's assigned a default name (Untitled-1, Untitled-2, and so on). The first time you choose File ⇨ Save, or press ⌘+S or Ctrl+S, the Save As dialog box appears.

NOTE As you use a template over time, you're likely to discover that you forgot to include something — perhaps a style, a repeating element on a particular master page, or an entire master page. To modify a template, you must open it, make your changes, and then use the Save or Save As command to save the file in the same place and with the same name as the original.

To modify a template, you have two options:

- **Open it as a normal file, make your changes, and then choose File ⇨ Save As (or press Shift+⌘+S or Ctrl+Shift+S) to save it again as a template.** To open a file as a normal file, be sure that Open Normal (Mac) or Normal (Windows) is selected at the bottom of the Open a File dialog box — this is the default option.

- **Open it as an original file (see Chapter 4), make your changes, and then choose File ⇨ Save (⌘+S or Ctrl+S) to save it again as a template.** To open a file as an original file, be sure that Open Original (Mac) or Original (Windows) is selected at the bottom of the Open a File dialog box — it's easy to forget to select this option, so most people end up using the previous technique to resave the template.

Creating documents from templates

It's very easy to create a document from a template: Just open a template file, and then save it with a new name, making sure that InDesign CS3 Document is selected in the Format pop-up menu (Mac) or Save as Type pop-up menu (Windows) — this the default setting. Work on your document and continue to save changes normally.

NEW FEATURE A more complicated way to create a document from a template is to choose File ⇨ New Document from Template. This opens the Adobe Bridge program, which can contain InDesign templates that you open and then save as documents. Chapter 35 covers Bridge in more detail.

Storing Objects in Libraries

If you're a savvy InDesign user, you should never need to build the same document twice. After all, that's what templates are for. Along the same lines, you never have to create the same object twice; that's what libraries are for. An InDesign *library* is a file — similar in some ways to a document file — in which you can store individual objects, groups and nested objects, ruler guides, and grids (ruler guides and grids are covered in the next section). For example, if you create a logo in InDesign and you want to use it in other documents, you can place it in a library. Once you save an object in a library, it's as though you have an endless supply of copies. Every time you need a copy, all you have to do is click and drag one out of the library.

You can also create files that contain pieces of your layout, called *snippets,* for use in other documents. Chapter 10 covers snippets in more detail.

Creating a library is easy: Choose File ➪ New ➪ Library, choose a location to save the library in, give the library a name, and click Save. InDesign automatically adds the filename extension .indl.

You can create as many libraries as you want and store them wherever is most convenient, including on a networked server so other InDesign users can share them. When it comes to naming and organizing libraries, the choice is yours. If you work for an advertising agency, for example, you may decide to create a separate library for each client; each library can contain logos, images, boilerplate text (disclaimers, copyright information, legal blurbs, etc.), and so on. If you work for an in-house art department, you can create separate libraries for corporate logos (black-and-white, grayscale, and two-color/four-color variations), house ads, frequently used graphics, and standing art.

TIP InDesign libraries are cross-platform. That is, you can open libraries created on a Mac using a PC and vice versa.

After you create a new library, an empty library panel is displayed, as shown in Figure 7.9. (Each library you open is in its own panel.) The name you assigned is displayed in its title bar. You add items by dragging them to the panel. You can group the panel with other panels (by dragging its tab onto another panel) or close it by clicking its close box or choosing Close Library from its flyout menu.

FIGURE 7.9

A library and its accompanying flyout menu

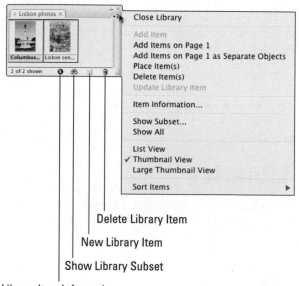

At this point, you're ready to begin placing objects into the library, after which you can begin copying the objects into other documents. Before I cover moving items into and out of libraries, here's a brief description of the controls in a library panel and the commands in the accompanying flyout menu (refer to Figure 7.9):

- **Numbers in the lower-left corner of the panel:** These indicate the number of objects currently displayed in the pane (although not necessarily visible, depending on the size of the panel) and the number of objects in the library. Search capabilities let you display a subset of the entire library.

- **Close Library:** This flyout menu command does the same thing as clicking a library panel's Close button.

- **Library Item Information iconic button and Item Information menu option:** However you access this feature, it displays the Item Information dialog box, shown in Figure 7.10. Here you can assign a name, type, and description to a library object. You can search for library objects based on these attributes.

FIGURE 7.10

The Item Information dialog box

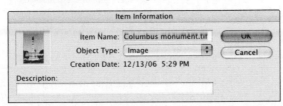

- **Show Library Subset iconic button and Show Subset menu option:** However you access this feature, it displays a dialog box that lets you locate and display objects that meet certain search criteria.

- **New Library Item iconic button and Add Item menu option:** However you access this feature, it lets you add selected objects on a document page to a library as separate items.

- **Add Items on Page:** This flyout menu option let you add all items on a document page to a library *as one library item*. You can also simply click and drag items together into the panel so they're added as a single library item.

- **Add Items on Page as Separate Objects:** This flyout menu option let you add all items on a document page to a library *as individual library items*.

- **Place Item(s):** This command lets you place copies of selected library objects into a document.

- **Delete Library Item iconic button and Delete Item(s) menu option:** However you access this feature, it lets you delete highlighted objects in the library.

- **Update Library Item:** Although you might think this menu option only updates the library item to reflect any changes made to the original item, that's not true. What this command really does is let you replace a library object, either a modified version of the original item or a completely different object. After you select the library object you want to replace, click whatever object you want to replace it with in your layout, and then choose Update Library Item.

- **Show All:** This command displays all library objects (rather than a subset identified by a previous search).

- **List View:** When this option is selected, library objects appear in a list rather than as thumbnails.

- **Thumbnails View:** When this option is selected, each library object appears in its own thumbnail window.

- **Sort Items:** This command lets you sort library items by Name, Oldest, Newest, and Type. If you sort by Oldest or Newest, items are arranged based on the order in which they were placed into the library.

To open an existing library, choose File ➪ Open or press ⌘+O or Ctrl+O.

NOTE   Multiple users can share a library, but only if it's locked (meaning people can use items in the library but not add new ones). To lock a library on the Mac, locate the library file in the Finder, select it, choose File ➪ Get Info, and select the Locked option. In Windows, locate the library file in its current folder, right-click the filename or icon, and then select Read-Only from the Properties contextual menu's General pane.

To delete a library, you must delete the file. Either click and drag the file icon to the Trash (Mac) or move the file icon to the Recycle Bin (Windows).

Adding and deleting library objects

In addition to placing individual objects, such as text and graphics frames, into a library, you can also place multiple-selected objects, groups, nested frames, ruler guides, guidelines, and all objects on a page.

There are several ways to add objects to a library. You can:

- Select one or more objects and then drag and drop them into an open library panel.

- Select one or more objects and then click the New Library Item button at the bottom of an open library panel.

- Select one or more objects and then choose Add Item from the flyout menu of an open library panel.

- Go to the desired page and then choose Add Items on Page from the flyout menu of an open library panel to add all selected objects on the current page or spread *as one library item*.

- Go to the desired page and then choose Add Items on Page as Separate Objects from the flyout menu of an open library panel to add all selected objects on the current page or spread *as individual library items*.

> **TIP** If you press and hold Option or Alt when adding an object to a library using any of the preceding methods, the Item Information dialog box appears. This dialog box lets you add searchable attributes to the object.

To delete a library object, click and drag its icon to the Delete Library Item iconic button (trashcan icon) at the bottom of the panel. You can also click on the object once and then choose Delete Item(s) from the library panel's flyout menu or just click the Delete Library Item iconic button. You can select a range of objects by clicking on the first one and then Shift+clicking on the last one. You can select multiple, noncontiguous objects by pressing and hold ⌘ or Ctrl and clicking on each icon that you want to delete.

When you place an object into a library, all its attributes are saved. For example, if you import a graphic into a document and then place a copy of the graphic into a library, the path to the original graphics file is saved, as are any transformations you've applied to the graphic or its frame (scale, rotation, shear, and so on). If you save text in a library, all formats, including styles, are retained.

Cataloging library objects

If your libraries contain only a few objects, finding the one you're looking for isn't very hard. But a library can hold as many objects as you want, and as a library becomes bigger, locating a particular object gets increasingly difficult. To make library objects easier to find, InDesign lets you tag them with several searchable attributes.

Library Caveats

Because the attributes of the original object are retained when you place a copy in a library, there are some pitfalls you have to watch out for:

- If you move, modify, or delete the original graphic files associated with a graphic you've placed in a library and then copy the library object into a document, the Links panel will report that the graphics file is modified or missing (just as it would if you imported the graphic and then moved, modified, or deleted the original). It's a good idea to store graphics files used in libraries in a common location, such as in a Standards folder on the network, so the graphics files aren't accidentally moved or deleted when you delete or archive a set of project files that happen to contain objects placed in libraries.

- If you copy a text frame from a library onto a document page, any styles or swatches in the library object that have the same name as styles or swatches in the target document are replaced by those in the target document. If the target document does not contain styles or swatches in the placed text, they're added to the document.

- If you copy a text frame from a library onto a document page, make sure that the fonts are available. If they're not available, you have to select alternate fonts.

To tag a library element, select it and then choose Item Information from the library panel's flyout menu. You can also display the Item Information dialog box by double-clicking on a library object or by clicking once on a library object and then clicking the Library Item Information iconic button at the bottom of the library panel. (Figure 7.10 shows the Item Information dialog box.) Now specify an Item Name, an Object Type, and/or a Description. In the Description field, it's a good idea to type one or more keywords that describe the object so that you can easily find it later. Click OK to close the dialog box and return to the document.

InDesign lets you search for library objects based on the information specified in the Item Information dialog box. For example, if you've placed several different corporate logos into a library that includes many other objects, you could search for the term *logo* in the Name or Description field. If you used the word *logo* in either of these fields for your logos, a search of these fields for the word *logo* will identify and display your logos. The ability to search for library objects based on name and description is a good reason to name your library objects carefully and consistently and to specify keywords in the Description field of the Item Information dialog box. Follow these steps:

1. **Choose Show Subset from a library panel's flyout menu or click the Show Library Subset iconic button (glasses icon) at the bottom of the panel.** The Show Subset dialog box, shown in Figure 7.11, appears.

FIGURE 7.11

The Show Subset dialog box with two search options specified

2. To search the entire library, click Search Entire Library; to search only the objects currently displayed in the page, click Search Currently Shown Items.

3. From the leftmost pop-up menu in the Parameters area, choose the Item Information category you want to search from the first pop-up menu: Item Name, Creation Date, Object Type, or Description.

4. From the next pop-up menu, choose Contains if you intend to search for text contained in the chosen category; choose Doesn't Contain if you want to exclude objects that contain the text you specify.

5. In the rightmost field, type the word or phrase you want to search for (if Contains is selected) or exclude (if Doesn't Contain is selected).

6. To add more search criteria, click More Choices; to reduce the number of search criteria, click Fewer Choices. You can add up to five levels of search criteria.

7. To display objects that match all search criteria, select Match All; to display objects that match any of the search criteria, select Match Any One. These options are available only if two or more levels of search criteria are displayed.

8. Click OK to conduct the search and close the dialog box.

All the objects that match the search criteria appear in the panel. The panel is empty if no objects match the search criteria. If you want to display all objects after conducting a search, choose Show All from the library panel's flyout menu.

Copying library objects onto document pages

Once you place an object into a library and, optionally, specify item information for the object, you can place copies of the library object into any document or into another library. To place a copy of a library object onto the currently displayed document page, click the object's icon in the library panel and drag it onto the page. As you drag, the outline of the library object appears. Release the mouse button when the outline is positioned where you want to place the object. You can also place a library object onto a document by clicking its icon and then choosing Place Item(s).

TIP You can copy an object from one library to another by clicking and dragging its icon from the source library panel and dropping it onto the target library panel. Press and hold Option or Alt when dragging and dropping an object between libraries to remove the original object from the source library (in effect moving it from one library to the other).

Using Ruler Guides and Grids

If you've ever seen a carpenter use a chalked string to snap a temporary line to use as an aid for aligning objects, you understand the concept behind guidelines. They're not structurally necessary and they don't show in the final product, yet they can still make your work easier. InDesign lets you create and display three types of nonprinting guidelines:

- **Ruler guide:** These are moveable guidelines that you can create by hand or automatically. They're helpful for placing items precisely and aligning multiple items.

- **Margin and column guides:** These guidelines are part of your page setup when you create or modify a document (see Chapter 4), providing the default margin around the sides of the page and the space between the default text frame's columns.

- **Baseline grid:** This is a series of horizontal lines that help you align lines of text and objects across a multicolumn page. When displayed, a baseline grid makes a page look like a sheet of lined paper.

■ **Document grid:** This is a crisscross of horizontal and vertical lines that aid in object alignment and placement.

■ **Frame-based grid:** This is like a page's baseline grid except that it is just for a specific text frame.

InDesign's grids and guides capabilities verge on overkill. Chances are you'll end up using a combination of ruler guides and the baseline or ruler guides and the document grid, but using all four is more complicated than necessary.

Ruler guides

InDesign lets you create individual ruler guides manually or a set of ruler guides automatically with the Create Guides command (Layout ➪ Create Guides).

Creating ruler guides manually

To create manual ruler guides, go to the page or spread onto which you want to place ruler guides. (If the rulers do not appear at the top and left of the document window, choose View ➪ Show Rulers or press ⌘+R or Ctrl+R.) Now click the horizontal ruler or vertical ruler, and drag the pointer onto a page or the pasteboard. Release the mouse button when the guideline is positioned where you want it. If you release the mouse when the pointer is over a page, the ruler guide extends from one edge of the page to the other (but not across a spread). If you release the mouse button when the pointer is over the pasteboard, the ruler guide extends across both pages of a spread and the pasteboard. If you want a guide to extend across a spread and the pasteboard, you can also press and hold down ⌘ or Ctrl as you drag and release the mouse when the pointer is over a page.

> **TIP** You can place both a horizontal and vertical guide at the same time by pressing ⌘ or Ctrl and dragging the ruler intersection point onto a page. You can also place a guide that extends across the page or spread and pasteboard by double-clicking the vertical or horizontal ruler.

Ruler guides are cyan in color (unless you change the color using Layout ➪ Ruler Guides) and are associated with the layer onto which they're placed. You can show and hide ruler guides by showing and hiding the layers that contain them. You can even create layers that contain nothing but ruler guides and then show and hide them as you wish.

> **TIP** If you want to create ruler guides for several document pages, create a master page, add the guides to the master page, and then apply the master to the appropriate document pages.

Creating a set of guides automatically

Follow these steps to create a set of ruler guides:

1. **If the document contains multiple layers, display the Layers panel (Window ➪ Layers or F7) and click the name of the layer to which you want to add guides.**

> **CROSS-REF** See Chapter 6 for more information about layers.

2. **Choose Layout ➪ Create Guides.** The Create Guides dialog box, shown in Figure 7.12, appears. Select the Preview option if you want to see the guides on the current document page as you create them.

3. **In the Rows and Columns areas specify the number of guides you want to add in the Number fields and, optionally, specify a Gutter width between horizontal (Rows) and vertical (Columns) guides.** Type 0 in the Gutter fields if you don't want gutters between guides.

4. **In the Options area, click the Margins option to fit the guides in the margin boundaries; click the Page option to fit the guides within the page boundary.**

5. **Click the Remove Existing Ruler Guides option to remove any previously placed ruler guides.**

6. **When you're done specifying the attributes of the ruler guides, click OK to close the dialog box.**

FIGURE 7.12

The Create Guides dialog box, along with the guides it created

Working with ruler guides

Once you've created ruler guides, you can show or hide them, lock or unlock them, and select and move, copy and paste, or delete one or more guides at a time. Here are a few pointers for working with ruler guides:

- To display or hide ruler guides, choose View ⇨ Grids & Guides ⇨ Show/Hide Guides or press ⌘+; (semicolon) or Ctrl+; (semicolon).

- To lock or unlock all ruler guides, choose View ⇨ Grids & Guides ⇨ Lock Guides or press Option+⌘+; (semicolon) or Ctrl+Alt+; (semicolon). (If the menu option has a check mark to its left, the ruler guides are locked.) By default, InDesign unlocks ruler guides.

- To select a ruler guide, click it with a selection tool. To select multiple guides, press and hold down Shift and click them. The color of a selected ruler guide changes from blue to the color of its layer.

- To select all ruler guides on a page or spread, press Option+⌘+G or Ctrl+Alt+G.

- To move a ruler guide, click and drag it as you would any object. (You can also change its coordinates in the Control panel or Transform panel.) To move multiple ruler guides, click and drag them. To move ruler guides to another page, select them, choose Edit ⇨ Cut or press ⌘+X or Ctrl+X, or choose Edit ⇨ Copy or press ⌘+C or Ctrl+C, display the target page, and then choose Edit ⇨ Paste or press ⌘+V or Ctrl+V. If the target page is the same shape as the source page, the ruler guides are placed in their original position.

- To delete ruler guides, select them and then press Delete or Backspace.

- To change the color of the ruler guides and the view percentage above which they're displayed (the default view threshold is 5 percent), choose Layout ⇨ Ruler Guides. The Ruler Guides dialog box, shown in Figure 7.13, appears. Modify the View Threshold value and choose a different color from the Color pop-up menu, and then click OK. If you change the settings in the Ruler Guides dialog box when no documents are open, the new settings become defaults and are applied to all subsequently created documents.

- To display ruler guides behind objects instead of in front, choose InDesign ⇨ Preferences ⇨ Guides & Pasteboard or press ⌘+K on the Mac, or choose Edit ⇨ Preferences ⇨ Guides & Pasteboard or press Ctrl+K in Windows, and check Guides in Back in the Guide Options section of the dialog box's Guides & Pasteboard pane.

- If the Snap to Guides command (View ⇨ Grids & Guides ⇨ Snap to Guides, or Shift+⌘+; [semicolon] or Ctrl+Shift+; [semicolon]) is selected, object edges snap to ruler guides when you drag them in the snap zone. To specify the *snap zone* (the distance — in pixels — at which an object snap to a guide), choose InDesign ⇨ Preferences ⇨ Guides & Pasteboard or press ⌘+K on the Mac, or choose Edit ⇨ Preferences ⇨ Guides & Pasteboard or press Ctrl+K in Windows, and type a value in the Snap to Zone field in the Guide Options section of the dialog box.

FIGURE 7.13

The Ruler Guides dialog box

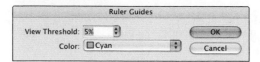

Working with column guides

You can also adjust column guides if your document has them, though you don't get the same flexibility in adjusting column guides as you do ruler guides. Column guides are created when you create a new document and set it up with multiple columns (see Chapter 3).

By default, column guides are locked. To unlock them (or relock them) choose View ➪ Grids & Guides ➪ Lock Column Guides. (If the menu option has a check mark to its left, the column guides are locked.)

To move a column guide, click and drag it. Note that the color of a selected column guide does not change as the color of a selected ruler guide does. Also note that you cannot select multiple column guides or move them to other pages.

The only way to add or delete column guides is to change the number of guides in the Margins and Columns dialog box (choose Layout ➪ Margins and Columns); adjusting the number of columns undoes any custom moves applied to column guides.

Working with the baseline grid

Every new document you create includes a baseline grid. If the document you're working on uses a multicolumn page layout, a baseline grid can be helpful for aligning text baselines across columns and for ensuring that object edges align with text baselines. Baseline grids aren't much use for small documents, like business cards and ads, and one-column designs. Here's how to create them:

1. **Choose InDesign ➪ Preferences ➪ Grids or press ⌘+K on the Mac, or choose Edit ➪ Preferences ➪ Grids or press Ctrl+K in Windows, and choose the Grids pane.** The Grids pane, shown in Figure 7.14, appears.

2. **Choose a color from the Color pop-up menu in the Baseline Grid area.**

3. **In the Start field, type the distance between the top of the page and the first grid line.** If you type 0, the Increment Every value determines the distance between the top of the page and the first grid line.

4. **Type the distance between grid lines in the Increment Every field.** Generally, the value you type in this field will be the same as the leading value you use for the publication's body text.

5. **Choose a View Threshold percentage from the pop-up menu or type a value in the field.** Generally, you don't want to display the baseline grid at reduced view percentages because grid lines become tightly spaced.

6. **Click OK to close the dialog box and return to the document.**

FIGURE 7.14

The Grids pane of the Preferences dialog box

A baseline grid is document-wide (that is, you can't change it from page to page), and grid lines are displayed behind all objects, layers, and ruler guides. The default baseline grid begins ½ inch from the top of a document page; the grid lines are light blue and placed 1 pica apart; and they are displayed at view percentages above 75 percent. If you change any of these settings when no documents are open, the changes are applied to all subsequently created documents; if a document is open, changes apply only to that document.

TIP The Show/Hide Baseline Grid command (View ➪ Grids & Guides ➪ Show/Hide Baseline Grid, or Option+⌘+' [apostrophe] or Ctrl+Alt+' [apostrophe]) lets you display and hide a document's baseline grid.

You set the baseline grid for a text frame in a very similar way. After selecting the text frame, choose Object ➪ Text Frame Options (⌘+B or Ctrl+B), and then go to the Baseline Options pane, shown in Figure 7.15. Select the Use Custom Baseline Grid option to enable the grid for this text frame, and then choose the rest of the settings as appropriate to it. The Offset, Start, Relative To, Increment Every, and Color options work the same way as in the Grids pane of the Preferences dialog box.

FIGURE 7.15

The Baseline Options pane of the Text Frame Options dialog box

Working with the document grid

Like the baseline grid, every document includes a default *document grid,* which is a set of horizontal and vertical lines. And like baseline grids, you may or may not find the document grid to be a useful aid for laying out pages. If you like working on graph paper in the real world, the document guide may be just your cup of tea. On the other hand, you may find document grids to be too constricting and opt not to use them. If you want to use document grids, follow these steps:

1. **Choose InDesign ➪ Preferences ➪ Grids or press ⌘+K on the Mac, or choose Edit ➪ Preferences ➪ Grids or press Ctrl+K in Windows.** The Grids pane appears (refer to Figure 7.14).

2. **Choose a color from the Color pop-up menu in the Document Grid area.**

3. **Type the distance between grid lines in the Gridline Every field.** If your basic measurement unit is an inch, you probably want to use the default value of 1 inch.

4. **Type the number of divisions between grid lines in the Subdivisions field.** If your basic measurement unit is an inch, you can specify a value of 6 to subdivide the grid into 1-pica squares. Or, if you prefer, you can type a value of 4, 8, 16, and so on to subdivide the grid into standard divisions of an inch.

5. **Click OK to close the dialog box and return to the document.**

TIP   The Show/Hide Document Grid command (View ➪ Grids & Guides ➪ Show/Hide Document Grid or ⌘+' [apostrophe] or Ctrl+' [apostrophe]) lets you display and hide the document grid.

Summary

If you want to be a true InDesign expert, you must take advantage of three of its most powerful features: master pages, templates, and libraries. All these features save time and ensure design consistency across documents. A master page is a preformatted page design that you can apply to document pages in a multi-page publication; a template is a preconstructed document that serves as the starting point when you need to create multiple versions of the same publication; and a library is a storage file in which you can save any object you've created with InDesign for use in other publications.

To help you place and align objects, InDesign lets you create three types of guidelines: ruler guides, the baseline grid, and the document grid. You can also move the column guides that InDesign creates automatically for you. You can show or hide guidelines, and you have the option to snap object edges to guidelines when you click and drag them in the specified snap zone.

Chapter 8

Defining Colors, Tints, and Gradients

Although color is most widely used by high-end publishers — people producing magazines and catalogs — color is becoming more accessible to all publishers thanks to the recent emergence of inexpensive color printers, color copiers, and leading-edge desktop-publishing programs. Whether you want to produce limited-run documents on a color printer, create newsletters using spot colors, or publish magazines and catalogs using process colors and special inks, InDesign offers the tools that you need to do the job well.

But color is a complex issue in printing, which involves both physics and chemistry. The inks that produce color are designed chemically to retain those colors and to produce them evenly, so your images don't look mottled or faded. How light reflects off of ink and paper to your eye determines the color you see, and many factors (particularly different textures of paper) can affect the physics of how the light carries the color.

You also have implementation issues to consider: How many colors can your printing press produce, and how much does it cost? When do you decide to go for the exact pure color, and when do you decide to go with a close-enough version that costs less to print?

Once you have figured out what your color capabilities are, you can get into the nitty-gritty of actually using color in your graphics or applying colors to text and layout elements (such as bars along the edge of a page). Or you can use color both ways. To a great extent, where you define and apply color determines what you can do with it.

CROSS-REF Chapter 29 covers color matching and other high-end color-output issues in depth. This chapter concentrates on how to create and apply colors within InDesign.

IN THIS CHAPTER

Getting acquainted with color terminology

Making sense of process and spot colors

Working with color models in InDesign

Defining colors and tints

Mixing colors

Importing colors from files

Sampling colors from images

Understanding color issues in imported graphics

Working with gradients

Editing, copying, and deleting swatches

Applying colors, tints, and gradients

Defining Color Terms

Color is an expansive (and sometimes confusing and esoteric) concept in the world of publishing. The following definitions, however, should start you on your way to a clear understanding of the subject:

- **Build:** Attempts to simulate a color-model color by combining the appropriate percentages of the four process colors.

- **CIE Lab:** A standard that specifies colors by one lightness coordinate and two color coordinates, green-red and blue-yellow. The first part of the name means Commission Internationale de l'Éclairage (International Committee on Illumination), an international standards group, and the second part refers to the mathematical approach used to describe the colors in a cubic arrangement: luminance, *a*-axis, and *b*-axis.

- **CMYK:** A standard that specifies colors as combinations of cyan, magenta, yellow, and black. These four colors are known as *process colors*.

- **Color gamut:** The range of colors that a device, such as a monitor or a color printer, can produce. Each color model has a different color gamut.

- **Color model:** An industry standard for specifying a color, such as CMYK or Pantone.

- **Color separation:** A set of four photographic negatives, one filtered for each process color, shot from a color photograph or image. When combined, the four negatives reproduce that original image.

- **Color space:** A method of representing color in terms of measurable values, such as the amount of red, yellow, and blue in a color image. The color space RGB represents the red, green, and blue colors on video screens.

- **Four-color printing:** The use of the four process colors in combination to produce most other colors.

- **Process color:** Any of the four primary colors in publishing — cyan, magenta, yellow, and black (known collectively as CMYK). A six-color, high-fidelity variant produced by Pantone is called Hexachrome.

- **RGB:** The standard used by monitors, and the abbreviation from the three colors in it: red, green, and blue. One of the biggest hurdles to producing color documents that look as you'd expect is that computers use RGB while printers use CMYK, and the two don't always produce colors at the same hue.

- **Spot color:** A single color applied at one or more places on a page, such as for a screen or as part of an illustration. You can use more than one spot color per page. Spot colors can also be process colors.

- **Swatchbook:** A table of colors collected together as a series of color samples. The printer uses premixed ink based on the color model identifier you specify; you look up the numbers for various colors in the table of colors in a swatchbook.

Understanding Process and Spot Color

In this section, I briefly explore the differences between spot and process colors, the two primary ways of indicating color in print documents.

Identifying methods of color printing

Several forms of color are used in printing, but the two most prevalent ones are process color and spot color.

Process color is the use of four basic colors — cyan, magenta, yellow, and black (known collectively as CMYK) — that are mixed to reproduce most color tones the human eye can see. A separate negative is produced for each of the four process colors. This method, often called *four-color printing*, is used for most color publishing.

> **NOTE**   Like CMYK, RGB and Lab are created by mixing colors; however, InDesign refers to RGB and Lab colors as *mixed colors*, leaving the term *process color* for CMYK because that's an industry-standard term for CMYK.

Spot color is any color ink — whether one of the process colors or some other hue — used for specific elements in a document. For example, if you print a document in black ink but print the company logo in red, the red is a spot color. A spot color is often called a *second color* even though you can use several spot colors in a document. Each spot color is output to its own negative (and not color-separated into CMYK). Using spot color gives you access to special inks that are truer to the desired color than any mix of process colors can be. These inks come in several standards, and include metallics, neons, and milky pastels. You even can use varnishes as spot colors to give layout elements a different gleam from the rest of the page. Although experienced designers sometimes mix spot colors to produce special shades not otherwise available, you probably won't need to do so.

There are several advantages to spot colors. You can use colors like metallic inks that are impossible to create with CMYK. Also, your printed results will be more consistent than with CMYK separations, which can suffer from *color shift* (variation in the hue produced) over the length of a long printed piece. But spot colors work only in objects that have distinct, continuous hue, such as a solid brick red, that can be printed with just one ink. To produce any image with multiple colors, such as a photograph, you need to use multiple inks, and because printing presses can traditionally print only four to eight colors on a page, you have to mix colors to create the range of hues in such multicolor objects.

> **TIP**   If you create spot colors, I suggest that you include the word *Spot* as part of the name, so you can quickly tell in a panel or menu whether a selected color will print on its own plate or be color-separated. InDesign does use an icon to tell you whether a color is process or spot, as well as what color model (CMYK, RGB, or Lab) in which it was defined (refer to Figure 8.1), but often it's easier to see the word than a tiny icon.

NOTE   Adobe programs, including InDesign, show that spot colors like Pantone, Toyo, and DIC (Dainippon Ink & Chemical) are based on the CMYK color model, even though they're not. It doesn't really matter, because if you print them as a spot color, they get their own plate and your printer will use the actual Pantone, Toyo, or DIC ink. And if you color-separate them into process colors, you'll get the CMYK values shown in the Swatch Options dialog box; or you can hold the mouse over the color name in the Swatches panel (if the Tool Tips option is enabled in the Preferences dialog box, as described in Chapter 3).

Mixing spot and process colors

Some designers use both process and spot colors in a document in a procedure known as using a *fifth color*. Typically, the normal color images are color-separated and printed using the four process colors, while a special element (such as a logo in metallic ink) is printed in a spot color. The process colors are output on the usual four negatives; the spot color is output on a separate, fifth negative and printed using a fifth plate, a fifth ink roller, and a fifth inkwell. You can use more than five colors, however; you're limited only by your budget and the capabilities of your printing plant. (Most commercial printers can handle six colors for each run through the press, and larger ones often can handle as many as eight colors.)

Converting spot color to process color

InDesign can convert spot colors to process colors. This handy capability lets designers specify the colors they want through a system with which they're familiar, such as Pantone, without the added expense of special spot-color inks and extra negatives. Conversions are never an exact match, but guidebooks are available that can show you in advance the color that will be created. And with several Pantone and HKS variations, designers can pick a Pantone or HKS color that color-separates predictably.

You can set InDesign to convert some spot colors in a document to process colors while leaving others alone: Just use the Color Mode pop-up menu in the Swatch Options dialog box, covered later in this chapter. (For example, you can keep a metallic silver as a spot color so it prints with a metallic ink, rather than be converted to a grayish color that is the closest the CMYK colors can produce to simulate a silver. But you would convert common colors like deep blue, purple, and green to process colors, because the CMYK inks can combine fairly accurately to reproduce them.) You can also leave all spot colors as spot colors or convert all spot colors to process colors.

CAUTION   Colors defined in one model and converted to another may not reproduce exactly the same because the physics underlying each color model differ slightly. Each model was designed for use in a different medium, such as with paper or on a video monitor.

Working with Color Models

Once you understand color terminology and the difference between process and spot colors, you can start thinking about the type of colors you create in InDesign. (You define colors in the Swatches panel, as I describe later in this chapter.) The color models fall into two broad classes:

- Those that let you define a color by selecting a color from a *color wheel* (which represents a spectrum of available colors) or by entering specific values for the color's *constituent colors* (the colors that make up the color), which include CMYK, RGB, LAB, and Multi-Ink.

- Those that have a predefined set of colors, which you select from a palette of swatches. These swatches include ANPA (American Newspaper Publishers Association), DIC (Dainippon Ink & Chemical), Focoltone, Toyo, Trumatch, 13 variants of Pantone, and 8 variants of HKS. There are also two sets of colors meant for use on the Web.

NOTE Most North American publishers use Pantone color models, also known as the Pantone Matching System (PMS). Focoltone, HKS, and Trumatch tend to be used in Europe. DIC, Focoltone, and Toyo tend to be used in Asia. ANPA is used by North American newspapers. And everyone uses CMYK.

NOTE Several of the swatch library names are in all uppercase in InDesign's menus and dialog boxes. That's because they're trademarked names, which some people (such as those at Adobe) like to indicate by using all caps. That's just a convention and means nothing per se. (Legally, the word need only be treated as a proper adjective, though the owner needs to use the ® or ™ symbols in its own materials to assert ownership.)

Keep in mind that the colors displayed are only on-screen representations; the actual colors may be different. The differences are particularly noticeable if your monitor is running in 8-bit (256 hues) color mode. Check the actual color in a color swatchbook for the model you are using. (Art and printing supply stores usually carry these swatchbooks. See the sidebar "Using Color Swatchbooks" for lists of other sources.) You can also calibrate your monitor display with tools from X-Rite (www.xrite.com); this keeps the colors as close as possible to actual output.

TIP InDesign uses the same swatch format as Illustrator, so you import color models into InDesign created in or for Illustrator. InDesign also supports the Adobe Swatch Exchange format that all Adobe CS2 and CS3 applications support for color exchange.

Using Color Swatchbooks

Anyone who uses a lot of color should have a color swatchbook handy. You probably can get one at your local art supply store or from your commercial printer (prices typically range from $50 to $100, depending on the color model and the type of swatchbook). But if you can't find a swatchbook, here's where to order the most popular ones:

- **Pantone:** Several Pantone swatchbooks are available, including ones for coated and uncoated paper, and for spot-color output and process-color output. If you are converting (called *building* in publishing parlance) Pantone colors to CMYK for four-color printing, I particularly recommend the *Pantone Process Color Imaging Guide: CMYK Edition* or the *Pantone Process Color System Guide* swatchbooks. Pantone, 590 Commerce Blvd., Carlstadt, NJ 07072-3098; phone: 201-935-5500; fax: 201-935-3338; Internet: www.pantone.com.

continued

continued

- **Hexachrome:** Pantone also created the Hexachrome standard that uses six colors rather than four to build truer-to-life colors. Pantone sells Hexachrome swatchbooks, as well as the $299 HexWare software that adds the Hexachrome output capability to Adobe Photoshop and Illustrator. Because InDesign uses Illustrator color swatch files, you can add Hexachrome support to InDesign via HexWare. (See the contact information for Pantone in the preceding bullet.)

- **Trumatch:** Based on a CMYK color space, Trumatch suffers almost no matching problems when converted to CMYK. Variants of the swatchbooks for coated and uncoated paper are available. Trumatch, 71 Hill St., Southampton, NY 11968; phone: 800-878-9100; fax: 631-204-0002; Internet: www.trumatch.com.

- **ANPA:** Designed for reproduction on newsprint, these colors also are designed in the LAB color space. Newspaper Association of America, 4401 Wilson Blvd. #900, Arlington, VA 22203; phone: 571-366-1000; fax: 571-366-1195; Internet: www.naa.org.

- **Focoltone:** Like Trumatch, this color model is based on the CMYK color space. A & P Publishing Network, No. 6 Aljunied Ave. 3 #01-02, Singapore 389932; phone: +65-6746-0188; fax: +65-6746-1890; Internet: www.apmedia.com.

- **HKS:** This color model is used mainly in Germany and other European countries, with variants for industrial printing such as on plastics. It uses various combinations of cyan, magenta, and yellow with black overlays to achieve different shades. Hostmann-Steinberg, Bremer Weg 125, D-29223 Celle, Germany; phone: +49-5141-591-0; fax: +49-5141-591-202; Internet: www.hks-colour.de.

- **Dainippon Ink & Chemical (DIC):** Like Pantone, the DIC color set is a spot-color–based system. Dainippon Ink & Chemical Americas, 222 Bridge Plaza South, Fort Lee, NJ 07024; phone: 201-592-5100; fax: 201-592-8232; Internet: http://dicwww01 .dic.co.jp/eng/index.html.

- **Toyo:** Similar to Pantone in that it is based on spot-color inks, this model is popular in Japan. Toyo Ink America, 710 W. Belden, Addison, IL 60101; phone: 630-930-5100; Internet: www.toyoink.com.

Understanding Paper Variation Models

Both the Pantone and HKS color models recognize that the type of paper on which you print affects how a color appears, so they have variations based on popular paper types. Here's how they work:

- **Pantone Process Coated:** Use this variant when you color-separate Pantone colors and your printer uses the standard Pantone-brand process-color inks on coated paper. Colors in this variant have the code DS added *before* the numerals in their names and the code C *after* the numerals.

- **Pantone Process Uncoated:** Use this variant when you color-separate Pantone colors and your printer uses the standard Pantone-brand process-color inks on coated paper. Colors in this variant have the code DS added *before* the numerals in their names and the code U *after* the numerals.

NOTE The *DS* code stands for digital SWOP, or Specifications for Web Offset Publications, a prepress standard for the web-offset printing process used by magazines, catalog, and most high-run printing presses.

- **Pantone Solid Coated:** Use this variant when your printer uses actual Pantone-brand inks (as spot colors) when printing to coated paper stock. Colors in this variant have the code C appended to their names.

- **Pantone Solid Matte:** This is the same as Pantone Coated but for paper with a matte finish. Colors in this variant have the code M appended to their names.

- **Pantone Solid Uncoated:** This is the same as Pantone Solid Coated but for uncoated paper. Colors in this variant have the code U appended to their names.

- **Pantone Metallic Coated:** This contains metallic colors designed for coated papers (which helps make them shine like metal). Colors in this variant have the code C appended to their names.

- **Pantone Pastel Coated:** This contains pastel colors designed for coated papers (which helps make them more lustrous). Colors in this variant have the code C appended to their names.

- **Pantone Pastel Uncoated:** This contains pastel colors designed for uncoated papers (which helps make them have the visual texture of eggshells). Colors in this variant have the code U appended to their names.

- **Pantone Color Bridge:** This contains Pantone solid colors that reproduce well with process colors, for use on coated paper. Colors in this variant have the code PC appended to their names.

- **Pantone Color Bridge Uncoated:** This contains Pantone solid colors that reproduce well with process colors, for use on uncoated paper. Colors in this variant have the code U appended to their names.

- **Pantone Color Bridge Euro:** This contains Pantone solid colors that reproduce well with process colors on European printing presses, for use on any paper. Colors in this variant have the code EC appended to their names.

NEW FEATURE The Color Bridge colors used to be called Solid to Process in previous versions of InDesign. (InDesign CS3 keeps the Solid to Process labels as well for familiarity.) Also, the uncoated version of this color model is new to InDesign CS3, as are the two Euro color models.

- **Pantone Solid to Process:** This contains Pantone solid colors that reproduce well with process colors, for use on any paper. Colors in this variant have the code PC appended to their names.

- **Pantone Solid to Process Euro:** This contains Pantone solid colors that reproduce well with process colors on European printing presses, for use on any paper. Colors in this variant have the code EC appended to their names.

- **HKS E:** Use this HKS variant for continuous-form stationery. Colors in this variant have the code E appended to their names.

- **HKS E Process:** Use this HKS variant for continuous-form stationery printed with process colors. Colors in this variant have the code E appended to their names.

- **HKS K:** Use this HKS variant for glossy art paper (highly coated). Colors in this variant have the code K appended to their names.

- **HKS K Process:** Use this HKS variant for glossy art paper (highly coated) printed with process colors. Colors in this variant have the code K appended to their names.

- **HKS N:** Use this HKS variant for natural paper (uncoated). Colors in this variant have the code N appended to their names.

- **HKS N Process:** Use this HKS variant for natural paper (uncoated) printed with process colors. Colors in this variant have the code N appended to their names.

- **HKS Z:** Use this HKS variant for newsprint. Colors in this variant have the code Z appended to their names.

- **HKS Z Process:** Use this HKS variant for newsprint printed with process colors. Colors in this variant have the code Z appended to their names.

 When printing on uncoated stock with any colors designed for use on coated stock, you will usually get weaker, less-saturated color reproduction.

Defining Colors and Tints

InDesign comes with a few predefined colors: [Black], [Registration] (black on each negative for the printing press), [Paper] (white), [None] (transparent), Cyan, Magenta, Yellow, Red, Green, and Blue. So you most likely want to add a few of your own.

Before you can apply any colors — whether to bitmap images or to layout elements such as strokes, text, frames, and shapes — you must first define the colors. InDesign offers three ways to create colors: via the Swatches panel, via the Colors panel, and by double-clicking the Fill or Stroke iconic button on the Tools panel. You can also import colors from other Adobe programs and from some color images.

No matter how you define colors, you have a couple of decisions to make first:

- Do you want to create your own color by mixing basic colors like red, green, and blue (called RGB and typically used for screen display), or cyan, yellow, magenta, and black (called CMYK or *process colors*, and typically used for printing presses)?

- Do you want to use a color from an ink maker like Pantone or Toyo? These colors — called *spot colors* — are typically used as an extra ink on your document but can also be converted to the standard four-process colors; therefore, they're handy when you know the color you want when you see it.

All of InDesign's color-creation tools support both process and spot colors. And all have access to the predefined colors like Pantone and Toyo as well as to the free-form color pickers for mixing CMYK or RGB colors. If you plan to print the color on its own plate, you need to use a predefined color, so you know the printer can reproduce it. If you plan to color-separate a color into the four CMYK plates, then it doesn't matter whether you use a predefined color or make one of your own. One advantage to using a predefined color is that it's easy to tell other designers what the color is; another is that you get very close matches if you start with a predefined color and then end up having it color-separated in some documents and kept as a spot color in others.

Creating colors the ideal way: the Swatches panel

The best way to create colors in InDesign is to use the Swatches panel. All colors in this panel get a unique name and are tracked by InDesign. That means each such color is available to be used on any object in your document, with no risk of having slightly different variants. Plus, you can modify a swatch and ensure that all objects using that swatch are updated, and you can delete a swatch and tell InDesign which color to use in its place. Furthermore, when you print, you have control over how each color is handled (whether it is printed to its own plate, whether it is printed at all, and whether there should be any adjustments to its ink density or screening angle.) Figure 8.1 shows the Swatches panel.

 You can drag the color from the Stroke or Fill iconic buttons onto the Swatches panel to create a swatch of that color.

 If no document is open when you create, edit, or delete colors, the new color palette becomes the default for all future documents.

 Because regular black can appear weak when it's overprinted by other colors, many designers create what printers call *superblack* or *rich black* by combining 100 percent black and 100 percent magenta. (Some use cyan instead of magenta.) You can define superblack as a separate color or redefine the registration color as 100 percent of all four-process colors, and use that as a superblack. Note that superblack should be used only in large areas — using it on type or small objects increases the chances of registration problems for those items.

Personalizing the Swatches Panel

You can change the appearance of the entries in the Swatches panel by using the three options in the Swatches panel's flyout menu: Name (the default), Small Name (a tighter list view), Small Swatch (no names, just small icons), and Large Swatch (no names, just larger icons).

Also, use the Hide Options menu to suppress the display of the Stroke, Fill, Formatting Affects Container, and Formatting Affects Text iconic buttons and the Tint field and pop-up menu; Show Options brings them back.

Finally, you can use the Show All Swatches, Show Color Swatches, and Show Gradient Swatches iconic buttons at the bottom of the panel to control which swatches appear.

FIGURE 8.1

The Swatches panel and its flyout menu

Show All Swatches

Show Color Swatches

Show Gradient Swatches

Delete Swatch

New Swatch

To create your own color, go to the Swatches panel (Window ➪ Swatches or F5) and select New Color Swatch from the flyout menu. You get the New Color Swatch dialog box shown in Figure 8.2. Now follow these steps:

1. **In the Swatch Name field, give your color a name that describes it, such as Lime Green or Bright Purple.** You can also select the Name with Color Value option, which uses the color values to make up the color name as done for the colors under [Registration] in Figure 8.1. This option is available only for CMYK, RGB, and LAB colors, not for swatch-based colors such as Pantone.

2. **In the Color Type pop-up menu, choose from Process or Spot.** These are covered earlier in this chapter; leave the color type at Process if you're not sure.

3. **In the Color Mode pop-up menu, choose the mixing system or swatch library (both are considered to be *color models*) you want to use: CMYK, RGB, Lab, or a swatch-based model.** (These are covered earlier in this chapter.)

4. **For the CMYK, RGB, and Lab models, use the sliders to create your new color.** A preview appears in the box at left. For the swatch-based models, scroll through the lists of colors and select one.

5. **If you want to create multiple colors, click Add after each color definition and then click Done when done.** To create just one color, click OK instead of Add. You can also click Cancel to abort the current color definition.

FIGURE 8.2

The New Color Swatch dialog box lets you define colors. (At top is the dialog box for CMYK color mixing; at bottom is the dialog box for the swatch-based spot colors such as Pantone colors.) An identical dialog box named Swatch Options lets you edit them.

How to Decide on a Color-Naming System

You can name a CMYK, RGB, or LAB color anything you want. (Colors defined in other models will use their official names, such as Pantone 147U or ANPA 1732-4 AdPro.) To make it easier to remember what a defined color looks like, you should use either descriptive names (such as Grass Green or Official Logo Blue) or use names based on the color settings. Choose one naming convention to keep things consistent.

The benefit of using descriptive names is that they have intrinsic meaning, which helps designers choose the right one. For example, there's no confusion that Official Logo Blue is the color to be used for the company logo, but the proper usage of the same color using a name based on its color values won't be so obvious.

The benefit of using color-value names is that designers who do a lot of color work know what that color is. Grass Green could be any of several colors, but C=30 M=0 Y=50 K=5 can be only one color.

A good strategy is to use the color-value names for all colors — with a twist: For colors that have specific usage, add that to the color name. For example, you might use a grassy green for a particular feature article, so you would just name it based on its color values (for example, C=30 M=0 Y=50 K=5). But your magazine logo color would be named something like Logo C=100 M=100 Y=20 K=25, so you have a reminder of this swatch's designated usage.

InDesign names colors based on their values automatically if you select the Name with Color Value option and choose Process as the Color Type when you define the color. For example, if you create a color in the CMYK model, you might give it a name based on its mix, such as *55C 0M 91Y 0K* for that grass-green color — composed of 55 percent cyan, 0 percent magenta, 91 percent yellow, and 0 percent black. (Believe it or not, this naming convention is how professionals specify colors on paste-up boards.) InDesign's Name with Color Value option would name this color *C=55 M=0 Y=91 K=0*. The same system applies to the RGB, HSB, and LAB models.

Creating tints

A *tint* is a shade of a color. InDesign lets you create such tints as separate color swatches, so they're easy to use for multiple items. The process is easy:

1. **In the Swatches panel, just select a color from which you want to create a tint.**
2. **Using the flyout menu, select New Tint Swatch.** You get the New Tint Swatch dialog box shown in Figure 8.3.
3. **Click and drag the slider to adjust the tint, or type a value in the field at right.**
4. **Click Add to create another tint from the same base color, and then click OK when you're finished.** (If you're adding a single tint, there's no need to click Add; just click OK when done.) Click Cancel to abort the current tint. Any new tint has the same name as the original color and the percentage of shading, such as Leaf Green 66%.

NOTE   You can create a tint from a tint, which can be confusing. Fortunately, InDesign goes back to the original color when letting you create the new tint. Thus, if you select Leaf Green 66% and move the slider to 33%, you get a 33 percent tint of the original Leaf Green, not a 33 percent tint of the Leaf Green 66% (which would be equivalent to a 22 percent tint of the original Leaf Green).

FIGURE 8.3

The New Tint Swatch dialog box lets you define colors; a nearly identical dialog box named Swatch Options lets you edit them. The difference is that, when editing, you can change all the other color values, not just the degree of tint.

TIP   You can also apply tints to objects without creating a separate swatch for each tint. After applying the color (described later in this chapter), select the object and change the value in the Tint field of the Swatches panel, or use its pop-up menu's predefined tint values.

Creating mixed colors

InDesign offers another type of color: mixed-ink color. Essentially, a mixed-ink color combines a spot color with the default process colors (cyan, magenta, yellow, and black) to create new color swatches. For example, you can combine 38 percent black with 100 percent Pantone 130C to get a darker version of Pantone 130C (called a *duotone*, though InDesign doesn't limit you to mixing spot colors with just black, as traditional duotones do).

To create a mixed-ink swatch, select the spot color you want to begin with and then choose New Mixed Ink Swatch from the Swatches panel's flyout menu. You get the dialog box shown in Figure 8.4, in which you select the percentages of the spot color and any or all of the default process colors you want to mix. You also give the new color a name. Click Add to add another mixed-ink swatch based on the current spot color, and then click OK when you're finished. If you're creating just one color, click OK instead of Add. You can click Cancel to abort the current mixed-ink color definition.

TIP   Be sure to test such mixes by creating a color proof first. They may not look as you expect when actually printed because of how printing presses handle a color overlapping other colors.

There's more to mixed-ink colors than creating them one by one. InDesign lets you create mixed-ink groups, which are a series of colors based on a spot color and one or more default process colors. Figure 8.5 shows the New Mixed Ink Group dialog box, in which you select the colors to mix as you do in the New Mixed Ink Swatch dialog box. This feature is handy to create a palette of colors within a color range, as well as to create color combinations known as *duotones* (a spot color mixed with black) and *tritones* (two spot colors mixed with black).

FIGURE 8.4

The New Mixed Ink Swatch dialog box lets you mix one or more spot colors with any or all of the default process colors to create new shades and variations.

But you do more than simply mix the colors. In this dialog box, you specify an initial tint for each color you want to mix, then how many times you want to create a color using it, as well as the increment of color for each creation. This can be confusing, so I walk you through the options in Figure 8.5.

The spot color Pantone 519 M is chosen with an Initial value of 0%, a Repeat setting of 3, and an Increment of 4%. Also chosen is the spot color Pantone 8201 M, with an Initial value of 50%, a Repeat setting of 5, and an Increment of 10%. This combination creates 24 mixed-ink swatches, as shown in the Swatch Preview section (click Preview Swatches to display the preview colors in the Swatch Preview section of the dialog box).

InDesign uses the settings and first mixes 0 percent of Pantone 519 M with 50 percent of Pantone 8201 M. That's one swatch. Then it mixes 0 percent of Pantone 519 M with 60 percent of Pantone 8201 M (adding the increment of 10%). It does so four more times, for 70, 80, 90, and 100 percent of Pantone 8201 M mixed with the 0 percent of Pantone 519 M because there was a Repeat setting of 5. Note that InDesign stops at 100 percent saturation even if the Increment results in a higher number.

So that's six mixed-ink swatches based on 0 percent of Pantone 519 M. InDesign now repeats this six sets of Pantone 80201 M mixed with the next increment of Pantone 519 M (4 percent, based on the Increment value of 4% for that color). That's six more. The process is repeated two more times, one for 8 percent and one for 12 percent, to meet the Repeat setting of 3. So that's a total of 24 swatches.

TIP To figure out how many swatches you can create using this feature, add 1 to the number in each of the Repeat fields, and then multiply the values. In the preceding example, you get 24 — (3+1) × (5+1), or 4 × 6, or 24. That's because the Repeat setting indicates how many more variations to create in addition *to* those with the base (Initial) value.

FIGURE 8.5

The New Mixed Ink Group dialog box lets you mix a selected spot color with any or all of the default process colors in user-defined increments to create a range of new shades and variations.

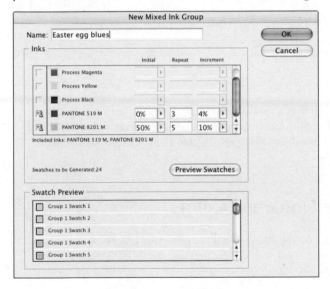

Using the Colors panel

Many people may try to use the Color panel (Window ➪ Color or F6) to define colors, but that can be a mistake. At first, you may not realize you can create colors from the Color panel. It shows a gradation of the last color used and lets you change the tint for that color on the current object. But if you go to the flyout menu and choose a color model (RGB, CMYK, or Lab), you get a set of mixing controls (refer to Figure 8.6).

So what's the problem? Colors created through the Color panel don't appear in your Swatches panel and so can't be used for other objects. Called *unnamed colors* because they don't appear anywhere, these can be dangerous for publishers to use. (Adobe added them to InDesign to be consistent with how Illustrator defines colors—a foolish consistency.)

First, you can't modify them later in the Swatches panel if you want to adjust the color for all objects using them.

TIP You can double-click the Stroke and Fill iconic buttons on the Tools panel to create colors, using a Photoshop-style color picker. You can add any colors created this way to the Swatches panel using the Add Swatch button. Otherwise, you run the same risk as creating colors through the Color panel.

FIGURE 8.6

The Color panel

Second, you can't specify the color to print as a spot color, which you might later decide is how you want to print a particular color. They print only as process colors and do not show up in the list of colors in the Color pane of the Print dialog box (see Chapter 31 for more details on this).

Managing Unnamed Colors

No matter how disciplined you are, chances are that you will get unnamed colors in your document. Fortunately, InDesign provides several ways to identify and convert those unnamed colors to swatches you can then edit, apply, and manage consistently:

- If you go to the Color panel and modify a color without thinking about it, choose Add to Swatches from the flyout menu to add the modified color to the Swatches panel.

- Choose Add Unnamed Colors from the Swatches panel's flyout menu, which adds all unnamed colors in one fell swoop.

- Drag an unnamed color from the Fill iconic button or Stroke iconic button on the Tools panel onto the Swatches panel to create a swatch.

- Use the Find/Change dialog box's Object pane to find unnamed colors in the Fill and/or Stroke panes in the Find Object Format Options dialog box and replace them with actual swatches. (See Chapter 11.) Note that this does not convert an unnamed color into a swatch but lets you eliminate the use of such colors.

InDesign CS3 Color Techniques

Adobe InDesign offers a strong set of tools for color creation and control, as Chapters 8, 12, and 30 show in detail. This special eight-page color section shows some of these tools in action, using InDesign's actual capabilities.

Inside Color Models

Color is made up of light, but the printing model and computer-monitor models act very differently. Color printing is based on how light reflects off paper through inks — the standard inks in printing are cyan, magenta, yellow, and black (CMYK), although there are specialty inks such as Pantone, Toyo, and Trumatch. The ink absorbs all colors but the one you see; for example, your eyes can see cyan because the ink has absorbed all the other colors that light would normally pick up. That's why mixing several inks produces a dark brown or gray — most of the light is absorbed by the multiple inks. By contrast, computer monitors use a model based on how the three colors of light — red, green, and blue (RGB) — combine. All three combine to make white, while having none of the three colors gives you black. Because the physics of the two models are different, what you see on-screen — or what your scanner or digital camera sees when capturing an image — doesn't necessarily match what is printed.

The CMYK model

The RGB model

CMYK color (far left) and RGB color (immediate left). For CMYK, the cube shows how cyan, magenta, and yellow combine in various percentages; the slider at the cube's right adds black, which has the effect of darkening the combination shown. In RGB, there's no slider since the three colors combine to produce all color shades (white is the absence of all colors). Below are example inks from specialty color libraries.

Pantone Solid swatches

ANPA swatches

Trumatch swatches

Focoltone swatches

DIC swatches

HKS-E swatches

Toyo swatches

Pantone Metallic swatches

Mixed Inks: Duotones and Beyond

A mixed-ink color combines spot colors and/or process colors to create a blended color. Such mixed-ink colors are mostly used for duotones and tritones, which combine one or two spot colors with black. A duotone (a spot color plus some black) is often used to simulate that dark brown of a very old photograph, for example. A tritone (two spot colors plus some black) creates richer or unusual colors that standard CMYK mixes can't create. But InDesign doesn't limit you to just duotones and tritones containing black; you can use yellow, cyan, and/or magenta as well — or create them solely from spot colors, with no process colors at all.

To create a mixed-ink color, you first must have created the spot colors you want to mix with the process colors. Then choose New Mixed Ink Swatch from the Swatches panel's flyout menu to get the New Mixed Ink Swatch dialog box. (Access the Swatches panel by choosing Window ➪ Swatches or pressing F5.) You can create solid colors, color tints, and gradients, as well as sets of color swatches using the mixed-ink capability. Here, you select the colors you want to mix and set the percentage of ink for each. Keep in mind that the more spot colors you use, the more it will cost to print the result (unless you convert them at print time to process colors).

Cyan	Magenta	Yellow	Black

1	2	3	4	5	6
P 227-2U	P 168-1U	P 13-1U	P 78-5U	P 263-1U	P 144-1U

3: 100% Y: 100%	3:100% K: 20%	4: 35% K: 10%	2: 100% K: 30%	1: 20% 2: 30% K: 20%	3: 100% 4: 100% K: 20%

1: 30% 5: 100%	1: 30% 3: 100% 5: 100%	1: 100% 3: 35% 6: 10%	3: 25% 4: 15% 6: 100%	3: 25% 4: 50% 5: 25%	3: 35% 4: 15% 6: 10%

You create mixed-ink swatches by combining colors at various percentages. The top row shows the four process colors (cyan, magenta, yellow, and black) and six Pantone uncoated colors. The middle row shows traditional duotones and tritones created with them, while the bottom row shows mixed-ink colors composed of multiple spot colors. The captions show the mixes, using the codes in the upper row to identify the colors used. Below is the New Mixed Ink Swatch dialog box where you actually mix the colors.

In addition to creating mixed-color swatches, InDesign can create a whole palette of related colors for you in one fell swoop, using the New Mixed Ink Group dialog box, shown at right. You get a swatch for each combination generated.

Copying Colors from an Image

Even if you have an excellent sense of color, matching colors by eye can be difficult. Because you may want to use a color from an image in your document — as a text color or for lines or strokes — an accurate color-matching tool is a necessity. Fortunately, InDesign has the Eyedropper tool to sample a color and then apply it to an object or to text. You can also create a color swatch from the sample for use later.

The color-selection process is simple: First, click the Fill iconic button or Stroke iconic button, in the Tools panel or the Swatches panel, to determine what will get the sampled color. Now select the Eyedropper tool in the Tools panel, and then click on any colored object in your document with the tool (circled in yellow above). The Fill or Stroke button displays the sampled color.

After clicking a color with the Eyedropper tool, the Eyedropper tool changes to the Marker tool, which applies the current fill and stroke to any text you highlight. For other objects, just click them with the Marker tool to apply the current fill to other objects (hold Shift to apply the stroke color to the current object's fill instead). You can toggle back to the Eyedropper tool to sample another color by holding the Option or Alt key.

To add the color to your Swatches panel, just Control+click or right-click the color in the Tools panel; the color will be added as an RGB-based process color. Or select New Color Swatch from the Swatches panel's flyout menu to be able to name the color and set options such as the color model and color type.

Sharing Colors with Others

Although you can't use the Eyedropper tool to sample colors in Photoshop or Illustrator documents, you can share colors with users of those programs, as well as with other InDesign users. In InDesign, select any swatches you want to export — only mixed-ink swatches cannot be shared this way — and choose Save Swatches from the flyout menu. Now save the swatches as an Adobe Swatch Exchange (.ase) file, which other Creative Suite applications can open. (These are also called ColorBook files.) In Photoshop and Illustrator, choose Save Swatches for Exchange from their Swatches panels' flyout menus. In all three programs, import colors using the Load Swatches flyout menu commands. To import mixed-color swatches across InDesign documents, you must open the document containing those swatches and then apply each of them, even if just temporarily, to an object in the new target document. That copies them to the target.

Working with Gradients

Gradients (also called blends) add a sense of motion or depth to a background or image. An image editor or illustration program such as Photoshop, Paint Shop Pro, Illustrator, or CorelDraw gives you very fine control over gradients, letting you control their shape and pattern. InDesign approaches the ability of such programs, and in some cases surpasses them. When combined with transparency and InDesign's light effects, you can really create some interesting effects, as shown in these two pages.

Two-color linear gradient	**Two-color radial gradient**
Even distribution, 0° angle	*Even distribution*
Even distribution, 30° angle	*75% midpoint*
45% start, 0° angle	*45% start*
Manual gradient	*Manual gradient*

Example gradients (at left), using various settings for the stop and start colors, as well as for the gradient midpoint and, for linear gradients, the angle. At bottom left is the New Gradient Swatch dialog box where you set the gradient's colors, stop points, angle, and other settings.

Use the Gradient Swatch tool to manually set the gradient angle and stop points (top image below). The length of the line determines how tight the gradient ramp is, while the angle of the line sets the gradient angle. (The line does not print.) The bottom image below shows the new Gradient Feather tool, which does essentially the same thing but blends to transparent.

Applying Color Tints and Transparency

Adding color to a grayscale image, whether at full strength or as a lighter tint, can greatly change its character. And applying transparency (by reducing its opacity from solid, or 100%) to text, images, and other objects can greatly change their look and feel.

Original grayscale image

Content: swatch applied

Content: duotone applied

Content: tritone applied

Content: 20% [Black]

Content: [Paper] (white)
Fill: [Black]

Content: 20% Plum
Fill: 10% Plum

Content: 100% Plum
Fill: 20% Yellow

From the Swatches panel, you can apply swatches to the contents of grayscale images to colorize them. (Be sure to select them with the Direct Selection tool before applying the color swatch.) By also coloring the fill (be sure to select it with the Selection tool), you can achieve interesting effects — especially when combined with tints. To do more-complex colorizing, use an image editor like Adobe Photoshop or Corel Paint Shop Pro.

Applied via the Effects panel, transparency can give new dimension to text and graphics. At left, I applied 60% opacity to the banners to give a vellum effect, then applied colored, partially transparent drop shadows to them.

Working with Lighting Effects

InDesign CS3 adopts a host of lighting effects that Photoshop has offered for a while (in its layer blending options), letting you create dimensional effects such as beveled edges and inner glows. Using the Effects panel, you can apply any of these effects (including several at once) to your choice of an object's fill, stroke, and/or contents. Below are several examples of the effects, as well as the panel's Effects dialog box, where you can find all the controls. Note that these effects rely on both transparency and color to carry out their design goals.

Example lighting effects. Top row: The original object, drop shadow, and inner shadow. Second row: Basic feather, directional feather, and gradient feather. Third row: Outer glow and inner glow. Bottom row: Bevel and emboss, and satin.

Normal	**Lighten**	**Normal**	**Lighten**
Multiply	**Difference**	**Multiply**	**Difference**
Overlay	**Exclusion**	**Overlay**	**Exclusion**
Soft Light	**Hue**	**Soft Light**	**Hue**
Hard Light	**Saturation**	**Hard Light**	**Saturation**
Color Dodge	**Color**	**Color Dodge**	**Color**
Color Burn	**Luminosity**	**Color Burn**	**Luminosity**
Darken		**Darken**	

The 15 blend modes affect how various lighting effects appear. At left, they are applied to the drop shadows of the text placed over a solid background. At right, the blend modes are applied to both the 80% opaque text and to its drop shadows over a 30% opaque image.

The Web's Limited Palette

Although the HTML supports thousands of colors, you can only count on 216 colors to display properly on popular Macintosh and Windows Web browsers. That's because most browsers play it safe and assume that people have just the basic video support on their computers: 8-bit color depth, which permits 256 colors. Of those 256, Windows reserves 40 for its interface, leaving 216 for the browser to use. Understanding this, InDesign comes with a Web-Safe swatch library that has only the colors that all browsers can display. Keep these limits in mind when you convert your print images to the Web's JPEG or GIF formats; whether you convert them using InDesign's Export to XHTML/Dreamweaver feature or in a program like Photoshop, expect the Web images' colors to shift and be less subtle.

The examples at left show how print-oriented colors (top row) are typically shifted when viewed in a Web browser (bottom row).

The InDesign swatch library at left shows all 216 Web-safe colors; by contrast, the number of colors that can be printed is in the millions.

Working with Traps

If you don't have your InDesign documents output to negatives or directly to plate and have them printed on a standard web offset press (SWOP, or Specifications for Web Offset Printing), you don't need to worry about trapping. But if you do such professional output, *trapping* is an issue you should be aware of. InDesign lets you control trapping in some situations, based on what kind of output device you are using. These controls are global — affecting everything in the document — so if you want to set specific trapping settings for graphics, for example, you need to do so as part of creating the illustration in a program like Illustrator or CorelDraw. The one local control InDesign does offer is whether strokes and fills overprint or trap.

Knockout (no overlap of abutting colors)

Overprint

Centering (light color and dark color move into each other)

Choke (dark color moves into light color)

Spread (light color moves into dark color)

Above: The various trapping methods you can use in InDesign. Except for overprinting, each method is applied to every object in your document.

Adjusting Color for Output

Like most professional design tools, InDesign uses color profiles (Edit ➪ Color Settings) to help ensure that your output matches as closely as possible the original image's colors (the capabilities and limits of your output device ultimately determine how close you can get). By applying color profiles and using InDesign's Rendering Intent color settings, you can change the output character of your images.

You should set your document to use the appropriate RGB color profile for your monitor or scanner, as well as the appropriate CMYK profile for your printer or printing press to get the most accurate color. A mismatch between the profile and the input and output devices can shift the color of your images. The images at left have the following settings, clockwise from upper left: default settings; NTSC with relative colorimetic rendering; CIE RGB/absolute colorimetric rendering; and Wide Gamut RGB/saturated.

That's why it's best to think *Swatches panel* when you think about adding or editing colors instead of the more obvious *Color panel*. And even better is to remove the Colors panel from your user interface by clicking its close box, so you don't get tempted to use it.

Importing and sampling colors

InDesign lets you add colors to your document from other sources, such as importing swatch files, adding colors from imported graphics automatically, and letting you sample a color from an imported image.

Importing swatches

You can import colors from other InDesign, Illustrator, and Illustrator EPS files by choosing Load Swatches from the Swatches panel's flyout menu. Plus, you can also import colors from Adobe Swatch Exchange library files this way. From the resulting dialog box, navigate to the file that contains the colors you want to import, select that file, and click Open.

TIP A quick way to import specific color swatches from another InDesign document or template is to click and drag the colors from that other file's Swatches panel into your current document or template.

QUARKXPRESS When you import color swatches from other documents or from Adobe Swatch Exchange files, InDesign brings in *all* the colors. You cannot choose specific colors to import, as you can in QuarkXPress.

So you can share those swatches with other Creative Suite 2 and 3 users, InDesign lets you save swatches into color library files. Just select the colors you want to save, and then choose Save Swatches from the Swatches panel's flyout menu. You're asked to give the Adobe Swatch Exchange file a name before you save it.

You can also import an Illustrator color library, adding its set of swatches to InDesign. To do so, create a new swatch as described earlier in this chapter. In the New Color Swatch dialog box, choose Other Library from the Color Mode pop-up menu. You get a dialog box from which you select any color, tint, or gradient swatch library file in the old Adobe Illustrator 8 format. (You can't use Illustrator's patterned swatches, but don't worry if the swatch file contains them; InDesign simply ignores them.)

Importing colors from graphics

When you import a graphic file in EPS format or in PDF, any named colors (swatches) in that file are automatically added to the Swatches panel. But sometimes the colors won't print accurately from InDesign:

- Even though InDesign does not support Hexachrome colors, it does retain any Hexachrome colors in an imported PDF file. These Hexachrome colors print as CMYK if you print from InDesign; note that many Hexachrome colors do not print properly when converted to CMYK. But if you export your InDesign file to a PDF file, those Hexachrome colors are retained and print as Hexachrone colors, assuming your printer can print PDF files directly.

- Colors in imported EPS files may not print as expected (you can minimize this chance by using popular programs such as the latest versions of Adobe Illustrator, CorelDraw, and Adobe Macromedia FreeHand). One of three things can happen:

  - Each color prints on its own plate (as if it were a spot color), even if you defined it as a process color.

  - A spot color is color-separated into CMYK even when you define it as a spot color in both the source program and in InDesign.

  - A color prints as black.

Sampling colors

Many types of graphics, such as bitmap images, don't use named colors or swatches. But InDesign lets you *sample* colors in such graphics, determining the RGB values and then letting you create a swatch from them. Here's how:

1. **In the Tools panel or Swatches panel, choose the Fill iconic button or Stroke iconic button.** It doesn't really matter which unless you will immediately create a shape or enter text after capturing the desired color; in that case choose whichever aspect you'll want the new object or text to have the color applied to.

2. **Select the Eyedropper tool and then click on the graphic where the desired color is used.** The Fill or Stroke iconic button will now have that color. (If the Eyedropper tool is not visible in the Tools panel, look for the Measure tool, then click and hold down its icon to get the pop-up menu that lets you select the Eyedropper tool.)

3. **The Eyedropper tool changes to the Marker tool.** Any object you select with the Marker tool has the color applied to its fill or stroke, depending on whether the Fill or Stroke iconic button is active. Note you can switch between the Eyedropper and Marker tool to select different colors and apply them by holding the Option or Alt key to get the Eyedropper tool back, then releasing it to switch to the Marker tool.

 If you apply a sampled color via the Marker tool, it will be an unnamed color. It's best to first create a swatch from your sampled color so you can ensure consistent color usage.

4. **To add the new, unnamed color to the Swatches panel, Control+click or right-click the Fill iconic button or Stroke iconic button (whichever has the captured color) and choose Add to Swatches from the contextual menu that appears.** (Or just drag the color to the Swatches panel.) Now you can edit and apply the captured color like any other color swatch.

Figure 8.7 shows a composite image that highlights the Eyedropper tool at center left and the Marker tool at right.

FIGURE 8.7

At left: sampling a color with the Eyedropper tool. At right: applying that sampled color to an object using the Marker tool.

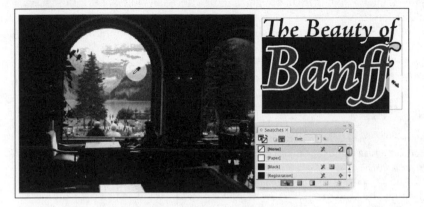

Color Considerations for Imported Graphics

When you work with imported graphics, whether they are illustrations or scanned photographs, color is part of the graphic file. So the responsibility for color controls lies primarily with the creator of the graphic. It is best to use color files in CMYK EPS or DCS format (for illustrations and vector art) or CMYK TIFF format (for scans and bitmaps). These standards are de facto for color publishing, so InDesign is particularly adept at working with them. (See Chapter 26 for details on preparing graphics files for import.)

Although printing uses CMYK, computers use RGB as the color model, since monitors use red, green, and blue electron guns to display images. The dilemma most designers face is that an RGB image displays properly on-screen but may appear with slightly adjusted hues in print, while a CMYK image may print correctly but appear incorrectly on-screen. Most designers get good at mentally shifting the colors from one model to another as they see the results of their work in print over time. Until that happens, rely on color proofs from your printer to see what your images actually look like when printed.

Do note that color files pasted via the Clipboard should print properly after they're pasted into an InDesign graphics frame. But problems, such as dropped colors or altered colors, sometimes occur depending on the applications involved and the amount of memory available. If you click and drag files from Photoshop or Illustrator directly into InDesign rather than using copy and paste, you should have no such problems.

Working with Gradients

A technique that has been popular for a long time among designers is the gradient, which blends two or more colors in a sequence, going from, say, green to blue to yellow to orange. InDesign has a powerful gradient creation feature that lets you define and apply gradients to pretty much any object you create in InDesign: Text, lines, frames, shapes, and their outlines (strokes).

 Gradients go by several names among artists. Included among them are *blends* and *graduated fills.*

Creating gradients

In the Swatches panel, where you define colors and tints you can also define gradients: Just use the New Gradient Swatch option in the flyout menu. You get the dialog box shown in Figure 8.8. The first two options are straightforward:

- **Type a name for the gradient in the Swatch Name field.** Picking a name is a bit more difficult than it is for a color, but use something like "Blue to Red" or "Bright Multihue" or "Logo Gradient" that has a meaning specific to the colors used or to its role in your document.

- **In the Type pop-up menu, choose Linear or Radial.** A linear blend goes in one direction, while a radial blend radiates out in a circle from a central point. (Later in this section, Figure 8.11 shows some example gradients.)

Now it gets a little tricky. Follow these steps:

1. **Select a stop point — one of the squares at the bottom of the dialog box, on either side of the gradient ramp that shows the gradient as you define it.** The stop points are essentially the from-and-to colors, with the from being the stop point at left and the to being the stop point at right. With a stop point selected, you can now define its color.

2. **Choose what color model you want to define the color in — select from CMYK, RGB, Lab, and Swatches in the Stop Color pop-up menu.** The area directly beneath the pop-up menu changes accordingly, displaying sliders for CMYK, RGB, and LabB, as well as a list of all colors from the Swatches panel for the Swatches option.

3. **Create or select the color you want for that stop point.**

 You can also click and drag swatches from the Swatches panel to the gradient ramp. (Use the [Paper] swatch for white.)

4. **Repeat Steps 1 and 2 for the other stop point.** Note that the color model for the two stop points don't have to be the same — you can blend from a Pantone spot color to a CMYK color, for example.

FIGURE 8.8

The New Gradient Swatch dialog box

You now have a simple gradient. But you don't have to stop there. Here are your options:

- You can change the rate at which the colors transition by sliding the diamond icon at the top of the gradient ramp.
- You can create additional stop points by clicking right below the gradient ramp. By having several stop points, you can have multiple color transitions in a gradient. (Think of them like tab stops in text — you can define as many as you need.) You delete unwanted stop points by clicking and dragging them to the bottom of the dialog box.

Notice that there's a diamond icon between each pair of stop points — that means each can have its own transition rate. Figure 8.9 shows a complex gradient being defined.

TIP   When you create a new gradient, InDesign uses the settings from the last one you created. To create a gradient similar to an existing one, click on that existing gradient before selecting New Gradient Swatch from the flyout menu. InDesign copies the selected gradient's settings to the new one, which you can then edit. One reason to use this is to create, say, a radial version of an existing linear gradient.

QUARKXPRESS   InDesign's gradient controls are much more sophisticated than QuarkXPress's simple two-color blend controls. Plus, InDesign lets you save your gradient settings as swatches for easy reuse; QuarkXPress does not.

The Swatches panel shows a preview of the actual gradient next to its name. You can also see the pattern in the Fill iconic button or Stroke iconic button in the Tools panel if that gradient is currently selected as a fill or stroke, as well as in the Gradient iconic button in that panel, whether or not it's currently applied as a fill or stroke.

If a gradient mixes spot colors and process colors, InDesign converts the spot colors to process colors.

FIGURE 8.9

A complex, multihued gradient being defined

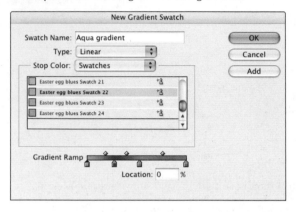

Creating unnamed gradients

Just as it does with colors, InDesign lets you create *unnamed gradients* — gradients that have no swatches. My caution on using this feature for colors applies less for gradients because all colors in a gradient are converted to process colors and/or use defined spot-color swatches — so there are no unnamed colors in their output. Here's how it works:

1. **Select the object to which you want to apply the gradient.** Make sure the stroke or fill, as appropriate, is active in the Tools panel.

2. **Go to the Gradient panel (Window ⇨ Gradient), shown in Figure 8.10.**

3. **Select a stop point.**

4. **Now go to the Color panel or Swatches panel.** The Color panel is usually in the same panel group as the Gradient panel, but choose Window ⇨ Color or press F6 to display it if not. Open the Swatches panel by choosing Window ⇨ Swatches or pressing F5.

5. **In the Colors panel, create a color using the CMYK, RGB, or Lab models.** (Use the flyout menu to choose the model.) Or click and drag a swatch from the Swatches panel onto the stop point.

6. **Repeat Steps 2 through 5 for the other stop point.**

7. **Create any additional stop points by clicking below the gradient ramp, and adjust the transition controls as desired.**

FIGURE 8.10

The Gradient panel is used for creating unnamed gradients and for adjusting the angles of linear gradients and the starting locations of any gradients.

Adjusting gradient angle and location

After you apply a linear gradient — whether via a gradient swatch or as an unnamed gradient — you can change the angle of the gradient, as done with the bottom middle gradient in Figure 8.11 (compare it to the otherwise identical object at the bottom right).

To rotate a gradient, you use the Gradient panel — you cannot set rotation in a gradient swatch itself. In the Gradient panel, type a value in the Angle field to rotate the gradient's direction. That's it! You can't rotate a radial gradient because it's circular and, thus, any rotation has no effect. That's why InDesign grays out the Angle field for radial gradients.)

You can adjust the location of a linear or radial gradient by entering a value in the Location field in the Gradient panel or using the Gradient Swatch tool in the Tools panel. The Location field lets you specify a precise location for where the gradient starts, but it's not visually intuitive for most designers to work this way.

NEW FEATURE The Gradient Swatch tool is the new name for the previous versions' Gradient tool. Its functionality is unchanged.

The Gradient Swatch tool provides a more visual approach. To use it, select the Gradient Swatch tool and draw a line in the object, as shown in Figure 8.12. The origination point, angle, and length of the line drawn with the Gradient Swatch tool determine the result. Shorter lines confine the color transition to a small area, while longer ones broaden it. Keep these points in mind when you use the tool:

- For a linear gradient, the start point corresponds to where you want the first stop point of the gradient to be, while the end point corresponds to the last point. This lets you stretch or compress the gradient, as well as offset the gradient within the object. Also, the angle at which you draw the line becomes the angle for the gradient.

- For a radial gradient, the line becomes the start and endpoint for the gradient, in effect offsetting it, as done in the upper-left gradient in Figure 8.11 (compare it to the standard gradient setting for the same object at upper right).

NEW FEATURE The new Gradient Feather tool — accessed from the Gradient Swatch tool's pop-out menu or via the shortcut Shift+G — works just like the Gradient Swatch tool except that it makes a gradient that goes from transparent to the chosen color, as Figure 8.12 shows. To remove a gradient feather effect, uncheck the Gradient Feather option in the Effects panel, as explained in Chapter 12.

FIGURE 8.11

Examples of gradients. Top row: A two-color linear gradient (left) with variations that have different transition controls. Second row: A four-color gradient (left) with variations that have different transition controls. Third row: The second row's gradients with various angles applied. Fourth row: A two-color radial gradient (left), the same gradient reversed (center), and with a different transition control (right). Bottom row: the fourth row's gradients modified using the Gradient Swatch tool (see Figure 8.12).

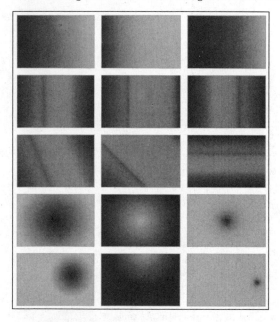

FIGURE 8.12

The Gradient Swatch tool (left) lets you set the offset, adjust the gradient length, and (for gradient blends) adjust the gradient angle. The origination point, angle, and length of the line drawn with the Gradient Swatch tool determine the result. The Gradient Feather tool (right) acts like the Gradient Swatch tool except that it starts with transparent as the initial "color."

Managing Swatches

When you create colors, tints, and gradients (described later in this chapter), you may find it easy to go overboard and make too many. You'll also find that different documents have different colors, each created by different people, and you'll likely want to move colors from one document to another. InDesign provides basic tools for managing swatches in and across documents.

TIP   To help simplify working with swatches, you can have InDesign show just color and tint swatches, just gradient swatches, or all swatches by using the iconic buttons at the bottom of the Swatches panel. Figure 8.1 illustrates which iconic button does what.

Editing swatches

Editing swatches is pretty easy in InDesign: For any swatch in the Swatches panel, just double-click the swatch's preview or the swatch's name, or choose Swatch Options from the flyout menu.

The Swatch Options dialog box (called Gradient Options for gradient swatches) will then appear. The dialog box will differ based on what type of swatch you are editing, but in all cases it is identical except for the dialog box name to the dialog box you used to create the swatch with in the first place, such as the New Color Swatch or New Tint Swatch dialog boxes shown earlier in this chapter.

Make any adjustments and click OK when you're done. Voilà! Your swatch is now changed.

CAUTION   When editing a tint, the Swatch Options dialog box also lets you change the other attributes of the color. If you change those settings in the tint, all other tints based on the original color, as well as the original color, are changed accordingly. If you want to change a setting of just the tint — such as making it a spot color while leaving the original color a process color — you need to duplicate the original color and make a tint from that duplicate.

Merging swatches

InDesign also lets you merge swatches — select multiple swatches and then choose Merge Swatches from the Swatches panel's flyout menu — but I suggest you avoid this. When InDesign merges swatches, it tries to calculate a new value based on the swatches' values, essentially weighting the CMYK values (RGB and other values are converted to CMYK first). But it's a crapshoot: You are not likely to get the color you expect. If you want a shade between two colors, I recommend you create it as a new swatch, manually entering the desired CMYK (or RGB or Lab) values.

Deleting swatches

InDesign makes deleting swatches easy: Just select the color, tint, or gradient in the Swatches panel. Then choose Delete Swatch from the flyout menu, or click the Delete Swatch iconic button at the bottom of the Swatches panel.

Well, that's not quite it. You then get the dialog box shown in Figure 8.13, which lets you assign anything using the deleted swatch to a new color (the Defined Swatch option) or leave the color on any object that happens to be using it, but delete the swatch from the Swatches panel (the Unnamed

Swatch option). (As I explain earlier in this chapter, unnamed colors should be avoided, so if your document is using a color, keep its swatch.)

CAUTION   If you delete a tint and replace it with another color, any object using that tint gets the full-strength version of the new color, not a tint of it.

Likewise, if you delete a color swatch that you've based one or more tints on, those tints are also deleted if you replace the deleted swatch with an unnamed swatch. However, if you delete a color swatch and replace it with another swatch, those tint swatches based on the original color swatch will remain but use the new color instead.

TIP   InDesign offers a nice option to quickly find all unused colors in the Swatches panel — the flyout menu's Select All Unused option. Then you can just delete them in one fell swoop.

NOTE   Remember that when you select swatches for deletion or duplication, you can ⌘+click or Ctrl+click multiple swatches to work on all of them at once. Note that Shift+clicking selects all swatches between the first swatch clicked and the swatch that you Shift+click, whereas ⌘+click or Ctrl+click lets you select specific swatches in any order and in any location in the panel.

TIP   If you delete a swatch and replace it with an unnamed swatch, you can recapture that deleted swatch later by choosing the Add Unnamed Colors menu item in the Swatches panel's flyout menu.

FIGURE 8.13

The Delete Swatch dialog box lets you replace a deleted color with a new one or leave the color applied to objects using it.

Duplicating swatches

To duplicate a swatch so you can create a new one based on it, use the Duplicate Swatch option in the Swatches panel. The word *copy* is added to its name, and you edit it — including its name — as you would any swatch.

Applying Colors, Tints, and Gradients

Applying colors, tints, and gradients to objects in InDesign is easy. Select the object, then click the Formatting Affects Text iconic button or Formatting Affects Container iconic button in the Swatches panel or Tools panel, as appropriate for what you want to apply the color to, and then click the appropriate swatch. In either case, you can also choose whether to apply the attribute to the object's fill or stroke by clicking the Fill or Stroke iconic button in the Swatches panel or Tools panel.

NOTE You can apply colors and tints to grayscale and black-and-white bitmapped images, such as those in the TIFF and Photoshop formats. But you cannot color vector-based graphics (such as those in the Illustrator and EPS formats) or color bitmapped images.

CROSS-REF Although you cannot apply a tint to a color bitmapped image, you can achieve a similar effect by making it (or any bitmapped image) partially or fully transparent, as explained in Chapter 12.

Once you've determined what you want to apply the color, tint, or gradient to, you can use the Swatches panel to select a swatch, or pick the last-used color and gradient from the Apply Color and Apply Gradient iconic buttons on the Tools panel. Figure 8.14 shows the panel. (You can't apply tints this way.)

For tints, you can also enter a tint value in the Swatches panel's Tint field. (You would use a swatch for tints you want to use repeatedly in your layout, such as for the background tint in sidebar boxes, to ensure consistency. You would use the Tint field for tints you are applying on the fly, typically for one-time use.)

You can also apply colors and tints (but not gradients) to *gaps* in strokes through the Stroke panel's fly-out options menu: Select Show Options and select a swatch from the Gap Color pop-up menu. You can apply a tint by entering a value in the Gap Tint field, or by choosing a value from its pop-up menu.

FIGURE 8.14

The Tools panel lets you choose what part of an object you want to color, as well as apply the last-used color or gradient.

Eyedropper tool

Swap Fill and Stroke button

Stroke button

Formatting Affects Contents button

Apply None button

Fill button

Apply Gradient button

Default Fill and Stroke button

Apply Color button

Formatting Affects Container button

Summary

Using color in publishing involves complex decisions. There are many ways to define colors, but they don't all result in the same colors when you finally print your documents. That's why choosing the color models for your documents up front is important.

Color can also be expensive to print, so you may need to weigh when you use color and how you apply it. A spot color — a single ink — is cheaper to print than full color (produced by combining four process colors) but, of course, it gives you less visual flexibility. You can also mix spot colors with process colors to add special colors such as pastels and metallics that process colors cannot produce.

Key to defining colors is choosing the appropriate color model: spot or process. A spot color prints on its own plate, while a process color is separated into the four basic colors used in traditional color publishing. If you define too many colors as spot colors, you're likely to create an impossible-to-print or a very expensive-to-print document. InDesign lets you convert colors from spot to process and vice versa, so you can choose the right output options for each document. Similarly, it's best to create color images in the color model you intend to use for output: CMYK for traditional printing and RGB for on-screen display.

InDesign uses swatches to contain defined colors (including colors made up of other colors), tints, and gradient blends; the use of swatches lets you apply colors repeatedly with the assurance it's the same color each time, much as character and paragraph styles ensure consistent text formatting. Although you can also apply colors without using these swatches, doing so can cause output problems, especially when you're using color separations.

To maintain consistency of colors, InDesign can import colors from other InDesign documents, as well as from Adobe swatch files known as Adobe Swatch Exchange files. InDesign also imports colors used in EPS and PDF files.

A powerful feature in InDesign is its capability to create gradient blends that can contain blends among multiple colors. No other layout program offers this level of control or flexibility on gradients, although image editors such as Photoshop go even further than InDesign does.

Part III

Object Fundamentals

IN THIS PART

Chapter 9
Adding Frames and Lines

Chapter 10
Manipulating Objects

Chapter 11
Transforming Objects

Chapter 12
Applying Effects to Objects

Chapter 13
Orchestrating Objects

Chapter 9

Adding Frames and Lines

IN THIS CHAPTER

Knowing how and when to create frames for text and graphics

Creating text frames

Creating graphics frames

Converting frames for specific content

Drawing straight lines

When you create a new InDesign document, you make several important decisions, including the page size, number of columns, and gutter width, that determine the basic structure of your publication. After you click OK in the New Document dialog box (File ➪ New ➪ Document, or ⌘+N or Ctrl+N), you're greeted with a blank first page. Much like an artist confronting an empty canvas, it's now time for you to add the text, graphics, and graphic elements (shapes and lines) that make up the final piece.

InDesign uses *objects* as the building blocks you manipulate to create finished pages. An object is a container that can (but doesn't have to) hold text or graphics, as well as attributes such as color, strokes, and gradients; when an object contains an imported graphic or text, or if an object is created as a placeholder for a graphic or text, it's referred to as a *frame*. A frame looks and behaves much the same as an object but has some additional properties:

- If you change the size or shape of a frame that contains text, you affect the flow of text in the frame and in any subsequent frames of a multiframe story.

- If you change the size or shape of a frame that contains an imported graphic, you also change the portion of the graphic that's visible.

Designing pages in InDesign is largely a matter of creating and modifying frames and modifying the text and graphics the frames contain. If, for example, you're creating a simple, one-page publication such as a business card, an advertisement, or a poster, you likely add several text frames to the page; each text frame holds a different piece of textual information. In the case of a business card, text frames would contain the company name, the name and title of the cardholder, the company address and phone numbers, and so on.

If you want to include photos or computer-generated illustrations in your piece — maybe you want to add an EPS version of a corporate logo to your business card or a scanned image to an ad — you must also add graphics frames. A graphics frame serves as the cropping shape for the graphic within.

In this chapter, I show you how to create and modify basic text frames, graphics frames, shapes, and straight lines. After you create a text frame, you can type text directly into it or you can place a text file from a word-processing program. (For information about importing, formatting, and flowing text through a document, see Part IV.) After you create a graphics frame, you can import a graphic into it and then crop, scale, or apply other effects to the graphic. (For more information about importing and modifying graphics, see Part V.)

InDesign offers tools to create both frames and shapes, which work the same way as each other. Visually, a graphics frame has an X placed through it, as a reminder that you can place contents into it (an ancient layout convention), while a shape — what InDesign calls an *unassigned frame* — does not, presumably because you are using it not as a container but as a printing object. (A text frame looks just like a shape.) But the difference between frames and shapes is artificial, because a shape can easily become a frame simply by placing text or graphics into it. So for all practical purposes, shapes and frames are the same thing. In this book, I use the word *frame* to mean either frames or shapes.

This chapter focuses on creating simple frames and straight lines. But InDesign also lets you create complex shapes and convert them to frames for holding text and graphics. And you can modify frames and other shapes. For more information about using InDesign's Pen tool to create free-form shapes and curved lines and to modify existing frames and shapes, see Chapter 28.

Creating frames and lines is also typically just an early step in the layout process. You want to modify and use those objects for various layout objectives. The Control panel provides the basic controls for objects all in one place, and Chapter 10 covers this versatile panel in more depth. Chapter 11 covers ways to modify objects, and Chapter 12 covers special effects you can apply to objects. InDesign also lets you save object styles so you can apply the same settings to multiple frames or lines and keep them in synch; Chapter 13 covers this feature in more detail.

> **TIP** When you create a frame or shape, you can align the frame edge with a guideline by clicking within the number of pixels specified in the Snap to Zone in the Guides & Pasteboard pane of the Preferences dialog box, as Chapter 3 explains.

Creating a Text Frame

All the text blocks, called *stories,* in an InDesign document are contained in text frames. Unlike a word-processing program, which doesn't let you do anything but type text, InDesign requires you to create a text frame before you can add text to a page using the keyboard. (If you want to import the text from a word-processing file onto a page, you don't have to create a text frame before you import.) After you create a new text frame, you can type and format text, move or resize the frame, and add graphic effects to the frame edge and the frame background.

CROSS-REF For information about importing text, see Chapter 14. Chapter 13 shows you how to anchor frames to text, so frames follow the text as it reflows, a useful feature for figures, tables, and sidebars.

The Tools panel contains several tools for creating both shapes and graphics frames, and because any shape or graphics frame can be converted into a text frame, you can use any of these tools to create a container that you intend to fill with text. However, in most cases, your text is contained within simple, rectangular text frames, and the quickest and easiest way to create such a frame is with the Type tool; it's the tool with a big T on it.

TIP If you want to place a particular piece of text on every page in a multipage publication (for example, the title of a book), you should place the text frame on a master page, as explained in Chapter 7.

Here's how to create a text frame:

1. **Select the Type tool by clicking it or by pressing T.**

2. **Move the I-beam pointer (also called the *text cursor*) anywhere within the currently displayed page or on the pasteboard.**

3. **Click and hold the mouse button, and while holding down the mouse button, drag in any direction.** As you drag, a cross-hair pointer appears in the corner opposite your starting point; a colored rectangle indicates the boundary of the frame, as shown in Figure 9.1. (The color is blue for objects on the default layer; objects on other layers have that layer's color. See Chapter 5 for more on layers.) You can look at the width and height values displayed in the Control panel or the Transform panel as you drag to help you get the size you want. Holding down the Shift key as you drag creates a square.

FIGURE 9.1

Creating a text frame with the Type tool is a simple matter of clicking and dragging until the rectangle that appears as you drag is approximately the size and shape of the intended text block.

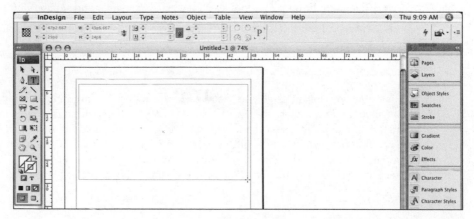

4. **When the frame is the size and shape you want, release the mouse button.** The flashing cursor appears in the finished frame, indicating that you can use the keyboard to type new text. Don't worry too much about being precise when you create a text frame: You can always go back later and fine-tune its size and position.

At this point, you can begin typing, or you can click and drag elsewhere on the page or pasteboard to create another text frame. You can create as many new text frames as you want. Just make sure not to click in an existing text frame when your intention is to create a new one. If you click within an existing frame when the Type tool is selected, the flashing cursor appears and InDesign thinks you want to type text.

CROSS-REF   Chapter 14 covers the methods to add text to frames.

You can type or import text into *any* empty frame, not just those created with the Type tool. When creating nonrectangular frames, you cannot use the Type tool but must use the Pen, Pencil, or one of the frame or shape tools.

Creating a Graphics Frame

Although you can use InDesign's illustration features to create the kind of vector graphics that can be created with dedicated illustration programs such as Illustrator, FreeHand, and CorelDraw, you may find yourself needing to import an illustration that you or somebody else created using another program. You may also want to add other kinds of digital images to a publication, such as a scanned photograph, a piece of clip art stored on a CD-ROM, or a stock photograph that you've downloaded from the Internet.

In InDesign, all imported graphics are contained within graphics frames. The Tools panel contains three tools for drawing graphics frames:

- **Ellipse Frame:** This tool lets you create oval and round frames.
- **Rectangle Frame:** This tool lets you create rectangular and square frames.
- **Polygon Frame:** This tool lets you create equilateral polygons and starburst-shaped frames.

There are three equivalent shape tools: Ellipse, Rectangle, and Polygon.

The first time you use InDesign, the Rectangle Frame tool is displayed in the Tools panel, as is the Rectangle tool for creating shapes that hold neither text nor graphics. (The frame tools have an *X* through their icons.) To access the other frame tools, click and hold on the Rectangle Frame tool to display a pop-out menu with the Ellipse Frame and Polygon Frame tools. Drag and release to select a different frame tool. When you do, it replaces the Rectangle Frame tool in the Tools panel until the next time you change the tool. (You have the same options for the shape tools.)

Here's how to add a new graphics frame:

1. **Select the Ellipse Frame tool, the Rectangle Frame tool (or press F), or the Polygon Frame tool.**

2. **Move the cross-hair pointer anywhere within the currently displayed page or on the pasteboard.**

3. **Click and hold the mouse button, and while holding down the mouse button, drag in any direction.** As you drag, the cross-hair pointer appears in the corner opposite your starting point and a blue shape indicates the boundary of the frame. You can look at the width and height values displayed in the Control panel or Transform panel as you drag to help you get the size you want. Holding down the Shift key as you drag creates a circle if the Ellipse Frame tool is selected, a square if the Rectangle Frame tool is selected, and an equilateral polygon or starburst if the Polygon Frame tool is selected.

4. **When the frame is the size and shape you want, release the mouse button.** Don't worry too much about being precise when you create a graphics frame. You can always go back later and fine-tune it. Figure 9.2 shows an oval graphics frame.

When any of the frame-creation tools is selected, you can create as many new frames as you want. Simply keep clicking, dragging, and releasing.

CAUTION Don't try to click a frame handle when a frame-creation tool is selected. Instead of moving the handle you are clicking, you end up creating a new frame. You have to switch to one of the selection tools to move or resize a graphics frame.

CROSS-REF See Part V for details on importing graphics and modifying imported graphics.

FIGURE 9.2

Creating a graphics frame with any of the frame-creation tools is the same as creating a text frame with the Type tool. Choose the appropriate frame tool, and then click, drag, and release. In this example, an elliptical graphics frame has just been created; its bounding box appears with resizing handles.

Creating Custom Polygons

You can configure the Polygon tool and the Polygon Frame tool to create either regular polygons or starburst shapes. Double-click either of the Polygon tools to display the Polygon Settings dialog box, shown below. The value in the Number of Sides field determines how many sides your polygons have. If you want to create a starburst shape, specify a value in the Star Inset field. As you increase the percentage value, the spikes become longer and pointier. When you change the values in the Polygon Settings dialog box, the new values are used for both versions of the polygon tool.

You cannot modify an existing polygon's attributes by selecting the polygon and then opening the Polygon Settings dialog box. You must either edit its shape with the Direct Selection tool, as covered in Chapter 28, or change attributes in the Polygon Settings dialog box and create a new polygon.

Note that you can set separate defaults for the Polygon Frame and Polygon tools, letting you have two default settings available at any time.

Converting Frames for Specific Content

It makes no difference whether you use a frame tool or a shape tool — or even the Type tool — to create a frame that you want to hold a graphic. Similarly, you don't have to use the Type tool to create a frame that will hold text. Just select an empty frame and import text or a graphic into it. InDesign automatically converts the frame into the appropriate type.

Note that if you import a graphic into a text frame that already has text in it, the graphic is added as an inline graphic within the text, as Chapter 13 explains. (You cannot add text to a graphics frame that already has a graphic in it.)

You can also choose Object ⇨ Content ⇨ Graphic to convert a shape or text frame to a graphic frame. Or choose Object ⇨ Content ⇨ Unassigned to convert a text frame or graphics frame to a shape. There's really little reason to do so, given that InDesign converts the frame automatically when you place content into it. But you might use these commands to convert empty frames into the desired type so it's clear later on what they're supposed to be used for.

Drawing Straight Lines

Although they're not as flashy or versatile as graphics shapes and frames, lines can serve many useful purposes in well-designed pages. For example, plain ol' vertical rules can be used to separate columns of text in a multicolumn page or the rows and columns of data in a table. Dashed lines are useful for indicating folds and cut lines on brochures and coupons. And lines with arrowheads are handy if you have to create a map or a technical illustration.

InDesign lets you create straight lines with the Line tool and zigzag lines, curved lines, and free-form shapes with the Pen and Pencil tools. In this chapter, I keep things simple and limit the coverage to the Line tool.

CROSS-REF For information about using the Pen and Pencil tools, see Chapter 28.

To draw a straight line:

1. **Select the Line tool (or press \).**
2. **Move the I-beam pointer anywhere within the currently displayed page or on the pasteboard.**
3. **Click and hold the mouse button, and while holding down the mouse button, drag in any direction.** As you drag, a thin, blue line appears from the point where you first clicked to the current position of the cross-hair pointer. Holding down the Shift key as you drag constrains the line to horizontal, vertical, or a 45-degree diagonal.
4. **When the line is the length and angle you want, release the mouse button.** Don't worry too much about being precise when you create a line. You can always go back later and fine-tune it. Figure 9.3 shows a new line.

TIP When you create a line, it takes on the settings in the Stroke panel (Window ⇨ Stroke or ⌘+F10 or Ctrl+F10). The default line width is 1 point. To change the width of a selected line, double-click the Line tool and adjust the Weight in the Stroke panel that appears. If you make this adjustment when no document is open, all new documents use the new settings.

When the Line tool is selected, you can create as many new lines as you want. Simply keep clicking, dragging, and releasing.

FIGURE 9.3

After you create a line with the Line tool, the active line appears either within a rectangular bounding box that has eight resizing handles (if the Selection tool was previously selected; left) or with anchor points at both ends (if the Direct Selection tool was previously selected; right).

Summary

Empty objects, frames that hold text and graphics, and lines are the fundamental building blocks of pages. InDesign's Tools panel contains several tools for creating these objects. The easiest way to create a text frame is by clicking and dragging a rectangle with the Type tool.

Frames created for text or graphics, or to hold nothing, can actually hold text or graphics; InDesign converts them to the appropriate frame type based on what you put in them.

The Line tool lets you draw straight lines.

Chapter 10

Manipulating Objects

The primary purpose of the text frames and graphics frames that you add to the pages of your InDesign documents is to hold text and graphics, and much of the time you spend using InDesign involves modifying the appearance of the text and graphics you put in your frames. However, like real-world containers — bags, boxes, cartons, and cans — text frames and graphics frames exist independently of their contents (they don't even have to have any contents), and you can modify the position, shape, and appearance of frames without affecting the text and graphics within.

In this chapter, you learn how to do perform basic manipulations on the objects that you add to your pages: select, move, copy, delete, and position. If you've ever worked with a page-layout or illustration program, many of the basic techniques for manipulating objects should seem very familiar.

CROSS-REF For information on resizing, rotating, and applying other transformations to objects, see Chapter 11. For information on applying strokes and other effects to objects, see Chapter 12. For information on working with the text within a frame, see Part IV. For information on working with imported graphics, see Part V.

IN THIS CHAPTER

Selecting objects and understanding tool differences

Moving, copying, and deleting objects

Working with snippets

Preventing objects from printing

Aligning and distributing multiple objects

Using gridlines and guidelines when positioning objects

Selecting Objects

If you want to manipulate or transform an object, you must first select it. To select an object, you must first choose a selection tool. InDesign offers three tools for selecting objects: the Selection tool (the solid arrow icon; shortcut V), the Direct Selection tool (the hollow arrow icon; shortcut A), and the Pointer tool (the crop-tool-and-hand icon; no shortcut).

When an object is selected, various commands and controls for changing its position and appearance become available depending on how you select it, what panels are open, and what the object is.

Understanding the selection tools

All InDesign objects — unassigned shapes, text and graphics frames, and straight and curved lines — have at least two levels of selection. You can select the object itself, or you can select the rectangular bounding box that encloses the object. (For rectangular objects, the bounding box and the shape are the same.) The tool that you choose — typically, either the Selection tool or the Direct Selection tool — determines what you can do to the object you select:

- **Selection tool:** This tool lets you select an entire object by clicking anywhere in it. This is the best tool to use if you want to move or resize an object's container. For a text object, resizing the frame does not affect the text size, but for a graphics object, both the frame and graphic are resized. (You can also resize objects with the Direct Selection tool.) When you click an object with the Selection tool, the object's bounding box is selected.

- **Direct Selection tool:** This tool lets you select any of the individual anchor points (and direction handles of free-form shapes and curved lines) on an object. If you click with the Direct Selection tool on an object that has a bounding box, the shape within is selected; the bounding box is not selected. You use this tool to work on the object independent of its container frame. You can also move a graphic within its frame by clicking within the object with the Direct Selection tool and then dragging the graphic.

Tool Differences: Selection versus Direct Selection

For QuarkXPress users, the difference between the Selection tool and the Direct Selection tool takes some getting used to. In terms of working with content, the Direct Selection tool is much like QuarkXPress's Content tool, but it also lets you edit the frame as if it were a Bézier object.

For example, if the Direct Selection tool is selected and you drag a point on the frame, you move that point and thus change the shape of the object — a rectangle — would be converted into a polygon because the lines immediately adjacent to the moved point move with the point, while the rest of the frame is not affected.

In QuarkXPress, if the Content tool is selected and you drag a point on the frame, you resize the frame (perhaps nonproportionally) but the entire side(s) adjacent to the point move with the point, so a rectangle would still be a rectangle. To change a frame in the way that QuarkXPress does with both the Content and Item tools, use the Selection tool in InDesign.

Finally, the Position tool in InDesign lets you crop and resize a frame by dragging its handles (like the Selection tool) or drag an object to reposition it (like the Direct Selection tool), depending on what you select.

CROSS-REF Chapter 16 covers how to select and work with text. Chapter 28 covers using the Direct Selection tool to select and change the shape of objects.

There's a third way to work with objects: the Position tool. (To access it, click and hold on the Direct Selection tool until the pop-out menu appears, and then choose the Position tool.) Essentially a renamed version of PageMaker's Crop tool, the Position tool combines some aspects of the Selection tool with some aspects of the Direct Selection tool:

- As with the Selection tool, you can resize an object's frame by clicking and dragging its handles.

- As with the Direct Selection tool, you can click a graphic and reposition it (crop it) within the frame by dragging.

Unless you're a PageMaker user who's totally mystified with the InDesign Selection and Direct Selection tools, you'll likely never use this tool. But if you do, note that you can change how quickly InDesign displays any masked portion of a selected graphic by double-clicking the tool and selecting the desired option from the dialog box that appears: After Short Delay, After Standard Delay, After Long Delay, Never, and No Delay.

Selecting objects

Here's how to select a frame, shape, line, or path — in other words, an object — with any of the selection tools:

1. **Select the desired selection tool by clicking it or, if the Type tool is not selected, by pressing V for the Selection tool or A for the Direct Selection tool.**

2. **Move the pointer anywhere within an object, and then click and release.** To select an object with no background color, you must click its edge. If you click within it, the object is not selected. (The exception: Text frames are selected if you click within them.)

Choose View ➪ Show Frame Edges or press Control+⌘+H or Ctrl+H to see object edges if they aren't already visible.

NEW FEATURE The shortcut for View ➪ Show Frame Edges has changed to Control+⌘+H in InDesign CS3 for the Mac. (The Windows shortcut of Ctrl+H is unchanged.)

If you're using the Selection tool or the Position tool, when you release the mouse button, the object you clicked — or the object's bounding box if it has one — appears with a colored outline (the color is based on which layer it resides; blue is the default), eight resizing handles (four on the corners and four on the midpoints of the sides), and the solid centerpoint (which you can click and drag to move the object), as shown in Figure 10.1.

If you're using the Direct Selection tool, when you release the mouse button, the object you clicked appears, with a colored outline (the color is based on which layer it resides; blue is the default), reshaping handles (called *nodes* and located at corners and any other transition points), and the hollow centerpoint (which you can click and drag to move the object). Note that you can also select any of the frame segments to reshape the object. Figure 10.2 shows the same graphics frame that Figure 10.1 does, but it's selected using the Direct Selection tool, with one of the points being dragged to reshape the frame.

FIGURE 10.1

When you select a frame with the Selection or Position tool (in this case an oval graphics frame), the bounding box appears with eight resizing handles.

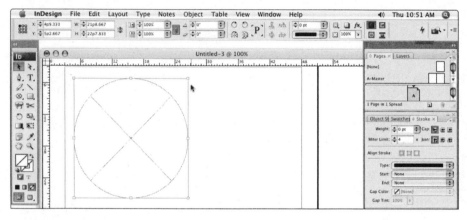

FIGURE 10.2

When you select a frame with the Direct Selection tool (in this case an oval graphics frame), the frame's reference points appear. Here, I am moving one of those points. Note how it reshapes — not resizes — the frame.

There are several tricks to know when selecting objects:

■ You can also select an object with the Selection tool by clicking and dragging a rectangle around it; this is called a *marquee*. Simply click in an empty portion of the page or pasteboard near the object you want to select and drag out a rectangle that intersects the object. (You don't have to enclose the entire object.) Clicking and dragging is a handy way to select multiple objects.

■ If an object is on a master page and you're working on a document page, you must Shift+⌘+click or Ctrl+Shift+click the object to select it. (If you try to select an object by clicking and it doesn't become selected, the object must be on a master page.) For more information about using master pages, see Chapter 7.

■ When you double-click an object other than a text frame, the selection tool switches between the Selection tool and the Direct Selection tool. If the Position tool is active, double-clicking the object switches to the Direct Selection tool, and double-clicking switches to the Selection tool. The only way to switch back to the Position tool is to select it from the Direct Selection tool's pop-out menu.

■ If you double-click a text frame, InDesign switches to the Type tool. Double-clicking again selects the text, as described in Chapter 15. If the Type tool is active, you can select the text frame by pressing Esc — a faster alternative to picking a selection tool and then selecting the frame with it.

■ If you want to select an object within a group, InDesign now lets you double-click the object to select just it. (Single-clicking selects the entire group.) Groups are covered in Chapter 13.

NEW FEATURE   The last three methods in the list above are new to InDesign CS3.

Selecting overlapping objects

You often have multiple objects overlapping in your layout, with some objects completely obscured by others. So how do you select them? InDesign gives you several options.

The Select submenu

One way to select overlapping objects is by choosing Object ➪ Select and then choosing the appropriate command. Figure 10.3 shows the Select submenu and its options.

The first four options let you select another object relative to the currently selected object:

■ **First Object Above** selects the topmost object.

■ **Next Object Above** selects the object immediately on top of the current object.

■ **Next Object Below** selects the object immediately under the current object.

■ **Last Object Below** selects the bottommost object.

FIGURE 10.3

The Select submenu in the Object menu

If no objects are selected, InDesign bases its selection on the creation order.

TIP You can also access these four selection options by Control+clicking or right-clicking an object and choosing Select from the contextual menu.

The Select submenu has four other options:

- If an object has content (text or graphic) and you've selected its content, choose Object ⇨ Select ⇨ Container to choose the frame. This is the same as selecting it with the Selection tool.

- If an object has content (text or graphic) and you've selected its frame, choose Object ⇨ Select ⇨ Content to choose the content within the object. This is basically the same as selecting it with the Direct Selection tool.

- If you have selected an object in a group of objects, using the Direct Selection tool, choose Object ⇨ Select ⇨ Previous Object in Group to navigate to the previous object in the group.

- Similarly, if you have selected an object in a group of objects, using the Direct Selection tool, choose Object ⇨ Select ⇨ Next Object in Group to navigate to the previous object in the group.

Object creation order determines what is "previous" or "next" in a group.

Keyboard shortcuts

You can use the keyboard shortcuts listed in this section. While this approach takes memorizing the commands, it's the fastest way to change your selection because you don't have to mouse around to the menus.

- Option+Shift+⌘+] or Ctrl+Alt+Shift+] selects the topmost object.
- Option+⌘+] or Ctrl+Alt+] selects the object immediately on top of the current object.
- Option+⌘+[or Ctrl+Alt+[selects the object immediately under the current object.
- Option+Shift+⌘+[or Ctrl+Alt+Shift+[selects the bottommost object.

Control panel selection buttons

The Control panel also provides iconic buttons — Select Previous Object and Select Next Object — to select the next or previous object, as well as the Select Contents and Select Container iconic buttons to select the content or container (frame). Figure 10.4 shows the buttons.

FIGURE 10.4

The Control panel's selection buttons

These iconic buttons now appear no matter which selection tool you use and whether or not the objects are grouped. In previous versions of InDesign, they appeared only if the objects were grouped and selected with the Direct Selection tool.

If you Shift+click either selection button, InDesign jumps past four objects and selects the fifth one. If you ⌘+click or Ctrl+click either button, InDesign selects the bottommost or topmost object, respectively.

If you use the Select Previous Object or Select Next Object buttons and reach the top or bottom of the object stack, InDesign CS3 now loops back from the top to the bottom object or from the bottom to the top object. In previous versions, there was no way to loop around.

Selecting multiple objects

When an object is selected, you can move or modify it. When several objects are selected, you can move or modify all the objects at once, saving you the time and drudgery of selecting and performing the same modification to several objects one at a time. You have several options for selecting multiple objects. You can:

- Choose the Selection tool and hold down the Shift key while clicking in succession on the objects you want to select.

- Choose any of the selection tools, and then click in an empty portion of the page and drag a rectangle (called a *marquee*) around any portion of each object you want to select. Make sure you don't click an item or you move it when you drag.

  - If you use the Selection or Position tool, the bounding box of each item is selected. You can resize any of the bounding boxes, but the anchor points and direction lines of the shapes within are not selected and cannot be moved.

  - If you use the Direct Selection tool, the anchor points and direction handles of the shapes in the bounding boxes are selected. You can change the shape of any of the objects by dragging an anchor point or a direction handle.

- If you want to select all items on a page or spread, choose Edit ⇨ Select All or press ⌘+A or Ctrl+A. (If the Type tool is selected and a text frame is active when you choose Select All, you highlight all the text, if any, in the frame.) If the Direct Selection tool is selected when you choose Select All, the anchor points and direction handles of the shapes in the selected objects' bounding boxes are selected. If any other tool is selected when you choose Select All, the bounding boxes of the objects are selected.

Deselecting objects

A selected object remains selected until you cause it to become deselected, and there are many reasons you might want to deselect an item. For example, you might want to deselect a text frame if you want to see how it looks when displayed without the frame's in and out ports visible. Or you might want to simply "let go" of an object you just finished working on. There are several ways to deselect a selected object. You can:

- Click in an empty portion of the page with any of the selection tools selected.

- Press and hold the Shift key with any of the selection tools selected and click the object you want to deselect.

- Choose any of the object-creation tools (the Pen, Pencil, Line, or any shape- and frame-creation tools), and then click and drag to create a new object.

- If you want to deselect all items on a page or spread, choose Edit ⇨ Deselect All or press Shift+⌘+A or Ctrl+Shift+A. (If the Type tool is selected and a text frame is active when you choose Deselect All, you'll deselect any text that's highlighted in the frame.)

Moving Objects

Before you can move an object, you must first select it. Once an object is selected, InDesign provides several methods for moving or copying it.

You can move a selected object by:

- **Clicking and dragging it to a different location:** When you drag an object, you can move it anywhere within the current page or spread, into an open library (see Chapter 7 for more information about libraries), or into another document (if another document is open and its window is visible). If you drag an object from one document to another, a copy of the object is placed in the target document and the original object remains unchanged in the source document.

 Press and hold down the Shift key as you drag to restrict the angle of movement to the nearest 45-degree angle based on the direction in which you're moving your mouse.

- **Pressing any of the arrow keys:** Each time you press an arrow key, the object is nudged by the distance specified in the Cursor Key field in the Units & Increments pane of the Preferences dialog box (choose File ➪ Preferences ➪ Units & Increments or press ⌘+K on the Mac, or choose Edit ➪ Preferences ➪ Units & Increments or press Ctrl+K in Windows). The default nudge value is 1 point. If you press and hold the Shift key when using arrow keys, the nudge increment is 10 points.

- **Selecting it with the Selection or Direct Selection tool, then double-clicking the tool to open the Move dialog box:** You enter the desired horizontal (X) and vertical (Y) coordinates, or the distance from the current location and the angle of the new location from the existing one. (This does not work with the Position tool.)

- **Selecting it with any of the selection tools, then choosing Object ➪ Transform ➪ Move:** You enter the desired horizontal (X) and vertical (Y) coordinates, or the distance from the current location and the angle of the new location from the existing one.

- **Changing the X and Y values in the Control panel or in the Transform panel:** These values determine the distance between an object's control point and the ruler origin, where the horizontal and vertical rulers intersect (usually the upper-left corner of a page or spread). (If the Control panel is not displayed, activate it by choosing Window ➪ Control or pressing Option+⌘+6 or Ctrl+Alt+6. If you want to use the Transform panel, activate it by choosing Window ➪ Object & Layout ➪ Transform.) Figure 10.5 shows the Control panel and Transform panel and their controls. If you want, change the object's control point — where the X and Y coordinates refer to.

Each of the preceding methods for moving objects has its merits. The method you choose depends on how you prefer to work.

CROSS-REF Chapter 2 explains how to set the control point.

FIGURE 10.5

The Control and Transform panels

CROSS-REF InDesign lets you move and copy entire pages between documents, as described in Chapter 5.

Creating Copies of Objects

Once you create something—a simple, rectangular frame or a complicated graphic made up of several dozen objects—InDesign makes it easy to reuse the original. InDesign provides many options for copying objects within documents as well as across them.

Copying objects within documents

Here are your options for copying objects within a document:

- **Copy and Paste commands (Edit ⇨ Copy, or ⌘+C or Ctrl+C; Edit ⇨ Paste, or ⌘+V or Ctrl+V):** Using these commands is a good choice if you have to copy something from one page to another. A great option is Paste in Place (Edit ⇨ Paste in Place, or Option+Shift+⌘+V or Ctrl+Alt+Shift+V), which pastes an object in the same place as the original object. It's very handy when copying an element from one page to another because it places the copy in the same location on the new page, saving you the effort of having to move it. (When copying among documents, Paste in Place uses the same X and Y coordinates as the original.)

- **Duplicate command (Edit ⇨ Duplicate, or Option+Shift+⌘+D or Ctrl+Alt+Shift+D):** The Duplicate command is quicker than using copy and paste. When you duplicate an object, the copy is placed one pica below and to the right of the original.

InDesign offsets a duplicate by whatever settings are in the Step and Repeat dialog box or by the distance and direction of the last Option+drag or Alt+drag copying of an object — whichever was done last.

- **Manual cloning:** When you drag and drop an object while pressing and holding Option or Alt, a copy of the selected object is created. If you're a drag-and-dropper, you may prefer this manual method to the Duplicate command.

- **Cloning with the transform tools:** If you press and hold Option or Alt while using any of the transform tools (Rotate, Shear, Scale, and Free Transform), a copy of the selected object is transformed. The selected item remains unchanged.

- **Control panel and Transform panel cloning:** If you press and hold Option or Alt when you exit the Control or Transform panels (by pressing Return or Enter or releasing the mouse after choosing an option from a menu), the transformation is applied to a copy of the selected item.

- **Step and Repeat command (Edit ➪ Step and Repeat, or Shift+⌘+U or Ctrl+Shift+U):** Think of the Step and Repeat dialog box (shown in Figure 10.6) as the Duplicate command on steroids. It lets you create multiple duplicates of selected objects and specify the horizontal and vertical offset of the duplicates. This command is handy if you have to create, for example, a vertical and/or horizontal grid of lines on a page. Simply draw a horizontal line at the top of the page or a vertical line along the left edge of the page. With the line selected, use the Step and Repeat command to place and evenly space as many additional lines as you need.

FIGURE 10.6

The Step and Repeat dialog box

The shortcut for Step and Repeat has changed in InDesign CS3 to Option+⌘+U or Ctrl+Alt+U. And the Step and Repeat dialog box now has a Preview check box so you can see the effects of the settings before actually applying them.

Figure 10.7 shows a typical task that's easily handled with the Step and Repeat command. First, the top row was built by creating two copies of the original; the rest of the rows were created by step-and-repeating the four grouped objects in the top row.

If you need to use an object or a group of objects repeatedly, storing them in a library is a good idea. Once you place something in a library, you can drag-copy as many clones as you want into any document. (Chapter 7 covers libraries.)

FIGURE 10.7

These business cards were created with two trips to the Step and Repeat dialog box. First, I copied the upper-left original to the right. Then I selected both cards and had them copied four times to fill out the page vertically.

Copying objects between documents

Occasionally, you'll want to use something you've created in one InDesign document in another document. For example, maybe you need an ad that ran in last month's newsletter again for this month's edition. Or perhaps you created a small illustration for an ad that you want to use in a companion brochure. InDesign offers several options for moving objects between documents. You can:

- Open the document that contains the objects you want to copy, select the objects, and then copy them to the clipboard with Edit ➪ Copy, or ⌘+C or Ctrl+C. Open the target document and use Edit ➪ Paste, or ⌘+V or Ctrl+V, to place the copied objects. You can also use Edit ➪ Paste in Place, or Option+Shift+⌘+V or Ctrl+Alt+Shift+V, to paste the object at the same X and Y coordinates as the original.

- If you need to use the objects in more than one document, you can copy them into a library, which lets you place as many copies as you want in any document. (Libraries are covered in Chapter 7.)

Working with Snippets

Working with XML snippets is easy: Just drag objects from InDesign to the desktop or a folder to create the snippet file. And drag the snippet file on to a layout to place the objects on it. But don't let that simplicity blind you to a couple cool attributes of snippets:

■ You can send snippets to other users on storage drives, via e-mail or over the network — like any other file.

■ New to InDesign CS3, you can control where a snippet's object are placed in your document. Select Position at Original Location or Position at Cursor Location in the Snippet Import section of the Preference dialog box's File Handling pane (choose InDesign ➪ Preferences ➪ File Handling or press ⌘+K on the Mac, or choose Edit ➪ Preferences ➪ File Handling or press Ctrl+K in Windows). The Position at Cursor Location option means the objects will be placed wherever you release the mouse when dragging the snippet.

■ A very easy way to share parts of your document is to select the desired objects and drag them out of your document window into the Mac or Windows desktop or into a folder. InDesign creates a file called an XML snippet file (with the filename extension .inds) that contains all the objects, formatting, and position information. You or another person can drag the file onto an InDesign document to place the objects, with all formatting intact.

NEW FEATURE The ability to control the position of a snippet in a new document is new to InDesign CS3.

■ You can open the source document (the one that contains the objects) and the target document and drag-copy the objects from the source document to the target document. (Choose Window ➪ Arrange ➪ Tile to display both document windows side by side.)

Deleting Objects

There are several ways to delete objects in InDesign. Most people either have a favorite method or use one that's easiest to adopt in their current state (such as using a mouse action to delete a frame when they're using the mouse already to size frames). No matter your preferred approach, be sure you select an object with the Selection tool. The methods are:

■ Choose Edit ➪ Cut or use the keyboard shortcuts ⌘+X or Ctrl+X to cut objects. Or choose the Cut command in the contextual menu you get when Control+clicking or right-clicking an object.

■ Choose Edit ➪ Clear or use the keyboard shortcuts ⌘+Delete or Backspace to delete (clear) the object.

■ Drag the object to the Mac's Trashcanor the Windows Recycle Bin; this clears the object.

Cut objects can then be pasted elsewhere, at least until the time an object is cut or copied. Cleared objects cannot be pasted back.

QUARKXPRESS If you're a QuarkXPress user, you may find yourself instinctively pressing ⌘+K or Ctrl+K to delete an object. In InDesign, this shortcut displays the Preferences dialog box. If you can't let go of the QuarkXPress shortcut, edit your keyboard shortcuts to assign ⌘+K or Ctrl+K to the Clear command, as Chapter 3 explains.

Preventing Objects from Printing

InDesign lets you prevent an object from printing. To do so, select the object, open the Attributes panel (Window ➪ Attributes), and then select the Nonprinting option. Figure 10.8 shows the panel. (The other settings in this panel control stroke settings, which Chapter 12 covers.)

FIGURE 10.8

The Attributes panel

You would use this feature for comments and other elements that should not print but that you need to have visible on-screen. Another approach to nonprinting objects is to place them all on a layer and make the entire layer nonprinting.

 Chapter 6 covers layers. Chapter 31 covers printing.

Aligning and Distributing Objects

InDesign lets you align and distribute objects, saving you the hassle of manually moving and placing each element, or figuring out the correct locations in the Control panel or Transform panel to do so. The Align panel is where InDesign offers these timesaving capabilities.

The Align panel (Window ➪ Object & Layout ➪ Align or Shift+F7), shown in Figure 10.9, has several iconic buttons that let you manipulate the relative position of multiple objects in two ways. (The buttons show the alignments they provide.)

TIP The Align panel's iconic buttons may also be available in the Control panel if you've selected multiple objects with the Selection tool, depending on how wide your screen is and how many buttons you've set the Control panel to display. (See Chapter 2 for how to customize the buttons it displays.)

FIGURE 10.9

The Align panel contains 14 iconic buttons that let you control the alignment and space among selected objects. If the two Distribute Spacing buttons do not appear at the bottom of the panel, choose Show Options from the flyout menu.

With the Align panel, you can:

■ **Line up objects along a horizontal or vertical axis.** For example, if you've randomly placed several small graphic frames onto a page, you can use the iconic alignment buttons in the Align panel to align them neatly — either horizontally or vertically. Figure 10.10 shows a before-and-after example of objects aligned with the Align panel.

FIGURE 10.10

The rectangles on the left were aligned along the left edge of the leftmost object by clicking the Align Left Edges iconic button in the Align panel. The result of the alignment operation is shown on the right.

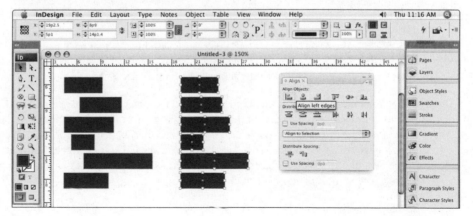

■ **Distribute space evenly among objects along a horizontal or vertical axis.** Here's a typical problem that's easily solved by using this feature: You've carefully placed five small graphics on a page so that the top edges are aligned across the page and there is equal space between each picture. Then you find out one of the graphics needs to be cut. After deleting the unneeded graphic, you could use the Align panel to redistribute the space among the remaining graphics so that they're again equally spaced. Figure 10.11 shows a before-and-after example of the Align panel's Distribute Spacing capability using a series of vertically arranged objects.

FIGURE 10.11

The objects on the left are unequally spaced. Clicking the Distribute Vertical Space iconic button in the Align panel repositions the objects so that the spaces between the objects are equal, as shown on the right.

> **NOTE**   The Align iconic buttons don't work with objects that have been locked with the Lock Position command. If the objects are on a locked layer, you need to unlock the layer. (Chapter 13 covers locking. Chapter 6 covers layers.)

When you click a button in the Align panel, selected objects are repositioned in the most logical manner. For example, if you click the Align Left Edges iconic button, the selected objects are typically moved horizontally (to the left, in this case) so that the left edge of each object is aligned with the left edge of the leftmost object. Along the same lines, if you click the Distribute Vertical Centers iconic button, the selected objects are moved vertically so that there's an equal amount of space between the vertical center of each object.

Spacing can appear uneven if you click the Distribute Horizontal Space or Distribute Vertical Space iconic buttons when objects of various sizes are selected. For objects of different sizes, you usually want to use the Distribute Spacing buttons (which make the space between objects even) rather than space objects based on their centers or sides (which is how the Distribute Object buttons work).

Using the Measure Tool and Info Panel

InDesign has two little-known methods to get dimension information about objects: the Measure tool and the Info panel. Because so much information about object size and position resides in the Control panel, these methods are little used. They're more vestiges of InDesign's pre-Control panel era. But they can be useful on occasion.

Available through the Eyedropper tool's pop-out menu or via the shortcut K, the Measure tool opens the Info panel and lets you draw a line whose dimensions appear in that panel (look for D1 in the upper left) so you can measure an arbitrary distance. You can measure the distance of two segments if you hold the Option or Alt key when dragging the tool for the second segment. Note that the second measurement must start where the first measurement left off — the two measurement lines must share a "corner." That second measurement displays in the D2 area, as shown in the figure.

Although you can see objects' dimensions in the Control, Transform, and Info panels, the value of the Measure tool is that it enables you to determine the distance between objects rather than the dimensions of objects. It can also come in handy when you're measuring the distance across multiple objects. The figure shows the tool and Info panel.

When you select an object, the Info panel also shows its width and height, as well as any rotation angle, gradient, or stroke applied. While these are all bits of information you can get from the Control panel or Transform panel, the Info panel does show one bit of unique information: In its upper-left quadrant, the panel shows the current position of the mouse, providing a handy way to ensure that your starting and ending points when drawing something are exactly where you want them.

NEW FEATURE A new, unnamed pop-up menu in InDesign CS3's Align panel lets you choose where selected objects align to: Align to Selection (the default behavior and what previous versions of InDesign did), Align to Margins, Align to Page, and Align to Spread.

TIP Although InDesign has no default shortcuts for them, you can create keyboard shortcuts for the alignment and distribution buttons, as explained in Chapter 3.

NOTE If the two Distribute Spacing iconic buttons do not appear at the bottom of the panel and you want to distribute objects, choose Show Options from the flyout menu or click the double-arrow icon to the left of the panel name.

Positioning Objects Precisely with Guides

Just as carpenters often use chalk lines to make sure things are straight when putting up the framework of a house, you can use guidelines and gridlines to help achieve precise object placement and alignment when building InDesign documents. InDesign lets you show or hide three kinds of guides: User-created vertical and horizontal guidelines, document gridlines, and baseline gridlines. You can tell InDesign to automatically snap object edges to guidelines and gridlines when you create, resize, or move an object within a user-specified distance.

CROSS-REF For more about creating and displaying guidelines and grids, see Chapter 7.

TIP Everyone should use the Control panel's coordinates, as well as guides, to make sure that objects are consistently placed from page to page. Many designers place objects by eye, using the mouse, but that typically means there are small position and size variations from page to page that shouldn't be there. Many readers won't notice if the differences are slight, but even small differences make small adjustments to text flow that can add up over pages. And it's all so unnecessary.

You can control which guidelines and grids objects snap to, as well as how close they have to be to snap to the guideline or grid. This snap-to feature makes it easier to sustain consistent object placement in your layout.

You set how close an object must come to a guideline or grid in the Guides & Pasteboard pane of the Preferences dialog box (choose InDesign ➪ Preferences ➪ Guides & Pasteboard or press ⌘+K on the Mac, or choose Edit ➪ Preferences ➪ Guides & Pasteboard or press Ctrl+K in Windows). In the Snap to Zone field, enter a value (in pixels) within which an object must be of a guideline or grid to snap to that guidelines or grid when you create, resize, or move the object.

But setting the snap-to zone is just the first step. You must enable snap-to in InDesign as well for whichever elements you want to snap to:

- For guidelines and baseline grids, be sure Snap to Guides is enabled. Choose View ➪ Guides & Grids ➪ Snap to Guides, or press Shift+⌘+; [semicolon] or Ctrl+Shift+; [semicolon]). Note that the guidelines must be visible for objects to snap to them; to make them visible, choose View ➪ Guides & Grids ➪ Show Guides, or ⌘+; [semicolon] or Ctrl+; [semicolon]. But the baseline grid need not be visible.

- For document grids, be sure that Snap to Document Grid is enabled. Choose View ⇨ Guides & Grids ⇨ Snap to Document Grid, or Shift+⌘+' (apostrophe) or Ctrl+Shift+' (apostrophe).

In both cases, if the menu option has a check mark to its left, it is enabled. Choosing it toggles between enabling and disabling the snap-to feature. Note that the grid need *not* be visible for objects to snap to them

NEW FEATURE On the Macintosh only, holding ⌘ when dragging overrides the Snap to Guides option, letting you place an object anywhere in the document, even off-grid.

If you want to align objects with text baselines *and* to align text baselines with the baseline grid, use the Grids pane in the Preferences dialog box to specify the same vertical spacing for the Document Grid as for the Baseline Grid. For example, specify an Increment Every value of 1 pica in the Baseline Grid area, and specify a Subdivisions value of 6 in the Document Grid area.

CROSS-REF Individual text frames also can have their own baseline grid, to which text can be set to snap, as described in Chapter 15.

Summary

After you create an object, you can move, modify, or delete it. If the object is a frame, you also have the option of modifying the text or graphic within it. Before you can modify an object, you must select it. When an object is selected, commands and controls for changing its position and appearance become available. To select an object, you must first choose one of the three selection tools.

You can create a single copy of any object by using the Copy and Paste commands, by using the Duplicate command, or by Option+dragging or Alt+dragging a clone of the original. The Step and Repeat command lets you create multiple copies of objects and position the copies relative to the originals. The Paste in Place command pastes an object on a new page at the same X and Y coordinates as the original object.

You can prevent selected objects from printing using the Attributes panel (Window ⇨ Attributes).

The Align panel (Window ⇨ Object & Layout ⇨ Align or Shift+F7) lets you align multiple objects and control the amount of space between them, while vertical and horizontal ruler guides and snap-to-grid features help you accurately position and align items. You can also distribute objects precisely using this panel.

Using grids and guidelines, you can have InDesign "snap" objects to the closest guideline or gridline, to minimize minute differences in the positions of objects placed via the mouse.

Chapter 11

Transforming Objects

IN THIS CHAPTER

Resizing and scaling objects

Rotating, shearing, and flipping objects

Repeating transformations

Replacing object attributes

O ne of the wonders of desktop publishing is how you can make fundamental changes to objects. You can make them smaller, bigger, and wider. You can rotate them, flip them, and skew them. Try that with a printed photograph or strip of type.

The most common transformations include resizing frames and resizing (scaling) their contents. The other basic transformations — rotating, shearing, and flipping — are used less often, with rotation being the most widely useful and the other two usually limited to special effects.

For all of these controls, InDesign offers multiple ways to achieve the desired transformation: menu options, tools, panels, and dialog boxes. When there's a choice, pick whichever is most convenient at the moment.

CROSS-REF Chapter 10 covers how to select objects, as well as how to move, copy, delete, and align them. Chapter 12 covers special effects such as adding strokes and lighting effects.

Resizing and Scaling Objects

Two closely related transformation features are resizing and scaling. The difference is that resizing affects just the container — the frame or path — while scaling affects both the container and its contents. (For lines, there is no difference between resizing and scaling, because there are no contents.)

Resizing methods

After you create a shape, frame, path, or line, you may find that it's too big or too small for your design. No problem. Resizing objects is as easy as moving them. And as is the case with repositioning objects, you have two basic options for resizing: the mouse or your choice of the Control or Transform panel.

Using the mouse

Click and drag the control handles on an object's bounding box using the Selection or Position tool. To change the width and height, drag a corner handle. To change only the width or height, drag a midpoint handle. If you press and hold Shift as you drag, the object's original proportions are retained.

> **TIP**   If you drag immediately after clicking a handle, only an object's bounding box is displayed as you drag. If you click and then pause until the pointer changes, the contents within are displayed as you drag.

Here's how the various selection tools act on objects — frames, paths, and lines — when you resize them via the mouse:

- **If you resize a graphics or text frame with the Selection tool, InDesign resizes just the frame.** Hold ⌘ or Ctrl to also scale the contents. For lines and paths, resizing the bounding box (the invisible "frame" that enclosed them) resizes the object but does not affect the thickness (weight) of any strokes unless you also hold the ⌘ or Ctrl key while dragging.

- **If you resize a graphics or text frame with the Position tool, InDesign resizes just the frame, as long as you selected the frame and not its contents.** If you selected the contents, InDesign resizes just the contents. The same is true when selecting paths. For lines, the Position tool acts like the Selection tool.

- **If you resize a graphic within a frame or path with the Direct Selection tool, only the graphic's size changes.** Just be sure that you select the graphic, not its frame. Hold ⌘ or Ctrl to also scale the frame (or the bounding box for a path).

- **If you resize a frame (rather than its contents) with the Direct Selection tool, the frame is reshaped.** If you select a path with the Direct Selection tool, its nodes appear so you can reshape the path (see Chapter 28). If you select a line, dragging on its nodes will simply move the line, not resize it.

Using the Control or Transform panel

As with using the mouse, how you select an object determines what is resized (see the previous section). After selecting an object in the desired way, modify the horizontal and/or vertical dimensions by changing the W (width) and/or H (height) values in the Control panel or Transform panel. For a frame or path containing graphics, if the contents are selected rather than the bounding box or path outline, the new size values apply to the contents rather than to the container. Otherwise, the container is resized.

If you want to have the X and Y values change by the same amounts when you enter a new value for either, be sure the Constrain Proportions for Width & Height iconic button shows a solid chain in the Control panel. If the button shows a broken chain, each dimension is changed independently. Toggle between the solid chain and broken chain by clicking the button. Note that the Transform panel does not have this button.

Note that resizing lines works a little differently: When a line is selected with any selection tool, the W and H fields are replaced by the L field, where you can enter the line's new length. This ensures the line's angle is not changed by the resize.

Scaling methods

There are similar ways to change the scale of an object's contents:

■ **Select the Scale tool.** If it's not already selected, click the object you want to scale, and then drag the mouse in the direction you want to scale the object, as shown in Figure 11.1. (You don't need to drag on any handles.) If you want, you can click and drag the reference point from its default location in the upper-left-hand corner of the bounding box to a different location. When the object grows or shrinks, the reference point doesn't move, but it does affect how InDesign interprets the direction and degree of scale desired as you move the mouse. Press and hold Shift and drag horizontally to apply only horizontal scale, vertically to apply only vertical scale, and diagonally to apply horizontal and vertical and keep the object's original proportions. Release the mouse button when the object is the size you want. (If you select the object with the Direct Selection tool, only its contents will scale, not its frame as well.)

FIGURE 11.1

Clicking and dragging with the Scale tool enlarges or reduces a frame. In this example, the Scale tool is being used to enlarge a frame.

291

■ **Choose the Free Transform tool, select an object handle, and drag in the direction you want to scale the object.** Selecting a corner handle scales in both dimensions, while selecting a side handle scales the contents only in that side's dimension.

■ **Using the Selection or Position tool, click and drag a handle to resize a graphics or text frame.** To change the content's scale as well as the frame size while doing this, hold down ⌘ or Ctrl.

■ **Select the object and then change the values in the Scale X Percentage and Scale Y Percentage fields in the Control panel or Transform panel**.

NOTE If you want to have the X and Y percentage values change by the same amounts when you enter a new value for either, be sure the Constrain Proportions for Scaling iconic button shows a solid chain in the Control or Transform panel. If the button shows a broken chain, each dimension is changed independently.

Here's how the Scale tool acts on objects based on what selection tool you used to select them:

■ If you selected a graphics or text frame with the Selection or Position tool, InDesign scales the frame and the contents.

■ If you selected a graphic within a frame with the Direct Selection or Position tool, only the content is scaled.

The Control Panel's Transformation Controls

The Control panel contains all sorts of transformation controls. The figure here identifies them. Among those added in InDesign CS3 are the flip, rotation, text-wrap, and lighting-effects buttons, as well as the rotation preview *P* icon.

NEW FEATURE When you select a scaled object with the Selection or Position tool, the Control or Transform panel may still show scale values of 100 percent. InDesign CS3 adds a control in the Preference dialog box's General pane to change that odd behavior, as Chapter 3 explains.

Performing Other Transformations

In addition to the essential mundane capabilities to move, copy, delete, resize, and scale objects, InDesign provides tools and several controls in the Control panel and Transform panel that let you perform more-dramatic effects on objects, such as rotation, mirroring, *shearing* (which distorts a shape by applying a combination of rotation and slant), and flipping.

For all these tools, keep these tips in mind:

- If you press Option or Alt as you drag, you work on a copy of the object.

- To get finer control as you drag, click farther from the active object's reference point.

- If you drag immediately after clicking on an object, the object appears in its original location and the object's bounding box moves as you drag. If you click and then pause until the cross hair changes to an arrowhead, the object is displayed as you drag.

- A key consideration is what you use to select an object before applying a transformation. If you use the Selection or Pointer tool, the transformation applies to the entire object. If you use the Direct Selection tool, the transformation applies to the selected node or side (or segment). For example, to flip or rotate just a side of an object, select it with the Direct Selection tool. To rotate the entire object, use one of the other tools.

- The Rotate and Shear tools rely on the object's control point — the black square in the matrix of nine reference points shown at the left of the Control and Transform panels — to determine where rotation and shearing are done from. You can also simply click anywhere in the document window with these tools to choose your own control point for the current operation. (This also applies to the Scale tool.)

- You can access all these functions by choosing Object ⇨ Transform and then choosing the desired option from the submenu. They're also available from the contextual menu you get when Control+clicking or right-clicking an object. You can also double-click the tools themselves to get the same dialog boxes that these menus provide.

How you use these transformations is up to you and is limited only by your imagination. As always, discretion is advised. Just because InDesign has some pretty cool features doesn't mean that you should use them in every publication you create.

Rotating objects

If you need to rotate an object, you can do it via the mouse or via your choice of the Control panel or Transform panel.

Using the Rotate tool

The Rotate tool is best used when you want to experiment with different angles quickly, or if you want to preview the rotation to see what looks right. Here's how:

1. **Select the Rotate tool.** If the Type tool isn't selected, you can also press R to select the Rotate tool.

2. **If it's not already selected, click the object you want to rotate.** When using the Selection or Position tool, you can click and drag the bounding box's control point (which matches the control point set in the Control or Transform panel) to a different location. The object rotates around the control point. Figure 11.2 shows a text frame being rotated around a repositioned control point (near the upper-left corner). When using the Direct Selection tool, select the side (or segment) or node you want to rotate.

When you rotate an object with the Rotate tool, a moving bounding box appears along with the original object if you drag immediately after clicking, as in this example.

3. **Move the pointer away from the control point, and then click and drag with a circular motion, clockwise or counterclockwise.** Press and hold Shift as you drag to constrain rotation increments to the nearest 45-degree angle.

4. **Release the mouse button when the object is at the angle you want.**

Using the panels

The Control panel and Transform panel give you both more exact control and the ability to rotate an object's contents. The two panels have the Rotation Angle fields, in which you can enter precise rotation amounts. If the object is selected via the Selection or Position tool — or if an edge is selected with the Direct Selection tool — the value entered here rotates the entire object around the current control point. If you select the object's contents with the Direct Selection tool, the content rotates within the frame. Either way, note how the preview *P* icon in the Control panel shows the current rotation.

Understanding the Panel Flyout Menu Options

Like almost all InDesign panels, the Control and Transform panels include a flyout menu that contains additional commands for transforming objects.

Note that all of these flyout menu options — except Clear Transformations — toggle between being enabled (a check mark appears to its left) and disabled (nothing appears to its left) when you choose them.

Here's what the options do:

- **Clear Transformations:** Choose this menu option to undo all transformations applied to an object. Note that you can also get this menu option by Control+clicking or right-clicking the *P* rotation preview in the Control panel.

- **Redefine Scaling as 100%:** Enable this option to make the current scale appear as 100 percent in all panels. For example, if you scaled an object to 75 percent and chose this option, all panels display its scale as 100 percent but leave the object at its current scale. Note this menu option is available only in the Transform panel.

- **Dimensions Include Stroke Weight:** If you enable this menu option, the width of any stroke is added to the frame dimensions, and the dimensions shown in the Control panel and Transform panel reflect the strokes' widths (see Chapter 12). This helps you with precise placement because frames extend beyond the frame, so adding a 6-point frame to a rectangle in effect increases its width and height by 12 points (6 points on each side).

- **Transformations Are Totals:** If you enable this menu option, InDesign adds up all rotation angles, scale values, and so on applied to an object as well as to any objects that contain the object. For example, if you paste an unrotated item into a frame that's been rotated 30 degrees, the angle of rotation for the nested item is reported as 0 degrees, even though its parent frame was rotated 40 degrees. Similarly, if you scale an object by 50 percent whose nested object had been previous scaled by 50 percent, the nested object's scale would still display as 50 percent. If you disable this menu option, the angle of rotation of a nested object is calculated relative to the horizontal/vertical orientation of the page, and the scale relative to its original size. Thus, for the previous examples, InDesign would report the nested object's rotation as 30 degrees and its scale as 25 percent, since it would take into account the transformations applied to the parent object.

- **Show Content Offset:** If enabled, this menu option shows the graphics content's position of the origin relative to the frame containing it in the X and Y fields in the Control panel and Transform panel. If you move a graphic within the frame, the offset will be positive as you move it to the right and/or down, and negative as you move it to the left and/or up. If disabled, the Control panel and Transform panel instead show the graphics content's absolute position on the page relative to the current control point.

- **Adjust Stroke Weight While Scaling:** If enabled, this menu option makes InDesign scale the frame's stroke as the frame is resized. For example, a frame with a 1-point stroke has its stroke scaled to 0.5 points if the frame is scaled to 50 percent. If this option is disabled, the stroke width is not affected when you scale the frame.

The Transform panel also lets you apply three predefined rotations to select an object through its flyout menu: Rotate 180°, Rotate 90° CW, and Rotate 90° CCW.

NOTE   Negative numbers rotate counterclockwise, positive numbers clockwise.

NEW FEATURE   You can also use the Rotate 90° Clockwise and Rotate 90° Counterclockwise iconic buttons in the Control panel. In previous versions of InDesign, these controls were in the Control palette's palette menu.

Using the Shear tool

When you shear an object with the Shear tool, you actually perform two transformations at once: rotation and slant. Because the contents within text frames and graphics frames are distorted along with the frames when you shear an object, you'll probably use this tool only for special effects.

QUARKXPRESS   The InDesign Shear tool is not the same as the QuarkXPress Skew tool — Shear both slants and rotates an object, while Skew just slants it. To simulate the QuarkXPress Skew tool, move the mouse horizontally when using the InDesign Shear tool; this ensures that there is no rotation.

TIP   If you want to just slant an object, just use the Shear X Angle field in the Control panel or Transform panel, or choose Object ➪ Transform ➪ Shear.

To shear an object with the Shear tool:

1. **Select the Shear tool.** If the Type tool isn't selected, you can also press O to select the Shear tool.

2. **If it's not already selected, click the object you want to shear.** If you want, you can drag the control point from its default location in the upper-left-hand corner of the bounding box to a different location. When you shear an object, the control point doesn't move.

3. **Move the pointer away from the control point, and then click and drag.** Hold the Shift key and drag to constrain rotation increments to multiples of 45 degrees. Figure 11.3 shows a frame being sheared.

Flipping objects

InDesign also lets you flip objects horizontally, vertically, or in both directions. As you would expect, there are several ways to do this:

■ Click the Flip Horizontal or Flip Vertical iconic buttons in the Control panel. (Notice how the new *P* preview icon shows you the currently applied flip setting.)

FIGURE 11.3

In this example, a frame is being sheared using the Shear tool.

- Choose Flip Horizontal or Flip Vertical from the Transform panel's flyout menu, choose Object ➪ Transform ➪ Flip Horizontal or Object ➪ Transform ➪ Flip Vertical, or choose Flip Horizontal or Flip Vertical from the contextual menu that appears when you Control+click or right-click an object.

- Drag an object's bounding box handle across and beyond the opposite corner or edge, as if you were resizing the object's frame. This also moves the object. (If you use the Direct Selection tool, the frame doesn't move, but the flipped contents move, usually outside the frame, so you'd need to reposition to contents in that case to make them visible again.)

Repeating Transformations

Whatever transformations you use, you can apply them repeatedly. InDesign remembers the effects you apply to frames with the Control panel, Transform panel, and transform tools.

Choose Object ➪ Transform ➪ Transform Again (or press Option+⌘+3 or Ctrl+Alt+3) to repeat the last transformation on the selected object (it can be a different object than you last applied a transformation to).

Or choose Object ➪ Transform ➪ Transform Sequence Again (or press Option+⌘+4 or Ctrl+Alt+4) to apply all recent transformations to a select object. That sequence of transactions stays in memory until you perform a new transformation, which then starts a new sequence, so you can apply the same set of transformations to multiple objects.

CROSS-REF Not only can you apply transformations repeatedly, you can also save transformations, strokes, and other object attributes as object styles, so they can be applied at any time. Chapter 13 covers this feature in detail.

Replacing Object Attributes

A really painstaking task in any layout is going through it to fix formatting to frames, lines, or other objects once the design standards have changed. InDesign has a very handy way to apply object formatting consistently to objects — the object styles feature described in Chapter 13 — but even if you use these styles, local formatting still applies to at least some objects. That's where the Object pane of the Find/Replace dialog box comes in, letting you replace attributes throughout your document, no matter what they are applied to. Figure 11.4 shows that pane.

FIGURE 11.4

The Object pane of the Find/Change dialog box

Include Locked Stories
Include Locked Layers
Include Hidden Layers
Include Footnotes
Include Master Pages

NEW FEATURE   The ability to search and replace object attributes is new to InDesign CS3.

Here's how it works:

1. **Open the Find/Change dialog box by choosing Edit ⇨ Find/Change, and then going to the Object pane.**

2. **Select the desired object attributes by clicking the Object Find Format Settings iconic button to the left of the Find Object Format list.** In the dialog box that displays (refer to Figure 11.5), select the attributes to search (choose one category at a time from

the list at left and then set the desired parameters in the pane that appears), and click OK when done. (This dialog box is nearly identical to the New Object Style dialog box covered in Chapter 13.) The attributes appear in that Find Object format list. (Highlight an attribute in the list and click the Clear Object Find Format Settings iconic button — the trashcan icon — if you want to remove an attribute from your search.)

FIGURE 11.5

The Find Object Format Options dialog box. (The Change Object Format Options dialog box is identical.)

3. **If you're replacing attributes, click the Object Format Settings iconic button to the right of the Change Object Format list.** These controls work like the Find Object Format controls.

4. **Limit or expand the search range by choosing an option from the Search pop-up menu: Selection, Document, and All Documents.** Also choose the type of frames to search in the Type pop-up menu: All Frames, Text Frames, Graphic Frames, and Unassigned Frames. Finally, to determine the scope of your search, select or deselect any of the six iconic buttons at the bottom of the pane (from left to right: Include Locked Layers, Include Locked Stories, Include Hidden Layers, Include Master Pages, and Include Footnotes). Note that the first two buttons apply only to finds; you cannot change the formatting of locked objects. (If an icon's background darkens, it is selected.)

5. **Click Find, Change, Change All, or Change/Find as desired to perform your search and/or replace operation.**

6. **Click Done when done.**

Summary

InDesign's resizing controls let you change the size of a frame without affecting its contents, while scaling affects its contents as well.

You can change an object's shape using the Rotate, Scale, or Shear tools or the corresponding fields in the Control panel or Transform panel. You can also resize objects' frames.

A handy feature in InDesign lets you apply a sequence of transformations over and over again to one or more objects. Another handy feature new to InDesign CS3 is the ability to search and replace object attributes.

Chapter 12

Applying Effects to Objects

InDesign has always been the leader when it comes to providing special effects, such as drop shadows and transparency, to layout elements, and accurately reproducing them in print. (That remains true even with QuarkXPress 7's addition of transparency and blending effects.) InDesign, in fact, has greatly blurred the role of a desktop publishing program, bringing in high-end graphics capabilities that had long been the province of image-manipulation programs such as Photoshop and illustration software such as Illustrator and FreeHand. The result is you have the ability to create more visually rich documents than you can with any other program.

InDesign's effects fall into two broad categories: strokes and lighting. The two types of effects are related in that they both interact with the edges of objects.

Strokes are the edges of all objects — frames, lines, and text — and InDesign lets you adjust their thickness, style, and color.

Lighting effects create a simulated three-dimensional appearance for objects, providing visual depth through drop shadows and embossing, for example. A related effect is transparency, which lets you control whether objects let elements below them show through, as well as create interesting fade effects.

CROSS-REF   Chapter 8 covers how to create and apply colors, gradients, and tints as fills within objects and to text. You apply these same colors, gradients, and tints the same way to strokes as you do to fills.

NOTE   Choose View ⇨ Show Frame Edges, or press Control+⌘+H or Ctrl+H, to see frame edges if they aren't already visible.

IN THIS CHAPTER

Adding strokes and fills to frames

Applying corner options

Applying transparency

Using drop shadows, glows, feathering, and other lighting effects

---

Working with Strokes

When you create a new frame or shape, there's not much to it. It has no content, no color (it's transparent or *none-colored* in InDesign's vocabulary), and no border. Text has color but no border. But both have strokes; they just happen to have a thickness of 0 points, so they are invisible at first. Lines (and paths) have an automatic stroke width of 1 point.

Adding strokes

In the old days of traditional paste-up, adding a simple, black border around a sidebar or a thin keyline around a graphic was a tedious and time-consuming process of laying out adhesive tape and then hoping that your meticulously placed rules remained straight and your perfectly square corners remained tight long enough to make it to the printer. If you were unlucky, your rules wound up on the floor or stuck to somebody's elbows. Nowadays, computers make adding borders to shapes an easy task. InDesign lets you quickly apply strokes to the shapes and text you create and modify the thickness, color, and style of strokes.

To add a stroke:

1. **Select any of the selection tools and click the frame, shape, line, or path to which you want to add a stroke.** For text, highlight the desired text with the Type tool.

2. **Click the Stroke iconic button in the Tools panel (see Figure 12.1) or in the Swatches panel.**

3. **You now can click a color, tint, or gradient from the Swatches panel, or click one of the three iconic buttons at the bottom of the Tools panel.** These buttons (from left to right) let you apply the last-selected color, last-selected gradient, or [None]. (Applying [None] removes the stroke's color, tint, and/or gradient.)

Note that if you don't see the stroke applied to the object, you may need to specify a stroke width, as I describe a little later in this section.

The controls in the Color panel (Window ⇨ Color or F6) let you change the tint of the color applied to a stroke, but I recommend you use the tint control on the Swatches panel (Window ⇨ Swatches or F5) instead, so you don't accidentally use unnamed colors (see Chapter 8 for more information on this issue). The Gradient panel (Windows ⇨ Gradient) gives you the option to apply either a linear or radial gradient to strokes. For linear gradients, you can specify the angle using the Angle field.

CROSS-REF   For information about adding colors, tints, and gradients to the Swatches panel, see Chapter 8.

TIP   You can type percentages in panel fields for size- and scale-oriented items such as stroke widths. For example, to change a 1-point stroke to a hairline (0.25 points), you can type 0.25 pt or 25%.

FIGURE 12.1

Three iconic buttons at the bottom of the Tools panel offer the quickest and easiest method of applying the last-used color or gradient to objects, or removing a color, tint, or gradient.

When you add a stroke, it's assigned by default a width of 1 point. You can change the width and several other characteristics of a stroke using the controls in the Stroke panel. Except when working with text, you can also change the stroke width and type in the Control panel.

When using the Stroke panel to modify a stroke:

1. **Select any of the selection tools and click the object whose stroke you want to modify.**

2. **If the Stroke panel is not displayed, show it by choosing Window ⇨ Stroke or pressing ⌘+F10 or Ctrl+F10.**

3. **To change the width of stroke, enter a new value in the Weight field.** You can also change the Weight value by choosing a new value from the field's pop-up menu or by clicking the up and down arrows. (Each click increases or decreases the stroke by 1 point.)

4. **Set the Miter Limit.** The default of 4 is fine for almost all frames.

NOTE The value in the Stroke panel's Miter Limit field determines when a corner point switches from *mitered* (squared off) to beveled. You'll rarely use this feature; it's useful when you have thick lines joining at sharp angles. In such cases, the lines may extend farther than needed, and the miter value (1 to 500, with 1 being the most conservative setting and 500 the most forgiving) tells InDesign when to change the squared-off corner to a beveled one, which prevents the problem.

NEW FEATURE The shortcut for the Stroke panel has changed to ⌘+F10 or Ctrl+F10 in InDesign CS3. The old F10 shortcut still works but may conflict with Mac OS X's Exposé program.

5. **Click any of the three Cap iconic buttons to specify how dashes will look if you create a dashed stroke (covered in Step 9).** Figure 12.2 shows how each of the cap styles affect a line.

FIGURE 12.2

The line in this illustration was selected with the Direct Selection tool. Each of the three available endcap styles — butt (left), round (center), and projecting (right) — is shown.

6. **Click any of the three Join iconic buttons to specify how corners are handled.** Figure 12.3 shows how each of the join styles affects a corner.

7. **Choose an Align Stroke option.** The default is the first iconic button, Align Stroke to Center, which has the stroke straddle the frame. You can also choose Align Stroke to Inside, which places the entire thickness inside the frame boundary, or Align Stroke to Outside, which places the entire thickness outside the frame boundary.

8. **You can also choose endpoints for your strokes (this affects lines only, not rectangles, ellipses, and other closed-loop shapes) using the Start and End pop-up menus.** Figure 12.4 shows the options.

FIGURE 12.3

The Stroke panel lets you apply mitered (left), rounded (center), and beveled (right) corners to shapes.

FIGURE 12.4

The Start options in the Stroke panel. (The End options are identical.)

9. **To create a dashed line instead of a solid line, choose an option from the Type pop-up menu.** (These are also available from the Control panel.) You see 18 types of predefined dashes and stripes, as shown in Figure 12.5. The Gap Color and Gap Tint fields at the bottom of the Stroke panel become active as well and let you choose a specific color and tint for the gaps in dashes and stripes.

 To see the full Stroke panel, click the dual-arrow icon to the left of the Stroke panel's label. By default, the panel shows only the Weight, Cap, Miter Limit, and Join options.

FIGURE 12.5

The predefined dash and stripe options in the Stroke panel's Type pop-up menu

> **TIP**   If you really want to turn heads, you can create reversed text within the frame by adding a fill color and lightening the text. But remember: Reversed text is harder to read, so keep the text size on the large side, and use this effect sparingly. You may want to make the reversed-out text boldface to aid in its readability.

Creating stroke styles

InDesign lets you create custom strokes, known as *stroke styles*, in any of three types: dashed, dotted, and striped lines. To create custom dashes or stripes, choose the Stroke Styles option in the Stroke panel's flyout menu. Figure 12.6 shows the Stroke Styles dialog box from which you can create new strokes, edit or delete existing ones, and import (load) strokes from a stroke styles file that you create by saving a document's strokes as a separate file for import into other documents by clicking the Save button; stroke style files have the filename extension .inst.

> **QUARKXPRESS**   The InDesign Stroke Styles feature looks and works very much like the QuarkXPress Dashes & Stripes feature. The major difference is that InDesign has a separate option for dotted lines.

Note that you cannot edit or delete the seven default stripe patterns shown in the figure, nor can you edit or delete the default dash patterns; they're not even available in the dialog box. When you edit or create a stroke pattern, you get the New Stroke Style dialog box, shown in Figure 12.7. In the Name field, you type a name for your stroke. In the Type pop-up menu, you can choose to create (or convert a stripe you are editing to) a dashed, dotted, or striped stroke.

FIGURE 12.6

The Stroke Styles dialog box

FIGURE 12.7

The dashes version of the New Stroke Style dialog box

For dashes, you can resize the dash component by clicking and dragging the down-pointing triangle at the end of the dash in the ruler section. You can add dash segments by simply clicking on the ruler and dragging a segment to the desired width. Or you can use the Start and Length fields to manually specify them. The Pattern Length field is where you indicate the length of the segment you're defining; this is then repeated to fill the frame or line the stroke is applied to. In the Corners pop-up menu, you tell InDesign whether to adjust how the dashes and gaps are handled at corners; the default is Adjust Dashes and Gaps, a setting you should keep — it makes certain that your corners have dash segments that extend along both sides of the corner, which look neater. (Your other options are Adjust Dashes, Adjust Gaps, and None.) You can also choose a cap style and the stroke weight. The preview section of the pane lets you see your dash as you create or edit it.

For dots, you get a dialog box similar to dashes, as Figure 12.8 shows. The Start and Length fields disappear and are replaced with the Center field that determines where any added dots are placed on the ruler. (The initial dot, shown as a half-circle, starts at 0 and cannot be moved or deleted.) The Caps field is also gone.

FIGURE 12.8

The dotted-line version of the New Stroke Style dialog box

 To delete a dash or dot segment, just click and drag it off the ruler to the left.

For stripes, you get the dialog box shown in Figure 12.9. The principle is the same as for dashes: You create segments (in this case vertical, not horizontal) for the stripes by dragging on the ruler. However, the stripes version of the dialog box expresses its values in percentages because the actual thickness of each stripe is determined by the stroke weight — the thicker the stroke, the thicker each stripe is in the overall stroke.

TIP In all three versions of the New Stroke Style dialog box, you click Add to add the stroke to your document, and then you can create a new one. When you're done creating strokes, click OK. (When editing a stroke, the Add button is not available.)

Adding Fills

The option to add a stroke to any shape becomes even more powerful when combined with the option to fill any shape with a color or tint. For example, adding a stroke around a text frame is an effective way to draw attention to a sidebar.

Adding a fill to a shape is much like adding a stroke, and the options available for specifying color and tint are identical. The only difference is that you click the Fill iconic button in the Tools panel or Swatches panel rather than the Stroke iconic button.

FIGURE 12.9

The stripe version of the New Stroke Style dialog box

> **TIP**   Note the use of the Preview Weight pop-up menu and field in Figures 12.7 through 12.9. This lets you increase or decrease the preview size so you can better see thin or small elements in your stroke.

Adding Corner Options

Anytime you're working on an object that has any sharp corners, you have the option to add a little pizzazz to the corners with InDesign's Corner Options feature (choose Object ⇨ Corner Options). Five built-in corner options, shown in Figure 12.10, are available. Note that if the shape contains only smooth points, any corner option you apply won't be noticeable.

FIGURE 12.10

The Corner Options dialog box lets you apply any of these six options to frame corners. From left to right: None, Fancy, Bevel, Inset, Inverse Rounded, and Rounded.

A word of caution about adding fancy corners: These effects are handy for such things as certificates and coupons, but don't get carried away and use them for everyday tasks such as frames for graphics and text unless you have a good reason. Few things kill a design like too much graphic embellishment.

NEW FEATURE   The Corner Options menu and dialog box had been called Corner Effects in previous versions of InDesign. The functionality has not changed.

QUARKXPRESS   The corner-options feature in InDesign is similar to the text-box and picture-box variants in QuarkXPress, which offer the same corners except for the Fancy option. In QuarkXPress, you create, or convert, a box to a variant that has one of these corner options, while in InDesign, you apply the corner options to a frame or line.

To add a corner option:

1. **Use any of the selection tools to select the object to which you want to add a corner option.** Then choose Object ➪ Corner Options to display the Corner Options dialog box.

2. **Choose an option from the Effect pop-up menu.**

3. **Type a distance in the Size field.** The Size value determines the length that the option extends from the corner.

4. **Click OK to close the dialog box and apply your changes.**

 Enable the Preview check box to view changes as you make them.

Using the Attributes Panel

One of InDesign's easily overlooked panels is the Attributes panel. It has two sets of controls: one set for controlling overprinting and one set (with just one control) for controlling whether an object prints. (The Nonprinting option is covered in Chapter 10.)

The three overprinting check boxes — Overprint Fill, Overprint Stroke, and Overprint Gap — control how any fills, strokes, and gaps in an object or its stroke are printed. By default, these are all unchecked, and InDesign knocks out any colors beneath (such as for an object the current object overlaps or for an imported graphic in the frame) so you get the pure color specified for your fill, stroke, and/or gap. If these options are checked, InDesign will print the specific color on top of whatever colors might be underneath, essentially blending the colors. (Chapter 31 explains overprinting and knockouts in detail.)

You typically enable overprinting as a special effect, where that blending is intentional, such as for a ghosting effect.

TIP If you can't see a corner effect after applying one, make sure that a color is applied to the stroke or try making the object's stroke thicker. Increasing the Size value in the Corner Options dialog box can also make a corner option more visible.

Applying Lighting Effects

InDesign offers sophisticated built-in drop shadow, feathering, and other options that let you create dimensional effects based on simulated lighting. It also lets you apply transparency to objects, so you can make them fade away or overlap so that the underlying object is somewhat visible.

NEW FEATURE InDesign CS3 adds a bevy of lighting effects, including inner shadows, outer and inner glows, beveling and embossing, satin finish, and two additional kinds of feathering.

QUARKXPRESS Most versions of QuarkXPress do not offer lighting-effects features, although there are third-party plug-ins to add many of these capabilities, and QuarkXPress 7 does have transparency and drop-shadow features included.

Using the Effects panel

You access InDesign's lighting effects from the Effects panel (Window ⇨ Effects, or Shift+⌘+F10 or Ctrl+Shift+F10). The panel itself offers controls for InDesign's transparency functions, but you can access the other lighting effects from it as well, either by choosing the desired option from the fly-out menu's Effects menu option or by clicking the Add an Object Effect pop-up menu (the *fx* icon) at the bottom of the panel.

> **NOTE**   The Add an Effect iconic pop-up menu is also available in the Control panel. And you can select the same options from the submenu when choosing Object ⇨ Effects. All of these open the Effects dialog box.

> **NEW FEATURE**   The Effects panel is the new name for the former Transparency pane, because it now includes additional lighting effects. Its shortcut has also changed to Shift+⌘+F10 or Ctrl+Shift+F10. (The old Shift+F10 shortcut still works but may interfere with Mac OS X's Exposé program.)

A cool capability in the Effects panel is the ability to apply effects from one object to other objects. In the panel, you see a list with four items: Object, Stroke, Fill, and Text. (If not, click the triangle to the left of Object to reveal the others.) Select the desired component in that list before applying the transparency settings (otherwise they apply to the entire object); if you are applying other effects, you can choose what to apply later on, as described later in this chapter.

If the selected object has any lighting effects applied to it, you see *fx* to the left of whichever object components (Object, Stroke, Fill, and Text) have these effects. If you hover the mouse over the *fx* symbol, InDesign lists what effects are applied. Click and drag the desired *fx* symbol to an object you want to apply the same effects to, releasing the mouse when it is over the desired object. (You of course can also use object styles, as described in Chapter 13, to apply multiple settings including lighting effects to objects, but this Effect panel drag-and-drop formatting provides a quick way for applying consistent formatting that you don't want to include in an object style.)

> **NOTE**   This ability to drag and drop lighting effects is not available if the only effect applied is transparency (including any blending mode settings).

The Effects panel's flyout menu also has two controls to undo your lighting effects: Clear Effects undoes lighting effects such as drop shadows for the selected object, while Clear All Transparency also removes the opacity settings for objects. These menu options have equivalent iconic buttons called Remove Effects and Clear all Effects and Make Opaque, respectively, as Figure 12.11 shows.

Applying transparency

One of InDesign's most sophisticated tools is its set of transparency options that lets you make items partially transparent. You apply transparency with the Effects panel (Window ⇨ Effects, or Shift+⌘+F10 or Ctrl+Shift+F10). Figure 12.11 shows example transparency settings for an image and text (the original objects are at left).

FIGURE 12.11

The Effects panel and its flyout menu, the effects-related iconic buttons in the Control panel, and an example of a transparency applied to both text and a photo

Opacity field and pop-up menu

Add an Object Effect pop-up menu

Drop Shadow

Apply Effects to Object pop-up menu

Blending Mode pop-up menu

Clear All Effects and Make Opaque

Effects pop-up menu

Opacity field and pop-up menu

Remove Effects

In the Opacity field of the Effects panel, the Control panel, or Effects dialog box's Transparency pane, enter a value or choose one from the unlabeled Opacity pop-up menu. A value of 0 is completely invisible, while a value of 100 is completely solid.

NEW FEATURE You can now apply transparency separately to an object itself, to just its stroke, to just its fill, and to just its text. To do so, select the desired element from the list at the center of the Effects panel (click the right-facing arrow if the list does not display) or use the Apply Effect to Object iconic pop-up menu in the Control panel. You cannot apply these effects to text selections or to layers.

NOTE If you remove an object from a group that had transparency applied (via cut and paste or copy and paste), that pasted object does not have the group's transparency settings applied to it.

There are 16 transparency types, called *blending modes,* available in the unlabeled Blending Mode pop-up menu at the upper left of the Effects panel. The differences among them can be subtle or extreme, depending on a variety of issues. (Photoshop and Illustrator users will recognize these options from those programs.) You should experiment with them to see what effect works best in each case. The 16 modes are:

- **Normal:** Colors the selection with the blend color, without interaction with the base color. This is the default mode.

- **Multiply:** Multiplies the base color by the blend color. The resulting color is always a darker color. Multiplying any color with black produces black. Multiplying any color with white leaves the color unchanged. The effect is similar to drawing on a page with multiple magic markers.

- **Screen:** Multiplies the inverse of the blend and base colors. The resulting color is always a lighter color. Screening with black leaves the color unchanged. Screening with white produces white. The effect is similar to projecting multiple slide images on top of each other.

- **Overlay:** Multiplies or screens the colors, depending on the base color. Patterns or colors overlay the existing artwork, preserving the highlights and shadows of the base color while mixing in the blend color to reflect the lightness or darkness of the original color.

- **Soft Light:** Darkens or lightens the colors, depending on the blend color. The effect is similar to shining a diffused spotlight on the artwork. If the blend color (light source) is lighter than 50 percent gray, the artwork is lightened, as if it were dodged. If the blend color is darker than 50 percent gray, the artwork is darkened, as if it were burned in. Painting with pure black or white produces a distinctly darker or lighter area but does not result in pure black or white.

- **Hard Light:** Multiplies or screens the colors, depending on the blend color. The effect is similar to shining a harsh spotlight on the artwork. If the blend color (light source) is lighter than 50 percent gray, the artwork is lightened, as if it were screened. This is useful for adding highlights to artwork. If the blend color is darker than 50 percent gray, the artwork is darkened, as if it were multiplied. This is useful for adding shadows to artwork. Painting with pure black or white results in pure black or white.

- **Color Dodge:** Brightens the base color to reflect the blend color. Blending with black produces no change.

- **Color Burn:** Darkens the base color to reflect the blend color. Blending with white produces no change.

- **Darken:** Selects the base or blend color — whichever is darker — as the resulting color. Areas lighter than the blend color are replaced, and areas darker than the blend color do not change.

- **Lighten:** Selects the base or blend color — whichever is lighter — as the resulting color. Areas darker than the blend color are replaced, and areas lighter than the blend color do not change.

- **Difference:** Subtracts either the blend color from the base color or the base color from the blend color, depending on which has the greater brightness value. Blending with white inverts the base color values; blending with black produces no change.

- **Exclusion:** Creates an effect similar to, but lower in contrast than, the Difference mode. Blending with white inverts the base color components. Blending with black produces no change.

- **Hue:** Creates a color with the luminance and saturation of the base color and the hue of the blend color.

- **Saturation:** Creates a color with the luminance and hue of the base color and the saturation of the blend color. Using this mode in an area with no saturation (a gray) produces no change.

- **Color:** Creates a color with the luminance of the base color and the hue and saturation of the blend color. This preserves the gray levels in the artwork and is useful for coloring monochrome artwork and for tinting color artwork.

- **Luminosity:** Creates a color with the hue and saturation of the base color and the luminance of the blend color. This mode produces the inverse of the Color mode.

NOTE The Difference, Exclusion, Hue, Saturation, Color, and Luminosity modes do not blend spot colors, just process colors.

NOTE InDesign's blending calculations differ based on whether the document is to be printed (usually in CMYK) or seen on-screen (as RGB). Be sure to choose the right blending space based on the intended output. To do so, choose Edit ➪ Transparency Blend Space ➪ Document CMYK or Edit ➪ Transparency Blend Space ➪ Document RGB, as appropriate.

You have two other transparency-related options in the Effects panel:

- **Isolate Blending:** This option restricts the blending modes to the objects in a group, instead of also applying them to objects beneath the group. This can prevent unintended changes to those underlying objects.

- **Knockout Group:** This option obscures any objects below the selected group. But those objects beneath the knocked-out group are still affected by any blend mode settings applied to the group, unless the Isolate Blending option is also selected.

CROSS-REF Chapter 31 explains printing issues when using transparency.

Applying drop shadows and inner shadows

A drop shadow casts its shadow away from the object, as if it were blocking the light. An inner shadow casts its shadow inside, as if the frame were a wall blocking light that falls inside the object. Figure 12.12 shows examples of these and the other lighting effects.

FIGURE 12.12

Various effects applied to a set of objects. Top row: the original object, drop shadow, and inner shadow. Second row: basic feather, directional feather, and gradient feather. Third row: outer glow and inner glow. Bottom row: bevel and emboss, and satin.

The Drop Shadow pane of the Effects dialog box, shown in Figure 12.13, is accessed by choosing Object ➪ Effects ➪ Drop Shadow or pressing Option+⌘+M or Ctrl+Alt+M. (You can also open this pane by choosing Effects ➪ Drop Shadow from the Effects panel's flyout menu, as well as from the Add an Object Effect pop-up menu [the *fx* iconic menu] in the Effects panel or Control panel. Even simpler: click the Drop Shadow iconic button in the Control panel.)

FIGURE 12.13

The Drop Shadow pane of the Effects dialog box

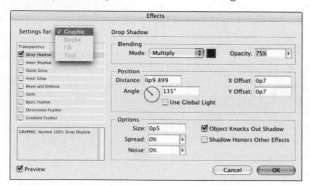

To apply a drop shadow to an object, you select it with a selection tool — you cannot apply the shadow to just highlighted characters. In the dialog box, you set the following options:

- Choose what component of the object to apply the drop shadow to by using the Settings For pop-up menu or by using the Apply Effect to Object iconic pop-up menu in the Control panel.

NEW FEATURE You can apply multiple drop shadows, one to each component of an object: Object, Fill, Stroke, and/or Text.

- Check the Drop Shadow option to turn on the drop shadow function for the selected component.

- Select a lighting type (technically, a blend mode) by choosing one of the 16 options in the Mode pop-up menu. These are the same blending modes used in transparencies and are covered earlier in this section.

- Choose a color source — Swatches, RGB, CMYK, and Lab — from the Color pop-up menu (the square swatch to the right of the Mode pop-up menu), and then select a color from the sliders or swatches below. You'll get sliders for RGB, CMYK, and Lab with which to mix a color if you selected RGB, CMYK, or Lab in the Color pop-up menu, and a set of previously defined color swatches if you selected Swatches in the Color pop-up menu.

- Specify the opacity by typing a value in the Opacity field; 0% is invisible, while 100% is completely solid.

- Specify the shadow's position relative to the object using the X Offset and Y Offset fields. A positive X Offset moves the shadow to the right, while a positive Y Offset moves the shadow down. Negative values go in the other direction.

- Specify the shadow's size by typing a value in the Distance field.

NEW FEATURE The Distance field had been called Blur in previous versions of InDesign.

- Set the light source angle by entering a value in the Angle field or by clicking a location in the circle. You can also check Use Global Light to use those settings, as described in the sidebar "What Is Global Light?"

- To control the shadow's appearance, use the controls in the Options area of the pane. The Size field lets you specify the width of the shadow's fuzzy edge. (A value of 0 gives it a hard edge, a value as great as Distance fades the shadow over the whole shadow.) The Spread field and slider let you control where the shadow begins to get fuzzy. (A value of 0 starts immediately at the object edge, while a larger value pushes the fuzzy part away from the object.) The Noise field and slider let you add visual noise to the shadow, making it less smooth as the value increases. The other two controls — the Object Knocks Out Shadow and Shadow Honors Other Effects check boxes — are self-explanatory.

- To see the effects to your selected object as you experiment with various settings, select the Preview option.

TIP Although traditionally associated with text, you can apply drop shadows to any objects, such as frames and shapes.

 NEW FEATURE The Drop Shadow dialog box from previous versions of InDesign is now a pane of the new Effects dialog box in InDesign CS3. Its menu option in the Object menu has also been moved to a submenu option you access through Object ⇨ Effects.

Applying inner shadows

The controls for the new inner shadow feature work almost exactly the same as the controls for drop shadows, with these exceptions:

- The Spread field in the Options area is called Choke. It does the same as Spread but applies inside the frame rather than outside of it.

- The Object Knocks Out Shadow and Shadow Honors Other Effects check boxes aren't available for inner shadows.

Applying feathering

A similar option to drop shadows is feathering, which essentially softens the edges of objects. Figures 12.14 through 12.16 show all three types of feathering.

NEW FEATURE InDesign CS3 offers three feathering variations; directional and gradient feathering are new to this version.

Applying basic feathering

To apply basic feathering, where the edges are blurred around all sides of an object, select the Basic Feather option. The controls are simple:

- In the Feather Width field, enter a value for the degree of feathering — smaller numbers have the least effect; larger numbers have the most effect. The featuring area starts at the outside edge of the object, so a larger number "eats into" the object, making it a wispier version of itself.

- The Choke field and pop-up menu let you set where the frame edge begins to get fuzzy (a value of 0 starts immediately at the object edge, while a larger value pushes the fuzzy part into the object).

- The Noise field and pop-up menu let you add visual noise to the shadow, making it less smooth as the value increases.

- The Corners pop-up menu gives you three options: Sharp, Rounded, and Diffused. The Sharp option retains the original corner shape as much as possible. The Rounded option rounds the corners of the object; it can distort the shape dramatically at larger Feather Width settings. The Diffused option creates a soft, almost smoky effect by making the object borders and corners more translucent.

FIGURE 12.14

The Basic Feather pane of the Effects dialog box

NEW FEATURE The Feather dialog box in previous versions of InDesign is now part of the Basic Feather pane of the new Effects dialog box in InDesign CS3. Its menu option in the Object menu has also been moved to be a submenu option you access through Object ⇨ Effects. Also, the Choke and Noise options are new to InDesign CS3.

Applying directional feathering

The Directional Feather controls act like a drop shadow in that there is an external light source that determines how the feathering's blur appears along an object's edges. The effect is more like a shadowy smear. The controls are similar to that of Basic Feather, with these exceptions:

- Rather than have one Width setting, there are separate settings for the Top, Bottom, Left, and Right. If the chain icon is a solid chain, then all edges have the same width; click it to get the broken-chain icon, which lets you control each edge independently.

- The Shape pop-up menu lets you choose which edges are feathered: First Edge Only (the ones specified in the Width fields), Leading Edges (any in the path of the light source), and All Edges.

- Set the light source angle by entering a value in the Angle field or by clicking a location in the circle.

FIGURE 12.15

The Directional Feather pane of the Effects dialog box

Applying gradient feathering

The Gradient Feather controls create the effect of having a strong light source near the object, washing out part of the object. Here's how the controls work:

- You set the gradient itself in the Gradient Stops area. You add stop points, choose opacity for each, and set the location for both gradient stops and transition points just as you do for any gradient (see Chapter 8). You can reverse the gradient's direction by clicking the iconic button to the right of the gradient ramp.

- In the Options area, you set the gradient type — Linear or Radial — and the lighting angle.

FIGURE 12.16

The Gradient Feather pane of the Effects dialog box

CROSS-REF You can also apply gradient feathering using the Gradient Feather tool, as described in Chapter 8.

Applying outer and inner glows

Glows are what they sound like: A lighting effect that makes it seem as if there is light behind an object that causes it to glow (an outer glow) or a light source within the object's frame that causes a glow inside (an inner glow). Figure 12.17 and Figure 12.18 show the panes.

Applying an outer glow

Here's how the controls for outer glow work (note that the first three options are the same as for transparency effects):

- Choose the blending mode in the Mode pop-up menu, the glow color in the Color pop-up menu (the square swatch to the right of the Mode pop-up menu), and the transparency level in the Opacity field or pop-up menu.

- Choose the glow's intensity by choosing Software or Precise in the Technique pop-up menu. The Precise option creates a more saturated, harsher glow.

- Choose how far away from the frame that the glow begins to dissipate by entering a value in the Spread field. A value of 0 starts the fade immediately.

- Choose the width of the glow in the Size field.

- Add visual noise to the shadow, making it less smooth as the value increases, by entering a value in the Noise field or choosing a value from the pop-up menu.

FIGURE 12.17

The Outer Glow pane of the Effects dialog box

Applying an inner glow

The controls for inner glows are nearly identical to those for outer glows, with these two exceptions:

■ The Spread field in the Options area is called Choke. It does the same as Spread but applies inside the frame rather than outside of it.

■ The Source options — Center and Edge — let you choose the light source's location relative to the object.

FIGURE 12.18

The Inner Glow pane of the Effects dialog box

Applying beveling and embossing

Beveling means to make an object appear to be above the plane of other objects, thus casting a shadow at the edges. *Embossing* is a variation of beveling where only the edges are raised; the contents are lowered back to the normal plane. Figure 12.19 shows the Bevel and Emboss pane.

FIGURE 12.19

The Bevel and Emboss pane of the Effects dialog box

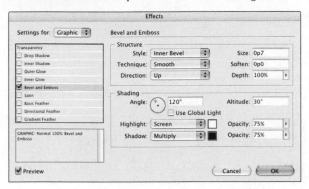

The controls for beveling and embossing combine controls from several other lighting effects:

- In the Structure area, choose the bevel or emboss style from the Style pop-up menu: Outer Bevel (the bevel extends outside the frame), Inner Bevel (the bevel extends inside the frame), Emboss, and Pillow Emboss (a shallower embossing).

- In the Technique pop-up menu, choose the type of shadow effects: Smooth, Chisel Hard, and Chisel Soft.

- Choose the apparent height of the effect by entering a value in the Depth field or using the Depth slider. Similarly, choose the shadow's thickness by entering a value in the Size field.

- Choose the direction of the effect by selecting either Up (raised) or Down (etched out) in the Direction pop-up menu.

- Adjust the shadow's intensity by entering a value in the Soften field.

- In the Shading area, choose the light source's direction by entering a value in the Angle field, clicking a point in the circle, or checking the Use Global Light option. Similarly, adjust the light source's height in the Altitude field.

- Adjust the blending mode applied to areas of the bevel or emboss that are "hit" by the light using the Highlight Mode pop-up menu and the blending mode applied to the shadowed areas using the Shadow Mode pop-up menu. In both cases, there is also a combination field and pop-up menu labeled Opacity where you can adjust the effect's transparency.

Applying satin effects

The satin effect is similar to a glow, except that it applies a shadow to the frame's edges, as if the object were made of satin cloth and bowed slightly out from its edges. Figure 12.20 shows the Satin pane.

FIGURE 12.20

The Satin pane of the Effects dialog box

To apply a satin effect:

- Choose the blending mode in the Mode pop-up menu, the glow color in the Color pop-up menu (the square swatch to the right of the Mode pop-up menu), and the transparency level in the Opacity field or pop-up menu.

- Choose the light source's direction by entering a value in the Angle field, clicking a point in the circle.

- Choose the width of the satin effect in the Size field.

- Specify the shadow's size by typing a value in the Distance field.

- To have the satin effect appear as if the object were sinking slightly from the edges (making it darker), check Invert.

Summary

If you have a frame or shape selected, you can add a stroke around its border or add a color to its background, as well as apply transparency to an object or its contents. You can further enhance these attributes with the corner-options capabilities. You can apply strokes (and colors) to lines and text as well.

InDesign CS3 has significantly expanded its set of lighting-effects capabilities, adding inner shadow, glow, feather, bevel, emboss, and satin effects to the transparency, drop shadow, and basic feathering effects from previous versions. You can apply these effects to entire objects, to just their frames, just their fills, or just their text.

Chapter 13

Orchestrating Objects

F rames, shapes, lines, and paths are the building blocks with which you construct InDesign pages. Becoming familiar with creating and modifying individual objects, which is the focus of Chapters 9 through 12, is a key step in learning how to create publications with InDesign. The next step is to learn how to use several features that let you manipulate multiple objects at once and quickly adjust the relationships among the various objects that make up a page. A good InDesign user can handle individual objects one at a time with ease, a virtuoso user can simultaneously juggle several objects with equal ease.

Think of it this way: As an InDesign user, you're much like an architect. You begin with a blueprint — perhaps a rough, felt-tip pen sketch or maybe just a graphic in your mind's eye — open a new document, and start construction. The settings you establish in the New Document dialog box (File ⇨ New ⇨ Document, or ⌘+N or Ctrl+N) — the page size, margin placement, column arrangement, and number of pages — serve as the foundation as you begin adding objects to your pages. You must then construct your building or rather, your publication, using four basic components: Text frames, graphics frames, shapes, and lines. You can tweak and twist each of those components in a nearly endless variety of ways while retaining basic properties. After all, a sheared (skewed) and mirrored text frame with a purple dashed stroke, a gradient background, and magenta text outlined in cyan is still just a text frame.

As a publication evolves, plans invariably change: An advertiser pulls out and a magazine article needs to be stretched an extra half-page by enlarging an InDesign-created illustration. A client loves his company's newsletter but wants the front-page graphic cropped differently. A new product is added to a catalog and half the pages reflow. If you build your documents soundly

IN THIS CHAPTER

Changing the stacking order of objects

Working with groups

Locking objects

Nesting objects

Inserting objects within a text thread

Anchoring objects to text

Setting text wrap

Working with object styles

Managing source links

from the ground up and use the features covered in this chapter, you should be prepared to handle even the most challenging page building—and rebuilding—tasks.

Stacking Objects

Each time you begin work on a new page, you start with a clean slate (unless the page is based on a master page, in which case the master objects act as the page's background; see Chapter 7 for more on master pages). Every time you add an object to a page—either by using any of InDesign's object-creation tools or with the Place command (File ➪ Place, or ⌘+D or Ctrl+D)—the new object occupies a unique place in the page's object hierarchy, or *stacking order*.

The first object you place on a page is automatically positioned at the bottom of the stacking order; the next object is positioned one level higher than the first object (that is, on top of and in front of the backmost object); the next object is stacked one level higher; and so on for every object you add to the page. It's not uncommon for a page to have several dozen or even several hundred objects.

TIP   When building pages, always try to keep the number of objects to a minimum. For example, instead of putting a headline in one text frame and a subhead in a separate text frame directly below the one that contains the headline, use a single text frame. Lean documents save and print more quickly and are less problematic to modify than bloated documents.

Although each object occupies its own level, if the objects on a page don't overlap, then the stacking order is not an issue. But some of the most interesting graphic effects you can achieve with InDesign involve arranging several overlapping objects, so it's important to be aware of the three-dimensional nature of a page's stacking order.

Because objects are added in back-to-front order, it makes sense to build your pages from back to front. For example, if you want to use a lightly tinted version of a scanned image as the background for a page, you would first place the image on the page, and then add other objects on top of or in front of the graphics frame.

In an ideal world, the first object you place on a page would remain forever the backmost, the last object would be the frontmost, and every object in between—created in perfect order from back to front—would relate correctly with every other object. In this perfect world, you would never have to worry about moving objects backward or forward.

But the world is not perfect, and you may change your mind about what you want to achieve in your layout after you've already placed objects in it. To change an object's position in a page's stacking order, use the Arrange menu option (Object ➪ Arrange), which offers four submenus:

- Bring to Front (Shift+⌘+] or Ctrl+Shift+])
- Bring Forward (⌘+] or Ctrl+])
- Send to Back (Shift+⌘+[or Ctrl+Shift+[)
- Send Backward (⌘+[or Ctrl+[)

For example, you might want to see how a piece of text looks in front of an illustration. But if you create the text frame before you create or place the illustration, you have to move the text frame forward (or the illustration backward) in the stacking order.

CROSS-REF In addition to letting you change the stacking order of objects on a page, InDesign also lets you create document-wide layers. Each layer contains a separate collection of stacked objects. For more information about using layers, see Chapter 6.

To change the stacking order of objects:

1. **Use any of the object-creation tools to create four overlapping shapes, as shown in Figure 13.1.** The numbers in parentheses indicate the order in which you should create the shapes.

FIGURE 13.1

The first shape you create is the backmost, the second is one level above, and so on. In this example, the three smaller boxes partially overlap each other and they are all in front of the largest box.

2. **If it's not already displayed, open the Swatches panel by choosing Window ⇨ Swatches or pressing F6.** You use this panel to change the shade of each object so you can easily tell them apart.

3. **Click the Selection tool, click the last object you created, and then use the color tools in the Tools panel or the Swatches panel to fill the object with a color.**

CROSS-REF See Chapters 8 and 12 for more information about applying fills and strokes to objects.

4. **Use the Swatches panel to fill each of the remaining boxes with a successively lighter tint of the color, as shown in Figure 13.2.** In the example, the remaining shapes are tinted at 25 percent, 50 percent, and 75 percent, respectively.

FIGURE 13.2

Applying tints to the shapes lets you see the stacking order of the four rectangles. Every InDesign object occupies one level in the stacking order.

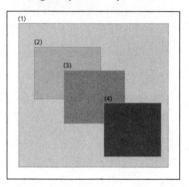

5. **Click the frontmost shape (the last one you created), and then choose Object ⇨ Arrange ⇨ Send Backward or press ⌘+[or Ctrl+[.** Notice that the Bring to Front and Bring Forward menu options are not available. That's because you can't move the front-most object any farther forward in the stacking order.

6. **Click the backmost shape (the first one you created), and then choose Object ⇨ Arrange ⇨ Bring Forward or press ⌘+] or Ctrl+].** When you bring the object forward, one of the objects becomes obscured.

7. **Choose Object ⇨ Arrange ⇨ Bring to Front or press Shift+⌘+] or Ctrl+Shift+].** The smaller shapes are now obscured by the largest one.

8. **Choose Object ⇨ Arrange ⇨ Send to Back or press Shift+⌘+[or Ctrl+Shift+[.** The hidden objects are once again visible.

To select an object that's hidden behind one or more other objects, press and hold ⌘ or Ctrl, and then click anywhere within the area of the hidden object. The first click selects the topmost object; each successive click selects the next lowest object in the stacking order. When the bottom object is selected, the next click selects the top object. If you don't know where a hidden object is, you can simply click the object or objects in front of it, then send the object(s) to the back.

Another way to select objects that are in a stack or group is to use the Select Previous Object or Select Next Object iconic buttons in the Control panel. If you Shift+click either button, InDesign jumps past four objects and selects the fifth one. If you ⌘+click or Contrl+click either button, InDesign selects to the bottommost or topmost object, respectively.

CROSS-REF   See Chapter 10 for more details on selecting objects.

Combining Objects into a Group

InDesign lets you combine several objects into a group. A group of objects behaves like a single object, which means that you can cut, copy, move, or modify all the objects in a group in a single operation. Groups have many uses. For example, you might create a group to:

- Combine several objects that make up an illustration so that you can move, modify, copy, or scale all objects in a single operation.

- Keep a graphics frame and its accompanying caption (text) frame together so that if you change your mind about their placement, you can reposition both objects at once.

- Combine several vertical lines that are used to separate the columns of a table so that you can quickly change the stroke, color, length, and position of all lines.

TIP If you want to manipulate a group, select any object in the group with the Selection tool. The group's bounding box appears. Any transformation you perform is applied to all objects in the group. If you want to manipulate a specific object in a group, choose the Direct Selection tool.

To create a group:

1. **Switch to a selection tool.**
2. **Select all the objects you want to include in your group.**
3. **Choose Object ⇨ Group or press ⌘+G or Ctrl+G.**

That's all there is to it. When you create a group from objects that do not occupy successive levels in the stacking order, the objects are shuffled as necessary so that the grouped objects are stacked on adjacent layers directly below the topmost object. If you create a group from objects on different layers, all objects are moved to the top layer and stacked in succession beneath the topmost object.

CROSS-REF See Chapter 6 for more about layers.

NOTE You cannot create a group if some of the selected objects are locked and some are not locked. All selected objects must be locked or unlocked before you can group them. (Locking and unlocking objects is covered later in this chapter.)

Using groups within groups

One nifty thing about groups is that you can include a group within a group. For example, all the objects in Figure 13.3 — five stars and two circles (a gray circle and a white circle form the moon) — have been grouped, making it easy to manipulate the whole illustration. But that's not all. The stars within the group are also a group. So are the two circles that make up the crescent moon. That is, first the stars were grouped together, then the two circles were grouped together, and finally then the group of stars was grouped with the circles that form the moon to create a larger group. Grouping the stars makes it easy to change all of them at once, as shown in Figure 13.4. And grouping the two circles that make up the crescent moon makes it easy to move the moon.

NOTE A group can contain as many levels of subgroups, or *nested* groups, as you want, but it's best to keep things as simple as you can. The more levels of nested groups you have within a group, the more work it is to ungroup the objects.

The bounding box indicates that all the objects within it have been grouped. What you can't tell from this illustration is that the five stars are a group within the larger group, which lets you move or modify all of them in a single operation, as shown in Figure 13.4.

The group selection tool (explained in the next section) lets you select a nested group. In this example, the nested group of stars was selected, and then a radial blend was applied to all of them at once.

Selecting objects within groups

The main reason you create groups in the first place is so that you can delete, copy, move, or modify all the objects at once. But sometimes, you may want to modify an object within a group. No problem. You don't have to ungroup objects to modify an individual object. InDesign offers several options for selecting objects — and nested groups — within groups. You can:

- Select an individual object by clicking it with the Direct Selection tool or Position tool.
- Double-click an object in a group with the Selection tool to select just that object. (This is new to InDesign CS3.)

- Select the bounding box of an individual object by clicking it with the Direct Selection tool or Position tool, and then switching to the Selection tool.

- If you have selected an object in a group of objects, choose Object ⇨ Select ⇨ Previous Object in Group to navigate to the previous object in the group, or choose Object ⇨ Select ⇨ Next Object in Group to navigate to the previous object in the group. Or use the Select Previous Object or Select Next Object iconic buttons in the Control panel.

- Select multiple objects within a group by Shift+clicking each object with the Direct Selection or Position tool.

- Select the bounding box of multiple objects within a group by Shift+clicking each object with the Direct Selection or Position tool, and then switching to the Selection tool.

- Select a nested group by clicking any object within the nested group with the Direct Selection or Position tool, and then pressing and holding Option or Alt and clicking the object again. Pressing and holding Option or Alt in this situation temporarily accesses the Group Selection tool, indicated by a small plus sign (+) below and to the right of the arrow pointer.

Ungrouping

After creating a group, you may eventually decide that you want to return the objects to their original, ungrouped state. To do so, simply click any object in the group with the Selection tool to select the entire group, and then choose Object ⇨ Ungroup or press Shift+⌘+G or Ctrl+Shift+G. If you ungroup a group that contains a group, the contained group is not affected. To ungroup this subgroup, you must select it, and then choose Ungroup again.

Locking Objects

If you're certain that you want a particular object to remain where it is, you can use Object ⇨ Lock Position, or ⌘+L or Ctrl+L, to prevent the object from being moved. Generally, you'll want to lock repeating elements such as headers, footers, folios, and page numbers so that they're not accidentally moved. (Such repeating elements are usually placed on a master page; you can lock objects on master pages, too.) A locked object can't be moved whether you click and drag it with the mouse or change the values in the X and Y fields in the Control panel or Transform panel. Not only can you not move a locked object, but you can't delete one, either. However, you can change other attributes of a locked object, including its stroke and fill.

To unlock an object, use Object ⇨ Unlock Position, or Option+⌘+L or Ctrl+Alt+L.

CROSS-REF You can also lock entire layers, as described in Chapter 6.

QUARKXPRESS QuarkXPress's lock feature is meant to prevent accidental repositioning or resizing by the mouse; it lets you modify the locked object through dialog boxes and the Measurements palette. By contrast, locking in InDesign is meant to truly lock the object from any changes, not just accidental ones.

Nesting Objects within Frames

Not only does InDesign let you combine several objects into a group, but you can also place an object within the boundaries of a frame. Just as a group that's embedded within a larger group is said to be a *nested* group, an object that's been placed within another frame is said to be a *nested* object. When you place an object within a frame, the containing frame acts as the cropping shape for the object within.

One of the more common uses of nested frames is for cropping imported graphics. When you place a graphic onto a page, the graphic is automatically placed within a frame. (You can also place a graphic within an existing frame.) You can reveal and hide different areas of the graphic by resizing or reshaping the container frame. Figure 13.5 shows an imported graphic that's been placed within a circular frame.

CROSS-REF   For more information about importing and modifying graphics, see Part VI.

FIGURE 13.5

In this example, the rectangle displayed with handles indicates the border of a graphic that's been placed into a triangular frame. Clicking the graphic with the Direct Selection tool selects the graphic rather than the round frame. To select the frame's bounding box instead of the graphic, click the graphic with the Direct Selection tool.

Nesting Frames within Other Frames

As you can with groups, you can place a frame within a frame within a frame and so on, to create as many nested levels as you want. The same caveat applies: Keep things as simple as possible to achieve the desired effect. To nest a frame within a frame:

1. **Use any selection tool to select the frame you want to nest within another frame.**

2. **Choose Edit ➪ Copy or press ⌘+C or Ctrl+C.**

3. **Select the frame into which you want to place the copied object, and then choose Edit ➪ Paste Into or press Option+⌘+V or Ctrl+Alt+V.** Figure 13.6 shows a before/after example of a squiggly line that's been pasted into a circular frame that serves as the masking shape for the line.

> **TIP** Selecting nested objects can be tricky. In general, the same selection techniques that work with groups also work with nested frames. If you need to modify text within a nested or grouped text frame, simply click within the frame with the Type tool.

> **QUARKXPRESS** InDesign's nested frames are similar to QuarkXPress's constrained boxes, though the QuarkXPress constrained boxes don't let you mask objects as InDesign's nested frames do — the entire nested box must fit within the enclosing box in QuarkXPress.

FIGURE 13.6

I created the squiggly line (left) with the Pen tool. I then copied and pasted it into (Edit ➪ Paste Into) a circular frame (right). Selecting the line with the Direct Selection tool shows the visible portion of the line within the oval cropping frame, as well as the parts of the line that are cropped.

Creating Inline Frames

In most cases, you want the objects you place on your pages to remain precisely where you put them. But sometimes, you want to place objects relative to related text in such a way that the objects move when the text is edited. For example, if you're creating a product catalog that's essentially a continuous list of product descriptions and you want to include a graphic with each description, you can paste graphics within the text to create inline graphics frames.

An inline frame is treated like a single character. If you insert or delete text that precedes an inline frame, the frame moves forward or backward along with the rest of the text that follows the inserted or deleted text. Although inline frames usually contain graphics, they can just as easily contain text or nothing at all.

There are two ways to create an inline frame: using the Paste command and using the Place command.

CAUTION Inline frames may interfere with line spacing in paragraphs with automatic leading. If the inline frame is larger than the point size in use, the automatic leading value for that line is calculated from the inline frame. This leads to inconsistent line spacing in the paragraph. To work around this, you can either apply a fixed amount of leading to all characters in the paragraph, adjust the size of inline frames, place inline frames at the beginning of a paragraph, or place inline frames in their own paragraphs.

QUARKXPRESS InDesign's inline frames are similar to QuarkXPress's anchored boxes, with two important differences: First, if an inline frame is wider than the containing text frame, InDesign hangs the extra width of the inline frame outside of the width of the text frame instead of causing a text overflow as it does in QuarkXPress. Second, QuarkXPress does not offer the same level of positioning control as InDesign does.

There are three ways to create inline frames. The first two are the simplest, but the third gives you more control over the inline frame when you create it.

NOTE You can set text wraps on inline frames using the standard Text Wrap panel (Window ⇨ Text Wrap, or Option+⌘+W or Ctrl+Alt+W), as described later in this chapter. But note that such wraps affect only text that appears on the same line or below the inline frame, not text above the inline frame or text in other frames.

Creating an inline frame with the Paste command

If you want to create an inline frame from an object you've already created, all you have to do is copy or cut the object and then paste it into text as you would a piece of highlighted text. Here's how:

1. **Use the Selection or Position tool to select the object you want to paste within text.** You can use any type of object: A line, an empty shape, a text or graphics frame, even a group of objects.

2. **Choose Edit ⇨ Copy or press ⌘+C or Ctrl+C.** If you don't need the original item, you can use the Cut command (Edit ⇨ Cut; ⌘+X or Ctrl+X) instead of the Copy command. An object that you cut or copy remains on the Clipboard until you cut or copy something else or you turn off your computer. If you intend to use the original object elsewhere, it's better to use the Copy command when creating an inline frame.

3. **Select the Type tool (or press T), and then click within the text where you want to place the copied object.** Make sure the cursor is flashing where you intend to place the inline frame.

4. **Choose Edit ⇨ Paste or press ⌘+V or Ctrl+V.** Figure 13.7 shows an example of an inline frame.

TIP Inline frames often work best when placed at the beginning of a paragraph. If you place an inline frame within text to which automatic leading has been applied, the resulting line spacing can be inconsistent. To fix this problem, you can resize the inline frame.

To change the position of an inline frame, choose Object ⇨ Anchored Object ⇨ Options. The Anchored Object Options dialog box that appears is the same as the Insert Anchored Object dialog box covered later in this section and shown in Figure 13.8.

Creating an inline frame with the Place command

In addition to using the Paste command to create an inline frame from an existing object, you can use the Place command to create an inline graphics frame from an external graphics file. (You can't use this technique for inline text frames.) Here's how:

1. **Select the Type tool (or press T), and then click within a text frame to establish the insertion point.**
2. **Choose File ⇨ Place or press ⌘+D or Ctrl+D.**
3. **Locate and select the graphics file you want to place within the text, and then click Choose or Open.**

 TIP You can use the transform tools (Rotate, Scale, Shear, and Free Transform) and the Control panel or Transform panel to modify an inline frame as you modify any other frame.

TIP To delete an inline frame, you can select it, and then choose Edit ⇨ Clear or Edit ⇨ Cut, or you can position the cursor next to it and then press Delete or Backspace.

FIGURE 13.7

The icon identifying a tip is placed in the text as an inline frame so that it moves up and down with the surrounding text.

Creating an inline frame using the Anchored Object command

You can also choose Object ➪ Anchored Object ➪ Insert to insert an inline frame. This option opens a dialog box, shown in Figure 13.8, that lets you control the positioning of the inline frame as you insert it.

> **NOTE** This method inserts a new frame in your text, in which you paste or place a graphic or text. To create an inline frame using an existing frame, use the cut-and-paste method described earlier in this section.

FIGURE 13.8

The Insert Anchored Object dialog box for inline frames

To create an inline frame with the Anchored Object command, follow these steps:

1. **Select the Type tool (or press T), and then click within a text frame to establish the insertion point.**

2. **Choose Object ➪ Anchored Object ➪ Insert.**

3. **Choose Inline or Line Above from the Position pop-up menu.** The Insert Anchored Object dialog box shown in Figure 13.8 appears.

4. **In the Object Options section, specify inline frame's settings.** You choose the type of frame (text, graphics, or unassigned) using the Content pop-up menu, apply an object style if desired using the Object Style pop-up menu, apply a paragraph style if desired using the Paragraph Style pop-up menu, and set the inline frame's dimensions using the Height and Width fields.

   Note that the Paragraph Style you choose, if any, applies to the inline frame, not to the paragraph in which the inline frame is embedded. Oddly, InDesign lets you apply a paragraph style to the inline frame even if it contains no text.

5. **In the lower part of the dialog box, set the desired position settings.** You have two basic choices for position:

   ▪ The Inline option, if selected, places the frame at the text-insertion point, setting it in the same line as that insertion point. You can adjust the inline frame's vertical position on that line by typing a value in the Y Offset field, which works like shifting the baseline of any text.

   ▪ The Above Line option, if selected, places the inline frame above the current line. Typically, you would use this when you want to place a frame above the first line of a paragraph. An example would be using graphics as the equivalent of headlines above specific paragraphs. You can adjust the alignment of the inline frame relative to the paragraph using the Alignment pop-up menu, as well as control how much space is above and below the inline frame using the Space Before and Space After fields.

   No matter which position you choose, selecting the Prevent Manual Positioning option ensures that the positions of individual frames can't be adjusted using InDesign's other text and frame controls (such as Baseline Shift). This forces users to use this dialog box to change the inline frame's position.

6. **Click OK to insert the inline frame.**

7. **Add any desired content to the inline frame as you would with any other frame.**

Anchored objects added by choosing Object ➪ Anchored Object ➪ Insert do not have text automatically wrapped around them. Use the Text Wrap panel (Window ➪ Text Wrap, or Option+⌘+W or Ctrl+Alt+W) to open this panel and set text wrap. Figure 13.9 shows an inline frame before and after text wrap has been applied.

But anchored objects created by pasting a graphic into text do automatically have text wrap around them.

FIGURE 13.9

Choosing Object ➪ Anchored Object ➪ Insert does not make InDesign wrap text around the resulting frame (top). Use the Text Wrap panel to set text wrap for such objects (bottom).

Adjusting inline frames

After you create an inline frame, you can adjust its position vertically or horizontally. Again, there are several methods.

A quick-and-easy trick to move an inline frame vertically is as follows:

1. **Use the Type tool to highlight the inline frame as you would highlight an individual text character.** In the Character panel or Control panel, type a positive value in the Baseline Shift field to move the inline frame up; type a negative value to move the frame down.

2. **Use a selection tool to select the inline frame, and then drag the frame up or down.**

A quick way to move an inline frame horizontally is as follows:

1. **With the Type tool selected, click between the inline frame and the character that precedes it.**

2. **Use the kerning controls in the Character panel or Control panel to enlarge or reduce the space between the inline frame and the preceding character.**

Note that these preceding methods work only if the Prevent Manual Positioning option remains unchecked in the Insert Anchored Object dialog box or Anchored Object Options dialog box. (This option is not selected by default.) You can also adjust the vertical (Y) position of an inline frame by choosing Object ➪ Anchored Object ➪ Options. The resulting Anchored Object Options dialog box is the same as the Insert Anchored Object dialog box covered previously in this section and shown in Figure 13.8, except the Anchored Object Options dialog box does not have the Object Options section.

Of course, you can also adjust its other attributes, such as strokes, fills, dimensions, rotation, and skew, as needed using the Tools panel, Control panel, and other panels.

Deleting inline frames

It's easy to delete an inline frame: Select the frame with the Selection or Direct Selection tool and then choose Edit ➪ Clear or press Delete or Backspace. If you want to remove the object but keep it in the Clipboard for pasting elsewhere, choose Edit ➪ Cut, or press ⌘+X or Ctrl+X.

Setting Up "Follow Me" Anchored Frames

InDesign offers another way to associate frames to text, and this one can make it easier to have sidebars, pull-quotes, info boxes, and other elements that relate to a specific piece of text remain near that text even as it reflows. The difference between an inline frame and an anchored frame is that an anchored frame is not embedded in the text frame — it is simply leashed to it.

 InDesign retains anchored frames set up in Microsoft Word documents. It also preserves anchored frames when exporting text as RTF files.

When to use anchored frames

Before I explain how to create anchored frames, it's important for you know when to use them. There are several caveats to consider:

- Because an anchored frame follows its text as it flows throughout a document, you need to ensure your layout retains clear paths for those anchored objects to follow. Otherwise, you could have anchored frames overlap other frames as those anchored frames move.

- Anchored frames should generally be small items and/or used sparingly. The more items you have anchored to text, the greater the chance that they will interfere with each other's placement. Likewise, you can move large items only so far within a page, so the benefit of keeping them close to their related text goes away.

- Items such as pull-quotes are obvious candidates for use as anchored frames. But in many layouts you want the pull-quotes to stay in specific locations on the page for good visual appearance. The InDesign anchored-frame function can accommodate that need for specific positioning on a page, but you need to be careful as you add or delete text so that you do not end up with some pages that have no pull-quotes at all because there is so much text between the pull-quotes' anchor points. Conversely, you need to make sure you don't have too many pull-quotes anchored close to each other, which could result in overlapping objects.

Typically, you would use anchored frames for small graphics or icons that you want to stay next to a specific paragraph. Another good use would be for cross-reference ("For More Information") text frames.

Figure 13.10 shows the Insert Anchored Object dialog box for an anchored object, while Figure 13.11 shows an example of an anchored frame in use.

Adding anchored frames

The process for adding an anchored frame is similar to that for inline frames (described in the previous section). But the controls over positioning are quite different.

Here are the steps:

1. **Select the Type tool (or press T), and then click within a text frame to establish the insertion point.**

2. **Choose Object ⇨ Anchored Object ⇨ Insert.**

3. **Choose Custom from the Position pop-up menu.** The Insert Anchored Object dialog box shown in Figure 13.10 appears.

4. **In the Object Options section, specify the inline frame's settings.** Choose the type of frame (text, graphics, or unassigned) using the Content pop-up menu; apply an object style, if desired, using the Object Style pop-up menu; apply a paragraph style, if desired, using the Paragraph Style pop-up menu; and set the inline frame's dimensions using the Height and Width fields.

   Note that the Paragraph Style you choose, if any, applies to the inline frame, not to the paragraph in which the inline frame is embedded. Oddly, InDesign lets you apply a paragraph style to the inline frame even if it contains no text.

5. **Decide whether to select the Relative to Spine option.** If this option is not selected, the anchored frame is placed on the same side of the text frame on all pages, whether left-facing or right-facing. If this option is selected, InDesign places the text frame on the outside of both pages or inside of both pages, depending on how the anchored position is set. In other words, if the anchored frame is set to be on the left of the reference text for a left-hand page, selecting this option puts the anchored frame to the right of the reference text on a right-hand page. If this option is not selected, InDesign places the anchored frame to the left of the text frame on both left-hand and right-hand pages.

6. **In the Anchored Object section of the dialog box, click one of the positioning points (the squares) to set up the text frame's relative position.** Note that you need to think about both the horizontal and vertical position you desire. For example, if you want the anchored frame to appear to the right of the text reference, click one of the right-hand points. (Remember that selecting the Relative to Spine option overrides this, making the right-hand pages' positions mirror that of the left-hand pages, rather than be identical to them.) If you choose the topmost right-hand point, the anchored frame is placed to the right of the text reference and vertically appears at or below that text reference. But if you choose the bottommost right-hand point, you're telling InDesign you want the anchored frame to appear vertically above the text reference.

   You need to experiment with your layout to see what works best in each case.

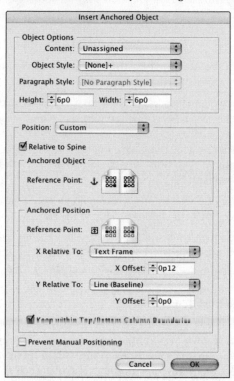

FIGURE 13.10

The Insert Anchored Object dialog box for anchored objects

7. **In the Anchored Position section of the dialog box, click one of the positioning points to set up the text reference's relative position.** (Position points are similar to the reference points in the Control and Transform panels, covered in Chapter 2.) Although there are nine points shown, the only three that matter are those in the middle row. Typically, you'd have the text reference be on the opposite side of the anchored frame; if you want the anchored frame to be to the left, you thus would indicate that the text reference is to the right. (If you set the text reference to be on the same side as the anchored frame, InDesign places the anchored frame over the text.) The reason there are three points (left, middle, and right) is to accommodate layouts where you want some anchored frames to appear to the left of the text and some to the right; in that case, choose the middle position here and select the right- or left-hand position in the Anchored Object section as appropriate to that object.

I mentioned that you can ignore the top and bottom row of position points in the Anchored Section. If you click any left-hand position point, InDesign sets the position as if you clicked the middle row's left-hand position point. If you click any right-hand position point, InDesign treats it as if you clicked the middle right-hand position point. The only reason the nine points are there is for consistency with the Anchored Object section's position points.

8. **There are three options in the Anchored Position section that you may need to set that give InDesign more precise instructions on how to place the anchored frames:**

   ■ The X Relative To pop-up menu tells InDesign from where the horizontal location is calculated, using the following options: Anchor Marker, Column Edge, Text Frame, Page Margin, and Page Edge. The right option depends both on where you want the anchored frames placed and whether you have multicolumn text frames (in which case Text Frame and Column Edge result in different placement, while in a single-column text frame they do not).

   You can also specify a specific amount of space to place between the chosen X Relative To point and the anchored frame by typing a value in the X Offset field.

   ■ The Y Relative To pop-up menu tells InDesign from where the horizontal location is calculated, using the following options: Line (Baseline), Line (Cap-height), Line (Top of Leading), Column Edge, Text Frame, Page Margin, and Page Edge.

   As you would expect, you can also indicate a specific amount of space to place between the chosen Y Relative To point and the anchored frame by typing a value in the Y Offset field.

9. **No matter which position settings you apply, you can select the Prevent Manual Positioning option to ensure that the positions of individual frames can't be adjusted using InDesign's other frame-positioning controls (such as the Control panel's or Transform panel's X and Y fields).** This forces users to use this dialog box to change the anchored frame's position.

10. **Click OK to insert the anchored frame.**

TIP   To see the results of various position options as you work in the Insert Anchored Object dialog box, enable the Preview check box. This greatly helps you to understand the results of various settings before you commit to them.

FIGURE 13.11

Example of an anchored frame

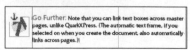

Converting existing frames to anchored frames

Once you get the hang of when and how to use anchored frames, you likely want to convert some frames in existing documents to anchored frames. There's no direct way to do that in InDesign, but there is a more circuitous path you can take:

1. **Use a selection tool to cut the existing frame you want to make into an anchored frame by choosing Edit ⇨ Cut or pressing ⌘+X or Ctrl+X.** You can also copy an existing frame by choosing Edit ⇨ Copy or pressing ⌘+C or Ctrl+C.

2. **Switch to the Type tool, and click in a text frame at the desired location to insert the text reference to the anchored frame.**

3. **Paste the cut or copied frame into that insertion point by choosing Edit ⇨ Paste or pressing ⌘+V or Ctrl+V.** You now have an inline frame.

4. **Choose Object ⇨ Anchored Object ⇨ Options to display the Anchored Object Options dialog box (refer to Figure 13.10).**

5. **Using the Position pop-up menu, choose Custom.** This converts the frame from an inline frame to an anchored frame.

6. **Adjust the position for the newly minted anchored frame as described in the previous section.**

7. **Click OK when done.**

Adjusting anchored frames

After you create an anchored frame, you can adjust its position.

A quick-and-easy trick is simply to click and drag anchored frames or use the Control panel or Transform panel to adjust their position. If the text the frame is anchored to moves, however, InDesign, of course, overrides those changes. You can't manually move an anchored frame if the Prevent Manual Positioning option is selected in the Insert Anchored Object dialog box or Anchored Object Options dialog box. This option is not selected by default.

For the most control of an anchored frame's position, choose Object ⇨ Anchored Object ⇨ Options. The resulting Anchored Object Options dialog box is the same as the Insert Anchored Object dialog box covered previously in this section and shown in Figure 13.10, except that the Anchored Object Options dialog box does not have the Object Options section.

And, of course, you can adjust its other attributes as needed, such as strokes, fills, dimensions, rotation, and skew.

Releasing and deleting anchored frames

If you no longer want an anchored frame to be anchored to a text location, you can release the anchor. To do so, select the anchored frame and then choose Object ⇨ Anchored Object ⇨ Release.

It's also easy to delete an anchored frame: Select the frame and then choose Edit ➪ Clear or press Delete or Backspace. If you want to remove the object but keep it on the Clipboard for pasting elsewhere, choose Edit ➪ Cut, or press ⌘+X or Ctrl+X.

Wrapping Text around Objects

In the days before personal computers and page-layout software, wrapping text around a graphic or other object was a time-consuming and expensive task. Text wraps were rare, found only in the most expensively produced publications.

Not any more. Not only do all page-layout programs let you create text runarounds, most programs, including InDesign, provide several options for controlling how text relates to graphics and other objects that obstruct its flow.

When a frame is positioned in front of a text frame, InDesign provides the following options. You can:

- Ignore the frame and flow the text behind it
- Wrap the text around the frame's rectangular bounding box
- Wrap the text around the frame itself
- Jump the text around the frame (that is, jump the text from the top of the frame to the bottom)
- Jump the text to the next column or page when the text reaches the top of frame
- Specify the amount of distance between the text and the edge of the obstructing shape
- Flow text within the obstructing shape rather than outside it

TIP   InDesign lets you wrap text around frames on hidden layers, as well as remove text wrap for objects on hidden layers. This is handy when you want to hide images or other distracting items but preserve the layout. See Chapter 6 for details on using layers.

If you want to wrap text around only a portion of a graphic — perhaps you need to isolate a face in a crowd — the best solution is to open the graphics file in its original program, create a clipping path around that portion, and then resave the file and import it and its clipping path into an InDesign document (clipping paths are explained in Chapter 28). Another option is to use the Pen tool to create a free-form shape within InDesign and then use the shape as both a frame and a clipping path.

Using the Text Wrap panel

The controls in the Text Wrap panel (see Figure 13.12) let you specify how a selected object will affect the flow of text behind it. Remember, the flow of text around an obstructing object is determined by the text wrap settings applied to the obstructing object.

> **TIP** You can override the text-wrap settings of objects that are in front of a text frame by telling the text frame to ignore them. To do so, click a text frame, and then choose Object ⇨ Text Frame Options or press ⌘+B or Ctrl+B. In the Text Frame Options dialog box's General pane, select Ignore Text Wrap, and then click OK.

> **NOTE** The Text Wrap panel has three options that may not display when you open it: Wrap Options, Contour Options, and Include Inside Edges. You can more easily hide/show these functions by double-clicking the double-arrow icon to the left of the Text Wrap label in the panel's tab or by choosing Hide Options/Show Options from the flyout menu.

Here's how to apply text-wrap settings to a frame or other object:

1. **If the Text Wrap panel is not displayed, choose Window ⇨ Text Wrap or press Option+⌘+W or Ctrl+Alt+W.**

2. **Click any of the selection tools.** If the Type tool isn't selected, you can press V to select the Selection tool or press A to select the Direct Selection tool.

3. **Click the object to which you want to apply text-wrap settings.** The object can be anywhere, but you probably want to position it on top of a text frame that contains text so you can see the results of the settings you apply.

4. **Click one of the five text-wrap iconic buttons at the top of the Text Wrap panel.** Figure 13.13 shows how each of these options affects a graphics frame.

5. **If you want, adjust the space between the surrounding text and the obstructing shape by typing values in the Top Offset, Bottom Offset, Left Offset, and Right Offset fields.** (These fields are not available if you click the No Text Wrap iconic button.) If the object is a rectangle, all four fields are available if you click Wrap around Bounding Box or Wrap around Object Shape. Only the Top Offset field is available if you click the Wrap around Object Shape iconic button for a free-form shape or the Jump to Next Column button. The Top Offset and Bottom Offset fields are available if you click Jump Object.

> **NEW FEATURE** The Text Wrap panel now has the Make All Settings the Same iconic button (the chain icon) in the area that contains the offset fields. If the chain is unbroken, changing any offset automatically changes the other offsets to the same value. If the chain is broken, you can adjust each offset independently. Click the button to toggle between the two modes.

> **NOTE** A bounding box is the dimension of the graphic, whether or not it is wholly contained in its frame. You use a bounding box if you want to have the wrap follow the graphic's dimensions rather than that of the frame containing it.

6. **Select Invert if you want to flow the text inside the obstructing shape.**

FIGURE 13.12

The Text Wrap panel and its flyout menu. Also, note the preview frame for the wrap area outside the graphics frame's bounding box.

FIGURE 13.13

Examples of the five text-wrap options (left to right, top to bottom): No Text Wrap, Wrap around Bounding Box, Wrap around Object Shape, Jump Object, and Jump to Next Column; as well as the Invert option selected for the Wrap around Bounding Box option

7. **If you choose the Wrap around Object Shape iconic button, you can also select from the Contour Options's Type pop-up menu.** There are six options (Figure 13.14 shows examples of each):

   ▓ Bounding Box determines the dimensions of the bounding box — the uncropped image, which may be larger or smaller than the graphics frame containing it — and uses them for the wrap boundary.

   ▓ Detect Edges tries to determine the graphic's outside boundary by ignoring white space; you would use this for bitmapped images that have a transparent or white background.

   ▓ Alpha Channel uses the image's alpha channel, if any, to create a wrapping boundary.

   ▓ Photoshop Path uses the image's clipping path, if any, to create a wrapping boundary.

   ▓ Graphic Frame uses the frame's boundary rather than the bounding box.

   ▓ Same as Clipping uses the clipping path for the graphic created in InDesign.

   User-Modified Path uses any modification to one of the above boundaries you have made by editing it with the Direct Selection tool. This option is grayed out unless you modify the wrap boundary yourself.

8. **You can control how text wraps around an object that splits a column by choosing an option from the Wrap To pop-up menu.** The options are Right Side, Left Side, Both Left and Right Sides, Side Towards Spine, Side Away from Spine, and Largest Area. You rarely choose Both Left and Right Sides, because unless the object is small, readers' eyes stop at the interposed object and not see the rest of the text on the other side of it. Use either of the spine options to have the text stay on the outside or inside of a page, relative to the object, based on whether the page is right-facing or left-facing. You often want to choose Largest Area, because that gives the text the most space next to the interposed object, which tends to be what looks good in many situations.

NEW FEATURE The Wrap To options are new to InDesign CS3. (Previous versions aligned the text to the left of the interposed object.)

9. **By selecting the Include Inside Edges option, InDesign lets text appear inside any interior "holes" in the graphic.** Use this technique rarely because in most cases it's hard for the reader to follow text that wraps around an image, flows inside it, and then continues to flow outside it. But if the interior is large enough and not too distant from the text that flows on the outside, this effect might be readable.

TIP If you specify text-wrap settings when no objects are selected, the settings are automatically applied to all new objects.

TIP To apply text-wrap settings to a master item on a document page, press and hold Shift+⌘ or Ctrl+Shift to select the item, and then use the controls in the Text Wrap panel as just described. If you don't want the text wrap applied to existing document items, just to new ones, choose Apply to Master Page Only in the Text Wrap panel's flyout menu.

FIGURE 13.14

The six contour options for text-wrap options (left to right, top to bottom): Bounding Box, Detect Edges, Alpha Channel, Photoshop Path, Graphic Frame, and Same as Clipping

Setting text-wrap preferences

There are several global text-wrap options you should be aware of, all of which are accessed via the Composition pane of the Preferences dialog box (choose InDesign ➪ Preferences ➪ Composition or press ⌘+K on the Mac, or choose Edit ➪ Preferences ➪ Composition or press Ctrl+K in Windows). Here are the options:

- **Justify Text Next to an Object:** This option is useful when you have left-aligned text that wraps around an object at the right. It also works if you have right-aligned text that wraps around an object at the left. This can lead to an awkward wrap, however, because InDesign doesn't try to make the text align precisely to the wrap's contour (because the text isn't justified). Use this option to justify the text just around the wrap, and then continue using the text's specified nonjustified alignment.

- **Skip by Leading:** This option makes text wrap below or above an object based on the text's leading, so there's at least a full line space between the text and the object, even if the object's text-wrap settings would allow less space.

■ **Text Wrap Only Affects Text Beneath:** This option, if selected, prevents text frames placed on top of an object from wrapping, while those behind the graphic frame are still allowed to wrap. This option allows some text to overlap the graphic and other text to wrap around it. Note this is a global setting, affecting all objects. To override wrap settings of individual text frames, choose Object ➪ Text Frame Options, or press ⌘+B or Ctrl+B, and enable the Ignore Text Wrap option.

Changing the shape of a text wrap

When you specify text-wrap settings for an object, an editable shape is created. If the text-wrap shape is the same shape as the object, the text-wrap boundary is superimposed on the object. You can modify a text-wrap boundary by clicking it with the Direct Selection tool, and then moving, adding, deleting, and changing the direction of anchor points and by moving direction lines. Figure 13.15 shows a text wrap before and after being manually reshaped.

CROSS-REF For more information about modifying free-form shapes, see Chapter 28.

FIGURE 13.15

The example at left shows a text wrap (outside outline) created by using the graphic's built-in clipping path (Wrap around Object Shape). The text wrap was modified by dragging and removing anchor points to create the variation at right.

Defining and Applying Object Styles

For many years, desktop-publishing programs have let designers save textual styles for easy reuse and application to text throughout a document. But of the major programs, only InDesign lets you create object styles, so you can ensure that multiple objects have the same attributes and that any changes to the style are made to all the objects using that style.

QUARKXPRESS   QuarkXPress 7's content-synchronization feature approximates InDesign's object styles but is much less flexible.

Designers should find the process of creating and applying object styles very familiar because the concept is the same as creating other types of styles, such as paragraph, character, and stroke styles.

CROSS-REF   Paragraph and character styles are covered in Chapter 20. Stroke styles are covered in Chapter 12. Table and cell styles are covered in Chapter 22.

There are no hard-and-fast rules about how best to implement them. Like handwriting, you should develop your own style. How many styles you create, the names you use, and whether you apply them with keyboard shortcuts or through the Object Styles pane are all matters of personal taste. One thing is indisputable: You should use object styles whenever you're dealing with multiple objects that need to be formatted the same way.

Creating object styles

You create object styles using the Object Styles panel (Window ⇨ Object Styles, or ⌘+F7 or Ctrl+F7), shown in Figure 13.16. You can also click the New Object Style iconic button (the turned-page icon) at the bottom of the panel. New styles are added at the bottom of the style list or, if a group is selected, at the bottom of the group's list.

TIP   The simplest way is to apply various attributes to an object (text frame, graphics frame, unassigned frame, or line) is to select it and then choose New Object Style from the Object Style panel's flyout menu. InDesign records all those settings automatically, so they're in place for the new object style.

Whether you start with an existing object or create a new object style completely from scratch, you use the New Object Style menu option that opens the New Object Style dialog box shown in Figure 13.17.

At the left side of the dialog box is a list of types of attributes that are or can be set. The checked items are in use for this style; you can uncheck an item so InDesign doesn't apply its settings to objects using the style. For example, if Fill is unchecked, the object style won't apply any Fill settings to objects using that style.

NEW FEATURE   Because there are so many panes, the New Object Style dialog box now breaks them into two sections: Basic Attributes and Effects. The Effects set of panes have the same functions as the Effects dialog box. For the details on the Effects panes' settings, see Chapter 12.

New to InDesign CS3's New Object Style dialog box are the Frame Fitting Options pane and the panes for the various new lighting effects.

To switch from one type of attribute to another, simply click the item name in the list at left of the dialog box for the type of attributes on which you want to work, such as Stroke or Transparency.

TIP   Be sure to enable the Preview check box to see the results of object styles on the currently selected object. Of course, you need to make sure the object is visible on-screen to see those effects.

FIGURE 13.16

The Object Styles panel and its flyout menu

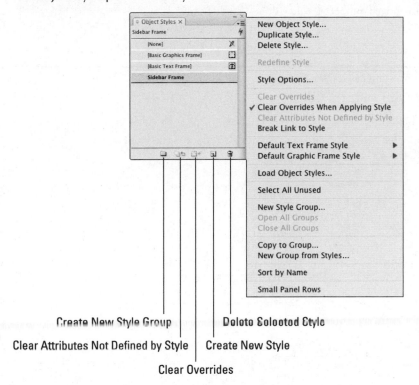

Create New Style Group

Clear Attributes Not Defined by Style | Create New Style

Clear Overrides

Delete Selected Style

The General pane

When you open the New Object Style dialog box, you see the General pane, which lets you create a style based on an existing object style (using the Based On pop-up menu), and which lets you assign a keyboard shortcut for fast application of this style (using the Shortcuts field).

You can use the Based On feature to create families of object styles. For example, you can create a style called Photo/Base for the bulk of your placed photographs, and then create variations such as Photo/Sidebar and Photo/Author. The Photo/Base style might specify a hairline black stroke around the photo, while Photo/Sidebar might change that to be a white stroke. But if you later decide you want the stroke to be 1 point and change it in Photo/Base, Photo/Sidebar automatically gets the 1-point stroke while retaining the white color.

The General pane also lets you see the current style settings. Click any of the arrows in the Style Settings section to get more details on how they are set for this object style.

CROSS-REF   Chapter 8 covers the definition and application of colors, gradients, and tints.

The other options are grayed out because they do not apply to fills.

FIGURE 13.17

The New Object Style dialog box and its General pane

The Fill pane

Shown in Figure 13.18, the Fill pane of the New Object Style dialog box lets you set colors for fills using whatever colors are defined in the Swatches panel. You can also set the tint and, if you select a gradient fill, the angle for that gradient. Finally, you can choose to have the fill overprint the contents of the frame by selecting the Overprint Fill option.

TIP   If you click the Stroke icon in the pane, you are taken to the Stroke pane of the New Object Style dialog box. This emulates the behavior of the Stroke and Fill iconic buttons in the Tools panel and the Swatches panel.

The Stroke pane

The Stroke pane in the New Object Style dialog box is identical to the Fill pane except that options specific to fills are grayed out and options available to strokes are made available. The color, tint, and gradient angle options are the same as for the Fill pane.

In the Stroke pane, you choose the type of stroke (solid line, dashed line, or dotted line) using the Type pop-up menu, and the thickness using the Weight field. You can also choose to overprint the stroke over underlying content by selecting the Overprint Stroke option. Finally, if your stroke is a dotted or dashed line, you can set the color, tint, and overprint for the gap in the Gap Color section.

TIP If you click the Fill iconic button in the pane, you are taken to the Fill pane of the New Object Style dialog box. This emulates the behavior of the Stroke and Fill iconic buttons in the Tools panel and the Swatches panel.

FIGURE 13.18

The Fill pane of the New Object Style dialog box

CROSS-REF Chapter 12 covers the use of strokes and settings such as gap.

The Stroke & Corner Options pane

Shown in Figure 13.19, the Stroke & Corner Options pane of the New Object Style dialog box lets you set stroke position and how corners and line ends are handled. It also lets you apply fancy corners to frames.

The Stroke Effects section is where you align the strokes to the frame edges, using the Stroke Alignment buttons. You also control how lines join at corners using the Join buttons. The End Cap buttons control how the lines end (such as immediately, or with a rounded or squared-off cap). You can also use the Miter Limit field to tell InDesign when a corner point should switch from *mitered* (squared off) to a beveled appearance, based on the sharpness of the corner's angle. Finally, you can select line endings such as arrowheads using the Line Start and Line End pop-up menus.

The Corner Options section is where you select from five fancy corners, such as Bevel and Rounded, using the Effect pop-up menu and where you specify the radius, or reach, of the corner using the Size field.

CROSS-REF Chapter 12 covers the use of strokes and settings such as alignment and line endings, as well as corner options.

FIGURE 13.19

The Stroke & Corner Options pane of the New Object Style dialog box

The Paragraph Styles pane

The Paragraph Styles pane of the New Object Style dialog box controls which paragraph style, if any, is applied to text in the frame. It has just two options:

- You choose the style from the Paragraph Style pop-up menu that you want automatically applied to any text typed into the frame.

- If that style is set to invoke another style for the next paragraph, be sure to select the Apply Next Style option; otherwise, the object style insists on making every paragraph use the style specified in the pop-up menu.

NOTE Chances are you won't use the Paragraph Styles pane except for frames that contain only consistent, very simple text, such as pull-quotes or bios.

CROSS-REF Chapter 20 covers paragraph styles in detail.

The Text Frame General Options pane

Shown in Figure 13.20, the Text Frame General Options pane of the New Object Style dialog box controls how text is handled within a frame. This essentially replicates the controls in the General pane of the Text Box Options dialog box (Object ⇨ Text Frame Options, or ⌘+B or Ctrl+B), including the number of columns, column width, gutter settings, inset spacing (how far from the frame edge text is placed), vertical justification (how text is aligned vertically in the frame), and whether text wrap settings are ignored when this frame overlaps other frames.

> **NOTE** You can set text frame options even if the current object is not a text frame. That's so you can have a consistent style for multiple kinds of objects, with the text attributes coming into play only for objects that actually are text frames.

> **CROSS-REF** Chapter 15 covers text frame options in detail.

FIGURE 13.20

The Text Frame General Options pane of the New Object Style dialog box

The Text Frame Baseline Options pane

The Text Frame Baseline Options pane of the New Object Style dialog box controls how text is handled within a frame. This essentially replicates the controls in the Baseline Options pane of the Text Box Options dialog box (Object ⇨ Text Frame Options, or ⌘+B or Ctrl+B), including how the text baseline is calculated for the frame and whether the text frame gets its own baseline grid.

> **CROSS-REF** These options are covered in Chapter 15.

The Story Options pane

The Story Options pane of the New Objects Style dialog box lets you enable optical margin alignment — its controls are the same as the Story panel (Type ⇨ Story). Optical margin alignment adjusts the placement of text along the left side of a frame so the text alignment is more visually pleasing.

 You can set optical margin alignment even if the current object is not a text frame. That's so you can have a consistent style for multiple kinds of objects, with the text attributes coming into play only for objects that actually are text frames.

CROSS-REF   Chapter 19 covers optical margin alignment in detail.

The Text Wrap & Other pane

Shown in Figure 13.21, the Text Wrap & Other pane of the New Object Style dialog box lets you set text wrap — mirroring the features of the Text Wrap panel (Window ⇨ Text Wrap, or Option+⌘+W or Ctrl+Alt+W), as well as make an object nonprinting (normally handled through the Attributes panel by choosing Window ⇨ Attributes).

FIGURE 13.21

The Text Wrap & Other pane of the New Object Style dialog box

NOTE   You can set text wrap even if the current object is not a text frame. That's so you can have a consistent style for multiple kinds of objects, with the text attributes coming into play only for objects that actually are text frames.

CROSS-REF Text wrap settings are covered earlier in this chapter. Chapter 10 covers nonprinting objects. Chapter 12 covers other Attributes panel options.

The Anchored Object Options pane

The Anchored Object Options pane of the New Object Style dialog box lets you set the attributes for inline and anchored frames, using the same settings as in the Anchored Object Options dialog box.

CROSS-REF Anchored objects are covered previously in this chapter.

The Frame Fitting Options pane

The New Object Style dialog box's Frame Fitting Options pane lets you set the offset values for imported graphics, by entering values in the Crop Amount area. You select what those offset (crop) settings are calculated from by selecting one of the reference points in the Alignment area. And you select the default frame-fitting behavior for imported graphics in the Fitting pop-up menu: None, Fit Content to Frame, Fit Content Proportionally, or Fill Frame Proportionally. Figure 13.22 shows the pane.

NEW FEATURE The Frame Fitting Options pane is new to InDesign CS3.

CROSS-REF Reference points are covered in Chapter 2. Setting offset values for frames are covered in Chapter 10. Frame-fitting options are covered in Chapter 27.

FIGURE 13.22

The Frame Fitting Options pane of the New Object Style dialog box

Managing object styles

The Object Styles panel's flyout menu of the New Object Style dialog box (refer to Figure 13.16) has several options for managing object styles:

- **Duplicate Style:** Click an object style's name, and then choose this menu option to create an exact copy. If you want to create an object style that's similar to one you've already created, you might want to choose New Object Style rather than Duplicate Style, and then use the Based On option to create a child of the original. If you choose Duplicate Style, the copy is identical to, but not based on, the original; if you modify the original, the copy is not affected. The panel also has the Create New Style iconic button (the turned-page icon) to create a new style.

- **Delete Style:** Choose this to delete selected object styles. To select multiple styles, press and hold ⌘ or Ctrl as you click their names. To select a range of styles, click the first one, and then press and hold Shift and click the last one. You can also delete styles by selecting them in the pane and then clicking the Delete Selected Style iconic button (the trash-can icon) at the bottom of the panel.

- **Redefine Style:** This option lets you modify an existing object style by first making changes to an object that already has an object style defined for it, and then choosing Redefine Style. The newly applied formats are applied to the object style.

- **Style Options:** This option lets you modify an existing object style. When a style is highlighted in the Object Styles panel, choosing Style Options displays the Object Style Options dialog box, which is identical to the New Object Style dialog box covered earlier.

- **Load Object Styles:** Choose this option if you want to import object styles from another InDesign document. You get a dialog box listing the styles in the chosen document, so you can decide which ones to import.

  If you import styles whose names match those in the current document, InDesign gives you a chance to let the imported style overwrite the current style or to leave the current style as is and give the imported style a new name. If there is an entry in the Conflict with Existing Style, you can click that entry for a pop-up menu that provides two choices: Auto-Rename and Use Incoming Style Definition. Figure 13.23 shows this Load Styles dialog box.

  Note that at the bottom of the dialog box is the Incoming Style Definitions window, which lists the style definitions to help you decide which to import, as well as which to overwrite or rename.

- **Select All Unused:** Select this option to highlight the names of all object styles that have not been applied to any objects. This is a handy way of identifying unused styles in preparation for deleting them (by choosing the Delete Style menu option).

- **Sort by Name:** This option alphabetizes your object styles.

■ **Small Panel Rows:** Click this option to reduce the text size in the Object Styles panel. Although harder to read, a panel with this option selected lets you access more styles without having to scroll. To return the panel to its normal text size, deselect this option.

NEW FEATURE InDesign CS3 lets you rearrange the order of style names in the Object Styles panel, by dragging them within the list.

FIGURE 13.23

The Load Styles dialog box

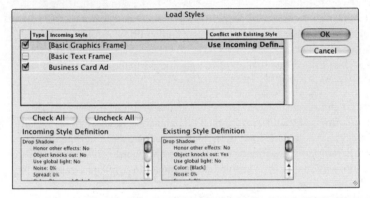

Using style groups

To help you find the desired style in documents that have dozens of them, InDesign lets you create style groups, which create a folder in the Object Styles panel's style list that you can open and close as desired. To create a group, choose New Style Group from the panel's flyout menu or click the Create New Style Group iconic button (the folder icon) on the bottom of the panel. Enter a name in the dialog box that appears and click OK.

NEW FEATURE Style groups are new to InDesign CS3.

To add styles to a group (which have a folder icon to the left of its name in the panel list), you have three options:

■ You can drag any desired styles into the group.

■ You can copy a selected style to the group by choosing Copy to Group and then selecting the target group in the dialog box that appears.

- If multiple styles are selected, you can create a group and move them into it in one fell swoop by choosing New Group from Styles in the flyout menu. (Note that this option is selected if any of the three predefined styles — [None], [Basic Graphics Frame], and [Basic Text Frame] — are selected.

 To quickly open all groups, choose Open All Groups in the panel's flyout menu. To quickly close them all, choose Close All Groups.

Understanding predefined styles

Note that InDesign comes with two predefined object styles — [Basic Text Frame], and [Basic Graphics Frame] — that you can modify as desired. Frankly, they're not necessary because it makes more sense for you to create object styles using your own naming conventions. Adobe's rationale is that there should be at least one style defined, so if you delete all other styles, there's still a style that can be applied to objects. While I don't buy that argument, it doesn't matter because you can easily ignore these default styles if you prefer.

You can set which object styles are automatically used for new text and graphics frames: In the Object Styles panel's flyout menu, choose Default Text Frame Style and then the desired style from the submenu to set a default text frame; choose Default Graphic Frame Style and then the desired style from the submenu to set a default graphics frame. To no longer have object styles automatically applied to new objects, choose [None] in the Default Text Frame and/or default Graphic Frame submenus.

Applying object styles

After you create an object style, applying it is easy. Just click an object, and then click the object style name in the Object Styles panel, or press its keyboard shortcut. (Windows users must make sure Num Lock is on when using shortcuts for styles.)

 InDesign has a Quick Apply panel that lets you apply any style — object, paragraph, or character — as well as other saved settings from one location. Chapter 2 covers this panel.

Handling existing formatting

When you apply an object style to selected objects, all local formats are retained. All other formats are replaced by those of the applied style. That is, unless you do one of the following:

- If you press and hold Option or Alt when clicking a name in the Object Styles panel, any local formatting that has been applied to the objects is removed. You can achieve the same effect by choosing Clear Attributes Not Defined by Style from the Object Styles panel's flyout menu or by clicking the Clear Attributes Not Defined by Style iconic button at the bottom of the panel.

- To have any existing formatting automatically removed when applying a style, be sure that Clear Overrides When Applying Style is checked in the flyout menu.

NEW FEATURE The Clear Overrides When Applying Style menu option is new to InDesign CS3.

■ If you want to override any local changes with the settings in the object style, choose Clear Overrides in the flyout menu or click the Clear Overrides iconic button at the bottom of the Object Styles panel. The difference is that Clear Attributes Not Defined by Style removes all attributes for which the object style contains no settings, while Clear Overrides imposes the object style's settings over conflicting attributes that you set manually.

If a plus sign (+) appears to the right of an object style's name, it means that the object has local formats that differ from those of the applied object style. This can occur if you apply an object style to an object text to which you've done some manual formatting or if you modify formatting for an object after applying an object style to it. (For example, you may have changed the fill color; that is a local change to the object style and causes the + to appear.)

Removing an object style from an object

To remove a style from an object, choose Break Link to Style from the Object Styles panel's flyout menu. The object's current formatting won't be affected, but it will no longer be updated when the object style is changed.

Managing Links

The Links panel (Window ⇨ Links, or Shift+⌘+D or Ctrl+Shift+D) is a handy place to manage the links to your graphics and text, particularly when you need to update them. (Figure 13.24 shows the Links panel.)

InDesign always creates links for graphics files. But it will create links to source text files (including Excel spreadsheets) only if the Create Links When Placing Text and Spreadsheet Files option is checked in the Type pane of the Preferences dialog box (InDesign ⇨ Preferences ⇨ Type or ⌘+K on the Mac, or Edit ⇨ Preferences ⇨ Type or Ctrl+K in Windows). This option is not checked by default, because many designers don't want to have text files easily updated in their layouts. That's because all the formatting they've done to the file in InDesign will be removed when the link to the source file is updated, causing the text to be replaced.

TIP If you can store all your linked files in a single location — not necessarily in a single folder, but perhaps within a folder hierarchy on your hard drive or a file server — you can minimize link problems. If you move, rename, or delete the original file after importing a graphic, you break the link, which causes printing problems. Keeping all graphics files in a single, safe place — a place that's backed up regularly — is a good idea.

The panel also shows the link status — current, missing, modified, or embedded — using the icons noted in Figure 13.24, so you can quickly tell what links might need to be managed.

FIGURE 13.24

The Links panel and flyout menu

Managing file relations

Most menu options in the Links panel's flyout menu handle the relationships between placed objects in InDesign and their source file, such as letting you reestablish links to missing and modified files, display an imported graphic or text file in the document window, open the program used to create a graphic or text file, and work on copies and versions of the source graphics and text:

- **Relink:** This menu option, and the Relink iconic button (the leftmost at the bottom of the panel), lets you reestablish a missing link or replace the original file you imported with a different file. When you choose Relink or click the button, the Relink dialog box is displayed and shows the original path name and filename. You can enter a new path name and filename in the Location field, but it's easier to click Browse, which opens a standard Open a File dialog box. Use the controls to locate and select the original file or a different file, and then click OK. (You can also drag and drop a file icon from the Mac OS Finder or Windows Explorer directly into the Relink dialog box.) If you want to restore broken links to multiple files, highlight their filenames in the scroll list, and then choose Relink or click the Update Link button.

NEW FEATURE InDesign CS3 now lets you relink all instances of a file in your layout. So you only have to do the operation once. The trick: In the Relink dialog box, be sure to check the new Relink All Instances option. You can now also relink an Excel spreadsheet.

NOTE When you open a document that refers to an outdated or missing source file — perhaps you edited the file or moved it to a different location — InDesign alerts you. You can update or relink the files as desired.

- **Go To Link:** Choose this menu option, or click the Go to Link iconic button (second from left) in the panel to display the highlighted file in the document window. If necessary, InDesign navigates to the correct page and centers the frame in the document window. You can also display a particular graphic or text file by double-clicking its name in the scroll list while holding down the Option or Alt key.

- **Edit Original:** If you want to modify an imported graphic or text file, choose Edit Original from the flyout menu or click the Edit Original iconic button (far right) at the bottom of the panel. InDesign tries to locate and open the program used to create the file. This may or may not be possible, depending on the original program, the file format, and the programs available on your computer.

- **Update Link:** Choose this menu option or click the Update Link iconic button (third from the left) at the bottom of the panel to update the link to a modified graphic or text file. Highlight multiple filenames, and then choose Update Link or click the Update Link button to update all links at once.

NOTE When you update missing and modified graphics, any transformations — rotation, shear, scale, and so on — that you've applied to the graphics or their frames are maintained. That is, unless you've deselected the new Relink Preserves Dimensions option in the File Handling pane of the Preferences dialog box, as shown in Chapter 3.

- **Copy Link(s) To:** Choose this menu option to copy the source graphic or text file to a new location and update the link so that it refers to this new copy.

- **Embed File:** This menu option — available for graphics only — lets you embed the complete file of any imported graphics file. (InDesign normally imports only a low-resolution screen preview when you place a graphic that is 48K or larger.) If you want to ensure that the graphics file forever remains with a document, you can choose to embed it; however, by embedding graphics, you produce larger document files, which means it takes you longer to open and save them. If you do use this option, an alert is displayed and informs you about the increased document size that will result. Click Yes to embed the file. Note that this menu option changes to Unembed File, so you can reenable the original link at any time.

- **Unlink:** This menu option — available for text files only — removes the link to the source text file, so it can't be updated. Note that this option cannot be undone from the Links panel; you have choose Edit ⇨ Undo, or press ⌘+Z or Ctrl+Z.

- **Purchase This Image:** If you use the online image catalog, Adobe Stock Photos, that ships with InDesign, you can purchase images by choosing this menu option. Otherwise, any graphics placed from this catalog will be low-resolution or watermarked.

Managing versions

Several flyout menu options relate to managing file versions created and updated using the Version Cue version-management tool that comes with the full Adobe Creative Suite:

- **Save Link Version:** This option lets you save a graphic altered by using the Editor Original menu option as a version in the Version Cue project.

- **Version:** This option lets you select an alternative version of an Adobe Creative Suite graphic file (if that graphic has been saved with at least one version). By default, a placed graphic displays the most recent version of itself in InDesign, so you would use this menu option to select a previous version of the file.

CROSS-REF See Chapter 4 for more details on the versioning functionality.

Navigating directly to files

Several flyout menu options let you navigate directly to files so you can, for example, move, copy, or rename them:

- **Reveal in Finder (Macintosh) and Reveal in Explorer (Windows):** This menu option opens a window displaying the contents of the folder that contains the source file.

- **Reveal in Bridge:** This menu option opens the Adobe Bridge program with a window displaying the contents of the folder that contains the source file, so you can use Bridge functions on the source file.

CROSS-REF See Chapter 35 for more details on Adobe Bridge.

Getting detailed information

Two flyout menu options are information-oriented:

- **Link Information:** This option displays the Link Information dialog box, which actually doesn't let you do much. (In the dialog box, the Previous and Next buttons let you display information about the previous and next files in the list, but that's about it.) But it does display 11 sometimes-useful bits of information about the highlighted file, including its name, status, creation date, file type, and location.

■ **Link File Info:** Available only for files that have X/Open Management Profile (XMP) context information associated to them (basically, files managed through Adobe Bridge and Creative Suite applications), this menu option displays the XMP information for the selected file.

Working with InCopy files

Three flyout menu options relate to the InCopy add-on program for which a limited version comes with InDesign: Check Out, Cancel Check Out, and Check In. All control whether files that are associated to an InCopy assignment are available for others (checked in) or in use exclusively by you (checked out).

 See Chapter 36 for more details on using Adobe InCopy.

Managing the panel itself

The rest of the flyout menu options are for panel housekeeping functions:

■ **Sort by Name:** This option lists all files in alphabetical order. (By default, objects are listed in the order they are placed.)

■ **Sort by Page:** This option lists imported files on page 1 first, followed by imported files on page 2, and so on.

■ **Sort by Type:** This option lists all files grouped by type of file (such as Word, JPEG, and TIFF).

■ **Sort by Status:** This option lists files with missing links first, followed by files that have been modified, and finally files whose status is okay.

■ **Small Panel Rows:** This option lets you reduce the size of text in the panel and decrease the space between entries so that you can see more entries at once. Of course, the reduced rows are also harder to read. To go back to the normal display size, simply select this option again.

Summary

Most InDesign pages are made up of several objects. Each object occupies a separate level in a page's stacking order. The first object you place on a page occupies the bottom later, and each new object you create or place occupies a new layer that's on top of all other layers. You can change a page's stacking order by moving individual items forward or backward in the stacking order. InDesign also provides several options for working with several objects at once. When multiple items are selected, you can combine them into a group that behaves like a single item. You can also place an object within a frame to create a nested object.

InDesign provides two ways to associate frames with text. One method lets you insert objects within a text thread to create inline frames that flow with the surrounding text. The other creates a link between a specific location in your text thread and an outside frame, so the frame moves along with that location as the text moves.

InDesign also lets you have text wrap around objects, with controls over the wrap's shape, location, and text flow.

InDesign lets you create object styles, which are named collections of attributes, that you can apply to objects to ensure consistent formatting and to easily update formatting across multiple objects, sort of the frame version of a paragraph style for text. You can also group frequently used styles into folders to make them easier to find in the Object Styles panel.

To manage the links to source files — such as to bring in an updated version or use a different version — use the Links panel. You can also get information about linked files.

Part IV

Text Fundamentals

IN THIS PART

Chapter 14
Importing Text Files

Chapter 15
Flowing Text through a Document

Chapter 16
Editing and Formatting Text

Chapter 17
Specifying Character Attributes

Chapter 18
Specifying Paragraph Attributes

Chapter 19
Creating Special Text Formatting

Chapter 20
Setting Up Styles

Chapter 21
Using Special Characters

Chapter 14

Importing Text Files

A lthough you can use InDesign as your primary word processor, doing so is a little like buying a Hummer for suburban errands — attention-getting but highly inefficient.

In publishing, at least the first draft of text is generally written in a word processor such as Microsoft Word. The key is to make sure you don't do work in your word processor that has no meaning to InDesign, resulting in wasted time or, worse, doing work in your word processor that requires extra effort in InDesign to undo or clean up.

Whether created in Word or not, text is imported into an InDesign publication to apply the layout and fine typographic formatting. Besides importing files into InDesign, you can drag text into your layout and, through the use of the Macintosh and Windows clipboards (copy and paste), you can import file formats, to a limited degree, that are not directly supported by InDesign.

IN THIS CHAPTER

Determining which formatting tasks to do in InDesign

Preparing files for import from word processors and spreadsheets

Pasting and dragging and dropping text from other programs

Importing text-only, Word, RTF, and Excel files

Exporting text

Working with tagged text

Determining Where to Format Documents

InDesign's import capabilities may tempt you to do a lot of your text formatting outside the program; however, it's not always wise to do so.

Because a word processor's formatting capabilities don't match all InDesign typographic features, it's often not worthwhile to do extensive formatting in your word processor. This is particularly true of layout-oriented formatting. Multiple columns and page numbers, for example, will be of a much higher standard in your final InDesign document than you could hope to create in a word processor. After all, even the sophisticated formatting features in today's word processors don't begin to approach those needed for true publishing.

It used to be true that layout programs ignored more sophisticated formatting, such as tables, during file import, but that's not true in InDesign. So you can produce your tables, footnotes, and even paragraph styles in Microsoft Word. However, I would not spend much time on such formatting, because you'll want to use InDesign's more sophisticated tools. Use InDesign for your layout and complex text formatting (fonts, leading, and hyphenation), and use your word processor for basic table setup (leave the high-end formatting to InDesign), footnotes, basic text editing, paragraph style assignments (identifying headlines, body copy, and so forth), and basic character formatting (boldface, italics, and other meaning-oriented formatting).

Preparing Text Files

What preparation do you possibly need to do for your word-processor files? They should just load into InDesign as is, right? This is not necessarily true, even if your word processor supports one of the InDesign text-import formats.

Limit your word-processor formatting to the type of formatting that enhances reader understanding or conveys meaning. Such formatting may include using italic and boldface to emphasize a word, for example, or using styles to set headlines and bylines in different sizes and typefaces. (See Chapter 20 for tips on using styles in word-processor text.) Let your editors focus on the words; leave presentation tasks to your layout artists.

One type of file preparation you may need to do is to translate text files into formats supported by InDesign. InDesign supports just Microsoft Word, Rich Text Format (RTF), and text-only (ASCII) formats. If you use Corel WordPerfect or Apple iWork Pages, you need to save in one of those other formats. Where possible, you should save in Microsoft Word format (up through the Office 12 version, better known as Office 2008 on the Mac and Office 2007 in Windows), because InDesign supports more Word formatting capabilities than it does RTF capabilities, and the text-only format preserves no formatting.

NOTE InDesign also imports InCopy files. InCopy is an add-on program from Adobe meant for copy editors, editors, and other non-layout artists that lets them do basic text editing of layout files without messing up the layout. Chapter 36 covers InCopy in more detail.

Preserving special features in text files

Today's word processors let you do much more than type and edit text. You also can create special characters, tables, headers and footers, and other document elements. Some of these features work when imported into a publishing program, but others don't.

InDesign imports the following Word formatting (from Mac version 98 and later and from Windows version 97 and later):

- All caps
- Boldface
- Bulleted lists
- Color
- Column breaks
- Condensed/expanded spacing
- Double strikethrough
- Double underlines
- Drop caps
- Font
- Footnotes and endnotes
- Indents
- Index and table-of-contents text
- Inline graphics (if in an InDesign-supported format)
- Italics
- Numbered lists
- Outline
- Page breaks
- Paragraph and character style sheets
- Point size
- Redlining/revisions tracking (for use in InCopy, not InDesign)
- Small caps
- Strikethrough
- Subscripts and superscripts
- Tables
- Text boxes, including any follow-me links to them
- Underlines
- Underline options

NEW FEATURE Newly supported text attributes in InDesign CS3 for importing include support for automatic bulleted and numbered lists (covered in Chapter 18) and Word's various underline options (covered in Chapters 17 and 19).

The following formats are partially supported or are converted during import:

- Embossed text (made into paper color, usually white)
- Engraved text (made into paper color, usually white)
- Word-only underline (converted to single underlines, including for spaces and punctuation)

The following formats are not supported, and any text using them is imported as plain text:

- Highlighting
- Shadow
- Text effects, such as blinking and Las Vegas Lights

The following formats are not supported, and any text using them is removed during import:

- Annotations and comments
- Hidden text (deleted during import)
- Section breaks
- Subscribed/OLE items
- Text-wrapping breaks

Tables

Word processors have developed very capable table editors, letting you format tabular information quickly and easily, and often rivaling dedicated spreadsheet programs. InDesign can import tables created in Word or Excel, as well as tables in RTF documents.

QUARKXPRESS InDesign does a good job of importing Word tables and Excel spreadsheets as tables, unlike QuarkXPress 6.0 and earlier.

CROSS-REF Chapter 22 covers tables in depth.

Headers and footers

Headers and footers are a layout issue, not a text issue, so there is no reason to include these elements in your word-processor document. Because page numbers change based on your InDesign layout, there's no point in putting the headers and footers in your word-processor document anyway. Note that if you do use them, they do not import into InDesign.

CROSS-REF Chapter 5 explains how to add headers and footers to your layout.

Footnotes and endnotes

If you use a word processor's footnote or endnote feature and import the text file, InDesign correctly places footnotes at the bottom of the column and endnotes at the end of the imported text. The superscripted numerals or characters in the notes usually translate properly as well.

Hyperlinks

Modern word processors, such as Word, let you include hyperlinks in their text, so when you export to XHTML, eBook, or PDF formats, the reader can click the link and jump to a Web page or to another PDF or eBook file. When you import text files with such hyperlinks, InDesign retains their visual formatting — hyperlinks usually display as blue underlined text — as well as the actual link.

 InDesign retains hyperlinks for documents that are exported as PDF, eBook, or XHTML files. Chapter 33 covers such documents in more detail.

Inline graphics and text boxes

Modern word processors typically support inline graphics, letting you import a graphic into your word-processor document and embed it in text. Word, for example, lets you import graphics, and InDesign, in turn, can import the graphics with your text, as long as they are in formats supported by InDesign. But graphics embedded in your word-processor document through Mac OS 9's Publish and Subscribe or through OLE (Object Linking and Embedding, available in both Windows and Mac OS) do not import into InDesign.

InDesign does import text boxes from a Word file (these are usually used for sidebars, captions, and pull-quotes) as separate text frames. If those Word text boxes are tied to a specific piece of text, so they flow with that text, InDesign honors those follow-me links and let you adjust them.

 Chapter 13 covers follow-me links and related anchoring features in more detail.

Avoiding text-file pitfalls

Sometimes, issues not related to the contents of a word-processor file can affect how files are imported into InDesign.

Fast save

Several programs (notably Microsoft Word) offer a fast-save feature, which adds information to the end of a word-processor document. The added information notes which text has been added and deleted and where the changes occurred. You can use this feature to save time because the program doesn't have to write the entire document to disk when you save the file. When you use the fast-save feature, however, text import into publishing programs — including InDesign — becomes problematic. I suggest that you turn off fast save, at least for files you import into InDesign. With today's speedy hard drives, the time you gain by using fast save is barely noticeable anyway. The vast majority of file corruption problems and bugs in Word are related to the fast-save feature and its use makes file recovery in the event of a crash problematic at best. To disable fast save in Word, choose Word ➪ Preferences on the Mac or Tools ➪ Options in Windows, go to the Save pane, and deselect the Allow Fast Saves option.

Software versions

Pay attention to the version number of the word processor you use. This caution may seem obvious, but the issue still trips up a lot of people. Usually, old versions (two or more revisions old) or new versions (newer than the publishing or other importing program) cause import problems. The

Fixing Microsoft Word's Bad Dashes

Several versions of Word — including Word X for Mac and Word 97 and Word 2000 for Windows — have a default setting that converts two hyphens to an en dash (–) rather than an em dash (—), which is simply wrong typographically. (Word 98, 2004, and 2008 for Mac and Word 2002/XP and 2007 for Windows don't have this problem.)

To solve this problem, I recommend that you turn off Word's automatic conversion of two hyphens to a dash (choose Tools ➪ AutoCorrect ➪ AutoFormat as You Type, then uncheck the Symbols option). Instead, go to the AutoCorrect pane, type two hyphens in the Replace field, put an em dash (shortcut Option+Shift+– [hyphen] on the Mac or Alt+0151 in Windows) in the With field, and then click Add. This causes Word to substitute the correct dash when you type two consecutive hyphens.

import filters either no longer recognize the old format (something has to go to make room for new formats) or were written before the new version of the word processor was released. InDesign supports Microsoft Word for Windows versions 97, 2000, 2002/XP, 2003, and 2007, and Microsoft Word for Mac versions 98, 2001, X, 2004, and 2008, as well as the same-numbered versions of Excel.

Adding Text

No matter where your text originates — in your mind, in e-mail, on the Web, or in a word processor — you can add it to an InDesign publication easily. You can type text directly in InDesign, paste it, drag and drop it, or import it.

InDesign works with text inside *frames* — holders for the copy — that you can create in advance or let InDesign create for you when you import text.

 If you click a frame that holds text or a graphic when importing text, the text replaces the existing text or graphic.

 All the text you import may not fit in the selected text frame. Chapter 15 explains how to make it flow to other text frames.

Using the Type tool

First, you can't do anything with text without the Type tool. Once the Type tool is selected, as shown in Figure 14.1, you can click in an existing block of text, or click and drag to create a new text frame. You can even click in any empty graphics frame or unassigned frame with the Type tool to convert it to a text frame.

You can't click in *master text frames* — text frames that are placed on the page by the master page in use — and simply start typing. To select a master text frame and add text to it, Shift+⌘+click or Ctrl+Shift+click it. (For more on master pages, see Chapter 7.)

NOTE What you can't do is simply click in your document and begin typing, as you can in PageMaker. InDesign is like other page-layout programs in that the text must be in a frame. Fortunately, you can create that frame just by clicking and dragging with the Type tool.

QUARKXPRESS InDesign does not require that you create a frame before importing text, unlike QuarkXPress.

FIGURE 14.1

When the Type tool is selected, you can click in a text frame and start typing.

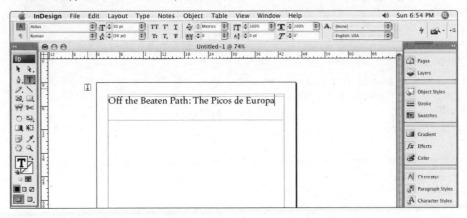

From this point, start typing to enter text, or bring text in from other programs (as covered in the following sections). If you want to add placeholder text — random text that you might use to try out formatting on, for example — choose Type ⇨ Fill with Placeholder Text. InDesign adds fake Latin text to the text frame until it is filled.

When you type new text, it takes on whatever style attributes are set for [Basic Paragraph Style], a predefined style in InDesign. You can modify this predefined style as you can any style you create.

CROSS-REF Chapter 20 covers styles in more detail.

Pasting text

When text is on the Mac or Windows Clipboard and the Type tool is active in InDesign, you can paste it at the location of the cursor (text-insertion pointer) or replace highlighted text with it. If no text frame is active, InDesign creates a new rectangular text frame to contain the pasted text.

InDesign uses standard menu commands and keyboard commands for cutting and copying text to the Clipboard, and for pasting text. On the Mac, press ⌘+X to cut, ⌘+C to copy, and ⌘+V to paste. In Windows, press Ctrl+X to cut, Ctrl+C to copy, and Ctrl+V to paste.

Keep Characters to a Minimum

If you're new to professional publishing, you have a few things to learn about the difference between typing on a typewriter or into a word processor and entering text for a high-end publication:

- Remember that there's no need to type two spaces after a period or colon (in either your word processor or InDesign). In fact, it causes awkward spacing and perhaps even text-flow issues.

- Don't enter extra paragraph returns for space between paragraphs and don't enter tabs to indent paragraphs — you accomplish both more consistently with paragraph attributes (see Chapter 18).

- When you need to align text in columns, don't enter extra tabs; place one tab between each column, and then align the tabs (see Chapter 22).

To see where you have tabs, paragraph breaks, spaces, and other such invisible characters, use the command Option+⌘+I or Ctrl+Alt+I, or choose Type ➪ Show Hidden Characters. Chapter 16 shows the icons for each character.

By default, pasted text retains any formatted, such as boldface and font size, it had in InDesign and in most other programs (a few don't preserve that formatting when you paste text from them). But InDesign lets you control whether pasted text retains its formatting:

- When pasting text from InDesign, you can strip out its formatting by choosing File ➪ Paste without Formatting (or pressing Shift+⌘+V or Ctrl+Shift+V).

- When pasting text from outside InDesign, you have the same Paste without Formatting option as when pasting text from InDesign and an option to always strip formatting automatically. To do so, go to the Clipboard Handling pane of the Preferences dialog box (InDesign ➪ Preferences ➪ Clipboard Handling or ⌘+K on the Mac, or Edit ➪ Preferences ➪ Clipboard Handling or Ctrl+K in Windows) and select the Text Only radio button for the Paste setting. Conversely, to ensure that formatting is retained in text copied from other applications, select the All Information (Index Marker, Swatches, Styles, Etc.) radio button.

NEW FEATURE The option to change the paste behavior has moved in InDesign CS3 to the new Clipboard Handling pane, from the File Handling pane.

Also, when you paste text, InDesign is smart enough to know to remove extra spaces or add them around the pasted text. You can disable this by deselecting the Adjust Spacing Automatically When Cutting and Pasting Words option in the Type pane of the Preferences dialog box.

Dragging and dropping text

You can also drag and drop text highlighted from text from another frame or document. If you press and hold Option or Alt while dragging, you drag a copy of the selected text rather than move the original text.

By default, InDesign allows drag-and-drop within the Story Editor. To enable drag-and-drop in your layout, go to the Type pane of the Preferences dialog box (InDesign ⇨ Preferences ⇨ Type or ⌘+K on the Mac, or Edit ⇨ Preferences ⇨ Type or Ctrl+K in Windows) and select the Enable in Layout View option. You can also drag-and-drop within the Story Editor by deselecting the Enable in Story Editor option.

CROSS-REF The Story Editor is covered in Chapter 16.

You can also drag text from external sources into InDesign:

- You can drag the icon of a text file or a supported word-processing file directly from the Windows Explorer (desktop or folder) or from the Mac Finder (desktop or folder) onto an InDesign page.

- You can drag highlighted text from a document created with another program (Microsoft Word, for example) into an InDesign document window.

In both cases, a new text frame is created, and any styles in the source files are also brought into InDesign. Unlike importing a file through the Place command (covered later in this chapter), you have no control over how this formatting is imported; instead, all formatting is imported or none of it is, based on your InDesign preference settings.

NOTE You can drag in only files that are in one of the supported formats (Word, Excel, InCopy, RTF, and text-only).

As with copy-and-paste, InDesign lets you control whether formatting is retained in dragged text:

- When dragging text within InDesign, hold Shift to remove the text's formatting. The text will then take on the formatting of the text it is dragged in to.

- When dragging text from outside InDesign, use the Text Only option in the Clipboard Handling pane of the Preferences dialog box, as described in the previous section, to strip out formatting for all dragged text.

Importing text with the Place dialog box

The Place dialog box (File ⇨ Place, or ⌘+D or Ctrl+D) gives you the most control over how text is imported. Figure 14.2 shows the dialog box.

Text imported via the Place dialog box is placed according to your current selection:

- If the cursor (text-insertion pointer) is active within text in a text frame, the text is inserted at that location.

- If a text frame is selected but you have not clicked within the frame's text, the text is imported into the frame, replacing any existing text.

- If two or more text frames are selected, a loaded-text icon appears.

- If no text frames are selected, a loaded-text icon (shown in Figure 14.3) lets you draw a rectangular text frame to contain the text, click in an existing empty frame, or click any empty area in your layout to create a text frame there with the text.

FIGURE 14.2

The Place dialog box

To place text:

1. **Choose File ⇨ Place, or press ⌘+D or Ctrl+D.**

2. **Locate the text file you want to import.**

3. **If you want to specify how to handle current formatting in the file, select the Place dialog box's Show Import Options option, shown in Figure 14.2, and click Open.** This opens the appropriate Import Options dialog box for the text file's format. Then click OK to import the graphic. (I cover the Import Options dialog box a little later in this section.) If you don't select the Show Import Options option, clicking Open imports the graphic using default settings.

FIGURE 14.3

The loaded-text icon (left). There are two variants — autoflow (center; press and hold Shift) and semiautoflow (right; press and hold Option or Alt) — that let text flow to other frames during import. At far right is the loaded-text icon when multiple files are selected.

If you prefer memorizing keyboard commands to simply checking boxes, press Shift while you open the file to display the import options.

4. **If you had not selected a frame before starting the text import, specify where to place the text by clicking and dragging the loaded-text icon to create a rectangular text frame, clicking in an existing frame, or clicking in any empty frame.**

You can select multiple files — text and/or graphics — in the Place dialog box by Shift+clicking a range or by ⌘+clicking or Ctrl+clicking multiple files one by one. InDesign lets you place each file in a separate frame. Just click once for each file imported, or Shift+⌘+click or Ctrl+Shift+click to have InDesign place all files on the page in separate frames. If you place more than one file at the same time, the loaded-text icon displays the number of files to be placed, as well as a mini-preview of each file, as Figure 14.3 shows.

 The ability to import multiple files at once is new to InDesign CS3.

 When you place multiple files at once, you can place them in any order. Just move among them using the keyboard left and arrow keys.

To cancel the entire text import, just select a different tool. To cancel a specific file in a multiple-file import, press Esc when that file's mini-preview is displayed. (The other files are still available to be placed.)

Import options for Microsoft Word and RTF files

InDesign offers a slew of options for controlling how Word and RTF files are imported through the Place dialog box. There are so many options that you can actually save your import preferences as a preset file for repeat use.

Figure 14.4 shows the Import Options dialog box for Microsoft Word. It has four groups of options. (The import options for RTF files are identical.)

At the top of the pane is the Preset pop-up menu, which lets you select from saved sets of import options. If you change any options in this dialog box, the pop-up menu shows [Custom], so you know that any selected preset's settings have been altered for this specific file import. You can save settings by clicking Save Preset. And you can set a preset as the default import behavior by clicking Save as Default; these settings are used for all Word file imports unless you choose a new default or make changes in this dialog box. This lets you avoid using the Import Options dialog box for your routine imports.

The next section, Include, lets you strip out specific types of text from the Word file: Table of Contents Text, Index Text, Footnotes, and Endnotes. Any selected items are imported. It's common not to import table-of-contents or index text because you typically create your table of contents and indexes in InDesign.

The third section, Options, has just one option: Use Typographer's Quotes. If selected, it converts keyboard quotes (' and ") to the curly typographer quotes (', ', ", and ").

FIGURE 14.4

The Microsoft Word Import Options dialog box

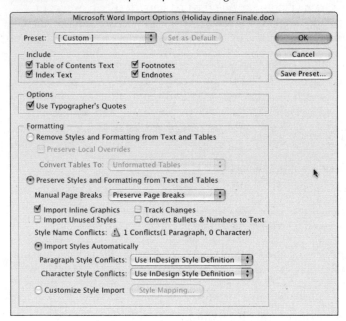

Unlike other layout programs, InDesign does not translate two consecutive hyphens (--) into an em dash (—) when you import text, even if you select the Use Typographer's Quotes option.

The fourth section, Formatting, is fairly complex.

To remove text formatting during import, so you have fresh text to which you can apply your InDesign styles, select the Remove Styles and Formatting option from Formatting section. Two additional controls become available if you select this option:

- **Preserve Local Overrides:** Selecting this option retains local formatting such as italics and boldface while ignoring the paragraph style attributes. You'd usually want this selected so that meaning-related formatting is retained.

- **Convert Tables To:** You can use this pop-up menu to choose how tables are unformatted during import. The Unformatted Tables menu item retains the table's cell structure but ignores text and cell formatting, while the Unformatted Tabbed Text menu item converts the table to tabbed text (with a tab separating what used to be cells and a paragraph return separating what used to be rows) and strips out any formatting. If you intend to keep tables as tables but format them in InDesign, choose Unformatted Tables.

To retain text formatting during import, so the InDesign document at least starts out using the settings done in Word, select the Preserve Styles from Text and Tables option. There are two reasons to select this option. The most common reason is because you are using style sheets in Word with the same names as in InDesign. This saves your designers from having to manually apply the correct styles when working on layouts (the editors basically do it in Word when editing). The other reason is your Word file is really a rough template of your eventual InDesign file, so you want to keep all that Word effort and use it as the basis for refinement in InDesign.

There are several controls for this option:

- **Manual Page Breaks:** This pop-up menu lets you retain page breaks entered in Word, convert them to column breaks, or strip them out. The break option you choose depends on how your layout is structured compared to the Word file's layout.

- **Import Inline Graphics:** This option, if selected, imports graphics placed in the Word text. (Chapter 13 covers inline graphics in more detail.)

- **Import Unused Styles:** This option, if selected, loads all Word style sheets into InDesign, rather than just the ones you actually applied to text in the file. You normally would not want to import all of Word's styles because the program has dozens of predefined styles that could clog up your InDesign Paragraph Styles and Character Styles panels.

- **Track Changes:** This option, if checked, saves all changes tracked by Word and makes them available to InCopy users who work on the InDesign file (see Chapter 36). You cannot see these tracked changes within InDesign itself.

- **Convert Bullets & Numbers to Text.** This option, if checked, removes any automatic bullet and numbering lists in Word, converting the bullets and numbers into the actual characters. If you select this option, and insert an item in an imported numbered list, the list doesn't renumber automatically, as it would if you leave this unchecked. (In previous versions of InDesign, bullets and numbers were converted, eliminating the automatic aspect.)

- **Style Name Conflicts:** If InDesign detects that the Word file has a style with the same name as your InDesign document, it notes how many to the right of the Style Name Conflicts label. You then have two ways of handling these conflicts, with separate pop-up menus for paragraph styles and character styles:

  - If you select the Import Styles Automatically option you get three options for both paragraph and character styles, using the two separate pop-up menus (Paragraph Style Conflicts and Character Style Conflicts). The Use InDesign Style Definition menu item preserves the current InDesign styles and applies them to any text in Word that uses a style sheet of the same name. This is the most common option because it lets your editors indicate what styles to use in InDesign but relies on InDesign's more precise typographic settings. If you choose the Redefine InDesign Style menu item, the Word style sheet's formatting permanently replaces that of InDesign's style. If you choose the Auto Rename menu item, the Word file's style sheet is renamed and added to the Paragraph Styles or Character Styles panel. This preserves your existing InDesign styles while also preserving the ones imported from the Word file.

■ If you select the Customize Style Import option, you can decide which specific InDesign styles override same-name Word styles, which Word styles override same-name InDesign styles, and which Word styles are renamed during import to prevent any overriding. Click Style Mapping to open the Style Mapping dialog box shown in Figure 14.5, where you make these decisions. You can also click Auto-rename Conflicts in that dialog box to rename all conflicting Word styles to new names. (This is the same as choosing Auto Rename in the Import Styles Automatically pop-up menus.)

NEW FEATURE The Track Changes and Convert Bullets & Numbers to Text options are new to InDesign CS3. (Previous versions of InDesign imported tracked changes, but InDesign CS3 now lets you strip them out by unchecking the Track Changes option.)

Import options for text-only files

The options for text-only (ASCII) files are much simpler, as Figure 14.6 shows:

■ **Character Set pop-up menu:** This lets you change the encoding type for the text file. There are 18 options, mainly for various languages and language groups such as Chinese, Central European, Greek, Baltic, and Japanese. In most cases, you leave the menu at its default of ANSI, which is what most North American PCs and Macs are set to. Choose another option only if you know the file is encoded in something else.

■ **Platform pop-up menu:** This lets you choose between Macintosh and Windows. Choose whichever is appropriate for the source file. The biggest differences are in how paragraph returns are specified and in some supported special characters.

FIGURE 14.5

The Style Mapping dialog box

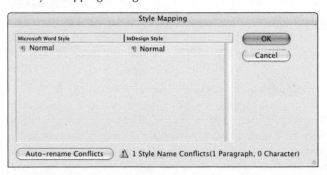

■ **Set Dictionary To pop-up menu:** This lets you assign the default spelling and hyphenation dictionary language. Unless you're publishing in multiple languages or regions (such as in English for use in the U.K., Canada, and the United States), you can leave this at the default setting, which is based on the language you selected when you installed InDesign.

■ **Extra Carriage Returns:** In this section, you can control how carriage returns are handled. Select the Remove at End of Every Line option if the source file has a return at the

Exporting Text

Unfortunately, you can't export text from InDesign into a word-processor format like Word; your options are RTF, InDesign Tagged Text, InCopy, and text-only formats. The best option is RTF if you want to send the file to someone using a word processor, and it's Tagged Text if you want to send it to another InDesign user with all InDesign settings retained.

After you click in a text frame with the Type tool, you export text by choosing File ➪ Export, which provides a dialog box very much like the Save As dialog box. Here, you choose the file format, filename, and file location. If you have selected a range of text in a text frame, only that text is exported; otherwise, the entire story is exported.

Be aware that if you export highly formatted InDesign files to RTF, then later reimport those RTF files into the same InDesign layout, you may get some odd effects, particularly around style names. That's because of how InDesign handles style names in groups versus how they are named during RTF export. The bottom line is that you may end up with several copies of the same style, perhaps with different settings, when you reimport that RTF file.

Note that you can export files to two InCopy formats: the InCopy format (filename extension .incx) used with InDesign 2.0 and the InCopy CS format (filename extension.incd) used with InDesign CS and later. InDesign CS3 and InCopy CS3 can import both formats.

end of each line (often the result of copying text from the Web or from a PDF file). Select the Remove Between Paragraphs option if the source file uses two hard returns to indicate new paragraphs. You can select neither, one, or both as appropriate to your source file.

- **Formatting:** In this section, you can select the Replace option to have several consecutive spaces converted to a tab (you specify the minimum number of spaces in the field that follows). You can also select the Use Typographer's Quotes option to convert keyboard quotes (' and ") to the curly typographer quotes (', ', ", and "). This option is normally selected.

FIGURE 14.6

The Text Import Options dialog box for a text-only file

InCopy files

There are no options when importing InCopy files. Because they contain formatting applied as part of an InDesign layout, InDesign imports them as is.

Import options for Microsoft Excel files

When importing Excel spreadsheets, you have several options, as Figure 14.7 shows. In the Options section, you can control the following settings:

- **Sheet pop-up menu:** You can choose which sheet in an Excel workbook to import. The default is the first sheet, which is usually named Sheet1 unless you renamed it in Excel. (If you want to import several sheets, you need to import the same spreadsheet several times, choosing a different sheet each time.)

- **View pop-up menu:** You can import custom views you have defined in Excel for that spreadsheet. If the Excel document has custom views, you can ignore custom views by choosing [Ignore View] from the pop-up menu. If you have no custom views, this pop-up menu is grayed out.

- **Cell Range pop-up menu:** You can specify a range of cells using standard Excel notation $Sx:Ey$, where S is the first row, x the first column, E the last row, and y the last column, such as A1:G89. You can type a range directly in the pop-up menu, which also acts as a text-entry field, or you can choose a previously entered range from the pop-up menu.

- **Import Hidden Cells Not Saved in View:** By selecting this option, you import any hidden cells. Be careful when doing so because they're usually hidden for a reason (typically, they show noncritical data sources or interim calculations).

In the Formatting section, you can control the following settings:

- **Table pop-up menu:** You choose the Formatted Table menu item, which imports the spreadsheet as a table and retains text and cell formatting; the Unformatted Table menu item, which imports the spreadsheet as a table but does not preserve formatting; or the Unformatted Tabbed Text menu item, which imports the spreadsheet as tabbed text (tabs separate cells and paragraphs separate rows) with no formatting retained.

- **Table Style pop-up menu:** Here, you can choose an InDesign table style to apply to the imported table, or leave it alone (by choosing [No Table Style]).

- **Cell Alignment pop-up menu:** You can tell InDesign how to align text within the cells. You can retain the spreadsheet's current alignments by choosing Current Spreadsheet or override them by choosing Left, Right, or Center.

- **Include Inline Graphics:** If selected, this option enables you to import any graphics placed in the Excel cells. (Chapter 13 covers inline graphics in more detail.)

NEW FEATURE The ability to apply a table style is new to InDesign CS3.

- **Number of Decimal Places to Include:** In this field, type how many decimal places to retain for numbers. For example, if you type 4 in this field and have a cell that contains the value for π, InDesign imports the numeral 3.1415, even though the Excel spreadsheet displays 10 decimal places (3.1415926535). Note that InDesign does not import any formulas, just their numeric or textual results.

- **Use Typographer's Quotes:** Select this option to convert keyboard quotes (' and ") to the curly typographer quotes (', ', ", and "). This option is normally selected.

FIGURE 14.7

The Microsoft Excel Import Options dialog box

Import options for Tagged Text files

InDesign offers a text-file format of its own: Adobe InDesign Tagged Text. Tagged Text actually is ASCII (text-only) text that contains embedded codes to tell InDesign which formatting to apply. You embed these codes, which are similar to macros, as you create files in your word processor.

CROSS-REF Chapter 4 explains how to export Tagged Text files. For a list of the Tagged Text codes themselves, check out the documentation that comes on the InDesign installation disc.

When importing Tagged Text files, there are a few options if you select the Show Import Options check box in the Place dialog box:

- **Use Typographer's Quotes:** If selected, it converts keyboard quotes (' and ") to the curly typographer quotes (', ', ", and ").

- **Remove Text Formatting:** If selected, all text formatting, including styles, is removed from the text.

- **Resolve Style Conflicts Using:** With this pop-up menu, choose Publication Definition or Tagged Text Definition. The former applies the document's style formatting to any imported text that uses styles with the same names, overriding the formatting saved with the Tagged Text file; the latter applies the Tagged Text file's style definitions to any imported text that uses styles with the same names, overriding the formatting specified in the document.

- **Show List of Problem Tags Before Place:** If selected, this option displays a dialog box listing any style sheets in the imported file whose names conflict with those in the document.

 See Chapter 23 for details on how to use the Tagged Text format to automate the creation of catalogs and other database-generated documents.

Summary

Because today's word processors are so powerful, there's a temptation to do a lot of sophisticated, layout-oriented formatting in them before bringing the files into a layout program like InDesign. But don't. No word processor has the typographic or layout capability of InDesign, and doing a lot of work in your word-processing file is simply a waste of time; you'd need to do it over again in InDesign in the context of your layout anyhow.

Focus on the meaning-oriented formatting in your word processor: use of style sheets to indicate headlines, bylines, quotation blocks, and so on, as well as local formatting like italics, superscripts, and font changes.

When you're done preparing your text, be sure to save it in a format compatible with InDesign. Even if your word-processor format is not compatible with InDesign, chances are it can save in one that is.

InDesign provides a variety of methods for getting text into your documents, including importing files through the Place dialog box, dragging and dropping files generated in a word processor, and pasting text from other sources.

You can export text from InDesign for use in a word processor or another InDesign user. Your options are RTF, InDesign Tagged Text, InCopy, and text-only.

Chapter 15

Flowing Text through a Document

It doesn't take much experience with InDesign to discover that all your text doesn't fit into the finite space individual frames provide. Consider these scenarios:

- If you're laying out a newsletter, you might receive an article in the form of a Microsoft Word document that you need to flow into several columns across a spread.

- A magazine might have an article that starts on page 20 and then continues on page 198, with the text originating in Apple iWorks Pages and saved as Rich Text Format (RTF) for import into InDesign.

- With catalogs, you might have a continuous file exported from a database that contains different product descriptions that are positioned below the items' pictures.

- In book publishing, each chapter may be imported as a separate word processing file and flowed continuously through many pages.

- The text of a simple advertisement, delivered by a client via e-mail, might flow through several text frames.

IN THIS CHAPTER

Creating text frames on master pages

Linking frames and flowing text through them

Breaking and rerouting text flow

Specifying and adjusting columns

Managing text-frame spacing and alignment

Creating forced breaks

Working with overset text

In all these cases, the benefits of frames — the ability to size, resize, reshape, and place them with precision — seem limiting. When the text doesn't fit in a frame, what are you supposed to do? Well, don't resort to cutting and pasting text into different frames. You need to keep the imported text together and link the frames that will contain the text. InDesign refers to the process of linking frames as *threading* and considers linked frames to be *threaded*. You can link frames on a single page, from one page to another no matter how many pages are in between, and automatically to quickly flow text while adding new pages with frames.

The text flowing through one or more threaded frames is considered a *story*. When you edit text in a story, the text reflows throughout the columns and threaded frames. You can also spell check and do search and replace for an entire story even though you have just one text frame active on-screen. Similarly, you can select all or some of the text in the story and change its formatting, copy it, or delete it.

CROSS-REF Chapter 9 explains how to create frames, while Chapter 14 explains what kind of text can be imported. Chapter 16 explains how to select, spell check, and search and replace text. Chapters 17 through 20 explain how to format text.

Working with Text Frames

On a simple layout such as a business card or advertisement, you might simply create text frames as you need them. In a newsletter, you might drag text frames for an article in from a library. But with a book or even a text-heavy magazine, text frames are usually placed on master pages — a template for document pages — so they automatically appear on document pages. Many publications can combine master frames, individual frames, and threaded frames, as shown in Figure 15.1.

CROSS-REF For detailed information about using libraries and master pages, see Chapters 5 and 7.

FIGURE 15.1

In this cookbook spread, the recipes are in a master text frame, which is threaded to other master text frames if needed on subsequent pages. The folios at bottom are also defined on the master pages. The sidebar on the left page is placed in a text frame created on the document page.

Creating text frames on master pages

Master pages—predesigned pages that you can apply to other pages to automate layout and ensure consistency—can contain several types of text frames. You can have the following:

- Text frames containing standing text such as a magazine's folio.
- Text frames containing placeholder text for elements such as figure captions or headlines.
- An automatically placed text frame for flowing text throughout pages. The automatically placed text frame is called the *master text frame* and is created in the New Document dialog box (File ➪ New ➪ Document, or ⌘+N or Ctrl+N).

Creating a master text frame

A master text frame is an empty text frame on the default master page that lets you automatically flow text through a document. When you create a new document, you can create a master text frame, which fits within the margins and contains the number of columns you specify. Here's how it works:

1. **Choose File ➪ New ➪ Document, or press ⌘+N or Ctrl+N.**

2. **Select the Master Text Frame option at the top of the New Document dialog box as shown in Figure 15.2.**

FIGURE 15.2

Selecting the Master Text Frame option in the New Document dialog box places a text frame on the default master page within the margins you specify.

3. **Use the Page Size area to set the size and orientation of the pages; select the Facing Pages option if your pages have a different inside and outside margin (as a book would).**

4. **Specify the size and placement of the master text frame by typing values in the Top, Bottom, Inside, and Outside fields (or the Left and Right fields if Facing Pages is deselected).** InDesign places guides according to these values and places a text frame within the guides. The text frame fits within the boundaries of these values and the guides on the master page.

5. **Type a value in the Number field in the Columns area to specify the number of columns in the master text frame.** To specify the amount of space between the columns, type a value in the Gutter field. InDesign places guides on the page to indicate the columns.

6. **Click OK to create a new document containing a master text frame.**

After you create a document with a master text frame, you see guides on the first document page indicating the placement of the frame.

Modifying master text frames

Although you set up the master text frame in the New Document dialog box, you're not confined to those settings. As you design a publication, you may need to change the size, shape, and/or number of columns in the master text frame. To display the master page, choose Window ➪ Pages, or press ⌘+F12 or Ctrl+F12. In the Pages panel that appears, double-click the master page's icon (it's usually in the upper portion of the panel; the default master page is called A-Master). Use the Selection tool to click the master text frame within the guides and modify it using the following options:

■ The Control panel and Transform panel let you change the placement of a selected master text frame using the X and Y fields, the size using the W and H fields, the angle using the Rotation field, and the skew using the Shear X Angle field. You can also type values in the Scale fields to increase or decrease the width and height of the text frame by percentages. You can also use the mouse to resize and reposition the text frame.

■ The Text Frame Options dialog box (Object ➪ Text Frame Options, or ⌘+B or Ctrl+B), shown in Figure 15.3, lets you change the number of columns and the space between them, specify how far text is inset from each side of the frame, specify how text aligns vertically within the frame, and specify the placement of the baseline grid. If you don't want text within this box to wrap around any items in front of it, select the Ignore Text Wrap option at the bottom of the dialog box.

CROSS-REF Chapter 13 covers all the options in the Text Frame Options dialog box except for the Columns section, which is covered later in this chapter.

■ Paragraph styles, character styles, object styles, Story panel settings, and other text attributes are applied in the master text frame to the document text you flow into that frame. You can always override those attributes by applying other styles or formatting to the flowed text on your master text page.

■ The Direct Selection tool lets you drag anchor points on the frame to change its shape.

QUARKXPRESS The InDesign master text frame is not the same as QuarkXPress's automatic text box on a master page. You cannot flow text into a QuarkXPress automatic text box while you're working on a master page; it is, instead, an empty text box that is placed on each of your layout pages for you automatically. Although you can have QuarkXPress flow text into automatic text boxes across pages as you add pages to your layout, you can also place text in these boxes individually, without them being linked. An InDesign master text frame is linked automatically from page to page and is not meant for holding text that does not flow from page to page.

FIGURE 15.3

To change the properties of a master text frame, select it on the master page and use the General pane of the Text Frame Options dialog box.

Drawing additional text frames

The master text frame is helpful for containing body text that flows through a document. You're likely to need plenty of other text frames on both master pages and document pages. Generally, these are smaller text frames intended to hold headlines, captions, or short paragraphs of descriptive copy.

Creating text frames on master pages

If you're going to add text frames to a master page for repeating elements such as headers and footers, you need to display the master page. Choose Window ⇨ Pages, or press ⌘+F12 or Ctrl+F12, to display the Pages panel. Then double-click the desired master page's icon, as shown in Figure 15.4. Any text frames you add to master pages appear on document pages based on that master page. To switch back to the document and view the text frames, double-click a page icon in the upper portion of the Pages panel.

FIGURE 15.4

To access a master page so you can add or modify objects, double-click a master-page icon in the Pages panel.

Text Frame Anatomy

Before you start threading text frames, you need to understand what a text frame is trying to tell you about its text. To get the message, you need to select the text frames with one of the selection tools; when the Type tool is selected, all you can see is overset text. The text frame provides the following indicators, as shown in the figure.

- **In port (empty):** A small white square on the upper-left corner of a text frame is the in port, indicating where a story enters the frame.

- **In port (with arrow):** Within a chain of threaded text frames, the in port might contain a right-facing arrow indicating that the story is continuing into this frame from elsewhere.

- **Out port (empty):** A small white square on the lower-right corner of a text frame is the out port, indicating that the story fits comfortably within the frame.

- **Out port (with arrow):** Within a chain of threaded text frames, the out port might contain a right-facing arrow indicating that the story is continuing into another frame.

- **Out port (with plus sign):** A small red plus sign in the out port indicates that more of the story exists than can fit in the text frame and that there is no subsequent text frame for the text to flow into.

- **Threads:** When you choose View ➪ Show Text Threads (or press Option+⌘+Y or Ctrl+Alt+Y), you can view threads, or lines, indicating the direction in which frames are threaded. (To see multiple text chains, Shift+click to select text frames from different threads.)

This spacious two-level condo, built in 1908 and extensively updated over the years, features 4 bedrooms and 2¼ bathrooms, with two bedrooms and one bathroom on each floor and an additional quarter bath on the main level.

Among the amenities in this light-filled home are:
- Flexible layout offers dining room or study off kitchen, plus living room with adjacent den or dining room as well as parlor/bedroom in front.
- Fireplace in living room.
- Close to Golden Gate Park.
- Hardwood floors throughout both levels.
- Period detail throughout.
- Modern amenities, including phone, Internet, and grounded electrical outlets.
- Open kitchen with plenty of storage, plumbed for gas.
- Kitchen appliances and in-unit washer and dryer are included.
- Recent remodeling of front exterior façade.
- Unit has deeded parking for two cars in shared garage, plus shared storage space.

- HOA dues of $220/mo.
- Shared backyard features brick patio, lush garden, and patio heater.
- Pets allowed (with size and number restrictions).
- Clean ($0) Markoff pest report provided by seller.
- Title records show living space of 1,818 square feet.
- Attic bedrooms and bath added by previous owner are unwarranted.

Offers as they come; no offers will be reviewed before April 28, 2007, at 5 p.m. E-mail agent for disclosure package. Include preapproval letter and disclosure acknowledgment with offers.

Showing Schedule	
Sun. 4/15, 4/22	2p-5p
Tue. 4/10, 4/17, 4/24	11:30a-1p
Thu. 4/19 *(by appt. only)*	6p-7p

In the figure, the top text frame's in port (at the upper-right corner of the frame) is empty, indicating that the text starts in this frame, rather than flows from another frame. An arrow icon in its out port (at the lower left of the frame) shows that the text flows elsewhere, and the thread from its out port shows that it flows to the frame below. That lower frame's in port shows an arrow icon, indicating that text is flowing to it. The out port of the lower frame shows the overset text icon (the red + symbol), indicating that all the text doesn't fit.

Creating rectangular and variable-shaped text frames

To create rectangular text frames on document pages or master pages, select the Type tool. Click and drag to create text frames, and use the Control panel or Transform panel to fine-tune the placement and dimensions. Figure 15.5 shows a rectangular text frame used for a magazine folio.

For variable-shaped text frames such as circles or Bézier shapes, use the Pen tool, Pencil tool, Ellipse tool, or Polygon tool to create an empty frame. Then convert the frame to a text frame by clicking it with the Type tool or a loaded text icon, or by choosing Object ➪ Content ➪ Text. (You get the loaded-text icon when you place a text file or when you flow text from an existing frame, which I describe later in this chapter.)

If you're working on a document page and want to type in a text frame placed on the page by a master page, select the Type tool and Shift+⌘+click or Ctrl+Shift+click the frame.

You can also edit an existing rectangular text frame with the Direct Selection tool as if it were a free-form shape, as described in Chapter 28.

FIGURE 15.5

A rectangular text frame used on a master page for a folio

Threading Text Frames

InDesign provides three options for *threading* (or linking) text frames: manual, semiautoflow, and autoflow. Each has its own icon, as shown in the sidebar "Threading Icons." The method you choose depends on how much text you're dealing with and the size and quantity of your text frames:

- You might use the manual method, in which you click the first text frame's out port and then the second text frame to link two text frames across several pages for an article continuation.

- The semiautoflow method lets you click on a series of text frames to flow text. It works well for linking a succession of text frames in something such as a catalog layout.

- The autoflow method adds text frames and pages as you import text and is intended for flowing long text files such as a book chapter or annual report.

Threading frames manually

To thread text frames manually, you simply use a selection tool to link out ports to in ports. You can prethread existing text frames by linking empty text frames, and add text later, or you can create threads from a text frame that contains text.

Linking manually from out port to in port works well for continuing a magazine article from one page to the next.

Oddly, you cannot thread frames while the Type tool is selected, so remember to switch to a selection tool.

To thread text frames:

1. **Create a series of frames or shapes through which you intend to flow text.** (Any empty non-text frames are converted to text frames as soon as you thread to them from a text frame. Thus, at least the first frame in this chain must be a text frame.) The frames do not need to be on the same page.

2. **Click any of the selection tools.**

3. **Click the out port of the first text frame in the thread.** The pointer becomes the loaded-text icon.

4. **Click the in port of the second text frame in the thread.** You can also click any empty frame or click and drag to draw a new text frame. How text flow behaves depends on the text frame's status:

   ▪ If the first frame holds no text, when text is later placed or typed into it, any text that does not fit that first text frame flows into the second frame.

   ▪ If the first frame holds text but is not already linked to another text frame, any overset text flows into the text frame you just selected.

   ▪ If the first text frame is already linked to another text frame, the text is now redirected to the text frame you just selected.

5. **Use the Pages panel to add or switch pages as necessary while you continue clicking out ports and in ports until your chain of threaded text frames is complete.** You can also switch pages using the page controls at the bottom left of the document window, by choosing Layout ➪ Go to Page, or pressing ⌘+J or Ctrl+J, as explained in Chapter 5.

6. **When you finish threading text frames, select another object on the page or another tool.** When you import a story into any text frame in this chain, it starts in the upper-right corner of the first frame and flows through the frames in the same order as the threads.

TIP   To see text threads easily while threading across pages, change the document view to 20 percent or so.

NOTE   Text flows in the order in which you select frames. If you move a frame, its order in the text flow remains unchanged, so if you're not careful, you could, for example, accidentally have text flow from a frame at the top of the page to one at the bottom of a page, and then to one in the middle of a page.

Threading frames semiautomatically

InDesign's semiautoflow method of threading text frames varies only slightly from the manual method. Follow the same steps for threading text frames manually, except press and hold Option or Alt each time you click in the next text frame. This lets you bypass the in ports and out ports and simply click from text frame to text frame to establish links. Note that if a text frame contains overset text, the overset text flows through the additional frames as you create the thread.

Remember to Option+click or Alt+click each text frame, or you revert to manual threading.

 While first placing a word-processing file, you can also Option+click or Alt+click in the first text frame to begin a semiautoflow process.

Threading frames and adding pages automatically

The autoflow method for threading frames is what lets you flow a lengthy story quickly through a document. You can either autoflow text into the master text frame or into automatically created text frames that fit within the column guides. InDesign flows the text into any existing pages, and then adds new pages based on the current master page. You can initiate autoflow before or after placing a word processing file.

Placing text while autoflowing

If you haven't imported text yet, you can place a file and have it automatically flow through the document. This method works well for flowing text into pages that are all formatted the same way, such as a book. Here's how it works:

1. **Confirm that the master page in use has a master text frame or appropriate column guides.**

2. **With no text frames selected, choose File ⇨ Place, or press ⌘+D or Ctrl+D.**

3. **Locate and select the word-processing files you want to be placed in the same story, and then click Open.**

4. **When the loaded-text icon appears, Shift+click in the first column that contains the text.** Be sure to Shift+click within a few pixels of the upper-left corner of that column so InDesign knows you want to place text in it; otherwise, InDesign will create a new text frame and place the text there instead of in your desired column. InDesign adds all the necessary text frames and pages, and flows in the entire story.

 InDesign CS3 lets you select multiple files in the Place dialog box. See Chapter 14 for details on how to control where the files are placed.

Autoflowing after placing text

If you've already placed a text file into a single text frame or even a threaded chain of text frames, you can still autoflow text from the last text frame. To do this, click the overset icon in the out port, and then Shift+click on any page to indicate where to start the autoflow.

 You might use the autoflow-after-placing-text method if you're placing the introduction to an article in a highly designed opener page, and then flowing the rest of the article into standard pages.

Threading Icons

While you're threading text, several icons provide visual cues as to the type of threading you're doing and what the results will be. (To view threads from a text frame selected with the Selection tool or Direct Selection tool, choose View ➪ Show Text Threads, or press Option+⌘+Y or Ctrl+Alt+Y.) The figure shows, from left to right, the loaded-text icon, the loaded-text frame-flow icon, the thread icon, the semiautoflow text-flow icon, and the autoflow text-flow icon. (A mini-preview of the contents displays under the icon, unless you turn this preview off, as I explain in Chapter 3.)

■ The *loaded-text icon* contains text that needs to be placed or overset text that needs to be threaded into a new text frame.

■ When the loaded-text icon is over a text frame, the icon changes so the icon appears in parentheses, becoming the *loaded-text frame-flow icon*. The same thing happens for the semiautoflow text-flow icon.

■ The *thread icon*, which looks like two links in a chain, appears while you're threading text frames manually. Specifically, the loaded-text icon changes to this icon when it's over an empty text frame to which you can thread the current text frame.

■ The *semiautoflow text-flow icon* appears when you Option+click or Alt+click text frames while threading a series of text frames.

■ The *autoflow text-flow icon* appears when you Shift+click on a page to initiate the autoflow process, in which InDesign adds text frames and pages to contain the entire story.

Breaking and rerouting threads

After text frames are threaded, you have three options for changing the threads: You can break threads to stop text from flowing, insert a text frame into an existing chain of threaded text frames, and remove text frames from a thread.

■ To break the link between two text frames, double-click either an out port or an in port. The thread between the two text frames is removed and all text that had flowed from that point is sucked out of the subsequent text frames and stored as overset text.

■ To insert a text frame after a specific text frame in a chain, click its out port. Then click and drag the loaded text icon to create a new text frame. That new frame is automatically threaded to the previous and next text frame.

■ To reroute text threads — for example, to drop the middle text frame from a chain of three — click the text frame with the Selection tool and press Delete or Backspace. The text frame is deleted and the threads are rerouted. You can Shift+click to multiple-select text frames to remove as well. Note that you cannot reroute text threads without removing the text frames.

Adjusting Columns

The placement of columns on the page and the amount of space between them has significant impact on readability. Column width, in general, works with type size and leading to create lines and rows of text that you can read easily. This means that you're not getting lost from one line to the next, accidentally jumping across columns, and getting a headache while squinting at the page.

> **TIP** As a rule of thumb: As columns get wider, the type size and leading increase. For example, you might see 9-point text and 15-point leading in 2½-inch columns, while 15-point text and 13-point leading might work better in 3½-inch columns.

InDesign lets you place columns on the page automatically, create any number of columns within a text frame, and change columns at any time.

Specifying columns in master frames

If you choose to create a *master text frame* — an automatically placed text frame within the margin guides — when you create a new document, you can specify the number of columns in it at the same time.

In the Columns area in the New Document dialog box shown in Figure 15.2, use the Number field to specify how many columns you need and the Gutter field to specify how much space to place between them. Whether or not you select the Master Text Frame option (which makes the frame appear on all pages), guides for these columns are still placed on the page and can be used for placing text frames and other objects.

Adjusting columns in text frames

After you create a text frame and flow text into it, you can still change the number of columns in it. First, select the text frame with a selection tool or the Type tool (or Shift+click to select multiple text frames and change all their columns at once). Then choose Object ➪ Text Frame Options, or press ⌘+B or Ctrl+B. You can also use the Control panel to quickly change the number of columns by entering a value in the Columns field when you've selected a text frame.

> **TIP** Although programs like InDesign and QuarkXPress have long offered multiple-column text frames, many designers still draw each column as a separate frame (a holdover from PageMaker's approach). Don't do that — creating individual frames for each column makes it easy to have columns of slightly different widths and slightly different positions, so text doesn't align properly. Plus, using this feature makes it easy to change the number of columns; no need to resize existing text frames or relink them.

Note that the options in the Columns area work differently depending on whether Fixed Column Width is selected or deselected:

- If it is not selected, InDesign subtracts from the text frame's width the space specified for the gutters, and then divides the remaining width by the number of columns to figure out how wide the columns can be. For example, a 10-inch-wide text frame with three

Forcing Column and Other Breaks

Most of the time, you want text to flow naturally from column to column and page to page, but sometimes, you want to take over the flow and dictate exactly when text starts on a new column or page. InDesign provides several ways to do so:

■ Choose one of the break options by choosing Type ➪ Insert Break Character and then selecting the desired option from the submenu. The choices are Column Break (which makes the text start at the top of the next column), Frame Break (which starts the text at the top of the next frame in the story chain), Page Break (which starts the text at the next page containing a text frame in the story chain), Odd Page Break (which starts the next in the next odd-numbered page in the story chain), and Even Page Break.

■ Use one of the keyboard shortcuts: keypad Enter for column break, Shift+keypad Enter for frame break, or ⌘+keypad Enter or Ctrl+keypad Enter for page break.

■ Specify a break at the current text location using the Keep Options dialog box's Start Paragraph pop-up menu: In Next Column, In Next Frame, On Next Page, On Next Odd Page, or On Next Even Page. You can access the Keep Options dialog box by pressing Option+⌘+K or Ctrl+Alt+K, choosing Keep Options from the flyout menu of the Control panel's ¶ pane, or choosing Keep Options from the flyout menu of the Paragraph panel (Type ➪ Paragraph, or Option+⌘+T or Ctrl+Alt+T).

■ Specify a break as part of the paragraph style, using the options in the Start Paragraph pop-up menu in the Keep Options pane of the New Paragraph Styles or Paragraph Style Options dialog box.

Note that if you apply a column break within a single-column text frame, InDesign considers the next frame in the story chain to be the next column. Likewise, if you apply a frame break within the sole text frame on a page, InDesign considers the next page that contains a frame in the story chain to be the next frame.

columns and a gutter of ½ inch ends up with three 3-inch columns and two ½-inch gutters. The math is $(10 - (2 \times 0.5)) \div 3$.

■ If it is selected, InDesign resizes the text frame to fit the number of columns you selected at the indicated size, as well as the gutters between them. For example, if in a 10-inch-wide text frame you specify a column width of 5 inches and a gutter of ½ inch and you choose three columns, you end up with a 15-inch-wide text frame containing three 5-inch columns and two ½-inch gutters. The math is $(5 \times 3) + (2 \times 2)$.

Select the Preview option to see the effects of your changes before finalizing them.

Placing rules between columns

The use of vertical rules (thin lines) between columns — called *intercolumn rules* — is an effective way to separate columns with small gutters. This is often done in newspapers, where columns and gutters are usually thin. It can also add visual interest and a sense of old-fashioned authority — it was a common technique for newspapers a century ago and is still used by the august *Wall Street Journal*, for example.

Unfortunately, InDesign does not provide an automatic method for creating intercolumn rules. To get around this lack, you need to draw lines on the page — in the center of the gutters — with the Line tool. Because you might resize text frames or change the number of columns while designing a document, you should add the vertical rules at the end of the process. In a document with a standard layout, such as a newspaper or magazine, you can place the rules between columns in text frames on the master page so they're automatically placed on every page. As always with such objects, you can modify them on individual document pages as needed (just be sure to Shift+⌘+click or Ctrl+Shift+click to select them when working in your document pages).

When drawing rules between columns, use the rulers to precisely position the lines. After you've drawn the lines, Shift+click to select all the lines and the text frames, and then choose Object ➪ Group, or ⌘+G or Ctrl+G. When the lines are grouped to the text frame, you can move them all as a unit. This also prevents someone from accidentally moving a vertical rule later.

TIP   Keep the width of intercolumn rules thin: usually a hairline (¼ point) or ½ point. Larger than that is usually too thick and can be confused with the border of a sidebar or other boxed element.

Managing Spacing and Alignment within Text Frames

The Text Frame Options dialog box lets you control several other key aspects of text placement within a frame, not just the number and size of columns. Two of these controls — both of which are in the General pane — affect the placement of text relative to the frame itself:

■ The Inset Spacing options let you bring text in from the frame boundary. Rectangular frames have four options: Top, Bottom, Left, and Right. Other frames just have one option that applies to the entire frame: Inset. You typically use Inset Spacing when you have a stroke around or a background behind the text frame, so the text does not print at the very edge of the frame.

NEW FEATURE   The Text Frames Options dialog box's General pane now has the Make All Settings the Same iconic button (the chain icon) in the area that contains the Inset Spacing fields. If the chain is unbroken, changing any offset automatically changes the other offsets to the same value. If the chain is broken, you can adjust each offset independently. Click the button to toggle between the two modes.

■ The Vertical Justification section lets you specify how text aligns vertically within the frame, but only if the frame is rectangular. Use the Align pop-up menu to choose the desired alignment: Top, Center, Bottom, or Justify. If you choose Justify, InDesign spreads the text out so it fills the frame from top to bottom, adding space between lines and paragraphs as needed to do so. You can control the maximum amount of space allowed between paragraphs by entering a value in the Paragraph Spacing Limit field, but note that this could result in InDesign adding more space between lines than between paragraphs if that's what it takes to fill the frame.

CROSS-REF For more details on the other Text Frame Options dialog box controls, see Chapter 13 for details on the Ignore Text Wrap check box and Chapter 10 for more on baseline grids. I cover the column settings in the previous section in this chapter.

Working with Overset Text

Even as you add text frames and pages, you can have more text than there is room for. Called *overset text*, this extra text doesn't appear anywhere in your layout. So how do you find overset text?

InDesign provides two ways:

- Look at the out port of the last text frame in a story chain. If it is a red cross, that means there is more text in the story that isn't placed in the layout. (If the out port is an empty black square, then there is no remaining unplaced text.)
- Open each story in the Story Editor, and look at the ruler along the left side of the text, just to the right of the list of currently applied paragraph styles. Overset text is indicated by a depth measurement of *OV* and is furthermore noted with a red line to the right of the text. (Chapter 16 explains how to use the Story Editor.)

Once you've identified your overset text, you then can edit the text to fit the space you do have; use tracking controls to tighten the spacing for a line here and there to get rid of widows that take up excess space; reformat it to fit the space you do have; add more space, such as through creating additional pages; or rebalance the space available by making some stories longer and others shorter. You can often use a combination of these techniques, in a process called *copyfitting*.

Summary

When text doesn't fit within a single text frame — the case in almost any multi-page publication — you need to link (or *thread*) the text frames. You can do this manually, threading one text frame to the next, or you can have InDesign automatically add pages containing threaded text frames. After frames are threaded, you can still reflow text by breaking text threads and rerouting the threads.

In addition to flowing text through the threaded frames, you can flow it through multiple columns within each frame. You can change the number of columns or their widths within a frame at any time. To distinguish columns more visually, you can draw vertical lines between columns and group them with the text frames.

To control when text starts at the top of a column, frame, or page, InDesign offers both local and style-based options to force breaks.

When your story has more text than you have room for in your layout — something you can identify by looking at a story's last text frame's out port or by using the Story Editor — you need to use a combination of editing, formatting, and layout techniques to make everything fit.

Chapter 16

Editing and Formatting Text

Most users do the bulk of their writing and editing in a word processor before bringing the files into InDesign for lay out.

But that doesn't mean you shouldn't do word-processor functions in InDesign. It makes a lot of sense to write captions, headlines, and other elements that need to fit a restricted area, as well as to take care of copy editing and minor revisions. InDesign lets you do such writing and editing in the actual layout, or in a built-in text editor that mimics the Mac's TextEdit or Windows' WordPad, except it does layout-specific things for you as well, such as tracking line counts.

Either way, you'll extensively use InDesign's editing, search-and-replace functions, and spell checker to refine your content.

Editing Text

When working in a layout, InDesign gives you the basic editing capabilities found in a word processor: cutting and pasting, and deleting and inserting text. These capabilities work very much like other text editors and word processors, so you should be able to use the techniques you already know to edit text within InDesign.

Controlling text view

But before you begin to edit text, you need to see it. In many layout views, the text is too small to work with. Generally, you zoom in around the block of text using the Zoom tool. For quick access to the tool, press Z. (Except

IN THIS CHAPTER

Editing text, including highlighting, cutting and pasting, and deleting

Using the Story Editor

Correcting mistakes as you type

Checking spelling as you type or all at once

Customizing the spelling and hyphenation dictionaries

Searching and replacing words and formats

Adjusting text appearance within text frames

Placing notes in text

when the cursor is in a block of text! In that case, you need to click the Zoom tool.) Then click to zoom in. To zoom out, press and hold Option or Alt when clicking.

Another way to zoom in is to use the keyboard shortcut ⌘+= or Ctrl+=. Each time you use it, the magnification increases. Zoom out by pressing ⌘+− [hyphen] or Ctrl+− [hyphen].

It's best to use the ⌘+= or Ctrl+= method when your text cursor (text-insertion pointer) is already on or near the text you want to zoom into; the cursor location is the center point for the zoom. Use the Zoom tool when your pointer is not near the text you want to magnify; then move the Zoom pointer to the area you want to magnify, and click once for each level of desired magnification.

TIP It helps to think of the zoom-in shortcut as ⌘++ [plus] or Ctrl++ [plus], but if you do, remember that you don't also press the Shift key, which technically is what you would need to do to get a plus sign.

In addition to seeing the text at a larger size, it also helps you see the spaces, tabs, and paragraph returns that exist in the text. Choose Type ➪ Show Hidden Characters or press Option+⌘+I or Ctrl+Alt+I (refer to Figure 16.1).

FIGURE 16.1

To help you see spaces, breaks, and other control characters, special symbols can display on-screen (they do not print). Top row, from left to right: regular space, nonbreaking space, fixed-width nonbreaking space, em space, en space, thin space, hair space, punctuation space, quarter space, third space, figure space, and flush space. Second row: tab and right tab. Third row: discretionary hyphen and nonbreaking hyphen. Fourth row: forced line break (new line), discretionary line break, paragraph return, column break, frame break, page break, even page break, and odd page break. Fifth row: note, indent to here, end nested style here, non-joiner, and end-of-story marker.

Navigating text

To work at a different text location, click in a different text frame or another location in the current text frame. You can also use the four arrow (cursor) keys on the keyboard to move one character to the right, one character to the left, one line up, or one line down. Add ⌘ or Ctrl to the arrow keys to jump one word to the right or left, or one paragraph up or down. The Home and End keys let you jump to the beginning or end of a line; add ⌘ or Ctrl to jump to the beginning or end of a story. (A *story* is text within a text frame or that is linked across several text frames, as described in Chapter 15.) Note that if your story begins or ends in a text frame on another page, InDesign brings you to that page.

Highlighting text

To highlight text, you can always use the old click-and-drag method. Or, you can add the Shift key to the navigation commands in the previous section. For example, while ⌘+right arrow or Ctrl+right arrow moves the cursor one word to the right, Shift+⌘+right arrow or Ctrl+Shift+right arrow highlights the next word to the right. Likewise, Shift+⌘+End or Ctrl+Shift+End highlights all the text to the end of the story.

For precise text selections, double-click to select a word and its trailing space (punctuation is not selected) and triple-click to select a paragraph. If you need the punctuation trailing a word, double-click, and then press Shift+⌘+right arrow or Ctrl+Shift+right arrow to extend the selection. To select an entire story, choose Edit ➪ Select All, or press ⌘+A or Ctrl+A.

To deselect text, choose Edit ➪ Deselect All, or press Shift+⌘+A or Ctrl+Shift+A. More simply, you can select another tool or click another area of the page.

Cutting, copying, and pasting text

After you've highlighted text, you can press ⌘+X or Ctrl+X to remove it from its story and place it on the Clipboard for later use. Use ⌘+C or Ctrl+C to leave the text in the story and place a copy on the Clipboard. Click anywhere else in text — within the same story, another story, or another document — and press ⌘+V or Ctrl+V. If you're menu-driven, the Edit menu provides the equivalent Cut, Copy, and Paste commands as well, plus the Paste without Formatting command.

Deleting and replacing text

To remove text from a document, you can highlight it and choose Edit ➪ Clear or press Delete or Backspace on the keyboard. Or you can simply type over the highlighted text or paste new text on top of it.

QUARKXPRESS Don't use ⌘+K or Ctrl+K to clear text. While that works in QuarkXPress, this shortcut opens the Preferences dialog box in InDesign.

Using the Story Editor

InDesign has a feature copied straight from Adobe PageMaker: the Story Editor. This window, shown here, lets you edit text without the distractions of your layout. It presents your text without line breaks or other nonessential formatting. You just see attributes such as boldface and italics, and, in a separate pane to the left, the names of the styles that have been applied. After clicking in a text frame, you open the Story Editor by choosing Edit ➪ Edit in Story Editor, or by pressing ⌘+Y or Ctrl+Y.

In the Story Editor, you use the same tools for selecting, deleting, copying, pasting, and searching and replacing as you would in your layout. The Story Editor is not a separate word processor, simply a way to look at your text in a less-distracting environment for those times your focus is on the meaning and words, not the text appearance.

Note that you set preferences for text size and font in the Story Editor Display pane of the Preferences dialog box (choose InDesign ➪ Preferences ➪ Story Editor Display or press ⌘+K on the Mac, or choose Edit ➪ Preferences ➪ Story Editor Display or press Ctrl+K in Windows), as detailed in Chapter 3. You can also set whether drag and drop is allowed for text within the Story Editor by using the Drag and Drop Text Editing controls in the Preference dialog box's Type pane. (By default, InDesign allows drag and drop within the Story Editor.)

The Story Editor can also identify overset text, as explained in Chapter 15.

If text is not highlighted, you can delete text to the right or left of the cursor. On the Mac, press Delete to delete to the left and press Del (sometimes labeled Clear) to delete to the right. In Windows, press Backspace to delete to the left and Delete to delete to the right.

> **TIP** If you double-click a text frame with any tool other than a drawing or frame tool, InDesign automatically switches to the Type tool and places the insertion point where you double-clicked. (This also works for text paths and table cells.) You can switch back to a selection tool by pressing Esc.

Undoing text edits

Remember to take advantage of InDesign's multiple undos while editing text. Choose Edit ➪ Undo and Edit ➪ Redo any time you change your mind about edits. The Undo and Redo keyboard commands are definitely worth remembering: ⌘+Z and Shift+⌘+Z or Ctrl+Z and Ctrl+Shift+Z.

Correcting Spelling Mistakes

Whether you're entering text directly in InDesign or importing text files from elsewhere, there are bound to be spelling mistakes. After all, we're all human. Fortunately, InDesign offers a few ways to take care of these misspellings.

InDesign's spell-check features flag three types of possible editorial problems: repeated words such as *an an*, words with odd capitalization such as the internal capitalization (called *intercaps*) in software and company names (like *InDesign*), and words not found in the spelling dictionary that may be spelled incorrectly. You can customize the spelling dictionary, and you can purchase other companies' spelling dictionaries to add words from disciplines such as law and medicine, as well as add dictionaries for other languages.

Fixing spelling on the fly

In my word processor, I've long taken it for granted that text can be corrected as I type. Microsoft Word, for example, has a feature called AutoCorrect that lets you specify corrections to be made as you type, whether they are common typos or the expansion of abbreviations to their full words (such as having Word replace *tq* with *thank you*).

Now, InDesign offers the same functionality, which it calls Autocorrect (with a lowercase *c*). You enable Autocorrect in the Autocorrect pane of the Preferences dialog box (choose InDesign ➪ Preferences ➪ Autocorrect or press ⌘+K on the Mac, or choose Edit ➪ Preferences ➪ Autocorrect or press Ctrl+K in Windows), as Figure 16.2 shows.

> **NOTE** Autocorrect works only for text you type in InDesign once you've turned Autocorrect on; it does not correct imported or previously typed text.

It's easy to configure Autocorrect:

1. **Select the Enable Autocorrect option to turn on this feature.**

You can also enable Autocorrect by choosing Edit ⇨ Spelling ⇨ Autocorrect.

2. **If you want InDesign to automatically fix capitalization errors, select the Autocorrect Capitalization Errors option.** Typically, this finds typos involving capitalizing the second letter of a word in addition to the first. For example, InDesign would replace *FOrmat* with *Format*.

3. **Choose the dictionary whose spelling and capitalization rules you want InDesign to use from the Language pop-up menu.** The default is based on the language you selected when you installed InDesign.

FIGURE 16.2
_____

The Autocorrect pane of the Preferences dialog box, as well as its Add to Autocorrect List dialog box

4. **To add your own custom corrections, click the Add button.** This opens the Add to Autocorrect List dialog box, also shown in Figure 16-2. Type the typo text or code you want InDesign to watch for in the Misspelled Word field and the corrected or expanded text you want InDesign to substitute in the Correction field. Click OK or press Enter when done, or click Cancel or press Esc to close the dialog box without adding anything.

 Oddly, you cannot use special symbols, not even InDesign's symbol codes (such as entering the ^+ code for an em dash), in the Correction field.

5. **Click OK to close the Preferences dialog box when done.**

The Importance of Capitalization in Autocorrection

The Misspelled Word and Correction fields are case-sensitive unless both entries are all lowercase. If you're not careful with how and when you capitalize text in these fields, you won't get the automated correction you expect.

The basic rule is this: Capitalize text in either field only if you are trying to fix capitalization errors. InDesign assumes you are fixing capitalization if you use any capital letters in these fields.

Thus, if you type *indesign* in the Misspelled Word field and *InDesign* in the Correction field, InDesign converts the *indesign, Indesign, inDesign*, and other miscapitalized variations to the properly capitalized *InDesign*. But if you type *Indesign* in the Misspelled Word field and *InDesign* in the Correction field, InDesign only corrects *Indesign*, not *indesign* and other miscapitalized variations.

Therefore, get in the habit of entering your text in lowercase in these fields. For example, type *portino* in the Misspelled Word field and *portion* in the Correction field, InDesign corrects *portino*, *Portino, POrtino*, and so on.

If you want to fix both spelling and capitalization errors at the same time, do it this way: Type the word in the Misspelled Word field in lowercase and the word in the Correction field as you want it capitalized. For example, type *indseign* in Misspelled Word and *InDesign* in Correction. This way, any instance of *indseign* — no matter how it is capitalized — is replaced with the properly spelled and capitalized *InDesign*.

To remove an autocorrection, just select it in the Autocorrect pane's Misspelled Word list and click Remove.

Checking spelling as you type

You can have InDesign check your spelling as you type by simply choosing Edit ➪ Spelling ➪ Dynamic Spelling. You can also choose Spelling ➪ Dynamic Spelling from the contextual menu if you are using the Type tool. If that menu option is selected, InDesign checks the spelling as you type, as well as the spelling of any text already in the document. Suspected errors are highlighted with red squiggle underlining, so you can correct them as needed.

NOTE There's no way to have InDesign help you correct misspellings with as-you-type spell checking; if you want InDesign to suggest proper spelling, you need to use the Check Spelling dialog box, which I cover in the next section.

Using the Check Spelling dialog box

The other method you can use to check spelling is the Check Spelling dialog box, which gives you more control. First, it lets you choose what part of the document to spell check. Second, it provides suggestions on correct spelling and lets you add correctly spelled words that InDesign doesn't know about to its spelling dictionary. So even if you use the new dynamic spell-checking feature, you still want to do a final spell-checking pass in the Check Spelling dialog box.

Specifying the text to check is a two-step process: First, set up the spell-check scope in the document; then specify the scope in the Search menu.

To set up the scope, highlight text, click in a story to check from the cursor forward, select a frame containing a story, or open multiple documents. Just as in search and replace, what you choose to open and select determines what scope options InDesign has for spell checking.

Then, open the Check Spelling dialog box (Edit ⇨ Spelling ⇨ Check Spelling, or ⌘+I or Ctrl+I) and choose an option from the Search pop-up menu: Document, All Documents, Story, To End of Story, and Selection. Figure 16.3 shows the dialog box. Depending on how you set up the scope, not all the options are available in the Search pop-up menu. For example, if you do not highlight text, the Selection option is not available. However, you can change the scope setup in the document while the Check Spelling dialog box is open. For example, you can open additional documents to check.

To check the spelling of a single word, double-click to highlight it and then open the spell-checker — the Check Spelling dialog box's Search pop-up menu is automatically set to Selection.

Control+click or right-click on a word, range of text, or a point in a text frame (using the Type tool) to get the contextual menu from which you choose Check Spelling.

FIGURE 16.3

Use the Search pop-up menu in the Check Spelling dialog box to specify which text to spell check.

When you first open the Check Spelling dialog box and text is selected or the text cursor is active, it immediately begins checking the spelling, going to the first suspect word. You can change the scope of the search using the Search pop-up menu at any time.

NEW FEATURE   The immediate spell-checking feature is new to InDesign CS3.

If text is not selected or the text cursor is not active, the Check Spelling dialog box displays "Ready to Check Spelling" at the top. To begin checking the text scope you specified in the Search pop-up menu, click Start.

When adjusting the scope of the spell check in the Search pop-up menu, your choices are All Documents, Document, Story, and To End of Story. You can also make the spell check case-sensitive by enabling the Case Sensitive check box.

When the spell checker encounters a word without a match in the dictionary or a possible capitalization problem, the dialog box displays "Not in Dictionary" at the top and shows the word. When the spell checker encounters repetition such as *me me,* the dialog box displays "Duplicate Word" and shows the repeated words. Use the buttons along the right side of the dialog box to handle flagged words as follows:

- To leave the current instance of a Not in Dictionary word or Duplicate Word unchanged, click Skip (this appears only after the spell check has started). To leave all instances of the same problem unchanged, click Ignore All.

- To change the spelling of a Not in Dictionary word, click a word in the Suggested Corrections list or edit the spelling or capitalization in the Change To field. To make the change, click Change.

- To correct an instance of a Duplicate Word, edit the text in the Change To field, and then click Change.

- To change all occurrences of a Not in Dictionary word or a Duplicate Word to the information in the Change To field, click Change All.

- To add a word flagged as incorrect — but that you know is correct — click Add to add the word to InDesign's spelling dictionary. (If you have multiple dictionaries, first choose the dictionary to add it to using the Add To pop-up menu.)

- To add a word flagged as incorrect to a specific dictionary, click Dictionary. The resulting Dictionary dialog box lets you choose which dictionary to add the word to, as well as what language to associate it with. You can also specify hyphenation settings. I cover the options in this dialog box later in this chapter.

- To close the Check Spelling dialog box after checking all the specified text, click Done.

While you're using Check Spelling, you can jump between the dialog box and the document at any time. This lets you edit a possibly misspelled word in context or edit surrounding text as a result of changed spelling. So if you find an instance of *a a* in front of *apple,* you can change the entire phrase to *an apple* rather than just replace the duplicate *a a* with *a* in the dialog box and have to remember to later change *a apple* to *an apple.*

Working with multiple languages

Each word in InDesign can have a distinct language assigned to it (English, French, Spanish, German, and so on). The word's language attribute tells InDesign which dictionary to consult when it's spell checking or hyphenating the word. For example, if you have the word *frères* in an

English sentence, you can change the language of that word so it is no longer flagged by the English spell checker — the French spell checker is used instead and recognizes that the word is correctly spelled.

Just because you have the ability to control language at the word level doesn't necessarily mean that you have to use it. In general, even when you're publishing for an international audience, full paragraphs or stories are in the same language. For example, if you have the same packaging for a product sold in the United States and France, you might have one descriptive paragraph in English and the other in French. The English dictionary also contains many common words with foreign origins such as *jalapeño, mélange,* and *gestalt.*

To assign a language to text, highlight the text and choose an option from the Language pop-up menu on the expanded Character panel, as shown in Figure 16.4. You can also set the language as part of a character or paragraph style (see Chapters 17 and 18 for more details). In the Check Spelling dialog box, a field above the Search menu shows the language of each word as it's checked. Unfortunately, you can't change the language in that dialog box.

FIGURE 16.4

The Language pop-up menu on the Character panel lets you choose a different language for hyphenating and spell checking highlighted text.

NOTE There's a language option called [No Language]; selecting it *prevents* spell checking and hyphenation.

NEW FEATURE InDesign CS3 adds language support for Ukrainian. It also supports the new Dutch: 2005 Reform in addition to previous Dutch (now called Dutch: Old Rules), the German: 2006 Reforms in addition to German1996 Reform and German: Traditional), and German: Swiss 2006 Reform in addition to German: Swiss. And Spanish: Castilian has been renamed just Spanish.

Customizing the Spelling and Hyphenation Dictionaries

A spelling dictionary can never cover all the bases — you always have industry-specific words and proper nouns not found in the dictionary in use. In addition, copy editors tend to have their own preferences for how to hyphenate words. What they consider correct hyphenation may vary, and some word breaks are preferred over others. To solve both these problems, you can customize InDesign's dictionaries by adding words and specifying hyphenation. InDesign handles both spelling and hyphenation in one dictionary for each language, so you use the same controls to modify both.

Changes made to a dictionary file are saved only in the dictionary file, not with an open document. So if you add words to the English: USA dictionary, the modified dictionary is used for spell checking and hyphenating all text in documents that use the English: USA dictionary.

TIP If you're in a workgroup, be sure to share the edited dictionary file so everyone is using the same spelling and hyphenation settings. (The file is located in the Dictionaries folder inside the Plug-ins folder inside your InDesign folder.) You can copy it for other users, who must then restart InDesign or press Option+⌘+/ or Ctrl+Alt+/ to reflow the text according to the new dictionary's hyphenation.

Customizing the spelling dictionary

While spell checking, you often find words that don't match those in the dictionary. If you know the word is spelled correctly and likely to appear in your publications often, you can add it to the dictionary. In the future, this word isn't flagged and you don't have to click Ignore to skip it; and you can be sure that when it's used, it is spelled as it is in the dictionary.

When adding words to the dictionary, you can specify their capitalization. For example, InDesign's dictionary prefers *E-mail*. You can add *e-mail* if you prefer a lowercase *e* or *email* if you prefer to skip the hyphen. If you're adding a word that may have variations (such as *e-mailing*) be sure to add those variations separately.

To add words to the dictionary:

1. **Choose Edit ➪ Spelling ➪ Dictionary**. The Dictionary dialog box shown in Figure 16.5 appears.

FIGURE 16.5

Type a new term in the Word field, and then click Add to include it in the spelling dictionary. Be sure to select the Case Sensitive option for proper names and acronyms.

2. **Choose whether the addition to the dictionary affects just this document or all documents.** To do so, use the Target pop-up menu, which lists the current document name as well as User Dictionary (to change the dictionary file). The advantage of making the spelling specific to the document is that all users, such as service bureaus, have the same spellings; the disadvantage is that other documents won't share this spelling.

3. **Choose the dictionary that you want to edit from the Language pop-up menu.**

4. **Type or paste a word in the Word field.** The word can include special characters such as accents and hyphens, spaces, and a capitalization pattern to follow.

5. **If you want InDesign to accept only the added word with the capitalization typed in the Word field, select the Case Sensitive option.** This lets you add proper names, for example, but have them still flagged when typed in all lowercase or with extra capital letters. For example, if you type **Healdsburg** in the Word field and select Case Sensitive, InDesign doesn't flag *Healdsburg* but does flag *healdsburg* and *HEaldsburg*.

6. **If you want to edit the hyphenation, click Hyphenate.** You can add, remove, or modify the number of tildes to change the hyphenation rules for the word, as covered in the next section.

7. **Click Add.**

8. **If you want to import a word list or export one for other users to import into their copies of InDesign, click Import or Export as appropriate.** You navigate to a folder and choose a filename in a dialog box similar to the Open a File or Save dialog boxes. Note that when you click Export, InDesign exports all *selected* words from the list. If no words are selected, it exports all the words in the list.

9. **Continue to add words, and when you're finished, click Done.**

When you're adding variations of words, you can double-click a word in the list to place it in the Word field as a starting place.

In addition to adding words through the Dictionary dialog box, you can click Add in the Check Spelling dialog box when InDesign flags a word that you know is correct, as I cover earlier in this chapter.

To delete a word that you added to the dictionary, select it in the list and click Remove. To change the spelling of a word you added, delete it and then re-add it with the correct spelling. You can see the words you've deleted since you opened the dialog box by choosing Removed Words from the Dictionary List pop-up menu, so you can add back any deleted by error.

Customizing hyphenation points

Industries and publications usually have internal styles on how words hyphenate, especially if the text is justified. For example, a bridal magazine that uses the term *newlywed* often may prefer that it breaks at the end of a line as *newly–wed*. But if that hyphenation would cause poor spacing, the publisher might let it break at *new–lywed* as well. InDesign lets you modify the hyphenation dictionary by specifying new, hierarchical hyphenation points.

When you customize the hyphenation points, be sure to add variations of words (such as the plural form *newlyweds*). InDesign sees each word as wholly unrelated and, thus, doesn't apply the hyphenation of, say, *newlywed* to *newlyweds*.

To specify hyphenation points:

1. **Choose Edit ⇨ Spelling ⇨ Dictionary.**
2. **Choose from the Language menu the dictionary that you want to edit.**
3. **Type or paste the word in the Word field; you can also double-click a word in the list.**
4. **If you want, click Hyphenate to see InDesign's suggestions for hyphenating the word.** You can then change the hyphenation according to Steps 5 and 6.
5. **Type a tilde (~, obtained by pressing Shift+`, the open single keyboard quote at the upper left of the keyboard) at your first preference for a hyphenation point.** If you don't want the word to hyphenate at all, type a tilde in front of it.
6. **Type tildes in other hyphenation points as well.** If you want to indicate a preference, use two tildes for your second choice, three tildes for your third choice, and so on. InDesign first tries to hyphenate your top preferences (single tildes), and then it tries your second choices if the first ones don't work out, and so on. Figure 16.6 shows an example.
7. **Click Add.**
8. **Continue to add words until you're finished, and then click Done.**

To revert a word to the default hyphenation, select it in the list and click Remove. To change the hyphenation, double-click a word in the list to enter it in the Word field, change the tildes, and then click Add. When you're adding variations of words, you can double-click a word in the list to place it in the Word field as a starting place.

> **TIP**   If a word actually includes a freestanding tilde (not as an accent, as in ñ), type \~ to indicate the character is part of the word. These are rare and happen mostly in World Wide Web addresses.

FIGURE 16.6

Type hyphenation preferences in the Word field, using tildes (~) to indicate hyphenation points; then click Add to include them in the spelling dictionary.

Setting spelling and hyphenation dictionary preferences

By default, when spell checking and hyphenating text, InDesign consults dictionaries created by a company called Proximity. Because spelling and hyphenation points vary from dictionary to dictionary, and you may prefer one dictionary over another, you can purchase and install other companies' dictionaries to use instead of Proximity's. However, it's very hard to find commercial alternatives to the Proximity dictionaries, so most users use the ones that come with InDesign and update them as needed.

To replace a dictionary:

1. **Place the dictionary file in the Dictionaries folder in the Plug-ins folder inside your InDesign folder.**

2. **Go to the Dictionary pane of the Preferences dialog box, shown in Figure 16.7.**
(Choose InDesign ⇨ Preferences ⇨ Dictionary or press ⌘+K on the Mac, or choose Edit ⇨
Preferences ⇨ Dictionary or press Ctrl+K in Windows.)

FIGURE 16.7

If you purchase and install different hyphenation and spelling dictionaries, you can
select them in the Dictionary pane of the Preferences dialog box. You can also add your
own dictionaries.

3. **From the Language pop-up menu, choose which language's dictionary you want to
replace.** Dictionary files associated with that language appear in the list below the pop-
up menu.

4. **Use the four buttons under the list of dictionary files to modify the dictionary files
associated with the language.** They are, from left to right:

   ▪ **Relocate:** This lets you select a replacement dictionary for the one selected in the list
   above. Navigate to the folder and dictionary file you want to use, and then click Open.

   ▪ **New:** This creates a new, empty dictionary file that you can then modify with the
   Dictionary dialog box covered earlier in this chapter. The result is a custom dictionary.

   ▪ **Add:** This lets you add a dictionary to the selected language. Thus, you can have multiple dictionaries per language, which is very useful for handling industry-specific
   terms or trademarked terms, for example.

■ **Remove:** This removes a dictionary associated to a language. Note that there must be at least one dictionary per language, so this button is grayed out when only one dictionary remains in the list.

TIP A fast way to fill a new custom dictionary with the desired words is to spell-check a bunch of documents containing those special words. Add the words InDesign does not recognize to your custom dictionary, as I describe earlier in this chapter.

5. **If you have multiple rules engines for hyphenation and spelling, choose the referred rules engine from the Hyphenation and/or Spelling pop-up menu.** Such rules engines are rare, so you typically have only the default choice of Proximity for these two pop-up menus.

6. **If you don't want to use the language's standard quotation characters, you can change them in the Double Quotes and Single Quotes pop-up menus.** You might change the default quotes if you are publishing in one language but have extensive phrases from other languages in them. For example, a French book that extensively uses English passages (perhaps a literary article) might want to apply French quotes to text tagged with one of the English languages.

7. **To regulate how hyphenation is handled, use the Compose Using pop-up menu.** Your choices are User Dictionary, which has InDesign ignore the hyphenation override settings that a user has made to this document (a great way to override someone's incorrect hyphenation changes); Document, which uses only the hyphenations specified in the document; and User Dictionary and Document, which uses hyphenation settings from the dictionary as well as any hyphenation specified in the document. This last setting is the default.

8. **To ensure consistent spelling and hyphenation, use the two options in the User Dictionary section:**

   ■ **Merge User Dictionary into Document:** If selected, this copies the user dictionary into the document, so if the file is used by someone else who doesn't have that user dictionary, the spelling and hyphenation rules are nonetheless retained.

   ■ **Recompose All Stories When Modified:** If selected, this rehyphenates and changes quote settings for all stories in the document, even those created before the user dictionary was modified or added.

9. **Click OK.**

TIP If you change Dictionary Preferences with no documents open, the new dictionary becomes a program default and applies to all new documents. If a document is open, the change applies only to that document.

Searching and Replacing

InDesign's Find/Change dialog box (Edit ➪ Find/Change, or ⌘+F or Ctrl+F) lets you do everything from, for example, finding the next instance of *curry* in an article so you can insert *extra spicy* in red, to finding all instances of a deposed chef's name in six different documents. If you know how to use the search-and-replace feature in any word processor or page-layout application, you should be comfortable with InDesign's Find/Change in no time.

NEW FEATURE InDesign CS3 adds a lot of new features to the Find/Change dialog box, including a new interface, the ability to essentially program your search by specifying conditions using the Greprep syntax, the ability to search for special characters (glyphs), the ability to search for object attributes (see Chapter 11), and the ability to save search/replace queries so you can use them repeatedly.

Searching and replacing text

The Find/Change dialog box comes in two forms: reduced for finding and changing just text, and expanded for including attributes in a search. Click More Options to expand the dialog box to include formatting options for your search and replace, and Fewer Options to reduce it.

Before starting a Find/Change operation, determine the scope of your search:

- To search within a text selection, highlight it.
- To search from a certain location in a story to the end of it, click in that location using the Type tool to place the text cursor (also called the text-insertion point) there.
- To search an entire story, select any frame or click at any point in a frame containing the story.
- To search an entire document, simply have that document open.
- To search multiple documents, open all of them (and close any that you don't want to search).

To search for text:

1. **Determine the scope of your search, as just described, open the needed documents, and insert the text cursor at the appropriate location.**

2. **Choose Edit ⇨ Find/Change, or press ⌘+F or Ctrl+F.** Go to the Text pane if it's not already displayed.

3. **Use the Search pop-up menu, as shown in Figure 16.8, to specify the scope of your search: Document, All Documents, Story, To End of Story, or Selection.** Options unavailable for the current search scope won't display.

TIP As you're using the Find/Change dialog box to search and replace text, you can jump into a text frame (just click it with the Type tool) and edit it as you please, and then return to Find/Change by clicking the Find/Change dialog box.

4. **Type or paste the text you want to find in the Find What field.** To search for special characters, type their codes (see Table 16.1) or use the pop-up list (the right-facing arrow icon) to select from a menu of special characters. (If you type the codes, note that they are case-sensitive.) To use special characters, use the Special Characters for Search pop-up list (the icon to the right of the Find What field) to select from a menu of special characters (see Figure 16.9).

FIGURE 16.8

Use the Search pop-up menu in the Find/Change dialog box to specify the scope of the text to search. The buttons below also provide scope options.

Include Locked Layers

Include Locked Stories

Include Hidden Layers

Include Master Pages

Whole Word

Case Sensitive

Include Footnotes

5. **Type or paste the replacement text into the Change To field.** To use special characters, use the Special Characters for Replace pop-up list (to the right of the Find What field). Alternatively, type their codes (see Table 16.1).

6. **Specify the parameters for your search by selecting or deselecting the seven iconic buttons at the bottom of the pane: Include Locked Layers, Include Locked Stories, Include Hidden Layers, Include Master Pages, Include Footnotes, Case Sensitive, and Whole Word.** If an icon's background darkens, it is selected.

7. **Specify whether to consider capitalization patterns in the Find/Change operation by selecting or deselecting the Case Sensitive option.** When selected, Find/Change follows the capitalization of the text in the Find What and Change To fields exactly.

8. **If you want to search for or replace with specific formatting, use the Format buttons.** These buttons are available only if you had clicked More Options. (I cover these buttons later in this chapter.)

9. **Click Find to start the search.** Thereafter, click Find Next (it changes from the Find button after you start the search) to skip instances of the Find What text, and click

Change, Change All, or Change/Find to replace the Find What text with the Change To text. (Change simply changes the found text, Change All changes every instance of that found text in your selection or story, and Change/Find changes the current found text and moves on to the next occurrence of it; it basically does in one click the actions of clicking Change and then clicking Find Next.)

10. Click Done when you're finished. Note that you can do several search-and-replace operations, which is why the dialog box stays open after completing a search.

NOTE If you use the Change All feature, InDesign reports how many changes were made. If the number looks extraordinarily high and you suspect the Find/Change operation wasn't quite what you wanted, remember you can use InDesign's undo function (Edit ⇨ Undo, or ⌘+Z or Ctrl+Z) to undo the search and replace so you can try a different replace strategy.

TIP InDesign records your last 15 entries in the Find What and Change To fields, so you can repeat previous Find/Change operations. That's why each field is a pop-up menu. Click the menu to open it, and use the down-arrow key to scroll through those recorded operations.

FIGURE 16.9

Click the right-facing arrow on the Find What and Change To fields to display a list of special characters.

Table 16.1: Text Codes for Search and Replace

Character	Code
Markers and Page Numbers	
Auto page number	^N
Next page number	^X
Previous page number	^V

continued

TABLE 16.1   (continued)

Character	Code
Markers and Page Numbers	
Any page number*	^#
Anchored object market*	^a
Footnote reference marker	^F
Index entry marker*	^I
Section marker	^x
End nested style marker	^h
Inline graphic marker*	^g
Indent to here	^I
Symbols	
Bullet (()	^8
Caret (^)	^^
Copyright (©) symbol	^2
Paragraph (¶) symbol	^7
Registered trademark (®) symbol	^r
Section (§) symbol	^6
Punctuation	
Double left quotation mark (")	^{
Double right quotation mark (")	^}
Double keyboard quote (")	^"
Any double keyboard quote*	"
Single left quotation mark (')	^[
Single right quotation mark (')	^]
Single keyboard quote (')	^'
Any single quote or apostrophe*	'
Em dash (—)	^_
En dash (–)	^=
Discretionary hyphen	^-
Nonbreaking hyphen	^~
Spaces	
Tab	^t
Right-indent tab	^y

Character	Code
Spaces	
Em space	^m
En space	^>
Flush space	^f
Nonbreaking space	^s
Nonbreaking fixed space	^S
Hair space	^|
Thin space	^<
Punctuation space	^.
Sixth space	^%
Quarter space	^4
Third space	^3
Non-joiner	^j
White space (any space or tab)*	^w
Breaks	
End of paragraph	^p
Forced line break	^n
Discretionary line break	^k
Column break	^M
Frame break	^R
Page break	^P
Odd page break	^L
Even page break	^E
Wild Cards	
Any character*	^?
Any digit*	^9
Any letter*	^$
Clipboard Contents	
Formatted contents**	^c
Unformatted contents**	^C

*Can be entered in the Find What field only

**Can be entered in Change To field only

What Is Grep?

In the Find/Change dialog box is a pane called Grep that looks to be the same as the Text pane. Grep is a utility in the Unix operating system (including variants such as Linux) that provides a powerful language for programming searches based on pattern-matching. The Grep dialog box brings this language to InDesign's search-and-replace functions without having to know the Grep syntax or codes. It works just like the Text pane except that there are additional options in the Special Characters for Search and the Special Characters for Replace pop-up menus next to the Find What and Change To fields, respectively.

Under the hood, Grep uses complex codes to perform its pattern-matching. Many of these codes are the same as internal InDesign codes, though with different meanings. To ensure that InDesign doesn't get confused, Adobe engineers had to create a separate Grep pane rather than add Grep features to the Text pane of the Find/Change dialog box.

In the Special Characters for Search pop-up menu, shown here, you can choose from several sub-menus: Location, Repeat, Match, Modifiers, and Posix. You can use as many of these as needed to define your search patterns.

In the Special Characters for Replace pop-up menu, there is just one additional menu option — Found — where you can select found text (from previous searches) to include in the replacement text.

Although InDesign simplifies access to Grep, using it still requires knowledge of what the Grep commands actually do and how they work (its syntax) — something that only a tiny minority of users will know, so don't feel bad if you don't end up using this feature. Adobe does include some documentation on Grep's syntax in its InDesign CD, and you can get an in-depth tutorial on Grep in many Unix books.

To search and replace regular spaces, type the number of spaces you want to find and change in the Find What and Change To fields, as if they were any other regular character.

If there are other characters not in InDesign's special-character menu that you want to search for or replace with, just type their keyboard codes (see Chapter 21) or paste them into the field. (You can paste them by first copying them to the Clipboard from your document text, or from a utility like Character Palette on the Mac, Character Map in Windows, or PopChar in either platform, as Chapter 21 explains.)

InDesign also provides three wild cards — Any Character, Any Digit, and Any Letter — that let you search for unspecified characters, numbers, or letters in other text. For example, if you want to change all the numbered steps in a document to bulleted lists, you might search for Any Digit and replace it with a bullet. Or you can search for variations of a word to find, say, *cafe* and *café* at the same time (in this case, you would type caf and then choose Any Letter, or type caf^$ if you prefer to use the codes).

Changing special characters

InDesign CS3 also lets you replace special characters (glyphs) through a separate Glyph pane in the Find/Change dialog box, shown in Figure 16.10. This makes it easier to actually enter the desired characters. The process is mostly straightforward (just ignore the parts of the pane not described in this section):

NEW FEATURE The Glyph pane is new to InDesign CS3's Find/Change dialog box.

1. **In the Find Glyph section, choose the font of the desired character in the Font Family pop-up menu, and its style in the Font Style pop-up menu.**

2. **To choose the character itself, click the pop-up menu icon to the right of the Glyph field.** You get a dialog box that mimics the Glyphs panel (see Chapter 21); choose the character from the panel by double-clicking it.

3. **Repeats Steps 1 and 2 using the controls in the Change Glyph section to select the replacement glyph.**

4. **Set the scope of your search using the Search pop-up menu and the Include Locked Layers, Include Locked Stories, Include Hidden Layers, Include Master Pages, and Include Footnotes iconic buttons, as described earlier in this chapter.**

5. **Execute the search and/or replace using the Find, Change, Change All, and Change/Find iconic buttons as described earlier in this chapter.**

6. **Click Done when done.**

 If you want to quickly wipe out the selected glyphs, click the Clear Glyphs button.

FIGURE 16.10

The Glyphs pane of the Find/Change dialog box

Searching and replacing formatting

To find and change formatting or text with specific formatting, you can use the expanded Find/Change dialog box. For example, you might find all the blue words in 14-point Futura Extra Bold and change them to 12-point Mrs Eaves Bold. Or you might find all instances of the words *hot and spicy* in 15-point body text, and then resize the text to 12 point and apply the font Chili Pepper.

To replace text formatting, follow these steps:

1. **To add formats to a Find/Change operation for text, click More Options in the Find/Change dialog box (if it was not clicked earlier).** The dialog box expands to include the Find Format Settings (see Figure 16.11) and Change Format Settings areas.

2. **Use the Format buttons to display the Find Format Settings and Change Format Settings dialog boxes, which let you specify the formats you want to find.** The two dialog boxes are identical, except for their names; refer to Figure 16.11 for the Find Format Settings dialog box.

3. **Use the menu at the top to specify the type of formatting: Style Options (paragraph and character styles), Basic Character Formats, Advanced Character Formats, Indents and Spacing, Keep Options, Bullets and Numbering, Character Color, OpenType Features, Underline Options, Strikethrough Options, and Drop Caps and Other.** You can change multiple attributes at once by making selections from as many panes as needed.

To search and replace formatting only — regardless of the text to which it is applied —
leave the Find What and Change To fields blank.

FIGURE 16.11

Clicking More Options in the Find/Change dialog box displays the Find Format Settings and Change Format
Settings areas. (More Options changes to Fewer Options.) Clicking Format opens either the Find Format
Settings dialog box (shown here) or Change Format Settings dialog box, depending on whether you click
Format in the Find Format Settings area or in the Change Format Settings area.

Locating and specifying all the formatting you want to find and change requires you to dig deeper
and deeper into the Find Format Settings and Change Format Settings dialog boxes. Unfortunately,
you can't really get a picture of all the formats you're selecting at once, and you have to keep jumping from one pane to the next. Fortunately, when you've finished selecting formats, the selected
options are summarized in the Find Style Settings and Change Style Settings areas.

Changing fonts globally

Sometimes, you need to replace a font throughout your document. You can't use the Find/Change
dialog box to do this because it requires that you specify specific text to find and replace. But you
can choose Type ➪ Find Font and use the Find Font dialog box shown in Figure 16.12 to replace
a specific font with another. The Fonts in Document section shows all fonts actually in use so you
can select the one you want to replace. You then choose the new font and style using the Font
Family and Font Style pop-up menus in the Replace With section.

NEW FEATURE New to InDesign CS3 is the Redefine Style When Changing All check box, which if selected ensures that any font replacement updates all paragraph and character styles to use the new font. In previous versions, the styles kept the old, unavailable font.

Two other buttons in the Find Font dialog box help you understand what font you're replacing:

- **Show in Finder (Mac) or Reveal in Explorer (Windows):** This button opens the folder that contains the font, which is handy if you have the same font in multiple folders and want to know which one InDesign is using.

- **More Info:** This button provides details on the selected font, such as any printing restrictions, the font version, the location, and the PostScript font name.

FIGURE 16.12

The Find Font dialog box with the More Info button clicked

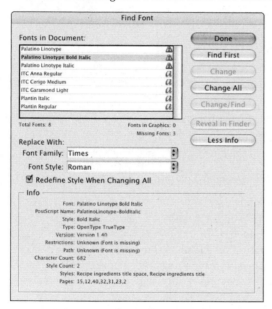

Working with saved search queries

If you plan to do the same search and/or replace operation repeatedly, you can now save queries in InDesign CS3. After entering the find and search information, click the Save Query iconic button, enter a name in the Save Query dialog box that appears, and click OK. That query will now appear in the Query pop-up menu in the Find/Change dialog box.

Managing Your Fonts

You typically replace fonts in your layout because you actually want to use a different font, not merely because you don't happen to have the fonts installed on your system that the document is using. After all, the design shouldn't change just because you don't happen to have the needed fonts on your computer.

In both Mac OS X 10.4 (Tiger) and 10.5 (Leopard), the easiest way to add fonts is by opening the Font Book program in the Applications folder, and then choosing File ➪ Add Fonts to install OpenType, Type 1 PostScript, and TrueType fonts. You can also do it manually by dragging fonts files to one of the following folders:

- **Fonts folder in the Library folder (Library:Fonts):** This is where you should place fonts that you want all users to have access to. Just drag them in, whether they're PostScript, TrueType, or OpenType.

- **Fonts folder in the user's Home folder's Library folder (Users/*user name*:Library:Fonts):** Any fonts dragged here are available only to that user.

- **Fonts folder in the System folder's Library folder (System:Library:Fonts):** This is where Apple places the default fonts for Mac OS X applications. You can add fonts here as well by dragging them, but I recommend you leave this folder alone. You can create a horrible mess on your system if you place your own font files here.

Any fonts installed in the Mac OS X folders are not available to Mac OS 9 applications (which older PowerPC-based Macs can run under Classic mode). You need to also maintain fonts in the System Folder's Fonts folder — note that the Mac OS 9 folder name is System Folder while the Mac OS X folder name is simply System — or use a Mac OS 9 font manager such as Adobe Type Manager.

In Windows XP and Vista, you add OpenType or TrueType fonts by opening the Fonts folder. In XP, choose Start ➪ Settings ➪ Control Panel and double-click the Fonts button; in Vista, choose Start ➪ Control Panel and click Classic View in the right-hand pane, then double-click the Fonts button. You can simply drag the new fonts into the window, or you can choose File ➪ Install Fonts. (In Vista, you may have to press and release the Alt key to see the menus.)

Note that Windows XP has built-in support for TrueType and OpenType fonts, while Windows Vista has built-in support for PostScript Type 1, TrueType, and OpenType fonts.

If you're using a font management utility such as Insider Software's FontAgent Pro or Extensis's Suitcase for Mac, or Adobe's Type Manager or Extensis's Suitcase for Windows, use their tools to add fonts, as well as to activate and deactivate the fonts that are installed. Activation and deactivation let you turn fonts on and off without actually having to install or delete them. This is a great feature if your documents use different font sets, because you can then quickly turn on or off just the correct fonts for the job you happen to be working on at the moment.

To run a saved query, just choose it from the Query pop-up menu. To delete a saved query, choose it from the Query pop-up menu and then click Delete Query iconic button.

NEW FEATURE   The ability to save search queries is new to InDesign CS3.

Adjusting Text Appearance in Text Frames

Although most adjustments to text frames—such as frame size, shape, and location—affect the layout, not the text, there are several text-frame attributes that do affect your text's appearance.

Setting text frame options

Most of these adjustments reside in the General pane of the Text Frame Options dialog box shown in Figure 16.13. You open the dialog box by selecting a frame and choosing Object ⇨ Text Frame Options, or pressing ⌘+B or Ctrl+B.

CROSS-REF   Chapter 9 covers the creation, modification, and deletion of text frames in more detail. Chapter 15 covers the Column settings in the Text Frame Options dialog box. The rest of Part IV covers formatting text.

FIGURE 16.13

The General pane (left) and Baseline Options pane (right) of the Text Frame Options dialog box.

These four sections of the General pane of Text Frame Options dialog box provide the following controls:

- **Columns:** The section lets you specify the number of columns, and column width and gutter settings, as explained in Chapter 15.

- **Inset Spacing:** This section creates an internal margin in the frame, putting space between the frame edge and the text. You can set the Top, Bottom, Left, and Right settings separately. To make the setting in one change the setting in all, be sure the Make All the Settings the Same iconic button appears as an unbroken chain; if the chain is broken, it is not enabled. Click the button to toggle between the two modes.

- **Vertical Justification:** This section controls the placement of text vertically in a text frame, similar to right-, center-, or left-aligning a paragraph horizontally. The Top, Center, and Bottom options in the Align pop-up menu move the text to the top, the center, or bottom of the text frame. The Justify option is a bit different: It permits variable spacing between paragraphs, so the text fits the full depth of the frame. If you choose Justify, the leading within paragraphs is unaffected, but InDesign adds as much space as needed between each paragraph — up to the value set in the Paragraph Spacing Limit field — to ensure that the last line of text in the frame is at the bottom of the frame. Because the default is 0p, text isn't vertically justified even if you choose Justify; you must also increase the Paragraph Spacing Limit value. Figure 16.14 shows some examples of this.

NOTE In a multicolumn text frame, vertical justification applies only to the last column.

- **Ignore Text Wrap:** This option is in its own untitled section. If selected, it lets text in the text frame overprint another object, even if text wrap is set for that object. You'll use this rarely. An example of when you might want to select this option is when you have a headline you want to overprint a graphic around which body text wraps.

FIGURE 16.14

This brochure shows examples of vertical justification, showing how the spacing changes as the number of lines changes. (Normal, top-aligned text is at left.)

The Baseline Options pane provides controls for where text baselines begin relative to the frame's top:

- **First Baseline:** This section lets you determine where the baseline for the first line of text in the frame rests. (The baseline is the invisible line on which characters rest and through which descenders, such as the lower portions of letters like *p* and *g*, "poke through.") You have five options in the Offset pop-up menu. How you use each of them depends on your aesthetic goals:

  - **Ascent:** This option puts the baseline as close to the top of the frame as possible, so the tops of characters graze the text frame's top (or the margin you set in the Inset Spacing section). This is the default.

  - **Cap Height:** The Cap Height adjusts the baseline so that it is a cap height's distance from the frame top. The cap height is the height of a capital letter *C*, but some fonts have characters that extend above that location, and these fonts will have characters that rise above the top of the frame if you choose Cap Height here.

  - **Leading:** This option places the baseline from the frame's top in the same amount as the text's leading. If leading is set to 13 points, for example, the baseline will be 13 points from the top of the frame, no matter if that makes characters rise above the frame top (such as if the text size is set at 15 points) or causes a gap (such as if the text size is set at 9 points).

  - **x Height:** This adjusts the baseline so that it is an x height's distance from the frame top. The x height is the height of a lowercase letter *x*. Selecting x Height ensures that capital letters and letters with ascenders (such as *d* and *h*) poke through the top of the frame.

  - **Fixed:** This option uses the value in the Min field to position the baseline. You use this if you want the baseline for all text frames to be the same no matter what the text size and appearance is. That's pretty rare. Standard practice is to have text positioned from the frame top relative to its size, which the other Offset options essentially do.

  You can override any of the settings described here by specifying an amount in the Min field. The Min field tells InDesign that the first baseline must be at least a specific distance from the frame top. InDesign first tries to position the baseline based on the Offset amount, but if that is closer to the frame top than the Min setting, the Min setting prevails.

- **Baseline Grid:** This section lets you set a baseline grid just for the selected text frame(s). The baseline grid provides a set of guidelines for your text, which helps ensure that columns stay aligned. Note that you can have your paragraphs snap to these guidelines if you enable baseline grid alignment in your paragraph formatting or paragraph styles. Also note that your document can have its own universal baseline grid, and selected text frames can have their own independent ones. You set the document baseline grid in the Grids & Guides pane of the Preferences dialog box and the text-frame-specific baseline grids here, by selecting the Use Custom Baseline Grid option.

CROSS-REF The various baseline grid settings are covered in Chapter 3. Setting paragraphs to align to baseline grids is covered in Chapter 18.

The other frame-oriented action you can take that affects text is resizing (scaling). Normally, when you resize a text frame, the text size is unaffected, and the text simply reflows in the new frame's dimensions. But you can also have the text resized along the same percentages as the frame itself. Chapter 11 covers these techniques.

Working with Notes

InDesign CS3 has adopted a feature previously available only if you bought the separate InCopy software: the notes feature. Notes are very handy to leave yourself reminders or pass on instructions or explanations to other users.

NOTE Notes are inserted into text; you cannot add them to other objects.

You can add notes using any of three interface choices:

- Click the Notes tool in the Tools panel, then click at the text location where you want to insert a note.
- Using the Type tool, click in the text where you want to add a note, then choose Notes ⇨ New Note to add a note.
- Using the Type tool, click in the text where you want to add a note, then open the Notes panel (Window ⇨ Notes) and choose New Note from the flyout menu or click the New Note iconic button at the bottom of the panel.

However you add them, notes are indicated in the document with a golden yellow dual-triangle character that looks somewhat like an hourglass. Called a *note anchor*, it is shown in Figure 16.15. (That assumes, of course, you are displaying hidden characters Type ⇨ Show Hidden Characters, or Option+⌘+I or Ctrl+Alt+I.) Neither the note nor its anchor will, of course, print.

If you select a string of text, InDesign won't display the New Note menu option; instead, it displays the Convert to Note option to make that text into a note. That's great if someone types a note directly into text, but it can be dangerous if you are trying to highlight an entire word, as you would do when adding notes in Adobe Acrobat. (If you accidentally convert a text select to a note, you can convert a note back to text by choosing Convert to Text from the Notes panel's flyout menu or from the Notes menu.)

You can use the Notes panel's flyout menu or the Notes menu to navigate through notes (choose Previous Note or Next Note), control notes' display (Expand Notes in Story and Collapse Notes in Story), remove notes (choose Delete Note, Remove Notes from Story, or Remove All Notes), move to the note's anchor (choose Go to Note Anchor), or split a note into multiple notes (choose Split Note).

The Notes panel and its flyout menu. In the text to the left of the Notes panel is the hourglass-shaped icon in text that indicates a note.

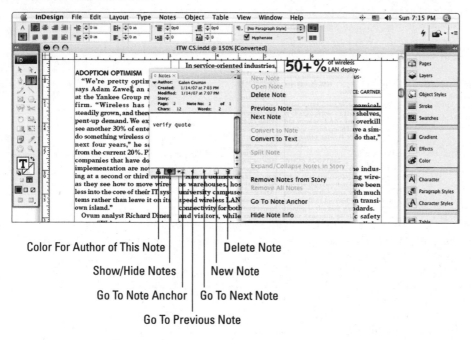

You can set note preferences in the Preference dialog box's Notes pane, shown in Figure 16.16. (To open that pane, choose InDesign ⇨ Preferences ⇨ Notes or press ⌘+K on the Mac, or choose Edit ⇨ Preferences ⇨ Notes or press Ctrl+K in Windows.) In addition to changing the note anchor's color, you can also tell InDesign whether to spell-check notes, search notes in find/change operations, and display a user color behind notes in text, as shown below. (Each user who edits a file gets assigned a unique color for easy identification, à la Microsoft Word's Track Changes feature.)

FIGURE 16.16

The Notes pane of the Preferences dialog box

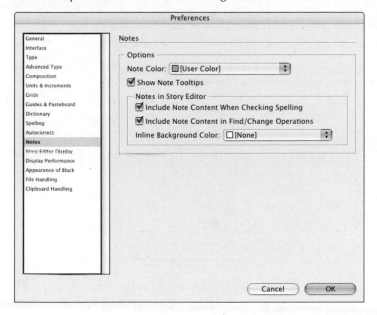

Summary

InDesign provides a variety of methods for getting text into your documents, including typing directly into a text frame, placing or dragging and dropping files generated in a word processor, and pasting text from other sources. You can also edit and type text in the Story Editor window.

You can export text from InDesign for use in a word processor or another InDesign user. Your options are RTF, InDesign Tagged Text, InCopy, and text-only.

InDesign can check spelling as you type, correct some errors as you type, and spell-check high-lighted text, a whole story, a whole document, or a group of open documents as you prefer. You can customize the spelling and hyphenation dictionary to include industry-specific words or proper nouns and to specify your preferences for how certain words are hyphenated. InDesign provides dictionaries for many languages to support international publishing, and it lets you create your own dictionaries.

InDesign's Find/Change dialog box lets you search and replace not only text but also text formatting and special characters. The dialog box now has several new panes to give you finer controls over your searches, as well as the ability to save searches for reuse later.

The Text Frame Options dialog box lets you adjust the spacing of text within text frames, such as the distance from the frame edge and the alignment of paragraphs within the frame.

InDesign also lets you place notes in your files to act as reminders, instructions, or explanations for other people as well as for yourself.

Chapter 17

Specifying Character Attributes

*T*ype is the visual representation of the spoken word. A *typographer* is a person who designs with type. As a user of InDesign, chances are you're going to be making lots of decisions about the appearance of the text in the publications you produce. You are, whether you consider yourself one or not, a typographer. And not only are InDesign users typographers, they're typographers who have an extensive arsenal of text formatting tools that let them tweak and polish their type in a nearly infinite variety of ways.

Of all the decisions an InDesign user makes when designing a publication, decisions about type are arguably the most important. Why? Because a publication can't be effective if the text is hard to read. The difference between good typography and bad typography is the same as the difference between clear speaking and mumbling. The intent of a clear speaker and a mumbler may be the same, but the effect on the listener is quite different. In publishing, the printed words are the containers in which the writer's message is transported to the reader. As the caretaker of those words, you hold great power. Whether or not the message is successfully transported depends largely on your typographic decisions.

As you learn to use InDesign's powerful type-formatting features, you should always remember the cardinal rule of typography: Type exists to honor content. By all means, you should take full advantage of the available tools, but sometimes knowing when not to use a fancy typographic feature is as important as knowing how to use the feature in the first place.

CROSS-REF This chapter focuses on modifying character-level typographic formats; Chapter 18 focuses on modifying paragraph-level formats.

IN THIS CHAPTER

Working with characters versus paragraphs

Changing font families, font styles, and font sizes

Applying other character formats

Controlling horizontal and vertical spacing

Working with Character Formats

Before you begin looking at InDesign's character-formatting features, you should be clear about a fundamental InDesign type-formatting concept: Using separate tools, InDesign lets you modify the appearance of highlighted characters or selected paragraphs:

- When characters are highlighted (or the text cursor is flashing), you can use the Character panel (Type ⇨ Character, or ⌘+T or Ctrl+T) shown in Figure 17.1 to change their appearance in several ways. (You can also choose Window ⇨ Type & Tools ⇨ Character.) If you choose Hide Options from the flyout menu, the Vertical Scale, Horizontal Scale, Baseline Shift, and Skew fields and the Language pop-up menu are not displayed. You can also use the double-arrow iconic button to the left of the panel name to toggle among showing the panel title, the basic options, and all options.

- When paragraphs are selected, the Paragraph panel (Type ⇨ Paragraph, or Option+⌘+T or Ctrl+Alt+T) lets you change how the paragraphs are constructed. (For more information about the Paragraph panel, see Chapter 18.)

The Character panel provides access to most of InDesign's character-formatting options. Three of the options — Font Family, Font Style, and Font Size — are also available in the Type menu, and several options have keyboard shortcuts. The Control panel offers all the formatting options of the Character panel plus others, as shown in Figure 17.2. (If the Control panel doesn't show the character formatting options shown in the figure, be sure to select text and click the **A** iconic button on the panel. If the Control panel is not visible (it almost always is), display it by choosing Window ⇨ Control or pressing Option+⌘+6 or Ctrl+Alt+6.)

> **TIP** If the Type tool is selected and no objects are active, the controls in the Character panel are still available. In this situation, any changes you make in the Character panel become the default settings for the document and are automatically used when you create new text frames. If you change character formats when the cursor is flashing and no text is selected, your changes are applied at the insertion point. When you begin typing, you see the results of your changes.

> **TIP** If you have a smallish monitor, set at 1024 by 768 pixels (the norm for a 17-inch display) the Character and Character Styles panels are shoved to the bottom of the panel dock; when they're selected, the only thing you see is their panel tabs and flyout menu icons. You have a few choices: Shorten other panel groups in the dock to make room for them, remove other panel groups to make room for them, or drag them out of the dock so they "float."

InDesign lets you apply character formats to highlighted text in two ways. You can:

- Use the local controls in the Character panel, the Control panel, or the Type menu; or use the keyboard shortcuts

- Create and apply character-level styles

FIGURE 17.1

The Character panel with all options shown, and its flyout menu

Either way, you can apply the same formatting. The difference is that a character style's settings are stored, so you can apply the exact same settings easily to other text. Plus, if you change a character style's settings, any text based on it automatically changes to reflect the new settings.

If you're working on a simple, one-page publication, such as a business card, a poster, or an ad, you'll probably use the Character panel to format the text elements. However, if you're producing a multi-page publication — a newsletter, magazine, catalog, or newspaper, for example — you should take advantage of styles. Using them saves you time and makes your job a whole lot easier.

FIGURE 17.2

The character formatting options in the Character (**A**) pane of the Control panel and its flyout menu

Character Formatting Controls (Character pane)

Font Family   Kerning   Vertical Scale

Underline   Horizontal Scale

Superscript   Manage Character Styles

All Caps   Character Style

Font Size   Go to Bridge

Leading   Skew

Small Caps   Baseline Shift

Subscript   Tracking   Language

Strikethrough   Quick Apply

Font Style   Flyout menu

Paragraph Formatting Controls (Paragraph pane)

CROSS-REF   For details about creating and applying character and paragraph styles, see Chapter 20.

Even if you do use styles for a particular publication, you'll probably also do some local formatting. For example, you would probably use the Character panel to format the type on the opening spread of a feature magazine article, and then use styles to quickly format the remainder of the article.

CROSS-REF   Some of the object-level controls in the Control and Transform panels let you change the appearance of all the text within a text frame. For more information about these controls, see Chapter 11.

NOTE   In InDesign (like most programs), you can select only contiguous text. So if you have, for example, several subheads to which you want to apply local character formatting, you can't select them all and apply the formatting in one fell swoop. You have to do each text segment separately. (That's one reason to use character styles instead of local formatting.)

Changing Font Family, Font Style, and Font Size

These days, the terms *font, face, typeface, font family, font style*, and *type style* are often used inter-changeably. When you're talking with friends or colleagues about typography, it doesn't matter which term you use as long as you make yourself understood, but if you're going to be setting type with InDesign, you should be familiar with the font-related terms in the menus and panes.

The term *font,* or typeface, usually refers to a collection of characters — including letters, numbers, and special characters — that share the same overall appearance, including stroke width, weight, angle, and style. For example, Helvetica Plain, Arial Bold, Adobe Garamond Semibold Italic, and ITC New Baskerville Italic are well-known fonts. A *font family* is a collection of several fonts that share the same general appearance but differ in stroke width, weight, and/or stroke angle. Some examples of font families are Adobe Caslon, Berthold Baskerville, Times New Roman, and Tekton.

In InDesign, each of the fonts that makes up a font family is referred to as a *font style* (though most designers call these *type styles*). For example, the Times Europa font family is made up of four font styles: Roman, Italic, Bold, and Bold Italic, as shown in Figure 17.3. When you choose a font family from the Character panel's Font Family menu, InDesign displays the family's font style variations in the accompanying Font Styles pop-up menu.

Unlike most word-processing and desktop-publishing programs, InDesign doesn't include built-in shadow and outline font styles. (These font styles are available only if a font includes them.) Most programs create these stylistic variations artificially by modifying plain characters. If you want to create outline text, you can use the Stroke panel (Window ➪ Stroke, or ⌘+F10 or Ctrl+F10) to apply a stroke. If you want to create a drop shadow for text, you can do so using InDesign's light-ing effects features. (Chapter 12 covers these features in detail.)

Similarly, bold and italic variations are available only for font families that include these font styles. This prevents you from applying, for example, italic to Trajan, a font family that doesn't include an italic variation. (InDesign does let you create false italics by skewing text, which I cover later in this chapter. However, you should avoid such heavy-handed shape twisting unless it's absolutely necessary.)

When you change from one font to another in InDesign, you can choose a new font family and font style independently in the Character panel. For example, changing from Arial Bold to Times Bold or from Arial Regular to Berthold Baskerville Regular is a simple change of font family. However, if you switch from Bookman Light to Century Schoolbook Bold Italic, you're changing both font family and font style.

NOTE InDesign can display previews of fonts when you select fonts through the Control panel, various text-oriented panels, and the Type menu. You turn on this capability in the Type pane of the Preferences dialog box, as covered in Chapter 3. But it can make your menus unwieldy.

FIGURE 17.3

The Gill Sans font family includes 15 font styles.

NOTE   When creating character styles, the font family, font style, and font size controls are available in the Basic Character Formats pane of the New Character Styles and New Paragraph Styles dialog boxes.

One Font, Many Names

InDesign sometimes displays a font name multiple times in various panes and dialog boxes, such as the Character panel. This occurs if you have multiple versions of a font on your computer — say, both a TrueType and PostScript version of Helvetica. (Version 2 and earlier of InDesign would show only one of these fonts, making the others inaccessible.)

You can tell which is which by the code that InDesign appends to the font name: (TT) for TrueType, (T1) for PostScript Type 1, and (OTF) for OpenType. You may also see icons instead: a stylized "TT" for TrueType, a stylized "a" for PostScript Type 1, and a stylized "O" for OpenType, as shown below.

You really shouldn't have multiple versions of a font on your computer because different versions can look dissimilar and be spaced differently, resulting in an inconsistent appearance that's hard to fix. If you notice such multiple versions because InDesign calls them to your attention, delete or deactivate the unneeded fonts. (Typically, you would keep the PostScript version — or the OpenType version, if it's supported by your service bureau.)

Selecting fonts

The Character panel and Control panel offer two methods for changing the font family applied to highlighted text. You can:

- Click the Font Family pop-up menu, and then choose a name from the list of available font families.

- Click in front of or highlight the font name displayed in the Font Family field, type the first few letters of the font family you want to apply, and then press Return or Enter. For example, typing `Ari` select Arial (if it's available on your computer).

If you use the Font submenu in the Type menu, you can type the first letter of a font to skip to font names beginning with that letter once you have highlighted any font in the submenu.

You can select just the font family, as Figure 17.4 shows. When you change the font family applied to selected text, InDesign tries to maintain the applied font style. If, for example, you switch from Adobe Garamond Bold Italic to Adobe Caslon, InDesign automatically uses Adobe Caslon Bold Italic, which is one of several font styles that make up this font family. But if you switch from Arial Bold Italic to Avant Garde, which doesn't include a bold italic variation, InDesign uses Avant Garde Book instead.

FIGURE 17.4

To select a font style from the Control panel, you can first choose the font family from the Font Family pop-up menu, and then choose a font style from the Font Style pop-up menu, which shows only the font styles available for the selected font family.

If a particular font family includes a submenu with font style variations, you can also choose a font style at the same time you choose a font family. If you choose only a font family when font styles are available in an accompanying submenu, no changes apply to the selected text. Figure 17.5 shows an example of choosing both at the same time.

CROSS-REF See Chapter 16 for details on how to search and replace formatting such as font attributes, as well as how to replace a font completely throughout a document.

FIGURE 17.5

You can also select both the font family and the font style at the same time using the submenus in the Font Family menu in the Control panel, Character panel, or Character Styles panel, or in the Type menu's Font submenu.

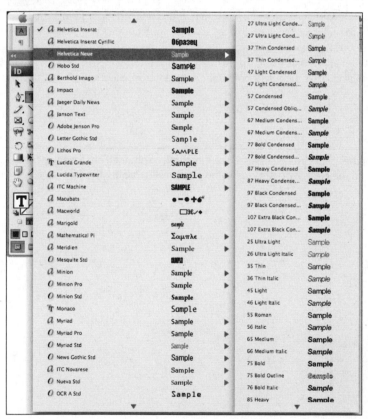

Changing font size

InDesign lets you specify font sizes (called *type sizes* by most publishers) from 0.1 point to 1,296 points (108 inches) in increments as fine as 0.001 point. Of course, even if it were possible to clearly print type as small as a thousandth of a point (that is, $^1/_{72,000}$ of an inch), which is beyond the capabilities of most printers, nobody could read it without a microscope anyway.

Use good judgment when choosing font sizes. For example, headlines should be larger than sub-heads, which in turn are larger than body text, which is larger than photo credits, and so on.

InDesign offers several methods for changing the font size of highlighted text. You can:

- Use one of several techniques in the Character panel and Control panel:
  - Choose one of the predefined sizes from the Size menu.
  - Highlight the currently applied font size displayed in the accompanying editable field, type a new size, and then press Return or Enter.
  - Use the up and down cursor keys to increase or decrease the size in 1-point increments. Pressing and holding Shift multiplies the increment to 10.
- Choose Type ⇨ Size, and then choose one of the predefined sizes listed in the Size submenu. If you choose Other from the submenu, the Size field is highlighted in the Character panel. Type a custom size, and then press Return or Enter.
- Control+click or right-click a text selection, and then choose a size from the Size submenu. If you choose Other from the submenu, the Font Size field is highlighted in the Character panel. Type a custom size, and then press Return or Enter.
- Use keyboard commands to adjust text size:
  - Press Shift+⌘+. (period) or Ctrl+Shift+. (period) to enlarge highlighted text in 2-point increments. (You can set a different increment in the Units & Increments pane in the Preferences dialog box, which you access by choosing InDesign ⇨ Preferences ⇨ Units & Increments or pressing ⌘+K on the Mac, or by choosing Edit ⇨ Preferences ⇨ Units & Increments or pressing Ctrl+K in Windows.)
  - Press Shift+⌘+, (comma) or Ctrl+Shift+, (comma) to reduce highlighted text.
  - Press Option+Shift+⌘+. (period) or Ctrl+Alt+Shift+. (period) to increase the text size in 10-point increments.
  - Press Option+Shift+⌘+, (comma) or Ctrl+Alt+Shift+, (comma) to decrease the text size in 10-point increments.

 It helps to think of these shortcuts as using the > and < characters, mnemonics for *more* and *less*, rather than as using the period and comma.

 If text is highlighted and the Size field is empty, it means that more than one font size is used in the selected text.

Labeling Paragraphs

Changing the formatting of the first few words in a paragraph can indicate the beginning of a story or a new topic. This is commonly used for *run-in heads* (short titles usually in boldface or italic, and often in a contrasting font) on the same line as the rest of the paragraph. Although you use this technique in paragraphs, you need to use local character formatting or character styles to change the look of the first part of each paragraph, so I'm explaining this technique here rather than in Chapter 18. You can also use the nested styles feature, described in this chapter, to apply the appropriate character style consistently to paragraphs that have such labels applied.

The following descriptions show frequently used label formatting. You use the appropriate controls in the Character panel or in the Character pane (press the **A** iconic button) of the Control panel.

- **Boldface**: Bold speaks the loudest, and is generally used for subheads in magazines, newspapers, and reports.

- *Italics*: If bold shouts, italics tend to whisper. They're a good choice for tertiary heads and to label bulleted items within a list.

- Underlines: For a typewriter effect, you might underline the text of a label.

- SMALL CAPS: For a subtle, classic look that blends well with the rest of the document, use small caps on labels. However, don't use small caps if you're using labels as subheads that allow readers to skim through a document and read only relevant portions.

- **Typeface change:** Rather than relying on different variations of a font, you can use a different font altogether, such as Futura Medium as used on this paragraph, for a label. To contrast with serif body text, you might choose a sans serif typeface that complements the look of your publication. Often, this will be a variation of your headline font.

- Scaled text: Scaling text horizontally — up 10 or 20 percent — quietly differentiates it from the remainder of the paragraph. (More severe scaling distorts the typeface and can look unprofessional.) Unlike bold or underline, the text doesn't pop off the page at you, but it is visually distinct. Scaling text vertically, however, can be too subtle unless you combine it with boldface or another style.

- Size change: Creating a label by simply bumping the size up a point or two is another subtle design choice. The labels blend well with the body text, but they don't announce their presence enough to be used as subheads for scanning.

A tip: To provide a little more space between the label and the text, you might want to use an en space or em space rather than a normal space.

Applying Other Character Formats

Font family, font style, and font size are the most commonly modified character formats, but the Character panel and Control panel contain several other controls for managing the appearance of type. Some of these controls are displayed in the panel window; others are available in the panels' flyout menu. The Control panel offers more formatting options than the Character panel.

In the Control panel, you can adjust all caps, small caps, superscript, subscript, underline, strikethrough, kerning, tracking, horizontal and vertical scale, baseline shift, skew, character style, and language. Through the flyout menu, you can also set ligatures, modify underline and strikethrough settings, control whether text may break (be hyphenated), select its case (such as all caps and small caps), and select OpenType features. Figure 17.2 shows the flyout menu for the Control panel's character formatting (**A**) pane.

In the Character panel, you can adjust kerning, tracking, horizontal and vertical scale, baseline shift, skew, and language. Through its flyout menu (refer to Figure 17.1), you can also set all caps, small caps, superscript, subscript, underline, strikethrough, ligatures, and underline and strikethrough settings, as well as control whether text may break (be hyphenated) and select OpenType features.

NOTE You must choose Show Options from the Character panel's flyout menu to display the Vertical Scale, Horizontal Scale, Baseline Shift, Skew, and Language options in the panel.

NOTE When you create character styles, the kerning, tracking, subscript, superscript, case, ligature, underlining, break, and strikethrough controls are available in the Basic Character Formats pane of the New Character Styles and New Paragraph Styles dialog boxes. The scale, baseline shift, skew, and language controls are in the Advanced Character Formats pane. OpenType controls are in the OpenType Features pane. Custom underline and strikethrough options, as covered in Chapter 19, are available in the Underline Options and Strikethrough Options panes, respectively.

Figure 17.6 shows the various effects in action.

FIGURE 17.6

Various character-formatting options applied to text are illustrated here. Top row: The word *InDesign* has a different font style applied, *incredible* has been scaled horizontally, and *control* is in all caps, while *over* has had each letter's baseline shifted by a different amount. Middle row: The word *text* has been skewed, *with* is in small caps, a gradient and underline are applied to *typographic*, a custom underline has been applied to *capabilities, and formatting* has been vertically scaled. Bottom row: Compare the baseline shifts in the top row to the true superscript and subscript following the words *most* and *people*. The word *never* has a custom strikethrough applied, while *even* uses a standard one. The word *heard* has a colored stroke applied and a fill of white.

Horizontal Scale and Vertical Scale

Some font families include condensed (that is, slightly squeezed) and/or expanded (slightly stretched) stylistic variations, but most don't. InDesign's Horizontal Scale option lets you create artificially condensed and expanded type by squeezing or stretching characters. Similarly, the Vertical Scale option lets you shrink or stretch type vertically.

Among typographers, there are two schools of thought about scaling type. One camp contends that such distortions of letter forms are taboo and should be avoided. The other side contends that a small amount of scaling doesn't adversely affect the original font and is acceptable. There's general agreement that overscaling should be avoided. For the most part, if you need to make text bigger or smaller, you should adjust font size; if you need to squeeze or stretch a range of text a bit, it's better to use InDesign's kerning and tracking controls (covered later in this chapter) because the letterforms are not affected. Only the space between letters changes when you kern or track text.

Unscaled text has a horizontal and vertical scale value of 100 percent. You can apply scaling values between 1 percent and 1,000 percent. If you apply equal horizontal and vertical scale values, you're making the original text proportionally larger or smaller. In this case, changing font size is a simpler solution. Keep in mind that when you scale text, you are not changing the font size. For example, 24-point type scaled vertically to 200 percent is 48 points tall, but its font size is still 24 points.

To change the scale of highlighted text, enter new values in the Horizontal and/or Vertical Scale fields in the Character panel or Control panel. If a value is highlighted in the Horizontal Scale or Vertical Scale field, you can also use the up and down cursor keys to increase and decrease the scaling in 1 percent increments; press and hold Shift to increase or decrease in 10 percent increments.

Baseline Shift

The *baseline* is an invisible horizontal line on which a line of characters rests. The bottom of each letter (except descenders, such as in *y, p, q, j*, and *g*) sits on the baseline. InDesign's Baseline Shift feature lets you move highlighted text above or below its baseline. This feature is useful for carefully placing such characters as trademark and copyright symbols and for creating custom fractions. (Unlike superscripts and subscripts, text whose baseline has shifted does not change size.)

To baseline-shift highlighted text, type new values in the Baseline Shift field in the Character panel or Control panel. You can also use the up and down cursor keys to increase the baseline shift in 1-point increments, or press and hold Shift when using the cursor keys to increase or decrease it in 10-point increments.

Skew (false italic)

For fonts that don't have an italic font style, InDesign provides the option to *skew,* or slant, text to create an artificial italic variation of any font. (You can also use it with fonts that have a natural italic; refer to Figure 17.6.) Like horizontal and vertical text scaling, skewing is a clunky way of creating italic-looking text. Use this feature to create special typographic effects, such as the shadow text shown in Figure 17.7, or in situations where a true italic style is not available.

FIGURE 17.7

Skewing and shading a copy of the black text creates this backlit shadow effect.

NOTE Skewing as a form of italics typically works better for sans serif typefaces than for serif typefaces because the characters are simpler and have fewer embellishments that can get oddly distorted when skewed.

To skew highlighted text, you have two options:

- Type an angle value between –85 and 85 in the Skew field in the Character panel or Control panel. Positive values slant text to the left; negative values slant text to the right.

- Click the accompanying up or down cursors when the cursor is in the Skew field to skew text in 1-degree increments. Pressing and holding Shift while clicking the cursors changes the increment to 45 degrees.

TIP You can also skew all the text in a text frame using the Shear tool or by changing the value in the Shear X Angle field in the Transform panel or Control panel after selecting the frame. Slanting text by shearing a text frame does not affect the skew angle of the text. You can specify a skew angle for highlighted text independently from the frame's shear angle. Chapter 11 covers this effect in more detail.

Language

The ability to correctly hyphenate and check the spelling of text in several languages is one of InDesign's most powerful features. The program uses dictionaries to accomplish these tasks. These dictionaries, each of which contains several hundred thousand words, also let you specify a different language for text on a character-by-character basis, although chances are that a single word is the smallest text unit to which you apply a separate language.

For example, an article about traveling in France might include the word *tabac* (the French term for a kiosk or small store selling cigarettes, phone cards, and various sundries). By applying the French language to this word, as shown in Figure 17.8, InDesign does not flag it when you check spelling. However, if you were to apply U.S. English to *tabac,* it would show up as a misspelled word (unless you add it to your dictionary, as explained in Chapter 16).

To assign a different language to highlighted text, choose the appropriate language from the Language pop-up menu in the Control panel or from the Character panel's flyout menu, as shown in Figure 17.8.

FIGURE 17.8

By applying the French language to *tabacs,* as shown here, InDesign uses the associated dictionary when checking the spelling of this word.

QUARKXPRESS The Passport edition of QuarkXPress has a similar feature to specify the hyphenation and spelling language. The standard version of QuarkXPress does not include this feature.

All Caps and Small Caps

When you choose All Caps, the uppercase version of all highlighted characters is used: Lowercase letters are converted to uppercase, and uppercase letters remain unchanged.

Similarly, the Small Caps option affects just lowercase letters. When you choose Small Caps, InDesign automatically uses the Small Caps font style if one is available for the font family applied to the highlighted text (few font families include this font style). If a Small Caps font style is not available, InDesign generates small caps from uppercase letters using the scale percentage specified in the Advanced Type pane of the Preferences dialog box (choose InDesign ⇨ Preferences ⇨ Advanced Type or press ⌘+K on the Mac, or choose Edit ⇨ Preferences ⇨ Advanced Type or press Ctrl+K in Windows). The default scale value used to generate small caps text is 70 percent (of uppercase letters).

You should avoid typing text in all capital letters, even if you think you want all caps. If you type lowercase letters, you can easily change them to uppercase by applying the All Caps format, but if you type uppercase letters, you can't change them to lowercase or to small caps without retyping them or having InDesign retype them for you. To have InDesign do the work, select the text and then choose Type ⇨ Change Case ⇨ Lowercase. You can also choose Title Case (which capitalizes each word in the highlighted text) or Sentence Case (which capitalizes the first letter in each highlighted sentence) as appropriate to the text. (You can convert selected text to all uppercase by choosing Type ⇨ Change Case ⇨ Uppercase.)

Superscript and Subscript

When you apply the Superscript and Subscript character formats to highlighted text, InDesign applies a baseline shift to the characters, lifting them above (for Superscript) or lowering them below (for Subscript) their baseline, and reduces their size.

The amount of baseline shift and scaling that's used for the Superscript and Subscript formats is determined by the Position and Size fields in the Advanced Type pane of the Preferences dialog box (choose InDesign ⇨ Preferences ⇨ Advanced Type or press ⌘+K on the Mac, or choose Edit ⇨ Preferences ⇨ Advanced Type or press Ctrl+K in Windows). The default Position value for both formats is 33.3 percent, which means that characters are moved up or down by one-third of the applied leading value. The default Superscript and Subscript Size value is 58.3 percent, which means that superscripted and subscripted characters are reduced to 58.3 percent of the applied font size. The Advanced Type pane lets you specify separate default settings for Superscript and Subscript.

For most newspaper and magazine work, I prefer a size of 65 percent for superscripts and subscripts, as well as a position of 30 percent for subscripts and 35 percent for superscripts. These values work better than the InDesign defaults in the small text sizes and tight leading of such publications.

 If you change these settings when no document is open, they become the default for all future new documents.

You can use the Superscript and Subscript formats to create, for example, custom fractions or numbers for footnotes or to reposition special characters such as asterisks. To apply the Superscript or Subscript format to highlighted text, choose the appropriate option from the Character panel's flyout menu. Figure 17.6 shows examples of text to which the default Superscript and Subscript settings have been applied.

 InDesign does not have an equivalent to QuarkXPress's superior format, which is like a superscript except that it aligns the top of the character to the text's cap height. This helps ensure that the leading is not changed. Some OpenType fonts, however, have superior characters, as I cover later in this chapter.

Underline and Strikethrough

The Underline and Strikethrough formats are holdovers from the days of typewriters and are not typographically acceptable for indicating emphasis in text; it's better accomplished using bold and/or italic font styles.

Underlines can be useful in kickers and other text above a headline, as well as in documents formatted to look as if they are typewritten. Strikethrough is rarely useful in a document, although in textbooks and other educational materials, you may want to use it to indicate incorrect answers, eliminated choices, or deleted text (when showing how to edit).

If you do use underlines and strikethrough, InDesign lets you specify exactly how they look through the Underline Options and Strikethrough Options dialog boxes available in the flyout menus of the Character panel and Control panel.

CROSS-REF   Chapter 19 covers these custom underline and strikethrough settings in detail.

NOTE   If you don't set a specific size for underlines and strikethroughs, the weight of an underline or strikethrough line is relative to the font size.

Ligatures

A ligature is a special character that combines two letters. Most early typefaces included five ligatures: ff, fi, fl, ffi, and ffl. Many newer fonts — especially TrueType ones — include just two ligatures: fi and fl. (InDesign will use whatever of these five ligatures are available in your fonts.) When you choose the Ligature option, InDesign automatically displays and prints a font's built-in ligatures — instead of the two component letters — if the font includes ligatures.

One nice thing about the Ligature option is that, even though a ligature looks like a single character on-screen, it's still fully editable. That is, you can click between the two-letter shapes and insert text if necessary. Also, a ligature created with the Ligatures option does not cause InDesign's spell checker to flag the word that contains it.

To use ligatures within highlighted text, choose Ligatures from the Character panel's or Control panel's flyout menu (Ligatures is set to On by default). Figure 17.9 shows a before-and-after example of text to which the Ligature option has been applied.

FIGURE 17.9

Ligatures are used in the top two lines but not in the bottom two. Notice the difference in space between the *fi* and *fl* letter pairs in *finally* and *float*.

finally, I
can float!

finally, I
can float!

QUARKXPRESS Unlike QuarkXPress for Windows, InDesign for Windows supports automatic ligatures in Windows fonts that have them.

For most Mac fonts that include ligatures, pressing Option+Shift+5 inserts the fi ligature, while Option+Shift+6 inserts the fl ligature. In Windows, you have to use a program like Character Map that comes with Windows (usually available by choosing Start ⇨ All Programs ⇨ Accessories ⇨ System Tools ⇨ Character Map) to access the ligature characters in fonts that support them. Either way, if you type ligatures yourself, InDesign's spell checker flags any words that contain them. For this reason, you typically want to let the program handle the task of inserting ligatures.

OpenType options

The OpenType font standard developed by Adobe and Microsoft supports many more character variations than the ones most publishers use. In OpenType, many variations of a character exist in the same font, and you specify which variant you want for highlighted text in the Character panel's or Control panel's flyout menu.

Figure 17.10 shows examples of the two kinds of numerals supported in OpenType. The OpenType menu in the Control panel's and Character panel's flyout menu has the following options:

FIGURE 17.10

The top row of numbers uses typical titling figures — all are the same height. The bottom row uses old-style numerals.

- **Discretionary ligatures:** This option creates ligatures whenever possible, rather than just for the standard fi, fl, ffi, and ffl combinations.
- **Fractions:** This option substitutes true fractions such as ½ for the text 1/2.
- **Ordinal:** This option raises the *st*, *nd*, and *th* portions of ordinal numbers such as *1st*, *22nd*, and *345th*.
- **Swash:** This option adds embellishments in front of the first character or at the end of the last letter of a word.

- **Titling Alternates:** This option uses variants of a font for use in titles. These variants are usually a little clearer than the body-text version so they work better as titles where surrounding white space can make the normal variations within body text look strange.

- **Contextual Alternates:** This option uses variants for specific characters to improve legibility in some contexts. For example, a contextual alternate for *t* might drop the left-side bar in the *t* so it doesn't bump against an adjacent letter.

- **All Small Caps:** This option replaces all the text with true small caps, not the scaled-down version that the standard InDesign Small Caps feature uses. True small caps are usually a little thicker than their scaled-down version, so they have the same visual weight as lowercase letters.

- **Slashed Zero:** This option adds a slash over a 0 character for fonts that support it. The slashed zero is often used in European writing to differentiate from the letter O.

- **Superscript/Superior:** This option replaces scaled-down raised text that InDesign uses to create superscripts with thicker characters placed where the font designers think works best. As with true small caps, this results in superscripts that have more visual weight.

- **Subscript/Inferior:** This option replaces scaled-down lowered text that InDesign uses to create subscripts with thicker characters placed where the font designers think works best. As with true small caps, this results in subscripts that have more visual weight.

- **Numerator:** Use this option to build the top of a fraction when the font does not have predefined ones, such as for $^7/_5$.

- **Denominator:** Use this option to build the bottom of a fraction when the font does not have predefined ones, such as for $^1/_n$.

- **Stylistic Sets:** This option lets you choose which sets of variants within a font to use. A very few OpenType fonts, such as Poetica Std, use stylistic sets that provide multiple variations of the same characters, letting you choose which variants to use.

- **Tabular Lining:** This option uses standard numeric characters (which start on the baseline and have no descenders or ascenders) spaced evenly for proper alignment in tables.

- **Proportional Oldstyle:** This option uses old-fashioned numerals with ascenders and descenders that are spaced like any other characters, based on their width, shape, and visual weight.

- **Proportional Lining:** This option uses standard numerals spaced like any other characters, based on their width, shape, and visual weight.

- **Tabular Oldstyle:** This option uses old-fashioned numerals spaced evenly for natural alignment in tables.

- **Default Figure Style:** This option does whatever the font's designers want it to do by default (one of the previous four settings).

Expert Fonts Explained

There is a type of Type 1 PostScript font called an *expert font* that includes old-style numerals, fractions, true small caps, and other special characters. You can use it as an adjunct to the regular version of the font, which lets you manually apply the special characters.

For example, if you used Garamond as your font, you could apply Garamond Expert to the numerals to get old-style numerals. This is a lot of work, so most people don't bother except for typographically sophisticated — and short — documents, such as ads.

Unfortunately, InDesign doesn't detect the availability of expert fonts (for when you don't have OpenType fonts) and therefore doesn't use them to apply OpenType-like attributes such as old-style numerals, true small caps, and true fractions when they are available. Instead, you have to apply them manually — or buy and use OpenType fonts instead.

CROSS-REF Chapter 21 covers OpenType in more detail, including examples of various effects.

For the vast majority of fonts in use today, applying an OpenType feature has no effect because most fonts in use are standard Type 1 PostScript or TrueType. Among OpenType fonts, there is wide variation in what variations they support; InDesign indicates unavailable options by enclosing them in brackets in the menu.

No Break

InDesign lets you prevent individual words from being hyphenated or a string of words from being broken at the end of a line. For example, you may decide that you don't want to hyphenate software names, such as InDesign, CorelDraw, or FreeHand. Or perhaps you don't want to separate the *J.* and the *P.* in *J. P. Morgan*. The No Break option was created for situations such as these.

To prevent a word or a text string from being broken, highlight it, and then choose No Break from the Character panel's or Control panel's flyout menu.

CAUTION If you apply the No Break option to a range of text that's longer than the width of the current column, InDesign tracks the text so that it fits on a single line — squeezing it unacceptably — and sometimes, InDesign refuses to display the rest of the text in the frame.

TIP You can prevent a word from being hyphenated by placing a discretionary hyphen (Shift+⌘+– [hyphen] or Ctrl+Shift+– [hyphen]) in front of the first letter.

Leaving Space between Characters and Lines

Typographers often pay as much attention to the space between characters, words, and lines of text as they do to the appearance of the characters themselves. Their concern about space is well justified. The legibility of a block of text depends as much on the space around it, called *white space,* as it does on the readability of the font.

InDesign offers two ways to adjust the space between characters — kerning and tracking — as well one way to adjust spacing between lines: leading.

CROSS-REF InDesign also provides a way to adjust the space between paragraphs; see Chapter 18. It also explains how to control the spacing between words, which is part of paragraph formatting.

Kerning

Kerning is the adjustment of space between a pair of characters. Most fonts include built-in kerning tables that control the space between pesky character pairs, such as *LA, Yo,* and *WA,* that otherwise could appear to have a space between them even when there isn't one. Particularly at small font sizes, it's safe to use a font's built-in kerning information to control the space between letter pairs. But for large font sizes, for example the front-page nameplate of a newsletter or a magazine headline, you may want to manually adjust the space between certain character pairs to achieve consistent spacing.

The Kerning controls in the Character panel and Control panel provide three options for kerning letter pairs: metrics kerning, optical kerning, and manual kerning:

- **Metrics kerning** uses a font's built-in kerning pairs to control the space between character pairs in the highlighted text.

- **Optical kerning** has InDesign look at each letter pair in highlighted text and add or remove space between the letters based on the shapes of the characters.

- **Manual kerning** is adding or removing space between a specific letter pair in user-specified amounts.

The kerning method you use depends on the circumstances. For example, some fonts include a large set of kerning pairs. Such fonts, especially at text font sizes (9 to 12 points) and lower, may look fine using the default metrics kerning option, which uses built-in kerning pairs. On the other hand, if the font applied to highlighted text has few or no built-in kerning pairs or if several different fonts are mixed together, the text may benefit from the optical kerning method. At display font sizes (36 points and larger), you may want to manually kern individual letter pairs to suit your taste.

When the flashing text cursor is between a pair of characters, the Kerning field displays the pair's kerning value. If metrics or optical kerning is applied, the kerning value is displayed in parentheses.

Understanding Units

InDesign lets you apply kerning and/or tracking to highlighted text in $1/1,000$-em increments called *units*. An em is as wide as the height of the current font size (that is, an em for 12-point text is 12 points wide), which means that kerning and tracking increments are relative to the applied font size.

QuarkXPress converts may be surprised at the seemingly large unit values produced by InDesign's kerning and tracking methods. That's because InDesign adjusts space in 0.001-em units ($1/1,000$th of an em), whereas QuarkXPress uses 0.005-em units ($1/200$th of an em). Because you're working with finer increments in InDesign, you need higher multiples than in QuarKXPress to achieve the same actual spacing.

To apply metrics or optical kerning to highlighted text, choose the appropriate option from the Kerning pop-up menu. To apply manual kerning, click between a pair of letters, and then type a value in the Kerning field or choose one of the predefined values. Negative values tighten; positive values loosen.

You can also use a keyboard shortcut to apply manual kerning. Press Option+left cursor or Alt+left cursor to decrease the kerning value in increments of 20 units. Press Option+right cursor or Alt+right cursor to increase the kerning value in increments of 20 units. If you add the ⌘ or Ctrl keys to these keyboard shortcuts, the increment is increased to 100 units. If you use the up and down cursor keys in the Kerning field in the Character panel or Control panel, you change the kerning in increments of 10; while pressing and holding Shift the increments increase to 25.

CAUTION A warning about kerning and tracking: InDesign happily lets you tighten or loosen text to the point of illegibility. If this is the effect you're after, go for it. But as a general rule, when letter shapes start to collide, you've tightened too far.

Tracking

Tracking is similar to kerning but applies to a range of highlighted text. Tracking is the process of adding or removing space among *all* letters in a range of text. You might use tracking to tighten character spacing for a font that you think is too spacey or loosen spacing for a font that's too tight. Or you could track a paragraph tighter or looser to eliminate a short last line or a *widow* (the last line of a paragraph that falls at the top of a page or column).

To apply tracking to highlighted text, type a value in the Character panel's Tracking field or choose one of the predefined values. Negative values tighten; positive values loosen (in 0.001-em increments). Use the same keyboard techniques as for kerning.

Leading

InDesign's leading (rhymes with *sledding*, not with *deeding*) feature lets you control the vertical space between lines of type. In the days of metal type, typesetters would insert thin strips of metal — specifically, lead — between rows of letters to aid legibility. In the world of digital typography, *leading* refers to the vertical space between lines of type as measured from baseline to baseline.

In the publishing world, leading is traditionally an attribute of paragraphs, but InDesign takes a nonstandard character-oriented approach. This means that you can apply different leading values within a single paragraph. InDesign looks separately at each line of text in a paragraph and uses the largest applied leading value within a line to determine the leading for that line.

That capability might have some utility in some cases, but for most publishers, the results are unevenly spaced lines that look unacceptably amateurish. Fortunately, you can make InDesign work like the rest of the world and apply consistent leading to entire paragraphs (using the largest leading value applied if several have been applied in a paragraph): Enable the Apply Leading to Entire Paragraphs option in the Type pane of the Preferences dialog box (choose InDesign ➪ Preferences ➪ Type or press ⌘+K on the Mac, or choose Edit ➪ Preferences ➪ Type or press Ctrl+K in Windows).

QUARKXPRESS Leading as a character format is a carryover from PageMaker (and not necessarily a good one). This will confuse recent QuarkXPress converts, who are used to seeing leading as a paragraph attribute (as it should be).

Auto Leading Mysteries

In many ways, InDesign makes once-mystical typographic processes easy to use by designers, honoring the rules and intricacies of typography historically known only to typographers. But when it comes to auto leading, InDesign has gone off in a mysterious direction.

For example, why is something that InDesign treats as a character format setting accessed through the Paragraph panel? (Easy answer: Leading should be a paragraph attribute in the first place, and whoever put the Leading control in the Character panel missed the Auto Leading control!) A harder mystery: Why is the Auto Leading control offered as part of the justification controls, for which it has no relationship? (Maybe that's how it got missed when Leading was put in the Character panel!)

Another mystery is why you cannot specify Auto Leading amounts in anything other than percentages. This will cause many QuarkXPress documents imported into InDesign to flow incorrectly because QuarkXPress lets you set the Auto Leading to a specific value, such as +2 (which adds 2 points to the text size rather than use a percentage like 120 percent that results in awkward leading amounts like 14.4 points). Being able to specify a specific additive value like +2 makes sense for many kinds of layouts, so the inability to specify such values is an unfortunate continued omission in InDesign.

By default, InDesign applies Auto Leading to text. When Auto Leading is applied, leading is equal to 120 percent of the font size. For example, if Auto Leading is applied to 10-point text, the leading value is 12 points; for 12-point text, Auto Leading is 14.4 points; and so on. As long as you don't change fonts or font sizes in a paragraph, Auto Leading works pretty well. But if you do change fonts or sizes, Auto Leading can result in inconsistent spacing between lines. For this reason, it's safer to specify an actual leading value.

Generally, it's a good idea to use a leading value that is slightly larger than the font size, which is why Auto Leading works in many cases. When the leading value equals the font size, text is said to be *set solid*. That's about as tight as you ever want to set leading unless you're trying to achieve a special typographic effect or working with very large text sizes in ad-copy headlines. As is the case with kerning and tracking, when tight leading causes letters to collide — ascenders and descenders are the first to overlap — you've gone too far.

You can change InDesign's preset Auto Leading value of 120 percent. To do so, choose Type ➪ Paragraph, or press Option+⌘+T or Ctrl+Alt+T, to display the Paragraph panel. Choose Justification in the flyout menu, type a new value in the Auto Leading field, and then click OK.

To modify the leading value applied to selected text, choose one of the predefined options from the Leading pop-up menu in the Character panel or Control panel, or type a leading value in the field. You can type values from 0 to 5,000 points in 0.001-point increments. You can also use the up and down cursor keys to change leading in 1-point increments.

Summary

As a user of InDesign, modifying the appearance of type is one of the more common tasks you'll perform. InDesign lets you modify the appearance of highlighted characters or selected paragraphs. When text is highlighted, you can use the controls in the Character panel or Control panel to change any of several character attributes: font family, font size, font style, leading, kerning, tracking, vertical and horizontal scale, baseline shift, and skew. You can also set the hyphenation and spell-checking language, apply all caps or small caps, superscripts or subscripts, underline, strikethrough, ligatures, and OpenType variations.

You also set line spacing (leading) as a character attribute, something that's normally applied to entire paragraphs in other programs. This can lead to uneven line spacing, something that fortunately InDesign lets you override to get consistent leading throughout a paragraph.

Chapter 18

Specifying Paragraph Attributes

M uch like an individual character, a paragraph in InDesign is a basic typographic unit. When you create a new text frame and begin typing, you create a paragraph each time you press Return or Enter. A paragraph can be as short as one character or word on a single line or many words strung out over many lines. When you press Return or Enter, the paragraph formats of the preceding paragraph are automatically used for the subsequent paragraph (unless you create styles that automatically change paragraph formats).

In general, paragraph formats control how the lines of text in the paragraph are constructed. Changing paragraph formats doesn't change the appearance of the individual characters within the paragraph. To do that, you must highlight the characters and modify character-level formats.

CROSS-REF This chapter focuses on modifying paragraph-level typographic formats; Chapter 17 focuses on modifying character-level formats. Chapter 20 covers the creation and use of styles for both characters and paragraphs.

IN THIS CHAPTER

Understanding paragraph fundamentals

Changing basic and advanced paragraph formats

Applying automatic bullets and numbering

Working with hyphenation and justification

Modifying other paragraph formats

Understanding Paragraph Basics

To select a paragraph, simply click within it using the Type tool. Any change you make to a paragraph-level format applies to all the lines in the paragraph. (Unlike character-level formats, you don't have to highlight all the text in a paragraph to modify a paragraph-level format.) If you need to change the paragraph formats of several consecutive paragraphs, you can highlight all the text in all the paragraphs, or you can click anywhere in the first paragraph, drag anywhere within the last paragraph, and then release the mouse button.

Just as you can't apply two different colors to a single character, you can't apply conflicting paragraph formats within a single paragraph. For example, you can't specify for one line in a paragraph to be left-aligned and the rest right-aligned. All lines in a paragraph must share the same alignment, indents, tab settings, and all other paragraph-level formats.

As is the case with character formats, there are two ways to apply paragraph formats:

- Use the controls in the Paragraph panel or Control panel's Paragraph (¶) pane, shown in Figures 18.1 and 18.2, or their keyboard shortcuts.
- Create and apply paragraph styles.

A paragraph style is essentially a text-formatting macro that lets you apply several paragraph formats to selected paragraphs in a single operation. If you're working on a multi-page publication such as a book, newspaper, magazine, or catalog that repeatedly uses the same basic text formats, you definitely want to use paragraph styles to handle the bulk of your formatting chores. But even if you use styles, you probably also use the Paragraph panel to do some manual paragraph formatting.

CROSS-REF Tab settings are also a paragraph-level format. See Chapter 22 for a detailed explanation of InDesign's tabs feature.

Figure 18.1 shows the Paragraph panel. There are three ways to open the Paragraph panel: Choose Type ⇨ Paragraph, choose Window ⇨ Type & Tables ⇨ Paragraph, or press Option+⌘+T or Ctrl+Alt+T.

The panel can have two appearances: If you choose Hide Options from the pop-up menu, the Space Before, Space After, Drop Cap Number of Lines, Drop Cap Number of Characters, Hyphenate, and Align to Baseline Grid, and Do Not Align to Baseline Grid controls are not displayed. You can use the double-arrow iconic button to the left of the panel name to toggle among showing the panel title, the basic options, and all options.

TIP If you have a smallish monitor, set at 1024 x 768 pixels — the technical norm for a 17-inch display — the Paragraph and Paragraph Styles panels are shoved to the bottom of the panel dock, and when selected all you see are their panel tabs and flyout menu icons. You have a few choices: Shorten other panel groups in the dock to make room for them, remove other panel groups to make room for them, or drag them out of the dock and make them floating.

You can also use the Control panel's paragraph formatting options, shown in Figure 17.2. (Be sure to click the ¶ iconic button to get the paragraph options.) These controls mirror those in the Paragraph panel, and using them instead of the Paragraph panel can reduce screen clutter. If the Control panel is not visible (it almost always is), display it by choosing Window ⇨ Control or pressing Option+⌘+6 or Ctrl+Alt+6.

In both the Paragraph panel and the Control panel, several of the options have keyboard shortcuts.

TIP If the Type tool is selected and no objects are active, any changes you make in the Control panel's Paragraph (¶) pane become the default settings for the document and are automatically used when you create new text frames.

FIGURE 18.1

The Paragraph panel

The Manage Paragraph Styles pop-up menu is new to InDesign CS3. It lets you edit and otherwise manage styles, though it has fewer controls than the Paragraph Styles panel's flyout menu. Chapter 20 covers styles in more detail.

Gone in the Control panel is the Toggle Paragraph and Paragraph Styles Panels iconic button. Use the keyboard shortcuts, dock, mouse, or Window menu to switch among them instead.

Using leading

Leading, or the space between lines in a paragraph, is treated by InDesign as a character format through the Character panel or Control panel, even though it's traditionally an attribute of the paragraph. However, you can override InDesign's character-oriented approach so it works like all other layout programs. To ensure that leading changes affect entire paragraphs, select the Apply Leading to Entire Paragraphs option in the Type pane of the Preferences dialog box (choose InDesign ➪ Preferences ➪ Type or press ⌘+K on the Mac, or choose Edit ➪ Preferences ➪ Type or press Ctrl+K in Windows).

For more details on how to apply leading, see Chapter 17.

When creating paragraph styles, you set leading in the Basic Character Formats pane of the New Paragraph Styles dialog box.

FIGURE 18.2

The Control panel's paragraph formatting options and flyout menu

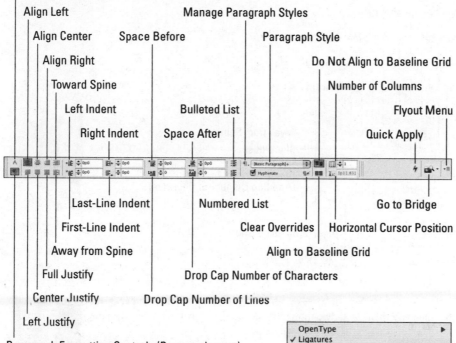

Character Formatting Controls (Character pane)

Align Left

Align Center   Space Before

Align Right

Toward Spine

Left Indent

Right Indent   Space After

Manage Paragraph Styles

Paragraph Style

Do Not Align to Baseline Grid

Number of Columns

Bulleted List   Flyout Menu

Quick Apply

Last-Line Indent

First-Line Indent

Away from Spine

Full Justify

Center Justify

Left Justify

Paragraph Formatting Controls (Paragraph pane)

Numbered List

Clear Overrides   Horizontal Cursor Position

Align to Baseline Grid

Drop Cap Number of Characters

Drop Cap Number of Lines

Go to Bridge

OpenType	▶
✓ Ligatures	
Underline Options....	
Strikethrough Options...	
No Break	
✓ Adobe Paragraph Composer	
Adobe Single-line Composer	
Only Align First Line to Grid	
Balance Ragged Lines	
Justification...	⌥⇧⌘J
Keep Options...	⌥⌘K
Hyphenation...	
Drop Caps and Nested Styles...	⌥⌘R
Paragraph Rules...	⌥⌘J
Bullets and Numbering...	
✓ Dock at Top	
Dock at Bottom	
Float	
Customize...	

The Paragraph Pane's Guest Functions

Two options in the Control panel's Paragraph (¶) pane are unrelated to paragraph formatting:

The Number of Columns field affects text frames and has the same effect as the same-named control in the Text Frame Options dialog box, as described in Chapter 15.

The Horizontal Cursor Position status indicator shows the horizontal position, relative to the frame's left inset, of the text cursor. This can be helpful when trying to measure where to draw vertical rules, set tab stops, or otherwise understand where specific text sits within a line so you can align or place something at the same horizontal location.

Controlling alignment and indents

The nine alignment icons at the top of the Paragraph panel and the four fields are always displayed; the four additional fields, two icons, and the Hyphenate option are also displayed when you choose Show Options from the flyout menu. InDesign refers to the top set of options as Basic Paragraph Formats; the additional seven options are Advanced Paragraph Formats.

The top set lets you control a paragraph's alignment and indents (left, right, first line, and last line). The additional options control paragraph spacing and drop caps, as well as lock or unlock text baselines to the baseline grid.

NOTE   When creating paragraph styles, you set alignments and indents in the Indents and Spacing pane of the New Paragraph Styles dialog box. Instead of buttons for aligning to the baseline grid, this pane has the Align to Grid pop-up menu, which has three options: None, All Lines, and First Line Only (this last option is also available in the Paragraph and Control panels' flyout menus).

Alignment

The nine alignment icons at the top of the Paragraph panel control how line beginnings and endings in selected paragraphs are placed relative to the left and right margins. (All but one are also available in the Control panel's Paragraph [¶] pane.) Here's a description of each alignment option (the icons do a pretty good job of showing what they do):

- **Align Left (Shift+⌘+L or Ctrl+Shift+L):** Places the left edge of every line at the left margin (the margin can be the frame edge, frame inset, left indent, or column edge) and fits as many words (or syllables, if hyphenation is turned on) on the line as possible. When a word (or syllable) won't fit at the end of a line, it's placed (flush left) on the next line. In left-aligned paragraphs, the right margin is said to be *ragged* because the leftover space at the right end of each line differs from line to line and produces a jagged edge.

  Some designers prefer to use this alignment for columns of text because they like the irregular, somewhat organic shapes that result; others prefer to align both left and right edges by adding space as needed between characters (called *justification*), which produces a more rigid, vertical look. Similarly, left-aligned text is sometimes hyphenated, sometimes not. (You can find more about hyphenation and justification later in this chapter.)

- **Align Center (Shift+⌘+C or Ctrl+Shift+C):** To create centered text, the leftover space of each line is divided in half. One-half of the leftover space is placed on the left end of the line; the other half is placed on the right end. The result is that both the left and right edges of the paragraphs are ragged, and the text is balanced along a vertical axis.

- **Align Right (Shift+⌘+R or Ctrl+Shift+R):** This is a mirror opposite of Align Left. The right edge is straight; the left edge is ragged. Columns of text are seldom set flush right because it's not as easy to read as flush-left text. Right-aligned text is sometimes used for such things as captions placed to the left of a picture, blurbs on magazine covers, and advertising copy.

- **Left Justify (Shift+⌘+J or Ctrl+Shift+J):** In justified text, the left and right ends of each line are flush with the margins. The flush-left/flush-right results are produced either by sprinkling the spaces of each line among characters and/or words or by reducing space between characters and/or words to accommodate additional characters (more about justification later in this chapter). Justified text is nearly always hyphenated (if you don't hyphenate justified text, spacing between letters and words is very inconsistent). Aligning the last line flush left is the traditional way of ending a paragraph, which is why Left Justify is the justified-text style most often used on paragraphs.

- **Center Justify:** This is the same as Left Justify except that the last line is center-aligned.

- **Right Justify:** This is the same as Left Justify except that the last line is right-aligned. Note that this iconic button is not available in the Control panel.

- **Full Justify (Shift+⌘+F or Ctrl+Shift+F):** This is the same as Left Justify except that the last line is also forcibly justified. This option can produce very widely spaced last lines. The fewer the characters on the last line, the greater the spacing.

  The previous three options are rarely used, and for good reason. People expect justified text to have the last line aligned left and the space at the end of the line to be a marker that the paragraph has ended. By changing the position of that last line, you can confuse your reader. So use Center Justify, Right Justify, and Full Justify options sparingly in special situations where the reader won't be confused — typically in brief copy like ads and pull-quotes.

- **Align Towards Spine:** This is similar to Left Justify or Right Justify except that InDesign automatically chooses a left or right alignment based on where the spine is in a facing-pages document. Essentially, this automatically creates right-aligned text on left-hand pages and left-aligned text on right-hand pages.

- **Align Away from Spine:** This is the same as Towards Spine, except that the alignment is reversed: Text aligns to the left on left-hand pages and to the right on right-hand pages.

To apply a paragraph alignment to selected paragraphs, click on one of the icons. (The hand pointer appears when the pointer is over a panel button.) You can also use the keyboard shortcuts in the preceding list.

Left-aligned and right-aligned paragraphs typically fit fewer characters per line than justified paragraphs. Most publications standardize on one of these two alignments for body copy; one factor is often how much copy needs to be squeezed in.

Indents

You can move the edges of paragraphs away from the left and/or right margins and indent the first line using the indent controls in the Paragraph panel or Control panel.

Left and right indents are often used for lengthy passages of quoted material within a column of text. Using indents is also handy way of drawing attention to pull-quotes and moving text away from a nearby graphic.

The options are:

- **Left Indent:** Type a value in this field to move the left edge of selected paragraphs away from the left margin. You can also use the up and down arrow keys. Each click increases the value by 1 point; pressing and holding Shift while clicking increases the increment to 1 pica.

- **Right Indent:** Type a value in this field to move the right edge of selected paragraphs away from the right margin. You can also use the up and down arrow keys.

- **First-Line Left Indent:** Type a value in this field to move the left edge of the first line of selected paragraphs away from the left margin. You can also press the up and down arrow keys. The value in the First-Line Indent field is added to any Left Indent value. For example, if you've specified a Left Indent value of 1 pica and you then specify a 1-pica First-Line Indent value, the first line of selected paragraphs is indented 2 picas from the left margin. If you've specified a Left Indent value, you can specify a negative First-Line Left Indent value to create a *hanging indent* (also called an *outdent*). But you cannot specify a First-Line Left Indent value that would cause the first line to extend past the left edge of the text frame (that is, the First-Line Left Indent value can't exceed that of the Left Indent value).

- **Last-Line Right Indent:** Type a value in this field to move the right edge of the last line of selected paragraphs away from the right margin. You can also press the up and down arrow keys. This function otherwise works just like the First-Line Left Indent function, so the Last-Line Right Indent value cannot exceed that of the Right Indent value.

Using a tab or spaces to indent the first line of a paragraph, which is what was done in the age of typewriters, is usually not a good idea. You're better off specifying a First-Line Indent. Similarly, you can indent an entire paragraph by inserting a tab or multiple word spaces at the beginning of every line in the paragraph, but both are typographic no-nos. Use the indent controls instead.

Hanging indents often have awkward measurements because they depend on the width of the bullet or other lead-in character. That can involve lots of experimentation to get the hang right. A simpler way is to insert the Indent Here character (Type ➪ Insert Special Character ➪ Other ➪ Indent to Here, or ⌘+\ or Ctrl+\). InDesign figures out the dimensions for you. Note that in this case, the Paragraph or Control panel will not show any indent values.

There is a risk with using Indent Here: You can have inconsistent hanging indents if the lead-in characters or space differ in your paragraphs, or if tracking or kerning of text before the indent-to-here characters varies from paragraph to paragraph.

Spacing Guidelines for Indents

The easy part of creating first-line indents and hanging indents is using the software. The hard part can be deciding how much space to use. For example, how do you decide how deep to make a first-line indent? Amateur publishers or designers, who are likely to be thinking in inches rather than points or picas, are likely to use too much space. They're tempted to use 0.25", 0.125", or another nice dividend of an inch for spacing rather than a more appropriate value such as 6 points. When deciding on spacing, consider the following:

- First-line indents that indicate new paragraphs should generally be one or two em spaces wide. The width of an em space is equal to the point size in use — so 10-point text should have a 10- or 20-point first-line indents. Opt for less space in narrower columns to avoid awkward space and more space in wider columns so the spacing is evident.

- As you remember from grade-school outlines, indents help organize information, with deeper indents indicating more detail about a topic. Professional publications, though, have many organizational options — such as headlines, subheads, and run-in heads — so they rarely have a need for more than two levels of indents. You might use indents on lengthy quotes, bulleted lists, numbered lists, kickers, and bylines. If you do, stick to the same amount of indent for each so the readers' eyes don't wander.

While these values give you a good starting point, you might need to modify them based on the typeface, font size, column width, design, and overall goals of the publication.

Lock to Baseline Grid

Every document includes a grid of horizontal lines, called the *baseline grid,* which can be displayed or hidden (View ➪ Grids & Guides ➪ Show/Hide Baseline Grid, or Option+⌘+' or Ctrl+Alt+') and used to help position objects and text baselines. A document's baseline grid is established in the Grids pane of the Preferences dialog box (choose InDesign ➪ Preferences ➪ Grids or press ⌘+K on the Mac, or choose Edit ➪ Preferences ➪ Grids or press Ctrl+K in Windows). Generally, a document's baseline grid interval is equal to the leading value applied to the body text.

You can ensure that lines of text align across columns and pages by locking their baselines to the baseline grid. To do so, click the Align to Baseline Grid iconic button in the Paragraph panel (the rightmost button on the bottom). To prevent such locking to the baseline, click the Do Not Align to Baseline Grid iconic button. These same buttons also exist on the right side of the Control panel's Paragraph (¶) pane.

You can also set individual baseline grids for specific text frames. You do so in the Baseline Options pane of the Text Frame Options dialog box (Object ➪ Text Frame Options, or ⌘+B or Ctrl+B). This is particularly handy for multicolumn text frames. InDesign aligns a paragraph to its text frame's baseline grid if it has one and to the document's baseline grid if not — assuming, of course, that Align to Baseline Grid is enabled.

CROSS-REF   Chapter 10 covers how to set up baseline grids in more detail.

Although you can use InDesign's Lock to Baseline Grid feature to align text baselines across columns and pages (or within text frames), you can produce the same results by combining uniform body text leading with other paragraph formats (Space Before and Space After). Some designers like the certainty and simplicity of the Lock to Baseline Grid feature; others prefer to control text alignment across columns themselves. Whichever works best for you is fine.

NOTE Keep in mind that when paragraphs are aligned to the baseline grid, the applied leading values are ignored.

The Only Align First Line to Grid option in the Paragraph panel's and Control panel's flyout menu aligns the first line of a paragraph to the baseline grid. It is a handy way to align multiline subheads so the first line stays on the grid, but the extra lines can fall naturally. You can use this for any paragraph that you want to be the rest point if your text gets off the baseline grid, without forcing every line to align to the grid.

Another option, Balance Ragged Lines in the Paragraph panel's and Control panel's flyout menus, ensures that the rag is balanced, that is to say, where the lines alternate short and long (when possible), rather than fall in a seemingly random pattern. This is designed to make headlines and other large copy (such as in ads) more visually pleasing. You wouldn't use this for body text, where the small text size and need to have efficient spacing makes this feature irrelevant. Unfortunately, this setting also forces hyphenation to achieve the balanced rag, which may be contrary to your intent.

Adding Space between Paragraphs

When you choose Show Options from the Paragraph panel's flyout menu, four additional fields appear, as shown earlier in Figure 18.1. They're also always in the Control panel. Two of these fields let you insert space before and/or after paragraphs.

When you need to format a lengthy chunk of text with multiple paragraphs, there are two ways to indicate a new paragraph. You can:

- Indent the paragraph's first line (by specifying a First-Line Left Indent value).
- Insert some extra space between the new paragraph and the preceding one.

NOTE There's no rule that says you can't use both spacing methods, but generally you use one or the other. What you don't want to do is insert extra returns between a paragraph, which is what was done in the days of typewriters.

To insert space before selected paragraphs, type a value in the Space Before field in the Paragraph panel or Control panel. You can also use the up and down arrow keys; each click increases the value by 1 point, while pressing and holding Shift increases the increment to 1 pica.

The Space After field works the same as the Space Before field but inserts space below selected paragraphs. Generally, you use Space Before or Space After to separate paragraphs. Combining both can be confusing.

NOTE When creating paragraph styles, you set paragraph spacing in the Indents and Spacing pane of the New Paragraph Styles dialog box.

Adding Drop Caps

A drop cap is created by *notching* a paragraph's first letter or letters into the upper-left corner of the paragraph. Drop caps are often used to embellish the first paragraph of a story, to draw attention to paragraphs, and to interrupt the grayness in columns of text. In the Paragraph panel or Control panel, InDesign lets you specify the number of letters you want to include in a drop cap and the number of lines you want to notch them.

To add one or more drop caps to selected paragraphs, type a number in the Drop Cap Number field in the Paragraph panel or Control panel. That's how many characters will be made into drop caps. To specify the number of lines a drop cap extends into a paragraph, type a value in the Drop Cap Depth field.

If the first character in a paragraph is a quotation mark (" or '), it can look odd as a one-character drop cap. If you don't like this look, you have a couple of options: You can either delete the opening quotation mark, an acceptable but potentially confusing practice, or you can use the first two characters in the paragraph as drop caps instead. Some publications simply prefer not to start paragraphs with quotes, preventing the problem from the editorial side.

After you create a drop cap, you can modify it by highlighting it and then changing any of its character formats — font, size, color, and so on — using a character style, the Character panel or Control panel, and other panels (such as Stroke and Swatches). Figure 18.3 shows some examples of drop caps.

A handy way to apply these settings is to use the Drop Cap & Nested Styles option in the Paragraph panel's or Control panel's flyout menu. You can also use the shortcut Option+⌘+R or Ctrl+Alt+R. Figure 18.4 shows the dialog box.

With this dialog box, you can set a character style that is applied to the paragraph. You can also use it to apply another character style to other text in the paragraph. To do so, click New Nested Style, and then choose from the three (unnamed) pop-up menus to specify how the style is to be applied. The first pop-up menu lets you choose the character style to apply, the second pop-up menu lets you choose Through or Up To (specify the number in the field to its right), and the third pop-up menu lets you determine what elements you're using, as the figure shows.

CROSS-REF Because this feature is most useful when coupled with a paragraph style (otherwise, it's easier to simply highlight some text in a paragraph and apply a character style to it), Chapter 20 covers drop caps and other nested styles in more detail.

NOTE When creating paragraph styles, the above controls are available in the Drop Caps and Nested Styles pane of the New Paragraph Styles dialog box.

FIGURE 18.3

The drop cap in the top-left example has a one-character drop cap three lines deep. The bottom-left paragraph has a two-line, four-character drop cap. In the top-right example, the font size of a one-letter, four-line drop cap has been enlarged to raise it above the first line of text. In the bottom-left example, a Left Indent value combined with a negative First-Line Left Indent value produced the one-character, three-line drop cap's hanging indent.

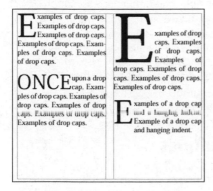

FIGURE 18.4

The Drop Caps & Nested Styles dialog box

Adding Automatic Bullets and Numbered Lists

Word processors have long been able to add automatic bullets and numbering to paragraphs. In the late 1980s, so could Ventura Publisher. Finally, InDesign can do it too. (QuarkXPress still cannot.) Automatic bullets and numbering are now available as a paragraph-level format, accessed in the Paragraph panel's and Control panel's flyout menus by choosing Bullets and Numbering Options.

CROSS-REF   Chapter 19 covers the setup and application of bullets and numbering in more detail. This feature is most useful when coupled with a paragraph style; otherwise, you have to apply these settings for each selection of paragraphs you want to make into a list. (Chapter 20 covers styles in more detail.)

Special Initial Cap Techniques

The three-line, single-letter drop cap is used so often that it's almost a cliché. Serviceable, yes, but very commonplace. But you can create all sorts of initial caps — large first letters such as drop caps and raised caps — in InDesign, as this example shows:

Creating raised caps

Raised caps are an alternative to drop caps, created by enlarging and raising the first few characters of the paragraph above the first line in the paragraph. Creating raised caps is simple — highlight the characters you want to raise with the Type tool and enlarge them using the Font Size field in the Character panel (Type ⇨ Character, or ⌘+T or Ctrl+T) or in the Character pane of the Control panel (press the A iconic button).

If you raise a word or phrase, you might need to track the raised words to tighten them. You also might need to kern between the raised text and the remainder of the line. Other options for raised caps include changing the font, color, and scale of the characters. If you plan to repeat the raised-cap formatting, save it as a character style.

You can also create partially raised caps by creating a drop cap and then enlarging the drop cap using the Character panel, the Character pane of the Control panel, or a character style.

Converting text to outlines for initial caps

You can convert drop caps, raised caps, or any character in any font to a graphic (actually, it's a frame, but you can work with it as if it were a graphic). You can then resize, scale, shear, fill, and stroke the character-shaped frame — even import a graphic into it. To do this, highlight the characters with the Type tool, and then choose Type ➪ Create Outlines, or press Shift+⌘+O or Ctrl+Shift+O. Frames are based on the size and outlines of the font in use and are automatically anchored in the paragraph so they flow with the text.

Note that when you convert text to outlines, the characters no longer exist as text. If you converted part of a word, the remaining portions of the word may be flagged during a spelling check. If you need to edit the converted text, delete the outlines, retype the word, and convert the characters again.

Using graphics as initial caps

Rather than using text for initial caps, you can use graphics. You can purchase clip art collections that consist of nothing but ornate capital letters to use as initial caps. To use a graphic as an initial cap, first delete the character you will replace with a graphic. Then, use the Place command (File ➪ Place, or ⌘+D or Ctrl+D) to import the graphic.

Size the graphic as appropriate, and then place it behind the paragraph, next to the paragraph, or anchored in the text of the paragraph. To anchor a graphic in text, select it with the Selection tool and choose Edit ➪ Cut, or press ⌘+X or Ctrl+X. Select the Type tool and click at the beginning of the paragraph; then choose Edit ➪ Paste, or press ⌘+V or Ctrl+V. The graphic is now anchored to the text, and you can apply InDesign's Drop Cap settings to it as if it were text. Similarly, you can resize it to create a raised cap from it. (Chapter 13 covers anchoring in more detail.)

In addition to importing graphics for use as initial caps, you can create your own graphics in InDesign. For example, you can place the initial cap character in its own text frame and create reverse type from it as I explain in this chapter. Or you can shade the character and place it slightly behind the paragraph.

Controlling Hyphenation and Justification

Hyphenation is the placement of hyphens between syllables in words that don't completely fit at the end of a line of text — a signal to the reader that the word continues on the next line. InDesign gives you the option to hyphenate or not hyphenate paragraphs, and if you choose to hyphenate, you can customize the settings that determine when and where hyphens are inserted.

As noted earlier, justification is the addition or removal of space between words and/or letters that produces the flush-left/flush-right appearance of justified paragraphs. InDesign's justification controls let you specify how space is added or removed when paragraphs are justified.

If your pages contain columns of text, you have to decide whether to use left-aligned or justified paragraphs and whether you want to hyphenate words that don't entirely fit at the end of a line. As mentioned earlier, if you justify paragraphs, you almost certainly want to hyphenate them, too. If you opt for left-aligned paragraphs, whether to hyphenate is a personal choice.

InDesign offers two hyphenation methods: manual and automatic.

 When creating paragraph styles, all the hyphenation controls are available in the Hyphenation pane of the New Paragraph Styles dialog box — except for the composer setting.

Manual hyphenation

If you want to break a particular word differently from the way InDesign would normally break the word, you can place a *discretionary hyphen* in the word. If the word falls at the end of a line in a hyphenated paragraph, InDesign uses the discretionary hyphen to split the word if the first syllable fits on the line. To insert a discretionary hyphen, use the shortcut Shift+⌘+– (hyphen) or Ctrl+Shift+– (hyphen) in the text where you want the hyphen to appear, or choose Type ➪ Insert Special Character ➪ Hyphens and Dashes ➪ Discretionary Hyphen.

You can prevent a particular word from being hyphenated either by placing a discretionary hyphen in front of the first letter or by highlighting the word and choosing No Break from the flyout menu of the Control panel or Character panel. (You need to select the A iconic button in the Control panel to get this option in its flyout menu.) But be careful: If you select more than a line's width of text and apply No Break, InDesign may not display the rest of the story's text.

TIP If you place a discretionary hyphen in a word, InDesign breaks the word only at that point (or does not break it at all). But you can place multiple discretionary hyphens within a single word; InDesign uses the one that produces the best results.

InDesign uses discretionary hyphens only if you select the Hyphenate option in the Paragraph panel or in the Control panel. If Hyphenate is not selected, neither manual nor automatic hyphenation is applied.

Likewise, if you want to force a hyphen that cannot be broken (meaning it cannot fall at the end of a line), insert the nonbreaking hyphen character (choose Type ➪ Insert Special Character ➪ Hyphens and Dashes ➪ Nonbreaking Hyphen, or press Option+⌘+– [hyphen] or Ctrl+Alt+– [hyphen]).

Automatic hyphenation

To automatically hyphenate selected paragraphs, all you have to do is select the Hyphenate option in the Paragraph panel or Control panel. (The Hyphenate option appears only if you choose Show Options from the flyout menu.)

If you choose to hyphenate paragraphs, you can control how hyphenation is accomplished through the Hyphenation option in the flyout menu. When you choose Hyphenation, the Hyphenation Settings dialog box, shown in Figure 18.5, appears.

NEW FEATURE The Hyphenate across Column option is new to InDesign CS3.

Here's a brief description of each option:

■ **Hyphenate:** This is a duplicate of the Hyphenate option in the Paragraph panel and Control panel. If you didn't select it before opening the Hyphenation dialog box, you can select it here.

The Hyphenation Settings dialog box

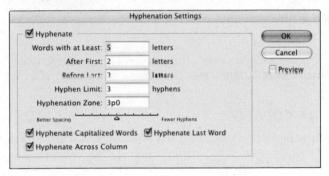

■ **Words with at Least ___ Letters:** Here, you specify the number of letters in the shortest word you want to hyphenate. For example, if you specify four letters, *mama* can be hyphenated, but *any* can't be.

■ **After First ___ Letters:** Here, you specify the minimum number of characters that can precede a hyphen. If you type 2, for example, the word *atavistic* can be broken after *at*. If you specify 3, *atavistic* cannot be broken until after *ata*.

■ **Before Last ___ Letters:** This field is similar to After First ___ Letters, but it determines the minimum number of characters that can follow a hyphen.

■ **Hyphenation Limit ___ Hyphens:** Specify the number of consecutive lines that can be hyphenated in this field. Some designers limit the number of consecutive hyphens to two or three because they believe that too many consecutive hyphens produce an awkward, ladder-like look. If the Hyphenation Limit value you enter prevents hyphenation in a line that would otherwise be hyphenated, the line may appear more spaced out than surrounding lines.

■ **Hyphenation Zone:** This field applies only to nonjustified text and only when the Adobe Single-Line Composer option is selected (in the Paragraph panel's or Control panel's fly-out menu). A hyphenation point must fall within the distance specified in this field to be used. Otherwise-acceptable hyphenation points that do not fall within the specified hyphenation zone are ignored. You can also click and drag the slider below the field to select a value rather than type a value in this field.

- **Hyphenate Capitalized Words:** Select this option to break capitalized words, such as proper names and the first word of sentences. If you don't enable this check box, a capitalized word that would otherwise be hyphenated will get bumped to the next line, possibly producing excessive spacing in the previous line.

- **Hyphenate Last Word:** Select this option to break the last word in a paragraph. Otherwise, InDesign moves the entire word to the last line and spaces the preceding text as necessary. Some typographers don't like having a word fragment as the last line, arguing that there's no need to break a word in two because there is clearly enough space to keep it together. I'm not so dogmatic.

- **Hyphenate across Column:** Enable this check box to let text hyphenate at the end of a column.

When you're done specifying hyphenation settings in the Hyphenation Settings dialog box, click OK to close the dialog box and return to your document.

Justifications controls

InDesign provides three options for controlling how justification is achieved. You can:

- Condense or expand the width of spaces, or *spacebands,* between words
- Add or remove space between letters
- Condense or expand the width of characters, or *glyphs*

The options in the Justification dialog box, shown in Figure 18.6, let you specify the degree to which InDesign adjusts normal word spaces, character spacing, and character width to achieve justification. You access this dialog box through the flyout menu in the Control panel or in the Paragraph panel, or by pressing Option+Shift+⌘+J or Ctrl+Alt+Shift+J. Although you can use the Justification controls on selected paragraphs, in most cases you specify Justification settings when you create styles, particularly your body-text styles.

FIGURE 18.6

The Justification dialog box

How Many Characters?

Consider changing the After First ___ Letters hyphenation setting to 2 if you have narrow columns or large text. Although many typographers object to two-letter hyphenation — as in *ab-dicate* or *ra-dar* — it often looks better than text with large gaps caused by the reluctance to hyphenate such words. Hyphenation also makes sense for many words that use two-letter prefixes such as *in-*, *re-*, and *co-*.

Although I advocate two-letter hyphenation at the beginning of a word, I prefer three-letter hyphenation at the end (set through Before Last ___ Letters). Except for words ending in *-ed* and sometimes *-al*, most words don't lend themselves to two-letter hyphenation at the end of the word. Part of this is functional, as it's easy for readers to lose two letters beginning a line. I prefer two-letter hyphenations at the end of a word only when the alternative is awkward spacing. As with all typography, this ultimately is a personal or house-style choice.

Regardless of the two- versus three-letter debate, words broken using minimum settings of 1 look awful. They also go against reader expectations because the norm is to have several letters after a hyphen. Never use a minimum setting of 1 for After First ___ Letters. If you do, you get hyphenations such as *A-sia*, *a-typical*, and *u-niform* that simply look terrible in print. They also don't provide enough context for the reader to anticipate the rest of the word. Likewise, never use a minimum of 1 for Before Last ___ Letters because you get hyphenations such as *radi-o*.

> **NOTE** When creating paragraph styles, all the justification controls are available in the Justification pane of the New Paragraph Styles dialog box.

Here's a brief description of each option:

- **Word Spacing:** Type the percentage of a spaceband character that you want to use whenever possible in the Desired field. (The default value is 100%, which uses a font's built-in width.) Type the minimum acceptable percentage in the Minimum field; type the maximum acceptable percentage in the Maximum field. The smallest value you can enter is 0%; the largest is 1000%. Some designers are adamant that only word spaces — not letter spaces — should be adjusted when justifying text. Others allow small adjustments to letter spacing as well.

- **Letter Spacing:** The default value of 0% in this set of three fields uses a font's built-in letter spacing. In the Desired field, type a positive value to add space (in increments of 1% of an en space) between all letter pairs; type a negative value to remove space. Type the minimum acceptable percentage in the Minimum field; type the maximum acceptable percentage in the Maximum field.

- **Glyph Scaling:** The default value of 100% uses a character's normal width. In the Desired field, type a positive value to expand all character widths; type a negative value to condense character widths. Type the minimum acceptable percentage in the Minimum field; type the maximum acceptable percentage in the Maximum field. Some designers adamantly contend that scaling characters is even more unacceptable than letter spacing, while others see no harm in scaling characters, as long as it's kept to a minimum. If you do apply glyph scaling, it's best to keep it to a range of 97 to 103 percent at most.

I suggest 85 percent minimum, 100 percent optimum, and 150 percent maximum for word spacing; and   5 percent minimum, 0 percent optimum, and 10 percent maximum for letter spacing. I prefer minimum settings that are less than the optimum because they help text fit more easily in narrow columns. These settings work well for most newsletters and magazines output on an imagesetter. At the same time, I usually leave the maximum word spacing at 150 percent.

NOTE   When specifying values in the Justification dialog box, Minimum values must be smaller than Desired values, which in turn must be smaller than Maximum values.

The Auto Leading field in the Justification dialog box lets you specify a custom value for Auto Leading. In InDesign, this is a character-level format, even though it rightfully should be a paragraph format. Although it's great that InDesign also makes it available in this paragraph-oriented dialog box, it's a bit hidden here. Plus, it's too bad you can't specify an actual number of points (such as +2 to indicate 2 points of leading more than the text size), which is how leading is traditionally calculated.

CROSS-REF   Leading is covered in detail in Chapter 17.

InDesign also lets you control what happens to words that end up taking a full line's width. In the Single Word Justification pop-up menu, you would normally keep the default Full Justification option, which spaces the word to fill the line. You could also choose Align Left, Align Center, or Align Right to avoid spacing out the word to fit. But that's a cure worse than the problem: Having a line of a different width than the others looks like either a new paragraph or a mistake, and both appearances are sure to confuse readers.

If you use the Adobe Paragraph Composer option (explained in the next section) for justified paragraphs, specifying a narrow range between minimum and maximum Word Spacing, Letter Spacing, and Glyph Scaling generally produces good-looking results. However, if you choose the Adobe Single-Line Composer option, a broader range between Minimum and Maximum gives the composer more leeway in spacing words and letters and hyphenating words and can produce better-looking results. The best way to find out what values work best for you is to experiment with several settings. Print hard copies and let your eyes decide which values produce the best results.

About Word Spacing

Word spacing—the space between words—is another important contributor to the aesthetics of a document. Think about it: If the words in a sentence are too close to one another, comprehension may be affected because of the difficulty in telling where one word ends and another begins. If the words are too far apart, the reader might have a difficult time following the thought that's being conveyed.

Here's a design rule I like to follow: The wider the column, the more space you can add between words. This is why books tend to have more word spacing than magazines. Like all other typographic issues, there's a subjective component to picking good word spacing. Experiment to see what works best in your documents.

NOTE A paragraph's justification settings are applied whether the paragraph is justified or not. However, for nonjustified paragraphs, only the Desired values for Word Spacing, Letter Spacing, and Glyph Scaling are used.

Composing text

The Paragraph panel's — but not the Control panel's — flyout menu offers two choices for implementing the hyphenation and justification settings you've established: the Adobe Single-Line Composer and the Adobe Paragraph Composer. (These are also available in the Justification dialog box I cover in the previous section.)

Adobe Single-Line Composer

Old-school programs like QuarkXPress and PageMaker use single-line composition methods to flow text. This method marches line by line through a paragraph and sets each line as well as possible using the applied hyphenation and justification settings. The effect of modifying the spacing of one line on the lines above and below is not considered in single-line composition. If adjusting the space within a line causes poor spacing on the next line, tough luck.

InDesign offers this traditional approach to composing text; just enable Adobe Single Line Composer in the Justification dialog box. When you use the Adobe Single-Line Composer, the following rules apply:

- Adjusting word spacing is preferred over hyphenation.
- Hyphenation is preferred over glyph scaling.
- If spacing must be adjusted, removing space is preferred over adding space.

Adobe Paragraph Composer

InDesign's Adobe Paragraph Composer (called the Multi-Line Composer in some earlier versions) is enabled by default. It takes a broader approach to composition by looking at the entire paragraph at once. If a poorly spaced line can be fixed by adjusting the spacing of a previous line, the Paragraph Composer reflows the previous line. The Paragraph Composer is governed by the following principles:

- The evenness of letter spacing and word spacing is the highest priority. The desirability of possible breakpoints is determined by how much they cause word and letter spacing to vary from the Desired settings.
- Uneven spacing is preferred to hyphenation. A breakpoint that does not require hyphenation is preferred over one that does.
- All possible breakpoints are ranked, and good breakpoints are preferred over bad ones.

The paragraph-level composer is more sophisticated than the single-line option, offering generally better overall spacing because it sacrifices optimal spacing a bit on one line to prevent really bad spacing on another, something the single-line method does not do.

However, there is one frustration in dealing with the paragraph-level composer: When you try to edit text or play with tracking to get rid of an orphan or widow, the Paragraph Composer keeps adjusting the text across several lines, often counteracting your nips and tucks. The Single-Line Composer doesn't do that.

 When creating paragraph styles, the composition controls are available in the Justification pane of the New Paragraph Styles dialog box.

Setting Other Paragraph Formats

The Paragraph panel's and Control panel's flyout menus contain two additional paragraph-formatting options:

■ **Keep Options:** This option lets you determine how and when paragraphs can be split when they fall at the bottom of a column or page.

■ **Paragraph Rules:** This option lets you place a horizontal line in front of or after a paragraph. Lines placed using the Paragraph Rules feature become part of the text and move along with surrounding text when editing causes text reflow.

Keep Options

A *widow* is the last line of a paragraph that falls at the top of a column (the poor thing has been cut off from the rest of the family). An *orphan* is the first line of a paragraph that falls at the bottom of a column (it, too, has become separated from its family). InDesign's Keep Options feature lets you prevent widows and orphans; it also lets you keep paragraphs together when they would otherwise be broken at the bottom of a column.

When you choose Keep Options from the Paragraph panel's or Control panel's flyout menu — or when you use the shortcut Option+⌘+K or Ctrl+Alt+K — the Keep Options dialog box, shown in Figure 18.7, appears.

The Keep Options dialog box provides several options for how paragraphs are managed as text breaks across columns and pages:

■ **Keep with Next ___Lines:** This option applies to two consecutive paragraphs. Specify the number of lines of the second paragraph that must stay with the first paragraph if a column or page break occurs within the second paragraph. This option is useful for preventing a subhead from being separated from the paragraph that follows.

■ **Keep Lines Together:** Select this option to prevent paragraphs from breaking and to control widows and orphans. When this box is checked, the two options below it become available. (The radio buttons present an either/or choice. One must be selected; At Start/End of Paragraph is selected by default.)

FIGURE 18.7

The Keep Options dialog box

- **All Lines in Paragraph:** Select this option to prevent a paragraph from being broken at the end of a column or page. When a column or page break occurs within a paragraph to which this setting has been applied, the entire paragraph moves to the next column or page.

- **At Start/End of Paragraph:** Select this option to control widows and orphans. When this option is selected, the two fields below it become available:

  - **Start ___ Lines:** This field controls orphans. The value you type is the minimum number of lines at the beginning of a paragraph that must be placed at the bottom of a column when a paragraph is split by a column ending.

  - **End ___ Lines:** This field controls widows. The value you type is the minimum number of lines at the end of a paragraph that must be placed at the top of a column when a paragraph is split by a column ending.

CAUTION Keep in mind that when you eliminate an orphan or widow using Keep Options, the line that precedes the widow line is bumped to the next column or page, which can produce uneven column endings on multicolumn pages.

- **Start Paragraph:** From this pop-up menu, choose In Next Column to force a paragraph to begin in the next column; choose In Next Frame to force a paragraph to begin in the next frame; choose On Next Page to force a paragraph to begin on the next page (such as for chapter headings). Your other choices are similar: On Next Odd Page and On Next Even Page. Choose Anywhere to let the paragraph begin where it would fall naturally in the sequence of text (no forced break).

NOTE When creating paragraph styles, all the above controls are available in the Keep Options pane of the New Paragraph Styles dialog box.

Paragraph rules

Usually, the easiest way to create a horizontal line is to use the Line tool. But if you want to place a horizontal line within text so that the line moves with the text when editing causes the text to reflow, you need to create a paragraph rule. A paragraph rule looks much like a line created with the line tool but behaves like a text character. Paragraph rules have many uses. For example, you can place one above or below a subhead to make it more noticeable or to separate the subhead from the paragraph that precedes or follows it. Or you can place paragraph rules above and below a pull-quote so that the rules and the pull-quote text move if editing causes text reflow.

Here's how to place a paragraph rule:

1. **Select the paragraph(s) to which you want to apply a rule above and/or a rule below, and then choose Paragraph Rules from the Paragraph panel's or Control panel's flyout menu, or use the shortcut Option+⌘+J or Ctrl+Alt+J.** You can also specify this as part of a paragraph style. The Paragraph Rules dialog box, shown in Figure 18.8, is displayed.

FIGURE 18.8

The Paragraph Rules dialog box

2. **Choose Rule Above or Rule Below, and then select the Rule On option.** You can add a rule above, below, or both. If you want to add rules above and below, you must select Rule On for both options and specify their settings separately. If you want to see the rule as you create it, select the Preview option.

3. **For Weight, choose a predefined thickness from the pop-up menu or type a value in the field.**

4. **Choose a rule type from the Type pop-up menu.** Typically, you'd use just a simple line, but InDesign offers 17 types of lines, including dashed, striped, dotted, and wavy.

5. **Choose a color from the Color pop-up menu, which lists the colors displayed in the Swatches panel (Window ➪ Swatches or F5).** If you choose (Text Color), InDesign automatically uses the color applied to the first character in the paragraph. If your ruling

line is not a plain line, you can also choose the Gap Color to determine what color goes between dashes, stripes, dots, and so on in your line. For both the Color and Gap Color options, you can specify a corresponding tint (shade) with the Tint and Gap Tint pop-up menus, respectively.

6. **From the Width pop-up menu, choose an option.** Choose Column if you want the rule to extend from the left edge of the column to the right edge of the column; choose Text if you want the rule to extend from the left edge of the frame or column to the line ending on the right.

7. **To indent the rule from the left and/or right edges, type values in the Left Indent and/or Right Indent fields.**

8. **To control the vertical position of the rule, type a value in the Offset field.** For a rule above, the offset value is measured upward from the baseline of the first line in a paragraph to the bottom of the rule; for a rule below, the offset is measured downward from the baseline of the last line in a paragraph to the top of the rule.

9. **Click the Overprint Stroke option if you want to print a rule on top of any underlying colors.** This ensures that any misregistration during printing does not result in white areas around the rule where the paper shows through. You typically use this for black or other dark colors. There's a similar Overprint Gap option for lines that have a Gap Color.

10. **To ensure that a rule over a paragraph at the top of a frame displays within the frame, check the Keep in Frame option.**

NEW FEATURE The Keep in Frame option is new to InDesign CS3. In previous versions, rules that appear over the first paragraph in a frame either did not display or displayed outside the frame, contrary to most users' expectations.

11. **Click OK to close the dialog box, implement your changes, and return to your document.**

To remove a paragraph rule, click in the paragraph to which the rule is applied, choose Paragraph Rules from the Paragraph panel's flyout menu, deselect the Rule On option, and then click OK.

TIP You can use the Paragraph Rules feature to place a band of color behind text by specifying a line thickness at least 2 points larger than the text size and offsetting the rule so it moves up behind the text.

NOTE When creating paragraph styles, all the above controls are available in the Paragraph Rules pane of the New Paragraph Styles dialog box.

Optical margin override

Additionally, the Paragraph panel's flyout menu contains a third option not available in the panel itself: Ignore Optical Margin, which tells InDesign not to apply optical margin alignment for specific paragraphs in a story that has optical margin alignment applied. (Chapter 19 explains this feature in depth.)

You can also control ignore optical margin alignment as a paragraph style setting, so any paragraphs with a certain style applied ignore the optical margin alignment set for the story. To do so, enable the Ignore Optical Margin check box in the Indents and Spacing pane of the New Paragraph Style or Paragraph Style Options dialog box. (Chapter 20 explains how to create and edit styles.)

NEW FEATURE   The ability to override optical margin alignment for individual paragraphs and via paragraph styles is new to InDesign CS3.

Summary

Much like character formats, InDesign's paragraph formats let you control the appearance of selected paragraphs. For example, you can control a paragraph's alignment and specify left, right, and/or first-line indents, and you can use drop caps to add space between paragraphs. If you want to hyphenate a paragraph, you can add hyphenation points manually to individual words, or you can have InDesign automatically hyphenate words as appropriate.

If you choose to use InDesign's justification controls to specify how space is added or removed between characters and/or words to achieve justification, you also have two options for composing text (controlling the spacing approach): the full-paragraph composition method that looks at several lines of text at once, and the single-line method that looks at each line in isolation.

Chapter 19

Creating Special Text Formatting

O nce you learn the basics of typefaces, character formats, and paragraph formats, you can achieve just about any look with text. The trick is combining and applying the skills you've learned to produce special effects that not only look professional but also enhance the meaning of the text.

Glance at any professional publication — a national magazine, direct-mail catalog, cookbook, or product brochure — and you see typographic techniques that set the publication apart from anything that can be easily produced in a word processor. (Even when word processors do offer a feature, they often lack the control necessary to really fine-tune an effect.) And skilled designers use these effects with a purpose — special bullet characters emphasize a theme, drop caps draw readers in, and pull-quotes tantalize the audience, for example.

Throughout this chapter, you learn how InDesign can produce special typographic effects and, more importantly, when to use them.

You can apply all sorts of formatting to text beyond those described here. For example, by using InDesign's object transformation tools, as covered in Chapter 11, you can change the look of entire text blocks such as through rotation and scaling.

By applying special object effects such as transparency and embossing — covered in Chapter 12 — you can really jazz up your layouts. InDesign's text-wrap feature (covered in Chapter 13) also lets you make text interact with surrounding objects.

IN THIS CHAPTER

Working with bulleted and numbered lists

Formatting fractions

Creating reverse type

Adding sidebars and pull-quotes

Specifying optical margin alignment

Creating custom underlines and strikethroughs

Converting text to graphics

Running text along a path

And for text selections, you can apply color (see Chapter 8), strokes (see Chapter 12), and various character and paragraph formatting (see Chapters 17 and 18).

Using Bulleted and Numbered Lists

Automatic bullets and numbering are available as a paragraph-level format in InDesign, accessed in the Paragraph panel and Control panel's flyout menus by choosing Bullets and Numbering Options. (Figure 19.1 shows the resulting dialog box.) There are additional bullet and number controls in the Type menu. And you can also apply these lists via paragraph styles.

Defining lists

The process for setting automatic bullets and numbered lists is almost identical; only the top part of the Bullets and Numbering dialog box differs, based on whether you select Bullets or Numbers from the List Type pop-up menu. (Choose None to remove the automatic bullets or numbers.)

FIGURE 19.1

In the Bullets and Numbering dialog box, note the top part changes based on whether you are formatting bullets (left) or numbered lists (right).

Follow these steps to set up a list (select the Preview option if you want to see the results of your choices before you finalize them):

    1a.   **For a bulleted list, choose a bullet character from the Bullet Character area.** The area shows bullet characters available for the current font; you can change the selection by changing the selected font or by clicking Add, which opens a dialog box similar to the Glyphs panel (see Chapter 21).

1b. For a numbered list, choose a numbering style in the Format pop-up menu, go through the following options.

   i. Specify the number's formatting in the Number field (you can select special characters and placeholder numbers in the pop-up menu to its right), and choose whether the numbers continue or start anew at this paragraph through the Mode pop-up menu (your choices are Continue from Previous Number and Start At).

   ii. In the Format pop-up menu, your options are 1, 2, 3, 4 ...; 01, 02, 03, 04 ...; I, II, III, IV ...; i, ii, iii, iv ...; A, B, C, D ...; and a, b, c, d ...

   iii. If you are using defined lists (covered later in this section), select the appropriate list type from the List Type pop-up menu. You can also choose New List to create a new list type.

   iv. If you are using sublists, also called *nested lists,* specify the current paragraph's list level by entering a value between 1 and 9 in the Level field. (This paragraph is part of a sublist under the paragraph 1b in the main list.) If you do use sublists, check the Restart Numbers at This Level After check box and enter a level — it must be higher than the current level — in the adjacent field or choose the Any Previous Level option from the adjacent pop-up to reset the numbering if this paragraph is at a different numbering level than previous ones in the list. Specifying a specific level means that the numbering will restart only if the previous numbered paragraph was at the specified level. Choosing Any Previous Level resets the numbering if the previous numbered paragraph was at any other level than this paragraph's.

   v. In the Number field, you can insert all sorts of special spaces and characters, giving you broad control on how numbers display, through the Insert Special Characters submenu. You can also choose number placeholders, which tell InDesign what numbers to insert in the list. For simple lists, choose Current Level from the Insert Number Placeholder pop-up submenu — the default. The other levels are used when you have sublists within lists. You can also choose Chapter Number to insert the chapter's number as part of the list item's placeholder number. (See Chapter 25 for more on specifying the chapter number.)

2. Set the font settings for the bullet or numbers using the Character Style pop-up menu to choose a character style. The default setting of [None] uses the paragraph's current formatting. Note that the look of the numerals is more a design decision than an editorial decision. If numerals are in a different typeface and/or in a different color, a period following the numeral might just look cluttered.

3. In the Bullet or Number Position section of the dialog box, set the indents for the list. Using the Alignment pop-up menu, choose Left, Center, or Right to determine where the bullet or numeral is positioned within its tab. You can set the hanging indent amount and the bullet's or numbers overhang by using the Left Indent, First Line Indent, and Tab Position fields.

4. Click OK when you are done with the settings.

NEW FEATURE InDesign CS3 changes the alignment options for bullets and numbers to give you more precise control of their placement.

Spacing Guidelines for Lists

The easy part of creating bulleted lists and numbered lists in InDesign is using the software. The hard part can be deciding how much space to use. For example, how much space goes between a bullet and the text following it? Amateur publishers or designers, who are likely to be thinking in inches rather than points or picas, are likely to use too much space. They're tempted to use 0.25", 0.125", or another nice fraction of an inch for spacing rather than a more appropriate value such as 6 points. When deciding on spacing, consider the following:

- In bulleted lists, use a hanging indent for a succession of two- or three-line bulleted paragraphs in wider columns. If your bulleted items are five or six lines long, especially in narrow columns, it might work better to use run-in heads to break up the information.

- Generally, the amount of space between a bullet and its text is equal to half the point size of the text. So if you're working with 11-point text, place 5.5 points between the bullet and text.

- When it comes to numbered lists, you need to decide whether you're going to include a period or other punctuation after the number and whether you'll ever have two-digit numbers. Numerals in most typefaces are the width of an en space, and they should be followed by the same amount of space the numbers and their punctuation take up. If you have a two-digit numeral, the numbers take up one em space and so should be followed by one em space.

While these values give you a good starting point, you might need to modify them based on the typeface, font size, column width, design, and overall goals of the publication.

Note that the Format menu is the new name for the previous version's Style menu. The 01, 02, 03, 04 ... option in the Format menu is also new. The Number field and its pop-up menu replace the previous version's Separator menu. And the Mode pop-up menu replaces the previous version's Start At field. The Character Style pop-up menu replaces the previous version's Font Family, Font Style, Size, and Color options.

InDesign gives you even more control over bulleted and numbered lists through the options you get by choosing Type ➪ Bulleted & Numbered Lists:

- The Apply/Remove Bullets and Apply/Remove Numbers submenu options quickly let you turn on or off the bullets or numbering for selected paragraphs. You can also use the iconic buttons for these controls on the Control panel.

- The Restart/Continue Numbering option is a handy way to control which paragraphs are numbered, such as when you have an unnumbered paragraph within a list. (This option is also available in the flyout menu of the Paragraph panel and Control panel.)

- The Convert Bullets to Text and Convert Numbering to Text options remove the automatic bullets or numerals in a paragraph but leave an actual bullet character or numeral at the beginning of the paragraph for you to do as you please. (These options are also available in the flyout menu of the Paragraph panel and Control panel.)

A more advanced option is the Define Lists option (available in three places: by choosing Type ⇨ Bulleted & Numbered Lists ⇨ Define Lists, by choosing Define Lists from the Paragraph panel's flyout menu, or by choosing New List in the List Type pop-up menu in the Bullets and Numbering dialog box). Here, you create list types with just two options: Continue Numbers across Stories and Continue Numbers from Previous Document in a Book. You access these list types when you create or edit paragraph styles using the style dialog boxes' Bullets and Numbering pane, or when you apply bullets and numbering through the Paragraph panel's or Control panel's flyout menu. (Either way, choose the appropriate style in the List Type pop-up menu.)

When you enable Continue Numbers across Stories, InDesign continues numbering text based on the last number used in the previous story rather than restarting the numbering at each story (the normal behavior). When you enable Continue Numbers from Previous Document in a Book, InDesign continues numbering text based on the last number used in the previous chapter of a book (see Chapter 23) rather than starting over again with this document (the normal behavior).

 The Bullet & Numbered Lists option in the Type menu is new to InDesign CS3, as are the controls for defining list types.

Applying lists

When you specify numbered or bulleted list settings in the Paragraph panel, these settings are immediately applied to any selected paragraphs. Likewise, any list settings specified in paragraph styles are automatically applied to any paragraphs using those styles.

But you can quickly default bulleted or numbered lists to selected paragraphs using these techniques:

- Click the Bulleted List or Numbered List iconic button in the Control panel.
- Choose Type ⇨ Bulleted & Numbered Lists ⇨ Apply Bullets or choose Type ⇨ Bulleted & Numbered Lists ⇨ Apply Numbers.

You can also unapply (remove) a bulleted list or numbered list from selected paragraphs by using the above formatting commands. For example, to make a bulleted list normal (no bullets or numbers), click the Bulleted List iconic button or choose Type ⇨ Bulleted & Numbered Lists ⇨ Apply Bullets. These commands act as toggles, turning the lists off and on.

Working with imported lists

But chances are you're not writing the bulk of your text in InDesign. Instead, the text was delivered in the form of a word-processing file, and the writer or editor made some decisions about bullets or numerals. A lot of times, writers simply type an asterisk followed by a space to indicate a bullet. Or maybe an editor typed a numeral followed by a parenthesis in front of each step. Other times, writers or editors use their word processor's automatic bullet or numbering feature.

If the writer used manual numerals or bullets, that's what you get. If the writer used automatic bullets or numbers, that's also what you get, unless you told InDesign to override them, as I cover in Chapter 14.

Bullet Character Options

Although you may not know what they're called, you're used to seeing en bullets, the small round bullet (•) included in most typefaces. But you're not limited to using this character. You can use any character in the body text font, or you can switch to a symbol or pi font and choose a more decorative character.

Zapf Dingbats and Wingdings are the most common symbol fonts, offering an array of boxes, arrows, crosses, stars, and check marks. These can be cute and effective, but cute isn't always a good thing. If you opt for a different bullet character, make sure you have a reason and that it works well with the rest of the design. Check-mark bullets in an election flyer might make sense; bulky square bullets in a to-do list for a wedding caterer might not make sense.

Note that you might want to reduce the size of the symbol slightly and that you might need to use different spacing values than you would use with an en bullet.

Don't limit yourself to these two common fonts either. You can purchase many different symbol fonts to support different content. For example, you might see leaf-shaped bullets in an herb article and paw-print bullets in a pet training article. To use your own drawing or a logotype as a bullet, convert the drawing to a font using a utility such as FontLab Studio (see the companion Web site www.InDesignCentral.com for links to this and other font utilities).

Formatting Fractions

Creating fractions that are formatted correctly can be handy. Compare the left fraction in Figure 19.2, which is not formatted appropriately, to the other fractions in the figure, which are correctly formatted. Although InDesign doesn't provide an automatic fraction maker, you can use OpenType typefaces, expert typefaces, or character formats to achieve professional-looking fractions.

 InDesign has no equivalent to QuarkXPress's fraction-building tool, although the use of OpenType fonts that support automatic fractions can provide similar functionality.

Applying a fraction typeface

Some expert typefaces include a variation, appropriately called *Fractions*, that includes a number of common fractions, such as ½, ⅓, ¼, and ¾. Adobe has Expert Collection variants for many of its popular Type 1 PostScript fonts; these collections include true small caps, true fractions, and other typographic characters. You can also use a symbol font, though the numerals may not exactly match the appearance of numerals in the rest of your text because symbol fonts typically use plain fonts like Helvetica as their basis.

To use a true fraction from an Expert Collection font, choose Type ➪ Glyph, select the font and face from the pop-up menus at the bottom of the panel shown in Figure 19.2, and then select the fraction you want to use.

FIGURE 19.2

From left to right: the ⅞ fraction unformatted, formatted via OpenType, formatted via an Expert Collection font, and formatted manually. Note that the rightmost fraction uses a regular slash, while the middle two use virgules. Also shown is the Glyph panel used to select the Expert Collection symbol.

If you have OpenType fonts, the process can be automated: Be sure that the Fraction option is enabled for the selected text, either as part of its character or paragraph style or by highlighting the text and adjusting the OpenType options directly:

- For styles, go to the OpenType Features pane when creating or modifying a paragraph or character style, and check Fractions.

- For local formatting, highlight the text containing the fraction and then choose OpenType ⇨ Fraction from the flyout menu of the Character panel or Control panel — be sure that Fraction is checked in the menu (choose it if not).

NOTE These OpenType options have no effect on non-OpenType fonts.

Formatting fractions manually

If you're dealing with a wide range of fractions in something like a cookbook, you probably won't find all the fractions you need in your Expert Collection font. Regular Type 1 Postscript and TrueType fonts certainly don't have the desired fractions. And although OpenType fonts have the necessary characters to create almost any fraction, many fonts are not available in OpenType format — and even when they are available, many publishers have not spent the money to replace them all. Therefore, most organizations opt for formatting all the fractions manually. But if you are a frequent fraction user, I strongly encourage you to switch to OpenType fonts.

The built-in fractions in expert fonts and the fractions generated by OpenType fonts are approximately the same size as a single character in that font; this size should be your goal in formatting a fraction manually. Usually, you achieve this by decreasing the size of the two numerals (perhaps by using the subscript and superscript formats), raising the numerator (the first, or top, number in the fraction) using the baseline shift feature, and kerning on either side of the slash as necessary. (Chapter 17 covers these controls.)

InDesign's default superscript and subscript size is 58.3 percent of the character's size (this odd value actually equals ⁷⁄₁₂, in keeping with typography's standard of using points, of which there are 12 in a pica, for text measurement). The numerator and denominator in a fraction should be the same size, so if you use InDesign's superscripts at its default settings, multiply the text's point size by 0.583 (just highlight the denominator text, go to the Font Size field in the Character panel or Control panel, and type *0.583 after the current size value). I recommend changing InDesign's superscript and subscript font styles to 65 percent to improve readability, especially at smaller sizes. You can change these default settings in the Advanced Type pane of the Preferences dialog box (choose InDesign ➪ Preferences ➪ Advanced Type or press ⌘+K on the Mac, or choose Edit ➪ Preferences-Advanced Type or press Ctrl+K in Windows).

 Mac fonts provide another option for refining fractions: a special kind of slash called a *virgule,* which is smaller and at more of an angle than a regular slash. Press Option+Shift+1 to enter a virgule, and then kern around it as you would a slash. Expert fonts and OpenType fonts also come with virgules, which they use in their fractions; Figure 19.2 shows the difference.

Unless you rarely use fractions, by all means save your manual formatting as character styles: one for the numerator, one for the denominator, and perhaps one for the slash or virgule. You can apply the formats with a keystroke or use Find/Change (Edit ➪ Find/Change, or ⌘+F or Ctrl+F) to locate numerals and selectively apply the appropriate character style.

Reversing Type out of Its Background

This is the reverse of what you usually see — rather than black type on a white background, white type appears on a black background. Of course, reverse type doesn't have to be white on black; it can be any lighter color on a darker color. You can often see reverse type in table headings, kickers (explanatory blurbs following headlines), and decorative elements. Reverse type, which brightens text and pulls readers in, works best with larger type sizes and bold typefaces so the text isn't swallowed by the background.

InDesign doesn't have a reverse type command or font style — but using this effect involves just a simple combination of basic InDesign skills. To lighten the text, highlight it with the Type tool, click the Fill iconic button on the Tools panel or Swatches panel, and choose a light color from the Swatches panel (Window ➪ Swatches or F5). For a dark background, you have three options: filling the text frame with a darker color, making the text frame transparent and placing it on top of darker objects, or using a ruling line behind the text.

For the first two options, select the text frame with any selection tool, and then click the Fill iconic button on the Tools panel. To fill the text frame with a color, click a darker color on the Swatches panel. To make the text frame transparent, click the Apply None iconic button on the Tools panel. Then place the text frame in front of a darker object or graphic.

For reverse-out type that is not in its own text frame, you use a ruling line of the appropriate width (at least a couple points larger than the text size) and move it into the text. If you use Rule Above, you move the line down behind the text; if you use Rule Below, you move it up. Figure 19.3 shows reversed-out type used as description headings, as well as the Paragraph Rules dialog box and the settings used to create the effect. (To access this dialog box, choose Paragraph Rules from the flyout menu of the Control panel or Paragraph panel, or press Option+⌘+J or Ctrl+Alt+J.)

FIGURE 19.3

This product guide uses reversed-out text created with ruling lines for its description titles.

When designing elements with reverse type, make sure the point size of the text is large enough to print clearly on the darker background. Consider the thinnest part of characters, especially in serif typefaces, when judging the size and thickness of reverse type. You often want to use a semibold or bolder version of a font so the text maintains its visual integrity.

 All paragraph formatting options in the Control panel are in the paragraph pane; be sure the ¶ iconic button is selected to display them.

Creating Sidebars and Pull-Quotes

Pick up almost any publication, from *Newsweek* magazine to your neighborhood newsletter, and you're almost guaranteed to see sidebars and pull-quotes. So basic that you can even create them with a modern word processor, these treatments aren't really typographic treatments — they're just page-layout techniques involving text elements you create by applying simple InDesign skills.

A *sidebar* is supplemental text, formatted differently, and often placed within a shaded or outlined box. Sidebars help break up text-heavy pages and call attention to information that is often interesting but not essential to the main story. Even in technical publications, it's helpful to pull in-depth information or related text into sidebars to provide visual relief. To create a sidebar, you usually place the text in its own frame, and then stroke the frame and optionally fill it with a tint, as I cover in Chapters 8 and 12. To inset the text from the edges of the frame, use the Text Frame Options dialog box (Object ➪ Text Frame Options, or ⌘+B or Ctrl+B), as I cover in Chapter 13.

A *pull-quote* is a catchy one- or two-line excerpt from a publication that is enlarged and reformatted to achieve both editorial and design objectives. On the editorial side, pull-quotes draw readers into articles with excerpts that do everything from summarize the content to provide shock value. On the design side, pull-quotes break up staid columns and offer opportunities for typographic treatment that emphasize the content (such as colors and typefaces that reflect the mood of an article). Although the design often dictates the use of and length of pull-quotes, an editorial person should select the text and indicate it on hard copy or within text files. To create a pull-quote, copy and paste the relevant text into its own text frame, and then reformat the text and frame as you want. Use the Text Wrap panel (Window ⇨ Text Wrap, or Option+⌘+W or Ctrl+Alt+W) to control how text in columns wraps around the pull-quote.

CROSS-REF   InDesign lets you anchor a sidebar, pull-quote, or other frame to a specific spot in the text so that it follows that text as the text reflows. Chapter 13 covers this capability in detail. It also covers text wrap in detail.

Optical Margin Alignment

When display type such as a pull-quote or a headline in ads is left-aligned or justified, the edges can look uneven due to the gaps above, below, or next to quotation marks, punctuation, and some capital letters, as shown in the text frame at right in Figure 19.4. To correct the unevenness, graphic designers use a technique called *hanging punctuation* — which InDesign calls *optical margin alignment* — in which they extend the punctuation slightly beyond the edges of the rest of the text as shown in the text frame at left in Figure 19.4.

FIGURE 19.4

Notice the difference between the text frame at right with Optical Margin Alignment enabled and the text frame at left with standard alignment.

Discover Undiscovered Spain: The Picos de Europa

Discover Undiscovered Spain: The Picos de Europa

The *edge* of text is defined by the edges of the text frame or any Inset Spacing specified in the Text Frame Options dialog box (Object ⇨ Text Frame Options, or ⌘+B or Ctrl+B).

InDesign's Optical Margin Alignment option automates hanging punctuation, extending punctuation and the edges of some glyphs (such as a capital *T*) slightly outside the edges of the text.

Unfortunately, you can't control how much the characters "hang" outside the text boundaries — InDesign decides that for you. And optical margin alignment applies to all the text frames in a story, rather than to just the highlighted text. This means you need to isolate into its own story any text for which you want hanging punctuation.

To specify optical margin alignment, select any text frame in a story and choose Window ⇨ Type & Tables ⇨ Story to open the Story panel. Enable the Optical Margin Alignment option, as shown in Figure 19.4.

NOTE In general, optical margin alignment improves the look of display type whether it's left-aligned, centered, justified, or even right-aligned. However, optical margin alignment actually causes columns of body text to look uneven (because they are).

You can disable optical margin alignment for specific paragraphs, while keeping it applied to the rest of the story's text by using either of the following techniques:

- For selected paragraphs, choose Ignore Optical Margin in the Paragraph panel's flyout menu.
- For all paragraphs using a specific paragraph style, enable the Ignore Optical Margin check box in the Indents and Spacing pane of the New Paragraph Style or Paragraph Style Options dialog box. (See Chapter 20 for details on creating and editing styles.)

NEW FEATURE The ability to override optical margin alignment for individual paragraphs and via paragraph styles is new to InDesign CS3.

End-of-Story Markers

In magazines, newsletters, and other publications with multiple stories, the text often continues from one page to the next. In news magazines, a story might meander from page to page, interrupted by sidebars and ads. In a fashion magazine, stories generally open on a splashy spread, and then continue on text-heavy pages at the back of the magazine. In either case, readers can get confused about whether a story has ended. Designers solve this by placing a *dingbat* (a special character such as a square) at the end of each story.

You can use any dingbat character — in Zapf Dingbats, DF Organics, Woodtype, or Wingdings, for example — or an inline graphic to mark the end of a story. The end-of-story marker should reflect the overall design and feel of a publication or emphasize the content. You might see a square used in a financial publication, a heart in a teen magazine, or a leaf in a gardening magazine. A derivative of the company's logo might even be used to mark the end of a story — you can easily envision the Nike swoosh used in this way.

To place a dingbat, first decide on the character and create a character style for it. If you're using a graphic, you might consider converting it to a font with a utility such as FontLab Studio so you can insert it as text and format it consistently using a character style. If you're using an inline graphic, you might store it in an InDesign library (see Chapter 7) so it's easily accessible. Make sure everyone working on the publication knows the keystroke for entering the dingbat or the location of the graphic.

Once you have the character established, you need to decide where to place it. Generally, the dingbat will be flush with the right margin or right after the final punctuation in the last line:

- To place the dingbat flush with the right margin, there are two ways to set a right-aligned tab:
  - One is to choose Type ⇨ Insert Special Character ⇨ Other ⇨ Right Indent Tab, or just press Shift+Tab.
  - The other way is to set a tab stop in the paragraph style you use for final paragraphs (see Chapter 22 for more details on setting tabs). Because InDesign offers an easier method to right-indent a dingbat, you should use this method only if you want to right-align the dingbat to a place in the column other than at the right margin — essentially, if you want to have it indented a little from the right margin.
- When placing the dingbat after the final punctuation, I recommend clearly separating the two with an en space by typing Shift+⌘+N or Ctrl+Shift+N, or with an em space by typing Shift+⌘+M or Ctrl+Shift+M.

Underline and Strikethrough Options

InDesign lets you create custom underlines and strikethroughs. While you'll use these sparingly, they can be effective for design-oriented text presentation, such as in the examples shown in Figure 19.5.

The Character panel's and Control panel's flyout menus provide the Underline Options and Strikethrough Options menu items to create custom versions. (You must have the Character pane of the Control panel selected to get these options; click the **A** iconic button to display it.) The process for the two is similar:

1. **Highlight the text to which you want to apply the custom underline or strikethrough.**

2. **Specify the thickness, type, color, and other settings for the line that makes up the underline or the strikethrough line.** Note that if you choose a line type that has gaps — such as dashed, dotted, or striped lines — you can also choose a gap color, such as was done for the top example in Figure 19.5. Figure 19.6 shows the Strikethrough Options and Underline Options dialog boxes.

3. **Apply the underline style through the Control panel or Character panel, or use the keyboard shortcut (Shift+⌘+U or Ctrl+Shift+U).** Apply the strikethrough style through the Control panel or Character panel, or use the keyboard shortcut (Shift+⌘+/ or Ctrl+Shift+/).

FIGURE 19.5

Examples of custom underlines and strikethroughs

A custom underline or strikethrough created and applied this way is in effect only for the first text to which an underline or a strikethrough is applied. InDesign reverts to the standard settings the next time you apply an underline or strikethrough using the Character panel or Control panel or by using the shortcuts Shift+⌘+U or Ctrl Shift+U for underlines and Shift+⌘+/ or Ctrl+Shift+/ for strikethroughs.

CROSS-REF If you want to use a custom underline or strikethrough setting repeatedly, you should define the setting as part of a character style, as described in Chapter 20.

FIGURE 19.6

The Strikethrough Options (top) and Underline Options (bottom) dialog boxes. In both, the Type pop-up menu at the right provides the list of line types available.

InDesign has no equivalent to QuarkXPress's Underline Styles. Instead, specify custom underlines and strikethroughs as part of a character style. First, add stripes and dashed lines as stroke styles in the Strokes panel (choose Window ➪ Stroke, or press ⌘+F10 or Ctrl+F10), and select the Stroke Styles option from the flyout menu, as described in Chapter 12. To use a stroke style as an underline option in the New Character Style or Character Style Options dialog box, go to the Underline Options pane and choose the stroke style from the Type pop-up menu.

Converting text into shapes

If you want to use the shape of a letter or the combined shapes of several letters as a frame for text or a graphic, you could test your skill with the Pen tool and create the letter shapes yourself. But getting hand-drawn characters to look just the way you want them to can take lots of time. A quicker solution is to use the Create Outlines command to convert text characters into editable outlines. The Create Outlines command is particularly useful if you want to hand-tweak the shapes of characters, particularly at display font sizes, or place text or a graphic within character shapes.

TIP If all you need to do is apply a stroke or fill to characters within text, you don't have to convert the characters into outlines. Instead, use the Stroke panel, as I explain in Chapter 12.

When you use the Create Outlines command, you have the choice of creating an inline compound path that replaces the original text or an independent compound path that's placed directly on top of the original letters in its own frame. If you want the text outlines to flow with the surrounding text, create an inline compound path. If you want to use the outlines elsewhere, create an independent compound path.

To convert text into outlines:

1. **Use the Type tool to highlight the characters you want to convert into outlines.** Generally, this feature works best with large font sizes.

2. **Choose Type ➪ Create Outlines, or press Shift+⌘+O or Ctrl+Shift+O (that's the letter O, not a zero).** If you hold down the Option or Alt key when you choose Create Outlines, or if you press Shift+Option+⌘+O or Ctrl+Alt+Shift+O, a compound path is created and placed in front of the text. In this case, you can use either of the selection tools to move the resulting compound path. If you don't hold down Option or Alt when you choose Create Outlines, an inline compound path is created: This object replaces the original text and flows with the surrounding text.

When you create outlines out of a range of highlighted characters, a compound path is created, and each of the characters becomes a subpath. You can use the Release (Compound Path) command (Object ➪ Paths ➪ Release Compound Path, or Option+Shift+⌘+8 or Ctrl+Alt+Shift+8) to turn each of the subpaths into independent paths, as described in Chapter 28.

After you create text outlines, you can modify the paths the same as you can modify hand-drawn paths — by selecting them with the Direct Selection tool and then adding, deleting, or moving anchor points; clicking and dragging direction handles; and converting smooth points to corner points and vice versa. You can also use the transformation tools, the Control panel (Window ➪ Control, or Option+⌘+6 or Ctrl+Alt+6), and the Transform panel (Window ➪ Transform) to change the appearance of text outlines. You cannot, however, edit text after converting it to outlines.

Additionally, you can use the Place command (File ⇨ Place, or ⌘+D or Ctrl+D) or the Paste Into command (Edit ⇨ Paste Into, or Option+⌘+V or Ctrl+Alt+V) to import text or a graphic into the frames created by converting text to graphics.

Making Text Follow a Path

InDesign lets you have text follow any open or closed path, such as a line or frame. Simply select the path or shape with the Type on a Path tool, which is available from the Type tool's pop-out menu. Now start typing (or paste or place) your text.

Once you have entered the text and formatted it with font, size, color, and so forth, you can apply special effects to it using the Type on a Path Options dialog box, which you access by choosing Type ⇨ Type on a Path ⇨ Options and then selecting from its options.

NEW FEATURE   You can also double-click the Type on a Path tool to open the Type on a Path Options dialog box.

Figure 19.7 shows the dialog box and several examples of its formatting. In the dialog box:

- Use the Effect pop-up menu to choose an effect (the options show previews of each one).
- Use the Align pop-up menu to choose what part of the text is aligned (Baseline, Center, Ascender, or Descender).
- Use the To Path pop-up menu to choose whether to align to the center, bottom, or top of the path.
- Flip the text by selecting the Flip option.
- Change the text's spacing by entering a value in the Spacing field (positive numbers space out the text, while negative ones contract it).

FIGURE 19.7

The Type on a Path Options dialog box lets you apply special effects, alignment, and flip to text following a path.

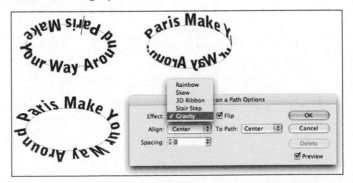

Summary

InDesign gives you the power to embellish and manipulate text in almost infinite ways. It's your responsibility to format text in ways that clarify and reinforce the content rather than simply decorate it.

Bulleted lists — often created with special character bullets — help break out information. So do numbered lists.

If your text uses fractions, you have several ways to format them, depending on the fonts you have: automatically with OpenType, by selecting the specific fraction in an Type 1 PostScript Expert Collection font or by manually creating the fraction using baseline shifts, size changes, and kerning on each character.

You can pull readers into a story with sidebars and pull-quotes, which also break up text-heavy areas. For display type, InDesign provides an automatic method for hanging punctuation outside the margins. The use of special characters at the end of the story is an effective way to let the reader know the story is complete; you can help these dingbats' visual appearance by preceding them with a special space or a right tab.

Underline and strikethroughs need not be the standard lines everyone uses; InDesign lets you create custom lines — dotted, dashed, multiline, and others — for a little extra pizzazz.

Desktop publishing has blurred the line between text and graphics, so it's no surprise you can convert text to frames, which lets you treat them as graphics. You can also have text follow the contours of a shape or line.

Chapter 20

Setting Up Styles

I f you were assigned the task of making 500 star-shaped cookies, the first thing you'd do is find a star-shaped cookie cutter. Of course, you could shape each cookie by hand, but not only would this take considerably more time than using a cookie cutter, no two cookies would look exactly the same. Think of styles as cookie cutters for formatting text. They save you time and ensure consistency. If you'll be using InDesign to create long documents that require considerable text formatting, styles are indispensable.

InDesign lets you create two types of textual styles:

- A *character style* is a set of character-level formats you can apply to range of highlighted text in a single step.

- A *paragraph style* is a set of both character- *and* paragraph-level formats you can apply to selected paragraphs in a single step.

> **NOTE** InDesign calls these *styles*, not *style sheets* as other programs such as Microsoft Word and QuarkXPress do. I personally prefer *style sheet* because that term has a longer history in publishing terminology and because *style* is also used to indicate font styles such as boldface and italics. But in this book, I'm sticking with the InDesign term *style*.

> **CROSS-REF** InDesign also lets you create styles for objects such as frames and lines, as Chapter 13 explains. And you can create styles for tables and cells, as covered in Chapter 22.

In one respect, styles are far superior to cookie cutters. If you use a cookie cutter to create hundreds of cookies and then find out your cookies are the wrong shape, you're out of luck. But if you use a style to format hundreds of pieces of text and then decide you don't like the look of the formatted text, you can simply modify the style. Any text you've formatted with a style is automatically updated if you modify the style.

IN THIS CHAPTER

Creating and applying paragraph and character styles

Working with nested styles

Modifying style-formatted text

Modifying styles

Importing styles

When it comes to using styles, it's as important to know when *not* to use them as it is to know *when* to use them. For short documents—especially one-pagers such as business cards, ads, and posters—that contain relatively little text and don't use the same formats repeatedly, you're probably better off formatting the text by hand.

Creating and Applying Styles

Before you can use a style to format text, you must create it. You can create styles whenever you want, but usually, creating styles is one of the first tasks you tackle when working on a long document. Also, you may want to create your paragraph styles first and then, if necessary, add character styles. In many cases, character styles are used to format text within paragraphs to which paragraph styles have already been applied.

Note that InDesign comes with a predefined default paragraph style called [Basic Paragraph] that text in a new frame automatically has applied to it. You can edit [Basic Paragraph] like any other style. Similarly, there's a predefined character style called [Basic Character].

Note that this chapter assumes you know how to use the character and paragraph formatting tools covered in Chapters 17 and 18, respectively. Also, text in your layout may already have styles applied, using styles defined in Microsoft Word, as explained in Chapter 14.

TIP If you have a smallish monitor, set at 1024x768 pixels—the norm for a 17-inch display—the Character Styles and Paragraph Styles panels are shoved to the bottom of the panel dock, and when selected the only thing you see is their panel tab and flyout menu icon. You have a few choices: Shorten other panel groups in the dock to make room for them, remove other panel groups to make room for them, or drag them out of the dock and make them floating.

Paragraph styles

Let's say you've been given the job of creating a newsletter. It will be several pages long and contain several stories. Each story will have the same text elements: a big headline, a smaller headline, an author byline, and body text. The stories will also include pictures, and each picture requires a caption and a credit line. Before you begin laying out pages and formatting text, you should create styles for all these repetitive text elements. The Paragraph Styles panel (Type ➪ Paragraph Styles, or ⌘+F11 or Ctrl+F11), shown in Figure 20.1, is where you need to go for both creating and applying styles.

NEW FEATURE The shortcut for accessing the Paragraph Styles panel has changed to ⌘+F11 or Ctrl+F11 in InDesign CS3 from just F11 in previous versions. The old shortcut still works but may interfere with the Mac OS X's Exposé program.

FIGURE 20.1

The Paragraph Styles panel and its flyout menu

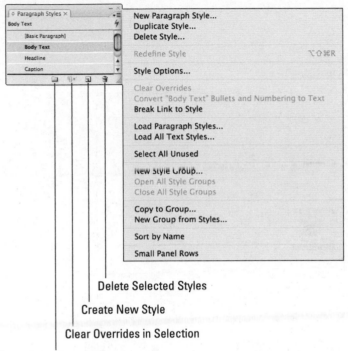

Delete Selected Styles

Create New Style

Clear Overrides in Selection

Create New Style Group

Creating paragraph styles

The easiest way to create a paragraph style is to manually apply character- and paragraph-level formats to a sample paragraph and then — with the sample paragraph selected — follow the next set of steps. If no text is selected when you create a style, you'll have to specify character- and paragraph-level formats as you create the style, which is more difficult than formatting a paragraph in advance. Here's how you create a paragraph style from a preformatted paragraph:

1. **If it's not displayed, show the Paragraph Style panel by choosing Type ⇨ Paragraph Styles, or pressing ⌘+F11 or Ctrl+F11.** You can also choose Window ⇨ Type & Tables ⇨ Paragraph Styles.

2. **Make sure you highlight a paragraph that's been styled with all the character and paragraph formats you want to include in your style, and then choose New Style from the Paragraph Styles panel's flyout menu, as shown in Figure 20.1.** The New Paragraph Style dialog box, shown in Figure 20.2, appears. You can also create a new style by clicking the Create New Style button (the page icon) at the bottom of the

Paragraph Styles panel. When you click this button, a new style with a default name (Paragraph Style 1, Paragraph Style 2, and so on) is added to the list. The formats applied to the selected paragraph are included in the new style; the New Paragraph Style dialog box is not displayed.

FIGURE 20.2

The New Paragraph Style dialog box

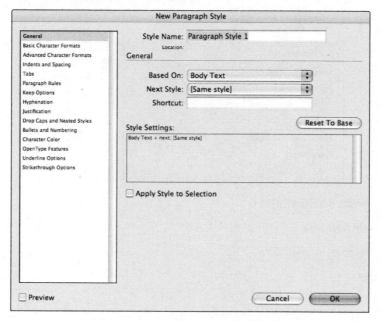

3. **Type a name for the style in the Style Name field.** Assign your style names with care; be descriptive. Imagine that somebody else will be using the document, and assign a name that conveys the purpose of the style. For example, anybody will know what a style called Body Copy is used for, but a style called Really Cool Style won't mean anything to anybody but you.

4. **Change character- or paragraph-level formats.** The scroll list to the left of the dialog box shows 15 options, as shown in Figure 20.2. If you want to change any character- or paragraph-level formats, choose the appropriate option to switch to the relevant pane, and then make your changes.

5. **Use the Based On pop-up menu, which displays the names of other paragraph styles, to create families of styles.** For example, you could create a style called Body Copy/Base for the bulk of your body text, and then create variations such as Body Text/Drop Cap, Body Text/No Indent, and Body Text/Italic. If you use the Based On pop-

up menu to base each of the variations on Body Text/Base and you then modify this parent style, your changes are applied to all the variations. By default, a new style is not based on anything, so [No Paragraph Style] displays in this pop-up menu.

TIP If you've created a style based on another, and you don't like the changes you've made, you can rest the style to be the same as its based-on style by clicking Reset To Base.

6. **To automatically switch from the style you are creating to another style as you type text, choose a style from the Next Style pop-up menu.** If you specify a Next Style for a style, it's automatically applied to a new paragraph when you press Return or Enter. If you choose [Same Style] (the default), the style you're creating continues to be applied to new paragraphs when you press Return or Enter while typing. Typically, you'd use the Next Style feature for things like headlines that are always followed by a specific kind of paragraph (like a byline). And you'd typically use [Same Style] for body text, where the next paragraph usually has the same formatting.

7. **Assign a keyboard shortcut.** If you want to (and you often should), you can assign a keyboard shortcut to a style (Windows users must make sure Num Lock is on). Press and hold any combination of ⌘, Option, and Shift, or Ctrl, Alt, and Shift, and press any number on the keypad. (Letters and non-keypad numbers cannot be used for keyboard shortcuts.)

8. **When you're done specifying the attributes of your style, click OK.**

NEW FEATURE If you want to apply a new style to text that is selected, be sure to check the Apply Style to Selection check box before clicking OK to save the new style.

Applying paragraph styles

After you create a paragraph style, applying it is easy. Just click within a paragraph or highlight text in a range of paragraphs, and then click on the style name in the Paragraph Styles panel or press its keyboard shortcut. (Windows users must make sure Num Lock is on when using shortcuts for styles.)

NOTE If your selected paragraphs have more than one paragraph style applied within the group, the Paragraph Styles panel displays the text *(Mixed)* at the lower left.

When you apply a style to selected paragraphs, all local formats and applied character styles are retained. All other formats are replaced by those of the applied style.

CROSS-REF InDesign has a Quick Apply panel that lets you apply any style — object, paragraph, or character — as well as other saved settings from one location. Chapter 2 covers this panel.

Overriding existing formatting

If you press and hold Option or Alt when clicking on a name in the Paragraph Styles panel, any character styles that have been applied within selected paragraphs are retained, as are the following character formats: Superscript, Subscript, Underline, Strikethrough, Language, and Baseline Shift. If you press and hold Option+Shift or Alt+Shift when clicking a style name, all local formatting, including any character styles, within the selected paragraphs is removed.

InDesign Styles for QuarkXPress Users

InDesign handles character formatting differently than QuarkXPress does in its style sheets. QuarkXPress lets paragraph style sheets get their character formatting from character style sheets. That lets character style sheets do double-duty: They can be the basis for character formatting in paragraph styles and also be used independently on text selections.

InDesign does not work this way—you specify the character formatting in the paragraph style, and use character styles only for text selections. This can be frustrating if you have several styles that use the same character formatting; if that basic formatting needs to change, InDesign forces you to update each paragraph style separately. In QuarkXPress, you can just update the underlying character style sheet.

But the downside to QuarkXPress's approach is that if the underlying character style sheet changes, *all* paragraph styles sheets using it are affected. InDesign, instead, has you define a simple paragraph style with the character attributes and then has similar paragraph styles based on that first style sheet. The new styles can have different character settings, so if the parent paragraph style sheet's character attributes change, only the children styles' non-overridden attributes also change.

You can also use the Clear Overrides button at the bottom of the panel or the Clear Overrides option in the flyout menu. Either way, you remove all formatting that conflicts with the style's formatting—unless you press and hold ⌘ or Ctrl, which clears character formatting only, or Shift+⌘ or Ctrl+Shift, which clears paragraph formatting only.

If you want to remove a style from a paragraph, so it's not changed if the style is later changed, choose Break Link to Style from the flyout menu. The upper left of the panel displays the text "(No Style)".

A few last words about paragraph styles: There are no hard-and-fast rules about how best to implement them. Like handwriting, you should develop your own style. How many styles you create, the names you use, whether you apply them with keyboard shortcuts or through the Paragraph Styles panel, and whether you use paragraph styles, character styles, or both are all matters of personal taste. One thing is indisputable: You should use styles whenever possible; they are a layout artist's best friend.

Managing paragraph styles

The Paragraph Styles panel's flyout menu, shown in Figure 20.1, displays 18 options for managing styles; three iconic buttons at the bottom of the panel let you reapply, create, and delete paragraph styles. Here's a brief description of each option:

- **New Paragraph Style:** This option creates a new paragraph style. When you choose New Paragraph Style, the New Paragraph Style dialog box appears. The panel also has an iconic button to create a new style.

- **Duplicate Style:** Click on a style name, and then click this button to create an exact copy. If you want to create a style that's similar to one you've already created, you can choose New Paragraph Style rather than Duplicate, and then use the Based On option to create a child of the original. If you choose Duplicate, the copy is identical to but not based on the original; if you modify the original, the copy is not affected.

- **Delete Style:** Choose this option to delete highlighted styles. To select multiple styles, press and hold ⌘ or Ctrl as you click on their names. To select a range of styles, click the first one, and then press and hold Shift and click the last one.

> **NOTE** InDesign gives you the option of replacing a deleted style with another style. You can also choose [No Paragraph Style] if you no longer want a style applied. In that case, select the Preserve Formatting option to convert the unapplied style's formatting to local formatting, or deselect it to make the text lose that formatting as well as its style.

- **Redefine Style (Option+Shift+⌘+R or Ctrl+Alt+Shift+R):** This option lets you modify an existing style. Highlight text to which the style you want to modify has been applied, change the formats as desired, and then click Redefine Style. The newly applied formats are applied to the style.

- **Style Options:** This option lets you modify an existing style. When a style is highlighted in the Paragraph Styles panel, choosing Style Options displays the Paragraph Style Options dialog box, which is identical to the New Paragraph Style dialog box.

- **Clear Overrides:** This option removes any local formatting such as boldface or small caps applied to the selected paragraphs. Note that the text within the paragraph that has the local overrides must be selected; you cannot simply just click anywhere in the paragraph. This is simply a more obvious alternative when clicking a style name to pressing and holding Option or Alt to remove local formatting (but retain any character styles applied) or to pressing and holding Option+Shift or Alt+Shift to remove both local formatting and applied character styles.

- **Convert "*current style name*" Bullets and Numbering to Text:** This option removes any automatic bullets or numbering defined through InDesign's bulleted and numbered lists feature from selected paragraphs (see Chapter 19). The paragraphs that this option is applied to still have bullets and numbers, but they are no longer updated if the style is changed or if paragraphs are added or deleted (this normally would add bullets and adjust numbering).

- **Break Link to Style:** This option removes the style from the paragraph but leaves it with the formatting, now converted to local formatting. That way, the selected paragraph won't be changed if the paragraph style is later changed. Once you remove a style from a paragraph, InDesign displays "(No Style)" at the bottom of the Paragraph Styles panel when the paragraph is selected.

- **Load Paragraph Styles:** Choose this option if you want to import styles from another InDesign document. (I discuss importing styles in detail later in this chapter.)

Applying a Sequence of Styles All at Once

InDesign has a neat capability that lets you apply multiple styles to selected text. First, define the various styles, and be sure that each style has a different style selected in the Next Style pop-up menu in the Paragraph Style Options or New Paragraph Style dialog boxes. For example, if you have Headline, Byline, and Body Copy styles, make sure that Headline has Byline selected in Next Style and that Byline has Body Copy selected in Next Style.

Then highlight all the text that uses this sequence of styles. Now Control+click or right-click Headline and select Apply "Headline" + Next Style from the contextual menu. InDesign will apply Headline to the first paragraph, Byline to the second paragraph, and Body Copy to the rest.

- **Load All Text Styles:** This option lets you import both paragraph and character styles from another InDesign document. (I discuss importing styles in detail later in this chapter.)

- **Select All Unused:** Select this option to highlight the names of all paragraph styles that have not been applied to any paragraphs. This is a handy way of identifying unused styles in preparation for deleting them (by choosing the Delete Style option).

- **The five style group options:** I cover these in the next section.

- **Sort by Name:** Normally, styles are added to the panel in the order you create them. To alphabetize the list, select this option.

- **Small Panel Rows:** Click this option to reduce the text size in the Paragraph Styles panel. Although harder to read, a panel with this option set lets you access more styles without having to scroll. To return the panel to its normal text size, select this option again.

NEW FEATURE   The Sort by Name option is new to InDesign CS3.

Using style groups

To help you find the desired style in documents that have dozens of them, InDesign lets you create style groups, which create a folder in the styles panel's style list that you can open and close as desired. To create a group, choose New Style Group from the panel's flyout menu or click the Create New Style Group iconic button (the folder icon) on the bottom of the panel.

Or you can select multiple styles in the panel and choose New Group from Styles in the flyout menu. (Note that this option is grayed out if you have selected any of the predefined styles — [None] and either [Basic Paragraph] or [Basic Character].)

Enter a name in the dialog box that appears and click OK.

NEW FEATURE   Style groups are new to InDesign CS3.

To add styles to an existing group (which will have a folder icon to the left of its name in the panel list), you have two options:

- You can drag any desired styles into the group.
- You can copy a selected style to the group by choosing Copy to Group and then selecting the target group in the dialog box that appears.

To quickly open all groups, choose Open All Groups in the panel's flyout menu. To quickly close them all, choose Close All Groups.

Character styles

Character styles are nearly identical in every respect to paragraph styles, but instead of using them to format selected paragraphs, you use character styles to apply character-level formats to a high-lighted range of text. For example, you can use a character style to:

- Modify the appearance of the first several words in a paragraph. For example, some publications, particularly magazines, use a type-style variation such as small caps as a lead-in for a paragraph. You can use a character style not only to switch the type style to small caps, but also to change size, color, font family, and so on.
- Apply formatting to part of a paragraph via a paragraph style. The paragraph style controls for drop caps, nested styles, automatic bullets, and automatic numbering all rely on character styles.
- Apply different formatting to such text elements as Web site, e-mail, and FTP addresses within body text.
- Create other body text variations for such things as emphasis, book and movie titles, product and company names, and so on.

Creating and applying character styles

Using character styles is much the same as using paragraph styles. First you create them; then you apply them. And you use the Character Styles panel (Type ➪ Character Styles, or Shift+⌘+F11 or Ctrl+Shift+F11), shown in Figure 20.3, to do both. As is the case with paragraph styles, the easiest way to create a character style is to apply the character-level formats you want to use in the style to some sample text, and then follow the steps in this section. You can create a character style from scratch (that is, without preformatting any text), but if you do, you'll have to set all the character formats when you create the style.

NEW FEATURE The shortcut for accessing the Character Styles panel has changed to Shift+⌘+F11 or Ctrl+Shift+F11 in InDesign CS3 from Shift+F11 in previous versions. The old shortcuts still work but may interfere with the Mac OS X's Exposé program.

NEW FEATURE If your selected text has more than one character style applied within the selection, the Character Styles panel displays the text "(Mixed)" at the lower left.

FIGURE 20.3

The Character Styles panel and its flyout menu

Create New Style Group | Delete Selected Styles

Create New Style

To create a character style from highlighted text:

1. **If it's not displayed, show the Character Style panel by choosing Type ⇨ Character Styles, or pressing Shift+⌘+F11 or Ctrl+Shift+F11.** You can also choose Window ⇨ Type & Tables ⇨ Character Styles.

2. **Make sure you highlight text that's been styled with all the character formats you want to include in your style, and then choose New Style from the Character Styles panel's flyout menu.** The New Character Style dialog box, shown in Figure 20.4, appears.

   You can also create a new style by clicking the Create New Style iconic button (the page icon) at the bottom of the panel. When you click this button, a new style with a default name (Character Style 1, Character Style 2, and so on) is added to the list. The formats applied to the selected text are included in the new style; the New Character Style dialog box is not displayed.

3. **Type a name for the style in the Style Name field.**

4. **Choose the appropriate option from the scroll list to the left of the Style Name field to open the relevant pane if you want to change any character-level formats.** The list displays seven options: General, Basic Character Formats, Advanced Character Formats, Character Color, OpenType Features, Underline Options, and Strikethrough Options.

5. **Use the Based On pop-up menu to create families of styles.** This menu displays the names of other character styles. For example, you could create a style called Body Copy/Base Character that uses the same character attributes as your base Body Copy paragraph style and then create variations such as Body Text/Emphasis, Body Text/URLs, and so on. If you use the Based On pop-up menu to base each of the variations on Body Text/Base Character and you modify this parent style, your changes are applied to all the variations.

FIGURE 20.4

The New Character Style dialog box

 If you've created a style based on another, and you don't like the changes you've made, you can rest the style to be the same as its based-on style by clicking Reset To Base.

6. **If you want (and you should), you can assign a keyboard shortcut to a style (Windows users should make sure that Num Lock is on).** Press and hold any combination of ⌘, Option, and Shift, or Ctrl, Alt, and Shift, and press any number on the keypad. (Letters and non-keypad numbers cannot be used for keyboard shortcuts.)

7. **When you're done specifying the attributes of your style, click OK.**

NEW FEATURE If you want to apply a new style to text that is selected, be sure to check the Apply Style to Selection check box before clicking OK to save the new style.

Overriding character styles

Overriding existing formatting via character styles does work differently than overriding formatting in paragraph styles in two ways.

First, when you remove the link to a character style, the Character Styles panel displays [None] as the current style in its style list. When you remove the link to a paragraph style, the Paragraph Styles panel shows no style in the style list but instead displays "(No Style)" at the bottom of the panel.

Second, there is no Clear Overrides iconic button in the Character Styles panel (nor does the shortcut of Option+Shift+clicking or Alt+Shift+clicking perform this function). Instead, you apply the [None] style to clear a character style from text. Note that if you later apply a paragraph style to text with [None] character style, the text will take on the paragraph style's formatting rather than retain its local formatting.

But as with paragraph styles, you can break the link of text to its character style by choosing Break Link to Style from the flyout menu.

Managing and grouping character styles

The options displayed in the Character Styles panel's flyout menu are the same as those for the Paragraph Styles panel's flyout menu, which are explained earlier in this chapter.

Similarly, style groups work the same way for character styles as they do for paragraph styles.

Working with Nested Styles

Often, you'll want to apply character formatting in a consistent manner to many paragraphs. For example, you may want to change the font for the first character in a bulleted list so that the correct symbol appears for the bullet. Or you might want to italicize the numerals in a numbered list. Or you might want the first four words of body text that appear after a headline to be boldface and in small caps. Or you might want the first sentence in instructional paragraphs to be in italics. InDesign lets you automate such formatting through the nested styles feature.

Figure 20.5 shows an example of nested styles in use, along with the Paragraph Style Options dialog box's Drop Caps and Nested Styles pane in which you create them. Here, you can see that the first sentence of the introductory paragraph's text is set to appear in italics.

Here's how the nested styles work:

1. **Define any character styles that you'll apply to text through a nested style.** Even if all you're doing is making text italic, you need to define a character style to do so. The nested styles feature cannot apply any attributes other than those available in a character style.

2. **Open the Paragraph Styles panel (Type ⇨ Paragraph Styles, or ⌘+F11 or Ctrl+F11), choose Style Options from the flyout menu to open the Paragraph Style Options dialog box, and go to the Drop Caps and Nested Styles pane.**

3. **Click New Nested Style.** An entry appears in the Nested Styles section of the dialog box. This is what will be applied to text.

4. **Click the style name in the Nested Styles section of the pane to choose from an existing character style.** When you click the style name, a list of other styles appears, including [None], which uses the paragraph style's default formatting.

You also have the [Repeat] option, which if selected lets you repeat a sequence of previous styles. (You choose the number in the third column.)

FIGURE 20.5

You can use a nested style to set the first sentence in the introductory paragraph in italics. The scope options, shown in the pop-down menu, for a nested style determine what text receives the specified formatting.

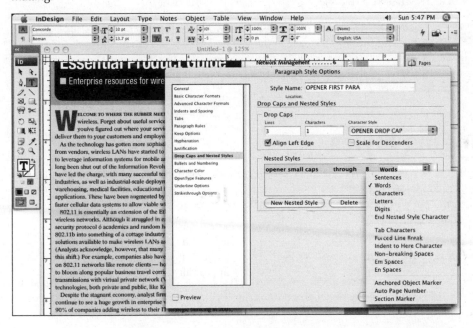

5. **Click in the second column to determine the scope end point.** Your choices are Through or Up To. For example, if you choose Through for a nested style that is set for four words, all four words will get the nested style. If you choose Up To, the first three words get the style and the fourth doesn't.

6. **In the third column, specify how many items you want InDesign to count in determining the scope's endpoint.** For example, if you want to have the first seven characters have the style applied, type 7. If you want to have the style applied up to the first tab, type 1.

7. **Click the item in the fourth column to specify the scope of text to which you're applying the nested styles.** Figure 20.5 shows the options. They break into three groups: a number of items (characters, words, and so on), a specific character (tab, em space, and so on), and a specific marker character (inline graphic marker, auto page number, and section marker). Whatever you choose needs to be consistent in all your text because InDesign will follow these rules slavishly.

8. **Create multiple nested styles in one paragraph with different rules for each.**
   Obviously, you may not need to do this, but the option exists. InDesign applies the styles in the order in which they appear in the dialog box, and each starts where the other ends. Use the up and down arrow iconic buttons at the bottom of the dialog box to change the order of nested styles.

9. **Select the Preview option to preview the formatting if you selected sample text before opening the dialog box.**

10. **Click OK when you're done.**

NOTE   The Nested Styles feature is included in the same dialog box as the Drop Caps feature. That's because a drop cap would be the first nested style in a paragraph and can never be anything but the first style. By combining the two into one dialog box, InDesign lets you treat a drop cap as part of a series of styles to be applied to a paragraph. If you want only a drop cap, you simply don't create a nested style.

Changing Styles

If you scratch your name into wet cement, you have only a few minutes to change your mind. After that, your formatting decisions are cast in stone, so to speak. Fortunately, styles are much more forgiving. Not only can you modify a style whenever you want, you're free to manually modify text to which styles have been applied.

Modifying styles

The most important thing to know about modifying a style is that all text to which a modified style has been applied is automatically updated. Additionally, if you modify a parent style, all children styles that were created by choosing Based On are also automatically updated.

There are three ways to modify an existing style. You can:

■ **Click the style name in the Character Styles or Paragraph Styles panel, and then choose Style Options from the panel's flyout menu.** The Character Style Options or the Paragraph Style Options dialog box appears.

■ Double-click a style name to display the Character Style Options or Paragraph Style Options dialog box.

■ **Control+click or right-click a style name and choose Edit "*style name*" from the contextual menu to display the Character Style Options or Paragraph Style Options dialog box.**

Either way, these dialog boxes are the same as the New Character Style and New Paragraph Style dialog boxes, respectively. Make whatever changes you want, and then click OK. Any text with the styles applied will be updated automatically with the new formatting.

The First Line Effect

About the only thing missing from the nested styles feature is, unfortunately, an effect favored by many designers: applying a format to the first line in a paragraph, usually a paragraph that follows a headline. The most common version of this has the first line formatted in all small caps and then switches to normal capitalization for the rest of the paragraph.

InDesign's nested styles feature doesn't support this effect because it requires a specific stop point (number of characters, words, or sentences, or a specific character such as a tab, line break, indent-to-here, em space, en space, or the end-nested-style character, which lets you set an arbitrary end). But there is no definite endpoint at the end of the line, as it depends on how InDesign flows and breaks the text, which is different for each paragraph's first line.

The best you can do is highlight these manually and apply the small caps attribute yourself, or use the nested styles feature and manually insert either the forced line break or the end-nested-style character at the end of each line. It's easier to enter a forced line break — just type Shift+Enter or Shift+Return instead of choosing Type ⇨ Insert White Space ⇨ Forced Line Break. If you prefer to use the end-nested-style character, you have to choose Type ⇨ Insert Special Character ⇨ Other ⇨ End Nested Style Here.

Modifying text that's been styled with a style

If you need to change the appearance of text that's been formatted using a style, all you have to do is highlight the text — characters or paragraphs — and then use the Control panel, Character panel (Type ⇨ Character, or ⌘+T or Ctrl+T), or the Paragraph panel (Type ⇨ Paragraph, or Option+⌘+T or Ctrl+Alt+T) to change the formats.

When you change any formats in text to which a style has been applied, you are making local changes (to make global changes, you would modify the style). When you change formatting in style-formatted text, a plus sign (+) appears next to the style name in the Character Styles or Paragraph Styles panel, as shown in Figure 20.6.

FIGURE 20.6

The plus sign (+) next to the style name in the Paragraph Styles panel indicates that local formatting has been applied within a paragraph, overriding the style's attributes. The Character Styles panel uses the same symbol to indicate the use of local formatting as well.

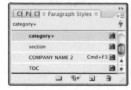

Importing Styles

If you create a style, you never have to re-create it, assuming you save the document that contains the styles. InDesign lets you import character and paragraph style from one document into another. Also, when you import text files from word processing programs that use style sheets, you can import the style sheets along with the text.

Importing styles from InDesign documents

The Paragraph Styles and Character Styles panels' flyout menus contain commands that let you move styles between documents. The Paragraph Styles panel lets you import only paragraph styles or both paragraph and character styles; the Character Styles panel lets you import only character styles or both character and paragraph styles. Here's how you do it:

1. **If it's not displayed, show the Paragraph Styles panel by choosing Type ⇨ Paragraph Styles, or pressing ⌘+F11 or Ctrl+F11; or show the Character Styles panel by choosing Type ⇨ Character Styles, or pressing Shift+⌘+F11 or Ctrl+Shift+F11.**

2. **Choose Load Paragraph Styles from the Paragraph Styles panel's flyout menu if you want to import selected paragraph styles. Likewise, choose Load Character Styles from the Character Styles panel's flyout menu if you want to import selected character styles.** You can also choose Load All Text Styles from either panel's flyout menu if you want to import both character and paragraph styles from that other document. Regardless of what kind of types of styles you choose to import, the Open a File dialog box appears.

3. **Use the controls in the Open a File dialog box to locate the InDesign document that contains the styles you want to import.**

4. **Double-click the document name or click the document name once and then click Open.** The Load Styles dialog box, shown in Figure 20.7, appears and lists the styles in the chosen document so you can decide which ones to import.

If you import styles whose names match those in the current document, InDesign gives you a chance to allow the imported style to overwrite the current style or to leave the current style as is and rename the imported style. If there is an entry in the Conflict with Existing Style column, you can click that entry for a pop-up menu that provides two choices: Auto-Rename and Use Incoming Definition (the default). If you choose Use Incoming Style Definition, the imported style overwrites the current document's style.

Note that there are two windows at the bottom of the dialog box that list the style definitions for the currently selected style to help you decide which styles to import, as well as which ones to overwrite or rename.

You can also use the Copy (Edit ⇨ Copy, or ⌘+C or Ctrl+C) and Paste commands (Edit ⇨ Paste, or ⌘+V or Ctrl +V) to move a style from one document to another. Simply copy some text in the source document to which the style you want to move has been applied. Then display the target document and use the Paste command to place the copied text into a text frame. The Character Styles and/or Paragraph Styles panels in the target document display the names of the new, "imported" styles.

FIGURE 20.7

The Load Styles dialog box

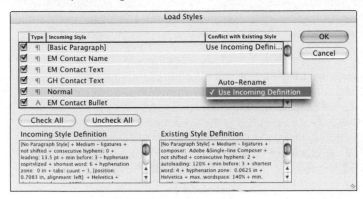

Working with style sheets in imported text files

In most workgroup publishing environments, writers generate text using Microsoft Word, and InDesign users place the text in a layout and add other design elements — imported pictures, illustrations, lines, and so on — to create a finished publication. Whether writers are producing short magazine articles or lengthy book chapters, chances are they're doing some text formatting as they write — perhaps as little as applying occasional bold or italic styles or as much as using a complete set of style sheets, if their word processor supports them.

NOTE I use the term *style sheet* to refer to the formatting capability in Microsoft Word, following Word's naming convention. And I use *style* when referring to the formatting capability in InDesign, per its naming convention. In the rest of this section, the use of the two terms should help you keep track of when I mean the style sheets from Word versus the styles in InDesign.

When you import a word processing file into InDesign, you can bring the formatting and style sheets along with the text.

A writer might use isolated formatting to indicate which styles should be applied in InDesign — for example, she might apply bold to one-line paragraphs that should be formatted as a subhead. However, if the writer applies appropriate paragraph styles to text in her word processor, much of the formatting in InDesign can be automated by importing the style sheets. To import style sheets with a word processing file, select the Retain Format option in the Place dialog box (File ➪ Place, or ⌘+D or Ctrl+D). You can determine which style sheets import and how to handle any conflicts between style names if you select the Show Import Options option in the Place dialog box.

CROSS-REF See Chapter 14 for a complete list of formatting options that will import from Word, as well as for more information about using the Place command to import text files and managing style-sheet import.

After you place a text file that contains style sheets, the Paragraph Styles panel and Character Styles panel display the names of all the imported styles.

Editing imported paragraph style sheets

If you import paragraph style sheets with text, you can simply use the style sheets specified in the word processor to format the text. This method works well for designs that do not follow a template — for example, brochures or feature stories. You might import the text, experiment with formatting it, and then edit the imported style sheets now available as styles in InDesign to reflect your design.

For example, say you import a magazine feature article that is formatted with three paragraph style sheets (Headline, Byline, and Body Copy) into an InDesign document that does not contain styles with those names. The three styles are added to InDesign's Paragraph Styles list and have similar specifications to what the same-named style sheets had in the word processor. However, because InDesign offers more formatting options, you might modify those styles to fine-tune the text formatting. To edit a paragraph style, select it in the Paragraph Styles panel, choose Style Options from the panel's flyout menu, and then make your changes in the Modify Paragraph Style Options dialog box.

Overriding imported paragraph styles

In documents that follow a template, you can provide writers with style-sheet names that must be applied to their text. For example, say you're working on a tri-fold brochure that is part of an entire series of similar tri-folds. The writer might format the text with five paragraph style sheets that also exist as styles in your InDesign document: Heads, Subheads, Body Copy, Bullets, and Quotes. The style-sheet specifications in the word processor don't matter — only the name counts — because the styles in an InDesign document override same-name style sheets in imported text files.

For example, the writer's style sheets use standard fonts such as Times and Helvetica along with bold and italic typestyles to distinguish the types of text. But when the word processing file is imported into InDesign, the style sheets are overridden with InDesign styles that have the same name but specify the actual fonts used by the designer and the many formatting options available in InDesign.

You can supply writers either with actual style sheets or with only style-sheet names:

- To supply style sheets, export text in InDesign from a similar story as a Rich Text Format (RTF) file, which writers can open in their word processor; the word processor adds the style-sheet names in the RTF file to its own style-sheet list. The writers can then save these style-sheet names to a template file and use that template for future documents. To export text, use the Export dialog box (File ➪ Export, or ⌘+E or Ctrl+E) and choose Rich Text Format from the Format pop-up menu (called Save as Type in Windows if you're not using the Version Cue interface described in Chapter 4).

- Or, you can simply give writers a list of style-sheet names that they can create themselves to their own specifications. In this case, it's particularly important that the style sheets created in the word processor have exactly the same names as those styles in the InDesign document.

Exporting styles

Although InDesign lets you export text (through the File ⇨ Export command), only a few file formats are supported: Text-only (ASCII), RTF, InCopy, and InDesign Tagged Text.

An exported RTF file keeps the style names but not the actual formatting, which can make further editing difficult in a word processor. An InDesign Tagged Text file retains the style definitions, but it does so as codes, so again it's hard to deal with in a word processor. So you really can't export styles to word processor users, just to other InDesign users.

Summary

If you're working on a document that uses the same text formats repeatedly, you can save time and ensure consistency by using styles. A style is essentially a macro for formatting text. InDesign lets you create character-level styles and paragraph-level styles. Character styles let you apply several character attributes — such as font, size, leading, kerning, and tracking — to highlighted text at once. Similarly, you can use paragraph styles to apply several paragraph formats — alignment, indents, drop caps, space before or after, and so on — simultaneously to selected paragraphs.

After you apply a style sheet to text, you can still manually modify the text by highlighting it and overriding the style's formats. And any modifications you make to the style are automatically applied to any text using it.

If you're importing a text file from Microsoft Word, you can import any applied styles along with the text, making them available as InDesign styles.

Chapter 21

Using Special Characters

InDesign is a real internationalist, supporting 27 languages and 12 variants in its spelling and hyphenation dictionaries and providing easy access to foreign characters.

Even if you publish everything in English, InDesign's linguistic flexibility is quite useful, as the same mechanism that gives you easy access to foreign characters also gives you easy access to all sorts of special symbols — such as ¢, £, ©, and ® — used in finance, mathematics, physics, and so on.

These symbols — whether regular letters, foreign characters, or special symbols — are called *glyphs*. InDesign offers menu options and keyboard shortcuts to use common glyphs, and the Glyphs panel to access specialty glyphs. Do note that many fonts have lots of glyphs available, which the Glyphs panel reveals, but you'll likely need to buy fonts, called *pi fonts*, to handle special characters used in specific fields.

 Mac and Windows fonts come with a wealth of special characters called glyphs, and Mac OS and Windows fonts often have different glyph collections. If you work across platforms, this makes it important to use the same symbol fonts on both platforms and to be sure that you know the glyphs you use are available in all the fonts you use.

IN THIS CHAPTER

Inserting special characters via menus, shortcuts, and the Glyphs panel

Creating and sharing glyphs sets

Working with OpenType character variants

Using other tools for accessing special characters

Understanding special spaces, dashes, and quotes

Working with foreign languages

Inserting Glyphs

InDesign provides three ways to insert glyphs into your text: using menus, using the Glyphs panel, and using keyboard shortcuts. Typically, you use keyboard shortcuts for the symbols you use repeatedly, the menus for ones you use less frequently (given they're organized into common usages such as spaces and dashes), and the Glyphs panel for those you use the least or that you can't access via shortcuts or menus.

Using keyboard shortcuts

Symbols are commonly used in all sorts of documents, from legal symbols to scientific ones. That's why most fonts have a selection of popular symbols built in that you can access via keyboard shortcuts. Table 21.1 shows the common symbols for Windows and Macintosh fonts. (Table 21.2, later in this chapter, shows the shortcuts for foreign characters such as accented letters.)

CROSS-REF   When you're searching and replacing text via the Find/Change dialog box, InDesign uses codes to indicate special symbols, as well as lets you paste the symbol into its Find What and Change To fields. Chapter 16 covers this in more detail.

TABLE 21.1

Shortcuts for Common Symbols

Character	Mac Shortcut	Windows Shortcut
Legal		
Copyright (©)	Option+G	Shift+Alt+C or Ctrl+Alt+C or Alt+0169
Registered trademark (®)	Option+R	Shift+Alt+R or Alt+0174
Trademark (™)	Option+2	Shift+Alt+2 or Alt+0153
Paragraph (¶)	Option+7	Shift+Alt+7 or Ctrl+Alt+; or Alt+0182
Section (§)	Option+6	Shift+Alt+6 or Alt+0167
Dagger (†)	Option+T	Shift+Alt+T or Alt+0134
Double dagger (‡)	Option+Shift+T	Alt+0135
Currency		
Cent (¢)	Option+4	Alt+0162
Euro (€)	Option+Shift+2	Alt+Ctrl+5
Pound sterling (£)	Option+3	Alt+0163
Yen (¥)	Option+Y	Ctrl+Alt+– (hyphen) or Alt+0165
Punctuation		
En bullet (•)	Option+8	Alt+8 or Alt+0149
Thin bullet (·)	*Not supported*	Alt+0183
Ellipsis (...)	Option+; (semicolon)	Alt+0133

Character	Mac Shortcut	Windows Shortcut
Measurement		
Foot (')	Control+'	Ctrl+'
Inch (")	Control+Shift+'	Ctrl+Alt+'
Mathematics		
One-half fraction (½)	*Not supported*	Ctrl+Alt+6 *or* Alt+0189
One-quarter fraction (¼)	*Not supported*	Ctrl+Alt+7 *or* Alt+0188
Three-quarters fraction (¾)	*Not supported*	Ctrl+Alt+8 *or* Alt+0190
Infinity (∞)	Option+5	*Not supported*
Division (÷)	Option+/	Alt+0247
Root (√)	Option+V	*Not supported*
Greater than or equal to (≥)	Option+>	*Not supported*
Less than or equal to (≤)	Option+<	*Not supported*
Inequality (≠)	Option+=	*Not supported*
Rough equivalence (≈)	Option+X	*Not supported*
Plus or minus (±)	Option+Shift+=	Alt+0177
Logical not (¬)	Option+L	Ctrl+Alt+\ *or* Alt+0172
Per mil (‰)	Option+Shift+R	Alt+0137
Degree (°)	Option+Shift+8	Alt+0176
Function (*f*)	Option+F	Alt+0131
Integral (∫)	Option+B	*Not supported*
Variation (∂)	Option+D	*Not supported*
Greek mu (μ)	Option+M	Alt+0181
Greek Pi (Π)	Option+Shift+P	*Not supported*
Greek pi (π)	Option+P	*Not supported*
Greek Sigma (Σ)	Option+W	*Not supported*
Greek Omega (Ω)	Option+Z	*Not supported*
Miscellaneous		
Apple logo (🍎)	Option+Shift+K	*Not supported*
Light (¤)	*Not supported*	Ctrl+Alt+4 *or* Alt+0164
Open diamond (◊)	Option+Shift+V	*Not supported*

Using menus

InDesign provides a set of menus to insert commonly used special characters, such as special spaces and dashes, as well as internal control characters such as Indent to Here and Column Break. There are three menu options, all in the Type menu, for inserting special characters:

- **Insert Special Characters:** This option has five submenus: Symbols, Markers, Hyphens and Dashes, Quotation Marks, and Other. The Symbols submenu includes things like ® and ©; the Markers submenu includes automatic page numbers, section markers, and footnote numbers; and the Other submenu includes tabs, Indent to Here, End Nested Style Here, and Non-joiner.

- **Insert White Space:** This option's submenu offers 12 types of fixed-size spaces as well as a nonbreaking version of variable-sized (regular) space.

- **Insert Break Character:** This option's submenu offers six types of break characters (such as column breaks and page breaks), a paragraph break (it's easier just to press Return or Enter to get this), and two types of line breaks (forced and discretionary).

CROSS-REF The spaces, dashes, and quotation marks characters are covered in this chapter. The hyphen and Indent to Here characters are covered in Chapter 18. The break characters are covered in Chapter 15. The ended-nested-style character is covered in Chapter 20. Automatic page and section markers are covered in Chapter 7. Footnotes are covered in Chapter 24. Tabs are covered in Chapter 22, while right tabs are covered in Chapter 20.

NEW FEATURE InDesign CS3 has added submenus to the Insert Special Characters menu to help organize its contents better.

Using the Glyphs panel

Inspired by Microsoft Word's Symbol dialog box (Edit ➪ Insert Symbol), InDesign's creators have created a flexible panel, the Glyphs panel, to access special symbols and characters in any font.

To open the panel, choose Type ➪ Glyphs or press Option+Shift+F11 or Alt+Shift+F11. The Glyphs panel, shown in Figure 21.1, displays. By default, the panel shows available characters for the current font, but you can change the font using the Font Family and Font Style pop-up menus at the bottom of the panel.

NEW FEATURE The Glyphs panel now has a keyboard shortcut: Option+Shift+F11 or Alt+Shift+F11.

It's unlikely that the Glyphs panel will show all available characters in its window, so use the scroll bar at right to move through all the characters. To show a subset of the font's characters, choose an option such as Entire Font or Currency from the Show pop-up menu (the options depend on how the font file is organized internally). You can also make the characters larger or smaller by clicking the Zoom Out or Zoom In iconic buttons at the panel's bottom right.

On-screen Special Characters

When you use special characters such as em spaces and nonbreaking hyphens, it can be hard to tell them apart from regular characters. That's why InDesign lets you display these spaces, tabs, hyphens, breaks, paragraph returns, and other control characters that exist in the text. Choose Type ⇨ Show Hidden Characters or press Option+⌘+I or Ctrl+Alt+I to turn on this display — and note these on-screen symbols will not print.

Here's what the symbols look like for the various control characters. Top row, from left to right: regular space, nonbreaking space, fixed-width nonbreaking space, em space, en space, thin space, hair space, punctuation space, quarter space, third space, figure space, and flush space. Second row: tab and right tab. Third row: discretionary hyphen and nonbreaking hyphen. Fourth row: forced line break (new line), discretionary line break, paragraph return, column break, frame break, page break, even page break, and odd page break. Fifth row: note, indent-to-here, end-nested-style, non-joiner, and end-of-story markers.

The Glyphs panel and its flyout menu

NEW FEATURE Recently used glyphs now display at the top of the Glyphs panel, making it easier to use them. You can hide these recently used glyphs by choosing Hide Options from the flyout menu or by clicking the double-arrow icon in the tab to the left of the panel's name.

InDesign CS3 also lets you change how the glyphs are sorted in the panel. Choose Sort Glyphs ⇨ By Unicode (the default) from the flyout menu to have them appear in order of the international Unicode standard's numbering scheme, or choose Sort Glyphs ⇨ By CID/GID to sort them based on the font's internal character and glyph IDs. There's really no reason to change this sort option from the Unicode default.

Creating glyph sets

For quick access to frequently used glyphs (from multiple fonts), InDesign lets you create glyph sets.

To create glyph sets:

1. **Click New Glyph Set from the Glyphs panel's flyout menu, as shown in Figure 21.1.** (Choose Type ⇨ Glyphs, or press Option+Shift+F11 or Alt+Shift+F11, to open the panel. You can also choose Window ⇨ Type & Tables ⇨ Glyphs.)

2. **Type a name in the New Glyph Set dialog box, and click OK.**

3. **Using the Insert Order pop-up menu, choose in what order you want added glyphs to appear.** Your choices are Glyph Value Order (such as the Unicode value), Insert at Front, or Insert at End.

4. **In the Glyphs panel, select the special character you want to add to your new set.** You may need to change the font and style using the pop-up menus at the bottom of the panel.

5. **In the panel's flyout menu, choose Add to Glyph Set ⇨ *set name* to add the symbol to the chosen set.**

6. **Repeat Steps 4 and 5 for each glyph you want to add.**

7. **When done adding glyphs, choose Edit Glyph Set ⇨ *set name* to edit the glyph set.** This opens the Edit Glyph Set dialog box shown in Figure 21.2. You can change the name and the glyph insertion order in this dialog box if you wish.

8. **If you want a specific font to be used for a glyph (which you need to do for symbols chosen from pi fonts, as opposed to common symbols like ™ available in most fonts), make sure that the Remember Font with Glyph option is selected.** You can also choose or change the font using the Font and Style pop-up menus in the dialog box.

9. **To delete a glyph, select it in the Edit Glyph Set dialog box, and then click Delete from Set.**

10. **Click OK when done.**

FIGURE 21.2

Editing a glyph set

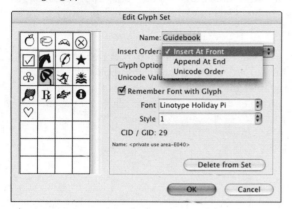

InDesign CS3 automatically creates a glyph set called Recent Glyphs, which are glyphs you've selected recently. You can edit and otherwise work with this automatic set just like any other set.

To access a glyph set, simply click the desired glyph set from the Show pop-up menu in the Glyph panel. Make sure the Type tool is active and that the text cursor (text-insertion point) is active in a text frame or path. Double-click the desired glyph in the Glyphs panel; InDesign inserts it at the text cursor location.

Sharing glyph sets

You can share glyph sets with other users. When you create a glyph set, InDesign creates a file in the Glyph Sets folder within the Presets folder that in turn resides within the folder containing the InDesign application. Just copy these files to other users' Glyph Sets folders to give them access to them.

The ability to share glyph set files is new to InDesign CS3.

Working with OpenType Variants

InDesign takes strong advantage of OpenType, but only if you let it. The OpenType font standard has been around for several years, but it is still not used very much. One reason is that it requires publishers to replace their older fonts, which costs money for enhancements that everyone has lived without for years.

But OpenType offers compelling value, at least for some fonts. What OpenType provides is a greater variety of glyphs and glyph attributes than a standard font. For example, small caps, old-fashioned numerals (the kinds with superiors and denominators), true fractions, true superiors (used for footnotes and mathematics), and true ordinals (the raised or superscript *th* in 4th) are just some of the examples.

What's key is that you don't have to manually style such attributes for every occurrence, as you do with the so-called expert-collection fonts. Instead, InDesign automatically applies the available attributes to selected text or to text whose paragraph style or character style uses the specified OpenType features. (Note that any OpenType attributes in brackets are unavailable for the current font.)

The results can be striking, as Figure 21.3 shows.

FIGURE 21.3

The text at the top has had several OpenType attributes enabled, as seen in the Character panel's flyout menu. The text at the bottom shows the same text with the normal attributes for the same font.

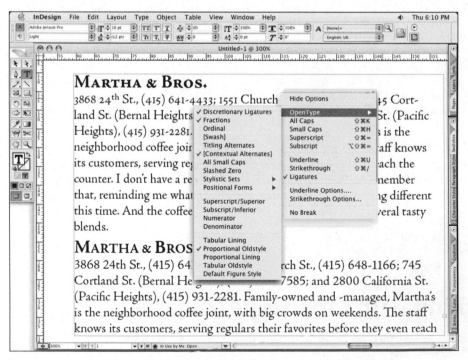

There are several types of OpenType attributes:

- **Discretionary ligatures:** This creates ligatures beyond the standard fi, fl, ffi, and ffl that InDesign uses (when available) in TrueType, Type 1 PostScript, and OpenType fonts when ligatures are enabled in the Character panel or in character styles, as Chapter 17 covers.

- **Fractions:** This substitutes true fractions such as ½ for the text *1/2*.

- **Ordinal:** This raises the *st*, *nd*, and *th* portions of ordinal numbers such as *1ˢᵗ*, *22ⁿᵈ*, and *345ᵗʰ*.

- **Swash:** This adds embellishments in front of the first character or at the end of the last letter of a word.

- **Titling Alternates:** This uses variants of a font for use in titles. These variants are usually a little clearer than the body-text version so they work better as titles, where as surrounding white space can make the normal variations within body text look strange.

- **Contextual Alternates:** This uses variants for specific characters to improve legibility in some contexts. For example, a contextual alternate for *t* might drop the left-side bar in the *t* so it doesn't bump against an adjacent letter.

- **All Small Caps:** This replaces all the text with true small caps, not the scaled-down version that the standard InDesign small-caps feature uses. True small caps are usually a little thicker than their scaled-down version, so they have the same visual weight as lowercase letters.

- **Slashed Zero:** This adds a slash over a 0 character for fonts that support it. The slashed zero is often used in European writing to differentiate from the letter *O*.

- **Superscript/Superior:** This replaces scaled-down raised text that InDesign uses to create superscripts with thicker characters placed where the font designers think works best. As with true small caps, this results in superscripts that have more visual weight.

- **Subscript/Inferior:** This replaces scaled-down lowered text that InDesign uses to create subscripts with thicker characters placed where the font designers think works best. As with true small caps, this results in subscripts that have more visual weight.

- **Numerator:** This is used to build the top part of a fraction when the font does not have predefined ones, such as for ⅞.

- **Denominator:** This is used to build the bottom part of a fraction when the font does not have predefined ones, such as for ¼.

- **Stylistic Sets:** This lets you choose which sets of variants within a font to use. A very few OpenType fonts, such as Poetica Std, use stylistic sets, which provide multiple variations of the same characters, letting you choose which variants to use.

- **Positional Forms:** This lets you choose which form of a character to use, for Arabic fonts and some Roman scripting fonts where the character's position within a word (beginning, middle, or end) determines its visual appearance.

- **Tabular Lining:** This uses standard numeric characters (which start on the baseline and have no descenders or ascenders) spaced evenly for proper alignment in tables.

- **Proportional Oldstyle:** This uses old-fashioned numerals with ascenders and descenders that are spaced like any other characters, based on their width, shape, and visual weight.

- **Proportional Lining:** This uses standard numerals spaced like any other characters, based on their width, shape, and visual weight.

- **Tabular Oldstyle:** This uses old-fashioned numerals spaced evenly for natural alignment in tables.

- **Default Figure Style:** This does whatever the font's designers want it to do by default (one of the above four settings).

NEW FEATURE Support for positional forms in OpenType fonts is new to InDesign CS3

The top text in Figure 21.3 shows the use of true small caps (in the name *Martha & Bros.*), ordinal numbers (the raised *th* in *24th*), and proportional old-style numerals (look at the address and phone numbers). The bottom text shows the same text without these effects.

Figure 21.4 shows the same text with a font that supports discretionary ligatures, contextual alternates, and swashes:

- You can see contextual ligatures in many *st* combinations, such as the word *staff* on the sixth line (which begins with the word *weekend*).

FIGURE 21.4

This is the same text as in Figure 21.3, but it has a different font that supports discretionary ligatures, contextual alternatives, and swashes (look for the embellishments that appear between characters and at the beginning and end of words).

Martha & Bros.
3868 24th St., (415) 641-4433; 1551 Church St., (415) 648-1166; 745 Cortland St. (Bernal Heights), (415) 642-7585; and 2800 California St. (Pacific Heights), (415) 931-2281. Family-owned and -managed, Martha's is the neighborhood coffee joint, with big crowds on weekends. The staff knows its customers, serving regulars their favorites before they even reach the counter. I don't have a regular, and the folks at Martha's even remember that, reminding me what I had last time so I can order something different this time. And the coffee is excellent, roasted by the family in several tasty

- You can see a contextual alternate by looking at the *t* in the abbreviation *St.* that begins the fourth line. Compare that embellished *t* with the *t* in the word *Heights* on the same line: the alternate used in *St.* extends the *t*'s bar to extend over the adjacent period, while the normal *t* in *Heights* does not.

- In this figure, many words use swashes at the end or beginning, such as in the last line's *And the coffee*, *roasted*, *the*, and *in several* text fragments.

Using Other Tools to Access Special Characters

Besides using the built-in InDesign tools for special characters, you can also use utility programs. You might do this because you want to use the same consistent tool for all your applications.

Mac OS X 10.4 (Tiger) and Mac OS X 10.5 (Leopard) each comes with two tools that are like a simple version of InDesign's Glyphs panel, as shown in Figure 21.5: the Character Palette and Keyboard Viewer. Both are available under the Keyboard Input menu item. Note that you might need to turn on the Keyboard Input menu item by choosing  ➪ System Preferences, and then going to the International control panel's Input Menu pane. Select the Show Input Menu in Menu Bar option.

FIGURE 21.5

Mac OS X's Character Palette and Keyboard Viewer

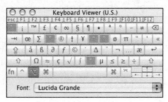

Similarly, Windows has a tool to access special symbols, as shown in Figure 21.6: In both Windows XP and Windows Vista, use the Character Map utility that comes with Windows. Character Map is usually installed in the Windows Start menu; choose Start ➪ All Programs ➪ Accessories ➪ System Tools ➪ Character Map. (If you use the Classic Start Menu interface, choose Start ➪ Accessories ➪ System Tools ➪ Character Map.)

FIGURE 21.6

Windows XP's Character Map utility (the Windows Vista version is identical).

On both platforms, you can also use a utility like Ergonis's PopChar, which adds a quick-access icon to the Mac and Windows menu bars. Figure 21.7 shows the Mac and Windows versions. Notice how the keyboard shortcut for each special character is shown at the bottom as a character is highlighted. (The companion Web site, www.InDesignCentral.com, has links to this and other utilities.)

If you don't want to use one of these utilities in all your applications but, instead, want to take advantage of your word processor's tools, note that the popular word processors have their own feature for special character access, as shown in Figure 21.8:

- In Microsoft Word (Mac or Windows), choose Insert ➪ Symbol. (It may also be accessible through the toolbar if you added this command to your toolbar; look for the button with the Ω character.)

- In Corel WordPerfect, choose Insert ➪ Symbol. (Use the Set pop-up menu to switch among different types of symbols.)

- In Apple iWork Pages, choose Edit ➪ Special Characters. (Use the list of symbol categories at left to switch among different types of symbols.)

FIGURE 21.7

The PopChar utility for Mac OS X (top) and Windows (bottom)

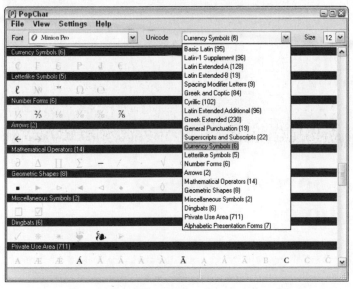

The tools for inserting special characters in Microsoft Word (top), Corel WordPerfect (bottom left), and Apple iWork Pages (bottom right)

Understanding Special Spaces, Dashes, and Quotes

Typographers have long had a wide arsenal of spaces, dashes, and hyphens to control text appearance. While word processors offer some of these characters, InDesign goes way beyond what most people even know exist.

Using special spaces

One way to carefully fine-tune spacing is to literally replace individual spaces with special spaces. Instead of narrowing and widening with tracking and justification settings, these special spaces maintain their widths. InDesign provides 13 special space options in two categories: nonbreaking spaces and fixed-width spaces.

Nonbreaking spaces

A *nonbreaking space* glues two words together, ensuring that a line doesn't wrap between two words if you don't want it to. For example, you might want to use a nonbreaking space in *OS X* so *OS* doesn't end on one line with *X* starting on the next line. Nonbreaking spaces are also handy if you put spaces on either side of your dashes; they make sure a dash is glued to the word before it. All are available by choosing the desired space from Type ⇨ Insert White Space's submenu.

InDesign has two types of nonbreaking spaces: the regular one, whose size is variable and thus can be adjusted like any other regular space in a line, and the fixed-width one, which essentially is a nonbreaking en space. The regular nonbreaking space is the one you'll use 99 percent of the time.

Fixed-width spaces

Fixed-width spaces keep their size intact no matter how much InDesign adjusts regular spaces elsewhere in your text as part of its text-flow and composition decisions.

The three most common fixed-width spaces are the em space (the width of a capital *M*, which also happens to be the same width as the type size), the en space (the width of a capital *N*, which happens to be half the width of an em space), and the thin space (the width of a lowercase *t*, which happens to be a quarter the width of an em space).

But InDesign's creators are control freaks, so they offer a lot more fixed-width space options than just the common em, en, and thin spaces:

- A punctuation space is the width of a comma or period, useful in aligning text in tables.
- A figure space is the width of a standard (tabular lining) numeral, also useful in aligning text in tables.
- A flush space is used to fill out a line between an end-of-story character and the text on the rest of line. But it works only if the paragraph is set to Full Justify. Frankly, it's easier to use a right tab (Shift+Tab) character, which does the same thing no matter what justification is applied to your paragraph.
- A hair space is essentially half a thin space, and is typically used instead of kerning to nudge slightly overlapping characters away from each other.
- The other spaces — third space, quarter space, and sixth space — are the specified fractions of an em space's width.

The non-joiner character is a zero-width "space" character that you'll hardly ever use, as it's really designed for languages such as Arabic and Devanagari, where letterforms get joined in some circumstances but not others. The non-joiner prevents the characters from being joined, overriding any automatic font options. In English, you might use this character to manually prevent automatic ligatures (the only circumstance where characters are joined together in English).

NEW FEATURE The third space, quarter space, sixth space, and nonbreaking fixed-width space are new to InDesign CS3, as is the non-joiner character.

TABLE 21.2

Shortcuts for Spaces, Dashes, Hyphens, and Quotes

Character	Mac Shortcut	Windows Shortcut
Em space ( )	Shift+⌘+M	Ctrl+Shift+M
En space ( )	Shift+⌘+N	Ctrl+Shift+N
Thin space ()	Option+Shift+⌘+M	Ctrl+Alt+Shift+M
Nonbreaking space	Option+⌘+X	Ctrl+Alt+X
Em dash (—)	Option+Shift+–	Alt+Shift+– or Alt+0151
En dash (–)	Option+–	Alt+– or Alt+0150
Nonbreaking hyphen	Option+⌘+–	Ctrl+Alt+–
Discretionary hyphen	Shift+⌘+–	Ctrl+Shift+–
" (open double quote)	Option+[	Shift+Alt+[
" (closed double quote)	Shift+Option+[	Shift+Alt+]
' (open single quote)	Option+]	Alt+[
' (closed single quote)	Shift+Option+]	Alt+]
" (keyboard double quote)	Option+shift+'	Ctrl+Alt+'
' (keyboard single quote/apostrophe)	⌘+'	Ctrl+'
` (keyboard open single quote)	`	`

Using dashes

Many people confuse the two types of dashes used in typography: the em dash and en dash.

All about em dashes

An em dash (so called because it is the width of a capital *M*) is the most common dash, and it's used to indicate break in sentence flow, either for an inserted phrase (sort of a supersize parenthesis) or to indicate a complete change in thought (which typically occurs in transcribed text).

When you import text from a word processor, InDesign converts two consecutive hyphens — the way you indicate a dash in a typewriter — to a real em dash. But InDesign doesn't do this when you type, so you must specify the em dash through the torturous menu command Type ⇨ Insert Special Character ⇨ Hyphens and Dashes ⇨ Em Dash or know its keyboard shortcut (Option+Shift+– [hyphen] or Alt+Shift+– [hyphen]).

Spacing em Dashes — or Not

Typographers are divided over whether you should put spaces around em dashes — like this — or not — like this. Traditionally, there is no space. But having space lets the publishing program treat the dash as a word, so that there is even space around all words in a line. Not having a space around dashes means that the publishing program sees the two words connected by the em dash as one big word. So the spacing added to justify a line between all other words on the line may be awkwardly large because the program doesn't know how to break a line after or before an em dash that doesn't have space on either side. Still, whether to surround a dash with space is a decision in which personal preferences should prevail.

PLATFORM DIFFERENCES Note that most Windows programs don't use the Alt+Shift+– shortcut for an em dash; if they don't have their own shortcut, you can use the universal Windows shortcut Alt+0151 (be sure to type the numbers from the numeric keypad, not from the keyboard). By the way, the universal Windows shortcut for an en dash is Alt+0150.

CAUTION Several versions of Word — including Word 97 and Word 2000 for Windows and Word X for Mac — have a default setting that converts two hyphens to an en dash (–) rather than an em dash (—), which is simply wrong typographically. Chapter 14 explains how to handle this.

All about en dashes

The en dash, so called because it is the width of a capital *N*, is traditionally used to:

- Separate numerals, as in a range of values or dates (pages 41–63)
- Label a figure (Figure 21–1), although publishers are divided on whether to do this (some just use a regular hyphen)
- Indicate a negative value (–45) as a minus sign
- Indicate an interrupted hyphenation (first– and business-class passengers)
- Indicate a multiple-word hyphenation (Civil War–era rifle)

Of course, many people don't use an en dash at all — or incorrectly use it instead of an em dash. While desktop publishing has made it easy for almost anyone to produce good-looking documents, most have no clue about the use of special characters that typographers and copy editors have traditionally applied to final documents.

Using quotes and apostrophes

By default, InDesign replaces the keyboard's typewriter-style, straight quotation marks (" and ') and apostrophe (') with the typographic, curly quotes — that is, as long as Use Typographer's Quotes is enabled in the Type pane of the Preferences dialog box (choose InDesign ⇨ Preferences ⇨ Type or press ⌘+K on the Mac, or choose Edit ⇨ Preferences ⇨ Type or press Ctrl+K in Windows). InDesign handles both quotes in imported text and as you type.

You can change the quotes that InDesign uses in the Dictionary pane of the Preferences dialog box, as Chapter 3 explains.

CAUTION   Do not use the keyboard open single quote key (`), in the upper-left corner of your keyboard to the left of the 1, as an open single quote. Instead, use the keyboard apostrophe (') key. If you use the open single quote keyboard key, you will get a different open single quote character than the standard typographic version.

Entering keyboard quotes

When Use Typographer's Quotes is enabled, you can enter the keyboard quotes — perhaps for use as foot marks (') and inch marks (") — by using keyboard shortcuts. Type Option+⌘+' or Ctrl+Alt+' for double quotes and ⌘+' or Ctrl+' for single quotes. They're also available by choosing Type ➪ Insert Special Character ➪ Quotation Marks.

NEW FEATURE   The ability to insert keyboard quotation marks is new to InDesign CS3.

Typing reverse single quotes

A reverse single quote — a close single quote, really — is often used to indicate an omission — for example, in '80s to mean the 1980s or in 'burbs to mean suburbs. You need to enter this type of reverse quote manually at all times (whether or not Smart Quotes is in use) by typing Option+] or Alt+].

Handling adjacent single and double quotes

When a single quote is followed immediately by a double quote, or vice versa, separate the two with your choice of a nonbreaking space, thin space, or punctuation space. For most fonts, I think the thin space provides the best visual result. For example:

- He told me, "I asked, 'Do you have time to help?' "
- " 'I am too busy' was her answer," he sighed.

Working with Foreign Languages

Adobe offers 18 language versions of InDesign, covering Brazilian Portuguese, Chinese (in both simplified and traditional versions), Czech, Danish, Dutch, English (providing both American and British English in the same version), Finnish, French, German, Greek, Italian, Japanese, Korean, Norwegian, Polish, Spanish (Castilian), and Swedish. WinSoft sells versions of InDesign in several other languages, including Arabic (both Middle Eastern and North African forms), Hebrew, Hungarian, Russian, and Turkish.

But you don't need one of those editions to work with these languages' characters and symbols. InDesign supports 27 languages and 12 additional variants no matter which version you use. Those language-specific editions from Adobe and WinSoft provide the user interface in a local language, but all are multilingual when it comes to the text they handle.

Many languages use the Roman alphabet, often with accent marks added. Western and Eastern European languages, for example, use the Roman alphabet, though some languages have extra characters such as the German ß, the Icelandic ð, the French «, and the Spanish ¡. For Western European languages, the majority of Roman-based fonts include these extra characters — but not all do, so do check before relying on a specific font. Fewer Roman-based fonts have the special accented letters common in Eastern European and Turkish languages such as the ğ and ş — so chances are you need to buy fonts designed specifically for these languages. And for languages with non-Roman scripts — such as Arabic, Chinese, Greek, Hebrew, Japanese, Korean, Thai, and Vietnamese — it's a sure bet you need to get language-specific fonts.

CROSS-REF InDesign comes with spelling and hyphenation dictionaries for the 27 languages it supports. Chapter 16 covers how to work with these dictionaries in more detail, as well as how to let InDesign know which language specific text is in, so it knows which dictionaries to use with it.

Although most American publishers don't produce work in other languages, they may still use accents in their work. (Canadian publishers, of course, often publish in English and French.) And, of course, many publishers do publish in other languages, such as Spanish, French, German, and Portuguese, because they do business with customers in multiple countries. Even all-English publishers may choose to use accents in foreign words like *café* to help pronunciation and show a bit of international flair.

See Table 21.3 for foreign-language characters used in Western European languages — the ones that most North American publishers are apt to use occasionally, without resorting to fonts designed for these languages. Note that Windows shortcuts involving four numerals (such as Alt+0157) should be entered from the numeric keypad while holding the Alt key.

TIP If your font doesn't have the accented characters you need, you may be able to create them by kerning accent marks over the letters. See Chapter 17 for detailed information on kerning.

TABLE 21.3

Shortcuts for Western European Accents and Foreign Characters

Character	Mac Shortcut	Windows Shortcut
acute (´)*	Option+E *letter*	' *letter*
cedilla (ç)*	*see Ç and ç*	' *letter*
circumflex (ˆ)*	Option+I *letter*	^ *letter*
grave (`)*	Option+` *letter*	` *letter*
tilde (~)*	Option+N *letter*	~ *letter*
trema (¨)*	Option+U *letter*	" *letter*
umlaut (¨)*	Option+U *letter*	" *letter*

continued

TABLE 21.3   *(continued)*

Character	Mac Shortcut	Windows Shortcut
Á	Option+E A	' A *or* Alt+0193
á	Option+E a	' a *or* Alt+0225
À	Option+` A	` A *or* Alt+0192
à	Option+` a	` a *or* Alt+0224
Ä	Option+U A	" A *or* Alt+0196
ä	Option+U a	" a *or* Alt+0228
Ã	Option+N A	~ A *or* Alt+0195
ã	Option+N a	~ a *or* Alt+0227
Â	Option+I A	^ A *or* Alt+0194
â	Option+I a	^ a *or* Alt+0226
Å	Option+Shift+A	Alt+0197
å	Option+A	Alt+0229
Æ	Option+Shift+'	Alt+0198
æ	Option+'	Alt+0230 *or* Ctrl+Alt+Z
Ç	Option+Shift+C	' C *or* Alt+0199
ç	Option+C	' c *or* Alt+0231 *or* Ctrl+Alt+,
Đ	*Not supported*	Alt+0208
đ	*Not supported*	Alt+0240
É	Option+E E	' E *or* Alt+0201
é	Option+E e	' e *or* Alt+0233
È	Option+` E	` E *or* Alt+0200
è	Option+` e	` e *or* Alt+0232
Ë	Option+U E	" E *or* Alt+0203
ë	Option+U e	" e *or* Alt+0235
Ê	Option+I E	^ E *or* Alt+0202
ê	Option+I e	^ e *or* Alt+0234
Í	Option+E I	' I *or* Alt+-205
í	Option+E i	' i *or* Alt+0237
Ì	Option+` I	` I *or* Alt+0204
ì	Option+` i	` i *or* Alt+0236
Ï	Option+U I	" I *or* Alt+0207
ï	Option+U i	" I *or* Alt+0239

Character	Mac Shortcut	Windows Shortcut
Î	Option+I I	^ I *or* Alt+0206
î	Option+I i	^ I *or* Alt+0238
Ñ	Option+N N	~ N *or* Alt+0209
ñ	Option+N n	~ n *or* Alt+0241
Ó	Option+E O	' O *or* Alt+0211
ó	Option+E o	' o *or* Alt+0243 *or* Ctrl+Alt+O
Ò	Option+` O	` O *or* Alt+0210
ò	Option+` o	` o *or* Alt+0242
Ö	Option+U O	" O *or* Alt+0214
ö	Option+U o	" o *or* Alt+0246
Õ	Option+N O	~ O *or* Alt+0213
õ	Option+N o	~ o *or* Alt+0245
Ô	Option+I O	^ O *or* Alt+0212
ô	Option+I o	^ o *or* Alt+0244
Ø	Option+Shift+O	Alt+0216
ø	Option+O	Alt+0248 *or* Ctrl+Alt+L
Œ	Option+Shift+Q	Alt+0140
œ	Option+Q	Alt+0156
Þ	*Not supported*	Alt+0222
þ	*Not supported*	Alt+0254
ß	Option+S	Ctrl+Alt+S or Alt+0223
∫	Option+B	*Not supported*
Š	*Not supported*	Alt+0138
š	*Not supported*	Alt+0154
Ú	Option+E U	' U or Alt+0218
ú	Option+E u	' u or Alt+0250 *or* Ctrl+Alt+U
Ù	Option+` U	` U or Alt+0217
ù	Option+` u	` u or Alt+0249
Ü	Option+U U	" U or Alt+0220
ü	Option+U u	" u or Alt+0252
Û	Option+I U	^ U or Alt+0219
û	Option+I u	^ u or Alt+0251

continued

TABLE 21.3	*(continued)*	
Character	**Mac Shortcut**	**Windows Shortcut**
Ý	*Not supported*	' Y or Alt+0221
ý	*Not supported*	' y or Alt+0253
Ÿ	Option+U Y	" Y *or* Alt+0159
ÿ	Option+U y	" y *or* Alt+0255
Ž	*Not supported*	Alt+0142
ž	*Not supported*	Alt+0158
Spanish open exclamation (¡)	Option+1	Ctrl+Alt+1 *or* Alt+-0161
Spanish open question (¿)	Option+Shift+/	Ctrl+Alt+/ *or* Alt+0191
French open double quote («)	Option+\	Ctrl+Alt+[*or* Alt+0171
French close double quote (»)	Option+Shift+\	Ctrl+Alt+] *or* Alt+0187

* On the Mac, enter the shortcut for the accent and then type the letter to be accented. For example, to get *é*, type Option+E and then the letter *e*. In Windows, if the keyboard layout is set to United States-International — via the Keyboard icon in the Windows Control Panel — you can enter the accent signifier and then type the letter (for example, type ` and then the letter *e* to get *è*). To avoid an accent (for example, if you want to begin a quote — such as *"A man"* rather than have *Ä man"* — type a space after the accent character — for example, type " and then a space, and then A, rather than typing " and then A.

European Languages and Accented Characters

Using accents in foreign words is great, but many Americans use them incorrectly, which is embarrassing. Although I can't tell you how to properly spell and accent every foreign word (a good dictionary for that language can!), I can tell you which accented characters are used in European languages. If you're using a word from one of the languages here and that word uses an accented character not shown for the language, you either have the wrong accent or that word is actually from a different language. I've also indicated which countries use the euro currency symbol (€) by including that symbol in their lists, and special currency symbols for other nations.

Many of the characters shown here are not available in standard PostScript and TrueType fonts. Most are available in OpenType fonts, though they're not in every case. You may need a special font for the specific language to get all the characters.

Albanian: ç, ë

Basque (Euskara): ñ, €

Breton: â, ê, è, ñ, ô, ù, ü, €

Catalan: à, ç, è, é, í, ï, l·, ò, ó, ú, ü, €

Croatian: ć, č, đ, š, ž

Czech: á, č, ď, é, ě, í, ň, ř, š, ť, ú, ů, ý, ž

Danish: å, æ, é, ø, ú

Dutch: á, â, è, é, ê, ë, í, ï, ij, ó, ô, ö, ú, û, €

English, American and Canadian: $, ¢

English, British: ö; £

English, Old: ð, þ

Estonian: ä, õ, ö, s, ž

Faroese: á, æ, ð, í, ó, ø, ú, ý

Finnish: ä, ö, €

French: à, â, æ, è, é, ê, ë, ç, î, ï, ñ, ñ, œ, ù, û, ü, ÿ, «, », €

Frisian: â, ê, î, ô, ú, û

Gaelic (Irish): á, é, í, ó, ú, €

Gaelic (Scots): à, á, è, é, ì, ò, ó, ù, £

German: ä, ö, ß, ∫, ü, €

Hungarian: á, é, i', ó, ö, ő, ú, ü, ű

Icelandic: á, æ, é, ð, í, ó, ö, þ, ú, ý

Italian: à, è, ì, í, ò, ó, ù, €

Latvian: ā, č, ē, ģ, ī, ļ, ņ, š, ū, ž

Lithuanian: ą, č, ę, ė, į, š, ų, ū, ž

Luxembourgean: ä, ë, é, ï, ö, ü, €

Maltese: à, ċ, è, ġ, ħ, î, ì, ò, ù, ż

Norwegian: å, ø, æ

Occitan (Provençal): á, à, ç, é, è, í, ó, ò, ú, €

Polish: ą, ć, ę, ł, ń, ó, ś, ź, ż

Portuguese: à, á, â, ã, é, ê, ç, í, ñ, ó, ô, õ, Ú, ü, €

Rhaeto-Roman: à, è, é, ì, î, ò, ù

Romanian: â, ă, î, ş, ţ

Slovak: á, ä, č, d', é, í, Í, l', ń, ó, ô, ŕ, š, ť, ú, ý, ž

Slovenian: č, š, ž, €

Spanish (Castilian, Galician): á, é, í, ñ, ó, ú, ü, ¿, ¡, €

Swedish: å, ä, é, ö

Turkish: â, ç, ğ, î, ı, ö, ş, û, ü

Welsh: à, á, â, ä, è, é, ê, ë, ì, í, î, ï, ò, ó, ô, ö, ù, ú, û, ü, ŷ, ý, ÿ

A great source for information on foreign characters and fonts is the Yamada Language Center, accessible on the Web at http://babel.uoregon.edu/yamada/fonts.html.

Summary

There are a multitude of special characters available for your documents. You can access common ones via keyboard shortcuts, less common ones through InDesign's Type menu, and all available characters through the Glyphs panel.

InDesign also automatically converts keyboard quotes into their typographic counterparts, plus it lets you select the quote style to be used, so you can use the right style for the language you are publishing in.

Part V

Business Document Fundamentals

IN THIS PART

Chapter 22
Setting Up Tabs and Tables

Chapter 23
Automating Text

Chapter 24
Footnotes, Indexes, and TOCs

Chapter 25
Creating Multi-Document Projects

Chapter 22

Setting Up Tabs and Tables

I f you ever used a typewriter, you may remember pressing the Tab key to indent each paragraph. And you may have pounded on it repeatedly to align columns of data. In InDesign, you use first-line indents to distinguish the first line of a new paragraph, and you reserve tabs for separating columns of data. Although InDesign has a built-in table editor, you can create simple tables using regular tabs quickly with the tabs feature. For more sophisticated tables, use the table editor.

In InDesign, tabs are part of paragraph formats — meaning that, when you set them, they apply to all the text in selected paragraphs rather than to selected characters within a paragraph. By default, when you start typing in a paragraph or you create a new paragraph style, there are invisible, automatic tab stops every half-inch. Regardless of the measurement system your rulers are set to use, when you press Tab you jump to the next 0.5-inch increment on the ruler.

As soon as you set a tab stop of your own, it overrides any of the automatic tab stops to its left. The automatic tab stops remain to the right until you override all of them.

> **TIP** Any tabs you set in the Tabs panel when no document is open are added to all future documents you create. Therefore, if tabs set at every quarter-inch are more useful to you, add them with no documents open.

IN THIS CHAPTER

Preparing tabbed text

Learning the Tabs panel

Creating tables

Formatting rows, columns, and cells

Working with table and cell styles

Converting text to tables

InDesign provides four different types of tabs so you can:

- Left-align text to the left at a tab stop (the default setting, and the one you'll use most often)

- Center text on either side of the tab stop (very useful in column headers)

- Right-align text at a tab stop (useful for columns of integers)

- Align a specific character in the text with the tab stop (such as a comma or period in a number)

Figure 22.1 shows examples of tabs.

FIGURE 22.1

Under the Item column, Trifle and Whip Cream are positioned with right-aligned tabs. The three other column headings — Ingredient, Amount, and Price — are positioned with center tabs. In the chart, the ingredients are left-aligned, the amounts are center aligned, and the prices are aligned on the dollar sign (top chart) and the decimal point (lower chart).

Item			Ingredient		Amount		Price
	Trifle		lemon juice		3/4 cup		$.89/20 oz.
			eggs		4		$1.99/dozen
			sugar		1 1/2 cups		$1.79/pound
			heavy cream		1 cup		$.99/quart
			strawberries		1 1/2 cups		$2.09/pound
			pound cake		1		$2.75 each
Whip Cream			heavy cream		1 1/2 cups		$.99/quart
			sugar		1/4 cup		$1.79/pound
Item			Ingredient		Amount		Price
	Trifle		lemon juice		3/4 cup		$.89/20 oz.
			eggs		4		$1.99/dozen
			sugar		1 1/2 cups		$1.79/pound
			heavy cream		1 cup		$.99/quart
			strawberries		1 1/2 cups		$2.09/pound
			pound cake		1		$2.75 each
Whip Cream			heavy cream		1 1/2 cups		$.99/quart
			sugar		1/4 cup		$1.79/pound

Using the Tabs Panel

To set tabs in InDesign you use the Tabs panel, which floats above your text so that you can keep it open until you're finished experimenting with tabs. To open the Tabs panel, choose Type ➪ Tabs, or press Shift+⌘+T or Ctrl+Shift+T. Figure 22.2 shows the Tabs panel along with a simple table created using one tab stop.

NEW FEATURE The menu sequence Window ➪ Type & Tables ➪ Tabs is no longer available to access the Tabs panel.

FIGURE 22.2

The Tabs panel and a simple table created with several tab stops

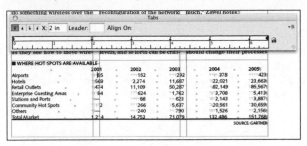

Tab style buttons

Four buttons on the Tabs panel let you control how the text aligns with the tab you're creating:

- **Left:** The default tab stops are left-aligned, which means that the left side of the text touches the tab stop as if it were a left margin. Most tabs you create for text will be left-aligned.

- **Center:** Centered tab stops are like the centered paragraph alignment, with text balanced evenly on either side of the tab stop. Center tabs are often used for table headings.

- **Right:** When you set right-aligned tabs, the right edge of text touches the tab stop. This is commonly used for aligning numbers that do not include decimals or for the last column in a table.

- **Align On:** By default, the last tab style button is for decimal tabs, which means that a period in the text aligns on the tab stop. If there's no period in the text, InDesign pretends that there is one after the last character. Instead of aligning on a period, you can specify a different character, such as a comma or dollar sign, for an Align On tab, and text aligns to that character. You do this using the Align On field, which is covered later in this section.

TIP If you need a tab flush with the right margin, for example, to position a dingbat at the end of the story, click the Right Tab iconic button and position it on the right side of the tab ruler. Then drag the right-aligned tab on top of the right indent arrow. (You can't actually click to place a tab on top of the arrow, but you can drag a tab on top of it.) An even faster way is to choose Type ➪ Special Character ➪ Other ➪ Right Indent Tab or press Shift+Tab.

X field

The X field of the Tabs panel lets you specify a position for a new tab stop. You can type a value in this field in 0.01-point increments, and then press Shift+Enter or Shift+Return to create a tab. InDesign positions tabs relative to the left edge of the text frame or column. Or you can just click the mouse on the ruler where you want the tab to be, as described later.

Preparing Text Files for Setting Tabs

When designers import text, the most common problem they encounter is that writers try to line up the text on their screens by using multiple tabs between columns rather than setting appropriate tab stops in the first place and having one tab between each "cell." That's because word processors also have default tab stops of 0.5", and most users use those defaults rather than figure out how to set tabs themselves. When you import the file with these tabs, the chances of items lining up in InDesign as they do in the word processor are pretty close to zero. That means a lot of cleanup work for the designers.

Before you start setting tabs in InDesign, take a look at the tabs already entered in the text. You can check this out in your word processor or in text that has been placed in InDesign. To view tab characters in InDesign, choose Type ➪ Show Hidden Characters, or press Option+⌘+I or Ctrl+Alt+I. The light-blue double French closed quote symbols (») are tabs.

To set effective tabs for columns of data, each line or row of information should be its own paragraph, and each column of data should be separated by only one tab character. If there's only one tab between each column, you need to set only one tab stop per column, and you can more carefully control a single tab stop rather than several.

Because the text is not in its final font or text frame, the current tab placement does not matter. But if necessary, the writer can change tab settings in Word to align the columns for proofreading or editing purposes.

As with multiple tabs stops, if there are extra paragraph returns between the rows or information, or if each line ends in a soft return or line break (Shift+Return or Shift+Enter) rather than a paragraph return (Return or Enter), you should fix these with search and replace in your word processor or using the Find/Change dialog box (Edit ➪ Find/Change, or ⌘+F or Ctrl+F) in InDesign, as described in Chapter 16.

It's best to insist that any word processor documents imported into InDesign be created so there is only one tab between each entry on a line, no matter how it looks in the word processor. Then you can set up the appropriate tab stops in InDesign.

If a text frame has Inset Spacing specified for its left edge in the General pane of the Text Frame Options dialog box (Object ➪ Text Frame Options, or ⌘+B or Ctrl+B), InDesign measures tabs from the text inset rather than from the frame.

TIP   Why type numbers when you can just use the mouse? The reason is to get more accurate positioning than using the mouse usually allows, especially when you know exactly where the tab stop should be. Of course, you can add a tab by using the mouse, and then click the field and type a more precise value in the X field.

As with other fields in InDesign, the X field can perform mathematical computations for you. So you can set a tab at half of 0.125" without figuring out that value, or you can move a tab by adding to or subtracting from its current value. It may seem unlikely that you would ever do this, but it's extremely handy for changing tab settings so they're, say, half as far apart as they used to be, or half as far apart plus 2 points to the right.

The operands for performing math in fields are + (addition), – (subtraction), * (multiplication), and / (division). If you want to combine these operands — for example, add 5 then subtract 2 — you have to remember back to middle school and Algebra I to type the operands in the correct order: multiply, divide, add, and then subtract.

Leader field

A tab leader is a character or series of characters that fills the white space between tabs, like the periods you see between a table of contents entry and its page number. They got the name *leader* because they lead your eyes across the page. Figure 22.3 shows a dot leader in use between the donor's name and the donation amount.

InDesign lets you specify up to eight characters, including special characters that repeat to fill any white space. When you set a leader for a tab stop, the leaders actually fill any space prior to that tab stop (between the previous text and the tab location).

To spread out the leader characters, type spaces between the characters you enter. Don't enter spaces before and after a single character though, as that results in two spaces between the characters when the pattern repeats (unless that's the look you're going for). You can't enter special types of spaces — such as thin spaces or hair spaces — in the Leader field; you always get em spaces.

NOTE The reason to use tab leaders is to help the reader. Unless the design is more important than the content, you probably shouldn't use eight-character tab leaders even though you can. A cacophony of characters draws too much attention and can be confusing. Because the pattern of leaders repeats, one space and a period are usually sufficient.

To enter special characters in the Leader field, use keyboard commands, InDesign's Glyphs panel, or a utility such as PopChar, Mac OS X's Character Palette, or Windows's Character Map. If you use InDesign's Insert Special Character menu option (Type ➪ Insert Special Character) or the Glyphs panel (Type ➪ Glyphs), you insert a character into your text, which you have to cut and paste into the Leader field. It isn't inserted directly in the Leader field as you would expect.

FIGURE 22.3

A right-aligned tab with dot leader is used here to create a table of contents.

Align On field

The Align On tab style defaults to a period, but you can replace the period with any character, including special characters. When that character is found in tabbed text, it aligns on the tab stop. If that character is not found, InDesign pretends that it follows the last character in the tabbed string. The most common characters entered in the Align On field include a comma (,), dollar sign ($), cents symbol (¢), and opening or closing parentheses ((and)).

 NOTE   If the Align On field is not visible in the Tabs panel, just widen the panel by dragging one of its sides so the field displays.

Tab ruler

Rather than typing values in the X field, you can position tabs by clicking on the ruler at the bottom of the Tabs panel. The Tab ruler has the following characteristics:

- **It displays in the same measurement system as the document, with 0 specifying the edges of the column.** If Inset Spacing is specified for the left edge of the text frame in the Text Frame Options dialog box (Object ⮑ Text Frame Options, or ⌘+B or Ctrl+B), the ruler starts after the text inset in the first column.

- **The ruler provides arrows for controlling and displaying the selected paragraph's first-line, left, and right indents.** Dragging the two left arrows changes both the paragraph's first-line and left indents, while dragging the top arrow changes only the first-line indent. Dragging the arrow at right changes the right indents. These arrows help you see indents in relation to tabs that you're setting. (They have the same effect as changing the indent settings in the Paragraph or Paragraph Styles panels, as covered in Chapter 18.)

- **Icons that match the tab styles display on the rulers to show you where and what type of tabs are already set.** You can drag these around to reposition existing tabs, and you can drag them off the ruler to delete tabs.

- **You can scroll through the ruler by clicking it and dragging to the left or right.** This lets you set tabs beyond the current column or text frame width, such as for text that flows into text boxes of different widths.

Position Panel above Text Frame button

Under the right circumstances, clicking the Position Panel above Text Frame iconic button (the magnet icon) in the lower-right corner of the Tabs panel snaps the panel and the ruler to the selected text frame or column. The idea is to make it easier to see the tab stops in relation to an actual area of text.

For this to work, you need to make sure the top of the text frame is visible on-screen, the Type tool is selected, and you've placed the cursor in text or highlighted text. If you don't meet all these prerequisites, nothing happens.

Once you manage to get the Tabs panel positioned correctly, it's quite useful. You can add and adjust tabs in relation to the text (provided that the text is at the top of the text frame!) and you

can always see from where the tabs are measured. Even better, if you move the cursor to another column in the text frame, you can click the Position Panel above Text Frame iconic (magnet) button again to position the Tabs panel over that column.

Flyout menu

In addition to setting tabs and indents in the Tabs panel, InDesign provides four additional options through the flyout menu:

- **The Clear All menu option deletes any tabs you've created**. Any text positioned with tabs reverts to the position of the default tab stops. (You can delete an individual tab stop by dragging its icon off the ruler.)

- **The Delete Tab menu option deletes the currently selected tab.** (Just click it first in the tab ruler.)

- **The Repeat Tab menu option lets you create a string of tabs across the ruler that are all the same distance apart.** When you select a tab on the ruler and choose this menu option, InDesign measures the distance between the selected tab and the previous tab (or, if it's the first tab on the ruler, the distance between the selected tab and the left indent/text inset). The program then uses this distance to place new tabs, with the same alignment, all the way across the ruler. InDesign repeats tabs only to the right of the selected tab, but it inserts tabs between other tab stops.

- **The Reset Indents menu option removes any changes to the left indent, right indent, or indent hang settings defined in the paragraph style currently applied to the text.**

 The Delete Tab and Reset Indents menu options are new to InDesign CS3.

 You can also delete tabs by dragging them off the tab ruler using the mouse.

Creating Tables

Whether you're working on yesterday's box scores for the sports pages, an annual report, or a fun, little parenting magazine, you've got numbers — numbers with dollar signs, numbers with decimals, numbers intermixed with text. You have to line the columns up correctly, not only so the information looks good but also so it's easy to read. Then you often need to add ruling lines to separate the material visually for the reader.

You can do all this with tab stops, ruling lines, and other InDesign tools. Or you can make your life easier and use InDesign's table editor, which lets you specify almost any attribute imaginable in a table through the Table panel and the Table menu.

CROSS-REF InDesign lets you import tables from Microsoft Word, RTF, and Microsoft Excel files, including some of their cell formatting. Likewise, you can convert their tables to tabbed

text using the options in the Import Options dialog box that's accessible when you place a file through the Place dialog box, as covered in Chapter 14.

Figure 22.4 shows the Table panel and Table menu, as well as a table. You access the Table panel by choosing Window ➪ Type & Tables ➪ Table or pressing Shift+F9.

FIGURE 22.4

The Table panel, the Table menu, and the Control panel when a cell is selected. This figure also shows the table that appears in Figure 22.2; however, this time it's been created using the table tools rather than via tabs.

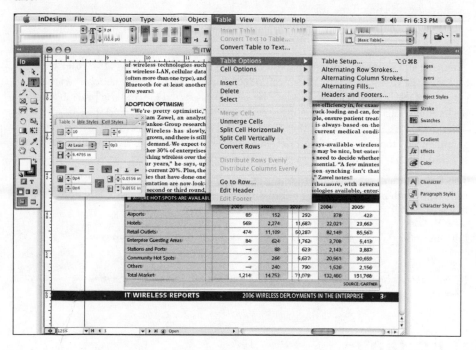

QUARKXPRESS Although both QuarkXPress and InDesign treat tables as collections of cells, InDesign offers more formatting options for cell strokes. InDesign has more controls for text and row placement. InDesign imports Word and RTF tables, while QuarkXPress does not. Only QuarkXPress 6.1 and later can import Excel spreadsheets, whereas all InDesign versions can. But QuarkXPress offers more control over the flow of text among cells in a table. InDesign doesn't let you flow text from one cell to another, much less control the order of that flow.

Creating a table

To create a table in InDesign, you first create or select a text frame with the Type tool and then choose Table ⇨ Insert Table or press Option+Shift+⌘+T or Ctrl+Alt+Shift+T. If you select an existing text frame, the table is inserted at the text cursor's location in the existing text.

That produces the Insert Table dialog box, where you type the number of body rows and columns and the number of header and footer rows. (Header and footer rows repeat on each page for tables that go across multiple pages.) Click OK to have InDesign create the basic table, which is set as wide as the text frame. The depth is based on the number of rows, with each row defaulting to the height that will hold 12-point text.

You can also apply a table style to the new table by selecting one from the Table Style pop-up menu. I cover how to create these styles later in this chapter.

With the basic table in place, you now format it using the Table panel and the Table menu. You can increase or decrease the number of rows and columns, set the row and column height, set the text's vertical alignment within selected cells (top, middle, bottom, and justified), choose one of four text-rotation angles, and set the text margin within a cell separately for the top, bottom, left, and right. Note that all the Table panel's options affect only the currently selected cells, except for the Number of Rows and Number of Columns fields. Figure 22.5 shows the Table panel with its flyout menu.

FIGURE 22.5

The Table panel and its flyout menu

TIP If you have a smallish monitor, set at 1024x768 pixels — the norm for a 17-inch display — the Table, Table Styles, and Cell Styles panels are shoved to the bottom of the panel dock, and when you select them, the only thing you see is their panel tab and flyout menu icon. You have a few choices: Shorten other panel groups in the dock to make room for them, remove other panel groups to make room for them, or drag them out of the dock and make them floating.

CROSS-REF You set cell text's horizontal alignment using the paragraph formatting controls covered in Chapter 18. You can apply other paragraph and character formatting to cell text as described in Chapters 17 and 19. You can also apply tabs within cells using the Tabs panel covered earlier in this chapter.

For more sophisticated table attributes, use the Table Options dialog box and its five panes, as shown in Figures 22.6 through 22.9. Access this dialog box using the Table Options menu item in the Table panel's flyout menu or by choosing Table ➪ Table Options. In both menus, you can select a specific pane using a submenu from the Table Options menu item.

To add items to a table, you can type text in any cell, paste text or graphics into a cell, or place text or graphics into a cell by choosing File ➪ Place or pressing ⌘+D or Ctrl+D.

NEW FEATURE InDesign CS3 lets you paste tabbed text into tables. The tabs are retained, and all the text is pasted into the same cell.

Table Setup pane

The Table Options dialog box's Table Setup pane (which has the keyboard shortcut Option+Shift+⌘+B or Ctrl+Alt+Shift+B and is shown in Figure 22.6) lets you adjust the rows and columns, as you can do in the Table panel. It's also where you specify the table border's weight, line type, color, tint, gap color and tint (if you choose a dashed, dotted, or striped line for the border), the space before and after the table, and whether row lines (which InDesign calls *strokes*) are placed on top of column lines or vice versa. If your table has cells with different line settings that would be overridden by the table border, you can preserve those cell settings by selecting the Preserve Local Formatting option.

You also can set how strokes draw in the Draw pop-up menu at the bottom of the pane; note that the InDesign 2.0 compatibility option essentially places rows in front but has them end inside the outside border, while the Row Strokes in Front has those strokes overprint the table border as well.

Row Strokes and Column Strokes panes

InDesign lets you have the lines between columns and rows alternate color, thickness, and even type. Figure 22.7 shows the Row Strokes pane; the Column Strokes pane is identical, except that it applies to column (vertical) strokes rather than to row (horizontal) strokes.

You can choose a predefined alternate pattern by using the Alternating Pattern pop-up menu, or by simply typing a number in the First and Next fields. The First field at the left of the pane specifies how many row strokes (or column strokes) get the formatting specified on the left side of the pane, while the Next field at the right side specifies how many get the formatting specified at the right. InDesign applies the formatting at left to the number of rows specified in its First field, and then switches to the formatting at right for the number of rows specified in that First field. If there are still more rows, InDesign switches back to the left side's formatting, repeating the alternating pattern until it runs out of rows. The Column Strokes pane works the same way.

FIGURE 22.6

The Table Setup pane of the Table Options dialog box

FIGURE 22.7

The Row Strokes pane of the Table Options dialog box, shown here, is identical to the Column Strokes pane.

In addition to specifying the line attributes, you can also have InDesign skip a specified number of top and bottom rows (or columns) using the Skip First and Skip Last fields. You can specify these so header and footer rows are excluded from the pattern.

Fills pane

The Fills pane, shown in Figure 22.8, is similar to the Row Strokes and Column Strokes panes. You set the color, tint, alternation pattern, and any skipped rows or columns — but not both — for fills you want applied to your table. The Alternating Pattern pop-up menu lets you pick from predefined numbers of columns or rows, depending on whether you want the fills to alternate from left to right or from top to bottom across the table.

FIGURE 22.8

The Fills pane of the Table Options dialog box

If you choose Custom Row, InDesign uses the alternation settings in the Row Strokes pane; if you choose Custom Column, InDesign uses the alteration settings in the Column Strokes pane. That ensures the line color and other settings change with the fills.

Headers and Footers pane

The Headers and Footers pane, shown in Figure 22.9, lets you change the number of header and footer rows, as well as specify how often the header and footer repeats. (If your Word or RTF file's table uses a heading row, InDesign designates it as a header row.) Your options are Every Text

Column, Once per Frame, and Once per Page. You'll usually use one of the latter options because it automatically repeats the header row for tables that break across text frames and/or pages.

FIGURE 22.9

The Headers and Footers pane of the Table Options dialog box

Working with rows and columns

InDesign's table editing tools work very much like those in Microsoft Word. To select a row or column, click on an outside edge; you can also click in a cell with the Type tool and choose Table ➪ Select ➪ Row (⌘+3 or Ctrl+3) or choose Table ➪ Select ➪ Column (Option+⌘+3 or Ctrl+Alt+3). The submenu in Table ➪ Select also lets you select all header rows, all footer rows, and all body (regular) rows.

To move to a specified row, you can choose Table ➪ Go to Row and type the row's number, but it's usually easier to use your mouse to move to the desired row. After all, how often do you know the row's number?

To quickly select header rows or footer rows, choose Table ➪ Edit Header or Table ➪ Edit Footer.

 Choose Table ➪ Select ➪ Table, or press Option+⌘+A or Ctrl+Alt+A, to select an entire table. Choose Table ➪ Delete ➪ Table to delete an entire table.

Adding and deleting

Insert or delete rows and columns using the Table menu or the Table panel's flyout menu. Both have Insert and Delete menu options. Selected rows or columns are deleted, while new rows or columns are inserted before any selected row or column. You can also use the shortcuts in Table 22.1.

Manipulating rows and columns

You can make the space between rows or columns even by choosing Table ⇨ Distribute Rows Evenly, or Table ⇨ Distribute Columns Evenly. But be careful — merging several cells increases the perceived column or row size and causes InDesign to excessively space rows or columns based on those merged cells' size.

You can also resize rows and columns by clicking any of the cell boundaries and dragging them — similar to how you can resize columns and rows in Microsoft Word's table editor.

InDesign also lets you control how rows break across frames and pages, and whether rows must be kept together. But to do so requires a dialog box oriented to cell formatting, which is covered later in this chapter.

TIP InDesign can convert regular (body) rows to header and footer rows, or vice versa. Select the row(s) you want to convert; then choose Table ⇨ Convert Rows; and then choose To Header, To Body, or To Footer as appropriate.

NOTE All the row and column options are available in both the Table menu and the Table panel's flyout menu, as well as through the contextual menu that appears when you select one or more cells and Control+click or right-click.

TABLE 22.1

Table-Editing Shortcuts

Command	Mac Shortcut	Windows Shortcuts
Select cell	⌘+/	Ctrl+/
Select row	⌘+3	Ctrl+3
Select column	Option+⌘+3	Ctrl+Alt+3
Select table	Option+⌘+A	Ctrl+Alt+A
Insert cell	Option+⌘+9	Ctrl+Alt+9
Insert row	⌘+9	Ctrl+9
Delete cell	Shift+Backspace	Shift+Backspace
Delete row	⌘+Backspace	Ctrl+Backspace

Working with cells

InDesign offers the Cell Options dialog box to manage the formatting of cells. It's accessible by choosing Cell Options from the Table menu or from the Table panel's flyout menu. Four panes are available, as shown in Figures 22.10 through 22.13.

Text pane

The Cell Options dialog box's Text pane, which is accessible through the shortcut Option+⌘+B or Ctrl+Alt+B and shown in Figure 22.10, addresses several options available in the Table panel covered earlier in this chapter, including the top, bottom, left, and right cell insets (margins), as well as vertical text alignment and text rotation. But it has several other options:

- **Paragraph Spacing Limit:** This option determines the maximum space between paragraphs in a cell when you choose Justify from the Align pop-up menu. This prevents too much space between paragraphs in a cell.
- **First Baseline:** This option determines how the text baseline is positioned from the top of a cell. The options are Ascent, Cap Height, Leading, x Height, and Fixed.

CROSS-REF Vertical alignment and baseline positioning work the same as they do for text frames, as covered in Chapters 15 and 10, respectively.

- **Clipping Contents to Cell:** This option displays only the amount of text that fits in the cell's current size — if checked, it prevents the cell from expanding to accommodate the text.

FIGURE 22.10

The Text pane of the Cell Options dialog box

Strokes and Fills pane

Shown in Figure 22.11, the Strokes and Fills pane lets you choose the weight, type, color, and tint of the strokes around a cell, as well as any gap color and tint (if you choose a striped, dashed, or dotted line as the stroke type).

FIGURE 22.11

The Strokes and Fills pane of the Cell Options dialog box

At the top of the pane is the representation of the selected cells, depending on whether you've highlighted one or multiple cells when you open this pane. Figure 22.11 shows the representation when multiple cells are selected across more than one row and more than one column. (If you select multiple cells in one row, you get two cells shown side by side; if you select multiple cells in one column, you get two cells, one on top of the other.)

Click on the cell boundary to which you want to apply the stroke formatting and then choose the formatting you want. You could have different formatting for each of the left, right, top, and bottom outside cell boundaries, as well as different formatting for the horizontal boundary between selected cells and for the vertical formatting for the vertical boundary between selected cells. Usually, you select all outside boundaries and apply stroke formatting to all of them simultaneously, and you may do the same for the interior boundaries as well.

NOTE   **InDesign does not show you the stroke formatting applied to the representation's segments, so you may not realize that different segments have different settings. Therefore, it's best to make sure the selected cells are visible and that you've checked the Preview option so you can see what you're actually applying to the cells.**

In this pane, you can also select a fill color for the selected cells, based on existing color swatches, as well as a tint.

You can set both cell strokes and fills as Overprint, which means the color prints on top of any underlying color, rather than knocking out that color. Overprinting can change the color the reader sees because it essentially mixes inks. Overprinting a blue fill on a yellow background, for example, results in a green fill.

Rows and Columns pane

The Row and Columns pane (see Figure 22.12) sets row height and column width, as well as keeps options for rows:

The Rows and Columns pane of the Cell Options dialog box

- **Row Height pop-up menu:** Use this to specify the height as either Exactly or At Least the measurement to the right of the menu. This is the same as what you can specify in the Table pane.

- **Column Width field:** This field is also the same option you have in the Table pane to set the column width.

- **Keep Options:** Use the Start Row pop-up menu to determine where the selected row starts. You can choose Anywhere, which means after the previous row (space permitting in the text frame, of course); In Next Text Column; In Next Frame; On Next Page; On Next Odd Page; or On Next Even Page. Select the Keep with Next Row option to keep rows together.

Diagonal Lines pane

A unique InDesign feature is the ability to place diagonal lines in table cells. Figure 22.13 shows the Diagonal Lines pane. It's similar to other panes involving strokes except for two specific options:

- You choose the type of diagonal line — top left to bottom right, bottom left to top right, or both — using the iconic buttons at the top of the pane.

- You determine whether the diagonal line appears on top of the cell contents or vice versa using the Draw pop-up menu.

FIGURE 22.13

The Diagonal Lines pane of the Cell Options dialog box

Other cell options

Most of the work you do with cells involves typing and editing text (or graphics), applying fills and strokes, and setting margins (as covered earlier in this chapter), as well as formatting text (as covered in Chapters 16 through 20) and formatting frames (as covered in Chapters 11 and 12). After all, a cell is essentially just a text or graphics frame that's contained in a table with other frames. But there are a few other things to know about working with cells:

- You can merge and unmerge cells by highlighting the cells and choosing Table ⇨ Merge Cells or Table ⇨ Unmerge Cells.

- You can split cells by highlighting the cells and choosing Table ⇨ Split Cell Horizontally or Table ⇨ Split Cell Vertically. To unsplit cells, you must merge them. (You can also choose Edit ⇨ Undo, or press ⌘+Z or Ctrl+Z, before taking another action.) Cells that are split take on the cell's current settings for text formatting, fill color, size, margins, and strokes.

- InDesign indicates text that does not fit in a cell with a large red dot in the cell, as Figure 22.14 shows.

- You can apply colors and gradients to cells, as well as strokes, using the standard InDesign Swatches, Gradient, and Stroke panels (all accessible through the Window menu). These have the same effect as using the equivalent Table menu and Table panel options.

FIGURE 22.14

InDesign indicates text that does not fit in a cell by displaying large red dots in the cell. Here, they appear in the rightmost column.

■ WHERE HOT SPOTS ARE AVAILABLE		2001	2002	2003	2004	2005
Airports		85	152	292	378	423
Hotels		569	2,274	11,687	22,021	●
Retail Outlets		474	11,109	50,287	82,149	●
Enterprise Guesting Areas		84	624	1,762	3,708	5,413
Stations and Ports		—	88	623	2,143	3,887
Community Hot Spots		2	266	5,637	20,561	●
Others		—	240	790	1,526	2,156
Total Market		1,214	14,752	71,079	132,486	●
					SOURCE: GARTNER	

- The Control panel offers easy access to several cell and table features, as Figure 22.15 shows. Note that these options appear only if at least one cell is selected — meaning the entire cell, rather than just some of its contents. Figure 22.15 also calls out table- and cell-specific controls.

TIP You can apply strokes to cells through the Stroke panel (Window ⇨ Stroke, or ⌘+F10 or Ctrl+F10). Use its flyout menu to select the Stroke Styles menu option, which provides a list of styles and the ability to create your own, as Chapter 12 explains.

Using table and cell styles

To make it easy to apply and update table formatting across a document, InDesign provides table and cell styles. They work like paragraph, character, and object styles, taking the table formatting features covered earlier in this section and bringing them together into the New Table Style and New Cell Style dialog boxes.

NEW FEATURE Table and cell styles are new to InDesign CS3.

To work with table styles, open the Table Styles panel by choosing Window ⇨ Type & Tables ⇨ Table Styles. To work with cell styles, open the Cell Styles panel by choosing Window ⇨ Type & Tables ⇨ Cell Styles. Choose New Table Style or New Cell Style from the appropriate panel's flyout menu, and then use the various panes to specify the desired formatting. The panes, and their options, are the same as described earlier in this chapter.

TIP   Whether creating a new table style or a new cell style, the easiest method is to format an existing table or cell the way you want it, select it, and then create a new table or cell style — InDesign picks up the existing formatting for the new style. Otherwise, you have to specify everything in the New Table Style or New Cell Style dialog box, where it's harder to see the effects of your settings.

FIGURE 22.15

The Control panel and its flyout menu when table cells are selected

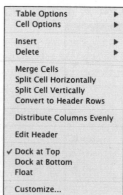

There are a few notes about creating table and cell styles — in the General pane of the New Table Style and New Cell Style dialog boxes, shown in Figures 22.16 and 22.17, respectively — that you should know before getting too far in to them:

- You give each style its own name. Choose names that should make sense a week or a month later, so you know what they are meant to be used for!

- You can base a new table style on an existing one, so changes to the parent style are automatically reflected in the children styles based on it.

- You can assign a keyboard shortcut to styles you use frequently.

When creating table styles, you can also have the table style automatically apply the cell styles of your choosing to the following table elements: header rows, footer rows, body rows, the leftmost column, and the rightmost column.

When creating cell styles, you can choose a paragraph style to be automatically applied to text in cells using the style.

FIGURE 22.16

The General pane of the New Table Style dialog box

CROSS-REF The controls for applying, modifying, and managing table and cell styles are the same as for paragraph and character styles, so refer to Chapter 20 for details on these common functions.

FIGURE 22.17

The General pane of the New Cell Style dialog box

Converting Tabs to Tables

Often, you'll have a table done using tabs—whether imported from a word processor or originally created in InDesign with tabs—that you want to convert to a real InDesign table. That's easy. Select the tabbed text you want to covert and choose Table ⇨ Convert Text to Table. You get the Convert Text to Table dialog box shown in Figure 22.18.

FIGURE 22.18

The Convert Text to Table dialog box

In the Convert Text to Table dialog box, you can choose a Column Separator (Tab, Comma, Paragraph, or a text string you type in the field) or a Row Separator (same options). Although most textual data uses tabs to separate columns and paragraphs to separate rows, you may encounter other data that uses something else. For example, spreadsheets and databases often save data so that commas separate columns rather than tabs. That's why InDesign lets you choose the separator characters before conversion.

During the conversion, InDesign formats the table using the standard settings, and the current text formatting and the default cell insets and stroke types. You can then adjust the table using the tools covered earlier in this chapter. Note that the conversion treats all rows as body rows.

You can also convert a table to text by selecting multiple cells or an entire table, as described earlier, and choosing Table ➪ Convert Table to Text. InDesign presents the same options as it does in the Convert Text to Table dialog box, so you can determine how the converted data appears.

QUARKXPRESS In one way, InDesign is savvier about text-to-table conversion than QuarkXPress because InDesign lets you choose any string as the column or row separator during conversion (just type that string in the appropriate field). But in another way, InDesign is less savvy: QuarkXPress lets you pivot data during conversion, so you can swap columns and rows for a better fit.

Summary

Unlike the typewriter days, creating tabs in a page-layout application provides various options for aligning text with a tab and creating tab leaders. The Tabs panel (Type ➪ Tabs, or ⌘+Shift+T or Ctrl+Shift+T) provides an interactive ruler for positioning tabs along with all the other controls you need. Your ultimate success with using the tabs feature depends on how well you prepared the text in the first place — the key is to position one tab correctly rather than entering several tabs to achieve the correct placement.

To create tables in InDesign, you use the Table panel (Window ➪ Type & Tables ➪ Table or Shift+F9) to create the table outline, format cells, merge and split cells, apply colors and ruling lines, and do other complex table editing. Table and cell styles let you apply this formatting consistently across multiple tables, as well as update multiple tables simultaneously as formatting changes.

You can also convert tabbed text into a table and vice versa.

Chapter 23

Automating Text

IN THIS CHAPTER

Using automatic page numbers and section names

Working with text variables

Creating mail-merged and other customized documents

Creating catalogs and other structured documents with Tagged Text files

A key area of improvement over the years in InDesign is the increased use of text automation. From the very beginning, InDesign offered automatic page numbers so your folios and cross-references would reflect the current pages as your layout changed. Later versions enhanced this with section markers, which let you create variable names in folios for your section titles. Still later came the ability to use data files and merge their contents into a layout to customize your output, similar to how word processors let you customize labels with their mail-merge feature. The newest version of InDesign adds to this mix a new option: variable text, which gives you more flexibility in where and how you can have InDesign update text automatically throughout a document.

Although not designed for variable text, another long-standing InDesign feature helps automate the creation of documents from sources such as databases. The Tagged Text format is a powerful way to create catalogs and other such layouts that have consistent formatting for content that varies from each edition — or even from entry to entry within a layout.

Altogether, these features have helped InDesign stake significant ground in reducing the labor and time of manual processes, such as search and replace, for text that changes predictably throughout the document.

Automating Page Numbers

You may often want page references in text — the current page number in a folio, for example, or the target page number for a "continued on" reference. You could type in a page number manually on each page of a multipage document, but that can get old fast. As I mention earlier in this book (see Chapters 5 and 7), if you're working on a multipage document, you should be using master pages. And if you're using master pages, you should handle page numbers on document pages by placing page-number characters on their master pages.

If you want to add the current page number to a page, you can choose Type ➪ Insert Special Character ➪ Markers ➪ Current Page Number, or press Option+Shift+⌘+N or Ctrl+Shift+Alt+N, whenever the Type tool is active and the text cursor (text-insertion point) is flashing. If you move the page or the text frame, the page-number character is automatically updated to reflect the new page number.

To create "continued on" and "continued from" lines, choose Type ➪ Insert Special Character ➪ Markers ➪ Next Page Number to have the next page's number inserted in your text, or choose Type ➪ Insert Special Character ➪ Markers ➪ Previous Page Number to have the previous page's number inserted. That next or previous page is the next or previous page in the story. (There are no shortcuts for these complex menu sequences — unless you assign your own, as explained in Chapter 3.)

One flaw in InDesign's continued-line approach is that the text frames must be linked for InDesign to know what the next and previous pages are. Thus, you're likely to place your continued lines in the middle of your text. But if the text reflows, so do the continued lines. Here's a way to avoid that: Create separate text frames for your continued-on and continued-from text frames. Now link just those two frames, not the story text. This way, the story text can reflow as needed without affecting your continued lines.

Using Section Markers

InDesign offers another marker called the section marker that lets you insert specific text into your document and update it by just changing the marker text.

The section marker is defined as part of a section start (see Chapter 5), and it's meant to be used in folios for putting in the section name or chapter name. But you can use it anywhere you want and for anything you want, not just for section or chapter labels.

To define a section marker (there can be only one per section, of course), open the Pages panel (Window ➪ Pages, or ⌘+F10 or Ctrl+F10) and choose Numbering & Section Options from the panel's flyout menu. In the resulting dialog box, type a text string in the Section Marker field. Then click OK.

To use the marker, have the text insertion point active in whatever text frame you want to insert it, and then choose Type ➪ Insert Special Character ➪ Markers ➪ Section Marker. That's it!

Using Text Variables

The section marker was clearly the inspiration for the new text-variable feature. Why stop at section markers? With text variables, you can define an unlimited number of text variables that InDesign happily updates across your documents whenever you change them, or they change with your layout.

NEW FEATURE　Text variables are new to InDesign CS3.

Creating text variables

To create a text variable, choose Type ➪ Text Variables ➪ Define. You'll get the Text Variables dialog box shown in Figure 23.1. It lists existing text variables, including the seven ones predefined in InDesign: Chapter Number, Creation Date, File Name, Last Page Number, Modification Date, Output Date, and Running Header. Any ones you create are added to this list.

Note that the source of the number used in the Chapter Number text variable is something you define as part of a book. For each document in a book, you can specify its chapter number using the Document Numbering Options dialog box accessed from the book panel's flyout menu.

CROSS-REF　Chapter 25 explains books and how to set the chapter number.

To create a new text variable, click New. You get the New Text Variable dialog box shown in Figure 23.2. Give the variable a name in the Name field, and choose the type of variable you want from the Type pop-up menu. Your choices are the eight predefined types — Chapter Number, Creation Date, File Name, Last Page Number, Modification Date, Output Date, Running Header (Character Style), and Running Header (Paragraph Style) — plus Custom Text, which lets you enter any text of your choosing.

Note that you can create more than one variable for, say, File Name or Modification Date — just give each its own name. You might do this because you want them formatted differently in different contexts. For example, you might want the modification date formatted as "Published on March 27, 2007" on a title page but as "Mod. Date: 03/27/07" in a footnote. Having two text variables using the Modification Date type lets you do this.

Also note that there are two types of running header text variables. You choose Running Header (Character Style) if you want to insert text derived from text using a certain character style; you choose Running Header (Paragraph Style) if you want to insert text derived from text using a certain paragraph style. The idea of a running header is to give the reader context for the current contents of a page as part of a folio. For example, an encyclopedia might display the name of the page's first entry in its left page folios and the name of the page's last entry in its right page folios to help the reader quickly zero into a specific topic as she thumbs through the pages. The options for formatting a text variable varies based on the type of variable it is.

TIP   If you create text variables when no document is open, these text variables will be available in all new documents you later create. You can also load text variables from other documents, as described later in this chapter.

FIGURE 23.1

The Text Variables dialog box

FIGURE 23.2

The New Text Variable dialog box, for a running header

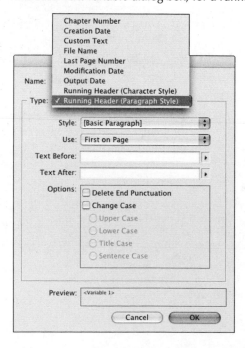

Formatting text variables

Three formatting options are available for more than one type of text variable:

- **Text Before and Text After:** These two fields — available for all types except Custom Text — let you add any text you want before or after the variable. For example, you might enter the word *Chapter* in the Text Before field for a Chapter Number variable. Note that both fields have an unnamed pop-up menu to their right from which you can select a variety of common symbols and spaces.

 Don't forget to add any needed leading or trailing spaces in the Text Before and Text After fields.

- **Style:** This pop-up menu lets you select the numbering style to apply in the Chapter Number and Last Page Number types, the character style for the Running Header (Character Style) type, and the paragraph style for the Running Header (Paragraph Style) type of text variables.

- **Date Format:** This field and its associated pop-up menu lets you choose the desired date and time formats for the Creation Date, Modification Date, and Output Date text variables. Examples include *MM/dd/yy* to get a date like 05/08/62 and *MMMM d, yyyy* top get a date like August 15, 1962. Don't worry about memorizing codes — just pick the desired options from the pop-up menu to the right of the Date Format field.

Several other variables have unique options:

- **Custom Text:** This has the fewest options. Just enter the desired text, including choosing special characters such as spaces and dashes from the unnamed pop-up menu to the right of the Text field. That's the only field to adjust for this text variable.

- **Last Page Number:** In addition to the Text Before, Text After, and Style formatting controls, this type includes one unique control: the Scope pop-up menu. Here, you choose between Section and Document to tell InDesign what you mean by last page number: if it's the section's last page or the document's last page.

- **File Name:** In addition to Text Before and Text After formatting controls, this type has two unique check boxes — Include Entire Folder Path and Include File Extension — to tell InDesign exactly how much of the filename to include. If both are unchecked, InDesign includes just the core filename, such as `Jun 07 TOC`. Checking the Include Entire Folder Path adds the file location before the core filename, such as `MacintoshHD:Projects:Jun 07 TOC` or `C:\Projects\Jun 07 TOC`. Checking the Include File Extension appends the filename extension, such as `June 07 TOC.indd`.

- **Running Header:** The formatting options for these two types are the most complex, as shown in Figure 23.2. The two Running Header menu options have two options not available to other Type pop-up menu options:
    - **Use:** Here, you determine which text to use: First on Page uses the first text on the page that has the specific style applied, while Last on Page uses the last text on the page that has the specific style applied.

■ **Options:** Here, you can control whether the punctuation of the source text is retained or not in the running header (check Delete End Punctuation to remove it) and whether the running header overrides the text of the source text's capitalization (check Change Case and then choose the appropriate capitalization option: Upper Case, Lower Case, Title Case, or Sentence Case).

Editing and managing text variables

Editing text variables is very much like creating them: Just select the variable to change in the Text Variables dialog box and click Edit. You get the Edit Text Variable dialog box, which is identical except for its name to the New Text Variable dialog box covered in the previous section.

You format text variables like any other text, applying styles and local formatting as you would with any other text.

You can also import text variables from other documents by clicking Load in the Text Variables dialog box, and then choosing the document to import the variables from. After choosing a document, you get the Load Text Variables dialog box, shown in Figure 23.3, where you can select which variables are imported and handle name conflicts.

To get rid of a text variable, select it from the list in the Text Variables dialog box and click Delete.

To convert a text variable in your document to the actual text, highlight it using the Type tool and either choose Type ⇨ Text Variables ⇨ Convert Variable to Text or, if you happen to be in the Text Variables dialog box, click Convert to Text.

Inserting text variables

Inserting text variables in your document uses the same essential process as inserting a special character such as a section market, except you use the Text Variable menu option: Choose Type ⇨ Text Variables ⇨ Insert Variable, and then choose the desired variable from the submenu. If you happen to be in the Text Variables dialog box, select the desired text variable from the list and click Insert.

Linguistic Smarts

InDesign's text-variable feature is smart enough to translate names of days and months into whatever language you've specified for the text (using the Language option in the Character panel or in your character or paragraph style). For example, **Monday, May 1, 2007 AD** becomes **mardi, mai 1, 2007 apr. J.-C.** in French and Τρίτη, Μαΐου 1, 2007 μ.Χ. in Greek.

But it is not smart enough to change the date format for the target language, such as changing the American English notation of 05/01/2007 to 01/05/2007 for most European languages.

FIGURE 23.3

The Load Text Variables dialog box

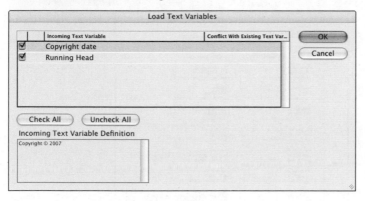

Working with Merged Data

Word processing programs such as Microsoft Word have long let you create forms with mail merge, so you can send a letter to lots of people, letting Word automatically print a copy for all recipients and insert their names, addresses, and so forth into their copies. (Some programs have called this capability *variable text.*) A decade ago, PageMaker 7 added a similar capability called *data merge*, which uses the same principle to handle variable text for form letters, catalogs, and other documents where the layout is identical but specific pieces are customized. InDesign's approach is based on the old PageMaker tool.

Merged-data documents fall into two basic classes, as Figure 23.4 shows:

- Form letters, where one layout is printed multiple times, with each copy having personalized information.

- Labels, where layout components are repeated several times in the same layout, but with different information. Usually just one copy is printed.

What InDesign's data-merge feature cannot do is let you create catalogs in which you have different, variable-sized records on one page. You can use the data-merge feature for catalog-type documents if your layout is highly structured and each record takes exactly the same amount of space (as address labels do).

CROSS-REF If you want to create catalogs or other documents with variable-sized records from databases or similar sources, use InDesign Tagged Text, as described later in this chapter.

FIGURE 23.4

Two types of merged-data documents: a form letter (left) and a set of mailing labels (right)

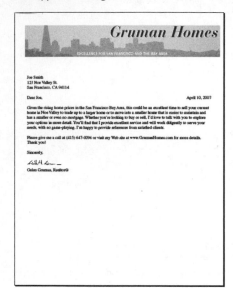

Setting up merged data

Regardless of which kind of merged documents you are creating, the setup is the same. Create a text file with the various data separated either by tabs or commas (use just one as your separator in the file, rather than mix the two). Start a new record by pressing Enter or Return (a new paragraph). The first row should contain the names of the fields. For example, for a local guidebook listing cafés, your data might look like this (I've put → characters to indicate the tabs):

```
name→address→phone
Martha & Bros.→3868 24th St.→(415) 641-4433
Martha & Bros.→1551 Church St.→(415) 648-1166
Martha & Bros.→745 Cortland St.→(415) 642-7585
Martha & Bros.→2800 California St.→(415) 931-2281
Diamond Corner Café→751 Diamond St.→(415) 282-9551
Farley's Coffeehouse→1315 18th St.→(415) 648-1545
```

This simple file has three fields per entry: the café name, its address, and its phone number. The file uses tabs as the separators.

 NOTE   Because the source file is a text-only file, it cannot contain any formatting such as boldface or italics.

To import graphics as inline graphics, precede the field name with @, such as *@photo*. The record fields need to provide the complete path to the graphic file, which must be in a supported format. For example, a file's complete path could be `MacintoshHD:Images:myphoto.tiff` on the Mac or `C:\Images\myphoto.tif` in Windows.

Creating pages with merged data

With the source file ready, create or go to the text frame in which you want to flow your data, selecting the text-insertion point with the Type tool.

TIP There's a real benefit to putting your fields on master pages: You can then update the layout if the source data file changes (choose Update Data Fields from the Data Merge panel's flyout menu). You cannot do this if you place the fields on a regular document page because InDesign would have created a new document containing the merged data.

Now follow these steps to insert the fields in that frame:

1. Open the Data Merge panel by choosing Window ➪ Automation ➪ Data Merge.

2. **Choose Select Data Source from the Data Merge panel's flyout menu, navigate to the desired file using the resulting dialog box, and click Open.** If your data file changes, you can import the most current version by choosing Update Data Source from the Data Merge panel's flyout menu. Choose Remove Data Source to remove a data file from the panel.

3. **The Data Merge panel now lists the data file and the fields it contains, as Figure 23.5 shows.**

FIGURE 23.5

The Data Merge panel and its flyout menu

Create Merged Document button

Controls for moving through records if Preview is enabled

4. **Click and drag the fields to the appropriate spots in your layout, or double-click a field name to insert it at the current text-insertion point.** For example, in a form letter, you might click and drag the Name field to a point right after the text *Dear* and before the comma in the salutation. The field names are enclosed in French quotation marks (« »). In your layout, this would look like

```
Dear «Name»,
```

You can use a field more than once in the layout. The panel shows which page numbers each field is used in (to the right of the field name).

5. **Format the fields as desired.** They take on any paragraph formatting applied to the paragraphs containing them. You can use character styles and/or other local formatting on the fields as desired.

6. **Click the Create Merged Document iconic button at the bottom right of the panel or choose Create Merged Document from the flyout menu to import the entire data file's contents into your layout.** The Create Merged Document dialog box shown in Figure 23.6 opens with the Records pane. In this pane, you have the following options:

FIGURE 23.6

The Records pane of the Create Merged Document dialog box

- In the Records to Merge section, choose which records to import. You can choose All, Single Record, or Range.

■ In the Records per Document Page pop-up menu, choose Single Record if you want a new page output per record (such as in a form letter) or Multiple Records if you want to print multiple copies of the same record on a page (such as for business cards). Note that InDesign copies the entire text frame containing the data fields when you choose Multiple Records. (See the next section for more details on placing multiple records per page.)

7. **Go to the Options pane and verify that the placement options work for your document.** Figure 23.7 shows the Options pane, whose options are:

■ In the Image Placement section, choose how to fit any imported graphics by choosing an option in the Fitting pop-up menu. You typically pick Fit Images Proportionally, which is the default setting. You can also select the Center in Frame option to center the imported graphics, and the Link Images option to link to the source graphics files rather than embed the graphic into the InDesign layout.

■ In the lower section of the pane, you can have InDesign remove blank lines created by empty fields by selecting the Remove Blank Lines for Empty Fields option. This is handy, for example, if your layout permits two address lines per recipient. Anyone with a single address line has no space between that address and the city name if this option is selected. You can also limit the number of pages in the merged document by selecting the Page Limit per Document option and typing a value in its field.

8. **Click OK. InDesign creates a new document based on the original layout and merged data.** The merged text is now editable and is no longer linked to its source data, so to update the document you need to regenerate it from the document that contains the data-merge records. (That's why InDesign creates a new document for the resulting data rather than replacing the source file.)

There is a key exception: If you place the records on a master page, the data-merge feature creates document pages based on the imported data within the current document, rather than creating an entirely new document. If you place the records on a master page, you can later update the records through the Data Merge panel and have the document pages updated as well.

TIP You can preview the data in your fields by enabling the Preview check box in the Data Merge panel (or choosing Preview from its flyout menu). You can go through the actual data by using the arrow buttons to the right of the Preview option or by typing a record ▪ ▪ in the preview field.

▪ ▪ can set placement options before creating a merged document by choosing Content ▪ ▪ ▪ ent Options from the Data Merge panel's flyout menu. Figure 23.7 shows the ▪ ▪ ▪ tions dialog box, which has the same options as the Options pane of the ▪ ▪ ▪ ent dialog box.

FIGURE 23.7

The Options pane of the Create Merged Document dialog box and the Content Placement Options dialog box offer the same options.

Working with multiple records per page

As I describe in the previous section, you can have InDesign create a new page for each record or place multiple records on the same page. Although the process for both adding fields and generating the pages via the Data Merge panel is the same for both, note that creating multiple records on a page may not quite work as you might expect:

- The various options pertaining to multiple records are grayed out if your document has other pages with content already placed on them. So if you want to have pages that contain other information, such as a title page, you need to create those pages after you have created the multiple records. Note that you can have other objects on the master page or document page that contains the frame from which the multiple records will be based, but not content on any other page.

- Keep in mind that InDesign copies the entire frame that your merged data is in, one for each of the record—*don't* copy the frames containing the data-merge text in your layout to fill out your page. So be sure you want everything in that frame copied and that the frame is as large as needed to hold the records but no larger (otherwise, you will get excessive white space). And be sure that this "master" frame should placed at the topmost and leftmost position in your layout.

■ Be sure that you leave blank the space in which the labels' fields are copied — the data-merge feature won't work around objects in the layout. Instead, it blindly follows the specs in the Multiple Record Layout pane, repeating fields until the page is full or until it runs out of fields.

Figure 23.8 shows a simple layout that is a typical example of where you would use the Multiple Records option. You set up the placement of these records in the Multiple Record Layout pane, shown in Figure 23.9.

FIGURE 23.8

Top: A layout with one record that will be copied multiple times on the page using the Data Merge panel's Multiple Record Layout functions. Bottom: A page created with six records from the frame at top.

The Multiple Records pane of the Create Merged Document dialog box, along with the records previewed

Using Tagged Text for Database Publishing

The InDesign Tagged Text format can be very handy as a start to database publishing. Its markup codes let you specify and even define the formatting in a document, so you can create a text file with the InDesign commands embedded in them. When InDesign imports the file, it applies all the formatting specified. If you can generate these codes from a database or other automation system, you can automate much of the creation of complex documents such as catalogs whose content changes frequently.

 Chapter 4 explains the Tagged Text format in more detail.

For example, say you have a product directory that lists the company name, URL, and product description. You'd have a text file with entries that look something like this:

```
<ASCII-WIN>
<pstyle:Company>Name 1
<pstyle:URL>Web address 1
<pstyle:Description>Descriptive text 1 goes here.
<pstyle:Company>Name 2
<pstyle:URL>Web address 2
<pstyle:Description>Descriptive text 2 goes here.
```

The `<ASCII-WIN>` (or `<ASCII-MAC>` if the file was created on a Mac) code appears only at the top of the file. The code `<pstyle:style name>` specifies the paragraph style to apply (for character styles, the code is `<cstyle:style name>`). Be sure that the name is an exact match, including any capitalization; otherwise, InDesign doesn't recognize the style you want to use.

The trick is to have your database or other information source add the codes before the content they export. Typically, you'd do this using a programming language that comes with or is compatible with your database or content source.

To use text coded this way, you open an existing document that is already set up with text frames and styles, and then place the Tagged Text file into the document. The coded text takes on the designated styles, making it easy, for example, to flow an updated catalog into a template. Figure 23.10 shows a document created this way.

FIGURE 23.10

A catalog created by importing a Tagged Text file

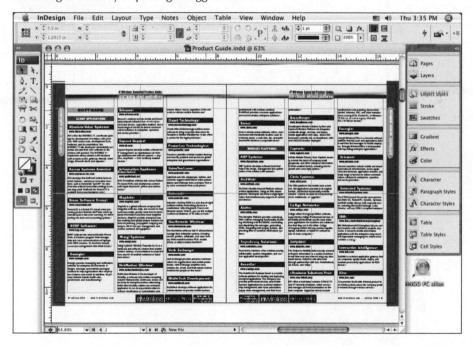

Summary

It's a lot of work to track page number references in a document as text reflows and the number of pages changes. The automatic page numbering characters in InDesign resolve that burden, tracking the current page numbers and the page numbers used in continued lines for you.

InDesign lets you specify all sorts of text variables — such as section names, current date, chapter numbers, and text you specify — to likewise remove the manual effort in keeping text that changes predictably up to date.

To help reduce labor, InDesign also lets you produce data-merge documents. Such documents contain variable text, such as the address in a form letter or pricing and names in a catalog.

Finally, consider using the InDesign Tagged Text format to specify sophisticated formatting, such as defining paragraph and character styles in InDesign, in your word processor or database. This requires a familiarity with programming or coding in formats like HTML but can be a powerful way to add formatting for highly predictable, structured documents in your word processor before you import the file into InDesign. Using it just to specify paragraph and style sheets is a great way to bring database-oriented data, such as catalogs, into an InDesign template.

Chapter 24

Working with Footnotes, Indexes, and TOCs

IN THIS CHAPTER

Adding footnotes

Indexing documents and books

Creating tables of contents and lists

Many business documents — books, reports, white papers, and so on — use features traditionally associated with academic book publishing: footnotes to cite sources, indexes to provide a map to where specific content is located in the document, and tables of contents (TOCs) to provide an overview of the document's structure and contents.

When you're working on any type of document — a report, a magazine, a textbook — you can easily spend more time manually creating tables of contents, keeping footnotes updated, and laboriously managing indexes than you spend designing the publication. InDesign helps reduce this labor while also ensuring that your footnotes, indexes, and TOC stay automatically updated as your document is revised.

CROSS-REF Although you can use the footnote, index, and TOC features in individual documents, they're also designed to work across multiple documents such as books. Chapter 25 covers how to manage such multi-document projects.

Working with Footnotes

Many kinds of document use footnotes — academic articles and journals, books, manuals, and even some magazines. So it makes sense for InDesign to support them as well.

InDesign imports footnotes from Microsoft Word files (see Chapter 14), as well as lets you add footnotes directly. The process is simple: Choose Type ➪ Insert Footnote, and InDesign adds a footnote to the bottom of the column that contains the footnote entry, as Figure 24.1 shows. InDesign handles the footnote numbering as you add and delete footnotes; you type the footnote text.

InDesign can help you find the footnoted text in your document. Using the Type tool, select all or part of the desired footnote text at the bottom of a column or text frame, and then choose Type ➪ Go to Footnote Reference. InDesign then goes to the page containing the original footnote reference, placing that text near the center of the window.

But footnotes are more complicated than that, so InDesign lets you control much of the appearance of footnotes by choosing Type ➪ Document Footnote Options to open the Footnote Options dialog box, whose two panes are shown in Figure 24.2.

FIGURE 24.1

A three-column text box with a footnote in the first column

FIGURE 24.2

The Footnote Options dialog box's two panes: Numbering and Formatting (left) and Layout (right)

> **CAUTION** InDesign also inserts footnotes at the bottom of a text frame, even if there are other frames overlapping that text frame with text wrap turned on. This means that you can inadvertently obscure a footnote under another frame because you understandably — but mistakenly — think that turning on text wrap causes InDesign to keep the footnote outside that other frame.

> **CAUTION** You cannot insert footnotes into tables. Instead, you have to handle them the old, manual way: inserting a footnote character as needed and typing your footnotes below the table, and updating the footnote as needed manually.

Numbering and Formatting pane

Use the Numbering and Formatting pane of the Footnote Options dialog box to control the formatting of the footnote text and footnote character in the current InDesign document. (To change these settings for future documents, open the dialog box with no document open and set your new defaults.)

You have these options in the Numbering section:

- **Style:** Choose the numbering style through the Style pop-up menu, which gives you seven numbering options:
  - *, **, *** . . .
  - a, b, c, d, . . .
  - A, B, C, D, . . .
  - *, †, ‡, §, ¶ . . .
  - i, ii, iii, iv . . .
  - I, II, III, IV . . .
  - 1, 2, 3, 4 . . .

- **Start At:** Choose the starting number by typing a value in the Start At field (the default is 1).

- **Restart Numbering Every:** If you want the numbering to restart on each page, spread, or section, select the Restart Numbering Every option and then choose Page, Spread, or Section from its pop-up menu.

- **Show Prefix/Suffix In:** If you want a prefix and/or suffix with the footnote number, select the Show Prefix/Suffix In option. Then choose where the prefix and/or suffix should be displayed with the adjoining pop-up menu. Its choices are Footnote Reference (that's the footnote in the text), Footnote Text (the actual footnote at the bottom of the column), and Both Reference and Text (at both locations).

  Type your prefix characters in the Prefix field and your suffix characters in the Suffix field. Use the pop-up menu to the right of the Prefix field to insert any of several special characters into the Prefix field: (, [, a hair space, and a thin space. All characters in the Prefix field precede the footnote character. Likewise, with the pop-up menu to the right of the Suffix field, you can insert a) or] in the Suffix field. All characters in the Suffix field follow the footnote character.

CROSS-REF   See Chapter 21 for details on special spaces such as hair spaces.

In the Formatting section, there are two subsections: Footnote Reference Number in Text and Footnote Formatting.

In the Footnote Reference Number in Text subsection, you have two options:

■ **Position:** Using the Position pop-up menu, specify how the footnote character is formatted; your options are Apply Superscript, Apply Subscript, and Apply Normal. Most documents use superscripts and don't have any suffixes or prefixes. But some documents enclose their footnotes in parentheses or brackets rather than superscript them; if that is your style, you would choose Apply Normal and type [in the Prefix field and] in the Suffix field in the Numbering section above.

■ **Character Style:** If you want to apply a character style to the footnote character in text, select the Apply Character Style option and then choose the style in the adjoining pop-up menu.

In the Footnote Formatting subsection, you have these options:

■ **Paragraph Style:** You can apply a specific paragraph style to the footnote text by choosing a style in the Paragraph Style pop-up menu. You typically should have a specific style for your footnotes.

■ **Separator:** Type in the Separator field the characters you want to separate the footnote number and its text. (This follows any text you typed in the Suffix field.) These are often various spaces, but they can also be a period or colon followed by a space. The pop-up menu below the field lets you choose several kinds of spaces (tab, em space, and en space).

NOTE   You can use the codes for various space characters in the Prefix, Suffix, and Separator fields. Common ones are ^t for a tab, ^m for an em space, ^> for an en space, ^< for a thin space, and ^\ for a hair space.

Layout pane

Use the Layout pane to control the placement of the footnote relative to the rest of the document.

In the Spacing Options section, you have these options:

■ **Minimum Space before First Footnote:** Set the space between the bottom of the column and the first footnote by typing a value in the Minimum Space before First Footnote field.

■ **Space Between Footnotes:** Set the space between footnotes by typing a value in the Space Between Footnotes field. You typically do not add a value here because you can better control spacing with your paragraph style used by the footnote text.

In the First Baseline section, you have these options:

- **Offset:** Set how the footnote's baseline should be determined; your options are Ascent, Cap Height, x Height, and Fixed.

- **Min:** You also can set the minimum distance from that location to the baseline by entering a value in the Min field.

CROSS-REF   See Chapter 10 for more on setting baselines.

In the Placement Options section, you have these options:

- **Place End of Story Footnotes at Bottom of Text:** Select the Place End of Story Footnotes at Bottom of Text option to override end-of-story footnotes (endnotes) generated in Microsoft Word so they appear at the bottom of text columns in InDesign.

- **Allow Split Footnotes:** If you don't want footnotes to break across columns, deselect the Allow Split Footnotes option.

In the Rule Above section, you have these options:

- **Rule On:** Select the Rule On option to place a ruling line above the footnotes. In the Rule Above pop-up menu to its left, choose First Footnote in Column or Continued Footnotes to determine which footnotes get the ruling line above them.

- **Weight, Color, Type, Tint, Overprint Stroke, Gap Color, Gap Tint, and Overprint Gap:** Use these controls to format the stroke that is used as the ruling line. (Chapter 12 covers these settings in detail.)

- **Left Indent, Width, and Offset:** Use these fields to control how the line is positioned relative to the text frame.

Indexing Documents and Books

If you've ever been unable to find information in a book that you knew was there, you can appreciate how important a good index can be. Short, simple documents can get by fine without indexes. But long books almost always need indexes to help the reader locate specific information. Indexing used to be a laborious process, involving lots of index cards. InDesign makes indexing much easier, while still relying on you to make key decisions about how the index will be formatted. The following sections show you how to do your part.

CROSS-REF   After reading this chapter, you may find that you need a more sophisticated indexing tool than InDesign provides. Check out Sonar Bookends InDex Pro by Virginia Systems, to which I have a link on the companion Web site (www.InDesignCentral.com). In addition, the company offers Sonar Bookends InXref for creating cross-references in text that update automatically.

Nested or Run-in Index?

There is no right way to index, but common sense should be a guide. Determine which index format you use by the number of levels in the index's hierarchy. If the index has only two levels, a run-in format works well, but an index with three or more levels requires a nested format for the sake of clarity.

Nested indexes look like this:

Kitchen Hardware

Buying, 191

Cost estimates, 242–248

Design guidelines 92–94, 96, 99–101

Hiring contractors, 275–284

Installation, 180–195

Sizing, 91–99

Standards, 24–28, 98, 133

Tools, 199–203, 224, 282–283

Run-in indexes look like this:

Kitchen Hardware: Buying, 191; Cost estimates, 242–248; Design guidelines 92–94, 96, 99–101; Hiring contractors, 275–284; Installation, 180–195; Sizing, 91–99; Standards, 24–28, 98, 133; Tools, 199–203, 224, 282–283

Although InDesign doesn't force you to make this decision until you actually build the index, you really need to make it before you get started. If you tag words for a four-level nested index, but then build a run-in index, your index will be too confusing for readers to make sense of trying to follow all those levels in a string of text.

Choosing an indexing style

Your approach to developing an index depends on the indexing style you want to use. Large publishers usually have their own house style guides for indexes. If you don't have a style guide for indexes, I recommend that you read through the indexing guidelines in *The Chicago Manual of Style*. Another option is to use an index you like as a model and then take the steps necessary in InDesign to achieve that index style. Before you begin indexing your document, ask yourself the following questions:

- Do you want to capitalize all levels of all entries, or do you just want sentence-style caps?
- Should headings appear in boldface?
- What type of punctuation will you use in your index?
- Should the index be nested or run-in style (see the sidebar "Nested or Run-in Index?")?

Once you make these decisions, it's a good idea to make a small dummy of your index. From the dummy, create a master page for index pages, paragraph styles for letter headings (A, B, C, and so on in the index), paragraph styles for each level of the index (including indents as appropriate), and character styles for any special formatting you want on page numbers or cross-reference text. InDesign doesn't do any of this for you — if you don't set up styles for your index, your multilevel index will simply look linear when it's built.

Using the Index panel

When a chapter or document is ready to be indexed, open the Index panel (Window ➪ Type & Tables ➪ Index or Shift+F8). You use this panel to add words to the index in up to four indent levels, edit or delete index entries, or create cross-references. The Index panel appears in Figure 24.3.

FIGURE 24.3

The Index panel and its flyout menu

Go to Selected Marker | Delete Selected Entry

Update Preview | Create New Index Entry

Generate Index

Understanding Reference and Topic modes

The Index panel has two modes, indicated by the radio buttons at the top: Reference and Topic. Reference mode is the mode you should be in when adding and editing entries from selected text.

NOTE If you're creating an index in a book (see Chapter 25), be sure to enable the Book check box in the Index panel.

The Topic mode is meant to give you a clean environment in which to enter the topic names and levels that you want your index to have. Then, when an indexer adds an index entry, she can use the topics that appear in the bottom of the New Page Reference dialog box and double-click the topic to use that topic definition rather than whatever she might enter herself in the dialog box. You don't have to use Topic mode if you don't want to — all index entries create *topics* (InDesign-speak for the entry text). Although a well-intentioned feature meant to help standardize index entries, the Topic mode's use is not intuitive, and most indexers simply ignore it, adding entries manually from selected text or by typing phrases into the Index panel when in Reference mode.

Note that only topics that have actual references (where text occurs on actual pages, not in the pasteboard, on a master page, or in overset text) or cross-references will appear in the final index. So don't worry about unused topic text appearing in your index.

The Index panel has the Book option. Enable this check box if you are creating an index for multiple chapters in a book. You must have a book open for this option to be available. If you do have a book open and do not select it, the index is saved with the current document and not opened with any chapter of the book. If it is selected, you can see all topics indexed across a book if you select the Topic radio button.

Entering index items via the Index panel

To add entries to your index, choose New Page Reference from the Index panel's flyout menu, or press ⌘+U or Ctrl+U, to get the dialog box shown in Figure 24.4. Here's how the controls work:

FIGURE 24.4

The New Page Reference dialog box. The middle portion changes if you select one of the cross-reference options such as See or [Custom Cross-Reference] in the Type pop-up menu, as shown in the right-hand dialog box.

- If you selected text first in your document, the text is entered automatically into Topic Level 1. Otherwise, type the text that you want to add to the index. The text is added to the Topic list and, if it is in the document, also to the list of index entries.

Indexing Differences for QuarkXPress Users

The InDesign index features are similar to those in QuarkXPress, though the InDesign Index panel and QuarkXPress Index palette are organized differently. (Furthermore, InDesign puts all its controls in the Index panel; there are no preferences to set in the Preferences dialog box as there are in QuarkXPress.)

Among the differences in functionality: QuarkXPress lets you automatically reverse the text in the Text field as you add it to the index. (For example, you can change *Classic Science Fiction* to *Science Fiction, Classic.*) InDesign does not have this feature, nor does it have a shortcut command for quick index-entry additions as QuarkXPress does.

But InDesign has the capability to generate custom cross-reference text and to specify the capitalization for topics. InDesign can also show index entries for all chapters in a book, not just for the current chapter. (Although QuarkXPress can index an entire book, its Index palette can show entries for the current chapter only, which may lead to different index formatting and word choices from chapter to chapter.) InDesign also has more formatting options for index-entry text elements and separators.

- You can type text that controls how the entry is sorted in the Sort By column. For example, if the highlighted text is *The Zango Group,* but you wanted it sorted as if it were *Zango Group, The* (so it appears with the *Z* entries in the index), type *Zango Group, The* in the Sorted By column. Similarly, you might have the movie title *2001: A Space Odyssey* sorted as *Two Thousand and One: A Space Odyssey* so the listing appears properly with the *T* entries in the index.

- More complex indexes take advantage of the four possible entry levels. You may want an index entry to appear under a higher-level topic. For example, you may want *2001: A Space Odyssey* to appear in the index under *Classic Science Fiction,* in which case you would enter *Classic Science Fiction* in the Topic Level 1 field and *2001: A Space Odyssey* in the Topic Level 2 field.

- You can apply a specific character style to an index entry's page number by enabling the Number Style Override check box and then choosing a character style from the pop-up menu to its right. InDesign lets you apply consistent formatting to all page numbers in an index, but this option is handy when you want to highlight specific page numbers to call special attention to them, such as having the definitional reference's page number appear in boldface.

NEW FEATURE The ability to apply a specific character style to an individual entry's page number is new to InDesign CS3.

- Use the Type pop-up menu to determine the page entries for the index entry. The pop-up menu has two basic sections, shown in Figure 24.5.

  - One section covers the entry's range — typically, you just want the current page number on which the text appears, but in some cases, you might want to indicate that a topic spans a number of pages, a document section, all text with a specific style, or one of the other options. For example, if you have a section about France in a world history book, you might want the main entry to indicate the whole section — such as *France, 167–203*, while leaving references in other sections (such as references in a section on Germany) to be for just the page on which it appears. If you choose For Next # of Pages or For Next # of Paragraphs, the dialog box displays the Number field for you to enter how many paragraphs or pages you want the index entry's range to span. Note that you can apply a character style to the page number generated in the index by selecting the Number Style Override option and choosing a character style in the pop-up menu to its right.

■ The other section covers cross-references, letting you choose from several types. The dialog box changes slightly, as shown in Figure 24.4, if you choose a cross-reference entry. It adds the Referenced text field for you to type the text that the index contains after the cross-reference. For example, you might choose a See reference so an entry for *secure login* appears in the index as *Secure login: See login ID*. You can create your own custom cross-references by choosing [Custom Cross-Reference]; InDesign displays the Custom text field and pop-up menu in which you type (or select from previously typed) text that you want InDesign to use. For example, you might want the cross-reference to say *Go to* rather than one of the defaults like *See*.

NOTE   Use *See* to point readers to the appropriate index entry; use *See Also* to point the readers to additional useful information elsewhere in the index; use *See Herein* to point readers to a subentry for this index entry; and use *See Also Herein* to point readers to additional useful information in a subentry to this index entry.

■ To add text within the range specified, click Add. (If the text entered is not in the specified range, the text will be added to the Topic list, but no index entry will appear for the text.) To add all occurrences of the text in the document (or book), click Add All.

FIGURE 24.5

The Type pop-up menu's options in the Page Reference Options dialog box (the New Page Reference dialog box is identical except for the name)

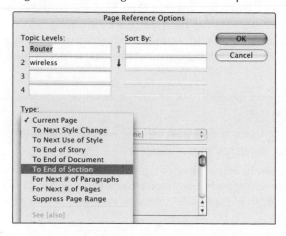

- To change previously defined index entries, choose Page Reference Options in the Index panel's flyout menu.

 In multiparagraph text selections, InDesign indexes each paragraph in that selection. The idea is that you can create lists this way.

At the bottom of both the New Page Reference and Page Reference Options dialog boxes is a list of letters as well as the entry Symbols. You can scroll through this list of headings to see what is already indexed under each letter. Although you might think clicking a letter forces the current index entry to appear in that letter's section of the index, it does not.

To see which text in your document is indexed, choose Type ➪ Show Hidden Characters, or press Option+⌘+I or Ctrl+Alt+I. Index entries will have a wide blue caret symbol before them, as Figure 24.6 shows.

FIGURE 24.6

If hidden characters are displayed, you can identify index entries by the light blue caret in front of the indexed text ("Keyboard," in this example).

Keyboard conventions¶

This book provides both the Macintosh and Windows shortcuts th
Mac shortcut first. In most cases, the Mac and Windows shortcuts
for the names of the keys, as follows:¶

• The Mac's Command key (⌘) is the most-used shortcut key. Its
is Ctrl.¶

Entering index items using keyboard shortcuts

To quickly add a word or text selection to an index, highlight the text and press ⌘+U or Ctrl+U to add the text to the New Page Reference dialog box (refer to Figure 24.4).

To index a word without opening that dialog box, just press Option+Shift+⌘+[or Ctrl+Alt+Shift+]. This adds the text to the index using its default settings. (You can always edit them later, as I describe in the next section.) And to enter an index entry as a proper name (last name, first name), use the shortcut Option+Shift+⌘+] or Ctrl+Alt+Shift+].

Editing index entries

You can edit an index entry by double-clicking its page number in the Index panel or by selecting a page number and choosing Page Reference Options from the flyout menu. You get the Page Reference Options dialog box, shown in Figure 24.5. It is identical to the New Page Reference dialog box shown in Figure 24.4, except for its name. To change the entry, just change the desired attributes in this dialog box and click OK.

Incorporating Indexing into a Workflow

If you're working on a document by yourself, or you're creating a fairly simple index in a work-group, you can pretty much index as you go. Or you can plan some time at the end of the editorial cycle to go through a document or chapters to index them.

But if your publication requires professional indexing — as would be the case for the multilevel index of a long book such as this one — deciding when to send your original InDesign files out for indexing is difficult. You might do it one chapter at a time, right after editorial approval and right before the file goes to production. Or you might send each chapter out for indexing before the last round of edits.

What you can't do is continue working on one copy of your InDesign documents while another copy is being indexed — there is no way to move the index tags to another file.

On a tight schedule, you may be tempted to move your InDesign documents into production while another copy of your files is indexed. You then generate the index, send that file to production, and then send the whole thing to print. The index is trapped in InDesign documents that aren't final — unfortunate, because the next time you edit the document, you would like to have the index tags in it. If you have to work this way, you need to decide whether to reindex the publication or redo the production work.

Working with the index

The Index panel's flyout menu has several options useful for fine-tuning and generating the index:

- **Duplicate Topic:** This option lets you duplicate a topic entry so you use the settings in one entry without having to reselect them all.

- **Delete Topic:** This option removes a topic (and any associated entries) from the index.

- **Import Topics:** This option lets you import topic lists from other InDesign documents — a very handy way to ensure consistent entry labels from chapter to chapter in a book, for example.

- **Go to Selected Marker:** This option causes InDesign to jump to the text that contains the selected index entry in the Index panel. This is a handy way of seeing if the reference in the text truly merits being listed in the index.

- **Topic Options:** This lets you edit the Level and Sort By settings for topic entries; these affect all index entries that use them. Note that this menu option becomes Page Reference Options if you have selected a specific entry's page number in the Index panel. And if the Topics radio button is selected in the Index panel, the Topic Options menu is renamed simply Options.

- **Capitalize:** This option lets you standardize the capitalization of topic entries — you can choose Selected Topic, Selected Topic and All Subtopics, All Level 1 Topics, and All Topics.

- **Update Preview:** This option updates the index entries in the Index panel to reflect page-number changes, new occurrences of index text occurrences, and deleted occurrences of indexed text. It does not change the actual index.

- **Generate Index:** This creates the actual index in your document, via the dialog box shown in Figure 24.7. Here, you specify the title for the index, the paragraph style for that title, whether a selected index is replaced with the new one, whether an entire book is indexed, whether layers on hidden layers are indexed, whether the index is nested or run-in (see the sidebar "Nested or Run-in Index?" earlier in the chapter), whether empty index headings and sections are included, what paragraph styles are applied to each level of index entry and what character styles are applied to different portions of index entries, and finally, the characters used as separators within index entries. (Click More Options to see the nested/run-in and later options.) After you generate an index, you get the standard InDesign loaded-text pointer (the paragraph icon); click an existing text frame into which you want to flow the index, or click anywhere in a document to have InDesign create the text frame for you and flow the index text into it.

> **TIP** Each time you edit text in a document or book chapter, it's a good idea to rebuild the index so the page numbers in it are updated. There is no dynamic link between a flowed and formatted index and the index markers in text.

- **Sort Options:** This lets you determine which alphabets — such as Roman, Cyrillic, and Greek — should be indexed and in what order they should appear in your index. This is quite handy for documents that use multiple alphabets. (Without this option, entries using foreign alphabets were grouped into the Symbols category in the index.)

- **Show Find Field:** This lets you find text within the entries and topics in the Index panel — it adds a Find field and ↓ (Search Forward) and ↑ (Search Backward) iconic buttons to the Index panel.

- **Show Unused Topics:** This highlights topics for which there are no index entries, so you can easily delete them.

FIGURE 24.7

The Generate Index dialog box, with all options displayed

NEW FEATURE   The Sort Options feature is new to InDesign CS3.

NOTE   For documents that contain foreign alphabets that you nonetheless want indexed all in one alphabet (such as Roman), be sure to use the desired alphabet's transliteration for the foreign term's entry in the index's topic list. For example, if your text uses the Greek letters for a fraternity name, such as ΦΓΔ, you would enter `Phi Gamma Delta` as the index entry.

Creating Tables of Contents

Long documents such as books and catalogs lend themselves to tables of contents (TOC) to give the reader a summary of the content and the locations for each section. In InDesign, a TOC is simply a list of paragraphs that are formatted with the same styles. After you create a book (or even a single document), InDesign can build a TOC by scanning the chapters for the paragraph styles you specify. For example, if you create a book, you might have paragraph styles named Chapter Title, Section, and Subsection that you apply to chapter titles, chapter sections, and chapter subsections. Using the Table of Contents feature, InDesign can generate a TOC that has all three levels.

If you want to use the Table of Contents feature, you have to use styles. Not only do styles guarantee consistent formatting, but they also tell InDesign what text you want to include in your TOC. The other thing to keep in mind for TOCs: They are linear, either listing from top to bottom the text in the order it appears in a document or in alphabetical order.

CROSS-REF   TOCs rely on paragraph styles. For more on styles, see Chapter 20.

Planning a TOC

Before you start whipping up a TOC in InDesign, decide what the content of your TOC will be: Is all the text tagged with Head and Subhead paragraph styles? (Be sure you apply styles consistently to generate an accurate TOC, so if you're not sure about that, look through the documents or chapters.)

You also need to create paragraph styles for the TOC itself. It's easy to forget that because TOCs usually have several levels themselves (a title, as well as formatting specific to each level of listing), and each level should usually have its own paragraph style. You likely also need some character styles for your TOC; for example, you might want the page numbers to be bold, in which case you'd need a character style that applies boldface to them.

After you decide what goes in your TOC, use a little bit of dummy text to format a sample TOC before you create the styles that will format the TOC itself. Your formatting should include any indents for different levels in your list and should include tabs and fill characters as necessary. When you're satisfied with the formatting of your sample TOC, create the TOC paragraph and character styles from it. Be sure to use clear names such as TOC-Level 1.

QUARKXPRESS Unlike QuarkXPress, InDesign can generate TOCs only based on paragraph styles, not on character styles. This means you can't create other kinds of lists, such as a list of companies in a magazine article or research report, based on the use of character styles. InDesign doesn't have a flexible lists feature as QuarkXPress does, but you can use the InDesign TOC feature to create some lists in addition to TOCs.

Defining a TOC

InDesign uses TOC styles to manage the formatting of TOCs. A TOC style defines the text you want in a TOC, in what order it appears, how page numbers are added, and how the various TOC elements are formatted. To create a TOC style, you choose the Layout ➪ Table of Contents Styles, which opens the dialog box shown in Figure 24.8.

FIGURE 24.8

The Table of Contents Styles dialog box

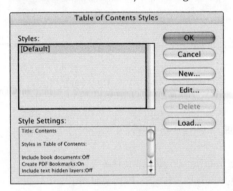

In the Table of Contents Styles dialog box, click New to create a new TOC style. You can also edit an existing style by clicking Edit, delete one by clicking Delete, and import one from another InDesign document by clicking Load.

Here's how to create a TOC style after clicking New and getting the dialog box shown in Figure 24.9 (be sure to click More Options to see everything in the figure):

1. **Type a name for the TOC style in the TOC Style field.** The default is TOC Style 1.

2. **In the Title field, type a heading for the TOC.** This is the actual text that will appear in your TOC.

3. **Use the Style pop-up menu to its right to choose the paragraph style that this title will have.** If you don't want a title, leave the Title field blank, but note that you still get an empty paragraph at the top of your TOC for this title. You can always delete that paragraph.

FIGURE 24.9

The New Table of Contents Style dialog box

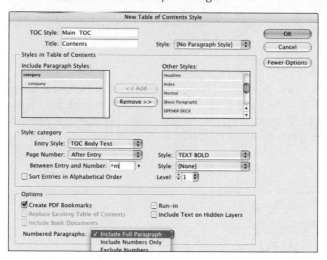

4. **In the Styles in Table of Contents section of the dialog box, click a paragraph style from the Other Styles list on the right that you want to appear in your TOC.** For example, you might click Chapter Title in a book. Click << Add to add it to the Include Paragraph Styles list at left. (Click Remove >> to remove any paragraph styles you don't want to be used in the TOC generation.)

5. **Now choose the formatting for the TOC entries that come from the selected paragraph style, using the Style section of the dialog box.** Here's where you apply the formatting to the text that appears in the TOC:

   ■ Use the Entry Style pop-up menu to select the paragraph style for the current TOC level.

   ■ Use the Page Number pop-up menu to determine how page numbers are handled: After Entry, Before Entry, and No Page Number (you might use this last option for alphabetically arranged categories in a catalog, where you want to list page numbers only for product classes and specific products). If you want the page numbers to have a character style applied, choose that style from the Style pop-up menu to the right of the Page Number pop-up menu. Use the Between Entry and Number field and pop-up menu to choose what appears between the TOC text and the page number. You can type any characters you want, as well as have multiple characters; use the pop-up menu to select special characters such as bullets and tabs. In most cases, you would select a tab; the paragraph style selected earlier for the TOC entry would include leader information, such as having a series of periods between the text and the number. You can also apply a character style to the characters between the text and the page numbers through the Style pop-up menu at right.

 If the Entry Style, Page Number, and other options don't appear, click More Options to see them.

Creating Other Lists

Although InDesign calls its list-generation feature the Table of Contents feature, you can use it for other kinds of lists. Basically, anything that is tagged with a paragraph style can be used to create a list. For example, if your captions all have titles that use their own paragraph style, you can generate a list of figures by creating a TOC style that includes just, say, the Caption Title paragraph style. An InDesign document can have more than one TOC, so you can have multiple lists in your document.

What InDesign cannot do is create a list based on *character* styles, so you can't create a list based on, say, names in a gossip column where the names use a character style to make them bold and perhaps change font as well. Nor can you create a list based on caption titles that are part of a paragraph also containing the caption; if you try to do so, your list will include the complete text of the captions as well as the embedded title.

But you may have to create your lists this way, getting the entire paragraph of, say, a caption, using the TOC feature to gather all those captions into a TOC-built list, and then removing all the text that you don't need. That still saves you time and gives you a better shot at having a complete list than entering all that text manually.

⬛ If you want the entries at this level to be sorted alphabetically, such as for a list of companies in a magazine article, select the Sort Entries in Alphabetical Order option.

NEW FEATURE You can change the alphabetization order by changing the Language option in the Character panel's flyout menu when no text or text frame is selected before having InDesign generate the TOC (described later in this chapter). The TOC will then take on the chosen language's rules for alphabetizing.

⬛ If you want to change the level of the current TOC entry, use the Level pop-up menu. Note that you do not have to manually rearrange the order of items in the Include Paragraph Styles list by clicking and dragging them if you change the level of entries — InDesign correctly sorts them when it creates the TOC, even if the levels seem out of order in the Include Paragraph Styles list.

⬛ Choose the appropriate options from the Options section of the dialog box. Select the Create PDF Bookmarks option if you're exporting the document as a PDF file and want the file to have *bookmarks* (which is essentially a clickable set of TOC links). Select the Run-in option if you want all entries at the same level to be in one paragraph; this is not common for TOCs but is used in indexes and lists of figures. Select the Replace Existing Table of Contents option if you want InDesign to automatically replace an existing TOC if the TOC style is changed. Select the Include Text on Hidden Layers option if you want text on hidden layers to be included in the TOC. Finally, select the Include Book Documents option if you have a book open and want InDesign to generate a TOC based on all chapters in that book. (InDesign shows the current open book's name.) You can control how numbered paragraphs are treated in the TOC by choosing an option from the Numbered Paragraph pop-up menu: Include Full Paragraph, Include Numbers Only, and Exclude Numbers.

NEW FEATURE The Numbered Paragraph pop-up menu is new to InDesign CS3.

6. **Continue this process for each paragraph style whose text should be in the TOC, such as Section and Subsection in a book.** Note that the order in which you add these styles determines the initial levels: The first paragraph style added is level 1, the second is level 2, and so on. But you can change the order by changing the Level setting, as I describe earlier.

QUARKXPRESS The level of formatting you can achieve over TOC entries in InDesign is greater than in QuarkXPress.

After you define a Table of Contents style, you can go to the Edit TOC Style dialog box — it's identical to the New Table of Contents Styles dialog box — and make any changes. Just choose Layout ➪ Table of Contents Styles, select the TOC style to edit, and click Edit.

With a TOC style in place and your document properly formatted with the paragraph styles that the TOC style looks for when generating a TOC, you're ready to have InDesign create the actual TOC for you. But before you do this, make sure you've saved space in the document for the TOC. This could consist of a single text frame or a series of linked text frames, or simply an empty page or set of pages (depending on how long your TOC is). When you're creating a TOC for a book, it might be useful to flow it into its own chapter.

To generate a TOC, choose Layout ➪ Table of Contents. A dialog box appears that is identical to the New Table of Contents Style dialog box shown in Figure 24.9. If desired, you can make changes to the TOC style settings. (If you want to save those changes for future TOCs generated by the TOC style, be sure to click Save Style.) Then click OK to have InDesign generate the TOC. You may also get a dialog box asking if you want to include items in *overset text* (text that didn't fit in your document after you placed it); click Yes or No as appropriate. It may take a minute or two for the program to generate the TOC. If you've selected a text frame (with or without text in it), InDesign places the TOC text in it. If no text frame is selected, InDesign displays the familiar text-insertion icon (the paragraph pointer) that it displays when you place a text file — either click a text frame to insert the TOC text in that frame or click on your document to have InDesign create a text frame in which to flow the TOC text.

Figure 24.10 shows a TOC generated by InDesign, in this case for a book.

You might need to generate a TOC just to see how long it really is, and then make the necessary space available in your document. If your TOC has its own set of page numbers, such as using Roman numerals in a separate section (as this book does), this is not an issue. But if the TOC's page numbers affect the numbering for the pages that follow, it's imperative that you generate a TOC and add the necessary pages, then generate the TOC again. Otherwise, if you have to add or delete pages based on the TOC length, the TOC will have the old page numbers, not the current ones. If you do need to update page numbering after flowing a TOC, simply rebuild the TOC by selecting the text frame holding the TOC and then choosing Layout ➪ Update Table of Contents. (Doing so skips the Table of Contents dialog box.)

NOTE If you applied local formatting to the TOC after it was generated and then later regenerate that TOC for any reason, you may need to reapply that local formatting to the updated TOC.

FIGURE 24.10

A sample TOC generated by InDesign

Summary

InDesign's book, TOC, and indexing features can significantly streamline your efforts when using these features in all sorts of business documents.

InDesign supports footnotes, both those imported from Microsoft Word and those created in InDesign. You have several options to control the formatting of the footnote text and its placement in your document.

InDesign also provides the ability to index your document, and control the formatting of those indexes. Although most users can make use of the simpler features — such as adding a First Level entry that consists of text highlighted in the document — the more complicated your index, the more you may need a professional indexer, even if he or she does the work in InDesign. If you do need a professional, be sure your schedule allows time for the indexer to take possession of your InDesign files.

The Table of Contents feature makes it easy to generate TOCs, and you can also use it for some other kinds of lists, as long as you tag the source text with consistent paragraph styles.

Chapter 25

Creating Multi-Document Projects

Longer projects such as books, catalogs, and magazines often consist of multiple InDesign documents, so multiple users can work on different pieces of the project simultaneously. Breaking up these projects into several documents also results in smaller, more manageable documents. If you're working on this type of document, by yourself or in a workgroup, InDesign provides the book feature for managing the document files, updating page numbers across documents, and ensuring consistency in the book.

In InDesign, a *book* is a special type of file that you create to track multiple documents for yourself or for a workgroup. A book file displays as a panel, and it lists each InDesign document — let's call them *chapters* to distinguish them from stand-alone documents — that you add to the book. Using these book panels, you can add, open and edit, rearrange, and print chapters of the book.

CROSS-REF Books are a natural venue for using the index and table of contents (TOC) features, given you can create a unified index or TOC across all chapters within a book in one fell swoop. Chapter 24 covers how to create indexes and TOCs. Books are also a natural way to contain files in a workgroup environment. See Chapter 35 for more details on workgroup workflow techniques.

IN THIS CHAPTER

Planning your multiple-document book project

Creating and opening books

Adding chapters to books

Managing style sources across chapters

Controlling page numbering, section variables, and chapter numbering

Printing and exporting books

The Pros and Cons of Books

Although designed for workgroups, the implementation of the book feature in InDesign has some flaws that may discourage you from using it that way. The problem is with how multiple users access book chapters:

- For a workgroup to access a book, the book itself must be stored on a shared server. Users can then open the book across the network and leave it open while they're working. To work on a document in the book, the user opens the document across the network as well. Not only can opening and saving the file be slow, but it leaves documents vulnerable to any instability in your network. (While you're working on the document, there is no local copy of it — unless you are using the Version Cue workgroup publishing tools described in Chapter 4.)

- If multiple users are working on a book or its constituent documents, they might end up saving different versions, overwriting each other, because there is no built-in document-management system for multi-user access. Or they might end up with multiple versions of the various elements. Using Version Cue can prevent people from overwriting each other's files, but you still could end up with multiple versions that someone will need to reconcile. However, InDesign indicates in the book panel whether someone else has a document open, so you can at least monitor usage before saving changes.

Despite these drawbacks, the book feature does provide advantages in a workgroup situation that may outweigh any concerns you have. These include the abilities to:

- See who is working on each chapter and when
- Update styles and swatches across documents for consistency
- Update page numbers across multiple documents
- Create a TOC and an index for multiple documents (In fact, using a book is the only way to generate a TOC and index for multiple documents.)
- Easily print all the chapters of a book with the same settings

If you need some of the benefits of using a book (such as a TOC for multiple documents), but you can't live with one of the drawbacks, you can start out with separate documents. Then, once the documents are close to their final form, you can combine them into a book on one computer and finish the project in book form.

None of this is meant to discourage the single user from managing longer projects using the book feature. If you're producing a book by yourself, and it consists of multiple InDesign documents, by all means take advantage of this feature. The only consideration is whether your output provider can handle the book file or requires you to combine the documents into a single document (or, more easily, export it to one production-quality PDF file).

Planning Your Book

If you decide that the book feature is appropriate and useful for a project, do some planning before you even create a book. Use the following guidelines before you begin building your book in InDesign:

- Organize your chapters in advance by deciding on the number, names, and order of the chapters. You can make changes to a chapter's number, name, and order at any time, but figuring out these basics ahead of time will save you time in the long run.

- Make decisions about the format of the book (styles, swatches, pagination style, and so on) at the chapter level, beginning with the first chapter.

- Pay attention to formatting. Formatting is important because if your chapters use different color swatch names, style names, and so on, synchronizing the formatting across the chapters will be difficult.

- Use templates and styles to format the chapters uniformly.

- Decide where to store the book file itself (this must be a shared server for a workgroup); store the documents in this folder as well. Set up the appropriate sharing through your operating system.

- Make sure members of the workgroup have access to any templates, libraries, graphics, fonts, plug-ins, and so on that are necessary to work on the project.

Creating and Opening Books

To create a new book, choose File ➪ New ➪ Book. The New Book dialog box, shown in Figure 25.1, lets you specify a location for the book and give it a name. If you're on a Mac and creating a book that may be used in Windows, you'll notice that InDesign automatically adds the .indb extension to the filename. Click OK to create and open the book.

To open an existing book, use the File ➪ Open command (⌘+O or Ctrl+O). Each book appears in its own panel. If several books are open, the panels are contained in a free-floating panel group.

If you're opening a book from a shared server, make sure to mount the server on your desktop first. You can also double-click a book's icon, which also shows the open book's panel. To close a book's panel, and any book documents that are in it, simply click its Close box.

> **TIP** Multiple users on the same platform (Mac or Windows) — but not users from multiple platforms — can open the same book panel at the same time. If another user makes changes to the book, those changes appear in your copy of the book when you click on the panel.

> **TIP** You can add several documents at once. If they are in the same folder, just click the first document and Shift+click the last to select all documents between them, or ⌘+click or Ctrl+click the individual documents if they are not listed contiguously.

FIGURE 25.1

To create a new book, choose File ⇨ New ⇨ Book.

Adding chapters to books

New book panes are empty — you need to add your carefully prepared documents to them. To do this, click the Add Document iconic button (the **+** icon on the bottom right of your book's panel) shown in Figure 25.2, or choose the Add Document menu option in the book panel's flyout menu. Either way, Use the Add Documents dialog box to locate and select the first document — or "chapter" — you want to add. Click the Open button to make this the first chapter in the book. Repeat this process to add to the book all the chapters you have ready. (You can also add more later.)

Opening and editing chapters

To work on a chapter in a book, first open the book. Then double-click the chapter name in the book's panel. The chapter opens in InDesign just like any other InDesign document opens. Note that to open a chapter, it must be available, as I discuss in the next section. When you finish editing a chapter, save and close it as usual. (Any open chapter documents will remain open in InDesign even if you close the book's panel.)

If you need to take a chapter home and work on it, you can edit a chapter outside the book. To do this, first move (not copy) the chapter's file to a different folder or disk so the chapter displays as Missing in the book panel. This keeps other users from editing it while you have it. When you finish editing the file, move the edited file back in its original location. The book panel shows this chapter as Modified. (To move a file across disks on the Mac, hold ⌘ when dragging it to its new location; in Windows, hold Shift.)

FIGURE 25.2

A book panel and its flyout menu. The icon to the left of a chapter's filename indicates the style source. The status column shows which chapters are open on your computer, which are in use by others, which are available to be opened, and which are missing.

You can replace an existing chapter with another document by selecting the chapter in the book panel, and then choosing Replace Document from the flyout menu. Navigate to a new document, select it, and click the Open button. InDesign replaces the selected chapter with the new document.

You can delete chapters from a book by choosing Remove Document from the flyout menu or by clicking the Remove Document iconic button (the – icon) from the bottom of the panel.

Finally, there are three other menu options in the flyout menu that come in handy for managing the book: You can save books by choosing Save Book, save to a new name by choosing Save Book As, and close the book by choosing Close Book. (Any changes to the book are not saved, though you get a warning box giving you the chance to save any unsaved books.)

Saving a book is separate from saving a document in a book. Any changes made to an open document are saved only if you save that document. But any changes you make through the book panel's flyout menu, such as synchronizing styles (covered in the next section), are automatically saved in the affected documents.

If the Automatic Document Conversion menu option is selected in the book panel's flyout menu, InDesign converts all chapters created in earlier versions of InDesign to the InDesign CS3 format. Otherwise, it saves any previous-version chapters to new InDesign CS3-format files with new names, leaving the originals untouched. (In this case, the book panel lists just the InDesign CS3-format files.)

Understanding a book panel's status reports

If you're using a book panel in a workgroup, it provides helpful status reports about each chapter, as shown in Figure 25.2. The statuses include:

- **Available:** The chapter can be opened, edited, or printed. Only one user at a time can open a chapter.

- **Open:** You have the chapter open and can edit it or print it. Nobody else can open the chapter at this time.

- **In Use:** Another user has the chapter open. In this case, you cannot edit or open the chapter.

- **Modified:** The chapter has been changed since the last time you opened the book panel. Simply click on the book panel to update it.

- **Missing:** The chapter's file has been moved, renamed, or deleted since it was added to the book. Double-click the chapter name to open a Find File dialog box and locate it.

There's also the Document Information menu option in a book panel's flyout menu. When you select a chapter and choose this option, InDesign shows you the file's modification date, location, and page range, as well as lets you replace it with a different document.

Working with Style Sources

The first chapter you add to the book is, by default, the style source, as indicated by the icon to the left of its filename. If the chapters of your book don't share common formatting, you don't need to worry about this feature. But with a book, that's rarely the case — usually you want the styles, swatches, and so on to remain the same. The style source in an InDesign book defines the styles and swatches that are common to all the chapters in the book. When you use the Synchronize feature, discussed in the next section, InDesign makes sure that the paragraph styles, character styles, object styles, table styles, cell styles, trap presets, TOC styles, master pages, numbered lists, text variables, and swatches in each chapter in the book match those in the style source.

NEW FEATURE   InDesign CS3 adds the ability to synchronize master pages across book chapters, as well as the new table styles, cell styles, numbered lists, and text variables.

If you decide to make a different chapter the style source, all you need to do is click in the column to the left of that chapter's filename. This moves the icon indicating the style source to that chapter (see Figure 25.2).

To help you make sure that common formatting remains consistent across the document, the book panel provides a Synchronize iconic button, as well as a Synchronize Selected Documents or Synchronize Book menu item (based on what is selected) in the flyout menu. Follow these steps to synchronize:

1. **Be sure you're satisfied with the styles in the style source and that all chapters are available for editing.**

2. **Choose the style source (the document whose styles you want to be used everywhere) by clicking the box to the left of the source chapter so that the style-source icon appears.**

3. **Choose Synchronize Options from the book panel's flyout menu, which opens the dialog box shown in Figure 25.3.** Make sure every type of item you want synchronized— Object Styles, TOC Style, Character Styles, Paragraph Styles, Trap Presets, Swatches, Master Pages, and so on—is selected.

FIGURE 25.3

The Synchronize Options dialog box

4. **Select the chapters you want to synchronize and click Synchronize or choose Synchronize Selected Documents from the flyout menu.** If no chapters are selected, InDesign assumes you want to synchronize all chapters; you see the Synchronize Book menu option in the flyout menu rather than Synchronize Selected Documents menu option in that case.

5. **Now compare the styles (character, paragraph, object, table, cell, and TOC), swatches (color, tint, and gradient), trap presets, master pages, and so on in the style source to those in each chapter.** If anything is different, the information in each

chapter is updated to match the style source. This means that if someone changes the typeface in a style in a chapter, it reverts to the typeface specified in the style source. If anything is missing from a chapter — for example, if you just added a swatch to the style source but not to other chapters — that information is added to each chapter.

By using the synchronization feature, each chapter has the same basic set of styles and swatches as the style source. I say "basic set" because you can still add more of these specifications to each chapter. When using the synchronization feature, you need to keep in mind the following:

- Synchronizing will *not* remove unique paragraph styles, character styles, object styles, TOC styles, swatches, trap presets, and so on from your chapters — as long as their names don't match those in the style-source document, of course. Therefore, you can implement special formatting needs in a chapter by creating unique styles in that chapter.

- Synchronizing cannot solve any problems related to using the template or styles incorrectly, or change any local formatting applied to text (such as font changes or italics) or local changes to master page items.

Clearly, synchronizing is no cure-all for the renegade formatting that often occurs when multiple users work on the same project. Be sure everyone knows what the standards are for the design, how to implement the standards properly, and how to make local changes appropriately.

Working with Page Numbers and Sections

A key reason to use the book feature is to let InDesign handle the page numbering within your book's chapters and sections, for folios, cross-references, index entries, and tables of contents.

When working with books, you have two choices for numbering pages: You can let the book panel number pages consecutively from one chapter to the next or you can add sections of page numbers, which carry through the book until you start a new section. In long documents, section page numbering is common because it lets you have page numbering such as 2.1–2.14 in, say, Chapter 2. (Plus, as Chapter 5 explains, creating a section start is the only way to start a document on a left-facing page, which is often necessary in magazines.)

Numbering pages consecutively

If the chapters you add to a book have no sections in them, you end up with consecutive page numbering: The first page number of each chapter follows the last page number of the previous chapter (so if one chapter ends on page 16, the next chapter starts on page 17). When working in a chapter, if you open the Section dialog box (choose Numbering & Section Options in the Pages panel's flyout menu), you see that Automatic Page Numbering is selected by default.

The consecutive page numbering works as follows:

- Whenever you add a chapter with no sections to a book, InDesign numbers pages consecutively throughout the book.

■ As you add and delete pages from chapters, the page numbers are also updated.

■ You can force repagination by choosing Update Numbering from the book panel's flyout menu.

■ You control the page numbering using the Book Page Numbering Options dialog box (choose Book Page Numbering Options from the book panel's flyout menu), shown in Figure 25.4. You can have the numbering pick up after the previous chapter's page number, skip to the odd page number that would follow the previous chapter's page number, or skip to the even page number that would follow the previous chapter's page number. These last two options are meant when you have chapters that always start on a right or left page (respectively) no matter where the previous chapter's last page falls. (You can also have InDesign automatically add a blank page as needed in these cases.) In this dialog box, you also can tell InDesign to update all page and section numbers for you to reflect any changes to the book's chapters, by checking the Automatically Update Page & Section Numbers option.

FIGURE 25.4

The Book Page Numbering Options dialog box

InDesign lists chapters alphabetically by filename in a book panel, so if your chapters don't have section starts, the automatic page numbering may not follow your desired chapter order. To fix this, click and drag the chapters within the book pane to the desired location in the pane, so the first chapter is in the top position, the next chapter is in the second position, and so on.

Numbering pages with sections

If any chapters you add to books already contain sections of page numbers (implemented through the Section dialog box, which you access via the Numbering & Section Options menu option in the Pages panel's flyout menu), the section page numbering overrides the book's consecutive page numbering.

The section page numbering carries through chapters of the book until InDesign encounters a new section start. So if one chapter ends on page iv, the next page starts on page v unless you start a new section. Note that it's fairly typical in magazines to assign the page number in each article's document file because there are usually ads between articles that are inserted later in the printing process.

CROSS-REF Using the options in the Section dialog box is covered in Chapter 5.

Manual numbering updates

Sometimes, having InDesign automatically update page and section numbering is a real pain, as you must wait for it to grind through all the chapters when you, for example, add or update a chapter near the beginning of the book's chapter list. In that case, uncheck the Automatically Update Page & Section Numbers in the Book Page Numbering Options dialog box, accessible from the book panel's flyout menu.

When it is time to repaginate the book, choose Update Numbering from the panel's flyout menu, and then choose the appropriate option from its submenu: Update Page & Section Numbers, Update Chapter & Paragraph Numbers, or Update All Numbers.

NEW FEATURE   The ability to separately control which numbers are updated is new to InDesign CS3.

CROSS-REF   Paragraph numbers refers to the new numbered lists capability described in Chapter 19. Section numbers are covered in Chapter 5.

Specifying chapter numbers

You can see and modify any chapter's page numbering settings by selecting the chapter in the book panel, and then choosing Document Numbering Options from the flyout menu. Figure 25.5 shows the dialog box. The top half of the dialog box is the same as the Pages panel's Section dialog box, while the bottom half — the Document Chapter Numbering area — lets you control the chapter numbering style and the chapter number itself.

FIGURE 25.5

The Document Numbering Options dialog box

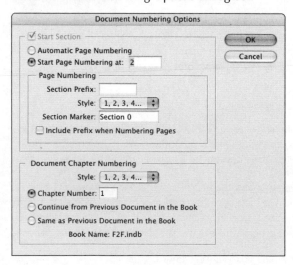

NEW FEATURE The Document Chapter Numbering controls in the Document Numbering Options dialog box are new to InDesign CS3.

You can force a chapter to have a specific number by selecting the Chapter Number option, have the chapter use the same chapter number as the previous document (such as when you break a chapter into two documents), and have InDesign automatically number the current document by incrementing from the previous document's chapter number.

CROSS-REF The chapter number defined here — whether manually overridden or automatically adjusted — is what the Chapter Number text variable uses, as explained in Chapter 23.

Printing Chapters and Books

If you want to print multiple chapters in the book with the same settings, you can print through the book panel. You can print any chapters with the status of Available or Open. Here's how:

1. **To print the entire book, make sure no chapters are selected.** To print a continuous range of chapters, Shift+click them. To print noncontiguous chapters, ⌘+click or Ctrl+click the chapters to select them.

2. **Click the Print Book iconic button or choose Print Book or Print Selected Documents in the book panel's flyout menu (the option displayed depends on whether chapters are selected in the book panel).** The standard InDesign Print dialog box opens. Note that the option to choose all pages or a range of pages is grayed out — you must print all chapters in the selected chapters.

3. **Make any adjustments in the Print dialog box.**

4. **Click Print to print the chapters.**

A related set of features includes the capability to output a book to PDF, using the Export Book to PDF or Export Selected Documents to PDF menu options in the flyout menu. They work like their equivalent Print menu options. You can also preflight a book or selected chapters and package a book or selected chapters for a service bureau. The Preflight Book/Preflight Selected Documents menu options in the book panel work like their equivalent menu options in the File menu.

NEW FEATURE InDesign CS3 adds the Merge Identically Named Layers on Export option to the book panel's flyout menu. If checked, InDesign unifies layers with the same name into one layer for exported PDF files generated from multiple documents in the same book, rather than create separate layers for each chapter's layer.

CROSS-REF For more on preflighting, packaging, printing, and output settings, see Chapters 30 through 32.

Summary

InDesign lets you control how page numbering, chapter numbering, and section numbering are handled and updated via the book panel's flyout menu. It also lets you control which chapters are printed or exported to PDF.

Part VI

Graphics Fundamentals

IN THIS PART

Chapter 26
Importing Graphics

Chapter 27
**Fitting Graphics and
Frames Together**

Chapter 28
**Drawing Free-Form Shapes and
Curved Paths**

Chapter 26

Importing Graphics

You can import graphics of all sorts into your InDesign documents several ways. InDesign is particularly adept at importing graphics created in popular Macintosh and Windows formats. And through the Mac and Windows Clipboards (copy and paste), you can import file formats — to a limited degree — that InDesign doesn't directly support.

Because InDesign has some built-in graphics features, as I describe in Chapters 27 and 28, you may be tempted to use InDesign as your graphics program. Don't. Its tools are fine for some work, such as creating shapes that text wraps around, borders, and gradations of color — but InDesign is not meant to be a professional graphics-creation tool. In fact, it's designed to work closely with such professional tools, especially Adobe's Illustrator and Photoshop.

Particularly for bitmap images such as scanned files and photographs, InDesign has few capabilities to apply special effects or otherwise manipulate the image's content, so you should do as much work as possible in your image editor before importing the file into InDesign. For example, you can resize, crop, rotate, and slant an imported image in InDesign, but you can't convert it from a full-color image into a duotone or change its line screen or brightness and contrast.

The bottom line is this: Use your graphics program for creating and editing original images and photos. Use InDesign's graphics features to embellish your layout, rather than create original artwork.

InDesign lets you easily open a graphics program to edit placed images from within InDesign. Press and hold Option or Alt, and then double-click the image. InDesign launches the program that created the graphic; if you don't own that program, InDesign launches a compatible program if you have one.

IN THIS CHAPTER

Preparing files for import from graphics programs

Understanding special considerations for supported graphics formats

Working with files across platforms

Understanding color issues

Using the Place dialog box to import graphics

Specifying import options for various graphics formats

Exporting graphics

Working with imported graphics' layers

Figuring out other ways to import graphics

For example, if you Option+double-click or Alt+double-click an Encapsulated PostScript (EPS) file in your layout that was created in Adobe Illustrator, but you use CorelDraw instead, InDesign launches CorelDraw on your system.

CROSS-REF   Transformations such as resizing, flipping, rotating, and skewing that you're likely to apply to imported graphics use the same tools as for any InDesign objects, so I cover all these transformations in one place: Chapter 11. I cover the effects that you can apply to any object, including graphics, in Chapter 12.

Preparing Graphics Files

InDesign offers support for many major formats of graphics files. Some formats are more appropriate than others for certain kinds of tasks. The basic rules for creating your graphics files are as follows:

- **Save line art in a format such as EPS, PDF, Adobe Illustrator, Windows Metafile (WMF), Enhanced Metafile (EMF), or PICT.** (These object-oriented formats are called *vector* formats. Vector files are composed of instructions on how to draw various shapes.) InDesign works best with EPS, PDF, and Illustrator files.

- **Save bitmaps (photos and scans) in a format such as TIFF, Adobe Photoshop, PNG, JPEG, PCX, Windows Bitmap (BMP), GIF, Scitex Continuous Tone (SCT), or PICT.** (These pixel-oriented formats are called *bitmap* or *raster* formats. They are composed of a series of dots, or pixels, that make up the image.) InDesign works best with TIFF and Photoshop files.

Note that PICT files can be in vector or bitmap format depending on the original image and the program in which it was created or exported from. If you enlarge a PICT image and it begins to look blocky, it's a bitmap. Similarly, EPS and PDF files can contain bitmap images as well as vector ones.

NEW FEATURE   InDesign CS3 can import InDesign files as if they were graphics — when importing a multi-page document, you choose the page you want to import, as you can with PDF files. Note that InDesign files imported as graphics cannot be edited in InDesign; you must update the original file instead.

I suggest that you make EPS and TIFF formats your standards because these have become the standard graphics formats in publishing. If you and your service bureau work almost exclusively with Adobe software, you can add the PDF, Illustrator, and Photoshop formats to this mix. (The Illustrator and PDF formats are variants of EPS.) If you use transparency in your graphics, it's best to save them in Photoshop, Illustrator, or PDF formats because other formats (particularly EPS and TIFF) remove much of the transparency layering data that will help an imagesetter optimally reproduce those transparent files.

Graphics embedded in text files

Modern word processors typically support inline graphics, letting you import a graphic into your word-processor document and embed it in text. Word, for example, lets you import graphics, and InDesign, in turn, can import the graphics with your text. But graphics embedded in your than one page) into your document as an uneditable graphic. You can crop, resize, and do other such manipulations common to any graphic, but you can't work with the text or other imported PDF file's components.

 Special PDF features, like sounds, movies, hyperlinks, control buttons, and annotations, are ignored in the imported file.

Other vector formats

If you're outputting to negatives for professional printing, you should avoid non-PostScript vector formats. But they're fine for printing to inkjet and laser printers.

PICT

The standard Macintosh format for drawings, PICT also supports bitmaps and is the standard format for Mac OS 8 and 9 screen-capture utilities. InDesign imports PICT files with no difficulty, but it cannot color-separate them for output to negatives. Because fonts in vector PICT graphics are automatically translated to curves, you need not worry about whether fonts used in your graphics reside in your printer or available at your service bureau.

Windows Metafile

The standard Windows format for drawing, Windows Metafile is similar to PICT in that it can contain bitmap images as well as vector drawings. But InDesign will ignore bitmap information in Windows Metafiles, stripping it out during import. Microsoft Office 2000 introduced a new version of this format, called *Enhanced Metafile*, which InDesign also supports.

Issues with bitmap formats

Bitmap (also called *raster*) formats are simpler than vector formats because they're made up of rows of dots (*pixels*), not instructions on how to draw various shapes. But that doesn't mean that all bitmaps are alike.

Professional-level bitmap formats

Although InDesign supports a wide variety of bitmap formats, there is usually just one to worry about if you're producing professional documents for output on a printing press: TIFF. (You may also use the Scitex CT format if you're using Scitex output equipment to produce your negatives.) I suggest you convert other formats to TIFF using your image editor (Corel Photo-Paint and Adobe Photoshop, the two top image editors, import and export most formats, as do other modern image-editing programs) or a conversion program like the Mac shareware program GraphicConverter, Equilibrium's DeBabelizer for Macintosh, the shareware program Advanced Batch Converter (for Windows), or DataViz's Conversions Plus (for Windows) and MacLinkPlus (for Macintosh).

 For links to graphics conversion tools, go to this book's companion Web site at www.InDesignCentral.com.

Photoshop

InDesign can import version 4.0 and later of this popular image editor's file format. When you place Photoshop files in InDesign, you can control how the alpha channel is imported—be sure to

---

word-processor document though Mac OS 8 and 9's Publish and Subscribe or Windows' OLE do not import into InDesign.

Inline graphics imports exactly as their preview images, not as the original formats. This means that in most cases, you get a much lower-resolution version in your InDesign layout. Despite their limitations, using inline graphics in your word processor can be helpful when you're putting together an InDesign document: Use the inline graphics whose previews are imported into InDesign as placeholders so that the layout artist knows you have embedded graphics. The artist can then replace the previews with the better-quality originals.

TIP **If you find yourself using several graphics as characters (such as a company icon used as a bullet), use a font-creation program such as FontLab Studio or FontLab Fontographer to create a symbol typeface with those graphics. Then both your word processor and layout documents can use the same high-quality versions.**

InDesign imports many file formats. If your graphics program's format is not one of the ones listed here, chances are it can save as or export to one. In the following list, the text in italics is the file-name extension common for these files on PCs.

The file formats InDesign imports include:

- **BMP:** The native Windows bitmap format. (*.BMP, .DIB*)
- **EPS:** The Encapsulated PostScript file format favored by professional publishers. A variant is called DCS, a color-separated variant whose full name is Desktop Color Separation. (*.EPS, .DCS*)
- **Flash animation:** For use in interactive documents, InDesign supports this Adobe-owned, cross-platform format. (*.SWF*) Chapter 33 covers the use of multimedia elements in more detail.

NEW FEATURE **The ability to import Flash files is new to InDesign CS3.**

- **GIF:** The Graphics Interchange Format common in Web documents. (*.GIF*)
- **JPEG:** The Joint Photographic Expert Group compressed bitmap format often used on the Web. (*.JPG*)
- **Illustrator:** The native format in Adobe Illustrator 5.5 through CS3 is similar to EPS. (*.AI*)
- **PCX:** The PC Paintbrush format that was very popular in DOS programs and early version of Windows; other formats have now largely supplanted it. (*.PCX, .RLE*)
- **PDF:** The Portable Document Format that is a variant of PostScript (as EPS is) and is used for Web-, network-, and CD-based documents. InDesign CS3 supports PDF versions 1.3 through 1.7 (the formats used in Acrobat 4 through 8). (*.PDF*)
- **Photoshop:** The native format in Adobe Photoshop 5.0 through CS3. .psd (*.PSD*) Note that InDesign cannot import the Photoshop Raw format (.RAW files).
- **PICT:** Short for *Picture*, the Mac's native graphics format until Mac OS X (it can be bitmap or vector) that is little used in professional documents and is becoming rare even for inexpensive clip art. (*.PCT*)

- **PNG:** The Portable Network Graphics format that Adobe introduced several years ago as a more capable alternative to GIF. (*.PNG*)

- **QuickTime movie:** For use in interactive documents, InDesign supports this Apple-created, cross-platform format. (*.MOV*) Chapter 33 covers the use of multimedia elements in more detail.

- **Scitex CT:** The continuous-tone bitmap format used on Scitex prepress systems. (*.CT*)

- **TIFF:** The Tagged Image File Format that is the bitmap standard for professional image editors and publishers. (*.TIF or .TIFF*)

- **Windows Metafile:** The format native to Windows but little used in professional documents. Since Office 2000, Microsoft applications create a new version called Enhanced Metafile. (*.WMF, .EMF*)

NOTE   Spot colors (called *spot inks* in Photoshop) are imported into InDesign when you place Photoshop, Illustrator, and PDF images into InDesign, as well as for InDesign documents imported as graphics. They appear in the Swatches panel, which I cover in Chapter 8.

InDesign does not support a few somewhat popular formats: AutoCAD Document Exchange Format (DXF), Computer Graphics Metafile (CGM), CorelDraw, Eastman Kodak's Photo CD, and Scalable Vector Graphics (SVG). DXF and CGM are vector formats used mainly in engineering and architecture, while CorelDraw is the native format of the leading consumer-oriented Windows illustration program, and Photo CD is a bitmap format meant for electronically distributed photographs.

CROSS-REF   Although InDesign cannot import SVG files, it can export them, as Chapter 4 explains. It can also export JPEG, EPS, and PDF files. (Chapter 32 covers PDF export.)

Issues with vector files

Vector images are complex because they can combine multiple elements — curves, lines, colors, fonts, bitmap images, and even other imported vector images. This means that you can unknowingly create a file that can cause problems when you try to output an InDesign layout file using it. Thus, when dealing with vector formats, you'll need to keep several issues in mind.

Embedded fonts

When you use fonts in text included in your graphics files, you usually have the option to convert the text to curves (graphics). This option ensures that your text prints on any printer. (If you don't use this conversion, make sure that your printer or service bureau has the fonts used in the graphic. Otherwise, the text does not print in the correct font; you likely get Courier or Helvetica instead.)

If your graphic has a lot of text, don't convert the text to curves — the image could get very complex and slow down printing. In this case, make sure that the output device has the same fonts as are in the graphic.

PostScript files: EPS, DCS, Illustrator, and PDF

PostScript-based files come in several varieties — EPS, DCS, Illustrator, and PDF — and because the format is a complex one, there are more issues to be aware of up front.

EPS

The usual hang-up with EPS files is the preview header. The preview is a displayable copy of the EPS file. Because EPS files are actually made up of a series of commands that tell the printer how to draw the image, what you see on-screen is not the actual graphic. Most programs create a preview image for EPS files, but many programs have trouble reading them, especially if the EPS file was generated on a different platform. In those cases, they display an X or a gray box in place of the image. (The EPS file prints properly to a PostScript printer.) That's why InDesign creates its own preview image when you import EPS files, lessening the chances of your seeing just an X or a gray box in place of the EPS preview.

When you import EPS files, InDesign lets you control some settings if you check Show Import Options in the Place dialog box, as covered later in this chapter. You can apply Photoshop clipping paths in the file (see Chapter 27), choose the preview format, convert the PostScript vector information into a bitmap (a process called *rasterization*), or embed links to OPI high-resolution source images (see Chapter 31 for details on OPI).

TIP   In CorelDraw 6.0 and later, and in Adobe Illustrator 6.0 and later, be sure to set the EPS creation options to have no preview header. This keeps your files smaller. (In CorelDraw, export to EPS. In Illustrator 6.0 and later, save as Illustrator EPS. Note that Illustrator 5.x's native format is EPS, so don't look for an export or save-as option.)

CAUTION   If you use transparency in your graphics, it's best to leave the files in Adobe Illustrator format rather than save them to EPS. Chapter 31 explains the issues in more depth.

DCS

The DCS variant of EPS is a set of five files: an EPS preview file that links together four separation files (one each for cyan, magenta, yellow, and black). Using this format ensures correct color separation when you output negatives for use in commercial printing. Service bureaus that do color correction often prefer these files over standard EPS files. One variation of the DCS file format, DCS 2.0, also supports spot color plates in addition to the standard plates for cyan, magenta, yellow, and black.

You should not use DCS files if you intend to create composite proof files or in-RIP separations from InDesign — InDesign will ignore the DCS separation files and just use the preview file for output. (RIP stands for raster-image processor.) Only use DCS files if you're outputting separations (but not in-RIP separations). Chapter 31 covers this in detail.

Illustrator

Adobe Illustrator files are very similar to EPS files, except they don't have a preview header, and they better support transparency settings in graphics. There are no special concerns for Illustrator files; just be sure to note the font and color issues I mentioned previously in this section. As I describe later in this chapter, InDesign can differentiate layers in an Illustrator file, letting you decide which ones to display in your layout.

PDF

PDF files can contain all sorts of elements — text, graphics, sounds, hyperlinks, and movies — presented as one or more pages with the visual richness of a print document. When you import a PDF file, InDesign treats it as a graphic and can place one or more of the PDF file's pages (if it has more select Show Import Options in the Place dialog box to get this control. You also can apply any embedded clipping paths (see Chapter 27) and import or exclude any embedded color profile. As I describe later in this chapter, InDesign can differentiate layers in a Photoshop image, letting you decide which one(s) to display in your layout.

CROSS-REF The Photoshop format also supports transparency very well, which helps avoid later printing problems, as Chapter 31 explains.

Scitex CT

The continuous-tone Scitex CT format is used with Scitex output high-resolution devices and is usually produced by Scitex scanners. If you're using this format, you should be outputting to a Scitex system. Otherwise, you're not going to get the advantage of its high resolution.

TIFF

The most popular bitmap format for publishers is TIFF, developed by Aldus (later bought by Adobe Systems) and Microsoft. TIFF supports color up to 24 bits (16.7 million colors) in both RGB and CMYK models, and every major photo-editing program supports TIFF on both the Macintosh and in Windows. TIFF also supports grayscale and black-and-white files.

The biggest advantage to using TIFF files rather than other formats that also support color, such as PICT, is that InDesign is designed to take advantage of TIFF. For example, in an image editor, you can set clipping paths in a TIFF file, which act as a mask for the image. InDesign sees a path and uses it as the image boundary, making the area outside of it invisible. That in turn lets you have non-rectangular bitmap images in your layout — the clipping path becomes the visible boundary for your TIFF image. InDesign also supports embedded alpha channels and color profiles in TIFF files.

CAUTION TIFF files do not handle images with transparency well. Even though the files will look okay on-screen, they may not print well or may cause printer errors. It's best to stick with the Adobe Photoshop format if you use transparency.

TIFF files have several variations that InDesign supports. But because other programs aren't as forgiving, follow these guidelines to ensure smooth interaction:

- You should have no difficulty if you use uncompressed and LZW-compressed TIFF files supported by most Mac and Windows programs. InDesign even supports the less-used Zip compression method for TIFF files. You should be safe using LZW-compressed TIFF files with any mainstream program, but if you do have difficulty, I recommend that you use uncompressed TIFF files. Also, always talk to your service bureau about LZW support before sending files for output. Many older imagesetters do not handle LZW compression and fail to output images that use it.

- Use the byte order for the platform for which the TIFF file is destined. Macs and PCs use the opposite byte order — basically, the Mac reads the eight characters that comprise a byte in one direction and the PC reads it in the other direction. Although InDesign reads both byte orders, other (typically older) programs may not, so why invite confusion? Of course, if only InDesign and Photoshop users will work on your TIFF files, the byte order doesn't matter.

Web-oriented bitmap formats

In recent years, several formats have been developed for use in the Hypertext Markup Language (HTML) documents found on the Web. These formats — GIF, JPEG, and PNG — achieve small size (for faster downloading and display on your browser) by limiting image and color detail and richness.

Although you can use any supported graphics format for documents you expect to export to the Web's XHTML document format, if you know your document is bound for the Web, you might as well use a Web graphics format from the start. (Note that InDesign converts all images to GIF or JPEG when you export to XHTML.)

GIF

GIF is the oldest Web format. To help keep file size down, it is limited to 256 colors. This reduces file size but also makes it unsuitable for photographs and graphics with color blends. But its compression approach doesn't lose any image detail, so it works well for sketches, cartoons, and other simple images with sharp details.

JPEG

The JPEG compressed color-image format is used for very large images and the individual images comprising an animation or a movie. Images compressed in this format may lose detail, which is why publishers prefer TIFF files. JPEG can even be used effectively on documents output to an inkjet printer because you can set the level of loss to none during export. But in professional printing, don't use JPEG images. That's because JPEG images use the RGB color model, not the CMYK model of standard printing. While it is possible to create CMYK JPEG files with Photoshop, those CMYK JPEGs won't display in and may even crash other applications and Web browsers.

When importing JPEG files, InDesign automatically scales the image to fit in the page. This helps deal with digital-camera graphics that tend to be very large and when imported end up taking much more than the width of a page. While you likely still need to scale the image to fit your layout, you can at least see the whole image before doing so.

JPEG is more useful on the Web, where the limited resolution of a computer monitor makes most of JPEG's detail loss hard to spot and provides an acceptable trade-off of slightly blurry quality in return for a much smaller file size. It's particularly well suited for photographs because the lost detail is usually not noticeable because of all the other detail surrounding it.

If you do use JPEG for print work, note that you can provide a clipping path for it in programs like Photoshop. The clipping path lets the image have an irregular boundary (rendering the rest of its background transparent) so you can use InDesign effects such as text wrap.

PNG

The PNG format is meant to provide GIF's no-loss compression but support 24-bit color so it can be used for photography and subtly colored illustrations on the Web. The PNG format's other significant attribute is full transparency support with an embedded alpha channel. (That is why InDesign lets you replace the transparency with white or keep the background color in the Image Import Options dialog box, as I cover later in this chapter.) The transparency also works in most recent Web browsers.

Other bitmap formats

The other supported formats are ones that you should avoid, unless you're printing to inkjet or laser printers. If you have images in one of these formats and want to use the format for professionally output documents, convert the images to TIFF before using them in InDesign.

- **BMP:** Like TIFF, the BMP Windows bitmap format supports color, grayscale, and black-and-white images.
- **PCX:** Like TIFF, PCX supports color, grayscale, and black-and-white images.
- **PICT:** PICT, the old standard Macintosh format for drawings, also supports bitmaps. InDesign imports PICT files with no difficulty.

Identifying Color Issues

It used to be that importing color from graphics files into publishing programs was an iffy proposition; colors would often not print properly even though they appeared correct on-screen. Those nightmares are largely a thing of the past, as modern page-layout software such as InDesign accurately detects color definitions in your source graphics, and modern illustration and image-editing programs are better at making that information accessible to page-layout programs. So, just note the following advice to ensure smooth color import.

If you create color images in an illustration or image-editing program, make sure that you create them using the CMYK color model or using a named spot color. If you use CMYK, the color is, in effect, preseparated. With InDesign, any spot colors defined in an EPS file are automatically added to the Swatches panel for your document and set as spot colors.

CROSS-REF See Chapter 8 for more on creating and editing colors.

If your program follows Adobe's EPS specifications (Adobe Illustrator, CorelDraw, and Adobe Macromedia FreeHand all do), InDesign color-separates your EPS file, no matter whether it uses process or spot colors. Canvas automatically converts Pantone spot colors to process colors in your choice of RGB and CMYK models. For other programs, create your colors in the CMYK model to be sure they print as color separations from InDesign.

Color systems

There are several color systems, or models, in use, and InDesign supports the common ones, including CMYK (process), RGB, Pantone, Focoltone, Dainippon Ink & Chemical (DIC), Toyo, Trumatch, and Web. A color system defines either a set of individual colors that have specially mixed inks (shown on swatchbooks, which have small samples of each color) or a range of colors that can be created by combining a limited number of inks (such as RGB for red, green, and blue and CMYK for cyan, magenta, yellow, and black).

Chapter 8 describes the various color models, but for file import, it's best to use just three — CMYK (process), RGB, and the Pantone Matching System — because they're universally used and tend to be the most reliable when passing information from one system to another.

NOTE The advice on color systems applies to just vector images because bitmap programs use CMYK or RGB as their actual color models, even if they offer swatchbooks of other models' colors.

Most layout artists use Pantone to specify desired colors, so keep a Pantone swatchbook handy to see which CMYK values equal the desired Pantone color. (One of the available Pantone swatchbooks, *The Pantone Process Color Imaging Guide CMYK Edition*, shows each Pantone color next to the CMYK color build used to simulate it.) This book's companion Web site (`www.InDesignCentral.com`) provides links to Pantone and other color swatchbooks.

Of course, you can simply pick a Pantone color from the electronic swatchbook in InDesign, and InDesign converts it to CMYK if you specify it to be a process color (the default setting). Many high-end illustration programs, including Adobe Illustrator, support Pantone and can do this instant conversion as well. If available (as it is in InDesign), use the Pantone Process Coated color model because it is designed for output using CMYK printing presses. But remember: What you see on-screen won't match what you get on paper, so it's a good idea to have the printed Pantone swatchbook.

Calibrated color

With InDesign's color management system (CMS) feature enabled, the program calibrates the output colors (whether they're printed to a color printer or color-separated for traditional printing) based on the source device and the target output device in an attempt to ensure that what you see on-screen comes close to what you'll see on the printed page. Although color calibration is a tricky science that rarely results in exact color matches across all input and output devices, it can help minimize differences as the image travels along the creation and production path.

Today, most image-editing programs let you apply color profiles that conform with the International Color Committee (ICC) standards. If you use color calibration, it's best to apply these ICC profiles in the images when you create them.

If you can't — or forget to — apply an ICC profile when creating your image, don't worry. You can add a profile (if you're creating images in a program that doesn't support ICC profiles) or apply a different one from InDesign.

 Chapter 29 covers color calibration in depth.

Exploring Methods for Importing Graphics

You can import a graphic into any kind of frame or shape (including a curved line created with the Pen tool) except a straight line, using the Place command, copy and paste, or drag and drop.

CAUTION But be careful: If the Type tool is selected when you use the Place dialog box to import a graphic into a selected text frame, you create an inline graphic at the text-insertion point (see Chapter 13 for information about creating and managing inline graphics).

When it's time to import a graphic, you're responsible for knowing where the file is — whether it's stored on a floppy disk that your friend gave you, on your hard drive, on a networked file server, or on a local or networked CD-ROM.

If you import a graphics file that's stored on any kind of removable media, such as a floppy disk, Zip disk, or CD, the link between the document and the graphics file will be broken when the media is removed. Generally, it's best to copy graphics files to your hard drive or to a networked file server before importing them into an InDesign document.

CROSS-REF Chapter 13 covers how to work with linked source files, such as how to update an imported file in InDesign if it is changed in another program.

Using the Place dialog box

Although there are several ways to add a graphics file to an InDesign document (all of which I explain in this chapter), the Place dialog box (File ⇨ Place, or ⌘+D or Ctrl+D) is the method you should use most often. When you use the Place dialog box, InDesign offers import options for various graphics file formats that are not available if you use other import methods. Figure 26.1 shows the Place dialog box.

When importing images, make sure Show Import Options is selected in the Place dialog box. Even if you're happy with the default import options, it's good to see what the import options are so when a non-default option does make sense, you're aware you have access to it.

FIGURE 26.1

The Place dialog box

Here's how to use the Place dialog box to import a graphic:

1. **Choose File ⇨ Place, or press ⌘+D or Ctrl+D.** If you want to import a graphic into an *existing frame*, select the target frame using either of the selection tools (either before you choose File ⇨ Place or afterward). If you want InDesign to create a *new frame* when you import the graphic, make sure no object is selected when you choose Place. Either way, the Place dialog box appears.

2. **Use the controls in the Place dialog box to locate and select the graphics file you want to import.**

3. **If you want to display import options that let you control how the selected graphics file is imported, either select Show Import Options, and then click Open; or press and hold Shift and double-click the filename, or Shift+click Open.** If you choose Show Import Options, the EPS Import Options, Place PDF, Place InDesign Document, or Image Import Options dialog box — depending on what kind of graphic you are importing — appears.

4. **Specify the desired import options, if any are applicable, and then click OK.** (I cover these options later in this chapter.)

5. **You can place the graphic in an existing frame or in a new frame, as follows:**
   - If an empty frame is selected, InDesign automatically places the graphic in the frame. The upper-left corner of the graphic is placed in the upper-left corner of the frame, and the frame acts as the cropping shape for the graphic.
   - If a frame already holding a graphic is selected, InDesign replaces the existing graphic with the new one if you selected the Replace Selected Item option in the Place dialog box. Otherwise, InDesign assumes you want to put the new graphic in a new frame.
   - To place the graphic into a new frame, click the loaded-graphic icon (shown in Figure 26.2) on an empty portion of a page or on the pasteboard. The point where you click establishes the upper-left corner of the resulting graphics frame, which is the same size as the imported graphic and acts as the graphic's cropping shape.
   - To place the graphic in an existing unselected frame, click in the frame with the loaded-graphic icon. The upper-left corner of the graphic is placed in the upper-left corner of the frame, and the frame acts as a cropping shape.

FIGURE 26.2

The loaded-graphic icon displays a preview image of the imported graphics, as well as the number of graphics ready to be placed.

You can select multiple files — graphics and/or text — in the Place dialog box by Shift+clicking a range or by ⌘+clicking or Ctrl+clicking multiple files one by one. InDesign will let you place each file in a separate frame. Just click once for each file imported, or Shift+⌘+click or Ctrl+Shift+click to have InDesign place all files on the page in separate frames. If you place more than one file at the same time, the loaded-text icon displays the number of files to be placed, as well as a mini-preview of each file, as Figure 14.3 shows.

 The ability to import multiple files at once is new to InDesign CS3.

TIP When you place multiple files at once, you can place them in any order. Just move among them using the keyboard left and arrow keys.

To cancel the entire graphics import, just select a different tool. To cancel a specific file in a multiple-file import, press Esc when that file's mini-preview is displayed. (The other files are still available to be placed.)

After you place a graphic, it's displayed in the frame that contains it, and the frame is selected. If the Selection tool is selected, the eight handles of its bounding box are displayed; if the Direct Selection tool is selected, handles are displayed only in the corners. At this point, you can modify either the frame or the graphic within, or you can move on to another task.

Using import options

If you've ever used a graphics application — for example, an image-editing program such as Adobe Photoshop or an illustration program such as Adobe Illustrator or CorelDraw — you're probably aware that when you save a graphics file, you have several options that control such things as file format, image size, color depth, preview quality, and so on. When you save a graphics file, the settings you specify are determined by the way in which the image will be used. For example, you could use Photoshop to save a high-resolution TIFF version of a scanned graphic for use in a slick, four-color annual report or a low-resolution GIF version of the same graphic for use on the company's Web page. Or you could use Illustrator or FreeHand to create a corporate logo that you can use in various sizes in many of your printed publications.

If you choose to specify custom import settings when you import a graphics file, the choices you make will depend on the nature of the publication. For example, if it's bound for the Web, there's no need to work with or save graphics using resolutions that exceed a computer monitor's 72 dpi. Along the same lines, if the publication will be printed, the image import settings you specify for a newspaper printed on newsprint on a SWOP (Specifications for Web Offset Publications) press are different than those you specify for a four-color magazine printed on coated paper using a sheet-fed press.

If you choose Show Import Options when you place a graphic, the options displayed in the resulting dialog boxes depend on the file format of the selected graphic. When you set options for a particular file, the options you specify remain in effect for that file format until you change them. If you don't choose Show Import Options when you place a graphic, the most recent settings for the file format of the selected graphic are used.

Import options for bitmap graphics

InDesign gives you two sets of import options for the following types of bitmap images: TIFF, GIF, JPEG, Scitex CT, BMP, and PCX. You get three options for PNG files, and a different set of three for Photoshop files. There are no import options for PICT or QuickTime movie files. Figure 26.3 shows the four possible panes for bitmap images.

QUARKXPRESS QuarkXPress can convert a color bitmap image to grayscale during import (just press and hold ⌘ or Ctrl when selecting the file) — all without affecting the source file. InDesign has no equivalent capability, so you'll need to convert any images to grayscale first in a program like Photoshop.

Image pane

If you import a Photoshop, TIFF, or EPS file that contains an embedded clipping path, the Image pane lets you apply any embedded clipping path and/or alpha channel to the image to mask, or cut out, part of the image. (Otherwise, these options are grayed out.) Select the Apply Photoshop Clipping Path option to import the clipping path along with the image; select an alpha channel from the Alpha Channel pop-up menu to import the alpha channel along with the image.

FIGURE 26.3

InDesign provides the Image and Color panes in the Image Import Options dialog box for most bitmap formats; PNG files have a third pane, PNG Settings; and Photoshop files also have a third pane, Layers.

CROSS-REF Chapter 27 covers clipping paths in more detail.

Color pane

In the Color pane, you can turn on color management for the image and control how the image is displayed.

Select the Enable Color Management option to enable color management. Using the Profile pop-up menu, choose a color-source profile that matches the color *gamut* (range) of the device (scanner, digital camera, and so on) or software used to create the file. InDesign tries to translate the colors in the file to the colors that the output device is capable of producing. (These profiles are installed in your operating system by other applications, not InDesign.)

CROSS-REF **See Chapter 28 for more information about using InDesign's color-management features.**

Use the Rendering Intent pop-up menu to determine how InDesign translates the color in the selected graphics file with the gamut of the output device. If the graphic is a scanned photograph, choose Perceptual (Images). The other options — Saturation (Graphics), Relative Colorimetric, and Absolute Colorimetric — are appropriate for images that have mostly areas of solid color, such as Illustrator EPS files that have been opened in Photoshop and saved as TIFFs.

PNG Settings pane

Use this pane — available only if you place a PNG file — to use the transparency information in a PNG file, assuming it has a transparent background. You have two choices for controlling transparency handling: White Background and File-defined Background Color. The former forces the transparent portion to display as white in InDesign; the latter uses whatever background color is specified in the PNG file itself.

This pane also lets you adjust the gamma value during import — the *gamma* is a setting that describes a device's luminance, and to ensure most accurate reproduction, you want the gamma setting for the PNG file to be the same as that of your output device (a printer or monitor). It is meant to correct for the file being created on a specific type of monitor. However, to use this feature, you need to know the gamma setting for the final output device. Otherwise, leave it alone.

Layers pane

Use this pane — available only if you place a Photoshop image (or Illustrator or PDF vector file) — to select which layers you want imported into InDesign. You can then control which imported layers display in InDesign, though you cannot change their order. You'd need to go back to Photoshop and change the layer order there.

NOTE **Although you can save an image file with layers as a TIFF, preserving those layers, InDesign does not give you the ability to manage which layers from a TIFF file import into InDesign.**

Use the Layer Comp pop-up menu to select from different layer comps — if any — in the source file. A layer comp is essentially a snapshot of the Photoshop Layers panel that lets you group different layer visibility settings and save them for later use. There's also an option, in the When Updating Link pop-up menu, to control how changes to the file are handled in terms of layer management: If you

Working with Imported Layers

As I describe elsewhere in this chapter, InDesign lets you choose which layers in a Photoshop, Illustrator, or PDF file are imported into InDesign. Once such images are placed in InDesign, you can change which layers display, though you cannot change the order of layers. Note that the controls for modifying layers are pretty much the same as for importing them.

To modify which layers display, select the object with the Selection or Direct Selection tool, and then choose Object ➪ Object Layer Options. You can also Control+click or right-click the graphic and choose Graphics ➪ Object Layer Options from the contextual menu. Either way, the Object Layer Options dialog box, shown here, appears.

In this dialog box, you click the check boxes to the left of the layer names that you want displayed — the eye icon indicates a visible layer. (Be sure to select the Preview option to see the effects of your layer-view changes.)

Your other options in the Object Layer Options dialog box are:

- **Layer Comp:** If your source file uses layer comps (a snapshot of the state of the Photoshop Layers panel that essentially lets you group different layer visibility settings and save them for later application), you can choose those from the Layer Comp pop-up menu.

- **When Updating Link:** In the When Updating Link pop-up menu, you have two options that affect layer display if you update the link to the source graphic. The Use Photoshop's Layer Visibility feature uses whatever layer views are set in Photoshop for the graphic, while Keep Layer Visibility Overrides retains the InDesign layer settings when you relink the source graphic. (If the source graphic is an Illustrator or a PDF file, the When Updating Link pop-up menu options replace the word *Photoshop* with the word *Illustrator* or *PDF*, as appropriate.)

choose Use Photoshop's Layer Visibility, InDesign makes all layers visible in Photoshop when you update the link to the graphic from InDesign. If you choose Keep Layer Visibility Overrides, InDesign imports only the layers chosen in this dialog box if you later update the graphic in Photoshop.

InDesign does let you continue to work with imported graphics' layers after you've imported the file, as I cover later in this chapter.

Import options for vector file formats

If you're importing vector files, selecting the Import Options check box results in one of several dialog boxes appearing, depending on what the vector file type is. If you import older-version Illustrator or EPS files, the EPS Import Options dialog box appears; if you import PDF and newer-version Illustrator files, the Place PDF dialog box, which has two panes, appears. (Both dialog boxes are shown in Figure 26.4.) There are no import options for Windows Metafile graphics.

FIGURE 26.4

The EPS Import Options and Place PDF dialog boxes. The Place PDF dialog box has two panes: General and Layers. (The Layers pane for PDF files is almost identical to the Layers pane for Photoshop files shown in Figure 26.3.)

NOTE   Illustrator CS and later use PDF as their native file format, even though the filename extension is .ai, so InDesign detects these as PDF files and provides the PDF options during import. In earlier versions of Illustrator, the native format was actually a variant of EPS.

Dealing with PDF Security

Some PDF files are protected with passwords or have printing, text editing, and other content-access functions disabled. If a PDF file is password-protected, you're prompted to type the required password; do so and click OK. Note that some PDF files have a second password, called a *permissions password*, that you also need in order to open it.

If the selected file was saved with any security restrictions (no text editing, no printing, and so on), you can't place any pages of the file into InDesign. Ask the person who produced the file for an unrestricted copy.

EPS Import Options dialog box

If you use an OPI-based proxy workflow — that is, if an OPI-based service provider supplies you with low-resolution versions of graphics files that will eventually be replaced by high-resolution files during output — select the Read Embedded OPI Image Links option if you want InDesign, rather than your service provider, to perform image replacement during output. You should also select this option if you import graphics files that contain OPI comments for other imported graphics files; for example, an EPS file that contains OPI information for an embedded TIFF graphic. Don't select this option if you don't use an OPI-based workflow or if you want your service provider to handle image replacement during output. When the Read Embedded OPI Image Links option is not selected, InDesign retains OPI comments but doesn't use them. When you print (or export) the document, the proxy image and the link information are sent.

Also use this pane to import any clipping paths embedded in images that are in the EPS file. Select the Apply Photoshop Clipping Path option to enable this.

Finally, use this pane to control how the EPS file appears on-screen in InDesign. If you select the Use TIFF or PICT Preview option, InDesign uses the low-resolution proxy image embedded in the EPS file for display on-screen and prints the graphic using the embedded high-resolution PostScript instructions. If you select the Rasterize the PostScript option, InDesign converts the PostScript file into a bitmap image during import. There's rarely a reason to rasterize an imported EPS file.

Place PDF dialog box

When you use the Place command to import a PDF file and you choose to Show Options, the Place PDF file dialog box shown in Figure 26.4 appears. It provides several controls for specifying how the file is imported. In the General pane:

- In the Pages section, select Previewed Page, All, or Range to determine which pages you want to import. You can change the previewed page by using the arrow buttons under the preview image at left or typing a specific page number in the field below the preview image. If you want to import a range, use commas to separate pages and a hyphen to indicate range; for example, if you type 3, 5-9, 13, pages 3, 5 through 9, and 13 are imported.

NOTE When you place the PDF in InDesign, you get a separate loaded-graphic icon for each page, so as you place each page, a new loaded-graphic icon appears for the next page until there are no more to place. You can tell you're placing multiple pages because the loaded-graphics icon has a plus sign in it.

■ In the Options section, select one of the cropping options from the Crop to pop-up menu. If you choose Bounding Box, the page's bounding box (or, if none is defined in the PDF file, a rectangle that encloses all items, including page marks) is used to build the graphics frame. Choosing Art places the area defined by the file's creator, if any, as placeable artwork. For example, the person who created the file might have designated a particular graphic as placeable artwork. Choosing Crop places the area displayed and printed by Adobe Acrobat. Choosing Trim places the graphic in an area equal to the final, trimmed piece. Choosing Bleed places the page area plus any specified bleed area. Choosing Media places an area defined by the paper size specified for the PDF document, including page marks.

Also in the Options section, select the Transparent Background option if you want the white areas of the PDF page to be transparent. Deselect this option if you want to preserve the page's opaque white background.

In the Layers pane:

■ You see a list of image layers. Any that have the eye icon import into InDesign, and you can select or deselect layers by clicking the box to the right of the layer name to make the eye icon appear or disappear. You can then control which imported layers display in InDesign, though you cannot change their order (you'd need to go back to Photoshop and change the layer order there).

■ Use the When Updating Link pop-up menu to control how changes to the file are handled in terms of layer management. If you choose Use PDF's Layer Visibility, InDesign makes all layers visible in Illustrator or Acrobat visible when you update the link to the graphic from InDesign. If you choose Keep Layer Visibility Overrides, InDesign imports only the layers you select in this dialog box if you later update the graphic in Photoshop.

Place InDesign Document dialog box

When you import InDesign files to use as a graphic, you have the same options as for PDF files. The Place InDesign Document dialog box is identical to the Place PDF dialog box I cover in the previous section, except of course, for the dialog box's name.

Using other ways to import graphics

If you want to specify custom import options for an imported graphics file, you must use the Place command. However, if you don't need this level of control, InDesign offers three other options for importing graphics:

■ You can use your computer's Copy (File ➪ Copy, or ⌘+C or Ctrl+C) and Paste (File ➪ Paste, or ⌘+V or Ctrl+V) commands to move a graphics file between two InDesign documents or from a document created with another program into an InDesign document.

- You can drag and drop graphics file icons from your computer's desktop into InDesign documents.

- For Illustrator files, you can drag or copy and paste objects directly from Illustrator into InDesign. Depending on your Clipboard preference, these objects may only be embedded PDFs, which are not editable in InDesign.

To set your preference for copying or dragging vector objects from Illustrator into InDesign, go to the File Handling pane of the Preferences dialog box (choose InDesign ➪ Preferences ➪ File Handling or press ⌘+K on the Mac, or choose Edit ➪ Preferences ➪ File Handling or press Ctrl+K in Windows). If you want to place fully editable vector objects in InDesign, go to the Clipboard section of the Clipboard Handing pane and deselect the Prefer PDF When Pasting option. Leave it selected if you prefer to copy or drag noneditable, embedded PDFs into InDesign instead.

NEW FEATURE   In InDesign CS3, the Prefer PDF When Pasting option has moved to the new Clipboard Handling pane of the Preferences dialog box from the File Handling pane in previous versions.

Placing editable vector objects can be especially useful if you need to place a vector logo graphic into a template. An editable vector object entirely contained within InDesign reduces the need to jump between graphic applications to make changes such as editing the logo's colors and vector shapes.

If you use these methods to add a graphic to an InDesign document, some of the attributes of the original graphic may not survive the trip. The operating system, the file format, and the capabilities of the originating application may all play roles in determining which attributes are preserved. If you want to be safe, use the Place command or use the method I described previously to move fully editable vector objects into InDesign.

Copy and paste

If you copy an object in an InDesign document and then paste it into a different InDesign document, the copy retains all the attributes of the original. In the case of a copied and pasted graphic, all import settings, frame modifications, and graphic modifications are retained, as is the link to the original graphics file.

When you copy and paste a graphic into an InDesign document, a link between the original graphics file and the InDesign document is not established. The graphic becomes part of the InDesign document, as though you created it using InDesign tools. A vector image, such as a pasted graphic, is editable only if you deselect Prefer PDF When Pasting in the Clipboard Handling pane of the Preferences dialog box, as I described in the previous section.

Drag and drop

When an InDesign document is open, you can import a graphics file in any supported file format by clicking and dragging the file's icon into the window of the InDesign document. When you drag and drop a graphics file into a document, a link between the original graphics file and the document is established, just as it would be if you had used the Place command.

If you drag and drop an Illustrator file icon into an InDesign document window, the graphic behaves the same as it would if you had used the Place command. That is, individual elements within the graphic are not selectable or modifiable within InDesign. However, if you drag and drop Illustrator objects from an Illustrator document window into an InDesign document window, each object becomes a separate, editable InDesign object, as though you had created it in InDesign.

NOTE For Illustrator objects to be editable in InDesign, be sure that Prefer PDF When Pasting is deselected in the Clipboard Handling pane of the Preferences dialog box, as I describe in an earlier section.

This is a handy way of moving objects that you may want to modify between Illustrator and InDesign. For example, you can create text along a path in an Illustrator document, and then drag and drop the object into an InDesign document. Each character is converted into an editable shape, which you can stroke, fill, distort, and so on, using InDesign features. However, you cannot edit text along a path after you've dragged and dropped it into InDesign. (You have to go back to Illustrator, edit the original text, drag and drop it again, and then redo all your modifications.)

Using the Copy and Paste commands to add Illustrator objects to InDesign documents is the same as dragging and dropping objects between the programs. The copied objects behave the same as objects created in InDesign when you choose Paste, and no links are established.

Summary

If you work with publishing-oriented graphics formats — EPS, PDF, Illustrator, TIFF, and Photoshop — created by mainstay programs like Adobe Photoshop, Adobe Illustrator, CorelDraw, Corel Photo-Paint, and Macromedia FreeHand, you likely have no difficulties importing graphics into or printing graphics from InDesign. But be sure to stick with common color models, particularly CMYK and Pantone.

And it's best to do any special effects in your graphics program; InDesign has limited abilities to manipulate graphics beyond layout-oriented functions like resizing, cropping, flipping, slanting, and text wrap. To ease access to your graphics programs, InDesign lets you open them from within InDesign.

InDesign lets you import graphics in any of several supported graphics file formats. The preferred method for importing graphics is the Place command (File ➪ Place, or ⌘+D or Ctrl+D) because it lets you customize various import settings that control how an imported graphic appears and prints. InDesign also lets you manage the visibility of layers in some imported graphics.

You can also import graphics into an InDesign document by dragging and dropping graphics file icons into a document window or by copying and pasting objects between InDesign documents or between documents created with other programs and InDesign documents.

If you need to use Illustrator-generated objects or graphics files in your InDesign documents, several options are available: the Place command, the Copy and Paste commands, file drag and drop, and inter-application drag and drop. When using Copy and Paste or drag and drop from Illustrator, be sure to check InDesign's File Handling preferences first to choose between creating editable vectors or embedded PDFs in your document.

Chapter 27

Fitting Graphics and Frames Together

G etting a graphic into your layout is one thing, but that's not the end of the story. At a minimum, you want to make sure the image fits in the layout.

The most common actions you'll probably take are cropping, repositioning, and resizing. *Cropping* is a fancy term for deciding what part of the picture to show by altering the dimensions of the frame holding the graphic. *Repositioning* is essentially the same as cropping, except that you move the graphic within its frame. And if you want to get really fancy, you might work with clipping paths to create "masks" around image portions or even cut the graphic into pieces. *Resizing* (also called *scaling*) changes the size of the graphic, either larger or smaller.

CROSS-REF Transformations such as resizing, flipping, rotating, and skewing that you're likely to apply to imported graphics use the same tools as for any InDesign objects, so I cover all these transformations in one place, Chapter 11. I cover other effects that you can apply to any object, including graphics, in Chapter 12.

IN THIS CHAPTER

Cropping and positioning graphics

Working with graphics in irregular shapes

Fitting graphics into frames and vice versa

Importing, creating, and using clipping paths

Fitting Graphics within Their Frames

Remember, when you import a graphic using the Place dialog box (File ➪ Place, or ⌘+D or Ctrl+D) or by clicking and dragging a graphics file into a document window, the graphic is contained in a graphics frame — either the frame that was selected when you placed the graphic or the frame that was automatically created if a frame wasn't selected. The upper-left corner of an imported graphic is automatically placed in the upper-left corner of its frame.

NOTE   In almost every case, you select graphics with the Direct Selection tool to work with the graphic itself, rather than the frame. If you use the Selection tool, the work you do will apply to the frame. The Position tool can act on either the contents or the frame. Chapter 10 explains all three.

Resizing a graphic's frame

The easiest way to crop a graphic is to resize the frame that contains it. To resize the frame, use the Selection or Position tool to drag the frame's handles to reveal the portion of the graphic you want to print (and to conceal the portion you don't want to print). Press and hold Shift as you drag to maintain the proportions of the frame. (See Chapter 11 for details.)

Moving a graphic in its frame

You can also click on a graphic with the Direct Selection tool and then drag the graphic in its frame to crop it, revealing and concealing different parts of the graphic. For example, you can crop the top and left edges of a graphic by clicking and dragging the graphic above and to the left of its original position (in the upper-left corner of the frame).

You can also crop a graphic by moving it relative to its frame using the X and Y options in the Control panel and Transform panel when the Direct Selection tool is active; this is more precise than using the mouse.

The advantage of moving the image within the frame is that, when you've positioned the frame in the desired location in your layout, resizing the frame to crop the image then requires you to move the resized frame back to the desired location.

If you want to *mask out* (hide) portions of an imported graphic, you have the option of using an irregular shape as the frame, a graphic's built-in clipping path (if it has one), or a clipping path you generated in InDesign, as I cover later in this chapter.

Using an irregular frame

If you want to use an irregular shape as the frame for a graphic that's currently cropped by a rectangular frame, here's what you do:

1. **Click the Direct Selection tool (or press A if the Type tool isn't selected).**
2. **Click the graphic you want to place in a free-form shape (don't click its frame), and then choose Edit ➪ Copy, or press ⌘+C or Ctrl+C.**
3. **Click the shape (or create one if you haven't already) you want to use as a cropping frame.** It can be any kind of object except a straight line.
4. **Choose Edit ➪ Paste Into, or press Shift+⌘+V or Ctrl+Shift+V.** Figure 27.1 shows an example.

CROSS-REF   For more information about creating and modifying free-form shapes, see Chapter 28.

If you select a frame with the Direct Selection tool instead of the Selection tool, handles are displayed only at the frame corners rather than at the bounding-box corners and midpoints. When you select a frame with the Direct Selection tool, you can reshape the frame, and thus crop the graphic differently, by clicking and dragging corner points, adding and deleting points, and so on.

FIGURE 27.1

In this example, I copied and pasted the map of North America (left) into a free-form frame that reveals only Canada (right). I created the free-form frame by using the Pen tool to trace the contour of Canada.

Of course, you could also create the irregular shape first, and then use the Place dialog box to place the graphic file directly into the shape. (Or choose File ➪ Place Into, or press Option+⌘+V or Ctrl+Alt+V, to paste a cut or copied graphic inside the shape.) Using an irregular shape to crop a graphic is similar to using a clipping path except that you create the irregular shape yourself using InDesign's object-creation tools while a clipping path is either built into a graphics file or generated by InDesign, as I describe later in this chapter.

Figuring Out the Fitting Commands

If you've placed a graphic in a frame that's either larger or smaller than the graphic, you can use the Fitting commands (Object ➪ Fitting) to scale the graphic to fit the frame proportionally or disproportionately or to scale the frame to fit the graphic. Another option lets you center the graphic in the frame.

You can also use the frame-fitting iconic buttons in the Control panel, shown in Figure 27.2. But note that these may not display in your Control panel; by default, InDesign shows them only if your monitor is set to a resolution whose width is 1280 or more pixels. You can make room for them at smaller resolutions by customizing the Control panel display: Choose Customize from the panel's flyout menu and then deselect some of the Object controls to make room, as Chapter 2 explains.

FIGURE 27.2

The frame-fitting iconic buttons in the Control panel

Here's a description of each of the six options:

- **Fit Content to Frame:** To scale a graphic to fill the selected frame, choose Object ⇨ Fitting ⇨ Fit Content to Frame, or press Option+⌘+E or Ctrl+Alt+E. If the frame is larger than the graphic, the graphic is enlarged; if the frame is smaller, the graphic is reduced. If the graphic and the frame have different proportions, the graphic's proportions are changed so that the image completely fills the frame. Note that this can distort the graphic.

- **Fit Frame to Content:** To resize a frame so that it wraps snugly around a graphic, choose Fit Frame to Content, or press Option+⌘+C or Ctrl+Alt+C. The frame is enlarged or reduced depending on the size of the graphic, and the frame's proportions change to match the proportions of the graphic.

- **Center Content:** To center a graphic in its frame, choose Center Content, or press Shift+⌘+E or Ctrl+Shift+E. Neither the frame nor the graphic is scaled when you center a graphic.

- **Fit Content Proportionally:** To scale a graphic to fit in the selected frame while maintaining the graphic's current proportions (preventing distortion), choose Object ⇨ Fitting ⇨ Fit Content Proportionally, or press Option+Shift+⌘+E or Ctrl+Alt+Shift+E. If the frame is larger than the graphic, the graphic is enlarged; if the frame is smaller, the graphic is reduced. If the graphic and the frame have different proportions, a portion of the frame background appears above and below or to the left and right of the graphic. If you want, you can click and drag frame edges to make the frame shorter or narrower and eliminate any portions of the background that are visible.

- **Fill Frame Proportionally:** To resize a frame to fit the selected graphic, choose Object ⇨ Fitting ⇨ Fill Frame Proportionally, or press Option+Shift+⌘+C or Ctrl+Alt+Shift+C. This guarantees that no space is left between the graphic and the frame. (The Fit Frame to Content option can result in such space at the bottom and/or right sides of a graphic.)
- **Frame Fitting Options:** To control the default fitting for either the selected frame or (if no frame is selected) for newly placed graphics, use the Frame Fitting Options dialog box, shown in Figure 27.3. Here you can set the amount of crop, choose the reference point for the imported graphic (see Chapter 10), and automatically apply your choice of the Fit Content to Frame, Fit Content Proportionally, and Fill Frame Proportionally options.

NOTE If no object is selected, any settings specified in the Frame Fitting Options dialog box will be applied to all graphics placed into new empty frames from that point on. If no document is open, the settings are applied to all documents later created.

InDesign CS3 offers a quick way to fit a frame to its content: Just double-click a frame handle. The handle you double-click determines how the frame is fitting: using a corner handle fits the frame's width and height, using a left or right side handle fits the frame to the object's width, and using a top or bottom handle fits the frame to the object's height.

NEW FEATURE The Frame Fitting Options menu item and dialog box are new to InDesign CS3. So is the ability to scale an object by double-clicking part of its frame.

For frames with strokes, the fitting options align the outer edge of a graphic with the center of the stroke. A stroke will obscure a strip along the graphic's edge that is half the width of the stroke. The wider the stroke is, the more of the graphic that gets covered up.

FIGURE 27.3

The Frame Fitting Options dialog box lets you set the default behavior for newly imported graphics.

Creating Clipping Paths in Photoshop

Creating a clipping path in Photoshop is simple, once you get the hang of the process. (See the *Photoshop Bible* series [Wiley Publishing] for more on creating clipping paths in Photoshop.) A path is essentially a selection, which you can create with any of the Photoshop selection tools, including tracing your own selection to hand-drawing a path. Once you make the selection, here's how you make a path:

1. **Open the Paths panel by choosing Window ➪ Paths.**

2. **Using the panel's flyout menu, choose Make Work Path.** You're asked to choose a Tolerance setting in pixels — the smaller the number, the finer the path's shape.

3. **Click OK to accept your setting.** A work path appears in the Paths panel, showing in white the area contained by the path.

4. **Convert the work path into a named path by double-clicking the work path in the panel or by choosing Save Path in the flyout menu.**

5. **Give the path a name, and then click OK.**

6. **Choose Clipping Path from the flyout menu.** You're asked to choose which path to use as a clipping path (you can have multiple clipping paths in a Photoshop file); next, choose a Flatness setting. As with the Tolerance setting, the smaller the number of pixels, the finer the path's contours.

7. **Click OK.**

That's it! The tricky part is creating the selection area to begin with.

Working with Clipping Paths

A clipping path is essentially a shape that acts like a cutout mask — anything inside the shape displays and anything outside does not. It's a very handy way of displaying just the pieces of a graphic that you want to display, such as masking out extraneous background or focusing on a specific portion of a larger image. Clipping paths are also frequently used to control text wrap around graphics.

InDesign can work with clipping paths that are already part of an imported TIFF, JPEG, Photoshop EPS, or Photoshop image, as I explained earlier in this chapter, or with clipping paths you create in InDesign. And no matter the source of the clipping path, InDesign lets you modify it.

Using a graphic's own clipping path

In an ideal world, any graphics that you want to have fit in an irregular shape come with their own clipping paths. In that situation, you would first be sure to import the clipping path when you place the graphic.

Using the clipping path as a mask

To use that clipping path to mask out part of an image, you must convert the clipping path to a frame (that frame then masks out everything that doesn't fit within it). The process is simple: Select the clipping path with the Direct Selection tool and choose Object ➪ Clipping Path ➪ Convert Clipping Path to Frame.

NEW FEATURE The submenu option in the Object menu to convert a clipping path to a frame is new to InDesign CS3. In previous versions, it was available only in the contextual menu if you Control+clicked or right-clicked an object that contained a clipping path.

Using the clipping path as a wrap boundary

If your goal is to wrap text around the contours of the clipping path, you don't create a frame from the clipping path. Instead, you have InDesign's Text Wrap panel access that clipping path for its text wrap. Here's how:

1. **Be sure to select the Show Import Options check box in the Place dialog box (File ➪ Place, or ⌘+D or Ctrl+D) when you import the graphic and select the Apply Photoshop Clipping Path option in the Image Import Options dialog box.**

2. **Open the Text Wrap panel (Window ➪ Text Wrap, or Option+⌘+W or Ctrl+Alt+W), as shown in Figure 27.4.**

3. **Select the graphic.**

4. **Click the Wrap Around Object Shape button (the third one from the left) at the top of the Text Wrap panel.**

5. **If you want, adjust the space between the surrounding text and the obstructing shape by typing values in the Top Offset field.**

6. **Now select the clipping source from the Type pop-up menu in the Contour Options section of the Text Wrap panel.** Choose from two relevant options:

   - Alpha Channel uses the image's alpha channel, if any, to create a wrapping boundary. (An *alpha channel* is another type of clipping path and is also created in the source program such as Photoshop.)

   - Photoshop Path uses the image's clipping path, if any, to create a wrapping boundary. Use the Path pop-up menu to select which path to use if your image has more than one embedded clipping path.

NEW FEATURE InDesign CS3 creates a simpler text-wrap shape when importing a graphic with an alpha channel. This results in fewer points you have to work with when modifying the text-wrap shape.

CROSS-REF See Chapter 13 for the details of text wraps. See Chapter 28 for details on how to edit irregular shapes such as text-wrap boundaries.

FIGURE 27.4

The Text Wrap panel and its Type pop-up menu. You can see a Photoshop-generated clipping path around the North American continent.

Creating a clipping path in InDesign

If you import a graphic that doesn't have its own clipping path, you have two sets of options to create a clipping path in InDesign.

The easiest is to use the Text Wrap panel as I describe in the previous section but instead choose one of the following options from the Type pop-up menu:

- **Detect Edges:** This option tries to determine the graphic's outside boundary by ignoring white space. You would use this for bitmapped images that have a transparent or white background.

- **Same as Clipping:** This option uses the clipping path for the graphic created in InDesign. You would use this when the desired clipping path can't be created through the Detect Edges option. (I cover this method of clipping-path creation shortly.)

You can further modify the clipping path by selecting the graphic with the Direct Selection tool. The text-wrap boundary appears as a blue line; you can make the boundary easier to select by setting offsets in the Text Wrap panel, which moves the boundary away from the frame edge. Now use InDesign's free-form editing tools, as covered in Chapter 28, to edit the text-wrap boundary.

A slightly more difficult way to create a clipping path — but one that gives you more control — is to use the Clipping Path command (Object ➪ Clipping Path ➪ Options, or Option+Shift+⌘+K or Ctrl+Alt+Shift+K) to generate one automatically:

1. **Select the graphic to which you want to add a clipping path.** It's best to use the Direct Selection tool, so that you can see the clipping path within the frame as you work.

2. **Choose Object ➪ Clipping Path ➪ Options, or press Option+Shift+⌘+K or Ctrl+Alt+Shift+K.** The Clipping Path dialog box appears, as shown in Figure 27.5.

NEW FEATURE In InDesign CS3, you create clipping paths through the new Options submenu. You choose Object ➪ Clipping Path ➪ Options, rather than Object ➪ Clipping Path, as you did in previous versions.

3. **To have InDesign detect the likely boundary of the image, as opposed to a white or other light background, choose Detect Edges from the Type pop-up menu.** You can use the other options to select Alpha Channel or Photoshop Path as the clipping path for graphics that have one or more of these. (InDesign can only use one alpha channel or Photoshop path as the clipping path, so use the Path pop-up menu to choose the one you want.)

4. **Type a value in the Threshold field or click and drag the field's slider to specify the value below which pixels will be placed outside the clipping path shape (that is, pixels that will become transparent).** Pixels darker than the Threshold value remain visible and thus are inside the clipping path shape. The lowest possible Threshold value (0) makes only white pixels transparent. As the value gets higher, less of the graphic remains visible. The lightest areas are removed first, then midtones, and so on. (Enable the Preview check box to see the results of your changes without closing the dialog box.)

5. **Type a value in the Tolerance field.** This value determines how closely InDesign looks at variations in adjacent pixels when building a clipping path. Higher values produce a simpler, smoother path than lower values. Lower values create a more complicated, more exact path with more anchor points.

6. **If you want to enlarge or reduce the size of the clipping path produced by the Threshold and Tolerance values, type a value in the Inset Frame field.** Negative values enlarge the path; positive values shrink it. (The Inset Frame value is also applied to the path's bounding box.)

7. **Enable the Invert check box to switch the transparent and visible areas of the clipping path produced by the Threshold and Tolerance values.**

8. **If you want to include light areas in the perimeter shape InDesign generates based on the Threshold and Tolerance values, enable the Include Inside Edges check box.** For example, if you have a graphic of a doughnut and you want to make the hole transparent (as well as the area around the outside of the doughnut), click Include Inside Edges. If you don't click Include Inside Edges, InDesign builds a single shape (in the case of a doughnut, just the outside circle). The portion of the graphic in the shape remains visible; the rest of the graphic becomes transparent.

9. **Enable the Restrict to Frame check box if you want InDesign to generate a clipping path from just the portion of the graphic visible in the graphic frame, as opposed to the entire graphic (such as if you cropped the graphic).**

10. **Enable the Use High Resolution Image check box if you want InDesign to use the high-resolution information in the original file instead of using the low-resolution**

proxy image. Even though using the high-resolution image takes longer, the resulting clipping path is more precise than it would be if you didn't check Use High Resolution Image.

11. **When you've finished specifying clipping path settings, click OK to close the dialog box and apply the settings to the selected graphic.**

FIGURE 27.5

The Clipping Path dialog box

CAUTION If you use the Clipping Path command to generate a clipping path for a graphic that has a built-in clipping path, the one that InDesign generates replaces the built-in path.

NOTE The Clipping Path command works very well for images that have a white or light background but no clipping path. It's less useful for graphics with backgrounds that contain a broad range of intermingling values.

Once you've created the clipping path, you can use it either to mask the image (by converting it to a frame) or to control text wrap — just as you can with an imported clipping path. Both are covered earlier in this chapter.

Figure 27.6 shows an image montage from ten images. A matrix of nine photos is on the bottom layer. The top layer is a frame created from a clipping path around the outline of the North American continent, into which a tenth photo has been placed, creating a masked copy that overlays the other nine. For added effect, I applied a gradient feather to the masked photo so it fades away toward the bottom and lets detail from the images below emerge.

Modifying clipping paths

Whether the path was imported or created in InDesign, you can change it by choosing a different option in the Text Wrap panel — Detect Edges, Alpha Channel, Photoshop Path, or User-Modified Path — than was selected previously.

And you can edit the clipping path manually, like any other freeform shape, as I cover in Chapter 28.

FIGURE 27.6

A montage involving a frame created from an imported graphic's clipping path

Deleting clipping paths

Whether the clipping path was imported or created in InDesign, you can remove it by choosing None as the Type in the Clipping Path dialog box. (For an imported graphic, deleting the clipping path in InDesign does not destroy the original path in the graphic's source file.)

Summary

It's very common to need to fit a graphic to its frame or a frame to its graphic, so InDesign provides several mechanisms to do so. Likewise, it provides several mechanisms to crop a graphic so you can control which parts of it display. Manual options include using the mouse and the Control panel. The Fitting command (Object ⇨ Fitting) provides four submenu options for positioning and scaling a graphic relative to its frame.

InDesign also lets you control what part of a graphic displays and/or how text wraps around it using clipping paths, which are either imported from Photoshop files or created within InDesign.

Chapter 28

Drawing Free-Form Shapes and Curved Paths

InDesign's basic drawing tools let you create basic shapes, such as straight lines, rectangles and squares, circles and ellipses, and equilateral polygons. But what about when you need to create shapes that aren't so basic, such as amoeba or a cursive version of your first name, perhaps? That's where InDesign's Pen tool comes in. You can use the Pen tool to create any kind of line or closed shape. And you can use anything you create with the Pen tool as an independent graphic element or as a frame for text or a picture.

If you've ever used an illustration program such as Illustrator, FreeHand, or CorelDraw, or a page-layout program such as PageMaker or QuarkXPress, you may already be familiar with Bézier drawing tools. (Bézier tools are named after Pierre Bézier, a French engineer and mathematician, who developed a method of representing curved shapes on a computer in the 1970s.) If you aren't familiar with Bézier tools, you should know in advance that getting the hang of using them takes a little time and patience. Even if you're a virtuoso when drawing with a piece of charcoal or a B6 pencil, you need to practice with the Pen tool for a while before your drawing skills kick in. The good news is that once you get comfortable using the Pen tool, you can draw any shape you can imagine. (Of course, if you can't draw very well in the first place, using the Pen tool won't magically transform you into a master illustrator!) If this is new terrain for you, start simply and proceed slowly.

If you intend to use InDesign extensively as a drawing tool, you might want to purchase a drawing tablet, which can make working with the Pen tool a bit easier than using a mouse or trackball. On both Macs and PCs, you can usually hook up multiple input devices, so you can switch from tablet to mouse or trackball and back as needed.

IN THIS CHAPTER

Understanding path basics

Drawing zigzag and wavy lines

Drawing closed shapes

Drawing free-form shapes

Working with anchor points

Modifying segments

Manipulating open paths

Manipulating closed paths

Creating compound paths

Applying corner options to paths

Finding Out All about Paths

Every object you create with InDesign's object-creation tools is a path. That includes:

- Straight lines created with the Line tool
- Lines and shapes created with the Pen tool or the Pencil tool
- Basic shapes created with the Ellipse, Rectangle, and Polygon tools
- Basic frames created with the Ellipse Frame, Rectangle Frame, and Polygon Frame tools

All of InDesign's object-manipulation features are available for all paths. This includes the transformation tools, the Control panel and the Transform panel, the Stroke and Swatches panels, and the option to place a text file or graphics file either on or within the path. (You can't place text within a straight line because there is not even a partial enclosure in which to create the bounds of a text frame.)

The properties of a path

Regardless of the tool you use to create a path, you can change its appearance by modifying any of four properties that all paths share: closure, stroke, fill, and contents.

Closure

A path is either *open* or *closed*. Straight lines created with the Line tool and curved and zigzag lines created with the Pen tool are examples of open paths. Basic shapes created with the Ellipse, Rectangle, and Polygon tools and free-form shapes created with the Pen and Pencil tools are examples of closed shapes. A closed free-form shape is an uninterrupted path with no endpoints. Figure 28.1 shows the difference between open and closed paths.

FIGURE 28.1

The five paths on the left are open; the five on the right are closed. A stroke and fill have been added to show how they affect open and closed paths.

Stroke

If you want to make a path visible, you can apply a *stroke* to it, as Chapter 12 describes. (An unselected, unstroked path is not visible.) When you stroke a path, you can specify the stroke's width, color, tint, and style. Figure 28.2 shows a path before and after a stroke was added.

FIGURE 28.2

The original path (left) is selected. At right, a 2-point stroke was added to a clone of the original path.

Fill

A color, color tint, or gradient applied to the background of an open path or a closed path is called a *fill*. Figure 28.3 shows some examples of fills. Chapter 8 explains how to apply them.

FIGURE 28.3

From left to right: a color fill (black), a color tint fill (50 percent black), and a gradient fill. The paths are selected and displayed in their bounding boxes.

Contents

You can place a text file or a graphics file in any path (with the exception of a straight line), as Chapters 14 and 26 explain. When a path is used to hold text or a picture, the path functions as a *frame*. Although InDesign can place text in an open path, placing text and pictures in closed paths is far more common than placing them in open paths. Figure 28.4 shows several examples of pictures imported into paths.

QUARKXPRESS For QuarkXPress users, the idea of placing text and pictures in lines (that is, in open paths) may seem strange at first. (In QuarkXPress, lines cannot contain text or pictures, although line-like text paths can contain text.)

FIGURE 28.4

Top row: The same picture was imported into three different paths. (A stroke has been added to the paths to make them more visible.) Bottom row: Text has been placed in clones of the paths on the top row.

The anatomy of a path

No matter how simple (a short straight line) or complicated (a free-form shape with several straight and curved edges) a path is, all paths are made up of the same components. Figures 28.5 through 28.7 show the parts that make up a path:

- A path contains one or more straight or curved *segments*, as shown in Figure 28.5.

- An anchor point is located at each end of every segment. The anchor points at the ends of a closed path are called *endpoints*. When you create a path of any kind, anchor points are automatically placed at the end of each segment. After you create a path, you can move, add, delete, and change the direction of corner points.

FIGURE 28.5

From left to right, each path contains one more segment than the previous path. (The top row shows straight segments and the bottom row shows curved segments.) The two rightmost paths each contain three segments.

■ There are two kinds of anchor points: *smooth points* and *corner points*. A smooth point connects two adjoining curved segments in a continuous, flowing curve. At a corner point, adjoining segments — straight or curved — meet at an angle. The corners of a rectangular path are the most common corner points. Figure 28.6 shows some examples of smooth and corner points.

FIGURE 28.6

The path on the left has only corner anchor points; the path in the center has only smooth anchor points; and the path on the right has both kinds of anchor points.

■ A *direction line* runs through each anchor point and has a handle at both ends. You can control the curve that passes through an anchor point by dragging a direction line's handles. Figure 28.7 shows how you can change the shape of a path by dragging a direction line handle.

FIGURE 28.7

The original path on the left is cloned and then the direction handle of the right endpoint is dragged to create the path on the right.

NOTE   Anchor points and direction lines do not print.

659

Reading about riding a bike is one thing; riding a bike is another. If you've read Chapter 9, you already know how to ride with training wheels — you can create basic shapes with the basic object-creation tools. Now that you know more about what paths are made of, you're ready to tackle more-complex shapes. You're ready to wield the Pen tool.

Drawing Lines with the Pen Tool

The Pen tool is very versatile. With it you can create lines (open paths) and shapes (closed paths).

Straight and zigzag lines

The simplest kind of path is a straight line (that is, an open path) with a single segment, which you can create with either the Line tool or the Pen tool. But the Pen is much mightier than the Line because it lets you draw zigzag lines with multiple straight segments, curvy lines, and lines that contain straight and curved segments. You can't draw those kinds of shapes with the Line tool, or any of the other object-creation tools, for that matter.

 Chapter 9 covers the Line tool.

To draw lines with straight segments:

1. **Select the Pen tool or press P if the Type tool isn't selected.**

2. **Move the Pen pointer to where you want to place one of your line's endpoints, and then click and release the mouse button (make sure you don't drag before you release the mouse button).** When you click and release the mouse button while using the Pen tool, you create a corner point. A small, filled-in square indicates the anchor point, which is also an endpoint of the open shape you're creating.

3. **Move the Pen pointer to where you want to place the next anchor point, and then click and release the mouse button.** When you create the second point, a straight line connects it with the first point, the first anchor point changes to a hollow square, and the second anchor point is filled in. (If you want to create a line with a single segment, you can stop drawing at this point by choosing another tool.)

4. **For each additional anchor point, move the Pen pointer, and then click and release the mouse button.** If you hold down the Shift key as you click, the angles you create are limited to multiples of 45 degrees. To reposition an anchor point after you click the mouse button but before you release it, hold down the spacebar and drag.

CAUTION If you drag before you press the spacebar, you create a smooth point and curved segments.

5. **To complete the path, press the ⌘ key or the Ctrl key and click on an empty portion of the page or choose another tool.** If you click on the page, the Pen tool remains selected and you can continue creating additional paths. Figure 28.8 shows a path in various stages of being drawn.

Drawing Tools

InDesign uses the same drawing tools as Adobe Illustrator and Adobe Photoshop, so if you're familiar with those, you should have no trouble using InDesign's tools. If not, it might help to get a refresher on the tools:

- **Pen tool:** This tool draws both segments and Bézier curves. It has several associated tools to add, delete, and convert corner points, which are the handles that you use to change the direction and curvature of a curve or line segment.

- **Pencil tool:** This is a free-form drawing tool that simply draws out your mouse motions. The result is a Bézier curve. A Pencil tool is great if you have a steady, accurate drawing hand; the Pen tool is better if you want to control each segment and curve as you create it.

- **Shape tools:** The shape tools create closed objects that aren't intended to hold text or graphics; they're basically shapes you can color and/or stroke. There are Rectangle, Polygon, and Ellipse versions, as described in Chapter 9.

- **Frame tools:** The frame tools are the same as the shape tools, except they're meant to create shapes that will contain text or graphics, though they can also be empty.

- **Type and Type on a Path tools:** The Type and Type on a Path tools let you add text in an object and on an object's stroke, respectively. (See Chapter 19.)

You can also complete the path by clicking on the first point you created, but if you do, you create a closed path. (I discuss closed paths in the next section.)

TIP   As you create a path, you can move any anchor point, direction line handle, or the entire path by pressing the ⌘ or Ctrl key, and then clicking and dragging whatever element you want to move.

FIGURE 28.8

As each anchor point was created (from left to right), a new, straight segment was added to the path. The finished open path is a zigzag line that contains four straight segments produced by clicking and releasing the mouse a total of five times.

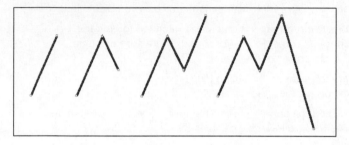

Curved lines

If all you ever need to create are zigzag lines with corner points and straight segments, the click-and-release method in the preceding section is all you need to know. But if you want to create curvy lines, you need to take the next step up the Bézier ladder and learn to add smooth points. Creating smooth points and curved segments is much like creating corner points and straight segments — with a twist. There are two ways of connecting curved segments when drawing a path: with smooth points and with corner points. I explain both methods in the steps that follow.

Curved segments connected by smooth points

If you want to draw a continuously curvy path that contains no corner points and no straight segments, you should create only smooth points as you draw. Here's how:

1. **Select the Pen tool or press P if the Type tool isn't selected.**

2. **Move the Pen pointer to where you want to place one of your line's endpoints, and then click and hold down the mouse button.** The arrowhead pointer is displayed.

3. **Drag the mouse in the direction of the next point you intend to create.** (Adobe suggests dragging about one-third of the way to the next point.) As you drag, the anchor point, its direction line, and the direction line's two handles are displayed, as shown in Figure 28.9. If you hold down the Shift key as you drag, the angle of the direction line is limited to increments of 45 degrees.

4. **Release the mouse button.**

5. **Move the Pen pointer where you want to establish the next anchor point, which ends the first segment, and then drag the mouse.** If you drag in approximately the same direction as the direction line of the previous point, you create an S-shaped curve; if you drag in the opposite direction, you create a C-shaped curve. Figure 28.10 shows both kinds of curves.

6. **When the curve between the two anchor points looks how you want it to look, release the mouse button.**

FIGURE 28.9

To create a smooth point when beginning a path, click and hold the mouse and drag in the direction of the next point. Here you see the direction line of a smooth endpoint created by clicking and dragging in the direction of the next anchor point.

FIGURE 28.10

A C-shaped curved segment (left); an S-shaped curved segment (right)

7. **Continue moving the Pen pointer, clicking and dragging, and then releasing the mouse button to establish additional smooth points and curved segments.**

8. **To complete the path, hold down the ⌘ key or the Ctrl key and click on an empty portion of the page or choose another tool.** If you click on the page, the Pen tool remains selected and you can continue creating additional paths.

You can also complete the path by clicking on the first point you created, but if you do, you create a closed path. Figure 28.11 shows a finished line that contains several curved segments.

TIP The two segments that form a smooth point's direction line work together as a single straight line. When you move a handle, the line acts like a teeter-totter; the opposite handle moves in the opposite direction. If you shorten one of the segments, the length of the other segment doesn't change. The angle and length of direction lines determine the shape of the segments with which they're associated.

FIGURE 28.11

This line contains five anchor points — all smooth points — and four curved segments. The two segments on the left are both C-shaped curves; the two on the right are both S-shaped.

Curved segments connected by corner points

Sometimes you may need to create a line with curvy segments that don't adjoin smoothly. Figure 28.12 shows an example of a line that's made up of several C-shaped curves that are connected with corner points. When adjoining segments — curved or straight — meet at a corner point, the transition is abrupt rather than smooth, as it is at a smooth point. To create this kind of shape, you need to be able to connect curved segments using corner points instead of smooth points. Here's how:

1. **Select the Pen tool or press P if the Type tool isn't selected.**

2. **Move the Pen pointer to where you want to place one of your line's endpoints, and then click and hold down the mouse button.** The arrowhead pointer is displayed.

3. **Drag the mouse in the direction of the next point you intend to create.** As you drag, the anchor point, its direction line, and the direction line's two handles are displayed. If you hold down the Shift key as you drag, the angle of the direction line is limited to increments of 45 degrees.

4. **Move the Pen pointer to where you want to establish the next anchor point, which ends the first segment, and then press Option or Alt and click and drag the mouse.** As you drag, the anchor point's handle moves and the direction line changes from a straight line to two independent segments. The angle of the direction line segment that you create when you drag the handle determines the slope of the next segment.

5. **Release the mouse button.**

6. **Continue moving the Pen pointer and repeat Step 4 and Step 5 to create additional segments joined by corner points.**

7. **To complete the path, hold down the ⌘ key or the Ctrl key and click on an empty portion of the page or choose another tool.** If you click on the page, the Pen tool remains selected and you can continue creating additional paths.

> **NOTE** A corner point that connects two curved segments has two direction lines; a corner point that connects two straight segments has no direction lines; and a corner point that connects a straight and curved segment has one direction line. If you drag a corner point's direction line, the other direction line, if there is one, is not affected. The angle and length of direction lines determine the shape of the segments with which they're associated.

Figure 28.12 shows a line with several curved segments joined by corner points.

FIGURE 28.12

Here, three corner points join four curved segments. The direction handles of the two rightmost segments are visible. The direction handles of a corner point are joined like a hinge; moving one handle doesn't affect the other handle.

Combining straight and curved segments

By combining the techniques for drawing straight segments and curved segments, you can create lines that contain both. Figure 28.13 shows three lines made up of straight and curved segments, as well as curved segments joined by smooth points and curved segments joined by corner points.

FIGURE 28.13

Three paths with both curved and straight segments, as well as corner points and smooth points

Here's how to draw a straight segment followed by a curved segment:

1. **While drawing a path, create a straight segment by clicking and releasing the mouse button, moving the Pen pointer, and then clicking and releasing the mouse button again.**

2. **Move the Pen pointer over the last anchor point you created in Step 1.** The Convert Point icon appears. (It looks like the regular Pen icon except that a small triangle missing its base appears at the icon's lower right.)

3. **Click, drag, and then release the mouse button to create the direction line that determines the slope of the next segment.**

4. **Move the Pen pointer to where you want to establish the next anchor point, and then click and drag to complete the curved segment.**

Figure 28.14 shows a step-by-step sequence of a curved segment being added to a straight segment. You can also follow a straight segment with a curved segment by simply clicking and dragging to create a smooth point. However, if you don't use the method I explain in the earlier steps, you are able to adjust the slope associated with only one of the curved segment's anchor points rather than both.

Follow these steps to draw a curved segment followed by a straight segment:

1. **While drawing a path, create a curved segment by clicking, dragging, and then releasing the mouse button, and then moving the Pen pointer, clicking, dragging, and releasing the mouse button again.**

2. **Move the Pen pointer over the last anchor point you created in Step 1.** The Convert Point icon appears.

3. **Click the anchor point to convert it from a smooth point to a corner point.**

4. **Move the Pen pointer to where you want to establish the next anchor point;** then click and release the mouse button to complete the straight segment.

FIGURE 28.14

(1) Draw a straight segment, as shown at left. (2) Click and drag to create a smooth anchor point. (3) Move the pointer to the next desired anchor point location and then click and drag to create a curved segment.

1   2   3

Figure 28.15 shows a straight segment being added to a curved segment.

FIGURE 28.15

(1) Draw a curved segment, as shown at left. (2) Move the pointer over the last anchor point and click on that anchor point. (3) Move the pointer to the next desired anchor point location, and then click and release the mouse button to create a straight segment.

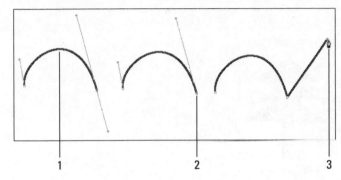

TIP When creating paths, use as few anchor points as possible. As you become more comfortable creating free-form paths, you should find yourself using fewer anchor points to create paths.

Drawing Free-Form Shapes

A closed path is an uninterrupted enclosure with no endpoints. When you apply a stroke to a closed path, there's no beginning or end. Generally, you'll create closed paths when you want to place text or pictures in free-form frames. Although you can place text or a picture in an open path, the result can look more than a little strange, especially if you add a stroke to the path. Then again, you can achieve some strange effects by using open paths as frames. If strange is your goal, go for it.

TIP For an easy way to draw free-form shapes, use the Pencil tool. It simply traces the movement of your mouse (or pen tablet) as you move it, much like a pencil works on paper. Although not as exact as the Pen tool, the Pencil tool does create Bézier curves that you can later edit.

When it comes to creating closed paths with the Pen tool, the process is exactly the same as it is for creating open paths, as I explained earlier in this chapter, with one difference at the end: If you click on the first endpoint you created, you create a closed path:

- To create a straight segment between the endpoint and the last anchor point you created, click and release the mouse button.

- To create a curved segment, click and drag the mouse in the direction of the last anchor point you created, and then release the mouse button.

667

Just like an open path, a closed path can contain straight and/or curved segments and smooth and/or corner points. All the techniques I explained earlier in this chapter for drawing lines with curved and straight segments and smooth and corner points apply when you're drawing closed paths. Figure 28.16 shows several closed paths used as graphic shapes, text frames, and graphics frames.

FIGURE 28.16

Closed paths of various shapes

If you draw a path and it turns out to be a little (or a lot, for that matter) different than you intended, don't worry. You can always modify it by moving, adding, deleting, and converting anchor points and by adjusting direction lines. You can also use the transformation tools, the Control panel, or the Transform panel to rotate, scale, shear, flip, and change the position of the path.

CROSS-REF See Chapters 10 and 11 for more information about manipulating shapes and using InDesign's transformation features.

Editing Free-Form Lines and Shapes

No matter how skillful you become using InDesign's Pen and Pencil tools to create free-form paths, it's difficult to create exactly what you want on your first attempt. For example, after creating a path, you may want to add detail, smooth out a rough spot, or turn a straight segment into a curved one. No problem. InDesign lets you modify the paths you create in several ways. You can:

■ Add or delete anchor points

■ Move anchor points

- Change corner points to smooth points and vice versa
- Modify direction lines
- Extend an open path
- Erase parts of the path or cut paths into segments
- Change a closed path to an open path and vice versa

The path-manipulation techniques I explain in this chapter apply to all types of paths, including open and closed paths created with the Pen tool, the Pencil tool, and the object-creation tools; text and graphic frames (which are simply paths that act as containers); clipping paths created with the Clipping Path command (Object ➪ Clipping Path ➪ Options, or Option+Shift+⌘+K or Ctrl+Alt+Shift+K) or built into imported graphics; and text-wrap paths created with the Text Wrap panel (Window ➪ Text Wrap, or Option+⌘+W or Ctrl+Alt+W).

CROSS-REF Chapter 27 covers clipping paths and text-wrap paths, while Chapter 13 covers the general use of the Text Wrap panel.

Generally, when you want to manipulate a path, you use one of the three variations of the Pen tool, all of which are displayed in a single pop-up menu in the Tools panel (shown in the sidebar "Drawing Tools" in this chapter):

- Both the Add Anchor Point tool and the Delete Anchor Point tool let you add and delete anchor points.
- The Convert Direction Point tool lets you change smooth points to corner points and vice versa.

You can also use the Pen tool with keyboard shortcuts to perform all the functions of the Add Anchor Point, Delete Anchor Point, and Convert Direction Point tools.

TIP If you find that you simply can't create a particular graphic effect within InDesign, you can always resort to your illustration program (assuming you have one). If you're an Adobe Illustrator user, you can easily drag and drop objects from Illustrator into InDesign documents.

Adding and deleting anchor points

If you want to add detail to an existing path, you need to add anchor points that give you more precise control over a portion of the path. Perhaps you've drawn the profile of a face and you want to add detail to the lips. Or maybe you've written your name longhand and you need to add a flourish that your original attempt lacks. In both cases, you can add smooth or corner points and then manipulate the curves associated with those points by moving them or manipulating their direction lines. (The next section explains how to move anchor points and manipulate direction lines.)

On the other hand, maybe you've created a path that's more complicated than necessary. Perhaps you drew a hand with six fingers instead of five or a camel with one too many humps. In these instances, you need to simplify the path by removing anchor points. InDesign lets you add and delete as many anchor points as you want.

You should always try to use as few anchor points as possible in the paths you create. The fewer points a path has, the less likely it is to cause printing problems.

When you want to modify the shape of a path, you should begin by selecting it with the Direct Selection tool rather than the Selection tool. If you select a path with the Selection tool, the path's bounding box is displayed with eight moveable handles. In this situation, you can modify the bounding box (thereby resizing the path), but you can't modify the path itself.

To add an anchor point:

1. **Select the path by clicking it with the Direct Selection tool.** You can also select multiple paths and then modify them one at a time.

2. **Select the Pen tool, the Add Anchor Point tool, or the Delete Anchor Point tool.** You can use any of these tools to add and delete anchor points. If the Type tool is not selected, you can select the Pen tool by pressing P, the Add Anchor Point tool by pressing =, and the Delete Anchor Point tool by pressing – (hyphen).

3. **Move the Pen pointer over the selected path at the point where you want to add an anchor point.**

4. **Click and release the mouse button.** A new anchor point is created where you click. If the Delete Anchor Point tool is selected, you must hold down the ⌘ or Ctrl key to add an anchor point. If you click on a straight segment between two corner points, a corner point is created. If you click on a curved segment between two smooth points or between a smooth point and a corner point, a smooth point is created. You can also click, drag, and then release the mouse button if you want to adjust the direction line of the point you create. Figure 28.17 shows a before and after example of a path to which a smooth anchor point is added.

FIGURE 28.17

The original path (left) is modified by adding a smooth point (second from left). Dragging the smooth point (third from left) produced the final shape (right).

After you add an anchor point, you can hold down the ⌘ or Ctrl key or switch to the Direct Selection tool and drag it or either of its direction handles to adjust the adjoining segments.

 Whenever you're working on a path, you can hold down the ⌘ or Ctrl key and then click and drag any element of the path—an anchor point, a direction line, or the entire path.

To delete an anchor point:

1. **Select the path by clicking it with the Direct Selection tool.** You can also select multiple paths and then modify them one at a time.

2. **Select the Pen tool, the Add Anchor Point tool, or the Delete Anchor Point tool.** You can use any of these tools to add and delete anchor points. If the Type tool is not selected, you can select the Pen tool by pressing P, the Add Anchor Point tool by pressing =, and the Delete Anchor Point tool by pressing – (hyphen) on the main keyboard or on the numeric keypad.

3. **Move the pointer over the anchor point that you want to delete, and then click.** If the Add Anchor Point tool is selected, you must hold down the ⌘ or Ctrl key to delete an anchor point. Figure 28.18 shows a before and after example of a path from which an anchor point has been deleted.

FIGURE 28.18

The curved segment of the original path (left) is removed by deleting the smooth anchor point (center) with the Delete Anchor Point tool. The resulting path is shown on the right.

Modifying segments

As you learned earlier in this chapter, a path is made up of one or more segments, and every segment is defined by a pair of anchor points. If you want to modify a segment, you can do so by dragging either or both of its anchor points, dragging the direction handles (if present) of the anchor points, or converting either of the anchor points from smooth to corner or vice versa. For example, you could drag an anchor point on a curvy path to increase or decrease the severity of a particular bump, or you could convert a straight-edged polygon into a curvy shape by converting all its corner points to smooth points.

Moving anchor points

When you select a path with the Direct Selection tool, its anchor points are displayed as small, hollow squares. When you click and drag an anchor point, the two adjoining segments change, but the direction handles, if present, are not affected. If you hold down the Shift key as you drag an anchor point, movement is restricted to increments of 45 degrees. Figure 28.19 shows how moving an anchor point affects adjoining curved and straight segments.

> **TIP** If all you need to do is resize a path — particularly a simple rectangle — rather than change its shape, you should select it with the Selection tool rather than the Direct Selection tool, and then click and drag one of its bounding box handles.

671

FIGURE 28.19

Top row: The arc of the curve (right) is reduced by clicking and dragging the smooth anchor point at the top of the curve (center). Bottom row: Dragging a corner (center) point changes the two adjoining segments (right).

Converting anchor points

If you want to change a wavy path that contains only curved segments to a zigzag path that contains only straight segments, you can do so by converting the smooth anchor points of the wavy path into corner points. Similarly, by converting corner points to smooth points, you can smooth out a path that contains straight segments. Figure 28.20 shows how straight and curved paths are affected as anchor points are converted.

FIGURE 28.20

Top row: The outer corner points of a straight-edged polygon path (left) were converted to smooth points to create the shape on the right. Bottom row: The zigzag path (right) was created by converting all the smooth points in the path on the left into corner points.

To convert an anchor point:

1. **Select the path by clicking it with the Direct Selection tool.**

2. **Choose the Convert Direction Point tool.** You can also perform the functions of this tool by holding down Option+⌘ or Ctrl+Alt when the Direct Selection tool is selected.

3. **Move the pointer over the anchor point you want to convert.** Depending on the point you want to convert, do one of the following:

   ▪ To convert a corner point to a smooth point, click the corner point, and then drag (direction lines are created and displayed as you drag).

   ▪ To convert a smooth point to a corner point without direction lines, click and release the mouse on the smooth point.

   ▪ To convert a smooth point to a corner point with independent direction lines, click and drag either of the smooth point's direction handles.

   ▪ To convert a corner point without direction lines to a corner point with direction lines, click and drag the corner point to create a smooth point, and then release the mouse button. Then click and drag either of the direction lines.

 When using the Convert Direction Point tool, you can temporarily switch to the most recently used selection tool by pressing ⌘ or Ctrl.

QUARKXPRESS QuarkXPress uses a very different approach to changing direction points from smooth to corner: It has iconic buttons in its Measurements palette that let you easily convert segment and corner types. The InDesign approach is more efficient in that it uses one tool and relies on a mouse-based tool (because you're likely using the mouse when you edit a shape), but it does require a bit more getting used to initially.

Manipulating direction handles

In addition to dragging and converting anchor points, you can adjust the shape of a curved segment by dragging any of the direction lines associated with the anchor points at either end of the segment. Figure 28.21 shows how moving direction lines affect a curved segment.

FIGURE 28.21

The top and bottom shapes on the right were created by dragging a direction line of a smooth point (center).

Remember, corner points between straight segments don't have direction handles. If you want to modify the segments associated with a corner point, simply click and drag the point.

To drag a curved segment's direction handle:

1. **Use the Direct Selection tool to select the path.**

2. **Click either of the two endpoints that define the curved segment.** Handles are displayed at the ends of the two lines that make up the selected point's direction line (and the lines make up what appears to be a single, straight line). The direction lines of the two adjoining segments (if present) also appear.

3. **Click and drag any available handle.** Press Shift as you drag to constrain movement to multiples of 45 degrees. As you drag, the handle at the opposite end of the direction line moves in the opposite direction like a teeter-totter. However, if you lengthen or shorten one side of a direction line, the other side is not affected.

4. **Release the mouse button when the shape is the way you want it.**

 If you use the Convert Direction Point tool to click and drag a smooth point's direction-line handle, the opposite portion of the direction line remains unchanged. This lets you adjust the segment on one side of a smooth point without affecting the segment on the other side.

Working with open and closed paths

If you've created an open path and subsequently decide that you want to extend the path at either or both ends, you can do so using the Pen tool. Along the same lines, you can use the Pen tool to connect two open paths and to close an open path. For example, if you've placed text or a graphic into an open path, you may decide that the path works better in a closed frame. And if you want to get even trickier, you can use the Scissors tool to split an open or closed path into two separate paths.

Extending an open path and connecting open paths

The steps required to extend an open path and to connect two open paths are very similar. Here's how you extend an open path:

1. **Use the Direct Selection tool to select the path you want to extend.**

2. **Move the Pen pointer over one of the path's endpoints.** When the Pen pointer is over an endpoint, a small, angled line appears below and to the right of the Pen.

3. **Click and release the mouse button.**

4. **Move the pointer to where you want to place the next anchor point.** If you want to create a corner point, click and release the mouse button. If you want to create a smooth point, click and drag, and then release the mouse button.

5. **Continue adding smooth and corner points until you're done extending the path.**

6. **Finish the path by holding down ⌘ or Ctrl and clicking on an empty portion of the page or choosing another tool.**

To connect two open paths, follow Steps 1 through 3 in the preceding list, and then click on the endpoint of another path (the other path doesn't have to be selected). Figure 28.22 shows a path before and after being extended; Figure 28.23 shows an open path produced by connecting two open paths.

FIGURE 28.22

The original path (left) was cloned to create the path on the right. The cloned path was then extended by clicking its right endpoint with the Pen tool, and then clicking four more times to create four additional corner points.

FIGURE 28.23

Connecting the two open paths on the left with the Pen tool produced the single path on the right.

If you hold down the Shift key when you click an endpoint with the Pen tool, an endpoint for a new path is created (that is, the selected path remains unchanged). In this situation, a small *x* is displayed below and to the right of the Pen pointer. This is useful if you want to create two paths that touch at a particular point. For example, you could draw a path and apply a 4-point black stroke to it, and then create another path that shares an endpoint with the first path. By adding a different kind of stroke to the second path, the two paths look like a single path to which two kinds of stroke have been applied.

Closing an open path

Closing an open path is much the same as extending an open path. The only difference is that you *complete* the path — that is, you close it — by clicking on the other endpoint. For example, if you slice a graphics frame into two pieces using the Scissors tool (I explain this in the next section of this chapter), two open paths are created. If you add a stroke to these open frames, a portion of the graphic edge (the nonexistent segment between the endpoints) is not stroked. If you close the path, the stroke completely encloses the graphic within. Figure 28.24 shows an open path that's been converted into a closed path.

FIGURE 28.24

The closed path on the right was created from a clone of the open path on the left.

InDesign provides two quick ways to close an open path after selecting it:

- Choose Object ➪ Paths ➪ Close Path.
- Click the Close Path iconic button on the Pathfinder panel (Window ➪ Object & Layout ➪ Pathfinder). Figure 28.31 later in this chapter shows the panel.

Opening a closed path

You can open a closed path in two ways, after selecting that path:

- Choose Object ➪ Paths ➪ Open Path.
- Click the Open Path iconic button on the Pathfinder panel (Window ➪ Object & Layout ➪ Pathfinder).

Either way, InDesign separates the start point into a start point and endpoint, letting you move either point or the segments attached to them independently.

NEW FEATURE When you choose Objects ➪ Paths ➪ Open Path or click the Open Path iconic button, InDesign CS3 now automatically selects the point where the path was opened, so you can immediately begin working with it (and know where it is).

Using the Scissors tool

The Scissors tool does precisely what its name suggests: It lets you slice things. Specifically, it lets you split paths — open and closed — into two pieces. There are a few things you should know about using the Scissors tool:

- It takes only one click with the Scissors tool to split an open path, but it takes two clicks to completely split a closed path.
- You can split graphics frames, but you can't split text frames that contain text. If you want to split a text frame that contains text, you must first cut the text and paste it elsewhere.

- If you split a graphics frame, a copy of the graphic is placed within both frames.

- When you split a path, all stroke and fill attributes of the original path are inherited by the two offspring. After you split a path, it looks the same as before you split it until you move or modify one of the resulting paths.

To split an open path, use the Scissors tool and move the cross-hair pointer over a path, and then click and release the mouse button. You can click on an open portion of a segment (that is, between anchor points) or on an anchor point. In both cases, two anchor points — endpoints of the two resulting paths — are created.

To split a closed path, use the Scissors tool and move the cross-hair pointer over a path; then click and release the mouse button. You can click an open portion of a segment or an anchor point. In both cases, two anchor points — endpoints of the two resulting paths — are created. Move the cross-hair pointer to a different position along the same path, and then click and release the mouse button.

After you split a path, you can switch to either of the selection tools and then select, move, or modify either of the two resulting paths as you wish. If you've split a closed path, you may want to close the two open paths (as I described in the previous section). Figure 28.25 shows a pair of open paths that were created using the Scissors tool on an open path. Figure 28.26 shows a closed graphics frame that's been split into two open frames.

FIGURE 28.25

The original path (left) was split into two pieces by clicking it with the Scissors tool (center). On the right, you see the two resulting paths after the one on the right has been moved.

FIGURE 28.26

The closed path (a graphics frame) on the left was cut twice with the Scissors tool (center). On the right, one of the resulting open paths has been moved with the Selection tool.

Working with Compound Paths

When more than one path is selected, you can use the Make (Compound Paths) command (Object ⇨ Paths ⇨ Make Compound Path, or ⌘+8 or Ctrl+8) to convert the paths into a single object. A compound path is similar to a group (Object ⇨ Group, or Ctrl+G or ⌘+G), except that when you create a group out of several objects, each object in the group retains its original attributes, such as stroke color and width, fill color or gradient, and so on. By contrast, when you create a compound path, the attributes of the backmost path are applied to all the other paths (that is, the attributes of the backmost path replace the attributes of the other paths).

NEW FEATURE InDesign CS3 makes a few changes to how you access various path commands. You access the Make Compound Path and Release Compound Path by choosing Object ⇨ Paths and then selecting the desired option, rather than choosing Object ⇨ Compound Paths and then the desired option. Finally, the shortcut for Release Compound Path has changed to Option+Shift+⌘+8 or Ctrl+Alt+Shift+8 (the Shift key has been added to the shortcut).

You can use a compound path to do such things as:

- **Create transparent areas within a path:** For example, by drawing a circular path in front of a graphic, you could then use the Make Compound Path command to poke a hole in the graphic and reveal the objects or the empty page behind the graphic. Figure 28.27 shows a compound path used as a graphics frame.

FIGURE 28.27

I created the graphic with the hole in it (right) by drawing a circular path (center) in front of a clone of the original graphics frame (left), and then creating a compound path from the graphics frame and the circular path. The background shape shows within the transparent hole.

- **Apply a single background color or place a single graphic within several shapes:** For example, you could use the Create Outlines command (Type ⇨ Create Outlines, or Shift+⌘+O or Ctrl+Shift+O) to convert text characters into a compound path, and then place a blend behind the path so that it extends across all characters. (I explain the Create Outlines command in Chapter 17.) Figure 28.28 shows an example of this.

FIGURE 28.28

I converted the text on the top into the editable outlines on the bottom. I then skewed the character outlines — which make up a compound path — by –30 degrees via the Shear X Angle field in the Control panel and applied a gradient fill.

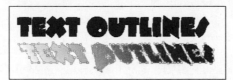

- **Quickly create complex shapes that would be difficult to create with the Pen tool:** For example, you could create the complex shape in Figure 28.29 by drawing each of the shaded areas as a separate, closed path. Or you could simply create a square, place four circles in front of it so that they overlap the edges of the square, and then choose Object ➪ Paths ➪ Make Compound Path — a process that takes only a few seconds.

That's only the beginning of what you can do with the Make Compound Path command. Mix in a little bit of your imagination and InDesign's other path-, graphic-, and text-manipulation features, and the possibilities become endless.

FIGURE 28.29

I converted the five closed paths on the left into a compound path by choosing Object ➪ Paths ➪ Make Compound Path to create the shape on the right. InDesign automatically applied the attributes of the original square path, which is the backmost path, to the resulting compound path. Notice that the four semicircular areas where the original shapes overlapped became holes after the shapes were converted to a compound path.

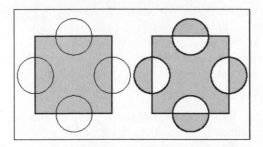

Creating compound paths

You can create a compound path out of any kind of path, including open and closed paths as well as text and graphics frames. When you create a compound path, all the original paths become subpaths of the compound shape and inherit the stroke and fill settings of the path that's farthest back in the stacking order. After you create a compound path, you can modify or remove any of the subpaths.

The direction of each subpath determines whether the subpath is filled or transparent. If a particular subpath is transparent instead of filled, or vice versa, you can use the Reverse Path command (Object ➪ Paths ➪ Reverse Path) or click the Reverse Path iconic button on the Pathfinder panel (Window ➪ Objects & Layout ➪ Pathfinder) to switch the behavior of a subpath. (Figure 28.31 later in this chapter shows the Pathfinder panel.)

If the results of choosing Object ➪ Paths ➪ Make Compound Path are not what you expected or want, you can undo the operation (Edit ➪ Undo, or ⌘+Z or Ctrl+Z). Paths often don't combine as expected because of how they are stacked; typically, an intervening object affects how InDesign combines the paths. To get a different result, try changing the stacking order, and then choose Object ➪ Paths ➪ Make Compound Path again.

To change an object's stacking order (to determine which path's attributes are used for the compound path), choose Object ➪ Arrange ➪ Send Backward, or ⌘+ [or Ctrl+], or choose Object ➪ Arrange ➪ Send Forward, or ⌘+ [or Ctrl+]. (Chapter 13 explains stacking order in more detail.)

If frames that contain text and/or graphics are selected when you choose Make Compound Path, the resulting compound path retains the content of the frame that's closest to the bottom of the stacking order. If the bottommost frame doesn't have any content, the content — text or graphic — of the next highest nonempty frame is retained in the compound path. The content of all frames above the frame whose content is retained is removed.

Editing compound paths

After you create a compound path, you can change the shape of any of the subpaths by clicking one with the Direct Selection tool, and then clicking and dragging any of its anchor points or direction handles. The Pen, Add Anchor Point, Delete Anchor Point, and Convert Direction Point tools work the same for subpaths as they do for other paths, which means that you can reshape them however you want.

The Stroke panel (Window ➪ Stroke, or ⌘+F10 or Ctrl+F10), Swatches panel (Window ➪ Swatches or F5), and Color panel (Window ➪ Color or F6) — as well as the transformation tools, the Control panel (Window ➪ Control, or Option+⌘+6 or Ctrl+Alt+6), and the Transform panel (Window ➪ Object & Layout ➪ Transform) — also let you change the appearance of a compound path. When you change the appearance of a compound path, the changes are applied uniformly to all subpaths.

Moving a subpath is a little tricky because you can't drag just that subpath. If you try, all the connected subpaths move. If you want to move an entire subpath, you must move each of the subpath's anchor points individually. In this case, it's probably easier to release the compound path, as I describe next, move the path as needed, and then re-create the compound path by choosing Object ➪ Paths ➪ Make Compound Path, or ⌘+8 or Ctrl+8.

If you want to delete a subpath, you must use the Delete Anchor Point tool to delete all its anchor points. If you delete an anchor point of a closed subpath, it becomes an open subpath.

NOTE
If the Selection or Position tool is active, you can't delete anchor points using the Cut command (Edit ⇨ Cut, or ⌘+X or Ctrl+X), the Clear command (or Edit ⇨ Clear, or Delete or Backspace), or the Del or Delete key. All of these keyboard commands remove the entire path. To work on those individual points, be sure the Direct Selection tool is active.

Changing a path's direction

When you create a path, it has a built-in direction — clockwise or counterclockwise — that is generally not noticeable but affects a compound path. Generally, you can't determine the direction of a path by looking at it. However, you can tell if paths' directions differ by how subpaths in a compound path interact:

- If a subpath in a compound path has the same direction as the backmost path, the area within the subpath is transparent.

- Conversely, if a subpath's direction is different than the backmost path, the area within the subpath will be filled.

If a subpath is filled in and you want it to be transparent, or vice versa, click the compound path with the Direct Selection tool, and then click the compound path whose direction you want to change and choose Object ⇨ Paths ⇨ Release Compound Path, or Option+Shift+⌘+8 or Ctrl+Alt+Shift+8, to separate the subpaths. Figure 28.30 shows how changing the direction of a subpath changes it from filled to transparent.

FIGURE 28.30

The gray square and circle on the left have been combined into a compound path, but the direction of the circular subpath causes it to be filled in instead of transparent. Changing the subpath's direction produced the results on the right: a transparent hole in the square shape.

Splitting a compound path

If you decide you want to deconstruct a compound path, you can do so by clicking anywhere within the compound path, and then choosing Object ⇨ Paths ⇨ Release Compound Path, or Option+Shift+⌘+8 or Ctrl+Alt+Shift+8. The resulting paths retain the attributes of the compound path.

NOTE
The Release command is not available if the selected compound path contains text or if it's nested within a frame.

Using the Pathfinder

Sometimes, you want to combine multiple paths. You can join them, as I describe earlier, or you can use the Pathfinder panel or menu options, as you prefer:

■ To use the Pathfinder panel and its iconic buttons, choose Window ➪ Object & Layout ➪ Pathfinder.

■ To use the menu options, choose Object ➪ Pathfinder, then choose the desired five options from the submenu: Add, Subtract, Intersect, Exclude Overlap, and Minus Back.

Figure 28.31 shows the Pathfinder panel and how each of the five options affects a group of closed paths (shapes).

FIGURE 28.31

Here are three closed paths (shapes) with the five Pathfinder options applied to them. Top row: the three original paths. Bottom row: from left to right, the same paths after applying after applying Add, Subtract, Intersect, Exclude Overlap, and Minus Back options. In the center is the Pathfinder panel, which has five iconic buttons for pathfinding tasks, nine for shape conversion, and three for opening, closing, and reversing paths.

Here's what the five Pathfinder options do:

- **Add:** This option adds all objects' shapes together.
- **Subtract:** This option subtracts all objects from the bottommost object in the stack.
- **Intersect:** This option creates an object where objects overlap. This works only on closed paths.
- **Exclude Overlap:** This option removes overlapping paths and keeps the nonoverlapping paths of all objects.
- **Minus Back:** This option subtracts all objects from the top object in the stack.

 The Pathfinder options are similar to QuarkXPress's Merge options.

Using Other Path Effects

InDesign provides several other functions to manipulate paths: the Convert Shape menu options, the Smooth tool, the Erase tool, and the Corner Options dialog box.

The Convert Shape options

While you can edit a shape with the Bézier tools I describe earlier in this chapter, it can be a lot of work for what should be a simple operation. InDesign gives you two easy ways to convert an object's shape:

- Choose Object ➪ Convert Shape and then choose one of the submenu options: Rectangle, Rounded Rectangle, Beveled Rectangle, Inverse Rounded Rectangle, Ellipse, Triangle, Polygon, Line, or Orthogonal Line.
- Click the iconic button in the Convert Shape section of the Pathfinder panel that corresponds to the desired Convert Shape submenu option. Choose Window ➪ Object & Layout ➪ Pathfinder to open the panel. (See Figure 28.31 to see the Pathfinder panel and its shape-conversion iconic buttons.)

QUARKXPRESS The Convert Shape options are similar to those in QuarkXPress's Item ➪ Shape menu option, though their options differ. For example, there's no Bézier shape or line option in InDesign's Convert Shape menu; instead you need to edit the Bézier points manually. But InDesign offers the triangle and polygon shapes, which QuarkXPress does not.

The Smooth tool

Available via the Pencil tool's pop-out menu is the Smooth tool, as shown in Figure 28.32. While it's a bit tricky to use, its concept is simple: It smoothes out corner points and the shapes of curved segments.

To use it, select the Smooth tool, and then move the pointer back and forth over a path (open or closed) that you want to smooth. If the path has multiple anchor points, it moves them to smooth out the curve, smoothing it more as you move the tool more. If the path is a corner such as for a frame, repeated movement of the Smooth tool converts the angular corner into a rounded corner.

FIGURE 28.32

The Smooth tool and Erase tool are available via the Pencil tool's pop-out menu in the Tools panel.

The Erase tool

Just as it has tools to create paths, InDesign has a tool to delete them: the Erase tool, which is accessible via the Pencil tool's pop-out menu.

To erase straight lines, first select the path to work with using the Selection tool. Then switch to the Erase tool and drag it alongside the path segment to cut — making sure not to cross the path — and then release the mouse. The segment disappears.

But for shapes, the tool takes some experimenting with. After selecting the shape with the Selection tool, switch to the Erase tool and then draw a path through the shape to erase part of it. The tool typically removes anchor points away from the direction of the mouse movement, causing part of the shape to disappear. Unfortunately, it's hard to predict what will be erased, so be patient and use the Undo command (Edit ➪ Undo, or ⌘+Z or Ctrl+Z) whenever the result is not what you want. Figure 28.33 shows two examples.

FIGURE 28.33

FIGURE 28.33

The Erase tool deletes path segments (at right) for the two originals (at left) in this composite image.

The Corner Options dialog box

When a path is selected, the Corner Options dialog box (Object ➪ Corner Options) lets you apply any of several graphical embellishments to its corner points (if the path has any corner points). Generally, corner options work best with rectangular shapes, but they can also produce interesting results when you apply them to free-form shapes and open paths. Figure 28.34 shows examples of corner options applied to a closed path and two open paths.

NEW FEATURE The Corner Options menu and dialog box is called Corner Effects in previous versions of InDesign.

CROSS-REF Chapter 12 shows all five corner options as applied to closed paths (shapes), as well as explains how to use the Corner Options dialog box.

FIGURE 28.34

The effects of corner options on one closed path and two open paths. Top row: The original paths. Bottom row: The modified paths.

Summary

If you need to create free-form paths—zigzag or curvy lines or complex closed shapes—you must use the Pen tool. All paths are made up of one or more segments, which begin and end in anchor points. Direction lines control the behavior or anchor points, which in turn control the transition between adjoining segments. When you create an open or a closed path using the Pen tool, you have the option of creating straight segments or curved segments, and corner points or smooth points.

When it comes to drawing with the Pen or Pencil tool, close is plenty good enough. That's because InDesign lets you modify paths in many ways—by moving, adding, and deleting anchor points; by switching smooth points to corner points and vice versa; and by clicking and dragging direction lines. You also have the option to extend either or both ends of an open path and to close open paths.

If a path requires more drastic surgery, you can use the Scissors tool, which lets you split any kind of path into two pieces.

Because InDesign is primarily a page-layout program, it doesn't contain the breadth of illustration-specific features that you would find in a dedicated vector-based drawing program. Although you may decide that you need a dedicated illustration program to handle your industrial-strength drawing tasks, InDesign does have several features for creating complex shapes.

For example, the Make Compound Path command lets you combine several paths into a single object. If you want to add a graphic flourish to the corners of a path, the Corner Options dialog box lets you apply any of several built-in corner styles and specify the size of the corner.

Part VII

Output Fundamentals

IN THIS PART

Chapter 29
Preparing for Color Prepress

Chapter 30
Preparing for Printing

Chapter 31
Printing Techniques

Chapter 32
Creating Prepress Files

Chapter 29

Preparing for Color Prepress

S ince their invention in the mid-1980s, desktop-publishing programs have broadened their features to cover more and more color publishing needs. Many of the color-oriented features have caused consternation among professional color separators and printers who have seen amateurs make a tough job worse or ruin an acceptable piece of work. This situation is familiar to anyone in desktop publishing in the early years when the typographic profession looked on in horror at amateurs publishing documents without understanding tracking, hyphenation, and many other fundamental areas.

Some programs have added more and more high-end color prepress features. InDesign is one of those, offering two types of trapping engines; the ability to control trapping of individual objects and pages; the ability to apply color models to imported pictures to help the printer adjust the output to match the original picture's color intent; and support for composite workflow, which creates files that have a version for output on a proofing printer such as a color inkjet and a version for output on an imagesetter as film negatives or directly to plate.

The perfect scenario for InDesign color output is that you're using all Adobe software in their latest versions: Photoshop CS3 (10.0), Illustrator CS3 (13.0), and a PostScript Level 3 output device or PDF/X export file. But most people won't have that perfect scenario, especially the PostScript Level 3 part, because it's new and the output devices that commercial printers use are expensive and not replaced often. And although companies like Adobe hope users upgrade all their software every two years when the new releases come, the reality is that people tend to upgrade the tools they use the most, letting the others slide. So, you might well use Photoshop CS3 and InDesign CS3 but Illustrator CS2 and Acrobat Professional 7.

IN THIS CHAPTER

Setting color calibration defaults

Setting up a monitor's color profile

Applying color profiles to imported images

Altering color profiles for objects and documents

Applying color profiles during printing

Proofing on-screen

Understanding color traps

Defining and applying trapping presets

Then there's the fact that not everyone uses Illustrator or Photoshop: Adobe Macromedia FreeHand is popular among professional artists, and CorelDraw has established a toehold among that group as well, especially among Windows users. Photoshop has less competition, though there are dedicated users of Corel Photo-Paint and Corel PaintShop Pro.

Having said that, don't panic if you're not using cutting-edge equipment and software. After years of user education and efforts by software developers like Adobe to build in some of the more basic color-handling assumptions into their programs, most desktop publishers now produce decent color output by simply using the default settings, perhaps augmented by a little tweaking in Photoshop or an illustration program. To really use the color-management and trapping tools in InDesign effectively, you should understand color printing. But if you don't, you can be assured that the default settings in InDesign will produce decent-quality color output.

CROSS-REF   The illustrations and figures in this chapter are in black and white. You need to look at your color monitor to see the effects of what I describe here, or download the image files from the companion Web site (`www.InDesignCentral.com`). Also take a look at the full-color examples in this book's special eight-page insert "Color Techniques."

Managing Color Management

InDesign comes with several color management system (CMS) options. A CMS helps you ensure accurate printing of your colors, both those in imported images and those defined in InDesign. What a CMS does is track the colors in the source image, the colors your monitor can display, and the colors your printer can print. If the monitor or printer does not support a color in your document, the CMS alters (recalibrates) the color to its closest possible equivalent.

Don't confuse InDesign's CMS capabilities with color *matching*. It is impossible to match colors produced in an illustration or paint program, or through a scanner, with what a printer or other output device can produce. The underlying differences in color models (which actually determine how a color is defined) and the physics of the media (screen phosphors that emit light versus different types of papers with different types of inks that reflect light) make color matching impossible. But a calibration tool like a CMS can *minimize* differences.

You can set the CMS settings in InDesign by choosing Edit ➪ Color Settings (there is no keyboard shortcut unless you assign one yourself; I explain how to do this in Chapter 3) to get the dialog box shown in Figure 29.1. (I get to these options a bit later in this chapter.)

If you're creating colors in a program and importing those colors into InDesign, it's important to calibrate them in the same way, or at least as closely as the different programs will allow. Other programs may have similar settings for calibrating their display against your type of monitor. Many of Adobe's Creative Suite 3 (CS3) applications have the same dialog box that appears in Figure 29.1:

- **Bridge CS3:** Choose Edit ➪ Creative Suite Color Settings, or press Shift+⌘+K or Ctrl+Shift+K.
- **Acrobat Professional 8:** Choose Acrobat ➪ Preferences or press ⌘+K on the Mac; choose Edit ➪ Preferences or press Ctrl+K in Windows, and then go to the Color Management

pane. Note that this pane's appearance differs from the appearance of other CS3 applications' Color Settings dialog boxes.

- **GoLive 9:** Choose Edit ➪ Color Settings. (No keyboard shortcut is available.)
- **Illustrator CS3:** Choose Edit ➪ Color Settings, or press Shift+⌘+K or Ctrl+Shift+K.
- **Photoshop CS3:** Choose Edit ➪ Color Settings, or press Shift+⌘+K or Ctrl+Shift+K.

Note that there are no CMS controls for Adobe Device Manager, Dreamweaver, or Flash Professional.

If you use Adobe Creative Suite 3, you can ensure that all CS3 programs use the same CMS, ensuring color consistency for elements that move among Photoshop, Illustrator, Acrobat, and InDesign. To select the CMS, open the Adobe Bridge CS3 application and choose Edit ➪ Creative Suite Color Settings; then select the desired CMS settings, and click Apply. I recommend you first select the Show Expanded List of Color Settings Files option before you click Apply. Figure 29.2 shows the dialog box.

FIGURE 29.1

The Color Settings dialog box lets you set application color defaults.

Note that if individual CS3 applications' color settings differ from the CS3-wide settings, you see a note to that effect at the top of the affected applications' Color Settings dialog box. Similarly, Bridge's Suite Color Settings dialog box will alert you (as shown in Figure 29.2) if CS3 applications use different CMS settings — and it lets you force the same setting on all of them.

TIP If you use a mix of CS3 and CS2 applications, set the same color settings in both Bridge CS3 and Bridge CS2, so all your applications have the same defaults. The CS2 applications have the same color setting options (and user interface) as CS3 applications, making this easy to do.

QUARKXPRESS InDesign and QuarkXPress have comparable color-calibration features, but there are some differences: QuarkXPress does not let you apply black-point compensation. And InDesign lets you save your color-management preferences for use in other documents.

FIGURE 29.2

Set a consistent color management profile for all Creative Suite 3 programs using Adobe Bridge.

Setting up your system

To achieve the best reproduction of printed colors on-screen, you need a closely controlled environment for your computer. Most people don't bother, relying instead on their brain's ability to mentally substitute the print color for what they see on-screen after they've had experience seeing what happens in actual printed documents. But the more you do to control the color viewing environment, the closer the match between what you see on-screen and what you see on the page.

These tips on setting up your system are in order from simplest to most complex:

- **Dim the lights.** Most people turn the brightness of their monitors too high, which distorts colors by overdoing the blues and underdelivering on the reds. Adjust the brightness level of the monitor to between 60 and 75 percent maximum. To make sure you can still see the screen, lower the amount of light in your workspace by using lower-wattage bulbs, turning off overhead lighting right above your monitor, and/or using translucent shades in nearby windows.

- **Change the color temperature of your monitor to 7,200 degrees on the Kelvin scale.** Most monitors have on-screen controls to do so.

- **If your monitor has a color profile, use it.** Where you manage profiles varies based on your operating system (note that some monitors or video cards come with their own color-setup software):

  - On the Mac, the Displays system preference has an option in its Color pane for setting color to a profile (stored in the System:Library:ColorSync:Profiles folder), or you can use the Color pane's Calibrate button to alter a profile based on your monitor's actual display.

  - In Windows XP, use the Display control panel; the Settings pane has an option called Advanced that will open a dialog box that has a Color Management pane. The profiles are stored in the Windows\System32\Spool\Drivers\Color folder. (Note that the Windows folder may have a different name on your computer, such as WinXP.)

  - In Windows Vista, use the Color Settings control panel and click the Add button in the Devices or All Profiles panes to add profiles. Change profiles in the Advanced pane. The profiles are stored in the Windows\System32\Spool\Drivers folder.

- **Use a calibration tool.** Tools such as X-Rite's Eye-One Display colorimeter and MonacoEZcolor software and Pantone's Huey calibrate your monitor and create a color profile specifically for it. These calibrators can cost $100 to $600, so they're typically purchased by graphics departments, not individual designers. Note that color calibration software without a hardware calibrator device is worthless; without being able to measure what colors actually come from your monitor, there's no way the software can meaningfully adjust the colors in your display. Also note that monitors vary their color display over their lifetime (they get dimmer), so you should recalibrate every six months. For most users, the variances in monitor brightness, color balance, and contrast — coupled with the varying types of lighting used in their workspace — mean that true calibration is impossible for images created on-screen and displayed on-screen. Still, using the calibration feature makes the on-screen color closer to what prints, even if it's not an exact match.

- **Work in a color-controlled room.** In such a room, the lighting is at 5,000 degrees Kelvin, so the light reflecting off your color proofs matches that of a professional prepress operation. Monitors should also be set with a white point of D65 (something done with calibration hardware and software). Also try to buy monitors with a neutral, light gray shade — or paint them that way — so your brain doesn't darken what you see on-screen to compensate for the off-white monitor frame right next to the screen image. Similarly, all furnishings should be neutral, preferably a light gray. Avoid having anything with a strong color in the room — even clothes.

> **NOTE**   There's long been a standard, the latest version of which is called ISO 3664, which has set 5,000 degrees Kelvin as the industry standard for proofing color printing. Basically, 5,000 degrees is filtered daylight where the red, green, and blue components are equal. The International Prepress Association (`www.ipa.org`) has a lot of standards information and resources related to color accuracy.

Adjusting the on-screen display

There are several factors that control how InDesign's CMS works in practice, some related to the operating system's settings and some to the settings in InDesign's Color Settings dialog box.

Setting monitor bit depth

To have color calibration in effect for a monitor, you must be displaying thousands of colors (16-bit color depth) or more colors (or a higher color depth, such as 24-bit). The process depends on your operating system:

- On the Mac, use the Displays system preference to change your monitor's bit depth.
- In Windows XP, use the Settings pane of the Display control panel.
- In Windows Vista, use the Display Settings control panel (which you typically access from the Personalization control panel).

Adjusting InDesign's color display settings

The Color Settings dialog box (Edit ➪ Color Settings) in InDesign is where you control how InDesign manages color display on-screen.

Select the monitor or color space in the RGB pop-up menu in the Working Spaces section of the Color Settings dialog box (refer to Figure 29.1). The monitor or color space that you select tells InDesign how to display imported images and colors defined within InDesign.

The first four options — Adobe RGB (1998), Apple RGB, ColorMatch RGB, and sRGB IEC61966-2.1 — are all neutral color spaces, meaning that they aren't adjusted for specific monitors. Adobe programs typically save their images with the sRGB (standard RGB) profile, which works well if you define colors based on swatches and use exact RGB settings or existing swatches.

The other options are monitor-specific profiles, which make sense to use if you choose your colors based on what you see on-screen. Which ones you get depend on what profiles are installed on your computer by the operating system and/or the software that came with your monitor.

The rest of the Color Settings dialog box's affect how InDesign manages color when printing your document.

Defining Color Models

Whether you define colors in InDesign or in your illustration or paint program, the method you use to define them is critical to ensuring the best possible output. Defining all colors in the same model as the target output device is best. Use the following guidelines:

- If your printer is RGB (this is rare), use the RGB model to define colors.

- If your printer is CMYK (such as an offset printer or most inkjets), use CMYK to define colors. However, InDesign is so good at converting RGB-based images — which is what monitors display best — to CMYK that many designers don't bother to define images they create as CMYK.

- If you're using Pantone colors for traditional offset printing, pick one of the Pantone solid models if your printer is using Pantone inks. Pick the Pantone Process Coated model if your printer is using inks from companies other than Pantone.

- If you're using Pantone colors for traditional offset printing, pick the Pantone Process Coated model if you will color-separate those colors into CMYK.

- Trumatch and Focoltone colors were designed to reproduce accurately whether they output as spot colors or are color-separated into CMYK. Other models (such as Toyo, ANPA, and DIC) may or may not separate accurately for all colors, so check with your printer or the ink manufacturer.

- If you're using any Pantone, Focoltone, Trumatch, Toyo, ANPA, or DIC color and outputting to a desktop color printer (whether RGB or CMYK), watch to ensure that the color definition doesn't lie outside the printer's gamut, as I explain in the next section.

- Never rely on the screen display to gauge any non-RGB color. Even with the InDesign CMS's monitor calibration, RGB monitors simply cannot match most non-RGB colors. Use the on-screen colors only as a guide, and rely instead on a color swatchbook from your printer or the color ink's manufacturer.

- InDesign's CMS does *not* calibrate color in EPS or PDF files. If you use EPS, I strongly recommend that you use the DCS (pre-separated CMYK) variant. If you use PDF files, embed the correct color profile in the application from which you create the PDF file or use Adobe Acrobat Distiller's options to set color profiles.

Adjusting color output settings

Setting how colors are displayed on-screen is just part of what you need to do to manage color in InDesign. You also have to tell InDesign how to handle colors during printing, which you do in a few locations. Most of the controls are in the Color Settings dialog box, though a few are in the Preferences dialog box.

Setting color management policies

The Color Management Policies section of the Color Settings dialog box (Edit ➪ Color Settings) is where you tell InDesign how to handle color calibration when printing.

But before you set these policies, you need to tell InDesign what your target printer or imagesetter is, so it knows what colors to aim for in its calibration. You do this in the CMYK pop-up menu of the dialog box's Working Spaces section.

Now you set how imported images' colors are managed in the Color Management Policies section of the dialog box. The RGB and CMYK pop-up menus let you manage how imported RGB and CMYK images are handled within InDesign.

- For the RGB pop-up menu, the default option is Preserve Embedded Profiles, which is the best option if your graphics sources have already had color profiles applied intentionally (such as in Illustrator of Photoshop) to help calibrate the output. Your other options are Off (no color management) and Convert to Working Space (which applies the setting in the Working Spaces section's RGB pop-up menu to all imported graphics, overriding their profiles).

- For the CMYK pop-up menu, the default option is Preserve CMYK Color Numbers, which ensures the actual CMYK values are preserved instead of any color profiles that may be applied. Your other options are Off, Convert to Working Space, and Preserve Embedded Profiles, which work for CMYK files the same as they do for RGB files in the RGB pop-up menu.

If your pictures are not usually color-managed at the source, it's best to override the embedded profiles for these two pop-up menus and choose either Convert to Working Space, which uses the color profiles selected in the Working Spaces section of the dialog box, or Off, which strips out any color profiles.

The Color Management Policies section also has options for when to notify you of profile mismatches (Ask When Opening and Ask When Pasting) and one to alert you to imported graphics have no profile applied (Ask When Opening). If you are color-managing your documents, you should enable all three check boxes. There is one exception to this advice: If you choose Convert to Working Space in the RGB and CMYK pop-up menus, you can deselect Ask When Opening for Missing Profiles because you won't be using any embedded profiles from the original graphic.

Understanding Profiles

The mechanism that a color management system (CMS) uses to do its calibration is the profile that contains the information on color models and ranges supported by a particular creator (such as an illustration program or scanner), display, and printer. InDesign includes dozens of such predefined profiles.

A CMS uses a device-independent color space to match these profiles against each other. A color space is a mathematical way of describing the relationships among colors. By using a device-independent color model (the CIE XYZ standard defined by the Commission Internationale de l'Éclairage, the International Commission on Illumination), a CMS can compare gamuts from other device-dependent models (such as RGB and the others). What this means is that a CMS can examine the colors in your imported images and defined colors, compare them against the capabilities of your monitor and printer, and adjust the colors for the closest possible display and printing.

Adjusting bitmap images' color

Use the Conversion Options section to control the display and printing of bitmapped images. (Make sure the Advanced Mode check box is enabled near the top of the Color Settings dialog box to display this section.) InDesign provides these controls for bitmap images to essentially compensate for the fact that, when photos are scanned or images saved, the color pixels may not accurately replicate the creator's intent. For example, a PowerPoint slide that has solid color areas may end up with slight variations in color among pixels — or perhaps with unexpectedly muted colors — when copied into Photoshop.

The first setting — the Engine pop-up menu — controls which adjustment engine to use: Adobe's or the one that comes with your operating system. Your choices are Adobe (ACE) and Apple CMM on the Mac, and Adobe (ACE) and Microsoft ICM in Windows. If you work in a cross-platform environment, choose Adobe (ACE); if you work in a Mac-only or Windows-only environment, pick whatever you prefer based on output tests you conduct with your service bureau.

The Intent pop-up menu is where you specify how you want your bitmap images' color to be adjusted. There are four options in the Intent pop-up menu:

■ **Perceptual:** This selection tries to balance the colors in an image when the adjustment engine translates from the original color range to the output device's color range under the assumption that it's a photograph and, thus, needs to look natural. This is appropriate for photographs.

■ **Saturation:** This selection tries to create vivid colors when the adjustment engine translates a graphic from the original color range to the output device's color range — even if doing so means some colors are printed inaccurately. This is appropriate for charts and other slide-like graphics whose colors are intended for impact rather than naturalness.

■ **Relative Colorimetric:** This selection shifts all the colors to compensate for the white point of the monitor as set in the operating system's display profile (essentially, adjusting the brightness of the output to compensate for any dimness or excess brightness in the monitor). It makes no other adjustments to the colors during output.

■ **Absolute Colorimetric:** This selection makes no adjustments to the colors during output. So it allows, for example, an image that uses two similar colors to end up being output as the same color because of the printer's limited color range.

Depending on what kinds of documents you produce, you likely want Perceptual or Saturation as your setting.

Adjusting blackness

You might think that black is black is black, but that's not true. So InDesign lets you control how black is treated during output as well.

In a bitmap image, for example, black is actually created by mixing red, green, and blue, so it's often really a very dark gray. The Conversion Options section of the Color Settings dialog box has the Black Point Compensation check box to look for those dark grays and convert them to true black. Enable this option (its default setting) to adjust the color range for maximum range, which permits truer colors in most cases and a more natural look with converted photographs. You should leave this option enabled, unless you know your source image has a small range (such as being mostly midtones), in which case black-point compensation can distort shadows and subtle colors in an effect similar to a moiré pattern.

InDesign also has controls for how black is treated in all elements of your layout, not just bitmap images. They reside in the Appearance of Black pane of the Preferences dialog box (choose InDesign ⇨ Preferences ⇨ Appearance of Black or press ⌘+K on the Mac, or choose Edit ⇨ Preferences ⇨ Appearance of Black or press Ctrl+K in Windows), which is shown in Figure 29.3. These controls affect how the [Black] swatch is treated during output, both for objects you create in InDesign and for those imported files (such as Illustrator, EPS, and PDF files) that have a black color swatch applied to their elements.

FIGURE 29.3

The Appearance of Black pane in the Preferences dialog box

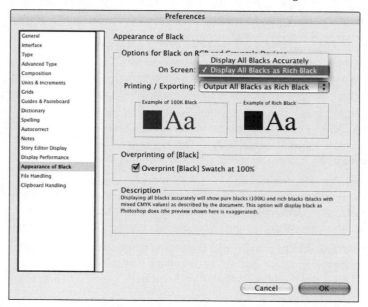

The Appearance of Black pane lets you control both the on-screen display of black and the output of black. Both the On Screen and Printing/Exporting pop-up menus offer the same two options:

- **Display (or Output) All Blacks Accurately:** This does exactly what it says, which can lead to weaker-looking blacks in documents that are otherwise rich in color.

- **Display (or Output) All Blacks as Rich Black:** This boosts the black output for better clarity, essentially by adding some magenta ink to make it appear darker. This helps black colors not look flat when surrounded by other rich colors.

By default, InDesign sets the On Screen pop-up menu to Display All Blacks as Rich Black and the Printing/Exporting pop-up menu to Output All Blacks as Rich Black.

I'm not sure you should stick with the Output All Blacks as Rich Black setting for output because you no longer get just black when you print. You can always use the [Registration] color swatch to get rich black (also known as *superblack*) and thus use that color specifically when you want to, rather than have all blacks automatically changed. While rich black helps blacks stand out when they're surrounded by other saturated colors, it can lead to overinking and bleedthrough in documents on thinner paper. You should experiment with your printing press and paper to see what works best for you.

Applying profiles to images

You can apply the desired profiles for individual images when you import them. Select Show Import Options when you place a graphic into InDesign in the Place dialog box (File ➪ Place, or ⌘+D or Ctrl+D). In the resulting Image Import Options dialog box, go to the Color pane and select the appropriate profile from the Profile menu, as well as the appropriate rendering intent from the Intent pop-up menu. Figure 29.4 shows the Image Import Options dialog box.

You can apply or change the profile to a placed image at any time by selecting it and choosing Object ➪ Image Color Settings. This opens the Image Color Settings dialog box, shown in Figure 29.5, in which you set a new profile and/or rendering intent. (You can also choose Graphics ➪ Image Color Settings from the contextual menu to open the Image Color Settings dialog box.)

FIGURE 29.4

You can apply color profiles when importing pictures through the Image Import Options dialog box.

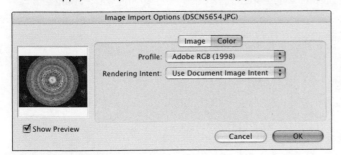

FIGURE 29.5

Using the Image Color Settings dialog box, you can apply color profiles to an object after it's placed in your document.

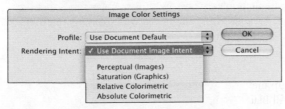

When you open a document, InDesign checks all the images imported into that document to see if they have a color-management profile embedded or applied. Based on the settings defined in the Color Settings dialog box (Edit ⇨ Color Settings), described earlier in this chapter, it may apply default profiles to them, do nothing, or ask you what to do. If there is no embedded color profile in the document and if the Ask When Opening check box is enabled in the Color Settings dialog box, the Missing Profile dialog box in Figure 29.6 appears when you open the document. When opening a document, you might get two such dialog boxes, one for RGB profile and/or one for CMYK profile, depending on what's embedded (if anything) in the documents' images.

Your choices are:

- **Leave as Is (Use Current Working Space):** This option uses the document's default profile to the image, as specified in the Color Settings dialog box, but does not embed that profile in the image.

- **Assign Current Working Space:** This option applied the document's default profile to the image, embedding that profile in the image so even if the document's default profile changes later the image's profile does not.

- **Assign Profile:** This option lets you choose the desired profile to be applied to and embedded in this image from the pop-up menu at right. Use this when there's a specific reason not to use the document's default profile.

FIGURE 29.6

You can set InDesign to alert you to missing profiles when opening a document, giving you a chance to apply them then.

Whichever method you use to apply profiles, only profiles appropriate for the image type appear in these pop-up menus — for example, only CMYK profiles (generally, these are output devices) appear for a CMYK TIFF file, even though the image may have been scanned using an RGB scanner and later converted to CMYK with Photoshop. This limitation exists because InDesign assumes that the image is designed for output to that specific printer and, thus, calibrates it with that target in mind. For RGB files, InDesign lets you apply monitor-oriented profiles and scanner-oriented profiles.

Changing document color settings

If you put together a document with specific color settings, as described earlier, but then decide you want to apply a new profile across your graphics or replace a specific profile globally in your document, you can.

Choose Edit ➪ Assign Profiles to replace the color management settings globally, as seen in Figure 29.7. You can set the RGB profile and CMYK profiles separately, as well as set the color intent for solid colors, bitmap images, and gradient blends using the Solid Color Intent, Default Image Intent, and After-Blending Intent pop-up menus.

Similarly, you can change the document's color workspace by choosing Edit ➪ Convert to Profile, which opens the Convert to Profile dialog box also shown in Figure 29.7. It also lets you change the CMS engine, rendering intent, and black-point compensation settings.

FIGURE 29.7

InDesign provides two dialog boxes — Assign Profiles (top) and Convert to Profile (bottom) — to change color-management preferences throughout a document. While their functions overlap, each has unique settings of its own.

There's real overlap in these two dialog boxes. Using the Assign Profiles dialog box to replace the document profile does the same as the Convert to Profile dialog box when it comes to replacing the profiles. The only difference is that the Assign Profiles dialog box can also remove profiles from the document. Both dialog boxes let you change the rendering intents for colors, though the Assign Profiles dialog box gives you several levels of control not available in the Convert to Profile dialog box. But the Convert to Profile dialog box lets you change the black-point compensation and the CMS engine. (These really could be combined into one dialog box.)

A related set of controls resides in the Profile or Policy Mismatch dialog box, which appears as you open a document if InDesign detects a mismatch between a document's color settings and those specified in InDesign's Color Settings dialog box. You can leave the document as is or assign a new profile to the document (using the Assign Profile pop-up menu) and, independently, choose whether to override the profiles applied to the document's images using the Placed Content pop-up menu. Figure 29.8 shows the dialog box.

FIGURE 29.8

If InDesign detects a mismatch between a document's color settings and those specified in InDesign's Color Settings dialog box, it displays the Profile or Policy Mismatch dialog box when you open that document.

Proofing On-Screen

Although nothing is as accurate as the final printed document — not even the printed proofs such as Matchprints that many service bureaus can provide — it can be useful to do an on-screen "soft proof" of your document before printing, especially if you are using new color settings or a new printer. InDesign lets you do such on-screen proofing.

First, specify your proofing setup by choosing View ➪ Proof Setup and choose the appropriate color space — the document and working spaces as defined in the Color Settings dialog box — or create a custom space by choosing Custom. The figure below shows the dialog box that results.

With the desired proofing setup enabled, turn on proofing by being sure a check mark appears to the left of View ➪ Proof Colors; if not, choose this menu option. If you want to also see how overprinting colors will appear, be sure a check mark appears to the left of View ➪ Overprint Preview; if not, choose this menu option or press Option+Shift+⌘+Y or Ctrl+Alt+Shift+Y. Now you can go from page to page and get an approximation of how your pages' colors will appear when printed.

InDesign provides two other preview options. One is the Flattener Preview panel that lets you see how transparency appears, as I cover in Chapter 31. The other is the Separations Preview panel (Window ➪ Output ➪ Separations Preview, or Shift+F6), which lets you turn on and off the display of specific color plates. The figure below shows the panel and its flyout menu. Choose Separations in the unnamed pop-up menu at upper left, then click the square to the left of each color plate to toggle the display on and off; if an eye icon appears, the plate is displayed. Then go from page to page to check the plates of interest to you.

The Separations Preview panel also lets you view the Ink Limit (choose Ink Limit from the pop-up menu at upper right and then the limit value in the unnamed pop-up menu at the upper right. InDesign will display in red any part of an object that exceeds that value. Again, go from page to page to see if any overinking is displayed.

The panel's flyout menu has several options. Enable the Show Single Plates in Black option to display individual plates in black rather than in their actual color (this is helpful when displaying light colors such as yellow, as it improves on-screen clarity). Enable the Desaturate Black option to better differentiate regular black from rich blacks such as [Registration]. The Ink Manager menu option opens the Ink Manager dialog box that Chapter 31 covers.

Managing color during output

When you're ready to output your document to a printer or other device, you set the profile and rendering intent for that destination device in the Color Management pane of the Print dialog box (File ⇨ Print, or ⌘+P or Ctrl+P), which has a Print Space section with a Profile pop-up menu and an Intent pop-up menu. Here you select the appropriate options for your output device.

CROSS-REF   Chapter 31 covers printing in more detail.

Saving color-management preferences

You can save and use color-management settings in other documents. The process is simple: Click Save in the Color Settings dialog box to save the current dialog box's settings to a file. If you want to use that saved color-settings information in another document, open that document and click Load in the Color Settings dialog box, and then browse for and select the color-settings file. That's it! This is a handy way to ensure consistency in a workgroup.

Working with Color Traps

Color trapping controls how colors overlap and abut when printed. InDesign offers moderate controls over trapping, enough to set the basics document-wide without getting into the expertise level of a commercial printer. It's also a feature that novice users can abuse terribly, which is one reason InDesign hides these options. If you don't know much about trapping, leave the features of the program at the default settings. Before you use InDesign trapping tools, study some books on color publishing, talk to your printer, and experiment with test files that you don't want to publish. If you're experienced with color trapping — or after you become experienced — you should find InDesign trapping tools easy to use.

You still want to use the trapping tools within the illustration product with which you create your EPS and PDF graphics because these tools help you to finely control the settings for each image's specific needs. Also, if you're using a service bureau that does high-resolution scanning for you and strips these files into your layout before output, check to make sure that the bureau is not also handling trapping for you with a Scitex or other high-end system. If it is, make sure you ask whether and when you should be doing trapping yourself.

If you print to a color laser, dye-sublimation, inkjet, or thermal wax printer, don't worry about trapping. You're not getting the kind of output resolution at which this level of image fine-tuning is relevant. But if you output to an imagesetter (particularly if you output to negatives) for eventual printing on a web-offset press or other printing press, read on.

Understanding trap methods

So what is trapping, anyway? Trapping adjusts the boundaries of colored objects to prevent gaps between abutting colors. Gaps can occur because of misalignment of the negatives, plates, or printing press — all of which are impossible to avoid.

Colors are trapped by processes known as *choking* and *spreading*. Both make an object slightly larger — usually a fraction of a point — so that it overprints the abutting object slightly. The process is called choking when one object surrounds a second object, and the first object is enlarged to overlap the second. The process is known as spreading when you enlarge the surrounded object so that it leaks (bleeds) into the surrounding object.

The difference between choking and spreading is the relative position of the two objects. Think of choking as making the hole for the inside object smaller (which in effect makes the object on the outside larger), and think of spreading as making the object in the hole larger.

TIP The object made larger depends on the image, but you generally bleed the color of a lighter object into a darker one. If you did the opposite, you'd make darker objects seem ungainly larger. Thus, choke a dark object inside a light one, and spread a light object inside a dark one. If the objects are adjacent, spread the light object.

Figure 29.9 shows the three types of trapping techniques. Spreading (upper right) makes the interior object's color bleed out; choking (lower left) makes the outside color bleed in, in effect making the area of the choked element smaller. The black lines show the size of the interior object; as you can see in the image at the upper right, when you choke a darker object into a lighter one, the effect is to change its size (here, the interior object gets smaller). At the upper left is an untrapped image whose negatives shifted slightly during printing, causing a gap.

InDesign supports a third type of trapping technique: *centering*, which both chokes and spreads, splitting the difference between the two objects. This makes traps look nicer (see the object in the lower right of Figure 29.9), especially between light and dark colors where regular choking and spreading can encroach on the light object.

Finally, InDesign offers a fourth trapping method, *neutral density,* that adjusts the trap as color hues and tints shift to minimize the possibility of darker lines where colors trap. But this can be dangerous; for a bitmap image, the neutral density method will most likely create an uneven edge as the trapping changes from pixel to pixel.

Specifying knockout and overprinting

In practice, trapping also involves controlling whether colors *knock out* or *overprint*. The default is to knock out — cut out — any overlap when one element is placed on top of another. If, for example, you place two rectangles on top of each other, they print like the two rectangles on the right side of Figure 29.10. If you set the darker rectangle in this figure to overprint, the rectangles print as shown on the left side of the figure. Setting colors to overprint results in mixed colors as shown on the left, while setting colors to knock out results in discrete colors as shown on the right.

FIGURE 29.9

Three kinds of traps: spreading (upper right), choking (lower left), and centering (lower right), with an untrapped image in the upper left that was misregistered during printing.

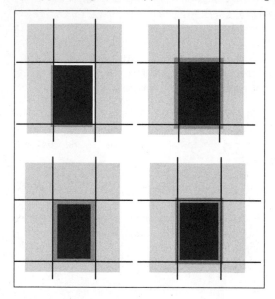

In InDesign, you use the Attributes panel (Window ➪ Attributes) for individual objects — text, frames, shapes, and lines — to pick from the panel's three trapping options: Overprint Fill, Overprint Stroke, and Overprint Gap. Having three options means you can separately control which parts of an object overprint or knock out. When these options are unchecked (the default), InDesign knocks out the objects. When checked, InDesign overprints them.

CROSS-REF The Attributes panel's Nonprinting option has nothing to do with trapping. Instead, it controls whether a specific object prints at all, as I explain in Chapter 10.

Most objects don't have all three trap-related settings available because not all objects have fills, gaps, and strokes, but all objects have Nonprinting available, which prevents the object from printing. All three options are normally deselected because you usually want objects' fills, gaps, and strokes to knock out. Figure 29.11 shows the panel.

FIGURE 29.10

The two kinds of untrapped options: overprint (left) and knockout

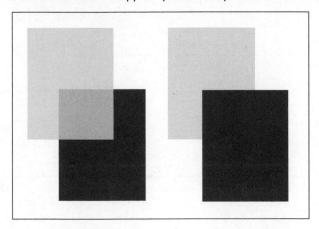

FIGURE 29.11

The Attributes panel lets you set whether objects' fills, strokes, and gaps overprint or knock out (the default, or deselected, status).

Specifying trapping presets

In InDesign, document-wide trapping settings are handled as part of the printing process (see Chapter 31). But you specify them like you do colors or other document attributes, through a panel. In this case, you use the Trap Presets panel (Window ➪ Output ➪ Trap Presets) that is shown in Figure 29.12. Choose New Preset from the panel's flyout menu to create a new preset, or select an existing preset and choose Preset Options to modify it. (Figure 29.13 shows the New Trap Preset dialog box.) You can also delete and duplicate trap presets from the flyout menu, as well as import them from other documents (through the Load Trap Presets option).

NOTE Consult your service bureau or commercial printer before changing the default settings. The people there will know what setting you should use based on the paper, inks, printing press, and image types you're using.

FIGURE 29.12

The Trap Presets panel

FIGURE 29.13

The New Trap Preset dialog box

Here are the settings you can change when creating or modifying a trap preset:

- **Name:** Type a name for the trap style in the Name field. Make sure it's a meaningful name, such as Choke, rather than New Preset 1, so in the future you'll know what it's for.

- **Trap Width:** Set your *trap width* (the amount of overlap you want between adjacent colors). The default is 0.25 point, a common setting. The Default field is for all colors except black and white. You set the trap width separately for black, using the Black field; this value is usually one and a half to two times as much as the regular trap settings because it controls how colors spread into black objects. The value is higher because you have more leeway with black — spreading a color into it doesn't change it from being black, while, for example, spreading yellow into blue makes a green, so you want to minimize that spreading.

- **Trap Appearance:** You can choose the type of joins and ends for traps, just as you do for strokes, with options of Miter, Round, and Bevel for both Join Style and End Style. In almost every case, you want to select Miter because this keeps the trap confined to the abutting images. If you choose another option, the choke or spread extends past the trapped objects a tad. If you think of the boundary of the trap as a line, then choosing Bevel or Round extends that line slightly past the objects. If the objects have white or a light color on either side, readers might notice that slight extension.

■ **Images:** InDesign lets you use several options to control how trapping is applied: Trap Placement plus four picture-specific settings, Trap Objects to Images, Trap Images to Images, Trap Images Internally, and Trap 1-bit Images.

   ▪ **Image Trap Placement:** This option determines how to handle trapping between an image and an abutting solid color. Your choices are Center, in which the trap straddles the edge between the image and the abutting color object; Choke, in which the abutting color object overprints the image by the Trap Width amount; Spread, in which the image overprints the abutting color object by the Trap Width amount; Neutral Density, which was defined earlier; and Normal, in which each pixel is trapped in the image individually and thus can result in an uneven edge between the image and the abutting object.

   ▪ **Trap Objects to Images:** This turns on trapping for images and any abutting objects such as text or graphics created in InDesign.

   ▪ **Trap Images to Images:** This turns on trapping for images and any abutting images.

   ▪ **Trap Images Internally:** This actually traps colors within the bitmap image. Use this only for high-contrast bitmaps, such as cartoons and computer screen shots, where the color has fewer gradations and more broad, consistent swaths.

   ▪ **Trap 1-bit Images:** This traps black-and-white bitmaps to any abutting objects (including those underneath). This prevents the appearance of white ghost areas around black portions if there is any misregistration when printing.

■ **Trap Thresholds:** These guide InDesign in how to apply your trapping settings:

   ▪ **Step:** This threshold value gives InDesign the color-difference threshold before trapping is implemented. The default is 10 percent, a value that traps most objects. A higher value traps fewer objects. The way this works is that the value represents the difference in color variance between adjacent objects, and you're telling InDesign not to worry about colors that are within the percentage difference. This is usually a low setting because it means you don't care if there are traps between similar colors because the human eye notices misregistration less between them, because they are, in fact, similar. In most cases, keep this value between 8 percent and 20 percent.

   ▪ **Black Color:** This defines at what point InDesign should treat a dark gray as black for the trap width in Black Width. For coarse paper, which usually absorbs more ink, dark tints and grays often end up looking like a solid color — 85 percent black appears as 100 percent black. Use Black Color Limit in such cases so that an 85 percent black object traps as it if were a 100 percent black object.

   ▪ **Black Density:** This is similar to Black Color Limit, except that it treats dark colors as black (like navy blue), based on their ink density. You can type a value of 0 to 10, with 1.6 being the default (0 is full black, while 10 is white).

■ **Sliding Trap:** This adjusts the way a choke or spread works. The normal value is 70 percent. When the difference in ink density (a good measure of color saturation) is 70 percent or more, this tells InDesign not to move the darker color so much into the lighter color. The greater the contrast between two colors, the more the lighter object is distorted as the darker color encroaches on it. At 0 percent, all traps are adjusted to the centerline between the two objects, while at 100 percent, the choke or spread is done at the full trap width.

■ **Trap Color Reduction:** This controls overinking that some traps can create. The default is 100 percent, which means that the overlapping colors in a trap are produced at 100 percent, which in some cases can cause the trap to be darker than the two colors being trapped, due to the colors mixing. Choosing a lower value in Trap Color Reduction lightens the overlapping colors to reduce this darkening. A value of 0 percent keeps the overlap no darker than the darker of the two colors being trapped.

Applying trapping to pages

Once you create trapping presets, you apply them. To do so, choose the Assign Trap Presets option in the Trap Presets panel's flyout menu. Figure 29.14 shows the dialog box.

 The [Default] preset, which you can modify, is applied to all pages by default.

FIGURE 29.14

The Assign Trap Presets dialog box

The process is simple: Choose the desired trap preset from the Trap Preset pop-up menu, and then select the pages to which the preset will be applied. Make your selection in the Pages section (select All or Range; if you select Range, type the page numbers in the Range field). Click Assign to complete the application of the trap preset to the selected pages. You can set multiple presets in a document to different page ranges, so if you want, select another trap preset and assign it to the desired pages. InDesign will show you which pages have which trap presets applied at the bottom of the dialog box. When you're finished, click Done.

NOTE   If your document uses sections, you can type page numbers in the Range field using the section numbering style (such as A-2, D-3, F-5-F-10) or by using absolute page numbers (+1, +5, +10-+15).

Summary

Although it's often impossible to precisely match colors from an electronic image when printing, InDesign can help make the color fidelity as high as possible through its support of color profiles and color management. It can also help make what you see on-screen and print on proofing devices look close to the final output, which helps you better gauge your actual colors.

If you use a compatible output device, InDesign also lets you control how adjacent colors print in a process known as *trapping*, which minimizes the chances of gaps appearing between colored objects. Fortunately, most users don't need to worry about fine-tuning trapping settings because InDesign's default settings handle most objects well.

Chapter 30

Preparing for Printing

O nce your document is created and all elements are perfectly in place, with the right colors, frame strokes, kerning, and so on, it's time to make tangible all that work you've done on-screen. You're ready to print the document.

Well, not quite. You may in fact be ready to just print your document, but if your document is at all complex or will be output at a service bureau or through your company's creative services group or print shop, you should take a few minutes and dot your i's and cross your t's. Little things can go wrong as you or your team work on a document — a font might deactivate, a picture might move or be renamed, or a new output device might be acquired.

That's where InDesign's preflighting and packaging capabilities come into play. The preflighting capability checks your document to make sure that all elements are available, while the packaging capability copies all required elements — from fonts to graphics — to a folder so you can give your service bureau all the pieces it needs to print your document accurately.

IN THIS CHAPTER

Setting up printers and drivers

Setting general printer options

Preflighting documents to find problems

Packaging documents for printing

Working with service bureaus

Setting up booklets

Making Initial Preparations

Before you can do anything, you need to make sure your system is set up with the right printer driver and printer description files — without these, your output is not likely to match your needs or expectations. It's important to set these up before you do any preflighting because preflighting checks your document against the printer settings you have active (such as color separations), and you can't have selected printer settings until the printer is set up.

The Mac and Windows platforms handle printing differently, so in this chapter I've divided all system-specific printing information, such as the coverage of drivers, into platform-specific sections.

Setting up Macintosh printers

Although you choose the printer type in the Setup pane of the InDesign Print dialog box, you still need to set up the printer on your Mac before you can use it.

In some cases, Mac OS X sets up the printer for you. In other cases, you may need to run an installation program that comes with the printer; sometimes, you need to run this software before you connect the printer to the Mac. Your printer documentation will explain the correct steps.

To see whether your printer is actually installed correctly, as well as to change its settings, you use the Print & Fax system preference by choosing ➪ System Preferences ➪ Print & Fax and then clicking Set Up Printers in the resulting Print & Fax system preference. The Printing pane should display by default (if not, go to it) and list any installed printers.

If you see the printer to which you want to print in the Print & Fax system preference, you've already installed your printer. Otherwise, make sure the printer you want to set up is connected to your Mac (directly or through the network) and turned on. (If you use a network printer, make sure the right network protocols, such as IP and AppleTalk, are turned on through the Network pane in the System Preferences dialog box, which you access by choosing ➪ System Preferences.) Then click the + iconic button below the printer list. What appears next depends on the version of the Mac OS you have:

- In Mac OS X 10.4 (Tiger), the Print Browser dialog box displays.
- In Mac OS X 10.5 (Leopard), an unnamed dialog box displays.

Both dialog boxes let you locate the printer, whether it's directly attached or available via the network. Select the desired printer and be sure the correct driver is selected in the Print Using pop-up menu. Click Add so the printer displays in your applications' Print dialog boxes.

Figure 30.1 shows the dialog boxes for adding a printer.

NOTE   You may need to install a PostScript Printer Description (PPD) file that contains specific details on your printer; this file should come on a disk or CD with your printer and is often installed with the printer's setup program. Otherwise, download it from the printer manufacturer's Web site. These files should reside in the PPD's folder in the Mac's System:Library:Printers folder. Note that Mac OS X preinstalls some PPDs for you, particularly those for Apple-branded printers and some Hewlett-Packard printers.

FIGURE 30.1

Top: Mac OS X 10.4 (Tiger)'s Print & Fax system preference and its Printer Browser dialog box show which printers are available and lets you add and configure them. Bottom: Mac OS X 10.5 (Leopard) has essentially the same interface except that the Printer Browser dialog box has no name.

If you're installing a printer not connected to your computer or network, such as the imagesetter used by your service bureau, you need to install the PPD files so InDesign knows what its settings are. Installing the printer software isn't necessary.

Mac OS X supports multiple printers, but it also lets you define the default printer — the one used unless you change it through a button or pop-up menu in an application's Print dialog box. (InDesign uses a pop-up menu called Printer to change the printer from the default setting.) In the Print & Fax dialog box, double-click the printer you want to be the default, which opens a job status dialog box for that printer. Choose Printer ⇨ Make Default or type ⌘+D (refer to Figure 30.2), and then close the job status dialog box. In the Print & Fax dialog box, the name of the default printer is displayed in bold in the printer list.

FIGURE 30.2

The job status dialog box for a specific printer lets you set that printer as the default printer for all applications.

Setting up Windows printers

The process for setting up printers varies based on the version of Windows you have.

Windows XP

In some cases, Windows XP sets up the printer for you. In other cases, you may need to run an installation program that comes with the printer; sometimes, you need to run this software before you connect the printer to the PC. Your printer documentation will explain the correct steps.

To see whether your printer is actually installed correctly, as well as to change its settings, you use Windows XP's built-in Printers control panel. The process to open this control panel depends on what version of Windows XP you have installed (Home or Professional) and whether you are running it in the Classic interface or not. Most people will use one of the following menu sequences to start the printer-installation process:

- Choose Start ➪ Settings ➪ Printers and Faxes
- Choose Start ➪ Control Panel ➪ Printers and Other Hardware.

Either way, you get a window with a list of existing printers and an icon labeled Add New Printer. Double-click the printer that you want to set up or double-click Add New Printer. (You likely need either a disk that came with the printer or the Windows CD-ROM if you add a new printer because Windows needs information specific to that printer).

NOTE If you're setting up a printer connected through the network, you usually should select the Local Printer option during installation. The Network Printer option is for printers connected to a print server, as opposed to printers connected to a hub or router. (A print server is a special kind of router, but it's typically used only for printers that don't have networking built in, such as many inkjet printers.) In some cases, even if your printer uses a print server, you'll still install the printer as a local printer, and then create a virtual port that maps to a network address (Hewlett-Packard uses this approach, for example).

If you're installing a printer not connected to your computer or network, such as the imagesetter used by your service bureau, you need to install the PPD files so InDesign knows what its settings are. You don't need to install the printer software.

When you open an existing printer, the dialog box shown in Figure 30.3 appears when you choose Printer ➪ Properties. One pane matters greatly: The Device Settings pane. Here you specify all the device settings, from paper trays to memory to how fonts are handled. (Note that some printers — such as Epson inkjet printers — do not have this pane, because they come with their own configuration software that handles these controls.)

For PostScript printers — the typical type of printer in a professional publishing environment — this pane has several key options:

- **Font Substitution Table:** This option opens a list of available fonts and lets you select how any TrueType fonts are translated to PostScript. The best (and default) setting is to have the printer translate TrueType fonts such as Arial to PostScript fonts such as Helvetica. (The Windows standards of Arial, Times New Roman, Courier New, and Symbol are set by default to translate to the PostScript fonts Helvetica, Times, Courier, and Symbol. PostScript fonts are set by default to Don't Substitute.)
- **Add Euro Currency Symbol to PostScript Fonts:** Be sure to select this option in this pane so the euro symbol (€) is available in all output.

NOTE You may need to install a PostScript Printer Description (PPD) file that contains specific details on your printer; this file should come on a disk or CD with your printer and is often installed with the printer's setup program. Otherwise, download it from the printer manufacturer's Web site. (Windows places PPD files in the Windows\System32\spool\drivers\w32x86 folder; note that the first folder may be named WinNT or WinXP instead of Windows.)

FIGURE 30.3

The Device Settings pane in Windows XP's setup for PostScript devices is the key pane in the Properties dialog box for a Windows printer. (Not all panes appear for all printers, depending on the printer type chosen and the network protocols installed.)

To set a printer as the default printer, right-click the printer in the Printers window (Start ➪ Settings ➪ Printers and Faxes), and select Set Default Printer from the contextual menu that appears. (Some Windows XP users will need to choose Start ➪ Control Panel ➪ Printers and Other Hardware.)

Windows Vista

The newest version of Windows, Vista, has a different interface for adding a printer, though the underlying process is the same as in previous versions.

Vista automatically adds USB printers that are powered on. For other printers, follow this process:

First, choose Start ➪ Control Panel, then click the Printer link in the Hardware and Sound section. (Or choose Start ➪ Control Panel, select Classic view from the left side of the dialog box and then double-click the Printers icon in the pane at the right.)

You get a window with a list of existing printers. Double-click the printer that you want to set up or click the Add a Printer button at the top of the pane (you likely need either a disk that came with the printer or the Windows CD-ROM if you add a new printer because Windows needs information specific to that printer).

If you're adding a printer connected through the network, you usually select the Add a Local Printer option during installation. The Add a Network, Wireless, or Bluetooth Printer option is for printers connected to a print server, as opposed to printers connected to a hub or router. (A print server is a special kind of router, but it's typically used only for printers that don't have networking built in, such as many inkjet printers.) In some cases, even if your printer uses a print server, you still install the printer as a local printer and then create a virtual port that maps to a network address (Hewlett-Packard uses this approach).

If you're adding a printer not connected to your computer or network, such as the imagesetter used by your service bureau, you need to install the PPD (PostScript Printer Description) file so InDesign knows what its settings are. (You don't need to install the printer software.) This file should come on a disk or CD with your printer and is often installed with the printer's setup program. Otherwise, download it from the printer manufacturer's Web site. (Windows places PPD files in the Windows\System32\spool\drivers\w32x86 folder.)

To configure a printer after it has been added, select it from the printer list, then click the Select Printing Preferences button at the top of the pane shown in Figure 30.4. The one pane you most need to pay attention to is the Advanced Options pane, which is where you specify all the device settings, from paper trays to memory to how fonts are handled. (Note that some printers — such as Epson inkjet printers — will not have this pane, since they come with their own configuration software that handles these controls.) You access this pane by clicking the Advanced button in the Layout pane of the Printing Preferences dialog box.

FIGURE 30.4

The Advanced Options pane in Windows Vista's setup for PostScript devices is the key pane in the Properties dialog box for a Windows printer. (Not all panes appear for all printers, depending on the printer type chosen and the network protocols installed.)

Another way to configure a printer is to double-click its icon in the pane to open the printer queue. Choose Printer ⇨ Properties and go to the Device Settings pane, which is nearly identical to the Windows XP setup pane of the same name (see previous section).

For PostScript printers — the typical type of printer in a professional publishing environment — this pane contains several key options in the PostScript Options section.

One option, TrueType Font Download Option, has a pop-up menu that lets you choose how TrueType fonts are handled. The default setting of Automatic should work in most cases, but if you are outputting to an imagesetter, check with your service bureau as to whether they'd prefer Outline instead (or, more rarely, Native TrueType).

The other PostScript Options settings should not be changed unless your service bureau requests it. Note that InDesign provides the three key controls in its own Print dialog box matching what you can do here: PostScript Language Level (the PostScript pop-up menu in the Print dialog box's Graphics pane), Mirrored Output (the Flip pop-up menu in the Output pane, and Negative Output (the Negative check box in the Output pane).

Preflighting Your Document

Now that your printers are set up, you can use InDesign's printing and preprinting checkup tools. The preflighting capability that's part of InDesign examines your document for any issues of concern and gives you a report on what may need to be fixed.

You might wonder why you need a preflight tool to check for things such as missing fonts and images, since InDesign lists any missing fonts and graphics when you open a document. The answer is that sometimes fonts and graphics files are moved after you open a file, in which case you don't get the alerts from InDesign. This is more likely to happen if you work with files and fonts on a network drive, rather than with local fonts and graphics. Preflighting also checks for other problematic issues, such as the use of RGB files and TrueType fonts.

Before you run the preflight tool, you should to set up your printer output so InDesign accurately checks your document's setup in anticipation of, for example, whether you plan to output color separations or spot colors. To do that, you need to go to the Print dialog box (File ⇨ Print, or ⌘+P or Ctrl+P), set your output settings, click Save Preset, provide a name in the Save Preset dialog box, and click OK, and then click Cancel to put them into effect *without actually printing the document.*

CAUTION   Don't confuse InDesign's print setup with the operating system's printer setup. In InDesign's Print dialog box is a button called Printer on the Mac and Setup in Windows that lets you change print settings for all applications — it's essentially a shortcut to the operating-system controls I described earlier in this section. You should only change these operating-system settings for output controls that InDesign's Print dialog box does not provide.

CROSS-REF   Selecting your output settings is covered in detail in Chapter 31.

Preflighting a document is easy. Choose File ⇨ Preflight, or press Shift+Option+⌘+F or Ctrl+Alt+Shift+F. In a few seconds, a dialog box appears that shows the status of your document. Here's a walk-through of what the six panes in the Preflight dialog box do:

- **Summary:** This pane (shown in Figure 30.5) shows you a summary of alerts. If your document has layers, you can select or deselect the Show Data for Hidden and Non-printing Layers option. If selected, layers that don't print are analyzed for font, image, and other issues. Select this option only if the person receiving your document plans on printing hidden layers. For example, in a French-and-English document, you may have hidden the French layer for proofing but still want it checked because the service bureau is instructed to print the document twice — once with the English layer on and the French layer off, and once with the English layer off and the French layer on.

FIGURE 30.5

The Summary pane of the Preflight dialog box

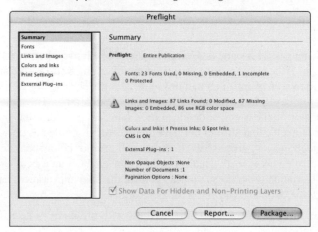

- **Fonts:** This pane (shown in Figure 30.6) shows the type of each font (Type 1 PostScript, OpenType, or TrueType), so you can spot any TrueType fonts before they go to your service bureau. (TrueType fonts usually don't print easily on imagesetters, so use a program like FontLab Studio Pro or FontLab Fontographer to translate them to PostScript instead.) The pane also shows any bitmap fonts, which you should replace if possible with another type, as bitmap fonts usually print poorly. (Fortunately, bitmap fonts are fairly rare.) And the pane shows if any fonts are missing from your system. You can search for specific fonts in the document by clicking Find Font.

  You can also limit the list of fonts to those with problems by selecting the Show Problems Only option.

FIGURE 30.6

The Fonts pane of the Preflight dialog box

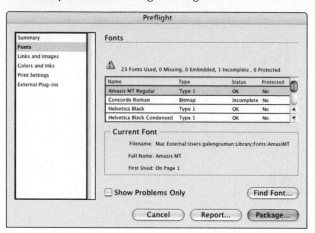

- **Links and Images:** This pane (shown in Figure 30.7) shows whether any graphics files are missing or if the original image has been modified since you placed it in your layout. Click Relink to correct any such bad links one at a time, or click Repair All to have InDesign prompt you in turn for each missing or modified file. The pane also shows whether a color profile is embedded in your graphics in case files that should have them don't or in case a file that should not have an embedded profile has one. It also alerts you if you use RGB images; although such images will print or color-separate, InDesign provides the warning because it's usually better to convert RGB images to CMYK in an image editor or illustration program so you can control the final appearance, rather than rely on InDesign or the output device to do the translation.

  You can also limit the list of linked files to those with problems by selecting the Show Problems Only option.

- **Colors and Inks:** This pane (shown in Figure 30.8) shows the inks used in the output, as well as their print settings. (If you are printing color separations, these correspond to the color plates that will eventually be used to print the document on a printing press.) You can't modify anything here; it's simply for informational purposes.

- **Print Settings:** This pane (shown in Figure 30.9) shows how the document is configured to print in the Print dialog box. That's why it's key to configure the output settings, as described earlier, before preflighting your document.

- **External Plug-ins:** This pane (shown in Figure 30.10) shows any plug-in programs required to output the file. Some third-party plug-ins make changes to the InDesign document that require the same plug-in to be installed at each computer that opens the file. This dialog box alerts you if you have such a dependency.

FIGURE 30.7

The Links and Images pane of the Preflight dialog box

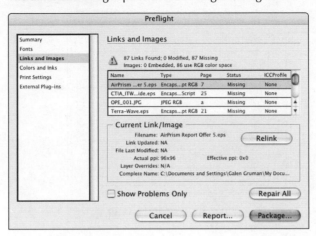

FIGURE 30.8

The Colors and Inks pane of the Preflight dialog box

TIP If you're working with the InDesign book feature (see Chapter 25), you can preflight the book's chapters from an open book's panel using the Preflight Book option in its flyout menu. (If one or more documents in the book are selected in the panel, the menu option changes to Preflight Selected Documents.) The options are the same as for preflighting individual documents.

FIGURE 30.9

The Print Settings pane of the Preflight dialog box

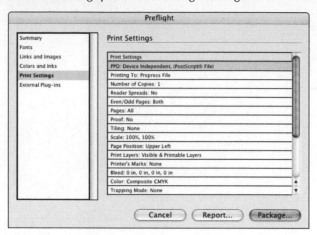

FIGURE 30.10

The External Plug-ins pane of the Preflight dialog box

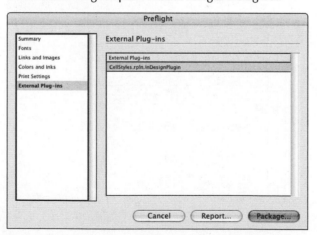

You can create a report of the preflight information by clicking Report. It generates a text file containing the information from the Preflight dialog box's panes, which you can give to your service bureau to check its settings and files against.

You can also click Package to gather all related fonts and files into one folder for delivery to a service bureau or other outside printing agency. The next section describes this option in more detail.

Click Cancel to exit the Preflight dialog box and go back to your document.

Creating a Document Package

If you've ever had the experience of giving a page-layout document to a service bureau, only to be called several hours later by the person who is outputting your document because some of the files necessary to output it are missing, you'll love the packaging capability in InDesign.

This capability, which you access by choosing File ⇨ Package, or pressing Option+Shift+⌘+P or Ctrl+Alt+Shift+P, copies into a folder all the font, color-output, and graphics files necessary to output your document. It also generates a report that contains all the information about your document that a service bureau is ever likely to need, including the document's fonts, dimensions, and trapping information. You can also create an instructions file that has your contact information and any particulars you want to say about the document.

When you run the packaging capability, InDesign preflights your document automatically and gives you the option of viewing any problems it encounters. If you elect to view that information, the Preflight dialog box appears (refer to Figures 30.5 through 30.10). You can continue to package your document from that dialog box by clicking Package once you're certain none of the problems will affect the document's output.

Before you can actually package the document, you need to save the current document, and then fill in the Printing Instructions form shown in Figure 30.11. You can change the default filename from Instructions.txt to something more suitable, such as the name of your print job.

CAUTION If you don't want to create an instructions form, don't click Cancel — that cancels the entire package operation. Just click Continue, leaving the form blank. Similarly, you must click Save at the request to save the document; clicking Cancel stops the package operation as well.

FIGURE 30.11

The Printing Instructions dialog box

The next step is to create the package folder. You do this in the dialog box that follows the Printing Instructions form, which on the Mac is called Create Package Folder and in Windows is called Package Publication. Figure 30.12 shows the Mac version, which except for the name at the top is the same as the Windows version.

FIGURE 30.12

The Create Package Folder dialog box for Mac InDesign is called the Package Publication dialog box in Windows.

In the dialog box, you can select what is copied: the fonts, color-output profiles, and *linked graphics* (graphics pasted into an InDesign document rather than imported are automatically included). You can also have InDesign update the graphics links for those graphic files that were modified or moved; if this option is not selected, any missing or modified graphics files will not be copied with the document.

You can tell InDesign to include fonts and links from hidden layers (which you would do only if you want the service bureau to print those hidden layers or if you were giving the document's files to a colleague to do further work).

You also can specify whether the document should use only the hyphenation exceptions defined within it. This often makes sense because it ensures that the printer's hyphenation dictionary — which may differ from yours — doesn't cause text to flow differently.

 See Chapter 16 for more details on these dictionaries. The next section of this chapter explains which files you should send to others using your documents.

You can also modify the instructions text file by clicking Instructions.

Finally, you can choose to view the report after the package is created — on the Mac, InDesign launches TextEdit and displays the report file, while on Windows, it launches Notepad and displays the report file.

Click Save (on the Mac) or Package (in Windows) when everything is ready to go. Your document is placed in the folder you specify, as is the instructions file (the report). There is also a folder called Fonts that includes the fonts, a folder called Links that has the graphics files, and a folder called Output Profiles that has the color output profiles.

TIP When you package document, any source files for objects on the pasteboard are not gathered. If you want such files included, increase the document's slug size (see Chapter 4) to encompass all the objects whose source files you want gathered in the package.

I strongly recommend using the packaging capability. It ensures that your service bureau has all the necessary files and information to output your document correctly.

Dealing with Service Bureaus

Service bureaus are great: Their staffs keep and maintain all the equipment, know the ins and outs of both your software and your printing press requirements, and turn jobs around quickly, at least most of the time. Working with a service bureau involves commitment and communication between both parties. It needs your business; you need its expertise and equipment.

To ensure that you get what you want (fast, accurate service) and that the service bureau gets what it wants (no-hassle clients and printing jobs), make sure that you both understand your standards and needs. Keep in mind that the service bureau has many customers, all of whom do things differently. Service bureaus likewise must not impose unreasonable requirements just for the sake of consistency, because customers can have good reasons for doing things differently.

Paying attention to a few basic issues can help you establish a productive relationship with your service bureau.

NOTE When I say *service bureau,* I also mean your company's production or prepress department and your commercial printer — the people who actually convert your files into the final product.

Sending documents versus output files

Because InDesign has the packaging capability, should you give the service bureau your actual InDesign documents or should you send a PostScript or PDF output file?

CROSS-REF Chapter 32 shows you how to create output files.

Often, your service bureau will have its requirements and preferences as to what kinds of output files it wants and when it wants output files rather than native InDesign files. You usually should provide what the service bureau wants, but there are times that your goals or concerns will override the service bureau's. Among the issues that play into deciding what files to provide are the following:

- A document file, even if the graphics files are copied with it, takes less space than an output file created from your document, which means fewer disks or cartridges to sort through and less time copying files from your media to the service bureau's (or transferring them over an FTP connection).

- A document file can be changed accidentally, resulting in incorrect output. For example, a color might be changed accidentally when the service bureau checks your color definitions to make sure that spot colors are translated to process colors. Or document preferences might be lost, resulting in text reflow.

- The service bureau cannot always edit an output file. So it may not be able to come to your rescue if you make a mistake such as forgetting to print registration marks when creating the output file or specifying landscape printing mode for a portrait document.

Basically, the question is: Where should the control ultimately be — with you or the service bureau? Only you can answer that question. But in either case, you can do two things to help prevent miscommunication: Provide the report file to the service bureau, and provide a proof copy of your document. The service bureau uses these tools to see if its output matches your expectations, regardless of whether you provide a document file or output file.

Determining output settings

A common area of miscommunication among designers, service bureaus, and printers is determining who sets controls over line screens, registration marks, and other output controls. (In some cases, when the printer is doing the film/plate output, it acts as both the service bureau and printer.) Whoever has the expertise to make the right choices should handle these options. And it should be clear to all parties who is responsible for what aspect of output controls — you don't want to use conflicting settings or accidentally override the desired settings:

- Assuming you're sending InDesign documents to the service bureau or printer, for output controls such as line screens and angles, the layout artist should determine these settings and specify them on the proof copy provided to the service bureau. That way the service bureau or printer can use its own PPD files rather than take the chance you have incorrect or outdated ones.

- If the publication has established production standards for special effects or special printing needs or if the job is unusual, I recommend that the layout artist determine the settings for such general printing controls as the registration marks and the printer resolution.

CROSS-REF   **InDesign print-control setup is described in Chapter 31.**

- For issues related to the service bureau's and/or printer's internal needs and standards, such as how much gap to have between pages and what trapping settings should be, I recommend that the service bureau and/or printer determine its own settings. If you're sending the service bureau or printer output files instead of InDesign documents, you have to type these settings in the Print dialog box pane before creating the file, so be sure to coordinate these issues with the service bureau and/or printer in advance.

- Coordinate issues related to the printing press (such as which side of the negative the emulsion should be on) with the printer and service bureau. Let the service bureau or printer determine this data unless you send output files.

In all cases, determine who is responsible for every aspect of output controls to ensure that someone does not specify a setting outside his or her area of responsibility without first checking with the other parties.

Smart service bureaus and printers do know how to edit an output file to change some settings, such as dpi and line screen, that are encoded in those files, but don't count on them doing that work for you except in emergencies. And then they should let you know what they did and why. And remember: Not all output files can be edited (such as EPS and PostScript files created as binary files), or they can be edited only in a limited way (such as PDF files).

The preceding issues often take the form of a conversation among the printer, the service bureau, and the designer. This conversation should touch on the topics of traps, ink spread, registration, and so forth. Relying on only the service bureau to get all the details correct without that three-way conversation can result in a less-than-optimal final printed product. Also, including the printer (and service bureau) earlier in the design phase of complex jobs can help avoid printing and production issues. All three parties bring an area of expertise to the job and so can educate each other a little about the goals of the piece. A designer with some production skills who knows the limitations of output and a given press can avoid excessive costs and poor output.

Ensuring correct bleeds

When you create an image that bleeds, it must actually print beyond the crop marks. There must be enough of the bleeding image that if the paper moves slightly in the press, the image still bleeds. (Most printers expect ⅛ inch, or a tad less than a pica, of *trim* area for a bleed.) In most cases, the document page is smaller than both the page size (specified in InDesign through the File ⇨ Document Setup menu option) and the paper size, so that the margin between pages is sufficient to allow for a bleed. If your document page is the same size as your paper size, the paper size limits how much of your bleed actually prints: Any part of the bleed that extends beyond the paper size specified is cut off. (This problem derives from the way PostScript controls printing; it has nothing to do with InDesign.)

NOTE This paper-size limit applies even if you set bleed and slug space in the Document Setup dialog box. These tell the printer how much of the material outside the page boundaries to output, so they're not cropped out automatically. But the paper, film negatives, or plates to which they are output must still be large enough to physically accommodate them.

Make sure that your service bureau knows that you're using bleeds and whether you've specified a special paper or page size, because that may be a factor in the way the operator outputs your job.

Sending oversized pages

If you use a paper size larger than U.S. letter size (8½ x 11 inches), tell the service bureau in advance because the paper size might affect how the operator sends your job to the imagesetter. Many service bureaus use a utility program that automatically rotates pages to save film because pages rotated 90 degrees still fit along the width of typesetting paper and film rolls. But if you specify a larger paper size to make room for bleeds or because your document will be printed at tabloid size, this rotation might cause the tops and/or bottoms of your document pages to be cut off.

I've worked with service bureaus that forgot that they loaded this page-rotation utility, so the operator didn't think to unload it for our oversized pages. It took a while to figure out what was going on because my publication's layout staff was certain that it wasn't doing the rotation (the service bureau assumed our staff had), and the service bureau had forgotten that it was using the rotation utility.

Setting up Booklets

One of the trickiest types of documents to print is a folded booklet, because you can't simply print the pages in sequence and have them end up on the right location on the final sheets of paper. When you fold them, the page order is rearranged due to the folding, especially in two-sided documents.

The tried-and-true approach is to use a booklet template that essentially provides a map of where pages should be — so when they are printed and folded, they end up in the right place — and then arrange your pages in that order via the Pages panel. Figure 30.13 shows the natural order (1–8) that you typically think a booklet has, as well as the actual page order (8,1; 2,7; 6,3; and 4,5) that it must be printed as, so after it is folded and stapled it appears to the reader in the sequence of 1 through 8.

NEW FEATURE The Print Booklet dialog box (and File menu option) replaces the InBooklet SE dialog box (and File menu option) from previous versions of InDesign. The capabilities are practically identical, though the user interface has changed.

There is an easier way: the Print Booklet dialog box (File ➪ Print Booklet). Here, you arrange your pages in the Pages panel in sequential order (1–8, in this case) and let the InDesign software figure out how to rearrange them for printing. Much easier! Figure 30.14 shows the Print Booklet dialog box's Setup pane.

FIGURE 30.13

Left: the logical order of pages for a folded, saddle-stitched booklet. Right: the order pages must be moved to so they print in the right sequence to be folded.

FIGURE 30.14

The Setup pane of the Print Booklet dialog box

Here are the key controls:

- **Booklet Type:** This pop-up menu is the key control. Here, you choose the type of booklet, which tells InDesign how to arrange the pages when printing so they are in the right sequence after folding. Your options are:

  - **2-up Saddle Stitch:** A folded sheet that contains two pages on each side, with the staples in the centerfold, between the pages. This is used in newsletters, smaller magazines, and many office documents.

  - **2-up Perfect Bound:** A folded sheet that contains two pages on each side, where the pages are stacked and folded, and then cut and held together with a glued backing or spine-based binding. This is typically used in books, larger magazines, and catalogs (because the square binding holds more pages than saddle-stitching does).

  - **2-up Consecutive:** A sheet that contains two pages on one side, with each page then cut and bound. This is essentially normal printing except that it uses a two-page sheet to print two pages at a time rather than a separate sheet for each page.

  - **3-up Consecutive:** This option is like 2-up Consecutive, except there are three pages on a sheet.

  - **4-up Consecutive:** This option is like 2-up Consecutive, except there are four pages on a sheet.

- **Space Between Pages:** (This option is not available for 2-up Saddle Stitch.) It lets you adjust the relative spacing among pages and objects, typically to provide additional white space around the folds.

- **Bleed Between Pages:** (This option is available for 2-up Perfect Bound only.) As with Space Between Pages, it lets you adjust the relative spacing among pages and objects, typically to provide additional white space around the folds.

- **Creep:** (This option is not available for the Consecutive options.) Creep shifts pages' contents away from the spine in increasing amounts as pages fall from the center of the booklet to the outside of it. Because outside pages have to fold over many inside pages, their content can end up obscured in the inside margins — their gutter is eaten up by folding over those other pages. Creep corrects this problem.

- **Signature Size:** (This option is available only for 2-up Perfect Bound.) Signature Size specifies how many pages are printed on each side of a sheet: 4, 8, 16, or 32.

- **Automatically Adjust to Fit Marks and Bleeds:** This option ensures that crop marks, bleeds, and other content that appears outside the page boundary is properly handled for the chosen booklet type. If the option is not checked, you can manually adjust these settings using the Top, Bottom, Left, and Right fields.

When using these features, consult with your commercial printer or service bureau for the appropriate settings. If you are printing the documents yourself, do a test run, and then fold, cut, and/or staple the sample document to make sure it works as expected before printing out lots of copies. The Preview pane, shown in Figure 30.15, helps to show the results of your choices, but doing a dry run is always the safest option.

When you're happy with your settings, choose Print to get the standard Print dialog box (covered in Chapter 31). You can also choose Print Settings to set up printer-specific controls (also covered in Chapter 31).

FIGURE 30.15

The Preview pane of the Print Booklet dialog box

Understanding Imposition

Layout artists may work on single pages or spreads, but printing presses rarely do. Sure, for short-run jobs, your printer may actually work with one page at a time, but typically, it works with forms, also called *signatures*. (In today's electronic age, the term *n-up printing* is now widely used to describe printing as signatures.)

Forms are groups of pages aligned so that when they are folded, cut, and trimmed they end up in proper numerical sequence. This act of arranging pages on a form is called *imposition*.

One popular printing method takes a huge sheet that encompasses anywhere from four to 64 pages, folds it, cuts it into pages, and trims the pages. This results in a stack of pages in the right order — a process known as *perfect binding*. This technique is used for square-backed publications such as books, many magazines, and many catalogs.

continued

continued

The other popular printing method also uses forms, but alignment is completed in a different way. Here, the form is broken into two-page spreads that are cut and trimmed, and then stacked separately. A page from each stack is added to a pile, and the pile is then folded to create the right page sequence—this is called a *booklet*. These folded spreads are stapled in the center in a process known as *saddle stitching*. Many magazines and catalogs use this approach.

Both approaches usually use large sheets of paper, called a *web*, which is why such commercial printing is known as SWOP, or Specifications for Web Offset Publications. (*Offset* refers to the way the ink is delivered to the page, with the ink offset to an intermediate roller between the color plate and the paper. This ensures that just the right amount of ink is placed on each sheet, sort of how an ink stamp works.)

Understanding how forms are configured will show you why what InDesign calls a *reader's spread*— the two adjacent pages that a reader sees when reading (and that a layout artist sees when designing on-screen)—is usually not how you want to output pages for use at a commercial printer. Printing reader's spreads makes more sense if you are, for example, wanting to show a client a mockup of the document, so you print spreads together on large paper (such as printing two 8.5-x-11-inch pages on an 11-x-17-inch sheet of paper).

The figure shows how a perfect-bound publication form is numbered, as well as a saddle-stitched form. Note that a form can have a number of pages other than 16 but must be in multiples of 4 pages.

734

To figure out the page sequence for a perfect-bound form, take a sheet of paper, and fold it in half as often as needed to create the number of pages on the form. You now have a booklet. Number the pages (front and back) with a pencil, and then unfold the paper to see how the form is put together. The front sides are one form, and the back sides are another.

To figure out the page sequence for a saddle-stitched form, you can take a sheet of paper for each spread, stack them, fold them once, and then number the pages (front and back) with a pencil, and then separate the sheets to see how the form is put together. The front sides are one form, and the back sides are another. Another way to do it is to realize that the bottom sheet contains page 1 and the final page on the back, and page 2 and the next-to-final page on the front. The sheet on top will have pages 3 and FP–2 (where FP is the final page number) on the front and pages 4 and FP–3 on the back, and so on until the middle sheet.

Summary

After you install the printer drivers for the various printers you'll use — both those on-site for proofing and those at a service bureau or prepress house — you should turn your attention to setting global printing defaults, the ones that affect all printing jobs, such as the use of paper trays and the handling of TrueType fonts.

Before you actually print, InDesign checks your document for possible output problems using its preflight tools. You also have the chance to create a print package — which collects all graphics, fonts, and a copy of the document file — to send to your service bureau or other output service.

Use the Print Booklets dialog box to have InDesign arrange pages correctly for *n*-up printing, such as saddle-stitched and perfect-bound documents in which several pages are printed on a single sheet of paper and then folded into the final configuration.

Chapter 31

Printing Techniques

Y our document is done. Your printers and printer options are set up, and you've preflighted your document, as described in Chapter 30. You're ready to see all that effort become reality by printing a proof copy or an actual version on a high-resolution imagesetter or printer.

The good news is that your hard work is over. Printing from InDesign is straightforward once everything has been set up. Just choose File ➪ Print, or ⌘+P or Ctrl+P, to go to the Print dialog box.

If you're working with the InDesign book feature (see Chapter 25), you can print the book's chapters from an open book's panel using the Print Book option in its flyout menu. (If one or more documents in the book are selected in the panel, the menu option changes to Print Selected Documents.) The setup options are the same as those for printing individual documents described in this chapter.

If you want to print booklets and have InDesign figure out the right printing order for their pages, use the File ➪ Print Booklet menu option that Chapter 30 describes. After you tell InDesign what kind of booklet you want so it can figure out the right page arrangement, you get the same printing options as described in this chapter.

And if you want to print to file, such as to create an EPS, PostScript, or PDF output file for use by a service bureau, set up the print options as described in this chapter and then use the output techniques that Chapter 32 covers.

IN THIS CHAPTER

Understanding the many print options

Saving printer settings for reuse

Specifying options used in imagesetters

Working with process and spot colors

Working with transparency and transparency flattening

Selecting InDesign Printing Options

The Print dialog box has eight panes as well as several options common to all the panes. Change any options and choose Print, and InDesign sends your document to the printer. Figure 31.1 shows the dialog box.

Common options

The common options available in the dialog box, no matter what pane is selected, are as follows:

- **Print Preset pop-up menu:** This pop-up menu lets you choose a previously defined set of printer settings. (See the sidebar "Using Printer Presets.")

- **Printer pop-up menu:** This pop-up menu lets you select the printer to use.

- **PPD pop-up menu:** This pop-up menu lets you select a PostScript Printer Description (PPD), which is a file that contains configuration and feature information specific to a brand and model of printer. PPD files are usually installed into your operating system using software that comes from your printer manufacturer, often as part of the printer installation process (see Chapter 30). If it finds no compatible PPDs, InDesign uses generic options. If it finds just one compatible PPD, it uses that one automatically; otherwise, it lets you select a PPD.

FIGURE 31.1

The General pane of the Print dialog box

■ **Setup button (Windows); Page Setup and Printer buttons (Mac):** These buttons give you access to printer-specific controls. Figures 31.2 and 31.3 show the resulting dialog boxes. You use these dialog boxes to specify options such as printing to file, paper sources, and printer resolution. Note that if you add a printer, you may need to quit InDesign and restart it for it to see the new printer.

FIGURE 31.2

Mac OS X's Page Setup and Printer dialog boxes (top and bottom, respectively)

 Windows and Mac OS X provide access to printer controls in different ways. In Windows, the Setup button gives you access to these, while on the Mac you use both the Page Setup and Printer buttons to access these controls.

■ **Save Preset button:** This lets you save Printer dialog box settings as a preset. (See the sidebar "Using Printer Presets.")

■ **Cancel button:** Clicking this button closes the Print dialog box without printing. Use this if you've clicked Save Preset but don't want to print, as well as when you have any reason not to print.

FIGURE 31.3

Windows XP's and Windows Vista's Print dialog boxes (top and bottom, respectively)

- **Print button:** Clicking this button prints the document based on the current settings.
- **Page preview subpane:** This subpane at lower left shows the current settings graphically. The page is indicated by the blue rectangle, while the direction of the large *P* indicates the printing orientation — in Figure 31.1's case, it's an unrotated portrait. The figure's subpane shows that the paper is the same size as the page. (If the page were larger than the paper, the overflow would be highlighted in light gray.) This preview changes as you adjust settings in the dialog box.

Using Printer Presets

InDesign lets you save printer settings as presets, so you can easily — and consistently — use them over and over. There are two ways to create them:

- In the Print dialog box, after setting up the various panes' options to the desired state, click the Save Preset button. This saves all the current settings into a preset whose name you specify in a dialog box that then appears.

- When not working in the Print dialog box, choose File ⇨ Print Presets ⇨ Define, or edit an existing preset by choosing File ⇨ Print Presets ⇨ *preset name*. When you click New or Edit in the resulting dialog box, a dialog box identical to the Print dialog box appears, except that the Print button becomes the OK button.

To apply a print preset when printing, choose it from the Print dialog box's Print Preset pop-up menu.

Note that if you have selected a print preset and then change settings in the Print dialog box, InDesign changes the name of the current preset in the Print Preset pop-up menu to [Custom] to remind you the settings have changed and are not saved. Click Save Preset to save these changes; a dialog box that appears in which you can use the existing preset name to update it with the new settings or specify a new name to save the changed settings as a new preset.

The General pane

The Print dialog box's General pane (refer to Figure 31.1) contains the basic settings for your print job:

- **Copies:** This text field is where you tell InDesign how many copies of the document you want to print. You can also select the Collate option to have InDesign print the pages in sequence. This is useful when you're printing multiple copies, so you get, for example, pages 1 through 16 printed in sequence and then printed again in sequence if you're making two copies. Otherwise, InDesign prints two copies of page 1, two copies of page 2, and so on, forcing you to manually collate them. If you select the Reverse Order option, InDesign prints from the last page to the first page, which is meant for printers that stack pages face up rather than the usual face down.

- **Pages:** These options let you choose to print all pages or a range of pages, in which case you type a range in the Range field. When specifying a range of pages, you can type non-consecutive ranges, such as 1–4, 7, 10–13, 15, 18, 20.

  If you want to print from a specific page to the end of the document, just type the hyphen after the initial page number, such as 4–. InDesign figures out what the last page is. Similarly, to start from the first page and end on a specified page, just start with the hyphen as in –11.

  InDesign lets you type absolute page numbers in the Range field. For example, typing +6–+12 would print the document's sixth through twelfth pages, no matter what their page numbers are.

- **Sequence:** The pop-up menu lets you choose from All Pages, Odd Pages Only, and Even Pages Only.

- **Spreads:** Selecting this option prints facing pages on the same sheet of paper; this is handy when you're showing clients comps, but make sure you have a printer that can handle that large paper size or that you scale the output down to fit (through the Setup pane, covered in the next section).

CAUTION You may not want to use the Spreads option when outputting to an imagesetter if you have bleeds because there will be no bleed between the spreads. If you use traditional *perfect-binding* (square spines) or *saddle-stitching* (stapled spines) printing methods, in which facing pages are not printed contiguously (see Chapter 29), do not use this option.

- **Print Master Pages:** Select this option if you want to print your master pages. This is handy for making reference copies available to page designers.

- **Options section:** There are three options in this section that are self-explanatory: Print Non-Printing Objects, Print Blank Pages, and Print Visible Guides and Baseline Grids. Print Blank Pages is usually used for collation, such as when blank pages divide sections of a manual. The other two are used typically by page designers to display hidden designer notes or wrap objects, as well as to ensure that objects really do align to the standard grids.

  The Print Layers pop-up menu in the Options section gives you additional control over how layers marked as nonprinting print. It used to be that if you marked a layer as non-printing, you would have to leave the Print dialog box to open the Layers panel to make it printable. Now, you can skip that step and override layers' nonprinting status using this pop-up menu. The default option, Visible & Printable Layers, honors your layers' printing status. Visible Layers prints all visible layers, including those marked as nonprinting. All Layers prints both visible and hidden layers, including those marked as nonprinting. (See Chapter 7 for more on layers.)

NEW FEATURE The Print Layers pop-up menu is new to InDesign CS3, as is its ability to control layer output when printing.

The Setup pane

The Setup pane, shown in Figure 31.4, is where you tell InDesign how to work with the paper (or other media, such as film negatives) to which you're printing. The options are straightforward.

Paper size and orientation

In the Paper Size section, choose the paper size using the Paper Size pop-up menu. You can also select the page orientation in the Orientation section by clicking any of the four iconic buttons that rotate the image as follows from left to right: 0 degrees (standard portrait), –90 degrees, 180 degrees, and 90 degrees (standard landscape).

FIGURE 31.4

The Setup pane of the Print dialog box

Choosing some printer models lets you choose the Custom option in the Paper Size pop-up menu, in which case you type the dimensions in the Width and Height fields, as well as position the output through the Offset and Gap fields. The latter two options are usually used when printing to a roll, such as in an imagesetter using photo paper (called *RC paper*, a resin-coated paper that keeps details extremely sharp), so you can make sure there is space between the left edge of the roll and the page boundary (the offset), as well as between pages (the gap). Most printers can't print right to the edge, thus the Offset setting; you also want to have a gap between pages for crop and registration marks, as well as room to physically cut the pages.

The Transverse option, if selected, rotates the output 90 degrees. This is done mainly for imagesetters whose paper and film negatives are usually about 12 inches wide. At that width, it's cheaper for the service bureau to rotate the pages 90 degrees in most cases (because most publications are usually no taller than 11 inches), packing more pages onto the RC paper or film.

CAUTION   Many service bureaus use a utility program that automatically rotates pages to save film, so check with your service bureau to make sure that selecting the Transverse option won't conflict with any rotation it might do. Also, if you specify a larger paper size to make room for bleeds or because your document will be printed at tabloid size, this rotation might cause the tops and/or bottoms of your document pages to be cut off. The basic rule: Discuss all output settings with your service bureau or prepress department first.

Potential Challenges for Page Positioning

Which Page Position option — Upper Left, Center Horizontally, Center Vertically, and Centered — you choose in the Print dialog box's Setup pane depends on what you are printing to. As a rule of thumb, use Centered for printing to paper. Use one of the other three choices for imagesetters. Talk to your service bureau to find out which one is best.

Here's the potential problem: On a proofing devices such as an inkjet, thermal wax, or laser printer, the Upper Left, Center Horizontally, Center Vertically options run the risk of putting part of the page outside the printer's imaging margin (a space of a pica or so from the paper edge in which the printer cannot print). That's why it's best to use the Page Position setting of Centered when printing to paper. This option also makes room available on all sides where possible for crop marks and bleeds.

But when you print to an imagesetter or platesetter, Centered may not be the best option. That's because your service bureau or commercial printer may not want the pages centered because it may be spacing them or rotating them to minimize waste of paper or film negatives. Imagesetters output to rolls of paper or film, so the service bureau or commercial printer has some control over the page's size. Always check first.

Scaling, positioning, and tiling options

The Setup pane also lets you set scaling, positioning, and tiling settings in the Options section.

The Scale settings are straightforward. You can choose separate Width and Height scaling settings to reduce or enlarge the page image. If the Constrain Proportions option is enabled, then a change in the Width field is applied to the Height field, and vice versa. To make a page fit the paper size, select the Scale to Fit option. InDesign will then display the actual percentage it will use. Note that Scale to Fit takes into account bleeds and crop marks, so even if the document page size is the same as the output device's paper size, Scale to Fit reduces it to make room for those elements.

The Page Position pop-up menu lets you choose how the page image is positioned on the paper to which you're printing. The default position is Centered, which centers the page image vertically and horizontally. You can also choose Center Horizontally, which aligns the top of the page image to the top of the paper and centers the page horizontally; Center Vertically, which aligns the left side of the page image to the left side of the paper and centers the page vertically; and Upper Left, which places the page image's upper-left corner at the paper's upper-left corner.

A very nice option is InDesign's Thumbnails check box and its adjoining pop-up menu. Here, you can have InDesign print *thumbnails* — miniature versions of pages, several to a sheet — for use in presenting comps, seeing whole articles at a glance, and so on. If you select the Thumbnails option, you then show many thumbnails you want per page from the adjoining pop-up menu. Its menu options are 1×2, 2×2, 3×3, 4×4, 5×5, 6×6, and 7×7. InDesign sizes the pages based on what it takes to make them fit at the number of thumbnails chosen per page, the page size, and the paper size.

QUARKXPRESS InDesign's Thumbnails option is more flexible than QuarkXPress's, letting you choose the number of thumbnails per page.

Use the Tile options to print oversized documents. If Tile is checked, InDesign breaks the document into separate pages called *tiles* that you later can assemble together. To turn on tiling, enable the Tile check box, and then choose the appropriate option from the adjoining pop-up menu:

- **Manual:** This lets you specify the tiles yourself. To specify a tile, you change the origin point on the document ruler, and that becomes the upper-left corner of the current tile. To print multiple tiles this way, you need to adjust the origin point and print, adjust the origin point to the next location and print, and so on, until you're done.

CROSS-REF Chapter 3 covers the origin point in more detail.

- **Auto:** This lets InDesign figure out where to divide the pages into tiles. You can change the default amount of overlap between tiles of 1.5 inches using the Overlap field. The overlap lets you easily align tiles by having enough overlap for you to see where each should be placed relative to the others.

- **Auto Justified:** This is similar to Auto except that it makes each tile the same size, adjusting the overlap if needed to do that. The Auto option, by contrast, simply starts at the origin point and then does as much of the page as will fit in the tile, which means the last tile may be a different width than the others. You can see the difference between the two by watching how the page preview window at left changes as you select each option.

The Marks and Bleeds pane

The Marks and Bleed pane, shown in Figure 31.5, lets you specify which printer marks are output with your pages, as well as areas to reserve for items that bleed off the page. The printer's marks are set in the Marks section, while the bleeds are set in the Bleed and Slug section.

Printer's marks

In most cases, you'd select the All Printer's Marks option and have all print on each sheet or negative. But you can select which marks you want to print. Here's what each option means:

- **Crop Marks:** These are lines at the corners of the page that tell a commercial printer where the page boundaries are, and thus to where the paper is trimmed.

- **Bleed Marks:** These add a very thin box around your page that shows the bleed area — where you expect items to print into, even though they're past the page boundary. (A *bleed* is an object that you want to be cut at the page boundary; the object needs to overshoot that boundary in case, during printing, the page is not trimmed exactly where it should be. Normally, 0p9, or 0.125 inches, is sufficient area for a bleed. You set the bleed area in the Marks and Bleeds pane, which I cover in the next section.

FIGURE 31.5

The Marks and Bleed pane of the Print dialog box

- **Registration Marks:** These are the cross-hair symbols used to ensure that the color negatives are properly aligned on top of each other when combined to create a color proof and to make sure that the colors are not misregistered on the final pages when they are lined up on a printing press.

- **Color Bars:** These print the CMYK colors and tints so a commercial printer can quickly check during printing whether ink is under- or oversaturated—the shades could be too light or dark. The CMYK colors also help a commercial printer know which color a particular negative is for (after all, negatives are produced using transparent film with black images).

- **Page Information:** This lists the filename and page number.

If a printer has options for printer's marks, they display in the Type pop-up menu, but most simply have one option: Default. You can also adjust the thickness of the printer's marks using the Weight pop-up menu settings of 0.125, 0.25, and 0.5 points; the default is 0.25 points (a hairline rule). You can also control the offset of crop marks from the page corners by adjusting the Offset value; the default of 0.833 inches (6 points) usually suffices. For all of these, check with your service bureau.

Because printer's marks print outside the page, it's possible your paper size may not be large enough to print the printer's marks. For example, if your page is 8½ x 11 inches and your paper is the same size, there's no room for the printer's marks. (The page preview subpane on the left of the

Print dialog box will show you if printer's marks fall outside the page's boundaries.) Be sure that your paper size is at least 1 inch wider and taller than your page size if you use printer's marks.

 When InDesign outputs PDF files, it is smart enough to automatically increase the paper size to add room for the printer's marks.

Bleeds and slugs

The Bleed and Slug area of the Marks and Bleed pane controls how materials print past the page boundary.

A bleed is used when you want a picture, color, or text to go right to the edge of the paper. Because there is slight variation on positioning when you print because the paper moves mechanically through rollers and might move slightly during transit, publishers have any to-the-edge materials actually print beyond the edge, so there are never any gaps. It's essentially a safety margin. A normal bleed margin would be 0p9 (⅛ inch), though you can make it larger if you want.

TIP You can control whether all bleed margins are changed if any of them is changed by clicking the Make All Settings the Same iconic button: If the chain icon is broken, each can be adjusted separately; if the chain icon is unbroken, changing one changes the others automatically. Click the button to toggle between the two behaviors.

A *slug* is an area beyond the bleed area in which you want printer's marks to appear. The reader never sees this, but the staff at the service bureau or commercial printer does, and it helps them make sure they have the right pages, colors, and so on. Like the bleed, the slug area is trimmed off when the pages are bound into a magazine, a newspaper, or whatever. (The word *slug* is an old newspaper term for this identifying information, based on the lead slug once used for this purpose on old printing presses.) The purpose is to ensure there is enough room for all the printer's marks to appear between the bleed area and the edges of the page. Otherwise, InDesign will do the best it can.

It's best to define your bleed and slug areas in your document itself when you create the document in the New Document dialog box (File ➪ New ➪ Document, or ⌘+N or Ctrl+N), as covered in Chapter 4. You can also use the Document Setup dialog box (File ➪ Document Setup, or Option+⌘+P or Ctrl+Alt+P). The two dialog boxes have the same options; if they don't show the Bleed and Slug section, click More Options to see them.

But if you didn't define your bleeds previously, you can do so in the Print dialog box's Marks and Bleed pane. You can also override those document settings here. To use the document settings, select the Use Document Bleed Settings option. Otherwise, type in a bleed area using the Top, Bottom, Inside, and Outside fields. (The Inside and Outside fields are labeled Left and Right, respectively, in a document composed of single pages rather than facing pages.)

If you want the bleed area to be the same on all four sides, click the broken-chain button to the right of the Top field; it becomes a solid chain, indicating that all four fields have the same value if any is modified. Any bleed area is indicated in red in the page preview subpane at the bottom left.

If you want to set the slug area, select the Include Slug Area option. InDesign reserves any slug area defined in the New Document or Document Setup dialog box. You cannot set up the slug area in the Print dialog box.

The Output pane

The next pane is the Output pane, which controls the processing of colors and inks on imagesetters, platesetters, and commercial printing equipment. You definitely want to check these settings with your service bureau. For proof printing, such as to a laser printer or inkjet printer, the only option that you need to worry about is the Color pop-up menu, seen in Figure 31.6.

 CAUTION These options should be specified in coordination with your service bureau and commercial printer — they can really mess up your printing if they're set incorrectly.

FIGURE 31.6

The Output pane of the Print dialog box

Here's what the options do:

- **Color:** Use this pop-up menu to choose how you want the document to print. Your options are Composite Leave Unchanged, Composite Gray, Composite RGB, Composite CMYK, Separations, and In-RIP Separations. (*RIP* stands for raster-image processor, the device in a printer or imagesetter that converts lines, curves, colors, and pictures into the tiny dots that make up printed output.)

  The Composite menu options are meant for proofing devices such as inkjets and laser printers. Most such printers are black-and-white or CMYK, so you usually choose Composite Gray or Composite CMYK. Choose Composite RGB for documents output to PDF format for display on screen. Composite Leave Unchanged is meant for proofing printers that support specialty ink swatches such as Pantone; very few do. (If your document uses colors like Pantone colors, you typically pick Composite CMYK, and your printer approximates the Pantone colors. Choose Composite Leave Unchanged only if your proofing printer has actual Pantone inks.)

Choose Separations if you're printing to an imagesetter to create film negatives or to a platesetter to create color plates. If your output device supports in-RIP separations — where the device creates the separate color plates, rather than having InDesign do it — choose In-RIP Separations. (Note that only a few printers' PPDs support this option.)

■ **Text as Black:** If you enable this check box, text appears in pure black, rather than being converted to gray or printed in a color (even if you apply a color to the text). This can make text more readable in a proof copy.

■ **Trapping:** Use this pop-up menu to select how color trapping is handled. (It is grayed out if Separations or In-RIP Separations are not selected in the Color pop-up menu.) The choices are Off, Application Built-In (meaning, as set in InDesign), and Adobe In-RIP (available only for printers that support Adobe's in-RIP separations technology).

> **NOTE** At this point, the publishing world has not standardized on PostScript Level 3 printing language or default trapping and color technologies. Therefore, you'll likely choose the standard Separations option that uses whatever settings you created in InDesign, or you'll choose the Off option and let your service bureau manage trapping directly. Check with your service bureau.

■ **Flip:** Use this pop-up menu and the associated Negative option to determine how the file prints to film negatives or plates. Service bureaus and commercial printers have different requirements based on the technology they use. They tend to use language such as *right reading, emulsion side up*, which can be hard to translate to InDesign's Flip settings. Type on the page is *right reading* when the photosensitive layer is facing you and you can read the text. Horizontally flipping the page makes it *wrong reading* (type is readable when the photosensitive layer is facing away from you). Check with your service bureau as to whether and how you should flip the output. Pages printed on film are often printed using the Horizontal & Vertical option in the Flip pop-up menu.

■ **Negative:** Enabling this check box creates a photographic negative of the page, which some commercial printers may request. This option is available only if Composite Gray, Separations, or In-RIP Separations is chosen in the Color pop-up menu.

■ **Screening:** This pop-up menu works differently depending on whether you choose Composite Gray or one of the separations options in the Color pop-up menu:

■ If you choose Composite Gray in the Color pop-up menu, your Screen pop-up menu choices are Default and Custom. If you choose Custom, you can specify the preferred line screen frequency and angle at the bottom of the pane using the Frequency and Angle fields.

■ If you choose Separations or In-RIP Separations in the Color pop-up menu, you get a series of options that vary based on the selected printer and PPD. But all show an lpi setting and a dpi setting. (See the sidebar on lpi and dpi in this chapter for more about these.) And the Frequency and Angle fields at the bottom of the pane display very precise angles optimized for the selected output device based on the chosen lpi/dpi settings. Although you can change the Frequency and Angle fields, you shouldn't.

The Inks section of the pane lets you see the frequency and angle settings for selected colors; you change a specific color plate's settings by first selecting the color and then altering the Frequency and Angle fields. You can also disable output of specific color plates by clicking the printer icons to the left of the colors — a red line is drawn through the icon for disabled plates — as well as control color plate output by clicking Ink Manager, which I cover later in this chapter.

The Simulate Overprint check box at the bottom of the Output pane lets InDesign overprint colors for printers that normally don't support this. (You would set an object to overprint another by selecting one of the Overprint options in the Attributes panel, as Chapter 29 explains.) This option is available only if the Color pop-up menu is set to Composite Gray, Composite CMYK, or Composite RGB.

What lpi and dpi Mean

The smallest dots on the physical output — paper, film, or press plate — are measured as dots per inch (dpi) and have a fixed size determined by the output device: a laser printer, imagesetter, or digital platemaker. An output device typically supports 600 to 3600 dpi, dots that are too small to reproduce on an offset press. To create a continuous-tone image that can be reproduced with ink on a press, these fixed-size dots are combined to form much larger, variable-sized dots called a *line screen*, measured as lines per inch (lpi). An image's line screen typically ranges from 80 lpi for a photo on newsprint to 250 lpi for high-end color art prints on coated paper.

Lines per inch specifies, in essence, the grid through which an image is filtered, not the size of the spots that make it up. Thus, a 100-lpi image with variably sized dots will, therefore, appear finer than a 100-dpi image. The figure shows an example, with a fixed-dot arrow at left and a variably sized–dot arrow at right.

The output device's dpi capabilities thus have a bearing on the lpi capabilities, and lpi is typically how a production person thinks of the desired output quality. A 300-dpi laser printer can achieve about 60-lpi resolution; a 1270-dpi imagesetter can achieve about 120-lpi resolution; a 2540-dpi imagesetter about 200-lpi resolution. Resolutions of less than 100 lpi are considered coarse, and resolutions of more than 120 lpi are considered fine.

But there's more to choosing an lpi setting than knowing your output device's top resolution. An often-overlooked issue is the type of paper the material is printed on. Smoother paper (such as *glossy-coated* or *super-calendared*) can handle finer halftone spots because the paper's coating (also called its *finish*) minimizes ink bleeding. Standard office paper, such as that used in photocopiers and laser printers, is rougher and has some bleed that is usually noticeable only if you write on it with markers. Newsprint is very rough and has a heavy bleed. Typically, newspaper images are printed at 85 to 90 lpi; newsletter images on standard office paper print at 100 to 110 lpi; magazine images print at 120 to 150 lpi; calendars and coffee-table art books print at 150 to 200 lpi.

Other factors affecting lpi include the type of printing press and the type of ink used. Your printer representative should advise you on preferred settings.

If you output your document from your computer directly to film negatives (rather than to photographic paper that is then shot to create negatives), inform your printer representative. Outputting to negatives allows a higher lpi than outputting to paper because negatives created photographically cannot accurately reproduce the fine resolution that negatives that output directly on an imagesetter have. (If, for example, you output to 120 lpi on paper and then create a photographic negative, even the slightest change in the camera's focus makes the fine dots blurry. Outputting straight to negatives avoids this problem.) Printer representatives often assume that you're outputting to paper and base their advised lpi settings on this assumption.

The Graphics pane

The Graphics pane, shown in Figure 31.7, controls how graphics are printed and how fonts are downloaded. The options here are meant for professional printing, such as when you send your files to imagesetters, where you're working with a service bureau or in-house printing department.

Your first option is the Send Data pop-up menu in the Images section. It has four options: All, Optimized Subsampling, Proxy (a low-resolution, 72-dpi version), and None. The Optimized Subsampling and Proxy options are meant to increase the speed of proof prints, with Proxy being the fastest. The None option is handy for quick proofs meant to focus on the layout and the text.

The Fonts options require that you understand how your output device is configured to handle fonts. Be sure to ask your service bureau what options it prefers. Here are the options available:

- **Download:** This pop-up menu specifies how fonts are downloaded to the printer, something you may need to do if the printer doesn't have its own store of fonts for use in printing text correctly. There are three choices:
  - **Subset:** Normally, when printing to a local printer, choose the Subset option, which sends font data to the printer as fonts are used. This means that if you use just one character of a font on a page, only that character is sent for that page, and if more characters are used on later pages, they are sent at that time. This is an efficient way to send font data to printers that don't have a lot of memory or hard drive space to store complete font information for many typefaces.

- **Complete:** If you're printing to a device that has a lot of font memory — or if your document has many pages and uses a font in bits and pieces throughout — choose this option from the Download pop-up menu. This sends the entire font to the printer's memory, where it resides for the entire print job. In cases such as those described, this is more efficient than the standard Subset method.

- **None:** Choose this option from the Download pop-up menu if you're certain all the fonts you use reside in the printer's memory or on a hard drive attached to the printer. Many service bureaus load all the fonts for a job into the printer memory, and then print the job. They then clear out the printer memory for the next job and load just the fonts that job needs. This is efficient when a service bureau has lots of clients who use all sorts of fonts. Alternatively, some service bureaus attach a hard drive loaded with fonts to their imagesetters, saving the font-loading time for them and for InDesign.

- **Download PPD Fonts:** If this check box is enabled, InDesign downloads any fonts specified as resident in the printer's PPD file. Normally, PPD files include lists of fonts that should reside in printer memory and thus don't need to be downloaded with each print job. Enabling this option overrides this behavior, and instead downloads those fonts from your computer even if they should reside in the printer's memory. You rarely need to enable this option; it's more of a safety when creating output files for printing by someone else.

FIGURE 31.7

The Graphics pane of the Print dialog box

Finally, you can specify what PostScript language is used and how PostScript data is transmitted. Although you set these up in the Mac OS X and Windows printer settings (refer to Figures 31.2 and 31.3), InDesign gives you the opportunity to override any defaults here, which can be handy when creating output files for printing elsewhere:

- From the PostScript pop-up menu, you can choose Level 2 or Level 3; choose whichever the output device supports. (Most still use Level 2.)

- The Data Format pop-up menu is grayed out unless you chose PostScript File in the Printer pop-up menu; your choices are ASCII and Binary. If you choose ASCII, the PostScript file is more likely to be editable in programs like Adobe Illustrator, but the file will be larger. Ask your service bureau which it prefers.

The Color Management pane

The Color Management pane, shown in Figure 31.8, is where you manage color output (apply color calibration). The options are straightforward.

CROSS-REF Chapter 29 covers the techniques for and issues of applying color profiles and other color management settings that the profiles in the Color Management pane use.

- **Document or Proof:** In the Print section, select one of these options based on whether you want to use the document's profile or a different profile for proofing. The Proof option is available only if you choose an output device such as an imagesetter, for which you might make a proof locally using an inkjet or other printer and then use the image-setter's PPD profile (as explained in Chapter 30) when producing your final output.

- **Color Handling:** In the Options section, use this pop-up menu to choose between Let InDesign Determine Colors and PostScript Printer Determines Color. The first option uses the color-management options set in InDesign, while the second lets the PostScript output device choose the color-management approach. This latter option is not available unless you have chosen a color PostScript printer as the destination. (If you choose Composite Leave Unchanged in the Output pane's Color pop-up menu, you have the No Color Management option in the Color Handling pop-up menu.)

- **Printer Profile:** Use this pop-up menu to select the device to which the document will ultimately be printed. This is by default the same as the profile selected in the Color Settings dialog box, which I cover in Chapter 29. But you can override that default here, such as when you are using a different printer temporarily.

Depending on which Color Handling and Printing Profile options you select, you may be able to use one or both of the following options:

- **Preserve CMYK Numbers:** When checked, this prevents the color management options from overriding the CMYK values in non-color-calibrated imported graphics.

- **Simulate Paper Color:** If you choose Proof of a Printing Condition as the Color Handling Method, enabling this check box makes InDesign simulate the typical color of the paper you've chosen for proofing (through View ➪ Proof Setup; see Chapter 29).

FIGURE 31.8

The Color Management pane of the Print dialog box

The Advanced pane

The options in the Advanced pane, shown in Figure 31.9, control printing of files as bitmaps, manage graphics file substitutions in an Open Prepress Interface (OPI) workflow, and set transparency flattening, which manages how transparent and semitransparent objects are handled during output.

Bitmap printing

For certain printers — mainly inkjet printers — InDesign lets you control the output resolution when you are printing the file as grayscale (by choosing Composite Gray in the Output pane's Color pop-up menu). To do so, enable the Print as Bitmap check box in the Advanced pane and select the desired dpi value from the pop-up menu at right.

Note that this feature is available only if you choose a compatible printer in the Printer pop-up menu *and* set the output to Composite Gray.

NEW FEATURE The bitmap printing capability is new to InDesign CS3.

OPI settings

If graphics files exist in high-resolution versions at your service bureau — typically, this occurs when the bureau scans in photographs at very high resolutions and sends you a lower-resolution version for layout placement — select the OPI Image Replacement option. This ensures that InDesign uses the high-resolution scans instead of the low-resolution layout versions.

The Omit for OPI section provides three additional related graphics file-handling options. You can have InDesign *not* send EPS, PDF, and bitmap images (such as TIFF files) by selecting the appropriate options. You would do so either to speed printing of proof copies, or when the service bureau has such files in higher-resolution or color-corrected versions and will substitute their graphics for yours. InDesign keeps any OPI links, so the graphics at the service bureau will relink to your document during output.

Transparency flattening

There are just two options in the Transparency Flattener section:

- **Preset:** This pop-up menu lets you choose a transparency preset (a saved set of options). At the least, InDesign provides the three default transparency-flattening options: [Low Resolution], [Medium Resolution], and [High Resolution].

- **Ignore Spread Overrides:** If this check box is enabled, any transparency settings you manually applied to document spreads are ignored and the selected preset is used instead for the entire document.

 Transparency settings and presets are covered later in this chapter.

FIGURE 31.9

The Advanced pane of the Print dialog box

The Summary pane

The final Print dialog box pane is the Summary pane, shown in Figure 31.10. It simply lists your settings all in one place for easy review. The only option — Save Summary — saves the settings to a file that you can include with your files when you deliver them to a service bureau or distribute them to other staff members; this way they know the preferred settings.

FIGURE 31.10

The Summary pane of the Print dialog box

Working with Spot Colors and Separations

When you print color separations, InDesign gives you expected control over how colors separate — which are converted to CMYK and which are printed on their own plates. But it goes much further, letting you control much of how those plates print, such as the order that plates print in and the angle of each color's line screens.

Managing color and ink output

Accidentally using spot colors such as red and Pantone 111 (say, for graphics and text frames) in a document that contains four-color TIFF and EPS files is very easy. The result is that InDesign outputs as many as six plates: one each for the four process colors, plus one for red and one for

Pantone 111, rather than convert red and Pantone 111 into CMYK mixes and thus output just the four CMK plates. But, you can avoid these kinds of mistakes.

That's exactly where the Ink Manager dialog box comes in. Accessed by clicking Ink Manager in the Output pane, this dialog box gives you finer control over how color negatives output. Figure 31.11 shows the dialog box.

If any colors should have been converted to process color but weren't, you have three choices:

■ **Click the spot-color iconic button:** You can override the spot color in the Ink Manager dialog box by clicking this iconic button (a circle) to the left of the color's name. That converts it to a process color and causes the iconic button to change to a four-color box that indicates a process color. (Clicking the four-color-box iconic button converts a process color back to a spot color, as well as changes the iconic button back to a circle.) This is the way to go for a quick fix.

FIGURE 31.11

The Ink Manager dialog box

■ **Make it a process color instead:** Do this by closing the Ink Manager and Print dialog boxes, and editing the color that was incorrectly set as a spot color in the Swatches panel (Window ➪ Swatches or F5), as covered in Chapter 8. This ensures that the color is permanently changed to a process color for future print jobs.

- **Convert all spot colors to CMYK process equivalents:** Do this by enabling the All Spots to Process check box. This is the easiest method to make sure you don't accidentally print spot-color plates for a CMYK-only document. (You can also use the All Spots Process option to quickly convert all spot colors to process, then convert back to spot colors just those colors you really do want on their own plates.)

The other Ink Manager options are for experts and should be changed only in consultation with your service bureau and commercial printer:

- **You can change the ink type in the Type pop-up menu.** Most inks — including the process inks — should be left at Normal. Use Transparent for varnishes and other finishes that let color through — you don't want InDesign to trap to such colors. If it did, no color would print under the varnish or finish. (A varnish is often used to highlight part of a page, such as making the text reflective in contrast to the rest of the page.) Use Opaque for metallics, pastels, and other thick colors; this setting lets adjacent colors trap to the edge of opaque objects, but it prevents trapping of underlying colors (because they will be totally covered over). Finally, use Opaque Ignore for inks that don't trap well with any other color — your service bureau or commercial printer tells you when you need to do this.

- **You can change the neutral density for each ink.** This tells InDesign how to handle the trapping of differently saturated inks. For example, a dark color (highly saturated) needs to be trapped more conservatively against a light color to prevent excess intrusion. In coordination with your commercial printer, you might want to override the default neutral density settings if you find that the defaults don't properly handle some trapping combinations. It's possible that your commercial printer is using a different brand of ink than is assumed in the settings, for example, and that could require a density adjustment.

- **Arrange the order in which color negatives print.** Sometimes commercial printers permit you to do this. It affects the trapping, because InDesign presumes that the colors are printed in the standard order — cyan, then magenta, then yellow, then black, then any spot colors — and factors that into its trapping adjustments. In some cases, changing the printing order improves a publication's color balance, because it happens to favor a range of tones that the standard order might not treat properly. For example, if there's a lot of black in the background, you might want to print black first. Other colors overprint it, giving it a warmer feel than if black is printed on top of the other colors as it is normally. To change the order of output used by InDesign's trapping calculations, select a color, and change its ink sequence number in the Trapping Sequence field; all other colors' sequences are automatically adjusted.

- **Apply a process color's settings to a spot color.** You can use the Ink Alias pop-up menu to do this, but I don't recommend you do this very often, as it makes the spot color print each dot over the dots of the selected process color, rather than be offset slightly so the color remains visible. You set an ink alias only if you are using a spot color in place of a standard process color — such as substituting a yolk color for standard yellow to create a special effect. In this case, the yolk color overprints the yellow color, replacing the yellow where both colors have been used.

- **Force one plate to be used for several versions of the same color.** Another case for using the Ink Alias feature is when your document has several color swatches that should be the same color. (Perhaps PDF files you placed used different names for the same color, such as PMS 175 and Pantone 175, so these multiple swatch names were all added to your document.) Ink Alias lets you have all these "colors" print on the same plate.

- **Force InDesign to substitute the basic CMYK process colors for the similar colors defined by the Pantone and HKS spot-color models.** Do this by selecting the Use Standard Lab Values for Spots option. In most cases, the substitute colors are almost identical, so no one will notice, but check with your printer first because the type of paper you use or other factors may cause a different output than expected.

CROSS-REF Chapter 8 covers how to create color swatches, how to specify which are to print as spot colors and which are to be converted to process colors, and how to use the various color models and ink libraries. Chapter 29 explains how to preview color separations on-screen.

Adjusting screen angles

When you print using color plates, each plate — cyan, magenta, yellow, and black, or any spot colors — is rotated slightly so its dots don't overprint the dots of other plates. This ensures that each color is visible on the paper and this is visible to the eye, which then blends them into various colors, simulating natural color. These rotations called *screening angles* determine how the dots comprising each of the four process colors are aligned so they don't overprint each other. Normally, you'd probably never worry about the screening angles for your color plates. After all, the service bureau makes those decisions, right? Maybe.

If you have your own imagesetter, or even if you're just using a proofing device, you should know how to change screen angles for the best output. If you're working with spot colors that have shades applied to them, you'll want to know what the screen angles are so that you can determine how to set the screening angles for those spot colors.

The rule of thumb is that dark colors should be at least 30 degrees apart, while lighter colors (for example, yellow) should be at least 15 degrees apart from other colors. That rule of thumb translates into a 15-degree angle for cyan, a 75-degree angle for magenta, no angle (0 degrees) for yellow, and a 45-degree angle for black.

But those defaults sometimes result in *moiré patterns*, which are distortions in the image's light and dark areas caused when the dots making up the colors don't arrange themselves evenly. With traditional color-separation technology, a service bureau has to adjust the angles manually to avoid such moirés — an expensive and time-consuming process. With the advent of computer technology, modern output devices, such as imagesetters, can calculate angles based on the output's lpi settings to avoid most moiré patterns. (Each image's balance of colors can cause a different moiré, which is why there is no magic formula.) Every major imagesetter vendor uses its own proprietary algorithm to make these calculations.

InDesign automatically uses the printer's PPD values to calculate the recommended halftoning, lpi, and frequency settings shown in the Output pane of the Print dialog box. But for spot colors, it's basically a guess as to what screening angle a color should get. The traditional default is to give it the same angle as yellow, because if a spot color's dots overprint yellow dots, the effect is less noticeable than if it overprinted, say, black dots. But if you have multiple spot colors, that approach doesn't work. In that case, choose a screening angle for the color whose hue is closest to the spot colors. Fortunately, InDesign calculates a recommended angle for you, so you don't have to make any guesses. As always, don't forget to consult your service bureau or printing manager.

Working with Transparency

InDesign lets you import objects with transparent portions, as well as create transparent objects using the Effects panel (see Chapter 12). Using features such as the Drop Shadow and Feather options in the Effects dialog box also might create transparency. But working with transparency can create unintended side effects in how overlapping objects actually appear when printed or viewed on-screen in a PDF file. To address that, InDesign gives you the ability to both control transparency on selected objects and groups, as well as control how transparency is handled during output.

QUARKXPRESS QuarkXPress 6 and earlier has no equivalent to InDesign's transparency
settings. QuarkXPress users instead must rely on such settings in programs such
as Adobe Photoshop and Illustrator for imported pictures and do without them for objects created
in QuarkXPress.

Using transparency the ideal way

The use of transparency can result in very cool effects in your layout, but it can also cause major problems when you print because transparency requires very complex calculations for the image-setter to handle, calculations that can be tripped up by how source files and other settings are applied.

So it's important to apply transparency wisely. Follow these techniques to get the best results when you print:

- All objects containing text should be stacked above any object with transparency effects. The flattening process can distort type unpleasantly when objects with effects are arranged above type objects. Obviously, arranging objects in this way is not always possible, but the difference in quality makes it worth the time to fix this when it is possible to do so.

- Similarly, keep transparent objects on their own layers when possible.

- Be sure to set the document's transparency blend space to match the type of output: RGB (for on-screen output such as PDF files) and CMYK (for printed documents). Do so by choosing either Edit ➪ Transparency Blend Space ➪ Document CMYK or Edit ➪ Transparency Blend Space ➪ Document RGB.

- Don't mix RGB and CMYK objects in the same layout if you use transparency; convert your source images to the same color model in their originating programs, such as Illustrator and Photoshop. Convert spot colors to CMYK in those programs as well, except, of course, for those that print on their own plates.

- Be careful when using Color, Saturation, Luminosity, and Difference blending modes with spot colors or gradients — they may not print correctly, so you may need a design alternative if such output problems occur.

- If your source files have transparency, neither flatten them in the program that created them or save them in formats that flatten them. That means you should keep files with transparency in these formats: PDF 1.4 or later, Illustrator 10 or later, and Photoshop 6 and later. Note that Illustrator Encapsulated PostScript (EPS) files keep their transparent areas separate when worked on in Illustrator but not when used by separate programs, so don't use the Illustrator EPS format for transparent objects if you can avoid it.

Flattening transparency during output

The more objects you have overlapping each other with transparency settings applied, the more complex the output calculations are to print those effects. This can prevent a document from printing because it can overwhelm the printer or other output device. That's why many commercial printers and prepress houses dread transparency.

Adobe PostScript Levels 1 and 2, EPS, and Adobe PDF 1.3 do not support Adobe's transparency technology in its native state. Therefore, transparency information must be flattened for export to EPS or Adobe PDF 1.3 format, or for printing to PostScript desktop printers, PostScript Level 2 raster-image processors (RIPs), and some PostScript 3 RIPs. (Although newer Adobe applications and the PDF 1.4 format do support transparency, many service bureaus and commercial printers use older imagesetters that do not, because their high cost requires they be used for many years so they can recoup its investment.)

Ideally, your service bureau or commercial printer handles the flattening of your files, so it can optimize the results for its equipment. If you send the service bureau native Creative Suite files or PDF 1.4 or later output, the bureau's staff should be able to work with the native transparency and do the flattening. Otherwise, it has to live with the flattening results you create, so be sure to test files to identify any issues early.

When InDesign flattens transparency, it converts the overlapping elements in a stack of transparent objects to a single, flat layer of distinct opaque graphics during output, creating a mosaic of pieces that produce the intended effect.

Creating flattener presets

InDesign comes with three transparency flattening settings — [Low Resolution], [Medium Resolution], and [High Resolution] — which you can edit in the Transparency Flattener Presets dialog box. To open this dialog box, shown in Figure 31.12, choose Edit ➪ Transparency Flattener Presets. The dialog box shows the settings for each preset as you select them. Use this dialog box to create, modify, delete, export (Save), and import (Load) presets. (You cannot modify or delete the three default presets.)

> **NOTE** InDesign uses pixels per inch, or ppi, rather than dpi in the Transparency Flattener Preset Options dialog box. They're equivalent measurements for computer-generated images. InDesign uses ppi for transparency because it's working with the pixels of your images rather than with the dots output by your printer.

FIGURE 31.12

The Transparency Flattener Presets dialog box

FIGURE 31.13

The Transparency Flattener Preset Options dialog box

Figure 31.13 shows the Transparency Flattener Preset Options dialog box, which appears when you create or modify a preset. There's a lot of trial and error in developing transparency flattener presets because the complexity of your documents and the capacity of your output devices will vary widely. But here are some guidelines:

- The most accurate transparency blends are achieved with a Raster/Vector Balance set to 100, which means you should use all vectors rather than convert blends to bitmap images. The [Low Resolution] preset is set at 75, which means that three-quarters of the blends are vectors and one-quarter is converted to bitmaps. The other options have higher vector proportions.

- Flattener resolution should be set to a value that corresponds with your output device's dpi. For Line Art and Text Resolution, 600 ppi or higher is fine, while 150 ppi is fine for gradients and meshes (overlapping transparencies). But the higher the output resolution of your output device, the higher you will make these values.

- If you apply transparency to objects that overprint or underprint text, you likely will select the Convert All Text to Outlines option; otherwise, InDesign may make the text that interacts with transparent objects thicker than text that doesn't.

- Convert Strokes to Outlines has the same effect on lines and strokes for InDesign objects that overlap or underlap objects with transparency.

- The Clip Complex Regions options apply only if the Raster/Vector Balance is less than 100. It corrects for a phenomenon called *stitching,* in which a transparent area has both vectors and bitmaps that create a blocky feel. This option isolates those areas and forces them to be all-vector.

Applying flattener presets

You can apply transparency flattener presets directly to a spread when working on a layout by selecting a spread in the Pages panel (Window ➪ Pages, or ⌘+F12 or Ctrl+F12), and then choosing Spread Flattening ➪ Custom from the flyout menu. You get a dialog box like the Transparency Flattener Presets dialog box (refer to Figure 31.12), except that any settings created here are applied only to the selected spread and are not saved as a preset for use elsewhere.

You can also apply transparency presets globally to your document — overriding any spread settings — in the Advanced pane of the Print dialog box as I describe earlier in this chapter.

Previewing flattener settings

InDesign lets you preview flattening settings, using the Flattener Preview panel. Shown in Figure 31.14, this panel lets you preview transparent objects and their flattening. To open the panel, choose Window ➪ Output ➪ Flattener Preview.

FIGURE 31.14

The Flattener Preview panel

In the panel, you can select what to preview in the Highlight pop-up menu. Your options are None, Rasterized Complex Regions, Transparent Objects, Affected Objects, Affected Graphics, Outlined Strokes, Outlined Text, Raster-Fill Text and Strokes, and All Rasterized Regions. (Note that the rasterized options display overlapping transparent objects that InDesign needs to convert to bitmaps during flattening—not simply any bitmap images in your document.) Choose the area you're concerned may not output at sufficient quality.

 If you enable the Auto Refresh Highlight check box, InDesign updates the preview if you change any settings; if not, you can update the preview by clicking Refresh.

You can also check the flattening results of different presets—just choose a preset from the Preset pop-up menu. Likewise, you can see what would happen to a spread that has a custom flattening applied if you were to override those custom settings—just enable the Ignore Spread Overrides check box.

If you like how the flattening looks, you can preapply them to the Print dialog box by clicking Apply Settings to Print.

Summary

In InDesign you have many options from which to choose to control exactly how your document prints. The right options depend on the document's contents and the output device you're using.

Be sure to define your colors as process colors unless you want them to print on their own plates. Although InDesign lets you convert all colors to process colors when you print, there are times when you want some colors to print on their own plate (these are called *spot colors*) and others to be converted to process, and the only way to make that happen is to define colors as process or as spot in the first place.

InDesign's transparency options let you control how overlapping objects print, as well as how those overlapping areas are handled during output to ensure both quality reproduction and speedy processing.

Chapter 32

Creating Prepress Files

I n this electronic age, there are many reasons not to print a document, at least not directly. You may want to deliver the document to readers in an electronic format, such as in HTML or as Adobe PDF. Or you may want to generate a prepress file that your service bureau can output for you at an imagesetter — one you may send over a network, through the Internet, on a high-capacity disk, or even as an electronic-mail attachment to a device that could be down the hall or in another state.

Selecting the Best Prepress File Option

InDesign has several options for creating prepress files:

- You can export to two variants of the PostScript printing language: Adobe Portable Document Format (PDF) or Encapsulated PostScript (EPS). Service bureaus typically prefer files exported this way.

- You can print to file using all the settings described in Chapter 31 — creating a PostScript output file — rather than output directly to a printer, creating a file tuned specifically to the printer driver that you selected. These output files can cause problems at a service bureau, so you're less likely to use this approach.

CROSS-REF InDesign can also export both individual objects and document pages as JPEG and Scalable Vector Graphics (SVG) graphics files. Chapter 4 explains how to do this.

IN THIS CHAPTER

Evaluating prepress output options

Creating Portable Document Format files

Creating Encapsulated PostScript files

Creating output files

Throughout this chapter, when I say "service bureau," I include commercial printers and internal printing departments.

The export option you pick has several advantages and consequences; here's a look at each choice separately.

Exporting to PDF

This option creates a file that can be linked to a Web page, whether on the Internet or on a corporate intranet. It can also be accessed from a CD or other disk medium, as long as the recipient has the free Adobe Reader program (available for download from www.adobe.com/acrobat). Finally, a service bureau can use a PDF file as the master file from which to print your documents.

This file can include some or all of the fonts, or expect the ultimate output device to have them. You also have control over the resolution of the graphics, which lets you, for example, create a high-resolution file for output on an imagesetter or a low-resolution version for display on the Web.

The PDF file won't have information on the specific printer, so a service bureau could use it on any available output devices. But not all service bureaus are geared to print from PDF files; while this is an increasingly popular option, it is by no means ubiquitous. To print a PDF file directly, the output device must be a PostScript 3 device; otherwise, the service bureau must open the PDF file in Adobe Acrobat or in a high-end PDF-oriented workflow publishing system to then print the file to the output device.

Exporting to EPS

This option creates files that can be sent to many output devices or edited by a PostScript-savvy graphics program like Illustrator, FreeHand, or CorelDraw. With InDesign, you can add a margin for bleeds, but you can't include printer's marks.

Most service bureaus can print directly from EPS files. But note that each page or spread in your InDesign document is exported as a separate EPS file, so a service bureau may prefer a prepress-oriented PostScript file or a PDF file that combines all pages into one file, which simplifies its output effort.

The lack of printer's marks might also bother your commercial printer because it needs them to properly combine film negatives. But some high-end workflow systems can add printer's marks and integrate high-resolution and color-corrected images — so EPS can remain a solid output option provided your service bureau has these capabilities.

If you're creating PDF files, it's best to export just the page or spread you want to use — otherwise, the file contains the data for all other pages, possibly and unnecessarily making its size unwieldy. (When exporting to EPS, a separate file is created for each page or spread, so this is not an issue.)

Using Prepress Files in Your Layout

Exported PDF or EPS files can be imported back into InDesign (or other programs, including QuarkXPress, PageMaker, FreeHand, Illustrator, CorelDraw, Photoshop, Canvas, and Photo-Paint) as graphics. This is handy if you want, for example, to run a small version of the cover on your contents page to give the artist credit, or if you want to show a page from a previous issue in a letters section where readers are commenting on a story. (Chapter 26 explains how to import these files into InDesign.)

Printing to EPS or PostScript files

If you know exactly what device your service bureau will use to output your document, and you know all the settings, you can create an EPS or PostScript output file. All your printer settings from the Print dialog are embedded in that file, making it print reliably only on the target printer.

NOTE Remember to work with your service bureau to understand what their needs and expectations are. Although some output files are fully or partially editable, it's usually not easy to know what might be incorrect in a document until you reach the expensive step of actually printing pages or negatives.

Creating PDF Files

Typically, you want to directly export your InDesign files as PDF files rather than create a PostScript file and translate to PDF using the separate Adobe Acrobat Distiller product. First, I show how to export, and then I explain how to print to PDF on those occasions when that's the better option.

Exporting PDF files

An easy way to create a PDF file from InDesign is to export it by choosing File ➪ Export, or pressing ⌘+E or Ctrl+E. The Export dialog box appears, which, like any standard Save dialog box, lets you name the file and determine what drive and folder it is to be saved in. The key control in the Export dialog box is the Formats pop-up menu, where you choose the format (in this case, Adobe PDF).

The fastest way to create a PDF file is to choose File ➪ PDF Export Presets and then select a preset from the submenu. There are seven presets optimized for different output needs. You can also add your own, as I explain a bit later in this chapter. When you select a preset from the submenu, you then see the Export dialog box. Choosing a preset defaults the Formats pop-up menu to Adobe PDF and preconfigures the PDF export settings covered in the following sections.

TIP If you're working with the InDesign book feature (see Chapter 25), you can export the book's chapters to PDF files from an open book's panel. The setup options are the same as they are for exporting individual documents.

After you've selected Adobe PDF in the Export dialog box's Formats pop-up menu and given the file a name and location, click Save to get the Export Adobe PDF dialog box shown in Figure 32.1. The dialog box has seven panes; General is the one displayed when you open the dialog box.

Common options

There are several common options that are accessible from all seven panes:

- **Adobe PDF Preset pop-up menu:** This pop-up menu lets you select from both predefined sets of PDF-export settings (similar to the printer presets covered in Chapter 31), as well as any presets you may have created. (I describe these presets later in this chapter.)

- **Standard pop-up menu:** This pop-up menu lets you choose which PDF interchange (PDF/X) format to use. For prepress workflow, you might choose one of the PDF/X-1a, PDF/X-3, or PDF/X-4 options in the Standard pop-up menu (the four-digit numbers at the end of the option names refer to the year that any revisions to the standard were added). PDF/X is a standard version of PDF, sanctioned by the International Organization for Standardization (ISO), meant to ensure consistent reproduction across a range of equipment. Irrelevant for on-screen viewing, PDF/X should be used if your service bureau is using compatible equipment. Otherwise, leave this pop-up menu at the default setting of None.

- **Compatibility pop-up menu:** This pop-up menu lets you choose which PDF file version to save the file as. Your options are Acrobat 4 (PDF 1.3), Acrobat 5 (PDF 1.4), Acrobat 6 (PDF 1.5), Acrobat 7 (PDF 1.6), and Acrobat 8 (PDF 1.7). Choosing Acrobat 4 (PDF 1.3) is the best option for documents what will be distributed on CD or over the Web because it ensures the broadest number of people will be able to view the file. But it also limits the ability to use some features, particularly those that protect the document from unauthorized usage, such as copying its contents. Choose a later version only if you're certain your intended recipients use that version of Acrobat or Acrobat Reader. For example, if your company has standardized on Acrobat 6 and the document will be used only internally, it's fine to pick the Acrobat 6 (PDF 1.5) option. Likewise, if you're sending the PDF file to a service bureau, use the version of Acrobat it uses because later versions of Acrobat support more features, especially for commercial printing. (PDF formats 1.5 and later, for example, support native transparency.)

NEW FEATURE Support for Acrobat 8's PDF 1.7 format is new to InDesign CS3.

- **Save Preset button:** Click this to save any settings made in the Export Adobe PDF dialog box as a new preset. (You can also define new PDF presets by choosing File ➪ PDF Export Presets.)

- **Cancel button:** Click this to cancel PDF export.

- **Export button:** Click this to create the PDF file based on the settings selected in the various panes.

The General pane

Use the General pane to determine what is exported. The pane has four sections: Description, Pages, Options, and Include.

In the Description field, type in the description text that you want to appear in the PDF file when it's opened in Adobe Acrobat. The description appears in the Description pane of Acrobat's Document Properties dialog box (File ⇨ Document Properties, or ⌘+D or Ctrl+D).

In the Pages section, you can set the following options:

- **All and Range:** Select All to print all pages or select Range to print a range. If you select Range, you type the desired page range in the Range field. When specifying a range of pages, you can type nonconsecutive ranges, such as 1–4, 7, 10–13, 15, 18, 20. If you want to print from a specific page to the end of the document, just type the hyphen after the initial page number, such as 4–. InDesign figures out what the last page is. Similarly, to start from the first page to a specified page, just start with the hyphen as in –11. InDesign also lets you type absolute page numbers in the Range field. For example, typing +6–+12 prints the document's sixth through twelfth pages, no matter what their page numbers are.

- **Spreads:** When this option is selected, the document prints facing pages on the same sheet of paper, which is handy when showing clients comps, but make sure you have a printer that can handle that large paper size.

TIP You may not want to use the Spreads option when outputting a PDF file for eventual printing on an imagesetter if you have bleeds, because there will be no bleed between the spreads. If you use traditional *perfect-binding* (square spines) or *saddle-stitching* (stapled spines) printing methods in which facing pages are not printed contiguously, do not use this option.

In the Options section, you can select the following options:

- **Embed Page Thumbnails:** Select this option if you're creating a PDF file to be viewed on-screen — these thumbnails help people using the Adobe Reader program navigate your document more easily. But if the PDF files are being sent to a service bureau or commercial printer for printing, there's no need to generate the thumbnails.

- **Optimize for Fast Web View:** Always select this option; this minimizes file size without compromising the output.

- **Create Tagged PDF:** Select this option to embed XML tag information into the PDF file. This is useful for XML-based workflows and Adobe eBooks.

- **View PDF after Exporting:** Select this option if you want to see the results of the PDF export as soon as the export is complete. Typically, however, you should not select this option because you likely have other things you want to do before launching Adobe Reader (or the full Adobe Acrobat program, if you own it) to proof your files.

- **Create Acrobat Layers:** If you selected Acrobat 6 (PDF 1.5) or later in the Compatibility pop-up menu, you can select this option, which outputs any InDesign layers to separate layers in Acrobat. (Acrobat 6 was the first version of Acrobat to support layers.) If you choose a different Compatibility option, Create Acrobat Layers is grayed out.

- **Export Layers:** This pop-up menu gives you additional control over how layers marked as nonprinting are exported to the PDF file. It used to be that if you marked a layer as nonprinting, you would have to leave the Export Adobe PDF dialog box to open the Layers panel to make it exportable. Now, you can skip that step and override layers' non-printing status using this pop-up menu. The default option, Visible & Printable Layers, honors your layers' printing status. Visible Layers exports all visible layers, including those marked as nonprinting. All Layers exports both visible and hidden layers, including those marked as nonprinting. (See Chapter 6 for more on layers.)

NEW FEATURE The ability to override layers' nonprinting status when exporting to PDF files is new to InDesign CS3.

FIGURE 32.1

The General pane of the Export Adobe PDF dialog box

In the Include section, you can select the following options:

- **Bookmarks:** This takes InDesign table-of-contents (TOC) information and preserves it as bookmarks in the exported PDF file.

- **Hyperlinks:** This preserves any hyperlinks added in InDesign. Otherwise, the hyperlinks are converted to standard text. (Chapter 33 explains how to create hyperlinks in InDesign.)

- **Visible Guides and Grids:** This includes the on-screen guides and grids in the output version — an option you'd use only when creating PDF files meant to be used as designer examples, not for readers or for prepress.

- **Non-Printing Objects:** This includes any objects marked as Nonprinting through the Attributes pane (Window ➪ Attributes), as Chapter 10 explains.

- **Interactive Elements:** This preserves interactive objects such as buttons rather than converting them to static graphics.

- **Multimedia:** This pop-up menu lets you control how embedded sound and video are handled. This option is available only if you choose Acrobat 6 (PDF 1.5) or later in the Compatibility pop-up menu and enable the Interactive Elements check box. The options are Use Object Settings, Link All, or Embed All. In InDesign, you can embed a sound or movie file, or link to one. This option lets you override the individual settings and make all such objects embedded or linked.

 Chapter 33 covers interactive documents, including the use of buttons and multimedia elements.

The Compression pane

All the options in this pane, shown in Figure 32.2, compress your document's graphics. For documents you're intending to print professionally, make sure that for Color, Grayscale, and Monochrome image types, the No Sampling Change option is selected (Figure 32.2 shows the option set to Bicubic Downsampling to), and that Compression is set to None. You don't want to do anything that affects the resolution or quality of your bitmap images if you're outputting to a high-resolution device.

But it's fine to select the Crop Image Data to Frames option because this discards portions of pictures not visible on-screen, reducing file size and reducing processing time during output (imagesetters and other devices usually have to process the entire image, even if only part of it is actually printed).

It's also fine to select the Compress Text and Line Art option. It compresses vector graphics (both imported and those created in InDesign) as well as text, but does so without affecting output quality.

The compression settings are more appropriate for documents meant to be viewed online, as I explain in the sidebar "Settings for On-Screen Usage" later in this chapter. You usually leave the image downsampling at 150 pixels per inch (ppi) for color and grayscale images, and at 300 ppi for black-and-white images. Even though a computer monitor's resolution is 72 ppi, you want enough resolution so when a reader zooms in, the images are still clear. A good rule of thumb for documents to be printed is that the downsampling or subsampling ppi for color and grayscale images should be at least double the printer's lpi. (I discuss downsampling and subsampling in the sidebar "Understanding Compression Methods" later in this chapter.)

For the Image Quality setting for images, Medium quality is fine for on-screen documents, but not for documents you intend to let readers print or that will be output at a service bureau. A rule of thumb is to choose High if the documents will be printed on an inkjet or laser printer, and Maximum if they will be printed at an imagesetter or other high-end output device.

FIGURE 32.2

The Compression pane of the Export Adobe PDF dialog box

Note that JPEG compression is *lossy*, meaning it discards data to save space. That's why its Image Quality settings are characterized with subjective terms like Low, Medium, and High. Zip compression is lossless, so no image detail data is discarded. Instead, you limit the color depth by choosing between 4-bit (16 colors) and 8-bit (256 colors).

When Compatibility is set to Acrobat 6 or later (format version 1.5 or later) and Compression is set to Automatic (JPEG 2000), a Tile Size field is available and determines the size of the tiles for progressive display. (For all other options, the tile size is automatically set, and restricted to, 128 pixels.) For large images, this option shows subsequent pieces, or tiles, of the image, until the full image has been displayed, so the reader has a visual indication that the page is in fact loading. You can change the size of the tile from the default of 256 pixels.

> **TIP** You can control whether all bleed margins are changed if any of them is changed by clicking the Make All Settings the Same iconic button: If the chain icon is broken, each can be adjusted separately; if the chain icon is unbroken, changing one changes the others automatically.

The Marks and Bleeds pane

Use the Marks and Bleeds pane, shown in Figure 32.3, to set the page bleed and printer's marks.

You typically set printer's marks only for files meant to be output on an imagesetter or other prepress device. Typically, you should select All Page Marks. Your Offset amount should be the same as or more than the bleed amount — if your Offset is less than the bleed, it's possible the marks could appear in your page's margins.

772

Understanding Compression Methods

The act of choosing a compression method for the color, grayscale, and monochrome images in a PDF is simple — you just pick something from a menu in the Compression pane of the Export Adobe PDF dialog box. The challenge is in knowing what to pick. Take a look at the type of images the compression for which the methods work best, and then choose the one that represents the bulk of the images in your layout.

- Zip compression is appropriate for black-and-white or color images with repeating patterns (usually screen shots or simple images created in paint programs).

- JPEG compression works well for continuous-tone photographs in grayscale or color. JPEG results in smaller files than Zip compression, because it throws out some image data, possibly reducing image accuracy.

- CCITT compression works for black-and-white images or 1-bit images. Group 4 works well for most monochrome images, while Group 3 is good for PDFs that will be faxed electronically.

Downsampling and subsampling accomplish similar goals, but use different mathematic techniques to do so. When you reduce the dpi, you're essentially throwing away image data to make it smaller — for example, replacing a 100-x-100-pixel image with a 25-x-25-pixel version reduces the file size to $1/16$th of its original size. Downsampling averages adjacent pixels' colors and replaces the cluster of adjacent pixels with one averaged pixel as it reduces the image size. (There are two methods for downsampling: bicubic and average. Bicubic usually, but not always, results in a truer image. Average downsampling tends to work better in nonphotographic images, with less minute detail.) Subsampling does no averaging; it simply throws away pixels in between the ones it retains. Downsampling looks better for photographic images with lots of detail and color; subsampling looks better for images with clear color differences and few intricate details.

For prepress purposes, the resolution should be one and a half to two times the line screen ruling used to print the file. For on-screen purposes, keep in mind that higher resolutions are better when users need to increase the view scale in the PDF (for example, if they need to see detail in a map). In the Acrobat support section of www.adobe.com, you can find more details about specific image resolutions that work well with printer resolutions.

If you have elements bleeding off the page, you want a Bleed setting of at least 0p9 (⅛ inch) — that builds in enough forgiveness so that when the pages are folded and trimmed, any elements that bleed off the page, in fact, do so even if there's a slip in the page alignment.

If you specified a slug area (which specifies space for the printing of printer's marks) in the New Document (File ➪ New ➪ Document, or ⌘+N or Ctrl+N) or Document Setup (File ➪ Document Setup, or Option+⌘+P or Ctrl+Alt+P) dialog boxes, select the Include Slug Area option to reserve that space in your PDF file.

Likewise, if you specified bleed settings in the New Document or Document Setup dialog boxes, you can have InDesign use those settings by selecting the Use Document Bleed Settings option.

FIGURE 32.3

The Marks and Bleeds pane of the Export Adobe PDF dialog box

CROSS-REF   **These marks, bleed, and slug options are the same as they are for direct printing and are covered in detail in Chapter 31.**

The Output pane

The Output pane, shown in Figure 32.4, has two sections — Color and PDF/X — where you control color calibration.

In the Color section, you have the following options:

- **Color Conversion:** This pop-up menu lets you choose from among No Color Conversion, which keeps the colors in whatever model in which they were defined; Convert to Destination, which converts them to the printer's color space (typically CMYK); and Repurpose, which converts only colors in objects that have color profiles assigned to them.

- **Destination:** This pop-up menu lets you choose the target output device.

- **Profile Inclusion Policy:** This pop-up menu lets you embed the color profile for the destination device in the PDF file or exclude it. You can choose from Don't Include Profiles, Include All Profiles, Include Tagged Source Profiles, and Include All RGB and Tagged Source CMYK Profiles. (A tagged profile is one that is set in InDesign, as opposed to an object imported with no profile. In other words, any images without profiles do not get the default profile assigned to them.)

FIGURE 32.4

The Output pane of the Export Adobe PDF dialog box

- **Simulate Overprint:** Enable this check box if you're exporting to Acrobat 4 (PDF 1.3) format and have objects overprinting each other (through the Attributes panel). This option is grayed out if you're exporting to Acrobat 5 or later format, because these formats support actual overprinting.

- **Ink Manager:** Click this button to change which color plates print, adjust ink density, and alter trapping sequence. (See Chapter 31 for more on this option, which is also offered when printing.)

In the PDF/X section, you have the following options:

- **Output Intent Profile Name:** If you're exporting with PDF/X compatibility, you can choose which output device or standard to be compatible with through this pop-up menu in the PDF/X section. (Note that whatever you choose here changes Destination popup menu's setting as well.)

- **Output Condition, Output Condition Identifier, and Registry Name:** Depending on the output device or standard you select, you may be able to add device-specific comments in the Output Condition, Output Condition Identifier, and/or Registry Name fields; consult with your service bureau.

CROSS-REF See Chapter 29 for more on color matching, rendering intent, and color trapping settings. See Chapter 31 for more on working with color plates, the Ink Manager, and ink density.

The Advanced pane

Use the Advanced pane, shown in Figure 32.5, to manage font embedding, Open Prepress Interface (OPI) image substitution, and transparency flattening.

The Fonts section lets you control which fonts are included in the PDF file. Including fonts increases the file size but ensures that the document displays or prints correctly, no matter if the recipient has the same fonts the document uses. The Subset Fonts When Percent of Characters Used Is Less Than field tells InDesign how to embed fonts in the exported PDF file. The default value of 100% tells it to include the entire font for each typeface used. This is the best option because it ensures that if your service bureau needs to edit the file later, the file will include all font information. If you choose a lower value and the service bureau changes some text, there's a chance that some characters used in the editing won't be in the file.

The value is a threshold, telling InDesign that if the file uses less than that percentage of the font's characters, to embed just the characters used; or, if the file uses more than that percentage, to embed them all. If your document uses many fonts but just a few characters in each, you might want to pick a value like 35%, because there is less chance that you will have typos in such documents (they tend to be ads and posters that are heavily proofed beforehand).

You can use a lower threshold for documents to be viewed solely on-screen because you don't expect readers to edit the files. In fact, you may lock the file to prevent such modification.

> **NOTE**   Some fonts can be locked, preventing their inclusion in PDF files. To avoid that problem, simply don't use them.

In the OPI section, use the three options in the Omit for OPI section to strip out EPS, PDF, and/or bitmap images — you would use this only if you had high-resolution or color-corrected versions of these files at a service bureau and wanted the bureau to substitute those files for the lower-resolution placeholder files you used during layout.

In the Transparency Flattener section, if you are exporting to Acrobat 4 (PDF 1.3) format, you can select a transparency preset, as well as override any transparency settings applied to individual spreads. Transparency flattening reduces the complexity of documents that have lots of transparent and semitransparent objects overlapping each other, which can dramatically increase output time and even prevent printing. If you are exporting to later versions of Acrobat, InDesign's flattening settings are passed on unchanged.

> **CROSS-REF**   See Chapter 31 for more on OPI and transparency flattening.

Finally, the Create JDF File Using Acrobat option essentially passes on the instructions for the PDF creation onto Adobe Acrobat Professional 7 or 8 (which must be installed on your system) and has it actually implement them. This gives the service bureau (or whoever is producing the final file) the job instructions separate from the underlying data, so the instructions can be changed as needed. Otherwise, the PDF file produced in InDesign cannot be changed unless you regenerate it in InDesign. Note that job definition files (JDFs) work only with the new Acrobat Professional 7 or 8 software, so this option is useless for organizations using earlier versions of Acrobat.

The Advanced pane of the Export Adobe PDF dialog box

The Security pane

The Security pane, shown in Figure 32.6, has no relevance to documents intended to be output at a service bureau or commercial printer, so make sure the Require a Password to Open the Document and the Use a Password to Restrict Printing, Editing, and Other Tasks options are not selected in that case.

These settings are useful if you're publishing the document electronically, because they control who can access the document and what they can do with the document once it's open. Here's how they work:

- **Encryption Level:** This section's options depend on the option set in the Compatibility pop-up menu; Acrobat 5 (PDF 1.4) or higher use High (128-Bit RC4) encryption, while earlier versions use 40-bit RC4.

- **Document Open Password:** In this section of the Security pane, you can require a password to open the exported PDF file by selecting this option and typing a password in the associated text field. If no password is typed here, you're forced to type one in a dialog box that appears later. To access protected content, recipients must use the Security pane in Acrobat (File ➪ Document Properties, or ⌘+D or Ctrl+D).

The Security pane of the Export Adobe PDF dialog box

- **Use a Password to Restrict Printing, Editing, and Other Tasks:** You can restrict recipients' actions by selecting this option and then specifying permissible actions by using the Printing Allowed and Changes Allowed pop-up menus, as well as selecting from among the options that follow. You can also require a password to allow editing of the file in another application.

  - **Printing Allowed:** You can choose None, Low-Resolution (150 dpi), and High Resolution.

  - **Changes Allowed:** You can choose None; Inserting, Deleting, and Rotating Pages; Filling in Form Fields and Signing; Commenting, Filling in Forms Fields, and Signing; and Any Except Extract Pages. (*Signing* means using digital signatures to verify sender and recipient identities.)

  - **Enable Copying of Text, Images, and Other Content:** If it's okay for recipients to use the PDF file's objects, enable this check box.

  - **Enable Text Access of Screen Reader Devices for the Visually Impaired:** If you are exporting to Acrobat 5 (PDF 1.4) or later and if you want the file to be accessible to visually impaired recipients that read text aloud, enable this check box. Note that this option is visible only if you are exporting to Acrobat 4 (PDF 1.3) or later.

  - **Enable Plaintext Metadata:** For documents with *metadata* — authoring information associated with XML documents and Web pages — you can make that metadata visible to Web-based search engines and similar applications by enabling this check box. Note that this option is visible only if you are exporting to Acrobat 6 (PDF 1.5) or later.

Settings for On-Screen Usage

If your output is destined for use on a monitor—such as from CD, on the Web, or in a corporate intranet—the settings you choose differ from the print-oriented ones described in the "Exporting PDF files" section. Here's what you need to do:

- In the PDF Options pane, change the Color pop-up menu to RGB, change the Images pop-up menu to Low Resolution, and select the Generate Thumbnails option. This optimizes the color and file size for on-screen display.

- In the Compression pane, choose Downsample to or Subsample to in all three image types' sections. The dpi value should be either 72 (if you intend people just to view the images on-screen) or 300 or 600 (if you expect people to print the documents to a local inkjet or laser printer—pick the dpi value that best matches most users' printers' capabilities). For the Compression pop-up menus, choose Automatic for the color and grayscale bitmaps, and CCITT Group 3 (the standard method for fax compression) for black-and-white bitmaps. Set Image Quality to Maximum for color and grayscale bitmaps. Finally, enable the Compress Text and Line Art check box.

- In the Marks and Bleeds pane, make sure no printer's marks are selected. Select Reader's Spreads if your facing pages are designed as one visual unit.

- In the Security pane, select User Security features and the options for which you want to add security. Use the Printing and Copying Text and Graphics options to prevent readers from copying and pasting your content, or to prevent printing—this is particularly aimed at Web-based readers of publicly distributed documents. The Changing the Document and Adding or Changing Notes and Form Fields options are meant for internally distributed documents, where you don't want a recipient who has the Acrobat program to modify the PDF file and then pass it on to someone else who might not realize it was altered. Similarly, you typically would use the passwords only for documents distributed internally, where you don't want all employees to have access to all documents. For Web-based documents, the presumption is that a page and its content are meant for public consumption unless the whole page has a password required, so these settings are usually irrelevant.

The Summary pane

The final Export Adobe PDF dialog box pane is the Summary pane shown in Figure 32.7. It simply lists your settings all in one place for easy review. The only option—Save Summary—saves the settings to a file so you can include it with your files when delivering them to a service bureau, or for distribution to other staff members so they know the preferred settings.

Using Distiller job options

In addition to setting up PDF export presets as I describe in the last section, InDesign lets you import such settings from Acrobat Distiller job-options files. You can load such job-option files by clicking Load in the Adobe PDF Presets dialog box (choose File ➪ PDF Export Presets ➪ Define) or simply by opening them in the Open a File dialog box (choose File ➪ Open, or press ⌘+O or Ctrl+O).

FIGURE 32.7

The Summary pane of the Export Adobe PDF dialog box

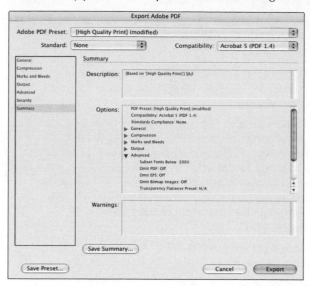

You can also create and edit these job-option files in this dialog box for sharing with Acrobat Distiller and other Creative Suite 2 or 3 users; click Save to save them for use by others. Figure 32.8 shows the dialog box.

Printing to PDF files

Sometimes, you may want to create a PDF file when printing, such as to save printer-specific options in the file. Note that, using this method, you need the $449 Adobe Acrobat Professional software to create a PDF file for prepress output, or the $299 Acrobat Standard for documents meant for display on-screen and printing on inkjet, laser, and other medium-resolution printers. Both include the Acrobat Distiller program that creates PDF files. (The free Adobe Reader is only for viewing PDF files and, in version 7 and later, for making comments viewable only by other version 7 or later users.)

CAUTION   Mac OS X can create PDF files without you having to buy Acrobat: Choose the PDF button in the Mac OS X's Print dialog box (get there by clicking Printer in InDesign's Print dialog box) to have the Mac OS create a generic-quality PDF file. But that file may not be print-quality, and you will not be able to set specific printer options as you can using the steps in this section.

FIGURE 32.8

The Adobe PDF Presets dialog box. When creating or editing these PDF presets, you get the same options described in the previous section for the Export PDF dialog box.

Set up your Print dialog box settings as described in Chapter 31, but don't click Print. Instead, follow these steps:

1. **Whether you use a Macintosh or a Windows PC, open the Acrobat Distiller program.** In Acrobat Distiller 4 and 5, choose Settings ⇨ Job Options to set the output options. In Acrobat Distiller 6 and later, choose a setting from the Default Settings pop-up menu in the Acrobat Distiller dialog box. Then go back to the InDesign Print dialog box.

2. **The process to actually print the file depends on your operating system:**

   ▪ In Mac OS X 10.4 (Tiger) and 10.5 (Leopard), click the Printer button, choose the Output Options menu item from the pop-up menu in the resulting dialog box, and then select the Save as File option, choose the file format (PDF) from the Format pop-up menu, and click Save. The Save to File dialog box appears.

   ▪ In Windows XP and Vista, select Acrobat Distiller from the Printer pop-up menu, and click Print. In a few seconds, a new window appears asking for a filename and file location.

3. **Choose the filename and location, and then click Save to save the file.**

You can also create PDF files by exporting to an EPS or a PostScript file, and then using the Acrobat Distiller program to convert the file to PDF. There's no need to do this if you have InDesign unless you happen to have EPS or PostScript files you've previously generated that you'd rather convert to PDF through Distiller than find the InDesign originals and export PDFs from InDesign. You can, of course, use Distiller to create PDFs from any PostScript or EPS file, no matter what program created it.

Exporting EPS Files

To create an EPS file from InDesign, choose File ➪ Export, or press ⌘+E or Ctrl+E. The Export dialog box appears, which, like any standard Save dialog box, lets you name the file and determine on what drive and in what folder the file is to be saved in. The key control in the Export dialog box is the Formats pop-up menu, where you choose the format (EPS, in this case).

After you've selected EPS in the Export dialog box's Formats pop-up menu, and given the file a name and location, click Save to get the Export EPS dialog box, shown in Figure 32.9. The dialog box has two panes; the General pane is displayed when you open the dialog box.

 PLATFORM DIFFERENCES The Formats pop-up menu is labeled Save as Type in Windows, but only if you are not using the Version Cue–style dialog boxes (see Chapter 4).

The General pane

Most export options are in the General pane.

FIGURE 32.9

The General pane of the Export EPS dialog box

Export EPS

| General | Advanced |

Pages
- ● All Pages
- ○ Ranges: a-28
- ☐ Spreads

PostScript®: Level 2
Color: CMYK
Preview: TIFF
Embed Fonts: Subset
Data Format: ASCII

Bleed
Top: 0 in   Inside: 0 in
Bottom: 0 in   Outside: 0 in

Cancel   Export

In the Pages section, you can set the following options:

■ **All Pages:** Select this option to print all pages in a document.

■ **Ranges:** Select this option when specifying a range of pages that you want to print. You can type nonconsecutive ranges, such as 1–4, 7, 10–13, 15, 18, 20. If you want to print from a specific page to the end of the document, just type the hyphen after the initial page number, such as 4–. InDesign figures out what the last page is. Similarly, to start from the first page to a specified page, just start with the hyphen as in –11. InDesign lets you type absolute page numbers in the Range field. For example, typing +6–+12 prints the document's sixth through twelfth pages, no matter what their page numbers are.

■ **Spreads:** Select this option to print facing pages on the same sheet of paper — this is handy when showing clients comps, but make sure you have a printer that can handle that large paper size.

TIP You may not want to use the Spreads option when outputting an EPS file for eventual printing on an imagesetter if you have bleeds because there will be no bleed between the spreads. If you use traditional *perfect-binding* (square spines) or *saddle-stitching* (stapled spines) printing methods in which facing pages are not printed contiguously, do not use this option.

The unnamed, middle section of the pane controls the handling of fundamental elements: PostScript version, graphics, and fonts. Here are the options:

■ **PostScript:** Use this pop-up menu to choose the version of the PostScript language to use in creating the EPS file: The Level 2 option works on a PostScript Level 2 or later printer (the majority in professional environments), while Level 3 works only on the newer PostScript 3 devices, which can include built-in color calibration, color separation, and trapping. Be sure to ask whoever is outputting your files which version to use.

■ **Color:** Use this pop-up menu to determine what happens to colors; your options are CMYK (for commercial printing), RGB (for online display), Gray (for black-and-white printing), or PostScript Color Management (which lets the output device figure out what to do with the colors based on the PostScript settings in the EPS file). For commercial printing, choose either CMYK or PostScript Color Management, depending on your service bureau's recommendations and the capabilities of its output devices. If your file uses spot colors, you want to use PostScript Color Management so they aren't converted to process colors, but the service bureau will need to have a printer that can handle that format.

■ **Preview:** This pop-up menu lets you choose the format for the EPS file's on-screen preview, which is what you see on-screen when you place an EPS file in a program like InDesign, Adobe Illustrator, QuarkXPress, or Macromedia FreeHand. Your options are None, TIFF, and — on the Mac only — PICT. TIFF is a safe option if you use recent versions of image editing, desktop publishing, and illustration programs. (You may need to select PICT to see the preview in older Mac programs.)

■ **Embed Fonts:** Use this pop-up menu to determine whether all fonts, no fonts, or just the characters used are embedded into the documents; the corresponding menu options are Complete, None, and Subset. Complete is the best option because it ensures that if your service bureau needs to edit the file later, the file includes all font information. If you choose Subset and the service bureau changes some text when editing the EPS file (such as to fix a typo), there's a chance that some characters used in the editing aren't in the file. Use None only if the service bureau has all the fonts you use and knows to load them into the printer before outputting this file.

- **Data Format:** Use this pop-up menu to select ASCII or Binary. The ASCII option creates a larger file but can be edited by someone who understands the PostScript language; the Binary option creates a smaller file that is not editable. The one you choose depends on whether you want or expect your service bureau or commercial printer to try to fix any problems in your file encountered during output. Be sure to talk to those people up front, so you and they agree on whether such efforts should be made.

In the Bleed section, you can set the bleed area for the Top, Bottom, Left, and Right sides of the page. If you have elements bleeding off the page, you want a bleed setting of at least 0p9 (⅛ inch); that builds in enough forgiveness so that, when the pages are folded and trimmed, any elements that bleed off the page will in fact do so, even if there's a slip in the page alignment.

NEW FEATURE You can now control whether all bleed margins are changed if any of them is changed by clicking the Make All Settings the Same iconic button. If the chain icon is broken, each can be adjusted separately; if the chain icon is unbroken, changing one changes the others automatically.

The Export EPS option does not let you use any bleed settings you may have set in the New Document (File ➪ New ➪ Document, or ⌘+N or Ctrl+N) or Document Setup (File ➪ Document Setup, or Option+⌘+P or Ctrl+Alt+P) dialog boxes. That's odd, because the Export PDF (File ➪ Export, or ⌘+E or Ctrl+E) and Print (File ➪ Print, or ⌘+P or Ctrl+P) dialog boxes *do* let you use those document settings.

The Advanced pane

The Advanced pane contains specialty settings affecting image substitution, transparency flattening, and color plates. Figure 32.10 shows the pane.

The options are:

- **Send Data:** In the Images section's Send Data pop-up menu, you can select either All or Proxy. Use the All option (the default) for all documents that will be printed, even if you're publishing the file electronically (on a CD or through the Web). Use Proxy (which sends a low-resolution, on-screen preview version of the document's images) only for documents that are viewed on-screen and not printed (or where you don't care that the printouts have low-quality graphics).

CROSS-REF See Chapter 31 for more on OPI and transparency flattening, as well as overprint simulation and the Ink Manager.

- **OPI Image Replacement:** In the OPI section, select the OPI Image Replacement option if you're using Open Prepress Interface (OPI) image substitution, in which the high-resolution files are stored elsewhere and the layout uses for-position-only versions to save drive space and save screen redraw time. You can also use the three options in the Omit for

OPI section to specify which images should be stripped out: EPS, PDF, and/or Bitmap Images. You would use this only if you have high-resolution or color-corrected versions of these files at a service bureau and want it to substitute those files for the lower-resolution placeholder files you used during layout. By omitting these graphics files from the EPS file, you make the EPS file much smaller.

- **Preset:** In the Transparency Flattener section, you can select a transparency preset as well as override any transparency settings applied to individual spreads. Transparency flattening reduces the complexity of documents that have lots of transparent and semitransparent objects overlapping each other, which can dramatically increase output time and even prevent printing. Select the Ignore Spread Overrides option to tell InDesign to ignore any transparency flattener overrides you may have made to specific spreads in the Pages panel (Window ➪ Pages, or ⌘+F12 or Ctrl+F12).

- **Ink Manager:** At the bottom of the pane, click Ink Manager to change which color plates print, adjust ink density, and alter trapping sequence.

FIGURE 32.10

The Advanced pane of the Export EPS dialog box

Creating Output Files

Service bureaus generally don't want to receive an output file, since they have little or no control over it, and mistakes you make could harm the output quality or even prevent printing. But sometimes, this option is what the service bureau wants, based on its equipment and expertise.

CAUTION   Do not send an output file to your service bureau unless the service bureau requests it and also provides the PPD file and output instructions.

To create an output file, you have two options. The simplest is to choose PostScript File from the Printer pop-up menu in the Print dialog box, as well as the appropriate PostScript Printer Description using the PPD pop-up menu (this should be the PPD for the ultimate output device). Then set the various options in the Print dialog's panes and click Save when done (the Print button becomes Save when you choose PostScript File in the Printer pop-up menu).

The other method is to print to file. *After* setting all the appropriate attributes in the Print dialog box (File ⇨ Print, or ⌘+P or Ctrl+P), do the following, as appropriate for your platform:

- In Mac OS X 10.4 (Tiger) and 10,5 (Leopard), click Printer, choose the Output Options menu item from the unnamed (third) pop-up menu in the resulting dialog box, then select the Save as File Option, choose the file format (PostScript, in this case) from the Format pop-up menu, and click Save. Note that not all printers have this Output Options menu item, so you may need to choose the PDF button instead in this dialog box to get a generic-quality PDF file.

- In Windows XP and Vista, click Setup and then enable the Print to File check box in the resulting dialog box and click Print.

Summary

In many cases, you want to generate an output file that ensures that your service bureau prints your document exactly as you want it, with no chance to accidentally make a change to your InDesign document. The service bureau's equipment dictates in most cases the format of these output files: EPS, PDF, or PostScript. Each option has pros and cons, and varying levels of controls, so be sure to use the option that gives you the most control and works with your service bureau's equipment.

Part VIII

Electronic Publishing Techniques

IN THIS PART

Chapter 33
Creating Electronic Documents

Chapter 34
Working with XML

Chapter 33

Creating Electronic Documents

In most respects, a document is a document is a document. But in today's electronic world, documents have evolved to include more than the text and graphics that have comprised documents for centuries. Not only can you print documents the traditional way, but also you can deliver them electronically as Adobe Portable Document Format (PDF) files, as files in the Web's XHTML format, and as Adobe eBook "digital edition" files. And that electronic delivery format permits a degree of interactivity never possible in printed documents, including hyperlinks, automated page actions, and the use of audio and video objects.

You create interactive documents just as you create print documents. InDesign's interactive functions work with those traditional capabilities — there's no special "interactive" mode to work under.

CROSS-REF Chapter 32 covers how to export InDesign documents to PDF files.

IN THIS CHAPTER

Working with hyperlinks

Creating bookmarks

Adding page actions

Working with audio and video objects

Exporting to Web pages

Exporting eBooks

Using Hyperlinks

The most common attribute you add to a print document to make it more useful when it's distributed electronically is hyperlinks. Web pages, eBook files, and PDF files can include these hot spots that, when clicked, direct a browser to open a new file or page. It's a whole new way to deliver related contents through an active cross-reference.

InDesign uses its Hyperlinks panel (Window ➪ Interactive ➪ Hyperlinks) to add, edit, and delete hyperlinks. In a sense, a hyperlink is a character attribute — it's applied to selected text. Figure 33.1 shows the Hyperlinks panel and its flyout menu.

FIGURE 33.1

The Hyperlinks panel and its flyout menu

Go to Hyperlink Source

Go to Hyperlink Destination

Create New Hyperlink

Delete Selected Hyperlinks

Creating hyperlinks

Although the process is straightforward, InDesign's terminology can make it a bit confusing on how to start. You first create a hyperlink destination — the place a hyperlinks goes to, or its *target* — by selecting the destination, such as text or an object, and then choosing New Hyperlink Destination from the Hyperlinks panel's flyout menu. Figure 33.2 shows the dialog box. You give the destination a name in the Name field and then choose from one of the three options in the Type menu:

- **Page:** This option lets you specify a specific page in a selected document. If you select this option, InDesign provides a Page field in which you specify the page number to open in the selected document, as well as the Zoom Setting pop-up menu, which lets you select how the page is displayed. (Options are Fixed, meaning at the default size in Adobe Reader; Fit View; Fit in Window; Fit Width; Fit Height; Fit Visible; and Inherit Zoom, which uses the current zoom setting in Adobe Reader.)

- **Text Anchor:** This option lets you specify a specific piece of text in the selected document. This would be the selected text.

- **URL:** This is a Web page address (the official name is Uniform Resource Locator), as shown in the New Hyperlink dialog box in Figure 33.2. If you select this option, InDesign displays the URL field in which you type the Web address.

With the destinations defined, you can now create the hyperlinks — the things that readers will actually click — to them. InDesign calls these the hyperlink *sources*. To create a hyperlink source:

1. **Select the text or object that you want to be a hyperlink's source, and then choose New Hyperlink from the Hyperlinks panel's flyout menu.** That opens the New Hyperlink dialog box, as shown in Figure 33.3.

FIGURE 33.2

The New Hyperlink Destination dialog box's three variants, selected via the Type pop-up menu, are (from top to bottom) URL, Page, and Text Anchor.

FIGURE 33.3

The New Hyperlink dialog box

Linking to Other Documents

The process for linking to other documents depends on whether those documents are on the Web or on a CD or internal server.

If you want to create a hyperlink to another document, such as on a CD or server, you can't use the New Hyperlink Destination dialog box. That's because the destination is not in your current document, so there is nothing to link to from within that document.

Instead, you must select the object that you are linking from in the New Hyperlink dialog box, using the Document pop-up menu to select Browse and then locate the destination file. Unintuitively, you must browse for the actual InDesign file to which you want to link — you cannot link to an existing PDF file. But the link is actually to the PDF version of that file, which means you must be sure to create the PDF of that other InDesign document and use the same filename, except for the filename extension. For example, if you link to ITWForm.indd, the link is actually to ITWForm.pdf. This approach severely limits your ability to link to external files.

But there is a workaround. You can set hyperlinks (as opposed to hyperlink destinations) that link to any object available on a Web server, including PDF files. Thus, you would simply create a hyperlink to a Web address, such as `www.InDesignCentral.com/i/Safer_Computing.pdf`, in the New Hyperlink dialog box. Note that such Web links cannot be made to specific pages inside a PDF file unless you have created a bookmark within that PDF file (using Adobe Acrobat Professional or InDesign). If such a bookmark exists, you treat it like a standard anchor link (adding *#name* after the URL, such as `www.InDesignCentral.com/i/Safer_Computing.pdf#help` to go to the text bookmarked as `help`).

2. **Type a name for the hyperlink source.** This lets you apply the same link to more than one location in your document — sort of a character style for hyperlinks. If the name already exists, an error message appears when you click OK — there's no way to know ahead of time if the name has already been used in the document.

3. **If the hyperlink is to another InDesign document, you can select that document by choosing Browse from the Document pop-up menu.**

4. **Use the Type pop-up menu to determine what you're hyperlinking to.** You have the same three options as in the New Hyperlink Destination dialog box's Type pop-up menu — Page, Text Anchor, and URL — as well as All Types, which, if chosen, displays previously defined hyperlinks in the document.

5. **Use the Name pop-up menu to select a previously defined hyperlink destination (target) or an anchor.** You can also create a hyperlink to an unnamed destination by leaving the Name pop-up menu set to [None].

CAUTION I advise against the method described in Step 5 because that hyperlink destination doesn't appear in the menu for future hyperlink sources, making it hard to modify later.

6. **In the Appearance section, you can control how the hyperlink appears on-screen:**

   ▪ Use the Type pop-up menu to choose Invisible Rectangle or Visible Rectangle. The Invisible Rectangle option gives no visual indication that the text contains a hyperlink, except that the mouse pointer becomes a hand icon when the reader maneuvers through the document. (You would typically pick this option when you've used blue underline as a character attribute for the hyperlink text to mirror the standard Web way of indicating a hyperlink.) The Visible Rectangle option puts a box around the text using the four settings I describe next (they are grayed out if Invisible Rectangle is selected).

   ▪ The Highlight pop-up menu lets you choose how the source text or frame is highlighted: None, Invert (reserves the foreground and background colors), Outline (places a line around the source), and Inset (places a line around the source, but inside any frame stroke; for text, it's the same as Outline.

   ▪ The Color pop-up menu displays Web-safe colors, as well as any colors you defined in the document.

   ▪ The Width pop-up menu lets you choose the thickness of the line used in the Outline and Inset options from the Highlight pop-up menu. The choices are Thin, Medium, and Thick.

   ▪ The Style pop-up menu lets you choose the type of line; the choices are Solid or Dashed.

TIP If your text includes a valid hyperlink, such as www.InDesignCentral.com, you can select it and create a URL hyperlink automatically by choosing New Hyperlink from URL in the Hyperlinks panel's flyout menu.

Once your hyperlink sources are defined, you can easily apply them by selecting text and clicking an existing hyperlink source from the Hyperlinks panel. You can also jump to the source or destination by selecting the desired hyperlink in the Hyperlinks panel and choosing either Go to Source or Go to Destination from the flyout menu, or by clicking the Go to Hyperlink Source or Go to Hyperlink Destination iconic buttons at the bottom of the panel. These make a handy way to verify the hyperlinks are correct.

Modifying and deleting hyperlinks

It's also easy to modify hyperlinks: Choose Hyperlink Options from the Hyperlinks panel's flyout menu to open the Hyperlink Options dialog box, which has the same options as the New Hyperlinks dialog box, shown in Figure 33.3, to modify the source. Similarly, to modify hyperlink destinations, choose Hyperlink Destination Options from the flyout menu to open the Hyperlink Destination Options dialog box, and then select the target from the Name pop-up menu. The Hyperlink Destination Options dialog box's options are the same as the New Hyperlink Destination dialog box shown in Figure 33.2.

You can change the source text or frame by selecting it, then clicking the hyperlink name in the Hyperlinks panel, and finally choosing Reset Hyperlink from the panel's flyout menu. To change the target for a hyperlink to an InDesign document, choose Update Hyperlink from the flyout menu (press and hold Option or Alt to select a file that is not open).

To delete a hyperlink destination, choose it in the Hyperlink Destination Options dialog box, and then click Delete. (Click Delete All to delete all destinations defined in the document.)

To delete a hypertext source, select it in the Hyperlinks panel and then choose Delete Hyperlink from the flyout menu or click the Delete Selected Hyperlinks iconic button at the bottom of the panel.

NOTE When you export your InDesign files to PDF files (as described in Chapter 32), be sure to select the Hyperlinks option in the Include section of the General pane in the Export PDF dialog box (File ➪ Export, or ⌘+E or Ctrl+E, and then choose Adobe PDF in the Format or Save as Type pop-up menu).

Creating Bookmarks

Bookmarks are an indexing mechanism used in Adobe PDF files. They typically act like tables of contents, letting you view the organization of a document through a set of clickable headings. Figure 33.4 shows an example file viewed in Adobe Reader.

InDesign has two ways to create bookmark entries. One is simply to create a table of contents using the standard InDesign table-of-contents tool. (Be sure that the Create PDF Bookmarks option is selected in the Table of Contents dialog box.) The other is to specify bookmarks to specific pages, objects, and/or text using the Bookmarks panel. Figure 33.5 shows the Bookmarks panel (Window ➪ Interactive ➪ Bookmarks) and its flyout menu.

CROSS-REF Chapter 24 covers the table of contents feature.

To create your own bookmark entries — either instead of or in addition to having InDesign use the table of contents — select what you want the bookmark to refer to (what will appear on-screen in the PDF file when a user clicks the bookmark in Acrobat or Adobe Reader). This can be a text selection or an object (frame or line); if nothing is selected, the bookmark is to the current page. Then choose New Bookmark from the Bookmarks panel's flyout menu, or click the Add Bookmarks iconic button — the page icon — at the bottom of the panel. After you create the bookmark, use the Rename Bookmark menu option to give it a meaningful name; this is the name that appears in the Bookmarks pane in Acrobat or Adobe Reader.

FIGURE 33.4

An example PDF document with bookmarks (at left)

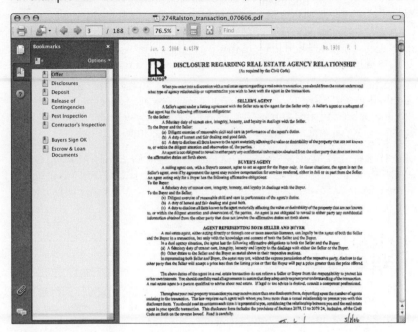

FIGURE 33.5

The Bookmarks panel and its flyout menu

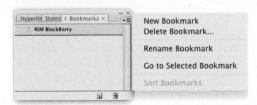

If you want a bookmark to be a subentry of another bookmark — the equivalent to a second-level or third-level headline in a table of contents — make sure that, before you create the bookmark, you select a bookmark in the Bookmarks panel. Any new bookmark is made a child of the selected bookmark.

The other Bookmarks panel flyout menu options are straightforward:

- Choose Delete Bookmark to delete any bookmarks selected in the panel. (You can also click the Delete Bookmarks iconic button — the trashcan icon — at the bottom of the panel.)

- Choose Go to Selected Bookmark to jump to that page in your InDesign document. An easier way is to simply double-click the bookmark entry in the pane.

- Choose Sort Benchmarks to sort benchmark subentries — this alphabetizes second-level, third-level, and other page-based subentries, and it sorts in order of appearance on the page any text- and/or object-based entries. It does not sort the top-level bookmarks, which appear in sequential order from the beginning of the document.

However you create your bookmarks, InDesign places them into your PDF file during PDF export — if you tell it to. In the PDF Export dialog box (choose File ➪ Export, or press ⌘+E or Ctrl+E, and choose Adobe PDF in the Format or Save as Type pop-up menu), make sure the Bookmarks check box is enabled in the General pane's Include section.

Creating Page Actions

One underused feature of the PDF format is the ability to set page actions. Most people simply create PDF files that are on-screen versions of the print document — static representations — but PDF files can include forms, buttons, and other interactive elements. One reason for the under use of page actions is that few tools let you create the placeholder items for them, and adding them in Acrobat Standard or Acrobat Professional is awkward — they really work best when they're created in the program that creates the whole document. InDesign addresses this reality with its support for interactive features.

Creating buttons

In InDesign, you use the States panel to create buttons and other objects that have actions associated with them.

The first thing you do is draw a button using the Button tool. A button is essentially a rectangular frame. Once it's created, you can resize and manipulate it like any other frame (including adding text and graphics), though you cannot create nonrectangular shapes.

> **TIP** You can convert an existing frame or shape — but not lines, open or closed paths, or text selections — to a button by choosing Object ➪ Interactive ➪ Convert to Button. This approach lets you use nonrectangular objects as your buttons.

After you create the button shape, you should immediately choose its appearance, using the Appearance pop-up menu in the States panel (Windows ➪ Interactive ➪ States). It's imperative that you choose the appearance now, because if you later change the appearance, any formatting (including text and graphics placement) you applied to the button are wiped out.

The Appearance pop-up menu options include None (to create a transparent button, such as a hot spot over part of an existing graphic), Drop Shadow, Glow, Bevel, and Custom.

 Choose Panel Options from the flyout menu to get a dialog box in which you choose the size of the button states' preview icons.

Creating states

If you selected any option other than None in the Appearance pop-up menu, InDesign has already created the states for you. Otherwise, once you've created your initial button, you create the states for the button by choosing New State from the States panel's flyout menu or by clicking the Create Optional State iconic button at the bottom of the panel. You always have an Up state when you create a button. You get a Rollover state the first time you choose New States and a Down state the second time. You can have only these three states for any button.

The states correspond to mouse actions:

- Up is what displays and occurs when you don't have the mouse over the button, or when you release the mouse button after pressing the button — the default appearance and action.

- Rollover is what displays and occurs when you pass the mouse over the button but you don't click the mouse onto the button.

- Down is what displays and occurs when you click the button with the mouse.

Note that you need to separately place text or graphics into each state of your button, as well as set any text frame options by selecting each state in the States panel (and then switching to the Type tool if needed to format that state). If you select a specific state's frame with something other than the Selection tool, reselect it with the Selection tool to see the states in the States panel (they disappear when you switch to other tools).

You can also use the panel's controls to place content in a selected state: In the flyout menu, choose Place Content into State, or click the Place Content into Selected State iconic button at the bottom of the panel. The Place dialog box opens, from which to choose a graphic or text file. (Note that the Appearance pop-up menu changes to Custom when you do this.) To remove placed content, choose Delete Content from State from the flyout menu or click the Delete Content of Selected State iconic button.

Figure 33.6 shows the States panel, the three standard states (Up, Rollover, and Down), and an example button.

You can disable or enable any state by deselecting or selecting the check box to its left in the panel. You can also select a state in the panel and choose State Options from the flyout menu to disable or enable the state.

Associating actions

Now comes the fun part: associating the action with the button. To do so, choose Button Options from the flyout menu. You'll get the Button Options dialog box, which defaults to the General pane. In this pane, you provide a name for the button and set the button's visibility in the PDF file you'll later export. The options are self-explanatory: Visible, Hidden, Visible But Doesn't Print, and Hidden But Printable. (You can also open the Button Options dialog box for a selected object by choosing Object ➪ Interactive ➪ Button Options.)

FIGURE 33.6

The States panel, its flyout menu, and an example button (top)

Delete Optional State and Its Content

Create New Optional State

Delete Content of Selected State

Place Content into Selected State

The real action association happens in the Behaviors pane, shown in Figure 33.7. Here, you first select the event that triggers the action using the Events pop-up menu:

- Mouse Up is when you release the mouse after clicking the button.
- Mouse Down is when you click the mouse button.
- Mouse Enter is when you move the mouse pointer over the button.
- Mouse Exit is when you move the mouse pointer away from the button after first passing over it.
- On Focus is when you tab into a form field (because a form field is simply a button, this is similar to Mouse Enter except that it detects keyboard access to the button).
- On Blur is when you tab out of a form field (because a form field is simply a button, this is similar to Mouse Exit except that it detects keyboard departure from the button).

NOTE   You may wonder what happens if you select a specific state before opening the Button Options dialog box. Nothing. It doesn't matter which state is selected in the pane — these are simply previews of the button's appearance based on the mouse status — because the behaviors selected in the Button Options dialog box affect the button as a whole.

FIGURE 33.7

The Button Options dialog box and its Behaviors pane

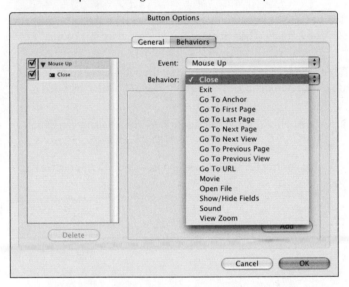

You then choose the action in the Behavior pop-up menu. Most are self-explanatory: Close, Exit, Go to First Page, Go to Last Page, Go to Next Page, Go to Preview Page, Go to Preview View, Go to Anchor, Go to URL, Move, Open File, Sound, and View Zoom. Some of these — Go to Anchor, Go to URL, Movie, Sound, Open File, and View Zoom cause other pop-up menus and fields to appear in the panel, such as to select a file to open or to select a hyperlink or anchor to jump to.

The Show/Hide Fields option is meant for Acrobat forms. InDesign considers every button to be a form field and provides a list of all buttons if you select this option. You can then decide which buttons (form-entry fields in this case) display on the mouse action — you would have only those display that you want to be used as form-entry fields. (To specify the order in which a reader tabs through form fields, select the fields in the form, and then choose Object ➪ Interactive ➪ Set Tab Order, which opens a dialog box in which you can sort the buttons in the order that you want the reader to move through as he or she presses Tab.)

Click Add to add a behavior to this state. You can add multiple behaviors to each state. And each event can have multiple behaviors — just select a new Behavior, and then click Add for each one.

Embedding Movies and Sound

In addition to having a button that opens a movie or sound, you can simply place a movie or sound file in your InDesign document. (Once you've placed the file, you can size it like any other placed graphic: You're essentially sizing the window in which the movie or sound plays.)

InDesign has several limits in what kind of movie and audio files it can import, as well as how those files can be used in exported files:

■ InDesign can open QuickTime (MOV files) and Microsoft AVI movies only, so be sure your movies are in one of those formats. These movies can be used only in exported PDF and eBook files.

■ InDesign also supports Adobe Flash animations (SWF files), though it can export those only to PDF files compatible with Acrobat 6 and later or for use in HTML pages and eBooks.

■ For sounds, it supports just the Apple AIFF and Microsoft WAV formats and can export them only to PDF files.

To control how a movie behaves and what control the reader has, choose Object ⇨ Interactive ⇨ Movie Options, as seen in Figure 33.8.

FIGURE 33.8

The Movie Options dialog box

A faster way to set movie and sound settings is to double-click the frame containing the movie or sound; the Movie Options dialog box or Sound Options dialog box appears, as appropriate.

The Movie Options dialog box

The options in the Movie Options dialog box are straightforward:

- In the Source section, select whether the movie file is copied into your document or simply linked to a URL on the Web or on a CD. If you're embedding the movie file and plan to export the InDesign document as a PDF file that won't be used on a computer with Internet access, be sure to select the Embed Movie in PDF option so everything the user needs is in the PDF file.

- In the Options section, you can change the Poster — the on-screen image inside the frame containing the movie. The default, Default Poster, lets Acrobat choose what displays (usually, it's the first frame of the move). You can also select None (for a blank frame), Standard (for the Adobe logo), Choose Image as Poster (in which case you select an image using the Browse button, such as perhaps the QuickTime logo), or Frame from Movie (to select a specific frame from the movie; not all movies will let you select this option).

- You also set the Mode — Play Once Then Stop, Play Once Stay Open, and Repeat Play — to determine the movie's playback action. Note that the Play Once Stay Open option lets the user choose to play the movie again.

- The Play on Page Turn option, if selected, plays the movie when a reader moves to the page containing it (as opposed to going directly to the page through a hyperlink).

- The Show Controller During Play option displays the QuickTime movie controller to adjust sound volume; pause and resume play; and rewind and fast-forward the movie.

- The Floating Window option puts the movie in a window that the reader can move. If selected, the dialog box also makes two pop-up menus accessible: Size, which determines the size of the window relative to the movie frame size, and Position, which places the floating window on the page.

The Sound Options dialog box

The options in the Sound Options dialog box (shown in Figure 33.9) are also straightforward:

- You can change the sound by clicking Choose to the right of the filename and then selecting a new sound.

- Using the Poster pop-up menu, you can change the placeholder image that appears on the page where you place the sound. Your options are None to have no placeholder image, Standard to have the Adobe logo, and Choose Image as Poster to use an image of your own choice (click Choose to the right of the Poster pop-up menu to select the image file).

FIGURE 33.9

The Sound Options dialog box

- If selected, the Play on Page Turn option automatically plays the sound when someone moves to this page in the exported PDF file.

- If selected, the Do Not Print Poster option hides the poster icon when someone prints the PDF page containing the sound.

- If selected, the Embed Sound in PDF option ensures that the PDF file exported from the InDesign document includes the sound file.

Exporting to the Web

InDesign CS3 lets you export your layouts to the XHTML format that Web editors such as Adobe's Dreamweaver and GoLive can open for further work. (Note that you usually want to do further work in a Web editor both to take advantage of Web-specific formatting options and to rework the layout to better fit the horizontal "page" size of a Web browser.) With InDesign CS3's newfound ability to export to the XHTML format — not just create an XML version specific to Adobe's GoLive Web editor, as in previous versions — you can more easily create Web pages based on print documents.

NEW FEATURE   The ability to export InDesign objects and pages to the Web's XHTML format is new to InDesign CS3.

XHTML is a structured version of the well-known HTML format that adds more consistent structure to make it easier to present pages consistently across Web editors and browsers. You may not have known that your Web editor was creating XHTML-formatted Web pages when you saved your pages — after all, the filename extension remains .htm or .html — but any Web editor worth its salt has been doing that for a few years now.

To export selected objects or the entire layout to XHTML format, simply choose File ➪ Cross-Media Export ➪ XHTML/Dreamweaver. (Despite the name, your files are not limited to use by Adobe's Dreamweaver software). If you want to export just specific items on a page, select them with one of the selection tools before choosing this menu option.

The Save As dialog box opens, where you choose the disk and folder to store the exported Web page, as well as the page's filename. After you click Save, the XHTML Export Options dialog box opens, shown in Figure 33.10, in which you specify how InDesign converts the layout to the Web format.

The following sections describe the options, though be sure to consult with your Web master on preferred settings if you're new to working on a specific Web site's pages.

FIGURE 33.10

The General pane of the XHTML Export Options dialog box

General pane

In the General pane, you choose whether to export the currently selected objects or the entire document by selecting the Selection or Document option. Note that Selection is available only if you had selected one or more objects in your layout before starting the file export.

The other major option in this pane is a set of controls for bulleted and numbered lists formatted using InDesign's bullet and numbering capabilities. The Bullets pop-up menu has two options:

- Map to Unordered Lists, which converts bulleted lists into the Web's bulleted lists (the <ul> type for HTML-savvy readers).
- Convert to Text, which treats the bulleted lists as regular paragraphs, inserting a hard-coded bullet character before each one.

The Numbers pop-up menu has three options:

- Map to Ordered Lists, which converts numbered lists into the Web's numbered lists (the <ol> type).

- Map to Static Ordered Lists, which converts numbered lists into the Web's numbered lists (the <ol> type, with each item's <li> tag specifying the specific number — such as <li value="1@dp> — so if the list items are reordered, the numbering does not change automatically).

- Convert to Text, which treats the numbered lists as regular paragraphs, inserting the numerals as regular characters at the beginning of each one.

Images pane

In the Images pane, shown in Figure 33.11, you choose how your images are converted to the Web's GIF and JPEG formats, selecting options such as image quality and color palette:

- **Copy Images:** Use this pop-up menu to determine how the InDesign document's images are converted when copied to the folder you are saving your XHTML pages to. Your options are Original, which leaves them untouched (meaning that they won't be converted into Web-compatible formats); Optimized, which converts them to the Web format specified in the Image Conversion pop-up menu; and Link to Server Path, which does not copy the file but instead inserts an image link <IMG SRC>) to the current location.

- **Formatted:** Enable this check box to export the images to reflect any modifications made to them in InDesign, such as cropping, transparency, or scaling. Otherwise, the "raw" source files are exported (under the assumption you will manipulate them further in a Web editor or image editor).

- **Image Conversion:** Use this pop-up menu to specify which format images are converted to GIF, JPEG, or Automatic (which selects the best format on a case-by-case basis).

- **GIF Options:** Use the Palette pop-up menu to choose the color palette for the image: Adaptive (No Dither), Web, System (Win), or System (Mac). For Web display, the first two are best; use the other two for pages meant to be displayed on a specific platform, such as pages available only on an internal company Web site. Enable the Interlace check box to speed up the initial screen display of the images while the page is loading, but note that this can slow down overall page loading, so you should use it only with very large images.

- **JPEG Options:** Use the Image Quality pop-up menu to select the image quality and thus the amount of compression (greater compression means lower quality): Low, Medium, High, or Maximum. Use the Format Method pop-up menu to control how the image displays as it loads on the Web page: Baseline (all at once) or Progressive. Note that choosing Progressive can slow down overall page loading, so you should use it only with very large images.

FIGURE 33.11

The Images pane of the XHTML Export Options dialog box

Advanced pane

In the Advanced pane, shown in Figure 33.12, you set how text formatting is converted to the Web's version of styles, called *cascading style sheets*, or *CSS*. The CSS options are:

- **Empty CSS Declarations:** This creates a CSS style list within the document but leaves the formatting unspecified, so your Web designer can specify the actual style specifications using a Web editor. Text that had styles applied have the styles indicated using <p class=> tags for paragraph styles and <span class=> tags for character styles.

- **No CSS:** This ignores style information in the InDesign file, thus placing just simple <p> tags at each paragraph, and stripping out any <span> tags. Essentially, you get unformatted text.

- **External CSS:** This option adds a <link href="name" rel="stylesheet" type="text/css"> tag in the <head> section of the exported file, using the style name specified in the field below the External CSS radio button. (Don't forge the .css filename extension!) This means that once someone creates the specified CSS style file, the document will know what formatting to apply to the text. (Text that had styles applied have the styles indicated using <p class=> tags for paragraph styles and <span class=> tags for character styles.) External CSS style files ensure consistency across multiple Web pages, all of which can call on the same style file. But note that InDesign does not create a style file for you based on your InDesign document's formatting — all style definitions must be done in your Web editing software.

The Advanced pane also lets you specify whether InDesign inserts a `<script type="text/javascript" src="name.js"></script>` tag in the `<head>` section of the exported file, using the script name specified in the field below the Link to External JavaScript check box, which must be enabled for this to work. (Don't forge the .js filename extension!) You must create your JavaScript elsewhere.

FIGURE 33.12

The Advanced pane of the XHTML Export Options dialog box

Working with exported files

After you've adjusted the XHTML Export Options dialog box's settings as desired, click Export to create the XHTML file.

The export process is simple, so it's easy to forget that converting print layouts to the Web's format is rarely a "point and shoot" activity. Expect your Web designer to do major work on those exported pages in his or her Web editing program, to optimize them for the Web environment. That's no reflection on you or InDesign, just the reality of working in different media. Figure 33.13 shows a fairly simple InDesign document and how it appears when exported to XHTML format and opened in Dreamweaver.

Essentially, InDesign is concerned with exporting the text so that the various stories are kept together, that the style names are retained (unless you say not to), and that the images are converted to Web format (unless you say not to). InDesign makes no attempt to preserve the layout — multiple pages are all poured into the one HTML file. Instead, it places each story and each graphic one after the other. Your Web designer then needs to do the layout and formatting work.

It's almost as if you gave the Web designer the original source files for your layout and suggested she start from scratch with those. The difference is that by exporting these files from InDesign, you can be sure that all text changes made in the layout are passed on to the Web designer and that all the graphics are Web-ready.

FIGURE 33.13

The original InDesign layout (top) and how the exported XHTML version appears in Dreamweaver (bottom)

Exporting eBooks

eBooks are essentially a hybrid between the PDF format and the Web HTML format, created by Adobe to make it easy to have visually rich pages on portable electronic book readers. The eBooks format has been around for a while, and previous versions of InDesign let you enable eBooks compatibility when you exported to PDF files.

But eBooks haven't really taken off, so Adobe is reinventing them as a way to get visually rich pages onto the Web, calling the new approach "digital editions." The company hopes the new approach will also make electronic books more palatable.

NEW FEATURE   InDesign CS3 is one of the first applications to support the new "digital editions" type of eBook.

You export InDesign files to the Books format by choosing File ➪ Cross-Media ➪ XHTML/Digital Editions. Choose a filename (the filename extension is automatically set to .epub) and location in the Save As dialog box that appears, then click Save. The XHTML/Digital Editions Export Options dialog box appears, where you specify how formatting and graphics are handled. Figure 33.14 shows the dialog box's two panes: General and Images. Most of these options mirror those you get when exporting to XHTML, as described in the previous section.

The General pane's options are straightforward:

- In the eBook section, enable the Include Metadata check box to include information about the document (set in the File Info dialog box, which you access by choosing File ➪ File Info, or pressing Option+Shift+⌘+I or Ctrl+Alt+Shift+I). This metadata can be helpful for search engines and other Web tools.

- In the CSS section, enable the Export Style Names Only check box to not create a cascading style sheet (CSS) file that contains the style definitions for your text. You would do this when you already have a CSS file created elsewhere whose formatting you want the exported document to use instead. (Of course, the names of the styles in that existing CSS file must match the style names in InDesign for the styles to be applied properly.) If this option is not checked, InDesign creates a CSS file using the style definitions in the InDesign file.

- The Bullets and Numbers section has the same options, and works the same way, as the Bullets and Numbers section of the General pane you see when exporting to XHTML, which the previous section describes.

- If enabled, the View eBook after Exporting check box opens an eBook editor or eBook-compatible browser (if you have one) to display the exported file so you can make sure it looks as you expected.

The Images pane has the same options you get when exporting to XHTML, so refer to the previous section for the details on these options.

After you've set the various options in the se two pages, click Export to create the eBook file.

FIGURE 33.14

FIGURE 33.14

Left: the General pane of the XHTML/Digital Editions Export Options dialog box Right: the Images pane

Summary

InDesign lets you create hyperlinks and anchors within your documents—to Web addresses, pages, and text in your InDesign document, and to pages and text in other InDesign documents— that are then clickable from a PDF file created from your InDesign file.

You can also create buttons that have associated actions—such as opening a movie file, closing a page, changing the zoom level, or moving to a new page—when exported as a PDF or eBook file. InDesign also lets you import movie and sound files that likewise play in exported PDF and eBook files, as well as Flash animations for export to PDF, eBook, or HTML files.

InDesign can export layouts or selected objects to the Web's XHTML format, converting graphics to Web-compatible versions and indicating style usage in text. But these exported files make no attempt to replicate the layout. Instead, InDesign ensures that the Web designer has the latest versions of all the document's contents in a format that the designer can work on directly using a Web editor such as Adobe Dreamweaver.

InDesign can also export entire layouts to the "digital editions" version of eBook files, which provide a richer visual experience than typical Web pages.

Chapter 34

Working with XML

IN THIS CHAPTER

Understanding XML

Creating XML tags in InDesign

Importing XML tags into InDesign

Exporting InDesign documents for use in XML documents

One of the most complex features in InDesign is its set of Extensible Markup Language (XML) features. XML is a structured language that essentially treats document components as data, so you can manage them through a database. The XML tools in InDesign let you treat InDesign documents as sources for XML databases, which are then linked into Web pages, PDF files, CD-ROMs, and so forth. They also let you create InDesign templates into which you flow data from XML files, all formatted and in the proper frames.

The key to XML is the fact that it's extensible. You create the tags, or labels, for various kinds of content (these are called *document type declarations,* or DTDs) based on what makes sense for your content. Then you specify what happens to each of the types of labeled content in terms of what's published, how it's presented, and so forth. Compare that to the more rigid HTML and PDF systems, where there are only certain tags available that cannot be changed, and the presentation is fixed based on the label chosen.

XML code is similar to HTML in the sense that there are tags surrounded by angle brackets (< and >) and that commands and labels are turned on and off (such as <standardHeader> at the beginning of a header item and </standardHeader> at the end of it). Comments begin with <!-- and end with >, while custom commands and declarations (called *processing instructions*) begin with <? and end with ?>. You don't have to understand this level of detail — just keep in mind that there are different codes to look for in examining XML code, if the need arises.

The use of XML will likely involve assistance from a Web master, content engineer, or other programming-savvy person. Page designers might also want to read *Beginning XML, 4th Edition*, or *Professional XML* (both from Wiley Publishing), depending on their level of experience. *Adobe InDesign CS3 Bible* limits itself to an overview of InDesign XML functions and is no substitute for a thorough understanding of XML.

Importing and Creating XML Tags

Chances are that most of the time, you export InDesign documents for use in XML databases, such as converting a publication's articles into a structured format used by a Web site's content management system. To export content properly, you need to apply tags to it. In InDesign, you can do that directly or have InDesign translate style tags into XML tags. You'll use both methods, because some content (such as images) won't have style tags associated with it but will need XML tags for proper processing in an XML database.

Those tags come from two sources: They're imported from a file provided by the Web site's content engineer, or they're created in InDesign by the page designer. Most of the time, you should use tags created by the content engineer, because that engineer is creating a standard set of tags for multiple page designers (both print- and Web-based). You might create your own tags when helping develop the initial tags in concert with that content engineer — or if you also are the content engineer, as well as page designer.

Importing tags

There are two places where you import tags: the Tags panel (Window ➪ Tags) and the Import XML dialog box (File ➪ Import XML). In the Tags panel, shown in Figure 34.1, you use the Load Tags option in the panel's flyout menu to import tags from an XML file or an InDesign document that has tags defined in it. All tags are imported when you choose Load Tags.

The other way to import XML tags is to choose File ➪ Import XML, which imports not only XML tags but also XML content from an XML file. This process works two ways, depending on how your document is set up:

- If your document has no content, importing an XML file adds the XML tags to the Tags panel and into the document's Structure window (covered later in this chapter). It also adds the content to the Structure panel, where you can click and drag it into InDesign frames in your layout.

- If your document has content, importing an XML file brings in the content to your document and places it in frames in your document that have the same tags already applied. This is a way to automatically populate a layout in InDesign.

FIGURE 34.1

The Tags panel and its flyout menu

Auto Tag | Delete Tag

New Tag

CAUTION The order of the tags in the XML file's tags definitions is important. If the XML file has three tags — defined in the order of Body, Head, and Caption — but the Structure pane in InDesign lists them in the order Head, Body, and Caption, InDesign imports only Body and Caption content. That's because it imports Body first and then looks for the first occurrence of the Body tag in the InDesign file. It then begins matching style tags at that point. Because Head is listed in InDesign before Body, Head is ignored. (All the tags are in the Structure pane, so you can manually place the imported Head content.)

When importing XML documents, you can control some of the import operations by ensuring that Show XML Import Options is selected in the Import XML dialog box. When you choose an XML document, and then click Open, a dialog box opens (see Figure 34.2) with the following import options:

- **Mode:** This pop-up menu gives you the options of merging the content into your InDesign document or appending it. Merge Content is the default and will match up content by tags during the import, overwriting content based on other options chosen in this dialog box. The other is Append Content, which simply adds the imported XML data after the current data, duplicating any similar hierarchies and same-named data. (The Import XML dialog box also offers these options via the Append Content and Merge Content radio buttons.)

- **Create link:** If this check box is enabled, InDesign adds a link to the XML file in the Links panel.

- **Apply XSLT:** If this check box is enabled, InDesign imports the XSLT style sheet either from the XML file or from a separate file; you specify which using the pop-up menu to its right. XSLT is the Extensible Stylesheet Language Transformation, a method for translating XML files from one structure (schema) to another, to enable movement of data across different XML databases. Think of it as a set of styles for the XML file's data structure.

XML Rules

The biggest change to XML in InDesign CS3 is invisible to the typical user. Adobe has made everything in InDesign scriptable. That not only makes it easier to write your own AppleScripts, VBScripts, or JavaScripts (see Chapter 38), but it also makes everything in InDesign accessible to XML-based programs. The result of all this is that both commercial and in-house XML developers can now create programs that essentially program an InDesign document as a set of XML rules.

These rules examine the source database and, based on the contents of the data, can then create the correct XML code that calls the appropriate InDesign functions to add pages, create frames, apply formatting, load text and graphics into specific frames, and so on. This takes the concept of Tagged Text files (see Chapter 23) and brings it to a whole new level of control and flexibility. Essentially, with XML rules, you can create the document on the fly based on the data in your database. (By contrast, Tagged Text is limited to the text itself and requires that the data be completely consistent so it fits in an existing InDesign template.)

The use of XML rules does require serious programming skills, which Adobe says 99 percent of users don't have and may never have. The company realized that XML is essentially programming, not designing, and so in this new version of InDesign it focused on making the XML capabilities more powerful and useful for programmers, rather than try to pretty up XML for designers. That's a good thing, and it is certain to be welcome news to the content engineers and developers at major media companies, academic publishers, and similar content-creation giants.

- **Clone Repeating Text Elements:** If this check box is enabled, the styles in the current InDesign document are preserved when importing content in the XML file that uses the same element names. In other words, it applies existing styles to new elements that use the same tags as existing elements.

- **Only import elements that match existing structure:** If this check box is enabled, elements in the imported file that vary from or are not defined by the existing InDesign document are stripped out.

- **Import text elements into tables if tags match:** If this check box is enabled, any text tagged in XML with the same tags as specified for cell contents in InDesign tables is imported into InDesign. Essentially, this lets users match XML data to specific table cells.

- **Do Not Import Contents of Whitespace-Only Elements:** If this check box is enabled, elements that consist of nothing but spaces are ignored, so these blank elements do not overwrite same-name elements in InDesign. It also eliminates extraneous spaces where one will do, such as in documents that have two spaces at the end of each sentence.

- **Delete Elements, Frames, and Content That Do Not Match Imported XML:** If this check box is enabled, any elements and items in the InDesign document that are not defined in the XML document are removed. In other words, this makes the imported XML document overwrite the InDesign document.

■ **Import CALS Tables as InDesign Tables:** If this check box is enabled, InDesign converts tables specified via the CALS standard to InDesign tables. CALS is essentially an extension to XML developed by the U.S. Defense Department's Continuous Acquisition and Life-Cycle Support project to specify table formatting in XML and SGML (another way of representing complex documents in database-oriented publishing systems).

NEW FEATURE   The Apply XSLT and Import CALS Tables as InDesign Tables options are new to InDesign CS3.

FIGURE 34.2

The XML Import Options dialog box

The Import XML dialog box also has three other options you should note:

■ **Import into Selected Element:** If this check box is enabled, InDesign brings the imported XML data into the currently selected object (typically a frame) rather than into a new frame.

■ **Merge Content:** If this check box is enabled, InDesign merges the XML file into the existing XML data, flowing into the same structure, overriding same-named data and adding new data. (This control is also available in the XML Import Options dialog box.)

■ **Append Content:** If this check box is enabled, InDesign simply adds the imported XML data after the current data, duplicating any similar hierarchies and same-named data. (This control is also available in the XML Import Options dialog box.)

Creating tags

You also create XML tags in the Tags panel using the New Tag flyout menu. A tag simply consists of the tag name and the tag color — its formatting is defined in the XML database or in a DTD file.

Note that a DTD may define several types of content that have their own subcontent types and rules. These are called *branches*. For example, there could be an AuthorInformation branch and a CustomerList branch that both contain tags named Name. You need to know which branch text tagged Name should go into, because XML won't know the context.

Mapping tags and styles

In the Tags panel's flyout menu, you can also map style tags to XML tags and vice versa using the Map Tags to Styles menu option and the Map Styles to Tags menu option, respectively. (They're also available in the Structure panel's flyout menu.) Figure 34.3 shows the Map Styles to Tags dialog box; the Map Tags to Styles dialog box is nearly identical, except the two columns are switched. Here's what they do:

FIGURE 34.3

The Map Styles to Tags dialog box

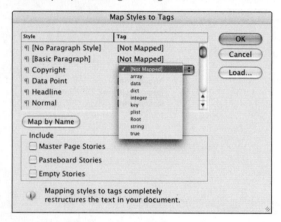

- Map Tags to Styles tells InDesign what XML tag to substitute for a specified character or paragraph style during XML export. The text retains its original InDesign style tags.

- Map Styles to Tags tells InDesign to immediately replace the specified styles with the XML tags. You see colored brackets around each string of text (paragraphs for paragraph styles and text selections for character styles) to indicate the text has an XML tag applied to it. The color corresponds to the tag color in the Tags panel. (You can change tag colors, as well as the tag name, using the Tag Options menu in the panel's flyout menu or simply by double-clicking the tag name in the panel.)

 InDesign checks to make sure that you include valid XML tag names according to XML standards. If you include a space or an illegal character in the tag name, an alert message appears when you click OK.

Applying Tags

It's easy to apply tags to text: Simply select the text and click the tag name in the Tags panel. If you want to replace the tag for selected text, be sure to select the Retag option in the Tags panel — otherwise, the original tag remains as well as the new tag applied. Unless they're style tags, multiple

XML tags can be applied to the same object or text. If you choose View ⇨ Structure ⇨ View Tag Markers, tagged text displays brackets around it in the color of the tag in the Tags panel. Similarly, if you choose View ⇨ Structure ⇨ Show Tagged Frames, tagged frames and lines also show a color indicator.

You can remove a tag by selecting the tagged text or object and then clicking the Untag button in the Tags panel.

It gets slightly more complex if you're using the Structure pane — which appears automatically on to the left of your document once you import XML data — to place tagged content imported from an XML file into InDesign objects. Figure 34.4 shows the Structure pane. (You can hide this pane by choosing View ⇨ Structure ⇨ Hide Structure, or pressing Option+⌘+1 or Ctrl+Alt+1 — or simply by clicking the double-arrow iconic button, Show/Hide Structure, at the bottom left of the document window.) The pane shows the document's tagged content, as well as the tags associated with it. The content appears in a hierarchy, reflecting any nesting in the tags (similar to how a character style can be thought of as a subset of a paragraph tag, because it applies to a component of a paragraph).

To apply XML content to a frame, simply click and drag the appropriate content (indicated with the Text Content icon) onto a frame. As you apply tags from the Tags panel to selected objects, you'll see icons for text and objects appear along with the name of the applied tags.

You can reorder the tags in the Structure pane to reflect the hierarchy of elements. Do this in coordination with your content engineer because the hierarchy in the InDesign file needs to match the hierarchy expectations in the XML database or content system.

Taking Advantage of Other XML Options

For the more XML-savvy, InDesign offers several controls in the Structure pane and its flyout menu, shown in Figure 34.4.

In the pane, you have these options:

- **Validate Structure:** This iconic button checks the current XML structure in the Structure pane and compares it against the DTD file imported with the XML data or imported later using the Import DTD option in the pane's flyout menu. There's a copy of the Validate Structure iconic button at the bottom of the pane, along with the View Errors List iconic button that shows any errors found.

- **Add an Attribute:** This iconic button lets you add an XML attribute, which is essentially a comment such as the revision date. It has no effect on the flow of information or the appearance or role of an element.

- **Add an Element:** This iconic button lets you add an XML element, which is a tag applied to text or an object.

- **Remove Selected Elements:** This iconic button removes any selected elements.

FIGURE 34.4

The Structure pane and its flyout menu. At right is the pane after validation, showing additional controls that appear if errors are found.

In the flyout menu, you have these options:

- The New Element, New Parent Element, New Attribute, New Comment, and New Processing Instruction menu items let you add those items.

- Delete deletes items.

- Edit edits items.

- Untag Element removes an elements XML tag.

- Go to Item lets you quickly move to the item with the selected tag.

- Validate from Root Element verifies the structure starting at the *root* (topmost) object against the DTD information.

- Validate from Selected Element starts the validation at the selected item.

- View List of Errors shows a dialog box with any validation errors found.

- Load DTD imports a document type declaration file, which defines the "role" of tags (such as indicating that the Head tag begins a section of a story).

- Delete DTD removes the DTD file from the InDesign document but leaves the structure untouched.

- DTD Options opens a dialog box in which you specify a specific element to validate the DTD from.

- View DTD shows a dialog box with the actual DTD information (similar to a code preview in an HTML editor).

- Import XML and Export XML duplicate the options in the File menu to import and export XML files.

- The Hide Attributes, Hide Comments, and Hide Processing Instructions menu options remove these noncontent markers from view in the Structure pane so you can concentrate on just the elements.

- Show/Hide Text Snippets shows or hides the first few words of text for each Text Content icon in the pane. Seeing these snippets is very helpful in knowing what each element actually contains.

- Add Untagged Items adds to the Structure pane all objects in the InDesign document that aren't already tagged with an XML tag. This helps ensure that you don't miss any object when reviewing the document structure.

- The Map Tags to Styles and Map Styles to Tags menu options match InDesign styles to XML tags, as I cover earlier in this chapter.

- Tagging Preset Options lets you specify the default mapping of tags to specific kinds of content: text frames, tables, and table cells. By choosing tags for each of these, you can specify globally how specific types of tagged content are assigned within InDesign.

NEW FEATURE   The New Parent Element flyout menu option is new to InDesign CS3.

Exporting XML Files

When the InDesign document has the proper elements properly tagged to the document's content, you're ready to export it to an XML file for use by a Web site's content-management system or other XML database. Choose File ➪ Export (⌘+E or Ctrl+E) — or the longer File ➪ Cross-Media Export ➪ Export XML menu sequence — to open the Export dialog box. In this dialog box, give the XML file a name in the Save As field (InDesign automatically adds the filename extension .xml), select a folder in which to place the file, and — most important — choose XML from the Format pop-up menu (called Save as Type in Windows if you are not using the Adobe Version Cue versions of dialog boxes). Then click Save.

NEW FEATURE The Export XML option is available as a submenu of the new File ➪ Cross-Media Export menu sequence and thus to have its own dialog box. It also continues to reside in the regular Export dialog box, which you access via File ➪ Export.

The Export XML dialog box appears. It opens with the General pane, shown in Figure 34.5. This pane is simple:

- **Include DTD Declaration:** Enable this check box to include the DTD information in the exported file. Otherwise, the XML database will need to import the DTD file separately.

- **View XML Using:** Enable this check box and select a Web browser or Web-supporting application in the adjacent pop-up menu to preview the XML file in that browser or program.

- **Export from Selected Element:** If an element is selected in the Structure pane, the Export from Selected Element check box will be available; if it's enabled, it exports the XML file only from that element on.

- **Export Untagged Tables as CALS XML:** To convert InDesign tables not tagged with XML attributes to the CALS XML format, enable this check box.

- **Remap Break, Whitespace, and Special Characters:** To convert special characters to their XML codes, enable this check box.

- **Apply XSLT:** If this check box is enabled, InDesign applies the XSLT style sheet either from the XML file or from a separate file; you specify which using the pop-up menu to its right.

- **Encoding:** Use this pop-up menu to choose the text encoding mechanism — a way of representing international characters across different computer systems. Your content engineer or Web master will tell you whether to select UTF-8, UTF-16, or Shift-JIS.

NEW FEATURE The Export Untagged Tables as CALS XML; Remap Break, Whitespace, and Special Characters; and Apply XSLT options are new to InDesign CS3.

In the Graphics pane, you tell InDesign how to handle the output of any tagged pictures. Figure 34.5 shows the pane. Your options are:

■ **Image Options section:** Here, you indicate which images to copy to the Images sub-folder that InDesign creates. Your choices are Original Images, Optimized Original Images, and Optimized Formatted Images. You can select any or all of these. The optimized images are converted to GIF or JPEG for use on the Web unless you specify GIF or JPEG in the Image Conversion pop-up menu rather than leave the default setting of Automatic; the formatted images crop the images to reduce file size.

FIGURE 34.5

The Export XML dialog box's General pane (at left) and Images pane (at right)

■ **GIF Options section:** Here, you choose the color palette in the Palette pop-up menu, with choices of Adaptive (No Dither), Web, System (Mac), and System (Win). Ask your Web master what to use; usually, you select Adaptive (No Dither). For very large images, interlacing can make on-screen display over the Web seem faster (by building the image line by line rather than waiting until the whole image has been transferred to the browser before anything is displayed); if you want to have such interlaced display of GIF files, select the Interlace option.

■ **JPEG Options section:** Here, you have options similar to those for GIF files. In the Image Quality pop-up menu, choose the desired image quality (Low, Medium, High, and Maximum). In the Format Method, choose Progressive to have the file displayed progressively (similar to the interlace option for GIF files) or Baseline to display it all at once. Unless your images are very large, keep the default Baseline.

When you export an XML file with graphics, InDesign automatically embeds XMP media management properties with the graphics' tags. You can view those properties by choosing File ➪ File Info (or pressing Option+Shift+⌘+I or Ctrl+Alt+Shift+I) and then choosing the Advanced pane. This information may be of interest to your content engineer but has no real meaning for the page designer. However, the content engineer may want to fill out the information in the File Info dialog box's other panes — Description and Origin — into which you can add comments, creator information and contact details, copyright information, credit and source information, keywords, and copyright URLs.

Summary

InDesign lets you tag content within documents with XML tags, so you can transfer that content to an XML database or Web content engine from which it can be used in a variety of media, formatted as appropriate for each. You can also import XML content into InDesign, automatically placing content into the appropriate frames if you've created an appropriate template and tagged it with the right XML tags. But InDesign's XML tools are only the beginning — you need an XML database and content-creation and content-presentation tools to use the XML data derived from InDesign documents.

For organizations creating complex content creation and management workflows using XML, InDesign CS3 exposes all of its functionality as XML rules that can be scripted, essentially letting you flexibly control the creation of InDesign files based on XML programming and XML data attributes.

Part IX

Workgroup Publishing Techniques

IN THIS PART

Chapter 35
Working with Others

Chapter 36
Workgroup Editing with InCopy

Chapter 35

Working with Others

Publishing is rarely a one-person enterprise. Chances are that the creators of your text and graphics are not the same people who do your layout. And in many environments, the chances are high that many people are involved in layout and production.

By its very nature, publishing is a group activity, so publishing programs must support workgroups. Yet a Mac or a PC is a *personal* computer, so it's easy to work on a Mac or PC without worrying about how your setup and work style might affect others. InDesign lets you create your own balance between the individual and the workgroup.

The key to working effectively in a workgroup environment is to establish standards and make sure they're easy to stick to. A basic way to accomplish this task is to place all common elements in one place so that people always know where to get the standard elements. This practice also makes it easy to maintain (add, modify, and delete) these elements over time, which is essential because no environment is static. How you do this depends on your computing environment:

- If you don't use a network, keep a master set of disks and copy elements from the master set in a folder with the same name on each person's computer. Update these folders every time a standard element changes on the master disk.

- If you do use a network, keep a master set of disks (networks do go down, so you'll want your files accessible when that happens) and create a folder for your standard elements on a network drive accessible to all users. Update this folder whenever a standard element changes on the master disk.

IN THIS CHAPTER

Sharing common elements with multiple users

Sharing document and general preferences with other documents

Transferring files safely between Mac and Windows versions of InDesign

Working with other CS3 applications

Unhiding the Windows Application Data Folder

The Application Data folder in Windows is hidden by default. To see it in Windows XP, open any folder in Windows, and then choose Tools ⇨ Folder Options to open the Folder Options dialog box. Go to the View pane and select the Show Hidden Files and Folders option. Click OK.

To see it in Windows Vista, choose Start ⇨ Computer, then choose Organize ⇨ Folder and Search Options in the dialog box that appears. Go to the View pane and enable the Show Hidden Files and Folders option. Click OK.

Sharing Elements with Other Users

Some standard elements can be accessed easily from a common folder because InDesign can import certain elements that are stored outside InDesign documents. These elements include graphics files, libraries, keyboard shortcut sets, and spelling dictionaries.

Other elements reside within documents and templates and cannot be saved in separate files. These elements include styles and master pages. But styles can be exported or imported from one document to another.

CAUTION   In several cases, multiple users can share the same preferences or other file using the Mac's alias feature or the Windows shortcut feature. (I note these where I cover specific features that permit this.) But keep in mind that, as with all over-the-network alias/shortcut solutions, there are some risks. For example, it is easier to corrupt the file. Also, the network and the host machine must be available at all times. Finally, if two users save changes to the file at the same time, only one user's changes will get through.

Where InDesign stores what

InDesign stores its building-block files, such as presets and preferences, in several locations.

Many of these files are stored in the folder containing the InDesign application:

- The Presets folder contains subfolders for several kinds of preference-related elements: Autocorrect, Find-Change Queries, InDesign Shortcut Sets, InDesign Workspaces, and Swatch Libraries. The Presets folder also includes the New Doc Sizes.txt file, which contains paper size definitions.

- Scripts available to all users of the computer are stored in the Scripts folder. This folder can contain a subfolder named Version 4.0 Scripts (just create it yourself if it doesn't exist), in which you can place InDesign CS2 scripts and ensure that they run in InDesign CS3.

- Plug-ins — both those that come with InDesign and those you buy from other companies — are stored in the Plug-ins folder, often in subfolders within it.

- The spelling and hyphenation exception dictionaries that come with InDesign are stored in the Dictionaries subfolder within the Plug-ins folder.

NEW FEATURE The AutoCorrect and Find-Change folders are new to InDesign CS3, providing a location for the presets for these new features. Also, the Scripts folder has moved out of the Presets folder into the main InDesign application folder.

Other files are stored with individual users' application preferences, so if users share a computer (switching from one user environment to another by logging in and out using the Windows or Mac OS X multiple-user feature), they can have different setups, even if they both use InDesign. To manage these different user environments, Mac OS X and Windows place many preference and related files in hard-to-find locations so users don't accidentally change them:

- On the Mac, the path is `Users:user name:Library:Preferences:Adobe InDesign:Version 5.0`.

- In Windows XP, the path is `Documents and Settings\user name\Application Data\Adobe\InDesign\Version 5.0`.

- In Windows Vista, the path is `Users\user name\AppData\Local\Adobe\InDesign\Version 5.0`.

Inside this Version 5.0 folder, the following presets and other preference files are stored:

- The InDesign preferences file (called InDesign Defaults).

- User-created spelling and hyphenation exception dictionaries are stored in the Dictionaries folder's Proximity subfolder.

- User-created menu sets are stored in the Menu Sets folder.

- User-created glyph sets are stored in the Glyph Sets folder.

- User-created keyboard shortcuts are stored in the InDesign Shortcut Sets folder; move the shortcut sets you want available to all users to the InDesign Shortcut Sets subfolder in the Presets folder in the application folder.

- User-created menu sequences are stored in the Menu Sets folder; move the menu sets you want available to all users to the Menu Sets subfolder in the Presets folder in the application folder.

- User-created workspaces are stored in the Workspaces folder; move all workspace sets you want available to all users to Workspaces subfolder in the Presets folder in the application folder.

- Scripts can be stored in the Scripts folder; store the scripts you want available to all users in the Presets folder in the application folder.

Trap presets, print presets, PDF export presets, transparency flattener presets, and stroke styles are *not* stored in files you can access—*unless* you explicitly store them using the Save commands in their dialog boxes or panels' flyout menus. Other presets and styles—such as text variables, and bulleted and numbered lists—are stored in the InDesign preference file (if no document was open when they were created) or in a specific document (if one was open when they were created).

 InDesign should not be open or running when you copy any of these building-block folders into the folders it uses. It sees only new files the next time you open the application.

Preference files

When no document is open and you change the preferences, add swatches and styles, modify tool settings (such as change the number of sides on the Polygon or Polygon Frame tool by double-clicking it), and modify the default settings of some panels and dialog boxes (such as Text Wrap and Text Frame Options), these changes are saved in the InDesign Defaults file.

Color definitions

Wanting to keep color, tint, and gradient definitions consistent across documents isn't unusual. This consistency helps you ensure, for example, that corporate identity colors, if you have them, are used instead of someone's approximations.

You can import swatches created in other documents (and templates) by having both documents open, and then clicking and dragging the swatch from the source document's Swatches panel (Window ➪ Swatches or F5) to anywhere in the other document's window. By creating a file that contains nothing but swatches, you can, in effect, create a color library for users.

You can't add swatches to a library, but any swatch used in a library element is copied to a document along with that element. So you could use a library that has a series of rectangles, each with a different swatch applied, as another way of creating a color library.

InDesign also lets you share swatch libraries, even across platform (just be sure the Adobe Swatch Exchange (also called ColorBook) swatch library file has the filename extension .ase if you're transferring a swatch library from the Mac to Windows).

 See Chapter 8 for more on creating swatches.

 On the Mac, color profiles are stored in the path `Users:user name:Library:` `ColorSync:Profiles`. In Windows XP, they're stored in the `Windows\System32\` `Spool\Drivers\Color` folder. In Windows Vista, they're stored in `Windows\` `System32\Spool\Drivers`.

Paragraph, character, table, cell, and object styles

The various style panels—Character Styles, Paragraph Styles, Table Styles, Cell Styles, and Object Styles—include an option in the flyout menu to import styles from other InDesign documents and templates. In the Character Styles and Paragraph Styles panels, you'll see flyout menu options to

Using a Common Settings Files

You can use the Mac's alias feature or the Windows shortcut feature to use an InDesign settings file stored in a folder other than the one in which InDesign resides. On a network, being able to use this technique means that everyone can share the same InDesign settings files, such as the InDesign Defaults file, keyboard shortcuts sets, spelling and hyphenation dictionaries, libraries, and swatch libraries. Note that if you're sharing these files across platforms, you need to create a Windows shortcut from Windows to these files as well as a Mac alias from the Mac.

But note that the InDesign Defaults file *cannot* be shared across platforms, so if you want to have a master copy on a network server for shared use, you'll need to maintain two masters — one for Mac and one for Windows. Because the files have the same name on both platforms (there is no filename extension for this file in Windows), you'll need to store them in separate directories or add something to the name such as "Mac" and "Windows." If you do change the name, note that the alias and shortcut on each user's system must simply be named InDesign Defaults.

import (load) just character styles or just paragraph styles, respectively, or both types of styles. Similarly, in the Table Styles and Cell Styles panels, you'll see flyout menu options to import just table styles or just cell styles, respectively, or both types of styles. The Object Styles panel's flyout menu simply has the Load Object Styles flyout menu option.

Note that the Load dialog boxes accessed through the various styles panels' flyout menus let you select which styles to load, as well as let you decide how to handle the import of styles that have the same names in the two documents.

TIP By importing styles with no document open, you copy all new styles into your global defaults (those stored in the InDesign Defaults file I cover earlier in this chapter). This technique is a handy way of bringing new styles into your default settings without affecting existing styles.

CROSS-REF See Chapter 20 for more on paragraph and character styles, Chapter 22 for more on table and cell styles, and Chapter 13 for more on object styles.

Spelling dictionaries

InDesign saves any spelling or hyphenation exceptions you add through Edit ➪ Dictionary, or when you're spell-checking, through Edit ➪ Check Spelling, or ⌘+I or Ctrl+I. You can copy these exception dictionaries from one computer to another (regardless of platform), or you can use an alias or shortcut from each computer to a central location on a server.

On both Mac and Windows, hyphenation exception files have the filename extension .not, while the spelling exception dictionaries have the extension .udc. The files will have the same name as the language dictionaries (but different filename extensions) to which they are associated, such as FREN.not for French hyphenation exceptions and USA.udc for U.S. English spelling exceptions.

CROSS-REF See Chapter 16 for more on hyphenation and spelling dictionaries.

Graphics and text files

Perhaps the most obvious elements to standardize are the *source elements* — the text and graphics that you use in your documents — especially if you have common elements, such as logos that are used in multiple documents.

The simplest method of ensuring that the latest versions of these common elements are used is to keep them all in a standard folder (either on each computer or on a network drive). This method works well when you first use a text or graphic element, but it does not ensure that these elements are updated in InDesign documents if the elements are changed after being imported.

For text and graphics files, using InDesign's links feature — when you keep common elements in a common location — can ensure consistency across documents. You can also use libraries and snippets to store commonly used graphics and text blocks (including any formatting for the text and its frame).

CROSS-REF See Chapter 13 for more on managing file links.

You can also share stroke styles if you save them from the Strokes Styles dialog box (open the Stroke panel by choosing Window ➪ Stroke, or press ⌘+F10 or Ctrl+F10, and then choose Stroke Styles from the flyout menu). Click Save to save the selected style; click Load to import a stroke style file (which has the filename extension .lnst).

CROSS-REF Chapter 12 covers strokes in more detail.

Libraries

InDesign libraries are a great aid for keeping documents consistent. Because libraries are stored in their own files, common libraries can be put in common folders. You can even access them across the network. If you want, you can keep an alias to a library elsewhere on the network on your computer's local drive.

For many people, libraries offer more flexibility than just links to graphics files because all attributes applied to graphics and their graphics frames are also stored in the library.

Libraries can be shared across platforms, and although Windows InDesign libraries have the filename extension .indl, that extension is not required for Windows InDesign to open and use Mac libraries.

CROSS-REF See Chapter 7 for more information on libraries.

Snippets

You can also share elements through snippets, which contain InDesign objects. Snippet files have the filename extension .inds and can be placed in an InDesign document like any graphic or text. They retain all their attributes, much like libraries, except that each snippet is stored in its own file.

Unlike library items, snippets retain their object coordinates, which can create some minor issues when you place a snippet made from a larger document into a second, smaller document. The objects don't fall off the pasteboard, but it may take some effort to find them.

CROSS-REF See Chapter 10 for more information on snippets.

Templates

In the course of creating documents, you're likely to evolve templates (called *stationery* in the Mac OS) that you want to use over and over. InDesign can save a document as a template. The only difference between a template and a document is that a template forces you to use Save As rather than Save in the File menu so that you don't overwrite the template but instead create new documents based on it.

Although the optimum approach is to design a template before creating actual documents, the truth is that no one can foresee all possibilities. Even if you create a template (and you should) with styles, swatches, and master pages intended for use in all new documents, you can expect to modify your template because working on real documents brings up the need for modifications and additions.

Whether or not you use templates, you still need to transfer basic layout elements like styles and master pages from one document to another, as I describe earlier in this chapter.

Templates can be shared across platforms, and although Windows InDesign templates have the filename extension .indt, that extension is not required for Windows InDesign to open and use Mac templates. (I still recommend that you always use the filename extensions, so the correct icons appear in your folders.)

CROSS-REF See Chapter 4 for more on templates.

Output settings

Several output-related settings — print presets, transparency flattener presets, and PDF export presets (also called *job-option files*) — can be shared by saving them to files and then loading them into other users' copies of InDesign. Print presets have the filename extension .prst; transparency flattener presets, .flst; and PDF export presets, .joboptions.

Another output-related setting — trap presets — is stored within InDesign documents and can be opened using the Load command from the Trap Presets panel's flyout menu. (Access this panel by choosing Window ➪ Output ➪ Trap Presets.)

CROSS-REF See Chapter 31 for more on print, transparency, and flattener presets. See Chapter 32 for more on PDF export presets. See Chapter 29 for more on trap presets.

Master pages

You can import master pages from one document to another by using the Load Master Pages flyout menu option in the Pages panel (Window ➪ Pages, or ⌘+F12 or Ctrl+F12). In the resulting dialog box, select the InDesign document whose master pages you want to import.

NEW FEATURE The ability to directly import master pages from other documents is new to InDesign CS3, eliminating the complex workaround of copying pages from one document to another that you had to do in previous versions.

CROSS-REF See Chapter 7 for more on master pages.

InDesign documents

An easy way to share InDesign documents with others is to use the Package feature (File ⇨ Package, or Option+Shift+⌘+P or Ctrl+Alt+Shift+P), which copies all files needed to one folder. This lets you place a complete package for others to work on in one location, whether on a network folder or on a removable medium such as a CD-RW.

CROSS-REF Chapter 30 covers the package feature.

Document presets and the New Doc Sizes.txt paper-size file can be shared as well. You can save and load document presets (filename extension .dcst) using the Document Presets dialog box. To share paper size definitions, copy the New Doc Sizes.txt file from the InDesign application folders' Presets subfolder on the computer containing the desired definitions to the Presets folder on other computers' InDesign applications folders.

CROSS-REF Chapter 4 covers document presets and paper size definitions.

If you're working on a network, the Version Cue file-version management software that comes with Adobe Creative Suite 3 applications, including InDesign CS3, can also help. It lets you create shared folders across the network that you save your files to once you're ready for others to work on them. Version Cue also retains earlier versions, so there is a history of changes that you can use to undo design directions that don't work out. A related tool is the InCopy CS3 software that Adobe sells separately; this software lets development editors and copy editors work on an InDesign document's text while the designer is working on the layout.

CROSS-REF Version Cue is covered in Chapter 4, while Chapter 36 provides an introduction to InCopy.

Interface preferences

You can share three types of interface settings as files: customized menus (filename extension .inms), custom keyboard shortcuts (.indk), and custom workspaces (.xml). They are available only to a specific user or to all users of a computer, depending on where you copy them to, as I described earlier in this chapter.

CROSS-REF These interface preference settings are covered in Chapter 3.

Mixing Mac and Windows Environments

As a cross-platform application, InDesign appeals strongly to all sorts of users who find that they must deal with "the other side." This includes corporate users whose various divisions have standardized on different platforms, service bureaus whose clients use different computers, and independent publishers or layout artists who deal with a range of clients.

InDesign differences

InDesign can read document files from either platform. However, the Windows version may not recognize a Mac-generated file as an InDesign file unless you do one of two things:

■ **Filename extension:** Add .indd for documents or .indt for templates to the Mac-generated file's name. InDesign does this automatically, so unless a user removed the filename extension, most files will have it. If the filename extension is missing, be sure to choose All Documents from the Enable pop-up menu (Mac) or Files of Type pop-up menu (Windows) in the Open a File dialog box. Table 35.1 lists the common filename extensions for the files InDesign typically works with.

■ **All Files:** Select this in the Enable pop-up menu (Mac) or File of Type pop-up menu (Windows) in the Open a File dialog box (File ➪ Open, or Ctrl+O) for cases when the document does not have its identifying filename extension.

On the Mac, you may not be able to double-click a PC-generated InDesign document (this is usually true when you see a PC icon rather than the InDesign icon for the file). When this happens, you'll need to open it from the InDesign Open a File dialog box (File ➪ Open, or ⌘+O).

TABLE 35.1

Filename Extensions

File	Filename Extension	File	Filename Extension
InDesign Files			
Document	.indd	Stroke styles	.lnst
Interchange	.inx	Document presets	.dcst
Template	.indt	Print presets	.prst
Library	.indl	Transparency flattener presets	.flst
Snippet	.inds	PDF export presets	.joboptions
ColorBook swatches	.ase	Customized menus	.inms
Hyphenation exception dictionaries	.not	Customized keyboard shortcuts	.indk
Spelling exception dictionaries	.udc	Customized workspaces	.xml

continued

TABLE 35.1	*(continued)*		
File	**Filename Extension**	**File**	**Filename Extension**
InCopy Files			
Document	.incd	Assignment	.inca
Interchange	.incx	Package	.incp
Other Files			
JavaScript	.js	EPS	.eps
Data type description	.dtd	Illustrator	.ai
XML	.xml	PDF	.pdf
XSLT	.xlst	SVG	.svg
GIF	.gif	ASCII text (text-only)	.txt
JPEG	.jpg, .jpeg	Rich Text Format	.rtf
Photoshop	.psd	Word	.doc
TIFF	.tif, .tiff	Excel	.xls

Which elements transfer

The following elements may be transferred across platforms, with any limits noted:

- **Color, tint, and gradient swatches:** These are retained and may also be imported across platforms, both directly from other documents and by loading individual swatch files. For Adobe Swatch Exchange swatch libraries copied from the Mac to Windows, be sure to add the filename extension .ase if it's not already there.

- **Color profile files:** Although these cannot be exchanged across the two platforms, both the Mac and Windows InDesign versions retain color-profile information from the other platform's files. And if both platforms have color profiles for the same device (monitor, scanner, printer, and so on), InDesign applies the correct color profiles. If a color profile is not available on the new platform, you can apply a new profile or ignore the issue. (If you ignore this issue, the correct profile will be in place when you bring the document back to the original platform.) If you print with a missing profile, InDesign substitutes the default profile based on the type of color model used (RGB or CMYK).

- **Paragraph, character, table, cell, and object styles; master pages; and trap presets:** These are retained and you may also import them from other documents across platforms.

- **Stroke styles, print presets, document presets, Adobe PDF export presets, and transparency flattener presets:** These are retained and you may also import them across platforms after saving them to their own files.

- **Hyphenation and spelling exceptions:** These are retained. The files use a filename extension on both the Mac and in Windows: .not for hyphenation additions, .udc for spelling additions.

- **Document preferences:** These are retained, but the InDesign Defaults file cannot be shared across platforms.

- **Plug-ins:** These files are not interchangeable across platforms. Plug-ins must be present on both platforms if you move documents that use the features of specific plug-ins. You'll need versions specific to each platform because these are essentially miniprograms that must be written to work on the Mac or Windows.

Which elements don't transfer

Adobe has removed most barriers between Mac and Windows in InDesign. Only the following elements cannot be moved across platforms:

- Shortcut sets

- Color profiles

- The InDesign Defaults preferences file

- AppleScripts and VBScripts (you can share JavaScripts)

Working with Multiple Versions of InDesign

Many designers have more than one version of InDesign installed on their computer so they can work with multiple clients' files in the same version of the software that the client uses, to ensure file compatibility and to prevent the use of features from a new version in the files of a client who has an older version.

When working with multiple copies of InDesign, double-clicking a filename from a folder launches the most recent version of InDesign installed, which may not be the one you want. So you typically have to launch the desired version of InDesign first and then open the file from within it.

On the Mac, there's a wrinkle. When you double-click a file with no filename extension, the Mac OS looks for a pair of attributes embedded in the file itself, called the *file type* and *file creator*, that pre-X versions of the Mac OS used instead of filename extensions. If it finds them, it launches the associated program. (But if the file has a filename extension, Mac OS X doesn't bother looking at the file type and creator.)

The file type and creator tell the Mac OS which version of the program to launch, so you can remove the filename extension for a file and then double-click it to have the proper version of InDesign launch and open the file for you. (There is no way to do this double-click trick in Windows.) Note that this trick won't always work, and that removing the filename extension also removes the InDesign logo from the file icon. If you use this trick, be sure to put the filename extension back (so the InDesign logo reappears) when done with the file.

Platform differences

There are also some general differences between Windows and Mac themselves that will add a few bumps along the road to cross-platform exchange.

Filenames

The most noticeable difference between Windows and Mac is the file-naming convention, and that difference is no longer so great since the advent of Mac OS X. To be cross-platform-compatible, restrict your filenames to 250 characters (including the filename extension), always use a filename extension, and do not use the following characters as part of the filename: : / | . * " < > ? / \. These restrictions conform to the Mac OS X standards but Windows users will need to make a couple of compromises:

- You can't use the full Windows filename size of 255 characters.
- You can't use the : / | . * " < > ? / \ characters in your filenames even though Windows supports all of them but : .

Although the Mac OS X supports filenames as long as 250 characters, you may have trouble copying Windows files to the Mac if the Windows filenames exceed 31 characters and you use the AppleTalk networking protocol to connect your Macs and PCs. That's because of limits in some of the software to make these cross-platform connections, which enforce pre–Mac OS X filename conventions on all files. It's easy enough to test whether your software is limiting you to 31 characters: Just transfer a file and see if either the software shortens the name or refuses to transfer the file. In either case, it's time to upgrade your networking software or switch to a protocol like IP.

CAUTION   If you rename your files in Windows or on the Mac OS X, either before transferring or while transferring them, you'll confuse InDesign. That's because InDesign's internal pointers to files such as graphics and swatch libraries retain the original name, so it keeps looking for those names. So it's best to make sure your filenames meet the cross-platform requirements before using them in InDesign.

Font differences

Although the major typeface vendors like Adobe Systems, Linotype, and Agfa offer their typefaces for both Windows and Mac users, these typefaces are not always the same on both platforms. Cross-platform differences are especially common among typefaces created a few years ago, when multiplatform compatibility was not a goal for most users or vendors.

Differences occur in three areas:

- **Internal font name:** The name used by the printer and type scalers (such as Extensis Suitcase, Insider Software FontAgent Pro, and Adobe Type Manager) is not quite the same for the Mac and Windows version of a typeface. This discrepancy results in an alert box listing the fonts used in the document that are not on your computer. The solution is to use the Find Font dialog box or the Find/Replace dialog box (both covered in Chapter 16) to replace all instances of the unrecognized font name with the correct one for the current platform.

Displaying Filename Extensions

Windows and Mac OS X (but not earlier versions of the Mac OS) use filename extensions to identify the file type. But they're typically not displayed to the user. Here's how to make filename extensions visible:

- In Mac OS X 10.4 (Tiger) and 10.5 (Leopard), choose Finder ➪ Preferences. (You have to be using the Finder, not be in an application, to see the Finder menu.) In the Preferences dialog box that appears, go to the Advanced pane, enable the Show All File Extensions check box, and close the dialog box.

- In Windows XP, open any folder and then choose Tools ➪ Folder Options. (You have to have a disk or folder open to have the View menu.) In the Folder Options dialog box that appears, go to the View pane. Uncheck the Hide Extensions for Known File Types check box, and then click OK

- In Windows Vista, choose Start ➪ Computer, then choose Organize ➪ Folder and Search Options in the dialog box that appears. Go to the View pane and enable the Show Hidden Files and Folders check box, then click OK.

- **Tracking, kerning, and character width:** These may vary between the two platforms even if typefaces use the same internal names, and could result in text reflow. The solution is to check the ends of all your stories to make sure text did not get shorter or longer.

- **Symbols:** Even when created by the same vendors, the character maps for each font file differ across platforms because Windows and the Mac use different character maps. This problem is complicated by the fact that some vendors didn't stick to the standard character maps for any platform or didn't implement all symbols in all their typefaces. The solution is to proofread your documents, note the symbols that are incorrect, and then use the Find/Change dialog box to replace them with the correct symbol. (Highlight the incorrect symbol, and use the copy and paste commands to put it in the Text field of the Find/Change dialog box rather than trying to figure out the right keypad code in Windows or the right keyboard shortcut on the Mac.) If you use OpenType fonts, you find far fewer issues with symbol translation than with PostScript Type 1 and TrueType fonts.

To minimize font problems, use a program like FontLab Fontographer or Studio Pro to translate your TrueType and PostScript files from Mac to Windows format or vice versa. This ensures that the internal font names, width information, and symbols are the same on both platforms. The companion Web site (www.InDesignCentral.com) includes links to these and other utilities.

CROSS-REF See Chapter 21 for more information on using special characters.

Transfer methods

Moving files between Macs and Windows PCs is easier now than ever before, thanks to the built-in support of Windows formats and networking in Mac OS X, the use of TCP/IP networking by both the Mac and Windows, and a selection of products on both platforms that let each machine read the other's disks (floppies, removable disks like CD-Rs, and even hard drives).

Working with Other Creative Suite Applications

One of the strengths of InDesign is that it is part of the Adobe Creative Suite, making it easy to work with graphics sources and other files directly in the environment used to create them. The integration is especially tight among InDesign, Photoshop, and Illustrator. You'll also see similar user interfaces and controls across the applications, letting you apply your skills in more than one context.

Working with graphics and colors

At the most basic level, InDesign can place Photoshop and Illustrator files directly, so there's no need to use an intermediate format such as TIFF or EPS. You can import the files using the Place dialog box, drag them (or pieces of them) directly into InDesign, or copy and paste them (or pieces of them). InDesign preserves any formatting such as layers and color swatches.

You can edit placed graphics files (not copied or dragged files) by choosing Edit Original from the contextual menu or from the Links panel's flyout menu. If the file has layers, you can manage those layers using Object Layers Options from the contextual menu or from the Object menu. You can also work with clipping paths and alpha channels in Photoshop files, because InDesign preserves them. If you drag or copy-and-paste graphics (but not place) from Illustrator, you can edit them directly in InDesign.

You can use the same color swatch libraries in InDesign, Photoshop, and Illustrator. These Adobe Swatch Exchange (ColorBook) files have the filename extension .ase, and you can save and load them using the Swatches panel in InDesign, Photoshop, and Illustrator. (Be sure to use the Save Swatches as ASE flyout menu options in Photoshop and Illustrator, and the Save Swatches flyout menu option in InDesign, to save these swatches, and the Load Swatches flyout menu item to import them in all three programs.)

CROSS-REF Part VI covers how to import and work with graphics files. Chapter 8 covers the process of creating colors and opening color libraries.

Working with Web content

You can export entire InDesign layouts or just selected objects in those layouts for use in Adobe Dreamweaver or GoLive, as Chapter 33 explains. InDesign creates XHTML files containing your text and basic formatting such as indicating paragraphs, styles used, and story boundaries, as well as converts any graphics to JPEG or GIF formats automatically. You can also simply export individual objects to JPEG format, as Chapter 4 explains.

Furthermore, GoLive 9 supports pasting InDesign contents into its pages and brings over the text as well as the style definitions; you can copy and paste InDesign frames to copy their contents or copy and paste text selections. You can also paste bitmapped images from InDesign into GoLive 9.

Dreamweaver's support of InDesign content via copy and paste is more limited: You can copy only text selections, not frames, and you cannot copy images into Dreamweaver from InDesign.

 In both Dreamweaver and GoLive, the Edit ➪ Paste Special menu command gives you some control over how pasted text is handled, such as how the text's line breaks are handled.

Working with Adobe Bridge

The Adobe Bridge application is meant to be a central command point for your Creative Suite documents and their component files, such as graphics and swatch libraries. You don't have to use Bridge — the standard Windows and Mac folder systems work perfectly well — but it does give you more context about your files, should you need it, as well as let you control some aspects of the Creative Suite's functionality.

File context

Figure 35.1 shows the Bridge's view of a folder containing a bunch of InDesign files. Note the previews of individual files, which help you know you're selecting the ones you want. And note the Filter panel at the left-hand side of the Bridge window; you can quickly use this to find files that match specific file types, creation dates, and modification dates, as well as control whether the files are sorted by name, document kind, creation date, dimensions, or any of seven other attributes.

Also note the Metadata panel at the right-hand side; this panel can include all sorts of information (metadata) about the file, such as the creator, that helps other members of a project get the right context so they know how and when to use the file. For example, the figure shows which fonts the selected layout uses, so you know which ones you'll need to work on it.

Some metadata information, such as creation date and fonts used, is automatically included in the files saved by Creative Suite applications. You can also modify and add metadata to a file within applications such as InDesign by choosing File ➪ File Info, or pressing Option+Shift+⌘+I or Ctrl+Alt+Shift+I.

You can add or modify this information later from Bridge by selecting a file in Bridge and choosing File ➪ File Info — or by right-clicking it or Control+clicking the filename in Bridge and choosing File Info from the contextual menu. Figure 35.2 shows the File Info dialog box, which is the same in Bridge as it is in InDesign.

In the Preferences dialog box's Metadata pane (Bridge CS3 ➪ Preferences), you can set which metadata properties you want to be displayed for all files by enabling the desired check boxes.

FIGURE 35.1

The Bridge folder view

FIGURE 35.2

The File Info dialog box lets you define or change a file's metadata.

Bridge interface

The Preferences dialog box (Bridge CS3 ⇨ Preferences) lets you control Bridge's user interface. Available controls include setting the color scheme and which folders display in the Favorites pane using the General pane, how thumbnail previews are generated using the Thumbnails pane, which applications are launched by double-clicking specific types of files using the File Type Associations pane, and how color management and language display are handled in Bridge using the Advanced pane.

Suite functionality

Bridge lets you set the default color management settings for all Creative Suite applications, to ensure consistent color representation as files move from one application to another. Choose Edit ⇨ Creative Suite Color Settings, or press Shift+⌘+K or Ctrl+Shift+K, to open the Suite Color Settings dialog box and choose the desired color settings.

You can also use Bridge to set up Version Cue projects, as well as check out files, promote versions over each other, and otherwise manage the files. The functionality here is the same as in individual Creative Suite applications, except that you can work on multiple types of project files from one location. Choose Tools ⇨ Version Cue to access these functions.

 Chapter 29 covers color management in detail. Chapter 4 covers Version Cue management in detail.

InDesign-specific functionality

Bridge also offers various utilities designed to augment individual Creative Suite applications. Most of these tools are for Photoshop, while a couple are for Illustrator. Just one is for InDesign: a tool that creates an InDesign file formatted as a contact sheet for selected images. To use it, first select the images in Bridge, and then choose Tools ⇨ InDesign Create InDesign Contact Sheet. Figure 35.3 shows the resulting Contact Sheet dialog box.

In this dialog box's Layout section, you set up how the images should be laid out, such as the number of columns and rows, space between images, whether images are rotated for better fit, and whether they have a gray frame placed around them.

The Caption section lets you control the captions that accompany each image. Click Define if the default caption of the filename is not what you want; this opens the Create or Modify Caption dialog box. You can change the caption by choosing the data aspects you want displayed from the Select from List pop-up menu, and then click the Add button immediately to the right of the pop-up menu to add them to the caption, and you can add your own text or modify the display as desired in the field above the pop-up menu. When you're satisfied, click the Add button to the right of this field to add the aspect to the caption's definition. (This means you can have *multiple* attributes form the caption.) A pane opens containing all aspects defined for the caption, and you can add, delete, or update them in this Create or Modify Caption dialog box. Click OK when you're done to return to the Contact Sheet dialog box.

You can also choose whether to use an existing InDesign template for your contact sheet, to save the contact sheet as a PDF file, or to save your settings as a preset for further use — the last option lets you create and use multiple contact sheet formats easily.

FIGURE 35.3

The Contact Sheet dialog box in Adobe Bridge

Summary

When working with other users, you can share preferences by copying or making aliases to just one InDesign Defaults file, ensuring that all users have the same preferences. But the InDesign Defaults file is not cross-platform–compatible, so Windows users cannot use a Mac user's file or vice versa.

Except for shortcut sets, color profiles, the InDesign Defaults preferences file, plug-ins, AppleScripts, and VBScripts, cross-platform users can share InDesign support documents. Otherwise, sharing files between PC and Mac users is very simple, thanks to a variety of disk- and network-based utilities now available for both platforms.

InDesign works well with several other Adobe Creative Suite 3 applications, including Photoshop and Illustrator. There is also some direct copy-and-paste support from InDesign to GoLive and Dreamweaver. The Bridge application is meant to act as a central hub and repository for all Creative Suite 3 applications, providing a unified location to store project files and to get information on files, such as creation date and fonts used. You can also set Creative Suite–wide color settings and manage Version Cue projects involving files from multiple programs.

Chapter 36

Workgroup Editing with InCopy

IN THIS CHAPTER

Preparing documents for workgroup editing

Working with story assignments

Using the InCopy program

ublishing is almost always a workgroup activity involving writers, editors, copy editors, layout artists, and production editors. Even when a person has multiple roles, most publications still involve multiple people. And that means that files go back and forth as edits are made, layouts are created, and text and other elements are adjusted to fit the available space. Just as its rival QuarkXPress has the CopyDesk companion product, InDesign has a companion product (called InCopy) to facilitate this constant "paper shuffling." InCopy is not as powerful as InDesign — it's not a layout tool — but it does let copy editors, editors, and other wordsmiths work on InDesign layouts to make sure headlines fit, stories fit, and captions can be written in context without needing a full copy of InDesign.

InCopy works best in a networked environment, where everyone shares files from a common folder (using Adobe's Version Cue or not, as you prefer). That way, a copy editor can work on a layout without worrying that the designer might be working on a local copy at the same time, for example.

InCopy is both a separate program that runs by itself for text editing stories in an InDesign layout and a plug-in that works within InDesign to provide shared editing capabilities.

Setting up Workgroup Assignments

InDesign comes ready out of the box to work with InCopy, in the form of the Assignments panel (Window ➪ Assignments), the various menu options available if you choose Edit ➪ InCopy, and the File ➪ User menu command.

NEW FEATURE   The inclusion of these InCopy features out of the box — making them always available — is new to InDesign CS3. In previous versions, they were visible only if you installed InCopy as well.

Identifying the user

The first thing you should do if you plan to use the InCopy features within InDesign is to set up your username so InCopy can track every change you make. Choose File ⇨ User to open the User dialog box shown in Figure 36.1. Enter a name for yourself and choose your preferred color from the Color pop-up menu. (InDesign and InCopy use the colors to help you quickly identify who made specific changes.) Then click OK.

FIGURE 36.1

The User dialog box

User
User Name: Galen Gruman
Color: ☐ Gold
ⓘ You must enter a user name in order to use features that require unique identification.
Cancel   OK

Preparing story files for InCopy

Before an InCopy user can work on a layout, an InDesign user has to InCopy-enable that layout. There are two ways to do that: using the Assignments panel, or exporting individual stories as InCopy files.

You should use the Assignments panel as the primary mechanism, since it gathers all files into one convenient group — an assignment — that is associated to this layout. You can create multiple assignments for the layout, grouping stories based on who should work on them or whatever division makes sense for your workflow.

Exporting InCopy files directly makes more sense when you want to share a specific story with an InCopy user, rather than have them work on stories relate to a particular layout in the context of that layout. It's essentially the same concept as sending an RTF file for an editor to work on in Word, except that an InCopy story retains all the InDesign text formatting so it can more easily be brought back into the layout.

But if you export stories this way, they're still available in the Assignments panel, so it's not a completely either/or approach between using the Assignments panel to create assignments versus exporting InCopy files. I prefer starting with the Assignments panel because I find it a simpler way to work.

Either way, an InCopy user can open an assignment and work on the text within a replica of the layout, to understand the relationships among stories and space constraints, for example. Yet that InCopy user cannot modify the layout or graphics, so designers don't have to worry about unexpected or accidental changes.

Creating story assignments

To create a new assignment, choose New Assignment from the Assignment panel's flyout menu. You see the New Assignment dialog box (refer to Figure 36.2) in which you name the assignment, enter who the text is assigned to and what color icon is associated with the assignment, establish a default location for all InCopy stories associated with that assignment, and determine which layout frames (and thus stories) are available to the InCopy user working on the assignment.

The four options related to layout frames are important to understand. The three radio buttons in the Include section do the following:

■ **Placeholder Frames:** The InCopy user sees just the layout "hole" containing the assigned stories' text; this provides the least visual context but keeps the file small.

■ **Assigned Spreads:** The InCopy user sees all spreads on which the story in the assignment exists. Other spreads are excluded, helping keep the file size manageable. All objects on those spreads, except for those containing stories in the assignment, are locked so the InCopy user cannot modify them (this applies to text frames, not just graphics, lines, and so forth).

■ **All Spreads:** The InCopy user sees the entire layout, providing the maximum content and the largest file size. But all objects other than those text frames containing stories in the assignment are locked.

There's a fourth option, the Linked Image Files When Packaging check box. When enabled, this option provides links to the source images, for maximum display quality. (The InCopy user will have to have access to those files, such as by using the same server or working in a Version Cue environment.) If this option is unchecked, the InCopy user gets only a low-resolution preview; typically, you would uncheck this option when the InCopy user will not have access to the graphics files and so having a low-resolution preview is better than having no preview at all.

When you create an assignment, InDesign creates an assignment file (with filename extension of .inca) that contains all the relationships of the stories to the layout and to each other.

You can modify an assignment's settings by choosing Assignment Options from the flyout menu. The Assignment Options dialog box is identical to the New Assignments dialog box.

NEW FEATURE The ability to specify a default location for an assignment's stories is new to InDesign CS3. This feature automatically moves stories to the appropriate location if they are moved from one assignment to another.

In addition to setting the default location for an assignment, you can also change an assignment file's location by selecting the assignment and choosing Change Assignment Location in the flyout menu. In the Select the New Location dialog box, choose a new folder and/or drive for the file, and then click Save. This is useful when working in a networked environment, so you can place the assignment file in the appropriate server folder for the current workflow stage.

NEW FEATURE To quickly see where an assignment file is, select it in the Assignments panel and choose Reveal in Finder (Mac) or Reveal in Explorer (Windows) from the flyout menu to open the folder on your computer. Or choose Reveal in Bridge to open the Bridge program and have it open the folder for you.

FIGURE 36.2

The New Assignment dialog box

Adding stories to assignments

An assignment by itself is an empty shell. It is useful only when it contains stories. To add a story to an assignment, select it (its frame or any of its text) and then choose Add to Assignment from the Assignments panel's flyout menu. (If you want to create a new assignment at the same time, just choose Add to Assignment ⇨ New from the flyout menu.) You can also add a story by selecting anywhere in its text frame and choosing Edit ⇨ InCopy ⇨ Add Selection. Figure 36.3 shows the Assignments panel with some stories in it.

NEW FEATURE You can now just add a story to an assignment by dragging its frame into the Assignments panel using any of the selection tools.

To change a story's assignment, select the assignment in the Assignments panel and then choose Add to Assignment from the flyout menu.

A story can have multiple assignments, to help you organize access to the constituent files based on whatever criteria you have. For example, you might create an assignment called Headlines and place the text of all headline-containing frames into that assignment to make them available as a group for use by a headline writer.

FIGURE 36.3

The Assignments panel and its flyout menu

Exporting InCopy story files

The other way to add stories to an assignment is to export the stories from InDesign to separate InCopy story files. (InCopy story files have a filename extension of .incx.)

To export stories, choose Edit ⇨ InCopy ⇨ Export. A dialog appears that lets you choose what to export: the selection, layer, all stories, all graphics, or all graphics and stories. (A story is all text in a text frame or path and any frames and/or paths linked to it.) After navigating to the folder where you want to store the InCopy file, click Export, and then click OK. (If you have not provided a username already, you must do so.)

But be careful when exporting all stories. This option likely won't act as you expect. That's because by *story*, InDesign means any text in any text frame. So, if your headlines are in separate frames and not linked to their body copy frames, the headlines will each be a separate story. Ditto for any captions or text in figures. This can create dozens of files in your project folder. So it's usually better not to choose Export All Stories and instead export each story individually that you want to be editable.

> **NOTE** The reason that InCopy exports all these separate story files is so multiple users can work on the same layout, but on different stories, at the same time. The concept of assignments provides the same benefit without having so many files.

All the exported stories are automatically added to an assignment called Unassigned InCopy Content. You can of course then move them into other assignments, as I describe in the previous section.

Packaging assignments

Tools like InCopy make a lot of sense when you're working in a network-connected workgroup. But what if one of the project members, such a freelance copy editor or a traveling editor, is offsite? You can collect all the relevant files for these project members and package them into one file that you can send via e-mail (or disk).

To do so, select the assignments you want to package in the Assignments panel and choose Package for InCopy from the flyout menu. (You can also choose Package for InCopy and Email, which packages the files and then launches your e-mail program.) InDesign will create the InCopy package file (with the filename extension .incp).

The recipient would choose Open Package from the flyout menu in InCopy's Assignments panel to open the file, and would then choose Package for InDesign to send you back all the files in one package.

NEW FEATURE   The ability to package assignments is new to InDesign CS3 and InCopy CS3.

Editing and manipulating assigned stories

When text is assigned, it is automatically checked in, making it unavailable for editing in the layout. To edit the text, you need to *check out* the story, making it available to you but to no one else. To do so, click on the frame containing the story you want to edit, and then choose Edit ⇨ InCopy ⇨ Check Out, or press ⌘+F9 or Ctrl+F9. To ensure that your changes are saved, I recommend you choose Edit ⇨ InCopy ⇨ Save Content periodically as you work.

TIP   A quick way to check out a story is to begin editing its text. InDesign will ask if you want to check out the story. Click Yes, and the story is checked out for you.

When done, choose either Edit ⇨ InCopy ⇨ Check In (Shift+⌘+F9 or Ctrl+Shift+F9) or Edit ⇨ InCopy ⇨ Check In All (Option+Shift+⌘+F9 or Ctrl+Alt+Shift+F9) to return the stories to use by others. (Or choose Edit ⇨ InCopy ⇨ Cancel Check Out to undo all your changes and leave the story unchanged.)

NOTE   You can keep doing design work on the frames associated to an assignment — such as resizing frames, adding graphics, and even changing the text's color — regardless of whether a story's text is checked in or out.

When you are working on a story, InDesign displays an icon indicating its status at the top of its text frame, as well as in the Assignments panel. These icons are:

    ✎   Checked In

    ▥   Checked Out

    ✗   Checked Out by Someone Else

    ▨   Checked In but Out of Date

If someone else is working on a story, you can have InDesign apply the current design changes to the layout on your screen by choosing Edit ➪ InCopy ➪ Update Story, or pressing Control+⌘+F5 or Ctrl+F5.

 InDesign CS3 has a new shortcut for the Mac for Update Story: Control+⌘+F5, compared to just ⌘+F5 in previous versions. The Windows shortcut of Ctrl+F5 is unchanged.

Using the InCopy Program

The stand-alone, separately purchased InCopy application looks and works very much like the InDesign Story Editor. You can also find a bevy of familiar panels — Notes, Scripts, Swatches, Tags, Tools, and the various text-editing panels — in the Window menu. You'll also find the standard Edit and Type menu options to change text attributes and do spell-checking. Plus, you find many of the standard InDesign preferences panes in the Preferences dialog box.

NOTE Just as in InDesign, you must set a username when working in InCopy, so it can track who has made what change. The User dialog box (File ➪ User) is the same as the one I cover earlier in this chapter for InDesign.

What's different? Plenty.

Story views

First, there are three panes in which to view the story:

- The Story pane (View ➪ Story View, or Option+⌘+G or Ctrl+Alt+G) is the plainest view, essentially the same as the InDesign Story Editor. Here, you work on text as if you are in a word processor, with applied styles shown at left. Figure 36.4 shows this view.

- The Layout pane (View ➪ Layout View, or ⌘+L or Ctrl+L) shows the story as it appears in InDesign.

- The Galley pane (View ➪ Galley View, or ⌘+G or Ctrl+G) is like the Story pane, except that each line breaks as it does in InDesign, so you can see where lines end and whether the last lines in paragraphs have room for more text or whether small text deletions could easily eliminate a short last line during copyfitting.

TIP You can quickly switch views by clicking the Galley, Story, and Layout tabs in the main story window.

 Note the Story and Galley panes, as well as the Assignments panel, will show all InCopy stories associated with an InDesign file — InCopy adds them all automatically if you open any of them. In any of these panes, you can display and hide stories by clicking the triangles to the left of the story name.

Story checkout, check-in, and saving

You can edit both individual InCopy story files (.incx) and InCopy assignment files (.inca) in InCopy. An assignment may contain multiple stories.

When you open an InCopy Interchange file or an InCopy assignment file in InCopy, you need to check stories out to edit them and check them in to make them available to others, as I described in the previous section for InDesign. To check out stories, go to the story in any of the panes, and then choose File ➪ Check Out, or press ⌘+F9 or Ctrl+F9. You check the story you are working on back in by choosing File ➪ Check In, or pressing Shift+⌘+F9 or Ctrl+Shift+F9.

You check back in all stories by choosing File ➪ Check In All, or pressing Option+Shift+⌘+F9 or Ctrl+Alt+Shift+F9. The Assignments panel (Window ➪ Assignments, or Option+⌘+F10 or Ctrl+Alt+F10) shows which stories are already checked out.

NEW FEATURE The keyboard shortcuts for checking stories in and out have changed to match those in InDesign.

You can also choose File ➪ Cancel Checkout to make a story available to others without saving any changes you made. Choose File ➪ Revert Story instead to undo changes you made since the last save but keep the story checked out for your use.

NEW FEATURE The names of the save commands have changed slightly, with *Story* changed to *Content* (such as Save Story now being called Save Content). The functionality is unchanged.

To save a story, you have four options in the File menu:

- Save Content, or ⌘+S or Ctrl+S, to save the current story.

- Save Content As, or Shift+⌘+S or Ctrl+Shift+S, to save the current story with a new name or in a new location. You have to import such a story into the InDesign layout.

- Save Content Copy, or Option+⌘+S or Ctrl+Alt+S, to save a copy of the current story, such as for archiving story versions.

- Save All Content, or Option+Shift+⌘+S or Ctrl+Alt+Shift+S, to save all stories — this helps ensure all changes are made to the InDesign document, no matter what stories the changes occurred in.

Revisions tracking

InCopy can track who made what changes to InDesign files — including changes made by the designer in the InDesign layout itself, not just changes made by InCopy users. To enable such revisions tracking, choose Changes ➪ Track Changes in Current Story, or press ⌘+Y or Ctrl+Y. If multiple stories are open (such as when you are working with an InCopy assignment), you can choose Changes ➪ Enable Tracking in All Stories.

NOTE InCopy CS3 can also show you revisions from your original Microsoft Word file (if you used its changes-tracking feature) — but only if you enabled the Track Changes option in the Import Options dialog box when you first placed the text file, as explained in Chapter 14.

FIGURE 36.4

Adobe InCopy CS3, with a layout viewed in the Story pane

Zoom tool

Hand tool   Info Column

Note tool   Command Bar panel

Position tool   Track Changes Toolbar panel

Type tool

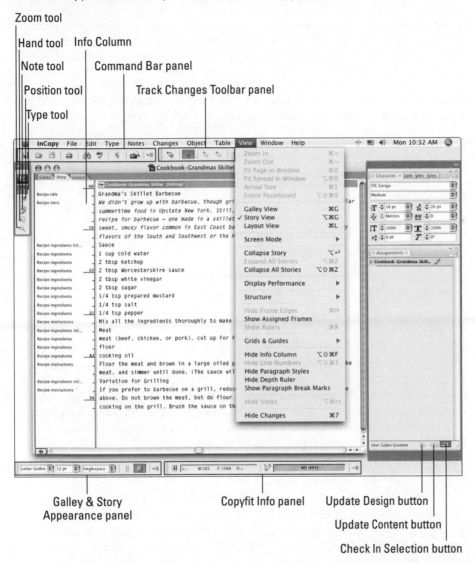

Galley & Story
Appearance panel   Copyfit Info panel   Update Design button

Update Content button

Check In Selection button

When reviewing changes, you can move from change to change by choosing Changes ⇨ Next Change, or pressing ⌘+down arrow or Ctrl+down arrow. You can move backward by choosing Changes ⇨ Previous Change, or pressing ⌘+up arrow or Ctrl+up arrow. You can accept individual changes by choosing Changes ⇨ Accept Change, or pressing Shift+⌘+O or Ctrl+Shift+O, and you can accept all changes by choosing Changes ⇨ Accept All Changes, or Option+Shift+⌘+O or Ctrl+Alt+Shift+O.

Likewise, you can reject changes individually by choosing Changes ⇨ Reject Change, or pressing Shift+⌘+; (semicolon) or Ctrl+Shift+; (semicolon), or globally by choosing Changes ⇨ Reject All Changes, or pressing Option+Shift+⌘+; (semicolon) or Ctrl+Alt+Shift+; (semicolon).

You can also use the Track Changes Toolbar panel to move among revisions and accept or reject changes. The iconic panel offers the following buttons from left to right: Track Changes in Current Story, Show/Hide Changes, Previous Change, Next Change, Accept Change, Reject Change, Accept All Changes, and Reject All Changes.

When reviewing changes, you can get information on who made the change and when by having the Change Info panel open (Window ⇨ Change Info, or Shift+⌘+F3 or Ctrl+Shift+F3).

 TIP You can hide changes as you make them by choosing View ⇨ Hide Changes, or pressing ⌘+7 or Ctrl+7. To review changes, you need to make changes visible.

Special features

The editing and formatting features are almost the same as in InDesign, so this chapter does not cover them. Likewise, the notes features are the same as those I describe in Chapter 16. But there are some specific InCopy features you should know about:

- You can transpose two letters by inserting the text-insertion pointer between them and choosing Edit ⇨ Transpose (Option+⌘+4 or Ctrl+Alt+4).

- You can create text macros in the Text Macros panel (Window ⇨ Text Macros, or Shift+⌘+F10 or Ctrl+Shift+F10). You add a macro by choosing New Macro from its fly-out menu or by pressing Option+⌘+F8 or Ctrl+Alt+F8.

- You can look up a word in an electronic thesaurus to find better alternatives. Choose Window ⇨ Thesaurus, or press Option+⌘+F7 or Ctrl+Alt+F7, to open the panel. If a word is selected, click the Load Word iconic button (the eyedropper icon) from the bottom of the panel to add it. Click the Lookup Word iconic button (the magnifying-glass icon) to look up alternatives. If you want one of the alternatives, select it and then click the Change Word iconic button (the dual-curved-arrows icon).

- The Command Bar panel (Window ⇨ Command Bar, or Shift+⌘+F2 or Ctrl+Shift+F2) provides iconic button access for, from left to right, New Document, Open Document, Save, Print, Find, Check Spelling, and Show/Hide Hidden Characters.

- The Galley & Story Appearance panel likewise provides Font, Size, and Text Preview Spacing pop-up menus to change the Story and Galley panes' text display, plus iconic buttons to Show/Hide Line Numbers and Show/Hide Paragraph Styles. You can also change these settings, plus the text cursor display, through the Galley & Story Display pane in the Preferences dialog box (choose InCopy ⇨ Preferences or press ⌘+K on the Mac, or choose Edit ⇨ Preferences or press ⌘+K in Windows). The pane is identical to the Story Editor preferences pane covered in Chapter 16. The show/hide options in the Galley & Story Appearance pane are also available in the View menu.

■ The Copyfit Info panel shows how many lines a story is over what fits in its text frames and/or paths, using the bar at its far right. As you delete text, the progress bar gets smaller and smaller until there is no runover. The panel also tracks the number of lines, words, characters, and column depth. The Update Copyfit Progress Info iconic button (the ruler icon) checks the current InDesign layout to see if changes to the layout have solved or created copyfitting problems, in which text overflows its text frames. The panel also has the Update Story Info iconic button (the downward arrow) at far left that updates the Change Info panel (File ➪ Change Info, or Shift+⌘+F3 or Ctrl+Shift+F3) with the name of the current reviser.

These last three panels, as well as the Track Changes Toolbar panel, are shown in Figure 36.4.

CROSS-REF The Quick Apply panel, which Chapter 2 covers, provides quick access via the keyboard to styles and other formatting controls. Given that InCopy users tend to do a lot of work via the keyboard, this panel can be a very handy tool for fast formatting.

Summary

InDesign CS3 comes out of the box with the tools needed to prepare stories for editing in a workgroup environment. The Assignments panel contains most of the tools you'll use to make stories available to others.

The separately purchased InCopy lets copy editors and other people who need access just to the layout's text revise that text (such as for copyfitting and headline writing) without needing the full InDesign program. By having such users work on text via InCopy, designers can also ensure that the layouts themselves are unchanged by nondesigners.

Part X

Extending InDesign

IN THIS PART

Chapter 37
Using Plug-Ins

Chapter 38
Using Scripts

Chapter 37

Using Plug-Ins

IN THIS CHAPTER

Using the default plug-ins

Purchasing special-purpose plug-ins

How plug-ins work within InDesign

Managing plug-ins

From the very get-go, the InDesign team engineered the software to be *extensible* — meaning you can extend its capabilities by adding more software. To do this, you use *plug-ins*, which are small software modules often developed by third parties. If you're a Photoshop user, you might be familiar with plug-ins such as Alien Skin's Eye Candy; or if you're a QuarkXPress user, you're probably familiar with the concept of add-on software through XTensions. Even if you're new to publishing, you may have purchased add-on software for your operating system, such as a custom screen saver or virus-protection software.

Extensible programs solve the one-size-fits-all nature of most software, letting you customize your tools to your workflow. If InDesign doesn't meet a need of yours — such as indexing, table editing, or imposition — you can look for a plug-in that does.

Using the Default Plug-Ins

Many core features in InDesign are actually implemented through plug-ins. When you launch the application, you may notice the words *Caching plug-ins* on the InDesign startup screen; this is when the plug-ins load. Structuring the software this way lets Adobe update or modify a finite area of the software and then distribute a new plug-in, instead of updating and distributing the entire application. Go to the Adobe Web site (www.adobe.com) periodically to look for both fixes and new plug-ins. There's also a directory of plug-ins at this book's companion Web site (www.InDesignCentral.com).

The default plug-ins are stored in a folder called Plug-Ins inside your InDesign application folder. If you open the Plug-Ins folder, as shown in Figure 37.1, you'll notice the plug-ins have been consolidated into special-purpose folders such as Filters and Text. You should leave the default plug-ins alone, for the most part.

QUARKXPRESS QuarkXPress users might be accustomed to removing XTensions to reduce launch time and consume less RAM. Don't use this technique with InDesign. Many core features of the application, such as the text handling, are implemented through plug-ins, and the program may not work at all if you remove required plug-ins.

FIGURE 37.1

The InDesign Plug-Ins folder stores the default plug-ins, as well as additional plug-ins you may install.

Purchasing Special-Purpose Plug-Ins

With the backing of a software and publishing giant like Adobe, InDesign has enticed a variety of proven developers to create special-purpose plug-ins.

Many plug-in developers provide a free evaluation copy so you can try before you buy. This is important because you can figure out if the plug-in really solves your problem, whether everyone in your workgroup needs it, and whether your service bureau needs it as well.

 To quickly find available InDesign plug-ins, go to the Plug-Ins page of this book's companion Web site (www.InDesignCentral.com).

Understanding How Plug-Ins Work within InDesign

To use a new plug-in, the first thing you need to do is install it. Many plug-ins include their own installers that search out your copy of InDesign and plant themselves in the Plug-Ins folder. If a plug-in doesn't include an installer or installation instructions, try clicking and dragging it into the Plug-Ins folder. Once a plug-in is in the correct location, you need to restart InDesign so the plug-in is recognized and its code is loaded. You cannot install a new plug-in while InDesign is running; you should always quit the application before changing anything in the Plug-Ins folder and then restarting.

If a plug-in cannot load with InDesign, an alert appears while the application is starting up. Usually, loading errors result from incompatible versions of InDesign and the plug-in. Check the plug-in's ReadMe file or contact the developer for assistance. To remove a plug-in, simply click and drag it out of the subfolder of the Plug-Ins folder and store it someplace else. (You might create a folder called Disabled Plug-Ins in which to store plug-ins that you're not using. Just be sure it's not stored in the Plug-Ins folder!)

Plug-ins are designed for specific platforms (Mac or Windows) as well as for specific versions of InDesign (1, 1.5, 2, CS, CS2, or CS3), so you need to get new versions of your plug-ins if you change platforms or upgrade to a new version of InDesign.

When a plug-in is loaded with InDesign, new controls appear in the interface. You might see entire menus, menu commands, dialog boxes, panels, and tools added to the application by a plug-in. No matter the combination of interface elements, when you're using the features of a plug-in, it should look and feel as if you're using InDesign. Some plug-ins meet this criteria; others do not.

For example, the MultiDocs plug-in from 65-Bit Software adds two menu options — Undo Multiple and Redo Multiple — to the Edit menu, permitting multiple levels of undo and redo from which the user can choose. Otherwise, InDesign's interface is unaffected. Other plug-ins might add panels or change other menus.

In some cases, plug-ins may add objects or information to documents that can be recognized only when the plug-in is loaded. If the plug-in is missing, you — or other users — may not be able to open the document, or the document may look different.

Managing Plug-Ins

After acquiring several plug-ins, you may have trouble managing all the features in InDesign because you'll have new panels, toolbars, and menu options throughout the program. Fortunately, InDesign has a tool to let you manage your plug-ins, so you can turn them on and off as needed, as well as save sets of plug-ins so you can turn on and off related plug-ins simultaneously.

To manage plug-ins, use the Configure Plug-ins dialog box shown in Figure 37.2. To open this dialog box, choose InDesign ➪ Configure Plug-Ins on the Mac or Help ➪ Configure Plug-Ins in Windows.

The default list of plug-ins will be very long because so many basic InDesign features are implemented through plug-ins. To help manage the display, you have six options at the bottom of the dialog box that filter what appears: Enabled, Adobe, Required, Disabled, Third Party, and Optional. Deselecting any of these options does not disable the plug-ins themselves; it simply removes them from the dialog box's list.

To manage plug-ins, you want to enable Third Party to see non-Adobe plug-ins and Optional to see plug-ins that can be turned off safely. Be sure that Enabled is also selected to see what is enabled or that Disabled is selected to see what plug-ins have been previously turned off. If neither Enabled nor Disabled is selected, you don't see any plug-ins in the list — you have to use these options in combination with each other. For example, selecting Enabled, Adobe, and Required shows only the required Adobe plug-ins that are enabled.

NOTE Required plug-ins have a lock icon to their left, while other plug-ins have a check mark to their left if enabled and nothing if disabled.

To enable and disable plug-ins, simply click to the left of the plug-in name. If checked, a plug-in is enabled when you relaunch InDesign. If unchecked, it is disabled. If you're not sure what a plug-in does, you can get more information (the name of the developer, the version, and a brief description) by clicking the plug-in name and then clicking Show Info.

When you first disable plug-ins, InDesign forces you to create a new *set* of plug-ins — sets are essentially a list of which plug-ins should be enabled and which should be disabled. You can copy, edit the name of, and delete sets using the Duplicate, Rename, and Delete buttons. You choose a set of plug-ins to put in use by using the Set pop-up menu at the top of the dialog box. You can also import and export plug-in sets by clicking Import and Export. Click OK when you're done or Cancel to leave the plug-ins as they were when you first opened the Configure Plug-ins dialog box.

You may want to turn specific plug-ins on and off as needed rather than have them in the way all of the time. A good way to do this is to create plug-in sets that you can then switch among. I recommend you create a set of plug-ins called Standard Plugs (at first, it would be the same as the All

Plug-ins set, including everything that comes with InDesign out of the box). Then, before you add any new plug-ins, first create a new set named after the new plug-in, and activate it in the Set menu. Then quit InDesign and install the new plug-ins. You can decide whether to switch between this plug-in set and Standard plug-ins using the Set pop-up menu or to save this new set as Standard Plug-ins, making the new plug-in part of your standard plug-in set.

FIGURE 37.2

The Configure Plug-ins dialog box

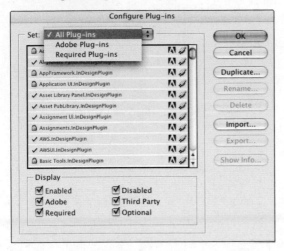

NOTE You must quit and relaunch InDesign for any changes to plug-ins to take effect.

Summary

Plug-ins are software modules that serve two purposes in InDesign: incorporating core features into the application and adding special functions. Plug-ins are stored in the Plug-Ins folder within the InDesign application folder. Many established developers of QuarkXPress XTensions and Photoshop plug-ins have developed InDesign plug-ins to provide additional features such as mathematical typesetting and page imposition. When purchasing and using plug-ins, consider whether other users of your workgroup and your service bureau need them as well. Finally, you can manage which plug-ins are in use through the Configure Plug-ins dialog box.

Chapter 38

Using Scripts

IN THIS CHAPTER

Installing and accessing scripts

Exploring JavaScript

Exploring AppleScript

Exploring VBA

Writing scripts

Learning more about scripting

Scripting automates many features in InDesign — it's essentially a way to program InDesign to do specific actions. Because InDesign uses standard script languages, you can also run scripts that work with multiple programs in concert, including InDesign. (All the applications must support the same scripting language, of course.) For example, you might use scripts to automate database publishing, such as to run a database search, export data to a text file, import that file into InDesign, and then apply the appropriate formatting.

InDesign supports three scripting languages:

- JavaScript on both Mac and Windows
- AppleScript on the Mac only
- Visual Basic for Applications (VBA), on Windows only

Because only JavaScript is supported by both platforms, I recommend you use it wherever possible, so your scripts can work in cross-platform environments. InDesign doesn't force you to choose just one scripting language, so you could keep using old AppleScript or VBA scripts created for previous versions of InDesign, as well as new scripts written in JavaScript.

As you become comfortable with scriptwriting, you're also likely to discover that virtually everything you do with InDesign is a repetitive task. The more you can free yourself of this kind of work by using scripts, the more time you have to be creative. The possibilities are endless. But before you get too excited, remember that scripting is programming, so most layout artists stay clear of it, using scripts only if they have a programmer available to write them.

Using Scripts

Accessing scripts is easy; they show up in the Scripts panel (Window ⇨ Automation ⇨ Scripts, or Option+⌘+F11 or Ctrl+Alt+F11) if you've placed scripts in the Scripts folder inside the folder that contains the InDesign application, as shown in Figure 38.1. Scripts don't have to be in the Scripts folder — they can be anywhere on your computer — but to use them outside this folder means you have to double-click them from your desktop rather than have access from within InDesign.

The Scripts panel in InDesign and its flyout menu

NEW FEATURE The shortcuts Option+⌘+F11 and Ctrl+Alt+F11 for opening the Scripts panel are new to InDesign CS3.

Script locations

Whether you create your own scripts or get them from vendors or other users, you need to save them so InDesign knows they exist. You have a choice of two locations:

- The Scripts folder inside the InDesign application folder (usually `Applications:Adobe InDesign CS3:Scripts` in Mac OS X 10.4 (Tiger) and 10.5 (Leopard), and `Program Files\Adobe\InDesign CS3\Scripts` in Windows XP and Vista). This makes the script available to all users of your computer. If you want the script to start when InDesign launches, place it in the Startup Scripts subfolder.

- The Script Panel folder; this makes the script available only that specific user (note that it will appear in a folder called User in your Scripts panel, as shown in Figure 38.1). The path varies based on your operating system:

  - On the Mac, the path is `Users:user name:Library:Preferences:Adobe InDesign:Version 5.0:Scripts:Script Panel`.
  - In Windows XP, the path is `Documents and Settings\user name\Application Data\Adobe\InDesign\Version 5.0\Scripts\Script Panel`.
  - In Windows Vista, the path is `Users\user name\AppData\Local\Adobe\InDesign\Version 5.0\Scripts\Script Panel`.

How Adobe Has Supercharged Scripts

Adobe has made several significant under-the-hood changes to scripting that increase both developers' and users' control over scripts.

First, everything within InDesign is now scriptable, giving you more control over the program and its contents.

Second, you can associate a script to a specific InDesign menu action so that when a user chooses that menu item, a script runs automatically (technically, by assigning a script to a MenuAction command's Prenotify or Postnotify property when writing the script's code). In InDesign, be sure that Enable Attached Scripts is also enabled in the Scripts panel's flyout menu.

Third, you can now undo all of a script's action by using the InDesign Undo command (Edit ➪ Undo, or ⌘+Z or Ctrl+Z) by ensuring that Undo Affects Entire Script is enabled in the Scripts panel's flyout menu. Otherwise, the undo command reverses just the last action within the script, requiring you to undo several times to "roll back" the complete script action.

Fourth, and last, by enabling the Enable Redraw flyout menu option, you can force InDesign to redraw the display while a script is running. This ensures that any changes to the document are immediately visible.

 The Scripts folder has moved up a level to the folder containing the InDesign application. It used to reside in the Presets folder within the InDesign application folder.

The script shows up in the Scripts panel. If it doesn't show up immediately, quit and reopen InDesign.

TIP To use scripts developed for InDesign CS2, create a new folder called Version 4.0 Scripts inside the Scripts or Script Panel folder and move your old scripts there. They then work in InDesign CS3.

Scripting principles

No matter what scripting language you use, there are several basic principles to observe. These fall into four basic categories:

- **Grammar:** All languages — including programming languages such as Pascal and C++, as well as scripting languages — include grammatical components that are used in standardized sequences. In English, we combine nouns, verbs, adjectives, adverbs, and so on to create sentences. Everybody knows the meaning of "The weather is especially nice today," because it uses common words in a sequence that makes sense. The sentence "Nice is the especially today weather," has the right components, but it's arranged in the wrong sequence, so the meaning is lost.

- **Statements and syntax rules:** In JavaScript, AppleScript, and VBA, verbs, nouns, adjectives, and prepositions are combined to create statements; statements are combined to form scripts. Verbs are also called *commands* and *methods*; nouns are called *objects*; and adjectives are called *properties*. Syntax rules specify how statements and scripts must be constructed so that a computer can understand them.

- **Object hierarchy:** All three scripting languages use a structural element called an *object hierarchy*. It's a fancy term for a simple concept. An object hierarchy works like a set of boxes within boxes. A large box contains a smaller box, which contains a smaller box, which contains a smaller box, and so on, until you reach the smallest box, which contains nothing and is the final level in the hierarchy of boxes.

- **InDesign hierarchy:** InDesign contains its own hierarchy, which lends itself nicely to scripting. A document contains pages, pages contain frames, and frames contain text and pictures. You can create scripts that perform actions at any of these levels. In other words, with scripts you can create documents, add pages, add items to pages, and modify the contents of frames, right down to a particular character in a text frame. You can think of this hierarchy in InDesign as a chain of command. You can't talk directly to an item that's at the bottom of the chain. Rather, you must first address the top level, then the next, and so on, until you've reached the item at the bottom of the chain. This is analogous to the way you use InDesign: You create new documents, add pages, place text and graphics on the pages, and, finally, modify the contents of the frames containing those items.

If you're thinking about dabbling with any of the scripting languages supported by InDesign, the following words of both caution and encouragement are in order. First the encouragement: You don't necessarily need programming experience, scripting experience, or a pocket protector to begin creating scripts. A bit of curiosity and a touch of patience will suffice. Now the caution: Scripting is essentially a euphemism for programming (that is, figuring out the right commands and then typing them for the application to execute). Writing scripts isn't a matter of choosing commands from menus, and clicking and dragging them, or entering values into fields; nor is it like writing a limerick. If you're starting from scratch, know in advance that you have to learn some new skills.

Learning to create scripts is like learning to swim: You can read books, documentation, and articles until your head spins, but eventually you have to get a little wet. The best way to learn about scripting is to write a script. So put on your swimsuit and dive in.

Be forewarned: There's something almost narcotic about creating scripts, and it's not uncommon for novice scriptwriters to get hooked. Don't be surprised if what starts out to be a 15-minute look-see turns into a multihour, late-night programming episode.

NOTE   Because scripting languages differ, you can't always duplicate the functionality of a specific script in one language into a script written in a different language.

NOTE   Adobe has a nearly 2,000-page scripting guide available as a PDF file. It comes with your InDesign or Creative Suite software, residing on the installation CD. You can find additional resources at www.adobe.com.

Exploring JavaScript

JavaScript is a scripting language developed by Netscape Communications, based on Sun Microsystems' Java language that was meant to let Web browsers manage resources on far-flung servers by running scripts to control the servers from a desktop. JavaScript soon became a popular scripting language because, like Java, it runs on so many types of computers, including Windows, Macintosh, and Unix. But because it is based largely on the object-oriented approach taken by professional computer languages such as C and C++, it can be difficult for nonprogrammers to use.

There are lots of JavaScript editor programs available. Most of these are developed by individuals and small firms, so the list is always changing. I recommend you use the Google search engine (www.google.com) and search for *JavaScript editor* to find the most current programs. A great script-editing program for Mac users is Bare Bones Software's venerable BBEdit; you can get more information at www.barebones.com.

Learning the language

JavaScript is a very complex language based on object-oriented programming, which abstracts items and attributes as objects that are then grouped, changed, or otherwise manipulated. This means that JavaScript is less "Englishlike" than other scripting languages because it requires you to spend a fair amount of time setting up the objects before you can manipulate them.

```
myObject.strokeTint = newValue;
```

This example shows that there is a current object named `strokeTint` that is being set to a new value; the actual value for `newValue` is set earlier in the script.

Getting More Information on JavaScript

Before you venture too far into scripting, you should review the JavaScript-related information provided with InDesign:

- **JavaScript documentation and tools:** Sun places the very technical JavaScript documentation on its Web site at http://java.sun.com/javascript/index.jsp

- **InDesign scripting documentation:** The InDesign installation CD contains a 2,000-plus-page PDF file that explains scripting for InDesign. This document, although a bit on the technical side, is a valuable resource. It includes an overview of JavaScript scripting and the object model, as well as a list of InDesign-specific scripting terms and scripting examples.

If you want still more information about JavaScript, several books are available, including *Beginning JavaScript, 2nd Edition,* by Paul Wilton and *JavaScript Bible, 6th Edition,* by Danny Goodman and Michael Morrison (both from Wiley Publishing).

What you need to write and run scripts

You need a program that can display, edit, and test your JavaScript — there is no bundled JavaScript editor in Windows or Mac OS X. Such editors typically format the JavaScript code for you, indenting it automatically, graying out comments, and highlighting certain keywords.

You can use a word processor or text editor to write and edit scripts, but such programs can't check the syntax or automatically format the script text to help show nested loops, conditional branches, and so forth. Also, you can usually use an HTML editor such as Macromedia Dreamweaver or Adobe GoLive in which to edit JavaScripts, though they also typically don't provide any debugging tools to help you track and fix coding (syntax) errors. (Figure 38.2 shows a JavaScript script being edited in Dreamweaver.) In this case, you need to open the error window in your browser as you test the code and see if it identifies the error location to help you find it in your HTML editor.

FIGURE 38.2

A JavaScript program viewed in Adobe Dreamweaver

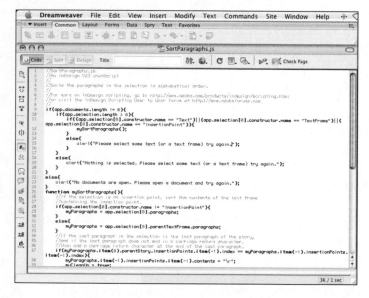

Running your script

The easiest way to run a script is to double-click it in the Scripts panel within InDesign. But you also can simply double-click the script file; note that InDesign may need to be open. Also, while you're developing the script, you can run the script directly from the application in which you created it — again, InDesign may need to be open. If you've done everything correctly, you see InDesign become the active program, and then the actions you put in your script take place. Voilà and congratulations! You can now call yourself a scripter without blushing. That's all there is to creating and running a script.

Saving your script

When you're finished writing and testing a script, choose Save from the script editor's File menu. Name your script and choose its storage location. Move or copy the saved script to one of the two locations I described earlier in this chapter.

Exploring AppleScript

AppleScript is a scripting language developed by Apple and initially released with System 7.5 that can be used to control Macs, networks, and scriptable applications, including InDesign. The AppleScript language was designed to be as close to normal English as possible so that average Mac users — specifically, those who aren't familiar with programming languages — can understand and use it.

 NOTE   InDesign can run text-only AppleScripts in addition to compiled (binary) ones.

Learning the language

Many of the actions specified in AppleScripts read like sentences you might use in everyday conversation, such as:

```
set color of myFrame to "Black"
```

or

```
set applied font of myCharacterStyle to "Times"
```

What you need to write and run scripts

The Script Editor provided with the Mac OS lets you write scripts. You find the Script Editor inside the AppleScript folder inside your Applications folder (at the root level of your hard drive). An uncompiled script is essentially a text file, so you can actually write scripts with any word processor. The Script Editor, however, was created for writing AppleScripts and includes several handy features for scriptwriters.

TIP   To see what AppleScript commands that InDesign supports, you can view the InDesign object model — the supported commands — within the Script Editor; just choose File ➪ Open Dictionary, and then scroll to the InDesign application icon and click Open.

Checking for syntax errors

The next step is to determine if the statements are correctly constructed. Click the Check Syntax button. If the Script Editor encounters a syntax error, it alerts you and highlights the cause of the error. If the script's syntax is correct, all statements except the first and last are indented, and a number of words are displayed in bold, as illustrated in Figure 38.3. Your script has been compiled and is ready to test.

Running your script

To run a script from InDesign, double-click the script in the Scripts panel. Alternatively, double-click the script file itself (InDesign may need to be open). When developing the script, click the Run button in the Script Editor; InDesign becomes the active program, and your script is running.

FIGURE 38.3

This Script Editor window contains sample AppleScript text. When you check the syntax of a script, the Script Editor applies formatting and indents.

If you have trouble getting a script to run, double-check the name that InDesign uses for itself. It might use InDesign® CS3 or simply InDesign® (yes, the name may include the registered trademark symbol). If you run a script from AppleScript (rather than just double-clicking it) and AppleScript can't find InDesign, it gives you a dialog box with which you find the InDesign program. When you've found and selected the InDesign application, AppleScript will find out what InDesign's filename is and use that in your script.

Saving your script

When you're finished writing and testing a script, choose Save from the Script Editor's File menu. Name your script, choose its storage location, and choose Compiled Script from the Format pop-up menu. Move or copy the saved script to one of the two locations I describe earlier in this chapter.

Getting More Information on AppleScript

Before you venture too far into scripting, you should review the AppleScript-related information provided with the Mac OS and with InDesign:

- **Mac scripting documentation and tools:** Apple places the AppleScript documentation on its Web site at www.apple.com/applescript. In your hard drive's Applications folder, you should have a folder called AppleScript that contains the Script Editor program, along with a folder of example scripts and the AppleScript Script Menu that adds the Script menu to the Finder. Apple also offers a professional AppleScript editor called AppleScript Studio for download at its developer Web site, www.apple.com/macosx/features/xcode/. Apple makes AppleScript Studio part of its Xcode scripting tool, so you need to get Xcode to get AppleScript Studio.

- **InDesign scripting documentation:** The InDesign CD contains a 2,000-plus-page PDF file that explains scripting, including AppleScript programming, for InDesign. This document, although a bit on the technical side, is a valuable resource. It includes an overview of Apple events scripting and the object model, as well as a list of InDesign-specific scripting terms and scripting examples.

If you want still more information about AppleScript, several books are available, including *AppleScript For Dummies, 2nd Edition*, by Tom Trinko and *Beginning AppleScript* by Stephen G. Kochan (both from Wiley Publishing).

If you save the script in Application format and want to edit your script later, you must open it by dragging and dropping it on the Script Editor application. This is because Application-format scripts are designed to immediately run when double-clicked. You would choose the Application format when creating scripts for use by others because chances are you don't want them to open the script in Script Editor but instead simply want them to use the script by double-clicking it like any other application. (It doesn't matter whether the script is in Application format if you run it from InDesign's Scripts panel.)

Locating more AppleScript tools

A few software utilities are also available for AppleScripters. The most widely used is Script Debugger, from Late Night Software ($199, www.latenightsw.com); it's an interface development tool that quickly creates AppleScript-based applications that have the standard Mac look and feel. Apple also offers its AppleScript Studio as a free download to developers who register at the Apple site (www.apple.com/macosx/features/xcode); this is more capable than the basic Script Editor that comes with Mac OS X. AppleScript Studio is part of Apple's Xcode scripting tool, so you need to get Xcode to get AppleScript Studio.

Exploring VBA

VBA, and its subset version VBScript, is Microsoft's technology for writing your own programs, both those that run in other programs (scripts) and those that run by themselves (custom applications). InDesign works with both VBA and VBScript. The Visual Basic language that underlies both VBA and VBScript is not meant for everyday computer users; knowledge of programming is very useful in taking advantage of this technology. Although based on the Basic language developed in the 1970s to help new users write their own programs, it has evolved a lot since then and is no longer so simple.

Learning the language

Many of the actions specified in VBA have some degree of English, such as:

```
set myTextFrame =
InDesign.Documents.Item(1).Spreads.Item(1).TextFrames.Add
```

or

```
mySelection.RotationAngle = 30
```

But as you can see, that degree of English is slight. The first code segment, for example, means to add a text frame to the first spread in the first document. The second means to rotate the selected object by 30 degrees.

What you need to write and run scripts

To use InDesign scripting in Windows, you need Microsoft Visual Basic or an application that contains VBA; these include Microsoft Office, Microsoft Visio, and AutoCAD. In Microsoft Office, you can run the Microsoft Script Editor by choosing Tools ➪ Macro ➪ Microsoft Script Editor, which lets you create scripts, edit them, test your code, and fix errors. Figure 38.4 shows the editor with a sample script. (Note that the script editor's dialog box has the self-important name Microsoft Development Environment rather than Microsoft Script Editor.)

You can also write scripts in VBScript, a VBA subset, in a text editor such as WordPad. You need Microsoft's free Windows Scripting Host (WSCRIPT.EXE), which is usually installed with Windows, and you can download it from Microsoft's Web site.

There's a third choice for your scriptwriting: You can also use the full Microsoft Visual Basic product from Microsoft.

 To use InDesign scripting in Windows, your user profile must have Administrator privileges.

TIP To see what Visual Basic commands InDesign supports, you can view the InDesign object model — the supported commands — within the Microsoft's Visual basic product; just choose Project ➪ References, and then select Adobe InDesign CS3 Type Library in the References dialog box and click OK.

Running your script

There are a few ways to run a VBScript. You can double-click the script in the Scripts panel within InDesign or double-click the script file itself from a folder. When developing scripts, you can run the script directly from the application in which you created a VBA or Visual Basic script, such as the Microsoft Script Editor. (VBScripts can be run from the Scripting Host application.) In all these cases, InDesign becomes the active program, and your script is running.

FIGURE 38.4

The Microsoft Development Environment window contains sample VBA text. When you work on a script, the Microsoft Development Environment applies indents automatically.

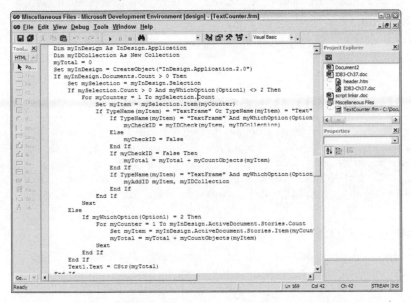

Saving your script

When you're finished writing and testing a script, choose Save from the script editor's File menu. Name your script and choose its storage location. Move or copy the saved script to one of the two locations I described earlier in this chapter.

Getting More Information on VBA

Before you venture too far into scripting, you should review the VBA related information provided by Microsoft and with InDesign:

- **Microsoft scripting documentation and tools:** Microsoft has a lot of information on VBA, VBScript, and Visual Basic on its Web site. Unfortunately, it's not well organized and is hard to find and understand. There's no tutorial that simply explains how a new scripter needs to get started. However, you can search on the Microsoft site for VBA, VBScript, and Visual Basic to get links to documents that may prove useful.

- **InDesign scripting documentation:** The InDesign CD contains a 2,000-plus-page PDF file that explains scripting in InDesign, including VBA programming. This document, although a bit on the technical side, is a valuable resource. It includes an overview of VBA scripting and the object model, as well as a list of InDesign-specific scripting terms and scripting examples.

If you want still more information about VBA and its two "sister" technologies, several books are available, including *VBScript Programmer's Reference, 2nd Edition,* by Adrian Kingsley-Hughes, Kathie Kingsley-Hughes, and Daniel Read; *VBA For Dummies, 5th Edition,* by John Paul Mueller; and *Mastering Microsoft VBA, 2nd Edition,* by Guy Hart-Davis (all from Wiley Publishing).

Creating and Running Scripts

At this point, I'm assuming that the appropriate scripting software is installed on your computer. If this is the case, you're ready to begin. For your first trick, you're going to make InDesign roll over — sort of. Actually, you're going to rotate an EPS graphic. First, you'll prepare InDesign for its role. Launch the program, and then create a new document (do not check Automatic Text Frame). In the middle of the first page, place an EPS graphic. Make sure that it remains active after you place it.

Writing simple scripts

The following three scripts, taken from Adobe's InDesign script examples, do the same thing in JavaScript, AppleScript, and VBA — they rotate an EPS graphic and its frame.

CROSS-REF All of the scripts in this chapter are available for download at `www.InDesignCentral.com`. Just cut and paste them from the text files into the appropriate scripting editor. Adobe's user forums are also a good place to go for scripting help.

Type the lines that follow this paragraph exactly as they're written for the scripting language you've chosen. Type a return character at the end of each line. Note also the use of straight quotation marks instead of curly typesetter's quotes (the script editor does this for you). Be very careful when you type the text: Typos are script killers.

NOTE In the code samples below, the ¬ symbol indicates where a line of code is broken to fit the page width; in the actual script, there would be no ¬ character and the line that follows would be combined with the line that now ends in ¬.

JavaScript

```
var myLink, myEPs, myFrame;
if(app.documents.length != 0){
 if(app.activeDocument.links.length != 0){
  for(var myLinkCounter = 0; myLinkCounter < ¬
  app.activeDocument.links.length; myLinkCounter ++){
   myLink = app.activeDocument.links.item(myLinkCounter);
   if(myLink.linkType == "EPS"){
    myEPS = myLink.parent;
    myFrame = myEPS.parent;
    myFrame.rotationAngle = 30;
    }
   }
  }
 }
```

This script first searches through all the items on the page and checks if any are EPS; if so, it sets the rotation of the item to 30. (Thanks to Adobe's InDesign scripting guru, Olav Martin Kvern, for developing the JavaScript code example.) Note the sequence of actions: First you verify that there is a nonempty document open, and then you check the content type of objects. For those objects that are of the EPS type, you activate the frame and then apply the rotation to that frame. JavaScripts require you to set your own variables (the `var` statements) that define what the object is. (Here, `myLink` is used for each object, `myEPS` is the object that contains the EPS attribute, and `myFrame` is the parent frame containing the EPS graphic.) You work with those variables to see what their attributes are and then change those attributes.

If you're in an adventurous mood, try substituting the statement `myFrame.rotationAngle = 30;` in the preceding script with each of the following statements:

```
myFrame.shearAngle = 30;
myFrame.verticalScale = 200;
```

If you want to get really fancy, combine all the `myFrame.` statements into a single script, so you can use the script to make all the changes at once.

AppleScript

```
tell application "Adobe InDesign CS3"
 activate
 set myPageItems to {EPS, oval, rectangle, polygon}
 set mySelection to selection
 if class of item 1 of mySelection is in myPageItems ¬
 and (count mySelection) > 0 then
  if class of item 1 of mySelection is EPS then
```

```
     set myFrame to parent of mySelection
   else
     set myFrame to item 1 of mySelection
   end if
   set rotation angle of myFrame to 30
 end if
end tell
```

NOTE Be sure that a document is open and that you have selected at least one frame of any type before starting the script. Also in the script itself, make sure to type the name of your InDesign program exactly as it appears in the Finder. Because you're free to rename your program, the name may not match the name in the first line of the script.

If you're in an adventurous mood, try substituting the statement set rotation angle of myFrame to 30 in the preceding script with each of the following statements:

```
set shear angle of myFrame to 30
set vertical scale of myFrame to 200
```

If you want to get really fancy, combine all the set statements into a single script, so you can use the script to make all the changes at once.

VBA

```
Dim myInDesign As InDesign.Application
Set myInDesign = CreateObject("InDesign.Application.CS3")
Set mySelection = myInDesign.Selection
If TypeName(mySelection.Item(1)) = "EPS" Then
 mySelection.Parent.RotationAngle = 30
Else
 mySelection.RotationAngle = 30
End If
```

If you're in an adventurous mood, try substituting the statement mySelection.RotationAngle = 30 in the preceding script with each of the following statements:

```
set the color of the current box to "Blue"
set the shade of the current box to 50
set the width of the frame of the current box to 10
set the box shape of the current box to ovular
```

If you want to get really fancy, combine all the set statements into a single script so you can use the script to make all the changes at once.

TIP Perhaps you noticed the chain of command used in the preceding scripts. First the script addresses InDesign, then the active document (layout), and finally the active frame. If you understand this concept, you'll be scripting like a pro in no time.

Labeling items

As you can see from the examples in the previous section, scripts often refer to items by their type and location in the document. But there's another way to refer to objects that makes sure you can select an item precisely: You can label, or name, an item. You do so in the Script Label panel (Window ➪ Automation ➪ Script Label). The process is easy: Select the object, and then type a name in the panel. That's it!

When writing scripts, you refer to the labeled object as follows. In these examples, the label is *TargetFrame*, and don't worry that the samples seem to do different things — they in fact are unrelated examples, not variations of the same command.

JavaScript

```
with(app.documents.item(0).pages.item(0)){
 myTargetFrame = textFrames.item("myTargetFrame");
}
```

AppleScript

```
select (page item 1 of page 1 of myTargetDocument whose ¬
label is "TargetFrame")
```

VBA

```
Set myAsset = myLibrary.Assets.Item("TargetFrame")
```

Writing conditional scripts

Some scripts simply automate a set of tasks in documents whose content is predictable. But more often than not, documents differ, and so you need conditional statements to evaluate certain things to see if they are true before applying a script's actions. Otherwise, you get an error message when something turns out not to be true. As a simple example, a script that does a search and replace needs to have a document open and a frame selected. If no frame is selected, the script won't know what to search, and the user will get an error message.

The same issue arises for repeated series of actions, where you want the script to do something for all occurrences. The script needs to know what to do when it can't find any more such occurrences. As an example, look at the following script, which counts all open documents. For it to work, at least one document has to be open, so the script checks first to see if in fact any documents are open and then delivers an error message that the user can understand if none is open. The rotate-EPS-graphic script earlier also used a conditional to make sure there was an EPS graphic in the document. Notice that in all three scripting languages, you use the command If to set up such conditionals.

JavaScript

```
if (app.documents.length==0){
 alert("No InDesign documents are open!");
}
```

 JavaScript uses == for comparing values (as in the example above) and = for assigning values. Visual Basic and AppleScript use = for both purposes.

AppleScript

```
tell application "Adobe InDesign CS3"
 activate
 set myNumberOfDocuments to (count documents)
 if myNumberOfDocuments = 0 then
  display dialog "No InDesign publications ¬
  are open!"
 end if
end tell
```

VBA

```
Dim myInDesign as InDesign.Application
 Set myInDesign = CreateObject ("InDesign.Application.CS")
 If myInDesign.Documents.Count
  MsgBox "No InDesign publications are open!"
 End If
End Sub
```

Another form of conditional is what's called a *control loop*, in which an action occurs either for a specified number of iterations or until a condition is met. The following scripts show an example of each for each language. Note the use of comments in the scripts — a handy way to document what you're doing for later reference. In JavaScript, a single-line comment begins with //, while a multiline comment begins with /* and ends with */. In AppleScript, a comment begins with -- and continues until you press Enter or Return. In VBA, it begins with Rem followed by a space, and it continues until you press Enter or Return.

JavaScript

```
for (var myCounter = 0; myCounter < 20; myCounter++){
 //do something
}
while (myStop == false){
 /* do something, at some point setting myStop to true
 to leave the loop. */
}
```

AppleScript

```
repeat with counter from 1 to 20
 --do something
end repeat

set myStop to false
repeat while myStop = false
 --do something, at some point setting myStop to true to ¬
 leave the loop.
end repeat
```

VBA

```
For counter = 1 to 20
 Rem do something
Next counter

Do While myStop = false
 Rem do something, at some point setting myStop to true ¬
 to leave the loop.
loop
```

Summary

If your workflow goes beyond original designs for each client and reaches into repetitive production, scripting is for you. Scripts are ideal for automating repetitive tasks — from importing pictures to creating and formatting entire documents. You can even link InDesign to other scriptable applications.

Because InDesign supports JavaScript on the Mac and Windows, as well as AppleScript on the Mac only and VBA on Windows only, you can choose the script language you're most familiar with and/or that is compatible with your other applications. Even better, you can use more than one scripting language with InDesign (though any individual script can use only one language).

Part XI

Appendixes

IN THIS PART

Appendix A
Installing or Upgrading InDesign

Appendix B
What's New in InDesign CS3

Appendix C
Switching from QuarkXPress

Appendix D
Switching from PageMaker

Appendix E
More Resources

Appendix F
Shortcuts Cheat Sheet

Appendix A

Installing or Upgrading InDesign

Installing InDesign CS3 is surprisingly easy, but before installing or upgrading, make sure your system meets the InDesign CS3 system requirements. The key requirements are that you are running Mac OS X 10.4 (Tiger), Mac OS X 10.5 (Leopard), Windows XP (with Service Pack 2 or later), or Windows Vista. Then use the steps in this appendix to make quick work of the installation process. If you're upgrading from an earlier version, you'll actually perform a new installation. But read the section on upgrading near the end of this appendix for information about making the transition to InDesign CS3.

IN THIS APPENDIX

Understanding CS3 system requirements

Installing InDesign CS3

Upgrading from prior versions of InDesign

Reinstalling or uninstalling InDesign

Understanding InDesign CS3 System Requirements

InDesign CS3 does not require extraordinary resources. If you have a Mac or PC that runs one of the required operating systems, you can run InDesign CS3. Just be sure to have enough hard-drive space and memory to be able to work with large images, many fonts, and multiple projects, as well, so you can have additional applications, such as Adobe Photoshop, open at the same time.

Here are the official requirements:

- For Macintosh systems, an Intel processor, or a PowerPC G3, G4, or G5 processor, running Mac OS X version 10.4 (Tiger) or 10.5 (Leopard).

- For Windows systems, an Intel Centrino (including Duo), Core (including Duo), Pentium (III or later), or Xenon processor — or

AMD K6, Athlon (any version), Opteron, Sempron, or Turion processor — running Windows XP (with Service Pack 2 or later) or Windows Vista.

- At least 350MB of free hard-drive space on the Mac and 625MB of free hard-drive space in Windows for installation (installation also requires free disk space on the startup drive, even if you install InDesign CS3 software on a different drive). (InCopy requires an additional 350MB on the Mac and 316MB in Windows.)

- A CD-ROM drive or DVD-ROM drive.

- At least 256MB of RAM. Realistically, you want at least 512MB (and more likely 1GB) in a production environment so you can run other programs responsively at the same time.

- Sixteen-bit color depth (thousands of colors) at 1024-x-768 monitor resolution. Realistically, you want to run InDesign at 24-bit color (millions of colors) at a higher monitor resolution — InDesign's user interface barely fits in the 1024-x-768 resolution typical of a 17-inch monitor.

- For PostScript printing, Adobe PostScript Language Level 2 or Adobe PostScript 3.

- For the multimedia features, QuickTime 7.

Installing InDesign CS3

Before beginning the installation process, make sure that you have your serial number provided by Adobe and that you have an Internet connection so you can activate the software after installation.

Running the installation program

Both the Mac OS and Windows installers for InDesign CS3 provide easy-to-follow on-screen instructions:

1. **Be sure that all other programs are closed.** InDesign typically does not install if other programs are running, even non-Adobe programs. (But it's fine to let your system utilities such as antivirus software continue to run.)

2. **Insert the CD in the CD-ROM or DVD-ROM drive or access the CD over the network.** If necessary, double-click the CD icon to open the CD.

3. **Double-click the installer program (Setup).** (On the Mac, you may be asked for a system password to allow the installation of new software.) The installer runs through an initialization step; be patient while it does so.

4. **Read the License Agreement, and click Accept to continue.** You can select a different language using the pop-up menu at the top of the dialog box.

5. **The InDesign installer asks you what language to install: English or English International.** Choose one and click Continue. *English* means the dialect of English used in the United States. *English International* means British English, the dialect used in the United Kingdom, Canada, Australia, and most former British colonies.

6. **The next dialog box gives you the opportunity to decide where to install InDesign.** If you have multiple disks attached to your computer, you see a list; select the desired disk. By default, the installer places InDesign in the Applications folder (Mac) or Program Files\Adobe folder (Windows) on your startup hard drive. If you want to change the location (for example, to your Applications folder), click the Browse button. Select or create another folder, and click Choose. When that's done, click Next>.

7. **In the next dialog box, type your name, company (leave it blank if you're an individual, such as a self-employed designer), and your serial number, and then click Continue.** A new dialog box appears where you can confirm your name, company, and serial number. If the information is correct, click Continue; if it's incorrect, click Back. You're also given the chance to register your copy of InDesign or to skip registration for a later time.

8. **InDesign presents the installation settings for final review.** Click Install> to accept them and begin the installation, or click <Back to change them. Click Finish once the installation is complete.

InDesign CS3 is now installed!

Activating and registering

You may have additional setup work to do if this is the first time you've installed InDesign CS3 on this computer:

1. **Launch InDesign, by double-clicking its icon from the application folder or from the dock (Mac) or Start menu (Windows) if the icon appears there.** You get a dialog box that has you reconfirm the license; click Accept to continue.

2. **In the Software Setup dialog box, enter your serial number, or select the I Want to Try Adobe InDesign Free for 30 Days option to run an unlicensed copy in tryout mode.** Click Next>. (You can also click the Product License Agreement hyperlink at the bottom of the dialog box to open the license in a browser window from which you can print it.)

3. **In the Activate dialog box that appears, choose whether to activate your software.** (You need an Internet connection to do so.) Click Activate Now to activate the software or Activate Later to run InDesign unactivated. If you click Activate Now, InDesign connects to the Adobe server to activate your software, and then displays the Activation Complete dialog box. Click Next> to continue on from that dialog box.

4. **The installer also asks if you want to register online.** If you have an Internet connection and are ready to register, click Yes. This launches your default browser and takes you through the registration process. After you register online, an alert may prompt you to restart your computer, depending on whether system-level files were installed. Unlike activation, registration is optional, and lets Adobe know who is entitled to technical support. (You can also register from within InDesign by choosing Help ➪ Register.)

The activation process downloads a unique ID from Adobe's servers to your computer, so if someone else installs InDesign, the Adobe server sees the additional installation and checks further.

(It does not transmit any information about you to Adobe.) You can upgrade major pieces of hardware without requiring reactivation, and you may install and activate the software on two computers (typically a desktop and a laptop) per the Adobe software license. If the Adobe server thinks you are trying to install a third copy, it requires you to call Adobe for reactivation, so a technician can determine whether you are simply trying to reinstall the program on a replacement computer or if you really are installing a third copy.

If you do not activate the software within 30 days of installation, it no longer runs. During those 30 days, InDesign asks you each time you launch it whether you want to activate the software. You can also choose Help ➪ Activate within InDesign to run the activation program.

> **TIP** To deactivate InDesign, so you can transfer the license to a different computer, choose Help ➪ Deactivate. Then activate the software on the new computer when you install it. Your license will be transferred. If you don't deactivate the old copy, the new installation counts as an additional installation. Remember: Adobe lets you have just two installations activated at any one time.

Finishing your setup

When you first launch InDesign after installing it, you get the dialog box that appears in Figure A.1. Its options include creating new documents, opening documents, and seeing information on new features. If you don't want one of these options, you can just go to the program by clicking Close. This is similar to quick-start dialog boxes in other programs, such as Microsoft Office, aimed at novice users. If you want to disable it so you go straight into InDesign, just enable the Don't Show Again check box.

FIGURE A.1

This Welcome Screen dialog box loads each time you open InDesign, unless you disable it.

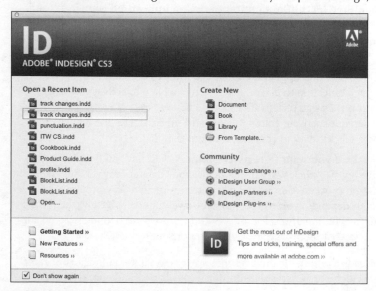

To see this dialog box again after disabling it, choose Help ⇨ Welcome Screen. If you uncheck the Don't Show Again option, it continues to appear each time you launch InDesign — until you check that option again, of course.

After you install InDesign CS3, there's one more setup step you should take: Tell InDesign CS3 how often to check for program updates via the Web. To do so, choose Help ⇨ Update. InDesign looks for any new updates and then displays a dialog box that has a button labeled Preferences. Click Preferences to open a dialog box in which you enable monthly update checks and tell InDesign whether to automatically install them or ask your permission first. You also select which Adobe software you want to have these settings applied to (not just InDesign).

Upgrading from Prior Versions of InDesign

All installations of InDesign CS3 are new installations; there is no option to upgrade a previous version. The installer creates a new folder and places your new copy of InDesign in it, regardless of whether you were using a previous version of InDesign. The only difference between purchasing a new product and upgrading is the price you pay for the software.

Installing new software has its good points and bad points. On the plus side, your existing, earlier-version copy of InDesign is available for future use. You never know when you need it — for example, for that new client who is still using InDesign CS, for which there is no back-saving capability from InDesign CS3 — so it can be worth keeping on your machine or at least storing on a CD or other removable disk. The drawback is, of course, that you need space in which to store this old software.

A bigger drawback to the fact that InDesign CS3 requires a new installation is that InDesign CS3 doesn't have any of the custom settings you've selected in your earlier version of InDesign; you often don't realize how many preferences you've set over time until you switch to a new version of the software.

If you did put some effort into customizing InDesign, when you start using InDesign CS3, do the following:

- Reset your preferences in the Preferences dialog box (choose InDesign ⇨ Preferences ⇨ General or press ⌘+K on the Mac, or choose Edit ⇨ Preferences ⇨ General or press Ctrl+K in Windows).

- Copy any color swatch libraries from the previous version of InDesign (as well as from Adobe Illustrator) to the Swatch Libraries folder in the Presets folder in your InDesign application folder.

- If you want to use InDesign CS2 scripts, create a folder called Version 4.0 Scripts, copy the scripts into it, and then move that folder to InDesign's scripts folder (see Chapter 38 for information on the two locations — global and local — for storing scripts).

- With no document open, set any preferences such as styles and color definitions that you want to be used in all future documents. You can also load such settings from other documents using the Load menu option in the various panels' flyout menus.

Although the customizing process can be tedious, it's definitely preferable to performing repetitive tasks such as creating the same style for each document.

Reinstalling and Uninstalling InDesign

If you had previously installed InDesign, you get a dialog box with two options when you run the Setup program:

- **Install or Reinstall:** Use this option to repair a damaged installation or install components you did not install the first time. (Check any unchecked items to have them installed.)

- **Uninstall Components:** Use this option to remove all or some of the InDesign application files. Then click Next>. The next dialog box lists all the installed components to reinstall or uninstall; click Modify> to begin the operation.

When the (re)installation or uninstallation is complete, click Finish.

If you uninstall InDesign, you are given the choice to remove the activation (as I cover earlier in this appendix) or leave it installed. Remove the activation if you are transferring your software to a new computer. If for some reason you don't get the deactivation option, cancel the uninstallation and deactivate the software within InDesign by choosing Help ➪ Deactivate. Then uninstall the software.

Appendix B

What's New in InDesign CS3

In its sixth major version (after 1.0, 1.5, 2.0, 3.0 [CS], and 4.0 [CS2]), InDesign 5.0 — known formally as InDesign CS3 — has become a very strong page-layout program offering a broad range of flexible, powerful tools.

You can find a host of updated features in this latest release, as well as some key new features. Although the chapters in this book identify new features as they come up in discussing publishing techniques, this appendix brings the whole list to you in one place for easy browsing. The new features are arranged in the same order as this book because that reflects the basic work-flow of publishing and the major functional divisions.

InDesign Interface

InDesign has revamped its user interface as part of a suite-wide change incorporating both Adobe and Macromedia approaches to standardize how all the applications work. Other interface changes are specific to InDesign and are meant to make things a little easier.

Tools, panels, and dialog boxes

In InDesign CS3, Adobe has revamped its palettes. Now called *panels*, they serve the same purpose and work pretty much the same way in terms of the functions they provide. But how you arrange them has changed, as well as some aspects of how they appear. The dock that many are placed into by default is also new to InDesign CS3.

IN THIS APPENDIX

Changes to the InDesign interface

What's enhanced for document and object functions

New text functions

Revisions to graphics functions

What's new in output functions

Revised scripting functions

Enhancements to XML functions

What's changed in workgroup editing functions

Adobe has changed how the Tools panel, as well as other panels, work. By default, the Tools panel is now encased in a dock, and you can drag it out so it's free-floating. When docked, the position of the Tools panel is fixed and the panel cannot overlap a document window; when it's free-floating, you can move the Tools panel anywhere, and it can obscure or be obscured by a document window. Also, the default layout for the Tools panel is now one icon wide, rather than two icons wide.

Adobe has made a few changes to the Tools panel's tools:

- The Gradient tool has been renamed the Gradient Swatch tool.
- The Gradient Feather tool is new.
- Gone is the Adobe tool (where the product logo is displayed); it used to launch the Adobe Web site.
- You now access the Shear tool from the Scale tool's pop-out menu, making space for a new tool: the Notes tool.
- A few tools — Button, Scissors, Gradient Swatch, Measure, and Eyedropper — have moved within the Tools panel.

The Control panel can now be customized, using the Customize flyout menu option. In the Customize Control Panel dialog box that appears, you can select and deselect sets of iconic buttons to control which ones display. These objects are grouped into five categories — Object, Character, Paragraph, Tables, and Other. You can control individual buttons within these categories by clicking the right-facing arrow icon to the left of each group's name; you get a list of options within that group that you can individually control.

The Control panel also adds several functions to its options if you have a widescreen monitor. For example, with a monitor set at 1280-pixel width, you see both the character and paragraph options at once, rather than have to toggle between them. When you've selected an object with the Selection tool at that resolution, you see extra controls such as frame alignment and frame fitting.

In the Control panel, the selection buttons now appear no matter what select tool you use and whether or not the objects are grouped. In previous versions of InDesign, these buttons appeared only if the objects were grouped and selected with the Direct Selection tool.

The Control panel now has iconic buttons for Rotate 90° Clockwise and Rotate 90° Counterclockwise. In previous versions of InDesign, these had been in the Control palette's palette menu, but they have been moved into the Control panel as iconic buttons in InDesign CS3.

The Control panel adds Manage Character Styles, Manage Paragraph Styles, and Manage Object Styles pop-up menus, depending on what type of object you've selected. It lets you edit and otherwise manage styles, though it has fewer controls than the corresponding styles panels' flyout menus.

Gone in the Control panel is the Toggle Character and Character Styles Palettes iconic button. Use the keyboard shortcuts, dock, mouse, or Window menu to switch among them instead.

In the Layers panel, the lock icon replaces the crossed-out pencil icon from previous versions of InDesign to indicate locked layers.

Changed and new panels include the following:

- The Effects panel replaces the Transparency panel and incorporates controls over many new lighting effects, as well as the previous drop shadow and feathering effects.
- The Cell Styles and Table Styles panels are new to InDesign CS3.
- The Assignments and Notes panels are new to InDesign CS3; previously they were available only if you bought the separate InCopy program.
- Recently used glyphs now display at the top of the Glyphs panel, making it easier to use them. You can hide these recently used glyphs by choosing Hide Options from the flyout menu or by clicking the double-arrow icon in the tab to the left of the panel's name.
- InDesign CS3 also lets you change how the glyphs are sorted in the Glyphs panel. Choose Sort Glyphs ⟶ By Unicode (the default) from the flyout menu to have them appear in order of the international Unicode standard's numbering scheme, or choose Sort Glyphs ⟶ By CID/GID to sort them based on the font's internal character IDs and glyph IDs. There's really no reason to change this sort option from the Unicode default.
- InDesign CS3 adds a lot more attributes to the Quick Apply panel, including menu commands, scripts, and text variables. (InDesign CS2 just had styles in this panel.) You can customize this panel to control which options display by choosing the unnamed pop-up menu at the top of the panel and deselect unwanted attributes (the check marks indicate attributes that will display).
- The Tabs panel is no longer available from the Window ⟶ Type & Tables submenu.
- The Command Bar in InDesign CS3 was called the PageMaker Toolbar in previous versions of InDesign.

The Step and Repeat dialog box now has a Preview check box so you can see the effects of the settings before actually applying them.

The Corner Options menu item (in the Object menu) and dialog box had been called Corner Effects in previous versions of InDesign.

The Drop Shadow dialog box in previous versions of InDesign has been made a pane of the new Effects dialog box in InDesign CS3. Its menu option in the Object menu has also been moved to be a submenu option when you choose Object ⟶ Effects. Also, what is now called the Distance field in the Drop Shadow pane was called Blur in previous versions of InDesign.

The Feather dialog box in previous versions of InDesign is now the Basic Feather pane of the new Effects dialog box in InDesign CS3. Its menu option in the Object menu has also been moved so it's a submenu option when you choose Object ⟶ Effects. Also, the Choke and Noise options in the Basic Feather pane are new to InDesign CS3.

New panes in InDesign CS3's New Object Style dialog box are the Frame Fitting Options pane and the panes for the various new lighting effects. Because there are now so many panes, the New Object Style dialog box breaks them into two sections: Basic Attributes and Effects. The Effects set of panes have the same functions as the Effects dialog box: Transparency, Drop Shadow, Inner Shadow, Outer Glow, Inner Glow, Bevel and Emboss, Satin, Basic Feather, Directional Feather, and Gradient Feather.

Shortcuts

Several shortcuts have changed in InDesign CS3:

- The Transform panel no longer has the keyboard shortcut F9.
- The Paragraph Styles panel now has a second shortcut — ⌘+F11 or Ctrl+F11 — in addition to the previous F11 shortcut.
- The Character Styles panel now has a second shortcut — Shift+⌘+F11 or Ctrl+Shift+F11 — in addition to the previous Shift+F11 shortcut.
- The Stroke panel has now has a second shortcut — ⌘+F10 or Ctrl+F10 — in addition to the previous F10 shortcut.
- The shortcut for the Effects panel (the new name for the old Transparency palette) has changed to Shift+⌘+F10 or Ctrl+Shift+F10.
- The Pages panel now has a second shortcut — ⌘+F12 or Ctrl+F12 — in addition to the previous F12 shortcut.
- The shortcut for Release Compound Path has changed to Option+Shift+⌘+8 or Ctrl+Alt+Shift+8.
- The hair space no longer has a shortcut.
- In the Macintosh version only, the shortcut for Hide/View Frame Edges has changed to Control+⌘+H (it remains Ctrl+H in Windows), and the shortcut for High Quality Display has changed to Control+Option+⌘+H (it remains Ctrl+Alt+H in Windows).

New shortcuts include the following:

- Type ➪ Glyphs: Option+Shift+F11 or Alt+Shift+F11.
- Type ➪ Insert Special Character ➪ Quotation Marks ➪ Straight Double Quotation Marks: Command+Shift+' or Alt+Shift+'.
- Type ➪ Insert Special Character ➪ Quotation Marks ➪ Straight Single Quotation Mark (Apostrophe): Command+' or Alt+'.
- Notes ➪ Notes Mode: ⌘+F8 or Ctrl+F8.
- Window ➪ Automation ➪ Scripts: Option+⌘+F11 or Ctrl+Alt+F11.

Menus

The File menu now includes the User option for use by InCopy, as well as the Export as XHTML option. The InBooklet SE menu has been renamed Print Booklet. The File menu no longer has the Package for GoLive option; that feature no longer exists. Also, the Save a Version option in previous versions of InDesign has been renamed Check In. And the Export XML option has moved to become a submenu of the new File ➪ Cross-Media Export menu sequence; it's also still available in the regular Export dialog box (File ➪ Export).

The Edit menu has some new options: One is the InCopy menu for setting up story assignments for use by InCopy. Another is the Menus option for customizing InDesign menus.

The Type menu adds two new menu options — Text Variables, and Bullets and Numbered Lists — to accommodate InDesign CS3's new text variables feature and to make bullets and numbering more accessible.

InDesign CS3 has added submenus to the Type ⇨ Insert Special Characters menu to help organize its contents better.

The Notes menu is new to InDesign CS3. This feature used to be available only if you bought the InCopy add-on.

In the Objects menu, the Effects option replaces the Drop Shadow and Feather options from the InDesign CS2 Object menu. The Compound Paths menu item in InDesign CS3's Object menu used to be provided through submenu items in the InDesign CS2 Paths menu.

The Object ⇨ Clipping Path ⇨ Convert Clipping Path to Frame menu option is new to InDesign CS3. In previous versions, it was available only in the contextual menu if you Control+clicked or right-clicked an object that contained a clipping path.

In InDesign CS3, you create clipping paths through the new Options submenu: Choose Object ⇨ Clipping Path ⇨ Options, rather than Object ⇨ Clipping Path as in previous versions.

InDesign CS3 makes a few changes to how you access various path commands. You access the Make Compound Path and Release Compound Path by choosing Object ⇨ Paths and then selecting the desired option, rather than choosing Object ⇨ Compound Paths and then the desired option.

The View menu adds the Show/Hide Assigned Frames and Show/Hide Notes options to accommodate the InCopy features added to InDesign CS3.

The Window menu adds the Assignments and Notes options, as well as the Cell Styles and Table Styles options to the Type & Tables submenu. It removes the Tabs option from the Type & Tables submenu. (You can still access the Tabs panel by choosing Type ⇨ Tabs.)

Preferences

The Interface and Clipboard Handling panes are new, taking controls previously available in the General and File Handling panes, respectively. The Notes pane is completely new.

The When Scaling area is new to the General pane of InDesign CS3's Preferences dialog box. This control used to be in the Type pane and called Adjust Text Attributes While Scaling. It now applies to both textual and graphics contents, not just text.

The Tool Tips display settings have moved from the General pane of the Preferences dialog box to the new Interface pane.

Using the File Handling pane, you can set whether snippets are positioned at their original location or relative to the current document's margins. Using the File Handling pane, you can ensure that when a file is relinked (as opposed to updated), all previously applied dimensions (such as scale and offset) are reserved. Use the new Relink Preserves Dimensions option to control this behavior.

In InDesign CS3, the Prefer PDF When Pasting option has moved from the File Handling pane in previous versions to the new Clipboard Handling pane of the Preferences dialog box.

The ability to customize menus is new to InDesign CS3; choose Edit ➪ Menus to do so.

Sharable files

You can now share glyph sets with other users. When you create a glyph set, InDesign creates a file in the Glyph Sets folder within the Presets folder that in turn resides within the folder containing the InDesign application. Just copy these files to other users' Glyph Sets folders to give them access to them.

The AutoCorrect and Find-Change folders are new to InDesign CS3, providing a location inside the Presets folder (itself inside the InDesign application folder) for the presets for these new features. Also, the Scripts folder has moved out of the Presets folder into the main InDesign application folder. All of these can be shared with other users by copying the files to the same-named folders.

Version Cue

Adobe has changed the Version Cue abled dialog boxes' Tools menu options considerably in Creative Suite 3. The Show File Info Area has been renamed Show Metadata Area, and Connect To has been renamed Connect to Server. The Refresh, Download, and Clear Local Files options are new. Gone are the old Share Project, Show Deleted Items, Delete, Restore, and Disconnect options. You manage most of these functions in one of two places: The Bridge program's Tools menu or in the Edit Properties dialog box (accessed by choosing Edit Properties in the Tools drop-down menu from a Version Cue–enabled dialog box).

In the Edit Properties dialog box, you can control whether a project is shared in the Edit Properties menu by checking or unchecking the Share This Project with Others option, and you access other Version Cue management features by clicking the Server Administration button.

When you save a new version of a layout using Version Cue, the saved file is much smaller, so your server is not filled as quickly. Adobe accomplished this by saving just the changes to the original file (much like how a differential backup is used to save space), not a copy of the original file and its modifications as before. There is no effect on the ability to work with versions, but you can no longer back up individual version files using the Version Cue system preference (Mac) or control panel (Windows) as in previous versions.

Document and Object Functions

InDesign CS3 has introduced several changes that affect documents and objects universally, with many of the revisions centered around page controls and object handling.

Measurements

InDesign now supports agates as a measurement option, using the code *ag*.

Page actions

InDesign CS3 now shows a preview image of your pages in the Pages panel, which makes it easier to know if you're selecting the right page. You can control the display by choosing Panel Options from the panel's flyout menu. In the Panel Options dialog box, select the desired icon size and make sure Show Thumbnails is checked. You can also set separate view settings for master pages.

As you drag pages and spreads around the Pages panel, InDesign CS3 now automatically scrolls through the pages. This means you don't have to increase the size of the panel to move pages across larger distances.

Also new to InDesign CS3 is that the mouse pointer changes to the grabber (hand) pointer when it's not over a page in the Pages panel. If you click and drag this pointer within the panel, InDesign scrolls the panel in the direction you move the mouse.

InDesign lets you import master pages across documents; choose Load Master Pages from the Pages panel's flyout menu.

When you drag a page from one document to another, InDesign now displays the Insert Pages dialog box, which lets you specify where to insert the page in the new document as well as whether to copy or move the page into the new document. (In previous versions, InDesign just copied the page in front of the current one.) To move a page rather than copy it, be sure to check the Delete Pages After Inserting option. Similarly, InDesign adds the Move To pop-up menu in the Move Pages dialog box (Layout ➪ Pages ➪ Move Pages).

InDesign now automatically scrolls the Pages panel's pages as you move pages up or down. Before, you had to enlarge the panel so the location you wanted to drag the pages to was visible.

Also new to InDesign CS3, the mouse pointer changes to the grabber (hand) pointer when it's not over a page in the Pages panel. If you click and drag this pointer within the panel, InDesign scrolls the panel in the direction you move the mouse.

The Pages panel's Allow Selected Pages to Shuffle flyout menu option used to be called Keep Spreads Together in previous versions of InDesign. This name change also changes InDesign's behavior: Now, you have to disable the Allow Selected Pages to Shuffle option to permit gatefold spreads rather than enable the Keep Spreads Together option.

In the Pages panel, the new Allow Master Item Overrides on Selection flyout menu option lets you change the item on document pages; you Shift+⌘+click or Ctrl+Shift+click it and change any attribute such as size, location, or color. If you deselect this option on the master page for any selected objects, then you cannot change the object on any document pages — a great way to prevent unauthorized changes for standard elements.

File exchange and sharing

The File ➪ New Document from Template menu option is new to InDesign CS3. It opens Adobe Bridge and lets you select a file to use as a template.

The Save as Alternate option has been removed from InDesign CS3, streamlining how the Version Cue management functions work.

You can now create InCopy story and assignment files from InDesign without having to buy the separate InCopy program.

The ability to export text to the InCopy format from the Export dialog box is new to InDesign CS3.

The ability to import Flash animation files is new to InDesign CS3.

Multi-document projects

InDesign CS3 adds the ability to synchronize master pages across book chapters, as well as to synchronize the new table styles, cell styles, numbered lists, and text variables.

Sometimes, having InDesign automatically update page and section numbering is a real pain, as you must wait for it to grind through all the chapters when you, for example, add or update a chapter near the beginning of the book's chapter list. In that case, uncheck the Automatically Update Page & Section Numbers in the Book Page Numbering Options dialog box, accessible from the book panel's flyout menu. When it is time to repaginate a book, choose Update Numbering from the panel's flyout menu, and then choose the appropriate option from its submenu: Update Page & Section Numbers, Update Chapter & Paragraph Numbers, or Update All Numbers. This ability to control which numbers are updated is new to InDesign CS3.

You can see and modify any chapter's page numbering settings by selecting the chapter in the book panel, and then choosing Document Numbering Options from the flyout menu. The Document Chapter Numbering area provides control over the chapter numbering style and the chapter number itself — both new capabilities in InDesign CS3.

Object selection

If you want to select an object within a group, InDesign CS3 now lets you double-click the object to select just it. (Single-clicking selects the entire group.)

In InDesign CS3, when you double-click an object other than a text frame, the selection tool will switch between the Selection tool and the Direct Selection tool. (If the Position tool is currently active, double-clicking the object switches it to the Direct Selection tool, and double-clicking again switches it to the Selection tool. The only way to switch back to the Position tool is to select it from the Direct Selection tool's pop-out menu.

If you double-click a text frame, InDesign now switches to the Type tool. Double-clicking again selects the text. If the Type tool is active, you can select the text frame by pressing Esc, as a faster alternative to picking a selection tool and then selecting the frame with it.

The ability to control whether a graphics or an unassigned frame is automatically converted to a text frame is new to InDesign CS3. (You specify the default behavior in the Type pane of the Preferences dialog box, using the Type Tool Converts Frames to Text Frames option.) In past versions, this behavior was automatic.

If you use the Select Previous Object or Select Next Object buttons and reach the top of bottom of the object stack, InDesign CS3 now cycles back. For example, if you reach the topmost object and click Select Previous Object, InDesign CS3 now moves to the bottommost object. In previous versions, you had to go all the way back to the bottom by using the Select Next Object button; there was no way to just loop around.

Object handling

You can now select multiple files — text and/or graphics — by Shift+clicking a range or by ⌘+clicking or Ctrl+clicking multiple files one by one. InDesign lets you place each file in a separate frame. Just click once for each file imported, or Shift+⌘+click or Ctrl+Shift+click to have InDesign place all files on the page in separate frames. If you place more than one file at the same time, the loaded-text icon or loaded-graphic icon shows the number of files to be placed, as well as a mini-preview of each file. You can also move among these files using the arrow keys, which enables you to place them in any order you prefer.

InDesign CS3 can import InDesign files as if they were graphics. When importing a multi-page document, you choose the page you want to import, as you can with PDF files. Note that you cannot edit InDesign files imported as graphics in InDesign; you must update the original file instead.

The ability to search and replace object attributes, using the new Objects pane in the Find/Change dialog box, is new to InDesign CS3.

InDesign CS3 no longer has the odd behavior of previous versions in which if you scale an object, the scale displayed in the Scale X and Scale Y fields always reverts to 100%, even though the size has clearly changed.

InDesign CS3 now lets you relink all instances of a file in your layout. So you only have to do the operation once. The trick: In the Relink dialog box (choose Relink from the Links panel's flyout menu), be sure to check the new Relink All Instances option.

The Text Wrap panel now has the Make All Settings the Same iconic button (the chain icon) in the area that contains the offset fields. If the chain is unbroken, changing any offset automatically changes the other offsets to the same value. If the chain is broken, you can adjust each offset independently. Click the button to toggle between the two modes.

The Text Wrap panel also has a new option — the Wrap To pop-up menu — that lets you control how text wraps around an object that splits a column. (Previous versions aligned the text to the left of the interposed object.)

The Text Frames Options dialog box's General pane now has the Make All Settings the Same iconic button (the chain icon) in the area that contains the Inset Spacing fields. If the chain is unbroken, changing any offset automatically changes the other offsets to the same value. If the chain is broken, you can adjust each offset independently. Click the button to toggle between the two modes.

A new, unnamed pop-up menu in InDesign CS3's Align panel lets you choose where selected objects align to: Align to Selection (the default behavior and what previous versions of InDesign did), Align to Margins, Align to Page, and Align to Spread.

On the Macintosh only, holding ⌘ when dragging overrides the Snap to Guides option, letting you place an object anywhere in the document, even off-grid.

Object effects

InDesign CS3 adds a bevy of lighting effects, including inner shadows, outer and inner glows, beveling and embossing, satin finish, and two additional kinds of feathering. It's also renamed the Transparency palette to the Effects panel, providing a single starting point for all these effects.

You can now apply lighting effects to your choice of an object, its stroke, or its contents.

The new Gradient Feather tool — accessed from the Gradient tool's pop-out menu or via the short-cut Shift+G — works just like the Gradient tool except that it makes a gradient that goes from transparent to the chosen color on the selected object. To remove a gradient feather effect, uncheck the Gradient Feather option in the Effects panel.

Text Functions

A third area of major focus for InDesign's revisions involves text handling, covering a wide range of functions.

Text import

Newly supported text attributes in InDesign CS3 for importing include support for automatic bul-leted and numbered lists, Word's various underline options, and tracked changes (for use in InCopy).

To remove the original formatting of text you drag and drop into InDesign CS3, hold the Shift key until you release the mouse button. The dropped text then takes on the formatting of the text you dragged it into.

Text editing

InDesign CS3 adds a lot of new features to the Find/Change dialog box, including a new interface, the ability to essentially program your search by specifying conditions using the Grep syntax, the ability to search for special characters (glyphs), and the ability to save search/replace queries so you can use them repeatedly.

The ability to add notes within text to documents is new to InDesign CS3. In previous versions, you had to buy the add-on InCopy program to have this capability. InDesign CS3 adds a capability called *text variables*, which automatically inserts specified text such as the current date, chapter number, and running header in your text and ensures it is always current.

InDesign CS3 automatically creates a glyph set in the Glyphs panel called Recent Glyphs, which are glyphs you've selected recently. You can edit and otherwise work with this automatic set just like any other set.

The third space, quarter space, sixth space, and nonbreaking fixed-width space — available by choosing Type ⇨ Insert White Space — are new to InDesign CS3.

The Non-joiner character (Type ⇨ Insert Special Character ⇨ Other ⇨ Non-joiner) is new to InDesign CS3. It's a zero-width "space" character that you'll hardly use, as it's really designed for languages such as Arabic and Devanagari, where letterforms get joined in some circumstances but not others. The non-joiner prevents the characters from being joined, overriding any automatic font options. In English, you might use this character to manually prevent automatic ligatures (the only circumstance where characters are joined together in English).

When Use Typographer's Quotes is enabled (in the Preference dialog box's Type pane), you can enter the keyboard quotes — perhaps for use as foot marks (') and inch marks (") — by using keyboard shortcuts. Type Option+⌘+' or Ctrl+Alt+' for double quotes and ⌘+' or Ctrl+' for single quotes. They're also available by choosing Type ⇨ Insert Special Character ⇨ Quotation Marks.

InDesign CS3 adds language support for Ukrainian. It also supports the new Dutch: 2005 Reform in addition to previous Dutch (now called Dutch: Old Rules), the German: 2006 Reforms in addition to German1996 Reform and German: Traditional), and German: Swiss 2006 Reform in addition to German: Swiss. And Spanish: Castilian has been renamed just Spanish.

Paragraph and character formatting

The Hyphenate Across Column option is new to InDesign CS3's Paragraph panel.

New to InDesign CS3's Find Font dialog box (Type ⇨ Find Font) is the Redefine Style When Changing All check box, which, if you select it, ensures that any font replacement updates all paragraph and character styles to the new font. In previous versions, the styles kept the old font.

The Keep in Frame option is new to InDesign CS3's Paragraph Rules capability, available in the Paragraph panel and Paragraph Styles panel. In previous versions, rules that appear over the first paragraph in a frame either did not display or displayed outside the frame, contrary to most users' expectations.

InDesign has enhanced its automatic bulleted and numbered lists feature several ways:

- The Format menu in the Bullets and Numbering dialog box is the new name for the previous version's Style menu.
- The 01, 02, 03, 04 ... option in the Bullets and Numbering dialog box's Format menu is new.
- The Number field and its pop-up menu replace the previous version's Separator menu in the Bullets and Numbering dialog box.
- The Mode pop-up menu in the Bullets and Numbering dialog box replaces the previous version's Start At field.

899

- The Character Style pop-up menu in the Bullets and Numbering dialog box replaces the previous version's Font Family, Font Style, Size, and Color options.

- And InDesign CS3 changes the alignment options for bullets and numbers in the Bullets and Numbering dialog box to give you more precise control of their placement.

InDesign CS3 lets you override optical margin alignment that is normally set for an entire story. You can enable the Ignore Optical Margin flyout menu option in the Paragraph panel, or enable the Ignore Optical Margin setting in the Indents and Spacing pane when creating or editing a paragraph style; this tells InDesign to use normal alignment against the text frame's left edge for the designated paragraphs, rather than use optical margin alignment.

InDesign now supports positional forms in OpenType fonts, such as for use in Arabic fonts and in some Roman script fonts.

Spelling and indexing

When you first open the Check Spelling dialog box while text is selected or the text cursor is active, InDesign CS3 now immediately begins checking the spelling, going to the first suspect word.

InDesign now lets you apply a specific character style to an individual index entry's page number in the New Page Reference dialog box by enabling the Number Style Override check box and then choosing a character style from the pop-up menu to its right. InDesign lets you apply consistent formatting to all page numbers in an index, but this option is handy when you want to highlight specific page numbers to call special attention to them, such as having the definitional reference's page number appear in boldface.

The new Sort Options feature in the Index panel's flyout menu lets you determine which alphabets — such as Roman, Cyrillic, and Greek — should be indexed and in what order they should appear. This is quite handy for documents that use multiple alphabets. (Without this option, entries using foreign alphabets were grouped into the Symbols category in the index.)

You can change the alphabetization order in a table of contents (TOC) by changing the Language option in the Character panel's flyout menu when no text or text frame is selected before having InDesign generate the TOC. The TOC then takes on the chosen language's rules for alphabetizing.

You can control how numbered paragraphs are treated in the TOC by choosing one of the options in the New Table of Contents Style dialog box's Numbered Paragraph pop-up menu: Include Full Paragraph, Include Numbers Only, and Exclude Numbers.

Tabs and tables

InDesign CS3 lets you create table and cell styles to reuse table and cell formatting.

You can now delete tabs and reset indents from the Tabs panel using the flyout menu's new Delete Tab and Reset Indents commands. (You can still delete tabs by dragging them off the tab ruler.)

InDesign CS3 lets you paste tabbed text into tables. The tabs are retained, and all the text is pasted into the same cell.

Styles

InDesign CS3 adds the Table Styles and Cell Styles panels to create reusable styles for table and cell formatting. Both are available by choosing Window ⇨ Type & Tables.

InDesign CS3 lets you rearrange the order of style names in the Object Styles, Character Styles, Paragraph Styles, Table Styles, and Cell Styles panels, by dragging them within the list.

You can now create style groups in InDesign CS3, providing a way to organize styles in the various style panels.

When working with the Object Styles panel, you now have the new flyout menu option Clear Overrides When Applying Style.

If you want to apply a new paragraph or character style to text that is selected, be sure to check the Apply Style to Selection check box before clicking OK to save the new style.

When creating nested styles via the Paragraph panel or Paragraph Styles panel, you now have the [Repeat] option, which if you select it, lets you repeat a sequence of previous styles.

If your selected text has more than one character style applied within the selection, the Character Styles panel will display the text (*Mixed*) at the lower left.

Color Functions

When you add Pantone colors in the Swatches panel, you'll see that the colors that were called Solid to Process in previous versions of InDesign are now labeled the Color Bridge colors. (InDesign CS3 keeps the Solid to Process labels as well for familiarity.)

Also, the uncoated version of this color model is new to InDesign CS3, as are the two Euro color models.

Graphics Functions

InDesign CS3 creates a simpler text wrap shape when importing a graphic with an alpha channel. This means you have fewer points you have to work with when modifying the text-wrap shape.

When you choose Objects ⇨ Paths ⇨ Open Path, InDesign CS3 now automatically selects the point where the path was opened, so you can immediately begin working with it (and know where it is).

Output Functions

InDesign has added several refinements to its controls for printing and output files. It has also added significant new capabilities for creating XHTML and eBook files from InDesign layouts.

Printing

The Print Booklet dialog box (and File menu option) replaces the InBooklet SE dialog box (and File menu option) from previous versions of InDesign. The capabilities are practically identical, though the user interface has changed. (The only real functional difference is that InBooklet SE lets you specify precisely which crop marks and related options to show, while Print Booklet relies on InDesign's Print dialog box to do so.) InBooklet SE was a trial version of the more capable InBooklet plug-in, but the company that made this plug-in was bought by Adobe's archrival Quark, which promptly ended plug-in support for InDesign. Adobe thus created its own Print Booklet feature to plug the gap.

In previous versions of InDesign, deselecting Show Layer in the Layers panel also prevented the layer from printing—and you had no way to override this from the Print dialog box. But InDesign CS3 has added a separate control in the Print dialog box, the Print Layers pop-up menu in the General pane, for controlling whether layers print so you can choose to have unhidden layers not print as well.

When printing a file as composite grayscale to certain types of printers, InDesign CS3 lets you print them as a bitmap and control their resolution through the new Print to Bitmap check box in the Print dialog box's Advanced pane.

PDF and EPS export

Similarly, you can control whether hidden layers are exported to PDF in the Output pane of the Export Adobe PDF dialog box's Print Layers pop-up menu.

InDesign CS3 adds the Merge Identically Named Layers on Export option to the book panel's fly-out menu. If checked, InDesign unifies layers with the same name into one layer for exported PDF files generated from multiple documents in the same book, rather than creating separate layers for each chapter's layer.

Support for Acrobat 8's PDF 1.7 format during export is new to InDesign CS3.

When exporting EPS files, you can now control whether all bleed margins are changed if any of them is changed by clicking the Make All Settings the Same iconic button: If the chain icon is broken, you can adjust each separately; if the chain icon is not broken, changing one changes the others automatically.

JPEG export

The ability to specify output resolution for JPEG files from the Export dialog box is new to InDesign CS3.

eBooks export

InDesign has added a new export option to produce the "digital editions" form of eBooks, a visually rich type of Web page; choose File ⇨ Cross-Media Export ⇨ XHTML/Digital Editions. Previous versions let you create eBooks as an option during PDF export, but Adobe has revised eBooks to be more Web-friendly and has thus created a separate set of controls over how InDesign exports files to the eBook format.

Web export

InDesign adds the ability to export files in the XHTML format used by Web editors (choose File ⇨ Cross-Media Export ⇨ XHTML/Dreamweaver). These exported files do not attempt to duplicate your layout. Instead, they convert the current document (or selected objects) into Web-ready formats for further work in Adobe Dreamweaver or other Web editing software. Gone is the ability to create an XML package of your document for use in Adobe GoLive.

Scripting Functions

Adobe has made several significant under-the-hood changes to scripting that increase both developers' and users' control over scripts.

- Everything within InDesign is now scriptable, giving you more control over the program and its contents.

- You can associate a script to a specific InDesign menu action so that when a user chooses that menu item, a script runs automatically (technically, by assigning a script to a MenuAction command's Prenotify or Postnotify property). In InDesign, be sure that Enable Attached Scripts is also enabled in the Scripts panel's flyout menu.

- You can now undo all of a script's action by using the InDesign Undo command (Edit ⇨ Undo, or ⌘+Z or Ctrl+Z) by ensuring that Undo Affects Entire Script is enabled in the Scripts panel's flyout menu. (Otherwise, the undo command reverses just the last action within the script, requiring you to undo several times to "roll back" the complete script action.)

- By enabling the Enable Redraw flyout menu option, you can force InDesign to redraw the display while a script is running. This ensures that any changes to the document are immediately visible.

The Scripts folder has been moved out of the Presets folder into the main InDesign application folder.

There is now a shortcut for the Scripts panel: Alt+ ⌘+F11 or Ctrl+Alt +F11.

To use scripts developed for InDesign CS2, create a new folder called Version 4.0 Scripts inside the Scripts or Script Panel folder and move your old scripts there. They then work in InDesign CS3.

XML Functions

You can now import XSLT style sheets either from the XML file or from a separate file.

InDesign CS3 provides an option during XML import to convert CALS tables to InDesign tables.

You can now designate parent elements in InDesign, using the New Parent Element flyout menu option in the Structure pane.

When exporting XML files, InDesign CS2 has added the Export Untagged Tables as CALS XML; Remap Break, Whitespace, and Special Characters; and Apply XSLT options.

Workgroup Editing Functions

InDesign CS3 has made itself InCopy-ready, so it's easier to prepare files for use in a workgroup environment. Adobe of course hopes this will sell more copies of InCopy by increasing awareness of it, but regardless of its motivation, the InCopy-related changes aid workgroup editing activities.

Within the InDesign program

InDesign CS3 includes the capabilities to create InCopy story files and InCopy assignment files without requiring you to purchase the separate InCopy software.

The ability to specify a default location for an assignment's stories is new to InDesign CS3. This feature automatically moves stories to the appropriate location if you move them from one assignment to another.

To quickly see where an assignment file is, select it in the Assignments panel and choose Reveal in Finder (Mac) or Reveal in Explorer (Windows) from the flyout menu to open the folder on your computer. Or choose Reveal in Bridge to open the Bridge program and have it open the folder for you.

You can now just add a story to an assignment by dragging its frame using any of the selection tools into the Assignments panel.

You can collect all the relevant files for these users and package them into one file that you can send via e-mail (or disk), using the new Package for InCopy and Package for InCopy and Email menu options in the Assignments panel's flyout menu.

InDesign CS3 has a new shortcut for the Mac for Edit ➪ InCopy ➪ Update Story: Control+⌘+F5, compared to just ⌘+F5 in previous versions. The Windows shortcut of Ctrl+F5 is unchanged.

Within the InCopy program

InCopy CS3 can show you revisions from your original Microsoft Word file (if you used its changes-tracking feature) — but only if you enabled the Track Changes option in InDesign's Import Options dialog box when you first placed the text file. (Previously, such tracked changes were automatically imported by InDesign and made available to InCopy. You now must enable this option to preserve those tracked changes.)

In InCopy CS3, the keyboard shortcuts for checking stories in and out have changed to match those in InDesign: ⌘+F9 or Ctrl+F9 to check out the current story, Shift+⌘+F9 or Ctrl+Shift+F9 to check in the current story, and Option+Shift+⌘+F9 or Ctrl+Alt+Shift+F9 to check in all stories.

In the File menu, the names of InCopy CS3's save commands have changed slightly; Story has changed to Content. (Thus Save Story is now called Save Content.) The functionality is unchanged.

Appendix C

Switching from QuarkXPress

IN THIS APPENDIX

Opening QuarkXPress documents

Dealing with conversion issues

Understanding tool differences

Converting keyboard shortcuts

Reconciling document differences

Working with text, tables, and graphics

Manipulating pages

Working with color

Learning to use new software, or even learning to use an upgrade of a familiar application, can be so intimidating that many users resist passionately. Even if an application is woefully out of date and lacking in functionality, you cling to it knowing you can accomplish your mission — even with workarounds — with less frustration than the untried, but powerful, new application. Users are particularly passionate about their choice of page-layout software — which is usually QuarkXPress — probably because they're involved with it for 8 to 12 hours a day. (A QuarkXPress user once said he spent more time with QuarkXPress than with his wife, so you can see where the dedication is coming from.)

But times, circumstances, and jobs change. Eventually, your old software won't run on your zippy, new machine or you switch jobs or you simply prefer another vendor. No matter what circumstances led you to choosing InDesign, this appendix is designed to help you let go and move forward, showing you the differences between your old layout application and InDesign, and pointing out a few benefits of InDesign as well.

NOTE All references to QuarkXPress apply to versions 3.x through 7.x unless I provide a specific version number.

So you can continue working with existing designs, in its very first version of InDesign, Adobe made sure it could open QuarkXPress files, recognizing the preeminence of QuarkXPress in the publishing world. Since then, Quark modified the QuarkXPress file format (starting in version 5) to prevent InDesign from opening its files, but because so many QuarkXPress users have stayed with version 4, the InDesign ability to open QuarkXPress files remains valuable.

Opening QuarkXPress Documents

The Open command (File ⇨ Open, or ⌘+O or Ctrl+O) lets you select and open documents and templates saved in QuarkXPress and QuarkXPress Passport versions 3.3 through 4.11 on Macintosh or Windows. (QuarkXPress Passport is the multilingual version of QuarkXPress.) You also can import QuarkXPress-created XML files into InDesign as XML documents. But, you can't open libraries or books from any version of QuarkXPress, nor documents or templates from QuarkXPress 5 and later.

> **TIP** Be sure to use QuarkXPress's Collect for Output function to copy all linked graphics to a single folder. This also ensures that all graphics files are available. If you don't do this, InDesign may not get all the linked graphics from the source QuarkXPress file.

All the text, graphics, items, master pages, styles, and more in the QuarkXPress document are converted to their InDesign equivalents. If the document contains items, content, or formatting that can't be converted, an alert notifies you of the issues. Once the document is converted, it appears as a new, untitled document.

Once you open a QuarkXPress file in InDesign, you can save it as an InDesign file only. InDesign automatically appends the .indd filename extension to the QuarkXPress filename, so unless you explicitly change the filename extension when saving, there's no chance of accidentally overwriting that original QuarkXPress file.

Dealing with Conversion Issues

Now that you know that InDesign is supposed to open QuarkXPress files, let's take a look at how well it actually does it. Yes, you can open QuarkXPress 3.3 and 4.x documents, save them as InDesign documents, and continue working with them. But the documents don't convert perfectly: You're likely to lose some formatting because InDesign doesn't have equivalent formatting, or its options work differently. In general, you can expect to use a QuarkXPress document as a starting point for a design — usually with a little repair work — but you should not expect to simply open a QuarkXPress document and have it look and print exactly the same way.

> **TIP** After realizing which QuarkXPress features are not supported or converted well, and considering how your own QuarkXPress documents are created, you can decide on a document-by-document basis whether conversion is worth the effort. In some cases, it might be easier to simply reconstruct a document, while in other cases you might be able to start working almost immediately.

When you convert QuarkXPress documents to InDesign, you can expect the following:

- Master pages are converted, including all items, content, and guides.
- All line and frame styles are converted to dashed or plain strokes.
- Text boxes are converted to text frames; picture boxes are converted to graphics frames.

- Text paths are converted.

- Because InDesign favors looser default text spacing than QuarkXPress, many stories will no longer fit in their text frames.

- All paragraph and character style sheets are converted to InDesign styles.

- Incremental auto-leading (such as +4, which adds 4 points to the largest font size on the line) is converted to InDesign's standard auto-leading.

- The Next Column (keypad Enter) or Next Box (Shift+keypad Enter) characters (which you use to bump text to the next column or next text box rather than resizing the box) are retained.

- The Bold and Italic font styles are converted to the appropriate typeface (if available), and Underline, Strike Thru, Superscript, Subscript, All Caps, and Small Caps are converted. Superior, Word Underline, Outline, and Shadow revert to plain text.

- Keyboard shortcuts assigned to character and paragraph styles are not retained, though you can assign keyboard shortcuts to your styles within InDesign.

- Index tags are not maintained, and you may have difficulty opening chapters of a book.

- If a picture is missing or modified in QuarkXPress, it won't appear in the InDesign document. If you want to retain the picture, you need to update the links in QuarkXPress (Utilities ➪ Usage ➪ Pictures) before converting it.

- Pasted (embedded) pictures, pictures imported using OLE or Publish and Subscribe, and pictures created with third-party XTensions do not convert.

- The customizable dashes in QuarkXPress are converted to solid and dashed lines; note that custom stripes do convert properly.

- Clipping paths created in QuarkXPress or imported with an image into QuarkXPress are not converted, so the image's display changes.

- The Same as Clipping Runaround feature in QuarkXPress leaves a runaround shape based on the clipping path in InDesign; but if you've resized the image in QuarkXPress, the runaround path stays at 100 percent in InDesign.

- Items for which Suppress Printout is checked are placed on a separate layer called Nonprinting layer. To view these objects in InDesign, view the layer.

- If a group contains an item for which Suppress Printout is selected, all the items are ungrouped and the suppressed items are placed on the nonprinting layer.

- Rotated items, typically when grouped, often are unrotated after conversion by InDesign.

- Pictures imported into QuarkXPress by holding ⌘ or Ctrl to import color images as grayscale or grayscale images and black and white lose that conversion and appear in their original color or grayscale in InDesign.

- The ICC-compliant color profiles used in QuarkXPress 4.0 and greater are retained, but the EfiColor profiles used in QuarkXPress 3.3x are not retained.

- Colors in QuarkXPress 3.3x documents are converted to InDesign swatches according to their CMYK values (except for HSB colors, which are converted to RGB swatches).

- Colors in QuarkXPress 4.*x* documents are converted to InDesign swatches according to their RGB values (except for HSB and LAB colors, which are converted to RGB swatches). Hexachrome colors are not converted.

- Blends are converted to linear or circular blends.

InDesign highlights any conversion issues as you open a QuarkXPress document, as Figure C.1 shows. You can save the warning's text to a text file by clicking the Save button, so you will have a reference to the issues to refer to later.

FIGURE C.1

The warning dialog box that InDesign presents when it cannot convert an element in a QuarkXPress file

Understanding Tool Differences

For the QuarkXPress veteran, the toughest thing about switching to InDesign is the set of tools. In your world, you've been using the Item tool (which you might call the pointer) and the Content tool (the little hand) for almost everything. Not only did you use them all the time, but the Item tool or Content tool was selected automatically for you most of the time (because object-creation tools snap back to the last-used selection tool). Over time, the two tools have evolved into almost one, so you might have been using the Content tool all the time, pressing ⌘ or Ctrl when you needed to manipulate an entire item.

You need to forget about this way of working entirely. In InDesign, you switch tools constantly. When you create an object, its tool remains selected so you can't move or resize the objects immediately after creation. The Selection tool only lets you move and resize objects, while the Direct Selection tool lets you reshape objects and work with graphics.

The difference between the Selection tool and Direct Selection tool takes some getting used to for QuarkXPress users. In terms of working with content, the Direct Selection tool is much like QuarkXPress's Content tool, but it also lets you edit the frame as if it were a Bézier object. For example, if the Direct Selection tool is selected and you click and drag a point on the frame, you move that point and thus change the shape of the object — a rectangle would convert into a polygon, because the lines immediately adjacent to the moved point move with the point while the rest of the frame is not affected. In QuarkXPress, if the Content tool is selected and you click and drag a point on the frame, you resize the frame (perhaps non-proportionally) but the entire side(s) adjacent to the point moves with the point, so the rectangle is still a rectangle. To change a frame in the way that QuarkXPress does with both the Content and Item tools, use the Selection tool in InDesign.

Think of the Type tool as a combination of the Rectangle Text Box tool and the Content tool for text. You must have the Type tool to work with text, but there's no moving or resizing of text frames while you're using it. However, you can hold ⌘ or Ctrl to temporarily change from the Type tool to the Selection tool. This is the same as pressing ⌘ or Ctrl while using the QuarkXPress Content tool, which allows you to manipulate the entire item. Release ⌘ or Ctrl to return to the Type tool.

This need to switch between the Type and Selection tools may seem restrictive at first — but the key is to embrace InDesign's single-letter shortcuts for selecting tools. (InDesign also provides QuarkXPress-like keyboard commands for temporarily activating tools, but it's easier to press a single letter to switch tools.)

As long as the Type tool isn't selected, you can activate any tool by pressing the letter that appears next to it in the tool's Tool Tip. In particular, you want to memorize the following:

- Press V for the Selection tool.
- Press A for the Direct Selection tool.
- Press T for the Type tool.
- Press H for the Hand tool. (You can also press the spacebar; when editing text, you can press Option or Alt.)
- Press Z for the Zoom tool. (You can also press ⌘+spacebar or Ctrl+spacebar and then click the mouse to zoom in, and Option+⌘+spacebar or Ctrl+Alt+spacebar and then click the mouse to zoom out.)

If you're also a Photoshop user, the single-letter shortcuts might be familiar to you, but it's an odd concept for a QuarkXPress-only user. Once you get the hang of it, however, you'll appreciate how fast and easy it is to switch tools.

A few overall interface differences between QuarkXPress and InDesign might hang you up initially. Keep in mind that many menu commands simply display a panel (which may already be open) rather than show a dialog box. Get used to deciphering icons or using Tool Tips on the panes because there are not as many dialog boxes containing named fields as you're used to in QuarkXPress's Character Attributes, Paragraph Attributes, and Modify dialog boxes. Contextual menus are implemented on a broader scale than in QuarkXPress, so you can Control+click or right+click objects, rulers, and more to make changes quickly.

InDesign CS3 also offers docking panes, whose tabs can be aligned to the left-hand and right-hand screen edges so they're not in the way. You can drag these docked panes to your document to make them floating panes à la QuarkXPress. Note that InDesign's panes can be rearranged and combined into multipane palettes by dragging them on top of each other; QuarkXPress's palettes are fixed and cannot be combined. Because InDesign has so many panes, it needs a way to manage them. Unlike QuarkXPress, InDesign lets you save these interface settings using its Workspaces feature (Window ➪ Workspace, whose submenu lets you select, create, and delete these workspaces).

InDesign uses all of QuarkXPress's measurement abbreviations, as well as its own. For example, InDesign accepts QuarkXPress's use of " to indicate inches, as well as InDesign's own standard of *in* and *inch*. Likewise, it accepts QuarkXPress's *mm* for millimeter as well as InDesign's own standard of *m*.

> **TIP** InDesign offers a set of keyboard commands similar to those in QuarkXPress (Edit ➪ Keyboard Shortcuts). I recommend that you avoid this set and learn the commands in InDesign. This will help you communicate about InDesign and work with other Adobe software.

Converting Keyboard Shortcuts

If you're switching from QuarkXPress and committed to learning InDesign's keyboard shortcuts, skim Table C.1 to see the primary differences.

TABLE C.1

Keyboard Shortcuts Translated from QuarkXPress to InDesign

Action	QuarkXPress Shortcut	InDesign Equivalent
Navigation		
Zoom in	Control or Ctrl	⌘+spacebar or Ctrl+spacebar
Zoom out	Control+Option or Ctrl+Alt	Option+⌘+spacebar or Ctrl+Alt+spacebar
Page grabber hand	Option or Alt	H, or Option or Alt
User Interface		
Preferences	Option+Shift+⌘+Y or Ctrl+Alt+Shift+Y	⌘+K or Ctrl+K
File Import		
Get Text/Picture	⌘+E or Ctrl+E	⌘+D or Ctrl+D (Place dialog box)
Text handling		
Paragraph formats	⌘+Shift+F or Ctrl+Shift+F	Option+⌘+T or Ctrl+Alt+T (Paragraph panel)
Character formats	⌘+Shift+D or Ctrl+Shift+D	⌘+T or Ctrl+T (Character panel)
Style Sheets palette	F11	⌘+F11 or Ctrl+F11 (Character Styles panel), Shift+⌘+F11 or Ctrl+Shift+F11 (Paragraph Styles panel)
Spelling (word)	⌘+L or Ctrl+W	⌘+I or Ctrl+I (Check Spelling dialog box)

Action	QuarkXPress Shortcut	InDesign Equivalent
Object handling		
Modify dialog box	⌘+M or Ctrl+M	*No equivalent*
Delete selection	⌘+K or Ctrl+K	Delete
Duplicate	⌘+D or Ctrl+D	Option+Shift+⌘+D or Ctrl+Alt+Shift+D
Step and Repeat	Option+⌘+D or Ctrl+Alt+D	Shift+⌘+U or Ctrl+Shift+U
Lock/Unlock	F6	⌘+L or Ctrl+L (lock), Option+⌘+L or Ctrl+Alt+L (unlock)
Ungroup	⌘+U or Ctrl+U	Shift+⌘+G or Ctrl+Shift+G
Space Align	⌘+, or Ctrl+,	Shit+F7 (Align panel)
Send to Back	Shift+F5	Shift+⌘+[or Ctrl+Shift+[
Send Backward	Option+Shift+F5 or Ctrl+Shift+F5	⌘+[or Ctrl+[
Bring to Front	F5	Shift+⌘+] or Ctrl+Shift+]
Bring Forward	Option+F5 or Ctrl+F5	⌘+] or Ctrl+]

Reconciling Document Differences

By and large, documents in InDesign and QuarkXPress are the same. You have master pages, layers, and pages. You can also set bleeds for objects that go beyond the page boundary. But there are some differences:

- InDesign lets you specify a slug area, which reserves space during printing for the printer's marks.

- QuarkXPress 6 and 7 permit several layouts in one document file, called a *project,* so you can mix layouts with different page sizes. InDesign does not permit that.

- The InDesign master text frame is not the same as QuarkXPress's automatic text box on a master page. You cannot flow text into a QuarkXPress automatic text box while you're working on a master page; instead, an empty text box is placed on each of your layout pages for you automatically. Although you can have QuarkXPress flow text into automatic text boxes across pages as you add pages to your layout, you can also place text in these boxes individually, without them being linked. An InDesign master text frame is linked automatically from page to page and is not meant for holding text that does not flow from page to page.

- QuarkXPress 5 through 7 support Web documents, which InDesign CS3 does not. But InDesign CS3 can export layouts to the Web's XHTML format.

- InDesign can generate TOCs only based on paragraph styles, not on character styles. This means you can't create other kinds of lists, such as a list of companies in a magazine article or research report, based on the use of character styles. InDesign doesn't have a flexible Lists feature as QuarkXPress does, just the Table of Contents feature that is essentially a subset of QuarkXPress's Lists feature. However, you can use the InDesign Table of Contents feature to create some lists besides TOCs. Also, the level of formatting you can achieve over TOC entries in InDesign is greater than in QuarkXPress.

- The InDesign index features are similar to those in QuarkXPress, though the InDesign Index panel and QuarkXPress Index palette have very different interfaces.

- The corner-style feature in InDesign (Object ➪ Corner Options) is similar to the text-box and picture-box variants in QuarkXPress, which offer the same selection of corners except for the Fancy option. In QuarkXPress, you create, or convert, a box to a variant that has one of these corner effects, while in InDesign, you apply the corner effect to a frame.

- InDesign's nested frames are similar to QuarkXPress's constrained boxes. The biggest difference is that, to nest a frame in InDesign, you paste a frame into another (Edit ➪ Paste Into, or Option+⌘+V or Ctrl+Alt+V). In QuarkXPress, you choose Item ➪ Constrain.

Working with Objects Rather Than Items

In QuarkXPress, you're used to items such as text boxes, picture boxes, lines, and maybe text paths. In InDesign, you have paths and frames, with the only difference being that frames contain graphics or text. You can, therefore, make a one-to-one relationship between text boxes and text frames, and picture boxes and picture frames. Just keep in mind that, with InDesign, you're not restricted to using frames for content; you can fill any path, even an open one, with text or graphics and have it become a frame. And if you don't make a frame (or the right kind of frame) up front, you can still import graphics and text in InDesign (unlike in QuarkXPress, which requires you to change the box type first).

While selecting and manipulating objects with tools, remember the following:

- Use the Selection tool to move objects or resize frames. It's kind of like QuarkXPress's Item tool.

- Use the Direct Selection tool to reshape objects, work with graphics, and change the endpoints of lines. It's kind of like QuarkXPress's Content tool.

- You can use the Position tool (a variation of PageMaker's Crop tool) to resize and move images and their frames, or reposition content in relation to their frames. It also blurs the QuarkXPress Content/Item dichotomy, acting like the Item tool in terms of resizing and moving frames and like the Content tools when it comes to repositioning the contents.

- When reshaping objects, you can use the Pen tool, Add Anchor Point tool, and Remove Anchor Point tool in addition to the Direct Selection tool.

- You can't just click master-page objects to select them on the document pages. Instead, use Shift+⌘+click or Ctrl+Shift+click to select them.

When modifying objects, remember the following:

- InDesign has a more-capable clone of QuarkXPress's Measurements palette (though QuarkXPress 7 has duplicated and expanded some of InDesign's innovations here), called the Control panel (Window ⇨ Control, or Option+⌘+6 or Ctrl+Alt+6). You can also use the Transform panel in InDesign (Window ⇨ Transform). Use these tools for the equivalent of QuarkXPress's Modify dialog box's Box and Line panes.

- In InDesign, when you scale a frame's contents using the Control panel or Transform panel, the scale value may jump back to 100% in the panel, even though the contents are indeed at the new size. This occurs when you have the Selection tool selected, because that causes InDesign to report the scale of the frame (stroke), not of the contents. If you switch to the Direct Selection tool, you see the proper scale for the contents in the Control panel or Transform panel.

- To specify runaround, choose Window ⇨ Text Wrap, or press Option+⌘+W or Ctrl+Alt+W, to open the Text Wrap panel.

- To specify attributes of text frames, choose Object ⇨ Text Frame Options, or press ⌘+B or Ctrl+B, to open the Text Frame Options dialog box.

- The InDesign Shear tool is not the same as the QuarkXPress Skew tool; Shear both slants and rotates an object, while Skew just slants it. To simulate the QuarkXPress Skew tool, hold the Shift key while you move the mouse horizontally when using the InDesign Shear tool. This ensures that there is no rotation. You can also use the Shear X fields in the Control panel or Transform panel to only slant an object.

Working with Text

InDesign works with text very differently than QuarkXPress in many cases, even though the fundamental capabilities are the same in both programs. Veteran QuarkXPress users are initially frustrated with InDesign's more laborious approach to text flow and formatting, but eventually appreciate some of InDesign's more powerful capabilities such as stroke formatting and nested styles.

Flowing text

Once you learn how to flow text in InDesign, you'll find it's easier and more flexible than QuarkXPress. It's easy to get stuck and to restrict yourself to QuarkXPress techniques. To prevent that, keep these differences in mind:

- To import a text file, use File ⇨ Place, or ⌘+D or Ctrl+D. You can also click and drag files and text from the desktop or any application that supports drag and drop. InDesign lets you import multiple text and/or graphics files at one time, with each placed in the frame of your choice or in a new frame.

- You do not need to create or select a text frame before you import text; you can create or select a text frame after choosing the file to import.

- InDesign does not have linking tools. To flow text from frame to frame, use a selection tool to click the out ports and in ports on text frames. (Make sure View ➪ Show Text Threads is selected.)

- To flow text and add pages automatically, click Master Text Frame in the New Document dialog box (File ➪ New ➪ Document, or ⌘+N or Ctrl+N). Then, you need to press Shift+⌘+click or Ctrl+Shift+click the master text frame on a document page. Finally, Option+click or Alt+click the loaded text icon.

CROSS-REF   See Chapter 15 for complete information about flowing text.

Editing text

A few minor differences exist when it comes to editing and selecting text:

- In QuarkXPress, clicking three times in text selects the line, and clicking four times selects the entire paragraph. In InDesign, clicking three times selects the paragraph.

- To type special characters such as ñ, •, or ¶, you can choose Type ➪ Glyphs to open the Glyphs panel rather than use system utilities or key combinations. (QuarkXPress 7 has a similar feature.)

- The control for showing invisible characters such as spaces, tabs, and paragraph returns is Type ➪ Show Hidden Characters, or press Option+⌘+I or Ctrl+Alt+I.

- InDesign lets you select from various Western European languages for spell checking and hyphenation. You first apply a language to text selections via the Character or Character Styles panels. The Passport edition of QuarkXPress has a similar feature to specify the hyphenation and spelling language, but not the standard version of QuarkXPress.

Formatting text

In general, formatting text in InDesign should feel comfortable to QuarkXPress users. You may miss those nice, big Character and Paragraph Attributes dialog boxes (featuring real words, not icons!), but you have most of the same power. Review these differences, and keep them in mind while formatting text:

- Use the Character panel (Type ➪ Character, or ⌘+T or Ctrl+T) to format highlighted characters. There are no buttons for selecting font styles (*type styles*, in QuarkXPress lingo) — InDesign requires you to choose the appropriate version of a typeface rather than attributes such as bold and italic, while other font styles are listed in the Character panel's flyout menu.

- Leading is a character-level format in InDesign; therefore the controls are in the Character panel rather than the Paragraph panel as you might have come to expect. Fortunately, you can change the leading behavior by selecting the Text pane of the Preferences dialog box and clicking the Apply Leading to Entire Paragraphs option. Clicking this box makes InDesign match the behavior of leading in QuarkXPress. Leading is always measured from baseline to baseline in InDesign.

- Unlike QuarkXPress, you can stroke and fill characters in InDesign.

- Use the Paragraph panel (Type ⇨ Paragraph, or Option+⌘+T or Ctrl+Alt+T) to format selected paragraphs; the flyout menu includes additional commands for adding rules and controlling hyphenation.

- InDesign lets you apply OpenType settings to OpenType fonts, using the flyout menus of the Character panel and Control panel, or the OpenType Features pane of the New Character Styles or Paragraph Style Options dialog boxes (accessed via the Paragraph Styles panel). QuarkXPress 6.1 and earlier can use OpenType fonts but apply only standard formatting to them; QuarkXPress 7 lets you apply OpenType features to text

- InDesign does not have H&J sets, so set up your hyphenation using the Paragraph panel and save your settings in paragraph styles.

- Use the Tabs panel (Type ⇨ Tabs, or Shift+⌘+T or Ctrl+Shift+T) to set tabs for selected paragraphs.

- To create styles, use the New Character Style and New Paragraph Style commands in the flyout menus of the Character Styles panel (Type ⇨ Character Styles, or Shift+⌘+F11 or Ctrl+Shift+F11) and the Paragraph Styles panel (Type ⇨ Paragraph Styles, or ⌘+F11 or Ctrl+F11). To share styles with other documents, use the Load commands in the same menus.

- Click Type ⇨ Find Font to replace fonts throughout your document; this works like the Font Usage dialog box in QuarkXPress (Utilities ⇨ Usage ⇨ Fonts).

- Unlike Windows QuarkXPress, InDesign for Windows supports automatic ligatures in Windows fonts that have them.

- InDesign has no equivalent to QuarkXPress's fraction-building tool, though it can build fractions automatically in OpenType fonts that support this capability.

- InDesign has no equivalent to QuarkXPress's Underline Styles. Instead, specify custom underlines and strikethroughs as part of a character style. To add stripes and dashed lines, open the Strokes panel (Window ⇨ Stroke, or ⌘+F10 or Ctrl+F10) and select the Stroke Styles option from the flyout menu.

- Those converting to QuarkXPress may be surprised at the seemingly large kerning and tracking values produced by all of the program's kerning and tracking methods. Keep in mind that InDesign lets you adjust space in 0.001-em units ($\frac{1}{1000}$ of an em). In QuarkXPress, for example, the kerning unit is 0.005 ems ($\frac{1}{200}$ of an em). So QuarkXPress users should not be surprised to see kerning and tracking values that are 10 to 20 times greater than you're used to — you're working with multiples of finer increments.

Working with Tables

Recent editions of QuarkXPress and InDesign have added significant table formatting capabilities. Among the differences:

- InDesign does a good job of importing Word tables and Excel spreadsheets as tables, unlike QuarkXPress versions through 6.0, which do not support tables during import without extra-cost add-on software. Also, InDesign can export tables in RTF format, enabling Word users to see and edit tables that you build in InDesign. This is very helpful for migrating tabular data into and out of InDesign for revision by Word users.

- InDesign tables and QuarkXPress tables have several differences. Although both treat tables as collections of cells, InDesign offers more formatting options for cell strokes than QuarkXPress does. InDesign has more controls for text and row placement than QuarkXPress offers. InDesign also imports Word, Excel, and RTF tables, while QuarkXPress does not. But QuarkXPress offers more control over the flow of text among cells in a table. InDesign doesn't let you flow text from one cell to another, for example, much less control the order of that flow.

- InDesign CS3 offers table and cell styles to simplify consistent formatting — and formatting revisions — across your document. QuarkXPress has no equivalent capability.

- In one way, InDesign is savvier about text-to-table conversion than QuarkXPress is because InDesign lets you choose any string as the column or row separator during conversion (just enter that string in the appropriate field). But in another way, InDesign is less savvy: QuarkXPress lets you "pivot" data during conversion, so you can swap columns and rows for a better fit.

Working with Graphics

Importing and manipulating graphics in InDesign is very similar to QuarkXPress. As long as you remember to use the Direct Selection tool to select a graphic rather than its frame, you and the InDesign graphics features will get along fine. Differences between the programs include the following:

- To import a graphics file in InDesign, use File ➪ Place, or ⌘+D or Ctrl+D. You can also click and drag files in from the desktop or other programs if InDesign supports their file formats. InDesign CS3 lets you import multiple graphics files at once.

- InDesign cannot convert color bitmap images to grayscale during import (while retaining the original file's colors) as QuarkXPress can. Thus, in InDesign, you need to convert the files in Photoshop or turn off color separation when printing.

- You do not need to create or select a graphics frame before you import a graphic; you'll be able to create or select a graphics frame after choosing the file to import.

- Use the Control panel (Window ⇨ Control, or Option+⌘+6 or Ctrl+Alt+6) or the Transform panel (Window ⇨ Transform) to rotate, scale, and skew graphics. You can create clipping paths by clicking Object ⇨ Clipping Path ⇨ Options or pressing Option+Shift+⌘+K or Ctrl+Alt+Shift+K.

- To automatically scale a graphic to fit within its frame — proportionally or not — use the Fitting commands in the Object menu, the iconic buttons in the Control panel, or their keyboard commands. As a bonus, you get a Fit Frame to Content command, a task you have to perform manually in QuarkXPress.

- The InDesign Stroke Styles feature (accessed via the Strokes panel's flyout menu) looks and works very much like the QuarkXPress Dashes & Stripes feature. The major difference is that InDesign has a separate option for dotted lines.

- Although InDesign doesn't have background, frame, and contents icons in its Swatches panel to let you select where color is applied, as QuarkXPress does, InDesign lets you determine what component of the image gets the color based on how you apply the color: Click and drag a color swatch onto an object to change the foreground color. Click a graphics frame and then the Fill or Stroke iconic button in the Tools panel or Swatches panel, and then select a color from the Swatches panel to change the background or frame color, respectively. Furthermore, you can use the Control panel's Select Container and Select Contents iconic buttons to choose whether the image background or contents, respectively, are colored when you click a swatch.

- InDesign offers a customizable drop-shadow tool (Object ⇨ Effects ⇨ Drop Shadow, or Option+⌘+M or Ctrl+Alt+M) that lets you determine the shadow angle, distance, and lighting effects. QuarkXPress's drop shadow is fixed to one setting. Although you can apply InDesign's drop shadow to any object, not just a text frame, you cannot apply it to selected text. By contrast, you can apply QuarkXPress's drop shadow only to selected text as a character attribute.

- InDesign lets you apply several other lighting effects, such as feathering and beveling, from the Effects panel or by choosing Object ⇨ Effects. QuarkXPress has no equivalent to any of these effects.

- QuarkXPress 6.1 and earlier has no equivalent to InDesign's transparency settings, which let you make objects transparent or semitransparent, allowing a wide variety of special effects. QuarkXPress users instead must rely on such settings in Adobe Photoshop and Illustrator for imported pictures and do without them for objects created in QuarkXPress. InDesign also provides controls for how overlapping transparent objects are output because they can sometimes interfere with printing.

- To track the location of graphics files, use the Links panel (Window ⇨ Links, or Shift+⌘+D or Ctrl+Shift+D).

- InDesign's relink function is not as smart as QuarkXPress's equivalent Picture Usage. If you have multiple broken links to the same file in an InDesign document, you must relink each one manually from the Links panel. QuarkXPress automatically fixes all links to the same file as soon as you correct any link to it. That's another reason to use InDesign's automatic fix when you open a document and InDesign identifies that links are broken or out of date. (You can relink a group of files at once by selecting them all in the Links panel [Window ➪ Links, or Shift+⌘+D or Ctrl+Shift+D], and choosing Relink in the flyout menu to relink them all at once.)

- QuarkXPress uses a very different approach to changing direction points from smooth to corner: It has iconic buttons in its Measurements palette that let you easily convert segment and corner types. The InDesign approach is more efficient in that it uses one tool and relies on a mouse-based tool (because you're likely using the mouse when you edit a shape), but it does require a bit more getting used to initially.

- InDesign's Pathfinder option to connect paths is similar to QuarkXPress's Merge options for paths.

Manipulating Pages

You'll find the controls for working with document pages and master pages to be quite similar to QuarkXPress — if not slightly better. Once you realize the differences and start working, you can take advantage of InDesign's improvements. The differences mostly relate to guides and using the InDesign Pages panel rather than the QuarkXPress Document Layout palette (the Page Layout palette in QuarkXPress 6 and later):

- InDesign provides three methods for creating guides: Click and drag them off the ruler as you do in QuarkXPress, double-click the ruler where you want a guide, or choose Layout ➪ Create Guides.

- To delete guides, you need to select them and click Delete. (To select all guides on a page, press Option+⌘+G or Ctrl+Alt+G.)

- Use the Pages panel (Window ➪ Pages, or ⌘+F12 or Ctrl+F12) as you would the QuarkXPress Document Layout palette (called the Page Layout palette in QuarkXPress 6 and later). To place more than two pages side by side, you need to use the Keep Spreads Together command in the panel's flyout menu.

- If you're missing the QuarkXPress Page menu, look for your favorite commands in the InDesign Layout menu and in the Pages panel's flyout menu. There's a bonus in the Type menu: a menu command so you don't have to remember the shortcut (Option+Shift+⌘+N or Ctrl+Alt+Shift+N). Choose Type ➪ Insert Special Character ➪ Markers ➪ Current Page Number.

- You can base one master page on another, the same way you can base styles on each other. QuarkXPress does not offer this capability.

- To share master pages among documents, you can load master pages from one document into another using the Load Master Pages command in the Pages panel's flyout menu. QuarkXPress cannot do this.

Working with Color

Not to intimidate you, but color can confound you (although Photoshop users should have an easier transition). Basically, try to forget everything you know about creating and applying colors in QuarkXPress. Here's what you need to know to work with colors in InDesign:

- Most of your work with colors happens through the Swatches panel (Window ➪ Swatches or F5) — not through the Colors panel as QuarkXPress users might think.

- To create colors, use the New Swatches command in the Swatches panel's flyout menu. You cannot create Hexachrome colors in InDesign.

- To apply colors, first click the Stroke or Fill iconic button on the Tools panel or Swatches panel to specify where the color goes on the selected object. Then click a color in the Swatches panel.

- Use the Swatches panel or Colors panel (Window ➪ Colors or F6) to specify a shade (tint) of a color; the Swatches panel is the best place to do this as you can create tints for reuse here as well as apply a tint to an existing color.

- InDesign's [Paper] color is equal to the QuarkXPress White color. Both programs use the color None for transparency, but InDesign provides None in both the Swatches panel and as an iconic button in the Tools panel.

- To share colors among documents, click and drag a colored object into another document window.

Printing and Output

InDesign and QuarkXPress offer many of the same output capabilities, such as print styles (called *print presets* in InDesign), PDF export, color calibration, and color separation support. But there are some notable differences beyond the different organization of their Print dialog boxes:

- To suppress printout of individual objects, use the Attributes panel (Window ➪ Attributes) and choose Nonprinting. You can also hide layers using the Layers panel (Window ➪ Layers or F7), which works pretty much like QuarkXPress's layers feature.

- InDesign's thumbnails option is more flexible than QuarkXPress's, letting you choose the number of thumbnails per page.

- Note that InDesign does not have any options to change image contrast or line-screen element for grayscale and black-and-white images, as QuarkXPress does. You'll need to apply such effects in an image editor.

- InDesign and QuarkXPress offer similar levels of color output controls, but InDesign does have several options QuarkXPress does not. One is setting ink density; another is automatically calculating screen angles for spot colors; and a third is providing you with the ability to more accurately preview documents with overprinting colors. InDesign also can apply black-point compensation as part of its color calibration during output. And InDesign lets you save your color-management preferences for use in other documents.

Appendix D

Switching from PageMaker

PageMaker has been dead since 2001, but it's taken the widespread adoption of Mac OS X on Macs that no longer run Mac OS 9—native applications such as PageMaker to get many users to switch to InDesign. And Windows users — who can still run PageMaker on their PCs — are finding fewer freelance designers and production editors skilled with PageMaker.

Fortunately for this PageMaker cadre, InDesign knows the PageMaker mentality, having adopted much of the PageMaker free-form approach since its very first version. (As InDesign has been updated, it has also taken on more of the structured QuarkXPress approach, but without removing its PageMaker-like roots.) So InDesign is a natural upgrade for PageMaker users.

IN THIS APPENDIX

Opening PageMaker documents

Examining the differences between PageMaker and InDesign

Looking at the Command Bar panel

Opening PageMaker Documents

The Open command (File ➪ Open, or ⌘+O or Ctrl+O) lets you select and open documents (what PageMaker calls *publications*) and templates saved in PageMaker 6.0, 6.5, or 7.0 format on Macintosh or Windows. (You can't open libraries, though.) All the text, graphics, elements, layers, master pages, styles, and more in the PageMaker document are converted to their InDesign equivalents. If formatting can't be converted, an alert notifies you of the issues. After the document is converted, it appears as a new, untitled document.

 See Chapter 4 for complete information about opening files.

Because InDesign and PageMaker are similar, documents from PageMaker usually convert reliably. However, you still shouldn't count on PageMaker documents appearing and printing exactly the same way once they're converted in InDesign. You may need to do a little repair work, depending on the type of formatting you use.

TIP   Be sure to copy all linked graphics to a single folder. (Do this by saving the publication to a new folder, with the All Linked Files option selected in the Save dialog box.) If you don't do this, InDesign may not get all the linked graphics from the source PageMaker file.

When you convert PageMaker documents to InDesign, you can expect the following:

- Master pages are converted, including all elements and content.
- Guides on master pages are placed on a separate layer called Guides.
- All line and stroke styles are converted to dashed or plain strokes.
- All styles are converted to InDesign styles.
- The Bold and Italic type styles are converted to the appropriate typeface (if available), Underline and Strikethrough are converted, while Outline, Shadow, and Reverse revert to plain text.
- Index tags are not maintained.
- If an imported graphic's link is not intact, it doesn't appear in the InDesign document. If you want to retain the graphic, you need to update the links in PageMaker (File ➪ Links Manager) before converting it.
- Pasted (embedded) graphics and graphics imported using OLE or Publish and Subscribe will not convert.
- Items for which Suppress Printout is checked are placed on a separate layer called Non-printing layer. To view these objects in InDesign, view the layer.
- If a group contains an item for which Suppress Printout is checked, all the items are ungrouped and the suppressed items are placed on the non-printing layer.
- PageMaker fill patterns are not supported.
- Tracking values are modified to InDesign's settings.
- Color profiles are converted.
- Colors are converted to InDesign swatches according to their CMYK values (except for HLS colors, which are converted to RGB swatches).

Examining the Differences between PageMaker and InDesign

As you might expect, because both PageMaker and InDesign come from the Adobe world, the transition from PageMaker to InDesign isn't that tough. The basic methods for working with frames, lines, and pages are the same in both programs. What you get with InDesign is more control, with improved tools for drawing, formatting text, and manipulating objects. And there's not much to miss about PageMaker, either.

Using tools and setting preferences

The basic selection, object-creation, and navigation tools in InDesign are similar to those in PageMaker. You need to remember that InDesign has three selection tools: the Selection tool for moving and resizing objects, the Direct Selection tool for reshaping objects and working with graphics, and the new Position tool, which is essentially the same as PageMaker's Crop tool.

Because you switch tools often, as you did in PageMaker, get in the habit of using the keyboard shortcuts. (Table D.1, later in this chapter, shows InDesign keyboard shortcuts that differ from PageMaker shortcuts. It's not a long list because the two programs share many shortcuts as part of Adobe's strategy to have a common interface across its creative programs, with the exception of Adobe Acrobat.) As long as the Type tool isn't selected, you can hop from tool to tool by simply pressing a letter on the keyboard. In particular, you want to memorize the following:

- Press V for the Selection tool.
- Press A for the Direct Selection tool.
- Press T for the Type tool.
- Press H for the Hand tool. (You can also press the spacebar; when editing text, you press Option or Alt instead of the spacebar.)
- Press Z for the Zoom tool. (You can also press ⌘+spacebar or Ctrl+spacebar to zoom in and Option+⌘+spacebar or Ctrl+Alt+spacebar to zoom out.) Remember you can zoom to 1600 percent in InDesign!

 There is no keyboard shortcut for the Position tool.

InDesign includes significantly more preferences than PageMaker. You definitely want to explore all the panes in the Preferences dialog box (choose InDesign ➪ Preferences ➪ General or press ⌘+K on the Mac, or choose Edit ➪ Preferences ➪ General or press Ctrl+K in Windows). You might find some power you've never had before (although you will be disappointed to see values for Superscript, Subscript, and Small Cap relegated to a document-wide preference in InDesign rather than something you can set as a character attribute for local formatting as they were in PageMaker).

InDesign also allows multiple levels of undo of the actions you performed in the current document. PageMaker required that you revert to the last mini-saved version. Both programs also let you revert to the last saved version of the file.

Working with objects rather than elements

As with other aspects of InDesign, when you work with objects, you gain more than you lose. The types of objects are similar: text frames, graphics frames, and lines. PageMaker is limited to creating closed frames and straight lines.

While selecting and manipulating objects with tools, remember the following:

- Use the Selection tool to move objects or resize frames.

- Use the Direct Selection tool to reshape objects, change the endpoints of lines, and work with objects in groups. The Direct Selection tool also works like PageMaker's Crop tool, letting you move graphics within a frame.

- You get Bézier curves in InDesign! Using the Pen tool, Add Anchor Point tool, and Remove Anchor Point tool, you can draw and manipulate curves to your heart's content.

- You can't just click master page objects: Press Shift+⌘+click or Ctrl+Shift+click to select them.

When modifying objects, remember the following:

- Look in the Object menu for familiar Elements menu commands.

- InDesign uses a more powerful version of the PageMaker Control palette, called the Command Bar panel (Window ➪ Objects & Layout ➪ Command Bar).

- To specify runaround, choose Window ➪ Text Wrap or press Option+⌘+W or Ctrl+Alt+W to display the Text Wrap panel.

- To specify attributes of text frames, use the Object ➪ Text Frame Options command, or ⌘+B or Ctrl+B.

- What PageMaker called *rounded corners* are called *corner options* in InDesign, accessible by choosing Object ➪ Corner Options.

- To align objects in InDesign, use the Align panel (Window ➪ Objects & Layout ➪ Align, or Shift+F7) or the iconic buttons in the Control panel. In PageMaker, you used the Align menu commands.

- To suppress printout of objects, put them on a different layer and hide the layer.

Working with text

When it comes to working with text, PageMaker users can feel comfortable, thanks to InDesign's Edit Story mode (choose Type ➪ Edit Story, or press ⌘+Y or Ctrl+Y) based on a feature that PageMaker users have long enjoyed.

If the display of graphics makes it difficult for you to edit text, go to the Display Preferences pane of the Preferences dialog box (choose InDesign ➪ Preferences ➪ Display Preferences or press ⌘+K on the Mac, or choose Edit ➪ Preferences ➪ Display Preferences or press Ctrl+K in Windows). Chapter 3 covers this pane.

Other differences between PageMaker and InDesign include:

- To type special characters such as ñ, •, or ¶, you can choose Type ➪ Glyphs (Option+Shift+F11 or Alt+Shift+F11) or Type ➪ Insert Special Character rather than use system utilities or key combinations.

- In PageMaker's Edit Story mode, you are only able to see invisible characters such as spaces and tabs. But you can see all hidden characters all the time in InDesign by choosing Type ⇨ Show Hidden Characters (Option+⌘+I or Ctrl+Alt+I).

- Use the Character panel (Type ⇨ Character, or ⌘+T or Ctrl+T) to format highlighted characters. Notice there are no font style buttons; InDesign requires you to choose the appropriate version of a typeface rather than apply bold and italic to the general typeface. Other font styles are listed in the Character panel's flyout menu.

- Unlike PageMaker, you can stroke and fill characters in InDesign using the Stroke panel (Window ⇨ Stroke, or ⌘+F10 or Ctr+F10) to set the stroke and the Swatches panel (Window ⇨ Swatches or F5) to apply the color.

- Use the Paragraph panel (Type ⇨ Paragraph, or Option+⌘+T or Ctrl+Alt+T) to format selected paragraphs. The flyout menu includes additional commands for adding rules and controlling hyphenation.

- Use the Tabs panel (Window ⇨ Type & Tables ⇨ Tabs, or Shift+⌘+T or Ctrl+Shift+T) to set tabs for selected paragraphs.

- To create styles, use the New Character Style and New Paragraph Style commands in the flyout menus of the Character Styles panel (Type ⇨ Character Styles, or Shift+⌘+F11 or Ctrl+Shift+F11) and the Paragraph Styles panel (Type ⇨ Paragraph Styles, or ⌘+F11 or Ctrl+F11). To share styles with other documents, use the Load commands in the same flyout menus.

- PageMaker offers just paragraph styles, while InDesign offers both paragraph and character styles.

TABLE D.1

Keyboard Shortcuts Translated from PageMaker to InDesign

Action	PageMaker Shortcut	InDesign Equivalent
Navigation		
Page grabber hand	F10 or Shift+F7	H, or Option or Alt
Text handling		
Paragraph Specifications dialog box	⌘+M or Ctrl+M	Option+⌘+T or Ctrl+Alt+T (Paragraph panel)
Styles pane	⌘+B or Ctrl+B	⌘+F11 or Ctrl+F11 (Character Styles panel), Shift+⌘+F11 or Ctrl+Shift+F11 (Paragraph Styles panel)
Indents/tabs dialog box	⌘+I or Ctrl+I	Shift+⌘+T or Ctrl+Shift+T (Tabs panel)
Edit in Story Editor	⌘+E or Ctrl+E	⌘+Y or Ctrl+Y
Spell-check	⌘+L	⌘+I or Ctrl+I

continued

TABLE D.1 *(continued)*		
Action	**PageMaker Shortcut**	**InDesign Equivalent**
User interface		
Control palette	⌘+' (apostrophe) or Ctrl+' (apostrophe)	Option+⌘+6 or Ctrl+Alt+6 (Control panel)
Colors pane	⌘+J or ⌘+J	F5 (Swatches panel)
Layers pane	⌘+8 or Ctrl+8	F7
Master Pages pane	Option+⌘+8 or Ctrl+Alt+8	⌘+F12 or Ctrl+F12 (Pages panel)
Hyperlinks pane	⌘+9 or Ctrl+9	none
Fill and Stroke dialog box	⌘+U or Ctrl+U	⌘+F10 or Ctrl+F10 (Stroke panel)
Align dialog box	Shift+⌘+E	Shift+F7 (Align panel)
Text Wrap dialog box	Option+⌘+E	Option+⌘+W or Ctrl+Alt+W (Text Wrap panel)

Working with graphics

InDesign and PageMaker are very much alike when it comes to importing and manipulating graphics. Differences include the following:

- You can click and drag graphics files into a layout in addition to using the Place command (File ➪ Place, or ⌘+D or Ctrl+D).

- You now get to create clipping paths; use the Object ➪ Clipping Path ➪ Options command (Option+Shift+⌘+K or Ctrl+Alt+Shift+K).

- InDesign can automatically scale pictures or frames for you. Use the Object ➪ Fitting commands — Fit Content to Frame, Fit Frame to Content, Center Content, and Fit Content Proportionally — or the equivalent iconic buttons in the Control panel.

- To track the location of graphics files, use the Links panel (Window ➪ Links, or Shift+⌘+D or Ctrl+Shift+D).

Manipulating pages

The one feature you might miss about PageMaker is those neat little page icons in the lower-left corner of the document window. In shorter documents especially, the icons provided a quick, easy method for jumping to pages. Get used to using the Page Number text field and arrows at the bottom of the document window or the icons in the Pages panel (Window ➪ Pages, or ⌘+F12 or Ctrl+F12) instead.

Other differences between InDesign and PageMaker's page handling include the following:

- To create columns in PageMaker, you create the text blocks after you create your document. In InDesign, you can create a document with columns already in place using the options in the New dialog box.

- Conversely, in PageMaker, you can set up page-numbering settings when you create a new document, while in InDesign you set up page numbers and sections after the document has been created.

- InDesign provides three methods for creating guides: clicking and dragging them off the ruler as you do in PageMaker, double-clicking the ruler where you want a guide, or choosing Layout ➪ Create Guides.

- To delete guides, you need to select them and click Delete. (To select all guides on a page, press Option+⌘+G or Ctrl+Alt+G.) Make sure that guides are not locked (View ➪ Grids & Guides ➪ Lock Guides, or Option+⌘+; [semicolon] or Ctrl+Alt+; [semicolon]).

- Use the Pages panel (Window ➪ Pages, or ⌘+F12 or Ctrl+F12) to create and apply master pages; to add, move, and delete document pages; and to display different pages.

- You can now place more than two pages side by side. Deselect the Allow Selected Spread to Shuffle command in the Pages panel's flyout menu to ensure they stay together if you add more pages later before them.

- Some of your favorite commands from the Layout menu seem to be missing (such as Insert Pages), but you can access similar commands from the Pages panel's flyout menu or from the Layout ➪ Pages submenu options.

- You can base one master page on another, the same way you can base styles on each other.

- To share master pages among documents, you can import them using the Load Master Pages command in the Pages panel.

Working with color

Although creating colors is somewhat different in InDesign, applying colors is fairly similar. You can create colors in the same color models, and you can manage colors in a similar way. Differences between PageMaker and InDesign include the following:

- Most of your work with colors happens through the Swatches panel (Window ➪ Swatches or F5), not through the Colors panel as PageMaker users might think.

- To create colors, use the New Swatches command in the Swatches panel's flyout menu.

- To apply colors, first click the Stroke or Fill iconic button on the Tools panel to specify where the color goes on the selected object. Then click a color in the Swatches panel.

- Use the Swatches panel or the Colors panel (Window ➪ Colors or F6) to specify a shade (tint) of a color; the Swatches panel is the best place to do this as you can create tints for reuse here as well as apply a tint to an existing color.

- Apply the color None to strokes and fills for transparency; you can also click the None iconic button on the Tools panel, or choose the [None] color in the Swatches panel.

- To share colors among documents, click and drag a colored object into another document window.

Looking at the Command Bar Panel

In addition to having the Position tool in InDesign that acts like PageMaker's Crop tool, InDesign also has the Command Bar panel, which provides 30 iconic buttons to permit quick access to various operations. You open and close this toolbar by choosing Window ➪ Objects & Layout ➪ Command Bar. Figure D.1 shows the panel and identifies each button's function.

FIGURE D.1

The PageMaker toolbar

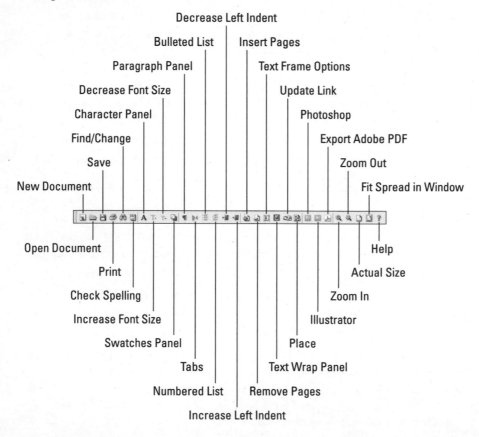

NEW FEATURE   The Command Bar panel is the new name for the PageMaker Toolbar in previous versions of InDesign. Also, the Package for GoLive iconic button has been removed from the panel, because InDesign CS3 no longer supports this feature.

The functions are self-explanatory. Note that some require that an object or a block of text be selected (for example, Update Link, Increase Left Indent, and Numbered List) while others do not (for example, Save, Help, and Export PDF).

Appendix E

More Resources

Technology doesn't stand still, especially in an area as dynamic as publishing, where multiple products work together. That's why I've created an independent Web site that helps InDesign users stay current on tools and techniques. Figure E.1 shows the site's home page. The www.InDesignCentral.com site provides the following resources:

- **Tools:** Links to plug-ins, scripts, utilities, and Adobe downloads

- **Tips:** My favorite tips, as well as reader tips

- **Resources:** Print publishing links, Web publishing links, Mac OS X links, and Windows XP links

- *InDesign Bible* **series and** *InDesign For Dummies* **series:** Excerpts from the books, including color versions of the screenshots from the chapters that cover color, as well as updates from after the books' release

Wiley Publishing, the publisher of this book, also offers a wide range of books to help layout artists and publications designers exploit the publishing tools to the fullest:

- *Adobe InDesign CS3 For Dummies* by myself, Galen Gruman, is a great way to quickly get up to speed on the newest version of InDesign.

- *Photoshop CS3 Bible* by Laurie Ulrich Fuller and Robert C. Fuller provides an in-depth look at how to make the most of Photoshop's extensive image-editing capabilities.

- *Photoshop CS3 Channels and Masks Bible* by Stephen Romaniello teaches how to make use of the valuable tools of channels and masks in Photoshop.

IN THIS APPENDIX

Web site for current tools and techniques

Books for further reference

- *Photoshop CS3: Top 100 Simplified Tips and Tricks* by Lynette Kent offers visual lessons in the latest update for Photoshop.

- *Illustrator CS3 Bible* by Ted Alspach includes in-depth coverage on using Illustrator for print and Web graphics, as well as information on how to integrate Illustrator with Photoshop.

FIGURE E.1

The home page for the InDesign Central Web site

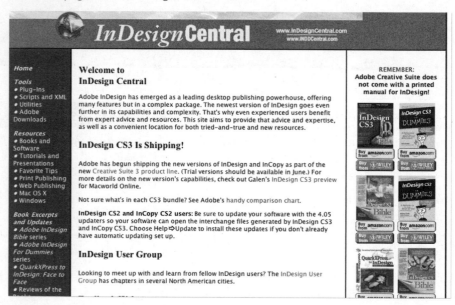

- *Adobe Acrobat 8 PDF Bible* by Ted Padova features complete coverage of using Acrobat and PDF for print prepress, the Internet, CD-ROMs, and all the new media.

- *Adobe Creative Suite 3 Bible* by Ted Padova and Kelly Murdock provides an all-in-one resource for users of Adobe's cornerstone tools (Photoshop, Illustrator, Acrobat Professional, and InDesign).

- *QuarkXPress to InDesign: Face to Face* by myself, Galen Gruman, provides a visual, side-by-side comparison of how to achieve in InDesign 2, CS, and CS2 the steps you would take in QuarkXPress versions 4, 5, and 6.

- *Digital Photography: Top 100 Simplified Tips & Tricks, 3rd Edition* by Rob Sheppard provides clear, illustrated instructions for 100 tasks that reveal cool secrets, teach time-saving tricks, and explain great tips to make you a better digital photographer.

- *Total Digital Photography: The Shoot to Print Workflow Handbook* by Serge Timacheff and David Karlins offers complete, end-to-end workflow advice from shoot to print in a full-color presentation.

Appendix F

Shortcuts Cheat Sheet

Shortcuts are essential to making the most of InDesign. Sure, you can access everything from a menu or pane, but shortcuts make the work much faster. This appendix covers InDesign's keyboard shortcuts and working with contextual menus, which lets you use the mouse to find out what options are available for specific objects.

Because there are so many keyboard shortcuts, I've broken them into functional areas to help you find them more easily in the following table. Note that shortcuts marked with an asterisk (*) have changed in InDesign CS3 or are new to InDesign CS3. Features marked with an asterisk are new to InDesign CS3.

Also note that these shortcuts are the default shortcuts for InDesign; you can edit these defaults by choosing Edit ➪ Keyboard Shortcuts, as covered in Chapter 3.

IN THIS APPENDIX

Using shortcuts in InDesign

Learning shortcuts new to InDesign CS3

TABLE F.1

InDesign Shortcuts

Action or Command	Mac	Windows
Opening/Closing/Saving		
New document	⌘+N	Ctrl+N
New default document	Option+⌘+N	Ctrl+Alt+N
Open document	⌘+O	Ctrl+O
Open library	Option+Shift+⌘+L	Ctrl+Alt+Shift+L
Browse Bridge	Option+⌘+O	Ctrl+Alt+O
Close document	⌘+W	Ctrl+W or Ctrl+F4
Close all documents	Option+Shift+⌘+W	Ctrl+Alt+Shift+W
Quit program	⌘+Q	Ctrl+Q or Alt+F4
Save document	⌘+S	Ctrl+S
Save document as	Shift+⌘+S	Ctrl+Shift+S
Save copy of document	Option+⌘+S	Ctrl+Alt+D
Export document	⌘+E	Ctrl+E
Place text and graphics	⌘+D	Ctrl+D
Viewing		
Hide/show panels	Tab	Tab
Hide/show all panes but Tools panel	Shift+Tab	Shift+Tab
Zoom in	⌘+=	Ctrl+=
Zoom out	⌘+− (hyphen)	Ctrl+− (hyphen)
Fit page/spread in window	⌘+0	Ctrl+0
Fit spread in window	Shift+⌘+0	Ctrl+Alt+0
Fit entire pasteboard in window	Option+Shift+⌘+0	Ctrl+Alt+Shift+0
Display actual size	⌘+1	Ctrl+1
Display at 50%	⌘+5	Ctrl+5
Display at 200%	⌘+2	Ctrl+2
Display at 400%	⌘+4	Ctrl+4
Overprint preview	Option+Shift+⌘+Y	Ctrl+Alt+Shift+Y
Switch between current and previous view	Option⌘+2	Ctrl+Alt+2
Set magnification	Option⌘+5	Ctrl+Alt+5
Set all pages to same view	⌘+percent in view percent menu	Ctrl+percent in view percent menu

Action or Command	Mac	Windows
Switch to previous document window	Shift+⌘+F6	Ctrl+Shift+F6
Switch to next document window	⌘+Y	Ctrl+F6
Show/hide text threads	Option+⌘+Y	Ctrl+Alt+Y
Show/hide frame edges	Control+⌘+H*	Ctrl+H
Show/hide rulers	⌘+R	Ctrl+R
Show hidden characters	Option+⌘+I	Ctrl+Alt+I
Fast display mode	Option+Shift+⌘+Z	Ctrl+Alt+Shift+Z
Typical display mode	Option+⌘+Z	Ctrl+Alt+Z
High-quality display mode	Control+Option+⌘+H*	Ctrl+Alt+H
Preference/Setup		
Preferences dialog box	⌘+K	Ctrl+K
Document setup	Option+⌘+P	Ctrl+Alt+P
File Info	Option+Shift+⌘+I	Ctrl+Alt+Shift+I
Tools		
Selection tool	V	V
Direct Selection tool	A	A
Position tool	Shift+A	Shift+A
Type tool	T	T
Type on a Path tool	Shift+T	Shift+T
Pen tool	P	P
Add Anchor Point tool	=	=
Delete Anchor Point tool	–	–
Convert Direction Point tool	Shift+C	Shift+C
Pencil tool	N	N
Ellipse tool	L	L
Rectangle tool	M	M
Rectangular Frame tool	F	F
Free Transform tool	E	E
Rotate tool	R	R
Scale tool	S	S
Shear tool	O	O
Scissors tool	C	C

continued

TABLE F.1 (continued)

Action or Command	Mac	Windows
Button tool	B	B
Measure tool	K	K
Hand tool	H	H
Temporary Hand tool	Shift+spacebar	Shift+spacebar
Zoom tool	Z	Z
Temporary zoom-in tool	⌘+spacebar	Ctrl+spacebar
Temporary zoom-out tool	Option+⌘+spacebar	Ctrl+Alt+spacebar
Gradient Swatch tool	G	G
Gradient Feather tool*	Shift+G	Shift+G
Eyedropper tool	I	I
Fill iconic button	X	X
Stroke iconic button	X	X
Swap Fill/Stroke iconic button	Shift+X	Shift+X
Default Fill/Stroke iconic button	D	D
Apply Color iconic button	, (comma)	, (comma)
Apply Gradient iconic button	. (period)	. (period)
Apply None iconic button	/	/
Panes		
Apply value in field	Option+Enter	Shift+Return
Show Control panel	Option+⌘+6	Ctrl+Alt+6
Show Links panel	Shift⌘+D	Ctrl+Shift+D
Show Layers panel	F7	F7
Show Pages panel	⌘+F12* or F12	Ctrl+F12* or F12
Show Swatches panel	F5	F5
Show Color panel	F6	F6
Show Glyphs panel	Option+Shift+F11*	Alt+Shift+F11*
Show Character panel	⌘+T	Ctrl+T
Show Paragraph panel	Option+⌘+T	Ctrl+Alt+T
Show Character Styles panel	Shift+⌘+F11* or Shift+F11	Ctrl+Shift+F11* or Shift+F11
Show Paragraph Styles panel	⌘+F11* or F11	Ctrl+F11* or F11
Show Object Styles panel	⌘+F7	Ctrl+F7

Action or Command	Mac	Windows
Show Quick Apply panel	⌘+Return	Ctrl+Enter
Show Text Wrap panel	Option+⌘+W	Ctrl+Alt+W
Open Text Frame Options dialog box	⌘+B	Ctrl+B
Show Index panel	Shift+F8	Shift+F8
Show Table panel	Shift+F9	Shift+F9
Show Tabs panel	Shift⌘+T	Ctrl+Shift+T
Show Align panel	Shift+F7	Shift+F7
Show Stroke panel	⌘+F10* or F10	Ctrl+F10* or F10
Show Effects panel*	Shift+⌘+F10	Ctrl+Shift+F10
Show Separations Preview panel	Shift+F6	Shift+F6
Show Scripts panel	Option+⌘+F11*	Ctrl+Alt+F11*
Show Info panel	F8	F8
Show Structure pane	Option+⌘+1	Ctrl+Alt+1
Switch to Notes mode*	⌘+F8	Ctrl+F8
Guides		
Show/hide guides	⌘+; (semicolon)	Ctrl+; (semicolon)
Lock/unlock guides	Option+⌘+; (semicolon)	Ctrl+Alt+; (semicolon)
Snap to guides on/off	Shift+⌘+; (semicolon)	Ctrl+Shift+; (semicolon)
Show/hide baseline grid	Option+⌘+"	Ctrl+Alt+"
Show/hide document grid	⌘+"	Ctrl+"
Snap to document grid on/off	Shift+⌘+"	Ctrl+Shift+"
Select all guides	Option+⌘+G	Ctrl+Alt+G
Create zero-point guidelines	⌘+click zero point when dragging guides	Ctrl+click zero point when dragging guides
Adding and Navigating Pages		
Add new page	Shift+⌘+P	Ctrl+Shift+P
Go to first page	Shift+⌘+PgUp	Ctrl+Shift+Page Up
Go back one page	Shift+PgUp	Shift+Page Up
Go forward one page	Shift+PgDn *or* ⌘+PgDn	Shift+Page Down *or* Ctrl+keypad PgDn
Go to last page	Shift+⌘+PgDn	Ctrl+Shift+Page Down

continued

TABLE F.1   (continued)

Action or Command	Mac	Windows
Go to last page viewed	⌘+PgUp	Ctrl+keypad PgUp
Go forward one spread	Option+PgUp	Alt+Page Up
Go back one spread	Option+PgDn	Alt+Page Down
Object Selection		
Select master page	Shift+⌘+click	Ctrl+Shift+click
Select topmost object	Option+Shift+⌘+]	Ctrl+Alt+Shift+]
Select object above current object	Option+⌘+]	Ctrl+Alt+]
Select bottommost object	Option+Shift+⌘+[	Ctrl+Alt+Shift+[
Select object below current object	Option+⌘+[	Ctrl+Alt+[
Go to last frame in thread	Option+Shift+⌘+PgDn	Ctrl+Alt+Shift+Page Down
Go to next frame in thread	Option+⌘+PgDn	Ctrl+Alt+Page Down
Go to first frame in thread	Option+Shift+⌘+PgUp	Ctrl+Alt+Shift+Page Up
Go to previous frame in thread	Option+⌘+PgUp	Ctrl+Alt+Page Up
Moving Objects		
Move selection 1 point	Left, right, up, and down cursors	Left, right, up, and down cursors
Move selection 10 points	Shift+left, right, up, and down cursors	Shift+left, right, up, and down cursors
Bring object to front	Shift+⌘+]	Ctrl+Shift+]
Bring object forward	⌘+]	Ctrl+]
Send object to back	Shift+⌘+[	Ctrl+Shift+[
Send object backward	⌘+[	Ctrl+[
Object Commands		
Cut	⌘+X	Ctrl+X
Copy	⌘+V	Ctrl+V
Paste	⌘+P	Ctrl+P
Paste into	Option+⌘+V	Ctrl+Alt+V
Paste in place	Option+Shift+⌘+V	Ctrl+Alt+Shift+V
Paste without formatting	Shift+⌘+V	Ctrl+Shift+V
Clear	Backspace	Backspace or Del
Duplicate object	Option+Shift+⌘+D	Ctrl+Alt+Shift+D
Step and repeat	Shift+⌘+U	Ctrl+Shift+U
Resize proportionately	Shift+drag	Shift+drag

Action or Command	Mac	Windows
Resize frame and content	⌘+drag	Ctrl+drag
Center content	Shift+⌘+E	Ctrl+Shift+E
Fill frame proportionally	Option+Shift+⌘+C	Ctrl+Alt+Shift+C
Fit content proportionally	Option+Shift+⌘+E	Ctrl+Alt+Shift+E
Fit content to frame	Option+⌘+E	Ctrl+Alt+E
Fit frame to content	Option+⌘+C	Ctrl+Alt+C
Decrease size/scale by 1%	⌘+, (comma)	Ctrl+, (comma)
Decrease size/scale by 5%	Option+⌘+, (comma)	Ctrl+Alt+, (comma)
Increase size/scale by 5%	Option+⌘+. (period)	Ctrl+Alt+. (period)
Duplicate	Option+drag, or Option+left, right, up, and down cursors	Alt+drag, or Alt+left, right, up, and down cursors
Group	⌘+G	Ctrl+G
Ungroup	Shift+⌘+G	Ctrl+Shift+G
Lock	⌘+L	Ctrl+L
Unlock	Option+⌘+L	Ctrl+Alt+L
Drop shadow	Option+⌘+M	Ctrl+Alt+M
Transform Again	Option+⌘+3	Ctrl+Alt+3
Transform Sequence Again	Option+⌘+4	Ctrl+Alt+4
Graphics Handling		
Convert text to outlines	Shift+⌘+O	Ctrl+Alt+O
Create outlines without deleting text	Option+Shift+⌘+O	Ctrl+Alt+Shift+O
Make clipping path	Option+Shift+⌘+K	Ctrl+Alt+Shift+K
Make compound path	⌘+8	Ctrl+8
Release compound path	Option+Shift+⌘+8*	Ctrl+Alt+Shift+8*
Text Selection		
Select all	⌘+A	Ctrl+A
Deselect all	Shift+⌘+A	Ctrl+Shift+A
Select word	double-click	double-click
Select one word to left	Shift+⌘+left cursor	Ctrl+Shift+left cursor
Select one word to right	Shift⌘+right cursor	Ctrl+Shift+right cursor
Select range	Shift+left, right, up, and down cursors	Shift+left, right, up, and down cursors

continued

TABLE F.1 (continued)

Action or Command	Mac	Windows
Select paragraph	triple-click	triple-click
Select one paragraph before	Shift+⌘+up cursor	Ctrl+Shift+up cursor
Select one paragraph after	Shift+⌘+down cursor	Ctrl+Shift+down cursor
Select to start of story	Shift+⌘+Home	Ctrl+Shift+Home
Select to end of story	Shift+⌘+End	Ctrl+Shift+End
Moving within Text		
Move left one word	⌘+left cursor	Ctrl+left cursor
Move right one word	⌘+right cursor	Ctrl+right cursor
Move to start of line	Home	Home
Move to end of line	End	End
Move to previous paragraph	⌘+up cursor	Ctrl+up cursor
Move to next paragraph	⌘+down cursor	Ctrl+down cursor
Move to start of story	⌘+Home	Ctrl+Home
Move to end of story	⌘+End	Ctrl+End
Text/Paragraph Formats		
Bold	Shift+⌘+B	Ctrl+Shift+B
Italic	Shift+⌘+I	Ctrl+Shift+I
Normal	Shift+⌘+Y	Ctrl+Shift+Y
Underline	Shift+⌘+U	Ctrl+Shift+U
Strikethrough	Shift+⌘+/	Ctrl+Shift+/
All caps on/off	Shift+⌘+K	Ctrl+Shift+K
Small caps	Shift+⌘+H	Ctrl+Shift+H
Superscript	Shift+⌘+=	Ctrl+Shift+=
Subscript	Option+Shift+⌘+=	Ctrl+Alt+Shift+=
Update character style based on selection	Option+Shift+⌘+C	Ctrl+Alt+Shift+C
Update paragraph style based on selection	Option+Shift+⌘+R	Ctrl+Alt+Shift+R
Drop caps and nested styles	Option+⌘+R	Ctrl+Alt+R
Paragraph rules	Option+⌘+J	Ctrl+Alt+J
Set horizontal scale to 100%	Shift+⌘+X	Ctrl+Shift+X
Set vertical scale to 100%	Option+Shift+⌘+X	Ctrl+Alt+Shift+X
Increase point size by 1 point	Shift+⌘+. (period)	Ctrl+Shift+. (period)

Action or Command	Mac	Windows
Increase point size by 10 points	Option+Shift+⌘+. (period)	Ctrl+Alt+Shift+. (period)
Decrease point size by 1 point	Shift+⌘+, (comma)	Ctrl+Shift+, (comma)
Decrease point size by 10 points	Option+Shift+⌘+, (comma)	Ctrl+Alt+Shift+, (comma)
Text Alignment and Spacing		
Align left	Shift+⌘+L	Ctrl+Shift+L
Align right	Shift+⌘+R	Ctrl+Shift+R
Align center	Shift+⌘+C	Ctrl+Shift+C
Justify full	Shift+⌘+F	Ctrl+Shift+F
Justify left	Shift+⌘+J	Ctrl+Shift+J
Justify right	Option+Shift+⌘+R	Ctrl+Alt+Shift+R
Justify center	Option+Shift+⌘+C	Ctrl+Alt+Shift+C
Autohyphenation on/off	Option+Shift+⌘+H	Ctrl+Alt+Shift+H
Hyphenation on/off (selected text)	Option+⌘+H	Ctrl+Alt+H
Set spacing and justification	Option+Shift+⌘+J	Ctrl+Alt+Shift+J
Set keep options	Option+⌘+K	Ctrl+Alt+K
Increase leading by 2 points	Option+up cursor	Alt+up cursor
Decrease leading by 2 points	Option+down cursor	Alt+down cursor
Increase leading by 10 points	Option+⌘+up cursor	Ctrl+Alt+up cursor
Decrease leading by 10 points	Option+⌘+down cursor	Ctrl+Alt+down cursor
Use autoleading	Option+Shift+⌘+A	Ctrl+Alt+Shift+A
Increase kerning/tracking by 20 units	Option+right cursor	Alt+right cursor
Increase kerning/tracking by 100 units	Option+⌘+right cursor	Ctrl+Alt+right cursor
Decrease kerning/tracking by 20 units	Option+left cursor	Alt+left cursor
Decrease kerning/tracking by 100 units	Option+⌘+left cursor	Ctrl+Alt+left cursor
Clear all kerning/tracking (set to 0)	Shift+⌘+Q	Ctrl+Shift+Q
Increase baseline shift by 2 points	Option+Shift+up arrow	Alt+Shift+up arrow
Increase baseline shift by 10 points	Option+Shift+⌘+up arrow	Ctrl+Alt+Shift+up arrow
Decrease baseline shift by 2 points	Option+Shift+down cursor	Alt+Shift+down arrow
Decrease baseline shift by 10 points	Option+Shift+⌘+down arrow	Ctrl+Alt+Shift+down arrow
Align to grid on/off	Option+Shift+⌘+G	Ctrl+Alt+Shift+G

continued

TABLE F.1   (continued)

Action or Command	Mac	Windows
Table Editing		
Insert table	Option+Shift+⌘+T	Ctrl+Alt+Shift+T
Insert column	Option+⌘+9	Ctrl+Alt+9
Insert row	⌘+9	Ctrl+9
Select table	Option+⌘+A	Ctrl+Alt+A
Select column	Option+⌘+3	Ctrl+Alt+3
Select row	⌘+3	Ctrl+3
Select cell	⌘+/	Ctrl+/
Delete column	Shift+Delete	Shift+Backspace
Delete row	⌘+Delete	Ctrl+Backspace
Table setup	Option+Shift+⌘+B	Ctrl+Alt+Shift+B
Set cell text options	Option+⌘+B	Ctrl+Alt+B
Find/Change Text, Spelling, and Indexing		
Edit in Story Editor	⌘+Y	Ctrl+Y
Find/change	⌘+F	Ctrl+F
Find next	Option+⌘+F	Ctrl+Alt+F
Search for selected text	Shift+F1	Shift+F1
Add selected text to Find What field	⌘+F1	Ctrl+F1
Add selected text to Change To field	⌘+F2	Ctrl+F2
Change current selection	⌘+F3	Ctrl+F3
Change current selection and search forward	Shift+⌘+F3	Ctrl+Shift+F3
Check spelling	⌘+I	Ctrl+I
Add new index entry	Option+Shift+⌘+]	Ctrl+Alt+Shift+]
Add new index entry (reversed)	Option+Shift+⌘+[	Ctrl+Alt+Shift+[
New index/open index entry dialog box	⌘+U	Ctrl+U
Special Characters		
Bullet (•)	Option+8	Alt+8
Ellipsis (...)	Option+; (semicolon)	Alt+; (semicolon)
Copyright ((c))	Option+G	Alt+G
Registered trademark ((r))	Option+R	Alt+R
Trademark ((tm))	Option+2	Alt+2

Action or Command	Mac	Windows
Paragraph (¶)	Option+7	Alt+7
Section (§)	Option+6	Alt+6
Keyboard double quote (")*	Control+Shift+'	Alt+Shift+'
Keyboard single quote/apostrophe (')*	Control+'	Alt+'
Switch between keyboard and typographic quotes	Option+Shift+⌘+"	Ctrl+Alt+Shift+"
Em dash (—)	Option+Shift+– (hyphen)	Alt+Shift+– (hyphen)
En dash (–)	Option+– (hyphen)	Alt+– (hyphen)
Nonbreaking hyphen	Option+⌘+– (hyphen)	Ctrl+Alt+– (hyphen)
Discretionary hyphen	Shift+⌘+– (hyphen)	Ctrl+Shift+– (hyphen)
Em space	Shift+⌘+M	Ctrl+Shift+M
En space	Shift+⌘+N	Ctrl+Shift+N
Thin space	Option+Shift+⌘+M	Ctrl+Alt+Shift+M
Nonbreaking space	Option+⌘+X	Ctrl+Alt+X
Soft return	Shift+Enter	Shift+Return
Column break	Keypad Enter	keypad Enter
Frame break	Shift+keypad Enter	Shift+keypad Enter
Page break	⌘+keypad Enter	Ctrl+keypad Enter
Indent to here	⌘+\	Ctrl+\
Right-indent tab	Shift+Tab	Shift+Tab
Insert current page number	Option+Shift+⌘+N	Ctrl+Alt+Shift+N
Printing and Output		
Print document	⌘+P	Ctrl+P
Preflight document	Option+Shift+⌘+F	Ctrl+Alt+Shift+F
Package document	Option+Shift+⌘+P	Ctrl+Alt+Shift+P
Miscellaneous		
Help	Help	F1
Undo	⌘+Z	Ctrl+Z
Redo	Shift+⌘+Z	Ctrl+Shift+Z

Index

SYMBOLS AND NUMERICS

 (Apple logo), 523

• (bullet)
    automatic, 472
    described, 480
    search and replace text code, 422
    shortcut, 942
    Word, converting to text, 381
· (bullet, thin), 522
^ (caret), 422
ç (cedilla), 539
¢ (cent), 522
^ (circumflex), 539
" (closed double quote), 536
' (closed single quote), 536
© (copyright)
    keyboard shortcut, 522
    search and replace text code, 422
    shortcut, 942
† (dagger), 522
° (degree), 523
÷ (division), 523
‡ (double dagger), 522
... (ellipsis), 522, 942
— (em dash)
    search and replace text code, 422
    shortcuts, 536, 943
    from Word, 374
• (en bullet), 522
– (en dash)
    search and replace text code, 422
    shortcuts, 536, 943
    from Word, 374
€ (euro), 522, 717
' (foot), 523
» (French close double quote), 542
« (French open double quote), 542
ƒ (function), 523
` (grave), 539
≥ (greater than or equal to), 523

β (Greek beta), 523
µ (Greek mu), 523
Ω (Greek Omega), 523
π (Greek pi), 523
Σ (Greek Sigma), 523
- (hyphen), 943
≠ (inequality), 523
∞ (infinity), 523
≡ (integral), 523
' (keyboard single quote/apostrophe), 536
≤ (less than or equal to), 523
¬ (logical not), 523
· (open diamond), 523
" (open double quote), 536
' (open single quote), 536
¶ (paragraph)
    search and replace text code, 422
    shortcut, 522, 943
‰ (per mil), 523
£ (pound sterling), 522
" (quotation mark)
    as first character after drop cap, 470
    search and replace text code, 422
    shortcut, 536, 943
® (registered trademark) symbol
    search and replace text code, 422
    shortcut, 522, 942
√ (root), 523
⊕ (rough equivalence), 523
§ (section symbol)
    search and replace text code, 422
    shortcut, 522, 943
¡ (Spanish open exclamation), 542
¿ (Spanish open question), 542
~ (tilde), 539
™ (Trademark), 522
∂ (variation), 523
¥ (yen), 522
¼ (one-quarter fraction), 523
½ (one-half fraction), 523
¾ (three-quarters fraction), 523

A

absolute colorimetric, bitmap images, 697

Absolute Numbering area, 85

absolute page number, 180

Acrobat files. *See* PDF files

Acrobat Professional, 690–691

actions, page, 798–799

activating and registering InDesign, 885–886

active layer objects, 192

Add Anchor Point tool (shortcut =), 45

adding and deleting objects to libraries, 218–219

adjacent single and double quotes, 538

Adjust View Settings area, Display Performance preferences, 110

Adobe Acrobat 8 PDF Bible (Padova), 932

Adobe Acrobat files. *See* PDF files

Adobe Bridge
    CMS, 690, 692
    documents file system, 148–149
    file context, 839–840
    interface, 841
    suite functionality, 841
    utilities for InDesign, 841–842

Adobe Creative Suite 3 Bible (Padova and Murdock), 932

Adobe Illustrator
    CMS, 691
    file import, described, 25
    format, 623
    PostScript files, importing, 624, 625

Adobe InDesign
    documents, sharing elements with other users, 832
    hierarchy, scripting, 866
    Interchange file format, 154
    Tagged Text format, 156

Adobe InDesign CS3 For Dummies (Gruman), 931

Adobe InDesign interface
    color functions, 901
    document and object functions
        effects, 898
        file exchange and sharing, 895
        handling objects, 897
        measurements, 894
        multi-document projects, 896
        page actions, 894–895
        selecting objects within group, 896
    graphics functions, 901
    menu, 68–69

output functions
    eBooks export, 903
    JPEG export, 902
    PDF and EPS export, 902
    printing, 902
    Web export, 903

scripting functions, 903

text functions
    editing, 898–899
    import, 898
    paragraph and character formatting, 899–900
    spelling and indexing, 900
    styles, 901
    tabs and tables, 900

tools, panels, and dialog boxes
    described, 889–891
    menus, 892–893
    preferences, 893–894
    sharable files, 894
    shortcuts, 892
    Version Cue, 894

workgroup editing functions
    within InCopy, 905
    within InDesign, 904

XML functions, 904

Adobe PageMaker
    Command Bar Panel, 930
    converting documents from other programs, 150
    differences from InDesign
        color, 929
        described, 924–925
        graphics, 928
        keyboard shortcut equivalents, 927–928
        manipulating pages, 928–929
        objects, 925–926
        text, 926–927
        tools and setting preferences, 925
    documents, opening, 923–924
    Story Editor feature, 406

Adobe Paragraph Composer, 479–480

Adobe Photoshop
    clipping paths, fitting graphics and frames, 648
    CMS, 691
    file import, described, 25
    format, 623
    graphics, importing, 626–627

Adobe Single-Line Composer, 479

Adobe tool, 43

Adobe Updater Preferences dialog box, 115–116
Advanced pane, printing techniques
    bitmap printing, 754
    described, 754
    OPI settings, 754–755
    Transparency Flattener, 755
agates measurement, 96
alerts, preflighting documents, 721
Align Away from Spine, 466
Align Center (Shift+⌘+C or Ctrl+Shift+C), 466
Align Left (Shift+⌘+L or Ctrl+Shift+L), 465–466
Align On field, 552
Align panel (Window ⇨ Object & Layout ⇨ Align or
        Shift+F7), 59
Align Right (Shift+⌘+R or Ctrl+Shift+R), 466
Align Towards Spine, 466
aligning
    objects, 282–284, 286
    paragraphs, 465–466
All Caps
    adjusting, 447
    characters, 450
All Small Caps, OpenType, 529
Allow Master Item Overrides on Selection, 204
alpha channel clipping path, 649
Alspach, Ted (Illustrator CS3 Bible), 932
anchor points
    adding and deleting, 669–671
    converting, 672–673
    moving, 671–672
anchored frame objects
    adding, 340–342
    adjusting, 343
    converting existing to, 343
    releasing and deleting, 343–344
    when to use, 339–340
Anchored Object command, creating with, 336–338
Anchored Object Options pane, 357
angle, gradient, 251–252
ANPA color
    printer model, 695
    swatchbook, 234
anti-aliasing text, 110
apostrophes
    adjacent single and double quotes, 538
    described, 537–538
    keyboard quotes, 538
    reverse single quotes, 538
Apple AIFF files, 800

Apple iWork Pages, 534
Apple logo (), 523
AppleScript
    conditional, writing, 878, 879
    described, 869
    labeling items, 877
    language, learning, 869
    resources, 871
    running, 870
    saving, 870–871
    support, 863
    syntax errors, checking for, 869
    writing and running, 869
    writing simple, 875–876
AppleScript For Dummies, 2nd Edition (Trinko), 871
application folder
    Plug-ins, 30–31
    Presets, 30
    Required, 31
Arabic fonts, 529
ASCII
    exporting, 519
    importing, 382–384
assignments
    user, identifying, 844
    workgroups, setting up, 843
Assignments panel
    benefits of using, 844
    described, 61, 64, 891
    exporting stories, 847
    new assignment, creating, 845–846
    packaging assignments, 848
    stories, adding to assignments, 846–847
Attributes panel, 61, 62
Auto-Collapse Icon Panels option, 87
Autocorrect feature
    described, 407–409
    find-change queries, 83
    preferences, 105–106
autoflow text-flow icon, 397
automatic bullets, 472
auto-recovery files, specifying folders for, 112
AVI movies, 800

B

background
    color compound paths, creating, 678
    layers, 189
    text, reversing out of, 492–493

baseline
    adjusting, 447
    superscript and subscript letters, 451
    text, setting, 432
baseline grid
    described, 225–227
    showing/hiding, 126
Baseline Grid area, 98–99
Baseline Shift
    characters, 448
    field, setting with keyboard, 98
Beginning AppleScript (Kochan), 871
beveling and embossing effects, 322–323
bitmap format (BMP)
    described, 623
    graphics, importing, 629
bitmap graphics
    BMP, 629
    CMS options, 697
    described, 626
    GIF, 628
    importing, 633–637
    JPEG, 628
    PCX, 629
    Photoshop, 626–627
    PICT, 629
    PNG, 628
    printing, 754
    professional-level, 626–628
    saving, 622
    Scitex CT, 627
    TIFF, 627
    Web-oriented, 628
black
    appearance of
        Overprint [Black] Swatch, 111
        pane displayed, 111
        on RGB and Grayscale Devices area, 110
    CMS options, 697–699
    text, printing, 749
bleeding
    Bleed and Slug area
        documents, creating, 141
        printing techniques, 747
    bleed marks, 745
    prepress files, 773–774
    service bureaus, preparing for, 729
blending modes, 314–315

BMP (Windows bitmap format)
    described, 623
    graphics, importing, 629
bold
    Story Editor feature, 406
    when to use, 446
booklets, printing
    described, 730–733
    imposition, 733–735
bookmarks
    electronic documents, 794–796
    prepress files, 770–771
Bookmarks panel (Window ⇨ Interactive ⇨ Bookmarks),
        66, 67
bounding box, 330
branches, 815
breaks, 423
Bridge (Adobe)
    CMS, 690, 692
    documents file system, 148–149
    file context, 839–840
    interface, 841
    suite functionality, 841
    utilities for InDesign, 841–842
build, color, 230
bullet (•)
    automatic, 472
    described, 480
    shortcut, 942
    search and replace text code, 422
    Word, converting to text, 381
· (bullet, thin), 522
bulleted and numbered lists
    applying, 489
    bullet characters, 480
    defining, 486–489
    imported, working with, 489
Button tool, 47
buttons, page actions, 796–797

C

calibration, CMS, 630
CALS tables, 815
Cap Height baseline, 432
capitalization
    hyphenated words, 476
    spelling corrections, 409
^ (caret), 422

carriage returns, 383
Cascading Style Sheets (CSS) text formatting, 805–806
cedilla (ç), 539
Cell Styles panel (Window ➪ Type & Tables ➪ Type Cell
    Styles), 61, 63
cells
    Excel, importing, 384, 385
    platforms, transferring across, 834
    styles
        described, 26
        sharing elements with other users, 828–829
    table
        colors, gradients, and strokes, 565
        Control panel, 565
        Diagonal Lines pane, 563–564
        formatting, 560
        merging and unmerging, 564
        overflowing text, 564
        splitting, 564
        Strokes and Fills pane, 561–563
        Text pane, 561
cent (¢), 522
Center Justify, 466
centering graphic in frame, 646
centimeters measurement, 96
chapters, multi-document projects, 610
Character panel (Type ➪ Character or Window ➪ Type &
    Tables ➪ Character or ⌘+T or Ctrl+T), 55
Character Set, importing text-only files, 382
Character Settings area, 91–92
Character Styles
    creating and applying, 27, 509–511
    first line effect, 515
    importing
        in imported text files, 517
        from InDesign documents, 516–517
    local changes, 515
    managing and grouping, 512
    modifying, 514
    overriding, 511–512
    panel (Type ➪ Character Styles or Window ➪ Type &
        Tables ➪ Character Styles or press Shift+⌘+F11
        or Ctrl+Shift+F11), 56, 57, 509
characters. *See also* special characters
    All Caps and Small Caps, 450
    Baseline Shift, 448
    bullet, 480
    Characters panel, 447
    Control panel, 446–447

defaults, 123
described, 437
drop caps, 470–471
expert font, 455
font family, font style, and font size
    described, 441–442
    labeling paragraphs, 446
    selecting, 443–444
    size, changing, 445
footnote style, 590
formats, 438–440
formatting, 899–900
Horizontal Scale and Vertical Scale, 448
language, 449–450
Ligatures, 452–453
No Break, 455
OpenType options, 453–455
platforms, transferring across, 834
scaling, 91
Skew (false italic), 448–449
space
    described, 456
    kerning, 456–457
    leading, 458–459
    tracking, 457
    units, 457
styles
    described, 501, 502
    sharing elements with other users, 828–829
Superscript and Subscript, 451
Underline and Strikethrough, 451–452
width, platform differences and, 837
Characters panel, 447
Check In
    document command, 152
    version control, 162
Check Spelling dialog box, 409–411
children master pages, 206–207
choking color trap process, 705
ciceros measurement, 96
CIE (International Committee on Illumination) Lab color
    standard
    described, 230
    profiles, 696
circumflex (ˆ), 539
Clipboard
    coloring imported graphics, 247
    PDF, 114
    search and replace text code, 423

Clipboard Handling pane
  Clipboard area, 114
  described, 113
  When Pasting Text and Tables from Other Applications
    area, 114
clipping path
  creating in InDesign, 650–652
  defaults, 124
  deleting, 653
  described, 648
  graphic's own, 648
  as a mask, 649
  modifying, 652–653
  Photoshop, 648
  as a wrap boundary, 649–650
cloning objects within documents, 279
Close (⌘+W, or Ctrl+W or Ctrl+F4) document command,
    152
closed double quote ("), 536
closed single quote ('), 536
closed path, opening, 676
closure, drawing free-form shapes and curved paths, 656
CMS (color management system)
  Acrobat Professional 8, 690–691
  bitmap images, 697
  blackness, 697–699
  Bridge, 690, 692
  calibration, 630
  color models, 695
  document color settings, 701–702
  InDesign color display settings, 694
  managing color during output, 704
  monitor bit depth, on-screen display, 694
  output settings, 695–699
  policies, 695–696
  preferences, saving, 704
  profiles, 696, 699–700
  proofing on screen, 702–703
  setting up, 692–694
CMYK color
  described, 231
  imported graphics, 247
  policies, 696
  printer model, 695
  standard, 230
  Trumatch swatchbook, 234
color
  applying, 254–255
  baseline grid area, 98
  blending mode, 315

capabilities, 229
Colors panel
    drawback to using, 243–244
    unnamed, managing, 244–245
converting spot to process, 232
creating with Swatches panel
    mixed colors, 241–243
    naming system, 240
    personalizing, 237
    steps, 237–239
    tints, 240–241
Creative Suite applications, 838
defaults, 127
defining, 236–237
definitions, sharing elements with other users, 828
document, creating and applying, 14–16
document grid, 100
dodge, blending mode, 314
EPS file, creating, 783
gradients
    angle and location, 251–252
    creating, 248–250
    described, 248
    unnamed, creating, 250–251
guide, 35
Guides & Pasteboard preferences, 100–101
importing
    color systems, 629–630
    described, 629
    formats, 247
    from graphics, 245–246
    swatches, 245
InDesign interface, 901
interface buttons, 49
layers, 192
mixing spot and process, 232
models, working with, 232–234
PageMaker, 929
paper variation models, 234–236
preflighting documents, 722, 723
printing
    methods, 231–232
    options, 748–749
    techniques, 756–759
profile files, cross-platform issues, 834
QuarkXPress, 921
sampling, 246–247
swatchbooks
    ANPA, 234
    DIC, 234

Focoltone, 234
Hexachrome, 234
HKS, 234
Pantone, 233, 630
Toyo, 234
Trumatch, 234
swatches
deleting, 253–254
duplicating, 254
editing, 253
merging, 253
transferring across platforms, 834
table cells, 565
terms, 230
color bars, 746
color burn blending mode, 314
color gamut, 230
color management, 120–121
Color Management pane, printing techniques, 753–754
color management system (CMS)
Acrobat Professional 8, 690–691
bitmap images, 697
blackness, 697–699
Bridge, 690, 692
calibration, 630
color models, 695
document color settings, 701–702
InDesign color display settings, 694
managing color during output, 704
monitor bit depth, on-screen display, 694
output settings, 695–699
policies, 695–696
preferences, saving, 704
profiles, 696, 699–700
proofing on screen, 702–703
setting up, 692–694
color model, 230
Color pane, importing bitmap graphics, 635
Color panel (shortcut F6), 61, 62
color prepress preparation
CMS options
bitmap images, 697
blackness, 697–699
color models, 695
described, 690–692
document color settings, 701–702
InDesign color display settings, 694
managing color during output, 704

monitor bit depth, on-screen display, 694
output settings, 695–699
policies, 695–696
preferences, saving, 704
profiles, 696
profiles, applying to images, 699–700
proofing on screen, 702–703
setting up, 692–694
color trapping
applying to pages, 710–711
described, 704
knockout and overprinting, 705–707
methods, 705
presets, specifying, 707–710
described, 689–690
color separation, 230
color shift, 231
color space, 230
color trapping
applying to pages, 710–711
described, 704
knockout and overprinting, 705–707
methods, 705
presets, specifying, 707–710
Colors panel
drawback to using, 243–244
unnamed, managing, 244–245
column guides, 225
columns
document setup, 122, 431
guides, 221
justified versus left-aligned paragraphs, 473
Layout Adjustment feature, 185
master pages, 209–210
table
adding and deleting, 559
manipulating, 559
text
master frames, specifying, 398
rule, placing between, 399–400
text frames, adjusting, 398–399
combining layers, 197
Command Bar panel (Window ➪ Object & Layout ➪
Command Bar)
described, 66, 67, 852
PageMaker, 930
previous name, 891
common settings file, sharing elements with other users, 829

composing text
    Adobe Paragraph Composer, 479–480
    Adobe Single-Line Composer, 479
Composition pane
    described, 92
    Highlight area, 93
    Text Wrap area, 94
compound paths
    creating, 679–680
    described, 678–679
    direction, changing, 681
    editing, 680–681
    Pathfinder panel or menu options, 682–683
    splitting, 681
Compression pane, PDF files, 771–772
conditional, writing, 877–879
Content tool (QuarkXPress), 270
context, OpenType
    alternates, 529
    described, 453
contextual menus, 77–79
Control panel and Transform panel, 294–296
Control panel (Option + ⌘ or Ctrl+Alt+6)
    customizing, 890
    described, 55, 292, 446–447
    objects, selecting, 275
    table cells, 565
Convert Shape path effect, 683
converting
    anchor points, 672–673
    documents from other programs
        generally, 149
        QuarkXPress, 150
    frames for specific content, 264–265
    images to GIF and JPEG formats, 804
    spot to process color, 232
copies, printing, 741
Copy and Paste commands (Edit ➪ Copy, or ⌘+C or Ctrl+C;
        Edit ➪ Paste, or ⌘+V or Ctrl+V), 278
Copy command, importing graphics, 639–640
Copyfit Info panel, 853
copying
    graphics, importing, 640
    images to GIF and JPEG formats, 804
    layer objects, 194
    and moving pages
        within document, 170–171
        shuffling, dangers of, 171, 173
        working across documents, 171–172

objects
    between documents, 280–281
    within documents, 278–280
    snippets, 281
    text, 405
copyright (©) symbol
    keyboard shortcut, 522
    search and replace text code, 422
    shortcut, 942
Corel WordPerfect special characters, 534
corner anchor point, 659
Corner Options
    defaults, 124
    described, 309–311
    dialog box, 685
    previous name for, 891
corner point, mitered and beveled, 304
Creative Suite workgroups
    Adobe Bridge
        file context, 839–840
        interface, 841
        suite functionality, 841
        utilities for InDesign, 841–842
    described, 838
    graphics and color, 838
    Web content, 838–839
creep booklet pages, 732
crop marks, 745
cropping
    graphics by adjusting frames, 644
    prepress files, 771
CSS (Cascading Style Sheets) text formatting, 805–806
curly quotes, 88
currency symbols, 522
Cursor Key field, selecting, 98
cursor movement options, 97
Cursor Options area, 108
curved line segments connected by corner points, 664–665
curved lines
    connected by smooth points, 662–664
    generally, 662
custom measurement, 96
custom strokes for characters, 25
custom text formatting, 575
cutting
    spacing, adjusting automatically, 89
    text, 405

D

dagger (†), 522

Dainippon Ink & Chemical (DIC) color
    printer model, 695
    swatchbook, 234

darken blending mode, 314

dash
    described, 307–308
    em dashes, 536–537
    en dashes, 537

data format, EPS file, 784

Data Merge panel (Window ⇨ Automation ⇨ Data Merge),
    61, 63

date format, 575

DCS PostScript files, 624, 625

decimal places, importing Excel file, 385

default figure style, positional forms, 530

degree (°), 523

Delete Anchor Point tool (shortcut - [hyphen]), 45

deleting
    color swatches, 253–254
    layers, 197–198
    objects, 281–282, 339
    objects from libraries, 218–219
    selected pages, 205
    text, 405, 407

denominator, OpenType, 453, 529

Detach Selection from Master flyout, 204

Diagonal Lines pane, table cells, 563–564

dialog boxes
    described, 889–891
    menus, 892–893
    preferences, 893–894
    sharable files, 894
    shortcuts, 892
    Version Cue, 894

DIC (Dainippon Ink & Chemical) color
    printer model, 695
    swatchbook, 234

dictionary
    changes to, 30
    customizing, 413–415
    preferences
        described, 102
        Hyphenation Exceptions area, 103–104
        installing dictionaries, 103
        language area, 102–103
        setting, 416–418
        User Dictionary area, 104

sharing with other users, 829

text-only files, importing, 382

*Digital Photography: Top 100 Simplified Tips & Tricks, 3rd
    Edition* (Sheppard), 932

dimension information, acquiring, 285

Direct Selection tool
    described, 270, 271–272
    multiple objects, 276
    QuarkXPress users, adapting, 910
    shortcut, 44

direction, changing compound paths, 681

direction handles, free-form shapes and curved paths,
    673–674

direction line, anchor point, 659

direction points, QuarkXPress, 673

discretionary hyphen
    described, 474
    search and replace text code, 422
    shortcuts, 536

discretionary ligatures, 453, 529

Display Performance preferences
    Adjust View Settings area, 110
    Options area, 109
    Scrolling area, 110

Distiller job options, prepress files, 779–780

distributing objects, 282–284

division (÷), 523

dock display, changing, 52–53

document
    Bridge file system, 148–149
    CMS options, 701–702
    colors, creating and applying, 14–16
    defaults, 121–123
    filename extensions, displaying, 146–147
    frames and pages, 4–7
    graphics, 17–18
    InDesign interface functions
        effects, 898
        file exchange and sharing, 895
        handling objects, 897
        measurements, 894
        multi-document projects, 896
        page actions, 894–895
        selecting objects within group, 896
    lines, 13–14
    master pages
        applying to, 210–212
        creating from, 207
        modifying master items on, 212–213
    new, creating, 2–4

document (*continued*)
opening, 142–145
opening versus opening templates, 147
other programs, converting
described, 149
PageMaker, 150
QuarkXPress, 150
versus output files for service bureau printing, 727–728
PageMaker, opening, 923–924
preferences, transferring across platforms, 835
presets, transferring across platforms, 834
printing composite, 19–20
QuarkXPress
differences, reconciling, 913–914
opening, 908
recovery after crash or power failure, 151
saving
commands, 151–152
documents versus templates, 152–154
export for document elements, 155–156
export to other formats, 154–155
exported tagged text files, 156–158
graphics, exporting files as, 158–159
reverting to last saved version, 154
special effects, 18–19
templates, creating from, 215
text, 7–12
versions, managing with Version Cue
described, 160
interface, understanding, 160–162
managing files, 164–165
working with, 162–163
views, 25
document grid
area, 100
frame based on, 222
layout standards, 227
showing/hiding, 126
Document Recovery Data area, 112
document snippets, 156
document window
interface
page field and pop-up menu, 38
page-turning buttons, 37
pasteboard, pages, and guides, 34–35
reference point, 35
scroll bars, 34
Show/Hide Structure button, 36
title bar, 31–34
Version Cue pop-up menu, 36–37
zero point, 34
Zoom field and pop-up menu, 36
Mac, 31
opening multiple, 132–133
Windows, 31
dots, 308
double dagger (‡), 522
dpi (dots per inch), 750–751
drag and drop
adding text, 376–377
graphics, importing, 640–641
text editing area, 89
Drag and Drop Text Editing area, 89
drawing frames, additional, 391–394
drawing free-form shapes and curved paths
compound paths
creating, 679–680
described, 678–679
direction, changing, 681
editing, 680–681
Pathfinder panel or menu options, 682–683
splitting, 681
described, 655, 667–668
editing
adding and deleting anchor points, 669–671
closing an open path, 675–676
converting anchor points, 672–673
described, 668–669
extending open path and connecting open paths, 674–675
manipulating direction handles, 673–674
moving anchor points, 671–672
opening a closed path, 676
Scissors tool, 676–677
lines with Pen tool
curved lines, generally, 662
curved lines connected by smooth points, 662–664
curved segments connected by corner points, 664–665
straight and curved segments, combining, 665–667
straight and zigzag lines, 660–662
path anatomy, 658–660
path effects
Convert Shape options, 683
Corner Options dialog box, 685
Erase tool, 684–685
Smooth tool, 684
path properties
closure, 656
contents, 657–658

fill, 657
    stroke, 657
Dreamweaver, 839
drop cap
    creating, 27
    quotation mark as first character after, 470
Drop Shadow
    described, 316–318
    dialog box, 891
drop shadows and inner shadows, 315–318
DTD declaration, XML files, 820
Duplicate command (Edit ⇨ Duplicate, or
        Option+Shift+⌘+D or Ctrl+Alt+Shift+D):, 278
duplicate page, 203
duplicate spread, 170–171, 203
duplicating color swatches, 254
Dynamic Spelling preferences, 104

E

eBooks
    exporting, 808–809
    output functions, 903
edges, clipping path, 650
Edit menu
    described, 70
    shortcut, 892
    Undo, 79
editing
    assigned stories, 848–849
    color swatches, 253
    drawing free-form shapes and curved paths
        anchor points, adding and deleting, 669–671
        converting anchor points, 672–673
        described, 668–669
        moving anchor points, 671–672
    free-form shapes and curved paths
        closing an open path, 675–676
        extending open path and connecting open paths,
           674–675
        manipulating direction handles, 673–674
        opening a closed path, 676
        Scissors tool, 676–677
    hyphenation, 414
    index entries, 597
    JavaScript, 868
    QuarkXPress text, 916
    text
        automation and managing, 576–577
        cutting, copying, and pasting, 405

        deleting and replacing, 405, 407
        highlighting, 405
        InDesign interface functions, 898–899
        navigating, 405
        Story Editor, 406
        text view, controlling, 403–404
        undoing, 407
    VBA scripts, 872–873
effects
    beveling and embossing, 322–323
    Corner Options, 309–311
    described, 301
    document, 18–19
    feathering
        basic, 319
        described, 318
        directional, 320
        gradient, 320–321
    lighting
        described, 311
        drop shadows and inner shadows, 315–318
        Effects panel, 312
        Global Light option, 318
        inner glow, 322
        outer glow, 321–322
        transparency options, 312–315
    overprinting options, 311
    satin effects, 323–324
    strokes
        adding, 302–306
        with fills, 309
        styles, creating, 306–309
Effects panel (shortcut Shift+⌘+F10 or Ctrl+Shift+F10)
    described, 64, 65, 891
    lighting effects, 312
electronic documents
    bookmarks, 794–796
    described, 789
    eBooks, exporting, 808–809
    hyperlinks
        creating, 790–793
        described, 789–790
        modifying and deleting, 793–794
    movies and sound, embedding
        described, 800–801
        Movie Options dialog box, 801
        Sound Options dialog box, 801–802
    page actions
        actions, associating, 798–799
        buttons, creating, 796–797

electronic documents (*continued*)
   described, 796
   states, creating, 797
   web, exporting to
      Advanced pane, 805–806
      described, 802–803
      files, working with, 806–807
      General pane, 803–804
      Images pane, 804–805
Ellipse Frame
   described, 262–263
   tool, 47
ellipse tool (shortcut L), 47
ellipsis (...), 522, 942
em dash (—)
   search and replace text code, 422
   shortcuts, 536, 943
   from Word, 374
em space
   search and replace text code, 423
   shortcuts, 536
Embed File option, 363
embedded fonts, 624
en bullet (•), 522
en dash (–)
   search and replace text code, 422
   shortcuts, 536, 943
   from Word, 374
en space
   described, 423
   shortcuts, 536
encryption level, prepress files, 777
endnotes, preserving, 372
end-of-story markers, 495–496
EPS (Encapsulated PostScript) file format
   described, 623
   display, 25
   export functions, 902
   exporting described, 782
   General pane, 782–784
   graphics, importing, 624, 625
   Import Options dialog box, 638
   prepress files
      exporting to, 766
      printing to, 767
Erase tool, 46, 684–685
Ergonis's PopChar, 532–533
euro (€), 522, 717
Excel (Microsoft) files, importing, 384–385
exclusion blending mode, 315

existing formatting and, 360–361
expert font characters, 455
exported tagged text files, 156–158
exporting
   files to JPEG or GIF, 158–159
   layers, blocking from, 196
Extensible Markup Language (XML)
   described, 811
   document snippets, 156
   exporting files, 820–822
   find-change queries, 83
   functions, 904
   rules, 814
   snippets, 113
   Structure pane options, 817–819
   tags
      applying, 816–817
      creating, 812, 815
      importing, 812–815
      Styles, mapping with, 816
eye icon, hiding layers, 195
Eyedropper tool
   dimension information, obtaining, 285
   Marker tool, switching to, 38
   sampling colors, 246–247
   shortcut, 48–49

F

facing-pages document, 208
false italic
   adjusting, 447
   characters, 448–449
fast save text files, 373
Feather dialog box, 891
feathering effects
   basic, 319
   described, 318
   directional, 320
   gradient, 320–321
file
   exchange and sharing, 895
   relations, 362–364
   versions, 364
   web, exporting to, 806–807
File Handling pane
   described, 111–112
   Document Recovery Data area, 112
   Images area, 113
   Saving InDesign files, 112

Snippet Import area, 113
Version Cue area, 113
file import
    Illustrator, 25
    Photoshop, 25
File menu
    described, 69–70
    shortcut, 892
filename
    extensions
        displaying, 146–147
        mixing Mac and Windows environments, 833–834
    formatting, 575
fill
    drawing free-form shapes and curved paths, 657
    overprinting, 311
    stroke effects with, 309
Fills pane
    styles, 352
    table, 558
find-change queries, XML, 83
first line effect, Character Styles, 515
First-Line Left Indent, 467, 468
fixed baseline position, 432
fixed-width spaces, 535–536
flagging text errors, 407
Flash animation (SWF files), 623, 800
Flattener Preview panel (Window ➪ Output ➪ Flattener), 65
flattening, printer
    images for spreads, 205
    presets
        applying, 763
        creating, 761–763
        previewing, 763–764
    transparency in prepress files, 776
flip settings, printing, 749
flipping objects, 296–297
Floating Tools Panel pop-up menu, 86
flowing text
    described, 387–388
    QuarkXPress, 915–916
Flush space, 423
Focoltone color
    printer model, 695
    swatchbook, 234
folders, auto-recovery files, 112
foldout spreads, 173–175
folios, layer, 190
follow-me anchored objects, 26

Font Downloading and Embedding area, 85–86
font substitution table, 717
FontLab Studio, 490
fonts
    changes, when to use, 446
    embedded, 624
    EPS file, creating, 783–784
    family, style, and size
        described, 441–442
        labeling paragraphs, 446
        selecting, 443–444
        size, changing, 445
    hidden layers, including, 726
    Mac, adding, 429
    Mac and Windows environments, mixing, 836–837
    platform issues, 837
    preflighting documents, 721
    preview size, 89, 90
    searching and replacing, 429
    shortcut, customizing, 117
    substituted, highlighting, 93
foot ('), 523
footers, preserving, 372
footnotes
    described, 26, 587–589
    Layout pane, 590–591
    numbering and formatting pane, 589–590
    positioning and character style, 590
    preserving, 372
foreign languages
    shortcuts (Mac and Windows), 539–542
    supported, 538–539
formatting
    characters, 438–440
    documents, exporting to other, 154–155
    fractions
        manually, 491–492
        typeface, 490–491
    index, 592
    Paragraph Styles, overriding, 505–506
    QuarkXPress text, 916–917
    table cells, 560
    Tagged Text files, importing, 386
    text
        described, 485–486
        importing text-only files, 383
        searching and replacing, 426–427
        variables, 575–576
four-color printing, 230

fractions
 formatting
  manually, 491–492
  typeface, 490–491
 OpenType, 453, 529
frame
 converting for specific content, 264–265
 cropping graphics, 644
 described, 28, 43, 259–260
 document, 4–7
 elements, showing and hiding, 126
 empty, converting to text frame, 88
 graphics, 262–263
 grid based on, 222
 limitations, 387
 nesting objects within, 332
 nesting objects within other, 332–333
 text
  adding, 374
  additional, drawing, 391–394
  appearance, 430–433
  creating, 260–262
  described, 388
  master pages, creating on, 389–391
  spacing and alignment, 400–401
frame, fitting
 clipping paths
  creating in InDesign, 650–652
  deleting, 653
  described, 648
  graphic's own, 648
  as a mask, 649
  modifying, 652–653
  Photoshop, 648
  as a wrap boundary, 649–650
 described, 643–644
 fitting commands, 645–648
 irregular frame, 644–645
 moving in frame, 644
 resizing frame, 644
Frame Fitting Options pane, 357
frame tools, 661
Free Transform tool, 48, 292
French close double quote (»), 542
French open double quote («), 542
Full Justify (Shift+⌘+F or Ctrl+Shift+F), 466
Fuller, Laurie Ulrich (*Photoshop CS3 Bible*), 931
function (*f*), 523

G
Galley pane, InCopy, 849
Galley & Story Appearance panel, 852
gap, overprinting, 311
gatefold (foldout) spreads, 173–175
General pane, object styles, 351–352
GIF (Graphics Interchange Format)
 converting images to, 804
 described, 623
 graphics, importing, 628
 XML, exporting, 821
global changes, searching and replacing text, 427–428
Global Light option, 318
global tools, 26–27
glyph scaling
 described, 25
 justification, 477
glyph sets, 83
glyphs
 creating sets, 526–527
 Glyphs panel, 524, 526
 keyboard shortcuts, 522–523
 menus, 524
 sharing sets, 527
 special characters, 521–522
 substituted, highlighting, 93
Glyphs panel (Type ➪ Glyphs or Window ➪ Type &
  Tables ➪ Glyphs, or press Option+Shift+F11 or
  Alt+Shift+F11)
 described, 58
 recently used glyphs, 891
GoLive 9, 691
Gradient Feather tool (shortcut Shift+G), 48
Gradient panel, 61, 62
Gradient Swatch tool (shortcut G), 48
gradients
 angle and location, 251–252
 creating, 248–250
 defaults, 125
 described, 248
 feathering effects, 320–321
 swatches, cross-platform issues, 834
 table cells, 565
 unnamed, creating, 250–251
grammar, scripting, 865
graphics
 coloring imported, 247
 Creative Suite applications, 838

document, 17–18
Excel inline, importing, 385
exporting files as, 158–159
flattening for spreads, 205
formats, 156
frames, 262–263
InDesign interface functions, 901
library files, 219
linked QuarkXPress files, 908
PageMaker, 928
PDF files, importing as, 149
QuarkXPress, 918–920
resizing methods, 290
sharing elements with other users, 830
Word inline, importing, 381
XML, exporting, 821–822
graphics and frames, fitting
    clipping paths
        creating in InDesign, 650–652
        deleting, 653
        described, 648
        graphic's own, 648
        as a mask, 649
        modifying, 652–653
        Photoshop, 648
        as a wrap boundary, 649–650
    described, 643–644
    fitting commands, 645–648
    irregular frame, 644–645
    moving in frame, 644
    resizing frame, 644
graphics, importing
    benefits of using dedicated program, 621–622
    bitmap formats
        BMP, 629
        described, 626
        GIF, 628
        JPEG, 628
        PCX, 629
        Photoshop, 626–627
        PICT, 629
        PNG, 628
        professional-level, 626–628
        Scitex CT, 627
        TIFF, 627
        Web-oriented, 628
    color
        calibrated color, 630
        color systems, 629–630

described, 629
    only, 245–246
copy and paste, 640
Copy command, 639–640
drag and drop, 640–641
embedded in text files, 622–624
limitations, 621
methods
    described, 630–631
    with Place dialog box, 631–633
options
    bitmap graphics, 633–637
    described, 633
    vector file formats, 637–639
preparing files, 622
vector files
    DCS PostScript files, 624, 625
    embedded fonts, 624
    EPS PostScript files, 624, 625
    Illustrator PostScript files, 624, 625
    PDF PostScript files, 624, 625–626
    PICT files, 626
    Windows Metafile format, 626
Graphics Interchange Format (GIF)
    converting images to, 804
    described, 623
    graphics, importing, 628
    XML, exporting, 821
Graphics pane printing techniques, 751–753
grave (`), 539
Grayscale Devices, appearance of black on, 110
greater than or equal to (≥), 523
Greek beta (β), 523
Greek mu (μ), 523
Greek Omega (Ω), 523
Greek pi (π), 523
Greek Sigma (Σ), 523
Greek Type view settings, 110
Grep Find/Change pane, Unix, 424
grids
    baseline, 432–433
    prepress files, 771
Grids preferences
    Baseline Grid area, 98–99
    Document Grid area, 100
grouped objects
    layers, 190
    selecting, 328

groups
    described, 359–360
    objects, combining into
        described, 329
        within groups, 329–330
        selecting within groups, 330–331
        ungrouping, 331
    Paragraph Styles, 508–509
Gruman, Galen
    Adobe InDesign CS3 For Dummies, 931
    QuarkXPress to InDesign: Face to Face, 24, 932
guide
    colors, 35
    columns, 221
    layers, controlling, 198
    margin, 221
    positioning objects precisely with, 286–287
    prepress files, 771
    QuarkXPress users, adapting, 920
    showing/hiding, 126
guideline, Layout Adjustment feature, 185
Guides & Pasteboard preferences
    Color area, 100–101
    described, 100
    Guide Options area, 101
    Pasteboard Options area, 102
gutter, in documents, 140

H

Hair space, 423
Hand tool, 49, 130–131
handling objects, InDesign interface, 897
hard light blending mode, 314
Headers and Footers pane, 558–559
headers and footers, preserving, 372
Help menu, 76–77
Hexachrome standard, 234
hidden objects, selecting, 328
hiding layers
    described, 195
    printing, 190
Highlight area, Composition pane, 93
highlighting text, 405
HKS swatchbook, 234
Horizontal Cursor Position status indicator, 465
Horizontal Scale and Vertical Scale, 448
hue blending mode, 315

hyperlinks
    electronic documents
        creating, 790–793
        described, 789–790
        modifying and deleting, 793–794
    prepress files, 770
    preserving, 373
Hyperlinks panel (Window ➪ Interactive ➪ Hyperlinks), 66, 67
hyphen (-), 943
hyphenation
    blocking for individual words, 455
    dictionary preferences, 103–104
    editing, 414
    exceptions, 726
    platforms, transferring across, 835
    points, customizing, 415–416
    text
        automatic, 474–476
        described, 473–474
        manual, 474
    violations, highlighting, 93

I

Illustrator (Adobe)
    CMS, 691
    file import, described, 25
    format, 623
    PostScript files, importing, 624, 625
Illustrator CS3 Bible (Alspach), 932
Image pane, importing bitmap graphics, 634
Images area, File Handling pane, 113
images, preflighting documents, 722, 723
importing
    Character Styles
        in imported text files, 517
        from InDesign documents, 516–517
    color
        from graphics, 245–247
        swatches, 245
    master pages, 207–208
    text functions, 898
imposition, printing preparations, 733–735
in port, text frame, 392
inches decimal measurement, 96
InCopy program
    described, 849
    files, linking, 365

revisions tracking, 850–852

special features, 852–853

story checkout, check-in, and saving, 850

story views, 849

indent, paragraph

  described, 465, 467

  left and right, 467

  spacing guidelines, 468

InDesign (Adobe)

  documents, sharing elements with other users, 832

  hierarchy, scripting, 866

  Interchange file format, 154

  Tagged Text format, 156

InDesign (Adobe) interface

  color functions, 901

  document and object functions

    effects, 898

    file exchange and sharing, 895

    handling objects, 897

    measurements, 894

    multi-document projects, 896

    page actions, 894–895

    selecting objects within group, 896

  graphics functions, 901

  menu, 68–69

  output functions

    eBooks export, 903

    JPEG export, 902

    PDF and EPS export, 902

    printing, 902

    Web export, 903

  scripting functions, 903

  text functions

    editing, 898–899

    import, 898

    paragraph and character formatting, 899–900

    spelling and indexing, 900

    styles, 901

    tabs and tables, 900

  tools, panels, and dialog boxes

    described, 889–891

    menus, 892–893

    preferences, 893–894

    sharable files, 894

    shortcuts, 892

    Version Cue, 894

  workgroup editing functions

    within InCopy, 905

    within InDesign, 904

  XML functions, 904

Index panel (Window ➪ Type & Tables ➪ Index or Shift+F8), 61, 63

indexing

  described, 591

  format, nested or run-in, 592

  Index panel

    described, 593

    editing entries, 597

    entering index items via, 594–597

    fine-tuning and generating, 598–600

    keyboard shortcuts, 597

    Reference and Topic modes, 593–594

  in QuarkXPress, 595

  style, choosing, 592–593

  text functions, 900

  workflow, incorporating into, 598

.inds files. *See also* snippets

  sharing elements with other users, 830–831

  XML, 113

inequality (≠), 523

Info panel (press F8), 66

infinity (∞), 523

initial caps, text, 472–473

ink

  output, printing, 756–759

  preflighting documents, 722, 723

Ink Manager

  output files, creating, 785

  prepress files, 775

inline frames

  adjusting, 338–339

  Anchored Object command, creating with, 336–338

  creating, 333–334

  deleting, 339

  Paste command, creating with, 334–335

  Place command, creating with, 335

inline graphics and text boxes, 373

inner glow lighting effects, 322

inner shadows, 315–318

Input Method Options area, 92

insert menu, 25

inserting

  pages, 203

  text automation, 576

Inset Spacing options, text frame, 400

inset spacing, text setup, 431

installation program, running, 884–885

installing InDesign

  activating and registering, 885–886

  finishing setup, 886–887

installing InDesign (*continued*)
    installation program, running, 884–885
    reinstalling, 888
    system requirements, 883–884
    uninstalling, 888
    upgrading from prior versions, 887
integral (≡), 523
interface. *See also* panel
    application folder
        Plug-ins, 30–31
        Presets, 30
        Required, 31
    color buttons, 49
    contextual menus, 77–79
    described, 29
    dock display, changing, 52–53
    document window
        described, 31
        page field and pop-up menu, 38
        page-turning buttons, 37
        pasteboard, pages, and guides, 34–35
        reference point, 35
        scroll bars, 34
        Show/Hide Structure button, 36
        title bar, 31–34
        Version Cue pop-up menu, 36–37
        zero point, 34
        Zoom field and pop-up menu, 36
    Edit menu
        described, 70
        Undo, 79
    File menu, 69–70
    Help menu, 76–77
    InDesign menu, 68–69
    Layout menu, 71
    Notes menu, 73–74
    Object menu, 74
    PageMaker users, adapting, 928
    panels, arranging, 50–52
    preferences, sharing elements with other users, 832
    QuarkXPress users, adapting, 912
    shortcuts, 72
    Table menu, 75
    tools
        Add Anchor Point tool (shortcut =), 45
        Button tool, 47
        Delete Anchor Point tool (shortcut - [hyphen]), 45
        described, 38
        Direct Selection tool (shortcut A), 44
        Ellipse Frame tool, 47
        Ellipse tool (shortcut L), 47
        Erase tool, 46
        Eyedropper tool (shortcut I), 48–49
        Free Transform tool (shortcut E), 48
        Gradient Feather tool (shortcut Shift+G), 48
        Gradient Swatch tool (shortcut G), 48
        Hand tool (shortcut H), 49
        Line tool (shortcut E), 46
        Measure tool (shortcut K), 49
        Note tool, 48
        panel, opening and closing, 40–41
        Pen tool (shortcut P), 45
        Pencil tool (shortcut N), 46
        Polygon Frame tool, 47
        Polygon tool, 47
        Position tool (no shortcut), 45
        Rectangle Frame tool (shortcut F), 47
        Rectangle tool (shortcut M), 47
        Rotate tool (shortcut R), 47
        Scale tool (shortcut S), 48
        Scissors tool (shortcut C), 47
        selecting, 41–42
        Selection tool (shortcut V), 43
        Shear tool (shortcut O), 48
        Smooth tool, 46
        Tool Tips and keyboard shortcuts, 39–40
        Type on a Path tool (shortcut Shift+T), 46
        Type tool (shortcut T), 45–46
        uses, understanding, 42–43
        Zoom tool (shortcut Z), 49
    Type menu, 71, 73
    view buttons
        Normal View Mode, 49
        Preview Mode, 49
    View menu, 75–76
    Window menu, 76
International Committee on Illumination (CIE) Lab color
    standard
    described, 230
    profiles, 696
ISO 3554 color printing proof, 694
Isolate Blending mode, 315
italic, false
    adjusting, 447
    characters, 448–449
italics. *See also* fonts
    Story Editor feature, 406
    when to use, 446

J

JavaScript
    conditional, writing, 878
    described, 867
    labeling items, 877
    language, learning, 867
    resources, 867
    running, 868
    saving, 869
    support, 863
    writing and editing tools, 868
    writing simple, 875
job-option files, 831
JPEG (Joint Photographic Expert Group) format
    converting images to, 804
    described, 623
    export
        files, 158–159
        output functions, 902
    graphics, importing, 628
    XML, exporting, 821
justification, text
    controls, 476–478
    described, 474
    left-aligned paragraphs versus, 473
    next to an object, 94
    setup, 431
    violations, highlighting, 93
justify text wrapped around object, 348

K

Kant, Lynette (*Photoshop CS3: Top 100 Simplified Tips and Tricks*), 931
Karlins, David (*Total Digital Photography: The Shoot to Print Workflow Handbook*), 932
Keep Options (widows and orphans) paragraphs, 480–481
kerning
    adjusting, 447
    platform issues, 837
    text with keyboard, 98
    violations, highlighting, 93
keyboard cursor movement options, 97
Keyboard Increments area, 96–98
keyboard quotes, 538
keyboard shortcuts
    default shortcuts, using and modifying, 116, 118–119
    described, 116

QuarkXPress, 119
    selecting objects, 275
    viewing and printing, 119
knockout color trapping, 705–707
Knockout Group blending mode, 315
Kochan, Stephen G. (*Beginning AppleScript*), 871

L

labeling JavaScript items, 877
language
    AppleScript, 869
    characters, 449–450
    dictionary preferences, 102–103
    JavaScript, 867
    layers, 190
    spelling corrections, 411–413
    translation, 576
    VBA scripts, 872
Last-Line Right Indent, 467
layers
    creating, 191–192
    described, 187–189
    manipulating
        combining, 197
        deleting, 197–198
        guides, controlling, 198
        hiding, 195
        locking, 195–196
        preventing from printing or exporting, 196
        rearranging, 196
        selecting, 194
    objects
        active layer, 192
        moving to different, 194
        placing, 193
        selecting, 193
    when to use, 189–190
Layers pane
    imported layers, working with, 636
    importing bitmap graphics, 635, 637
Layers panel
    described, 59, 60
    lock icon, 890
layout
    adapting, 200
    baseline grid, 225–227
    column guides, 225
    document grid, 227

layout *(continued)*
  libraries, storing objects in
    adding and deleting, 218–219
    cataloging, 219–221
    copying onto document pages, 221
    described, 215–218
    pitfalls, 219
  master pages
    applying to document pages, 210–212
    basing on another, 206–207
    described, 199, 200–201
    document pages, creating from, 207
    importing, 207–208
    laying out, 208–210
    modifying master items on document pages, 212–213
    new, creating, 205–206
    Pages panel, 201–205
  pages, 183–185
  prepress files, 767
  ruler guides and grids
    automatically creating set of guides, 222–223
    creating manually, 222
    described, 221–222
    manipulating, 223–224
  templates
    creating, 213–214
    described, 199, 201
    documents, creating from, 215
    modifying, 215
Layout Adjustment feature, 184–185
Layout menu, 71
Layout pane, InCopy, 849
leader field, 551
leading
  baseline, 432
  characters, 458–459
  described, 89
  paragraphs, 463–464
  setting with keyboard, 98
  text wrap area, 94
  text wrapped around object, 348
left alignment, 465–466
left, center, right, and Align On buttons, 549
Left Indent, 467
Left Justify (Shift+⌘+J or Ctrl+Shift+J), 466
left page, starting documents on, 172–173
legal symbols, 522
less than or equal to (≤), 523
letter spacing, justified, 477

letters, two combined, 452–453. *See also* ligatures
library
  master pages, 200
  sharing elements with other users, 830
  storing objects in
    adding and deleting, 218–219
    cataloging, 219–221
    copying onto document pages, 221
    described, 215–218
  swatch, 233, 828
ligatures, 452–453
lighten blending mode, 314
lighting effects
  described, 26, 311
  drop shadows and inner shadows, 315–318
  Effects panel, 312
  Global Light option, 318
  inner glow, 322
  outer glow, 321–322
  transparency options, 312–315
line art, saving, 622
Line tool, 46, 265–267
linear gradient, 251
lines
  document, 13–14
  erasing, 684
  straight, drawing, 265–266
  of type, selecting, 89
lines per inch (lpi) printing, 750–751
links
  described, 28
  electronic documents
    creating, 790–793
    described, 789–790
    modifying and deleting, 793–794
  hidden layers, including, 726
  objects
    detailed information, getting, 364–365
    file versions, 364
    InCopy files, 365
    navigating directly to files, 364
    panel housekeeping functions, 365
    status, 361–362
  preflighting documents, 722
  prepress files, 770
  preserving, 373
Links area, 89
Links panel (shortcut Shift+⌘+D or Ctrl+Shift+D), 55

lists
  bulleted and numbered
    applying, 489
    bullet characters, 472
    defining, 486–489
    imported, working with, 489
  numbered, 472
  tables of contents, 603
loaded-text frame-flow icon, 397
loaded-text icon, 397
local changes, Character Styles, 515
local tools, 27
location, gradients, 251–252
lock guides, showing and hiding, 126
lock icon, Layers panel, 890
locking
  layers, 195–196
  objects, 331
  paragraphs to Baseline Grid, 468–469
logical not (¬), 523
lossy compression, 772
lpi (lines per inch) printing, 750–751
luminosity blending mode, 315

M

Macintosh. *See also* AppleScript
  document windows, 31
  filename extensions, viewing, 147
  folders, opening, 143, 145
  fonts, adding, 429
  fractions, 492
  InDesign Defaults file location, 82
  ligatures, 453
  monitor bit depth, setting, 694
  Page Setup and Printer dialog boxes, 739
  PDF files, creating, 780
  printing
    initial preparations, 714–716
    PDF files, 781
    printer output file, 786
  saving documents versus saving templates, 152–153
  Snap to Guides option, 287
  spaces, dashes, hyphens, and quotes shortcuts, 536
  special characters, 531–534
  symbols, shortcuts for, 522–523
  system requirements, 883
  text-only files, importing, 382
  Version Cue interface, 160–161
  versions, 835

western European accents and foreign character
    shortcuts, 539–543
Windows environments, mixing for workgroups
  described, 833
  filename extensions, 833–834
  filenames, 836
  font differences, 836–837
  multiple versions of InDesign, 835
  nontransferable elements, 835
  transfer methods, 838
managing, 358–359
manual kerning, 456–457
margin
  document
    creating, 140
    setup, 122
  guides, 221
  Layout Adjustment feature, 185
  master pages, 209
  optical alignment, 356, 494–495
Marker tool, switching from Eyedropper tool, 38
markers, search and replace text codes, 422
Marks and Bleeds pane
  Bleed and Slug area, 747
  printing techniques
    described, 745
    Printer's marks, 745–747
marquee, 273
mask, clipping paths as a, 649
master frames, specifying, 398
master page
  applying to document pages, 210–212
  described, 199, 201
  frames, 389–391
  icon, 202
  jumping to, 38
  laying out, 208–210
  layout standards
    basing on another, 206–207
    described, 200–201
    document pages, creating from, 207
    importing, 207–208
    new, creating, 205–206
    Pages panel, 201–205
  modifying master items on, 212–213
  platforms, transferring across, 834
  printing, 742
  Save As, 203
  sharing elements with other users, 831–832

master text frames, 374–375
mathematics symbols, 523
Measure tool (shortcut K), 49
measurement symbols, 523
menu
  InDesign interface, 892–893
  navigating pages with, 180–181
  preferences files, 120
merged data, automating
  described, 577–578
  multiple records per page, 582–584
  pages, creating, 579–582
  setting up, 578–579
merging
  color swatches, 253
  table cells, 564
metrics kerning, 456
Microsoft Excel files, importing, 384–385
Microsoft Windows
  document windows, 31
  em dash shortcut, 537
  folders, opening, 143, 145
  fonts, adding, 429
  ligatures, 453
  Mac environments, mixing for workgroups
    described, 833
    filename extensions, 833–834
    filenames, 836
    font differences, 836–837
    multiple versions of InDesign, 835
    nontransferable elements, 835
    transfer methods, 838
  Print dialog boxes, 740
  printer output file, 786
  printing PDF files, 781
  saving documents versus saving templates, 152–153
  spaces, dashes, hyphens, and quotes shortcuts, 536
  special characters, 531–534
  symbols, shortcuts for, 522–523
  system requirements, 883–884
  text-only files, importing, 382
  Version Cue interface, 160–161
  versions, 835
  western European accents and foreign character
    shortcuts, 539–543
Microsoft Windows Vista
  application data folder, 826
  filename extensions, viewing, 146
  InDesign Defaults file location, 82

monitor bit depth, setting, 694
  printing preparations, 718–720
Microsoft Windows XP
  application data folder, 826
  filename extensions, viewing, 146
  InDesign Defaults file location, 82
  monitor bit depth, setting, 694
  printing preparations, 716–718
Microsoft Word
  importing text, 379–382
  special characters, 534
millimeters measurement, 96
mixed colors, Swatches panel, 241–243
monitor bit depth, CMS on-screen display, 694
mouse, resizing objects with, 290
movies and sound, embedding
  described, 800–801
  Movie Options dialog box, 801
  Sound Options dialog box, 801–802
moving
  anchor points, 671–672
  graphics in frame, 644
  layer objects, 194
  objects, 277–278
multi-document projects
  book feature, pros and cons of, 608
  creating and opening books
    adding chapters, 610
    book panel status reports, understanding, 612
    described, 609–610
    opening and editing chapters, 610–612
  described, 607
  InDesign interface, 896
  page numbers and sections
    chapter numbers, specifying, 616–617
    consecutively numbering pages, 614–615
    sections, numbering pages with, 615
    updates, manual numbering, 616
  planning, 609
  printing chapters and books, 617
  style sources, 612–614
multimedia prepress files, 771
multi-page documents
  adding pages, 168–170
  deleting pages, 170
  described, 167–168
  speedy page actions, 170
multiple records per page, merged data, 582–584
multiply blending mode, 314
Murdock, Kelly (*Adobe Creative Suite 3 Bible*), 932

N

naming system, creating color with, 240
navigating directly to files, links, 364
navigation
   PageMaker users, adapting, 927
   pages
      with menus and shortcuts, 180–181
      with Navigator panel, 181–183
      by page number, 179
      with Pages panel, 181
      special page numbers, 180
   QuarkXPress tools, adapting, 912
   text, 405
Navigator panel, 59–60, 131, 181–183
nested styles, paragraphs, 512–514
nesting objects
   within frames, 332
   within other frames, 332–333
network workgroups, 825
new pages, 203
No Break characters, 455
noise, feathering, 319
nonbreaking hyphen
   search and replace text code, 422
   shortcuts, 536
nonbreaking spaces
   described, 423
   shortcuts, 535, 536
non-joiner space, 423
non-printing objects, prepress files, 771
Normal View Mode, 49
Note tool, 48
Notes menu, 73–74, 892
Notes panel, 61, 64, 891
Notes preferences, 106–107
notes, text, 433–435
number, navigating pages by, 179
Number of Columns field, paragraphs, 465
numbered lists
   applying, 489
   bullet characters, 480
   described, 472
   formatting, 486–489
   imported, working with, 489
numbering
   pages, 175–176
   Prefix/Suffix, 589
   sections differently in one document, 204

special page, 180
Word, converting to text, 381
numerator, OpenType, 453, 529

O

object
   aligning and distributing, 282–284, 286
   anchored frames
      adding, 340–342
      adjusting, 343
      converting existing to, 343
      releasing and deleting, 343–344
      when to use, 339–340
   combining into groups
      described, 329
      within groups, 329–330
      selecting within groups, 330–331
      ungrouping, 331
   copying
      between documents, 280–281
      within documents, 278–280
      snippets, 281
   deleting, 281–282
   dimension information, acquiring through Measure tool
         and Info panel, 285
   flipping, 296–297
   hierarchy, scripting, 866
   InDesign interface functions
      effects, 898
      file exchange and sharing, 895
      handling objects, 897
      measurements, 894
      multi-document projects, 896
      page actions, 894–895
      selecting objects within group, 896
   inline frames
      adjusting, 338–339
      Anchored Object command, creating with, 336–338
      creating, 333–334
      deleting, 339
      Paste command, creating with, 334–335
      Place command, creating with, 335
   links
      detailed information, getting, 364–365
      file relations, 362–364
      file versions, 364
      InCopy files, 365
      navigating directly to files, 364

object (*continued*)
  panel housekeeping functions, 365
  status, 361–362
locking, 331
moving, 277–278
nesting
  within frames, 332
  within other frames, 332–333
pages, 183–185
positioning precisely with Guides, 286–287
printing, preventing from, 282
QuarkXPress
  manipulating, 914–915
  users, adapting handling tools, 913
replacing attributes, 298–299
resizing
  with Control or Transform panel, 290–291
  described, 289
  with mouse, 290
rotating
  Control panel and Transform panel, 294–296
  Rotate tool, 294
scaling
  Control panel, 292
  described, 289
  Free Transform tool, 292
  Scale tool, 291
  Selection or Position tool, 292
  Transform panel, 292
selecting
  Control panel buttons, 275
  described, 269–270
  deselecting, 276
  keyboard shortcuts, 275
  methods, 271–273
  multiple, 276
  overlapping objects, 273–275
  tools, 270–271
Shear tool, 296
stacking, 326–328
styles
  Anchored Object Options pane, 357
  creating, 350–351
  described, 349–350
  existing formatting and, 360–361
  Fill pane, 352
  Frame Fitting Options pane, 357
  General pane, 351–352
  groups, 359–360
  managing, 358–359

Paragraph Styles pane, 354
  predefined, 360
  removing, 361
  Story Options pane, 356
  Stroke & Corner Options pane, 353–354
  Stroke pane, 352–353
  Text Frame Baseline Options pane, 355
  Text Frame General Options pane, 355
  Text Wrap & Other pane, 356–357
styles, sharing elements with other users, 828–829
text, wrapping around
  options, 344
  preferences, 348–349
  shape, changing, 349
  Text Wrap panel, 344–348
transformation
  repeating, 297
  tips, 293
Object menu, 74
object styles, 26, 124
Object Styles panel (Window ➪ Object Styles, or press ⌘+F7 or Ctrl+F7), 56, 57
old-fashioned numerals, proportional
  expert fonts, 455
  OpenType, 453
one-half fraction (½), 523
one-quarter fraction (¼), 523
online file format, 155
online resources, 931
open diamond (·), 523
open double quote ("), 536
open single quote ('), 536
open path
  closing, 675–676
  extending connecting, 674–675
Open Prepress Interface (OPI)
  image replacement, 784–785
  printing techniques, 754–755
OpenType
  characters, 453–455
  variants, 527–531
optical font size, 89
optical kerning, 25, 456
optical margin
  alignment
    described, 25
    text, 494–495
  override for paragraphs, 483–484
ordinal, OpenType, 453, 529
out port, text frame, 392–393

outer glow lighting effect, 321–322
output files
    eBooks export, 903
    JPEG export, 902
    PDF and EPS export, 902
    printing, 902
    QuarkXPress, 921
    service bureau printing preparations, 727–729
    sharing elements with other users, 831
    Web export, 903
overlapping objects
    layers, 190
    selecting, 273–275
overlay, blending mode, 314
Overprint [Black] Swatch, 111
overprinting
    color trapping, 705–707
    fills, strokes, and gaps, 311
    layers, 190
    prepress files, 775
overrides, importing Word, 380
overset text
    identifying and editing, 401
    Story Editor feature, 406
    table cells, 564
oversized pages, service bureau printing preparations, 730

P

package
    assignments, 848
    described, 28
Padova, Ted
    Adobe Acrobat 8 PDF Bible, 932
    Adobe Creative Suite 3 Bible, 932
page
    adding to multi-page documents, 168–170
    breaks, importing from Word, 381
    copying and moving
        within document, 170–171
        shuffling, dangers of, 171, 173
        working across documents, 171–172
    deleting from multi-page documents, 170
    document, 4–7
    electronic document actions
        actions, associating, 798–799
        buttons, creating, 796–797
        described, 796
        states, creating, 797
    gatefold (foldout) spreads, 173–175

hyperlink, 790–791
    InDesign interface, 894–895
    inserting, 203
    layouts and objects, 183–185
    left page, starting documents on, 172–173
    merged data, 579–582
    multi-page documents, working with
        adding pages, 168–170
        deleting pages, 170
        described, 167–168
        speedy page actions, 170
    navigating
        with menus and shortcuts, 180–181
        with Navigator panel, 181–183
        by page number, 179
        with Pages panel, 181
        special page numbers, 180
    numbering, 175–176
    positioning challenges for printing, 744
    printing, 741
    QuarkXPress, manipulating, 920
    sections, dividing documents into, 176–179
    size
        documents, creating, 140
        Layout Adjustment feature, 185
    speedy actions for multi-page documents, 170
    transparency alert, 179
    turning with buttons, 37
page field and pop-up menu, 38
Page Numbering area, 85
page numbers
    automatically placing, 209
    consecutively numbering pages, 614–615
    search and replace text codes, 421–422
    text automation, 572
PageMaker (Adobe)
    Command Bar Panel, 930
    converting documents from other programs, 150
    differences from InDesign
        color, 929
        described, 924–925
        graphics, 928
        keyboard shortcut equivalents, 927–928
        manipulating pages, 928–929
        objects, 925–926
        text, 926–927
        tools and setting preferences, 925
    documents, opening, 923–924
    Story Editor feature, 406
Pages panel (shortcut ⌘+F12 or Ctrl+F12), 59, 60

pane, 28. *See also individual panes listed by name*
panel. *See also individual panels listed by name*
   active, characteristics of, 53–54
   described, 28
   interface
      described, 50–52, 889–891
      menus, 892–893
      preferences, 893–894
      sharable files, 894
      shortcuts, 892
      Version Cue, 894
   opening and closing, 40–41
panel group, 28
Pantone color printer model, 695
Pantone Matching System (PMS), 233
Pantone Process Coated paper, 234
Pantone Process Uncoated paper, 234–235
Pantone Solid Coated paper, 235
Pantone Solid Matte paper, 235
Pantone Solid Uncoated paper, 235
Pantone swatchbooks, 233, 630
paper
   color variation models, 234–236
   size and orientation, printing, 742–743
paragraph, 899–900
paragraph composer, 25
Paragraph Composer (Adobe), 479–480
Paragraph panel (Type ⇨ Paragraph or Window ⇨ Type &
      Tables ⇨ Paragraph, or press Option+⌘+T or
      Ctrl+Option+T), 56, 57
paragraph styles
   defaults, 123
   described, 501
   footnotes, 590
   sharing elements with other users, 828–829
Paragraph Styles panel
   applying, 505
   creating, 503–505
   existing formatting, overriding, 505–506
   exporting, 519
   first line effect, 515
   groups, 508–509
   illustrated, 56, 57, 503
   importing
      in imported text files, 517–518
      from InDesign documents, 516–517
   local changes, 515
   managing, 506–508
   modifying, 514

nested styles, 512–514
objects, 354
QuarkXPress, 506
paragraph symbol (¶)
   search and replace text code, 422
   shortcut, 522, 943
paragraphs
   alignment, 465–466
   Horizontal Cursor Position status indicator, 465
   indents
      described, 465, 467
      left and right, 467
      spacing guidelines, 468
   Keep Options (widows and orphans), 480–481
   labeling, 446
   leading, 463–464
   Lock to Baseline Grid, 468–469
   Number of Columns field, 465
   optical margin override, 483–484
   platforms, transferring across, 834
   rules, 482–483
   selecting, 461–463
   spacing, 469–470
password, prepress files, 777–778
Paste command, creating with, 334–335
Pasteboard Options area, 102
pasteboard, pages, and guides, 34–35
paste-up board. *See* master page
pasting
   adding text, 375–376
   graphics, importing, 640
   spacing, adjusting automatically, 89
   text, 405
path
   anatomy, drawing free-form shapes and curved paths,
      658–660
   described, 28
   effects
      Convert Shape options, 683
      Smooth tool, 684
   properties
      closure, 656
      contents, 657–658
      fill, 657
      stroke, 657
   text, following, 499
Pathfinder panel, 64, 65
Pathfinder panel or menu options, compound paths,
      682–683

PCX (PC Paintbrush)
    format described, 623
    graphics, importing, 629
PDF (Portable Document Format) files
    Clipboard area, handling, 114
    described, 28, 623
    graphics, importing as, 149
    PostScript files, importing graphics, 624, 625–626
    prepress files
        Advanced pane, 776–777
        compression methods, 773
        Compression pane, 771–772
        exporting described, 767–768
        Marks and Bleeds pane, 772–774
        on-screen usage, 779
        Output pane, 774–775
        printing to, 780–782
        Security pane, 777–778
        Summary pane, 779
    prepress files, exporting to, 766
    presets, transferring across platforms, 834
Pen tool
    curved lines, generally, 662
    described, 45
    straight and zigzag lines, 660–662
Pencil tool, 46, 661
per mil (‰), 523
perceptual color, bitmap images, 697
photographs, saving, 622
Photoshop (Adobe)
    clipping paths, fitting graphics and frames, 648
    CMS, 691
    file import, described, 25
    format, 623
    graphics, importing, 626–627
Photoshop CS3 Bible (Fuller), 931
Photoshop CS3 Channels and Masks Bible (Romaniello), 931
Photoshop CS3: Top 100 Simplified Tips and Tricks (Kant), 931
Photoshop Path clipping path, 649
pica measurement
    changing measurement system, 33–34
    described, 95
PICT (Mac Picture) format
    described, 623
    graphics, importing, 626, 629
pictures
    coloring imported, 247
    Creative Suite applications, 838
    document, 17–18

Excel inline, importing, 385
exporting files as, 158–159
flattening for spreads, 205
formats, 156
frames, 262–263
InDesign interface functions, 901
library files, 219
linked QuarkXPress files, 908
PageMaker, 928
PDF files, importing as, 149
QuarkXPress, 918–920
resizing methods, 290
sharing elements with other users, 830
Word inline, importing, 381
XML, exporting, 821–822
pictures and frames, fitting
    clipping paths
        creating in InDesign, 650–652
        deleting, 653
        described, 648
        graphic's own, 648
        as a mask, 649
        modifying, 652–653
        Photoshop, 648
        as a wrap boundary, 649–650
    described, 643–644
    fitting commands, 645–648
    irregular frame, 644–645
    moving in frame, 644
    resizing frame, 644
pictures, importing
    benefits of using dedicated program, 621–622
    bitmap formats
        BMP, 629
        described, 626
        GIF, 628
        JPEG, 628
        PCX, 629
        Photoshop, 626–627
        PICT, 629
        PNG, 628
        professional-level, 626–628
        Scitex CT, 627
        TIFF, 627
        Web-oriented, 628
    color
        calibrated color, 630
        color systems, 629–630
        described, 629
        only, 245–246

pictures, importing (*continued*)
copy and paste, 640
Copy command, 639–640
drag and drop, 640–641
embedded in text files, 622–624
limitations, 621
methods
described, 630–631
with Place dialog box, 631–633
options
bitmap graphics, 633–637
described, 633
vector file formats, 637–639
preparing files, 622
vector files
DCS PostScript files, 624, 625
embedded fonts, 624
EPS PostScript files, 624, 625
Illustrator PostScript files, 624, 625
PDF PostScript files, 624, 625–626
PICT files, 626
Windows Metafile format, 626
Place command, creating with, 335
place, defined, 28
Place dialog box, importing text, 377–379
Place InDesign Document dialog box, 639
Place PDF dialog box, 638–639
placing objects on layers, 193
plaintext metadata, prepress files, 778
plug-ins
default, using, 857–858
described, 28
installing, 859
managing, 860–861
platforms, transferring across, 835
preflighting documents, 722, 724
special-purpose. purchasing, 859
storage, 827
plug-ins folder, spell-checking, 30
PMS (Pantone Matching System), 233
point size, setting with keyboard, 98
Point/Pica Size area, 96
points measurement, 95
Polygon Frame tool, 47, 262–263
Polygon tool
defaults, 125
described, 47
polygons, creating custom, 264
Portable Document Format files. *See* PDF files

Portable Network Graphics (PNG) format
described, 623
graphics, importing, 628
Settings pane, importing bitmap graphics, 635
Position Panel above Text Frame button, 552–553
Position tool (no shortcut), 45
positional forms, OpenType, 529
positioning
footnote, 590
objects precisely with Guides, 286–287
printing setup, 744–745
PostScript files
EPS file, creating, 783
prepress files, printing to, 767
PostScript Printer Description (PPD) file, 717, 738
pound sterling (£), 522
predefined, 360
Preferences dialog box
described, 83–84
Font Downloading and Embedding area, 85–86
General pane options listed, 84
Page Numbering area, 85
Reset All Warning Dialogs button, 86
Scripting area, 86
When Scaling area, 86
preferences files
Adobe Updater Preferences dialog box, 115–116
Auto-Collapse Icon Panels option, 87
Autocorrect preferences, 105–106
black, appearance of
Overprint [Black] Swatch, 111
pane displayed, 111
on RGB and Grayscale Devices area, 110
Clipboard Handling pane
Clipboard area, 114
described, 113
When Pasting Text and Tables from Other
Applications area, 114
color and style defaults, 127
color management, 120–121
Composition pane
described, 92
Highlight area, 93
Text Wrap area, 94
Defaults file, 82
described, 81
Dictionary preferences
described, 102
Hyphenation Exceptions area, 103–104
installing dictionaries, 103

language area, 102–103
User Dictionary area, 104
Display Performance preferences
Adjust View Settings area, 110
Options area, 109
Scrolling area, 110
document defaults, 121–123
File Handling pane
described, 111–112
Document Recovery Data area, 112
Images area, 113
Saving InDesign files, 112
Snippet Import area, 113
Version Cue area, 113
Floating Tools Panel pop-up menu, 86
Grids preferences
Baseline Grid area, 98–99
Document Grid area, 100
Guides & Pasteboard preferences
Color area, 100–101
described, 100
Guide Options area, 101
Pasteboard Options area, 102
keyboard shortcuts
default shortcuts, using and modifying, 116, 118–119
described, 116
QuarkXPress, 119
viewing and printing, 119
menus, 120
Notes preferences, 106–107
object defaults, 124–125
Preferences dialog box
described, 83–84
Font Downloading and Embedding area, 85–86
General pane options listed, 84
Page Numbering area, 85
Reset All Warning Dialogs button, 86
Scripting area, 86
When Scaling area, 86
Presets folder, 82–83
reverting, 127
sharing elements with other users, 828
Show Thumbnails on Place option, 87
Spelling preferences
Dynamic Spelling area, 104
Spelling area, 104, 105

Story Editor Display preferences
Cursor Options area, 108
described, 107
Text Display Options area, 107–108
text defaults, 123
Tool Tips pop-up menu, 86
Type Pane
Advanced Type pane, 91
Character Settings area, 91–92
Drag and Drop Text Editing area, 89
Input Method Options area, 92
Links area, 89
Type options, 87–89
Units & Increments preferences
Keyboard Increments area, 96–98
Point/Pica Size area, 96
Ruler Units area, 94–96
View menu, 125–126
Prefix/Suffix numbering, 589
preflighting document, 720–724
prepress files
described, 765–766
Distiller job options, 779–780
EPS files
Advanced pane, 784–785
exporting described, 782
exporting to, 766
General pane, 782–784
printing to, 767
layout, using, 767
output files, creating, 785–786
PDF files
Advanced pane, 776–777
compression methods, 773
Compression pane, 771–772
exporting described, 767–768
exporting to, 766
General pane, 769–771
Marks and Bleeds pane, 772–774
on-screen usage, 779
Output pane, 774–775
printing to, 780–782
Security pane, 777–778
Summary pane, 779
PostScript files, printing to, 767
presets
color trapping, 707–710
folder

interface, 30
    preferences files, 82–83
    viewing, 826
    print, transferring across platforms, 834
preview
    EPS file, creating, 783
    fonts, 89, 90
Preview Mode, 49
print presets, transferring across platforms, 834
print settings, preflighting documents, 722
Printer's marks, 745–747
printing
    Advanced pane
        bitmap printing, 754
        described, 754
        OPI settings, 754–755
        Transparency Flattener, 755
    color, 231–232
    Color Management pane, 753–754
    common options, 738–740
    composite document, 19–20
    described, 737
    gatefold spreads, extra cost for, 174
    General pane, 741–742
    Graphics pane, 751–753
    hiding layers, 190
    InDesign interface, 902
    keyboard shortcuts, 119
    layers, blocking from, 196
    lip and dpi, 750–751
    Marks and Bleeds pane
        Bleed and Slug area, 747
        described, 745
        Printer's marks, 745–747
    objects, preventing from, 282
    Output pane, 748–750
    pages using transparencies, 179
    to PDF files, 780–782
    preset options, 741
    QuarkXPress, 921
    Setup pane
        page positioning challenges, 744
        paper size and orientation, 742–743
        scaling, positioning, and tiling options, 744–745
    spot colors and separations
        color and ink output, 756–759
        described, 756
        screen angles, adjusting, 759–760

Summary pane, 756
    text over transparent elements, 190
    transparency
        applying flattener presets, 763
        applying wisely, 760–761
        creating flattener presets, 761–763
        described, 760
        previewing flattener settings, 763–764
printing preparations
    booklets
        described, 730–733
        imposition, 733–735
    described, 713
    initial
        described, 713
        Macintosh, 714–716
        Windows Vista, 718–720
        Windows XP, 716–718
    package, creating document, 725–727
    preflighting document, 720–724
    service bureaus
        bleeds, ensuring correct, 729
        described, 727
        documents versus output files, 727–728
        output settings, 728–729
        oversized pages, 730
process color
    described, 231
    mixing with spot color, 232
    spot, converting from, 232
    standard, 230
production file format, 154
profiles, CMS, 699–700
proofing on screen, CMS, 702–703
proportional lining, positional forms, 530
proportional oldstyle, positional forms, 530
publication
    basic questions before beginning work on, 137–138
    setting up new
        creating new documents, 139–142
        described, 138–139
        types, creating your own, 142
pull-quotes, 493–494
punctuation
    search and replace text codes, 422
    symbols, 522
Punctuation space, 423

Q

QuarkXPress
color, 921
compatibility with, 907
conversion issues, 908–910
converting documents from other programs, 150
direction points, 673
document differences, reconciling, 913–914
documents, opening, 908
graphics, 918–920
indexing documents and books, 595
keyboard shortcut equivalents, 912–913
keyboard shortcuts, 119
objects, manipulating, 914–915
pages, manipulating, 920
Paragraph Styles, 506
printing and output, 921
tables, 918
text
editing, 916
flowing, 915–916
formatting, 916–917
tool differences, 910–912
XTensions plug-in
importing documents, 150
removing, 858
QuarkXPress to InDesign: Face to Face (Gruman), 24, 932
quarter space, 423
Quick Apply panel (Edit ➪ Quick Apply, or ⌘+Return or
Ctrl+Enter)
described, 66, 67
shortcut, 891
usefulness, 68
QuickTime movie format, 623
QuickTime movies, 800
quotes and apostrophes
adjacent single and double quotes, 538
closed double quote ("), 536
closed single quote ('), 536
described, 537–538
keyboard quotes, 538
open double quote ("), 536
open single quote ('), 536
quotation mark
as first character after drop cap, 470
search and replace text code, 422
shortcut, 536, 943
reverse single quotes, 538
shortcuts, 943

R

radial gradient, 251
reader's proof, 734
rearranging layers, 196
recovering documents after crash or power failure, 151
Rectangle Frame tool, 47, 262–263
Rectangle tool (shortcut M), 47
rectangular and variable-shaped text frames, creating,
393–394
reference point, 35
Registered trademark symbol (®)
search and replace text code, 422
shortcut, 522, 942
registration marks, 746
reinstalling InDesign, 888
relative colorimetric, bitmap images, 697
Relink file option, 362–363
Remove All Local Overrides and the Remove Selected Local
Overrides, 204
removing, 361
replacing
object attributes, 298–299
text
codes, 421–423
cutting, copying, and pasting, 405
deleting, 407
described, 418–419
formatting, 426–427
global changes, 427–428
method, 419–421
other characters, 425
saved queries, working with, 428, 430
scope, determining, 419
special characters, 425–426
Required folder, 31
Reset All Warning Dialogs button, 86
resizing
frame, fitting graphics, 644
objects
with Control or Transform panel, 290–291
described, 289
resources
AppleScript, 871
books, 931–932
JavaScript, 867
online, 931
VBA scripts, 874
restart numbering, 589
reverse single quotes, 538

reversed text, 306
reverting to last saved version of document, 154
revisions tracking, InCopy program, 850–852
RGB color
    black, appearance of, 110
    described, 231
    imported graphics, 247
RGB color (*continued*)
    policies, 696
    printer model, 695
    standard, 230
Rich Text Format (RTF)
    exporting text, 383, 519
    importing text, 379–382
    style sheets, 518
Right Indent, 467
Right Justify, 466
right-indent tab, search and replace text code, 422
Roman scripting fonts, positional forms, 529
Romaniello, Stephen (*Photoshop CS3 Channels and Masks Bible*), 931
root (√), 523
Rotate tool, 47, 294
rotating objects
    Control panel and Transform panel, 294–296
    Rotate tool, 294
rough equivalence (⊕), 523
Row Strokes and Column Strokes panes, 556, 557
rows and columns, table
    adding and deleting, 559
    manipulating, 559
RTF (Rich Text Format)
    exporting text, 383, 519
    importing text, 379–382
    style sheets, 518
rule
    columns, placing between, 399–400
    paragraph, 482–483
ruler
    document window, 33–34
    guides, document setup, 122
    guides and grids
        automatically creating set of, 222–223
        creating manually, 222
        described, 221–222
        manipulating, 223–224
    Layout Adjustment feature, 185
    showing/hiding, 126
    tabs, 552
ruler point. *See* zero point

Ruler Units preferences, 94–96
running
    AppleScript, 869, 870
    JavaScript, 868
    VBA scripts, 873
running header, formatting, 575

S

saddle stitching, 734
sampling color, 246–247
satin effects, 323–324
saturation color
    bitmap images, 697
    blending mode, 315
Save a Copy
    document command, 152
    version control, 163
Save As (Option+⌘+S or Ctrl+Alt+S)
    document command, 152
    master document, 203
    version control, 163
Save (⌘+S or Ctrl+S)
    document command, 152
    version control, 162
saved queries, text search and replace, 428
saving
    AppleScript, 870–871
    bitmaps, 622
    documents
        commands, 151–152
        export to other formats, 154–155
        exported tagged text files, 156–158
        graphics, exporting files as, 158–159
        reverting to last saved version, 154
        templates versus, 152–154
    files, 112
    JavaScript, 869
    scans, 622
    templates, 152–154
    VBA scripts, 873
Scale tool, 48, 291
scaled text
    adjusting, 447
    different, when to use, 446
scaling objects
    Control panel, 292
    described, 289
    Free Transform tool, 292
    printing setup, 744–745

Scale tool, 291
Selection or Position tool, 292
Transform panel, 292
scans, saving, 622
Scissors tool, 47, 676–677
Scitex CT format
described, 623
graphics, importing, 627
screen angles, adjusting for printing, 759–760
screen blending mode, 314
screening options, 749
Script Debugger (Late Night Software), 871
Script Label panel (Window ⇨ Automation ⇨ Script
        Labels), 64
Scripting area, 86
scripts
accessing, 864
AppleScript
conditional, writing, 878, 879
described, 869
labeling items, 877
language, learning, 869
resources, 871
running, 870
saving, 870–871
syntax errors, checking for, 869
tools, finding more, 871
writing and running, 869
writing simple, 875–876
conditional, writing, 877–879
described, 863
functions, InDesign interface, 903
JavaScript
conditional, writing, 878
described, 867
labeling items, 877
language, learning, 867
resources, 867
running, 868
saving, 869
writing and editing tools, 868
writing simple, 875
labeling items, 877
locations, 864–865
principles, 865–866
VBA
conditional, writing, 878, 879
described, 872
labeling items, 877

language, learning, 872
resources, 874
running, 873
saving, 873
writing and editing, 872–873
writing simple, 876
writing simple, 874–876
Scripts folder, 826
Scripts panel (Window ⇨ Automation ⇨ Scripts, or press
        Option+⌘+F11 or Ctrl+Alt+F11), 62
scroll bars, 34
Scrolling area, Display Performance preferences, 110
scrolling view
described, 128
Hand tool, 130–131
Navigator panel, 131
Zoom field and pop-up menu, 130
Zoom options in the View menu, 128–130
Zoom tool, 128
searching and replacing text
codes, 421–423
described, 418–419
formatting, 426–427
global changes, 427–428
method, 419–421
other characters, 425
saved queries, working with, 428, 430
scope, determining, 419
special characters, 425–426
searching for library objects, 220–221
section markers, text automation, 572
Section Numbering area, 85
section page number, 180
section symbol (§)
search and replace text code, 422
shortcut, 522, 943
sections
consecutively numbering pages, 614–615
dividing documents into, 176–179
numbering differently in one document, 204
Security pane, PDF prepress files, 777–778
selecting objects
Control panel buttons, 275
within group, 896
keyboard shortcuts, 275
from layers, 193
methods, 271–273
overlapping objects, 273–275
tools, 270–271

Selection or Position tool, 292
Selection tool
　described, 43, 270
　QuarkXPress users, adapting, 910
　Type tool, switching from, 43
semiautoflow text-flow icon, 397
separations, printing techniques
　color and ink output, 756–759
　described, 756
　screen angles, adjusting, 759–760
Separations Preview panel (Window ➪ Output ➪
　　　　Separations or Shift+F6), 65
separator, footnote, 590
sequence, printing, 742
service bureau printing preparations
　bleeds, ensuring correct, 729
　described, 727
　documents versus output files, 727–728
　output settings, 728–729
　oversized pages, 730
shapes
　erasing, 684–685
　text, converting to, 498–499
　tools, 661
Shear tool, 48, 296
Sheppard, Rob (Digital Photography: Top 100 Simplified Tips &
　　　　Tricks, 3rd Edition), 932
shortcuts
　described, 72
　navigating pages with, 180–181
　sets, 82
Show Hidden Characters
　defaults, 123
　described, 525
Show Thumbnails on Place option, 87
Show/Hide Structure button, 36
shuffling pages
　dangers of, 171, 173
　described, 204
sidebars, 493–494
signatures, 733–734
Single-Line Composer (Adobe), 479
sixth space, 423
size, scaling characters, 91
skew
　adjusting, 447
　characters, 448–449
slug area, prepress files, 773
small caps

characters, 450
OpenType, 453
when to use, 446
Small Caps characters, 92
small monitor
　character format icons, viewing, 438
　paragraph formatting icons, viewing, 462
　Table, Table Styles, and Cell Styles panels, viewing, 556
smooth anchor point, 659
Smooth tool
　described, 46
　path effects, 684
snap to grids, showing and hiding, 126
snap to guides
　described, 101
　Mac option, 287
snippets
　sharing elements with other users, 830–831
　XML, 113
soft light blending mode, 314
software versions, text files, 373–374
source elements, 830
space
　characters
　　described, 456
　　leading, 458–459
　　tracking, 457
　　units, 457
　search and replace text codes, 422–423
spacing
　adjusting automatically, 89
　paragraph indents, 468
　paragraphs, 469–470
　word, 478
Spanish open exclamation (¡), 542
Spanish open question (¿), 542
special characters
　Apple iWork Pages, 534
　Corel WordPerfect, 534
　cross-platform issues, 521
　dashes
　　em dashes, 536–537
　　en dashes, 537
　Ergonis's PopChar, 532–533
　fixed-width spaces, 535–536
　foreign languages
　　accented characters, 542–543
　　shortcuts, 539–542
　　supported, 538–539

glyphs
  creating sets, 526–527
  described, 521–522
  Glyphs panel, 524, 526
  keyboard shortcuts, 522–523
  menus, 524
  sharing sets, 527
insert menu, 25
Mac Keyboard Viewer and Character Palette, 531
Microsoft Word, 534
nonbreaking spaces, 535
OpenType variants, 527–531
quotes and apostrophes
  adjacent single and double quotes, 538
  described, 537–538
  keyboard quotes, 538
  reverse single quotes, 538
searching and replacing text, 425–426
Show Hidden Characters, 525
special spaces, 534
Windows Character Map, 531–532
special spaces, 534
spell-checking. *See also* dictionary
  capitalization, 409
  Check Spelling dialog box, 409–411
  described, 26
  exceptions, transferring across platforms, 835
  fixing on fly, 407–409
  flagging errors, 407
  hyphenation
    points, customizing, 415–416
    preferences, setting, 416–418
  multiple languages, 411–413
  Plug-ins folder, 30
  text function interface, 900
  as you type, 409
spelling preferences
  Dynamic Spelling area, 104
  Spelling area, 104, 105
splitting compound paths, 681
spot color
  converting to process, 232
  described, 230
  mixing with process color, 232
  printing techniques
    color and ink output, 756–759
    described, 756
    screen angles, adjusting, 759–760
  usefulness, 236

spread
  described, 201
  prepress files, 769
  printing, 742
spreading color trap process, 705
stacked objects, selecting, 328
stacking order, layers, 187
Start At numbering, 589
statements, scripting, 865–866
states, page actions, 797
States panel (Window ➪ Interactive ➪ States), 66, 67
stationery, 831
status, link, 361–362
Step and Repeat command (Edit ➪ Step and Repeat, or Shift+⌘+U or Ctrl+Shift+U)
  objects within documents, 279–280
  Preview, 891
story
  Assignments panel, 846–847
  checkout, check-in, and saving, 850
  defaults, 123
  editing and manipulating, 848–849
  exporting, 847
  text blocks, 260
Story Editor
  Display preferences
    Cursor Options area, 108
    described, 107
    Text Display Options area, 107–108
  editing text, 406
story files, preparing for InCopy, 844–848
Story Options pane, 356
Story panel (Type ➪ Story or Window ➪ Type & Tables ➪ Story), 58, 849, 851
story views, 849
straight and curved segments, combining, 665–667
straight and zigzag lines, drawing with Pen tool, 660–662
strikethrough text, 451–452, 496–498
stripe patterns, 306
stripes, 308
stroke
  defaults, 125
  described, 28, 301
  drawing free-form shapes and curved paths, 657
  effects
    adding, 302–306
    with fills, 309
    styles, creating, 306–309
  overprinting, 311

styles, transferring across platforms, 834
table cells, 565
Stroke & Corner Options pane, 353–354
Stroke pane, objects, 352–353
Stroke panel (shortcut ⌘+F10 or Ctrl+F10), 61, 62
Strokes and Fills pane, table cells, 561–563
Structure pane options, XML, 817–819
style. *See also* Character Styles; paragraph styles
    conflicts
        Tagged Text files, 386
        Word files, importing, 381–382
    defaults, preference files, 127
    index, 592–593
    multi-document projects, 612–614
    numbering, 589
    objects
        Anchored Object Options pane, 357
        creating, 350–351
        described, 349–350
        existing formatting and, 360–361
        Fill pane, 352
        Frame Fitting Options pane, 357
        General pane, 351–352
        groups, 359–360
        managing, 358–359
        Paragraph Styles pane, 354
        predefined, 360
        removing, 361
        Story Options pane, 356
        Stroke & Corner Options pane, 353–354
        Stroke pane, 352–353
        Text Frame Baseline Options pane, 355
        Text Frame General Options pane, 355
        Text Wrap & Other pane, 356–357
    platforms, transferring across, 834
    table
        described, 26
        panel, 565–568
    text
        character, 501, 502
        paragraph, 501, 502
    Word, importing, 381
style sheets, RTF, 518
stylistic sets, OpenType, 453, 529
subscript
    characters, 451
    OpenType, 453, 529
Summary pane printing technique, 756

superscript
    characters, 91, 447, 451
    OpenType, 453, 529
SVG, exporting files to, 158–159
swash, OpenType, 453, 529
swatch libraries
    described, 82
    uppercase, 233
swatchbooks, color
    ANPA, 234
    described, 230
    DIC, 234
    Focoltone, 234
    Hexachrome, 234
    HKS, 234
    Toyo, 234
    Trumatch, 234
swatches
    color
        deleting, 253–254
        duplicating, 254
        editing, 253
        merging, 253
        transferring across platforms, 834
    defaults, 125
    gradients without, 250–251
    importing, 245, 828
Swatches panel (shortcut F5)
    described, 61, 62
    mixed colors, 241–243
    naming system, 240
    personalizing, 237
    steps, 237–239
    tints, 240–241
symbols
    platform issues, 837
    search and replace text codes, 422
syntax
    errors, checking AppleScript for, 869
    rules, scripting, 865–866

T
table
    cells
        colors, gradients, and strokes, 565
        Control panel, 565
        Diagonal Lines pane, 563–564
        formatting, 560

merging and unmerging, 564
overflowing text, 564
splitting, 564
Strokes and Fills pane, 561–563
Text pane, 561
creating
described, 553–556
Fills pane, 558
Headers and Footers pane, 558–559
Row Strokes and Column Strokes panes, 556, 557
Table Options dialog box, 557
Table Setup pane, 556
Excel, importing, 385
panel, 61, 63
platforms, transferring across, 834
QuarkXPress, 918
rows and columns
adding and deleting, 559
manipulating, 559
styles
described, 26
panel, 565–568
panel (Window ➪ Type & Tables ➪ Table Styles),
61, 63
sharing elements with other users, 828–829
tabs, converting to, 568–569
Word, importing, 380–381
Table menu, 75
Table Options dialog box, 557
Table Setup pane, 556
tables of contents
defining, 601–605
described, 600
lists, creating other, 603
planning, 600–601
tabs
described, 547–548
functions, 900
panel
Align On field, 552
described, 56, 548–549
flyout menu, 553
leader field, 551
left, center, right, and Align On buttons, 549
loading, 891
Position Panel above Text Frame button, 552–553
ruler, 552
X field, 549–551
ruler, 552

search and replace text code, 422
tables, converting from, 568–569
tabular lining
OpenType, 453
positional forms, 530
tabular oldstyle, positional forms, 530
Tagged Image File Format (TIFF)
described, 623
graphics, importing, 627
Tagged Text files, importing, 386
tagged text for database publishing, 584–585
tags
library element, 220
XML
applying, 816–817
creating, 812, 815
importing, 812–815
Styles, mapping with, 816
Tags panel, 66, 67
team workgroups
assignments, setting up
described, 843
editing and manipulating assigned stories, 848–849
story files, preparing for InCopy, 844–848
user, identifying, 844
Creative Suite applications, other
Adobe Bridge file context, 839–840
Adobe Bridge interface, 841
Adobe Bridge suite functionality, 841
Adobe Bridge utilities for InDesign, 841–842
described, 838
graphics and color, 838
Web content, 838–839
editing functions
within InCopy, 905
within InDesign, 904
effectiveness, key to, 825
InCopy program
described, 849
revisions tracking, 850–852
special features, 852–853
story checkout, check-in, and saving, 850
story views, 849
Mac and Windows environments, mixing
described, 833
filename extensions, 833–834
filenames, 836
font differences, 836–837
multiple versions of InDesign, 835

nontransferable elements, 835
transfer methods, 838
transferable elements, 834–835
sharing elements with other users
color definitions, 828
common settings files, 829
described, 826
graphics and text files, 830
InDesign documents, 832
interface preferences, 832
libraries, 830
team workgroups *(continued)*
locations, 826–828
master pages, 831–832
output settings, 831
paragraph, character, table, cell, and object styles,
828–829
Preference files, 828
snippets, 830–831
spelling dictionaries, 829
templates, 831
Windows Application Data folder, viewing, 826
template
booklets, 730–733
creating, 213–214
described, 199
layers, 190
modifying, 215
opening versus opening documents, 147
saving, 152–154
sharing elements with other users, 831
text. *See also* characters; paragraphs
anti-aliasing, 110
automatic bullets and numbered lists, 472
black, printing, 749
blocks, 260
bulleted and numbered lists
applying, 489
bullet characters, 480
defining, 486–489
imported, working with, 489
columns
master frames, specifying, 398
rule, placing between, 399–400
text frames, adjusting, 398–399
composing
Adobe Paragraph Composer, 479–480
Adobe Single-Line Composer, 479
CSS formatting, 805–806

document, 7–12
editing
cutting, copying, and pasting, 405
deleting and replacing, 405, 407
highlighting, 405
navigating, 405
Story Editor, 406
text view, controlling, 403–404
undoing, 407
end-of-story markers, 495–496
flowing, 387–388
formatting, 485–486
formatting fractions
manually, 491–492
typeface, 490–491
frame
adding, 374
additional, drawing, 391–394
appearance, 430–433
creating, 260–262
defaults, 124
described, 388
library files, 219
master pages, creating on, 389–391
resizing methods, 290
spacing and alignment, 400–401
functions
editing, 898–899
import, 898
paragraph and character formatting, 899–900
spelling and indexing, 900
styles, 901
tabs and tables, 900
handling
PageMaker users, adapting, 927
QuarkXPress users, adapting, 912
hyphenation
automatic, 474–476
described, 473–474
manual, 474
initial caps, 472–473
justification
controls, 476–478
described, 474
next to an object, 94
kerning with keyboard, 98
notes, 433–435
optical margin alignment, 494–495
overflowing

identifying and editing overset, 401

Story Editor feature, 406

table cells, 564

path, following, 499

printing over transparent elements, 190

QuarkXPress

editing, 916

flowing, 915–916

formatting, 916–917

reversing out of background, 492–493

searching and replacing

codes, 421–423

described, 418–419

fonts, 429

formatting, 426–427

global changes, 427–428

Grep, 424

method, 419–421

other characters, 425

saved queries, working with, 428, 430

scope, determining, 419

special characters, 425–426

shapes, converting to, 498–499

sidebars and pull-quotes, 493–494

spelling corrections

capitalization, 409

Check Spelling dialog box, 409–411

dictionary, customizing, 413–415

fixing on fly, 407–409

flagging errors, 407

hyphenation points, customizing, 415–416

multiple languages, 411–413

spelling and hyphenation dictionary preferences,
    setting, 416–418

as you type, 409

styles

character, 501, 502

paragraph, 501

threading frames

autoflowing after placing text, 396

breaking and rerouting, 397

described, 394

icons, 397

manually, 394–395

placing text while autoflowing, 396

semiautomatically, 395–396

threads, showing and hiding, 126

underline and strikethrough, 496–498

view, controlling, 403–404

word spacing, 478

wrapping around objects

options, 344

preferences, 348–349

shape, changing, 349

Text Wrap panel, 344–348

text anchor, hyperlink, 790–791

text automation

described, 571

merged data

described, 577–578

multiple records per page, 582–584

pages, creating, 579–582

setting up, 578–579

page numbers, 572

section markers, 572

tagged text for database publishing, 584–585

text variables

creating, 573–574

editing and managing, 576, 577

formatting, 575–576

inserting, 576

language translation, 576

text correction. *See* spell-checking

Text Display Options area, 107–108

text files

adding text

dragging and dropping, 376–377

Excel files, 384–385

InCopy files, 384

pasting, 375–376

with Place dialog box, 377–379

Tagged Text files, 386

text-only files, 382–384

Type tool, 374–375

Word and RTF files, 379–382

fast save, 373

formatting location, 369–370

preparing, 370

sharing elements with other users, 830

software versions, 373–374

special features, preserving

described, 370–372

footnotes and endnotes, 372

headers and footers, 372

hyperlinks, 373

inline graphics and text boxes, 373

Text Frame Baseline Options pane, 355

Text Frame General Options pane, 355

Text pane, 561
text styles. *See* character style; paragraph style
text variables
  automation
    creating, 573–574
    editing and managing, 576, 577
    formatting, 575–576
    inserting, 576
    language translation, 576
  described, 26
text wrap
  area, 94
  defaults, 124
text wrap (*continued*)
  ignoring, 431
  layers, 190
  layers, hiding, 195
Text Wrap & Other pane, 356–357
Text Wrap panel, 897
Text Wrap panel (shortcut Option+⌘+W or Ctrl+Alt+W), 58
text-only files
  exporting, 519
  importing, 382–384
thesaurus, electronic, 852
thin bullet (·), 522
thin space
  described, 423
  shortcuts, 536
third space, 423
thread, 28
thread icon, 397
threading frames
  autoflowing after placing text, 396
  breaking and rerouting, 397
  described, 394
  icons, 397
  manually, 394–395
  placing text while autoflowing, 396
  semiautomatically, 395–396
three-quarters fraction (¾), 523
thresholds, color trap settings, 709
thumbnails
  prepress files, 769
  printing, 744
TIFF (Tagged Image File Format)
  described, 623
  graphics, importing, 627
tilde (~), 539
tiling, 744–745

Timacheff, Serge (*Total Digital Photography: The Shoot to Print Workflow Handbook*), 932
tint swatches
  cross-platform issues, 834
  panel, 240–241
title bar, 31–34
titling, OpenType
  alternatives, 529
  described, 453
Tool Tips
  keyboard shortcuts, 39–40
  pop-up menu, 86
tools
  AppleScript, finding more, 871
  interface
    Add Anchor Point tool (shortcut =), 45
    Button tool, 47
    Delete Anchor Point tool (shortcut [hyphen]), 45
    described, 38
    Direct Selection tool (shortcut A), 44
    Ellipse Frame tool, 47
    Ellipse tool (shortcut L), 47
    Erase tool, 46
    Eyedropper tool (shortcut I), 48–49
    Free Transform tool (shortcut E), 48
    Gradient Feather tool (shortcut Shift+G), 48
    Gradient Swatch tool (shortcut G), 48
    Hand tool (shortcut H), 49
    Line tool (shortcut E), 46
    Measure tool (shortcut K), 49
    Note tool, 48
    panel, opening and closing, 40–41
    Pen tool (shortcut P), 45
    Pencil tool (shortcut N), 46
    Polygon Frame tool, 47
    Polygon tool, 47
    Position tool (no shortcut), 45
    Rectangle Frame tool (shortcut F), 47
    Rectangle tool (shortcut M), 47
    Rotate tool (shortcut R), 47
    Scale tool (shortcut S), 48
    Scissors tool (shortcut C), 47
    selecting, 41–42
    Selection tool (shortcut V), 43
    Shear tool (shortcut O), 48
    Smooth tool, 46
    Tool Tips and keyboard shortcuts, 39–40
    Type on a Path tool (shortcut Shift+T), 46
    Type tool (shortcut T), 45–46

uses, understanding, 42–43

Zoom tool (shortcut Z), 49

Tools panel, 55

Total Digital Photography: The Shoot to Print Workflow Handbook (Timacheff and Karlins), 932

Toyo color

printer model, 695

swatchbook, 234

Track Changes, importing from Word, 381

tracking

adjusting, 447

characters, 457

platform issues, 837

violations, highlighting, 93

Trademark (™), 522

Transform panel, 292

Transform panel (Window ➪ Object & Layout ➪ Transform), 58

transformation, object

clearing, 295

repeating, 297

tips, 293

translation, layer, 190

transparency

alert, 179

compound paths, creating, 678

described, 26

flattening in prepress files, 776

lighting effects, 312–315

platforms, transferring across, 834

printing techniques

applying flattener presets, 763

applying wisely, 760–761

creating flattener presets, 761–763

described, 760

flattening during output, 761–764

previewing flattener settings, 763–764

proofing, 703

Transparency Flattener printing technique, 755

transparency preset, prepress, 785

transparent elements, printing text over, 190

Trap Presets panel (Window ➪ Output ➪ Trap Presets), 65

trap presets, transferring across platforms, 834

trap width, setting, 708

trapping, color

applying to pages, 710–711

described, 704

knockout and overprinting, 705–707

methods, 705

presets, specifying, 707–710

trapping, color printing, 749

Trinko, Tom (*AppleScript For Dummies, 2nd Edition*), 871

Trumatch color

printer model, 695

swatchbook, 234

Type menu, 71, 73, 892

Type on a Path tool (shortcut Shift+T), 46

Type on a Path tools, 661

Type Pane

Character Settings area, 91–92

Drag and Drop Text Editing area, 89

Input Method Options area, 92

Links area, 89

Type options, 87–89

type size, when to use different, 446

Type tool

adding text, 374–375

described, 45–46

QuarkXPress users, adapting, 911

rectangular and variable-shaped text frames, creating, 393–394

switching to Selection tool, 43

Type tools, 661

typeface fractions, formatting, 490–491

typefaces

changes, when to use, 446

embedded, 624

EPS file, creating, 783–784

family, style, and size

described, 441–442

labeling paragraphs, 446

selecting, 443–444

size, changing, 445

hidden layers, including, 726

Mac, adding, 429

Mac and Windows environments, mixing, 836–837

platform issues, 837

preflighting documents, 721

preview size, 89, 90

searching and replacing, 429

shortcut, customizing, 117

substituted, highlighting, 93

typographer's quotes

Excel files, importing, 385

formatting, 88

Tagged Text files, importing, 386

U

umlaut, 539
underlining text
    described, 451–452, 496–498
    when to use, 446
Undo text editing, 79, 407
uninstalling InDesign, 888
units, character, 457
Units & Increments preferences
    Keyboard Increments area, 96–98
    Point/Pica Size area, 96
    Ruler Units area, 94–96
Unix, Grep Find/Change pane, 424
unmerging table cells, 564
upgrading InDesign from prior versions, 887
uppercase swatch libraries, 233
URL hyperlink, 790–791
user, workgroup, 844
User Dictionary preferences, 104
user interface. *See* interface

V

Variation (∂), 523
VBA (Visual Basic for Applications)
    conditional, writing, 878, 879
    labeling items, 877
    scripts
        described, 872
        language, learning, 872
        resources, 874
        running, 873
        saving, 873
        writing and editing, 872–873
        writing simple, 876
    support, 863
VBScript, 872
vector graphic files, importing
    DCS PostScript files, 624, 625
    embedded fonts, 624
    EPS PostScript files, 624, 625
    Illustrator PostScript files, 624, 625
    options, 637–639
    PDF PostScript files, 624, 625–626
    PICT files, 626
    Windows Metafile format, 626
version, layers, 190

Version Cue
    document versions, managing with
        interface, understanding, 160–162
        managing files, 164–165
        working with, 162–163
    File Handling pane, 113
    pop-up menu, 36–37
Vertical Justification section, text frame, 400–401
view
    customizing, 127
    interface buttons
        Normal View Mode, 49
        Preview Mode, 49
    keyboard shortcuts, 119
    object display options, 131–132
    zooming and scrolling
        described, 128
        Hand tool, 130–131
        Navigator panel, 131
        Zoom field and pop-up menu, 36, 130
        Zoom options in the View menu, 128–130
        Zoom tool, 128
View menu, 75–76, 125–126
virgule, 492
Visual Basic for Applications. VBA

W

web, exporting to
    electronic documents
        Advanced pane, 805–806
        files, working with, 806–807
        Images pane, 804–805
    generally, 802–804
Web content, Creative Suite applications, 838–839
Web export/output functions, 903
Web site, launching Adobe, 43
Web-oriented graphics, importing, 628
When Pasting Text and Tables from Other Applications area,
        Clipboard, 114
When Scaling area, 86
white space, 423
wild cards, search and replace text code, 423
window, document
    interface
        page field and pop-up menu, 38
        page-turning buttons, 37
        pasteboard, pages, and guides, 34–35

reference point, 35
scroll bars, 34
Show/Hide Structure button, 36
title bar, 31–34
Version Cue pop-up menu, 36–37
zero point, 34
Zoom field and pop-up menu, 36
Mac, 31
opening multiple, 132–133
Windows, 31
Window menu, 76
Windows Application Data folder, viewing, 826
Windows Metafile format, 623, 626
Windows (Microsoft)
document windows, 31
em dash shortcut, 537
folders, opening, 143, 145
fonts, adding, 429
ligatures, 453
Mac environments, mixing for workgroups
described, 833
filename extensions, 833–834
filenames, 836
font differences, 836–837
multiple versions of InDesign, 835
nontransferable elements, 835
transfer methods, 838
Print dialog boxes, 740
printer output file, 786
printing PDF files, 781
saving documents versus saving templates, 152–153
spaces, dashes, hyphens, and quotes shortcuts, 536
special characters, 531–534
symbols, shortcuts for, 522–523
system requirements, 883–884
text-only files, importing, 382
Version Cue interface, 160–161
versions, 835
western European accents and foreign character
shortcuts, 539–543
Windows Vista (Microsoft)
application data folder, 826
filename extensions, viewing, 146
InDesign Defaults file location, 82
monitor bit depth, setting, 694
printing preparations, 718–720
Windows XP (Microsoft)
application data folder, 826
filename extensions, viewing, 146

InDesign Defaults file location, 82
monitor bit depth, setting, 694
printing preparations, 716–718
Word (Microsoft)
importing text, 379–382
special characters, 534
word processing
document format, 155
formatting capabilities, 369–370
word spacing
justification, 477
text, 478
workgroups
assignments, setting up
described, 843
editing and manipulating assigned stories, 848–849
story files, preparing for InCopy, 844–848
user, identifying, 844
Creative Suite applications, other
Adobe Bridge file context, 839–840
Adobe Bridge interface, 841
Adobe Bridge suite functionality, 841
Adobe Bridge utilities for InDesign, 841–842
described, 838
graphics and color, 838
Web content, 838–839
editing functions
within InCopy, 905
within InDesign, 904
effectiveness, key to, 825
InCopy program
described, 849
revisions tracking, 850–852
special features, 852–853
story checkout, check-in, and saving, 850
story views, 849
Mac and Windows environments, mixing
described, 833
filename extensions, 833–834
filenames, 836
font differences, 836–837
multiple versions of InDesign, 835
nontransferable elements, 835
transfer methods, 838
transferable elements, 834–835
sharing elements with other users
color definitions, 828
common settings files, 829
described, 826

graphics and text files, 830
InDesign documents, 832
interface preferences, 832
libraries, 830
locations, 826–828
master pages, 831–832
output settings, 831
paragraph, character, table, cell, and object styles, 828–829
Preference files, 828
snippets, 830–831
spelling dictionaries, 829
templates, 831
Windows Application Data folder, viewing, 826
worksheet, Excel, 384
workspaces, 83
wrap boundary, clipping paths as a, 649–650
writing
AppleScript, 869
JavaScript, 868
VBA scripts, 872–873

X

X field, 549–551
x height, baseline, 432
X value
moving objects, 277
resizing objects, 291
scaling objects, 292
zero point, 34
XML (Extensible Markup Language)
described, 811
document snippets, 156
exporting files, 820–822
find-change queries, 83
functions, 904
rules, 814
snippets, 113

Structure pane options, 817–819
tags
applying, 816–817
creating, 812, 815
importing, 812–815
Styles, mapping with, 816
XSLT style sheet, importing, 813, 815
XTensions plug-in, QuarkXPress
importing documents, 150
removing, 858

Y

Y value
moving objects, 277
resizing objects, 291
scaling objects, 292
zero point, 34
yen (¥), 522

Z

Zapf Dingbats and Wingdings, 490
zero, OpenType slashed, 453
zero point
determining, 94
X value, 34
Y value, 34
zigzag lines, drawing, 660–662
Zoom field and pop-up menu, 36, 130
Zoom options in the View menu, 128–130
Zoom tool, 49, 128
zooming and scrolling views
described, 128
Hand tool, 130–131
Navigator panel, 131
Zoom field and pop-up menu, 130
Zoom options in the View menu, 128–130
Zoom tool, 128